Law of the European Convention on Human Rights

Law of the European Convention on Human Rights

DJ Harris LLM, PhD (London)
Professor of Public International Law,
University of Nottingham

M O'Boyle LLB (Belf), LLM (Harvard)
Barrister-at-Law (Inn of Court of
Northern Ireland), Senior Legal Officer
at the European Court of Human Rights

C Warbrick MA, LLB (Cantab), LLM (Michigan)
Senior Lecturer in Law,
University of Durham

Butterworths
London, Dublin, Edinburgh
1995

United Kingdom	Butterworths a Division of Reed Elsevier (UK) Ltd, Halsbury House, 35 Chancery Lane, LONDON, WC2A 1EL, and 4 Hill Street, EDINBURGH EH2 3JZ
Australia	Butterworths, SYDNEY, MELBOURNE, BRISBANE, ADELAIDE, PERTH, CANBERRA and HOBART
Canada	Butterworths Canada Ltd, TORONTO and VANCOUVER
Ireland	Butterworth (Ireland) Ltd, DUBLIN
Malaysia	Malayan Law Journal Sdn Bhd, KUALA LUMPUR
New Zealand	Butterworths of New Zealand Ltd, WELLINGTON and AUCKLAND
Singapore	Reed Elsevier (Singapore) Pte Ltd, SINGAPORE
South Africa	Butterworth Publishers (Pty) Ltd, DURBAN
USA	Michie, CHARLOTTESVILLE, Virginia

Any Crown copyright material is reproduced with the permission of the Controller of Her Majesty's Stationery Office.

© Reed Elsevier (UK) Ltd 1995

Reprinted 1996

A CIP Catalogue record for this book is available from the British Library.

ISBN 0 406 25930 5

Typeset by Doublestruck Limited, London
Printed and bound in Great Britain by Ashford Colour Press, Gosport, Hampshire

Preface

We have written this book primarily for law students and practitioners whose need for knowledge about the Strasbourg system has long demanded a greater variety of textbooks in the English language.

The law of the European Convention on Human Rights has grown significantly over the last two decades. The European Commission and Court of Human Rights have established themselves as a major source of influence in the legal development of the thirty-one contracting states which have so far ratified the Convention and agreed to accept as binding the judgments of the Court and the decisions of the Committee of Ministers. The Court has, at the date of writing, handed down 514 judgments which, when added to the many hundreds of Commission reports and thousands of admissibility decisions, amounts to an impressive corpus of human rights law dealing with problems in practically every department of the law. Legislators, civil servants, practitioners and law students are now obliged by the growth and relevance of this area of law to inform themselves about, and keep abreast of, the principles underlying the Strasbourg case-law.

Since 1989 the actual and potential influence of the Convention system has undergone a quantum leap as an increasing number of Eastern and Central European states have been admitted to the Council of Europe and ratified the Convention. Cases can now be brought *inter alia* against Hungary, Bulgaria, the Czech Republic, Poland, Romania, Slovenia and Slovakia. It has been estimated that the Convention community could grow to as many as 40 to 45 contracting parties over the next decade. As can be imagined, the case-law of the institutions has had, and will continue to have, an important influence on legal reform in these new democracies. However, the elementary point must be made that the digestion and reception of Convention norms by these countries presupposes that efforts will be made by the states concerned and the Council of Europe to translate the leading decisions of the Commission and Court into the respective languages.

Nor should we forget that the courts in many Commonwealth countries and the new Constitutional courts in Russia and South Africa follow Strasbourg developments with a particularly interested eye.

In the United Kingdom one has to look no further than the daily newspaper for an indication of the range of domestic problems that are being litigated in Strasbourg. The current docket of the Court is also eloquent in this respect. Pending before it are cases against the United Kingdom concerning the right to silence (John Murray), freedom from self-incrimination (Saunders), the use of lethal force against terrorists in Gibraltar (McCann *et al*), marital rape (SW and CR), the procedural rights of children detained at Her Majesty's pleasure (Singh and Hussain), the adequacy of the scope of judicial review (Bryan), the determination that a video was blasphemous (Wingrove), the fairness of criminal proceedings in Scotland (Pullar), detention for failure to pay the poll tax (Benham) and denial of access to Court due to the operation of the rules of prescription (DW). As is illustrated throughout this book, important changes have already been brought about in the United Kingdom *inter alia* in civil and criminal law, family law, freedom of the press, immigration law, mental health law and prison law, as a result of complaints which have been examined by the Strasbourg institutions.

Inevitably, the nagging question is being asked: why do we have to go to Strasbourg to have these issues litigated? The United Kingdom is one of the very few countries where the Convention has not been incorporated into national law. The growth of support for a bill of rights in the United Kingdom creates the possibility that the provisions of the Convention could in the foreseeable future be directly applicable by our own courts which would then be empowered to hear Convention argument in cases such as those noted above. If this were to come about, the law of the Convention would be thrust to the fore of university legal curricula and would achieve an immediacy and relevance which would dynamise, if not revolutionise, the United Kingdom's constitutional system. There is also the possibility that the European Union might decide to adhere to the Convention in keeping with the expressed desire of the Brussels Commission.

Of course, the Strasbourg system is invasive. Episodically, the Court determines that some aspect of national law or practice is incompatible with a provision of the Convention, not infrequently in areas of particular sensitivity such as prisons, immigration matters or the administration of justice. Politicians and media commentators frequently complain, in strident tones of indignation, of interference in the domestic affairs of the state by uninformed and ill-qualified foreign jurists. Not unnaturally, the tones change somewhat where political freedoms and freedom of the press are at stake. Two inter-linked questions therefore arise: why do states continue to accept the operation of this system – after all, Article 65 enables them to denounce the Convention – and why has it been so successful over the years?

In response to these queries it is useful to recall the rationale for this regional system of human rights protection. Firstly, the Convention established such a system based on the concept of a collective guarantee of an agreed set of human rights standards by all contracting parties. It is an essential feature of this notion that the community of states, jointly and severally, has the right to supervise the protection of human rights in the jurisdiction of any contracting party. The price for a system of inter-nationally enforceable standards is that the manner in which human rights are protected within a Convention country is no longer exclusively a matter of national sovereignty and may be challenged either by way of an individual or an inter-state petition before the Strasbourg institutions. In other words, states are prepared to accept the competence of an international tribunal to examine issues emerging from their own law and practice because they have committed themselves, after the horrors and atrocities of the Second World War, to the observance of minimum human rights standards throughout Europe. The Convention system thus institutionalises a democratic commitment by like-minded European states attached to constitutional values and the rule of law.

Secondly, the system has taken root in legal systems throughout Europe and the notion of a long-stop protection now enjoys popular support. It has provided a frame of reference for national discussion of human rights issues and has contributed to the formation of a sensitised and informed public conscience on matters which are often controversial and which stir public passions like little else. A state that were to denounce its Convention obligations or withdraw its acceptance of the jurisdiction of the Commission and Court would risk serious internal criticism. Is it an exaggeration to suggest that the system has developed to the point that no European state could seriously contemplate resiling from the Convention?

Thirdly, the Convention system has not stood still. It has constantly been adapted to bring it up-to-date with contemporary notions of human rights protection. Thus, new rights have been added by the First, Fourth and Seventh Protocols, the individual has acquired the right to bring his case before the Court (the Ninth Protocol), and the problem of delay in the proceedings has been addressed by the procedural reforms contained in the Eighth Protocol and, most recently, the Eleventh Protocol. At the same time the philosophy of a post-war collective guarantee has matured, with the full consent of all the contracting parties, into a fledgling constitutional system with the European Commission and the Court of Human Rights at its centre.

Lastly, both the Commission and the Court have rightfully earned the confidence of contracting parties by carrying out their tasks with the objectivity of judicial bodies and have earned a world-wide reputation for fairness, balance and intellectual rigour.

The Eleventh Protocol, by providing for the creation of a single permanent Court to take the place of the existing organs, will undoubtedly revolutionise the enforcement system of the Convention by speeding up the examination of cases. By all accounts the new Court is likely to be in place by the end of the century. At the same time it should be borne in mind that the new Court will inherit the case-law of the existing organs, both as regards substantive issues and questions of admissibility. Moreover, it can be expected that the working methods and procedures of the Commission and Court which represent an important part of the *acquis conventionnel* will find an appropriate reflection in the workings of the new Court. Our account of the operation of the existing Commission and Court will thus, it is hoped, count for something more than the historical record.

Finally, it is worth pointing out that the account of the law of the Convention given in the following pages is an interweave of the judgments of the Court and the decisions as to admissibility and opinions on the merits of the Commission over the whole period of the life of the Convention without any clear distinction necessarily being made. When assessing the value of any particular case that is relied upon, it is necessary to be aware that the Court often disagrees with the Commission so that Commission decisions or opinions are in a sense provisional and have certainly to be read in the light of later Court pronouncements in the area of law concerned.

We would like to express our sincere thanks to Paul Mahoney, the Deputy Registrar of the Court, who was one of the originators of this project and whose considerable initial work served as a springboard for its completion. Thanks are also due to Karen Reid of the Commission's secretariat and Søren Prebensen of the Registry of the Court who read different chapters of the book with enthusiasm and made helpful suggestions; to Ed Bates and Chris Cole, who read the proofs; and to Rebecca Weaver and Angela Doul, who typed part of the manuscript. We also wish to thank Dr Anne Lister, research assistant in the University of Nottingham Human Rights Law Centre, for undertaking the huge task of checking the many citations in the manuscript.

Chapter 2 is the revised text of an article published in 1 Maastricht Journal of European and Comparative Law 122 (1994).

Our families have borne the brunt of all our endeavours to produce this work and to bring it as up-to-date as humanly possible. We thank them for their patience and support and the lack of complaint for too many weekends away from home and family chores.

We have endeavoured to state the law as it stood at the beginning of 1995 and occasionally, where possible, later.

The views expressed in this book are personal to the authors and do not represent those of any institution.

David Harris
Michael O'Boyle
Colin Warbrick

May 1995

Contents

Note on the citation of Strasbourg cases

1. COURT REPORTS

Citations of Court judgments in this book refer to the official publications of the European Court of Human Rights, published by Carl Heymanns Verlag in English and French. There are two series of publications: Series A (Judgments and Decisions) and Series B (Pleadings, Oral Arguments and Documents). The Series B volumes are some years behind, with only volumes for the first 100 or so cases published as yet.

Court cases are cited as follows:

- *Soering v UK* A 161 para 91 (1989) refers to paragraph 91 of the Court judgment in that case in volume 161 of Series A.
- *Soering v UK* A 161 (1989) Com Rep para 91 refers to para 91 of the Article 31 Commission Report in that case. As of 1984, extracts from the Commission Report in any case referred to the Court are printed in the Series A volume together with the Court judgment.
- *Buchholz v FRG* B 37 (1980) Com Rep refers to para 37 of the Commission's 1980 Article 31 Report in that case.

Note. The Commission's Article 31 reports in cases that have been referred to the Court are available on request from the Council of Europe in 'blue cover' form; they are not published in any official series pending the Court judgment.

2. COMMISSION DECISIONS AND REPORTS

CD   Collection of Decisions of the European Commission of Human Rights. This series (volumes 1-46, 1959-1974) was published by the Council of Europe. It was superseded by the Decisions and Reports series. In English or French.

DR   Decisions and Reports of the European Commission on Human Rights. This series (volume 1- , 1975-) is published by the Council of Europe. It reprints in English and in French selected Commission decisions as to admissibility; Commission friendly settlement reports under Article 28; and Commission Reports on the merits under Article 31 where the case is not referred to the Court. In the case of an Article 31 report, the Committee of Ministers Resolution that completes the case is also printed. As of volume 76, the volumes are published as volumes 76-A and 76-B, etc, with the A volume containing the original language of the decision etc, and the B volume, which is published later, containing the translation. This allows cases to be published much more quickly in at least one language.

3. OTHER REPORT SERIES

Digest   Digest of Strasbourg Case-Law Relating to the European Convention on Human Rights, Vols 1- , 1984- . This series results from a joint project of the Council of Europe and the Europa Instituut of the University of Utrecht. It contains extracts by Convention Article in digest form from the case-law of the European Commission and Court of Human Rights, including extracts from Commission cases not reported elsewhere. It is published by Carl Heymanns Verlag.

EHRR   The European Human Rights Reports publishes in English the judgments of the European Court of Human Rights and certain of the Commission's reports and decisions, particularly in the early years. There is now a Commission Supplement EHRR CD (volumes 15- , 1993-) that contains summaries and extracts of and from Commission decisions. The Reports are published by Sweet and Maxwell.

YB   The Yearbook of the European Convention on Human Rights contains selected Commission decisions as to admissibility. The earlier volumes contain extracts from Commission reports and Court judgments. In English and French.

Unreported cases   Some admissibility decisions are referred to in footnotes in this book as 'unreported'. This means that there are no plans to report them or that they have not been reported as yet in the Decisions and Reports series or any other of the above report series. Such decisions may, if copies remain available, be obtained on request in typed form from the Commission Secretariat. They are also now held in a Council of Europe computer database to which some national institutions have access.

List of abbreviations

A	Series A, Publications of the European Court of Human Rights (see Note on Citations, p xv)
ACHR	American Convention on Human Rights
AEL	Collected Courses of the Academy of European Law
AFDI	Annuaire Français de droit international
Ago Essays	International Law at the Time of its Codification, Vols 1-4, 1987
AJCL	American Journal of Comparative Law
AJIL	American Journal of International Law
B	Series B, Publications of the European Court of Human Rights (see Note on Citations, p xv)
BRC	British Review of Criminology
BYIL	British Yearbook of International Law
CD	Collection of Decisions of the European Commission of Human Rights (see Note on Citations, p xv)
CE	Council of Europe
CLJ	Cambridge Law Journal
CLP	Current Legal Problems
CLR	Commonwealth Law Reports
CM	Committee of Ministers, Council of Europe
Cm, Cmd, Cmnd	UK Command Papers
CMLR	Common Market Law Review
COD	Crown Office Digest
Cohen-Jonathan	*La Convention européenne des droits de l'homme, 1989*
Collected Texts	*European Convention on Human Rights: Collected Texts*, CE Publication, 1994
Com Rep	Commission Report
Conn ILJ	Connecticut International Law Journal
Corn ILJ	Cornell International Law Journal
Crim LR	Criminal Law Review
CWRIJL	Case Western Reserve International Law Journal
Digest	Digest of Strasbourg Case-Law (see Note on Citations, p xvi)
DR	Decisions and Reports of the European Commission of Human Rights (see Note on Citations, p xv)

ECR	European Court Reports
EHRR	European Human Rights Reports (see Note on Citations, p xv)
EJIL	European Journal of International Law
ELR	European Law Review
Ermacora Festschrift	Nowak, Steurer, Tretter, eds, *Progess in the Spirit of Human Rights*, 1988
ETS	European Treaty Series
Eur Comp L	European Competition Law Review
European System	Macdonald, Matscher and Petzold, eds, *The European System for the Protection of Human Rights*, 1993
F Sett	Friendly Settlement
Fawcett	The Application of the European Convention on Human Rights, 2nd edn, 1987
GAOR	General Assembly Official Records
GJICL	Georgia Journal of International and Comparative Law
GYIL	German Yearbook of International Law
Harv HRYB	Harvard Human Rights Yearbook
Harv LR	Harvard Law Review
HRC	Human Rights Committee
HRLJ	Human Rights Law Journal
HRJ	Human Rights Journal
HRQ	Human Rights Quarterly
HRR	Human Rights Review
ICCPR	International Covenant on Civil and Political Rights
ICJ Rep	International Court of Justice Reports
ICLQ	International and Comparative Law Quarterly
IHRR	International Human Rights Reports
IJFL	International Journal of Family Law
ILJ	Industrial Law Journal
ILM	International Legal Materials
ILR	International Law Reports
Imm AR	Immigration Appeal Reports
IR	Irish Reports
Israeli YBHR	Israeli Yearbook of Human Rights
Jacobs	*The European Convention on Human Rights*, 1975
JSWL	Journal of Social Welfare Law
JT	Journal des Tribunaux
Legros Mélanges	Elst, ed, *Mélanges offerts a Robert Legros*, 1985
LIEI	Legal Issues of European Integration
LQR	Law Quarterly Review
MJ	Maastricht Journal of European and Comparative Law
MJIL	Michigan Journal of International Law
MLR	Modern Law Review
NCJM Bulletin	Nederlands Tijdshrift voor de Mensenrechten
Neth QHR	Netherlands Quarterly of Human Rights
NILR	Netherlands International Law Review

NJW	Neue Juristische Wochenschrift
NLJ	New Law Journal
NYULR	New York University Law Review
OHLJ	Osgoode Hall Law Journal
Parl Ass	Parliamentary Assembly
PL	Public Law
RBDI	Revue Belge de droit international
RC	Hague recueil: Recueil des cours de l'academie de droit international
RDIDC	Revue de droit international et comparé
RDP	Revue de droit public
Rev ICJ	Review of the International Commission of Jurists
RGDIP	Revue général de droit international public
RSCDPC	Revue de science criminelle et de droit penal compare
RTDE	Revue trimestrielle de droit international
RTDH	Revue trimestrielle des droits de l'homme
RUDH	Revue universelle des droits de l'homme
SDHRC	Selected Decisions of the Human Rights Committee
SLT	Scots Law Times
Stavros	*The Guarantees for the Accused Person under Article 6 of the European Convention on Human Rights*, 1993
TLQ	Temple Law Quarterly
TP	Collected Edition of the Travaux Préparatoires of the European Convention on Human Rights, 8 vols, 1975-1985.
UKTS	United Kingdom Treaty Series
UNTS	United Nations Treaty Series
Van Dijk and Van Hoof	*Theory and Practice of the European Convention on Human Rights*, 2nd edn, 1990
Van Panhuys	Kuyper and Lammers, *Essays on the Development of the International Legal Order: In Memory of Haro F Van Panhuys*, 1980
Velu and Ergec,	*La Convention européenne des droits de l'homme*, 1990
VJIL	Virginia Journal of International Law
Wiarda Mélanges	Matscher and Petzold, eds, *Protecting Human Rights: the European Dimension*, 1988
YB	Yearbook of the European Convention on Human Rights (see note on Citations, p xvi)
YBILC	Yearbook of the International Law Commission
YEL	Yearbook of European Law
YJIL	Yale Journal of International Law

Table of statutes

Table of European legislation and international/UN conventions

List of
European Court of Human Rights cases

This list contains references to all Series A and Series B reports in the European Court of Human Rights Reports

Alphabetical list of
European Commission of Human Rights cases

Numerical list of
European Commission of Human Rights cases

List of other cases

CHAPTER 1

The European Convention on Human Rights in context

1. BACKGROUND

The European Convention on Human Rights[1] was adopted in 1950. It was drafted within the Council of Europe, an international organisation that was formed after the Second World War in the course of the first post-war attempt to unify Europe. The Convention institutions are based in Strasbourg, where the Council has its headquarters. The reason for the Convention was partly the need to elaborate upon the obligations of Council membership.[2] The importance of the Convention's role in giving meaning to these obligations has been highlighted in recent years by the fact that acceptance of the Convention, and of the right of individual petition and the jurisdiction of the European Court of Human Rights, is now a political obligation of membership of the Council.

More generally, the Convention was a response to current and past events in Europe. It stemmed from the wish to provide a bulwark against communism, which had spread into states in Central and Eastern Europe after the Second World War. The Convention provided both a symbolic statement of

---

1 87 UNTS 103; ETS 5; UKTS 38 (1965), Cmnd 2643. See generally Beddard, *Human Rights and Europe*, 3rd edn, 1993; Berger, *Case Law of the European Court of Human Rights*, Vols 1-3, 1992-1995; Cohen-Jonathan, *La Convention européenne des droits de l'homme*, 1989; Fawcett, *The Application of the European Convention on Human Rights*, 2nd edn, 1987 (hereafter Fawcett); Frowein, in Clapham and Emmert, eds, *Collected Courses of the Academy of European Law*, Vol 1, Bk 2, 1992, pp 267–358; Frowein and Peukert, *Europäische Menschenrechts Konvention: EMRK-kommentar*, 1985; Higgins, in Meron, ed, *Human Rights in International Law*, 1984, ch 13; Jacobs, *The European Convention on Human Rights*, 1975 (hereafter Jacobs); Janis and Kay, *European Human Rights Law*, 1990; Kempees, *Systematic Guide to the Case-law of the European Court of Human Rights*, 1995; Macdonald, Matscher and Petzold, eds, *The European System for the Protection of Human Rights*, 1993 (hereafter *European System*); Matscher and Petzold, eds, *Protecting Human Rights: The European Dimension*, 1988 (hereafter *Wiarda Mélanges*); Robertson and Merrills, *Human Rights in Europe*, 3rd edn, 1993; Van Dijk and Van Hoof, *Theory and Practice of the European Convention on Human Rights*, 2nd edn, 1990, English trans; Velu and Ergec, *La Convention européenne des droits de l'homme*, 1990 (hereafter Velu and Ergec); Villiger, *Handbuch der Europäischen Menschenrechtskonvention*, 1993. On the drafting of the Convention, see Teitgen, *European Supervision*, Ch 1, and Marston, 42 ICLQ 796 (1993).

2 Under Article 3, Statute of the Council of Europe 1949, 87 UNTS 103; ETS 1; UKTS 51 (1949), Cmnd 7778, a member state 'must accept the principles of the rule of law and of the enjoyment by all persons within its jurisdiction of human rights and fundamental freedoms'.

the principles for which Western European states stood and a remedy that might protect those states from communist subversion. It was also a reaction to the serious human rights violations that Europe had witnessed during the Second World War. It was believed that the Convention would serve as an alarm that would bring such large-scale violations of human rights to the attention of other Western European states in time for action to be taken to suppress them. In practice, this last function of the Convention has remained largely dormant, coming to life in just a small number of inter-state applications so far.[3] The Convention has instead been used primarily to raise questions of isolated violations of human rights in legal systems that basically conform to its requirements and are representative of the 'common heritage of political traditions, ideals, freedoms and the rule of law' to which the Convention Preamble refers. Increasingly, it has evolved into a European bill of rights, with the European Court of Human Rights having a role akin to that of a constitutional court in a federal legal system.

The Convention entered into force in 1953 and has now been ratified by 31 of the 36 member states of the Council of Europe.[4] The substantive guarantee in the Convention has been supplemented by the addition of further rights by the First,[5] Fourth,[6] Sixth[7] and Seventh[8] Protocols to the Convention that are binding upon those states that have ratified them. There have also been other Protocols that have amended the enforcement machinery[9] and provided the Court with a limited power to give advisory

3   See below, p 587.
4   The 36 members are Albania, Andorra, Austria, Belgium, Bulgaria, Cyprus, Czech Republic, Denmark, Estonia, Finland, France, Germany, Greece, Hungary, Iceland, Ireland, Italy, Latvia, Liechtenstein, Lithuania, Luxembourg, Malta, Moldova, Netherlands, Norway, Poland, Portugal, Romania, San Marino, Slovak Republic, Slovenia, Spain, Sweden, Switzerland, Turkey and the UK. Albania, Andorra, Estonia, Latvia and Moldova, members only as of 1993 or later, have yet to ratify the Convention.
5   213 UNTS 262; ETS 9; UKTS 46 (1954), Cmd 9221. Adopted 1952. In force 1954. Twenty-eight parties: all Convention parties except Liechtenstein, Lithuania and Switzerland.
6   ETS 46; Misc 6 (1964), Cmnd 2309. Adopted 1963. In force 1968. Twenty-three states are parties: Austria, Belgium, Cyprus, Czech Republic, Denmark, Finland, France, Germany, Hungary, Iceland, Ireland, Italy, Lithuania, Luxembourg, Netherlands, Norway, Poland, Portugal, Romania, San Marino, Slovakia, Slovenia and Sweden.
7   ETS 114. Adopted 1983. In force 1985. Twenty-three states are parties: Austria, Czech Republic, Denmark, Finland, France, Germany, Hungary, Iceland, Ireland, Italy, Liechtenstein, Luxembourg, Malta, Netherlands, Norway, Portugal, Romania, San Marino, Slovakia, Slovenia, Spain, Sweden and Switzerland.
8   ETS 117. Adopted 1984. In force 1988. Eighteen states are parties: Austria, Czech Republic, Denmark, Finland, France, Greece, Hungary, Iceland, Italy, Lithuania, Luxembourg, Norway, Romania, San Marino, Slovakia, Slovenia, Sweden and Switzerland.
9   Third Protocol 1963, ETS 45, UKTS 106 (1970), Cmnd 4552; Fifth Protocol 1966, ETS 55, UKTS 48 (1972), Cmnd 4963; Eighth Protocol 1985, ETS 118, UKTS 51 (1990), Cm 1136; Ninth Protocol 1990, ETS 140; and the Tenth Protocol 1992, ETS 146. The first three of these entered into force for all Convention parties in 1970, 1971 and 1990 respectively. The Ninth Protocol, which allows individuals to refer a case to the Court, is optional. In force in 1994. Eighteen parties: Austria, Cyprus, Czech Republic, Finland, Germany, Hungary, Ireland, Italy, Luxembourg, Netherlands, Norway, Poland, Romania, San Marino, Slovakia, Slovenia, Sweden and Switzerland. The Tenth Protocol, which amends the Committee of Ministers voting rule, requires ratification by all of the parties to the Convention to enter into force (21 ratifications so far).

opinions.[10] However, the Protocols referred to in the last sentence (but not those adding to the substantive guarantee) will all be replaced when the 1994 Eleventh Protocol,[11] which provides for a fundamental reform of the enforcement machinery of the Convention, enters into force. The Convention is a part of a network of international human rights treaties of universal or regional application. It is the regional counterpart to the International Covenant on Civil and Political Rights 1966 (ICCPR),[12] to which most Convention parties are also parties.[13] At the regional level, it has a common field of application with the American Convention on Human Rights 1969[14] and the African Charter on Human and Peoples' Rights 1981.[15] Like all of these treaties, the Convention protects rights first spelt out in the Universal Declaration of Human Rights 1948.[16]

2. THE SUBSTANTIVE GUARANTEE

The human rights in the Universal Declaration are commonly divided into civil and political rights, on the one hand, and economic, social and cultural rights, on the other. Civil and political rights are those that derive from the natural rights philosophy of the late eighteenth century in Europe. Economic, social and cultural rights[17] appeared with the emergence of socialist governments in the early twentieth century. The European Convention protects predominantly civil and political rights.[18] This was a matter of priorities and tactics. While it was not disputed that economic, social and cultural rights required protection too, the immediate need was for

10 Second Protocol 1963, ETS 44; UKTS 104 (1970), Cmnd 4551. In force 1970. Ratified by all Convention parties.
11 ETS 155. Requires ratification by all parties (12 so far). For an outline of the Protocol, see below, Ch 26.
12 999 UNTS 171; UKTS 6 (1977), Cmnd 6702. See McGoldrick, *The Human Rights Committee: its Role in the Development of the International Covenant on Civil and Political Rights*, 1991, and Nowak, *UN Covenant on Civil and Political Rights: CCPR Commentary*, 1993, English translation. The Convention differs from the ICCPR, however, by virtue of its emerging role as a European constitutional bill of rights.
13 All except Greece, Liechtenstein and Turkey. The ICCPR provides for an optional right of individual communication. All of the parties to the Convention that are parties to the Covenant have accepted the ICCPR right of communication except for Switzerland and the UK. As to the interrelationship between the Covenant and Convention rights of petition, see below, pp 626-627.
14 1144 UNTS 123. In force 1978. Twenty-five parties.
15 21 ILM 59 (1981). In force 1986. Forty-six parties.
16 GA Res 217A (III), GAOR, 3rd Sess, Part 1, Resns, p 71.
17 Examples of each are the rights to work, health and education respectively.
18 The Convention strays into the field of economic, social and cultural rights with its guarantees of the rights to property and education (Articles 1 and 2, First Protocol). There are also certain overlaps between the two categories in the case of freedom from forced labour (Article 4, Convention), the right to respect to family life (Article 8, Convention) and freedom of association (Article 11). In *Airey v Ireland* A 32 para 26 (1979) the Court stated that there is no 'watertight division' separating Convention rights from economic and social rights.

a short, non-controversial text which governments could accept at once, while the tide for human rights was strong. Given the values dominant within Western Europe, this meant limiting the Convention for the most part to the civil and political rights that were 'essential for a democratic way of life';[19] economic, social and cultural rights were too problematic and were left for separate and later treatment.[20] The Convention protects most civil and political rights, but not all. Most significantly, it does not guarantee the right of persons in detention to be treated with 'humanity' and 'dignity',[1] the rights of members of minority groups[2] and the right to equality before the law generally.[3] In addition, it does not guarantee freedom from racist or other propaganda or the right to recognition as a person before the law. All of the above rights are protected by the ICCPR,[4] which contains fuller guarantees of the rights to a fair trial,[5] family and children's rights and the right to participate in public life as well. The ICCPR also prohibits derogation from its obligations in time of war or public emergency in the case of more rights than does the European Convention.[6] In addition, some Convention guarantees are found only in optional protocols which not all parties have accepted. However, the generally worded guarantees in the Convention text

19 M Teitgen, CE Consult. Ass., Debates, 1st Session, p 408. 19 August 1949.
20 Economic and social rights are now protected by the 1961 European Social Charter. 529 UNTS 89; ETS 35; UKTS 38 (1965), Cmnd 2643. See Harris, *The European Social Charter*, 1984. The Charter has 20 parties. The missing Council members are the nine new members from Central and Eastern Europe and Liechtenstein, San Marino and Switzerland.
1   This is the terminology of Article 10, ICCPR. Article 3, Convention covers only the more extreme cases. A proposal for a Convention protocol on the rights of persons in detention is under consideration at Strasbourg.
2   The non-discrimination guarantee in Article 14 of the Convention applies only to some extent: see next note. A Convention protocol on the cultural rights of minorities and others is under consideration at Strasbourg. See also the Council of Europe Framework Convention for the Protection of National Minorities, ETS 157; 2 IHRR 217 (1995). Not in force. Twelve parties required (one so far). And see the European Charter for Regional or Minority Languages 1992, ETS 148. Not in force. Five parties required (one so far). In contrast with the ICCPR, Article 1, the Framework Convention does not guarantee the right to self-determination.
3   Contrast Article 26, ICCPR. Article 14, Convention prohibits discrimination between individuals on various grounds but only in areas of conduct covered by the rights protected in the Convention. For example, it prohibits discrimination in respect of freedom of religion (protected by Article 9) but not the right to housing. See also the guarantee of equality between spouses in Article 5, Seventh Protocol to the Convention. A proposal for a Convention protocol on the right to sexual equality is under consideration at Strasbourg. European Union law prohibits discrimination on grounds of sex and nationality in employment: see Lester and Joseph, in Harris and Joseph, eds, *The International Covenant on Civil and Political Rights and UK Law*, 1995, Ch 17.
4   The American Convention on Human Rights also contains a more extensive guarantee than the Convention. See Frowein, 1 HRLJ 44 (1980).
5   Some 'fair trial' omissions in Article 6, Convention are made good by the Seventh Protocol for the parties to it. Even with that Protocol, the Convention contains a less extensive 'fair trial' guarantee for juveniles and right to appeal in criminal cases.
6   See Article 4, ICCPR. Most significantly, derogation is not permitted from the guarantees of the right to freedom of thought, conscience and religion. These Article 4 prohibitions may, however, apply under the Convention by virtue of Article 15(1): see below, p 502.

can be interpreted purposively so as to remedy some, at least, of these defects.[7]

3. THE STRASBOURG ENFORCEMENT MACHINERY

Compared to most other international human rights treaties, the Convention has very strong enforcement mechanisms. It provides for both state and individual applications.[8] Under Article 24, any party may bring an application alleging a breach by another party simply on the basis that each has ratified the Convention. In addition, and considerably more important in practice, under Article 25 a party may make a declaration accepting the right of an individual, regardless of nationality, who claims to be a victim of a breach of the Convention to bring an application against it. Both state and individual applications go to the European Commission of Human Rights, which is a body of independent experts. The Commission decides whether the application should be admitted for consideration on the merits. If it is admitted, the Commission examines the facts and the legal arguments and, if a friendly settlement is not possible, adopts a report indicating its findings of fact and its opinion as to whether the defendant state has infringed the Convention. Following the adoption of the report, which is not legally binding, the case may be referred by the Commission or a party with a recognised interest in it to the European Court of Human Rights.[9] If it is not so referred, the case will be decided by the Committee of Ministers of the Council of Europe, which is composed of government representatives of all of the member states. In either case, the outcome is a decision that is binding in international law.

4. THE INTERPRETATION OF THE CONVENTION[10]

i. The general approach

As a treaty, the Convention must be interpreted according to the international law rules on the interpretation of treaties. These are to be found in

7 Eg, freedom from self-incrimination (in Article 14(3)(g), ICCPR) has been read into the 'fair hearing' guarantee in Article 6 (*Funke v France* A 256-A (1993)) and the precise threshold of ill-treatment contrary to Article 3 is a matter of judgment.

8 There is also provision for occasional reports by states on their compliance with the Convention (see Article 57), but the procedure has seldom been used. Reports have been called for on five occasions, most recently in 1988. See Mahoney, *Wiarda Mélanges*, p 370. See also the Committee of Ministers 1994 Declaration on Compliance with Commitments Accepted by Member States of Council of Europe, 2 IHRR 250 (1995), which provides for action to be taken, including the collection of information and the making of recommendations, on human rights compliance.

9 This court, which administers the European Convention at Strasbourg and operates within the framework of the Council of Europe is distinct from the European Court of Justice, which is the court of the European Union and is based in Luxembourg.

10 See Bernhardt, *Wiarda Mélanges*, p 65; Duffy, 4 HRR 98 at 111-8 (1979); Golsong, *European System*, Ch 8; Matscher, id, Ch 5; Van der Meersch, *Legros Mélanges*, 1985, p 207.

the Vienna Convention on the Law of Treaties 1969.[11] The basic rule is that a treaty 'shall be interpreted in good faith in accordance with the ordinary meaning to be given to the terms of the treaty in their context and in the light of its object and purpose'.[12] A good example of the use of this rule is the case of *Luedicke, Belkacem and Koç v FRG*.[13] There the Court adopted the 'ordinary meaning' of the words 'gratuitement' and 'free' in the two authentic language texts[14] of Article 6(3)(e), which it found 'not contradicted by the context of the sub-paragraph' and 'confirmed by the object and purpose of Article 6'.

ii.   Emphasis upon the object and purpose of the Convention

In accordance with the Vienna Convention, considerable emphasis has been placed in the interpretation of the Convention upon a teleological approach, ie one that seeks to realise its 'object and purpose'. This has been identified in general terms as 'the protection of individual human rights'[15] and the maintenance and promotion of 'the ideals and values of a democratic society'.[16] As to the latter, it has been recognised that 'democracy' supposes 'pluralism, tolerance and broadmindedness'.[17] The primary importance of the 'object and purpose' of the Convention was strikingly illustrated in *Golder v UK*.[18] There the Court read the right of access to a court into the fair trial guarantee in Article 6. It did so, in the absence of clear wording in the text to the contrary, mainly by reference to guidance as to the 'object and purpose' of the Convention to be found in its Preamble.[19] This indicated, *inter alia*, that the drafting states were resolved to 'take the first steps for the collective enforcement of certain of the rights stated in the Universal Declaration' in furtherance of the rule of law. As the Court stated, one could

11 1155 UNTS 331, UKTS 58 (1980), Cmnd 7964. See Articles 31–33. The rules of interpretation in the Vienna Convention are accepted as indicating rules of customary international law binding upon all states, whether parties to the Vienna Convention or not. The Vienna Convention is followed in the interpretation of the Convention: see *Golder v UK* A 18 para 29 (1975) and *Johnston v Ireland* A 112 para 51 (1986).
12 Article 31, Vienna Convention. The 'context' of a treaty includes its preamble and any agreement or instrument relating to and made in connection with it: Article 31(2). The subsequent practice of the parties to a treaty and any relevant rules of international law shall be taken into account 'together with the context': Article 31(3).
13 A 29 para 46 (1978).
14 Ie the English and French texts. Where, as was not the case in the *Luedicke* case, the two authentic texts of the Convention differ in their meaning, they must be interpreted in such a way as to 'reconcile them as far as possible': Article 33(4), Vienna Convention. If they cannot be reconciled, the 'object and purpose' becomes decisive: see *Wemhoff v FRG* A 7 p 23 (1968) and *Brogan v UK*, at p 134, below.
15 *Soering v UK* A 161 para 87 (1989). Cf the *Belgian Linguistics* case A 6 p 31 (1968).
16 *Kjeldsen, Busk Madsen and Pedersen v Denmark* A 23 para 53 (1976). Both of the considerations mentioned in the above sentence are confirmed by the Convention Preamble. The Preamble also identifies 'the achievement of greater unity between its Members' as the aim of the Council of Europe.
17 *Handyside v UK* A 24 para 49 (1976). Cf *Dudgeon v UK* A 45 para 53 (1981).
18 A 18 (1975).
19 The Court also referred to the emphasis upon the rule of law in the Statute of the Council of Europe (Preamble, Article 3).

not suppose compliance with the rule of law without the possibility of taking legal disputes to court.

The Court also confirmed in the *Golder* case its earlier pronouncement in *Wemhoff v FRG*[20] that '[g]iven that it is a law-making treaty, it is also necessary to seek the interpretation that is most appropriate in order to realise the aim and achieve the object of the treaty, and not that which would restrict to the greatest possible degree the obligations undertaken by the parties'. This approach was forcefully opposed by Judge Fitzmaurice in his separate opinion in the *Golder* case. Judge Fitzmaurice argued, *inter alia*, that the 'heavy inroads' made by the Convention into an area previously within a state's domestic jurisdiction, viz the treatment of its own nationals, demanded 'a cautious and conservative interpretation'. Such an argument, which emphasises the character of the Convention as a contract by which sovereign states agree to limitations upon their sovereignty, has now totally given way to an approach that focuses instead upon the Convention's law-making character and its role as a bill of rights that must be interpreted so as to permit its development with time.

It is in this last connection that statements to the effect that the Convention represents 'the public order of Europe'[1] are relevant. They signify that in the interpretation and application of the Convention the overriding consideration is not that the Convention creates 'reciprocal engagements between contracting states', but that it imposes 'objective obligations' upon them for the protection of human rights in Europe,[2] with the Convention evolving as Europe's constitutional bill of rights.[3]

iii. Dynamic or evolutive interpretation

It follows from the emphasis placed upon the 'object and purpose' of the Convention that it must be given a dynamic or evolutive interpretation.[4]

---

20 A 7 p 23 (1968). Cf *Delcourt v Belgium* A 11 para 25 (1970), concerning Article 6 in particular.
1 *Austria v Italy No 788/60*, 4 YB 112 at 140 (1961). Cf *Ireland v UK* A 25 para 239 (1978); *Soering v UK* A 161 (1989); *Chysostomos, Papachrysostomou and Loizidou v Turkey Nos 15299/89, 15300/89 and 15318/89*, 68 DR 216 at 242 (1991) (the Convention is a 'constitutional instrument of European public order in the field of human rights'); and *Loizidou v Turkey (Preliminary Objections)* A 310 para 93 (1995). See generally, Frowein, loc cit at note 1, above.
2 *Ireland v UK* A 25 para 239 (1978). The 'objective' character of the obligations manifested itself in *Austria v Italy*, previous note, in that Austria was permitted to question Italian conduct that occurred before Austria became a party to the Convention.
3 On the translation of the Convention from a purely international law instrument to a constitutional guarantee in a quasi-federal Europe, see Warbrick, 10 MJIL 698 (1989).
4 See Mosler, *Van Panhuys Essays*, p 149 and Sorensen, *Proceedings of the Fourth International Colloquy on the European Convention on Human Rights*, 1976, p 86. The term 'evolutive', rather than 'dynamic', is used in *Johnston v Ireland* A 112 para 53 (1986) and by a number of writers. On the interpretative and lawmaking role of the Commission and the Court generally, see Gearty, 52 CLJ 89 (1993); Mahoney, 11 HRLJ 57 (1990); Morrison, *The Dynamics of Development in the European Human Rights Convention System*, 1981, Ch 1; and Stavros, *The Guarantees for Accused Persons under Article 6 of the European Convention on Human Rights*, 1993, pp 340–350 (hereafter Stavros).

Thus, in *Tyrer v UK*,[5] the Court stated that the Convention is 'a living instrument which, as the Commission rightly stressed, must be interpreted in the light of present day conditions'. Accordingly, the Court could not 'but be influenced by the developments and commonly accepted standards in the penal policy of the member states of the Council of Europe' when considering whether judicial corporal punishment was consistent with Article 3. What was determinative, the Court stated, were the standards currently accepted in European society, not those prevalent when the Convention was adopted. In terms of the intentions of the drafting states, the emphasis is therefore upon their general rather than their particular intentions in 1950.[6] Other decisions that follow the *Tyrer* approach have reflected changed social attitudes towards children born out of wedlock[7] and homosexuals.[8] However, the Convention will not be interpreted to reflect change so as to introduce into it a right that was not intended to be included when the Convention was drafted. For this reason, Article 12, which guarantees the right to marry, could not be interpreted as including a right to divorce, even though such a right is now generally recognised in Europe.[9] In this way, a line is sought to be drawn between judicial interpretation, which is permissible, and judicial legislation, which is not. Mahoney[10] has suggested that, with this distinction in mind, the Court tends to emphasise incremental, rather than sudden change. The closed shop cases[11] are good examples of this gradualist approach. However, as in national law, the line between judicial interpretation and legislation can be a difficult one to draw, particularly in the case of generally worded provisions. Decisions can be seen either as instances of judicial creativity that move the Convention into distinct areas beyond its intended domain or as the elaboration of rights that are already protected. For example, the Court's finding of positive obligations for states in Article 8[12] and its application of Article 3 to cases of expulsion[13] can be seen as the discovery of obligations that were always implicit in the guarantees concerned or as the addition of new obligations for states.

When deciding a case by reference to the dynamic character of the Convention, the Court must make a judgment as to the point at which a new social standard has achieved sufficiently wide acceptance to affect the meaning of the Convention. In the course of doing so, the Court has

5   A 26 para 31 (1978).
6   Cf Mahoney, 11 HRLJ 57 at 70 (1990).
7   *Marckx v Belgium* A 31 (1979).
8   *Dudgeon v UK* A 45 (1981). See also *Soering v UK* A 161 (1989) (change in death penalty practice) and *Sigurjónsson v Iceland* A 264 (1993) (changes concerning the closed shop). The Convention enforcement machinery provisions are likewise to be interpreted dynamically: *Loizidou v Turkey (Preliminary Objections)* A 310 para 71 (1995).
9   *Johnston v Ireland* A 112 (1986). *Quaere* whether the sensitive nature of the divorce question in Ireland may have been another factor in the *Johnston* case.
10 11 HRLJ 57 at 60 (1990). Mahoney draws an analogy with the judicial activism and judicial restraint distinction found in commentary on the practice of the US Supreme Court.
11 See the *Young, James and Webster*, and *Sigurjónsson* cases, below, pp 627-628. Cf the gradual extension of Article 6(3) to pre-trial criminal proceedings: see below, pp 249-250.
12 See eg *Rees v UK* A 106 para 35 (1986).
13 See *Soering v UK* A 161 (1989).

generally been cautious, preferring to follow state practice rather than to precipitate new standards. For example, it has not yet been satisfied that there is a common new European standard concerning the rights of transsexuals; standards are still in transition with 'little common ground between the contracting states'.[14] But the Court does not necessarily wait until only the defendant state remains out of line before it recognises a new standard.[15] For example, in *Marckx v Belgium*[16] the Court applied a new approach to the status of children born out of wedlock that had been adopted in the law of the 'great majority', but certainly not all, of Council of Europe states.

iv. Reliance upon European national law standards

The question whether the Strasbourg authorities should be influenced by the law in European states in its interpretation of the Convention is relevant not only in contexts in which social standards are changing. The question may arise when the Court has to decide how rigorously to interpret the requirements of the Convention in other circumstances also. Here, too, any European consensus that exists has had a considerable impact upon the Strasbourg authorities' jurisprudence. For example, the Court's ringing pronouncements on the importance of freedom of speech and of the press in a democratic society[17] stem from a confident conviction as to values that generally underpin European society. Equally clearly, the easy incorporation into Article 1, First Protocol of a compensation requirement for the taking of the property of nationals followed from the 'legal systems of the contracting states'.[18] Former Judge Van der Meersch[19] has pointed to the paradox of taking standards in national law into account when interpreting an international treaty whose purpose is to control national law. The convincing justification that he provides is that there is a necessarily close relationship between the Convention standards and the European 'common law' by which they are inspired. Generally, the Court's reliance upon any European consensus is acceptable in that it is likely to be in accordance with recognised human rights standards, as in the case of the emphasis placed upon freedom of speech. Even so, the Court needs to be aware that government and individual interests do not always coincide and that a practice may not be acceptable in human rights terms simply because it is generally followed. What will be interesting to see is the effect that the

14 *Cossey v UK* A 184 para 40 (1990). Cf *Rees v UK* A 106 (1986) and, most recently, *B v France* A 232-C (1992).
15 A state that is entirely on its own is particularly at risk of an adverse judgment if its practice offends otherwise common European standards relevant to human rights: see, eg, the *Tyrer* case on judicial corporal punishment.
16 A 31 para 41 (1979). Cf *Dudgeon v UK* A 45 (1981).
17 See *Lingens v Austria* A 103 para 41 (1986).
18 *James v UK* A 98 para 54 (1986).
19 1 HRLJ 13 at 15 (1980). As Stavros, p 346, notes, another policy reason is that an interpretation that deviated substantially from general European practice would undermine state confidence in the Convention and threaten its continued success or even existence.

extension of the Convention's remit into Central and Eastern Europe will have upon the assessment of European standards.

In the absence of a European consensus, the Court has tended to reflect national law by applying a lowest common denominator approach or to accommodate variations in state practice through the margin of appreciation doctrine[20] when deciding upon the meaning of a Convention guarantee. The result is that a state's law or conduct may well escape condemnation if it reflects a practice followed in a number of European states or where practice is widely varied. For example, the fact that members of a linguistic minority may not be able to vote for election candidates whose language is theirs[1] or that civil servants may sit as expert members of a tribunal[2] does not present problems for the rights to free elections (Article 3, First Protocol) and an independent and impartial tribunal (Article 6) respectively, given that such situations are common in European states. Widespread differences in practice in respect of abortion may lead to a similar result.[3] Other examples can be found in connection with the right to a fair trial, where there is much diversity of practice resulting, most clearly, from the differences between civil and common law systems of criminal justice. Thus, when interpreting the Article 6(1) requirement that judgments be 'pronounced in public', the Court has taken account of the fact that courts of cassation in civil law jurisdictions commonly do not deliver their judgments in public.[4] Similarly, the Court has been influenced in its approach to the 'trial within a reasonable time' guarantee in Article 6(1) by the characteristics of civil law criminal justice systems.[5]

It is encouraging, however, that, faced with a diversity of practice, the Court has sometimes acted positively in the interests of protecting human rights. This is the case, for example, in the Court's application of Article 6(1) to administrative justice and its strict reading of the requirement of an impartial tribunal that is found in the same provision.[6] It has also become more prepared to condemn delays in judicial proceedings that stem not from structural considerations but simple inefficiency.[7] More controversial perhaps is the balance that the Court has struck between the rights of parents and their children. The policy of some states of permitting their child care authorities to intervene to protect children at the expense of parental rights more than most European states do so has led to findings of

---

20 As to this doctrine, see below, p 12.
1   *Mathieu-Mohin and Clerfayt v Belgium* A 113 para 57 (1987) ('a good many states').
2   *Ettl v Austria* A 117 para 40 (1987) ('domestic legislation . . . of member states affords many examples').
3   See *H v Norway*, discussed below, p 42.
4   See below, p 221.
5   See below, p 228. Cf the 'four day' rule in the Commission's jurisprudence under Article 5(3), which reflects a diversity of practice in European states: see below, p 136. Note also the absence of any need for jury trial, which is not found generally across Europe. For other examples of differing practice concerning the law of evidence and trial in absentia, resulting in a low common denominator, see Stavros, pp 238 and 265–266.
6   See below, pp 192 and 235.
7   But it is still not as strict as it might be: see below, p 230.

breaches of the Convention in several cases.[8] Finally, it is interesting to consider the evidence that the Court has available to it when it acts by reference to the standards in European national law. In practice, the Court does not have the time or resources to undertake or commission comparative studies of relevant areas of law. Instead, it relies upon the collective knowledge of its members and its registry and upon the *amicus curiae* briefs of non-governmental organisations and others.[9] The contribution of judges is obviously valuable but is curtailed by the Court's practice of hearing cases in chambers and the fact that judges are unlikely to claim expertise in all areas of their national law.[10]

v. The principle of proportionality[11]

The principle of proportionality is a recurring theme in the interpretation of the Convention. As the Court stated in *Soering v UK*,[12] 'inherent in the whole of the Convention is a search for a fair balance between the demands of the general interest of the community and the requirements of the protection of the individual's fundamental rights'. The achievement of such a balance necessarily requires an approach based, *inter alia*, upon considerations of proportionality. Reliance on the principle of proportionality is most evident in areas in which the Convention expressly allows restrictions upon a right. Thus, under the second paragraphs of Articles 8–11, a state may restrict the protected right to the extent that this is 'necessary in a democratic society' for certain listed public interest purposes. This formula has been interpreted as meaning that the restriction must be 'proportionate to the legitimate aim pursued'.[13] Similarly, proportionality has been invoked when setting the limits to an implied restriction that has been read into a Convention guarantee.[14] The principle has also been introduced into the non-

---

8 These have mostly concerned Sweden: see eg *Andersson (M&R) v Sweden* A 226-A (1992).
9 As to third party interventions, see below, p 668.
10 For doubts as to whether the Court makes a thorough investigation of the law of European states when relying on common standards, see eg the dissenting opinion of Judge Matscher in *Öztürk v FRG* A 73 (1984) and, among writers, Bernhardt, *European System*, p 35; Helfer, 26 Corn ILJ 133 at 138–140 (1989); and Mahoney, 11 HRLJ 57 at 79 (1990).
11 See Eissen, *European System*, Ch 7.
12 A 161 para 89 (1989). Cf *Belgian Linguistic* case A 6 p 31 (1968); *Sporrong and Lönnroth v Sweden* A 52 para 69 (1982); and *Fayed v UK* A 294-B (1994).
13 *Handyside v UK* A 24 para 49 (1976). Cf the approach to restrictions upon the right to property in Article 1, First Protocol: *James v UK* A 98 para 50 (1986). The doctrine has also been applied to restrictions permitted by Article 5 (see *Winterwerp v Netherlands* A 33 para 39 (1979)) and Article 12 (see *F v Switzerland* A 128 (1987)). See also the 'absolutely necessary' test in Article 2(2), where the test is one of 'strict proportionality'. As to this test and the principle's possible use in connection with the death penalty under Article 2, see below, pp 47 and 46.
14 *Mathieu-Mohin and Clerfayt v Belgium* A 113 para 52 (1987) and *Fayed v UK* A 294-B para 71 (1994). In the former case the Court also stated that a restriction must not impair the 'essence' of the right: ibid. Cf *Ashingdane v UK* A 93 para 57 (1985) (Article 6(1)). The Court not uncommonly uses this last idea when vetting a restriction under any of the headings discussed above, whether as an element of 'proportionality' or as a separate requirement.

discrimination rule in Article 14, so that for its prohibition of discrimination to be infringed there must be 'no reasonable relationship of proportionality between the means employed and the aim sought to be pursued'.[15] In addition, the principle is relied upon when interpreting the requirement in Article 15 that measures taken in a public emergency in derogation of Convention rights must be 'strictly required by the exigencies of the situation'.[16] Finally, proportionality is important when interpreting the positive obligations that parties have under Article 8 of the Convention.[17]

vi. The doctrine of a margin of appreciation[18]

A doctrine that plays a crucial role in the interpretation of the Convention is that of the margin of appreciation. In general terms, it means that the state is allowed a certain measure of discretion, subject to European supervision, when it takes legislative, administrative or judicial action in the area of a Convention right. The doctrine was first explained by the Court in *Handyside v UK*.[19] This was a case concerning a restriction upon a right within the Articles 8–11 group of rights. In the *Handyside* case, the Court had to consider whether a conviction for possessing an obscene article could be justified under Article 10(2) as a limitation upon freedom of expression that was necessary for the 'protection of morals'. The Court stated:

> 'By reason of their direct and continuous contact with the vital forces of their countries, state authorities are in principle in a better position than the international judge to give an opinion on the exact content of those requirements [of morals] as well as on the "necessity" of a "restriction" or "penalty" intended to meet them . . .
>
> Nevertheless, Article 10(2) does not give the contracting states an unlimited power of appreciation. The Court, which, with the Commission, is responsible for ensuring the observance of those states' engagements, is empowered to give the final ruling on whether a

15 *Belgian Linguistic* case A 6 p 34 (1968). Cf the recourse to proportionality when interpreting the term 'forced labour' in Article 4: *Van der Mussele v Belgium* A 70 para 37 (1983).

16 See *Lawless v Ireland* (Merits) A 3 (1961) and *Ireland v UK* A 25 (1978). Although the term proportionality is not mentioned in these judgments, the principle is applied in fact.

17 *Rees v UK* A 106 para 37 (1986). The Court here uses the 'balancing' formula which it later used more generally, and less convincingly, in the *Soering* case in the context of Article 3: see above, p 11.

18 See Higgins, 49 BYIL 281 at 296–315 (1976–77); Macdonald, *Ago Essays*, p 187; id, in *European System*, Ch 6; Mahoney, 11 HRLJ 57 at 78–85 (1990); Merrills, *The Development of International Law by the European Court of Human Rights*, 2nd edn, 1993, Ch 7; Morrison, 6 HRJ 263 (1970); O'Donnell, 4 HRQ 474 (1982); Van der Meersch in *Wiarda Mélanges*, p 201; and Youron, 3 Conn JIL 111 (1987).

19 A 24 paras 48–49 (1976). It had in effect been relied upon by the Court earlier, following the Commission, in *Lawless v Ireland* (Merits) A 3 para 28 (1961), in the context of Article 15. On the use of the doctrine in Articles 8–11, see further below, Ch 8.

"restriction" or "penalty" is reconcilable with freedom of expression as protected by Article 10. The domestic margin of appreciation thus goes hand in hand with a European supervision.'

The doctrine has since been applied in the above sense to a number of other Convention articles. As with Article 10, it has been relied upon when determining whether an interference with other rights in the Articles 8–11 group of rights is justifiable on any of the public interest grounds permitted by paragraph (2) of the Article concerned.[20] The doctrine is also used extensively when assessing whether a state has done enough to comply with any positive obligations that it has under these[1] and other Articles[2] and when determining whether a state's interference with the right to property protected by Article 1, First Protocol is justified in the public interest.[3] A margin of appreciation is also allowed in the application of other guarantees where an element of judgment by the national authorities is involved, such as Article 5[4] and 14.[5] It has been instrumental as well in the application of Article 15 when deciding whether there is a 'public emergency' and, if so, whether the measures taken in response to it are 'strictly required by the exigencies of the situation'.[6] As will be apparent, these Articles largely coincide with those to which the principle of proportionality spelt out in the *Handyside* case applies, the point being that in assessing the proportionality of the state's acts, a certain degree of deference is given to the judgment of national authorities when they weigh competing public and individual interests in view of their special knowledge and overall responsibility under domestic law. Finally, it should be noted that national courts are allowed considerable discretion, either under an implied doctrine of a margin of appreciation or under the fourth instance doctrine (see below), in the conduct of trials in respect of such matters as the admissibility or evaluation of evidence. Thus the Court has stated that Article 6(3)(d) generally 'leaves it to the competent authorities to decide upon the relevance of proposed

20 Most of the cases have concerned Articles 8 and 10. See below, Ch 8.
1 See eg *Abdulaziz, Cabales and Balkandali v UK* A 94 para 67 (1985) and *Keegan v Ireland* A 290 para 49 (1994).
2 See eg *Mathieu-Mohin and Clerfayt v Belgium* A 113 paras 52, 54 (1987) (free elections: Article 3, First Protocol). See also *H v Norway* No 17004/90 (1992) unreported, in which a margin of appreciation was allowed in respect of the positive obligation to protect life by law in the context of abortion. Cf the *National Union of Belgium Police* case A 19 (1975), where an Article 11 obligation in respect of trade union rights was interpreted as leaving such a wide discretion to states as to amount almost of an obligation of result, rather than of conduct.
3 See eg *James v UK* A 98 (1986).
4 See *Winterwerp v Netherlands* A 33 (1979)(person of unsound mind); *Weeks v UK* A 114 (1987)(release on parole); *Brogan v UK* A 145-B (1988) (terrorist suspects). As to a margin of appreciation in connection with the 'absolutely necessary' test in Article 2 and its possible application in the *Kröcher and Möller* case under Article 3, see below, pp 53 and 70 respectively.
5 *Belgian Linguistic* case A 6 p 35 (1968) and *Rasmussen v Denmark* A 87 para 40 (1984).
6 *Ireland v UK* A 25 (1978). See also the judgment in the *Lawless* case, above, p 12, n 16, and the speech by Sir Humphrey Waldock) for the Commission at the Court hearing in that case.

evidence'[7] and that 'it is for the national courts to assess the evidence before them'.[8] An interference with a right that has been ordered or approved by the objective decision of a national court following a full examination of the facts will also benefit from a margin of appreciation in its favour.[9]

The doctrine of the margin of appreciation is applied differentially, with the degree of discretion being allowed to the state varying according to the context. A state is allowed a considerable discretion in cases of public emergency arising under Article 15, in some national security cases[10] and in the protection of public morals[11] and generally when 'there is little common ground' between the contracting parties.[12] At the other extreme, the margin of appreciation is reduced almost to vanishing point in certain areas, as where the justification for a restriction is the protection of the authority of the judiciary.[13]

The doctrine of the margin of appreciation reflects the subsidiary role of the Convention in protecting human rights.[14] The overall scheme of the Convention is that the initial and primary responsibility for the protection of human rights lies with the contracting parties.[15] The Strasbourg authorities are there to monitor their action, exercising a power of review comparable to that of a federal constitutional court over conduct by democratically elected governments or legislatures within the federation.[16] The margin of appreciation doctrine serves as a mechanism by which a tight or slack rein is kept on state conduct, depending upon the context. The doctrine is none the less a controversial one. When it is applied widely, so as to appear to give a state a blank cheque or to tolerate questionable national practices or decisions,[17] it may be argued that the Convention authorities have abdicated their responsibilities. However, the doctrine has its counterpart in the context of judicial review in national systems of administrative law and serves as a lubricant at the interface between

7 *Engel v Netherlands* A 22 para 91 (1976).
8 *Isgrò v Italy* A 194-A para 31 (1991). Also under Article 6, a state is allowed a margin of appreciation in deciding whether an accused must be legally represented: *Croissant v Germany* A 237-B para 27 (1992)
9 See eg *Handyside v UK* A 24 (1976).
10 See eg *Leander v Sweden* A 116 para 67 (1987).
11 See eg the *Handyside* case, n 9 above.
12 *Rees v UK* A 106 para 37 (1986) (transsexuals) and *Rasmussen v Denmark* A 87 para 40 (1984) (fathers' rights).
13 *Sunday Times v UK* A 30 (1979). The Court may have been influenced to some extent in this case by the fact that there was disagreement within the relevant UK institutions as to the need for the restriction.
14 See Matscher, *European System*, Ch 5 at p 76. On the principle of 'subsidiarity' in the context of the Convention generally, see Petzold, *European System*, Ch 4.
15 *Belgian Linguistic* case A 6 p 34 (1968) and *Handyside v UK* A 24 para 48 (1976). Thus Article 1 requires the contracting parties to 'secure' the rights in the Convention. See also Articles 13 and 60, Convention.
16 Similarities can be found in this regard between the jurisprudence of the European Court and the US Supreme Court: see eg Mahoney, 11 HRLJ 57 at 65 (1990).
17 See, eg, *Barfod v Denmark* A 149 paras 28–36 (1989).

individual rights and public interest.[18] It may also be essential to retain state confidence in the operation of the system. In its absence, Strasbourg might well be seen as imposing solutions from outside without paying proper regard to the expertise and responsibilities of local decision-makers. The difficulty with the doctrine lies not so much in allowing it as in deciding precisely when and how widely to apply it on the facts of particular cases.

vii. The fourth instance (quatrième instance) doctrine

From the outset, the Strasbourg authorities have made it clear that they do not constitute a further court of appeal, ie a fourth instance, from the decisions of national courts applying national law. An application that merely claims that a national court has made an error of fact or law will be declared inadmissible *ratione materiae*.[19] In addition, where an application alleges that national law violates the Convention, the Strasbourg authorities will not normally question the interpretation of that law by the national courts.[20] However, where it is a part of a Convention requirement that national law be complied with (eg an arrest must be 'lawful': Article 5(1)), the Strasbourg authorities do claim a power to review the observance of national law by the national authorities. Even so, they are most unlikely to disagree with any decision by a national court upon the matter.[1]

viii. Effective interpretation

A recognised consideration in the interpretation of the Convention, which assists in realising its 'object and purpose', is the need to ensure the effective protection of the rights guaranteed. In *Artico v Italy*,[2] the Court stated that 'the Convention is intended to guarantee not rights that are theoretical or illusory but rights that are practical and effective'. There the Court found a breach of the right to legal aid in Article 6(3)(c) because the legal aid lawyer appointed by the state proved totally ineffective. The Court has relied upon the principle of effectiveness in other cases also when interpreting positive obligations.[3] In other contexts, the Court has emphasised the need to ensure the effectiveness of the Convention when interpreting the term 'victim' in Article 25[4] and when giving the Convention extra-territorial reach under Article 3.[5]

---

18 Note, however, that the doctrine has played little part in the application of the ICCPR. The only case in which it has been expressly referred to is *Hertzenberg v Finland* 1 SDHRC 124 (1982).
19 See eg *X v FRG No 254/57*, 1 YB 150 at 152 (1957).
20 *X and Y v Netherlands* A 91 para 29 (1985).
1 *Winterwerp v Netherlands* A 33 para 46 (1979).
2 A 37 para 33 (1980). Cf *Airey v Ireland* A 32 (1979).
3 *Klass v FRG* A 28 para 34 (1978).
4 *Marckx v Belgium* A 31 (1979).
5 *Soering v UK* A 161 para 86 (1989).

ix. Limits resulting from the clear meaning of the text

Although the Strasbourg authorities rely heavily upon the 'object and purpose' of the Convention, they have occasionally found that their freedom to do so is limited by the clear meaning of the text. Thus in *Wemhoff v FRG,*[6] it was held that Article 5(3) does not apply to appeal proceedings because of the wording of Article 5(1)(a). Remarkably, in *Pretto v Italy,*[7] the Court went against the clear wording of the Convention text in order to achieve a *restrictive* result. There it held that the unqualified requirement in Article 6(1) that judgments be 'pronounced publicly' (*rendu publiquement*) does not apply to a court of cassation. The Court considered that it must have been the intention of the drafting states (although there was no clear evidence in the *travaux préparatoires*)[8] to respect the 'long-standing tradition' in many Council of Europe states to this effect. For this reason, the Court did not 'feel bound to adopt a literal interpretation' and preferred a more flexible approach that it felt was not inconsistent with the basic 'object and purpose' of Article 6.

In *Soering v UK,*[9] the Court raised the possibility of informal amendment of the text of the Convention. Faced with wording in Article 2 which expressly permits capital punishment, the Court stated that '(s)ubsequent practice in national penal policy, in the form of a generalised abolition of capital punishment, could be taken as establishing the agreement of the contracting states to abrogate the exception provided for under Article 2(1)'. In fact, it found that this had not happened as the Convention parties had recently seen the need to adopt the Sixth Protocol, which abolishes the death penalty for those parties that accept it.[10]

x. The autonomous meaning of Convention terms[11]

As with any treaty, the terms in the Convention have their 'ordinary meaning'.[12] Accordingly, words such as 'degrading' (Article 3) have been understood in their dictionary sense.[13] Legal terms that might be considered as referring back to the meaning that they have in the national law of the

---

6   A 7 (1968).
7   A 71 para 26 (1983). See further, below, p 222.
8   The Court's approach may have been influenced by the fact that the text of Article 6 was probably drafted with only trial court proceedings in mind.
9   A 161 para 103 (1989). See also *Cruz Varas v Sweden* A 201 para 100 (1991).
10   This illustrates the risk that an optional protocol to the Convention may foreclose a broad interpretation of the original Convention, which is binding upon all parties. See, however, *Ekbatani v Sweden* A 134 para 26 (1988) in which the Court stated that the addition of a right in a protocol was not to be taken as limiting the scope of the meaning of the original Convention guarantee.
11   See Matscher, *European System*, Ch 5 at pp 70–73, and Van der Meersch, *Wiarda Mélanges*, p 201.
12   Article 31(1), Vienna Convention. See above at p 6.
13   *Tyrer v Ireland* A 26 (1978).

state concerned have not been so interpreted. Instead, they have been given an autonomous Convention meaning. This includes terms such as 'criminal charge', 'civil rights and obligations', 'tribunal' and 'witness' in Article 6.[14] The words 'law' and 'lawful', however, have a mixed national law and Convention meaning. They both require that there be a national law basis for what is done and are imbued with a Convention idea of the essential qualities of law. As to the latter, a 'law' must not be arbitrary; it must also be consistent with the general principles of the Convention, publicly available and have a reasonably predictable effect.[15]

xi. Recourse to the *travaux préparatoires*

Recourse may be had to the *travaux préparatoires*, or preparatory work, of the Convention[16] in order to confirm its meaning as established in accordance with the rule in Article 31 of the Vienna Convention or where the application of that rule leaves its meaning 'ambiguous or obscure' or 'leads to a result which is manifestly absurd or unreasonable'.[17] In practice, the Strasbourg authorities have made only occasional use of the *travaux préparatoires*.[18] This is partly because the *travaux* are not often helpful[19] and partly because of the emphasis upon a dynamic and generally teleological interpretation of the Convention that focuses where relevant upon current European standards rather than the particular intentions of the drafting states.[20]

xii. The interpretative roles of the Commission and the Court

The interpretation of the Convention is the role of the Commission and the Court. The Committee of Ministers makes no attempt to interpret the Convention when it acts under Articles 32 or 54. The Commission gives reasoned decisions at the admissibility stage, particularly when it declares an application to be inadmissible.[1] The interpretation of the Convention rules as to the admissibility of applications in Articles 26 and 27 is to be found

14 See below, pp 166, 175, 230, 267. Cf the autonomous interpretation of the terms 'vagrant' and 'persons of unsound mind' in Article 5(1)(d): see below, p 121.
15 See below, pp 105 and 286, concerning Articles 5 and 8-10.
16 For the *travaux préparatoires* of the Convention, see *Collected Edition of the Travaux Préparatoires of the European Convention on Human Rights*, 8 vols, 1975–85 (hereafter TP).
17 Article 32, Vienna Convention.
18 See eg *Johnston v Ireland* A 112 para 52 (1986) and *Lithgow v UK* A 102 para 117 (1986).
19 See eg *Cruz Varas v Sweden* A 201 para 95 (1991) (*travaux préparatoires* 'silent').
20 Remarkably, in *Young, James and Webster v UK* A 44 (1981) and *Sigurjónsson v Iceland* A 264 (1993) the Court resorted to the *travaux préparatoires* only to reject the evidence that it found: see below, p 427.
1 Admitted applications are sometimes admitted on the basis that they raise complex issues of fact and law that require consideration on the merits; in such cases, there is no reasoning at the admissibility stage.

mostly in the Commission's jurisprudence at this stage. In addition, the Commission's Article 31 reports on the merits of admitted applications are fully reasoned and are important sources of interpretation of the Convention.[2] However, it follows from the scheme of the Convention that in practice the 'last word'[3] as to the meaning of the Convention rests with the Court. If the Court interprets the Convention differently from the Commission, the Court's view prevails; once the Court speaks the Commission must and does, if sometimes slowly, change its mind.[4] In this respect, the relationship between the two institutions can be depicted as that between a lower and a higher court in a national legal system, with the interpretations adopted by the Commission in its decisions as to admissibility and its Article 31 reports being important indicators as to the meaning of the Convention in the absence of a Court pronouncement. Although the Court's jurisprudence has developed substantially in recent years, there remain many points of interpretation which only the Commission has considered.[5] Finally, there is no common law distinction between *ratio decidendi* and *obiter dicta* at Strasbourg. Any statement by way of interpretation by the Commission or the Court is significant, although inevitably the level of generality at which it is expressed or its centrality to the decision on the material facts of the case will affect the weight and influence of any pronouncement. Nor is there a doctrine of binding precedent in the sense that the Commission and the Court are bound by their previous interpretations of the Convention.[6] In *Cossey v UK*,[7] the Court stated that 'it usually follows and applies its own precedents, such a course being in the interests of legal certainty and the orderly development of the Convention case-law'. However, it continued, the Court is free to depart from an earlier judgment if there are 'cogent reasons' for doing so, which might include the need to 'ensure that the interpretation of

2   In contrast, Commission reports (and Court judgments) on friendly settlements contain little or no interpretation of the Convention.
3   Mosler, in *Van Panhuys Essays*, p 152. In theory, the contracting parties to the Convention have the 'last word' as to the meaning of their treaty and could, if they were all agreed (either when meeting within the Committee of Ministers or otherwise), adopt an interpretation that would prevail over that of the Court.
4   Eg the Commission adopted (see eg its Report in *Buchholz v FRG* B 37 (1980) Com Rep para 95) the Court's approach to the interpretation of the reasonable time requirement in Article 5(3) following the Court's rejection of the Commission's approach in *Wemhoff v FRG* A 7 (1968).
5   This is particularly true of interpretations adopted when declaring an application inadmissible as being 'incompatible with the provisions of the Convention'. Eg, the jurisprudence *constante* of the Commission excluding tax decisions from consideration under Article 6 has been an important factor in delaying the question reaching the Court: see below, p 183.
6   Cases in which the Court has reversed an earlier ruling by it are *De Wilde, Ooms and Versyp v Belgium*, below, p 147; *Huber v Switzerland*, below, p 133; and *Borgers v Belgium*, below, p 208. See further below, p 658.
7   A 184 para 35 (1990), in which the Court declined to depart from its judgment in *Rees v UK* A 106 (1986).

the Convention reflects societal changes and remains in line with present day conditions'.

5. NEGATIVE AND POSITIVE OBLIGATIONS AND *DRITTWIRKUNG*[8]

Article 1 of the Convention requires the contracting parties to 'secure' the rights and freedoms included in it. Together with the text of later articles dealing with particular rights, this wording in Article 1 has been interpreted as imposing both negative and positive obligations upon states. A negative obligation is one by which a state is required to abstain from interference with, and thereby respect, human rights. For example, it must refrain from torture (Article 3) and impermissible restrictions upon freedom of expression (Article 10). Since such obligations are typical of those that apply to civil and political rights, it is not surprising that most of the obligations that a state has under the Convention are of this character.

A positive obligation is one whereby a state must take action to secure human rights. Positive obligations are generally associated with economic, social and cultural rights[9] and commonly have financial implications, as, for example, with an obligation to provide hospitals in realisation of the right to health. However, they can also be imposed in respect of civil and political rights. In the case of the Convention, a number of positive obligations are expressly indicated by, or necessarily follow from, the text itself. There are, for example, obligations to protect the right to life by law (Article 2(1)); to provide prison conditions that are not 'inhuman' (Article 3); to provide courts, legal aid and translators in connection with the right to a fair trial (Article 6); and to hold free elections (Article 3, First Protocol).

Other such obligations have been read into the Convention. This process finds its source in the Court's jurisprudence in *Marckx v Belgium*.[10] There the Court stated, in the context of the right to 'respect for family life' in Article 8, that 'it does not merely compel the state to abstain from such interferences: in addition to this primary negative undertaking, there may be positive obligations inherent in an 'effective respect' for family life'. In that case, a positive obligation had been infringed, *inter alia*, because Belgian family law did not recognise a child born out of wedlock as a member of the mother's family, thus not allowing the mother and child 'to lead a normal family life'. In *Airey v Ireland*,[11] the same approach was used to establish a

---

8   See Alkema, in *Wiarda Mélanges*, p 33; Clapham, *Human Rights in the Private Sphere*, 1993, Ch 7 (based on Clapham, *European System*, Ch 9); and Drzemczewski, *European Human Rights Convention in National Law*, 1983, Ch 8.

9   See Van Hoof, in Alston and Tomasevski, eds, *The Right to Food*, 1984, p 97.

10 A 31 para 31 (1979). Cf *Abdulaziz, Cabales and Balkandali v UK* A 94 para 67 (1985) and *Rees v UK* A 106 (1986). See also the *National Union of Belgian Police* case A 19 para 39 (1975).

11 A 32 para 32 (1979). Cf *Powell and Rayner v UK* A 106 (1990).

positive obligation, this time one involving public expenditure,[12] under the same Article 8 guarantee to provide for effective access to a court for an allegedly battered wife to obtain an order of judicial separation.

In the *Marckx* and *Airey* cases, the state's positive obligation was, in the state's relations with individuals, to grant them the legal status, rights and privileges to ensure that their Convention rights are 'secured' (Article 1). In a related line of cases, the Court has established that there may not only be an obligation to provide a satisfactory legal framework of the kind described above; there may also be an obligation to protect an individual's rights against interference by other private persons. The first indication of this possibility came in *Young, James and Webster v UK*.[13] There the Court held that there was a breach of the right not to join a trade union protected by Article 11 when the law permitted an employer to dismiss the applicants for their refusal to join a trade union as required by a closed shop agreement. The state was held responsible on the basis that 'the domestic law in force at the relevant time . . . made lawful the treatment of which the applicants complained'. The Court found it unnecessary to consider whether British Rail, a public corporation, was a public or a private employer as there was liability in either event. If there was, as the Court supposed, liability in the latter situation, it resulted by implication from a positive obligation to control the conduct of private employers. Then, more clearly, in *X and Y v Netherlands*,[14] a state was held liable because its criminal law did not provide a means by which a sexual assault upon a mentally handicapped young woman could be the subject of a criminal prosecution. In the words of the Court, the Article 8 obligation to respect an individual's privacy imposed positive obligations that 'may involve the adoption of measures designed to secure respect for private life *even in the sphere of the relations of individuals themselves*'. The same formula was later used in *Plattform 'Arzte für das Leben' v Austria*,[15] in which the Court held that a state must take reasonable and appropriate measures to protect demonstrators from interference by other private persons intent upon disrupting their demonstration in breach of the right to freedom of assembly protected by Article 11.

However, the Court did not adopt this kind of reasoning in *Costello-Roberts v UK*,[16] a case concerning corporal punishment in a private school. Instead it noted that the case fell within the ambit of a right – the right to education – that was protected by the First Protocol to the Convention.[17] It stated that 'the state cannot absolve itself from responsibility' to secure a Convention right 'by delegating its obligations to private bodies or

---

12 For another case involving public expenditure, see *Bouamar v Belgium* A 129 (1988).
13 A 44 para 49 (1981).
14 A 91 para 23 (1985). Italics added.
15 A 139 para 32 (1988).
16 A 247-C (1993).
17 The Court indicated that the right to education included school discipline and applied without discrimination to state and private schools.

individuals'.[18] Accordingly, the Court held that, although the act of a private person, the treatment complained of could engage the responsibility of the defendant state under Article 3. It is likely that the approach in the *Costello-Roberts* case was particular to its facts and does not signal a departure from the earlier precedents concerning positive obligations outlined above.

The full extent to which the Convention places states under positive obligations to protect individuals against infringements of their rights by other private persons has yet to be established. Invasions of privacy by the press (Article 8)[19] and ill-treatment in private prisons (Article 3)[20] are other obvious areas to which an obligation to protect individuals against interferences with their rights by other private persons could extend. Deprivation of liberty by terrorists or other kidnappers (Article 5) is another.[1] The question of the protection under the Convention of individuals against other private persons is sometimes spoken of, misleadingly, in terms of the concept of *drittwirkung*. This concept, which is most developed in German legal thinking and law,[2] supposes that an individual may rely upon a national bill of rights to bring a claim against a private person who has violated his rights under that instrument.[3] Given that this involves the liability of private individuals, or the horizontal application of law, it can have no application under the Convention at the international level,[4] because the Convention is a treaty that imposes obligations only upon states.[5] Insofar as the Convention touches the conduct of private persons, it does so only indirectly through such positive obligations as it imposes upon a state. As noted earlier, the basis for the state's responsibility under the Convention in the case of such obligations is

---

18 A 247-C para 27 (1993). On the delegation point, the Court referred to *Van der Mussele v Belgium* A 70 (1983), in which, in a case alleging 'forced labour' contrary to Article 4 of the Convention, it had rejected the defendant state's argument that it was not responsible for the conduct of a private professional body, the *ordre des avocats*, concerning legal aid when the defendant state relied upon the arrangements for legal aid made by the *ordre* so as to comply with the obligation to provide legal aid in Article 6(3)(c).

19 But see *Winer v UK No 10871/84*, 48 IR 154 (1986), discussed below, p 326.

20 Ill-treatment in private prisons could be dealt with on the narrow 'delegation' basis applied in the *Van der Mussele* and *Costello-Roberts* cases.

1 See below, p 102. For the Strasbourg jurisprudence on racist speech and blasphemy by private persons, see below, pp 360 and 374.

2 For its meaning in German law, see Lewan, 17 ICLQ 571 (1968).

3 This is the concept of direct *drittwirkung*. For indirect *drittwirkung*, which likewise does not refer to positive obligations of the kind that exist under the Convention, see Lewan, loc cit at n 2, above.

4 What may happen, however, is that in a state in which the Convention is a part of national law, the Convention guarantee may be treated, like a national bill of rights, as generating rights vis-à-vis private persons: see Drzemczewski, *European Human Rights Convention in Domestic Law*, 1983, Ch 8, particularly concerning Germany (p 210). The Court's jurisprudence on Article 11, as to which, see below, pp 425ff, suggests that the Convention freedom of association guarantee would be particularly likely to have this potential.

5 See Article 1. Accordingly, as explained below, p 630, an application may not be brought under Article 25 against a private person and Article 24 supposes only inter-state applications.

that, contrary to Article 1, it has failed to 'secure' to individuals within its jurisdiction the rights guaranteed in the Convention by not rendering unlawful the acts of private persons that infringe them.

6. RESERVATIONS[6]

Article 64 of the Convention allows a party on signature or ratification 'to make a reservation in respect of any particular provision of the Convention to the extent that any law then in force in its territory is not in conformity with the provision'. Reservations have been made by most of the parties to the Convention.[7] They have been invoked successfully in several cases to prevent a claim being heard.[8] The only limitation upon the power to make a reservation to the Convention indicated in Article 64 is that it be not 'of a general character'.[9] In *Belilos v Switzerland*,[10] the Court stated that a reservation falls within this prohibition if it is 'couched in terms that are too vague or broad for it to be possible to determine their exact meaning and scope'. In that case, having confirmed its competence to rule on the validity of reservations, the Court held that a Swiss reservation concerning the scope of Article 6 was contrary to Article 64 on the basis of this test. The Court also held that the requirements had not been met in a second respect, viz non-compliance with the requirement in Article 64(2) that any reservation 'made under this Article shall contain a brief statement of the law concerned'.[11] Since this is 'not a purely formal requirement but a condition of substance',[12] non-compliance with it renders a reservation invalid without more. The outcome of the Court's decision in the *Belilos* case was that Switzerland was bound by (and found in breach of) Article 6 without the shield of the reservation. Although the Commission has held that a

6   See Frowein, *Wiarda Mélanges*, p 193. The rules on reservations in the Vienna Convention on the Law of Treaties. Articles 2(1)(d) and 19–23, apply to the Convention as customary international law: *Temeltasch v Switzerland* 5 EHRR 417 at 432 (1983) Com Rep.

7   For the text of reservations and declarations, see the *Yearbooks of the European Convention on Human Rights; Collected Texts*, pp 61ff; and the *Human Rights Information Sheets*, published regularly by the Council of Europe.

8   See eg *Chorherr v Austria* A 266-B para 18-22 (1993) and *K v Finland No 19823/92*, 16 EHRR CD 47 (1993).

9   On the question whether restrictions may be attached to Articles 25 or 46 declarations, see the *Loizidou* case, discussed below, p 581.

10 A 132 para 55 (1988). See Bourguignon, 29 VJIL 347 (1989); Macdonald, 21 RBDI 429 (1988); and Marks, 39 ICLQ 300 (1990).

11 The 'brief statement' need not include a summary of the law concerned; an indication of its subject-matter and a reference to an official source in which the text may be found is sufficient: *Chorherr v Austria* A 266-B para 21 (1993).

12 Id. para 59. The requirement was 'both an evidential factor' and contributed to 'legal certainty'; generally it was intended to ensure that a 'reservation does not go beyond the provisions expressly excluded by the state concerned': ibid. Cf *Weber v Switzerland* A 177 para 38 (1990) in which another Swiss reservation (one called a reservation, not an 'interpretative declaration': see below) was held to be invalid for non-compliance with Article 64(2).

reservation need not refer expressly to the article of the Convention to which the reservation has been made,[13] it has since indicated that its decision on this matter could 'usefully be reconsidered'.[14] A question that remains to be decided is whether a reservation to a provision such as Article 15, which applies to the Convention guarantee as a whole, might be of a 'general character' also.[15]

In the *Belilos* case, the Court also held that an instrument deposited on signature or ratification may qualify as a reservation even though it is not described as such; it is sufficient that the state intended it to be a reservation. In that case, Switzerland had deposited on ratification what it described as two 'interpretative declarations', including the instrument in issue, and two 'reservations'. The Court held that the 'interpretative declaration' concerned was a reservation for the purposes of Article 64 (although it proved not to be a valid one) in the light of the evidence in the Swiss *travaux* as to Switzerland's intentions. The Court's approach can be criticised as not taking account of the need for certainty in this regard and the reasonable expectation that a state knows the distinction in international law between a reservation and an interpretative declaration, particularly when it uses both terms in the instrument that it deposits.[16]

7. THE CONVENTION IN NATIONAL LAW[17]

i. The application of the Convention by national courts

International human rights guarantees are most valuable when they are enforceable in national law. Even in the case of as successful an international guarantee as the European Convention on Human Rights, a remedy in a national court will inevitably be more convenient and efficient than recourse to an international procedure. Accordingly, if the Convention can be relied upon in a party's national courts, an important extra dimension is added to its effectiveness, particularly in a state that lacks its own national bill of rights. Contrary to a commonly held view, however, the

13 See eg *X v Austria No 1452/62*, 6 YB 268 at 276 (1963).
14 *X v Austria No 8180/78*, 20 DR 23 at 27 (1980).
15 Eg the French reservation to Article 15 restricts the competence of the Strasbourg authorities to question the French government's judgment as to the need for emergency measures. See below, p 506.
16 Note, however, that Article 2(1)(d), Vienna Convention on the Law of Treaties defines a reservation as a 'unilateral statement, *however phrased or named*'. Emphasis added.
17 See Bernhardt, *European System*, Ch 3; Buergenthal, *The European Convention on Human Rights*, ICLQ Supp No 11, 1965, p 79; Drzemczewski, *European Human Rights Convention in Domestic Law*, 1983; Evans, in *Proceedings of the 1978 Athens Colloquy about the ECHR in Relation to other International Instruments for the Protection of Human Rights*, 1979, p 109; Gardner, ed, *Aspects of Incorporation of the European Convention of Human Rights into Domestic Law*, 1993; Polakiewicz and Jacob-Foltzer, 12 HRLJ 65, 125 (1991); Ress, in Maier, ed, *Protection of Human Rights in Europe*, 1982, p 209; id, *European System*, Ch 36; and Sorensen, in Robertson, ed, *Human Rights in National and International Law*, 1968, Ch 1.

number of applications to Strasbourg from states that have not incorporated the Convention into their law is not disproportionately large when population is taken into account.[18] Under Article 1 of the Convention, the parties undertake to 'secure' the rights and freedoms in the Convention to individuals within their jurisdiction. This does not require a party to incorporate the Convention into its law.[19] Although compliance with this obligation finds 'a particularly faithful reflection in those instances where the Convention has been incorporated into domestic law',[20] a party may satisfy Article 1 instead by ensuring, in whatever manner it chooses,[1] that its law and practice is such that an individual's Convention rights are guaranteed. In fact, the Convention has been incorporated into the law of the great majority of the contracting parties.[2] In the few states in whose law it has not been incorporated, the Convention plays a part in the national legal order only indirectly through, for example, the operation of rules as to the interpretation of statutes or in the development of judge-made law.[3]

Although incorporation of the Convention into national law is desirable, it does not by itself ensure a remedy in a national court for a breach of the Convention. This will only exist if the Convention guarantee as a whole, or the relevant article or part of it, is regarded by the national court concerned as self-executing.[4] By this is meant that the court accepts that the relevant provision creates a right that can be relied upon directly before it without further steps being needed by way of legislative or other state action.[5] National courts have differed in their assessment of the self-executing character of Convention provisions. For example, the Austrian and Swiss courts have generally applied Convention provisions as self-executing. In Belgium, whereas the negative obligation under Article 8 not to interfere with family life was held to be self-executing, the positive obligation to create an appropriate legal status for children born out of wedlock required legislation.[6] Less enthusiastically still, the Italian Court of Cassation

---

18 Krüger, in Gardner, op cit at n 17 above, pp 25-26.
19 See eg *Observer and Guardian v UK* A 216 (1991).
20 *Ireland v UK* A 25 para 239 (1978).
1   *Swedish Engine Drivers' Union* case A 20 (1976).
2   All 31 parties except Ireland and the UK. See the survey in Polakiewicz and Jacob-Foltzer, 12 HRLJ 65 at 125 (1991).
3   On the position in UK law, see Bratza, in Gardner, op cit at n 17, above, Ch 6; Clapham, *Human Rights in the Private Sphere*, 1993, Chs 1-3; Duffy, 29 ICLQ 585 (1980); and Jacobs, *Wiarda Mélanges*, p 273. On the possibility of the Convention being incorporated indirectly via European Community law, see Grief, 1991 PL 555.
4   Another factor is the precise status that the Convention has in the constitutional law of the state concerned in relation to other national laws that contradict it. In the law of some parties, the Convention has only the status of an ordinary law. In others it prevails over subsequent as well as prior inconsistent legislation or, as in Austria, it may even have the status of constitutional law. See the survey in Polakiewicz and Jacob-Foltzer, 12 HRLJ 65 at 125 (1991). In the Netherlands, the Convention is superior to constitutional law: see *Oerlemans v Netherlands* A 219 (1991).
5   On self-executing treaty provisions, see Brownlie, *Principles of Public International Law*, 4th edn, 1990, p 52.
6   See *Vermeire v Belgium* A 214-C para 11 (1991).

regards the Convention as a whole as stating only programmatic rules for the guidance of the legislature.[7] Even if a Convention provision is regarded as self-executing, it does not necessarily follow that national courts will actually make use of what is seen as 'foreign' law. Most noticeably, where a state, such as Germany, has its own well-established national bill of rights, the Convention has tended to be given only a limited role, with the local courts preferring to rely upon the bill of rights in the national constitution. In contrast, courts in some other states have emphasised the Convention because of its constitutional status (Austria) or the absence of a detailed national bill of rights (Switzerland).[8] There has, however, generally been a marked increase in reliance upon the Convention in recent years.[9] With the dramatic increase in the extent and impact of the European Court's jurisprudence, national courts have become all too aware that their decisions may find their way to Strasbourg to be scrutinised there by reference to Convention standards.[10] When the Convention is relied upon by a national court, the question arises whether, although not bound to do so, it will follow the interpretation of it that has been adopted at Strasbourg. In practice, national courts have usually done so, although there have been exceptions.[11] Where a point of interpretation has not been ruled upon in a Strasbourg case, the national courts will have no choice but to adopt their own interpretation. Insofar as they do so, it is possible that courts in different legal systems may interpret the Convention differently, particularly as there is no procedure for the reference of a case to Strasbourg for a definitive ruling.[12]

Whether a state incorporates the Convention into its law or not, it is required by Article 13 to provide an 'effective remedy' under its national law for a person who has an arguable claim under the Convention. Thus, for example, a wife whose husband has been excluded from a state's territory because of an immigration law that may infringe the Convention must have an effective remedy under national law by which to challenge the legality of the husband's exclusion.[13] The Court's jurisprudence suggests that a state that does not make the Convention directly enforceable in its national law is especially at risk of being in breach of Article 13.

---

7 See Polakiewicz and Jacob-Foltzer, 12 HRLJ at pp 66, 70, 83, 136 (1991) for the above examples.
8 See Polakiewicz and Jacob-Foltzer, id, pp 67 and 136, for the above examples. The Convention may not be pleaded in the German Constitutional Court: Krüger, loc cit at p 24, n 18, p 26.
9 For example, the French and Dutch courts make use of it more frequently: see Polakiewicz and Jacob-Foltzer, id, pp 75 and 128. The Convention is also increasingly referred to in jurisdictions, eg in the UK, where it is relevant only in the interpretation of statutes or the development of the common law.
10 Cf Polakiewicz and Jacob-Foltzer, id, p 141.
11 Polakiewiecz and Jacob-Foltzer, ibid, refer to rulings by Austrian, Belgian and French courts on the scope of Article 6(1) as the only ones in which the Strasbourg Court has been 'openly defied'.
12 Contrast the provision made under Article 177, Treaty of Rome for the reference of cases to the European Court of Justice for the interpretation of European Union law.
13 *Abdulaziz, Cabales and Balkandali v* A 94 para 93 (1985).

ii. The enforcement of Strasbourg decisions in national law

A Court judgment is 'essentially declaratory' and 'cannot of itself annul or repeal' inconsistent national law or judgments.[14] The Court may award an applicant 'just compensation' – a power which has been understood to permit the award of monetary compensation and legal costs.[15] The judgments of the Court and the decisions of the Committee of Ministers arising out of applications to Strasbourg are binding in international law upon the parties to them.[16] However, a court is not obliged to give them direct effect in the national law of the defendant state, which is free to implement them in accordance with the rules of its national legal system.[17] The record of states in executing Court judgments and Committee of Ministers' decisions has been described as 'remarkably good'.[18] This is true of the payment of compensation and costs, the restitutive steps taken to remedy a wrong done to an individual applicant and the amendment of legislative and administrative practices found contrary to the Convention.[19] There is no case as yet in which the Committee of Ministers, which is seised with the task of supervising the execution of judgments and decisions,[20] has found that a state has not complied with its obligations. However, it has to be said that the Committee, being a political body composed of representatives of member states, is not the best equipped or motivated body to question whether the steps taken go far enough.[1] Moreover, for political or other reasons, it has sometimes taken a state a number of years to effect any required reforms in its law or practice[2] or to pay compensation.[3]

14 *Marckx v Belgium* A 31 para 58 (1979). The same is true of Committee of Ministers' decisions.
15 Article 50. See below, p 682. The Committee of Ministers has a comparable power under Article 32: see below, p 699.
16 See Articles 53 and 32, Convention respectively.
17 See eg *Vermeire v Belgium* A 214-C (1991). Under Malta's European Convention Act 1987, its Constitutional Court is empowered to enforce judgments of the Strasbourg Court. In other national legal systems, practice varies as to whether legislative or administrative action is required or whether the national courts are competent, where appropriate, to act, eg by quashing a national court decision, including a criminal conviction, found at Strasbourg to be in breach of the Convention. In Spain the courts can so act; in Germany they cannot: see Bernhardt, *European System*, Ch 3 at p 38. See generally, *The European Convention on Human Rights: Institution of Relevant Proceedings at the National Level to Facilitate Compliance with Strasbourg Decisions*, Council of Europe Committee of Experts Study, 13 HRLJ 71 (1992).
18 Leuprecht, *European System*, Ch 35 at p 800.
19 On this last point, see below, p 30.
20 Articles 54 and 32(2), Convention respectively.
1   See Leuprecht, *European System*, Ch 35 at p 798.
2   See below, p 30.
3   On the reason for the non-payment of Article 32 compensation by Italy in some 'trial within a reasonable time' cases, see Leuprecht, *European System*, Ch 35 at p 796. Following delays in the payment of compensation, the Court now sets a three-month time limit: see, eg *Moreira de Azevedo v Portugal* (Article 50), A 208-C (1991).

8. THE CONVENTION AND THE EUROPEAN UNION[4]

The European Union has jurisdiction over its employees and other private persons (whether individuals or legal persons). As to the latter, it has, for example, a power to fine for a breach of Union competition law. The Union also adopts regulations and directives that must be made applicable directly or indirectly to private persons as a part of the national law of member states and it may act in the field of foreign policy to the detriment of individuals' Convention rights. In addition, the European Court of Justice at Luxembourg may determine the rights and obligations of private persons under Union law. When exercising jurisdiction in these ways, it is possible that Union institutions may infringe Convention rights. The question therefore arises as to whether they must comply with the Convention when they act. A related question is whether member states are responsible under the Convention for the effect on private persons of their legislation or other public acts that are a consequence of their Union membership.

As to the position of the Union, it cannot be directly liable at Strasbourg under the Convention for any conduct on the part of its institutions because the Union is not a party thereto.[5] Although the question of the Union's accession to the Convention has been debated over many years,[6] no formal application to accede has been made; whereas the Commission and the Parliament have supported accession, the necessary political will among the member states has been absent. The Convention does, however, control Union conduct in that it has been incorporated into Union law. The Maastricht Treaty[7] states that the 'Union shall respect fundamental rights, as guaranteed by the European Convention . . . as general principles of law'. This way of subjecting the Union institutions to the Convention is comparable to its incorporation into the national law of a state and falls short in its impact of Union accession to the Convention. In particular, as noted, it does not allow an individual to make an application to Strasbourg against the Union. Moreover, insofar as the Convention is applied as a part of Union law, it is far from clear that the Convention would prevail over a

---

4 From a large literature, see Clapham, *Human Rights and the European Community: A Critical Overview*, 1991; id, 10 YEL 309 (1990); Dauses, 10 ELR 398 (1985); Jacque, *European System*, Ch 39; Lawson, 5 LJIL 99 (1992); Lenaerts, 16 ELR 367 (1991); Mendelson, 1 YEL 121 (1981).

5 An Article 25 application against the EC was declared inadmissible for this reason in *CFDT v European Communities No 8030/77*, 13 DR 231 (1978). The same is true of other European institutions: *Heinz v Contracting States also Parties to the European Patent Convention No 21090/92*, 76A DR 125 (1994) (European Patent Office).

6 See, eg, McBride and Brown, 1 YEL 167 (1981) and more recently Gardner, in Beddard and Hill, eds, *Emerging Rights within the New Europe*, Southampton Papers in International Policy, No 2, 1992, p 8.

7 Article F(2). On its effect, see Krogsgaard, LIEI 1993/1, p 99. The Treaty confirms the jurisprudence of the European Court of Justice: see, eg, *Hoecht AG v Commission, Cases 46/87 and 227/88*, [1989]-3 ECR 2859, para 13.

conflicting provision of Union primary (ie treaty) law[8] and the interpretation and application of the Convention remains a matter for the European Court of Justice, not the Convention authorities.[9] Generally, the present situation is not satisfactory. Given the developing status of the Convention as a European bill of rights, with Strasbourg providing the constitutional court that interprets and applies it, Union accession to the Convention is overdue.

With regard to the position of member states, it has been held in one context that an application under the Convention cannot be brought against a Union member[10] in respect of legislation or other action taken by it in fulfilment of its Union obligations. In *M and Co v FRG*,[11] the Strasbourg Commission held that an application could not be brought against a state for action required of it by Union law to enforce a fine imposed by the Brussels Commission on the basis of a procedure that allegedly did not comply with the Convention right to a fair trial.[12] The Strasbourg Commission stated that 'the transfer of powers to an international organisation is not incompatible with the Convention provided that within that organisation fundamental rights will receive an equivalent protection'. Such protection was afforded under Union law, so that the object and purpose of the Convention was not subverted. However, the decision may not apply beyond its particular facts. In particular, a different conclusion might be reached in a case that involved the application of national law that resulted from Union membership, rather than the enforcement of Union decisions. None the less, the case involves a disappointing surrender of competence by the Strasbourg Commission, which would have done better to have followed its general approach by which Convention parties remain responsible 'for all acts and omissions of their domestic organs allegedly violating the Convention regardless of whether the act or omission in question is a consequence of domestic law or regulations or of the necessity to comply with international obligations'.[13]

9. ACHIEVEMENTS AND PROSPECTS

i. Contribution to the international law of human rights

In terms of international law, the Convention was an important landmark in the development of the international law of human rights. For the first time,

---

8 The potential for conflict was apparent on the facts of *Grogan, Case C 159/90*, [1991] ECR I-4685. Secondary legislation (regulations and directives) must be read subject to the Convention.

9 See Jacque, *European System*, Ch 39 at pp 894–895.

10 All fifteen Union members are parties to the Convention, although not to all of its Protocols.

11 *No 13258/87*, 64 DR 138 at 145 (1990).

12 As to the standards with which the Brussels Commission procedure would have to comply under Article 6, see *Société Stenuit v France* A 232-A (1992), in which French competition law five procedures were found by the Strasbourg Commission to infringe Article 6. Case struck off Court list when applicant withdrew.

13 *M and Co v FRG No 13258/87*, 64 DR 138 at 144 (1990), citing *Hess v UK No 6231/73*, 2 DR 72 (1975). See also the *Heinz* case, loc cit at n 5, above.

sovereign states accepted legally binding obligations to secure the classical human rights for all persons within their jurisdiction and to allow all individuals, including their nationals, to bring claims against them leading to a binding judgment by an international court finding them in breach. This was a revolutionary step in a law of nations that had been based for centuries on such deeply entrenched foundations as the idea that the treatment of nationals was within the domestic jurisdiction of states and that individuals were not the subject of rights in international law. If it has since been joined by other regional and universal treaty-based guarantees of human rights, the Convention remains the most advanced instrument of this kind. It has generated the most sophisticated and detailed jurisprudence in international human rights law and its enforcement mechanisms are unrivalled in their effectiveness and achievements. Its contributions to the jurisprudence of international human rights law mostly concern the meaning of the particular rights it protects, the development of key concepts of general application (eg the principle of proportionality and the meaning of the term 'law') and its approach to the interpretation of human rights treaties generally. In addition, it has contributed to other areas of international law, particularly the law on the functioning of international courts (eg the local remedies rule and provisional measures).[14]

ii. Impact on the protection of human rights in Europe

a. *Influence upon national law*

The Convention has had a considerable effect upon the national law of the contracting parties. It has served as a catalyst for legal change that has furthered the protection of human rights and has, in so doing, assisted in the process of harmonising law in Europe. So far, it has been as an agent of law reform in the context of particular breaches of human rights rather than a means of controlling human rights violations on a grand scale that the Convention has made its mark. Changes in the law have occurred mostly following judgments or decisions[15] in cases to which the state amending its law has been a party. Insofar as a judgment or decision involves a determination that a national law or administrative practice is inconsistent with the Convention,[16] the defendant state is required by international law to change its law or practice in order to comply with its treaty obligation in Article 1 of the Convention to 'secure' the rights and freedoms guaranteed. In compliance with this obligation, the parties to the Convention as a whole have made many changes in their law and practice following decisions or

---

14 See generally Merrills, *The Development of International Law by the European Court of Human Rights*, 2nd edn, 1993.

15 States have also undertaken to change their law or administrative practice in some cases of friendly settlements: see the examples below, p 601.

16 This will not always be the case. For example, the failure to try a person 'within a reasonable time' as required by Article 6(1) may have resulted from negligence on the facts not requiring any legislative or administrative adjustments.

judgments against them.[17] In a number of cases, a Strasbourg judgment or decision has provided a government with a lever to help overcome local opposition to law reform, as with the change in the law on homosexuality in Northern Ireland following *Dudgeon v UK*.[18] Sometimes, however, it is uncertain whether the steps taken by the defendant state go far enough.[19] In other cases, a state may be slow in putting the necessary measures in place. Thus it took fifteen years before the Isle of Man Tynwald legislated[20] to abolish judicial corporal punishment, thereby bringing the United Kingdom fully into line with its obligations under Article 3 following the *Tyrer* case.[1] Prior to the 1993 legislation, in the context of the special constitutional position of the Isle of Man,[2] the UK government had informed the Manx government after the *Tyrer* case that judicial corporal punishment would be contrary to the Convention and the case was brought to the attention of the local courts by the Manx authorities. Although this was considered sufficient by the Committee of Ministers, acting under Article 54, to comply with the *Tyrer* judgment,[3] it would appear that the United Kingdom's obligation to 'secure' the rights and freedoms in the Convention required that it go further and for the relevant law to be amended. The only clear case in which a state has refused point blank to change its law or practice to comply with a judgment or decision is *Brogan v UK*.[4] There the UK informed the Committee of Ministers that it did not feel able to change the prevention of terrorism legislation that had been held to be contrary to Article 5 of the Convention and would make an Article 15 declaration

---

17 For details, see European Court of Human Rights, *Survey of Activities 1959-1992*, 1993. See generally Ress, in *European System*, pp 812ff and Polakiewicz and Jacob-Foltzer, 12 HRLJ 65, 125 (1991). As to the UK, see Churchill and Young, 62 BYIL 283 (1992). For the amendment to Scottish legal aid practice following *Granger v UK* A 174 (1990), see *Boner v UK* A 300-B para 30 (1994).

18 A 45 (1981).

19 As Churchill and Young, 62 BYIL 283 at 346 (1992) point out, it may be unclear what steps are required by a judgment or decision or whether legislation read *in abstracto* goes far enough. As to whether the UK Contempt of Court Act 1991 and the Interception of Communications Act 1985 go far enough, see the Commission decisions at pp 390 and 339 below. Legislation intended to comply with a judgment or decision should clearly be interpreted by national courts so as to comply with this objective if possible.

20 Criminal Justice (Penalties, etc) Act 1993.

1 A 26 (1978). Belgium took nearly eight years to amend its law to comply with *Marckx v Belgium* A 31 (1979). In *Vermeire v Belgium* A 214-C (1991), it was held that the fact that law reform to comply with *Marckx* was pending was not a defence to an application that arose in the interim challenging the same law. See also Mahoney and Prebensen, *European Supervision*, Ch 26 at p 636.

2 The Isle of Man is a Crown possession that by convention is not subject to the legislative powers of Westminster on most internal matters.

3 CM Res DH (78) 39. There was no case in which a sentence of judicial corporal punishment was executed prior to its abolition in 1993. In *Teare v O'Callaghan*, 4 EHRR 232 (1981) a post-*Tyrer* sentence of corporal punishment was quashed by the Isle of Man High Court on the ground that it was contrary to Isle of Man international obligations and should be imposed only if other forms of punishment are unsuitable.

4 A 145-B (1988).

instead.[5] In a number of cases, states have acted to amend their law or practice to bring it into line with the Convention following decisions in cases to which they have not been a party.[6] For example, the Netherlands amended its legislation on children born out of wedlock as a consequence of *Marckx v Belgium*.[7] There have also been instances of a state changing its law in order to comply with the Convention or a Protocol before becoming a party.[8] The Convention's influence upon the law of states that are not parties to a case illustrates the following general point. The real achievement of the Convention system can be said to go beyond the statistical tally of cases and the provision of remedies for individuals. It resides in the deterrent effect of an operational system. States, confronted with a system that works, must keep their law and administrative practices under review. As happens in Whitehall, new legislation must, as far as foreseeable, be 'Strasbourg proofed'. In this way the Convention radiates a constant pressure for the maintenance of human rights standards and for change throughout the new Europe. A judgment of the Court in a case brought by one person may have an impact on 30 or so national jurisdictions.[9] Finally, it may be noted that the Convention has also influenced national law outside of Europe. Its text is echoed in the bills of rights of a number of states that were formerly colonies[10] and the jurisprudence of the Convention organs has been relied upon or cited in cases decided in the national courts of non-European states.[11]

b. A remedy for individuals

As far as individuals who claim to be victims of human rights violations are concerned, the primary effect of the Convention has been to provide a remedy before an international court of justice when all national remedies have failed. 'We will now take our case to Strasbourg' is a familiar refrain that may mean more than just blowing off steam.

5 This was also considered sufficient by the Committee of Ministers: see CM Res DH (90) 23. See *Brannigan and McBride v UK* A 258-B para 51 (1993).
6 Although, as non-parties, they are not legally bound by the judgment or decision, they are bound to 'secure' the rights protected by the Convention.
7 A 31 (1979). The Netherlands also amended its law concerning the time-limit within which a suspect must be brought before a court in the light of the *Brogan* case: see Myjer, NCJM-Bulletin 1989, p 459. The Danish law on the closed shop was amended following *Young, James and Webster v UK* A 44 (1981): see Bernhardt, *European System*, Ch 3 at p 39, n 41. France amended its law on interpretation costs because of *Luedicke, Belkacem and Koç v FRG* A 29 (1978): see French decree no 87–634 of 4 August 1987. For other examples, see Polakiewicz and Jacob-Foltzer, 12 HRLJ 125 (1991).
8 See Polakiewicz and Jacob-Foltzer, 12 HRLJ 65, 125 (1991), for examples concerning Finland, Luxembourg and Switzerland.
9 Cf Judge Ryssdal, *European System*, p xxvii.
10 Eg Nigeria: see Elias, *Nigeria: the Development of its Laws and Constitution*, 1967, p 142. Cf *Minister of Home Affairs v Fisher* [1980] AC 319 at 328, PC (Caribbean states).
11 See eg *State v Ncube* 90 ILR 580 (1992) (a Zimbabwean case referring to the *Tyrer* case). See also *Pratt v AG for Jamaica* [1993] 4 All ER 769, a Privy Council case which cites *Soering v UK* A 161 (1989). For other examples, see Mahoney and Prebensen, *European Supervision*, Ch 26 at p 637.

One measure of the undoubted value of the Convention remedy from the individual's point of view is the large number of admitted applications that have led to a favourable outcome for the applicant before the Court or the Committee of Ministers or by way of a friendly settlement.[12] Another is the wide variety of cases in which breaches have been found. Most violations have concerned the right to a fair trial. Cases under Article 6 have brought to light many delays in the hearing of cases in breach of the right to 'trial within a reasonable time'. Other common infringements have concerned the rights to an independent and impartial tribunal, to judicial review of executive action, to due process in disciplinary proceedings and to legal aid. The next most problematic guarantee for states has been that of freedom of the person. Many breaches of Article 5 have concerned various aspects of defendants' rights, such as the information required upon arrest, the right to bail, the length of detention on remand and the practice concerning discretionary life sentences. Other cases have involved the preventive detention of terrorists and the detention of the mentally disordered, vagrants, children and deportees. Claims relying upon the right to respect for family life, privacy, etc, in Article 8 have been almost equally successful. It is in this context that the Court has made most use of its 'dynamic' approach to the interpretation of the Convention and the idea that there may be positive obligations upon states, requiring them, for example, to legislate so as to respect the rights of homosexuals and children born out of wedlock in accordance with current social values. Cases under Article 10 have confirmed the fundamental importance attached to freedom of expression, particularly freedom of the press. Several violations of Article 3 have been found, in such diverse areas as the ill-treatment of persons in detention, judicial corporal punishment and extradition to face the death row phenomenon. At the other extreme, the guarantees of freedom from slavery and forced labour (Article 4), the right to free elections (Article 3, First Protocol) and all of the rights in the Fourth and Seventh Protocols have yet to lead to an adverse ruling.

Analysing the Strasbourg case-law from another perspective, the blind-spots revealed by the Convention have varied from one state to another. For example, in the United Kingdom the Convention has thrown a spotlight on prisons, causing an antiquated system of prison administration to be brought up to date. It has also provided checks upon state conduct in such diverse contexts as the Northern Ireland emergency and discretionary life sentences. In the Netherlands and Sweden, the Convention has highlighted the absence of judicial control over executive action in such areas as the licensing of commercial activities. In Italy, as well as in a number of other civil law jurisdictions, it has uncovered repeated delays in the administration of justice.

12 To date, a breach of at least one article of the Convention has been found by the Court in over two-thirds of the cases that it has decided on the merits. For friendly settlement figures, see below, p 599. Note, however, that only 9% of registered applications for which decisions as to admissibility had been taken by the end of 1994 had been declared admissible.

If the Convention may thus provide a valuable remedy in respect of human rights violations over a wide range of government activity, the Strasbourg procedures none the less have certain limitations or disadvantages from the applicant's standpoint. Some of these are inherent in all international remedies. Recourse to Strasbourg is inevitably less convenient than to a local court for obvious reasons such as language, distance and cost. Similarly, any international remedy will be less efficient because of procedural weaknesses, such as the absence of a power to sub-poena witnesses or to enforce or execute properly interlocutory injunctions or judgments respectively.

Other limitations are particular to the Strasbourg system as it functions at present. By far the most serious of these is the length of proceedings at Strasbourg, which is considered below. As has often been pointed out, it is somewhat ironic that the Strasbourg authorities could well be considered to infringe the trial within a reasonable time guarantee which they enforce against others. Another limitation results from the fact that some cases are decided finally not by a court, but by a political body – the Committee of Ministers – that is singularly ill-equipped in its composition and procedures to make final pronouncements as to compliance with an international human rights guarantee such as the Convention. A further problem is that the jurisdiction of the Commission and the Court to hear cases resulting from individual applications remains optional in law. However, although some states have been known on occasion to question whether the Strasbourg authorities have been too demanding in their interpretation of the Convention, it would be difficult in the prevailing political climate for any state not to renew its Article 25 and 46 declarations. In the one (marginal) case in which this has happened, for some twelve years the United Kingdom did not renew its Article 25 declaration for the Isle of Man following the decision in *Tyrer v UK* on corporal punishment.[13]

Given the importance now attached to the Convention system as providing a remedy for individuals, it is interesting to note how matters have progressed in this regard beyond the intentions of the drafting states. The original purpose of the Convention was not primarily to offer a remedy for particular individuals who had suffered violations of the Convention but to provide a collective, inter-state guarantee that would benefit individuals generally by requiring the national law of the contracting parties to be kept within certain bounds. An Article 25 application was envisaged as a mechanism for bringing to light a breach of an obligation owed by one state to others, not to provide a remedy for an individual victim. In accordance with this conception of the Convention, no provision was made for individuals to refer their case to the Court or to take part in proceedings before it. This, however, is not how the Convention has evolved. The individual has been brought more to the centre of the stage by allowing him

---

13 The Article 25 declaration, which had been allowed to expire in 1981, was renewed in 1993, following Manx legislation abolishing judicial corporal punishment and reforming the criminal law on homosexuality in the light of the *Dudgeon* case. See Edge, 144 NLJ 770 (1994). The Convention was extended to the Isle of Man under Article 63.

a right of audience before the Court and also, for those states that become parties to the Ninth Protocol, the right to refer his case to the Court.[14] The Commission's constructive use of the friendly settlement procedure, which usually leads to an immediate remedy for the applicant (compensation, pardon, etc), and the Court's application of Article 50 to award an applicant compensation and costs have also enhanced the value of the Convention remedy from the standpoint of the individual.[15]

iii. Prospects

Already the Convention has achieved a great deal in its first 40 years. Its future lies in the consolidation and further development of its jurisprudence and of its role as a European bill of rights. The momentum of the Court's work has increased rapidly in the last decade, with the Court giving detailed meaning to many different parts of the Convention guarantee. Recent reassuring examples of the Court's continued willingness to read the Convention in a positive, teleological way are its ruling that the Convention has an extra-territorial reach under Article 3[16] and that the right to respect for one's home and private and family life extends to protection from environmental pollution.[17] While it is to be hoped that the Court will continue to conceive of its function as the guardian of human rights in a dynamic and probing way, it must at the same time take care to respect the rich diversity of law in the legal systems of the contracting parties and not lose touch with common European values.

There is much that the contracting parties could do to improve the Convention's impact. They could immediately increase its effect by withdrawing such reservations as they have made and by ratifying the Protocols that they have not yet accepted. The bringing to fruition of various pending proposals for further Protocols adding to the rights protected would be welcome.[18] A Protocol bringing appropriate economic and social rights within the Convention system of individual petitions would also be valuable.[19] Although member states constantly acknowledge that

14 The Ninth Protocol, which entered into force in 1994, will be overtaken and improved upon by the 1994 Eleventh Protocol, as to which see below, Ch 26.
15 See further, below, pp 599 and 682.
16 *Soering v UK* A 161 (1989).
17 *Lopes Ostra v Spain* A 303-C (1995).
18 There are proposals for protocols on the rights of persons in detention, on sexual equality and on cultural rights (see next note) under consideration at Strasbourg. The Parliamentary Assembly, Recommendation 1246/1994, has proposed a protocol abolishing the death penalty in wartime.
19 On previously unsuccessful attempts to add a Convention protocol protecting economic, social and cultural rights, see Berchtold, in Matscher, ed, *The Implementation of Economic and Social Rights*, 1991, p 355. As noted above, there is a pending proposal for a Convention Protocol on cultural rights, particularly those of minorities. The European Social Charter, which protects economic and social rights, provides only for a reporting system. In 1995, a Charter Protocol was adopted (not yet in force) that provides for collective complaints by trades unions, NGOs, etc, but no provision is made for individual complaints. See generally on the Convention and economic, social and cultural rights, Pellonpaa, *European System*, Ch 37.

economic and social rights are indivisible from and just as important as civil and political rights,[20] states lack the necessary conviction to establish rights of individual petition for the former, even though they are familiar with judicial remedies for the breach of obligations concerning economic and social rights in Union law and their own national law.[1] But much more urgent are the problems besetting the Convention's enforcement machinery.[2] Paradoxically, the large number of applications to the Commission and of cases referred to the Court that are testimony to the success of the Convention could also be its undoing. In 1994, 2,944 applications were registered by the Commission, more than double the number just five years before.[3] Whereas it took the Court over 30 years to decide its first 200 cases, the second 200 required only three years.[4] The reasons for these startling changes are the increased awareness on the part of individuals and non-governmental organisations of the guarantees in the Convention and the chances of winning a case, the growth in the number of contracting parties[5] and the fact that they all now accept the right of individual petition and the jurisdiction of the Court. Recent reforms of the Commission's functioning have helped to expedite proceedings,[6] but there remains a considerable backlog at the admissibility stage.[7] Moreover, the spiralling number of admitted applications also inevitably delays the hearing of cases on their merits by both the Commission and the Court.[8] It can take two years for a decision as to admissibility to be reached and it will usually be five years before the various stages of proceeding are completed and a final decision given.[9] Such timescales are unacceptable and are 'in danger of undermining public confidence in the system of the Convention'.[10] In consequence, it has

---

20 See, eg, the *Final Resolution of Council of Europe Ministerial Conference on the European Social Charter*, Turin, 1991, para 2.
1 See eg the Community case-law under Article 119 concerning sexual discrimination in employment and national law remedies before industrial and social security courts of tribunals.
2 For a gloomy prognosis of the future in the absence of reform, see Tomuschat, 13 HRLJ 401 (1992).
3 Over 9,000 provisional files were opened in 1994: see below, Appendix II. One applicant is known to have applied for the French stamps.
4 Judge Ryssdal, *European System*, p xxvii. The number of cases decided by the Court on the merits annually was in single figures until 1984; it is now 50 and more cases a year. These figures are to some extent distorted by the large number of very similar 'trial within a reasonable time' cases against Italy in recent years.
5 The present number may increase further if the new European states that have applied for Council of Europe membership are admitted. The current applicants are Belarus, Croatia, FYR Macedonia, Russia and Ukraine. Russia's application was put on hold in 1995 because of Chechnya.
6 As to the new procedures under the Eighth Protocol, see below, p 575. Note, however, that delays in the Commission's work have resulted from pressure upon the secretariat as well as Commission members.
7 For details see below, p 707.
8 At the end of 1994, there were more than 54 cases pending before the Court.
9 A small number of cases can be expedited if necessary: eg *Soering v UK* A 161 (1989) took just one year.
10 Mme Lalumière, Secretary General of the Council of Europe, *European System*, p xvii.

become imperative to streamline and otherwise reform a cumbersome and lengthy procedure. The remedy that has been agreed is the merger of the Commission and the Court, with the new Court being composed of *full-time* judges. This proposal and other important improvements are incorporated in the Eleventh Protocol to the Convention, which was adopted in 1994. If, as is likely, the Eleventh Protocol, which requires ratification by all of the contracting parties, enters into force in the next three or four years, a radically improved system of supervision, operated by just one body, should be in operation by the end of the century.[11] The Convention's future is also bound up with that of the new Europe. Providing both a statement of European human rights values and machinery for their enforcement, it is set to play a key role in the on-going process of European integration. This is a role that will take on an extra dimension as cases arrive from the new Council of Europe member states in Central and Eastern Europe. The Convention's relationship with other European institutions or mechanisms for the protection of human rights will require further consideration. The fact that the member states of the European Union are subject to the Convention, but that the supra-national institutions to which they have transferred certain of their powers are not, is a weakness in the arrangements for securing human rights in Europe that should be remedied by the accession of the Community to the Convention. The Organisation on Security and Cooperation in Europe (CSCE) raises different issues.[12] Although devised in the context of the Cold War, its Human Dimension Mechanism, which provides for inter-state complaints but with no binding outcome, is still of value in areas, such as the protection of minorities, where the Convention's writ does not as yet run or where a remedy of a political rather than a legal kind is more suitable.

---

11 For a full account of the reforms contained in the Eleventh Protocol, see below, Ch 26.
12 On the OSCE and human rights, see Bloed and Van Dijk, *The Human Dimension of the Helsinki Process*, 1991; McGoldrick, 39 ICLQ 923 (1990); id, 42 ICLQ 411 at 431 (1993).

CHAPTER 2

Article 2: The right to life

'**Article 2**
1. Everyone's right to life shall be protected by law. No one shall be deprived of his life intentionally save in the execution of a sentence of a court following his conviction of a crime for which this penalty is provided by law.
2. Deprivation of life shall not be regarded as inflicted in contravention of this article when it results from the use of force which is no more than absolutely necessary.
   (a) in defence of any person from unlawful violence;
   (b) in order to effect a lawful arrest or to prevent the escape of a person lawfully detained;
   (c) in action lawfully taken for the purpose of quelling a riot or insurrection.'

The first right guaranteed in the Convention, in Article 2, is the right to life, the most basic human right of all.[1] The fundamental nature of the right is recognised by the fact that Article 2 is one of the few Convention Articles that cannot be derogated from in time of war or other public emergency.[2] Article 2 places upon states both a positive obligation to protect the right to life by law and a negative obligation not to take life, other than in certain exceptional cases. As yet, no case under Article 2 has been decided by the Court: the *McCann* case (below) is pending before it. In *Cyprus v Turkey*,[3] which is the only case in which a breach of Article 2 has been found, the case was decided by the Committee of Ministers.[4] Other important Article 2 cases have arisen out of killings in the Northern Ireland emergency or have concerned the question of abortion.

1 On the right to life in Article 2, see O'Boyle, 'The Use of Lethal Force under Article 2 of the European Convention on Human Rights', CE Doc DH-ED-COLL (90), and Opsahl, *European System*, Ch 11. See also the discussion of Article 2 in various chapters of Ramcharan, ed, *The Right to Life in International Law*, 1985.
2 See Article 15(2), Convention. Exceptionally, derogations may be made from Article 2 'in respect of deaths resulting from lawful acts of war': ibid.
3 (First and Second Applications), 4 EHRR 482 (1976) Com Rep; CM Res DH (79) 1.
4 Irrespective of other considerations, the case could not have been referred to the Court because Turkey had not accepted its jurisdiction.

1. THE OBLIGATION TO PROTECT THE RIGHT TO LIFE BY LAW

The first sentence of Article 2(1) states that 'everyone's right to life shall be protected by law'. This establishes a positive obligation for states to make adequate provision in their law for the protection of human life. It follows from this obligation that the taking of life must generally be illegal under a state's law. The kind (criminal, civil) or degree (in criminal law, for murder, manslaughter, etc) of liability is not specified. The principle of proportionality suggests that what is required will vary with the circumstances so that, for example, the negligent taking of life by careless driving may be treated less harshly than a premeditated case of poisoning. It can be supposed that criminal responsibility at the level of homicide is generally required for the intentional taking of life. In any case, the 'law' that protects the right to life should be 'formulated with sufficient precision to enable the citizen to regulate his conduct'.[5] Liability for the taking of life should extend under a state's law to the acts of both private persons[6] and persons acting for the state.

A state need not, however, make every taking of life illegal. Certain permissible exceptions are indicated in or may be inferred from the text of Article 2. Capital punishment is expressly permitted by Article 2(1), as is the taking of life by the state in the cases listed in Article 2(2). There are other cases in which the taking of life does not usually give rise to liability under European national law. Examples are killings in self-defence committed by private persons (and hence not within Article 2(2)) and accidental deaths in sporting contests. More problematic, and arguably not allowed by Article 2, are laws that permit a private person to use deadly force to defend his property or to effect a citizen's arrest. Causing death by omission also generally escapes liability. A controversial case in national law is euthanasia. It has been held by the Commission that Article 2 does not require that passive euthanasia, by which a person is allowed to die by not being given treatment, be a crime.[7] A different answer would be likely in the case of active euthanasia, whereby death is accelerated by a positive act.[8] The consent of the patient may be relevant in this connection; it is not clear that Article 2 *requires* that a state's law prohibit active euthanasia (or complicity in suicide generally) at the patient's request. As in the case of abortion (see

---

5 *Sunday Times v UK (No 1)* A 30 para 49, interpreting the word 'law' in Article 10, Convention.
6 See eg *W v UK No 9348/81*, 32 DR 190 (1983).
7 *Widmer v Switzerland No 20527/92* (1993), unreported. In that case, it was sufficient that Swiss law provided criminal liability for negligent medical treatment causing death.
8 However, in an early West German case, it was held that a doctor did not infringe Article 2 by giving an overdose of drugs to the terminally ill: Decision of the *Verwaltungsgericht*, Bremen of November 8 1959, NJW (1960), 400, cited in Fawcett, p 36. The turning off of a life support system is probably not to be regarded as a positive act but as part of an act of omission by which steps are not taken to keep a person alive: cf *Airedale NHS Trust v Bland* [1993] 1 All ER 821, HL (the Hillsborough football disaster case).

below), a wide margin of appreciation would be allowed if it could be shown that national practice varied a lot.

The positive duty to protect the right to life 'by law' includes the effective enforcement of the law. Accordingly, the state has an obligation to take reasonable steps to prevent the taking of life by providing police and security forces. But there are limits to the state's obligation in this regard. A claim that a person in fear of his life from the IRA was entitled to continued special protection by the Irish authorities was rejected on the ground that 'Article 2 cannot be interpreted as imposing a duty on a state to give protection of this nature, at least not for an indefinite period'.[9] Obviously, the fact that a killing occurs does not of itself entail a breach of Article 2; there can be 'no positive obligation to exclude any possible violence' against the person.[10] These words come from a case in which the applicant claimed that not enough was being done by the United Kingdom to protect individuals against threats to their lives from terrorism in Northern Ireland. Noting the number of armed and security forces in place, the Commission found, without considering that it was called upon under Article 2 to examine in detail the 'appropriateness and efficiency' of the preventive measures taken in Northern Ireland, that there was no breach of the Convention on the facts. The Commission's jurisprudence accepts, however, that there is an obligation to provide a reasonable level of protection against the acts of terrorists and others that place the lives of individuals at risk.

The duty to enforce the law to protect life also requires the proper investigation of all suspicious deaths (including deaths in custody)[11] and the prosecution of both public[12] and private offenders, subject to the normal rules as to prosecutorial discretion.[13] As to the investigation of deaths, Article 2 can be taken to require the investigation of the disappearance of individuals, including political 'disappearances', in circumstances that may suggest death.[14] In *McCann, Farrell and Savage v UK* (the *Gibraltar* case),[15] the Commission stated that the obligation to protect life contained a 'procedural aspect' which included 'the minimum requirement of a mechanism whereby the circumstances of a deprivation of life by the agents

---

9 *X v Ireland No 6040/73*, 16 YB 388 at 392 (1973). Special protection had been provided for a while.
10 *W v UK No 9348/81*, 32 DR 190 at 200 (1983). Cf *No 9825/82*, 8 EHRR 49 (1985) and *M v UK and Ireland No 9837/82*, 47 DR 27 (1986).
11 See Opsahl, *European System*, Ch 11 at p 211.
12 Legal immunity of the defendant state's agents from liability or prosecution would be a breach of Article 2. Cf *Guerrero v Colombia*, 1 SDHRC 112 (1982) (Article 6, ICCPR).
13 It was held in an early case, *No 809/60*, cited in Fawcett, p 37, that an application could not be brought under Article 25 for the failure to prosecute a person for an offence resulting in death, although it is not clear whether the case fell within the normal limits of prosecutorial discretion.
14 Cf the HRC's First General Comment on Article 6, ICCPR, para 4, GAOR, 37th Sess, Supp 40, n 93 (1982), reprinted in 1-2 IHRR 4 (1994): 'States should establish effective facilities and procedures to investigate thoroughly cases of missing and disappeared persons in circumstances which may involve a violation of the right to life.'
15 *No 18984/91* Com Rep para 193 (1994). For the facts, see below, p 49.

agents of a state may receive public and independent scrutiny'. On the facts of the case, the Commission concluded that the inquest into the killing of terrorist suspects, and the preceding police investigation into the deaths, met this requirement. An amnesty for persons convicted or suspected of homicide is not inconsistent with Article 2 provided that it reflects a proper balance between the interests of the state in the particular circumstances in which the amnesty is declared and the general need to enforce the law to protect the right to life.[16]

A difficult question is whether a state must forcibly feed a prisoner on hunger strike to save his life. When deciding that the forced feeding of a prisoner on hunger strike was not a breach of Article 3,[17] the Commission noted that the obligation under Article 2 to secure the right to life 'should in certain circumstances call for positive action on the part of the contracting parties, in particular an active measure to save lives when the authorities have taken the person in question into their custody'. Although the Commission would appear to have taken the view that such action included forced feeding, it is submitted that a state should not be liable under Article 2 for an omission that respects the will and physical integrity of an individual who is capable of taking a decision as to matters of life and death. As Opsahl[18] suggests, there is a duty to make food and water available to persons in custody, but no more.

Another question is whether the positive obligation in the first sentence of Article 2 extends beyond the protection of life against human acts or omissions of the kinds considered above to deaths within the general public resulting from circumstances such as lack of food or medical attention, unsafe roads or workplaces and environmental pollution, insofar as such circumstances may be attributed to the state. The question was raised, but left unanswered, in the context of medical care in a case in which the parents of a severely disabled child claimed that their daughter had not been allowed free medical treatment by the state.[19] In another case, it was alleged that the operation of a voluntary public vaccination scheme, which had led to the deaths of some young children, was a breach of Article 2. The Commission stated that the first sentence of Article 2(1), 'enjoins the state not only to refrain from taking life *intentionally* but, further, to take appropriate steps to safeguard life'.[20] This could be read very widely, so as to require a state to take positive 'steps' to make adequate provision for medical care, or for food and shelter or a healthy working or living environment. Alternatively, it could mean only that where a state takes on a responsibility such as that

---

16 *Dujardin v France No 16734/90* (1991) unreported.

17 *X v FRG No 10565/83*, 7 EHRR 152 at 153 (1984). Article 3 prohibits 'inhuman or degrading treatment'.

18 *European System*, Ch 11 at p 221. See also the facts of *Marcella and Robert Sands v UK No 9338/81*, cited by Opsahl, id, note 63.

19 *X v Ireland No 6839/74*, 7 DR 78 (1976). The question was not pursued because the child had in fact received assistance and her life had not been endangered. On medical treatment as a requirement under Article 3, see below, p 71.

20 *X v UK No 7154/75*, 14 DR 31 at 32 (1978).

involved in the operation of a public vaccination scheme, it will be liable under Article 2 for any negligence that results in death.[1] On the facts, the application was declared inadmissible on the ground that 'appropriate steps' had been taken with a view to the safe administration of the scheme.[2] In a later case, the 'appropriate steps' dictum was relied upon in a different context to raise, again without deciding, the question whether a state would be in breach of Article 2 if it imprisoned a convicted person when this would cause his wife to commit suicide.[3] The Commission has also considered, once again without deciding, whether Article 2 obliges a state to impose a legal duty upon members of the public to assist others in a case of medical emergency.[4] In a very early case the question whether the threat resulting from nuclear testing and the disposal of radioactive waste could involve liability under Article 2 was raised but not examined.[5]

The interpretation of Article 2 so as to establish positive obligations of the kind just described would present problems of causation on the facts of particular cases and would probably take the Convention further in the direction of protecting social rights[6] than was intended by the drafting states. However, other Convention guarantees have been interpreted dynamically[7] and have been so interpreted without regard to any economic costs.[8] A reading of Article 2(1) that developed the positive obligation in its first sentence in the direction suggested and that respected standards in the law of the contracting parties generally would be consistent with the object and purpose of the Convention and would be in step with the interpretation of the equivalent 'right to life' guarantee in the International Covenant on Civil and Political Rights.[9]

The first sentence of Article 2 states that 'everyone's' right to life must be protected. The question whether the word 'everyone' requires that the right

1 On this basis it is arguable that under Article 2 a state should provide adequate protection against the risk of infection with AIDS from a negligently administered blood transfusion.
2 See also *Tavares v France* No *16593/90* (1991) unreported, in which the applicant's wife had died in hospital in childbirth and a civil claim in the national courts had failed in the absence of fault by the hospital. The application was declared inadmissible on the basis that the hospital had procedures in place which it had followed. The Commission declined to examine the hospital procedures in detail.
3 *Naddaf v FRG* No *11604/85*, 50 DR 259 (1986). In that case, the Commission also referred to *X v FRG* No *5207/71*, 14 YB 698 (1971), in which it had considered, again without deciding, whether a forced eviction that endangered life was in breach of Article 2.
4 *Hughes v UK* No *11590/85*, 48 DR 258 (1986). Such an obligation would run counter to the general approach in national law whereby omissions do not engage criminal liability.
5 *No 715/60*, Recueil (1960) ii, cited in Fawcett, p 37.
6 Social rights within the Council of Europe framework are protected by the 1961 European Social Charter. In contrast with the Convention, however, the Charter does not provide a right of petition.
7 On the dynamic interpretation of the Convention, see *Tyrer v UK* A 26 (1978).
8 See *Airey v Ireland* A 32 (1979).
9 See the HRC's First General Comment, cited at p 39, n 14 above, para 5. Cf Opsahl, *European Supervision*, Ch 11 at p 212, who favours a reading of Article 2 that would impose an obligation to provide medical treatment to secure life. See, however, Fawcett, p 37, who refers to an interpretation of Article 2 along these lines as 'extravagant', and Dinstein, in Henkin, ed, *The International Bill of Rights*, 1981, Ch 5.

to life of an unborn child be protected has yet to be fully resolved.[10] In practice, the question has arisen in the context of abortion.[11] In *Paton v UK*,[12] the Commission ruled that the abortion of a ten-week-old foetus under British law to protect the physical or mental health of a pregnant woman was not in breach of Article 2. In doing so, it stated that Article 2 does not recognise an *absolute* right to life of an unborn child. However, the Commission left open the controversial question whether Article 2 does not protect the unborn child at all[13] or whether the foetus has a right to life under it subject to certain implied limitations. It was able to do so because, even if the latter were the position, the facts of the case came within one such limitation, viz the protection of the pregnant woman's health.[14]

The Commission's position was further clarified in *H v Norway*.[15] There a lawful abortion of a fourteen-week-old foetus on the statutory ground that the 'pregnancy, birth or care for the child may place the woman in a difficult situation of life'[16] was held not to be contrary to Article 2. This goes beyond the *Paton* case in that the abortion was later in time and for social, rather than health, reasons. The key to the Commission's decision in *H v Norway* was its understanding that 'national laws on abortion differ considerably' within the states parties to the Convention. In view of this, it considered that 'in such a delicate area the contracting states must have a certain discretion'. It then held that the defendant state's law, as it was applied to the facts of the case, did not exceed this 'discretion'. Whether the Commission would have reached the same conclusion if the case had involved that part of the defendant state's law that gave the pregnant woman an unlimited right to abortion during the first twelve weeks of pregnancy is not clear.[17] In this

---

10 On the question of the protection of the unborn child by Article 2, see Peukert, in *Wiarda Mélanges*, p 511.

11 Other 'right to life' issues concerning the unborn child include those arising out of embryonic and foetal research and the taking of hazardous drugs by pregnant women. As to the former, see the Council of Europe's 1992 Draft Convention for the Protection of Human Rights with Regard to Applications of the Life Sciences. As yet, such issues have not been considered in any reported Convention case. See Byk, *Medical and Biological Progress and the European Convention on Human Rights*, CE Doc, 1992.

12 *X v UK No 8416/78*, 19 DR 244 (1980).

13 As the Commission noted, the textual evidence supports this interpretation. Thus the wording of Article 2 beyond the first sentence of Article 2(1) can only apply to persons already born and in most other Convention articles in which the word 'everyone' appears it has the same limited meaning. The Commission also contrasted Article 2 with Article 4, American Convention on Human Rights (ACHR), which expressly states that the right to life 'shall be protected by law, and, in general, from the moment of conception'. Article 4 has, however, been interpreted in a limited way: see the *Baby Boy* case, 2 HRLJ 110 (1981).

14 The question was not directly in issue and the Court found no need to consider it in *Open Door Counselling and Dublin Well Woman v Ireland* A 246-A para 63 (1993).

15 *No 17004/90* (1992), unreported.

16 English translation of the Norwegian abortion statute in the Commission's decision.

17 Beyond the first 12 weeks, the Norwegian law provided that until the 18th week an abortion had to be authorised by two doctors by reference to several criteria, consisting most significantly of the pregnant woman's life or health or her 'difficult situation of life'. An abortion after 18 weeks could only be authorised in exceptional cases and provided that the foetus was not viable.

connection, it is interesting to note that, while again finding that it did not have to decide the question whether Article 2 protected the unborn child at all, in *H v Norway* the Commission did state that it 'will not exclude that in certain circumstances' it does offer such protection, without indicating what those 'circumstances' were. As matters stand, the ground for an abortion that was approved in *H v Norway* would appear to be very wide and capable of covering most cases.

A claim alleging that an abortion is in breach of Article 2 may only be brought by a 'victim' in the sense of Article 25, who must be someone personally affected. The 'potential father' qualifies as a 'victim' for this purpose so that he can bring a claim where the woman seeks or obtains an abortion without his consent.[18] An ordinary member of the public who opposes legislation permitting abortion is not so affected.[19] Nor is a church minister, even though he loses his office for refusal to carry out his functions as a result of his opposition.[20]

Cases involving abortion issues may well be brought, not by someone seeking to prevent an abortion under Article 2, but by a pregnant woman under Article 8, arguing for an abortion as a part of her right to privacy.[1] Insofar as such cases are successful, there are inevitable ramifications for Article 2, since an abortion that is protected by Article 8 cannot at the same time be contrary to Article 2. In contrast, an unsuccessful claim to a 'right to an abortion' under Article 8 on the basis of respect for private life[2] does not necessarily have consequences for Article 2.

In an early case,[3] the Commission expressed the opinion that in certain circumstances a sterilisation operation might be contrary to Article 2, presumably by denying a person the possibility even of conception. The application was dismissed on its facts because the operation was for medical reasons and the sterilised person had given her consent.[4] The question has not arisen since under Article 2 and would seem to come more properly within Articles 3 and 8.

A question that has not been considered directly is whether the state must provide adequate protection against acts (eg the pregnant woman's taking of drugs harmful to the foetus) that may reduce the 'quality of life' of a child without actually causing loss of life. The Commission has in other contexts

---

18 *Paton v UK No 8416/79*, 19 DR 244 (1980) (husband) and *H v Norway No 17004/90* (1992), unreported (partner).
19 *X v Austria No 7045/75*, 7 DR 87 (1976). Cf *X v Norway No 867/60*, 6 CD 34 (1961).
20 *Knudsen v Norway No 11045/84*, 42 DR 247 (1985).
1 See, in particular, *Brüggemann and Scheuten v FRG No 6959/75*, 10 DR 100 (1978). In that case, the Commission found it unnecessary to decide, in the context of an Article 8 claim, whether an unborn child is a person having a right to life for the purposes of Article 2. See Mr Fawcett's dissenting opinion.
2 In the *Paton* case, the husband's claim to respect for family life under Article 8 failed because of the 'rights of others' restriction in Article 8(2) (the wife's rights).
3 *No 1287/61*, cited in Fawcett, p 36.
4 The applicant was in fact the husband who unsuccessfully alleged a breach of Article 2 on the basis that he had not given his consent.

required that there be evidence of a danger to life, not just of ill-health, for Article 2 to apply.[5]

2. PROHIBITION OF THE TAKING OF LIFE

i. The general rule

Article 2 imposes liability for the actual taking of life where it is not justified by any of the four exceptions permitted by its text. Given that they are exceptions and that Article 2 is a provision from which derogation is not permitted in time of war or public emergency under Article 15,[6] they are 'exhaustive and must be narrowly interpreted'.[7] Liability applies to the taking of life by the state (by the police,[8] soldiers,[9] prison officers,[10] etc). It does not makes a state responsible for the taking of life by private persons.[11] A state's obligation in such cases is limited to the provision of legal protection in accordance with the first sentence of Article 2(1). The need to exhaust local remedies before a claim is brought arising out of deaths caused by state agents can be avoided if it can be shown that the deaths are the consequence of an 'administrative practice'; if they follow instead from a particular incident or incidents that are not the result of any official policy or practice, resort must first be had to the local courts.[12]

Cyprus v Turkey[13] is the one case in which a state has been found to have infringed Article 2 by the taking of life. There the Commission, having interviewed eye witnesses, found that twelve Greek Cypriot civilians had been killed in Northern Cyprus contrary to Article 2(1) by Turkish soldiers under the command of an officer following the 1974 invasion of northern Cyprus by Turkey. From other oral and written evidence given to the Commission, it also concluded that killings in breach of Article 2(1) had happened 'on a larger scale' than this. In addition, the Commission was satisfied that a number of Greek Cypriots who had been declared to be missing had been taken prisoner by Turkish troops following the invasion. Although accepting that there was a 'presumption of Turkish responsibility

---

5 *De Varga-Hirsch v France No 9559/81*, 33 DR 158 (1983) and *M v FRG No 10307/83*, 37 DR 113 (1984). Cf *X v Austria No 8278/78*, 18 DR 154 (1980).
6 See above, p 37, n 2.
7 *Stewart v UK No 10044/82*, 39 DR 162 at 169 (1984).
8 See eg *X v Belgium No 2758/66*, 12 YB 174 (1969).
9 See eg *Stewart v UK No 10044/82*, 39 DR 162 (1984).
10 For a case in which it was unsuccessfully claimed that Article 2 had been infringed because prison officers at Parkhurst Prison had a licence to kill, see *X v UK No 4203/69*, 34 CD 48 (1970).
11 Cf *Stewart v UK No 10044/82*, 39 DR 162 at 169 (1984).
12 *Ireland v UK* 41 CD 3 (1972).
13 (First and Second Applications) 4 EHRR 482 at 535–536 (1976) Com Rep. In 1979, the Committee of Ministers took note of the Commission's report and found that 'events which occurred in Cyprus constitute violations of the Convention': CM Res DH (79) 1. These included the violations of Article 2 established by the Commission.

for the fate of persons shown to have been in Turkish custody',[14] the Commission considered itself unable to reach any conclusion as to liability under Article 2 in the absence of evidence of the fact or circumstances of their deaths.[15]

A party to the Convention would appear to be responsible under Article 2 if it deports or extradites a person to another state when 'substantial grounds have been shown for believing that the person concerned . . . faces a real risk' on his return of being killed in circumstances that amount to a breach of Article 2.[16] This is the test adopted in *Soering v UK*[17] in respect of possible breaches of Article 3 resulting from the return of a fugitive offender to another state to face the death row phenomenon. It is submitted that it should apply so as to engage the returning state's responsibility for possible breaches of Article 2 also. The rule in the *Soering* case applies to a real risk of any breach of Article 2 following deportation or extradition, not just one involving the death penalty.

ii. Permitted exceptions

a. Capital punishment

The first exception concerns the death penalty, which is expressly permitted by Article 2(1). It may be imposed as a 'sentence of a court following . . . conviction for a crime for which this penalty is provided by law'. The use of the death penalty had to be allowed when the Convention was drafted because it was then generally provided for in the law of West European states. Practice has changed radically since, to the point where provision for the death penalty is very much the exception and, where it is available, is not carried out.[18] Accordingly, the Sixth Protocol to the Convention[19] abolishes the death penalty in peacetime for the parties to it. None the less, Article 2 remains the governing provision for those parties to the Convention that have not ratified the Sixth Protocol.[20] In *Soering v UK*,[1] the Court stated

14 Cf *Tomasi v France* A 241-A (1992), in which the Court stressed the defendant state's failure to explain injuries suffered in police detention when finding a breach of Article 3.
15 4 EHRR 482 at 535 (1976). This was partly due to the fact that the Commission was refused access by Turkey to the places of detention of Greek Cypriot prisoners: id 534. The Turkish Government also declined to respond to any of the allegations of killings. Cf *Cyprus v Turkey (Third Application)*, 15 EHRR 509 (1983).
16 Cf the facts of *Lynas v Switzerland No 7317/75*, 6 DR 141 (1976) (allegation that CIA agents would kill the applicant if he was extradited to the US).
17 A 161 (1989). In practice it may not matter whether a breach of Article 2 or 3 is established.
18 Cf *Soering v UK* A 161 para 102 (1989). On the invariable practice of commuting the death penalty in Belgium, see *No 17232/90* (1992) unreported. Article 2 does not in its terms prevent a state re-introducing the death penalty or re-commencing executions. Contrast Article 4, ACHR.
19 ETS 114. Adopted 1984. In force 1988. See below, p 564.
20 Of the 31 parties to the Convention 23 have ratified it. The UK has indicated its intention not to sign the Protocol. The death penalty remains the sentence in the UK for treason and in England and Wales for piracy with violence.
1 A 161 para 103 (1989).

that it would have been possible for the parties to the Convention informally to have 'abrogated' the exception provided for in Article 2(1) by the 'generalised abolition of capital punishment' in their national law. However, given the adoption of the Sixth Protocol as recently as 1983, the Court considered that this had not occurred. The position was, therefore, that the Article 2 exception continued in being, although the 'circumstances relating to a death penalty' might give rise to an issue under Article 3, both in respect of its application by the defendant state and by a state to which the defendant state deports or extradites a fugitive offender.[2] Likewise, it is submitted that its imposition is subject to the fair trial guarantee in Article 6, Convention and the prohibition of retroactive criminal punishment in Article 7, Convention, as well as to the non-discrimination requirement in Article 14, Convention.[3]

On its face, Article 2 permits the death penalty for any 'crime'. However, the principle of proportionality must apply, so that it should be permissible only for 'the most serious crimes'.[4] It is likely that the word 'crime' has an autonomous meaning in Article 2, as it has in Article 6.[5] Similarly, the meaning of the term 'court' developed for the purposes of Article 5[6] is relevant.

b.   Deaths resulting from the use of force for permitted purposes

Article 2(2) lists three other situations in which the taking of life by the state is justified. These are when it results from the use of force which is no more than absolutely necessary:

(i)   in self-defence or the defence of another;
(ii) to effect an arrest or prevent an escape; and
(iii) to quell a riot or insurrection.

At one stage in the drafting, a fourth exception was permitted:[7] where force is used to prohibit 'entry to a clearly defined place to which access is forbidden on grounds of national security'. This wording was finally omitted so that the taking of life on this basis was not intended to be allowed.

2   In the *Soering* case, the Court held that the UK would infringe Article 3 by extraditing the applicant to the US.
3   Opsahl, *European System*, Ch 11 at p 218, points out that it would it would be preferable to read such fair trial and other requirements into Article 2 rather than treat them as separate requirements in other articles since Article 2, unlike some other articles, cannot be derogated from in time of war or public emergency.
4   Cf *Soering v UK* A 161 para 104 (1989). Article 6, ICCPR and Article 4, ACHR, permit the death penalty only for 'the most serious crimes'. In the ACHR, it is also prohibited for 'political offences or related common crimes'. In the ICCPR, the imposition of the death penalty must not be contrary to the Genocide Convention (ie it must not be imposed so as to effect genocide).
5   See *Engel v Netherlands* A 22 (1976).
6   See the *Vagrancy* cases A 12 (1971).
7   See 3 TP 282 and 4 TP 58.

Article 2(2) permits the taking of life only when it results from the use of force which is 'no more than absolutely necessary' for one or more of the authorised purposes. In *Stewart v UK*,[8] the Commission stated that force is 'absolutely necessary' if it is 'strictly proportionate to the achievement of the permitted purpose'. The Commission continued:

> 'In assessing whether the use of force is strictly proportionate, regard must be had to the nature of the aim pursued, the dangers to life and limb inherent in the situation and the degree of risk that the force employed might result in the loss of life. The Commission's examination must have due regard to all the relevant circumstances.'

In the *Stewart* case, the applicant's thirteen-year-old son died after being hit on the head by a plastic bullet fired by a British soldier in Belfast. The son had been one of a crowd of 150 people who were throwing stones and bottles at an eight-man patrol. The patrol officer ordered a soldier to fire a baton round of plastic bullets at a leader among the rioters. As he did so, aiming at the youth's legs, the soldier was struck by missiles which caused him to hit the applicant's son instead.[9] In deciding that the force used was 'absolutely necessary', the Commission noted that public disturbances involving a loss of life were common in Northern Ireland; that riots such as that on the facts were sometimes used as cover for sniper fire against soldiers; that the detailed evidence presented to the Commission indicated that plastic bullets, although dangerous, were less dangerous than alleged;[10] that the soldier who was ordered to fire was trained and experienced in the use of plastic bullets; and that the eight soldiers were under attack by a hostile and violent crowd. These circumstances justified the ordering of the baton round to quell the riot. The death then resulted accidentally from the deflection of the soldier's aim.

In the *Stewart* case, it was argued by the defendant state that Article 2 was concerned only with the intentional taking of life, so that it did not regulate unintentional killings. The Commission rejected this argument, stating that:

> 'the text of Article 2, read as a whole, indicates that paragraph 2 does not primarily define situations where it is permitted intentionally to kill

---

8 *No 10044/82*, 39 DR 162 at 171 (1984). In interpreting Article 2(2) in this case, the Commission applied the Court's jurisprudence on the meaning of 'necessary' in Articles 8–11, as to which see *Handyside v UK* A 24 (1976). It added the word 'strictly' because of the word 'absolutely' in Article 2(2). In *Kelly v UK, No 17579/90* (1993) unreported, the Commission stated that the word 'absolutely' 'indicates that a stricter and more compelling test of necessity must be applied than in the context of other provisions of the Convention'.

9 These were the facts as found in civil proceedings in tort in the Northern Ireland courts. The Commission accepted these findings, which differed considerably from the account presented by the applicant, in accordance with its usual practice of accepting the facts as found by national courts. The civil claim failed on the basis that the force used was lawful under s 3(1) of the Criminal Law Act (NI) 1967: for the text, see below, p 50, n 4.

10 On the use of plastic bullets, see Jason-Lloyd, 140 NLJ 1492 (1990) and Robertson, 141 NLJ 340 (1991). On the use of CS gas, see *No 7126/75* (1977) 1 Digest 87.

an individual, but defines the situations where it is permissible to 'use force' which may result, as the unintended outcome of the use of force, in the deprivation of life.'[11]

In fact, cases that have arisen under Article 2(2) have concerned both intentional and unintentional killings.[12]

While it must be permissible for the police and security forces to use deadly weapons when confronted with dangerous criminals or terrorists who are reasonably believed to be armed, the 'absolutely necessary' test dictates caution. Questions and considerations that arise include the following:

> 'Is it proportionate to continue to fire even when the suspect has been wounded or appears to be neutralised in order to ensure that no residual threat remains? Under what circumstances may firearms be used to deal with persons armed with less dangerous weapons? The concept of proportionality must also take into account the possibility of reasonable error on the part of the actor. For example a policeman believes that he is confronted with a real weapon when, in fact the assailant is only armed with a toy gun or an unloaded weapon. The proportionality of his response must be judged in the light of the perceived facts as they occurred (against the background of the law concerning police use of firearms) as opposed to the facts established *ex post facto*.'[13]

IN SELF-DEFENCE OR THE DEFENCE OF ANOTHER

Article 2(2)(a) allows the use of force by the state in self-defence or the defence of another; it does not permit it in defence of property. It justifies the use of force in self defence only if the 'absolutely necessary' test is satisfied. This test was found to have been complied with in *Wolfgram v FRG*.[14] There the police arrested five men whom they reasonably (and correctly) suspected to be armed with dangerous weapons and on their way to commit an armed robbery. When one of the men detonated a grenade, the police opened fire, killing two of the men. The Commission found that the force used could be justified as being 'absolutely necessary' both in self-defence and to effect a lawful arrest. The Commission reached the same conclusion on the facts in *Diaz Ruano v Spain*,[15] in which an accused was

---

11 *Stewart v UK No 10044/82*, 39 DR 162 at 170 (1984). The Commission did not follow its earlier decision in *X v Belgium No 2758/66*, 12 YB 175 (1969) on this point.

12 There was no intent to kill in the *Stewart* case. For cases of intentional killing, see the *Farrell* and *Kelly* cases, below. It is not clear from the report whether the police shot with intent to kill in the *Wolfram* case, below.

13 O'Boyle, loc cit at p 37, n 1, above, p 5. Other considerations are whether the lives of innocent bystanders are placed at risk and the time available to the actor to assess the situation.

14 *No 11257/84*, 49 DR 213 (1986).

15 A 285-B (1994) Com Rep. F Sett before Court.

killed in police custody. The accused, a 21-year-old young man with no criminal record, was being questioned by two police officers at a police station in the absence of a lawyer while under arrest on suspicion of robbery. Becoming agitated, the accused seized one policeman's revolver and fired at the other policeman. The shot missed, but the policeman fired at took out his revolver and shot the accused dead. The policeman's conviction for manslaughter was overturned on appeal on grounds of self-defence. The Commission concluded that the killing fell within Article 2(2) as being 'absolutely necessary' in the policemen's defence. In a dissenting opinion, Mr Trechsel, joined by four other Commission members, emphasised that, in contrast with the national court prosecution against the policeman, under the Convention it was for the state to justify its agent's conduct under Article 2(2), and there were sufficient elements of doubt on the facts to lead to the conclusion that it had failed to do so.

The same problem of assessing what happened in fact was relevant in *McCann, Farrell and Savage v UK*.[16] In that case, three members of the Provisional IRA were shot dead on the street by SAS soldiers in Gibraltar. The persons killed were suspected of having on them a remote control device to be used to explode a bomb that was believed to be in a car parked in a public place, the explosion of which would have caused a 'devastating loss of life'.[17] In fact, the suspects did not have such a device on them and there was no bomb in the car. The Commission was of the opinion, by 11 to 6, that the shooting was justified under Article 2(2). It stated that:

> 'given the soldiers' perception of the risk to the lives of the people of Gibraltar – that a car bomb could be and was about to be detonated by the activation of a remote control device – the shooting of the three suspects can be considered as absolutely necessary for the legitimate aim of the defence of others from unlawful violence.'[18]

Although the shooting was with intent to kill, this could be justified on the basis that it was the only way to be sure that the suspects would not press the button that would cause the bomb to explode. In this connection, the Commission stated that 'a policy of shooting to kill terrorist suspects in preference to the inconvenience of resorting to the procedures of criminal justice would be in flagrant violation of' the Convention rights to life and to a fair trial.[19] However, no such policy was found to exist on the facts. In reaching its conclusion on the merits of the case, the Commission did not find it necessary to consider whether the Gibraltar Constitution, which permits the taking of life by such force 'as is reasonably justifiable' for the defence of any person from violence,[20] went further than Article 2 allowed;

16 *No 18984/91* (1994) Com Rep para 233. Case pending before the Court.
17 Id para 233.
18 Ibid.
19 Id para 206.
20 Cf the test in Northern Ireland law, below, p 51.

it was sufficient that on the facts the force used was 'absolutely necessary' as required by Article 2. In its conclusions, the Commission considered the proportionality of the defendant state's conduct at the level of operational responsibility as well as at the level of the conduct of the soldiers at the time of the incident. It indicated that the state was responsible under Article 2 not only for the conduct of the soldiers, but also for the way in which the operation had been planned. On the facts, the Commission concluded that, in the light of the good intelligence information that the authorities had received, their 'planning and execution of the operation' did not 'disclose any deliberate design or lack of proper care which might render the use of lethal force . . . disproportionate to the aim of defending other persons from unlawful violence'.[1]

TO EFFECT AN ARREST OR PREVENT AN ESCAPE

The use of force to effect an arrest (Article 2(2)(b)) was in issue in the two Northern Irish cases of *Farrell v UK*[2] and *Kelly v UK*.[3] In the *Farrell* case, four soldiers were placed on a rooftop at night as a result of intelligence suggesting that a bomb attack would be made by three men on a bank opposite. When three men were seen attacking (in fact robbing) two other men who were depositing money in the bank's night safe, the soldier in charge shouted 'Halt! I am ready to fire'. When the three men ran away, they were fired on with intent to kill in order to effect their arrest in the mistaken belief that they were terrorists. All three men, who were not believed to be armed, were killed. It was established in civil proceedings in the Northern Ireland courts that the soldiers had no means of contact with their base and were left in a situation where the only way of stopping the men escaping was to fire at them. The jury found that the soldiers had used force that was 'reasonable in the circumstances' to effect a lawful arrest or in the prevention of crime and hence lawful under s 3(1) of the Criminal Law Act (NI) 1967.[4] The case resulted in a friendly settlement before the Commission so that the Strasbourg authorities did not decide whether Article 2 had been infringed. In the *Farrell* case, the applicants had claimed not only that the shootings by the soldiers in the circumstances that confronted them were a breach of Article 2 but also that there was liability on the part of the defendant state because the whole operation had been negligently planned (the soldiers having no communications with their base, etc) at a higher level. This second claim was rejected as inadmissible for non-exhaustion of local remedies as it had not been raised in the national courts.

---

1 Id para 250.
2 *No 9013/80*, 30 DR 96 (1982) Decn Admiss; 38 DR 44 (1984) F Sett.
3 *No 17579/90*, (1993) unreported.
4 Section 3(1) is identical to s 3(1) of the Criminal Law Act 1967, which applies in England and Wales. Section 3(1) reads: 'A person may use such force as is reasonable in the circumstances in the prevention of crime, or in effecting or assisting in the lawful arrest of offenders or suspected offenders or of persons unlawfully at large.'

Were this not the case, the allegedly negligent planning of the operation by the authorities would, in terms of the *Stewart* test, have been a 'relevant circumstance' to have taken into account when considering the defendant state's responsibility under Article 2.[5]

The question of shooting with intent to kill to effect a lawful arrest was also raised in the *Kelly* case. There a seventeen-year-old joyrider was shot dead by soldiers in Northern Ireland who opened fire when he tried to evade an army checkpost. Prior to the application being made, a civil claim for compensation in tort had failed in the Northern Ireland courts because the use of force had been lawful under s 3(1) of the Criminal Law Act (NI) 1967, as being 'reasonable in the circumstances in the prevention of crime'. The national court relied upon the 'prevention of crime' justification for the use of force in s 3(1); it did not refer to the 'lawful arrest' ground for the use of force which s 3(1) also allowed. In assessing the facts, the trial court judge took into account that the soldiers had a genuine and reasonable belief that the youth was a terrorist; that they had shot at the driver with intent to kill or seriously injure him, this being the only way to stop the car; and that if the driver and the other youths in the car escaped they would probably commit other terrorist acts later. Applying the balancing test to be used in the application of s 3(1),[6] the judge held that the harm to be averted by preventing the occupants of the car from escaping so as to commit such acts was 'even graver' than that of shooting at them when there was a high probability of killing or seriously injuring them.

In its decision as to admissibility on the claim under Article 2, the Commission first decided that the soldiers had fired 'in order to effect a lawful arrest'. Having established this, the Commission found it unnecessary to consider the trial court judge's 'prevention of crime' justification for the shooting. As it noted, prevention of crime is a justification that is not permitted by the text of Article 2. Referring to the findings of fact of the trial court, the Commission stated that the use of force could be justified under Article 2 as being to effect a 'lawful arrest' because 'the shooting in this case was for the purpose of apprehending the occupants of the stolen car, who were reasonably believed to be terrorists, in order to prevent them carrying out terrorist activities'. The Commission's decision is open to criticism. Given that 'lawful' in Article 2(2)(b) means in part lawful under the law of the defendant state, it is to be noted that the Commission's decision was based on a mistaken view of Northern Irish law. Although force may be used under that law to prevent an offence, soldiers have no power of arrest on the ground of prevention of crime in a factual situation such as that in the *Kelly* case. As Smith[7] states, 'the Commission dismissed Mr Kelly's

---

5 Cf the *McCann* case, above, at p 49.
6 The test was spelt out by Lord Diplock in the *A-G for Northern Ireland's Reference (No 1 of 1975)*, [1977] AC 105 HL. The *Kelly* case went further on its facts than the *Attorney-General's Reference* case in which the supposition was that the escaping suspected terrorist who was killed would at once join others to ambush the army patrol.
7 144 NLJ 354 at 356 (1994).

application on the assumption that there existed in Northern Ireland a power of arrest which the Northern Irish courts had not recognised and which does not appear to exist'. The Commission's decision is also open to criticism if, as is submitted, 'lawful' in Article 2(2) means lawful under the Convention[8] as well as under national law. The arrest was not consistent with Article 5 of the Convention, which protects freedom of the person. Whereas under Article 5(1)(c) a person may be arrested 'when it is reasonably considered necessary to prevent his committing an offence', this supposes that he is about to commit a particular offence and that the intention upon arrest is to bring him before the 'competent legal authority' with a view to prosecution. On the facts of the *Kelly* case, there was no indication that the soldiers had grounds for believing that any particular terrorist offence was about to be committed or that the driver would be prosecuted upon arrest; the Commission's decision, like the judgment of the trial court, was in terms of the prevention of future terrorist acts at large.

Both the *Farrell* and *Kelly* cases raise the question whether the use of force with intent to kill can ever be justified to effect an arrest in accordance with a 'strict proportionality' test. If the person shot is about to kill another person, the shooting can be justified in terms of self-defence. To intend to kill is not consistent with the purpose of arrest under the Convention, which is to bring a person before the appropriate authorities, and ignores the possibility of a later arrest. The same reasoning applies to the use of deadly force against a person who is escaping from prison or other custody.

As to whether the force used in the *Kelly* case was 'absolutely necessary',[9] the Commission reasoned as follows:

> 'The Government have submitted, and the applicant has not disputed, that the only course of action open to the soldiers was either to open fire or to allow the car to escape. Neither before the domestic courts, nor before the Commission, was it contended that it would have been possible to immobilise the car by shooting at the tyres or the engine block. The Commission notes that the High Court judge commented that there was a high probability that shots fired at the driver would kill him or inflict serious injury. The situation facing the soldiers, however, had developed with little or no warning and involved conduct by the driver putting them and others at considerable risk of injury.[10] Their conduct must be assessed against the background of the events in Northern Ireland, which is facing a situation in which terrorist killings have become a feature of life. In this context the Commission recalls the judge's comments that, although the risk of harm to the occupants was high, the kind of harm to be averted (as the soldiers reasonably

---

8 Cf the interpretation of 'lawful' in Article 5: see eg *Bozano v France* A 111 (1986).

9 The Commission did not comment on the discrepancy between the Convention's 'absolutely necessary' test and the less strict 'reasonable in the circumstances' in England and Wales and Northern Ireland.

10 Ed. But no claim of self-defence was made.

thought) by preventing their escape was even greater, namely the freedom of terrorists to resume their dealings in death and destruction.'

Thus the Commission held that in the context of the Northern Ireland emergency soldiers may shoot with intent to kill or cause serious injury[11] in circumstances in which death is a probable result where this is the only way of preventing the escape of persons who it is reasonably suspected are terrorists who will commit further terrorist acts against the community. The Commission's approach can, again, be criticised. Its reliance upon the particular circumstances in Northern Ireland must be judged against the fact that Article 2 cannot be derogated from in time of public emergency[12] and the Commission's own view that exceptions to the right to life must be narrowly interpreted.[13] As to the use of force to effect an arrest to prevent future terrorist offences (supposing this to be 'lawful'), whereas the use of deadly force might be permissible to prevent the imminent use of such force by another person (in which case, as suggested above, the self-defence justification is more convincing), it is submitted that deadly force should never be considered as being 'absolutely necessary' to prevent future, undefined criminal acts. Given the importance of the issues involved in the case, it is regrettable that the *Kelly* case was dismissed as manifestly ill-founded and not allowed to proceed for a final decision on the merits.

TO QUELL A RIOT OR INSURRECTION

The terms 'riot' and 'insurrection' in Article 2(2)(c) have an autonomous Convention meaning. This was held in the *Stewart* case in respect of the term 'riot' and can be taken to be true of 'insurrection' also. In that case, the Commission declined to define the term 'riot', deciding only on the facts of the case that 'an assembly of 150 persons throwing missiles at a patrol of soldiers to the point that they risked serious injury must be considered, by any standard, to constitute a riot'.[14] In that case also, the Commission established that there is no obligation to retreat when quelling a riot. As in the case of the other permitted exceptions, the strict interpretation of the 'absolutely necessary' requirement adopted in the *Stewart* case is important in ensuring caution on the part of law enforcement officers when dealing

---

11 The *Kelly* case illustrates one kind of situation that has led to the allegation of a 'shoot to kill' policy in Northern Ireland, ie the situation in which the security forces are permitted by the general law (rather than as a result of any official policy within the law) to use deadly force to prevent suspected terrorists escaping. The other situation is that in which the security forces are allegedly (this has not been proven) authorised or instructed to kill suspected terrorists they seek out or happen upon. See generally on the 'shoot to kill' issue, Jennings, in Jennings, ed, *Justice under Fire*, 1988, Ch 5. Such a policy would be in breach of Article 2: see above, p 49.

12 The case may be distinguished on this basis from *Brogan v UK* A 145-B (1988), in which the Court relied upon the emergency situation when applying Article 5, from which derogation is permitted.

13 See above at p 47, n 6.

14 39 DR 162 at 172 (1984).

with large crowds at public meetings and demonstrations that get out of control. In *X v Belgium*,[15] the shooting of an innocent bystander by a policeman acting to quell a riot was not excused as being within Article 2(2)(c) because his use of firearms had not been 'lawful' under Belgian law for the reason that the required authorisation had not been given.

3. CONCLUSION

The meaning of the right to life in Article 2 of the Convention has been the subject of a number of cases before the European Commission of Human Rights, but has not as yet been considered by the European Court of Human Rights. The Commission has explored the meaning of the positive obligation upon the state in Article 2 to protect life, although it has still to answer a number of questions as to the scope of this obligation in respect of such matters as the provision of medical care and a healthy environment. In this regard, Article 2 has not as yet been given as broad a meaning as it has, at least on paper, in the practice of the Human Rights Committee interpreting the equivalent guarantee in the International Covenant on Civil and Political Rights.[16]

With regard to the taking of life by the state, the most important case to be decided on its merits has been *Cyprus v Turkey* in which the Commission and the Committee of Ministers did not shrink from finding that the defendant state was responsible for large-scale violations of Article 2. Insofar as it authorises the intentional taking of life by capital punishment, Article 2 has been eclipsed for most parties to the Convention by their acceptance of the Sixth Protocol to it. The other exceptional circumstances in which the taking of life is permitted by Article 2 have been interpreted by the Commission in several cases concerning Northern Ireland. Whereas an appropriately limited meaning of 'absolutely necessary', has been adopted, the reasoning of the Commission in the *Kelly* case and the dismissal of that application at the admissibility stage can be criticised.

Finally, the Commission has made some cautious progress on the contentious question of the right to life of the unborn child. It has so far found that abortions for broad health or social reasons are permitted, although it is not clear that it would go as far as to allow an unqualified right to abortion for the pregnant woman along the lines of the celebrated case of *Roe v Wade*.[17]

---

15 *No 2758/66*, 12 YB 174 (1969). Declared inadmissible on other grounds.
16 See Nowak, *UN Covenant on Civil and Political Rights: CCPR Commentary*, English translation, 1993, pp 103ff.
17 410 US 113 (1973).

CHAPTER 3
Article 3: Freedom from torture or inhuman or degrading treatment or punishment

'**Article 3**

No one shall be subjected to torture or to inhuman or degrading treatment or punishment.'

1. INTRODUCTION[1]

Article 3, which applies to human beings but not other legal persons,[2] contains an absolute guarantee of the rights it protects. It has been said to do so in two senses.[3] Firstly, it cannot be derogated from in time of war or other public emergency.[4] It is this, as well as the historical background to the Convention, that has led to the argument that it should not be trivialised, ie understood to prohibit other than the most serious forms of ill-treatment.[5] As Judge Fitzmaurice has pointed out, the temptation to lower the threshold of Article 3 is great since 'the Convention contains no prohibition covering intermediate forms of maltreatment . . . [so] that, if they are not actually caught by the strict language of the Convention, they deserve to be . . . because . . . they are nevertheless irreconcilable with the high ideal of human rights. . . .'[6]

Secondly, Article 3, unlike most Convention articles, is expressed in unqualified terms. This can be understood as meaning that ill-treatment within the terms of Article 3 is never permitted, even for the highest reasons of public interest. On this basis, it has been held that the need to fight

---

1 On Article 3 generally, see Cassese, *European System*, Ch 11; Doswald-Beck, 25 NILR 24 (1978); and Duffy, 32 ICLQ 316 (1983). On the treatment of detained persons under Article 3 and other articles of the Convention, see Reynaud, *Human Rights in Prisons*, CE Pub, Human Rights File No 5, 1986, and the reports for the 7th International Colloquy on the European Convention on Human Rights, on the Human Rights of Persons Deprived of their Liberty, 1990. See also Rodley, *The Treatment of Prisoners under International Law*, 1987. As to whether Article 3 applies to socio-economic conditions, see Cassese, 2 EJIL 141 (1991)

2 *Kontakt-Information-Therapie and Hagen v Austria No 11921/86*, 57 DR 81 (1988).

3 *Ireland v UK* A 25 para 163 (1978).

4 Article 15(2), Convention.

5 See eg the joint partially dissenting opinion of Messrs Schermers, Batliner, Vandenberghe and Hall in *Warwick v UK, No 9471/81*, 60 DR 5 at 20 (1986) Com Rep; CM Res DH (89) 5.

6 *Ireland v UK* A 25 (1978). Separate opinion.

terrorism cannot justify violations of physical integrity[7] or the use of psychological interrogation techniques[8] causing suffering above the threshold level of Article 3. However, there are recognised exceptions to the absolute nature of Article 3 in this second sense. As Fawcett has indicated,[9] if the taking of life by the state is not contrary to Article 2 of the Convention in certain circumstances (eg on grounds of self-defence), 'it must follow *a fortiori* that severe wounding is in such circumstances justifiable'. Similarly, conditions of detention that might otherwise be in breach of Article 3 may also be justified by reference to the need to prevent escape or suicide.[10] In addition, considerations of penal policy may lead to the different treatment of conduct causing the same level of suffering. For example, whereas judicial corporal punishment is degrading punishment contrary to Article 3,[11] imprisonment in normal prison conditions, which is just as degrading, is not. Finally, the absolute nature of the guarantee in Article 3 is qualified by the fact that consent may negative liability under Article 3, at least in some cases of medical treatment.[12]

Ill-treatment 'must attain a minimum level of severity' if it is to fall within Article 3. The threshold level is a relative one:

> '. . . it depends on all the circumstances of the case, such as the duration of the treatment, its physical or mental effects and, in some cases, the sex, age and state of health of the victim, etc.'[13]

These factors are relevant both when determining whether the suffering caused is sufficient to amount to inhuman or degrading treatment or punishment and when distinguishing between these lesser kinds of ill-treatment proscribed by Article 3 and torture. Where the facts of a case have warranted this, the Commission and the Court have commonly, but not always,[14] sought to distinguish between the different categories of ill-treatment listed in Article 3.[15] Although there is no need to draw such distinctions in the sense that Article 3 is infringed whatever the precise category of ill-treatment concerned, the boundary between torture and other forms of ill-treatment is relevant both to the question of compensation that

---

7   *Tomasi v France* A 241-A para 115 (1992).
8   *Ireland v UK* A 25 para 163 (1978).
9   *Ireland v UK* B 23-I, p 502 Com Rep (1976). Separate opinion. Cf *Hurtado v Switzerland* below, p 65 (proportionate force).
10 See *Kröcher and Möller v Switzerland No 8463/78*, 34 DR 24 (1982) Com Rep; CM Res DH (83) 15.
11 *Tyrer v UK* A 26 (1978).
12 See *X v Denmark No 9974/82*, 32 DR 282 (1983) and below, p 73. On self-inflicted conditions of detention, contrast *McFeeley v UK* ('dirty protest'), below, p 66, and *Soering v UK* (prolongation of time on death row by appeals), below, p 76.
13 *Ireland v UK* A 25 para 162 (1978). As to the relevance of the sensitivity of the particular applicant in a case of 'degrading' punishment, see *Campbell and Cosans v UK* A 48 para 30 (1982).
14 In *Soering v UK* the question whether the ill-treatment was 'treatment' or 'punishment' was not considered.
15 On the close inter-relationship between inhuman and degrading treatment or punishment, see below, p 81.

may be awarded under Article 50 and to a state's reputation. With regard to the latter, the United Kingdom's concession before the Court in *Ireland v UK*[16] that the 'five techniques' were torture, not just inhuman or degrading treatment, proved to be ill-conceived when the Court held that only the latter had occurred.

An important question is whether a state is responsible under Article 3 for the acts of its servants or agents that are *ultra vires*. In *Cyprus v Turkey*,[17] the Commission found the defendant state to be responsible for rapes committed by its soldiers because adequate measures had not been taken to prevent them or to effect disciplinary measures after the event. In *Ireland v UK*,[18] the Court considered whether a state might claim not to be responsible on the basis of ignorance of the conduct of its servants of agents. It stated that where the conduct in breach of Article 3 amounted to a practice incompatible with the Convention, it was 'inconceivable that the higher authorities of a state should be, or at least be entitled to be, unaware of the existence of such a practice'. Moreover, 'under the Convention those authorities are strictly liable for the conduct of their subordinates; they are under a duty to impose their will on subordinates and cannot shelter behind their inability to ensure that it is respected'.

A further issue is whether the state is responsible under Article 3 for failing to 'secure' (Article 1 of the Convention) an individual's rights by not providing legal protection against ill-treatment by private persons. In *Costello-Roberts v UK*,[19] the Court held that such responsibility does exist in the case of disciplinary corporal punishment in private schools. However, the Court reached this conclusion on very narrow grounds. It noted that there was an obligation in Article 2, First Protocol to the Convention, which the defendant state had accepted, to secure for children the right to education – a right that included appropriate limits on school discipline and that supposed no distinction between state and private schools. In the Court's view, a state could not avoid liability under the Convention by delegating its obligations to 'secure' a right protected by it to private bodies or individuals. Whether the Court would limit the responsibility of a state under Article 3 to control private conduct to situations where ill-treatment is in the sphere of another Convention right that the state has undertaken to guarantee has yet to be determined.[20] In

16 A 25 (1978). On *Ireland v UK*, see Bonner, 27 ICLQ 897 (1978); Cohn, 11 CWRJIL 159 (1979); Martin, 83 RGDIP 104 (1979); Mertens, 13 RBDI 10 (1977); O'Boyle, 71 AJIL 674 (1977); Pelloux, 24 AFDL 379 (1978); Spjut, 73 AJIL 267 (1979).
17 *Nos 6780/74 and 6950/75 (First and Second Applications)* 4 EHRR 482 at 537 (1976) Com Rep; CM Res DH (79) 1.
18 A 25 para 159 (1978).
19 A 247-C (1993).
20 In *X and Y v Netherlands* A 91 (1985) the Court found it unnecessary to consider a claim that the defendant state had infringed Article 3 by failing to provide the applicant with adequate legal protection against sexual abuse by a private person. The Commission found that there was an obligation to provide such protection under Article 8, but not under Article 3. However, the obligation upon a state not to return persons to another state to face a risk of ill-treatment by (private) terrorists, see below, p 78, n 18, might suggest that steps must be taken to prevent ill-treatment by terrorists at home.

the *Costello-Roberts*[1] case, the Commission adopted a broader basis for its opinion, arguing that Article 3 imposed 'a positive obligation on High Contracting Parties to ensure a legal system which provides adequate protection to children's physical and emotional integrity'. The United Kingdom was accordingly liable, in the opinion of the Commission, because the English legal system had authorised and provided no effective redress against the punishment that had been inflicted on the facts. The Court's more cautious approach may have been motivated by the possible ramifications of the Commission's reasoning for state responsibility under Article 3 in other areas of private ill-treatment. However, a reading of Article 3 by which parties were under a positive obligation to secure individuals against *all* private ill-treatment otherwise contrary to Article 3 would be consistent with the human rights 'object and purpose' of the Convention and with the existence of such an obligation in certain other Convention guarantees.[2] It would, for example, provide a means of controlling domestic violence or racial discrimination by private persons. Ill-treatment in private prisons could also be made subject to Article 3 on this basis.

A claim under Article 3 may raise an issue under another article of the Convention as well. In practice, this overlap has occurred mostly in the areas covered by Articles 3 and 8, particularly in connection with the rights to respect for family and private life. In such cases, the approach has been to concentrate primarily upon the claim under Article 8.[3] If Article 8 is not infringed, it is unlikely that there will be a breach of Article 3.[4]

Article 3 contrasts with the equivalent Article 7 of the ICCPR insofar as it omits any reference to 'cruel' treatment or punishment. This is not significant. The prohibition of 'cruel' treatment or punishment have been subsumed under the existing terms of Article 3.[5]

Article 3 is supplemented by the European Convention for the Prevention of Torture and Inhuman and Degrading Treatment or Punishment 1987.[6] Whereas the European Convention on Human Rights provides a remedy for a state or an individual victim after the event when Article 3 is infringed, the Prevention of Torture Convention establishes a preventive system whereby an independent committee of experts is authorised to visit public places of detention in states parties to the Convention to examine their treatment

---

1 A 247-C (1993) Com Rep para 37. Cf *Y v UK* A 247-A (1992) Com Rep para 36 (another school corporal punishment case).
2 See pp 19-22, above.
3 See eg *Marckx v Belgium* A 31 (1979) and *X and Y v Netherlands* A 91 (1985).
4 Eg a decision to take a child into public care is unlikely to be a breach of Article 3 if consistent with Article 8: *Olsson v Sweden (No 1)* A 130 (1988). Cf *Hendriks v Netherlands No 8427/78*, 29 DR 5 (1982) Com Rep; CM Res DH (82) 4.
5 See eg *Ireland v UK* A 25 (1978).
6 ETS 126; UKTS 5 (1991), Cm 1634. The Convention has been ratified by 29 parties, all of which are parties to the ECHR. On the Convention, see Cassese, 83 AJIL 128 (1989); Evans and Morgan, 41 ICLQ 590 (1992); id 34 BRC Special Issue 141 (1994); Murdoch, 5 EJIL 220 (1994). See also the UN Torture Convention 1984, 6 EHRR 259; 23 ILM 1027; 24 ILM 535.

'with a view to strengthening, if necessary, the protection of such persons from torture and from 'inhuman or degrading treatment or punishment' (Article 1). The Committee has visited places of detention (police stations, prisons, mental hospitals) of its choice in all of the states parties to the Convention.[7] It adopts national reports in which it indicates its findings and makes recommendations and suggestions as to improvements for the protection of detained persons. If a state refuses to co-operate or to act upon the Committee's recommendations, it is empowered, as its only sanction, to issue a public statement.[8] The national reports are confidential, except that they may be published at the request of the state concerned. In practice, most states have requested publication. It is noticeable from these that the Prevention of Torture Committee has tended to read the wording inhuman or degrading treatment or punishment more widely than the Court.[9] Although the European Court has not so far made use of evidence of ill-treatment contained in the Prevention of Torture Committee's reports, individual judges have referred to them.[10]

2. TORTURE

In *Ireland v UK*,[11] the Court defined torture as 'deliberate inhuman treatment causing very serious and cruel suffering'. Applying this test, it held that neither the use of the 'five techniques'[12] nor the physical assaults that had occurred in that case were torture. By 'deliberate' the Court meant that suffering must be inflicted intentionally.[13] It is possible to read the

7 See the Committee's annual and national reports. These are all available from the Council of Europe.
8 It has done so once: see the 1992 Public Statement on Turkey, 15 EHRR 309 at 315; 2 IHRR 251 (1995), in which the Committee indicated its conclusion that 'the practice of torture and other forms of severe ill-treatment of persons in police custody remains widespread'.
9 See Murdoch, 5 EJIL 220 (1994).
10 See the dissenting opinions of Judges Pettiti and Spielmann in *Klaas v Germany* A 269 (1993).
11 A 25 para 167 (1978). The Court referred to the definition of torture in the 1975 UN Declaration on Torture, etc, GA Resn 3452 (XXX), GAOR, 30th Sess, Supp 34, p 91: 'Torture constitutes an aggravated and deliberate form of cruel, inhuman or degrading treatment or punishment'. See also the more recent definition in the UN Torture Convention 1984, Article 1: 'For the purposes of this Convention, the term "torture" means any act by which severe pain or suffering, whether physical or mental, is intentionally inflicted on a person for such purposes as obtaining from him or a third person information or a confession, punishing him for an act he or a third person has committed or is suspected of having committed, or intimidating or coercing him or a third person, or for any reason based on discrimination of any kind, when such pain or suffering is inflicted by or at the instigation of or with the consent or acquiescence of a public official or other person acting in an official capacity. It does not include pain or suffering arising only from, inherent in or incidental to lawful sanctions.'
12 For the 'five techniques', see below, p 65.
13 The distinction between deliberate and reckless or negligent conduct has yet to be considered. As to premeditation, see below, p 62, n 8.

Court's judgment as meaning that, in contrast with inhuman treatment or punishment, the infliction of suffering must be for a purpose in order to amount to torture.[14] This certainly was the view of the Commission in the *Greek* case[15] where it stated that torture was an aggravated form of inhuman treatment 'which has a purpose, such as the obtaining of information or confession, or the infliction of punishment'. Provided that the sadistic infliction of suffering can be regarded as being for a purpose,[16] this additional requirement probably makes no difference in practice. Because of the absolute nature of Article 3, the causing of 'very serious and cruel suffering' cannot be saved from being torture on the ground, for example, that its purpose is to extract information from terrorists that will protect innocent lives.[17]

The only Strasbourg case in which torture has been held to have occurred as a matter of final decision is the *Greek* case,[18] in which the Commission's finding was confirmed by the Committee of Ministers. In that case, the Commission concluded that political detainees had been subjected by the Athens security police to an administrative practice of 'torture and ill-treatment' contrary to Article 3.[19] This had most often taken the form of *falanga*[20] or severe beatings of all parts of the body with a view to extracting confessions and other information as to the political activities of subversive individuals.[1] The Court held that torture had not occurred in *Ireland v UK* because the intensity of the suffering inflicted was insufficient. Remarkably, the unanimous opinion of the Commission in that case that the use in combination of the 'five techniques' had amounted to torture was rejected by the Court by a large majority. The Court would appear to have applied a more rigorous test for suffering to amount to torture; it is also possible that

---

14 The Court pointed out, para 167, that the purpose of the 'five techniques' and the assaults had been to obtain confessions and other information. Judge Fitzmaurice 'firmly rejected' any such requirement: footnote 19 of his separate opinion.

15 12 YB (the *Greek* case) 1 at 186 (1969) Com Rep; CM Res DH (70) 1. Cf *Ireland v UK* B 23-I, p 388 Com Rep (1976). See also the 'purpose' requirement in the UN Torture Convention 1984, Article 1, above, p 59, n 11.

16 In *Ireland v UK*, Judge Matscher suggested that it could. In any case, most cases of ill-treatment will involve other clear purposes, such as obtaining information.

17 See the Court's emphasis in *Ireland v UK* upon the 'absolute' nature of Article 3 and the irrelevance of the 'victim's conduct'. Although the UK Parker Committee Report, Cmnd 4901, had justified the conduct of the security forces in Northern Ireland in terms of its anti-terrorist purpose, the UK made no such argument in *Ireland v UK*.

18 12 YB (the *Greek* case) 1 at 504 Com Rep; CM Res DH (70) 1.

19 The Commission also characterised as 'torture *or* ill-treatment' (italics added) certain other instances of ill-treatment: see below, p 62.

20 Beating of the feet by a wooden stick or metal bar causing excruciating pain and leaving no marks.

1   There are a number of examples of physical assaults of various kinds constituting torture in the practice of the HRC under the ICCPR: see eg *Motta v Uruguay*, GAOR, 35th Sess, Supp 40, p 132. Other graphic, hypothetical examples are given by Judge Fitzmaurice in his separate opinion in *Ireland v UK*. See also the allegations in *Sargin and Yacci v Turkey Nos 14116-7/88*, 61 DR 250 (1989); 76A DR 5 (1994) F Sett.

it was less impressed than the Commission by the effects of psychological methods of interrogation.[2] However, as has been pointed out, the Court's ruling was surprising 'given that the Commission had found convincing evidence of weight loss, mental disorientation and acute psychiatric symptoms during interrogation in some of the 14 suspects subjected to these techniques'.[3] Both the Commission and the Court considered that the physical assaults of detainees in the same case caused insufficient suffering to amount to torture, although, like the use of the 'five techniques', they did constitute inhuman treatment.

It is implicit in *Ireland v UK*[4] that mental anguish alone may constitute torture provided that the resulting suffering is sufficiently serious; suffering caused by bodily injury is not essential.[5] In the *Greek* case,[6] the Commission referred to 'non-physical torture', which it described as 'the infliction of mental suffering by creating a state of anguish and stress by means other than bodily assault'. Evidence which the Commission considered under this heading, without concluding that any amounted to torture on the facts, involved mock executions and threats of death, various humiliating acts and threats of reprisal against a detainee's family.

3. INHUMAN TREATMENT

Ill-treatment 'must attain a minimum level of severity' if it is to amount to inhuman treatment contrary to Article 3.[7] In contrast with torture, inhuman

---

2 Note Judge Evrigenis' concern in *Ireland v UK*, A 25 (1978) that the Court's judgment might be read as excluding from torture 'new forms of suffering which have little in common with the bodily pain caused by the conventional torments' and which aim 'at inducing even temporarily the disintegration of the human personality, the destruction of man's mental and psychological balance and the annihilation of his will'.

3 Amnesty International, *Torture in the Eighties*, 1984, p 15.

4 See also *Tyrer v UK* A 26 (1978); *Campbell and Cosans v UK* A 48 (1982); and *Soering v UK* A 161 (1989).

5 In some cases, mental suffering will be pain resulting from bodily injury. Although the test of liability under Article 3 is consistently expressed by the Commission and the Court in terms of suffering, in *Cyprus v Turkey Nos 6780/74 and 6950/75 (First and Second Applications)*, 4 EHRR 482 at 540 (1976) Com Rep; CM Res DH (79) 1, inhuman treatment was found to have occurred upon proof of bodily injury by itself. It is not clear whether this was on the basis of assumed suffering or that bodily injury is a separate head of liability. The former would be more consistent with the theory of Article 3.

6 12 YB (the *Greek* case) 1 at 461 Com Rep; CM Res DH (70) 1 (1969).

7 *Ireland v UK* A 25 (1978). Cf above, p 56, on the threshold for breaches of Article 3 generally. The threshold requirement has led to the rejection of a number of claims where the suffering experienced clearly fell short of that required by Article 3: see eg *X v UK No 9261/81*, 28 DR 177 (1982) (expropriation of home); *X v FRG No 8819/79*, 24 DR 158 (1981) (police questioning of children); *X v UK No 10165/82*, 5 EHRR 516 (1983) (close supervision of prison visits); *Hogben v UK No 11653/85*, 46 DR 231 (1986) (change in penal policy delaying prisoner's release); *Wakefield v UK No 15817/89*, 66 DR 251 (1990) (transfer to distant prison); *M v France No 10078/82*, 41 DR 103 (1984) (restriction on place of residence); and *Kotalla v Netherlands* 14 DR 238 (1988) (no possibility of early release for life prisoner).

treatment need not be intended to cause suffering,[8] although in practice it is likely that such an intention will be present. As the Court has emphasised,[9] the crucial distinction lies in the degree of suffering caused. Clearly, less intense suffering is required than in the case of torture. A threat of torture, provided that it is 'sufficiently real and immediate', may generate enough mental suffering to be inhuman treatment.[10] Conduct giving rise to inhuman treatment may take various forms, including physical assault,[11] the use of psychological interrogation techniques, the detention of a person in inhuman conditions and the deportation or extradition of a person to face a real risk of inhuman treatment in another country. In *Tanko v Finland*,[12] the Commission stated that it 'does not exclude that a lack of proper medical care in a case where someone is suffering from a serious illness could in certain circumstances amount to treatment contrary to Article 3'.

i.   Assaults

Most cases of assault have concerned persons in detention. Assaults that were sufficiently serious in terms of the suffering caused to have amounted to inhuman treatment were unanimously held to have occurred in *Ireland v UK*. In one group of cases, four detainees were found by a prison doctor to have contusions and bruising which were caused by severe beatings by members of the security forces in Northern Ireland during interrogation at Palace Barracks.[13] In the *Greek* case,[14] assaults by Greek security police upon political detainees in the course of interrogation during the Regime of the Colonels were 'torture or ill-treatment' contrary to Article 3. In addition to *falanga* and severe beating of all parts of the body,[15] these included 'the application of electric shock, squeezing of the head in a vice, pulling out of

---

8   *Ireland v UK* A 25 para 167 (1978). Note, however, this is not the view of the Commission which requires that inhuman treatment be 'deliberate' also: the *Greek* case, 12 YB (the *Greek* case) 1 at 186 (1969). In *Soering v UK* A 161 para 100 (1989) the Court stated that in *Ireland v UK* it had found the use of the 'five techniques' to be inhuman 'because it was *premeditated* . . . and caused . . . intense . . . suffering' (italics added). Although the Court did find premeditation on the facts of *Ireland v UK*, para 167, it is not clear from the judgment in that case that premeditation is required for either inhuman treatment or torture. See, however, Cassese, *European System*, Ch 11 at p 246.

9   *Ireland v UK* A 25 para 167 (1978).

10 *Campbell and Cosans v UK* A 48 para 26 (1982).

11 But an assault resulting in death cannot be 'inhuman treatment' in breach of Article 3 if it is justified under Article 2: *Stewart v UK No 10044/82*, 39 DR 162 (1984).

12 *No 23634/94* (1994), unreported. On the requirement of medical treatment for detainees, see below, p 71.

13 The Court focused upon this group of cases to establish that there had been an administrative practice contrary to Article 3. It also drew attention to, but did not rule upon, other assaults during transit or interrogation that 'must have been individual violations of Article 3': A 25 para 182 (1978).

14 12 YB (the *Greek* case) 1 (1969) Com Rep; CM Res DH (70) 1. The term 'ill-treatment' was used to refer generally to treatment in breach of Article 3 other than torture.

15 These are described as 'torture *and* ill-treatment' (italics added) elsewhere in the report: see above, p 60.

hair from the head or pubic region, or kicking of the male genital organs, dripping water on the head, and intense noises to prevent sleep'.[16] In *Cyprus v Turkey*,[17] incidents of rape and assaults upon prisoners (in one case leading to death) by Turkish soldiers following the invasion of Cyprus by Turkey were both considered to be inhuman treatment contrary to Article 3. It is probable that a single act of rape is inhuman and degrading treatment of the victim, although there is no case-law on the point. There would be a breach of Article 3 in such a case where the offender was a state agent or where the act was not a crime under national law.[18]

A number of claims of inhuman treatment have been made in individual applications arising out of alleged assaults of persons during arrest or in detention on remand or following conviction. In *Tomasi v France*,[19] the applicant was arrested for a murder related to Corsican terrorist activities. The Court upheld his claim that he had been assaulted to the point of ill-treatment in breach of Article 3 while in custody at a police station. The Court relied upon separate medical certificates and reports by four doctors that attested to 'the large number of blows inflicted upon Mr Tomasi and their intensity'.[20] This by itself was sufficient to establish suffering at the level and of the kind required to amount to both inhuman and degrading treatment contrary to Article 3. On the question of causation, in the face of denials by the police officers concerned that they had assaulted the applicant and in the absence of evidence from witnesses, the Court noted that the defendant government had not suggested any alternative explanation for the marks which the doctors had each found on the applicant's body and identified as having been caused during the period of detention. The Court also noted that the applicant had at once drawn attention to the marks when brought before a judge. In the light of this evidence and on the basis that it was for the state to show that its agents were not responsible, the Court considered it proven that the injuries had been suffered at the hands of the police during custody.[1] As to any possible justification for the use of

---

16 12 YB (the *Greek* case) 1 at 500 (1969) Com Rep; CM Res DH (70) 1.
17 Nos 6780/74 and 6950/75 *(First and Second Applications)* 4 EHRR 482 at 537 (1976) Com Rep; CM Res DH (79) 1.
18 Such cases may, however, be dealt with under Article 8. In *X and Y v Netherlands* A 91 (1985) the question whether the suffering of a sexual assault victim was sufficient to establish inhuman or degrading treatment was not considered where a breach of the right to respect for private life under Article 8 had been found.
19 A 241-A (1992). On the *Tomasi* case, see Tompkins, 52 CLJ 9 (1993). For a claim of assault of a convicted prisoner, see *Reed v UK No 7630/76*, 19 DR 113 (1979).
20 A 241-A para 115 (1992). The medical evidence established remaining superficial abrasions and bruises on the face, arm and chest and injury to an ear.
1 Cf the approach to responsibility for the fate of persons in custody under Article 2: *Cyprus v Turkey*, above, p 44. See, however, *Diaz Ruano v Spain* above, p 48, in which the Commission found it not established beyond a reasonable doubt that marks on a person's body had been caused by the police at a police station. In the *Tomasi* case, the applicant's civil claim for assault failed in the French courts, *inter alia*, because it was not possible to identify any particular person who had committed an offence. Under Article 3, there is no need to identify a culprit; it is sufficient if it must have been a person whose acts engage state responsibility.

violence by the police in the case, the Court stated that 'the undeniable difficulties inherent in the fight against crime, particularly with regard to terrorism, cannot result in limits being placed on the protection to be afforded in respect of the physical integrity of individuals'.[2]

The outcome of the *Tomasi* case is to be contrasted with that in *Klaas v Germany*.[3] In the latter case, a woman driver suffered injuries in the course of being arrested by the police for a blood test for alcohol. Whereas the applicant argued that the injuries had been caused by excessive police force, the defendant state claimed that the applicant had injured herself while resisting a lawful arrest. Faced with this conflict of evidence, a German court had rejected a civil claim for compensation against the police because the applicant, who had the burden of proof on this point, had not satisfied the national court that the injuries had been caused by the use of excessive force. Accepting the findings of fact by the national court, the European Court held that Article 3 had not been infringed because it had not established that the injuries were caused by the use of excessive force by the police. In a brief passage, the Court distinguished the *Tomasi* case. Whereas in that case 'certain inferences could be made from the fact that Mr Tomasi had sustained unexplained injuries during forty-eight hours spent in police custody', in the *Klaas* case no 'cogent elements have been provided which could lead the Court to depart from the findings of fact of the national courts'.[4] However, this statement does not make it clear that the national court had found that the evidence as to whether excessive force had been used was inconclusive and decided against the applicant because she had failed to satisfy the burden of proof, which fell upon her, not the police. The judgment of the European Court supposes that, as under German law, in a claim under Article 3 such as that in the *Klaas* case it is for the applicant to satisfy the Court that the suffering complained of is the responsibility of the state.

The Court's approach was criticised by Judge Walsh in his dissenting opinion on the ground that under Article 3 the burden of proof should always be placed upon the police in respect of injuries to any person under arrest.[5] However, the Court's decision can be justified on the basis that a distinction can be drawn between the situation where injuries occur to an arrested person while out of sight in a police station and where they occur during an 'on the street' incident. The argument for a more rigorous approach, requiring a reversal of the burden of proof in all cases of alleged police violence against persons, would be that in such cases it is always difficult for a citizen to marshall evidence sufficient to convince a court of police misconduct. Such an argument, which would apply whether the applicant was legally under arrest or not, is not supported by the law in

---

2   A 241-A para 115 (1992).
3   A 269 (1993).
4   Id para 30.
5   This was also the approach of the Commission, which had found a breach of Article 3 by 10 votes to 5.

European states, in which there is no such general reversal of the burden of proof in civil proceedings for assault against the police.[6]

It is noticeable that the suffering caused to the applicant in the *Klaas* case[7] was not said by the Court to have fallen below the threshold level of Article 3. Whereas the Strasbourg authorities have not reached the point suggested by Judge De Meyer in the *Tomasi* case that any unjustified physical force used against a person in custody is a breach of Article 3, the level of suffering required for a breach of Article 3 would appear from the *Klaas* case to be less than that which resulted from the Palace Barracks assaults that were found to amount to inhuman treatment in *Ireland v UK*. On the other side of the line, the suffering caused by three strokes of the birch in *Tyrer v UK*[8] was not inhuman. Similarly, in the *Greek* case,[9] the Commission found that rough treatment consisting only of 'slaps or blows of the hand on the head or face', was not contrary to Article 3, although it did so for the surprising reason that they were tolerated by detainees. A proportionality test applies when assessing the degree of force used to effect an arrest. In *Hurtado v Switzerland*,[10] a stun grenade and physical force were used in the arrest of a potentially violent suspected drug trafficker, resulting in a fractured rib and bruises. The Commission concluded that the force was not disproportionate in the circumstances.

ii. Use of psychological interrogation techniques

Intense suffering not resulting from physical assaults of an old fashioned 'beating up' kind was found to have been caused in *Ireland v UK* by the use of 'five techniques' during the interrogation of persons placed in preventive detention in connection with acts of terrorism.[11] The techniques were described by the Court as follows:[12]

> '(a) *wall standing*: forcing the detainees to remain for periods of some hours in a 'stress position', described by those who underwent it as being "spreadeagled against the wall, with their fingers put high above the head against the wall, the legs spread apart and the feet back, causing them to stand on their toes with the weight of the body mainly on the fingers";

6 As to English law, for example, see Clayton and Tomlinson, *Civil Actions Against the Police*, 2nd edn, 1992, Ch 4.
7 The medical evidence established that the applicant had suffered a serious and probably long-term injury to her shoulder and a grazed forehead.
8 It was a degrading punishment contrary to Article 3: see below, p 84.
9 12 YB (the *Greek* case) 1 at 501 (1969) Com Rep; CM Res DH (70) 1.
10 A 280-A (1994) Com Rep. F Sett before Court.
11 Several of the techniques did, however, involve illegal assault.
12 A 25 para 96 (1978). The techniques had previously been used by the UK authorities against terrorists in colonial situations.

(b) *hooding*: putting a black or navy coloured bag over the detainees' heads and, at least initially, keeping it there all the time except during interrogation;

(c) *subjection to noise*: pending their interrogations, holding the detainees in a room where there was a continuous loud and hissing noise;

(d) *deprivation of sleep*: pending their interrogations, depriving the detainees of sleep;

(e) *deprivation of food and drink*: subjecting the detainees to reduced diet during their stay at the centre and pending interrogations.'

These methods 'were applied in combination, with premeditation and for hours at a stretch; they caused, if not actual bodily injury, at least intense physical and mental suffering to the persons subjected thereto and also led to acute psychiatric disturbances during interrogation'.[13] They were accordingly 'inhuman treatment' contrary to Article 3.[14]

iii. Conditions of detention

a. Conditions generally

The conditions or treatment of persons in a place of detention may be such as to amount to inhuman treatment.[15] The conditions in which many political detainees were kept in the *Greek* case[16] were held to be inhuman treatment by reference to overcrowding and to inadequate heating, toilets, sleeping arrangements, food, recreation and provision for contact with the outside world. These deficiencies were found in different combinations and were not all present in each of the several places of detention where breaches of Article 3 were found. In *Cyprus v Turkey*,[17] the withholding of food and water and medical treatment from detainees was inhuman treatment. In *Guzzardi v Italy*,[18] the preventive detention of a Mafia suspect in dilapidated, insanitary buildings in a restricted part of an isolated island was not.

A number of issues concerning a state's responsibility for prison conditions were addressed in *McFeeley v UK*.[19] In that case, as a part of their 'dirty protest' campaign to obtain 'special category status', convicted

---

13 Id para 167.

14 The ruling was by 16 votes to 1. For Judge Fitzmaurice, who dissented, the evidence of the effects of the use of the 'five techniques' did not prove suffering of the required severity.

15 This subsection does not consider ill-treatment in the form of physical assault or inadequate medical treatment, which are considered in other subsections.

16 12 YB (the *Greek* case) 1 (1969) Com Rep; CM Res DH (70) 1.

17 *Nos 6780/74 and 6950/75 (First and Second Applications)*, 4 EHRR 482 at 541 (1976) Com Rep; CM Res DH 79 (1).

18 A 39 (1980). Cf *Ireland v UK*, A 25 (1978) (conditions at Ballykinler not inhuman treatment).

19 *No 8317/78*, 20 DR 44 (1980). As to the Commission's rejection in this case of a 'close body search' claim (neither inhuman nor degrading), see below, p 83.

IRA prisoners defiled their cells with waste food and urine and smeared their faeces on the cell walls. Refusing to wear prison uniform, they were allowed to wear blankets in their cell but could not leave their cells except naked. The Commission considered that the resulting cell conditions would, if imputable to the state, have amounted to inhuman treatment. On the same basis, the prisoners' need to go naked if they left their cells would have raised a 'serious question' of compliance with Article 3. But a state is not generally responsible under Article 3 for self-imposed conditions of detention[20] and for this reason the United Kingdom was not liable. The Commission did suggest, however, that prison authorities must, despite a prisoner's obstructive attitude, exercise their custodial role in a humane and flexible way, reviewing the situation constantly in order to protect the health and well-being of a person in their custody but with due regard for the ordinary and reasonable requirements of imprisonment.[1] The Commission also seemed to suggest that, exceptionally, there may be liability under Article 3 in a case of self-induced conditions where the detained person's action is in protest against a breach of his Convention rights.[2] Finally, the Commission made the important point that when assessing conditions of detention, account is to be taken of the cumulative effect of conditions, as well as of specific allegations.[3]

There have also been cases concerning conditions of detention in mental hospitals. In *B v UK*,[4] the Commission visited Broadmoor Hospital, where the applicant was detained. It noted that there was 'deplorable over-crowding' in the dormitory accommodation and that the sanitary conditions in certain places were 'less than satisfactory'. Overall, however, although considering that the facilities at Broadmoor were generally 'extremely unsatisfactory', the Commission determined, somewhat surprisingly, that there was not inhuman treatment contrary to Article 3. In another Broadmoor case, the applicant complained of the conditions in a secure single cell in which he had been segregated, as a seriously disturbed patient. A friendly settlement was reached by which the United Kingdom agreed to pay compensation and to make various improvements in the conditions of detention of segregated patients.[5] A friendly settlement was also agreed in

---

20 Cf *McQuiston v UK No 11208/84*, 46 DR 182 (1986).
1 See also *B v FRG No 13047/87*, 55 DR 271 (1988).
2 20 DR 44 at 80 (1980). On the facts, the IRA claim to 'political prisoner' status was not justified by Article 9. Cf *X v UK No 8231/78*, 28 DR 5 (1982) (Sikh refusal to wear prison clothes on religious grounds not justified under Article 8). *Quaere* whether protest at illegal government conduct under *national* law would come within this exception and whether there is any limit as to the reasonableness of the form that the protest may take.
3 20 DR 44 at 83 (1980). Cf *Hilton v UK No 5613/72*, 3 EHRR 104 at 127 (1978) Com Rep; CM Res DH (79) 3 and *Herczegfalvy v Austria* A 244 (1992) Com Rep para 254 (administration of medical treatment). See also Mr Opsahl's dissent in *B v UK*, below, n 4.
4 *No 6870/75*, 32 DR 5 (1981) Com Rep pp 29-30; CM Res DH (83) 8. Messrs Opsahl, Tenekides, Kiernan and Melchior wrote dissenting opinions. Mr Opsahl criticised the Commission's 'disjunctive' approach in this case.
5 *A v UK No 6840/74*, 3 EHRR 131 (1980); F Sett.

Simon-Herold v Austria,[6] in which a remand prisoner was transferred for physical examination to a hospital where he was kept for over a week in a closed ward with violent, mentally ill patients, several of whom died in his presence. By the terms of the settlement, Austria conceded that the transfer to such a ward of a prisoner who was not suspected of mental illness might be inhuman treatment, and indicated steps it had taken to prevent such transfers in future.

An interesting question is the relationship between the standards of Article 3 concerning conditions of detention and the requirements of other European texts. The fact that conditions of detention do not comply with the 1973 Council of Europe Standard Minimum Rules for the Treatment of Prisoners (now replaced by the 1987 European Prison Rules)[7] does not necessarily mean that there is a breach of Article 3.[8] Nor is there an equivalence between the standards of Article 3 and of the European Prevention of Torture Convention. Murdoch[9] concludes that the latter has a lower threshold in that the Prevention of Torture Committee criticises states in its reports about conditions in places of detention that it visits that would probably not give rise to a successful application under the European Convention on Human Rights.[10] In the reverse situation, the Commission has referred to a finding of the Prevention of Torture Committee that living conditions in a special transit area at an airport in which aliens refused admission were temporarily housed were acceptable as supporting the Commission's own conclusion that the conditions in the area did not amount to ill-treatment contrary to Article 3[11].

b. Solitary confinement

Solitary confinement, or segregation, of persons in detention,[12] is not in itself a breach of Article 3. It is permissible for reasons of security or discipline or to protect the segregated prisoner from other prisoners or vice versa.[13] It may also be justified in the interests of the administration of justice, eg to prevent collusion between prisoners in respect of pending

6   *No 4340/69,* 14 YB 352 (1971); F Sett of 19 December 1972.
7   Appendix to CM Rec R (87) 3; 9 EHRR 513 (1987). For the 1973 Rules, which are replaced by the 1987 Rules, see CM Res (73) 5.
8   *Eggs v Switzerland No 7341/76,* 6 DR 170 (1976).
9   5 EJIL 220.
10 For an unsuccessful claim under Article 3 that relied upon a Prevention of Torture Committee report, see the *Delazarus* case, below, p 71.
11 *S M and T v Austria No 19066/91* (1993).
12 Most of the case-law on solitary confinement concerns remand or convicted prisoners. The following section applies *mutatis mutandis* to other persons in detention, such as mental patients (see *A v UK No 6840/74,* 3 EHRR 131 (1980) F Sett and *Dhoest v Belgium* 55 DR 5 (1987) Com Rep; CM Res DH (88) 1) and persons in preventive detention (see the *Second Greek Case No 4448/70,* 34 CD 70 (1970)).
13 *Ensslin, Baader and Raspe v FRG Nos 7572/76, 7586/76 and 7587/76,* 14 DR 64 (1978); *McFeeley v UK No 8317/78,* 20 DR 44 (1980); *Kröcher and Möller v Switzerland No 8463/78,* 34 DR 24 (1982) Com Rep; CM Res DH (83) 15.

proceedings.[14] In each case, 'regard must be had to the surrounding circumstances, including the particular conditions, the stringency of the measure, its duration, the objective pursued and its effects on the person concerned'.[15] Generally, prolonged solitary confinement is undesirable, particularly where the prisoner is on remand.[16]

None of the arrangements for the solitary confinement of remand or convicted prisoners in criminal justice systems that have been challenged in Strasbourg cases have been found to be in breach of Article 3. Thus in cases concerning restrictions imposed in the United Kingdom on both Category A prisoners[17] and on prisoners segregated under Rule 43, Prison Rules[18] 'inhuman treatment' had not occurred. Nor was a strict security regime imposed on terrorist prisoners in the FRG. In *Ensslin, Baader and Raspe v FRG*,[19] the risk that the Red Army Faction would make further armed attacks to secure the applicants' release justified their complete segregation from other prisoners in a secure prison area for about three years, either on remand or after their conviction until their group suicide. Their conditions of detention (which generally permitted radio and television and outdoor exercise) did not involve unacceptable sensory deprivation and the applicants were allowed to mix with each other and to have visitors. Medical reports confirmed that the conditions had no serious adverse consequences. In other cases, special solitary confinement arrangements to control uncooperative and disruptive behaviour by detained persons have been found to be justified on the facts.[20]

It is recognised, however, that 'complete sensory isolation coupled with complete social isolation can no doubt destroy the personality'.[1] At that point, Article 3 is infringed however strong the justification for segregation may be. The case which has come closest to the limits set by Article 3 in this regard is *Kröcher and Möller v Switzerland*.[2] In that case, two West Germans were detained on remand in Switzerland on charges of attempted murder following terrorist activities. In order to prevent their suicide or escape, the applicants were detained in separate, isolated cells. The windows were frosted over and lights burnt continuously in their cells. They were placed under constant television surveillance and allowed 20 minutes' exercise a

14 *X v FRG No 6038/73*, 44 CD 115 (1973).
15 *Ensslin, Baader and Raspe v FRG No 7572/76*, 14 DR 64 at 109 (1978).
16 *X v FRG No 6038/73*, 44 CD 115 (1973).
17 *X v UK No 8158/78*, 21 DR 95 (1980) and *X v UK No 10117/82*, 7 EHRR 140 (1984).
18 See eg *Reed v UK No 7630/76*, 19 DR 113 (1979); *X v UK No 9813/82*, 5 EHRR 513 (1983); and *X v UK No 8231/78*, 28 DR 5 (1982).
19 *No 7572/76*, 14 DR 64 (1978). See also *X v FRG No 6038/73*, 44 CD 115 (1973) (another Red Army Faction case).
20 For an extreme case, see *M v UK No 9907/82*, 35 DR 130 (1983), in which a convicted murderer who had killed two prisoners was segregated for six years in a specially adapted cell.
1 *Ensslin, Baader and Raspe v FRG Nos 7572/76, 7586/76 and 7587/76*, 14 DR 64 at 109 (1978). Cf *R v Denmark No 10263/83*, 41 DR 149 (1985).
2 *No 8463/78*, 34 DR 25, 57 (1982) Com Rep; CM Res DH (83) 15. For another borderline case, see *Treholt v Norway No 14610/89*, 71 DR 168 (1991).

day outside of their cell on weekdays only. Newspapers, radio and television were prohibited and the applicants' watches and diaries were removed. They were not allowed contact with each other, with other prisoners or with lawyers. These conditions prevailed for a month; some of them were relaxed during the remaining five months of detention on remand. The Commission accepted that the West German terrorist climate of late 1970s justified severe security measures.[3] While expressing doubts as to some of the measures taken in the first month, the Commission was of the opinion that because of (i) the gradual relaxation of the conditions of sensory and social isolation and the medical evidence as to their effect and (ii) their refusal to take advantage of certain opportunities for outside contact, the applicants had not been 'subjected to a form of physical or moral suffering designed to punish them, destroy their personality or break their resistance' in breach of Article 3. In a joint dissenting opinion, four members of the Commission[4] took the view that the Commission should have focused more upon the conditions in the first month and that these amounted to 'inhuman treatment', however great the security need.

The *Kröcher and Möller* case illustrates graphically the wide margin of appreciation allowed to national authorities in respect of conditions in places of detention in a terrorist context. Other cases concerning the detention of remand or convicted prisoners in more normal circumstances demonstrate, on the one hand, the genuine problems of control that certain detainees pose for prison authorities and, on the other hand, the difficulties of proof that prisoners may have in substantiating their claims of ill-treatment.[5] An approach by which the Strasbourg authorities applied Article 3 more rigorously so as to bring it closer into line with the standards in the 1987 European Prison Rules would not be to 'trivialise' it in an area in which the individual is very much within the control of the state.[6] The hesitation that the Commission and the Court[7] have had in converting their doubts and concerns about conditions of detention in cases arising under Article 3, whether in cases of solitary confinement or otherwise, into findings that a breach has occurred underlines the value of the complementary reporting mechanisms of the European Prevention of Torture Convention. Problems of evidence, the *quatrième instance* doctrine and the need for an applicant to prove that he in particular is a victim present difficulties in the context of individual applications that are not found in a supervisory system that is based upon regular inspections and the assessment of conditions generally. Certain of these points were demon-

---

3 The suicides in the *Ensslin, Baader and Raspe* cases, above, had occurred and there had been dramatic kidnapping and hijackings.

4 Messrs Tenekides, Melchior, Sampaio and Weitzel. The decision was taken by 8 to 5.

5 See eg *Hilton v UK No 5613/72*, 3 EHRR 104 (1978) Com Rep; CM Res DH (79) 3.

6 For criticism of the Commission's jurisprudence on conditions of detention, see Cassese, *European Supervision*, pp 232–41.

7 See the Court's doubts in the *Herczegfalvy* case (a mental patient case), below, p 72. In that case the Commission did find a breach of Article 3.

strated in *Delazarus v UK*.[8] There a prisoner in solitary confinement complained, *inter alia*, of the general conditions of detention at Wandsworth Prison. Relying upon reports of the European Prevention of Torture Committee and the Chief Inspector of Prisons in England and Wales, the Commission referred in particular to overcrowding, the confinement of prisoners to their cells for 23 hours a day and the use of chamberpots in cells. The Commission declared the claim inadmissible, however, because, the applicant, being in solitary confinement, could not complain of overcrowding and was less affected by the need to use chamberpots.

c.   Medical treatment

There is an obligation to provide adequate medical treatment (including psychiatric care) for persons in detention.[9] In *Hurtado v Switzerland*,[10] it was infringed when a person who had been forcibly arrested was not given an X-ray, which revealed a fractured rib, until six days after he requested it. Generally, the obligation includes a requirement to review arrangements for detention continuously in the interest of a prisoner's health and well-being.[11] Medical treatment must be provided in the place of detention or the detainee must be released at least temporarily to allow it to be obtained elsewhere, for example in a specialist clinic. Failure to adopt either course may amount to inhuman treatment contrary to Article 3 where the result of that failure is to cause serious injury to health.[12] The fact that imprisonment is incompatible with a prisoner's health is not of itself sufficient to require his release to avoid liability under Article 3 since imprisonment following conviction or on remand is obviously permissible.[13] Article 3 may, however, require 'humanitarian measures' in exceptional cases.[14]

Different questions arise in respect of compulsory medical treatment of persons in detention. The compulsory administration of treatment that is in

8   *No 17525/90* (1993) unreported.
9   See, in addition to the cases cited below, the *Greek* case, 12 YB (the *Greek* case) 1 (1969) Com Rep; CM Res DH (70) 1, and *Cyprus v Turkey Nos 6780/74 and 6950/75 (First and Second Applications)*, 4 EHRR 482 (1976) Com Rep; CM Res DH (79) 1. In both of these cases the failure to ensure adequate medical care was a factor in the ruling that inhuman treatment had occurred.
10 A 280-A (1994) Com Rep. F Sett before Court.
11 See the *McFeeley* case, above, p 67.
12 *Bonnechaux v Switzerland No 8224/78*, 18 DR 100 (1979) Com Rep; CM Res DH (80) 1 (treatment for a man in his 70s suffering from cardio-vascular disorders and diabetes during nearly three years' detention on remand satisfactory) and *Chartier v Italy No 9044/80*, 33 DR 41 (1982) Com Rep; CM Res DH 83 (12) (treatment of a convicted murderer for chronic hereditary obesity satisfactory). For criticism of the *Chartier* decision on its facts, see Cassese, *European Supervision*, p 237. See also *Kotälla v Netherlands No 7994/77*, 14 DR 238 (1978). In assessing liability, account may be taken of the applicant's refusal of prison treatment (*De Varga-Hirsch v France No 9559/81*, 33 DR 158 (1983)) or to permit a medical examination (*RSA and C v Portugal Nos 9911/82 and 9945/82*, 36 DR 200 (1984)).
13 *X v FRG No 9610/81*, 6 EHRR 110 (1983). The imposition of a sentence of imprisonment may none the less be inhuman punishment if other appropriate punishments are available.
14 *Chartier v Italy No 9044/80*, 33 DR 41 (1982) Com Rep; CM Res DH (83) 12. See also *X v Ireland No 9554/81*, 6 EHRR 336 (1983).

accordance with 'established principles of medicine' to a detained mentally disordered person unable to take decisions for himself is neither inhuman nor degrading treatment, even though it may involve the use of physical force. Thus in *Herczegfalvy v Austria*,[15] the Court held that the forcible administration of food and drugs to a violent, mentally-ill patient on hunger strike was not in breach of Article 3. The Court stated that in such cases 'the position of inferiority and powerlessness which is typical of patients confined in psychiatric hospitals calls for increased vigilance' when reviewing compliance with the Convention. None the less compulsion and force could be justified 'to preserve the physical and mental health of patients who are entirely incapable of deciding for themselves and for whom ... [the medical authorities] are therefore entirely responsible'. A separate aspect of the case, which the Court found 'worrying', was the fact that the applicant had been handcuffed and strapped by his ankles for two weeks because of the 'danger of aggression and the death threats' that he was making. Despite hesitation, the Court found unanimously that the evidence before it was 'not sufficient to disprove the government's argument that, according to the psychiatric principles generally accepted at the time, medical necessity justified the treatment in issue'.[16]

The *Herczegfalvy* case concerned a person who was incapable of taking decisions. Whether the compulsory medical treatment of convicted prisoners or other persons in detention who are not in this condition is consistent with Article 3 is not clear.[17] At the least, it is likely that Article 3 permits the compulsory treatment by the state in accordance with the 'standards accepted by medical science' of all persons in its custody where this is necessary to save them from death or serious injury.[18] This would include the feeding by force of persons on hunger strike and the compulsory administration of medicine. Such treatment would not be inhuman or degrading just because of the lack of consent or the manner of its administration. As to the latter, the Commission has held that although forced feeding may be humiliating in the way that it is administered, the state's obligation under Article 2 to secure the right to life of a person in its custody prevails over considerations relating to Article 3.[19] However,

---

15 A 244 para 82 (1992). Cf *X v FRG No 8518/79*, 20 DR 193 (1980). See also *B v UK No 6870/ 75*, 32 DR 5 (1981), in which, despite 'certain reservations', the psychiatric treatment of a Broadmoor patient was held not to be in breach of Article 3. And see *Dhoest v Belgium No 10448/83*, 55 DR 5 (1987) Com Rep; CM Res DH (88) 1 and the *Winterwerp* case, below, pp 124-125.

16 A 244 para 83 (1992). The Commission had unanimously found that the manner in which the treatment was administered (handcuffed, etc) was in breach of Article 3. The use of drugs for control, not medical reasons, is probably a breach of Article 3: for an allegation of such use, see *Freeman v Home Office (No 2)* [1984] QB 524.

17 For doubts as to whether convicted prisoners or detained mental patients are ever in a position to consent freely to medical treatment, see *Kaimowicz v Michigan Dept of Mental Health* 42 US Law Week 1013 at 2063 (1973).

18 See *Herczegfalvy v Austria A 244* (1992) Com Rep para 242.

19 *X v FRG No 10565/83*, 7 EHRR 152 (1984).

experimental medical treatment[20] may be inhuman treatment, if not torture, in the absence of consent.[1] Compulsory sterilisation was understood to be contrary to the Convention during its drafting.[2]

iv. Extradition or deportation[3]

The Convention does not guarantee a right not to be extradited or deported.[4] Nor is there a right to political asylum.[5] *A fortiori*, the refusal to allow aliens to enter a state's territory in non-asylum cases is not in breach of Article 3.[6] With regard to extradition, it is not *per se* contrary to Article 3 to extradite a fugitive offender in breach of an extradition treaty or of national extradition law: it is not the function of the Strasbourg authorities in this context 'to supervise the correct application of extradition law'.[7] Nor is it contrary to Article 3 to extradite a person for a political offence.[8] As to deportation, the exercise of the state's sovereign power to deport aliens is not generally in breach of Article 3.[9]

None the less, although generally permitted by the Convention, extradition or deportation may be inhuman treatment or some other form of ill-treatment[10] contrary to Article 3 in certain exceptional cases.[11] For example, if a person is ill, his extradition or deportation may cause him such suffering as to amount to inhuman treatment.[12] Where deportation separates a person from his family, the mental suffering caused will probably not reach the threshold level required by Article 3 (although this might not be so in some cases, for example the separation of a mother and young child); the case is more likely to fall within Article 8 instead.[13] The deportation of stateless or other persons who will not be received

---

20 Although this is a matter not limited to the ill-treatment of persons *in detention*, experimental medical treatment is most likely to occur in detention and is considered here for convenience.
1 See *X v Denmark No 9974/82*, 32 DR 282 (1983).
2 1 TP 116-7.
3 See Allweldt, 4 EJIL 360 (1993).
4 See *Vilvarajah v UK* A 215 (1991).
5 Ibid. On asylum and the Convention, see 2 IJRL 261 (1990).
6 See eg *X, Y, Z, V and W v UK No 3325/67*, 10 YB 528 (1967). See also *Abdulaziz, Cabales and Balkandali v UK* A 94 (1985). As to the admission of nationals, see Article 3, Fourth Protocol, below, p 562.
7 *Altun v FRG No 10308/83*, 36 DR 209 at 231 (1983).
8 Ibid.
9 Exceptionally, Article 4, Fourth Protocol prohibits the collective expulsion of aliens.
10 A few claims have been expressed in terms of degrading treatment: see eg *X v Switzerland No 9012/80*, 24 DR 205 (1980) (racial discrimination by receiving state).
11 As may the refusal to admit a national or an alien: see the *East African Asians* cases, below, p 81 (nationals).
12 See *Bulus v Sweden No 9330/81*, 35 DR 57 (1984); 39 DR 75 (1984) F Sett (mental illness). See also the claims in *X v Belgium No 984/61*, 6 CD 39 (1961) and *X v Switzerland No 9012/80*, 24 DR 205 (1980).
13 See eg *Berrehab v Netherlands* A 138 (1988); *Moustaquim v Belgium* A 193 (1991); and *Beldjoudi v France* A 234-A (1992).

elsewhere[14] and deportation where this is out of proportion on the facts of the case[15] may raise issues under Article 3.

In the remarkable case of *Amekrane v UK*,[16] the first applicant fled to Gibraltar seeking political asylum after an unsuccessful *coup d'état* in Morocco. At Morocco's request, he was handed back the following day as a prohibited immigrant. He was then convicted by a Moroccan military court and executed by firing squad for his part in the plot. The case was terminated when the UK paid £35,000 compensation by way of friendly settlement to the second applicant, the first applicant's widow. The Article 3 claim was not that it was inhuman treatment to return a political offender, whether by extradition or, as on the facts, by a doubtful application of national immigration law.[17] Instead, it was argued that it was inhuman treatment to do so in a situation in which the applicant faced a real risk of death without first giving him the chance to question his return in court or to seek sanctuary in another, more sympathetic country.

Most decided cases have concerned the consequences for the applicant of being extradited or deported to a particular state. Such cases involve claims that the applicant will be ill-treated at the hands of the public authorities of the receiving state or by private groups (eg guerillas) or individuals within its territory.[18] In practice, in a large number of applications, the claim has been withdrawn before any decision as to admissibility following an informal settlement by which the applicant has been permitted to remain in the country.

In the leading case of *Soering v UK*,[19] the Court held that it would be contrary to Article 3 for a party to the Convention to return a person to

14 *Harabi v Netherlands No 10798/84*, 46 DR 112 (1986) and *Giama v Belgium No 7612/76*, 21 DR 73 (1980).

15 Eg deportation for breach of an annual registration requirement by an established alien with many years of employment and local dependants. See *Agee v UK No 7729/76*, 7 DR 164 (1976) (claim of arbitrary, disproportionate deportation rejected on the facts).

16 *No 5961/72*, 16 YB 356 (1973); F Sett Report of 19 July 1974.

17 The case has been regarded as one of 'disguised extradition'. There was no extradition treaty with Morocco and, in any event, the 'political offence' defence would have been available in national law.

18 That account is to be taken of the risk of ill-treatment by private groups or individuals has been held in several Commission cases: see *Altun v FRG No 10308/83*, 36 DR 209 (1983); *X v FRG No 10040/82* 1 Digest Supp 3.0.3.4, p 14 (1983); and *Kirkwood v UK No 10479/83*, 37 DR 158 (1984). The point has, however, been left open in other Commission cases: see *X v FRG No 7216/75*, 5 DR 137 (1976); *X v UK No 8581/79*, 29 DR 48 (1980); and *YH v FRG No 12461/86*, 51 DR 258 (1986). As formulated in the *Soering* and *Vilvarajah* cases (below), the rule restricting return does not distinguish between ill-treatment at government and private hands.

19 A 161 (1989). On the *Soering* case, see Breitenmoser and Wilms, 11 MJIL 845 (1990); Finnie, (1990) SLT 53; Gappa, 20 GJICL 463 (1990); Lillich, 85 AJIL 128 (1991); O'Boyle, in O'Reilly, ed, *Human Rights and Constitutional Law*, 1992, p 93; Quigley and Shank, 30 VJIL 241 (1989); Schabas, 43 ICLQ 913 (1994); Shea, 17 YJIL 85 (1992); Steinhardt, 11 HRLJ 453 (1990); Van Der Meersch, 1 RTDH 5 (1990); Warbrick, 11 MJIL 1073 (1990); Wyngaert, 39 ICLQ 757 (1990). See also *Aylor-Davis v France No 22742/93* 76A DR 164 (1994), in which the applicant's extradition to Texas was not in breach of Article 3 because of US and Texan assurances that the death penalty would not be sought.

another state 'where substantial grounds have been shown for believing that the person concerned, if extradited, faces a real risk of being subjected to torture or to inhuman or degrading treatment or punishment in the requesting country'.[20] Although the rule applies to a risk of all kinds of ill-treatment contrary to Article 3, it is considered for convenience at this point under the heading of inhuman treatment.[1]

In the *Soering* case, which has a strong claim to being the most influential case that the Court has decided, the United Kingdom Home Secretary signed a warrant for the extradition of the applicant, a West German national, to face capital murder charges in the state of Virginia in the United States. He was accused of killing the parents of his girlfriend. The European Court held unanimously[2] that the return of the applicant would be a breach of Article 3.[3] The Court first held that there was a real risk of the death penalty being imposed if the applicant were extradited. This was because there was a real risk that he would be convicted, having admitted the killings,[4] and because the policy of the Virginia courts was such that the death penalty was likely in view of the vileness of the murders. This was so despite mitigating factors that the court might take into account[5] and the fact that, in satisfaction of the terms of the UK–US extradition treaty, the United Kingdom had been given an undertaking that the prosecuting attorney in Virginia would make a representation to the trial court that the British Government did not want the death penalty imposed. The Court gave little weight to this last point, however, because the attorney had indicated that he would none the less press for the death penalty.

The Court's reasoning was not that the imposition of the death penalty *per se* would result in a breach of Article 3. The applicant did not claim this and, in any event, it could not have been so because of the continued presence in Article 2 of the Convention of a provision permitting the death penalty.[6] However, the return of a fugitive offender to face the death penalty could involve a breach of Article 3 in the particular circumstances of a case.

---

20 A 161 para 91 (1989).
1   Neither the Commission nor the Court indicated whether the facts involved treatment or punishment, finding a breach of Article 3 generally instead. On the facts, there were probably elements of both.
2   The Commission, by 6 votes to 5, had found no breach of Article 3. Cf its earlier decision in *Kirkwood v UK No 10479/83*, 37 DR 158 (1984).
3   After the Court's judgment, the UK refused extradition on the charges of capital murder but surrendered the applicant on charges of non-capital murder: see CM Res (90) 8. The applicant was then convicted in Virginia of the two murders and given two life terms. The applicant's girlfriend was already serving a long term of imprisonment for the murders when he was convicted.
4   Although there was a possible defence of insanity, overall there remained a real risk of conviction.
5   These included the applicant's youth, lack of criminal record and mental state.
6   As to the position under Article 2 and under the Sixth Protocol to the Convention prohibiting the death penalty for the parties thereto, see above, pp 45 and 564. See also *Y v Netherlands No 16531/90*, 68 DR 299 (1991).

In this connection, the Court stated that the 'manner in which it is imposed or executed, the personal circumstances of the condemned person and a disproportionality to the gravity of the crime committed, as well as the conditions of detention awaiting execution, are examples of factors capable of bringing the treatment or punishment received by the condemned person within the proscription under Article 3'.[7]

In terms of the factors set out in the above list, the Court's decision on the facts of the *Soering* case turned mainly on a combination of the 'conditions of detention' and the 'personal circumstances' of the applicant. As to the conditions of detention, the crucial consideration was the exposure to the 'death row phenomenon' that the applicant would face. A condemned person in Virginia spent six to eight years subject to a stringent security regime and severe mental stress awaiting execution. In this connection, the Court discounted the fact that much of this time resulted from the convicted person's resort to the appeal procedures available because it was 'part of human nature that the person will cling to life by exploiting those safeguards to the full'.[8] The Court's approach on this point can also be supported on the basis that the conditions that a condemned man must suffer on death row while appealing, which provide the basis for the claim under Article 3, are the responsibility of the state. This distinguishes the situation from that of the 'trial within a reasonable time' guarantee in Article 6(1), concerning which the Court has always held that the state is not responsible for delay caused by the applicant.[9]

In terms of his 'personal circumstances', the applicant in the *Soering* case was only 18 when the offence was committed[10] and there was psychiatric evidence supporting the view that he was not mentally responsible for his acts.[11] Moreover, when assessing the United Kingdom's responsibility under Article 3, it was relevant that West Germany had also requested the return of its national to face trial there for the murder without the risk of the death penalty.[12]

---

7   A 161 para 104 (1989).
8   Id para 105. Contrast *Barrett and Sutcliffe v Jamaica*, GAOR, 47th Sess, Supp 40, p 254 (1992), in which the Human Rights Committee held that the state was not to be responsible under the ICCPR for the conditions on death row during time attributable to appeals.
9   See below, p 224.
10 The Court referred to the prohibition of the death penalty for persons under 18 (and hence less responsible for their acts than older persons) in Article 6, ICCPR and Article 4, ACHR. The standards in these later instruments 'at the very least' indicated that as a general principle the youth of the person concerned was a circumstance which is liable, with others, to put in question the compatibility with Article 3 of measures connected with the death penalty': id para 108. Cf *Thompson v Oklahoma* 487 US 815 (1988).
11 Although the Court did not develop this point, the evidence was such that the applicant might have had a defence of diminished responsibility in English law – a defence that was not available under Virginia law. See O'Boyle, loc cit at p 74, n 19, p 103.
12 This can be seen as a personal circumstance or as a separate factor additional to those listed by the Court that may be relevant. The UK gave the US request priority because it was made earlier and demonstrated a *prima facie* case, which the German request did not.

With regard to the other factors listed in the *Soering* case, the absence of a fair trial[13] and the form that the death penalty takes[14] are relevant to the 'manner in which it is imposed or executed' respectively. As to 'proportionality', the kind of offence for which the death penalty is imposed[15] and the facts of the particular case may be a consideration under both Articles 2 and 3.

The rule in the *Soering* case does not only apply to death penalty cases. Considerations such as the risk of an unfair trial and proportionality must be relevant under Article 3 where a person is returned for trial for a non-capital offence also. Similarly, the Commission has indicated that it may be 'inhuman treatment' to extradite a person for an offence where there is good reason to believe that the extradition process is being abused by the requesting state in order to prosecute him, contrary to the principle of speciality, for a political offence 'or even simply because of his political opinions'.[16] The 'inhuman treatment' in such cases would result from the risk that such proceedings would lead to an 'unjustified or disproportionate sentence'.[17] However, the mere fact that a person extradited or deported to another state may on his return face prosecution for a criminal offence that carries a severe sentence or one that is more severe than would apply in other European states does not in itself amount to a breach of Article 3.[18]

The basis for liability under the rule in the *Soering* case is that the extraditing state has 'taken action which has as a direct consequence the exposure of an individual to proscribed ill-treatment'.[19] The returning state is 'not being held directly responsible for the acts of another state but for the facilitation, through the process of extradition, of a denial of the applicant's rights by that other state'.[20] On the basis of this approach, a state could be liable under the Convention if a person's deportation or extradition presented a real risk of the infringement of any Convention Article, not just Article 3.[1] As the Court noted, the situation is an unusual one in that liability normally arises under the Convention only where a violation has in fact occurred; the prospect of a breach, however probable, is normally not sufficient. The Court explained its extension of liability to a case involving

---

13 Cf *X v Spain No 10292/83*, 6 EHRR 146 (1983). But see *Altun v FRG No 10308/83*, 36 DR 209 (1983). In the *Soering* case itself a fair trial claim was argued, and for that reason decided, under Article 6, not Article 3: see below, p 257.

14 Cf the ICCPR case of *Ng v Canada* 1 IHRR 161 at 177 (1993) (imposition of the death penalty by gas asphyxiation is 'cruel and inhuman treatment' because it did not involve the 'least possible physical and mental suffering').

15 For the kinds of offences to which the death penalty applies world-wide, see Schabas, *The Abolition of the Death Penalty in International Law*, 1993 (index: crimes). As to the death penalty in the UK, see above, p 45, n 20.

16 *Altun v FRG No 10308/83*, 36 DR 209 at 232-3 (1983).

17 Id at 233.

18 *C v FRG No 11017/84*, 46 DR 176 (1986). Nor is the return of a person to face prosecution for desertion from the armed forces inhuman treatment: *Kilic v Switzerland No 12364/86*, 50 DR 280 (1986).

19 A 161 para 91 (1989).

20 O'Boyle, loc cit at p 74, n 19, above, p 97.

1 Cf the pre-*Soering* discussion by Vogler, *Wiarda Mélanges*, p 663.

only the risk of a violation on the basis that 'where an applicant claims that a decision to extradite him would, if implemented, be contrary to Article 3 by reason of its foreseeable consequences in the requesting country, a departure from this principle is necessary in view of the serious and irreparable nature of the alleged suffering risked, in order to ensure the effectiveness of the safeguard provided by that Article'.[2] This reasoning carries most weight in a case where the receiving state is not a party to the Convention; in other cases, it is possible to bring a claim under the Convention against the receiving state itself if it has accepted the right of individual petition.[3] As far as a receiving state that is not a party to the Convention is concerned, although it cannot be held liable under the Convention for infringing Article 3, there is no doubt, as the Court acknowledged in the *Soering* case, that the Court's approach involves an element of assessment, and by implication judgment, of its national law and practice.[4]

A final point that emerges from a consideration of the *Soering* case is that insofar as Article 3 prohibits the extradition of a person when this is required by an extradition treaty, the requested state is placed in a position to which the rules as to inconsistent treaty obligations[5] apply.

The rule in the *Soering* case applies to deportation as well as extradition. In *Cruz Varas v Sweden*,[6] the applicants were a Chilean national who had been refused asylum in the defendant state, and his wife and child. The first applicant alleged that he had been ill-treated contrary to Article 3 by the Chilean police because of his political activities and that there was a real risk of this happening again if he were deported to Chile. The Court applied the rule in the *Soering* case but decided that it had not been shown on the facts that there were substantial grounds for believing that there was a real risk that the applicant would be ill-treated if returned. In particular, the Court was not convinced by the applicant's story of previous ill-treatment by the government. Although there was evidence that someone had ill-treated him, it was not established that it was the government. Unusually, the Court disagreed on this point with the findings of fact by the Commission. The Court also noted that in any event the political situation in Chile had improved, leading to the voluntary return of refugees from Sweden and

---

2 A 161 para 90 (1989).
3 When assessing the liability of the returning state, the Commission takes into account whether the receiving state is both a party to the Convention *and* has accepted the right of individual petition: *K and F v Netherlands No 12543/86*, 51 DR 272 (1986). In *Altun v FRG No 10308/83*, 36 DR 209 (1983), the Commission attached 'a certain importance' to the fact that the requesting party had not made an Article 25 declaration.
4 The receiving state, whether a party to the Convention or not, can file an *amicus curiae* brief under Rule 37(2), Rules of Court or present expert witnesses to ensure that its national law and practice is correctly understood.
5 See Article 30, Vienna Convention on the Law of Treaties 1969. The UK was *not* in this position in the *Soering* case: see s 11 of the Extradition Act 1870 and Articles IV and V(2), UK-US Extradition Treaty 1972, UKTS 16 (1977), Cmnd 6723.
6 A 201 (1991).

elsewhere.[7] In addition, the Court was influenced by the fact that the defendant state had considerable experience of assessing Chilean asylum claims and had examined the facts of the present case closely.[8]

The *Cruz Varas* case addressed the question of the evidence to be taken into account when assessing liability in cases of extradition or deportation in which the applicant has already been returned when the case is decided at Strasbourg.[9] The Court stated that in such a case the presence of a real risk of ill-treatment contrary to Article 3 is to be judged 'primarily' by reference to what the defendant state knew or ought to have known at the time of the return. The Court may take into account, however, information that comes to light subsequently in order to confirm or refute the defendant state's assessment of the situation or the applicant's fears.[10] Thus in the *Cruz Varas* case account was taken of the fact that following his return the applicant had been unable to produce witnesses or other evidence in support of his claim of prior ill-treatment. The Court did not mention the fact that the applicant had not been ill-treated following his return.

As indicated above, for there to be a breach of Article 3, the risk of ill-treatment must be a 'real risk', not just a 'mere possibility'. This point was clearly made on the facts of *Vilvarajah v United Kingdom*.[11] There the five applicants were Sri Lankan Tamils who claimed to be at risk of ill-treatment contrary to Article 3 by state security forces in the conflict between the Sri Lankan government and the Tamil liberation movement. The applicants were refused asylum by the defendant state and returned to their national state. The Court held that their return was not a breach of Article 3. Earlier there had been considerable government violence against the Tamil community as a whole, triggered off by the activities of the liberation movement, so that it might then have been accepted that there would be a real risk that any member of the community would have been ill-treated upon his return. However, the position had improved to the point where large numbers of Tamils were returning to Sri Lanka of their own volition. Whereas there remained the 'possibility' that the applicants, as Tamils, might be detained and ill-treated, this was not sufficient to establish a breach

7 It was for this reason that the Commission did not find a breach of Article 3.
8 Cf the Court's reliance on UK experience in dealing with Sri Lankan claims and its detailed treatment of the particular claims in the *Vilvarajah* case, below.
9 In the *Cruz Varas* case, the defendant state did not comply with a request by the Commission not to return the applicant: as to whether this was breach of the Convention, see below, p 668. Cf *Mansi v Sweden No 15658/89*, 64 DR 242 (1989); id 253 (1990) F Sett, where a Commission request not to deport was ignored and the applicant was tortured on return. In the *Soering* case, the defendant state respected such a request.
10 In the *Soering* case, in which the applicant had not been returned, the Court assessed the situation by reference to the facts as they were known to it, and to that extent by the defendant state, at the time of the Court's judgment.
11 A 215 para 111 (1991). The Commission has rejected a number of cases at the admissibility stage because it has not been satisfied on the basis of the evidence produced by the applicant that he would really be at risk if returned: see eg *Kozlov v Finland No 16832/90*, 69 DR 321 (1991) and *A and FBK v Turkey No 14401/88*, 68 DR 188 (1991). Return to face military service is not inhuman treatment: *A and FBK* case.

of Article 3. In the situation that prevailed, it was necessary to show that the applicants were especially at risk, which was not the case.[12] The Court was not influenced in its decision by the fact that three of the applicants were in fact subjected to ill-treatment on their return since 'there existed no special distinguishing features in their cases that could or ought to have enabled the Secretary of State to foresee that they would be treated in this way'.[13]

4. INHUMAN PUNISHMENT

Although there has been very little jurisprudence specifically on inhuman punishment, its meaning may be gauged from cases concerning other elements of Article 3. The same general considerations apply.[14] Thus, in assessing whether a punishment is inhuman, regard must be had to the physical or mental suffering, which must reach the level to which a person of the applicant's sex, age, health, etc, of normal sensibilities would be subject in the circumstances. The birching in *Tyrer v UK*[15] was not inhuman punishment because this threshold level was not reached on the facts. Consideration must be given to the 'nature and context' of the punishment and to the 'manner and method' of its execution.[16] As in the case of degrading punishment, account must be taken of the fact that certain kinds of punishment may be less acceptable, and hence more suspect, than others despite an equivalence of suffering.[17]

5. DEGRADING TREATMENT

For the purposes of Article 3, 'degrading' has its ordinary dictionary meaning. Degrading treatment, therefore, is treatment that humiliates or debases. As with other parts of Article 3, there is a minimum, threshold level of humiliation or debasement that must be reached.[18] Degrading treatment in the sense of Article 3 is conduct that 'grossly humiliates',[19] although

12 In an earlier case, the Commission had stated that extradition 'to a particular country in which, due to the very nature of the regime in that country or to a particular situation basic human rights such as are guaranteed by the Convention might be either grossly violated or entirely suppressed' would infringe Article 3: *X v FRG No 1802/63*, 6 YB 462 at 480 (1963). Cf *X v FRG No 4162/69*, 32 CD 87 (1969) (deportation). Such an approach survives the *Vilvarajah* case only insofar as the level of general risk is high enough for there to be a 'real risk' for all persons. Otherwise an applicant must provide evidence that he is especially at risk. See *R v Denmark No 16381/90* (1991) unreported, in which the Commission, after referring to Amnesty International reports, concluded that it would not be 'inhuman treatment' to deport an Iranian national to Iran on the basis only of the general situation there.
13 A 215 para 112 (1991).
14 For these, see above, p 56.
15 A 26 (1978).
16 Ibid.
17 See the discussion of the *Tyrer* case, below, p 84.
18 *Tyrer v UK* A 26 para 30 (1978). The statements in that case on degrading punishment apply *mutatis mutandis* to degrading treatment also.
19 The *Greek* case 12 YB (the *Greek* case) 1 at 186 (1969) Com Rep; CM Res DH (70) 1.

causing less suffering than torture. The question is whether a person of the applicant's sex, age, health, etc, of normal sensibilities would be grossly humiliated in all the circumstances of the case. In *Abdulaziz, Cabales and Balkandali v UK*[20] the Court appeared to require that there be an intention to humiliate for there to be degrading treatment. In that case, when considering Immigration Rules which distinguished between the spouses of husbands and wives, the Court found that it could not be degrading because 'it was not designed to, and did not, humiliate or debase but was intended solely to achieve' specified non-discriminatory aims. A requirement of intention runs counter to the Court's general reading of Article 3, by which, other than in cases of torture, the test of liability is solely in terms of the suffering caused. Such a requirement would mean that some cases of indirect discrimination could not be degrading treatment contrary to Article 3.[1]

The same treatment may be both degrading and inhuman, as in the case of resort to the 'five techniques' in *Ireland v UK*[2] and physical assault in *Tomasi v France*.[3] In these cases, it was relevant that it is humiliating to oblige a person by force to answer questions (or otherwise act) against his will or to violate his physical integrity. In the *Greek* case,[4] the Commission supposed that 'all torture must be inhuman and degrading treatment, and inhuman treatment also degrading'. However, all degrading treatment or punishment is not necessarily inhuman as well.[5]

Racial discrimination was found to be degrading treatment contrary to Article 3 in the *East African Asians* cases.[6] In those cases, 25 East African Asians had retained their status as United Kingdom citizens when Kenya and Uganda became independent rather than take the local nationality. They did so on the understanding that this would allow them continued access to the United Kingdom free from immigration control.[7] Following the adoption of a policy of Africanisation by the Kenyan and Ugandan governments and in order to control immigration from those states, legislation was enacted at Westminster terminating the right of entry of United Kingdom citizens lacking ancestral or 'place of birth' connections with the United Kingdom. The Commission considered in its opinion on the

20 A 94 para 91 (1985). Cf *Albert and Le Compte v Belgium* A 58 para 22 (1983).
1   As to indirect discrimination, see below, p 477.
2   A 25 (1978). This ruling was criticised by Judge Fitzmaurice who questioned whether most of the techniques were humiliating. He gave the following examples of treatment that was degrading: '. . . having one's head shaved, being tarred and feathered, smeared with filth, pelted with muck, paraded naked in front of strangers, forced to eat excreta, deface the portrait of one's sovereign or head of state, or dress up in a way calculated to provoke ridicule or contempt'.
3   A 241-A (1992). In *Ireland v UK*, the Court did not consider whether the physical assaults at Palace Barracks were degrading treatment, merely confirming the Commission's opinion that they were inhuman treatment.
4   12 YB (the *Greek* case) 1 at 186 (1969).
5   *Tyrer v UK* A 26 para 29 (1978).
6   3 EHRR 76 (1973) Com Rep; CM DH (77) 2.
7   The Commission did not find that there had, as argued, been an express undertaking to admit citizens who retained their nationality and left open the question whether there was an implied one.

merits that this legislation was racially discriminatory and that the applicants' subjection to it, with the attendant publicity and in the special circumstances of their cases, was an affront to their dignity to the point of being 'degrading treatment' in breach of Article 3.[8] The special circumstances were the refusal to admit nationals who had remained such in the expectation of admission; their reduction to the status of second class citizens; and the hardship which they had suffered by exclusion from the one state on which they had some claim to admission. Confirming its opinion in the *East African Asians* cases, in *Abdulaziz, Cabales and Balkandali v UK*[9] the Commission stated that although a state has a sovereign power to admit persons to its territory, by virtue of Article 3, 'the state's discretion in immigration matters is not of an unfettered character, for a state may not implement policies of a purely racist nature, such as a policy prohibiting the entry of any person of a particular skin colour'.

It might be inferred from the Commission's emphasis in the *East African Asians* cases upon the public nature of the discrimination and upon the special circumstances of the cases that more ordinary cases of racial discrimination[10] would not be degrading in breach of Article 3. The better interpretation is that the Commission's opinion in the *East African Asians* cases was tailored by the facts and that single instances or practices of direct or indirect[11] racial discrimination, which must be inherently degrading, are contrary to Article 3. Such an interpretation is consistent with the probability that the drafters of the Convention had anti-Semitism in mind when prohibiting degrading treatment. It is also supported by *Hilton v UK*[12] in which the Commission stated in its decision as to admissibility that an allegation of racial discrimination by prison officers against a prisoner raised an issue under Article 3. So also is the statement in *Tyrer v UK*[13] that an act does not necessarily have to occur in public to be degrading. If Article 3 did not apply to ordinary cases of racial discrimination, they would not be in breach of any part of the Convention unless Article 14 could be invoked. Article 14, however, provides just a partial remedy because it applies only where there is racial discrimination in the protection of a right guaranteed by the Convention. Hence it has no application in important areas of

8   The Committee of Ministers did not rule on the question of a breach. After much delay and after all of the applicants had been admitted to the UK, it decided that 'no further action' was called for: CM Res DH (77) 2.
9   A 94 (1985) Com Rep para 113.
10 For the meaning of discrimination in Article 14 of the Convention, see below, p 475.
11 Indirect discrimination results from a rule or practice that is neutral on its face (eg limiting employment to persons of a certain height) that, whether intended or not, has an unjustifiably discriminatory effect in its operation.
12 No 5613/72, 4 DR 177 (1976). The allegations that were considered in the Commission's opinion on the merits of the case concerned racial abuse by prison officers, which is also potentially degrading contrary to Article 3, rather than acts of racial discrimination. No breach was found on the facts: 3 EHRR 104 Com Rep; CM Res (79) 3 (1979). See also *Glimmerveen and Hagenbeek v Netherlands Nos 8348/78 and 8406/78*, 18 DR 187 at 195 (1979) and *X v Switzerland No 9012/80*, 24 DR 205 (1980).
13 *Tyrer v UK* A 26 para 32 (1978).

conduct, such as employment and housing. In the case of discrimination by private persons, responsibility would be based upon a positive obligation upon the state to ensure that private individuals may not lawfully interfere with other individuals' rights.[14]

A further question is whether discrimination on grounds other than race is subject to Article 3. Although the Commission stated in the *East African Asians* cases that it is 'generally recognised' that 'a special importance should be attached to discrimination based on race',[15] this was not necessarily intended to suggest that there might not be other such important categories. Legislation discriminating against illegitimate children and their parents[16] was held in *Marckx v Belgium* not to be degrading treatment contrary to Article 3. However, since the *Marckx* case, discrimination against children born out of wedlock has been identified as a kind of discrimination given special protection by Article 14, as has sexual discrimination.[17] It is arguable that discrimination on any of these grounds, all of which concern personal characteristics, is degrading contrary to Article 3.

A number of allegations of degrading treatment have concerned persons in detention. In *Hurtado v Switzerland*,[18] the applicant had defecated in his trousers because of the shock caused by a stun grenade used in his arrest. The Commission concluded that there had been degrading treatment when he was not able to change his clothing until the next day and after he had been transported between buildings and questioned. The condition of the cells of IRA prisoners participating in the 'dirty protest' campaign was also degrading, but did not give rise to liability on the part of the United Kingdom because it was self-imposed.[19] In *Ireland v UK*,[20] conditions at the Ballykinler military camp were 'discreditable and reprehensible' but not such as to amount to degrading treatment. Insistence that a convicted prisoner wear a prison uniform is not degrading treatment.[1] Nor is the transportation or other appearance in public of a remand or convicted prisoner in handcuffs or in uniform.[2] Intimate body searches of the same prisoners were not sufficiently humiliating to be in breach of Article 3.[3] However, intimate body searches in a non-terrorist context might be treated

---

14 See *X and Y v Netherlands*, discussed above, p 20. However, if racial discrimination involves a lack of respect for an individual's private life, the claim would probably be best brought under Article 8: ibid.

15 3 EHRR 76 at 86 (1973) Com Rep; CM Res DH (77) 2.

16 A 31 para 66 (1979).

17 See below, p 481.

18 A 280-A (1994) Com Rep. F Sett before Court.

19 *McFeeley v UK No 8317/78*, 20 DR 44 at 85-6 (1980). In B v UK No 6870/75, 32 DR 5 (1981), it was concluded that sanitary conditions and overcrowding at Broadmoor hospital did not amount to 'degrading treatment'.

20 A 25 para 181 (1978).

1 *McFeeley v UK No 8317/78*, 20 DR 44 at 81 (1980).

2 *X v Austria No 2291/64*, 24 CD 20 (1967). See also *Campbell v UK No 12323/86*, 57 DR 148 at 156 (1988).

3 *McFeeley v UK No 8317/78*, 20 DR 44 at 85-6 (1980). See also the *Greek* case, 12 YB (the *Greek* case) 1 at 461, 463, 465 (1969) Com Rep; CM Res DH (70) 1 (detainees stripped naked). As to forced feeding of prisoners, see above, p 72.

differently. Degrading treatment contrary to Article 3 may be shown by reference to particular incidents or the general regime of treatment to which prisoners are subjected.[4]

Claims of degrading treatment have been considered in various other diverse contexts. Allegations that the lips of Kurdish villagers were smeared with human excrement by Turkish security forces were admitted for consideration on the merits under Article 3.[5] A requirement that an accused person submit to a psychiatric examination was not degrading.[6] Nor does a state's failure to recognise a transsexual's new sex involve 'degrading' treatment.[7] Although the Convention does not protect the right to a reputation, it may be, in an exceptional case, that the humiliation suffered by defamatory remarks made by a public authority might qualify as degrading treatment.[8] Constant surveillance by the police could also, exceptionally, amount to degrading treatment.[9] As with claims of inhuman treatment, claims concerning private or family life cases that involve allegations of degrading treatment are more likely to succeed under Article 8. Thus the omission by a state to provide adequate criminal sanctions in the case of a sexual assault by a private person was not considered upon under Article 3 in respect of the humiliation suffered by the victim because liability had been established under Article 8.[10] In *Lopes Ostra v Spain*,[11] the noise and smells from a waste treatment plant near the applicant's family home did not give rise to degrading treatment.

6. DEGRADING PUNISHMENT

'Degrading' has the meaning that it has in connection with degrading treatment. In *Tyrer v UK*,[12] the Court characterised a degrading punishment as follows:

---

4   *Hilton v UK No 5613/72*, 3 EHRR 104 (1979), Com Rep; CM Res DH (79) 3.
5   *Gurdogan, Mustak, Mustak and Mustak v Turkey Nos 15202-5/89*, 76A DR 9 (1989) F Sett.
6   *X v FRG No 8334/78*, 24 DR 103 (1981).
7   *B v France* A 232-C (1992) Com Rep.
8   Cf the *East African Asians* cases 3 EHRR 76 at 80 (1973) Com Rep; CM Res DH (77) 2 (an action 'which lowers a person in rank, position, reputation or character' may be degrading if sufficiently severe). But see the dissenting opinion of Mr Fawcett in that case. An allegation of 'public defamation' was rejected without discussions in *Agee v UK No 7729/76*, 7 DR 164 (1976).
9   *D'Haese, Le Compte v Belgium No 8930/80*, 6 EHRR 114 (1983) (no breach on the facts). The facts would need to be extreme.
10 *X and Y v Netherlands* A 91 (1985). Cf *Hendriks v Netherlands No 9427/78*, 29 DR 5 (1982): Com Rep; CM Res DH (82) 4. As to cases of rape, see above, p 63, under inhuman treatment.
11 A 303-C (1994). A claim under Article 8 succeeded.
12 A 26 (1978). See Zellick, 27 ICLQ 665 (1978). On corporal punishment under Article 3 generally, see Phillips, 43 ICLQ 153 (1994). As to the steps taken to comply with the *Tyrer* decision, see above, p 30.

'. . . in order for a punishment to be 'degrading' and in breach of Article 3, the humiliation or debasement involved must attain a particular level and must in any event be other than that usual element of humiliation referred to in the preceding sub-paragraph (ie that which follows from the very fact of being convicted and punished by a court).[13] The assessment is, in the nature of things, relative: it depends on all the circumstances of the case and, in particular, on the nature and context of the punishment itself and the manner and method of its execution.'

Applying this test to the facts of the case, the Court held that a judicial sentence of three strokes of the birch imposed by an Isle of Man juvenile court on a 15-year-old boy for assault and executed by a police constable at a police station was a degrading punishment contrary to Article 3. With regard to the 'manner and method of its execution', the Court noted that medical and other safeguards[14] had been applied and that the birching had occurred in private. As to the private character of the birching, the Court stated that whereas publicity 'may be a relevant factor' in assessing whether a punishment is degrading, it did not consider that 'the absence of publicity will necessarily prevent a given punishment from falling into that category: it may well suffice that the victim is humiliated in his own eyes, even if not in the eyes of others'.[15] Also relevant was the three-week delay in administering the punishment pending an appeal and the fact that the birching was effected by a stranger. Finally, the 'indignity of having the punishment administered over the bare posterior aggravated to some extent the degrading character of the applicant's punishment', although 'it was not the only or determining factor'.[16]

What was crucial in deciding the case, however, were considerations concerning the 'nature and context' of judicial corporal punishment generally. The Court emphasised that such punishment was 'institutionalised violence' imposed by one individual upon another in the name of the state, the individual being 'treated as an object in the power of the authorities'; it was 'an assault on precisely that which it is one of the main purposes of Article 3 to protect, namely a person's dignity and physical integrity'.[17] Moreover, it was irrelevant that Manx public opinion favoured the birch on grounds of deterrence; a punishment did not cease to be degrading because it was or was believed to be effective and Manx public opinion was in any event out of step with 'commonly accepted standards in the penal policy' in Council of Europe states.[18] Adopting its 'dynamic'

---

13 Cf the 'usual element of humiliation' in military, prison, school and professional discipline cases: see *Albert and Le Compte v Belgium* A 58 (1983) (striking doctor off the list not sufficiently humiliating).
14 There was a prior medical examination and a doctor and the boy's father were present.
15 A 26 para 32 (1978).
16 Id para 35.
17 Id para 33. The Court added, somewhat inconclusively, that it could not 'be excluded that the punishment may have had adverse psychological effects': ibid.
18 Id para 31.

approach to the interpretation of the Convention, by which the Convention is to be interpreted in 'the light of present day conditions',[19] the Court considered that such standards were to be taken into account.

Although the *Tyrer* case did not in terms declare judicial corporal punishment to be degrading *per se*, it is unlikely, given present day Western European penal policy, to pass muster however administered. The case also makes the point that the Convention contains a distinction between acceptable and unacceptable *kinds*, as well as *degrees*, of degradation. In the case of imprisonment, which is obviously not in itself in breach of Article 3, the fact of incarceration and the conditions that necessarily go with it mean that the level of humiliation must be at least as high as that which accompanies a single use of the birch.

There have also been several cases concerning disciplinary corporal punishment in schools.[20] In *Costello-Roberts v UK*,[1] the Court held, by 5 votes to 4, that a disciplinary measure at a private boarding school by which a seven-year-old boy was given three 'whacks' on the bottom with a gym shoe over his trousers by the headmaster with no one else present was not a degrading punishment. The Court distinguished the *Tyrer* case by reference to the fact that the applicant in the *Costello-Roberts* case was much younger; that the punishment was less severe and resulted in no visible bruising; that it was not administered to the boy's bare bottom; and that the delay in executing it (three days) was much shorter.[2] The Court also distinguished between the official state violence involved in the execution in a police station of a judicial sentence and the informal administration of a private school disciplinary code. The four dissenting judges[3] gave the following reasons for disagreeing: 'After a three-day gap, the headmaster of the school "whacked" a lonely and insecure seven-year old boy. A spanking on the spur of the moment might have been permissible, but, in our view, the official and formalised nature of the punishment meted out, without the adequate consent of the mother, was degrading'. In contrast with the *Costello-Roberts* case, in which neither the Court nor the Commission[4] considered that Article 3 had been infringed, in two other cases – *Warwick v United Kingdom*[5] and *Y v United Kingdom*[6] – the Commission was of the

---

19 Ibid. As to the Courts' 'dynamic' approach, see above, p 7.
20 See on the earlier cases, Ghandi, 33 ICLQ 488 (1984)
1   A 247-C (1993). As to the basis on which Article 3 applies to private schools, see above, p 20.
2   The Court noted further that in the *Tyrer* case the applicant was 'held by two policemen whilst a third administered the punishment, pieces of the birch breaking at the first stroke': id para 31.
3   Judges Ryssdal, Vilhsalmsson, Matscher and Wildhaber. As to 'adequate consent', in *Costello-Roberts* the school prospectus stated that a high standard of discipline was maintained, but did not mention corporal punishment.
4   The Commission did, however, find a breach of the right to respect for private life under Article 8. The Court found no breach of Article 8.
5   No 9471/81, 60 DR 5 (1986) Com Rep; CM Res DH (89) 5. There have been several other UK cases. See eg *X v UK No 7907/77*, 24 YB 402 (1981), in which the UK made an ex gratia payment of £1,200 compensation and £1,000 costs where a 14-year-old girl at a state school had been caned.
6   A 247-C (1993). Com Rep.

opinion that there had been a breach of Article 3. In the *Warwick* case, a 16-year-old girl at a state school who had been caught smoking a cigarette was given one stroke of the cane on the hand, causing bruising, by the headmaster in his office in the presence of the deputy headmaster and another similarly delinquent girl immediately after being reported. The Committee of Ministers could not decide whether Article 3 had been infringed, being unable to obtain a two-thirds majority either way.[7] In *Y v United Kingdom*, a 15-year-old schoolboy at a private school was given four strokes of the cane on his bottom through his trousers, resulting in heavy bruising. The caning was administered by the headmaster in private as soon as the pupil was sent to him for defacing another boy's file. A county court claim in assault had been unsuccessful on the basis that the parents had agreed by contract to caning as a disciplinary punishment and the force used was reasonable. The case was not decided by the Court, having been struck off its list following a friendly settlement.[8] It is noticeable that, like the majority of the Court in the *Costello-Roberts* case, the Commission did not discuss in these cases the question of parental consent, which would not appear to prevent liability under Article 3. In the one other case on school corporal punishment that has reached the Court, it was held in *Campbell and Cosans v United Kingdom*[9] that the *threat* of corporal punishment (resulting from its availability in a state school) did not cause sufficient suffering or degradation to be 'inhuman' or 'degrading' *treatment*.

Generally, the conclusion to be drawn from the jurisprudence of the Court and the Commission is that the imposition of disciplinary corporal punishment in state or private schools is suspect from the standpoint of Article 3, particularly where physical harm is inflicted or where the manner of its administration is humiliating. Bearing in mind that the problem would appear to be uniquely British, it should be noted that United Kingdom disciplinary corporal punishment cases will become less frequent following legislative changes. Corporal punishment of all pupils in state schools and of publicly funded (but not other) pupils in independent schools in Great Britain has been abolished.[10] In addition, independent boarding schools in England and Wales with less than 50 boarders are required under the Children Act 1989, s 60, to register as children's homes and, as such, are prohibited from using corporal punishment.

As yet there has been no ruling as to corporal punishment administered by parents or child-minders.[11] The decisions in the *Costello-Roberts* and *Y v UK* cases, in which the Commission and the Court noted the *in loco parentis*

---

7 It is likely that the voting was influenced in favour of the defendant state by the changes in the law referred to at n 10, below, of which the Committee was informed. The Committee did, however, recommend that the UK pay the applicants' costs.

8 The UK government agreed to pay £8,000 compensation and £9,000 in costs.

9 A 48 (1982). There was a breach of Article 2, First Protocol in this case: see below, p 546.

10 Education (No 2) Act 1986, s 47 and the Education (Scotland) Act 1980, s 48A.

11 As to punishment by child-minders in English law, see *Sutton LBC v Davis*, [1994] 2 WLR 721.

basis for the school's disciplinary power, suggests that it is likely that a modest use of force at the *Costello-Roberts* level as a parental disciplinary measure in the home would not infringe Article 3. Responsibility under Article 3 for more extreme parental disciplinary measures permitted by national law would require positive obligation[12] reasoning of the kind adopted by the Commission in the *Warwick* and *Y* cases. The Court's approach in the *Costello-Roberts* case would not be sufficient in a non-educational context.

7. CONCLUSION

Article 3 has proved a difficult provision to interpret because of the generality of its text. The terms 'inhuman' and 'degrading' especially have no clear legal meaning and tend to be over-used in ordinary speech. As a result, Article 3 has led to an extraordinary variety of complaints. Correspondingly, it offers a considerable opportunity for judicial creativity, and in some respects the Strasbourg authorities have not disappointed. Most strikingly, Article 3 has been interpreted as controlling extradition or deportation to face ill-treatment abroad. The reasoning of the Court's judgment in the *Soering* case leaves open the possibility that extradition or deportation to face a real risk of breaches of other Convention articles (eg Article 6) might be controlled too. Article 3 has also been invoked in a number of important inter-state applications (the *Greek* case, *Cyprus v Turkey*, *Ireland v UK*) in which serious allegations of ill-treatment in a political or emergency context have been upheld. At a different level, Article 3 has been used to condemn various forms of corporal punishment. Paradoxically, while the Court has used its freedom under Article 3 to condemn judicial corporal punishment, the Convention continues to permit capital punishment in at least some cases by virtue of the clear wording of Article 2.

Although the dynamic or broad interpretations of Article 3 adopted by the Court in several of the above cases would scarcely have been anticipated by the drafters of the Convention, they are none the less in tune with present-day European standards. Similarly, the decision in the *Tomasi* case represents an important development that reflects international human rights standards as to the burden of proof concerning physical assault in detention. In some other respects, Article 3 has not been so rigorously applied. In particular, while not infrequently expressing doubts or concern, the Strasbourg authorities have hesitated to find that conditions of detention in prisons or mental hospitals fall below the standards set by the Convention. Given the absence of any other provision in the

---

12 As to positive obligations under the Convention, see above, p 19.

Convention[13] that could be used to protect persons vulnerable to ill-treatment in the custody of the state, a more demanding interpretation might be adopted that would not devalue or 'trivialise' Article 3.[14] Any such development might be prompted by the example given by the Prevention of Torture Convention.

13 The right to respect for privacy in Article 8 might apply in some cases. There is, however, no equivalent to Article 10, ICCPR, which requires that 'persons deprived of their liberty shall be treated with humanity and with respect for the inherent dignity of the human person'.
14 A proposal for a Convention protocol on the rights of persons in detention is under consideration at Strasbourg.

CHAPTER 4

Article 4: Freedom from slavery, servitude or forced or compulsory labour

'**Article 4**
1. No one shall be held in slavery or servitude.
2. No one shall be required to perform forced or compulsory labour.
3. For the purpose of this Article the term "forced or compulsory labour" shall not include:
   (a) any work required to be done in the ordinary course of detention imposed according to the provisions of Article 5 of the Convention or during conditional release from such detention;
   (b) any service of a military character or, in case of conscientious objectors in countries where they are recognised, service exacted instead of compulsory military service;
   (c) any service exacted in case of an emergency or calamity threatening the life or well-being of the community;
   (d) any work or service which forms part of normal civic obligations.'

Article 4 has generated comparatively little case-law. The few cases that have been considered on their merits have concerned the treatment of convicted prisoners or have resulted from attempts to extend the concept of forced labour to situations in which persons have been required by the state to provide their professional services to the community. No breach of Article 4 has yet been found.

1. FREEDOM FROM SLAVERY AND SERVITUDE

Article 4(1) requires that no one 'shall be held in slavery or servitude'. Its importance is underlined by the fact that it cannot be derogated from in time of war or public emergency.[1] Slavery has not been defined in any Strasbourg case. It is likely that the Strasbourg authorities would be guided

1 See Article 15(2), below, p 503.

by the meaning that the term has in the 1926 Slavery Convention.[2] There slavery is defined as 'the status or condition of a person over whom any or all of the powers attaching to the right of ownership are exercised'. In Roman law, a slave was the property of another and lacked the legal capacity of other human beings.[3]

The status or condition of servitude does not involve ownership and differs from slavery on that count. Distinguishing servitude from forced labour, the Commission stated in the *Van Droogenbroeck* case:[4]

'. . . it may be considered that in addition to the obligation to provide another with certain services the concept of servitude includes the obligation on the part of the "serf" to live on another's property and the impossibility of changing his condition.'

In that case, the Commission was of the opinion that the applicant was not held in 'servitude' when a court, having convicted him of a criminal offence, ordered that on completion of his prison sentence he should be placed at the disposal of the state for a number of years, during which time he could be recalled for detention. The Commission noted that the applicant was placed at the disposal of the state for only a limited period of time; that any recall decision would be subject to judicial review; and that the resulting detention would be compatible with Article 5 of the Convention. In the light of these considerations, the applicant's condition did not amount to 'that particularly serious form of deprivation of liberty' that constituted servitude.[5] As the Court stated in the same case, the compatibility of any detention with Article 5 does not by itself prevent it involving 'servitude' contrary to Article 4(1).[6]

The prohibitions of servitude and forced or compulsory labour in Article 4 overlap in that the 'work' or 'service' required of a person in servitude in breach of Article 4(1) may also be forced or compulsory labour contrary to Article 4(2) (see below). However, the degree of overlap is limited by the fact that certain kinds of work that might contribute towards servitude do not count as forced labour because of Article 4(3). Thus in the *Boy Soldiers* cases,[7] while considering that the applicants' military service could not be forced labour because it was excluded by Article 4(3), the Commission none

---

2 60 LNTS 253; UKTS 16 (1927), Cmd 2910. Article 1. Twenty-five of the parties to the European Convention, including the UK, are parties to the Slavery Convention. The Court has referred to other such treaties when interpreting Article 4: see below, p 92.

3 See Buckland, *A Manual of Roman Private Law*, 2nd edn, 1957, p.37.

4 B 44 (1980) Com Rep para 79. The Commission's approach is based upon the definition of 'serfdom' in the 1956 Supplementary Convention on the Abolition of Slavery, etc, Article 1,266 UNTS 3, UKTS 59 (1957), Cmnd 257.

5 B 44 Com Rep para 80 (1980).

6 A 50 para 58 (1982). The Court held that there was no breach of Article 4(1) on the facts, referring to the Commission's report in other respects.

7 *W, X, Y and Z v UK Nos 3435/67–3438/67*, 28 CD 109 (1968).

the less assessed it on the merits before deciding that it did not amount to servitude in the sense of Article 4(1).

2. FREEDOM FROM FORCED OR COMPULSORY LABOUR

Under Article 4(2), no one 'shall be required to perform forced or compulsory labour'. Such labour (hereafter referred to just as forced labour) does not include a requirement that a lawyer give his services free to assist indigent defendants. In *Van der Mussele v Belgium*,[8] the applicant, a pupil advocate, was called upon to provide such services. As the Court noted, this was part of a long-standing tradition in Belgium and certain other Convention parties by which legal aid was provided on a voluntary basis by the legal profession rather than through the publicly funded legal aid schemes which were now coming to replace such arrangements. The Court held that the work required of the applicant was labour in the sense of Article 4(2). Labour ('*travail*' in the French text) extended beyond physical work to all kinds of 'work or service', as became clear from the wording of Article 4(3). As to the meaning of forced or compulsory labour, the Court adopted – at least as a starting point and subject to the dynamic character of the Convention – the definition of this phrase in the ILO Forced Labour Convention 1930 (ILO Convention 29),[9] viz 'all work or service which is exacted from any person under the menace of any penalty and for which the said person has not offered himself voluntarily'. On the facts of the case, although the applicant committed no criminal offence by not participating, he would have run the risk of being struck off the roll of pupils. This was sufficient to amount to a 'penalty' for the purposes of Article 4(2). As to whether the applicant had 'offered himself voluntarily', the fact that he had given his prior consent when he became a pupil advocate was not conclusive. However, in a case of prior consent it required a 'considerable and unreasonable imbalance between the aim pursued'[10] – here entry to the legal profession – and the obligations accepted as a condition of achieving that

8   A 70 (1983). Cf *Gussenbauer v Austria No 5219/71*, 15 YB 558 (1972), which concerned an arrangement by which Austrian lawyers were required on pain of disciplinary sanctions to provide free legal aid for indigent defendants in return for which the state paid the Austrian Bar Associations an annual contribution to their pension funds. A friendly settlement was reached by which the legal aid system and pension fund arrangements were modified and a payment made to the applicant for expenses: F Sett Rep (1974). See also *X v FRG No 4653/ 70*, 46 CD 22 (1974) and *X v FRG No 8682/79*, 26 DR 97 (1981) (not forced labour to pay low fees to lawyers for legal aid work). And see *X and Y v FRG No 7641/76*, 10 DR 224 (1976).

9   39 LNTS 55; 134 BFSP 449; Cmd 3693. Article 2. The Court adopted the Forced Labour Convention definition because Article 4 had been drafted by reference to it. It was also relevant that nearly all of the Convention parties, including the defendant state, were parties to it. The Court also referred to the 1957 Abolition of Forced Labour Convention (ILO Convention 105), 320 UNTS 291, Cmnd 328, which prohibits the use of forced labour for defined purposes in supplementation of ILO Convention 29.

10 A 70 para 40 (1983).

aim for there to be forced labour. In determining whether that imbalance existed, it was necessary to look at 'all the circumstances of the case'. In the present case, the question was whether the service imposed a 'burden which was so excessive or disproportionate to the advantages attached to the future exercise of [the legal] profession that the service could not be treated as having been voluntarily accepted'.[11] In answering this question in the negative, the Court took into account the fact that the required service was not unconnected with the profession in question; that in return for it, advocates generally received certain advantages, including the exclusive right of audience in the courts; that the work contributed to a pupil advocate's professional training; that the requirement related to a right guaranteed in the Convention (the right to legal aid: Article 6(3)(c)) and was similar to the 'normal civic obligations' exception allowed by Article 4(3)(d); and that the burden imposed upon the applicant, involving in particular work without remuneration, was not such as to leave him without sufficient time for paid work.[12]

In the small number of other cases in which Article 4(2) has been applied, it has been held that it was not forced labour to require a notary to charge less for work done for non-profit-making organisations (eg churches),[13] to require an employer to deduct social security payments or income tax from an employee's salary[14] or to require an unemployed person to accept a job offer on pain of losing his unemployment benefit.[15]

Article 4 imposes not only a negative obligation upon states not to require forced labour of individuals (as on the facts of the cases in the preceding paragraph); it may also oblige states not to permit individuals lawfully to subject other individuals to such labour (or slavery or servitude). In the *Van der Muselle* case, the obligation of pupil advocates to provide free legal aid was to be found in rules freely adopted by the *Ordre des avocats*, which was a private professional body. Rejecting the argument of the defendant state that it was not responsible for these rules under the Convention, the Court noted that under Belgian law the state had laid the general obligation to provide legal aid upon the *Ordre des avocats* and that a state could not avoid

---

11 Id para 37.
12 The Court adopted a different, somewhat broader definition of forced labour from that earlier used by the Commission in *Iversen v Norway No 1468/62*, 6 YB 278 (1963). There the Commission had ruled inadmissible an application by a dentist who was required by Norwegian law on pain of criminal sanction to take paid work on qualifying in the public dental sector for a year and in a part of the country in which dentists were in short supply. Four members of the majority of the Commission found that the facts did not amount to forced labour. It is probable that the same result would follow from an application of the Court's approach in the *Van der Mussele* case, since the work was paid and for a short period only. On the *Iversen* case, see Schermers, 11 NILR 366 (1964).
13 *X v FRG No 8410/78*, 18 DR 216 (1979).
14 *Four Companies v Austria No 7427/76*, 7 DR 148 (1976). The question whether Article 4 could protect a company was left open.
15 *X v Netherlands No 7602/76*, 7 DR 161 (1976). Although this and the other Commission decisions referred to in this paragraph were taken before the Court's decision in the *Van der Mussele* case, it is unlikely that they would be decided differently under the Court's test.

its responsibility under the Convention to provide legal aid (Articles 6(1) and (3)(c)) by delegating it to others.[16] This very limited reasoning, which supposes that Article 4 applied because the rules in question operated in an area of a Convention right which the state was obliged to protect, would not assist, for example, an individual (eg a domestic servant) who claimed to have been subjected to forced labour by a private employer in circumstances that were lawful under national law. The Commission, however, was not unsympathetic to a broader view, which it is to be hoped would be adopted by the Strasbourg authorities, in a case involving a transfer system for professional footballers that was organised by a private football association. Without deciding the point (because the system did not meet the *Van der Muselle* test of forced labour), the Commission noted that 'it could be argued that the responsibility of the Netherlands government is engaged to the extent that it is its duty to ensure that the rules, adopted, it is true, by a private association, do not run contrary to the provisions of the Convention'.[17]

3.   PERMITTED WORK OR SERVICES

Article 4(3) excludes certain kinds of work or service from the prohibition of forced labour in Article 4(2). These kinds of work or service are not restrictions on the exercise of the right protected by Article 4(2), in which case they would be interpreted narrowly; instead they are part of the definition of forced labour in Article 4(2) and so serve as an aid to interpretation of that paragraph.[18]

i.   Work during detention

Article 4(3)(a) excludes from the prohibition of forced labour 'work required to be done in the ordinary course of detention imposed according to the provisions of Article 5' or 'during conditional release from such detention'. This exception includes work required in the course of any kind of detention that is permitted by Article 5(1) of the Convention. It includes, therefore, not only work during detention following conviction by a court of law,[19] which will be the most common case, but also work required of a detained minor[20] or vagrant.[1] The fact that a person whose detention is permitted by Article 5(1) is, in breach of Article 5(4), not provided with a

---

16 Reasoning of this kind was later used in the *Costello-Roberts* case concerning private school corporal punishment: see above, p 20.
17 *X v Netherlands No 9322/81*, 32 DR 180 at 182 (1983).
18 *Van der Mussele v Belgium* A 70 (1983).
19 This includes work done by a convicted prisoner for a private firm as well as work done in prison: *Twenty One Detained Persons v FRG No 3134/67 et al* 11 YB 528 (1968).
20 *X v Switzerland No 8500/79*, 18 DR 238 (1979).
1 *X v FRG No 770/60*, 6 CD 1 (1960).

remedy to challenge the legality of his detention does not render any work required of him in detention forced labour.[2] Article 4(3)(a) refers to work required during 'the ordinary course of detention'. This wording refers not only to the work that the state concerned ordinarily requires of a detained person; it also incorporates a European standard by which a particular state's practice can be measured. Such scrutiny relates to the purpose of the work required, as well as its nature and extent. Thus in the *Vagrancy* cases,[3] work in a vagrancy centre had not exceeded the limits set by Article 4(3)(a) because it was aimed at the rehabilitation of vagrants and was comparable to that in several other Council of Europe member states.

ii. Military service or substitute civilian service

Article 4(3)(b) excludes 'any service of a military character or, in case of conscientious objectors in countries where they are recognised, service exacted instead of compulsory military service'. There has been no case yet in which the length or conditions of compulsory military service, in those European states that retain it,[4] has been considered. 'Service of a military character' includes voluntary enlistment in the armed forces as well as compulsory military service. This was held in the *Boy Soldiers* cases[5] in the light of the drafting history of Article 4. In those cases, the four applicants had, at the age of 15 or 16 and with the consent of their parents, enlisted in the armed forces until the age of 18 and for a nine-year term thereafter. They could apply for release from the armed forces in certain exceptional circumstances (eg compassionate grounds) and had a statutory right to buy themselves out in the first three months of service. Since voluntary as well as compulsory military service fell within Article 4(3)(b), the applicants were not able to argue that the terms of their service amounted to forced labour. Otherwise, the question whether there was a 'considerable and unreasonable imbalance', as required by the Court in the *Van der Mussele* case, on the facts of the *Boy Soldiers* cases would have been a difficult one to answer. Article 4(3)(b) also excludes from the definition of 'forced labour' compulsory civilian work in substitution for conscription. A conscientious objector who refuses to do such work may be kept in detention for the period of military service. Since the Convention recognises in Article 4(3)(b)

2 *De Wilde, Ooms and Versyp v Belgium* (*Vagrancy* cases) A 12 para 89 (1971). Cf *Van Droogenbroeck v Belgium* A 50 (1982). The Commission had held in the *Vagrancy* cases that it did.

3 A 12 para 90 (1971). Cf *Van Droogenbroeck* case A 50 (1982). See also *X v Switzerland No 8500/79*, 18 DR 238 (1979) (work not abnormally long or arduous for a juvenile). In the *Vagrancy* cases, the Court did not consider the size of the 'allowances' or 'wages' paid to detainees which, in common with normal European practice, were small. The Commission has consistently regarded the 'extremely small' amounts commonly paid to working prisoners as consistent with Article 4(3)(a): see eg *Twenty One Detained Persons v FRG No 3134/67 et al*, 11 YB 528 (1968).

4 These constitute a majority of Council of Europe members: see CM Rec R (87) 8.

5 *W, X, Y and Z Nos 3435/67–3438/67*, 28 CD 109 (1968).

that a conscientious objector may be required to do substitute civilian work, a state may take measures to ensure that such work is done or impose sanctions for non-compliance.[6]

iii. Community service in a public emergency

Article 4(3)(c) excludes 'any service exacted in case of an emergency or calamity threatening the life or well-being of the community'. It was on this basis that two members of the majority of the Commission in the *Iversen* case[7] were of the opinion that the requirement that the applicant serve a year in the public dental service in northern Norway was not forced labour. Noting that the Norwegian government had enacted the law imposing the requirement because, in the government's opinion, the shortage of volunteer dentists had created an emergency that threatened the well-being of the community in northern Norway, the two members, applying the margin of appreciation doctrine, accepted the government's assessment of the situation. In another case, the Commission decided that a requirement that a person holding shooting rights over land take part in the gassing of foxholes as a measure of control over rabies was within Article 4(3)(c).[8]

iv. Normal civic obligations

Finally, Article 4(3)(d) excludes from the prohibition in Article 4(2) 'any work or service which forms part of normal civil obligations'. This includes compulsory fire service.[9] Having held that it did not amount to forced labour, the Court found it unnecessary in the *Van der Mussele* case to decide whether unpaid legal aid work required of pupil advocates came within Article 4(3)(d). In other cases, the Commission has ruled the following to be 'normal civic obligations': obligations imposed by the state upon a lessor to arrange for the maintenance of his building,[10] upon a holder of shooting rights to participate in the gassing of foxholes[11] and upon an employer to deduct taxes from an employee's income.[12]

---

6 *Johansen v Norway No 10600/83*, 44 DR 155 (1985). See also *Grandrath v FRG No 2299/64*, 10 YB 626 (1967) Com Rep; CM Res DH (67) 1 (Jehovah's Witness refusal to do military or substitute civilian service). See further on conscientious objection Article 9, p 368, below.
7 *No 1468/62*, 6 YB 278 (1963).
8 *S v FRG No 9686/82*, 39 DR 90 (1984).
9 *Schmidt v Germany* A 291-B para 22 (1994)
10 *X v Austria No 5593/72*, 45 CD 113 (1973).
11 *S v FRG No 9686/82*, 39 DR 90 (1984).
12 *Four Companies v Austria No 7427/76*, 7 DR 148 (1976).

CHAPTER 5

Article 5: The right to liberty and security of the person

1. ARTICLE 5(1): GENERALLY[1]

Article 5(1) protects the 'right to liberty and security of person'. By 'liberty' is meant physical liberty of the person.[2] The Court's jurisprudence contains several statements affirming the importance of this right in a democratic society[3] and explaining that the overall purpose of Article 5 is to ensure that no one should be dispossessed of his liberty in an 'arbitrary fashion'.[4] The essence of Article 5 is that, although the right to liberty is not an absolute one, a person must be detained only on a basis of law and that the law relied upon must be consistent with recognised European standards.

Article 5 also safeguards the individual against the illegal deprivation of liberty contrary to Article 5 by requiring that a person in detention be provided with a remedy or remedies by which he can challenge the legality of his detention and obtain compensation if it is not lawful. All kinds of detention by the state are controlled by Article 5. If most cases that have arisen have concerned arrest and detention in the context of criminal proceedings, there have been many other important cases on such matters as the detention of minors, the mentally disordered and persons being deported or extradited.

i. The meaning of arrest or detention

Arrest or detention[5] in the sense of Article 5 is an extreme form of restriction upon freedom of movement, which is generally protected by Article 2, Fourth Protocol to the Convention.[6] There have been several cases in

---

1   See Murdoch, 42 ICLQ 494 (1993); Kohl, 108 JT 485 at 505 (1989); Trechsel 1 HRLJ 88 (1980); id, *European System*, Ch 13.
2   *Engel v Netherlands* A 22 para 58 (1976).
3   See eg *Winterwerp v Netherlands* A 33 para 37 (1979).
4   See eg *Engel v Netherlands* A 22 para 58 (1976) and *Bozano v France* A 111 para 54 (1986).
5   No legal consequence turns upon the distinction between these two terms or the use of both terms in some sub-paragraphs of Article 5(1) and only the term 'detention' in others. Generally speaking, a person is first arrested and then placed in detention. The following pages mostly refer only to detention.
6   See below, p 559.

different factual contexts in which the Strasbourg authorities have had to draw the line between these two provisions.

The classic case of detention in the sense of Article 5 occurs when a person is kept securely in a closed prison. A more borderline case occurred in *Guzzardi v Italy*.[7] There the applicant was required by a judicial compulsory residence order to live for sixteen months on a remote island off the coast of Sardinia on suspicion of illegal mafia activities. He was restricted to a hamlet in an area of the island of some 2.5 sq kms that was occupied solely by persons subject to such orders, although the applicant's wife and child were allowed to live with him. While the applicant could move freely within the area and there was no perimeter fence, he could not visit other parts of the island. Islanders were allowed to enter the area, but seldom did so. The applicant had to report twice daily and was subject to a curfew. Drawing an analogy with the conditions typically found in a modern-day open prison, the Court held, by 11 to 7, that the applicant's conditions involved a sufficient degree of deprivation of liberty to fall within Article 5. The ruling was crucial as there was no sub-paragraph of Article 5(1) that could justify the applicant's detention and Italy was not at the relevant time a party to the Fourth Protocol.

In the *Guzzardi* case, the Court gave some general guidance as to the approach that should be followed when setting the parameters of Article 5. It stated that the distinction between restrictions upon freedom of movement serious enough to fall within it and others subject only to the Fourth Protocol is 'merely one of degree or intensity, and not one of nature or substance'.[8] When assessing whether the required 'degree or intensity' of restriction exists, regard must be had to 'a whole range of criteria such as the type, duration, effects and manner of implementation of the measure in question'.[9] As to the duration of detention, in other cases the Commission has correctly regarded very short periods of detention as falling within Article 5 in typical cases of close arrest by the police and other public authorities.[10] As the *Guzzardi* case demonstrates, however, as the degree of physical constraint lessens (for example, from that in a prison cell to that in a hamlet), so considerations such as social isolation and the other circumstances of detention identified by the Court come into play.[11]

There have been a number of other cases in which the degree of restriction upon freedom of movement required by Article 5 have been explored. In the context of the occupation of northern Cyprus by Turkish troops, the

---

7   A 39 (1980).

8   Id, para 93.

9   Id, para 92, adopting the language of *Engel v Netherlands* A 22 para 59 (1976). Cf *Ashingdane v UK* A 93 (1985).

10 See below, p 100.

11 In *Guzzardi v Italy No 7960/77* (1977) unreported, in which the applicant in the *Guzzardi* case had been transferred and restricted to an inhabited village on the mainland where his living conditions were the same as those of other residents of the village, except that he was subject to reporting conditions, it was held that there was no deprivation of liberty. Cf *Raimondo v Italy* A 281 (1994). See also *Cyprus v Turkey (First and Second Applications)*, below at n 13.

confinement of Greek Cypriots to detention centres which they were not free to leave, or to private houses where they were held under guard in conditions similar to those in detention centres, was detention within Article 5, as was their confinement in a hotel which they could not leave without permission or an escort.[12] In contrast, a limitation upon freedom of movement by which Greek Cypriots could not leave a village was subject to the Fourth Protocol, not Article 5.[13] In *Ashingdane v UK*,[14] a person kept compulsorily in a mental hospital under a detention order was protected by Article 5, even though he was in an 'open' (ie unlocked) ward and was permitted to leave the hospital unaccompanied during the day and over the weekend. The position would have been different if, although still subject to a detention order, he had been provisionally released.[15] It has also been held that the housing in a transit area at an airport of persons seeking asylum pending a decision on their claims does not give rise to detention in the sense of Article 5 if they are free to leave the defendant state's territory at any time.[16]

As far as restrictions upon the freedom of movement of members of the armed forces are concerned, in *Engel v Netherlands*[17] the Court stated that restrictions that follow from 'normal conditions of life within the armed forces of the contracting states' do not involve a deprivation of liberty. However, further constraint, including that which results from a sentence imposed for a military disciplinary offence, may be such as to fall within Article 5. Thus in the *Engel* case it was held that the 'strict arrest' of soldiers, by which they were locked in a cell in army barracks and accordingly unable to carry out their normal duties, fell within Article 5. *A fortiori*, their committal to a military disciplinary unit was subject to Article 5. In contrast, their 'aggravated arrest', by which soldiers continued with their normal duties but were confined during off-duty hours to a specially designated building within army premises, but not locked up, did not.[18] This is not wholly convincing reasoning; physical constraint within a building is

---

12 *Cyprus v Turkey (First and Second Applications) Nos 6780/74 and 6950/75*, 4 EHRR 482 at 529 (1976) Com Rep; CM Res DH (79) 1. Since these detentions did not fall within any of the exceptions allowed by sub-paragraphs (a)-(f) of Article 5(1), they were found to be in breach of Article 5. Cf *Cyprus v Turkey (Third Application)* 15 EHRR 509 (1983) Com Rep; CM Res DH (92) 12. House arrest was found to be subject to Article 5 in the *Greek* case: 12 YB (the *Greek* case) at 134-5 Com Rep; CM Res DH (70) 1.

13 *Cyprus v Turkey*, loc cit at n 12 above, p 524. Cf *Aygun v Sweden No 14102/88*, 63 DR 195 (1989) (restriction to Stockholm not subject to Article 5) and *SF v Switzerland No 16360/90*, 76A DR 13 (1994) (restriction to Italian enclave surrounded by Switzerland not subject to Article 5).

14 A 93 para 42 (1985). Contrast *Nielsen v Denmark*, below at p 100.

15 *W v Sweden No 12778/87*, 59 DR 158 (1988) and *L v Sweden No 10801/84*, 61 DR 62 (1988). Cf *Weeks v UK* A 114 (1987) in which the Court rejected an argument that the question of a deprivation of liberty in the sense of Article 5 did not arise when the applicant was recalled to hospital because he was only out on licence; for the purposes of Article 5, 'liberty' was a question of fact, and the applicant was free when recalled.

16 *S v Austria No 19066/91* (1992) unreported.

17 A 22 para 59 (1976).

18 Cf the ruling that a curfew by itself is not a deprivation of liberty in the sense of Article 5(1)(a): *Cyprus v Turkey (First and Second Applications)*, loc cit at n 12 above.

in itself sufficiently close confinement to be detention during the period to which it applies.

In practice, most cases of arrest or detention occur at the hands of the police in connection with criminal proceedings. It can be taken that where a policeman, by physical restraint or by words or conduct, indicates to a person that he is not free to leave, there is an arrest for the purposes of Article 5. The Commission has held that whether a person who is taken to a police station for questioning is deprived of his liberty depends upon the intention of the police.[19] The facts of the case were that a 10-year-old schoolgirl was taken to a police station for two hours for questioning in connection with a school theft and placed in an unlocked cell. The Commission held that there was no deprivation of liberty because the object had been to question, not to arrest. It is doubtful whether this is the best test in a case of this kind. It is not clear from the report whether the girl was requested and consented to go to the police station or whether she was made to believe that she was obliged to go. In the latter case, it is submitted, there would be an arrest in the sense of Article 5. Similarly, a person who is made to believe that he is obliged to remain when stopped on the street or elsewhere by the police for the purpose of being questioned, searched or subjected to a test in the administration of the criminal law should be protected by Article 5.[20] It is relevant in this last connection that Article 5 applies even though the period of detention may be very brief. Detention for a period of less than two hours for the purpose of deportation[1] has been held to qualify, as has an even shorter period of restraint for the purpose of effecting a blood test.[2]

Since Article 5 protects children as well as adults, the question arises as to the relationship between Article 5 and an exercise of parental rights that results in a child's detention. In *Nielsen v Denmark*,[3] a state hospital placed a 12-year-old boy in a closed psychiatric ward at the request of his mother, who had sole parental rights, for treatment for his neurotic condition. The son, acting through his father, claimed that the resulting detention was a deprivation of his liberty against his will contrary to Article 5. The Court saw the case as one of the exercise of parental rights by the mother, not one involving a restriction upon freedom of movement by the state. It noted that the exercise of such rights was a fundamental element of family life, respect for which was recognised as a right in Article 8 of the Convention,[4] and that parental rights in the law of the contracting parties to the Convention included parental competence 'to decide where the child must reside and also impose, or authorise others to impose, various restrictions on the child's

---

19 *X v FRG No 8819/79*, 24 DR 158 (1981).
20 Such arrests or detention may be justified under Article 5(1)(b): see below at p 114.
1   *X and Y v Sweden No 7376/76*, 7 DR 123 (1976).
2   *X v Austria No 8278/78*, 18 DR 154 (1979). Although problems may arise in complying with the procedural guarantees in Article 5 if it applies to very short periods of detention (see Trechsel, *European System*, p 288), they are not insuperable.
3   A 144 (1988).
4   See below, pp 329ff.

liberty'.[5] These restrictions, the Court stated, included rules which a child must comply with in 'a school or other educational or recreational institution'[6] and decisions as to hospitalisation for medical treatment. They presumably also include disciplinary measures taken by parents involving detention at home. Although such parental restrictions might appear to fall within Article 5, the Court held that Article 5 was simply not intended to apply to them, provided that they were imposed for a 'proper purpose'.[7] This was the case on the facts of the *Nielsen* case as the mother had consented to her child's hospitalisation for the protection of his health, not as a means of keeping him away from his father, as had been suggested.

The Court also seemed to say that, in any event, the restriction involved in the applicant's placement in a 'closed' psychiatric ward, which 'did not, in principle, differ from those obtaining in many hospital wards where children with physical disorders are treated', was not a deprivation of liberty in the sense of Article 5.[8] This is both doubtful and inconsistent with the Court's decision concerning detention in a mental hospital in the *Ashingdane* case.[9] The better and, it is submitted, acceptable[10] rationale for the Court's decision is that stated above, viz that there is an implied limitation to the right to liberty in Article 5 that follows from the conjunction of Articles 5 and 8. This approach distinguishes such a limitation from implied limitations generally, which are not permitted because the list of exceptions in Articles 5(1)(a)-(f) – within which parental rights do not fit easily[11] – is exhaustive. The Court's judgment was by 12 votes to 7. The seven dissenting judges,[12] like the Commission, considered that there had been a sufficient restriction upon the son's freedom of movement to make the case one of detention within Article 5 and that, although the case involved parental consent, the state was responsible for the detention, having 'associated itself with it through the action and assistance of its organs and officials'. Supposing that there was detention in the sense of Article 5 and that it otherwise applied, the better approach might have been to have tackled the

---

5 A 144 para 61 (1988).
6 Note, however, that the obligation to attend school and to accept disciplinary rules, which may permit detention as a punishment, will usually be one imposed by law by the state, rather than a matter of parental consent. See below, pp 543-544. The taking of a child into public care or placing it in a children's home is not in itself detention: see *Family T v Austria No 14013/88*, 64 DR 176 (1989). However, any acts by the state amounting to the detention of children in care must fall within Article 5.
7 Cf the requirement of lack of 'arbitrariness' in respect of the exceptions to the 'right to liberty' permitted by Article 5(1)(a)-(f): see below, p 105. The exercise of parental rights would also need to be lawful under the applicable municipal law.
8 A 144 para 72 (1988).
9 Above, p 99.
10 But for criticism of the Court's judgment, see Murdoch, 42 ICLQ 494 at 498 (1993) and Trechsel, *European System*, p 287.
11 The *Nielsen* case would not have fallen within Article 5(1)(e) because the applicant was not mentally disordered, only disturbed.
12 Judges Thor Vilhjalmsson, Pettiti, Russo, Spielman, De Meyer, Carrillo Salcedo and Valticos.

case as one of private detention,[13] rather than through an extended concept of state action, as suggested by the dissenting judges. The question would then have been whether Article 5 imposed a positive obligation upon states[14] to control private detention.

As a result of its approach, the majority of the Court did not find it necessary in the *Nielsen* case to examine this last question. In the context of the detention of children by parents, such a positive obligation would require a state to protect a child by law from parental detention that went beyond the bounds of the guarantee of respect for family life in Article 8 and that could not be justified under Article 5. A positive obligation to protect individuals from detention by private persons could arise in other contexts also, such as kidnapping by terrorists,[15] the detention of convicted persons in private prisons under arrangements for 'privatisation' and the arrest by a private person of a suspected criminal. The imposition of a positive obligation in such areas could be justified by the importance of the right to liberty involved and would be consistent with practice in European legal systems. In the case of 'privatised prisons', it would be surprising if a state could avoid its obligations under Article 5 by the expedient of arranging for the detention in a private prison of persons arrested in the public interest.

Article 5 applies even though the detained person surrenders himself for detention; the right to liberty is too important in a democratic society to conclude otherwise. Thus in *De Wilde, Ooms and Versyp v Belgium*,[16] the fact that a vagrant gave himself up to the police for detention did not mean that he was not entitled to the guarantees in Article 5.

Article 5 may extend to the arrest or detention of a person by a state's agents outside of its territory. Thus in *Reinette v France*,[17] it applied to the detention of an accused by the French police abroad after he had been handed over by the local authorities for return to France in custody on a French military aircraft; as soon as he was handed over 'the applicant was effectively subject to French authority and consequently to French jurisdiction'.

ii.   Conditions of detention not controlled by Article 5

Article 5 is generally concerned only with the fact of detention, not the conditions in which a person is detained: the latter are a matter for Article 3.[18]

---

13 That surely was the case in the *Nielsen* case; if the mother withdrew her consent, the child would have been released.
14 As to positive obligations, see above, p 19.
15 Cf Treschel, *European System*, p 280.
16 A 12 para 65 (1971).
17 *No 14009/88*, 63 DR 189 at 193 (1989). As to unlawful abduction or surrender, see below p 107.
18 *Ashingdane v UK* A 93 para 44 (1985). However, the requirement that detention be 'lawful' meant that a mentally disordered person must be kept in an institution that was authorised for that purpose: ibid.

Thus the fact that greater restrictions are placed upon the freedom of movement of a person already detained in the sense of Article 5 does not give rise to a new question of detention under that Article.[19] Although this is probably the correct interpretation, the result is a gap in the coverage of the Convention insofar as Article 3 covers only cases of serious ill-treatment or punishment.[20]

iii. The right to security of person

Article 5(1) guarantees the 'right to liberty *and security* of person'. However, the italicised words have not, as yet, been given any separate meaning;[1] the phrase instead is to be read as a whole. 'Security of person' must be understood in the context of physical liberty[2] so that it cannot be interpreted as referring to quite different matters such as a right to social security[3] or to submit a civil claim to a court.[4] Nor does it impose an obligation upon the state to give someone personal protection from an attack by others.[5] Instead, as the Court indicated in *Bozano v France*,[6] in its only pronouncement on the matter, the function of the wording 'security of person' is to require that an arrest or detention not be 'arbitrary'. Accordingly, the guarantee of 'security of person' serves merely to underline a requirement that the Strasbourg authorities have already developed when interpreting the 'right to liberty' in Article 5.[7] In view of this, the fact that a person's 'security' is, unlike his 'liberty', not subject to any exceptions in the text of Article 5(1)[8] is not significant.

---

19 *X v Switzerland No 7754/77*, 11 DR 216 (1977) and *D v FRG No 11703/85*, 54 DR 116 (1987). However, an extension of the period of detention by virtue of a prison disciplinary sentence would raise a question under Article 5: see *Campbell and Fell v UK* A 80 (1984) (loss of remission).

20 See above, p 61.

1 It could be used as a basis for challenging over-broadly formulated powers of arrest in the absence of any actual deprivation of liberty. Cf the *Klass* case concerning telephone tapping, below, p 337. However, the requirement of 'lawfulness' (below) can be used to the same effect.

2 *East African Asians v UK* 3 EHRR 76 at 89 (1973) Com Rep; CM Res DH (77) 2.

3 *X v FRG No 5287/71*, 1 Digest 288 (1972).

4 *Dyer v UK No 10475/83*, 39 DR 246 at 256 (1984).

5 *X v Ireland No 6040/73*, 16 YB 388 (1973). See, however, Article 2, above, p 39. As to the 'security' of stateless persons seeking immigration, see *X and Y v UK No 5302/71*, 44 CD 29 at 46 (1974). The equivalent 'security of the person' guarantee in Article 9 of the ICCPR has been interpreted to cover threats to the physical security of non-detained persons: *Chiko Bwalya v Zambia (314/1988)*, 1-2 IHRR 98 (1993).

6 A 111 paras 54 and 60 (1986). Cf *East African Asians* case loc cit at n 2 above and *Arrowsmith v UK No 7050/75*, 19 DR 5 at 18 (1978). See also *Dyer v UK No 10475/83*, 39 DR 246 at 256 (1984) and *Adler and Bivas v FRG Nos 5573/72 and 5670/72*, 20 YB 102 at 146 (1977).

7 As to the requirement that a deprivation of liberty must not be 'arbitrary' in order to be 'lawful', see below, p 105.

8 See *Kamma v Netherlands No 4771/71*, 18 YB 300 at 316 (1975) Com Rep; CM Res DH (1975) 1.

2. CASES IN WHICH DETENTION IS PERMITTED

i. Generally

Article 5 recognises that the 'right to liberty' cannot be absolute. It lists in Article 5(1), sub-paragraphs (a) to (f), circumstances in which the state[9] may detain an individual in the public interest. The exceptions listed in Article 5 are not mutually exclusive: the detention of a person in a mental hospital as a result of a conviction by a court may, for example, come within both Articles 5(1)(a) and (e). The list of exceptions is 'exhaustive' and, since it consists of restrictions, is to be given a 'narrow interpretation'.[10] However, this last consideration has not always prevailed.[11] The 'right to liberty' is also not absolute in the different sense that Article 5 can be derogated from in time of emergency under Article 15 of the Convention.[12]

a. *Limitations must be in accordance with a procedure prescribed by law*

Article 5(1) requires that any deprivation of liberty must be effected 'in accordance with a procedure prescribed by law'. The term 'procedure' includes the procedure followed by a court when ordering detention[13] and rules governing the making of arrests.[14] In *Winterwerp v Netherlands*,[15] the Court indicated that the requirement meant that the procedure followed must (i) be in conformity with the applicable municipal law and the Convention, including the 'general principles' contained in the latter; and (ii) not be 'arbitrary'.[16]

As far as compliance with municipal law is concerned, it is 'in the first place for the national authorities, notably the courts, to interpret and apply the law'.[17] If a national court rules[18] or a defendant state concedes in argument in a Strasbourg case[19] that the procedures required by municipal law have not been complied with, the Strasbourg authorities are most unlikely to disagree. In other cases too, they are likely to accept the interpretation and

9   The question whether Article 5 imposes a positive obligation upon states to control detention by private persons in any circumstances has yet to be decided: see the *Nielsen* case, above, p 102.
10 *Winterwerp v Netherlands* A 33 para 37 (1979).
11 See *Monnell and Morris v UK*, below, p 109 and *McVeigh, O'Neill and Evans v UK*, below, p 113.
12 See Article 15(2). This was significant in *Lawless v Ireland* A 3 (1961) and *Ireland v UK* A 25 (1978).
13 *Van der Leer v Netherlands* A 170-A (1990).
14 *Fox, Campbell and Hartley v UK* A 182 para 29 (1990).
15 A 33 para 45 (1979).
16 For the meaning of 'arbitrary', see the discussion of 'lawful' below, p 105. In *Winterwerp v Netherlands*, id, para 39, the Court linked the requirement of 'non-arbitrariness' with Article 18, Convention, which must be read with Article 5. The 'general principles' referred to include the rule of law.
17 *Winterwerp v Netherlands* id, para 46 and *Bozano v France* A 111 para 58 (1986).
18 See eg *Bonazzi v Italy* No 7975/77, 15 DR 169 (1978).
19 See eg *Naldi v Italy* No 9920/82, 37 DR 75 (1984). Cf *Schuurs v Netherlands* No 10518/83, 41 DR 186 (1985) F Sett.

application of its municipal law suggested by the defendant state.[20] Where, however, the national authorities can clearly be seen to have infringed municipal law, the Strasbourg authorities will intervene on their own initiative.[1] As the Court has stated, it must, as a supervisory body, have this ultimate power to interpret and apply national law when, as in Article 5, the Convention requires that a state comply with its national law.[2]

b. Limitations must be lawful

In addition to the requirement in the introductory wording of Article 5(1) that any deprivation of liberty be 'in accordance with a procedure prescribed by law', the wording of each sub-paragraph of Article 5(1) supposes that it is also 'lawful'. These two requirements could have been understood as complementary, distinguishing between the procedure followed in detaining a person and the grounds for detention. Instead, 'lawful' has been interpreted as referring to both procedure and substance, so that the two requirements overlap.[3] In practice, the Court sometimes merges its consideration of the two requirements, treating procedural, as well as substantive, regularity by reference to the single requirement that a deprivation of liberty be 'lawful'.[4] It follows that the Court has developed the same meaning for the two requirements. Thus the requirement of 'lawfulness' has also been understood to mean that any detention must be in accordance with the applicable municipal law[5] and the Convention[6] and must not be 'arbitrary'.[7]

With regard to the first requirement, as in the case of the requirement that any deprivation of liberty be 'in accordance with a procedure prescribed by law',[8] it is in the first place for the national authorities, particularly the courts, to decide whether the relevant municipal law has been complied with.

The prohibition of 'arbitrariness' provides the Strasbourg authorities with a vehicle by which to review restrictions upon the right to liberty in a manner similar to the way in which they act under Articles 8-11 using 'necessary in a democratic society' formula.[9] Thus a detention is 'arbitrary' if it is 'not in conformity with the purpose' of the particular sub-paragraph

---

20 See *Winterwerp v Netherlands* A 33 (1979) and *Wassink v Netherlands* A 185-A (1990).
1 See *Van der Leer v Netherlands* A 170-A (1990) and *Koendjbiharie v Netherlands* A 185-B (1990) Com Rep.
2 *Winterwerp v Netherlands* A 33 para 46 (1979).
3 Id, para 39.
4 See eg *Van der Leer v Netherlands* A 170-A (1990). In *Bouamar v Belgium* A 129 (1988) they were considered separately.
5 Municipal law includes directly applicable EEC law: *Caprino v UK No 6871/75*, 12 DR 14 at 19 (1978). This Commission case has not yet been confirmed by the Court. Although argument was based on an EEC directive in *Bozano v France* A 111 (1986) the Court did not refer to it. As to whether Nazi law was 'law', see *X v FRG No 4324/69*, 14 YB 342 (1971).
6 *K v Austria* A 255-B (1993) Com Rep. F Sett before Court.
7 *Winterwerp v Netherlands* A 33 para 39 (1979).
8 See above, p 104. The comments made there apply *mutatis mutandis* to the requirement of 'lawful'.
9 This has been pointed by Murdoch, 42 ICLQ 494 at 499 (1993) and Trechsel, *European System*, p 291. As to Articles 8-11, see below, Ch 8.

concerned or with Article 5 generally.[10] For example, detention ostensibly for the purpose of deportation that is really aimed at illegal extradition would be 'arbitrary'.[11] There is authority in respect of certain sub-paragraphs of Article 5(1) to the effect that a detention is also 'arbitrary' if, although properly motivated, it is not proportionate to the attainment of the sub-paragraph's purpose.[12] Such an approach is not taken, however, in respect of all sub-paragraphs. Instead, the closeness with which the Strasbourg authorities are prepared to control a state's conduct by means of a requirement of 'arbitrariness' varies from one context to another. For example, while being willing to consider whether an order for a person's detention as being of 'unsound mind' is taken on the basis of reliable evidence as to a person's medical condition and is otherwise warranted on the facts,[13] the Strasbourg authorities are unlikely to look behind a criminal conviction resulting in a sentence of imprisonment to see if the accused was properly convicted or sentenced.[14] Although such differences can be rationalised by reference to the wording of particular sub-paragraphs or the perception that some sub-paragraphs contain only formal guarantees,[15] in reality the matter is one of judgment by the Strasbourg authorities as to the degree of European supervision that is appropriate. To the extent that they do, so far exceptionally,[16] review decisions taken by a state's national authorities by reference to their proportionality, the Strasbourg authorities will allow those authorities a certain discretion or 'margin of appreciation' in their assessment of the situation.[17] In the context of Article 5(1)(f), the Commission has suggested that 'lawful' also incorporates the requirement that the municipal law upon which the detention is based must be accessible and foreseeable in its application.[18] There would appear to be no contextual reason why such a requirement should not apply to all sub-paragraphs of Article 5(1).[19]

---

10 See eg *Winterwerp v Netherlands* A 33 para 39 (1979) and *Bouamar v Belgium* A 129 para 50 (1988). Cf Article 18, Convention, which 'confirms' this interpretation: *Winterwerp* case, ibid.

11 See *Bozano v France*, below, p 125.

12 *Winterwerp v Netherlands* below, p 122 (Article 5(1)(e)). Cf *Caprino v UK*, below, p 127, n 10 ('necessity or proportionality') (Article 5(1)(f), in connection with the length of detention only) and *Van Droogenbroeck v Belgium*, below, at p 104 (Article 5(1)(a), applying a reasonableness test concerning one particular element of that provision only).

13 See *Winterwerp v Netherlands*, below, p 122.

14 See *Krzycki v FRG*, below, p 107.

15 See Trechsel, 1 HRLJ 88 at 107 (1980).

16 The examples given in n 12, above, are the only clear ones. The general tendency is to emphasise the need for a state to provide a national remedy in accordance with Article 5(4) to challenge an illegal detention, rather than to provide an international one through Article 5(1). Considerations of local knowledge, problems of proof and the *quatrième instance* doctrine lead to such an approach.

17 *Winterwerp v Netherlands* A 33 para 40 (1979) and *Weeks v UK* A 114 para 50 (1987).

18 *Zamir v UK No 9174/80*, 40 DR 42 (1983) (Article 5(1)(f)). This idea was introduced into the interpretation of the Convention in the *Sunday Times* case: see below, p 287 (Article 10(2)). Cf *Arrowsmith v UK* at p 103, n 6, above, in the context of the 'right to security of person'.

19 There is also no reason why the meaning given to 'lawfulness' in Article 8(2) in *Olsson v Sweden* (No 2), below, p 341, should not apply to Article 5.

A person who is detained on the territory of a contracting party in accordance with its law may none the less be detained 'unlawfully' by it contrary to Article 5(1) if he has been abducted from another state's territory.[20] Where, however, the contracting party has been handed custody of the person by the authorities of the other state, no question of a breach of Article 5 by the receiving state will arise even though the return might amount to 'disguised extradition' or otherwise be illegal under the returning state's law.[1] However, if the returning state is a party to the Convention it would be in breach of its Article 5 obligations in the above circumstances.[2]

ii. Detention following conviction by a competent court

Article 5(1)(a) permits 'the lawful detention of a person after conviction by a competent court'. Article 5(1)(a) concerns only the fact of detention; it does not control the place or conditions of detention. Thus transfer from prison to Broadmoor, as permitted by the court sentence, did not raise an issue under Article 5(1)(a).[3]

The requirement in Article 5(1)(a) that the detention be 'lawful' means that it must be in accordance with the applicable municipal law and with the Convention. This means that there must be a court judgment that justifies it and that the procedure that is followed to effect the detention is lawful. On the basis that Article 5(1)(a) does not require a 'lawful conviction' but only 'lawful detention', the Strasbourg authorities have held that Article 5(1)(a) does not permit them to review the legality of a conviction[4] or sentence[5] imposed by a national court. Nor can Article 5(1)(a) be relied upon to challenge the length or appropriateness of a sentence of imprisonment.[6] The reluctance of the Strasbourg authorities to review municipal court decisions is understandable both in terms of their long standing and sound policy of not acting as a court of appeal from national courts and of the likely flood of cases that would otherwise result. However, the better approach would be for them to claim the power to review the legality under municipal law of a conviction or sentence, but to acknowledge, as is their normal practice, that it will only be exercised in clear cases of illegality.[7] It would be surprising if a breach of Article 5(1)(a) were not found if the defendant state were to concede that a conviction or sentence was contrary to its law. On a separate point, detention will not be rendered retroactively 'unlawful' for the

20 *Stocké v Germany* A 199 (1991) Com Rep; point not considered by Court.
1 *Altmann v France No 10689/83*, 37 DR 225 (1984) (the *Klaus Barbie* case).
2 See *Bozano v France*, below, p 125.
3 See *X v UK No 7977/77*, 1 Digest 305 (1981).
4 *Krzycki v FRG No 7629/76*, 13 DR 57 at 61 (1978).
5 *Weeks v UK* A 114 para 50 (1987).
6 In *Weeks v UK*, below, p 108, the Court referred to the prohibition of inhuman punishment in Article 3, not to Article 5, when referring to the harsh life imprisonment in that case.
7 Cf above, at p 104. A case of abuse of power, as in the *Bozano* case, below, p 125, would be hardly likely to arise in the case of the judiciary.

purposes of Article 5(1)(a) because the conviction or sentence upon which it is based is overturned by a higher municipal court on appeal.[8]

The requirement of 'lawfulness' also supposes that the detention is not 'arbitrary', which in the context of Article 5(1)(a) means only that its purpose must be the execution of the sentence of imprisonment imposed by the court. Detention is not 'arbitrary' because the period of time spent in detention awaiting extradition from another state to serve a sentence in prison following escape is not taken into account as a part of that sentence.[9]

The reference to detention 'after' conviction implies a causative link, not just one of chronology. This is relevant in cases in which a person convicted of an offence is sentenced by a court first to a term of imprisonment and thereafter to possible further detention as a result of an administrative decision. Article 5(1)(a) applies to any such later administrative detention provided that there is a 'sufficient connection' between that detention and the initial court sentence.[10] The Strasbourg authorities may review the merits of an administrative decision ordering detention in such a case, but will allow the national authorities a 'margin of appreciation' in assessing the factual situation when doing so.

This interpretation of Article 5(1)(a) was established in *Van Droogenbroeck v Belgium*.[11] In that case, the applicant had been sentenced by a court to two years' imprisonment for theft and, on grounds of recidivism, 'placed at the Government's disposal' for ten years thereafter, the two parts of the sentence constituting under Belgian law 'an inseparable whole'.[12] On completion of his two-year sentence, the applicant was released from prison, but detained by administrative decision for much of the next few years on the basis of the original court sentence. The Court held that these further periods of detention fell within Article 5(1)(a). Although they occurred several years after the sentence, they were authorised by it and were intended to achieve its purpose. The connection with the sentence would have been broken, so that Article 5(1)(a) would not have applied, if the decision to recall the applicant had been 'based upon grounds that had no connection with the objectives of the legislature and the court or on an assessment that was unreasonable in terms of those objectives'.[13] In that case, a detention that was lawful at the outset would have become 'arbitrary' and hence incompatible with Article 5.

The approach in the *Van Droogenbroeck* case was applied in *Weeks v UK*[14] to the system of discretionary life sentences in English law. In that case, the applicant, aged 17, was given a life sentence for armed robbery. In

---

8 *Krzycki v FRG No 7629/76*, 13 DR 57 at 61 (1978). But see *Artico v Italy No 6694/74*, 8 DR 73 at 89 (1977). As to the position under Article 5(1)(f), see below, p 126.
9 *C v UK No 10854/84*, 43 DR 177 (1985).
10 Such a 'connection' also exists where a death sentence imposed by a court is commuted to one of imprisonment by executive act: *Kotälla v Netherlands No 7994/77*, 14 DR 238 (1978).
11 A 50 para 35 (1982).
12 Ibid.
13 Id, para 40.
14 A 114 (1987). As to discretionary life sentences, see below, p 152.

fact, he had stolen 35 pence from a pet shop after threatening the owner with a starting pistol. As the European Court stated, on first impression the life sentence was extremely harsh and arguably an 'inhuman punishment' contrary to Article 3 of the Convention. However, it was given because the applicant, who was characterised by the trial court judge as a 'very dangerous young man', could be released on licence when no longer a threat to the community or himself, which might be much sooner than would be the case if he were sentenced to a particular term of imprisonment appropriate to the offence. In fact, the applicant's condition remained such that he was not released on licence for nearly ten years. He was then recalled by the Home Secretary a year after his release, following incidents involving minor offences. The Court considered that the case was comparable to the *Van Droogenbroeck* case in that here too the purpose of the recall, which was the act of detention in question, was the legitimate one of social protection and the rehabilitation of the offender. Moreover, despite the considerable time that had elapsed, the causal link between the recall and the original sentence had not been broken: the Home Secretary's intention in recalling the offender was consistent with the objectives of the sentencing court. As to the justification for recalling the applicant on the facts, the Court noted that there was evidence of unstable and aggressive behaviour such as to give the Home Secretary grounds to act and that national authorities were allowed a 'margin of appreciation' in assessing such evidence.[15]

A sufficient 'causal connection' between a conviction and detention was also found in the very different situation in *Monnell and Morris v UK*.[16] In that case, the two applicants, ignoring the advice of their lawyers, applied in person to the Court of Appeal for leave to appeal. Leave was refused and the Court of Appeal directed that 28 and 56 days respectively of the applicants' detention pending appeal would not, as normal, count as a part of their sentences because they had wasted the Court's time. Somewhat surprisingly, the Strasbourg Court held that the days lost by the applicants could be justified under Article 5(1)(a) because the statutory power exercised by the Court of Appeal was intended to prevent abuse of the right of appeal, which was an aim that could be legitimately pursued by way of 'detention of a person after conviction by a competent court'. There was accordingly a 'sufficient causal connection'[17] between the detention of the applicants and their convictions.

The Court's judgment was strongly influenced by the fact that in the legal systems of certain states parties to the Convention detention pending appeal is regarded as a continuation of detention on remand.[18] In such states, the convicted person does not start to serve his sentence until appeal proceedings are over, at which point the appellate court determines the sentence and may count the time spent in detention on remand as a part of

15 On the application of Article 5(1)(a) to administrative recalls of mentally disordered offender patients, see *X v UK*, below, p 110, n 4.
16 A 115 para 46 (1987).
17 Id, para 40.
18 See *Wemhoff v FRG* A 7 p 23 (1968), and below, p 138.

the sentence, possibly omitting any time spent in detention on remand pending appeal if the appeal is without merit. The difference between such systems, which do not run the risk of a breach of Article 5(1)(a), and the English system was regarded by the Court as 'one of form and not of substance as far as the effect on the convicted person is concerned'[19] so that liability under the Convention should not depend upon it.

In Article 5(1)(a), a 'conviction' means a 'finding of guilt' in respect of an offence that has been found to have been committed.[20] Accordingly, it does not include detention as a preventive or security measure.[1] It does include cases in which a person is found guilty of an offence and, instead of being given a sentence of imprisonment by way of punishment, is ordered to be detained in a mental institution for treatment as mentally disordered.[2] Sub-paragraphs (a) and (e) overlap in applying to such cases,[3] at least initially.[4] Where, however, an accused is acquitted of an offence and then ordered to be detained in a mental institution, only Article 5(1)(e) applies.[5] Article 5(1)(a) applies to 'convictions' for disciplinary, as well as criminal, offences under municipal law provided that the outcome of the proceedings is the convicted person's detention.[6]

A 'conviction' is a conviction by a trial court, so that any detention pending appeal is to be justified by reference to Article 5(1)(a), not Article 5(1)(c).[7] This interpretation is necessary to permit the detention pending his appeal of an accused who is on bail before his conviction.[8] It also follows from the fact that an accused would not be detained following his trial in the absence of his conviction by the trial court, which is thus the cause of any detention pending appeal.[9]

---

19 *Monnell and Morris v UK* A 115 para 47 (1987).
20 Contempt of Parliament or a breach of parliamentary privilege determined by the United Kingdom House of Commons, which has historically led to detention, would be a conviction under this test, and is regarded as such in United Kingdom law: see Harris, 1966 Crim LR 205 at 212.
1 *Guzzardi v Italy* A 39 para 100 (1980).
2 *X v UK* A 46 para 39 (1981).
3 The claim in *Ashingdane v UK* A 93 (1985) was made and considered under Article 5(1)(e). The particular basis for the claim may dictate the sub-paragraph that is most appropriate. See *M v FRG No 10272/83*, 38 DR 104 (1984).
4 In *X v UK* A 46 para 39 (1981), the Court, which supposed that both paragraphs applied to the initial detention, expressed doubt as to whether Article 5(1)(a) continues to apply in a case in which a person ordered to be detained in a mental institution is released and then recalled to the institution by an administrative decision. The *Van Droogenbroeck* case, at p 108, above, suggests that it would do so provided that there was a 'sufficient connection' between the recall and the initial court sentence.
5 *Luberti v Italy* A 75 para 25 (1984). Cf *Dhoest v Belgium No 10448/83*, 55 DR 5 (1987) Com Rep; CM Res DH(88) 1.
6 *Engel v Netherlands* A 22 para 68 (1976).
7 *Wemhoff v FRG* A 7 p 23 (1968). The Court stated that Article 5(1)(a) takes over from Article 5(1)(c) even in legal systems, such as that in Germany, in which detention pending appeal is treated as a continuation of detention on remand. For criticism of the Court's decision, see Trechsel, *European System*, p 297.
8 *Wemhoff v FRG* A 7 p 23 (1968).
9 *B v Austria* A 175 para 39 (1990).

A 'conviction' exists so as to justify any detention based upon it even though the judgment, giving the reasons for the conviction, has not been yet delivered.[10] The 'conviction' may be that of a foreign court, whether a party to the Convention or not.[11] This is relevant to the situation in which an offender is transferred to a party to the Convention to serve a sentence of imprisonment.[12]

A 'competent' court is one with jurisdiction to try the case.[13] As with the same term in Article 5(4), 'court' in Article 5(1)(a) means a body that is independent of the executive and the parties and that provides 'adequate judicial guarantees'.[14] The 'adequate judicial guarantees' required by Article 5(1)(a) are 'not always co-extensive with those of Article 6'; account must be taken of the particular circumstances.[15] For example, whereas a 'public hearing' might be required in a criminal case,[16] the same might not be true in military disciplinary proceedings.[17] To the extent that there is an overlap between Article 5(l)(a) and Article 6, a breach of Article 6 in the trial of a person sentenced to imprisonment following his conviction might also mean that the detention is not justified by Article 5(1)(a).

The above jurisprudence on the meaning of a 'court' is relevant to the situation where a person is detained in a contracting state following a conviction by a court in another jurisdiction. In *Drozd and Janousek v France and Spain*,[18] following their conviction by an Andorran court, the applicants served their sentence of imprisonment in a French prison in accordance with a long standing custom. Faced with an argument that the applicants had been convicted in Andorra in breach of Article 6 of the Convention, the Court held that the detention in a French prison would be justified by Article 5(1)(a) unless the conviction in Andorra, which was not a party to the Convention, was 'the result of a flagrant denial of justice'.[19] Although there was a strong argument to the effect that the Andorran court had not been independent as required by Article 6(1) and had infringed Article 6 in other respects, the Court held that there was no breach of its 'flagrant denial' test on the facts. The decision that there had been no breach of Article 5(1)(a) was taken by 12 votes to 11. Whereas the majority stressed that it was not for the Convention parties to impose the standards of the Convention on non-parties, certain of the dissenting judges referred to the

---

10 *Crociani v Italy No 8603/79*, 22 DR 147 (1980).
11 *X v FRG No 1322/62*, 6 YB 494 at 516 (1963).
12 See *Drozd and Janousek v France and Spain* below, at n 18.
13 *X v Austria No 2645/65*, 11 YB 322 at 348 (1968) and *X v Austria No 4161/69*, 13 YB 798 at 804 (1970).
14 *De Wilde, Ooms and Versyp v Belgium* A 12 para 78 (1971) and *Engel v Netherlands* A 22 para 68 (1976). As to the invariable need for 'independence', see *Eggs v Switzerland No 7341/76*, 15 DR 35 at 62 (1978) Com Rep; CM Res DH (79) 7 (chief military prosecutor not a 'court'). As to the meaning of 'court' in Article 5(4), see below, p 146.
15 *Engel v Netherlands* A 22 para 68 (1976).
16 *Wemhoff v FRG* A 7 p 23 (1968).
17 *Engel v Netherlands* A 22 (1976).
18 A 240 para 110 (1992). Cf *Iribarne Perez v France No 16462/90*, 76A DR 18 (1994).
19 Cf the approach in *Soering v UK*, below, p 257.

Explanatory Report on the 1970 European Convention on the International Validity of Criminal Judgments[20] which states that a condition of the enforcement of foreign criminal judgments is that the decision must have been rendered in accordance with Article 6, European Convention on Human Rights.

iii. Detention for non-compliance with a court order or an obligation prescribed by law

Article 5(1)(b) permits 'the lawful arrest or detention of a person for non-compliance with the lawful order of a court or in order to secure the fulfilment of any obligation prescribed by law'.

The first limb of Article 5(1)(b) authorises the detention of a person who has failed to comply with a court order already made against him, as in cases of civil contempt. It includes failure to pay a court fine[1] or maintenance order and refusal to undergo a medical examination ordered by a court.[2] Detention for non-compliance with a court order for the enforcement of a contractual obligation merely because the person has been unable to comply with the order (eg for lack of funds) would be a breach of Article 1, Fourth Protocol to the Convention,[3] but not Article 5. For detention to be consistent with the first (and the second) limb of Article 5(1)(b), it must be 'lawful'.[4] In *K v Austria*,[5] the Commission stated that this means that it must be lawful under municipal law and the Convention and not be 'arbitrary'. In that case there was a breach of Article 5(1)(b) when the applicant was imprisoned for failure to comply with a court order to give evidence in court. This was because the court order infringed the applicant's freedom of expression, which was protected by Article 10 of the Convention.

The second limb covers the situation where a person is detained 'to compel him to fulfil a specific and concrete obligation which he has until then failed to satisfy'.[6] Examples of such obligations, which must be consistent in their nature with the Convention,[7] include an obligation to do military, or

---

20 ETS 70. In force 1974. Nine parties. See the joint dissenting opinion of Judges Pettiti, Valticos, Lopes Rocha, approved by Judges Walsh and Spielmann.
1 *Airey v Ireland No 6289/73*, 8 DR 42 (1977).
2 *X v FRG No 6659/74*, 3 DR 92 (1975). See also *No 6944/75*, 1 Digest 355 (1976) (failure to hand over property); *X v Austria No 8278/78*, 18 DR 154 (1979) (failure to take blood test); *Freda v Italy No 8916/80*, 21 DR 250 (1980) (failure to observe residence restriction); and *X v FRG No 9546/81*, 1 Digest Supp para 5.1.4.2. (1983) (failure to make a declaration of assets).
3 See below, p 559.
4 Article 5(1)(b) states that the court order must also be 'lawful'.
5 A 255-B (1993) Com Rep. F Sett before Court.
6 *Engel v Netherlands* A 22 para 69 (1976).
7 *McVeigh, O'Neill and Evans v UK Nos 8022/77, 8025/77 and 8027/77*, 25 DR 15 at 39 (1981) and *Johansen v Norway No 10600/83*, 44 DR 155 (1985). For example, an obligation to complete a census return must be consistent with the right to respect for privacy in Article 8 of the Convention.

substitute civilian, service;[8] to carry an identity card and submit to an identity check;[9] to make a customs or tax return;[10] or to live in a designated locality.[11] An obligation imposed upon a mafia suspect to 'change your behaviour' is not sufficiently 'specific or concrete'.[12] Article 5(1)(b) does not extend to obligations to comply with the law generally, so that it does not justify preventive detention of the sort that a state might introduce in an emergency situation.[13] Such a possibility would be inconsistent with the rule of law.[14]

Nor does Article 5(1)(b) apply to the ordinary enforcement of the law after breaches have occurred. If a person is detained on reasonable suspicion of having committed a crime, Article 5(1)(c), with its attendant Article 5(3) safeguards, applies, not Article 5(1)(b). An obligation imposed in connection with the enforcement of the criminal law may, however, come within Article 5(1)(b), if it is 'specific and concrete'. In *McVeigh, O'Neill and Evans v UK*,[15] the obligation in question was one on the part of persons entering Great Britain to submit to 'further examination' at the point of entry. Under the Prevention of Terrorism (Supplemental Temporary Provisions) Order 1976, all persons entering or leaving Great Britain could be examined to determine whether they had been involved in acts of terrorism. If suspicions were aroused, a person examined under the Order could be obliged to submit to 'further examination'. The three applicants, who were British or Irish nationals entering Great Britain from Ireland, were required to submit to 'further examination' and were detained under the Order for this purpose. After being questioned, searched, photographed and fingerprinted, the applicants were released after 45 hours' detention and were never charged with any criminal offence. The Commission held that the detention could be brought within Article 5(1)(b). It drew a distinction between the obligation in the 1976 Order and that in Regulation 10, made under the Civil Authorities (Special Powers) Act (NI) 1922, that was in issue in *Ireland v United Kingdom*.[16] Under Regulation 10, any person could be detained at any time in Northern Ireland for interrogation 'for the preservation of the peace and maintenance of order'. Regulation 10 was held in *Ireland v United Kingdom* not to impose an obligation in the sense of Article 5(1)(b). The Commission considered that whereas the Regulation 10 obligation was an example of 'a general obligation to submit to questioning or interrogation on any occasion, or for any purpose', the obligation under

---

8   *Johansen v Norway No 10600/83*, 44 DR 155 (1985). Any work or service listed in Article 4(3) of the Convention that is required of a person presumably qualifies.

9   *Reyntjens v France No 16810/90* (1992) unreported and *B v France No 10179/82*, 52 DR 111 (1987).

10 See *McVeigh, O'Neill and Evans v UK Nos 8022/77, 8025/77 and 8027/77*, 25 DR 15 at 40 (1981).

11 *Ciulla v Italy* A 148 para 36 (1989).

12 Ibid.

13 *Lawless v Ireland* A 3 p 51 (1961) and *Guzzardi v Italy* A 39 para 101 (1980).

14 *Engel v Netherlands* A 22 para 69 (1976).

15 Loc cit at n 7, above. See Warbrick, 32 ICLQ 757 (1983). Followed in *Harkin v UK No 11539/85*, 48 DR 237 (1986) and *Lyttle v UK No 11650/85*, 9 EHRR 381 (1986).

16 A 25 para 195 (1978).

the 1976 Order was significantly more 'specific and concrete' in that it applied only upon entering and leaving Great Britain to check the particular matters set out in the Order.

The *McVeigh* case establishes that in certain 'limited circumstances of a pressing nature' Article 5(1)(b) extends not only to cases in which there has been a prior failure to comply with an obligation, but also to cases in which short-term detention is considered necessary to make the execution of an obligation effective at the time that it arises. The Commission spelt out the test to be applied as follows:[17]

'In considering whether such circumstances exist, account must be taken . . . of the nature of the obligation. It is necessary to consider whether its fulfilment is a matter of immediate necessity and whether the circumstances are such that no other means of securing fulfilment is reasonably practicable. A balance must be drawn between the importance in a democratic society of securing the immediate fulfilment of the obligation in question, and the importance of the right to liberty. The duration of the period of detention is also a relevant factor in drawing such a balance.'

Considering the facts of the case, the Commission noted that the obligation 'to submit to further examination' was a part of a border security check aimed at controlling the well recognised problem of terrorism in Northern Ireland, in which context there was a 'legitimate need to obtain immediate fulfilment of the obligation to submit to such checks'.[18] Noting that examinations were made as far as possible without resort to detention and that, to be effective, it was necessary for any 'further examination' to take place subject to a limited period of detention, the Commission found that the applicants' detention was justified by Article 5(1)(b).[19] Although the *McVeigh, O'Neill and Evans* case concerned an emergency situation on its facts, it provides a means of justifying various powers of temporary detention exercisable by the police (eg random breath tests, road blocks, powers of stopping and searching) to enforce obligations in connection with the administration of the criminal law to which Article 5(1)(c) would not extend.

For Article 5(1)(b) to apply, the detention must be to 'secure the fulfilment' of the obligation concerned. Accordingly, detention that is a punishment for the breach of an obligation, rather than a device for fulfilling it, cannot be justified under Article 5(1)(b).[20] For the same reason,

17 25 DR 15 at 42 (1981).
18 Ibid. The problems posed in an emergency situation such as that in Northern Ireland can be tackled differently by derogating from Article 5 under Article 15 of the Convention. The UK relied upon such a derogation in *Ireland v UK*, but not in the *McVeigh* case. In the latter case, the Commission ruled that the detention did not fall within Article 5(1)(c) or any other part of Article 5, so that there would have been a breach of Article 5 had Article 5(1)(b) been held not to apply.
19 Ibid. Cf *B v France No 10179/82*, 52 DR 111 (1987).
20 See eg *Eggs v Switzerland No 7341/76*, 15 DR 35 (1978) Com Rep; CM Res DH (79) 7 and *Johansen v Norway No 10600/83*, 44 DR 155 (1985).

Article 5(1)(b) cannot justify detention that may be connected with an obligation, but that occurs before the obligation arises.[1]

iv. Detention on suspicion of having committed a criminal offence, etc

Article 5(1)(c) permits 'the lawful arrest or detention of a person effected for the purpose of bringing him before the competent legal authority on reasonable suspicion of having committed an offence or when it is reasonably considered necessary to prevent his committing an offence or fleeing after having done so'.

Article 5(1)(c) governs the arrest or detention of suspects in the administration of criminal justice. It is the first of three provisions (see also Articles 5(3) and 6) that trace the steps that are followed, supposing an arrest, in the course of investigating and prosecuting a person for a criminal offence.[2] It should be said at the outset that these provisions, both separately and as inter-related, present considerable difficulties of interpretation. This results partly from curious drafting, especially of Articles 5(1)(c) and (3). Although the Strasbourg authorities have done much, sometimes paying only limited respect to the text, to give these provisions a meaning that reflects the essentials of the administration of criminal justice in Europe, their task has been complicated by the fundamental differences between the systems of criminal procedure in civil and common law jurisdictions.[3] Certain of the Court's judgments make more sense in their rulings and in their wording for one kind of criminal justice system than for another.[4] Moreover, the Court has sometimes found it difficult to strike a proper balance between insistence upon a common European standard in the interests of procedural justice and respect for diverse national traditions by which the same end is achieved in different ways.

An 'offence' for the purpose of Article 5(1)(c) is one under criminal law.[5] Given that 'offence' must have an autonomous Convention meaning,[6] it could be interpreted as setting limits to the seriousness of the offence for which a state may authorise an arrest.[7] It is submitted that Article 5(1)(c) should set such limits, either through an interpretation of 'offence' or of the

1 *Ciulla v Italy* A 148 para 36 (1989) (detention prior to decision imposing an obligation restricting freedom of movement).
2 Article 5(1)(c) does not regulate the questioning of suspects, either after or before arrest. Only Article 3 of the Convention would appear to apply. Questions of surveillance and search and seizure of the person or property come within Article 8 of the Convention.
3 As to which, see below, p 165.
4 See eg the discussion of *Monnell and Morris v UK*, above, p 109, and *B v Austria*, below, p 138.
5 See eg *Ciulla v Italy* A 148 para 38 (1989).
6 See above, p 6.
7 In English law, for example, an arrest without a warrant is permitted in respect of 'arrestable offences', ie offences for which the possible sentence on first conviction is five years' imprisonment or is fixed by law: Police and Criminal Evidence Act 1984, s 24(1). Arrests by warrant depend upon particular statutory powers.

word 'lawful'[8] in order to prevent arrest in connection with minor offences in respect of which the public interest does not justify it.

Military *criminal* proceedings fall within Article 5(1)(c).[9] There is no indication yet that it extends also to disciplinary or regulatory offences. This may be because such proceedings do not normally commence with the arrest of the accused. However, military *disciplinary* proceedings may do so and may lead to 'convictions' in the sense of Article 5(1)(a).[10] It is submitted that an arrest in connection with such proceedings should be subject to Articles 5(1)(c) and (3).[11] At the very least, an autonomous Convention meaning of 'offence' in Article 5(1)(c) ought to include the more serious instances of military, and possibly other, disciplinary, offences as 'offences'.[12]

The term 'offence' was interpreted in *Brogan v UK*.[13] The case concerned a statutory power to arrest any person 'concerned in the commission, preparation or instigation of acts of terrorism', where the definition of 'terrorism' was the 'use of violence for political ends'. Although such involvement was not itself a criminal offence, the power of arrest was held to be justified under Article 5(1)(c). The definition of 'acts of terrorism' was 'well in keeping with the idea of an offence'[14] and, following their arrest, the applicants had at once been questioned about specific offences of which they were suspected. Whereas the first consideration mentioned by the Court might suggest that it was applying an autonomous Article 5 meaning of 'offence', it would seem from the second that the Court decided the point on the basis that involvement in 'acts of terrorism' indirectly meant the commission of specific criminal offences under Northern Irish law, which would appear to be the better approach on the facts.

Insofar as arrests by private persons to apprehend suspected criminals are permitted by the law of a contracting party, as they commonly are in European legal systems,[15] Article 5(1)(c) should arguably be interpreted as containing a positive obligation requiring that contracting parties ensure that they are permitted under its law only within the limits set by that sub-paragraph.[16]

Article 5(1)(c) permits the arrest or detention of a person only if 'it is effected for the purpose of bringing him before a competent legal authority'. The meaning of 'competent legal authority' is the same as that of 'judge or

8 See above, p 105.
9 See *De Jong, Baljet and Van Den Brink v Netherlands* A 77 (1984).
10 See above, p 110.
11 Article 5(1)(c) is not relevant to the segregation of convicted prisoners in connection with prison disciplinary offences since they are detained under Article 5(1)(a). As to regulatory offences, see below, p 169.
12 Cf the inclusion of some disciplinary offences as 'criminal' charges in Article 6(1), below, p 167.
13 A 145-B (1988).
14 Id, para 51. Cf *Ireland v UK* A 25 para 196 (1978).
15 In English law a private person may arrest a person who is reasonably suspected of being in the act of committing an 'arrestable' offence or is reasonably suspected of having committed an 'arrestable' offence that has in fact been committed: Police and Criminal Evidence Act 1984, sub-ss 24(4), 24(5).
16 As to positive obligations under the Convention, see above, p 19.

other officer authorised to exercise judicial power' in Article 5(3).[17] In terms of English law, the 'competent legal authority' would be a magistrate. The fact that a person who is detained is not eventually charged or taken before a 'competent legal authority' does not necessarily mean that the 'purpose' required by Article 5(1)(c) is not present when he is arrested; provided that 'reasonable suspicion' exists, a person may be arrested in good faith for questioning with a view to establishing the evidence needed to bring a charge without the arrest falling foul of Article 5(1)(c) because such evidence is not forthcoming.[18]

The scheme of Articles 5(1)(c) and (3), which must be read together,[19] makes it clear that Article 5(1)(c) is limited to the arrest or detention of persons for the purpose of enforcing the criminal law. Accordingly, the Court has held that the detention of a person to bring him before a 'competent legal authority' in connection with court proceedings for a compulsory residence order (on suspicion of involvement in mafia activities) is not justified by Article 5(1)(c) since the detention is not related to proceedings that could lead to conviction for a criminal offence.[20]

The fact that Article 5(1)(c) concerns only detention in the enforcement of the criminal law is relevant to the interpretation of the three grounds for arrest that it permits. Whereas the scope of the *first* of these grounds – suspicion of having committed an offence – is clear from its text, that of the second and third is less certain. As to the *second*, at first sight it could be read as authorising a general power of preventive detention. This interpretation was rejected in *Lawless v Ireland*,[1] as 'leading to conclusions repugnant to the fundamental principles of the Convention'.[2] Ruling that the wording 'for the purpose of bringing him before the competent legal authority' applied to all three of the limbs of Article 5(1)(c), the Court rejected the defendant government's argument that the detention of the applicant, a suspected IRA activist, under a statute that permitted the internment of persons 'engaged in activities . . . prejudicial to the . . . security of the state', could be justified as being 'necessary to prevent his committing an offence'. This was because the detention of an interned person under the statute was not effected with the purpose of initiating a criminal prosecution.[3] The Court's judgment, which is in accordance with the rule of law and European standards concerning preventive detention, as well as with the criminal law context of Article 5(1)(c), make it difficult to give any meaning to the second 'preventive' limb of Article 5(1)(c). Conduct that amounts in municipal law to the offence of

17 *Schiesser v Switzerland* A 34 para 29 (1979). See further, below, p 132.
18 *Brogan v UK* A 145-B para 53 (1988) and *Murray v UK* A 300-A para 67 (1994).
19 *Ciulla v Italy* A 148 (1989).
20 Ibid.
1 A 3 (1961).
2 Id, pp 51-53. Cf *Guzzardi v Italy* A 39 para 102 (1980): '... the phrase under examination is not adapted to a policy of general prevention directed against an individual or a category of individuals who, like mafiosi, present a danger on account of their continuing propensity to crime; it does no more than afford the contracting parties a means of preventing a concrete and specified offence.'
3 Cf *Ireland v UK* A 25 (1978) and *Guzzardi v Italy* A 39 (1980).

attempting to commit an offence is itself an 'offence', so that the first limb of Article 5(1)(c) applies. At common law, the second limb might be seen as covering the power of arrest to prevent murder[4] or any 'breach of the peace'[5] where either is about to occur. In terms of Article 5(1)(c), the purpose in either case might be to bring the person before a magistrate to be bound over. As to the *third* limb of Article 5(1)(c), this appears redundant, since a person who is 'fleeing after having' committed an offence can in any event be arrested under the first limb.

The first limb of Article 5(1)(c) permits the arrest of a person when there is a 'reasonable suspicion' that he has committed an offence. For there to be a 'reasonable suspicion', it is clearly not necessary to show that an offence has been committed or, if it has, to prove that the arrested person has committed it.[6] Instead, as the Court stated in *Fox, Campbell and Hartley v UK*,[7] 'reasonable suspicion' supposes 'the existence of facts or information which would satisfy an objective observer that the person concerned may have committed the offence'.[8] What may be regarded as 'reasonable' will 'depend upon all of the circumstances'.[9] In this connection, it is permissible to take into account that the case concerns the investigation of terrorist activities, so that allowance may be made for the need the police have to act urgently and not to place their informants at risk. Even so, in such a case 'the respondent government has to furnish at least some facts or information capable of satisfying the Court that the arrested person was reasonably suspected of having committed the alleged offence'.[10] In the *Fox* case, the accused were arrested in Northern Ireland by a constable exercising a statutory power allowing him to arrest for up to 72 hours 'any person whom he suspects of being a terrorist'.[11] This had been interpreted by the House of Lords as incorporating a 'subjective' test, so that an arrest was permissible if the policeman had an 'honestly held suspicion'; it was not necessary to show that a person in his position would have had a 'reasonable suspicion'.[12] Since it did not adopt an 'objective' test, the power of arrest was capable of permitting an arrest that did not comply with Article 5(1)(c). However, the question for the Court was not whether the statute concerned was invalid *in abstracto*, but whether there had on the facts been a 'reasonable suspicion' in the sense of that sub-paragraph. The only evidence produced by the

4 See *Handcock v Baker* (1800) 2 Bos & P 260, which extends beyond the attempt situation.
5 A 'breach of the peace' is not a criminal offence, although its occurrence will involve the commission of such offences. See Smith and Hogan, *Criminal Law*, 7th edn, 1992, p 437.
6 *X v Austria No 10803/84*, 11 EHRR 112 (1987). Cf *Ferrari-Bravo v Italy No 9627/81*, 37 DR 15 at 37 (1984).
7 A 182 para 32 (1990).
8 Ibid.
9 Ibid. The circumstances are those as they were known at the time of the arrest: *Nielsen v Denmark No 343/57*, 1 Digest 388 (1961). A confession is likely to give rise to a 'reasonable suspicion': *Vampel v Austria No 4465/70* (partial decision), 38 CD 58 at 60 (1970).
10 *Fox, Campbell and Hartley v UK* A 182 para 34 (1990).
11 Northern Ireland (Emergency Provisions) Act 1978, s 11. This power of arrest was abolished by the Northern Ireland (Emergency Powers) Act 1987.
12 *McKee v Chief Constable for Northern Ireland* [1984] 1 WLR 1358, HL.

defendant government was that the applicants had, some seven years previously, been convicted of terrorist offences and that they were, on arrest, questioned about specific terrorist acts, the government arguing that it could provide no further information for fear of endangering the lives of others. While accepting that some allowance could be made for the difficulties faced by the police in the emergency situation, the Court concluded that the evidence that had been provided was insufficient to establish that there was a 'reasonable suspicion', objectively determined, as Article 5(1)(c) required. As a result, Article 5(1) had been infringed. In contrast, there was sufficient evidence to satisfy the *Fox* case's discounted 'reasonable suspicion' test in terrorist cases in *Murray v United Kingdom*.[13]

The arrest or detention must be 'lawful'. As with other sub-paragraphs of Article 5(1), this means that it must be lawful under the applicable municipal law and the Convention and that the law in question, or action taken under it, is not 'arbitrary', ie is consistent with the purpose of Article 5(1)(c).[14] Likewise, in the absence of any indication of 'arbitrariness', the fact that one accused is lawfully detained while others are not is not by itself contrary to Article 5(1)(c).[15] Nor is the fact that a person is investigated in respect of one offence while detained on reasonable suspicion of another.[16]

The requirement of 'lawfulness' can provide the basis for controlling the modalities of arrest, such as the need for an arrest warrant. As noted earlier, Article 5(1)(c) has not so far been used to regulate the kind of offences for which arrest is permitted or the circumstances in which a private person may be empowered to arrest. It has been accepted, however, that arrest without a warrant is permitted by Article 5 in at least some cases.[17]

Although the Strasbourg authorities are competent to decide that the applicable municipal law concerning arrest has not been complied with, they will, in recognition of the primary competence of the national authorities, particularly the courts, intervene only in cases where there has been a clear breach of it.[18]

As with other sub-paragraphs of Article 5(1),[19] Article 5(1)(c) does not generally control the conditions of detention. It does not require, for example, that remand prisoners be segregated from convicted prisoners.[20]

---

13 A 300-A paras 56, 61-62 (1994). There was evidence from national court proceedings in the case and corroborative evidence about terrorist activity by other family members. The fact that the maximum length of detention in this case was only four hours was also 'material to the level of suspicion required'.

14 *De Jong, Baljet and Van Den Brink v Netherlands* A 77 para 44 (1984). See also *Wassinck v Netherlands* A 185-A para 24 (1994) and *Kemmache v France (No 3)* A 296-C para 42 (1994).

15 *X v Austria* No 4622/70, 40 CD 15 (1972).

16 *Kamma v Netherlands* No 4771/71, 18 YB 300 (1974) Com Rep; CM Res DH (75) 1.

17 *X v Austria* No 7755/77, 9 DR 210 (1977) and *X v Austria* No 9472/81, 1 Digest Supp 5.1.5.2., p 3 (1982). The fact that the power of arrest concerned did not require a warrant was not commented upon in *Fox, Campbell and Hartley v UK*, above, p 118.

18 *X v Austria* No 10803/84, 11 EHRR 112 (1989). See further, above p 104.

19 See above, p 106.

20 *X v FRG* No 1015/61, 1 Digest 276 (1961).

v.   Detention of minors

Article 5(1)(d) permits 'the detention of a minor by lawful order for the purpose of educational supervision or his lawful detention for the purpose of bringing him before the competent legal authority'. As in the case of other Article 5(1) terms,[1] 'minor' has an autonomous Convention meaning.[2] In the light of European standards, all persons under 18 can be taken to be minors.[3] Whether a state with an age of majority higher than 18 would find that its detention of a person of 18 years or more was justified under Article 5(1)(d) is unclear. In the case of both grounds for detention allowed by Article 5(1)(d), the detention must be 'lawful', which, as elsewhere in Article 5(1),[4] requires compliance with municipal law and the Convention and supposes that any deprivation of liberty is 'in keeping with the purpose of Article 5, namely to protect the individual from arbitrariness'.[5]

The first of the two permitted grounds, viz detention 'for the purpose of educational supervision', applies when the detention results from a 'lawful order', which may be made by an administrative authority or by a court. This ground for detention would appear to authorise the legal obligation normally found in state law requiring children to attend school.[6]

In *Bouamar v Belgium*[7] it was held that Article 5(1)(d) authorises the detention of a minor in a reformatory 'for the purpose of educational supervision' or in a remand prison as a preliminary to his transfer 'speedily' to such an institution. In that case, the defendant state was held to be in breach of Article 5(1)(d) when the applicant, a seriously disturbed and delinquent 16-year-old, was detained by court order in a remand prison, which provided no educational facilities, for periods amounting to 119 days' detention during most of one year. The orders were made under a 1965 Act, the policy of which was that juveniles who committed criminal offences should normally be placed in juvenile reformatories rather than be convicted by a criminal court. The orders for the applicant's detention were made under a provision of the Act that permitted a juvenile's detention in a remand prison for up to 15 days when it was 'materially impossible' to place him in a reformatory immediately. In the applicant's case, the problem was that the open reformatories that provided the required educational facilities were not willing to take him because of his difficult behaviour and there were no closed

1   Cf the interpretation of 'vagrant', etc in Article 5(1)(e), p 122, below.
2   *X v Switzerland No 8500/79*, 18 DR 238 (1979).
3   In 1972, the Committee of Ministers of the Council of Europe recommended that member states reduce the age of majority to 18: CM Res (72) 29. In *X v Switzerland No 8500/79*, 18 DR 238 (1979), it was noted that in no party to the Convention was the age of majority less than 18.
4   See above, p 105.
5   *Bouamar v Belgium* A 129 para 47 (1988).
6   As to cases involving parental consent, see *Nielsen v Denmark*, above, p 100. *Quaere* whether after hours detention in a state school as a punishment falls within Article 5(1)(d) as being ancillary to educational supervision. There would not be a 'competent court' for the purposes of Article 5(1)(a).
7   A 129 para 50 (1988).

reformatories with such facilities in his French-speaking region. The Court accepted that the applicant might be detained briefly in a remand prison pending his early placement elsewhere. On the facts, however, the period of prison detention was too long and was not for the permitted purpose. As to its purpose, the applicant's detention was an expedient adopted by the authorities in the absence of 'appropriate institutional facilities which met the demands of security and the educational objectives of the 1965 Act'.[8] If, for commendable policy reasons, Belgium had decided not to dispose of seriously disturbed juveniles through the criminal courts (in which case their detention could be justified following conviction under Article 5(1)(a)), it could only detain them consistently with Article 5 in institutions that offered the necessary educational supervision required by Article 5(1)(d). Should this involve the building of appropriate reformatories, the resulting commitment was, the Court made clear,[9] one that Belgium would have to undertake despite the cost involved. How comprehensive and 'school-like' the regime of 'educational supervision' provided by a reformatory for disturbed juveniles has to be is not clear. The Court merely stated that the required educational regime must be provided 'in a setting (open or closed) designed and with sufficient resources for the purpose'.[10]

The second of the two permitted grounds for the detention of a minor is 'his lawful detention for the purpose of bringing him before the competent legal authority'. The *travaux préparatoires* indicate that this wording was intended to cover the situation where a minor is detained with a view to being brought before a court not on a criminal charge (so that Article 5(1)(c) would apply) but 'to secure his removal from harmful surroundings'.[11] Thus the detention of a minor accused of a crime during the preparation of a psychiatric report necessary to the taking of a decision in his case is permitted,[12] as is detention pending the making of a court order placing a child in care.[13]

vi. Detention of persons of unsound mind, vagrants, etc

Article 5(1)(e) permits 'the lawful detention of persons for the prevention of the spreading of infectious diseases, of persons of unsound mind,[14]

---

8 Ibid.
9 It did this by referring to *Guincho v Portugal*, below, p 227, and *De Cubber v Belgium*, below, p 240, in which it had made no allowance for the financial cost of complying with the Convention in other contexts.
10 A 129 para 50 (1988). As to the English Children (Secure Accommodation) Regulations 1991, SI 1991/1505, under the Children Act 1989, see the facts of *Abbott v UK No 15006/89*, 67 DR 290 (1990). Case struck off; application withdrawn following government financial offer.
11 3 TP 724, quoted in Fawcett, p 90.
12 *X v Switzerland No 8500/79*, 18 DR 238 (1979) (detention for the remarkably long period of eight months for observation justified on this basis).
13 Cf *Bouamar v Belgium* A 129 para 46 (1988).
14 As to the relationship between Articles 5(1)(a) and (e) when a person is detained by a court as mentally disordered following his conviction, see above, p 236.

alcoholics or drug addicts or vagrants'. Each of the terms listed can be taken to have an autonomous Convention meaning.[15] The reason why persons within certain of these categories may be detained consistently with the Convention 'is not only that they have to be considered as occasionally dangerous for public safety but also that their own interests may necessitate their detention'.[16]

The meaning of 'persons of unsound mind' was considered in *Winterwerp v Netherlands*.[17] It is not a term that can be given a 'definitive interpretation' because the medical profession's understanding of mental disorder is still developing. What is clear is that the detention of a person cannot be justified under Article 5(1)(e) 'simply because his views or behaviour deviate from the norms prevailing in a particular society'.[18] Beyond that, when determining whether a person is of 'unsound mind', it is a matter of referring to the relevant municipal law, which need not define or list the categories of mental disorder to which it extends, and its application in the particular case in the light of current psychiatric knowledge.[19]

The term 'vagrants' was examined in *De Wilde, Ooms and Versyp v Belgium* (the *Vagrancy* cases).[20] The Court noted that in the Belgian Criminal Code 'vagrants' were defined as 'persons who have no fixed abode, no means of subsistence and no regular trade or profession'. It commented that a person who came within this definition was 'in principle' a 'vagrant' for the purposes of Article 5(1)(e). Although the Court did not expressly state that the Convention meaning was co-terminous with that in Belgian law, it is likely that the latter reflects the generally understood meaning of the term. In *Guzzardi v Italy*,[1] the Court rejected a government argument that suspected mafia members who lacked any identifiable sources of income were vagrants.

As to the other categories of persons who may be detained under Article 5(1)(e), there have been no reported cases in which the terms 'infectious diseases', 'alcoholics' or 'drug addicts' have been interpreted or the grounds for detention to which they relate called in question. However, as suggested below, the rules developed in the context of persons of unsound mind should apply *mutatis mutandis*.

For detention to be justified under Article 5(1)(e), it must be 'lawful'. This requires that the detention be in conformity with the applicable municipal law, both as to the grounds for detention and the procedure followed.[2] As to

15 This has been established to be true of 'persons of unsound mind' and 'vagrants': see the *Winterwerp* and *Vagrancy* cases, below.
16 *Guzzardi v Italy* A 39 para 98 (1980). The Court referred to persons of unsound mind, alcoholics and drug addicts.
17 A 33 para 36 (1979). On this case, see Muchlinski, 5 HRR 90 (1980).
18 Id, para 37.
19 Id, para 38.
20 A 12 (1971).
1   A 39 para 98 (1980).
2   *Winterwerp v Netherlands* A 33 para 39 (1979). In the latter respect, the requirement overlaps with that in the introductory wording to Article 5(1): see above, p 105. The detention must also comply with the Convention.

the latter, in *Van Der Leer v Netherlands*,[3] the Court held that a person had been detained 'unlawfully' contrary to Article 5(1)(e) when a court had ordered her detention as mentally ill without hearing her in person, as required by Dutch law. In addition, detention will not be 'lawful' if it is · 'arbitrary'. In other words, as the Court stated in *Winterwerp v Netherlands*,[4] it must in 'conformity with the purpose of the restrictions permitted by Article 5(1)(e)' and must also be warranted on the facts of the case. In more detail, in the *Winterwerp* case the Court held that, in the context of the detention of persons of 'unsound mind', the requirement of lack of 'arbitrariness' meant that three minimum conditions have to be satisfied:

(i)   the individual concerned must be 'reliably shown' by 'objective medical expertise'[5] to be of 'unsound mind';
(ii) the individual's 'mental disorder must be of a kind or degree warranting compulsory confinement'; and
(iii) the disorder must persist throughout the period of detention.

Although the Strasbourg authorities have the final word as to whether these conditions are met, the defendant state is allowed a certain 'margin of appreciation' when making its own initial assessment of the situation.[6] In this connection, it is accepted that when deciding whether a detained person's condition has improved to the point where he can be released, the national authorities are entitled to exercise caution where the person may be a danger to the public.[7] When applying the *Winterwerp* conditions, the Strasbourg authorities have not always agreed as to the outcome. In *Herczegfalvy v Austria*,[8] the Court unanimously found that the applicant's detention was justified by Article 5(1)(e) after the Commission had unanimously found that it was not.

The first of the *Winterwerp* conditions does not apply in emergencies. In the *Winterwerp* case itself, the applicant, who was later diagnosed as suffering from a mental illness, was committed to a psychiatric hospital by a

---

3   A 170-A para 22 (1990). See also *Koendjbiharie v Netherlands* A 185-B (1990) in which the state failed to renew the applicant's detention order within the legal time-limit. The Court found a breach of Article 5(4) ('speedily'), but did not (Judge Bernhardt dissenting) consider the case under Article 5(1).
4   A 33 para 39 (1979).
5   This will include a personal medical examination, other than in an emergency situation: see *X v UK*, below, p 124. In *Schuurs v Netherlands No 10518/83*, 41 DR 186 (1985), a certificate for the detention of a mentally disordered person was issued by a general practitioner, not a psychiatrist. The case led to a friendly settlement in which the question whether this was sufficient to comply with the *Winterwerp* conditions was left unresolved.
6   *Winterwerp v Netherlands* A 33 para 40 (1979); *X v UK* A 46 para 43 (1981); and *Luberti v Italy* A 75 para 27 (1984).
7   *Luberti v Italy* A 75 para 29 (1984) (delay in releasing a convicted murderer justified). Cf *Gordon v UK No 10213/82*, 47 DR 36 (1985) and *Dhoest v Belgium No 10448/83*, 55 DR 5 (1987) Com Rep; CM Res DH (88) 1.
8   A 244 (1992).

burgomaster after being found lying naked in a police cell following his arrest for theft. As was legally possible, the burgomaster acted without obtaining prior medical advice since the circumstances did not permit this.[9] The Court held that the applicant's emergency detention was 'lawful', although it expressed 'some hesitation' because the detention had lasted six weeks before being replaced by detention complying with the Court's three conditions. The Court's hesitation is understandable; while circumstances might permit the emergency detention of a mentally disordered person without prior medical examination or any medical advice in an emergency, it is to be expected that at least provisional confirmation by a psychiatrist of the need for detention would occur in a very short while.

The *Winterwerp* case was applied to another emergency situation in *X v UK*.[10] There, the applicant, who had been convicted of an offence involving a violent attack upon a workmate and shown signs of paranoid psychosis, had been detained in Broadmoor under a restricted offender patient order. After he had been allowed out on licence for three years, his wife reported circumstances that suggested to the applicant's consultant psychiatrist that there was an immediate danger that the applicant's mental state was such that he might resort to violence. Acting on the consultant's advice, but without a prior medical examination or check of the wife's information, the Home Secretary, acting under s 66 of the Mental Health Act 1959, at once recalled the applicant. The Court held that this action was consistent with Article 5(1)(e) as an emergency case. The Court took into account that persons subject to restricted offender patient orders are persons who have been considered to be a danger to the public on the basis of medical evidence and that in emergency cases it may be impracticable to arrange a medical examination before the person is detained. The Court also noted that upon re-admission to Broadmoor the applicant was medically examined in accordance with the *Winterwerp* conditions.

The requirement that detention under Article 5(1)(e) be 'lawful' in the sense of not 'arbitrary' does not concern conditions of detention or the provision of suitable treatment. These are matters for Article 3, not Article 5. However, as indicated in *Ashingdane v UK*,[11] this general rule is subject to the qualification that in the case of a 'person of unsound mind', his detention must be in a 'hospital, clinic or other appropriate institution authorised for' the detention of such persons. The *Ashingdane* case concerned the question of the conditions of detention of a mentally disordered person. The applicant's transfer from Broadmoor to the more liberal regime of an ordinary mental hospital was delayed for 19 months after the time when his mental condition warranted it because, in effect, of opposition by trade unions. It was held that although an earlier transfer would have assisted his recovery, the applicant would still have been

9   Dutch law was changed in 1972 so that a burgomaster must now always obtain prior psychiatric advice or, if that is not possible, the advice of a general practitioner.
10 A 46 (1981).
11 A 93 para 44 (1985).

detained at the ordinary hospital in the sense of Article 5(1), so that his continued detention at Broadmoor did not raise an issue under that provision. There was also no breach of Article 17 of the Convention since his Convention rights were not limited to a greater extent at Broadmoor.

As to treatment, in the *Winterwerp* case the Court rejected the applicant's argument that Article 5(1)(e) carried with it an implied 'right to treatment' appropriate to the person's mental state during the period of detention.[12] It stated that the detention of a mentally disordered person must be in the interest of the safety of the applicant or of others, but that medical treatment is not required. However, the failure to provide medical treatment to a person in detention under Article 5(1)(e) could amount to 'inhuman treatment' contrary to Article 3.[13] It could also cast doubt in a particular case on whether the second and third *Winterwerp* conditions were complied with.

The general approach to the interpretation of Article 5(1)(e) that has been explained in this subsection was spelt out in the context and in terms of the detention of 'persons of unsound mind'. Presumably, a similar degree of scrutiny should *mutatis mutandis* accompany detention on any other ground permitted by Article 5(1)(e). For example, the *Winterwerp* conditions should apply to the detention of persons with infectious diseases and there should be evidence that the spread of disease will be contained by a policy of detention. A public health policy of detaining persons who are HIV positive might be counter-productive by driving the problem underground – thus giving rise to questions concerning the necessity and justification of such a policy.

vii. Detention pending deportation or extradition, etc

Article 5(1)(f) permits 'the lawful arrest or detention of a person to prevent his effecting an unauthorised entry into the country or of a person against whom action is being taken with a view to deportation or extradition'. In practice, Strasbourg cases have mostly concerned the detention pending deportation or extradition[14] of persons (almost always aliens)[15] already in a contracting state, not the detention of persons seeking to enter illegally.[16] Article 5(1)(f) requires that the detention is 'lawful'. This means that it must be lawful under the applicable municipal law of the state concerned and the Convention and not 'arbitrary'.[17]

These requirements were in issue in *Bozano v France*.[18] In that case, a French court refused to order the extradition to Italy of the applicant, an

12 A 33 para 51 (1979).
13 See above, p 71.
14 A procedure for the return of deserting military personnel is akin to extradition and within Article 5(1)(f): *C v UK No 10427/83*, 47 DR 85 (1986).
15 Some states, eg the UK, permit the extradition of nationals.
16 For an illegal immigrant case, see *Zamir v UK No 9174/80*, 40 DR 42 (1983). In *McVeigh, O'Neill and Evans v UK*, loc cit at p 112, n 7, above, it was held that the detention of persons at a port of entry for 'further questioning' fell within Article 5(1)(b), not Article 5(1)(f).
17 See above, p 105.
18 A 111 (1986). See Cohen-Jonathan, 23 RTDE 255 (1987) and Sudre, 91 RGDIP 533 (1987).

Italian national convicted of murder, because he had been tried *in absentia*. The French government then made a deportation order against him. Despite knowledge of his whereabouts, the order was not served upon the applicant until a month later, when he was arrested suddenly one night. Without being given an opportunity to contact his wife or a lawyer (who might have taken legal steps to challenge the deportation) or to nominate a country of deportation (Spain was by far the nearest), the applicant was forcibly taken the same night by police officers by car across France to the Swiss border, where he was transferred to Swiss police custody. He was later extradited from Switzerland to Italy to serve his life sentence, on the basis of an Italian request for extradition initiated in Switzerland before the applicant's deportation from France. Subsequently, the deportation order against the applicant was declared invalid by a French court as being, *inter alia*, an abuse of power contrary to French law. The French court determined that the circumstances of the deportation demonstrated that the order's purpose had not been to cause the applicant's removal for reasons of a kind associated with deportation but to effect an illegal extradition. In the light of the order's invalidity and of indications that French law might have been infringed when the applicant was handed over, the European Court expressed the 'gravest doubts whether the contested deprivation of liberty satisfied the legal requirements in the respondent state'.[19] As to the question of 'arbitrariness', the Court 'attached great weight to the circumstances in which the applicant was forcibly conveyed to the Swiss border'.[20] Considering the facts as a whole, relating both to the indications of non-compliance with French law and, particularly, of 'arbitrary' executive action, the Court concluded that the applicant's detention had not been 'lawful' as required by Article 5(1)(f). It was instead an element in a process designed to achieve 'a disguised form of extradition'[1] that could not be justified by that provision.

A question that arose in the *Bozano* case was whether the ruling by the French court that the deportation order was invalid had retroactive effect so as to render the applicant's detention for the purpose of detention contrary to the applicable municipal law and hence unlawful for the purposes of Article 5(1)(f). Since this is a matter of the interpretation and application of municipal law, the question was, in the first place, one for the national authorities.[2] The Court's judgment seems to suppose that, in the absence of any ruling at the national level, the Strasbourg authorities were competent to make their own determination.[3] In this connection, the Court drew a distinction between the situation in which a state's agents, acting in good faith, are later found to have acted illegally and that in which there is evidence of abuse of power *ab initio*, as was true on the facts of the *Bozano* case. The Court seemed to

---

19 A 111 para 58 (1986).
20 Id, para 59.
1   Id, para 60.
2   See above, p 104.
3   Although there was no ruling at the national level in the *Bozano* case on the question of the retroactive effect of the order's invalidity, the Court made no finding of its own, preferring to emphasise the 'arbitrary' nature of the detention.

suggest that it would be much more likely that a finding of retroactive effect would be made in national law (and perhaps by the Court) in the latter case than in the former. In *Caprino v UK*,[4] in which there was no allegation of bad faith, the Commission had earlier taken the view that the invalidity of a deportation order did not affect the lawfulness of detention based upon it because it would still be the case that the detention was 'action ... being taken with a view to' the applicant's deportation. On the basis of this very restrictive approach, the fact that a deportation order is declared invalid, as in the *Bozano* case, would never render the detention contrary to Article 5(1)(f).

The Commission has taken the view that its competence under Article 5(1)(f) is limited to determining, whether there is a legal basis for the detention and whether the purpose of the detention is an 'arbitrary' one; as in the context of most parts of Article 5(1) the requirement of 'non-arbitrariness' does not to allow it to go further and, in this case, question the decision to deport the applicant on its facts. In *Zamir v UK*,[5] the Commission drew a distinction between cases arising under Article 5(1)(e) concerning mentally disordered persons and cases arising under Article 5(1)(f). Whereas in the *Winterwerp* case,[6] the Court was prepared under Article 5(1)(e) to consider whether the applicant's detention was warranted on the facts, in the *Zamir* case the Commission stated that its powers under Article 5(1)(f) did not extend that far. The *Bozano* case does not contradict this limited approach; the decision of the Court in that case was to the effect that the detention by the state was 'arbitrary' by reference to its purpose, which was extradition, not deportation.[7]

However, the Commission has expanded the scope of its powers under Article 5(1)(f) in a different direction by ruling that although Article 5(1)(f) sets no 'reasonable time' or other express limit as to the length of a person's detention (contrast Article 5(1)(c)), deportation or extradition proceedings must be conducted with 'requisite diligence'.[8] At the outset, the need for 'requisite diligence' was regarded as an element of the requirement that the detention be 'lawful'.[9] More particularly, it was seen as a part of the requirement that detention must not be 'arbitrary' in the sense that it should be proportionate.[10] Although subsequent cases would appear to treat it as a separate, implied requirement, the principle of proportionality provides a convincing basis for insistence upon 'reasonable diligence'.

In assessing whether the requirement has been met, the conduct of the applicant, as well as that of the authorities, is taken into account. As the

4 *No 6871/75*, 22 DR 5 at 12 (1980). Cf *Krzycki v FRG*, above, p 107, under Article 5(1)(a).
5 *No 9174/80*, 40 DR 42 (1983).
6 Above, p 123.
7 See A 111 para 59 (1986).
8 *Lynas v Switzerland No 7317/75*, 6 DR 141 (1976) (extradition). For deportation cases, see *X v UK No 8081/77*, 12 DR 207 (1977) and *Z v Netherlands No 10400/83*, 38 DR 145 (1984).
9 *Lynas v Switzerland No 7317/75*, 6 DR 141 (1976). The Commission's approach has been endorsed by the Court: see eg *Kolompar v Belgium* A 235-C (1992).
10 See the reading of the *Lynas* case in *Caprino v UK No 7317/75*, 22 DR 5 at 13 (1980). Contrast the Commission's refusal to consider the proportionality of a decision to deport or extradite: see above, at n 5.

Strasbourg authorities are aware, an applicant may often wish to delay proceedings in order to avoid the unpleasant consequences of his eventual return. There is no absolute limit to the time that proceedings may last; the test is one of diligence appropriate to the circumstances. In *X v FRG*,[11] 22 months' detention during extradition proceedings was held to be justifiable since the delay resulted from attempts by the West German government to obtain undertakings from the Turkish government to the effect that the applicant would not be subjected to the death penalty if extradited and there was no evidence of dilatoriness by the West German authorities.[12] In *Kolompar v Belgium*,[13] the Court found no breach of Article 5(1)(f) when the applicant had in various ways delayed proceedings or impliedly consented to their prolongation for nearly three years.

In addition to the above requirements, the Commission has suggested that the national law authorising the detention must be accessible and foreseeable in its application. Following the *Sunday Times* case,[14] it has taken the view that the meaning of the word 'law' in the phrase 'prescribed by law' in Article 10(2) of the Convention also applies to the word 'lawful' in Article 5(1)(f). This further requirement was applied in *Zamir v UK*[15] when the applicant's claim that he could not reasonably have foreseen the consequences under United Kingdom immigration law of failing to reveal on entry into the country the fact that he was married was rejected. Although the Court did not list this requirement in the *Bozano* case, it may be that it considered that the requirement did not call to be applied on the facts.

Detention may be justified by Article 5(1)(f) even though a formal request or an order for extradition has not been issued, provided that enquiries have been made, since the enquiries amount to 'action' being taken in the sense of that provision.[16] Likewise, detention may be within Article 5(1)(f) even though deportation or extradition does not in fact occur.[17]

3. ARTICLE 5(2): REASONS FOR ARREST TO BE GIVEN

Article 5(2) requires that everyone 'who is arrested shall be informed promptly, in a language which he understands, of the reasons for his arrest

---

11 *No 9706/82*, 5 EHRR 512 (1983).
12 Eventually, the applicant was not extradited in the absence of such assurances. There was regular judicial review of the need for his detention while the matter was pending. Cf *X v UK No 8081/77*, 12 DR 207 (1977) (eleven months' delay attributable to the need to obtain evidence from Pakistan and the applicant's own conduct).
13 A 235-C (1992) (the applicant had also requested postponement of a hearing). See also *S v France No 10965/84*, 56 DR 62 (1988). In *Osman v UK No 15933/89* (1991) unreported, over five years' detention pending extradition was acceptable given the applicant's conduct and determination not to be extradited.
14 See below, p 287.
15 *No 9174/80*, 40 DR 42 at 55 (1983). Cf *X v UK No 9403/81*, 28 DR 235 (1982).
16 *X v Switzerland No 9012/80*, 24 DR 205 (1980). The word 'action' was substituted for 'proceedings' because of the diversity of kinds of extradition and deportation proceedings – executive, judicial – in the drafting states: Fawcett, p 95.
17 See eg *X v FRG No 9706/82* at n 11, above.

and of any charge against him'. This requirement applies to arrest on any ground, not just arrest in connection with criminal proceedings.[18] It extends to cases in which a person is recalled after release, as well as to cases of initial detention.[19]

Article 5(2) provides 'the elementary safeguard that any person arrested should know why he is deprived of his liberty'.[20] He must be told 'in simple, non-technical language that he can understand, the essential legal and factual grounds for his arrest, so as to be able, if he sees fit, to apply to a court to challenge its lawfulness in accordance with' Article 5(4).[1] 'Lawfulness' means 'lawfulness' under both municipal law and the Convention so that the information required must address the legality of a person's detention in terms of Article 5 of the Convention as well as the applicable municipal law.[2] A further purpose of Article 5(2) is to enable the person arrested to deny the offence and hence obtain his release without resorting to court proceedings.[3]

The fact that the reasons need not be given at the time of arrest but only 'promptly' thereafter, permits a stricter requirement as to the detail in which the reasons for the arrest must be given. Whether sufficient is told to the arrested person is a matter to be determined on the facts of each case. In *Fox, Campbell and Hartley v UK*,[4] persons arrested on suspicion of terrorist offences were told at the time of arrest that they were being arrested under a named statutory provision. Later, they were interrogated about specific criminal acts. The Court held that although the information given at the time of arrest was insufficient because it was limited to the legal basis for the arrests, this deficiency was made good[5] by the indications as to the factual basis for the arrests that the applicants could infer from the nature of the questions put to them by the police during the subsequent interrogation.[6] The *Fox* case confirms that a person need not be expressly informed of the reasons for his arrest insofar as these are apparent from the surrounding circumstances.[7] It is submitted, however, that the decision on the facts in the

---

18 *Van Der Leer v Netherlands* A 170-A para 27 (1990). The case concerned a 'person of unsound mind' on its facts, but the Court's reasoning extends to all cases of arrest or detention. The Court rejected an argument to the effect that the wording 'and of any charge' implied that Article 5(2) was limited to Article 5(1)(c) cases.

19 *X v Belgium No 4741/71*, 43 CD 14 at 19 (1973). Cf *X v UK* A 46 para 66 (1981).

20 *Fox, Campbell and Hartley v UK* A 182 para 40 (1990).

1 Ibid.

2 *McVeigh, O'Neill and Evans v UK*, loc cit at p 112, n 7, above.

3 *X v UK No 8010/77*, 16 DR 101 at 114 (1979).

4 A 182 para 41 (1990). See Finnie, 54 MLR 288 (1991).

5 Cf *Murray v UK* A 300-A para 77 (1994). Contrast *Ireland v UK* A 25 para 198 (1978), in which, contrary to Article 5(2), some arrested persons were told only that they were being arrested under emergency legislation and given no further details.

6 In *X v Belgium No 1103/61*, 5 YB 168 (1962), the Commission held that 'you are accused of corruption' was sufficient. *Quaere* whether the *Fox, Campbell and Hartley* case now requires more detailed reasons. For the requirement in English criminal law, see Police and Criminal Evidence Act 1984, s 28.

7 Cf *Neumeister v Austria No 1936/63*, 7 YB 224 (1964); *Freda v Italy No 8916/80*, 21 DR 250 (1980); and *B v France No 10179/82*, 52 DR 111 (1987).

Fox case involves an unacceptable dilution of a basic guarantee. Article 5(2) requires that an arrested person be 'informed' of the reasons for his arrest, not that he be able to gather them from the drift of the interrogation, which may involve the putting of various alternative assertions.

In a case arising under Article 5(1)(c), there is no need to indicate all of the charges that may later be brought against an arrested person; it is sufficient that enough information is provided to justify the arrest.[8] There was a breach of Article 5(2) when a voluntary patient in a mental hospital, who had not received any official communication, learnt only by accident that a court order had been made for her compulsory detention.[9] Where a mentally disordered person cannot understand the information that is given to him, it must be given to a lawyer[10] or other person authorised to act for him. Whether a person who is detained pending deportation or extradition needs to be told the reasons for the proposed action against him as well as the fact that he is detained for such a purpose must depend upon the information that he needs under municipal law to be able to challenge the legality of his detention.[11]

The reasons must be given to the arrested person 'in a language which he understands'. In a case in which the arrest warrant for a French-speaking person was in Dutch, this requirement was held to be complied with on the basis that the subsequent interrogation, during which the reasons became apparent, was in French.[12]

Article 5(2) does not require that the reasons for an arrest be given in any particular way,[13] eg in the text of any warrant or other document authorising the arrest[14] or in writing at all.[15] Nor does it guarantee a right of access to a lawyer for an arrested person.[16]

An arrested person must be given the required information 'promptly'. In *Fox, Campbell and Hartley v UK*[17] the Court stated that this does not mean that it must be given 'in its entirety by the arresting officer at the very moment of the arrest'; provided that the arrested person is informed of the required legal and factual grounds for his arrest, whether at one time or in stages, within a sufficient period following the arrest, Article 5(2) is complied with. Whether this has occurred is to be assessed by reference to the facts of the particular case.[18] In the *Fox, Campbell and Hartley* case,

---

8   *X v UK No 4220/69*, 14 YB 250 at 278 (1971) (told of burglary charge, but not others that were later brought). As to the details of charges required in extradition cases, see *K v Belgium No 10819/84*, 38 DR 230 (1984).
9   *Van Der Leer v Netherlands* A 170-A para 31 (1990).
10 *X v UK* B 41 (1980) Com Rep para 111.
11 See Trechsel, *European System*, p 316.
12 *Delcourt v Belgium No 2689/65*, 10 YB 238 at 270 (1967). As to whether the costs of translation can be charged to the detainee, see Trechsel, *European System*, p 318.
13 *X v Netherlands No 2621/65*, 9 YB 474 at 480 (1966).
14 Ibid.
15 *X v Netherlands No 1211/61*, 5 YB 224 at 228 (1962).
16 *X v Denmark No 8828/79*, 30 DR 93 at 94 (1982).
17 A 182 para 40 (1990).
18 Ibid. Cf *X v Denmark No 8828/79*, 30 DR 93 (1982).

intervals of up to seven hours between the arrests and the giving of all of the information required by Article 5(2) were found to meet the requirement of 'promptness'. Surprisingly, a delay of two days was regarded as acceptable in an earlier Commission case.[19] In contrast, a delay of ten days has been held to be in breach of Article 5(2).[20] A delay in informing a person of a court order for his detention is not attributable to a state where the person's whereabouts are not known; it is sufficient that he is informed 'promptly' of the order once he makes contact or, presumably, when his whereabouts otherwise have become known.[1]

The requirement in Article 5(2) overlaps with that in Article 5(4) in that the latter also requires that a person be told 'promptly' the reasons for his detention.[2] In criminal cases, the requirement in Article 5(2) overlaps to some extent with the obligation in Article 6(3)(a) by which an accused person, whether detained pending trial or not, must be told promptly of the nature and cause of the accusation against him. The two obligations differ in purpose: whereas Article 5(2) is intended to facilitate a challenge to the legality of a person's detention, Article 6(3)(a) seeks to provides an accused with the information he needs to marshall his defence. Given these different purposes, the information required by Article 6(3)(a) will be 'more specific and more detailed' than that called for under Article 5(2).[3]

4. ARTICLE 5(3): PRE-TRIAL DETENTION AND TRIAL WITHIN A REASONABLE TIME[4]

Article 5(3) provides:

'Everyone arrested or detained in accordance with the provisions of paragraph 1(c) of this Article shall be brought promptly before a judge

---

19 *Skoogström v Sweden No 8582/79*, 1 Dig Supp, para 5.2.2.1 (1981). See also *X v Denmark No 6730/74*, 1 Digest 457 (1975) (24 hours apparently acceptable) and *Delcourt v Belgium No 2689/65*, 10 YB 238 at 252, 272 (1967).

20 *Van der Leer v Netherlands* A 170-A para 31 (1990).

1 *Keus v Netherlands* A 185-C para 22 (1990)(mentally disordered person absconded; sufficient that he was told when he telephoned the hospital). The Court would appear to have rejected an argument in this case that the applicant's lawyer should have been informed 'promptly' in the interim. Article 5(2) presumably requires that reasonable efforts be made to communicate with a person against whom a detention order is made. Article 5(2) was complied with when a person who was semi-conscious when arrested was told of the reasons for his arrest as soon as he recovered: *X v UK No 7125/75*, 1 Digest 458 (1977).

2 *X v UK* A 46 para 66 (1981). In that case, the Court applied Article 5(4) only.

3 *Nielsen v Denmark No 343/57*, 2 YB 412 at 462 (1959) and *GSM v Austria No 9614/81*, 34 DR 119 (1983).

4 On Article 5(3), see Pouget, 1989 RSCDPC 78. On pre-trial detention in European states, see Grosz, McNulty and Duffy, Rev ICJ No 23, 35 (1979). For a full statement of the principles concerning custody pending trial that the Council of Europe recommends that member states apply in their law and practice, see CM Rec R(80) 11 on Custody Pending Trial. The principles are generally consistent with, but not identical to, those in the Strasbourg jurisprudence under Article 5.

or other officer authorised by law to exercise judicial power and shall be entitled to trial within a reasonable time or to release pending trial. Release may be conditioned by guarantees to appear for trial.'

Article 5(3) is 'intended to minimise the risk of arbitrariness' by providing, in accordance with the concept of the 'rule of law', '[j]udicial control of interferences by the executive with the individual's right to liberty'[5] in the criminal process. It thus requires that a person arrested in accordance with Article 5(1)(c) on suspicion of having committed an offence be brought promptly before a judge or similar officer to determine the legality of his arrest and his continued detention pending further investigation and trial.[6] In addition, Article 5(3) requires that a person detained on remand be tried within a reasonable time.

i.   Right to be brought promptly before a judge or other officer

a.   Brought before a judge or other officer authorised to exercise judicial power

Article 5(3) requires that a person arrested under Article 5(1)(c) be brought before a judge or other comparable officer. It is for the state to take the initiative in this regard; it is not sufficient that an arrested person will be brought before an appropriate officer only if he appeals against his detention.[7] As Trechsel[8] points out, this is a guarantee that is 'particularly important in states in which there exists an actual danger of police brutality or torture', especially since methods of ill-treatment may be used that do not leave long-lasting marks.

The wording 'judge or other judicial officer authorised by law' has the same meaning as 'competent legal authority' in Article 5(1)(c).[9] As in that provision, in English law the requirement is satisfied by bringing an accused before a magistrate. Whereas the meaning of 'judge' has not caused difficulty,[10] the phrase 'other officer authorised to exercise judicial power' has, particularly where the person before whom an arrested person is brought also plays a part later in the prosecution of the case. In *Schiesser v Switzerland*,[11] the Court stated that the first characteristic of such an 'officer' is his 'independence of the executive and of the parties'. As to the officer's relationship with the parties, which in more recent cases has come

---

5   *Brogan v UK* A 145-B para 58 (1988).
6   Article 5(3) (particularly its trial within a reasonable time guarantee) does not extend to a person who, although subject to an order for detention on remand, is also serving a prison sentence following conviction for another offence: *X v FRG No 8626/79*, 25 DR 218 (1981).
7   *McGoff v Sweden No 9017/80*, 31 DR 72 (1982).
8   *European System*, p 333.
9   *Schiesser v Switzerland* A 34 para 29 (1979).
10 See the discussion of the meaning of 'court' in Article 5(4), below, p 146.
11 A 34 para 31 (1979).

to be expressed in terms of his 'impartiality',[12] an officer will not be impartial, as required by Article 5(3), if he is not only competent to decide on the accused's pre-trial detention, but may also later act as a prosecutor in the case. The two functions of investigation and prosecution must be kept separate; a prosecutor cannot be impartial as between the parties if he is one of them. Moreover, it was held in *Huber v Switzerland*[13] that it is not sufficient that the 'officer' does not *in fact* later serve as a prosecutor in the case so long as it is possible that he might do so: 'impartiality' involves an objective, as well as a subjective, element so that the 'officer's' impartiality must not be open to doubt. Whereas the Court had held in the *Scheisser* case that Article 5(3) only required that the officer not take part later in the prosecution of the case, in the *Huber* case the Court reversed its earlier decision on this point.[14] In introducing an objective element, the Court brought its Article 5(3) jurisprudence in ordinary criminal cases[15] into line with its interpretation of the 'impartiality' requirement in the fair trial guarantee in Article 6(1).[16] In the *Scheisser* case,[17] the Court also held that the fact that the officer is subordinate to a superior who is competent in law to give the officer instructions as to whether bail should be allowed does not compromise the officer's independence since such instructions were never given in practice. The question whether this ruling survives the introduction of an objective element to the requirement of 'impartiality' was not considered in the *Huber* case. It is submitted that it should; that the requirement can be met by a practice that is invariably followed.[18]

b. *Function of officer and procedure to be followed*

The function and the procedure that a judge or similar officer must exercise and follow respectively to comply with Article 5(3) was indicated in the *Scheisser* case. As to the former, his role is that of 'reviewing the circumstances militating for and against detention, of deciding, by reference to legal criteria, whether there are reasons to justify detention and of

12 On the overlapping nature of requirements as to independence and impartiality, see below, p 234.
13 A 188 para 43 (1990). Cf *Brincat v Italy* A 249-A (1992) (a public prosecutor who *might* later take part in the prosecution did not satisfy Article 5(3)).
14 Both cases concerned the Zurich District Attorney (Bezirksanwalt) who did not meet the requirements of Article 5(3): *Huber* case.
15 The Court had earlier imposed an objective impartiality requirement under Article 5(3) in military criminal proceedings: see *De Jong, Baljet and Van Den Brink v Netherlands* A 77 (1984) and *Pauwels v Belgium* A 135 (1988). These cases concerned the *auditeur-militair/ auditeur militaire* in the Dutch and Belgian systems respectively: neither complied with Article 5(3). A Dutch court martial does comply: *Koster v Netherlands* A 221 (1991) Com Rep (point not considered by Court). See also *J v Belgium No 14292/88*, 63 DR 203 (1989).
16 See below, p 234.
17 A 34 para 35 (1979). Cf *Pauwels v Belgium* A 135 para 37 (1988).
18 Cf the Court's reliance upon actual practice in *Engel v Netherlands*, below, p 232, n 20. In the pre-*Huber* case of *De Cubber v Belgium No 12607/86*, 60 DR 208 (1989), the Commission held that a Belgian investigating judge met the requirements of Article 5(3) on the present point.

ordering release if there are no such reasons'.[19] In this connection, the officer must be able to take a legally binding decision as to the lawfulness of the accused's detention; it is not sufficient that his recommendations are invariably followed.[20] As to the latter, the officer is simply under an 'obligation of himself hearing the individual brought before him'.[1] He is not obliged to allow the accused's lawyer to be present at the hearing.[2] This modest requirement may be contrasted with the procedure of a 'judicial character' that must be provided by way of remedy under Article 5(4).[3] A question that has been left open is whether, for the purposes of Article 5(3), an officer must have any particular qualifications or training.[4]

c. Promptly

Article 5(3) requires that an arrested person is brought 'promptly' before a judge or other officer. The Strasbourg authorities have not set any upper time limit to the meaning of 'promptly', preferring to decide each case on its facts.[5] In *Brogan v UK*,[6] the Court held that a delay of four days and six hours in bringing a person before a judge did not comply with Article 5(3). In that case, the four applicants were arrested by the police in Northern Ireland as persons reasonably suspected of involvement in acts of terrorism. After being questioned for periods ranging from four days and six months to over six days, all four were released without being charged with any offence or being brought before a magistrate. When determining the meaning of 'promptly', the Court stated that the use in the equivalent French text of '*aussitôt*', which literally meant immediately, confirmed that 'the degree of flexibility attaching to the notion of "promptness" is limited'.[7] The Court continued:[8]

---

19 *Schiesser v Switzerland* A 34 para 31 (1979). As to 'legal criteria', see *Skoogström v Sweden* B 68-A (1983) Com Rep.

20 *Ireland v UK* A 25 para 199 (1978) (Advisory Committee on Internment did not qualify). Cf the military criminal cases of *De Jong, Baljet and Van Den Brink v Netherlands* A 77 (1984); *Van der Sluijs, Zuiderveld and Klappe v Netherlands* A 78 (1984); and *Duinhof and Duijf v Netherlands* A 79 (1984).

1 *Schiesser v Switzerland* A 34 para 31 (1979). Cf *Skoogström v Sweden* B 68-A (1983) Com Rep.

2 *Schiesser v Switzerland* A 34 para 36 (1979). Cf the military criminal case of *De Jong, Baljet and Van Den Brink v Netherlands* A 77 para 47 (1984) (Article 5(3) satisfied by 'either a judge sitting in court or an official in the public prosecutor's department').

3 See below, p 147. In *Brannigan and McBride v UK* A 258-B para 58 (1993), the Court stated that a 'procedure that has a judicial character' must be followed. It cited the *Schiesser* and *Huber* cases for this proposition.

4 See *Schiesser v Switzerland* A 34 para 31 (1979).

5 *Ireland v UK* A 25 para 199 (1978).

6 A 145-B (1988). On the *Brogan* case, see Tanca, 1 EJIL 269 (1990).

7 Id, para 59. Given that the two language texts were equally authentic, the Court had to interpret them 'in a way that reconciles them as far as possible and is most appropriate in order to realise the aim and achieve the object of the treaty': ibid.

8 Ibid.

'Whereas promptness is to be assessed in each case according to its special features, the significance to be attached to those features can never be taken to the point of impairing the very essence of the right guaranteed by Article 5(3). . .'

Applying this approach to the facts of the case, the Court accepted that, 'subject to adequate safeguards, the context of terrorism in Northern Ireland has the effect of prolonging the period during which the authorities may, without violating Article 5(3), keep a person suspected of serious terrorist offences in custody before bringing him before a judge or other judicial officer'.[9] However, even in the light of these 'special features', the Court held, by 12 to 7, that the requirement of 'promptness' could not properly be stretched so as to permit a delay of four days and six hours or more. Implicit in the Court's reasoning is that, beyond a certain time, the remedy for a state faced with an emergency is to make a derogation under Article 15, rather than for Article 5(3) to be interpreted beyond its proper limits. In *Brannigan and McBride v UK*,[10] the defendant state conceded that the detention of IRA suspects under the same power as in the *Brogan* case and for longer periods was contrary to Article 5(3). However, there was no breach of the Convention because the defendant state had made a valid emergency derogation under Article 15. In another 'special features' context, viz that of military criminal law, the Court held that 'even taking into account the demands of military life and justice', a delay of five days was in breach of Article 5(3).[11]

If four days and six hours were too long in the *Brogan* case in the emergency situation of Northern Ireland, it must clearly be so in ordinary criminal cases. In the only other Court case concerning an ordinary criminal case, the Court predictably ruled that 15 days' delay was too long.[12] In its jurisprudence, the Commission has found that four days' delay in an ordinary criminal case is consistent with Article 5(3).[13] It is not certain that the Court would agree with the Commission that four days is acceptable in such a case.[14] In the *Brogan* case, the Court left the question open, stating

9 Id, para 61.
10 A 258-B (1993). See the discussion of this case under Article 15, below, p 498.
11 *Koster v Netherlands* A 221 (1991) (delay caused by foreseeable military manoeuvres not a good excuse). Cf *De Jong, Baljet and Van Den Brink v Netherlands* A 77 para 53 (1984) and *Duinhof and Duijf v Netherlands* A 79 (1984). See also *Van Der Sluijs, Zuiderveld and Klappe v Netherlands* A 78 (1984).
12 *McGoff v Sweden* A 83 (1984).
13 *X v Netherlands No 2894/66*, 9 YB 564 (1966). Cf *Egue v France* 57 DR 47 at 70 (1988) (four days 'in principle' permissible) and *C v Netherlands No 19139/91* (1992) unreported. In *X v Belgium No 4960/71*, 42 CD 49 at 55 (1972), a delay of nearly five days before bringing an accused before a judge was, exceptionally, permissible because he had been ill in hospital during this period. See also the facts of *Skoogström v Sweden Nos 12867/87 and 14073/88*, 59 DR 227 (1989) F Sett (six days) and *Sargin and Yagci v Turkey Nos 14116/88 and 14117/88*, 76A DR 5 (1991) Com Rep; CM Res DH (93) 59 F Sett (19 days).
14 The Court took a more rigorous approach on the particular facts of the *Brogan* case than the Commission; whereas the Court found a breach of all four terrorist cases, the Commission found one only in respect of the two applicants detained for over five days.

that it was not deciding whether in an ordinary criminal case 'any given period, such as four days, in police or administrative custody would as a general rule be capable of being compatible with' Article 5(3).[15] It is submitted that in the administration of the ordinary criminal law a much shorter period of time than four days should be the maximum. This would be consistent with the plain meaning of the word 'promptly' and with the purpose of Article 5(3), which, as noted, is to minimise the risk of 'executive arbitrariness'.[16]

ii.   The right to bail

Under Article 5(3), an arrested person is 'entitled to trial within a reasonable time or to release pending trial'.[17] On the face of it, this wording obliges a state either to try a detained accused within a reasonable time or, if it does not do so, to release him. Sensibly, in *Wemhoff v FRG*,[18] the Court rejected this reading, which it called the 'purely grammatical interpretation', on the ground that it would allow a state to avoid trying a person within a reasonable time at the cost of releasing him. This could not have been the intention of the parties and would, moreover, have been 'flatly contra-dictory' to the guarantee of 'trial within a reasonable time' for all accused persons, whether detained or not, provided by Article 6(1). In the view of the Court, the key to understanding Article 5(3) was to recall that it is part of a guarantee of freedom of the person. Accordingly, 'it is the provisional detention of accused persons' – not the trial – 'which must not . . . be prolonged beyond a reasonable time'. Such prolongation occurs, in breach of Article 5(3), when: (i) there is no good reason in the public interest to continue the accused's detention pending trial; or (ii) it is extended in time because the investigation and trial are conducted less expeditiously than might reasonably be expected. As far as the second possibility is concerned, the outcome of the Court's interpretation of Article 5(3) leads to the same result as the 'purely grammatical interpretation' which the Court rejected, in that a person in detention must be tried within a reasonable time. But, by providing a basis for questioning the grounds of detention pending trial, the first possibility goes further by adding a guarantee of a right to bail for

---

15 A 145-B para 60 (1988). The Netherlands has introduced a four-day limit in ordinary criminal cases following the *Brogan* case.

16 Id, para 58 (1988). A study conducted within the Commission in connection with the *Brogan* case indicated that many parties have a limit of less than four days. In the English law applicable to non-terrorist cases, under the Police and Criminal Evidence Act 1984, ss 41-46, a person arrested by the police may be detained for up to 24 hours or, in the case of serious arrestable offences, 36 hours before being charged and must then be brought before a magistrates' court 'as soon as is practicable' thereafter, which means not later than the next magistrates' court sitting. The periods of 24 and 36 hours' police detention before a charge may be extended up to a maximum of 96 hours, but only by a magistrate, who would be a judge in the sense of Article 5(3).

17 On this part of Article 5(3), see Harris, 44 BYIL 87 (1970) and Wilkinson and Daintith, 18 AJCL 326 (1970).

18 A 7 pp 21-22 (1969).

persons detained pending trial, without which Article 5 would be seriously deficient.

Before the right to bail is considered in detail, the following points concerning Article 5(3) should be noted. Firstly, while the persistence of a reasonable suspicion that the person arrested has committed an offence remains a condition of the accused's continued detention under Article 5(1)(c), once Article 5(3) comes into play, such a suspicion is not enough.[19] Article 5(3) supposes that there also are 'relevant and sufficient' public interest reasons to justify further interference with the 'right to liberty' of a person presumed to be innocent.[20]

Secondly, the different roles of the national courts and the Strasbourg authorities in the application of the right to bail in Article 5(3) have been explained by the Court as follows. When the national courts take their decision 'they must examine all the facts arguing for and against the existence of a genuine requirement of public interest justifying, with due regard to the principle of the presumption of innocence, a departure from the rule of respect for individual liberty and set them out in their decisions on the applications for release'.[1] It is then 'essentially on the basis of the reasons given in these decisions and of the true facts mentioned by the applicant' when pursuing his remedies for release at the national level that the Strasbourg authorities must make their judgment.[2] As to the last point, however, the Strasbourg authorities do take into account arguments put by the defendant state when an application is considered that were not relied upon by the national courts when bail was refused,[3] as the word 'essentially' in the above quotation allows. What is striking is that the Court has no hesitation in disagreeing with the national court's assessment of the need for detention on remand; there is little indication that a 'margin of appreciation' doctrine applies in this context.

Thirdly, there is the matter of the stages of the criminal process to which Article 5(3) applies. In *Wemhoff v FRG*,[4] it was held that Article 5(3) covers the period from the arrest of the accused on suspicion of having committed a criminal offence[5] to his acquittal or conviction by the trial court. The Court's

19 *Stögmuller v Austria* A 9 pp 32-3 (1969) and *Letellier v France* A 207 para 35 (1991).
20 *Letellier v France* A 207 para 35 (1991). The Court has left open the question whether the legal basis for continued detention shifts from Article 5(1)(c) to Article 5(3) once the latter applies: *Stögmuller v Austria* A 9 pp 32-3 (1969) and *De Jong, Baljet and Van Den Brink v Netherlands* A 77 para 44 (1984). The position would seem to be that it is Article 5(1)(c) as read with Article 5(3).
1 *Letellier v France* A 207 para 35 (1991). The Court also emphasised that in a case in which the final decision is taken on appeal, the appeal court should state 'clear and specific' reasons for reversing a decision to release by a lower court that is in a better position to assess the facts and the personality of the accused: id, para 52.
2 Id. Cf *Neumeister v Austria* A 8 p 37 (1968).
3 See *Stögmuller v Austria* A 9 p 44 (1969). See also *Letellier v France* A 207 para 42 (1991).
4 A 7 pp 23-24 (1968).
5 In *Herczegfalvy v Austria* A 244 (1992), in which the applicant was already in detention on another basis when the order for his detention on remand was made, it was held by the Commission that Article 5(3) began to run only when the remand order was made. The point was not reconsidered before the Court.

reason for deciding that Article 5(3) ceases to apply following conviction by the trial court was that thereafter the basis for detention becomes Article 5(1)(a) ('detention . . . after conviction'), not Article 5(1)(c), so that the pre-condition for the application of Article 5(3) no longer existed. 'Conviction' in Article 5(1)(a) had to mean 'conviction' by the trial court because otherwise there would be no basis in Article 5(1) for the arrest following his conviction by the trial court of a person remanded on bail pending trial. In *B v Austria*,[6] the Court was asked by a minority of the Commission[7] to reconsider its ruling in the *Wemhoff* case on this point. The argument for re-consideration was that in the criminal justice systems of a number of contracting parties, including that in Austria, the detention pending appeal of a person convicted by the trial court is not based upon his conviction and sentence of imprisonment, but is regarded instead as an extension of his detention on remand. Accordingly, the accused's detention pending appeal should, at least in such legal systems, be regarded as continuing to be based on Article 5(1)(c), not Article 5(1)(a), so that Article 5(3) should still apply. The Court, however, confirmed its *Wemhoff* ruling. Although the detention pending appeal might be seen in some contracting parties as a continuation of detention on remand, it fell within Article 5(1)(a) as having been caused by the 'conviction',[8] in the absence of which the accused would have been released. Moreover, it was no longer possible to regard the applicant as continuing to be detained with a view to being brought before the 'competent legal authority' in respect of an offence, as required by Article 5(1)(c), when he had already been convicted of it by the trial court. The Court's judgment is a reasonable interpretation of the text of Article 5. Unfortunately, since it means that Article 5(3) does not cover detention pending appeal, it is not possible under that provision to challenge the grounds for detaining a convicted person during his appeal or to question the 'diligence' with which appeal proceedings are conducted, which is scarcely consistent with the bias in Article 5 in favour of the 'right to liberty'. However, release pending appeal will not normally be such an important issue as release pending trial. Moreover, the length of the appeal proceedings may be questioned under the 'reasonable time' guarantee in Article 6(1).[9]

Other considerations to be borne in mind when applying Article 5(3) are that if the accused is detained for two or more separate periods pending trial, they are to be cumulated when applying the reasonable time guarantee in Article 5(3).[10] If proceedings are still pending before the national trial court when an application claiming a breach of Article 5(3) is heard at Strasbourg, the period of detention after an Article 25 application is made may be taken into account up to the date that the Commission adopts its

---

6 A 175 (1990).
7 After resisting the Court's ruling for some time (see, eg the Commission's opinion in the *Ringeisen v Austria* B 11 p 44 (1970) Com Rep), the majority of the Commission had come to accept it by the time of *B v Austria*.
8 On the need for a causative link, see *Van Droogenbroeck v Belgium*, at p 108, above.
9 See below, p 222.
10 *Kemmache v France* A 218 para 44 (1991).

report; any period of detention thereafter, which the Commission will not have examined, must be made the subject of a new application.[11] A period of detention that does not count as a part of the period to be taken into account under Article 5(3) (eg because local remedies have not been exhausted or the defendant state was not a Convention party at the time) may none the less be relevant as a part of the general context within which the reasonableness of the period of detention may be assessed.[12] A period of detention prior to extradition to the defendant state is likewise not subject to control under Article 5(3), although it too is relevant as a part of the general context.[13]

a.   Grounds for refusing bail

It is well established that a person must be released pending trial unless the state can show that there are 'relevant and sufficient' reasons to justify his continued detention.[14] The Court has identified four grounds upon which the refusal of bail may be justified: the danger of flight, interference with the course of justice, the prevention of crime and the preservation of public order.

DANGER OF FLIGHT

Most cases have concerned the danger of flight. The general test the Court applies when assessing the refusal of bail on this ground is found in the *Stögmuller* case,[15] where it said:

'[T]here must be a whole set of circumstances . . . which give reason to suppose that the consequences and hazards of flight will seem to him to be a lesser evil than continued imprisonment.'

As to the 'circumstances' that are relevant, clearly the severity of the sentence that the accused may expect if convicted is important. Insofar as the sentence is imprisonment, its significance is reduced as the length of the period of pre-trial detention increases if it can be assumed that this period will be treated as a part of the sentence.[16] However, although important, the severity of the likely sentence does not constitute a separate ground for refusing bail and cannot by itself warrant detention on remand on the ground of the danger of the accused absconding.[17] In the *Neumeister* case,[18]

11 Ibid.
12 *Neumeister v Austria* A 8 p 37 (1968) and *Vallon v Italy* A 95 (1985) Com Rep para 49. But see *Stamoulakatos v Greece* A 271 para 33 (1993) (an Article 6 case).
13 *X v Italy and FRG No 5078/71*, 46 CD 35 (1972).
14 *Wemhoff v FRG* A 7 p 24 (1968).
15 A 9 p 44 (1969).
16 See eg *Neumeister v Austria* A 8 p 37 (1968).
17 *Letellier v France* A 207 para 43 (1991). Nor can bail be refused on any ground on the basis that the accused is anyway likely to be sentenced to imprisonment: id, para 51.
18 A 8 p 39 (1968).

the Court also took into account the probable civil liability that would fall upon the accused under Austrian law in respect of the loss of property that would be attributed to him if convicted. Other relevant factors are 'those relating to the character of the person involved, his morals, his home, his occupation, his assets, his family ties and all kinds of links with the country in which he is being prosecuted'.[19] So also are the 'accused's particular distaste for detention',[20] indications that he has links with another country that will enable him to escape or that he is actually planning to escape[1] and the threat of further proceedings.[2] In the *Wemhoff* case, the Court held that it followed from the final sentence of Article 5(3) that where the danger of the accused not appearing for trial is the sole justification for detention, 'his release pending trial must be ordered if it is possible to obtain from him guarantees that will ensure such appearance'.[3] In the *Neumeister* case, one of the reasons for finding the defendant state in breach of Article 5(3) was that it had failed to give proper consideration to an offer of financial guarantee by the defendant in return for his release.[4]

INTERFERENCE WITH THE COURSE OF JUSTICE

A justifiable fear that the accused will interfere with the course of justice is another permissible ground for detention.[5] This includes destroying documents,[6] warning or collusion with other possible suspects[7] and bringing pressure to bear upon witnesses.[8] A general statement that the accused will interfere with the course of justice is not sufficient; supporting evidence must be provided.[9] The longer the detention continues and the more the investigation makes progress, the less likely that interference with justice will remain a good reason for detention.[10]

PREVENTION OF CRIME

In *Matznetter v Austria*,[11] the Court held, by 4 votes to 3, that the detention of the applicant on the basis of the prevention of crime was compatible with Article 5(3) 'in the special circumstances of the case'. In that case, the

---

19 *Neumeister v Austria* A 8 p 39 (1968). In *Yagci and Sargin v Turkey Nos 16419/90 and 16426/90*, Com Rep (1994); case before the Court, the Commission took into account when finding a breach of the right to bail that the accused had returned voluntarily to resume residence in Turkey.
20 *Stögmuller v Austria* A 9 p 44 (1969).
1 *Matznetter v Austria* A 10 p 32 (1969).
2 *X v Switzerland No 8788/79*, 21 DR 241 (1980).
3 *Wemhoff v FRG* A 7 p 25 (1968). Cf *Letellier v France* A 207 para 46 (1991).
4 *Neumeister v Austria* A 8 p 40 (1968).
5 *Wemhoff v FRG* A 7 p 25 (1968).
6 Ibid. Cf *W v Switzerland* A 254-A (1993).
7 *Wemhoff v FRG* A 7 p 25 (1968).
8 *Letellier v France* A 207 (1991).
9 *Clooth v Belgium* A 225 para 44 (1991)
10 Id, para 43 (1991).
11 A 10 p 33 (1969).

Austrian courts took into account the applicant's 'very prolonged continuation of reprehensible activities, the huge extent of the loss sustained by the victims and the wickedness of the person charged' and the fact that the accused's 'experience and great skill . . . were such as to make it easy for him to resume his unlawful activities'. The Court considered that these were all circumstances relevant to a refusal of bail on the ground of the prevention of crime. More generally, the Court's judgment, which has been followed in later cases,[12] suggests that the public interest in the prevention of crime may justify detention on remand where there are good reasons to believe[13] that the accused if released will commit an offence or offences of the same serious kind with which he is already charged. It is not necessary that there be a reasonable suspicion that any particular, identifiable offence will be committed. Where, however, the ground for believing that an accused charged with murder may commit other offences of violence if released is his mental condition, his detention should not be continued without steps being taken to give the accused the necessary psychiatric care.[14]

The three dissenting judges in the *Matznetter* case expressed concern at permitting the detention of an accused who was presumed to be innocent on the ground, in effect, that he would if released commit other offences. Judge Zekia in particular noted that in the *Lawless* case[15] the Court had ruled that the second limb of Article 5(1)(c), which authorises detention 'to prevent' a person 'committing an offence', does not permit preventive detention.[16] A line can, however, be drawn between the general power of preventive detention, unconnected with pending criminal proceedings against the detainee, which was in issue in the *Lawless* case and the detention on remand of a person who is already reasonably suspected of having committed a very serious offence and in respect of whose case there are other 'special circumstances' of the kind present on the facts of the *Matznetter* case.

PUBLIC ORDER

The final ground for detention recognised by the Court is the preservation of public order. In *Letellier v France*,[17] the Court accepted that, in

---

12 See *Toth v Austria* A 224 (1991); *B v Austria* A 175 (1990); and *Clooth v Belgium* A 225 (1991).
13 In *Clooth v Belgium* A 225 para 40 (1991) the Court used a different, possibly less strict, formula, stating that the danger of repetition must be a 'plausible' one.
14 Ibid.
15 See above, p 117.
16 Judge Balladore Pallieri considered that prevention of crime could be a ground for detention where there was reason to believe that a particular, identifiable offence would be committed. Judge Cremona required a 'real likelihood' that a similar, unidentified offence would be committed, which was not present on the facts. The Irish Supreme Court has ruled that refusal of bail on the ground of prevention of crime is unconstitutional as being contrary to the presumption of innocence: *People (Att Gen) v O'Callaghan* [1966] IR 501 Ir S Ct.
17 A 207 para 51 (1991). Cf *Kemmache v France* A 218 para 52 (1991) and *Tomasi v France* A 241-A (1992).

exceptional circumstances, 'by reason of their particular gravity and public reaction to them, certain offences may give rise to a social disturbance capable of justifying pre-trial detention, at least for a time'; this is so provided that the municipal law concerned recognises the ground and there is evidence that the accused's release 'will actually disturb public order'. This test is not satisfied where, as in the *Letellier* case, the decision to refuse bail on this ground takes into account only the gravity of the offence in the abstract. In that case, the French courts, whose law recognised that certain offences may lead to a risk of public disorder justifying pre-trial detention, had only taken into account the fact that the offence (accessory to murder) was a very serious one, without considering whether the accused's release would be likely to cause a public disturbance on the facts. Although the threat to public order may justify detention on remand at the outset, it may cease to do so as time passes.[18]

b. Conditions of bail

Article 5(3) states that if an accused is released on bail his release 'may be conditioned by guarantees to appear for trial'. In the *Neumeister* case,[19] Austria was held to have violated Article 5(3) partly because the amount of bail set had been calculated 'solely in relation to the loss imputed to' the applicant. This, the Court held, was contrary to Article 5(3) because the 'guarantee provided by that Article is designed to ensure, not the reparation of loss, but rather the presence of the accused at the hearing'. Using the maxim expression *unius est exclusio alterius*, which has been used in the interpretation of treaties,[20] Article 5(3) can be read as meaning that the only conditions that can be attached to release pending trial are those relating to appearance at trial. However, it would be unsatisfactory if Article 5(3) did not allow any considerations other than appearance at trial to be taken into account when allowing bail. Such an approach might work to a person's disadvantage in that it might prevent his release altogether if, for example, a condition as to the suppression of evidence or the prevention of crime were not permissible.[1] In the *Wemhoff* case,[2] the Court confirmed that financial guarantees to ensure appearance at trial may be set. In the *Stögmuller* case,[3] it implied that the surrender of a passport for the same purpose may also be required. Where the guarantee is a monetary one, the amount set must be assessed 'principally by reference to him [the accused], his assets and his relationship with the persons who are to provide the security', the purpose

---

18 *Tomasi v France* A 241-A para 91 (1992).
19 A 8 p 40 (1968).
20 See eg the *Life Insurance Claims (US v Germany)* 7 UNRIAA 91, 111 (1924).
1   For example, a not uncommon condition set by magistrates in England is that a person accused of assault or a public order offence stay away from a particular person or place.
2   A 7 p 25 (1968).
3   A 9 pp 43-44 (1969). Cf *Schmid v Austria No 10670/83*, 44 DR 195 at 196 (1985) (surrender of passport permissible, as were the surrender of a driving licence and a residence requirement).

being to ensure that there is 'a sufficient deterrent to dispel any wish on his part to abscond'.[4] It is probable that the setting of an amount that is more than sufficient to achieve this would be a violation of the right to bail under this provision.[5] The danger of the accused absconding, however, may be such as to make any amount of bail insufficient.[6]

iii. Trial within a reasonable time

As the Court has held many times, an accused's detention on remand may be continued during the whole of the pre-trial period if there are 'relevant and sufficient' grounds of the kind listed above that justify it. However, even though such grounds continue to exist, Article 5(3) may still be infringed if the accused's detention is prolonged beyond a 'reasonable time' because the proceedings have not been conducted with the required expedition.[7] This 'reasonable time' guarantee in Article 5(3) overlaps with that in Article 6(1), which applies to all accused persons, whether in detention or not. The guarantee in Article 5(3) requires that in respect of a detained person the authorities show 'special diligence in the conduct of the proceedings'.[8] The same, higher standard of diligence would appear to apply under Article 6(1) when the accused is in detention.[9] In practice, 'reasonable time' claims brought by persons remanded in custody that just concern the stages of the proceedings to which Article 5(3) apply, viz from arrest to conviction by the trial court,[10] are considered just under that provision, not under Article 6(1).[11] Reasonable time claims that extend in time beyond the accused's conviction to include appeal proceedings are either considered under both

---

4   *Neumeister v Austria* A 8 p 40 (1968). The accused must make available the information as to his assets needed for a proper assessment of the amount of security that should be set: *Bonnechaux v Switzerland No 8224/78*, 18 DR 100 at 144 (1979) Com Rep; CM Res DH (80) 1.
5   The Commission has stated that the authorities are under a duty to make a careful assessment of the information as to the accused's resources in their possession so as not to set a recognisance at too high a level: *Schertenlieb v Switzerland No 8339/78*, 23 DR 137 at 196 (1980) Com Rep; CM Res DH (81) 9.
6   *Neumeister v Austria* A 8 p 40 (1968).
7   In practice, the Court usually only goes on to consider whether the reasonable time guarantee in Article 5(3) has been infringed if it has first found no breach of the right to bail. In *Tomasi v France* A 241-A (1992) the Court went on to consider the reasonable time guarantee in a borderline case on the right to bail.
8   *Herczegfalvy v Austria* A 244 para 71 (1992). Cf the earlier formulation in *Wemhoff v FRG* A 7 p 26 (1968): 'an accused person in detention is entitled to have his case given priority and conducted with particular expedition'.
9   *Abdoella v Netherlands* A 248-A para 24 (1992). See further below, p 226. This negates earlier statements by the Court that Article 5(3) imposed a stricter 'reasonable time' standard than Article 6 in detention cases: see *Stögmuller v Austria* A 9 p 40 (1969) and *Matznetter v Austria* A 10 p 34 (1969).
10 See above, p 137.
11 The *Abdoella* case, above, n 9, concerned appeal proceedings, to which Article 5(3) does not extend.

Articles 5(3) (for the stages to which it applies) and Article 6(1)[12] or just under Article 6.[13]

As to the considerations to be taken into account in assessing whether trial within a reasonable time has occurred, the same ones apply for both Articles 5(3) and 6(1). Thus, as with Article 6(1), relevant factors are the complexity of the case, the conduct of the accused and the efficiency of the national authorities. These considerations are examined later under Article 6(1).[14]

As under Article 6(1), there is no absolute ceiling to the time that a person may be remanded in detention if there remain 'relevant and sufficient reasons'; the reasonableness of the length of proceedings depends on the facts of the case. Thus in *W v Switzerland*,[15] the Court held, by 5 to 4, that proceedings resulting in a four-year period of pre-trial detention were not in breach of Article 5(3). Rejecting the contrary view expressed by the Commission, the Court confirmed its long-standing position[16] that Article 5(3) does not set any maximum length of pre-trial detention. In the *W* case, the Court was satisfied with the assessment of the Swiss Federal Court that there were good reasons to refuse bail on the facts (danger of flight and interference with justice) and there were no delays attributable to the authorities in an extremely complicated case of company fraud. The case can be distinguished from others in which a breach of Article 5(3) has been found in respect of a long period of pre-trial detention during the investigation stage[17] on the basis that in those cases there were identifiable periods when little or nothing happened. In a strong dissenting opinion in the *W* case, Judge Pettiti[18] noted that the Court had never previously tolerated under Article 5(3) a period of four years' pre-trial detention[19] for a person presumed to be innocent and that the permitted or actual length of pre-trial detention in criminal justice systems in Europe generally is now

12 *B v Austria* A 175 (1990) (no breach of Article 5(3), but a breach of Article 6(1) in respect of post-conviction proceedings).
13 *Neumeister v Austria* A 8 (1968) and *Kemmache v France* A 218 (1991). In both of these cases, the Court had already found a breach of the right to bail in Article 5(3).
14 See below, p 223. Note that where, in English practice, a charge is ordered to 'lie upon the file' (rather than be prosecuted) while a conviction for a more serious offence remains in force, the 'reasonable time' guarantee in Article 5(3) does not apply: *L v UK No 16006/90*, 65 DR 325 (1990).
15 A 254-A (1993).
16 See *Wemhoff v FRG* A 7 p 24 (1968).
17 In *Toth v Austria* A 224 (1991) (two years and one month's detention on remand), there were periods of inactivity totalling eleven months resulting largely because of a disinclination to photocopy the official file. In *Tomasi v France* A 241-A (1992) (five years and seven months), the public prosecutor admitted to long periods in which no progress was made. See also *Birou v France* A 232-B (1992) Com Rep (five years' delay unreasonable; F Sett before Court).
18 See also the joint dissenting opinion of Judges Walsh and Loizou and the dissenting opinion of Judge De Meyer. The Commission had found a breach of Article 5(3) by 19 to 1.
19 It had tolerated three years and five months: *Wemhoff v FRG* A 7 (1968). In *Vakalis v Greece No 17841/91* (1993), unreported, the Commission found three years and four months not to be in breach of Article 5(3). In a UK case involving complex fraud offences, nineteen months was not too long: *Di Stefano v UK No 12391/86*, 60 DR 182 (1989).

much less than four years.[20] Judge Pettiti's opinion suggests, with much force, that there should be an absolute limit to the length of pre-trial detention and that very strong evidence indeed is necessary to justify both the refusal of bail and the time taken to investigate and try a case over a period lasting as long as four years.

5. ARTICLE 5(4): REMEDY TO CHALLENGE THE LEGALITY OF DETENTION

Article 5(4) provides:

> 'Everyone who is deprived of his liberty by arrest or detention shall be entitled to take proceedings by which the lawfulness of his detention shall be decided speedily by a court and his release ordered if the detention is not lawful.'

Article 5(4) is the *habeas corpus* provision of the Convention. It requires that a person in detention be provided in the municipal legal system concerned with a judicial remedy by which he can test the legality of his detention and obtain his release if his detention is unlawful. The obligation applies whatever the ground for detention (criminal offence, deportation, etc). A state must provide recourse to the courts in all cases, whether the detention is justified by Article 5(1) or not. Accordingly, an Article 5(4) claim must be considered even though the detention has been found to be lawful under the Convention.[1] Article 5(4) is a *lex specialis* in relation to the 'less strict' general remedy required by Article 13 of the Convention; if the Court finds a breach of Article 5(4), it is unlikely to consider a claim by a detained person under Article 13.[2] However, since the purpose of the remedy required by Article 5(4) is to facilitate a detained person's release, it is no longer required once he is lawfully free.[3] Even if the person is only out on licence, Article 5(4) no longer applies; instead, Article 13 applies, requiring that a remedy be provided by which the released person may challenge the consistency with the Convention of his earlier detention.[4] Where a person in

---

20 For some indication of recent lengths of criminal proceedings, see *Delays in the Criminal Justice System: Reports presented to the 9th Criminological Colloquium* (1989), Council of Europe Press, 1992.

1 *De Wilde, Ooms and Versyp v Belgium* A 12 para 73 (1971). In this case, the Court held that Article 5(4) was infringed even though Article 5(1) was not. Although Articles 5(1) and (4) do contain separate requirements, if the Court finds one to be infringed, it does not always consider it necessary to rule on compliance with the other: contrast *Van Der Leer v Netherlands* A 170-A (1990) and *Koendjbiharie v Netherlands* A 185-B (1990).

2 *De Jong, Baljet and Van Den Brink v Netherlands* A 77 para 60 (1984).

3 *X v Sweden No 10230/82*, 32 DR 303 (1983). A released person may none the less challenge under Article 5(4) the 'speediness' of any remedy available to him: *X v UK No 9403/81*, 28 DR 235 (1982). A person who absconds remains entitled to a remedy under Article 5(4) because he is still deprived of his liberty in law: *Van Der Leer v Netherlands* A 170 (1990).

4 *L v Sweden No 10801/84*, 61 DR 62 at 73 (1988) Com Rep; CM Res DH (89) 16.

detention is released 'speedily' while his application for release is pending, the question whether the remedy that he has sought complies with Article 5(4) will not be pursued by the Court on the ground that it serves no purpose. Thus in *Fox, Campbell and Hartley v UK*,[5] two of the applicants sought *habeas corpus* the day after their arrest but were released within the next 24 hours, before their application was heard. Given that the applicants had already been released 'speedily', the Court declined to consider whether the *habeas corpus* proceedings would have complied with Article 5(4). As with Article 13, Article 5(4) is of great importance because a municipal law remedy will be of more immediate effect and convenient to obtain than one via Strasbourg for a breach of the international guarantee in Articles 5(1).[6]

Although Article 5(4) only requires a remedy at one level of jurisdiction, in *Toth v Austria*[7] the Court held that if a party provides a right of appeal against a decision by a first instance 'court' rejecting a claim for release, the appellate body must 'in principle' comply with Article 5(4). The position is comparable to that concerning appeal courts in the right to a fair trial guarantee in Article 6(1).[8]

i.   Remedy before a court

The detained person must have access to a 'court'. This does not have to be a 'court of law of the classic kind integrated within the standard judicial machinery of the country'.[9] It must, however, be a body that has a 'judicial character' and that provides the 'guarantees of procedure appropriate to the kind of deprivation of liberty in question'.[10]

a.   Judicial character

To be of a 'judicial character', a body must be 'independent both of the executive and the parties to the case'.[11] Bodies that have predictably been held not to meet this requirement are a public prosecutor,[12] the medical officer of a 'person of unsound mind'[13] and a government minister.[14] In *Weeks v UK*[15] the English Parole Board was found to have the necessary judicial character. In that case, the Court found the Board to be 'independent of the executive *and impartial* in the performance of their

---

5   A 182 (1990).
6   Cf Trechsel, *European System*, p 319, who emphasises the subsidiary character of the remedy under the Convention, as to which, see above, p 14.
7   A 224 para 84 (1991). Cf *Navarra v France* A 273-B (1993).
8   See below, p 240.
9   *Weeks v UK* A 114 para 61 (1987).
10 *De Wilde, Ooms and Versyp v Belgium* A 12 para 76 (1971).
11 Id, para 77.
12 *Winterwerp v Netherlands* A 33 para 64 (1979).
13 *X v UK* A 46 para 61 (1981).
14 Ibid. Cf *Keus v Netherlands* A 185-C para 28 (1990).
15 A 114 para 62 (1987). Italics added.

duties'.[16] The distinction being drawn was between 'independence' of the executive and 'impartiality' as between the parties. As to impartiality, in *K v Austria*,[17] a court of law did not satisfy Article 5(4) because the judge who ruled on the applicant's detention for failing to pay a fine had earlier imposed the fine.

An investigating judge in a civil law system is a 'court'.[18] This decision has been criticised on the basis that, although 'independent', an investigating judge is not 'impartial' as between the parties since he has a responsibility to bring the investigation successfully to an end and hence has an incentive to detain the accused to avoid him absconding or tampering with evidence.[19]

A 'court' must also have a 'judicial character' in the sense of being competent to take a legally binding decision leading to the person's release. Thus in *X v UK*,[20] a Mental Health Review Tribunal, although independent of the executive and the parties, did not qualify because it could only make advisory recommendations for release to the Home Secretary. In *Weeks v UK*[1] the Parole Board qualified insofar as it could make recommendations for the release of recalled life sentence prisoners that were binding upon the Home Secretary, but failed to do so in respect of other powers to make recommendations that were not.[2] In *E v Norway*,[3] the Court was satisfied that whereas the Norwegian courts would normally just declare an administrative decision to be illegal without ordering that any remedial steps be taken, they could go further and order a person's release in a case of illegal detention, as Article 5(4) requires. In *Van Droogenbroeck v Belgium*[4] it was insufficient that a court could convict the responsible government official for illegal detention but could not order the detained person's release.

b. Procedural guarantees

In the early case of *Neumeister v Austria*,[5] a chamber of the Court held that all that Article 5(4) required was that a 'court' be of a 'judicial character'; it 'in no way relates to the procedure to be followed'. Later, in *De Wilde, Ooms and Versyp v Belgium*,[6] the plenary court reversed this ruling. It held that Article 5(4) obliges a 'court' to provide 'guarantees of judicial procedure',

---

16 Cf the Court's change in approach in respect of the meaning of 'officer' in Article 5(3), above, p 133.
17 A 255-B (1993) Com Rep. F Sett before Court.
18 *Bezicheri v Italy* A 164 (1989).
19 Trechsel, *European System*, p 327,
20 A 46 (1981). A Tribunal now has a power of decision: Mental Health Act 1983, ss 72-74.
1   A 114 para 64 (1987).
2   See now Criminal Justice Act 1991, s 34, by which the Parole Board may *direct* the Home Secretary to release the prisoner.
3   A 181-A (1990).
4   A 50 (1982).
5   A 8 para 24 (1968). The Court found support for its view in the fact that the decision must be taken 'speedily', which militated against elaborate procedural rules.
6   A 12 para 78 (1971).

although when determining 'whether a proceedings provides adequate guarantees, regard must be had to the particular nature of the circumstances in which the proceedings take place.'[7] Applying this differential approach, the Strasbourg authorities have established a number of procedural requirements that may be relevant. Generally, the Court has indicated that where a lengthy deprivation of liberty might result from the detention, resembling that which might be imposed by a court in criminal proceedings, the procedure followed must provide guarantees not 'markedly inferior' to those in the criminal courts of Council of Europe member states.[8] Thus in the *De Wilde, Ooms and Versyp* case, the defendant state was found in breach of Article 5(4) because the procedure before a magistrate by which persons provisionally arrested as vagrants could be ordered to be detained for periods of up to a year or in some cases longer, fell well short of those associated with a criminal trial. Although the applicants were heard in person at a public hearing and could request an adjournment, they were denied other defendants' rights provided in the Belgian Code of Criminal Procedure. At the other extreme, less strict standards are permitted where a person is detained in an emergency for just a short period of time.[9]

AN ORAL HEARING

A person who is detained as being 'of unsound mind' under Article 5(1)(e) must be allowed 'to be heard either in person or, where necessary, through some form of representation'.[10] A minor detained under Article 5(1)(d) is also entitled to be heard in person and provided with effective legal assistance.[11] In *Sanchez-Reisse v Switzerland*,[12] the Court noted that its previous jurisprudence had 'tended to acknowledge the need for a hearing before the judicial authority' in cases arising under Article 5(1)(c). In the same case, however, the Court held that written proceedings were sufficient under Article 5(1)(f), at least on the facts before it. In that case, the applicant's request for release was, in accordance with Swiss law, made via the Federal Police Office, which attached its own opinion on the merits of the request. The Federal Court rejected the request on the basis solely of the written documents, without giving the applicant an opportunity to respond to any new points of fact or law raised in the Police Office's opinion. The Court held that an oral hearing was not required since there was 'no reason

---

7 Ibid.
8 Id, para 79. The guarantees found in Council of Europe member states can be taken to be those in the guarantee of the right to a fair trial in Article 6.
9 *Wassink v Netherlands* A 185-A (1990).
10 *Winterwerp v Netherlands* A 33 para 60 (1979). As the Court indicated, legal representation will be vital where a 'person of unsound mind' does not understand what is happening. Cf *Keus v Netherlands* A 185-C (1990). See also *Merkier v Belgium No 11200/84*, 57 DR 38 (1988) F Sett.
11 *Bouamar v Belgium* A 129 para 60 (1988).
12 A 107 para 51 (1986), referring to the *Schiesser* case. See contra *Neumeister v Austria* A 8 p 44 (1968), which can now be disregarded. In *X v Switzerland No 8485/79*, 22 DR 131 (1981), the Commission had earlier held that written proceedings were sufficient.

to believe that the applicant's presence could have convinced the Federal Court that he had to be released.'[13] In *Farmakopoulos v Belgium*,[14] however, the Commission stated in the context of an Article 5(1)(f) case that Article 5(4) generally requires that the detained person or his representative participate in the court proceedings, by which it meant participation in a hearing. Given the origins of Article 5(4) in the writ of *habeas corpus*, the better view is that the 'body' should be produced before the court and the detained person allowed to argue for release in all cases of detention.[15]

LEGAL ASSISTANCE

As apparent from the preceding paragraph, there are indications that Article 5(4) requires that an applicant be allowed legal assistance when pursuing his claim to release where this is necessary for the remedy to be effective. In *Bouamar v Belgium*,[16] it was held in an Article 5(1)(d) case that a minor was entitled to 'the effective assistance of his lawyer' at the hearing at which his detention was challenged. Similarly, in *Megyeri v Germany*,[17] it was held in an Article 5(1)(e) case that a person detained as being mentally disordered was entitled to legal representation at the hearing unless there were special circumstances suggesting otherwise. In that case it was also held, in a ruling that should apply to minors too, that the person concerned should not be required to take the initiative to obtain legal representation. In both of these cases, the applicant was not fully in a position to act for himself. In *Woukam Moudefo v France*,[18] in which the applicant had been arrested on suspicion of a criminal offence (Article 5(1)(c)), the Commission had occasion to consider the right to legal assistance more generally. It was of the opinion that the 'fundamental procedural guarantees' required by Article 5(4) included the provision of 'legal assistance', including assistance before the hearing as well as representation at it, wherever this was necessary to render the application effective. In that case, there was a breach of Article 5(4) when an accused was not allocated a lawyer for his appeal to the French Court of Cassation for release when the appeal involved points of law.

The right to legal assistance spelt out in these cases involves the provision of legal aid in case of indigency where this is necessary for the remedy to be effective.[19] In *Zamir v UK*,[20] the Commission accepted that free legal aid

---

13 A 107 para 51 (1986).
14 A 235-A (1992) Com Rep para 46. The Commission relied on the Court judgment in the *Keus* case, which concerned a hearing in a mental patient case.
15 Cf the concurring opinions in the *Sanchez-Reisse* case of Judges Ganshof, Van Der Meersch and Walsh.
16 A 129 para 60 (1988).
17 A 237-A (1992).
18 A 141-B (1988) Com Rep paras 86-91. F Sett before Court. Cf *K v Austria* A 255- B (1993) Com Rep. F Sett before Court . See also *S v Switzerland* A 220 para 53 (1991).
19 Cf the test for legal aid in civil cases in Article 6(1), below, p 198. Given that Article 5(4) proceedings do not involve the determination of a criminal charge, the more generous 'interest of justice' test in Article 6(3)(c), as to which see below, p 261, does not apply.
20 *No 9174/80*, 40 DR 42 (1983). The *Megyeri* and *Woukam Moudefo* cases involved officially appointed lawyers paid for by the state.

was required for an illegal immigrant detained pending deportation in view of the complexity of the proceedings and his limited English.

Whereas there would appear to be a right to legal assistance as described above, a detained person is not necessarily entitled to present his case himself. In *Sanchez-Reisse v Switzerland*,[1] the Court considered that in extradition proceedings it was acceptable for the remedy to consist of exclusively written proceedings that necessitated legal assistance and in effect prevented the applicant from participating in the presentation of his case.

ADVERSARIAL PROCEEDINGS

Article 5(4) also incorporates the principle of adversarial proceedings, which has been developed under Article 6(1).[2] There it means that all evidence must be produced before the parties with a view to adversarial argument. In the context of Article 5(4), the relevant cases have mostly concerned 'equality of arms',[3] which is a distinct procedural right that can be subsumed within the general principle of adversarial proceedings. It was on the basis of the latter principle that a breach of Article 5(4) was found in *Toth v Austria*[4] because the prosecuting authority was present during the appeal hearing on the question of the applicant's detention when the applicant was not.[5] The Court also found that there was a breach of the principle in *Lamy v Belgium*[6] when an accused detained under Article 5(1)(c) was, unlike the Crown counsel opposing him, not allowed access to the official file on his case when applying for bail. Similarly, in *Weeks v UK*,[7] which arose under Article 5(1)(a), the Court held that Article 5(4) was not complied with because the prisoner seeking release was not entitled to full disclosure of adverse material in the Parole Board's possession. However, in *Wassink v Netherlands*[8] it was not necessary to allow the applicant or his counsellor to read the statements given over the telephone to the judge by witnesses about the applicant's mental state to satisfy the requirement of an adversarial procedure in the context of Article 5(1)(e); it was sufficient that the judge allowed the applicant's counsellor to comment on a summary.

TIME AND FACILITIES TO PREPARE AN APPLICATION

A detained person must be allowed the necessary time and facilities to prepare his case.[9] As to time, a detained person must be allowed a

---

1 A 107 para 46 (1986).
2 See below, p 214.
3 As to which, see below, p 207. The ruling in the *Neumeister* case A 8 p 43 (1968) that 'equality of arms' was not required can be disregarded.
4 A 224 (1991).
5 Cf *Sanchez-Reisse v Spain*, facts above, p 148, in which the Court held that the applicant should have been allowed an opportunity to respond to the opinion of the Police Office.
6 A 151 (1989). Cf *Toth v Austria* A 224 (1991). See also *Byloos v Belgium No 14545/89*, 69 DR 252 (1991). F Sett.
7 A 114 para 66 (1987). Cf *Thynne, Wilson and Gunnell v UK* A 190-A para 80 (1990).
8 A 185-A (1990).
9 *K v Austria* A 255-B (1993) Com Rep. F Sett before Court. Cf Article 6(3)(b), below, p 252.

reasonable period of time to present his application. In *Farmakopoulos v Belgium*,[10] the Commission stated that any time limit upon its use 'must not be so short as to restrict the availability and tangibility of the remedy'. In the same case, the Commission indicated that although Article 5(4) does not require that a detained person be informed of the remedy available, the failure to give such information is relevant when assessing the acceptability of any time limit.

As to facilities, he must be told the reasons for his detention because this is information which is essential in order to challenge its legality.[11] Several of the cases considered in the preceding section on the principle of adversarial proceedings could also be regarded as concerning to the right to facilities to prepare one's case.

NO GENERAL RIGHT TO A PUBLIC HEARING

Article 5(4) does not generally require a public hearing. Thus none is needed before a tribunal considering the release of a mental patient[12] and an investigating judge, taking his decision privately in his office, has been held to be a 'court' under Article 5(4).[13] However, there was a public hearing in the *Vagrancy* cases[14] and it may be that proceedings that are akin to criminal proceedings in the length of deprivation of liberty at risk should be in public, as in criminal cases.

ii. The incorporation rule

The theory underlying Article 5(4) is that a judicial remedy should be available to review the legality of an administrative act of detention. If, therefore, the initial decision to detain is taken by a 'court', Article 5(4) becomes redundant; the required supervision is 'incorporated in the decision' of the court that ordered the detention.[15] This is most clearly the case when a person has been 'convicted by a competent court' consistently with Article 5(1)(a). It applies equally, however, to other situations where detention is ordered by a 'court'.[16] The meaning of 'court' for this purpose is the same as it otherwise is under Article 5(4).

---

10 A 235-A (1992) Com Rep (24-hour limit too short on the facts). Case withdrawn by applicant before Court.
11 *X v UK* A 46 para 66 (1981). This is also required under Article 5(2), with which Article 5(4) overlaps.
12 *Dhoest v Belgium No 10448/83*, 55 DR 5 at 26 (1987), Com Rep; CM Res DH (88). Cf *X v Belgium No 6859/74*, 3 DR 139 (1975).
13 *Bezicheri v Italy* A 164 para 20 (1989). Cf *Neumeister v Austria* A 8 p 44 (1968).
14 See above, p 147.
15 *De Wilde, Ooms and Versyp v Belgium* A 12 para 76 (1971). Cf *Engel v Netherlands* A 22 para 77 (1976).
16 See *Winterwerp v Netherlands* A 33 (1979).

iii. A continuing remedy at reasonable intervals

The fact that the initial decision to detain a person is taken by a 'court' or that an administrative detention is subsequently ratified by such a body will not suffice to comply with Article 5(4) where 'the very nature of the deprivation of liberty under consideration would appear to require a review of lawfulness at reasonable intervals'.[17] In cases, that is, where the circumstances that provide the basis in law for detention may cease to exist, it becomes necessary to provide the detained person with a continuing remedy at reasonable intervals. This requirement was applied in *X v UK*,[18] in which the applicant had been ordered by the trial court following his conviction to be detained at Broadmoor as a restricted offender patient on the statutory grounds that he was mentally disordered and a danger to the public. Although the initial judicial supervision required by Article 5(4) was 'incorporated in the decision' of the trial court, which was clearly a 'court' in the sense of that provision, the possibility that the applicant's mental condition might improve so as no longer to warrant detention meant that Article 5(4) required that he be provided with further possibilities, either by way of 'automatic periodic review of a judicial character' or by the opportunity for him to 'take proceedings at reasonable intervals before a court', to challenge the lawfulness of his continued detention.[19] Other situations in which a continuing remedy may be required are cases of the preventive detention of recidivists,[20] the detention of minors[1] and the refusal of bail to an accused person.[2]

Another situation of this kind is that of the discretionary life sentence in English law.[3] A discretionary life sentence may be imposed in certain cases where the offence is grave and the offender is a danger to the public. In such a case, the sentence will include a punitive or tariff period that is assessed by reference to the seriousness of the offence. Once the tariff period has expired, there remains a discretionary period of detention for security reasons, during which the offender may be released if he ceases to be a danger to the public. In *Thynne, Wilson and Gunnell v UK*,[4] the Court held that Article 5(4) requires a continuing remedy during the discretionary period by which the convicted person is able to challenge, on the ground that he is no longer dangerous, the legality of his continued detention. Similarly, it was held in the same case that when a person subject to a

17 Id, para 55 (1979). In other terms, a continuing remedy is required if 'new issues affecting the lawfulness of the detention might subsequently arise': *X v UK* A 46 para 51 (1981).
18 A 46 (1981).
19 Id, para 52. For a case of 'automatic periodic review' see *Keus v Netherlands* A 185-C para 24 (1990).
20 *Van Droogenbroeck v Belgium* A 50 (1982) and *E v Norway* A 181-A (1990).
1 *Bouamar v Belgium* A 129 (1988).
2 *Bezicheri v Italy* A 164 (1989).
3 *Weeks v UK* A 114 (1987) and *Thynne, Wilson and Gunnell v UK* A 190-A (1990). On these cases, see Richardson, 1991 PL 34.
4 A 190-A (1990), following and developing the decision in *Weeks v UK* A 114 (1987), as to which see above, p 108.

discretionary life sentence is released on licence, he is entitled under Article 5(4) to a remedy to challenge the lawfulness of his re-detention. Later, in *Wynne v UK*,[5] the Court confirmed the position that it had taken in the *Thynne, Wilson and Gunnell* case that, in contrast with a discretionary life sentence, there is no requirement of a continuing remedy in the case of a mandatory life sentence, even though the latter will also contain a notional tariff period which is relevant to the question of release on licence. This is because a mandatory life sentence is 'imposed automatically as the punishment for the offence of murder irrespective of considerations pertaining to the dangerousness of the offender.' Although there has been no ruling on the point, the Court's reasoning in the above cases suggests that, given that it does not relate to the dangerousness of the offender, there is also no requirement of a continuing remedy during the tariff period of detention of a discretionary life sentence either.

What is meant by a remedy at 'reasonable intervals' depends on the kind of case. A period of one month has been held to be a 'reasonable interval' in the context of detention on remand, the nature of which is such as to call for a remedy at 'short intervals'.[6] Although a longer interval may be acceptable in the case of a 'person of unsound mind', a period in excess of one year has been held to be in breach of Article 5(4).[7] Where there is clear evidence of a change in a person's mental condition, a hearing within a shorter period may be required.[8] Arrangements for 'automatic periodic review' must follow the same standards as to frequency.[9]

iv. The lawfulness of the detention

A remedy in the sense of Article 5(4) is one that permits the detained person to challenge the 'lawfulness' of his detention. In this connection, 'lawful' has the same meaning as it has in Article 5(1), so that the detained person must have the opportunity to question whether his detention is consistent both with the applicable municipal law and the Convention, including its general principles, and is not arbitrary.[10] With regard to the requirement that the detention not be arbitrary, the nature of the remedy required will vary according to the meaning that this term has in the particular sub-paragraph of Article 5(1) (or part of it) within which the case comes.[11] As noted

---

5 A 294 para 35 (1994).
6 *Bezicheri v Italy* A 164 para 21 (1989). See also *X v Netherlands No 11155/85*, 9 **EHRR** 267 (1985) (review after eleven days satisfactory).
7 *Herczegfalvy v Austria* A 244 (1992).
8 *M v FRG No 10272/83*, 38 DR 104 (1984).
9 See *Keus v Netherlands* A 185-C para 24 (1990).
10 *Van Droogenbroeck v Belgium* A 50 para 48 (1982). As to 'lawful' under Article 5(1), see above, p 105.
11 *Bouamar v Belgium* A 129 para 60 (1988). See also *Zamir v UK No 9174/80*, 40 DR 42 at 58 (1983) Com Rep; CM Res DH (85) 3 and *Whitehead v Italy No 13930/88*, 60 DR 272 at 283 (1989) (an Article 5(1)(f) case).

earlier,[12] in respect of most sub-paragraphs the Strasbourg authorities only look to see whether the detention is consistent with its purpose. In a few cases, however, it introduces considerations of 'proportionality'. Thus, in a case concerning the detention of a 'person of unsound mind', it must be possible for the 'court' to determine whether the detention is warranted on medical grounds, since compliance with Article 5(1)(e) requires that the person's detention as being of 'unsound mind' is medically justified.[13] It was because no such possibility existed that *habeas corpus* proceedings in English law were held not to provide a sufficient remedy in *X v UK*.[14] As interpreted by the English courts, *habeas corpus* may be used to challenge the procedural regularity, but not the medical grounds, for the detention of a mentally disordered person.[15] Repairing the damaged reputation of *habeas corpus*, the Court did note that it would provide a sufficient remedy in a case of the detention of a 'person of unsound mind' in an emergency since the legality of detention under Article 5(1)(e) then does not depend upon a medical assessment.[16] *Habeas corpus* also constitutes a sufficient Article 5(4) remedy by which to challenge the detention of an accused person within Article 5(1)(c), since it allows the reasonableness of the grounds for suspicion, as well as the procedural legality of the detention, to be reviewed.[17]

In a different context, in *Weeks v UK*[18] it was held that the scope of judicial review in English law was not sufficient to provide a basis for an Article 5(4) remedy in the case of a person detained under a discretionary life sentence. In such a case, the 'lawfulness' of continued detention consistently with Article 5(1)(a) turns upon whether the prisoner remains a danger to the public, which is a matter for the Home Secretary to decide. His decision is subject only to limited review by the courts. Of the three grounds for judicial review listed by Lord Diplock in *Council of Civil Service Unions v Minister for the Civil Service*,[19] the most relevant, the European Court stated, was 'irrationality'. But this, the Court observed, applies only to a 'decision that is so outrageous in its defiance of logic or of accepted moral standards that no sensible person who had applied his mind to the question to be decided could have arrived at it'.[20] There are, however, signs that a

12 See above, p 106.
13 See the *Winterwerp* case, above, at p 123.
14 A 46 para 58 (1981).
15 See Sharpe, *The Law of Habeas Corpus*, 2nd edn, 1989, p 159. English judges have preferred to leave the question of the mental state of an individual entirely to doctors.
16 *X v UK* A 46 para 58 (1981).
17 *Brogan v UK* A 145-B para 65 (1988). *Habeas corpus* was also held to be a sufficient remedy in an Article 5(1)(f) case since the applicant's claim that the length of the detention was excessive could have been considered: *No 9088/80*, 28 DR 160 (1982). But see *Caprino v UK No 6871/75*, 22 DR 5 at 13 (1980). In *McVeigh, O'Neill and Evans v UK Nos 8022/77, 8025/77 and 8027/77*, 25 DR 15 at 47 (1981), *habeas corpus* was a sufficient remedy in an Article 5(1)(b) case.
18 A 114 (1987). On discretionary life sentences, see above, p 152.
19 [1985] AC 374, HL. The other grounds were illegality and procedural impropriety.
20 A 114 para 69 (1987).

ground of 'proportionality' may emerge in English administrative law as a further ground of judicial review,[1] which would strengthen judicial review as a remedy in a case as the *Weeks* case.

Since Article 5(4) extends only to the 'lawfulness' of a person's detention consistently with Article 5(1), it does not require a remedy that allows a detained person to challenge the conditions in which he is held.[2] Thus there was no breach of Article 5(4) when a person detained at Broadmoor lacked a remedy by which he could claim that he should have been transferred to a hospital more appropriate to his improved condition.[3]

Article 5(4) may be complied with by the provision of two or more separate remedies that together allow the applicant to test all aspects of the legality of his detention.[4] It is also sufficient that a remedy exists; it does not matter that the applicant finds it inadvisable to use it in his particular circumstances.[5] In *Van Droogenbroeck v Belgium*,[6] the Court held that the availability and scope of the remedy or remedies must be ' sufficiently certain' in the minds of the detained person or his lawyer to ensure the 'accessibility and effectiveness' that an Article 5(4) remedy supposes. However, this requirement would not appear to be a strict one, at least as applied in *E v Norway*.[7] There a unanimous Court Chamber, disagreeing with a unanimous Commission, accepted as 'sufficiently certain' a judicial power to overturn a decision to detain and order a person's release based upon general principles of judicial review, not a specific statutory power, that had never been used in this way in any actual case.

v. Decision must be taken speedily

Article 5(4) requires that a decision be taken 'speedily'. For this purpose, time normally begins to run when Article 5(4) proceedings are instituted.[8] However, if a person has to exhaust an administrative remedy before having recourse to a 'court', the period of time to be considered runs from the time that the administrative authority is seized of the case.[9] Moreover, there may be a breach of Article 5(4) where a detained person simply has to wait for a period of time before a remedy is available. Thus where a soldier held on a charge of having committed a military penal offence could only appeal to a

1 See *R v Secretary of State for the Home Department, ex p Brind* [1991] 1 AC 696, HL.
2 Article 5(1) generally concerns the fact, but not the conditions, of detention: see above, p 124.
3 *Ashingdane v UK* A 93 para 52 (1985). Cf *Roux v UK No 12039/86*, 48 DR 263 (1986).
4 *Weeks v UK* A 114 para 69 (1987).
5 *Keus v Netherlands* A 185-C para 28 (1990).
6 A 50 para 54 (1982).
7 A 181-A para 60 (1990). Cf *Keus v Netherlands* A 185-C para 28 (1990), in which the Court, by 5 to 4, accepted as sufficient a remedy that the defendant government only discovered in time to plead before the Court (not the Commission). The test was applied more rigorously in the earlier *Van Droogenbroeck* case.
8 *Van Der Leer v Netherlands* A 170-A (1990).
9 *Sanchez-Reisse v Switzerland* A 107 para 54 (1986). There is no right of direct access to a 'court': id, para 45. See also *Ireland v UK* A 25 para 200 (1978).

military court six days after his detention had begun, there was a breach of Article 5(4), even allowing for the 'exigencies of military life and military justice'.[10] Likewise a remedy available to a mental patient before an English Mental Health Review Tribunal only after he had been recalled for six months was not a 'speedy' remedy.[11] It appears from the two cases establishing these last propositions that Article 5(4) contains two separate requirements: one by which a detained person must have access to a remedy immediately upon detention or 'speedily' thereafter and another by which a remedy, once availed of, must proceed 'speedily'.[12] An application for legal aid in connection with Article 5(4) must also be conducted 'speedily'.[13]

The relevant period ends when the final decision as to the detention of the applicant is made; surprisingly, it is not, in the case of a person whose detention is found to be illegal by the national court, the date of his release.[14] Where a state provides the possibility of an appeal, the time taken before the decision on appeal must be taken into account.[15] Where a decision is not delivered in public, the period ends when it is communicated to the detained person or his lawyer.[16]

When considering whether a decision has been taken 'speedily', the approach to be followed is similar to that when assessing whether the 'trial within a reasonable time' guarantees in Articles 5(3) and 6(1) are satisfied.[17] There is no absolute limit to the time that a decision may take. The matter is to be determined 'in the light of the circumstances of each case'.[18] Consideration must be given to the diligence of the national authorities and any delays brought about by the conduct of the detained person,[19] as well as any other factors causing delay that cannot engage the state's responsibility. Where the length of time appears *prima facie* 'incompatible with the notion of speediness', it is for the state to explain the reason for any apparent delay.[20] Delay because the responsible judge is on holiday is not a good explanation; the state must 'make the necessary administrative arrangements, even during a vacation, to ensure that urgent matters are

---

10 *De Jong, Baljet and Van Den Brink v Netherlands* A 77 para 58 (1984). Where a 'continuing remedy' is called for, it must be provided at 'reasonable intervals', as to which, see above, p 152.

11 *X v UK* B 41 para 138 (1980) Com Rep.

12 An alternative interpretation is that, as in the case where an administrative remedy has to be exhausted, the time before and after the remedy becomes available are treated as a whole when considering whether a decision is taken 'speedily'. The Commission's report in *X v UK* does not support such an interpretation.

13 *Zamir v UK No 9174/80*, 40 DR 42 (1983) (seven weeks to hear *habeas corpus* application a breach for this reason).

14 *Luberti v Italy* A 75 (1984) (eleven days' gap).

15 Ibid. See also *Letellier v France* A 207 (1991).

16 *Koendjbiharie v Netherlands* A 185-B para 28 (1990).

17 See above, p 143, and below, p 222.

18 *Sanchez-Reisse v Switzerland* A 107 para 55 (1986).

19 Eg a state will not be responsible for any delay resulting from a detained person's disappearance (*Luberti v Italy* A 75 (1984)) or delay in filing an appeal (*Navarra v France* A 273-B (1993)).

20 *Koendjbiharie v Netherlands* A 185-B paras 28-30 (1990).

dealt with speedily', given that the 'right to liberty' is at stake.[1] Nor is the fact that a judge has an excessive workload an excuse, a state being under a general obligation to organise its court system efficiently.[2] When determining whether the time taken to decide an application for release infringes Article 5(4), account may be taken of the fact that the detained person was under the applicable municipal law able to make other applications that were disposed of with reasonable expedition.[3] The fact that a decision is about to be reached on the applicant's extradition is not a good reason for postponing a decision on his continued detention.[4] In extradition cases, the same considerations that are relevant to 'requisite diligence' requirement of Article 5(1)(e)[5] may apply to the 'speedy' remedy requirement of Article 5(4).[6]

In terms of the lengths of time that have been ruled upon in actual cases, a delay of five-and-a-half months in an Article 5(1)(c) case was not acceptable.[7] A period of five days was permissible in another Article 5(1)(c) case.[8] In a case in which persons detained on suspicion of having committed terrorist offences under Article 5(1)(c) were released 44 hours before their applications for *habeas corpus* were determined, there was also no breach of the 'speedy' decision requirement.[9] Periods of up to five months to decide on detention of a minor under Article 5(1)(d) were too long[10] as was a delay of four months in the case of a 'person of unsound mind' under Article 5(1)(e).[11] Periods of 31 and 46 days taken to rule on the release of a person detained pending extradition under Article 5(1)(f) were also in breach of Article 5(4).[12] In contrast, sixteen days to decide on the continued long-term detention of an habitual offender under Article 5(1)(a) was considered 'speedy'.[13]

For persons arrested under Article 5(1)(c) on suspicion of having committed an offence, Article 5(4) applies concurrently with the requirement in Article 5(3) that they be brought 'promptly before a judge or other

1   *E v Norway* A 181-A para 66 (1990).
2   *Bezicheri v Italy* A 164 para 25 (1989). Cf *Sanchez-Reisse v Switzerland* A 107 (1986).
3   *Letellier v France* A 207 para 56 (1991).
4   *Sanchez-Reisse v Switzerland* A 107 (1986).
5   See above, p 128.
6   *Kolompar v Belgium* A 235-C para 46 (1992).
7   *Bezicheri v Italy* A 164 para 24 (1989). See, however, *Navarra v France* A 273-B para 29 (1993) (seven months not in breach on the facts: applicant's delay and possibility of other appeals).
8   *Egue v France No 11256/84*, 57 DR 47 at 70 (1988). As noted above, six days was too long in the *De Jong* military criminal proceedings case.
9   *Fox, Campbell and Hartley v UK* A 182 para 45 (1990).
10 *Bouamar v Belgium* A 129 para 63 (1988).
11 *Koendjbiahrie v Netherlands* A 185-B paras 28-30 (1990). See also *Luberti v Italy* A 75 (1984) (eighteen months too long). In *Boucheras and Groupe Information Asiles v France No 14438/88*, 69 DR 236 (1991), nearly three months was acceptable where the delay resulted partly from the applicant's own conduct.
12 A 107 para 57 (1986). Ten days were acceptable in an Article 5(1)(f) case in *A v Sweden No 11531/85*, 53 DR 128 (1987).
13 *Christinet v Switzerland No 7648/76*, 17 DR 35 (1979).

officer authorised by law to exercise judicial power'.[14] English law is consistent with both requirements in that an accused may challenge his detention by applying for *habeas corpus* in the High Court while in police custody and for bail when he is brought before a magistrate. The two guarantees in Article 5(3) and (4) may be compared in this context as follows. Whereas they may both call for remedies that may lead to the applicant's release (soon after arrest and at regular intervals thereafter),[15] the questions that may arise when considering the 'lawfulness' of the accused's detention under Article 5(4) are 'often of a more complex nature' than those that arise under Article 5(3), when the issue is solely whether there remain good grounds to refuse bail.[16] Possibly for this reason, the Court has stated that 'the notion of promptly (*aussitôt*) . . . indicates greater urgency than that of speedily (*à bref délai*).'[17] An important point of difference is that the procedural guarantees required by Article 5(3) are less rigorous than those in Article 5(4)[18]. However, where the procedures in fact followed under Article 5(3) meet the requirements of Article 5(4), the judicial control required by the latter is 'incorporated in' any confirmation of an accused's detention made by a 'judge or other officer' made under the former.[19]

6. ARTICLE 5(5): RIGHT TO COMPENSATION FOR ILLEGAL DETENTION

Article 5(5) provides that everyone 'who has been the victim of arrest or detention in contravention of the provisions of this article shall be entitled to an enforceable right to compensation'.

Article 5(5) is the only provision in the Convention that provides for a right to compensation at the national level for a breach of a particular Convention right.[20] There is, for example, no comparable Convention obligation to provide compensation under national law for torture in breach of Article 3.[1] The remedy that Article 5(5) requires is one before a court, leading to a legally binding award of compensation to a person who has

---

14 *De Jong, Baljet and Van Den Brink v Netherlands* A 77 para 57 (1984).
15 The obligation under Article 5(3) to consider the grounds for an accused person's continued detention at reasonable intervals follows from the requirement that he be released if there are no longer good reasons to detain him. As to the same requirement in Article 5(4), see *Bezicheri v Italy* A 164 (1989) (interval of one month acceptable).
16 *E v Norway* A 181 para 64 (1990).
17 Ibid. Note, however, that the times that have been permitted under each provision so far are of the same order, and that the word 'promptly' in Article 5(3) relates only to the time when the detained person must be brought before a judge – it does not allow for the extra time taken making a decision.
18 See above, pp 133 and 147.
19 *De Jong, Baljet and Van Den Brink v Netherlands* A 77 para 57 (1984).
20 Article 3 of the Seventh Protocol provides for compensation for miscarriages of justice, which may indirectly involve a breach of the Convention right to fair trial.
1 However, compensation may be called for under the general right to an effective remedy under Article 13.

been arrested or detained contrary to Article 5.[2] A remedy before some body other than a court (eg an ombudsman) or an *ex gratia* payment by the government is not sufficient. Although it 'may be broader in scope than mere financial compensation', compensation in the sense of Article 5(5) does not include the detained person's release, since this is provided for by Article 5(4).[3] In practice, it will normally be financial compensation. Article 5(5) does not prohibit a state from requiring proof of damage resulting from the breach of Article 5 before compensation is available. As the Court has stated, although a person may be a 'victim' of such a breach in the sense of Article 5(5) even though he has not suffered any damage thereby, 'there can be no question of 'compensation' where there is no pecuniary or non-pecuniary damage to compensate'.[4] As to the amount of compensation, it is likely that states are allowed a wide margin of appreciation.[5]

Article 5(5) requires a remedy only when the applicant has been arrested or detained in 'contravention' of Article 5, by which is meant any one or more of paragraphs (1) to (4).[6] A question which arises is *when* a 'contravention' of Article 5 must be established so as to bring Article 5(5) into play. Where an applicant alleges in his application a violation of Article 5(5) at the same time as he claims a breach of some other part of Article 5, the Strasbourg authorities will proceed to examine the Article 5(5) claim in the course of considering that application if they find that another paragraph of Article 5 has been infringed.[7] They will do so without requiring the applicant to go back and exhaust local remedies to see whether he could in fact obtain the compensation that Article 5(5) requires under municipal law.[8] Instead, a state will be found to comply with Article 5(5) if it can show 'with a sufficient degree of certainty' that a remedy of the kind required by Article 5(5) is available to the applicant.[9] In this connection, where the Convention has been incorporated into the law of the defendant state and it can be shown with 'sufficient . . . certainty' that Article 5(5) can be directly relied upon in the national courts as the basis for a claim to compensation, this will suffice.[10] In other cases, the remedy must be shown

2   *Brogan v UK* A 145-B para 67 (1988) and *Fox, Campbell and Hartley v UK* A 182 para 46 (1990). There is no jurisprudence indicating the meaning of 'court' in this context; for its meaning elsewhere in Article 5, see above, pp 111 and 146.
3   *Bozano v France No 9990/82*, 39 DR 119 at 144 (1984). The Commission did not give any indication of the other forms of 'compensation' that it had in mind.
4   *Wassink v Netherlands* A 185-A para 38 (1990). Non-pecuniary damage includes moral damage (pain, emotional distress, etc).
5   See Trechsel, *European System*, p 344.
6   See eg *Wassinck v Netherlands* A 185-A (1990).
7   *Ciulla v Italy* A 148 paras 43-45 (1989).
8   Note, however, the dissenting opinion in the *Ciulla* case of Judge Valticos, with whom three other judges agreed, to the effect that an issue can only arise under Article 5(5) after a final Strasbourg determination in an earlier application that a breach of some other part of Article 5 has occurred, following which the applicant has unsuccessfully sought compensation in the national courts.
9   *Ciulla v Italy* A 148 paras 43-45 (1989). As to when the remedy should be available, it suffices that the remedy exists 'either before or after the findings by the Court': *Brogan v UK* A 145-B para 67 (1988). Cf *Fox, Campbell and Hartley v UK* A 182 para 46 (1990).
10   *Ciulla v Italy* A 148 paras 43-45 (1989).

with sufficient certainty to exist under national law by some other means. Thus in a common law jurisdiction it might take the form of an action in tort for false imprisonment where the breach of Article 5 is because the detention is unlawful in English law.[11]

The Commission has adopted a different approach where an application claims a breach of Article 5(5) but does not at the same time allege that some other part of Article 5 has been violated. The Commission will consider such a claim only if a final decision on a previous application has been taken by the Strasbourg authorities to the effect that a breach of some part of Article 5(1)-(4) has occurred or if the national courts of the defendant state have already decided, either directly or indirectly, that some part of Article 5(1)-(4) has been infringed.[12] In the absence of such a decision, the Commission will declare the application inadmissible.[13] This makes sense since the Commission will, in such a case, not have received any pleadings going to the question of a breach of Article 5(1)-(4), when such a breach is a precondition of the application of Article 5(5). The Court has not had such a case to consider. In practice, a claim under Article 5(5) alone will be exceptional in the absence of a prior decision as to non-compliance with Article 5(1)-(4) at either the national or the Convention level.

A final question is the relationship between the rights to 'compensation' in Article 5(5) for a breach of Articles 5(1)-(4) and to 'just satisfaction' in Article 50 for a breach of the Convention, including any part of Article 5. If compensation for damage is not available nationally in respect of a breach of Article 5(1)-(4), so that Article 5(5) has been infringed, there is the possibility of compensation under Article 50 for that infringement.[14] So far, however, the Court has not found that compensation under Article 50 was appropriate in any case in which it has found a breach of Article 5(5). It must also be the case that the fact that it is possible to obtain 'compensation' in national law as required by Article 5(5) should not prejudice the award of 'just satisfaction' for a breach of any obligation in Article 5(1)-(4).

7. CONCLUSION

Article 5 has been the subject of a considerable amount of jurisprudence interpreting what is a confusing text. The understandable wish of some of

---

11 In *Brogan v UK* A 145-B para 67 (1988) neither false imprisonment nor any other remedy was available because the breach of Article 5(3) involved was not in breach of UK law.
12 *Eggs v Switzerland No 10313/83*, 39 DR 225 at 235 (1984). See also *Huber v Austria No 6821/74*, 6 DR 65 at 69 (1976). An indirect ruling would be one in which, for example, a UK court were to find that there was no 'reasonable grounds' to suspect that X was guilty of the offence for which he was arrested where this finding would also involve a breach of Article 5(1)(c).
13 *X v Austria No 7950/77*, 19 DR 213 (1980).
14 See *Brogan v UK* A 145-B para 67 (1988), where the Court stated that its finding of a breach of Article 5(5) because compensation was not available was 'without prejudice' to its competence under Article 50.

the drafting states to have express confirmation of all of the circumstances in which they might detain an individual, rather than just a general prohibition of 'arbitrary' detention,[15] has caused predictable problems. Whereas the list in Article 5(1) offers some degree of certainty, its wording does not easily accommodate all of the recognised cases of arrest and is curiously old-fashioned in other respects. However, Article 5(1)(b) has been interpreted in the *McVeigh, O'Neill and Evans* case so as to allow short-term detention for such purposes as stopping and searching on the street that do not fit easily into the text of Article 5(1) and the *Winterwerp* and other cases have introduced some controls as to proportionality that can be applied to the detention of drug addicts, etc under Article 5(1)(d).

A separate problem has been that Articles 5(1)(c) and (3) are imperfectly drafted. In practice, they have been interpreted constructively so that Article 5(1)(c) is understood in a way that properly reflects the criminal process and Article 5(3) incorporates a right to bail. Quite apart from their drafting, these two provisions are also difficult to apply uniformly to the different civil and common law systems represented among the contracting parties. Much of the jurisprudence that has emerged in criminal cases is a response to the particular features of the common law[16] or, more usually, civil law system[17] concerned. If the aim of the Court has properly been to emphasise substance rather than form, the result can sometimes be a rule that does not always apply easily to all kinds of legal system.[18] In the context of criminal justice, the Commission and the Court have also had to consider under Article 5 – as under Article 6 – the speed with which the authorities should act. The standards that they have applied when determining under Article 5(3) whether an arrested person has been brought 'promptly' before a court[19] or has been tried within a 'reasonable time'[20] are not as strict as they might be.

On a more positive note, the requirement in Article 5(1) that detention be 'lawful' has been interpreted in an imaginative way that is in harmony with the reading of similar wording elsewhere in the Convention. In particular, the inclusion within it of a requirement that detention must not be 'arbitrary' is important. For example, it provided a basis for findings of breaches of Article 5 by reference to the purpose for which an individual was detained in the *Bozano* and *Bouamar* cases concerning the improper use of powers of deportation and short-term detention of juveniles respectively. Article 5(1) has also provided a mechanism for the setting of detailed and rigorous procedural standards concerning the detention of the mentally

---

15 Contrast Article 9(1), ICCPR, which simply prohibits 'arbitrary arrest or detention', leaving this phrase to be interpreted.

16 See the *Monnell and Morris* case, above, p 109.

17 See eg the *Schiesser* and *Huber* cases, above, p 133.

18 See eg the Court's interpretation of the relationship between Articles 5(1)(a) and (3) in the *Wemhoff* case, above, p 138.

19 See above, p 135.

20 See *W v Switzerland*, above, p 144.

disordered. Of more general importance has been the interpretation of Article 5(4) in such a way as to impose a demanding obligation upon states to provide a judicial remedy by which an individual may challenge the legality of his detention. One striking result of this has been that United Kingdom procedures concerning the release of mental patients and persons given discretionary life sentences have been revised following Strasbourg cases so as shift the decision-making power from the Home Secretary to a 'court' in several respects.

A number of cases concerning Northern Ireland have presented the Strasbourg authorities with difficult questions concerning the application of Article 5 to emergency situations. It is arguable that the remedy within the Convention system for a state faced with the very real problems posed by a terrorist threat is to derogate under Article 15 from its Convention obligations, rather than to argue that Article 5 be tempered to meet its needs. However, the Court has been prepared to make some allowance for the Northern Ireland situation in cases that have reached it under Article 5. If such an approach is to be followed, it is better for the rule that emerges to be expressly limited to the terrorist situation,[1] rather than be to stated in unqualified terms that might be applied to non-emergency situations also.[2] Terrorist cases should not be allowed to reduce minimum Convention standards of general application.

1 See the *Brogan* judgment, above, p 134.
2 This was not done in the *Fox, Campbell and Hartley* case, above, p 129, on the Article 5(2) point.

CHAPTER 6
Article 6: The right to a fair trial[1]

'**Article 6**

1. In the determination of his civil rights and obligations or of any
    criminal charge against him, everyone is entitled to a fair and
    public hearing within a reasonable time by an independent and
    impartial tribunal established by law. Judgment shall be
    pronounced publicly but the press and public may be excluded
    from all or part of the trial in the interest of morals, public order or
    national security in a democratic society, where the interests of
    juveniles or the protection of the private life of the parties so
    require, or to the extent strictly necessary in the opinion of the
    court in special circumstances where publicity would prejudice the
    interests of justice.
2. Everyone charged with a criminal offence shall be presumed
    innocent until proved guilty according to law.
3. Everyone charged with a criminal offence has the following
    minimum rights:
    (a) to be informed promptly, in a language which he understands
         and in detail, of the nature and cause of the accusation against
         him;
    (b) to have adequate time and facilities for the preparation of his
         defence;
    (c) to defend himself in person or through legal assistance of his
         own choosing or, if he has not sufficient means to pay for legal
         assistance, to be given it free when the interests of justice so
         require;
    (d) to examine or have examined witnesses against him and to
         obtain the attendance and examination of witnesses on his
         behalf under the same conditions as witnesses against him;

---

1   On Article 6, see Grotian, *Article 6 of the European Convention on Human Rights: The Right
    to a Fair Trial*, Council of Europe Human Rights File No 13, 1993. On Article 6 in criminal
    cases, see Poncet, *La protection de l'accuse sur la Convention européenne des droits de
    l'homme*, 1977; and Stavros, *The Guarantees for Accused Persons under Article 6 of the
    European Convention on Human Rights*, 1993 (hereafter Stavros). On the right to a fair trial
    generally, see Fawcett, in Andrews, ed, *Human Rights in Criminal Procedure: A Comparative
    Study*, 1982, Ch 2.

> (e) to have the free assistance of an interpreter if he cannot understand or speak the language used in court.'

1. ARTICLE 6: GENERALLY

The right to a fair trial has a position of pre-eminence in the Convention, both because of the importance of the right involved and the great volume of applications and jurisprudence that it has attracted. As to the former, the Court has more than once referred to 'the prominent place which the right to a fair trial holds in a democratic society within the meaning of the Convention',[2] a consequence of which is that 'there can be no justification for interpreting Article 6(1) of the Convention restrictively'.[3] As to the latter, more applications to Strasbourg concern Article 6 than any other provision. The cases concern mostly criminal and civil litigation before the ordinary courts, both at the trial court and appellate levels. They also involve, to an extent that could not have been predicted, proceedings before disciplinary and administrative tribunals and administrative decisions on an individual's rights and obligations.

The application of Article 6 has presented the Strasbourg authorities with various problems. A delicate question is the closeness with which they should monitor the functioning of national courts. In practice, the Strasbourg authorities have meticulously and properly followed the *'quatrième instance'* doctrine,[4] not questioning the merits of decisions on the facts taken at the national level. They also allow states a wide margin of appreciation as to the manner of their operation, for example in the rules of evidence that they use. A consequence of this last point is that in certain contexts the provisions of Article 6 are as much obligations of result as of conduct, with national courts being allowed to follow whatever particular rules they choose so long as the end result can be seen to be a fair trial.

In criminal cases, the interpretation of Article 6 is complicated by the basic differences that exist between the common law and civil law systems of criminal justice.[5] The adversarial and inquisitorial systems that these respectively entail and the dissimilar methods of investigating crime that they use necessarily makes for difficulties in the interpretation of a text that provides a framework for legal proceedings throughout Europe. It has not proved easy to meet the needs and circumstances of very different legal systems and still set appropriately high standards for a human rights guarantee of a fair trial.

---

2 *De Cubber v Belgium* A 86 para 30 (1984).
3 *Moreira de Azevedo v Portugal* A 189 para 66 (1990). Cf *Delcourt v Belgium* A 11 para 25 (1970). These statements can be taken to apply to Article 6 as a whole, not just Article 6(1).
4 As to this doctrine, see above, p 15.
5 See Crombag, in de Witte and Forder, eds, *The Common Law of Europe and the Future of Legal Education*, 1992, p 397.

In this connection, it may be helpful by way of introduction to outline very briefly the essential differences between the common and civil law systems for the investigation of crime. In common law jurisdictions, as exemplified by English and Irish law, the investigation of a criminal offence is conducted entirely by the police[6]. In the typical civil law jurisdiction,[7] the case is first investigated by the police, but then, when attention has focused on a particular suspect, handed over to an investigating judge, public prosecutor or other officer who questions the suspect and other witnesses, going over to some extent the ground already covered by the police. The accused person is often detained during this preliminary investigation, which can be a very lengthy process. When it is complete, the investigating judge will decide whether a prosecution should be brought.[8] A merit of the civil law approach is that the investigating judge is independent of the police and hence brings a fresh mind to the case. A disadvantage is that the investigation, during which an accused may spend several years in detention, tends to take longer than the investigation just by the police in a common law system.

Another problem has resulted from the application of Article 6 to administrative justice. If the Commission and the Court have commendably acted to fill a gap by reading Article 6 as requiring that administrative decisions that determine an individual's right, for example, to practise as a doctor or to use his land, are subject to Article 6, they have yet to establish a coherent jurisprudence spelling out the nature of the resulting obligations for states.

The above problems have been compounded in civil as well as criminal cases by the need to apply a text that was designed as a template for trial courts of the classical kind both to appellate courts and to disciplinary and other special courts, where the same procedural guarantees may not have such full application.[9]

Finally, it is relevant to note that in some contexts a breach of Article 6 will only be found to have occurred in criminal cases upon proof of 'actual prejudice' to the defence. This is the case in the application of the residual fair hearing guarantee in Article 6(1),[10] and is true of some Article 6(3)

---

6   As to the position in Scotland, see Kilbrandon, in Coutts, ed, *The Accused: A Comparative Study*, 1966, Ch 4. Some non-common law jurisdictions adopt the same system: see *Hauschildt v Denmark*, below, p 236. On English criminal procedure in the light of the Convention, see Leigh, 3 RSCDPC 453 (1988).

7   As to the position in France and Germany, see Vouin and Jescheck, in Coutts, id, Chs 15 and 18. See also Chatel (Belgium), Tsoureli (Greece), and Madlener (Germany) in Andrews, loc cit at n 1, above, Chs 8-10. See generally, Van den Wyngaert, ed, *Criminal Procedure Systems in the European Community*, 1993.

8   In England and Wales, this decision is normally taken by the Crown Prosecution Service on the basis of the case prepared by the police; the Service does not conduct its own investigation.

9   See Stavros, p 328. In *Nortier v Netherlands* A 267 para 38 (1993), the Court left open the question whether Article 6 applied to juvenile criminal proceedings in the same way as it applied to adult cases.

10 See below, p 203.

guarantees. That an 'actual prejudice' requirement has sometimes been applied in this way is explained by Stavros[11] as follows:

'. . . a detailed examination of the case-law does demonstrate that the Convention organs have often relied on the link between the fairness of the hearing and the more specific rights of Article 6 to require proof of actual prejudice before concluding on a violation in respect of the latter. This tendency has manifested itself in the context of Article 6(3)(a), (b) and (d) and sometimes in the context of the right to an impartial tribunal. This is not, however, always the case. The Convention organs appear to regard the presence of actual prejudice inherent in the failure to observe other guarantees,[12] pronouncing automatically the breach of the Convention.'

2. FIELD OF APPLICATION

i.   In the determination of a criminal charge

The rights guaranteed by Article 6(1) apply, firstly, when a 'criminal charge' is being determined. 'Criminal' has an autonomous Convention meaning.[13] Otherwise, if the classification of an offence in the law of the defendant state were regarded as decisive, a state would be free to avoid the Convention obligation to ensure a fair trial (as well as the guarantee against retroactive offences in Article 7) in its discretion. It would also result in an unacceptably uneven application of the Convention from one state to another. Article 6(1) applies only when the applicant is charged with an offence,[14] it does not extend to cases in which he brings a private prosecution in the enforcement of the criminal law.[15] Nor does Article 6(1) apply just because the applicant's property is affected by a criminal charge against a third party.[16] It also does not apply to proceedings that may result in the applicant being placed under police supervision with a view to the prevention of crime.[17]

---

11 Stavros, p 44. Footnotes omitted.
12 Ed. The author refers to the *Artico* and *Luedicke* cases, below, pp 264 and 270, concerning Articles 6(3)(c) and (e) respectively. The same must be true of the Article 6(1) guarantees of trial within a reasonable time and a public hearing in view of the purposes they serve. The requirement of 'actual prejudice' is most vividly illustrated by the ruling that an accused who is acquitted is no longer a 'victim' and so cannot complain of a breach of Article 6: *Stromillo v Italy No 15831/89*, 69 DR 317 (1991).
13 *Engel v Netherlands* A 22 (1976).
14 Article 6 does not apply to committal proceedings against a person charged with a criminal offence: *Mosbeux v Belgium No 17083/90*, 71 DR 269 (1990).
15 *Helmers v Sweden* A 212-A (1991).
16 *AGOSI v UK* A 108 (1986).
17 *Guzzardi v Italy* A 39 para 108 (1980) and *Raimondo v Italy* A 281-A (1994). Proceedings for confiscation of property to prevent its illegal use are likewise not 'criminal' (*M v Italy No 12386/86*, 70 DR 59 (1991)), although they may concern 'civil rights': see the *Raimondo* case, above.

Finally, Article 6 does not apply to extradition proceedings.[18] However in *Soering v UK*,[19] the Court did not exclude the possibility that 'an issue might exceptionally be raised under Article 6 by an extradition decision in circumstances where the fugitive has suffered or risks suffering a flagrant denial of a fair trial in the requesting state'. Thus, applying its reasoning concerning Article 3 by analogy,[20] the Court left open the possibility that where a person is extradited to another state, the sending state may be liable for a 'flagrant denial of a fair trial' by the requesting state.

a. *The meaning of 'criminal'*

When deciding whether an offence with which an individual is charged is criminal in the sense of Article 6(1), three criteria apply: the classification of the offence in the law of the defendant state; the nature of the offence; and the degree of severity of the possible punishment.[1] The first is crucial in that if the applicable national law classifies an offence as criminal,[2] it is automatically such for the purposes of Article 6 too. This is because the legal and social consequences of having a criminal conviction make it imperative that the accused has a fair trial. In cases in which the offence is not classified as criminal in national law, the other two criteria listed above – the nature of the offence and the possible punishment – come into play. In practice, this 'one-way' autonomous meaning of 'criminal' in Article 6(1) has been important in cases of offences characterised as disciplinary or regulatory or that are otherwise analogous to criminal offences without being classified as such in municipal law.

The idea of an autonomous concept was introduced in *Engel v Netherlands*[3] in the context of military disciplinary proceedings.[4] Elaborating upon the meaning of the second and third criteria referred to above, the Court stated that, in terms of its nature, an offence that concerned only the internal regulation of the armed forces was in principle disciplinary. With regard to the possible punishment, where it was the deprivation of liberty, an offence belonged to the criminal sphere unless the 'nature, duration or manner of execution of the imprisonment' was not such that its effect could be 'appreciably detrimental'.[5] The Court then found that disciplinary offences involving the publication of a periodical tending to undermine army discipline and the driving of a jeep irresponsibly that could each lead

---

18 *Farmakopoulos v Greece No 11683/85*, 64 DR 52 (1990).
19 A 161 para 113 (1989). The allegation concerning legal aid did not raise a 'flagrant denial' issue on the facts. The same 'flagrant denial' of Article 6 standard was used in the *Drozd and Janousek* case, above, p 111.
20 See above, p 75.
1 *Engel v Netherlands* A 22 (1976).
2 In French law customs offences are a special branch of criminal law and within Article 6 as criminal under national law: *Funke v France* A 256-A (1993).
3 A 22 (1976).
4 On disciplinary offences and Article 6, see Kidd, 36 ICLQ 856 (1987).
5 A 22 para 82 (1976).

to several months' imprisonment were criminal for the purposes of Article 6(1). In contrast, offences of being absent without leave that carried possible penalties of just two or three weeks imprisonment were not.[6]

The *Engel* case was applied to prison disciplinary proceedings in *Campbell and Fell v UK*.[7] There offences of mutiny, incitement to mutiny and gross personal violence to a prison officer were regarded, in terms of their nature, as offences involving generally anti-social conduct that made them not 'purely disciplinary'.[8] As to the possible punishment, the Court held that the loss by a prisoner of the remission of a part of his sentence could be regarded as imprisonment. Although not a deprivation of liberty in law (because in English law remission was a privilege, not a right), in practice remission was invariably allowed unless forfeiture had been imposed in disciplinary proceedings, so that it was tantamount to imprisonment.[9] The Court then held that a possible punishment of nearly three years' loss of remission (and an actual loss of over 18 months' remission),[10] together with the criminal 'colouring' of the offences themselves meant that they were criminal, so that Article 6 applied.[11]

Given the particular importance attached by the Court in the *Engel* and *Campbell and Fell* cases to the fact that the possible penalty was imprisonment, it would be possible to conclude that only military and prison disciplinary offences would qualify as criminal for the purpose of Article 6. Disciplinary proceedings in the medical and other liberal professions and in the police and the civil service are unlikely to carry a possible penalty of imprisonment. They may be subject to Article 6 in some cases on the basis that 'civil rights and obligations' are being determined.[12]

---

6 Cf *Eggs v Switzerland No 7341/76*, 15 DR 35 (1978) Com Rep; CM Res DH (79) 7 (five days' solitary confinement for military offence of disobeying orders insufficient).

7 A 80 (1984).

8 Id, para 71. These offences were abolished in English law in 1989.

9 Contrast *Kiss v UK No 6224/73*, 7 DR 55 (1976) where the Commission had earlier considered that loss of remission was not imprisonment because remission was not a 'right'.

10 The Court has sometimes looked to see what penalty was imposed. Most of its pronouncements, however, have, correctly, considered what the possible penalty was.

11 See also *Delazarus v UK No 17525/90* (1993), unreported (Article 6 applied where a prisoner risked a 'substantial loss' of remission). Under present English law, the disciplinary role of Boards of Visitors has been abolished. Criminal offences may be referred to the ordinary criminal courts. Prison governors may hear less serious cases and are competent to impose sentences of up to 42 additional days (the term 'remission' is no longer used). It is unlikely that this would be a sufficient possible penalty to bring a case within Article 6. In *Pelle v France No 11691/85*, 50 DR 263 (1986), the risk of 18 days' loss of remission for threatening to kill a warder was insufficient.

12 As eg in *Albert and Le Compte v Belgium* A 58 (1983), in which claims by doctors concerning professional disciplinary proceedings in which the applicants were at risk of being struck off the roll or suspended from practice were treated as being within Article 6 as concerning 'civil rights and obligations': see further, below, p 192. Whereas in that case the Court left open the question whether there was a 'criminal' offence, the Commission, applying the *Engel* requirement of imprisonment, held that there was not. The Court did hold that the two limbs of Article 6(1) were not mutually exclusive. See also *McFeeley v UK No 8317/78*, 20 DR 44 (1980) and *Ginikanwa v UK No 12502/86*, 55 DR 251 (1988).

Insofar as they are not, as generally in the case of persons employed by the state,[13] there would be an unfortunate gap in the protection of the right to a fair trial in the Convention since the penalties that may be imposed (dismissal,[14] transfer[15] or the loss of pension rights[16]) may have serious consequences for the person concerned. Moreover, a restriction in military and prison disciplinary proceedings to cases that may lead to imprisonment would constitute an unsatisfactory limitation upon the due process requirements of the Convention since penalties such as the loss of privileges or, in the case of prisoners, cellular confinement may be regarded as having severe consequences also.[17] It may be, however, that the Court's later jurisprudence (see the *Weber* and *De Demicoli* cases, below), which stress the importance generally of what is 'at stake' for the applicant may lead to a different conclusion.

Apart from disciplinary offences, the autonomous concept of a 'criminal' offence in Article 6 has, since the *Engel* case, been used to apply the fair trial guarantee in Article 6(1) to regulatory and certain other offences that, although not classified as criminal in national law, have criminal law characteristics. The leading case on regulatory offences is *Öztürk v FRG*.[18] There the Court held that an offence of careless driving, which was classified as regulatory, not criminal, under German law, was none the less 'criminal' for the purpose of Article 6. Despite the decriminalising steps that had been taken when such road traffic offences ceased to be criminal in Germany,[19] the offence retained characteristics that were the hallmark of a criminal offence: it was of general application (ie applicable to the public at large or a section of it – road users – and not just to members of a particular group) and carried with it a sanction – a fine – of a punitive and deterrent kind.[20] It was also relevant that although some Western European states had taken steps to decriminalise road traffic offences (to which the Court was not opposed provided that Article 6 was complied with), the great majority of

13 See below, p 182.
14 See *X v UK No 8496/79*, 21 DR 168 (1980) (policeman) and *Dimitriadis v Greece No 13877/ 88*, 65 DR 279 (1990). In both cases, the Commission found Article 6(1) inapplicable.
15 *Saraiva de Carvalho v Portugal No 9208/80*, 26 DR 262 (1981) (soldier transferred to the reserve: Article 6 inapplicable).
16 See *Kremzow v Austria No 16417/90*, 67 DR 307 (1990). In this case, Article 6 did not apply to proceedings in which a tribunal merely imposed a disciplinary sanction on the basis of a criminal court conviction without considering the merits.
17 In the *Campbell and Fell* case, the Court found it unnecessary to decide whether other possible punishments, including loss of privileges and cellular confinement, at least in the context of offences that were to some extent criminal in nature, might be sufficient to render an offence 'criminal'.
18 A 73 (1984). See also *Duhs v Sweden No 12995/87*, 67 DR 204 (1990) (de-criminalised car parking fines: question whether 'criminal' left open).
19 As well as allowing an official rather than a court to convict, West German law provided that the conviction should not be entered on the judicial criminal record and that the convicted person should not be liable to imprisonment for failure to pay the fine unless it could be shown that he had the means to do so.
20 Cf *X v Austria No 8998/80*, 32 DR 150 (1983) (administrative offence limiting the hours of work of young persons was 'criminal').

Convention parties continued to treat minor road traffic offences as criminal. In contrast with the position of disciplinary offences, the Court was not concerned by the 'relative lack of seriousness of the penalty at stake' (a modest fine as opposed to imprisonment) because the second element of the *Engel* test was very clearly satisfied.

Other offences that have been regarded as 'criminal' in the sense of Article 6 and that may, more or less convincingly, be placed within the category of regulatory offences are those under price-fixing regulations,[1] rules of competition in tendering for contracts,[2] police regulations forbidding public demonstrations[3] and a customs code.[4] In an important decision, in *Bendenoun v France*,[5] the Court ruled that offences imposing large financial penalties for tax evasion were 'criminal' in the sense of Article 6. In terms of the *Engel* criteria, they applied to all citizens as taxpayers and carried serious penalties, including the possibility of imprisonment for non-payment, that were intended to punish.

The Court has also applied the *Engel* criteria to offences relating to the administration of justice and parliamentary privilege so as to find them subject to Article 6 in some cases. In *Weber v Switzerland*,[6] the applicant had lodged a complaint initiating criminal proceedings against another person. He was convicted under Swiss law of the offence of revealing information in breach of confidence about the conduct of the judicial investigation resulting from his complaint. Although the offence was not classified as a criminal offence in Swiss law, it was held to fall within Article 6 because it applied to the whole population and carried an appropriate sanction of a fine or possible imprisonment.[7] In contrast, in *Ravnsborg v Sweden*[8] it was held that offences of disturbing the good order of court proceedings, whose criminal or non-criminal law character in national law was unclear, were not criminal under Article 6. The control of improper oral or written remarks was essentially an internal matter of discipline by a court to ensure its functioning and, in the case in question, the possible penalty was a modest fine, although it could be converted into a prison sentence of up to three months for failure to pay. In *Demicoli v Malta*,[9] the applicant, a journalist,

---

1 *Deweer v Belgium* A 35 (1980).
2 *Société Stenuit v France* A 232-A (1992) Com Rep. Applicant withdrew case before Court. In EEC law competition proceedings are classified as administrative, not criminal: see eg Regulation 17/62, Article 15(4). In *Al Jubail v Council* Case C-49/88 [1991] ECR I-3187 the ECJ recognised a duty to harmonise the EEC and ECHR notions of a fair trial.
3 *Belilos v Switzerland* A 132 (1988).
4 *Salabiaku v France* A 141-A (1988).
5 A 284 (1994). As to whether decisions on tax matters concern 'civil rights and obligations', see below, p 183.
6 A 177 (1990). See also *Les Travaux du Midi v FRG No 12275/86*, 70 DR 47 (1991) (fine for non-meritorious appeal: question whether Article 6 applied left open).
7 Imprisonment was possible if the fine was not paid. The case would have been one of criminal contempt in English law.
8 A 283-B (1994). See also *K v Austria* A 255-B (1993) Com Rep, F Sett before court (fine for refusal to give evidence not within Article 6). In English law, criminal contempt of court is a criminal offence and so would fall within Article 6 under the first *Engel* criterion.
9 A 210 (1991).

was convicted by the Maltese House of Representatives of breach of parliamentary privilege for publishing an article ridiculing two Members of Parliament. Whereas breach of parliamentary privilege was not a crime in Maltese law, it applied, like the offence in the *Weber* case, to the whole population and was enforced with a fine or imprisonment. In both of these cases, the European Court drew a distinction between the offences as they applied to members of the legal profession and Members of Parliament respectively and as they applied to members of the public. As far as the former situation was concerned, the offences could be seen as disciplinary offences and might come within Article 6 only in so far as it applied to such offences in accordance with *Engel*. In both cases also, the Court insisted that the possible penalty that was 'at stake' for the applicant was 'sufficiently important to warrant classifying the offence . . . as a criminal one'.[10]

In various contexts, a licence may be withdrawn by the competent authorities for failure to comply with its conditions without there being any regulatory or other offence with which the licence holder is charged. Although the sanction is a severe one, the revocation of a licence in these circumstances is not the determination of a 'criminal charge'.[11]

b.   *The meaning of 'charge'*

For Article 6(1) to apply, a person must be subject to a 'charge'. The point at which this begins to be the case has been developed mostly in connection with the 'trial within a reasonable time' guarantee, for which it will always need to be established.[12] Even so the precise date on which Article 6 begins to apply, whether for the 'reasonable time' guarantee or otherwise, will not be very significant if the possible dates that may be chosen involve a difference of only a few days.

Like the word 'criminal', 'charge' has an autonomous Convention meaning.[13] It is 'the official notification given to an individual by the competent authority of an allegation that he has committed a criminal offence' or some other act which carries 'the implication of such an allegation and which likewise substantially affects the situation of the suspect'.[14] 'Charge', however, is to be given a 'substantive', not a 'formal', meaning, so that it is necessary 'to look behind the appearances and investigate the realities of the procedure in question'.[15] When doing so, the test is whether the applicant is 'substantially affected' by the steps taken against him.[16] In practice, a person has been found to be subject to a

10 *Weber v Switzerland* A 177 para 34 (1990) and *Demicoli v Malta* A 210 para 34 (1991).
11 *Tre Traktörer Aktiebolag v Sweden* A 159 (1989) (revocation of a liquor licence). But it may be the determination of 'civil rights and obligations': ibid.
12 It also has relevance for the right of access to a criminal court: see *Deweer v Belgium* A 35 (1980).
13 *Deweer v Belgium* A 35 para 42 (1980).
14 *Corigliano v Italy* A 57 para 34 (1982).
15 *Deweer v Belgium* A 35 para 44 (1980).
16 The 'substantially affected' test, which was first adopted by the Commission, was incorporated into the Court's jurisprudence in *Deweer v Belgium* A 35 para 46 (1980).

'charge' when arrested for a criminal offence;[17] when officially informed of the prosecution against him;[18] when, in a civil law system, a preliminary investigation has been opened in his case and, although not under arrest, the applicant has 'officially learnt of the investigation or begun to be affected by it';[19] when authorities investigating customs offences require a person to produce evidence and freeze his bank account;[20] when his shop has been closed pending the payment of a sum by way of friendly settlement or the outcome of criminal proceedings that would be instituted if the sum were not paid;[1] and when the applicant has appointed a defence lawyer after the opening of a file by the public prosecutor's office following a police report against him.[2] In the case of an MP with parliamentary immunity, the relevant date was that on which the prosecuting authorities requested Parliament to lift the immunity.[3]

Most of the case-law on the meaning of 'charge' has concerned civil law systems of criminal justice. With regard to English law, applicants have been held to be subject to a 'charge' when they have been arrested[4] or charged by the police.[5] Presumably, the issuing of a summons would be sufficient. In one case,[6] an applicant already serving a prison sentence for one offence was found to be subject to a 'charge' in respect of a second offence from the time of his first conviction because from that moment, as the applicant was aware, 'immediate consideration' was being given to the possibility of further charges against him. From that moment onwards the uncertainty and anxiety that the applicant felt about his future and the need for him to prepare his defence meant that he was 'substantially affected'. This raises the question whether a person other than a prisoner is 'substantially affected' while the police are questioning or otherwise investigating him as a suspect but before he is arrested or charged. An answer in the affirmative would be consistent with the 'substantive', rather than 'formal', meaning of 'charge' that the Court has adopted. It would mean, however, that the point at which

---

17 *Wemhoff v FRG* A 7 (1968). In *Foti v Italy* A 56 (1982) the date on which two of the applicants were formally charged was chosen, not that of their arrest two or three days earlier. Yet a person must be 'substantially affected' from the time of his arrest. In *Boddaert v Belgium* A 235-D para 10 (1992), the date that the arrest warrant was issued was chosen, not the later date when the applicant surrendered to the authorities.

18 *Neumeister v Austria* A 8 p 41 para 18 (1968).

19 *Eckle v FRG* A 51 para 74 (1982). In accordance with the 'substantially affected' test, it is the date of notification or of otherwise first being affected by the investigation that is crucial, not the date on which the decision to open the investigation is taken: *Corigliano v Italy* A 57 (1982) (in that case there was a gap of several months between the two).

20 *Funke v France* A 256 A (1993).

1 *Deweer v Belgium* A 35 (1980).

2 *Angelucci v Italy* A 196-C para 13 (1991) (preliminary investigation not commenced until later). See also *P v Austria No 13017/87*, 71 DR 52 (1989) Com Rep; CM Res DH 91 (33) (Article 6 applied as of the request for inquiries against the applicant, not when the investigation opened later).

3 *Frau v Italy* A 195-E para 14 (1991).

4 *X v UK No 8233/78*, 17 DR 122 (1979).

5 *X v Ireland No 9429/81*, 32 DR 225 (1983) and *Ewing v UK No 11224/84*, 10 EHRR 141 (1986).

6 *X v UK No 6728/74*, 14 DR 26 (1978).

Article 6 began to apply in common law systems (as is sometimes already the case in civil law systems) would become a very uncertain one since there would be no formal occurrence that would clearly signify it.

Article 6 continues to apply until the 'charge' against the applicant is finally determined. It covers 'the whole of the proceedings in issue, including appeal proceedings'.[7] Although the Convention does not guarantee a right of appeal, Article 6 applies to any appeal proceedings that are in fact provided.[8] Applications for leave to appeal are also subject to it.[9] Article 6 governs appeals on the law or the facts[10] and appeals against conviction or sentence. It also applies to any separate sentencing hearing by a trial or appeal court that follows an appeal.[11] Constitutional court proceedings involving claims alleging a violation of constitutional rights are included insofar as they are decisive for the outcome of the criminal case.[12] If criminal proceedings are discontinued without the applicant being brought to trial, Article 6 ceases to apply as of the date of their discontinuance.[13]

Article 6 does not apply to proceedings that concern a person who is already convicted of an offence, and hence is no longer 'charged' with it, or that are otherwise not determinative of the 'charge'. Thus Article 6 does not apply on a 'criminal charge' basis[14] to proceedings concerning the appointment of a legal aid lawyer,[15] the assessment of costs in criminal cases,[16] the revocation of a suspended sentence,[17] an application for clemency[18] or conditional release,[19] the classification of a prisoner,[20] payment for prison work[1] or the inscription of an offence on a person's record.[2] Nor does Article 6 guarantee a convicted person a right to a re-trial.[3]

---

7 *Eckle v FRG* A 51 para 76 (1982).
8 See further, below, p 240. A reference of a case to the Court of Appeal by the Home Secretary under the Criminal Appeal Act 1968, s 17 is an appeal subject to Article 6: *Callaghan v UK No 14739/89*, 60 DR 296 (1989).
9 *Monnell and Morris v UK* A 115 (1987).
10 *Delcourt v Belgium* A 11 (1970).
11 *Eckle v FRG* A 65 (1983) and *Ringeisen v Austria* A 13 (1971).
12 This has been established in civil rights and obligations cases: see below, p 190, and must be true of criminal cases also.
13 *Eckle v FRG* A 51 para 78 (1982); *Orchin v UK No 8435/78*, 6 EHRR 391 (1983) (proceedings terminated by *nolle prosequi*). Although charges are left on file, Article 6 ceases to apply if the prosecution undertakes not to proceed with them (*X v UK No 8233/78*, 17 DR 122 (1979)) or it is the established practice not to do so (*X v UK No 3034/67*, 25 CD 76 (1967); *X v UK No 9550/81*, 5 EHRR 508 (1983)).
14 Nor does it apply on a 'civil rights and obligations' basis: see below, p 183.
15 *X v UK No 8715/79*, 5 EHRR 273 (1982).
16 *X v FRG No 4438/70*, 39 CD 20 (1971).
17 *X v FRG No 2428/65*, 25 CD 1 (1967).
18 *X v Austria No 1127/61*, 8 CD 9 (1961).
19 See eg *X v Austria No 1760/63*, 9 YB 166 (1966) and *Aldrian v Austria No 16266/90*, 65 DR 337 (1990).
20 *X v UK No 8575/79*, 20 DR 202 (1979) (Category A classification).
1 *Detained Persons v FRG No 3134/67*, 11 YB 528 (1968).
2 *X v FRG No 448/59*, 3 YB 254 (1960).
3 *Callaghan v UK No 14739/89*, 60 DR 296 (1989).

ii.   In the determination of civil rights and obligations[4]

a.   *The meaning of 'civil rights and obligations'*

Some of the more perplexing problems in the interpretation of the Convention concern the application of Article 6(1) to non-criminal cases. According to its text, Article 6(1) applies 'in the determination' of an individual's 'civil rights and obligations'. In their early jurisprudence, the Strasbourg authorities established that the phrase 'civil rights and obligations' incorporated, by the use of the word 'civil', the distinction between private and public law, with civil rights and obligations being rights and obligations in private law.[5] This distinction has long been significant in civil law systems for jurisdictional and other purposes[6] and has recently become important in United Kingdom administrative law.[7] On the basis of it, rights and obligations in public law (eg concerning nationality or the right to vote) are not 'civil' rights and obligations, so that Article 6 does not apply to their determination. Criminal law is in a special position. Decisions taken in the 'determination of . . . any criminal charge' are included by a separate part of the wording of Article 6(1).[8] Ancillary decisions relating to criminal proceedings not within this wording[9] are not otherwise subject to Article 6 as decisions determinative of civil rights and obligations. They are excluded both because of the distinction between private and public law and also, as the Court has preferred to emphasise, because if certain decisions in criminal proceedings are specifically covered by Article 6(1), others, by inference, are not.[10]

It follows from the above that the Convention does not guarantee an individual a fair trial in the determination of all of the rights and obligations that he may arguably claim in national law. However, as will be seen, the gaps in the coverage of Article 6 have been significantly, if somewhat confusingly, reduced by interpretation in recent years. Indeed, whereas the Strasbourg authorities still refer to 'civil rights and obligations' as meaning those in private law,[11] recent jurisprudence, by which more and more rights and obligations have been brought within Article 6, is not easy to explain in

---

4   See Bradley 21 OHLJ 609 (1983); Van Dijk, *Wiarda Mélanges*, p 131, and *European Supervision*, Ch 14. For studies of the early jurisprudence see Harris, 46 BYIL 157 (1974-75) and Rasenack, 3 HRJ 51 (1970). On the drafting history of 'civil rights and obligations', see Newman, 1967 PL 274 and Velu, 1961 RDIDC p 129.
5   *Ringeisen v Austria* A 13 para 94 (1971) and *König v FRG* A 27 para 95 (1978).
6   See Schlesinger, Baade, Damaska and Herzog, *Comparative Law*, 5th edn, 1988, pp 498ff.
7   See Wade and Forsyth, *Administrative Law*, 7th edn, 1994, pp 680-695.
8   A particular factual situation may concern both a criminal charge and civil rights and obligations, although the case will normally be dealt with under one head only: see *Albert and Le Compte v Belgium* A 58 para 30 (1983). Where a person injured by a crime may claim damages in the criminal prosecution of the offender, his 'civil rights' are being determined so that Article 6 applies: *Tjibaou v France No 13814/88*, 66 DR 198 (1990).
9   See above, p 173.
10 *Neumeister v Austria* A 8 p 43 (1968) (right to bail not a 'civil right' for this reason).
11 See, eg, the passage from the Court's judgment in *H v France*, below, p 176, n 19. In many cases, however, the Court simply classifies a right as a civil right or obligation without more.

terms of any distinction between private and public law that is found in European national law.

Before examining further the Strasbourg authorities' use of the idea of private law rights and obligations, it should be noted that in two early cases the Court left open the question whether there is an exact equation between civil rights and obligations and rights and obligations in private law. In particular, in *König v FRG* it stated that it did not have to decide 'whether the concept of "civil rights and obligations" . . . extends beyond those rights which have a private nature'.[12] It is not clear what the Court had in mind by this. One possibility is that human rights protected by the Convention that are public law rights (eg the right to legal aid) might be civil rights in the sense of Article 6.[13] However, although the Court has not expressly retracted the statements made in the *König* case, it has not repeated them since the *Le Compte* case in 1981 or ever applied them in practice.

The adoption of a private law meaning of civil rights and obligations, which would not have been immediately obvious to a common lawyer, raises the question of the boundary between private and public law. The precise point at which the line is drawn raises difficult questions because different states classify borderline cases differently. One approach would be to apply a doctrine of renvoi by which the Strasbourg authorities simply accepted the classification in the defendant state's legal system of a particular right or obligation as falling within private or public law. This, however, would lead to the application of Article 6 differentially between the contracting parties in an important respect.[14] In fact, the Court has, as with the parallel concept of a criminal charge, held that 'civil' has an autonomous Convention meaning, so that the defendant state's classification is not decisive.[15] In a particular case, therefore, a right that is treated as a matter of public law in the legal system of the defendant state may be regarded as being a private law, and hence a civil, right for the purposes of Article 6,[16] and vice versa.

Although adopting an autonomous Convention meaning of civil rights and obligations, the Court has refrained from formulating any abstract definition of the term, beyond distinguishing between private and public law.[17] It has instead preferred an inductive approach, ruling on the particular facts of cases as they have arisen. Even so, there are certain

---

12 A 27 para 95 (1978) and *Le Compte, Van Leuven and De Meyere v Belgium* A 43 para 48 (1981).

13 See the *Alam and Khan v UK* Nos 2991/66 and 2992/66, 10 YB 478 (1967) line of cases, concerning the right to family life, discussed in Harris, 46 BYIL 157 at 167 (1974-75), in which the Commission seemed for a while to adopt such an approach. Note that this approach concentrates on the rights, as opposed to the obligations, part of civil rights and obligations.

14 This does happen in other ways under Article 6: see eg *James v UK*, discussed below at p 186.

15 *König v FRG* A 27 para 88 (1978).

16 This happened in the context of social security rights in the *Feldbrugge* and *Deumeland* cases, below, pp 180-181.

17 In *Benthem v Netherlands* A 97 para 34 (1985), the Court declined the Commission's invitation, id, Com Rep para 91, to give guidance on the matter.

general guidelines that emerge from the cases. Firstly, 'only the character of the right at issue is relevant'.[18] The 'character of legislation which governs how the matter is to be determined (civil, commercial, administrative law, etc) and that of the authority which is invested with jurisdiction in the matter (ordinary court, administrative body, etc) are therefore of little consequence'.[19] This guideline has minimal significance for cases involving disputes between private persons which will invariably be governed by national private law and usually be within the jurisdiction of the ordinary courts. It is, however, of critical importance in cases that involve the relations between an individual and the state. In municipal law systems that traditionally have made use of the distinction between private and public law, the classification of such cases generally turns upon whether the public authority concerned is acting in a sovereign or non-sovereign capacity in its dealing with the individual.[20] For the purpose of Article 6, however, whether the state has 'acted as a private person or in its sovereign capacity is . . . not conclusive';[1] instead, the focus is entirely upon the 'character of the right'.

Secondly, when determining the 'character of the right', the existence of any 'uniform European notion' that can be found in the law of the contracting parties generally is influential. This inference can be drawn from the *Feldbrugge* and *Deumeland* cases.[2] There the Court found that there was no 'uniform European notion' (which by implication would have been followed) as to the private or public law character of the social security rights before it and was forced to make a choice in respect of rights it considered to have a mixed private and public law character.[3]

Thirdly, although the classification of a right or obligation in the law of the defendant state is not decisive, that law is none the less relevant in that it necessarily determines the content of the right or obligation to which the Convention concept of civil rights and obligations is applied. For example, whether the right to practise medicine is a matter of private or public law will depend upon whether, in the law of the defendant state, the services

18 *König v FRG* A 27 para 90 (1978). The wording quoted is phrased only in terms of 'rights', omitting 'obligations'. This tends to happen because most of the cases under Article 6 are brought by claimants, not defendants. For 'obligations' cases, see *Mulydermans v Belgium* A 214-A (1991) Com Rep (F Sett before Court) and *Schouten and Meldrum v Netherlands* A 304 (1994).

19 *Ringeisen v Austria* A 13 para 94 (1971), quoted in the *König* case A 27 para 90 (1978). A formula used in several recent cases is: 'Article 6(1) applies irrespective of the parties' status, be it public or private, and of the nature of the legislation which governs the manner in which the dispute is to be determined; it is sufficient that the outcome of the proceedings should be "decisive for private law rights and obligations"': *H v France* A 162 para 47 (1989).

20 For example, the state will be acting in a sovereign capacity when it exercises a power of deportation or expropriation. It will be acting in a non-sovereign capacity when it does something that a private person might do, such as buying chairs for an office. An act such as the purchase of guns for the army raises more difficult problems.

1 *König v FRG* A 27 para 90 (1978).

2 *Feldbrugge v Netherlands* A 99 (1986), and *Deumeland v FRG* A 100 (1986). Cf *König v FRG* A 27 para 89 (1978). See also *Detained Persons v FRG* No 3134/67, 11 YB 528 at 562 (1968).

3 Cf *Muyldermans v Belgium* A 214-A (1991) Com Rep para 56.

offered by the medical profession are made a part of a public service or are, although subject to state regulation, essentially a matter of contract between doctor and patient.[4] For this reason, despite the autonomous nature of civil rights and obligations, it would be possible for the same civil right or obligation to be subject to Article 6 as it exists in one legal system but not as it is found in another.

Applying their inductive approach, the Strasbourg authorities have developed an extensive jurisprudence classifying rights and obligations as being civil or not for the purposes of Article 6. As was to be expected, they have found that the rights and obligations of private persons in their relations *inter se* are in all cases civil rights and obligations. Thus cases concerning such relations in the law of contract,[5] commercial law,[6] insurance law,[7] the law of tort,[8] the law of succession,[9] family law,[10] employment law[11] and the law of personal[12] and real[13] property have been regarded as falling within Article 6. In such cases, the conception of private law in Article 6 and in European national legal systems exactly coincide.

The position is more complicated in cases which concern the individual in his relations with the state. In accordance with its approach in the *König* case,[14] the Court looks solely to the character of the individual's right or obligation in question. On this basis, a number of rights some expressed in very general terms,[15] have been recognised as civil rights for the purposes of Article 6.

The right to property is one such right. As a result, state action that is directly decisive[16] for property rights is determinative of civil rights and hence subject to the right to a fair trial in Article 6. Thus decisions concerning the granting of permission to purchase or retain the ownership of land,[17] the extraction of water from a well,[18] the expropriation[19] or confiscation[20] of land, land consolidation proceedings,[1] the husbandry of

4 See *König v FRG* A 27 para 89 (1978).
5 See the cases arising out of private employment contracts and contracts for the sale of land, below, pp 227, 189, respectively.
6 *Barthold v FRG No 8734/79*, 26 DR 145 (1981) (unfair competition).
7 Implied in *Feldbrugge v Netherlands* A 99 (1986) and *Deumeland v FRG* A 100 (1986).
8 Eg *Axen v FRG* A 72 (1983) (negligence) and *Golder v UK* A 18 (1975) (defamation).
9 See *X v Switzerland No 7211/75*, 7 DR 104 (1976).
10 *Airey v Ireland* A 32 (1979) (judicial separation) and *Rasmussen v Denmark* A 87 (1984) (paternity proceedings).
11 Eg *Buchholz v FRG* A 42 (1981) (unfair dismissal).
12 *Bramelid and Malmström v Sweden Nos 8588/79 and 8589/79*, 38 DR 18 (1983) (share valuation) Com Rep; CM Res DH (84) 4.
13 Eg *Pretto v Italy* A 71 (1983) (sale of land) and *Langborger v Sweden* A 155 (1989) (landlord and tenant).
14 See above at p 176.
15 In Hohfeldian terms, they are more accurately described as privileges rather than rights.
16 As to this requirement, see the *Le Compte* case, below, p 190.
17 See eg *Ringeisen v Austria* A 13 (1971) and *Håkansson and Sturesson v Sweden* A 171 (1990).
18 *Zander v Sweden* A 279-B (1993).
19 See eg *Sporrong and Lönnroth v Sweden* A 52 (1982).
20 *Raimondo v Italy* A 281-A para 43 (1994).
1 See eg *Poiss v Austria* A 117 (1987).

land,[2] the application of nature conservation[3] and planning laws[4] and the refusal of permission for a person to live in his home[5] have been held to be subject to the right to a fair hearing. With regard to personal property, decisions as to the withdrawal of goods from circulation,[6] bankruptcy[7] and the capacity to administer property[8] and decisions in disputes concerning expropriated shares,[9] patent rights[10] and liability to repay money lost[11] are similarly controlled by Article 6. Where the decision is taken by an administrative authority, there must be the possibility of challenging it before a tribunal that functions in accordance with Article 6.

The right to engage in a commercial activity is also a civil right. Hence state action by way of the withdrawal of an alcohol licence from a restaurant,[12] of a public service transport licence from a private passenger carrier[13] and of a licence to run a medical clinic[14] have been held to fall within Article 6. So has the refusal to issue a licence to operate a liquid petroleum gas installation[15] and to grant permission to run a private school.[16] Similarly, the right to practice a liberal profession,[17] such as medicine,[18] the law,[19] or architecture,[20] has also been held to be controlled by Article 6. In cases involving the right to engage in a commercial activity, there will often be an overlap between that right and the right to property.[1]

2   *Denev v Sweden No 12570/86*, 66 DR 45 (1989) Com Rep; CM Res DH (90) 241 (forestry).
3   See eg *Oerlemans v Netherlands* A 219 (1991) and *De Geouffre de la Pradelle v France* A 253-B (1992).
4   See eg *Skärby v Sweden* A 180-B (1990) (permit to build house).
5   *Gillow v UK* A 109 (1986).
6   *RR and GR v Netherlands No 14216/88*, 69 DR 219 (1991).
7   *Anca v Belgium No 10259/83*, 40 DR 170 (1984).
8   *Winterwerp v Netherlands* A 33 (1979) (result of decision to detain a mentally disordered person).
9   *Lithgow v UK* A 102 (1986)(compensation) and *Ruiz-Mateos v Spain* A 262 (1993) (restitution).
10 *X v Austria No 7830/77*, 14 DR 200 (1978). See also *Smith Kline and French Laboratories Ltd v Netherlands No 12633/87*, 70 DR 137 (1991) F Sett.
11 *Muyldermans v Belgium* A 214-A (1991) Com Rep.
12 *Tre Traktörer Aktiebolag v Sweden* A 159 (1989). As to managing a public house, see *X v Belgium No 8901/80*, 23 DR 237 (1980).
13 *Pudas v Sweden* A 125-A (1987). See also *Axelsson v Sweden No 12213/86*, 65 DR 99 (1989) (refusal of taxi licence).
14 *König v FRG* A 27 (1978).
15 *Benthem v Netherlands* A 97 (1985). See Van Dijk, 34 NILR 5 (1987).
16 *Jordebo Foundation v Sweden No 11533/85*, 61 DR 92 (1987) Com Rep; CM Res DH (89) 15.
17 This is considered as an aspect of the right to engage in a commercial activity for the present purpose.
18 See eg *König v FRG* A 27 (1978) and *Kraska v Switzerland* A 254-B (1993). Practice as a business agent, or property manager is also a civil right: *Jaxel v France No 11282/84*, 54 DR 70 (1987); 59 DR 42 (1989) F Sett. The question whether the right to practise as an accountant is a civil right was left open in *Van Marle v Netherlands*, discussed below, p 188.
19 *H v Belgium* A 127 (1987) and *De Moor v Belgium* A 292 para 43 (1994). Cf *Ginikanwa v UK No 12502/86*, 55 DR 251 (1988).
20 *Guchez v Belgium No 10027/82*, 40 DR 100 (1984).
1   Eg in the *Benthem* case, para 36, the Court noted that the licence had a proprietary character (being assignable) and that its grant was 'closely associated with the right to use one's possessions'.

Article 6 applies to the *grant* of a licence to undertake a commercial activity as well as a decision to withdraw it. In the *König* case,[2] the Court had emphasised that the case was one of the *continued* exercise of a right to practise medicine and to operate a clinic, distinguishing between a discretionary decision to grant a licence in the first place and the legitimate expectation that a licence holder has in its continuance. In the *Benthem* and later cases,[3] however, Article 6 has been applied to applications for new licences, the *König* distinction being abandoned.

The rights to property and to engage in a commercial activity share a common pecuniary character. Consistently with such a link, the Court's jurisprudence also recognises as a civil right the right to compensation for pecuniary loss resulting from illegal state acts. In *X v France*,[4] the Court held that a claim for damages for contracting AIDS from a blood transfusion because of government negligence fell within Article 6. Although the case concerned the exercise of a general regulatory power by a Minister and hence was clearly a matter of public law in France, its outcome was 'decisive for private rights and obligations', namely those concerning pecuniary compensation for physical injury.[5] The same approach was adopted in *Editions Périscope v France*.[6] There the applicant company had ceased trading because of pecuniary losses caused by an illegal decision by a public authority refusing it a tax concession. The Court held that the decision of an administrative court on the applicants' claim for compensation for damage sustained through the fault of the public authority determined the applicants' civil rights and obligations. In a brief statement of reasons, the Court noted that 'the subject matter of the applicant's action was "pecuniary" in nature and that the action was founded on an alleged infringement of rights which were likewise pecuniary rights', so that the right in question was a civil one. The Court's approach in these cases, which involves finding a pecuniary interest in a very general sense and supposing that such interests have a private law character, suggests that, as a general proposition, public law cases before administrative courts[7] in which compensation is claimed are

---

2 A 27 (1978).
3 *Benthem v Netherlands* A 97 (1985). Cf *Allan Jacobsson v Sweden* A 163 (1989) and *Kraska v Switzerland* A 254-B (1993).
4 A 234-C (1992). Cf *Adler v Switzerland No 9486/81*, 46 DR 36 (1985) Com Rep; CM Res DH (86) 4.
5 Cf *H v France* A 162-A (1989) (administrative court compensation claim for public hospital negligence within Article 6).
6 A 234-B (1992). Cf *Neves e Silva v Portugal* A 153-A (1989) (claim for pecuniary loss suffered by illegal refusal by public authority to grant manufacturing licence) and *Baraona v Portugal* A 122 (1987). In the latter case, an illegal arrest warrant caused the applicant to flee, leading to the loss of his business and other assets. The applicant's right to compensation for injury caused by a public official was private because 'it embodies a personal and property interest and is founded on an infringement of rights of this kind, notably the right to property': id, para 44. See also *Stran Greek Refineries and Stratis Andreadis v Greece* A 301-B (1994) (a pecuniary claim arising out of contract with the state was a 'civil right' whatever the public or private law nature of the contract under national law).
7 The same would be true of claims against a public authority in the English High Court.

within Article 6.[8] In this way, a very large area of public law litigation becomes subject to Article 6, despite the divide between public and private law.[9] None the less, as explained below, not all pecuniary disputes between the individual and the state fall within Article 6.[10]

A right of a non-pecuniary character to which Article 6 applies is the right to respect for family life. Thus state action that is directly decisive for this right, such as decisions placing children in care[11] or concerning parental access to children[12] or adoption[13] or fostering,[14] has been held to be regulated by Article 6.

One of the most controversial decisions taken by the Court concerns the classification of rights to social security and social assistance. In *Feldbrugge v Netherlands*,[15] the applicant's sick pay under a Dutch social security law was withdrawn on the ground that she was fit for work. Although the benefit was treated in Dutch law as a public law right, the Court held otherwise for the purposes of Article 6. Noting there was no 'uniform European notion' as to the classification of health insurance benefits, which it would probably have followed, the Court examined the nature of the benefit in Dutch law and found it to have mixed public and private characteristics, but with the latter predominating. In brief, although accepting that it was a part of a state health insurance scheme, the Court was persuaded by the fact that the allowance was a statutory right, rather than one in the discretionary gift of the state; that it had important economic consequences for an unemployed person, going to a person's very subsistence; that it was funded partly by employee contributions and could be seen as a substitute for salary due under a private law contract of employment onto which it was grafted; and that the scheme had many features of a private insurance scheme.

The Court's decision in the *Feldbrugge* case was by a majority of 10 votes to 7. In a strong joint dissenting opinion, the minority saw the balance differently, emphasising that the benefit derived from a collective scheme of social protection established by the state and had only limited private law connections. Since the benefit was therefore essentially a creature of public law, the question for the minority was whether the Court should move beyond its long-established position as to the scope of Article 6 based upon

8   See also *Beaumartin v France* A 296-A para 28 (1994) (dispute before administrative court about compensation under lump sum settlement agreement within Article 6) and *Ortenberg v Austria* A 295-B para 28 (1994) (landowner's 'civil right' in issue when she objected in an administrative court to permission to build on adjacent land because of effect on market value). 'Pecuniary rights' involved in both cases.

9   Court proceedings by an individual that do not involve a claim for compensation (eg a claim for an injunction against a public authority to prevent it destroying an historic site: *Martin v Ireland* No 8569/79, 42 DR 23 (1985)) remain outside Article 6.

10 *Schouten and Meldrum v Netherlands* A 304 para 50 (1994): see below, pp 181-182.

11 *Olsson v Sweden (No 1)* A 130 (1988).

12 *W v UK* A 121 (1987) and *Eriksson v Sweden* A 156 (1989).

13 *Keegan v Ireland* A 291 para 57 (1994).

14 *Eriksson v Sweden* A 156 (1989).

15 A 99 (1986).

the distinction between public and private law. In the light of the intentions of the drafting states, the diversity of approach across Europe as to whether judicial procedures were called for in disputes concerning social security benefits and the judicial, rather than legislative, role of the Court, the minority considered that it should not.

The Court's elaborate and not wholly convincing reasoning as to the private law character of the particular social security benefits before it in the *Feldbrugge* case and its companion case of *Deumeland v FRG*[16] suggested that the classification of other social security rights would be a matter of close scrutiny with, for example, a non-contributory benefit that was not linked to a private law employment contract perhaps falling outside Article 6. However, this has not proved to be the case. Instead, having taken a bold decision in the first two cases on their particular facts, the Court has since established that 'the development in the law [in Council of Europe states] that was initiated by those judgments and the principle of equality of treatment warrant taking the view that today the *general rule* is that Article 6(1) does apply in the field of social insurance, including even welfare assistance'.[17] Accordingly, the Court has held that Article 6 applies to a policeman's claim to a public service pension,[18] which, in contrast with the *Feldbrugge* and *Deumeland* cases, was clearly not linked to a private contract of employment. Moreover, the Court has extended Article 6 beyond social security rights to social assistance rights for persons in need.[19] In the case of benefits of either kind, the test, it seems, is whether the grant of the benefit lies within the discretion of the state or is a statutory right provided by law.[20] In the latter case, Article 6 applies and there is no need to engage in the detailed scrutiny of the public or private law nature of the right of the kind that was undertaken in the *Feldbrugge* case.

However, the Court continues to apply its *Feldbrugge* balancing approach in the case of disputes concerning an obligation to pay social security *contributions* where the relevant considerations when deciding whether a 'civil obligation' is being determined are not identical to those that apply in the case of a right to a state benefit. In *Schouten and Meldrum v*

16 A 100 (1986). In that case, using similar reasoning, the Court held, by 9 votes to 8, that an industrial injuries benefit under West German social security law was a private law right.

17 *Schuler-Zgraggen v Switzerland* A 263 para 46 (1993). Cf *Salesi v Italy* A 257-E para 19 (1993). Italics added.

18 *Lombardo v Italy* A 249-B (1992). It has also been applied, more closely in line with the facts of the *Feldbrugge* and *Deumeland* cases, to a disability benefit (see eg *Nibbio v Italy* A 228-A (1992)) and an invalidity pension (*Schuler-Zgraggen v Switzerland* A 263 (1993)). See also *Minniti v Italy No 9630/81*, 59 DR 5 (1987) Com Rep; CM Res DH (89) 7 and *Lo Giacco v Italy No 10659/83*, 69 DR 7 (1989) Com Rep; CM Res DH (91) 13.

19 *Salesi v Italy* A 257-E (1993). The distinction between social security and social assistance is not wholly clear, but generally persons receive differing amounts of social assistance on the basis of individual need, rather than the same amount for all qualifying persons.

20 *Lombardo v Italy*, above, n 18, and *Salesi v Italy*, above, n 17. It was a statutory right in both cases. Note that the members of the Court chambers that decided these cases who had participated and dissented in the *Feldbrugge* and *Deumeland* cases did not dissent from the unanimous decisions in these later cases.

Netherlands,[1] the Court held that Article 6 applied to a dispute concerning the applicant employer's contributions in respect of his employees to various Dutch social security schemes,[2] which were a matter of Dutch public law. In doing so, it balanced the public law and private law aspects of the contributions in the same way it had done for benefits in the *Feldbrugge* case. One difference between the two cases was that the contributions in the *Schouten* case were 'as a rule . . . not of crucial importance' to the employer's livelihood in the way that benefits for unemployed persons were likely to be. None the less, on balance the Court decided that the private law aspects of the obligation to pay contributions were of greater significance, emphasising the similarities between state and private insurance and the fact that the contributions were grafted on to the private law contract of employment.

In accordance with the private law reading of civil rights and obligations, claims concerning a number of other rights have been rejected as falling outside Article 6.[3] Rights concerning employment in the public sector fall within this category,[4] although recent court judgments have eroded the scope of this limitation. In *Lombardo v Italy*,[5] while recognising that 'disputes relating to the recruitment, employment and retirement of judges are as a general rule outside the scope of Article 6(1)', the Court held that a dispute concerning a judge's pension to which he was entitled by statute concerned a civil right. As in recent social security cases, the Court drew a distinction between the exercise of discretion by the state and the performance of a statutory obligation:

> 'In performing this obligation the state is not using discretionary powers and may be compared, in this respect, with an employer who is a party to a contract of employment governed by private law'.

1 A 304 para 57 (1974).
2 They were compulsory health insurance, medical assistance, unemployment insurance and occupational disability insurance schemes.
3 Most of the jurisprudence consists of admissibility decisions by the Commission. The Court has yet to find a right admitted for consideration by the Commission not to be within Article 6.
4 Claims by public employees in civil law systems concerning appointment, dismissal, conditions of service and discipline have been rejected at the admissibility stage in cases concerning members of the armed forces (*X v Portugal No 9208/80*, 26 DR 262 (1981)), civil servants (*Leander v Sweden No 9248/81*, 34 DR 78 (1983)); judges (*X v Portugal No 9877/82*, 32 DR 258 (1983)), clergymen in a state-regulated church (*X v FRG No 9501/81*, 27 DR 249 (1981)), state school teachers (*X v Italy No 8686/79*, 21 DR 208 (1980)) and public corporation employees (*X v Belgium No 3937/69*, 32 CD 61 (1969)). But Article 6 does apply to public employees employed under an ordinary contract of employment: see *Darnell v UK No 15058/89*, 69 DR 306 (1991);A 272 (1993) (NHS employee) and *C v UK No 11882/85*, 54 DR 162 (1987) (state school janitor). In *X v UK No 8496/79*, 21 DR 168 (1980), a claim by an English policeman was held not to fall within Article 6 because police officers 'are exclusively subordinated to governmental authorities and do not enter into contractual relationships'.
5 A 249-B para 17 (1992). Article 6 also applied in *Scuderi v Italy* A 265-A (1993) (civil servant salary claim) and *Muti v Italy* A 281-C (1994) (State Counsel's Office employee's invalidity pension).

The same result might have been achieved by focusing, as in other kinds of cases (see above), on the property or pecuniary interest of the public employee.[6]

Decisions determining a person's liability to pay tax[7] or eligibility for fiscal advantages[8] have long been regarded by the Commission as a matter of public law. Interestingly, in *Editions Périscope v France*[9] the Court held that a claim for compensation for pecuniary loss resulting from an illegal refusal to allow a tax exemption fell within Article 6 because of the claim's 'pecuniary nature', hence affecting the claimant's right to property. In doing so, the Court referred to the Commission's jurisprudence, followed in its report in that case, excluding tax or fiscal cases from the scope of Article 6 without confirming or rejecting it.

However, in *Schouten and Meldrum v Netherlands*,[10] a chamber of the Court did, *obiter dicta*, take a stance on the matter, confirming the Commission's position concerning obligations arising under tax legislation. It indicated that some pecuniary obligations vis-à-vis the state are 'to be considered as belonging exclusively to the realm of public law and are accordingly not covered by the notion of "civil rights and obligations"'. It mentioned as obligations that would thereby be excluded from Article 6 criminal law fines and cases where the obligation 'derives from tax legislation or is otherwise part of normal civic duties in a democratic society'.

Other kinds of public law cases that the Commission has regarded as being outside the scope of Article 6 are cases concerning immigration and nationality,[11] liability for military service,[12] legal aid in civil cases,[13] the reporting of court proceedings,[14] state funding of research,[15] the right to state education,[16] patent applications,[17] the disciplining of prisoners,[18] the rights of tenants associations,[19] compensation claims out of a public

6 Cf *Muyldermans v Belgium* A 214-A (1991) Com Rep; F Sett.
7 *X v France No 9908/82*, 32 DR 266 (1983). Cf *S and T v Sweden No 11189/84*, 50 DR 121 (1986) (tax on corporate profits).
8 *X v Austria No 8903/80*, 21 DR 246 (1980) (export incentive tax exemption).
9 Discussed above, p 179. See also the *Bendenoun* case, above, p 170 (penalties imposed for tax evasion within Article 6 on a criminal charge basis).
10 A 304 para 50 (1994).
11 Cases have concerned entry (*X, Y, Z, V and W v UK No 3325/67*, 10 YB 528 (1967)), including asylum (*P v UK No 13162/87*, 54 DR 211 (1987)), deportation (*Agee v UK No 7729/76*, 7 DR 164 (1976)) and nationality (*S v Switzerland No 13325/87*, 59 DR 256 (1988)).
12 *Nicolussi v Austria No 11734/85*, 52 DR 266 (1987).
13 *X v FRG No 3925/69*, 32 CD 56 (1970).
14 *Atkinson Crook and The Independent v UK No 13366/87*, 67 DR 244 (1990).
15 *X v Sweden No 6676/74*, 2 DR 123 (1974).
16 *Simpson v UK* 64 DR 188 (1989) (elementary education) and *X v FRG No 10192/83*, 7 EHRR 141 (1984) (university).
17 *X v Austria No 7830/77*, 14 DR 200 (1978). Disputes as to patent rights once granted are within Article 6: see above, p 178.
18 *McFeeley v UK No 8317/78*, 20 DR 44 (1980). The disciplining of prisoners (and soldiers) may involve a 'criminal charge': see above, pp 167-168.
19 *X v Sweden No 9260/81*, 6 EHRR 323 (1983). See also *K Association v Sweden No 10144/82*, 33 DR 276 (1983).

fund,[20] the right to state medical treatment,[1] the right to an hereditary peerage,[2] the right to stand for public office[3] and the validity of parliamentary elections.[4] Certain of these precedents may require re-examination in the light of the Court's recent jurisprudence.

As will be apparent, although the Court has maintained its private law meaning of civil rights and obligations, its jurisprudence in the past few years has led to a position in which Article 6 regulates many more kinds of disputes between the individual and the state than that meaning might suggest. Thus cases concerning public control of land, the licensing or other regulation of commercial or professional activities, compensation for illegal public acts and social security and assistance rights now fall within the bounds of the right to a fair trial. This results partly from the extensive interpretation given by the Court to the word 'determination'[5] in Article 6(1), but also from the Court's increasingly dynamic understanding of what amounts to a private law right for the purposes of Article 6. The ingenious use of such all-embracing concepts as the rights to property or to engage in commercial activities, as well as the distinction between legal rights and discretionary powers, has engineered considerable inroads into the realms of public law and administrative justice – sometimes to the point where the Court's attempt to explain its decisions in terms of public and private law appears artificial and unconvincing.[6]

It is arguable that the Court might do better to reformulate its approach in terms of an abstract definition of civil rights and obligations that starts from a different premise[7] or, alternatively, to add other categories beyond the private law meaning of the phrase.[8] Should it formulate a general test, the Court might ground its definition in the idea of individual freedom that is implicit in European law and society. This was the basis for the definition proposed by Messrs Melchior and Frowein in their dissenting opinion in the *Benthem* case.[9] They suggested that 'all those rights which are individual rights under the national legal system and fall into the sphere of general individual freedom, be it professional or any other legally permitted activity,

---

20 *Berler v FRG No 12624/87*, 62 DR 207 (1989) (compensation for Nazi persecution); *B v Netherlands No 11098/84*, 43 DR 198 (1985) (criminal injuries compensation); *Nordh v Sweden No 14225/88*, 69 DR 223 (1990) (natural disaster fund).

1 *L v Sweden No 10801/84*, 61 DR 62 (1988) Com Rep para 87; CM Res DH (89) 16.

2 *X v UK No 8208/78*, 16 DR 162 (1978) (claimed as a basis for entry to the House of Lords, not as a property right).

3 *Habsburg-Lothringen v Austria No 15344/89*, 64 DR 210 (1989) (office of head of state).

4 *Priorello v Italy No 11068/84*, 43 DR 195 (1985) and *IZ v Greece No 18997/91*, 76A DR 65 (1994).

5 See below, p 189.

6 The Court itself sometimes appears uncertain as to its approach, taking refuge in a very brief statements of reasons or just a conclusion without reasons: see eg *X v France* A 234-C (1992).

7 For criticism of the Court for not doing this, see Van Dijk, *European Supervision*, p 376.

8 The Court allowed this possibility in *König v FRG*: see above, p 175.

9 B 80 para 10 (1983). In argument before the Court, Mr Melchior substituted 'any other activity which is not absolutely prohibited by law' for 'any other legally permitted activity': id, p 103.

must be seen as civil rights'. However, they allowed important exceptions concerning the 'public service, fiscal matters, military service, immigration matters, electoral matters'.

Should, as is very likely, the Court continue with its present inductive approach, its jurisprudence already contains the seeds of further expansive decisions. For example, it is difficult to square the Commission's rulings excluding taxation disputes with the Court's reliance upon the property and pecuniary interests of individuals.[10] And, as noted, the Court has already made important inroads upon the rule that decisions involving employment in the public sector fall outside Article 6. Moreover, it would also be possible, quite consistently with the Melchior-Frowein 'individual freedom' approach, to add to the list of very general rights that have been recognised by the Court as civil rights (property, respect for family life, etc), for example by including other human rights in the Convention itself. These could include[11] freedom from inhuman treatment, freedom of expression[12] and freedom of conscience and religion.[13] The Court's reliance in some contexts on the distinction between legal entitlement and administrative discretion also offers considerable potential, even if it would seem to bear more upon the meaning of 'rights and obligations' than their 'civil' character. If Article 6 were to apply to the determination of all legal rights or obligations that an individual arguably has in national law, this would be likely to reinforce the view that some taxation disputes should be included and to bring within the purview of Article 6 other areas of public law (eg immigration and nationality law) to the extent that legal rights and obligations have been established in them. A further pragmatic extension to the Court's approach would be to consider that insofar as states have courts or administrative tribunals in place to determine cases concerning rights and obligations (of whatever kind) that an individual arguably has under its law, these should comply with Article 6.[14] The satisfactory end result would be

10 But see the *Schouten and Meldrum* case, above at pp 181-182.
11 One likely omission is the right to liberty of the person, in view of the particular provision for a judicial remedy in cases of deprivation of liberty in Article 5(4). This is the view of the Commission: see *Keus v Switzerland* A 185-C (1990) Com Rep and *Van der Leer v Netherlands* 11 EHRR 413 (1988) Com Rep. Cf *Neumeister v Austria* A 8 (1968) on the particular question of detention on remand. The Court has not ruled generally on the question whether the right to liberty is a 'civil right'. A claim for compensation for illegal detention (see *K v FRG No 11352/85*, 45 DR 273 (1985) (inadmissible)) would raise the same question in view of Article 5(5).
12 But see *Fryske Nasionale Partu v Netherlands No 11100/84*, 9 EHRR 261 (1985); *Hodgson v UK No 11553/85*, 10 EHRR 503 (1987) and *Clavel v Switzerland No 11854/85*, 54 DR 153 (1987) in which Article 6 claims concerning freedom of speech or the right to receive information were declared inadmissible.
13 But see *X v Denmark No 7374/76*, 5 DR 157 (1976) (dispute about religious faith or practice not within Article 6) and *Johansen v Norway No 10600/83*, 44 DR 155 (1985) (conscientious objector).
14 Cf the approach by which the appeal courts that states happen to have are regulated by Article 6: see below, p 240. *Quaere* whether some of the Court's judgments eg those concerning claims against public authorities in administrative courts (see eg *X v France*, above, p 179) and the social security and assistance cases, may in fact be explained in this way.

that an individual would be guaranteed a 'right to a court' in the sense of Article 6: (i) to assert or question any arguable legal 'right or obligation' that he has under national law;[15] or (ii) to challenge by means of judicial review a discretionary decision that is taken by the state that directly affects him. While it may not have been intended that the right to a fair trial in Article 6 should have such a wide application, an extensive reading along these lines would not be inconsistent with European law generally.

b.   A 'contestation' or dispute concerning civil rights and obligations

For Article 6 to apply there must be a 'dispute' at the national level between two private persons or between the applicant and the state the outcome of which is determinative of the applicant's civil rights and obligations. The need for a 'dispute' follows from the use of the word *'contestation'* in the French text of Article 6. In *H v Belgium*,[16] the requirement was explained as follows:

> 'Article 6(1) extends only to 'contestations' (disputes) over (civil) "rights and obligations" which can be said, at least on arguable grounds, to be recognised under domestic law; it does not in itself guarantee any particular content for (civil) "rights and obligations" in the substantive law of the contracting states.'

Thus for Article 6 to apply, the applicant must have an arguable claim to put before a national tribunal on a matter arising under national law, the decision on which will be determinative of his 'civil rights and obligations' in the Convention meaning of that term. The requirement is only that the applicant have a 'tenable' argument, not that he will necessarily win.[17]

The fact that the state has a very wide discretion in responding to an applicant's claim (eg when granting a licence) will not prevent Article 6 applying if, as is probable, there are administrative law principles that control the exercise of administrative discretion that the applicant can rely upon.[18]

According to the above quotation from *H v Belgium*, Article 6 does not control the content of a state's national law; it is only a procedural guarantee of a right to a fair hearing in the determination of whatever substantive legal rights and obligations a state in its discretion provides. For example, in *James v UK*,[19] the applicants had been deprived of their ownership of certain properties by the exercise by the tenants of a right to acquire the properties given to them by the statute. The applicants had no

---

15 Any restriction on his access to a court would have to be consistent with the *Ashingdane* and *Fayed* cases: below, pp 199-201.

16 A 127-B para 40 (1987). Cf *Neves e Silva v Portugal* A 153 para 36 (1989) in which the Court looked for a dispute as to '[civil] rights which can be said, at least on arguable grounds, to be recognised under domestic law, *irrespective of whether they are also protected under the Convention*'. Italics added. See also *W v UK* A 121 para 73 (1987).

17 *Neves e Silva v Portugal* A 153-A para 37 (1989).

18 See eg *Pudas v Sweden* A 125-A paras 32-34 (1987).

19 A 98 para 81 (1986).

remedy in court by which to challenge the exercise of this right once the terms of the statute were satisfied. Although the case concerned their right to property, which was a 'civil right', the absence of a remedy was not a breach of Article 6. Similarly, in *Powell and Rayner v UK*,[20] the statutory exclusion of liability in trespass and nuisance for aircraft overflight and noise did not raise an issue under Article 6.

However, a limit to this approach was set in *Fayed v UK*.[1] There the applicants wanted to bring a claim in defamation arising out of a government inspector's report under the Companies Act 1985 which found that they had been dishonest. Whereas the law of defamation extended to cover the facts of their claim, it would, as was generally agreed, have been successfully met by a defence of absolute or qualified privilege. After referring with approval to its approach in the *James* and *Powell and Rayner* cases, the Court drew a distinction between substantive and procedural limitations:

'Whether a person has an actionable domestic claim may depend not only on the substantive content, properly speaking, of the relevant civil right as defined under national law but also on the existence of procedural bars preventing or limiting the possibilities of bringing potential claims to court. In the latter kind of case Article 6(1) may have a degree of applicability. Certainly the Convention enforcement bodies may not create by way of interpretation of Article 6(1) a substantive civil right which has no legal basis in the state concerned. However, it would not be consistent with the rule of law in a democratic society or with the basic principle underlying Article 6(1) – namely that civil claims must be capable of being submitted to a judge for adjudication – if, for example, a state could, without restraint or control by the Convention enforcement bodies, remove from the jurisdiction of the courts a whole range of civil claims or confer immunities from civil liability on large groups or categories of persons . . . '

Thus, in the 'no legal basis' kind of case, the reasoning in the *James* and *Powell and Rayner* cases continues to apply so that, for example, if a state's law simply deprived a landowner of his right to his property or did not guarantee a right to privacy, Article 6 would not apply; there would be no basis for a ruling that such rights must be restored or provided.[2] In the 'removal from jurisdiction' or 'immunities' kind of case, however, the rule of law dictates some degree of Convention 'restraint or control'. If, for example, national law excused the state from legal liability in respect of all claims concerning 'civil rights and obligations' brought by individuals

20 A 172 (1990). Cf *Lawlor v UK No 12763/87*, 57 DR 216 (1988) (no right of access to grandchildren).
1 A 294-B para 65 (1994).
2 The absence of a substantive right may, however, be an infringement of another Convention guarantee (eg the right to property or the right to privacy).

against it, the Strasbourg authorities might be able to intervene under Article 6.

The vehicle for providing this 'restraint or control' would, the Court indicated in the *Fayed* case, be the right of access to a court that Article 6 guarantees. As explained below, in that case the Court, acting on the basis that Article 6 did otherwise apply,[3] concluded that the restriction upon the right of access presented on the facts of that case by the privilege defence to a defamation claim could be justified as having a legitimate aim and as being in proportion to its attainment.[4]

Generally, the Court has interpreted the 'dispute' requirement in such a way that it is not a significant hurdle. It has held that *'contestation'* should not be 'construed too technically' and that it should be given a 'substantive rather that a formal meaning'.[5] This approach is adopted as being in accordance with the spirit of the Convention and because the term *'contestation'* has no counterpart in the English text, a fact that has led to hesitation as to its importance.[6] A dispute may concern a question of law or of fact.[7] It need not concern the actual existence of a right, but may relate instead to its 'scope . . . or the manner in which the beneficiary may avail himself' of it.[8] The dispute must be 'genuine and of a serious nature'.[9] The word 'genuine' may exclude cases of a hypothetical kind, such as a case raising the question whether a proposed statute would, if enacted, infringe the applicant's rights or cases that have become moot. It is not necessary, however, that damages be claimed; a request for a declaratory judgment is sufficient.[10] The requirement that the dispute be of a 'serious nature' is not a significant obstacle, although it may disqualify cases in which the interference with a 'civil right' is *de minimis*. In *Oerlemans v Netherlands*,[11] there was a 'serious dispute' when the designation of the applicant's land as a 'natural site' meant that certain restrictions (eg no herbicides) might be imposed upon his farming.

A 'dispute' for the purposes of Article 6 must be justiciable, ie it must be one that inherently lends itself to judicial resolution. For this reason in *Van Marle v Netherlands*[12] the Court held, by 11 to 7, that Article 6 was not applicable to a dispute concerning the applicants' registration as accountants. According to the reasoning in the Court's judgment, this was

---

3   The Court found no need to decide this point.
4   See below, p 201.
5   *Le Compte, Van Leuven and De Meyere v Belgium* A 43 para 45 (1981).
6   In *Moreira de Azevedo v Portugal* A 189 (1990), the Court cast some doubt upon the very existence of the requirement ('if indeed it does' exist). Cf the joint dissenting opinion of six judges in *W v UK* A 121 (1987) and the dissenting opinion of Judge de Meyer in *Kraska v Switzerland* A 254-B (1993).
7   *Albert and Le Compte v Belgium* A 58 (1983).
8   *Le Compte, Van Leuven and De Meyere v Belgium* A 43 para 49 (1981).
9   *Benthem v Netherlands* A 97 para 32 (1985). Cf the 'case or controversy' requirement in US constitutional law: see eg *Poe v Ullman*, 367 US 497 (1961).
10 *Helmers v Sweden* A 212-A (1991).
11 A 219 (1991).
12 A 101 (1986).

because the dispute was concerned essentially with the assessment of the applicants' competence as accountants which was more akin to examining than judging, whereas Article 6 is aimed at regulating only the latter. Curiously, however, this reasoning is only that of a minority of the Court. Three of the eleven judges who voted for the holding that Article 6 did not apply did so, according to their joint concurring opinion, on the basis that there *was* a 'dispute', but that the evaluation of professional competence by a public authority did not concern a civil right.[13] The seven dissenting judges were of the opinion both that there was a 'dispute' and that its outcome was determinative of a civil right, viz the right to exercise a profession. Even so, a requirement of justiciability is a sensible one that is in accordance with European national law.[14]

c. When are civil rights and obligations being determined?

Supposing that a dispute exists, it is still necessary to show that civil rights and obligations are being 'determined' by the proceedings to which it is sought to apply Article 6(1). This will be the case when the outcome of the proceedings is 'directly decisive' for the civil rights and obligations concerned.[15] This requirement is clearly met where the determination of the applicant's civil rights and obligations is the primary purpose of the proceedings. Thus Article 6 undoubtedly applies to a personal injuries claim in tort before the ordinary courts between private individuals[16] and to a claim before an administrative court for negligence by a state hospital.[17]

In addition, it was held in *Ringeisen v Austria*[18] that Article 6 extends to proceedings which do not have the determination of 'civil rights and obligations' as their purpose but which none the less are decisive for them. In that case, the applicant had entered into a contract to buy land from third parties. The sale was subject to the approval of an administrative tribunal which refused permission because the land would be used for non-agricultural purposes. The object of the proceedings before the tribunal – the granting of permission by reference to the public interest – clearly pertained to public law. None the less, the Court held that civil rights and obligations were being determined:

'Although it was applying rules of administrative law, the Regional Commission's decision was to be decisive for the relations in civil law (*de caractère civil*) between Ringeisen and the Roth couple.'[19]

13 This point was left open by the Court.
14 Eg in English law the courts will not review the assessment of examinations: *Thorne v University of London* [1966] 2 QB 237.
15 *Ringeisen v Austria* A 13 (1971); *Le Compte, Van Leuven and De Meyere v Belgium* A 43 (1981).
16 See eg *Guincho v Portugal* A 81 (1984).
17 *H v France* A 162 (1992).
18 A 13 (1971).
19 Id, para 94.

In *Ringeisen v Austria*, the Court stated only that for Article 6 to apply the proceedings must be 'decisive' for civil rights and obligations. It was in *Le Compte v Belgium*[20] that the Court established that they must be '*directly decisive*' and that a 'tenuous connection or remote consequences do not suffice'. In that case, the applicants were Belgian doctors who had been temporarily suspended from medical practice by the competent disciplinary bodies. The Court accepted that the primary purpose of the disciplinary proceedings was to decide whether breaches of the rules of professional conduct had occurred. None the less, the proceedings were 'directly decisive' for the applicants' private law right to practise medicine because the suspension of the applicants' exercise of that right was a direct consequence of the decision that breaches of the rules had occurred.

Before the *Le Compte* case, it had been possible to imagine that the effect of the *Ringeisen* case was to undermine the Article 6 distinction between private and public law to a very great extent indeed. For example, the decision to deport an alien might be thought to be subject to Article 6 if the alien had private law rights under a contract of employment to be performed in the deporting state for which that decision was decisive. The *Le Compte* case makes clear that Article 6 would not apply in such a case; the connection between the public law decision to deport and the applicant's private law contract rights would be too tenuous or remote.[1] An interesting question is whether Article 6 would apply in such a case if the decision were to refuse a work permit, not to deport. In that case, it is submitted, the effect of the decision on the alien's contract of employment would be sufficiently direct to cause the case to fall within Article 6.

Despite the limiting effect of the *Le Compte* case, the impact of the *Ringeisen* case in extending Article 6 to cases in which the 'determination' of civil rights and obligations is a consequence, but not the purpose, of the proceedings has been considerable. In particular, it has provided the basis upon which cases involving decisions by administrative tribunals or the executive regulating private rights in the public interest are brought within the reach of Article 6.[2]

Proceedings before a constitutional court may involve the determination of civil rights and obligations where they involve a decision on a point of

---

20 A 43 para 47 (1981). Italics added. Disciplinary proceedings that lead only to a reprimand, not suspension, are not within Article 6: *No 10331/83*, 6 EHRR 583 (1983).

1 Cf *X v UK No 7902/77*, 9 DR 224 (1977), in which the Commission, anticipating the *Le Compte* case, held that on such facts the deportation decision was not sufficiently closely linked with the applicant's contract rights for the *Ringeisen* case to apply. Cf *Zelisse v Netherlands No 12915/87*, 61 DR 230 (1989) (call up for conscription in effect ended employment). Other deportation proceedings might come within Article 6 on the wider reading of Article 6(1) discussed above, p 175.

2 The consequences have been particularly striking where there has been no tradition of recourse at all to a judicial body against executive regulatory decisions: see eg the *Benthem* and *Ravnsborg* cases, below, p 192, n 17. As a result of the 'access to a court' requirement of Article 6, such recourse must be provided.

constitutionality that is decisive for those rights.[3] An appeal to the French Conseil d'Etat that challenges a government decree as *ultra vires* that has no direct effect on the applicant's rights is not within Article 6.[4] However, any preliminary decision in a case that is crucial to the applicant's claim is determinative of his civil rights and obligations and hence is subject to Article 6. Thus where a claim concerning a person's employment depends upon the validity of his dismissal, Article 6 requires a fair hearing on the preliminary question of the validity of the dismissal as well as on the substance of the claim.[5]

Article 6 applies not only to the proceedings in which liability is determined but also to any separate court proceedings in which the amount of damages is assessed.[6] Article 6 does not apply, however, to ancillary court proceedings concerning an application for interim relief,[7] the enforcement of a judgment,[8] the award of costs,[9] the re-opening of a case or leave to appeal.[10]

Nor does Article 6 apply to a report that results from an official investigation making findings of fact that bear upon an individual's 'civil rights and obligations'. This question arose in *Fayed v UK*[11] in which an inspector had been appointed by the government to investigate the affairs of a public company on suspicion of fraud. The inspector's report contained findings that were detrimental to the applicants' right to a reputation, which was a 'civil right' for the purposes of Article 6. Drawing a distinction between investigation and adjudication, the Court held that Article 6 none the less did not apply to the inspector's investigation; although it resulted in a finding that the applicants had been dishonest, this finding was not 'dispositive of anything' in terms of legal rights and duties in the way that a 'determination' in the sense of Article 6 needed to be.

A criminal prosecution brought by an applicant will involve the determination of his civil rights and obligations where such a prosecution is the remedy provided in national law for the enforcement of a civil right,

---

3   *Deumeland v FRG* A 100 (1986). In *Ruiz-Mateos v Spain* A 262 (1993), the Court declined to give a general ruling as to the applicability of Article 6(1) to constitutional court proceedings, deciding that in the particular case the Court's ruling on the constitutionality of an expropriation measure would be decisive for the applicants' right to property. See also *Kraska v Switzerland* A 254-B (1993) and *Lombardo v Italy* A 249-C (1992).

4   *Krafft and Rougeot v France No 11543/85*, 65 DR 51 (1990). Cf *Giesinger and Kopf v Austria No 13062/87*, 70 DR 152 (1991)

5   *Obermeier v Austria* A 179 (1990) (applicant's claim to have been suspended illegally necessarily failed if his dismissal valid).

6   *Silva Pontes v Portugal* A 286-A para 33 (1994).

7   *X v UK No 7990/77*, 24 DR 57 (1981) and *Alsterlund v Sweden*, below, n 9.

8   Ibid. It applies, however, if the proceedings raise new issues concerning the applicant's rights: see *K v Sweden No 13800/88*, 71 DR 94 (1991) and *Jensen v Denmark No 14063/88*, 68 DR 177 (1991).

9   *Alsterlund v Sweden No 12446/86*, 56 DR 229 (1988).

10   *X v Austria No 7761/77*, 14 DR 171 (1978) (re-opening) and *Porter v UK No 12972/87*, 54 DR 207 (1987) (leave to appeal).

11   A 294-B para 61 (1994). The purpose of the investigation was to establish the facts for the purpose of any legal proceedings that might later be brought by some other body.

as, for example, is the case in some legal systems in connection with the right to a reputation.[12] Article 6 also applies on the basis that civil rights and obligations are being determined when the victim of a crime joins a criminal prosecution as a civil party claiming compensation for injury caused by the crime.[13]

d.   The application of Article 6(1) in the context of administrative decisions[14]

Many decisions that are determinative of an individual's civil rights and obligations are taken by the executive or some other body that is not a tribunal in the sense of Article 6. Where this is so, Article 6 requires, in accordance with the right of access to a court,[15] that the state provide a right to challenge the decision before a tribunal that offers the guarantees in Article 6(1).[16] The question which then arises is whether the tribunal must have full appellate jurisdiction on the law and the facts of the case or whether it is sufficient that it only has a power of judicial review by which it may decide on the legality of the administrative act. Such pronouncements as the Court has made[17] suggest that the tribunal must have full appellate jurisdiction, at least in cases that do not involve matters of general policy.

The first cases in which the Court expressed a clear opinion on the matter concerned decisions by professional disciplinary bodies rather than governmental administrative authorities. In *Albert and Le Compte v Belgium*,[18] in which the applicant doctors wished to challenge disciplinary decisions against them on their merits, the decisions themselves were taken by a professional association, with a right of appeal to another such body and finally to the Belgian Court of Cassation. The European Court stated that the Convention required either that the associations met the requirements of Article 6 or 'they do not so comply but are subject to subsequent control by a judicial body that has full jurisdiction and does so provide the guarantees of Article 6(1)'. Article 6(1) was not complied with on the facts because the professional associations, which could rule on the merits, did not sit in public and because the Court of Cassation, which met all of the procedural demands of Article 6(1), could only consider points of law.

Then, in *W v UK*,[19] the Court held that the availability of judicial review was insufficient in a case in which parents wished to challenge on the merits

---

12 See eg *Helmers v Sweden* A 212 (1991).
13 See eg *Tomasi v France* A 241-A (1992). Cf *Moreira de Azevedo v Portugal* A 189 (1990).
14 See Boyle 1984 PL 89.
15 As to which, see below, p 196.
16 *Le Compte, Van Leuven and De Meyere v Belgium* A 43 para 51 (1981).
17 Sometimes the Court has not gone into detail, finding a breach of the right of access to a court in the absence of any possibility of recourse to a tribunal on any ground at all: see eg *Benthem v Netherlands* A 97 (1985) and *Ravnsborg v Sweden* A 283-B (1994).
18 A 58 para 29 (1983). In the *Le Compte* case, A 43 para 51 (1981), in a brief passage the Court stated that the appeal should 'cover questions of fact just as much as questions of law'. The judgment in the expropriation case of *Sporrong and Lönnroth v Sweden* A 52 para 86 (1982) was less clear.
19 A 121 (1987).

a local authority decision restricting access to a child in care. The Court stated that in 'a case of the present kind', ie one concerning access to children, Article 6 required that the tribunal have 'jurisdiction to examine the merits'.[20] As the Court noted, in United Kingdom administrative law, 'on an application for judicial review, the courts do not review the merits of the decision but confine themselves to ensuring, in brief, that the authority did not act illegally, unreasonably or unfairly'.[1] A similar decision was taken in an employment context in *Obermeier v Austria*.[2] There was no appeal to a tribunal on the merits against the decision of a government body to the effect that the applicant's dismissal had been 'socially justified'. Although it was possible to appeal to the Austrian Administrative Court on the ground that the government body had exercised its discretion in a manner incompatible with the object and purpose of the law, such a 'limited review' did not comply with Article 6(1).

In contrast, the remedy provided in *Oerlermans v Netherlands*[3] was adequate. There the applicant's land was designated by government order as a protected natural site, thereby restricting his farming activities. The applicant was able to bring proceedings before the civil courts for a full review of the lawfulness of the administrative decision. Under Dutch law, the courts could rule that the decision violated the applicant's legal rights or was contrary (i) to a rule of international or domestic law which protected his interests or (ii) to general principles of proper administration, which forbade any abuse of power and encompassed the principles of proportionality and reasoned decisions, as well as requiring relevant considerations to be taken into account. Although the court had no power to annul the decision, it could award damages for an infringement of the applicant's rights or grant an injunction to prevent the execution of the decision, thereby rendering it inoperative. This the Court held was sufficient to comply with Article 6(1) on the facts.

Crucial to the *Oerlermans* decision was that the applicant was able to have decided by the courts all of the relevant points of law and fact that he wanted to raise, especially a claim that an appeal to the Crown did not offer guarantees of a fair procedure. That this is all Article 6 requires in a particular case was spelt out more fully in *Zumtobel v Austria*[4] in which it held that, when assessing whether the right of access to a court with 'full jurisdiction' is complied with, regard must be had to the 'nature of the complaints' made by the applicant. In that case, the applicants' right of appeal to the Austrian Administrative Court against an order made by a government office for the expropriation of his land in order to build a road complied with Article 6 because the Court was able to consider 'on their

20 Id, para 82.
1 Ibid. Cf *Weeks v UK*, in which judicial review was insufficient for Article 5(4): above, p 154.
2 A 179 para 70 (1990).
3 A 219 (1991).
4 A 268-A para 32 (1993). Cf *Ortenberg v Austria* A 295-B paras 33-34 (1994) (administrative court had jurisdiction to examine all applicant's objections to planning permission to build next door; no breach of Article 6 right of access).

merits' all of the submissions that the applicant had earlier made to the office. That being so, it did not matter in that case that the Court's jurisdiction was limited to the question of the lawfulness of the administrative action and did not extend to full jurisdiction on all questions of law and fact.

The *Zumtobel* case is of importance in another respect. A problem with the application of Article 6 to administrative decision-making is that in some areas there are policy considerations that suggest that the final decision on the merits should rest with the executive, rather than a court, despite the impact upon an individual's civil rights and obligations that the decision may have. Decisions concerning the expropriation of land for a road or for public housing are obvious cases where this can be argued. Whereas the Court's jurisprudence concerning decisions on such matters as the disciplining of doctors, access to children and the dismissal of employees require a right of appeal to a tribunal with 'full jurisdiction', it is noticeable that in the *Zumtobel* case, concerning expropriation, the Court stated that Article 6 was complied with, regard being had, *inter alia*, 'to the respect which must be accorded to decisions taken by the administrative authorities on grounds of expediency'.[5] This statement may indicate a willingness to accept some limit to the requirement of 'full jurisdiction' in cases in which policy considerations apply.[6] Certainly an appeal in such cases from a decision by a minister or other administrative authority for a final decision on the merits by a tribunal that complies with Article 6 is not always provided for in the national law of the Convention parties generally at present.[7] It may be that all that Article 6 requires in such cases is a fully developed system of judicial review.[8]

The *Zumtobel* case was interpreted in this sense in *IKSCON v UK*.[9] In that case, a local authority served an enforcement notice on the applicant society for using its land in breach of the planning laws. On appeal, the Secretary of

---

5   A 268-A para 32 (1993). The question did not arise on the facts in *Sporrong and Lönnroth v Sweden* A 52 (1982). In that case, there was a breach of Article 6 in the absence of judicial review to challenge the time limits for the expropriation permits, which is what the applicants wanted; they did not seek to challenge the decision to build the roads for which the expropriation orders were made.

6   Cf the concurring opinion of Sir Basil Hall in the *Zumtobel* case, A 268-A (1993) Com Rep. See also the Commission Report in *Feldbrugge v Netherlands* A 99 (1986) Com Rep paras 101-103.

7   Cf *Kaplan v UK* 4 EHRR 64 (1980) Com Rep, in which the Commission stated that an 'interpretation of Article 6(1) under which it was held to provide a right to a full appeal on the merits of every administrative decision affecting private rights would . . . lead to a result which was inconsistent with the existing, and long-standing, legal position in most of the contracting states'.

8   This would be likely to include the principle of proportionality, as to which in UK law, see below, p 453. What is required by way of judicial review in a particular case would depend upon the nature of the applicant's complaint. The effectiveness of judicial review, will in any case depend on the extent to which the administrative discretion allowed in the case is circumscribed by law.

9   *No 20490/92*, 76A DR 90 at 111 (1994). See also *B v UK No 10471/83*, 45 DR 113 (1985).

State confirmed the enforcement notice, following an inspector's inquiry and report. The only judicial remedy then available to the applicant in respect of the resulting interference with their property rights was recourse to the English High Court 'on a point of law';[10] the High Court did not have a full right of appeal on the law and the facts. The Commission held that this limitation on the High Court's jurisdiction did not infringe Article 6. The applicant society had appealed to the High Court and had been able to put and have considered by the Court all of the arguments that it wished to make. Rejecting the applicant's argument that the High Court had lacked the 'full jurisdiction' that Article 6 required, the Commission stated that it is 'not the role of Article 6 to give access to a level of jurisdiction which can substitute its opinion for that of the administrative authorities on questions of expediency and where the courts do not refuse to examine any of the points raised'.

e.   The stages of proceedings covered by Article 6(1)

Article 6 normally begins to apply in cases involving the determination of a person's civil rights and obligations when court proceedings are instituted.[11] But, just as in criminal cases the guarantee may apply before the competent court is seised, so too in civil cases it may begin to run before the writ is issued.[12] This has been held to be the case in trial within a reasonable time claims[13] in which the applicant must exhaust a preliminary administrative remedy under national law before having recourse to a court or tribunal[14] or where he objects to a draft plan for land consolidation that deprives him of his land.[15] In the first situation, the Court emphasised that, since the applicant had to exhaust such a remedy, it was only fair to require that it proceed expeditiously. In the second situation, the Court's reasoning was that a dispute or '*contestation*' concerning civil rights and obligations arose when the objections to the draft plan were officially lodged, not later when the applicants instituted tribunal proceedings after being served with notice of the decision to deprive him of his land. The question whether the reasonable time guarantee applies to a pre-trial application for legal aid in respect of civil litigation has been left open.[16]

10 Town and Country Planning Act 1990, s 289.
11 See eg *Guincho v Portugal* A 81 (1984).
12 *Golder v UK* A 18 (1975).
13 Although the point at which Article 6 begins to run or ceases to apply in 'civil rights and obligation' cases will mostly be relevant in trial within a reasonable time cases, the question is dealt with here rather than in the context of that particular guarantee since other guarantees in Article 6(1) may also apply in the pre-trial phase (eg the right of access to a lawyer: see *Golder v UK*, below, p 196).
14 *König v FRG* A 27 (1978). Cf *Schouten and Meldrum v Netherlands* A 304 para 62 (1994) (if a public decision requires confirmation before it may be appealed, Article 6 applies once confirmation is requested).
15 *Erkner and Hofauer v Austria* A 117 para 64 (1987). Cf *Wiesinger v Austria* A 213 (1991). Article 6 does not apply, however, to private negotiations to solve a dispute before it is referred to arbitration: *Lithgow v UK* A 102 para 199 (1986).
16 *H v France* A 162 para 49 (1989).

As in criminal cases,[17] Article 6 ceases to apply only when the case is finally determined. Accordingly, it applies to appeal and judicial review proceedings.[18] Proceedings for the assessment of damages that are separate from the proceedings determining liability are also subject to Article 6, as may be proceedings before a constitutional court concerning any question as to constitutionality that is decisive for the applicant's civil claim.[19] Similarly, the reasonable time guarantee applies until the time for an appeal by the parties expires and the judgment becomes final.[20]

3.   ARTICLE 6(1): GUARANTEES IN CRIMINAL AND NON-CRIMINAL CASES

i.   The right of access to a court

One of the most creative steps taken by the European Court in its interpretation of any article of the Convention has been its ruling in *Golder v UK*[1] that Article 6(1) guarantees the right of access to a court. In that case a convicted prisoner was refused permission by the Home Secretary to write to a solicitor with a view to instituting civil proceedings in libel against a prison officer. The Court held that the refusal raised an issue under Article 6(1) because that provision concerned not only the conduct of proceedings in court once they had been instituted, but also the right to institute them in the first place. Although there was no express mention of the right of access in Article 6, its protection could be inferred from the text.[2] It was also a key feature of the concept of the 'rule of law', which, as the preamble to the Convention stated, was a part of the 'common heritage' of Council of Europe states. Moreover, any other interpretation would contradict a universally recognised principle of law and would allow a state to close its courts without infringing the Convention. Despite cogent arguments to the contrary by the dissenting judges,[3] the Court's judgment has long been unquestioned and provides a secure foundation for the full guarantee of the 'right to a court'.[4]

---

17 See above, p 173.
18 *König v FRG* A 27 para 98 (1978). In *Pretto v Italy* A 71 para 30 (1983) the 'reasonable time' guarantee ran until the Court of Cassation judgment was deposited with the court registry, whereupon it became public.
19 On these two points, see above, p 191.
20 *Pugliese v Italy (No 2)* A 206 para 16 (1991). See also *Lorenzi, Bernardini and Gritti v Italy* A 231-G (1992).
1   A 18 (1975).
2   The wording '*à ce que sa cause soit entendue*' in the French text provided the clearest indication.
3   See the judgments of Judges Verdross, Fitzmaurice and Zekia. For example, the last two of these judges noted that in at least some other instruments in which it had been intended to include the right of access, a separate provision had been inserted in addition to the equivalent of Article 6. On Judge Fitzmaurice's generally restrictive approach to the interpretation of the Convention, see above, p 7.
4   By this term is meant the right of access to a court and the guarantees in Article 6 once proceedings are instituted: *Golder v UK* A 18 para 36 (1975).

The right of access to a court was established and retains most of its significance in connection with the determination of 'civil rights and obligations'. Cases may concern private litigation, as in the *Golder* case, or claims against the state, including claims arising out of executive decisions.[5] But it also applies to criminal cases, where it means that the accused is entitled to be tried on the charge against him in a court.[6] The right of access does not include the right to bring a private criminal prosecution since Article 6 is concerned only with a charge against an individual.[7] Nor does it include a right of access to the European Court of Justice under Article 177 of the Treaty of Rome.[8]

The right of access means access in fact, as well as in law. It was for this reason that there was a breach of Article 6(1) in the *Golder* case.[9] Whereas the applicant was able in law to institute libel proceedings in the High Court, the refusal to let him contact a solicitor impeded his access to the courts in fact. It did not matter that directly the applicant's complaint was of an interference with his right of access to a solicitor, not the courts,[10] that he might have made contact with his solicitor other than by correspondence, that he might never have instituted court proceedings at all or that the applicant would have been able to have written to his solicitor before his claim became statute barred after his release from prison. A partial or temporary hindrance may be a breach of the right of access to a court.

As the ruling in the *Golder* case also indicates, the right is a right of effective access to the courts. This was demonstrated in *Airey v Ireland*[11] in which a wife, who was indigent, was refused legal aid to bring proceedings in the Irish High Court for an order of judicial separation. Given the particular nature of the proceedings[12] the Court held that, for the applicant's access to the court to be effective, she required legal representation, which for an

---

5 See eg *Sporrong and Lönnroth v Sweden* A 52 (1982) (no appeal to a court against expropriation permit) and *Keegan v Ireland* A 291 para 59 (1994) (no appeal to a court against an adoption decision). As to whether the court to which a person is entitled to have access to challenge an executive decision concerning his 'civil rights and obligations' must be competent to rule on the merits of the decision or just act by way of judicial review, see above, pp 192-195.

6 *Deweer v Belgium* A 35 (1980).

7 See above, p 166. Nor does an accused have a right to have criminal proceedings instituted against a third person: *T v Belgium No 9777/82*, 34 DR 158 (1983).

8 *Societe Divagsa v Spain No 20631/92* (1993) unreported.

9 Similar breaches of the right of access have found in other UK prisoner cases involving restrictions on contact with solicitors (*Silver v UK* A 61 (1983) (correspondence) and *Campbell and Fell v UK* A 80 (1984) (visits)). The letter must, however, be directly related to court proceedings: see *Grace v UK No 11523/85* Com Rep; CM Res DH (89) 21, 62 DR 22 (1988). The prior ventilation rule, by which prisoners were required to exhaust prison complaints procedures before resorting to the courts, also infringed it: *Campbell and Fell v UK*, above.

10 As the Court noted, it is possible for a prisoner to institute court proceedings without recourse to a solicitor.

11 A 32 (1979). See Thornberry, 29 ICLQ 250 (1980)

12 The Court emphasised the complexity of the proceedings, the need to examine expert witnesses and the emotional involvement of the parties.

indigent person meant legal aid.[13] The Court rejected the defendant government's argument that the right of access to a court does not impose positive obligations upon states, particularly ones with economic consequences for the state such as that to provide legal aid. The Court stressed, however, that it was not deciding that the right of access in Article 6(1) provided a full right to legal aid in civil litigation comparable to that specifically provided by Article 6(3)(c) in criminal cases, which extends to all cases in which 'the interests of justice so require'.[14] Legal aid is required by the right of access in civil cases, the Court stated, only in situations in which a person cannot plead his case effectively himself or where the law makes legal representation compulsory. Even in such cases, legal aid is not required in connection with all kinds of 'civil rights and obligations'[15] or where there is no 'reasonable prospect of success'.[16] As well as the absence of legal aid, the high cost of civil proceedings may be such as to infringe the right to effective access to the courts,[17] although no case has yet been admitted on the merits on this basis.

To be effective, the right of access also requires that a person be given personal and reasonable notice of an administrative decision that interferes with his 'civil rights and obligations' so that he has time to challenge it in court. In *De Geouffre de la Pradelle v France*,[18] a landowner was unable to challenge a decree declaring his land to be environmentally protected because the time period for an appeal had expired before he had been directly informed of its adoption. Although the decree had been published nationally in the Official Gazette in good time, the eight landowners affected could reasonably infer from the government's earlier involvement of them in the matter that 'the outcome of the proceedings . . . would likewise be

13 Interestingly, Ireland had made a reservation concerning criminal legal aid, which is expressly provided for in Article 6(3)(c). It did not anticipate the *Airey* judgment.

14 On the meaning of this phrase in Article 6(3)(c), see below, p 261.

15 Thus in *Munro v UK No 10594/83*, 52 DR 158 (1987) a distinction was drawn between Irish judicial separation proceedings and English defamation proceedings (no legal aid available for defamation). Although the latter were 'extremely complex' (seemingly sufficiently so as to satisfy the *Airey* test), a person's reputation was not of the same importance as the family relationships involved in judicial separation proceedings. A second consideration was that the applicant had already had an opportunity to raise the substantive issues that would be involved in defamation proceedings in his unfair dismissal claim before a tribunal. Cf *Winer v UK No 10871/84*, 48 DR 154 (1986).

16 In *X v UK No 8158/78*, 21 DR 95 (1980), the Commission stated that a refusal of legal aid because the claim lacked 'reasonable prospects of success' would 'not normally constitute a denial of access to court unless it could be shown that the decision of the administrative authority was arbitrary'. Cf *No 9649/82*, 2 Digest Supp 6.1.1.4.3.2.1., p 2 (1982) and *Webb v UK No 9353/81*, 33 DR 133 (1983). The existence of 'reasonable prospects' would not by itself be sufficient to require legal aid according to the Court in the *Airey* case: the question would then be whether the case was so complicated, etc, as to require a lawyer: cf *X v UK No 9444/81*, 6 EHHR 136 (1983).

17 *X and Y v Netherlands No 6202/73*, 1 DR 66 at 71 (1975) and *X v UK No 9194/80*, 2 Digest 333 (1981). These cases refer to lawyers' fees as well as the costs of proceedings. As to the deposit of security for costs, see *X v Sweden No 7973/77*, 17 DR 74 (1979).

18 A 253-B para 33 (1992).

communicated to each of them without their having to peruse the Official Gazette for months or years on end'.[19]

The right of access to a court is not an absolute one. Restrictions may be imposed since the right of access 'by its very nature calls for regulation by the state, regulation which may vary in time and place according to the needs and resources of the community and of individuals'.[20] In imposing restrictions, the state is allowed a certain 'margin of appreciation'. However, as indicated in *Ashingdane v UK*,[1] any restriction must not be such that 'the very essence of the right is impaired'. In addition, it must have a 'legitimate aim' and comply with the principle of proportionality, ie there must be 'a reasonable relationship of proportionality between the means employed and the aim sought to be achieved'.[2] In the *Ashingdane* case, the applicant instituted civil proceedings challenging the Secretary of State's decision under the Mental Health Act 1959 in effect to continue to detain him in a secure mental hospital. There was no liability under the Act for acts done under it in the absence of bad faith or reasonable care. Moreover, a claim in respect of such an act could not be brought unless the High Court gave leave, which it could do only if it was satisfied that there were 'substantial grounds' for believing that this condition was met. The Court held that these limitations on the right of access to a court as applied to the applicant's case were not in breach of the right. The limitation of liability under the Act had the 'legitimate aim' of preventing those caring for mental patients from being unfairly harassed by litigation and the availability of a claim in a case of bad faith or lack of reasonable care both left intact the essence of the right to institute proceedings and was consistent with the principle of proportionality.

In accordance with the *Ashingdane* approach, restrictions upon access to the courts by minors,[3] vexatious litigants,[4] prisoners[5] or bankrupts[6] have been allowed or countenanced in principle. Reasonable time limits in respect of proceedings are permitted,[7] as is the imposition of a 'civil fine' for making an abusive appeal to a higher court,[8] and a requirement that an appeal be lodged by a lawyer (not the applicant)[9] or for the payment of security for costs.[10] It is also permissible to deny a person whose telephone is tapped

19 Ibid.
20 *Golder v UK* A 18 para 38 (1975).
1 *Ashingdane v UK* A 93 para 57 (1985). Cf *Winterwerp v Netherlands* A 33 para 75 (1979). The 'very essence' requirement overlaps with the 'effective' right requirement: see *De Geouffre de la Pradelle v France*, at p 198 above, where the Court used both terms.
2 *Ashingdane v UK* A 93 para 57 (1985). Cf *Lithgow v UK* A 102 para 194 (1985).
3 *Golder v UK* A 18 (1975).
4 *H v UK No 11559/85*, 45 DR 281 (1985) (applicant subject to a vexatious litigant's order and hence needed judicial permission to bring a case).
5 *Campbell and Fell v UK* A 80 para 113 (1984) (limits on access to solicitor for security reasons). Cf *Campbell v UK No 12323/86*, 57 DR 148 (1988).
6 *M v UK No 12040/86*, 52 DR 269 (1987).
7 *X v Sweden No 9707/82*, 31 DR 223 (1982).
8 *Gillow v UK* A 109 (1986).
9 *Grepne v UK No 17070/90*, 66 DR 268 (1990) (*cautio judicatum solvi*).
10 *P v France No 10412/83*, 52 DR 128 (1987) and *Les Travaux du Midi v France No 12275/86*, 70 DR 47 (1991).

under a system that is consistent with Article 8 of the Convention a court remedy to question the legality of the tapping while it continues; such a restriction is justifiable in order to ensure the effectiveness of the system.[11] Where a company is nationalised, it is permissible to provide for an appropriate collective right of action concerning compensation in place of rights of action by individual shareholders in order to avoid a multiplicity of claims.[12] In contrast, a rule by which a claim in respect of fees for work done by a professional person cannot be brought by him, but must be subrogated to a professional organisation, which then has control over its exercise, robs him of the 'essence' of what is a personal right.[13] Similarly, a law that barred certain Greek monasteries from bringing legal proceedings in respect of their property, giving the right to bring proceedings to the Greek Church instead, was a breach of the monasteries' right of access to a court, even though the Church had an obvious interest in defending the property.[14]

A procedural bar to the successful bringing of a claim in the form of an immunity or defence that may be pleaded by the defendant is also to be seen as a restriction upon the right of access to a court. It will be permissible if it meets the *Ashingdane* requirements indicated above. This approach was adopted by the Court in *Fayed v UK*.[15] In that case, the Court held that a defence of privilege available in an action for defamation that might be brought by the owners of a company concerning allegations of fraud in a government inspector's report on the company was a permissible restriction on the right of access. It had a legitimate aim (to facilitate the investigation of public companies in the public interest) and, in the light of the defendant state's margin of appreciation, was not disproportionate on the facts.[16] The same approach could be used in a particular case to justify parliamentary,[17] diplomatic or state immunity from suit. In *Dyer v UK*,[18] the applicant soldier had been prevented from suing the Crown in negligence because s 10 of the Crown Proceedings Act 1947 excluded Crown liability in tort in respect of his injuries arising out of service in the armed forces. The Commission declared the application inadmissible on the basis that Article 6 was not applicable because there was no dispute or contestation concerning the applicant's civil rights and obligations under national law in view of the statutory immunity.[19] Whereas a state could not introduce such a limitation

---

11 *Klass v FRG* A 28 (1978).
12 *Lithgow v UK* A 102 (1986).
13 *Philis v Greece* A 209 (1991).
14 *Holy Monasteries v Greece* A 301-A (1994). The monasteries concerned had separate legal personality.
15 A 294-B (1994).
16 The Court noted, *inter alia*, that businessmen who enter the public sphere lay themselves open to close scrutiny; that the applicants had themselves sought to bring the matters commented upon into the public domain; and that judicial review of the inspector's activities provided some remedy.
17 See *X v Austria No 3374/67*, 12 YB 246 (1969).
18 *No 10475/83*, 39 DR 246 (1984). Cf *Wallace-Jones v UK No 10782/84*, 47 DR 157 (1986).
19 On the need for a dispute or contestation for Article 6 to apply, see above, p 186.

'arbitrarily', this was not the case on the facts; the special circumstances of armed forces employment coupled with the UK armed forces substitute pension scheme of a kind common to the law of other contracting parties meant that the limitation was justifiable. Following the *Fayed* case, the *Dyer* case would be considered in terms of the right of access under Article 6, rather than the question whether Article 6 was applicable.[20] One can imagine, however, that the outcome would be the same.

The right of access may be restricted in criminal, as well as non-criminal cases. Thus a decision may be taken not to prosecute or proceedings may be discontinued.[1] A practice whereby there is no hearing as to guilt or innocence (only as to the sentence) if an accused pleads guilty at the beginning of his trial is consistent with Article 6(1) provided that adequate safeguards exist to prevent abuse.[2] It is also permissible to issue a penal order by which a person is convicted and sentenced in respect of a minor criminal offence without any court hearing, provided that the person has sufficient opportunity to request a hearing. In *Hennings v Germany*,[3] the accused was convicted and fined by penal order of two offences without a hearing. Although properly critical of the fact that the applicant was given very short notice to object to the order, the Court found no breach of the right of access because the accused had negligently failed to take advantage of the opportunities he had been given to object.

A person may waive his right of access in both criminal or non-criminal cases, as, for example, by a contract clause by which the parties agree to arbitration rather than recourse to the courts.[4] In *Deweer v Belgium*,[5] the Court stated that a claim of waiver should be subjected to 'particularly careful review'. In that case, a butcher chose to pay an out of court fine for an 'over-pricing' offence rather than wait for trial. A waiver was found not to have occurred because his decision to waive his right to a trial was subject to constraint. In particular, the accused was faced with the provisional

---

20 In the *Fayed* case, the defendant state had argued that the case should be treated not as a right of access case – the applicants could freely go to court – but as a case concerning the applicability of Article 6. In its view, the privilege defence set a limit to the applicants' substantive rights and meant that there was no dispute or *contestation* concerning them. While drawing a distinction between substance and procedure (see the passage quoted above, p 187), the Court found it unnecessary to decide the question on the facts. As it stated, 'it is not always an easy matter to trace the dividing line between procedural and substantive limitations of a given entitlement under domestic law': A 294-B para 67 (1994).
1 *Deweer v Belgium* A 35 para 49 (1980). See also *X v UK No 8233/78*, 3 EHRR 271 (1979). Where the discontinuance of proceedings may imply guilt, there may be a breach of Article 6(2): see below, p 246.
2 *X v UK No 5076/71*, 40 CD 64 at 67 (1972). The adequate safeguards in that case were that 'the judge is satisfied that the accused understands the effect of his plea and the accused's confession is recorded'.
3 A 251-A (1992). Cf *X v FRG No 4260/69*, 35 CD 155 (1970).
4 *Deweer v Belgium* A 35 para 49 (1980). See also *R v Switzerland No 10881/84*, 51 DR 83 (1987).
5 A 35 para 49 (1980). Cf the requirement that a waiver be 'unequivocal' used in later cases in respect of other waivable Article 6 rights: see below, p 220.

closure of his shop pending prosecution, with consequential economic loss, if he elected to go for trial.

Finally, the right of access to a court overlaps with the right to an effective national remedy in respect of a breach of a Convention right that is guaranteed by Article 13.[6] The overlap exists insofar as the Convention right is also a 'civil right' in the sense of Article 6(1). The right of access provides a stricter guarantee than Article 13 in that it requires a remedy before a court.[7]

ii. The right to a fair hearing

In contrast with the other more precise guarantees in Article 6(1), the right to a 'fair hearing' has an open-ended, residual quality. It provides an opportunity both for adding other specific rights not listed in Article 6 that are considered essential to a 'fair hearing' and for deciding whether a 'fair hearing' has occurred on the particular facts of a given case when the proceedings are looked at as a whole. In criminal cases, it has to be read together with the specific guarantees in Articles 6(2) and (3). Whereas the latter are subsumed within the former, the general guarantee of a fair hearing in Article 6(1) has elements that supplement those specified in Articles 6(2) and (3). Where a case falls within one of the specific guarantees in Articles 6(2) or (3), it is sometimes considered by the Strasbourg authorities under that guarantee by itself or in conjunction with Article 6(1). Where the case has elements that go beyond a specific guarantee, the case is considered under both provisions or just under the general 'fair hearing' guarantee in Article 6(1).

Although the right to a 'fair hearing' applies in civil as well as criminal cases, 'the contracting states have a greater latitude when dealing with civil cases concerning civil rights and obligations than they have when dealing with criminal cases'.[8] Thus although certain of the guarantees listed in Article 6(3) (eg the right to legal assistance or to examine or cross-examine witnesses) may in principle be inherent in a 'fair hearing' in civil as well as criminal cases, they may not apply with quite the same rigour or in precisely the same way in civil proceedings as they do in criminal ones.[9] The same is true of such rights as the right to be present at the trial and to 'equality of arms' that flow exclusively from Article 6(1) in both criminal and civil cases.[10]

A number of specific rights have, in effect, been added to Article 6(1) through the medium of the fair hearing guarantee. The best established of these are the rights to an oral hearing in person and to equality of arms.

---

6   On the inter-relationship between the two guarantees, see *Golder v UK* A 18 para 33 (1975). See also *Powell and Rayner v UK* A 172 (1990) and the joint Separate Opinion of Judges Pinheiro Farinha and De Meyer in *W v UK* A 121 (1987). As to Article 13, see below, Ch 14.
7   See *De Geouffre de la Pradelle v France* A 253-B para 37 (1992).
8   *Dombo Beheer v Netherlands* A 274 para 32 (1993).
9   Ibid.
10   Ibid and *Hendrich v France* A 296-A (1994).

Others considered below are in the process of crystallisation. A breach of such a specific right may by itself amount to a breach of the right to a fair hearing in Article 6(1) without any need to consider other aspects of the proceedings.

In cases not involving a breach of such a specific right, the Court may none the less find a breach of the right to a fair hearing on a 'trial as a whole' basis. Thus in *Barberà, Messegué and Jabardo v Spain*,[11] involving the prosecution of alleged members of a separatist Catalan organisation for terrorist offences, the Court identified a number of features of the trial that cumulatively led it to conclude that there had not been a fair hearing. The Court referred to the fact that the accused had been driven over 300 miles the night before the trial, the 'unexpected changes' in the court's membership, the 'brevity' of the trial and, 'above all' the failure to adduce and discuss important evidence orally in the accused's presence as considerations that taken 'as a whole' rendered the hearing unfair contrary to Article 6(1).

Whereas the 'trial as a whole' approach may thus lead to a finding of the *absence* of a fair hearing on a cumulation of events basis, it may also work against an applicant where a particular, acknowledged deficiency is not thought to have prejudiced the accused when the proceedings are looked at *in toto*. In *Stanford v UK*,[12] it was not disputed that the accused was unable to participate effectively in the proceedings because he had not been able to hear the witnesses. However, when the proceedings were looked at 'in their entirety', including the fact that the accused had an experienced counsel with whom he had been able to communicate and who had clearly defended him well, the Court concluded that he had received a fair trial.

a. A hearing in one's presence

Although not expressly provided for in Article 6, the right to an oral hearing is implicit in the obligation in Article 6(1) to ensure a 'public hearing' and is considered below under that heading.[13] A rule providing for an oral hearing may just permit the presence of a lawyer. The present section is concerned with the right of a person who is a party to a case to attend the hearing himself.

As far as criminal cases are concerned, 'it flows from the notion of a fair trial that a person charged with a criminal offence should, as a general principle, be entitled to be present at the trial hearing'.[14] Clearly, the accused has an interest in witnessing and monitoring proceedings that are of great importance to him. Moreover, his right to be present at the trial hearing is

---

11 A 146 paras 68, 89 (1988).
12 A 182-A para 24 (1994). In the Commission's jurisprudence, see *Nielsen v Denmark* 343/57, 4 YB 494 at 548-50 (1961) Com Rep; CM Res DH (61); *Can v Austria* A 96 (1985) Com Rep para 48; *F v UK No 11058/84*, 47 DR 230 (1986); and *Harper v UK No 11229/84*, unreported, quoted in Stavros, p 44.
13 See below, p 218.
14 *Ekbatani v Sweden* A 134 para 25 (1988).

implicit in the right to 'participate effectively' in the conduct of his case;[15] an accused needs to be there to give evidence and to advise his lawyer on the presentation of his case or to present his case in person.[16] There is a close inter-relationship between the right to an oral hearing in one's presence and the right to adversarial proceedings. A trial in which the evidence accumulated during the investigation of the case is admitted to the record without being adduced in court in the presence of the accused is not consistent with either.[17]

It follows from the right of an accused to be present at his trial that where the state has custody of the accused, it must ensure that he is able to attend, provided that the accused gives the prison authorities any necessary information.[18]

In contrast with criminal cases, whereas there is a general right to an oral hearing the right of a party *to be present* at the hearing has been held by the Commission to extend to only certain kinds of non-criminal cases.[19] These include cases where the 'personal character and manner of life' of the party concerned is directly relevant to the decision[20] or where, as is likely, the case involves an assessment of the applicant's 'conduct'.[1] In other cases it will be sufficient that there is an oral hearing at which the party is represented by a lawyer.[2] However, the recognition of the right to an adversarial procedure[3] suggests that the right of a party to civil proceedings to be present should be more generally recognised.[4]

A party to a criminal or non-criminal case may waive his right to be present at an oral hearing, provided that the waiver is 'established in an unequivocal manner' and is 'attended by minimum safeguards commensurate to its importance'.[5] This may be done impliedly, by not attending the hearing, having been given effective notice of it.[6] It is not clearly established

15 *Stanford v UK* A 280-A para 26 (1994). Cf *Colozza and Rubinat v Italy* A 89 para 25 (1985). See also Articles 6(3)(c), (d), (e) which suppose the accused's presence.
16 In the *Colozza* case, Com Rep para 116 (1983), the Commission identified the importance of the 'personality of the accused' to the court's decision as a further reason for his presence.
17 *Barberà, Messequé and Jabardo v Spain* A 146 para 81 (1988).
18 *Goddi v Italy* A 76 (1984). In this case under Article 6(3)(c), the Court placed the burden on the accused, who had received notice of the proceedings, to inform the prison authorities. See also the facts of *Widmaier v Netherlands No 9573/81*, 48 DR 14 (1986) F Sett (extradition prevented appearance at appeal hearing).
19 See *Håkansson v Sweden* A 171-A para 66 (1990) and *Fredin v Sweden (No 2)* A 283-A para 21 (1994).
20 *X v Sweden No 434/58*, 2 YB 354 at 370 (1959). Child access cases fall within the above category (ibid), but see *X v Austria No 8893/80*, 31 DR 66 (1983). So may some commercial cases (*X v FRG No 1169/61*, 6 YB 520 at 572 (1963)). In later cases, the Commission has suggested that 'personal character and manner of life' cases are the only such cases: see eg *No 10754/84*, 2 Digest Supp 6.1.1.4.4.1 (1984).
1   *Muyldermans v Belgium No 12217/86*, A 214-A (1991) Com Rep para 64.
2   It is for the applicant to show that his presence is necessary: X v Switzerland No 7370/76, 9 DR 95 (1977).
3   See below, p 214.
4   Cf *Feldbrugge v Netherlands* A 99 (1986).
5   *Poitrimol v France* A 277-A (1993). Cf *Colozza and Rubinat v Italy* A 89 para 28 (1985).
6   *C v Italy No 10889/84*, 56 DR 40 (1988). As to effective notice, see below at p 205, n 10.

whether a party who has not been given such notice but who has absconded to evade court proceedings has thereby waived his right. In *Colozza and Rubinat v Italy*,[7] the Commission stated that there was no waiver in this situation as the right to a fair trial was absolute and applied to accused persons on the run as well as to others who had not indicated that they had waived their right. The Court, however, expressly left the point open. It is submitted that by absconding an accused or other party to a case has 'unequivocally' shown a wish not to be present.[8]

As well as in cases of waiver, trial *in absentia* is also permitted where the state has acted diligently, but unsuccessfully, to give an accused[9] effective notice of the hearing.[10] In *Colozza and Rubinat v Italy*,[11] the Court stated that this is because the 'impossibility of holding a trial by default may paralyse the conduct of criminal proceedings, in that it may lead, for example, to the dispersal of evidence, expiry of the time-limit for prosecution or a miscarriage of justice.' On the facts of the *Colozza* case, the Court found a breach of Article 6(1) because the authorities had not acted diligently. They had sent the summons to the applicant's previous address, which he had changed without informing the authorities as required by law. The Court found that the authorities had not been diligent in the steps they had taken to locate the applicant's new address and that trial *in absentia* was a disproportionate penalty for failure to report a change of address.[12]

In a case where a trial is permitted *in absentia* under the rule in the *Colozza* case, should the accused later learn of the proceedings,[13] he must be able to obtain 'a fresh determination of the merits of the charge'.[14] The right to such a rehearing adequately overcomes the 'fair' trial problems that may result from the accused's absence at the original trial.[15] The Court has stated that it is 'open to question' whether the right to a rehearing applies where the accused has waived his right to be present at the initial hearing.[16] In any event, it would be unlikely that the Court would hold that an accused who had absconded had a right to a re-hearing.[17]

---

7   A 89 para 28 (1985) Com Rep para 123. See also *B v France No 10291/83*, 47 DR 59 (1986).
8   Cf Stavros, p 265.
9   The cases have concerned criminal prosecutions. The notice must be given in person: *Stamoulakatos v Greece* A 271 (1993) Com Rep para 61. Court declined jurisdiction on *ratione temporis* grounds.
10 To be effective for this purpose, notice must be given in reasonable time (Cf *Goddi v Italy* A 76 (1984), an Article 6(3)(c) case) and in a language that the accused understands (*Brozicek v Italy* A 167 (1989)). Notice means official notice; the fact that the accused has 'indirect knowledge' of the proceedings is not sufficient: *T v Italy* A 245-C (1992).
11 A 89 para 29 (1985).
12 Cf *F C B v Italy* A 208-B (1991) and *T v Italy* A 245-C (1992).
13 In view of *T v Italy*, above, he may have to be given official notice.
14 *Colozza and Rubinat v Italy* A 89 para 29 (1985). The possibility must be available without the accused having to prove that he was not seeking to evade justice or *force majeure*: ibid.
15 Cf *B v France No 10291/83*, 47 DR 59 (1986).
16 *Poitrimol v France* A 277-A para 31 (1993).
17 A re-hearing is generally not permitted by European states where the accused has absconded: cf the European standard suggested in the Council of Europe Criteria Governing Proceedings held in the Absence of the Accused, CM Res (75) 11.

In addition to cases in which it has not proved possible to inform the applicant of the proceedings, a trial may also proceed in the absence or consent of the accused in the interests of the administration of justice in some cases of illness. Thus in *Ensslin, Baader and Raspe v FRG*,[18] the accused had, by going on hunger strike, reduced themselves to the point where they were medically unfit to attend the hearing for more than a limited number of hours each day. The decision to continue the trial during their absence was held by the Commission not to be a breach of the right to an oral hearing in person, taking into account the need for the proceedings not to grind to a halt, the presence of the applicants' lawyers at the hearing and their unrestricted opportunities to consult with their clients. Obviously also, an accused who seeks to delay proceedings by claiming unsubstantiated illness may be tried in his absence.[19]

Although Article 6 applies to such appeal proceedings as a state chooses to provide,[20] there are limits to the right to a public, and hence oral, hearing on appeal.[1] In some cases written proceedings will suffice, so that the question of the right to be present does not arise. In cases where an oral hearing is required, the presence of a legal representative may be sufficient. A pre-condition of any dispensation from the applicant's right to be present is that there has been an oral hearing at first instance at which he has been entitled to be present in accordance with the rules indicated above; beyond that, the right to be present depends on the role of the appellate court and the particular facts of the case.[2] For example, in *Monnell and Morris v UK*,[3] it was held that the applicants were not entitled to an oral hearing in person in proceedings before the English Court of Appeal in their applications for leave to appeal to that court against conviction and sentence; it was sufficient that they were permitted to make written submissions or representations through a lawyer whom they might appoint.[4] This was so even though the Court of Appeal might order that a part of the time spent in prison awaiting the outcome of an unmeritorious application should not count towards the applicant's sentence. Relevant considerations were that the trial proceedings had involved an oral hearing in the applicant's presence and that the Court of Appeal did not re-hear the facts of the case or call witnesses.

'In other cases concerning the hearing of an appeal on its merits, it has been held that where the court is competent only to consider points of law, it is unlikely that an oral hearing at which the applicant (as opposed to his lawyer) is entitled to be present is required, and it may well be that written proceedings are sufficient.[5]'

18 *Nos 7572/76, 7586/76 and 7587/76*, 14 DR 64 (1978).
19 *X v UK No 4798/71*, 40 CD 31 (1972).
20 See below, p 240
1   See below, p 220.
2   *Ekbatani v Sweden* A 134 para 27 (1988).
3   A 115 (1987).
4   An appellant is entitled to be legally represented at an oral hearing in such leave to appeal proceedings, although, as in the *Monnell* and *Morris* cases, he may not be allowed legal aid in the absence of arguable grounds for appeal.

Where the appeal court may hear the case *on the facts as well as the law*, the need for an oral hearing at which the applicant is entitled to be present depends on both the court's need for the applicant's presence in order to determine the facts and the importance of what is at stake for him. Thus in *Ekbatani v Sweden*,[6] in which the accused appealed to the Swedish Court of Appeal against his conviction, arguing that he had not committed the act in question, the European Court held that the applicant's presence was required: the court needed to hear the applicant in order to assess his credibility. In contrast, in *Jan-Åke Andersson v Sweden*,[7] the same Court of Appeal could determine the applicant's guilt or innocence from the case-file without hearing him. In *Kremzow v Austria*,[8] the presence of the applicant at the hearing of an appeal to consider whether his sentence should be increased to life imprisonment and whether he should serve it in an institution for mentally deranged offenders *was* required in view of what was at stake. Whether an oral hearing is required *at all* in appeals on questions of fact and law depends on the circumstances. In the *Andersson* and *Fejde* cases, written proceedings were sufficient.

b. Equality of arms

The right to a 'fair hearing' also requires compliance with the principle of 'equality of arms'.[9] The Commission has expressed the principle, in respect of both criminal and non-criminal cases, as entailing that 'everyone who is a party to such proceedings shall have a reasonable opportunity of presenting his case to the court under conditions which do not place him at substantial disadvantage vis-à-vis his opponent'.[10] In criminal cases, the principle of equality of arms included in Article 6(1) overlaps with the specific guarantees in Article 6(3).[11] It has, however, a wider application than this, applying to all aspects of the proceedings.[12]

---

5 *Axen v FRG* A 72 (1983) and *Sutter v Switzerland* A 74 (1984) (written proceedings sufficient in both). Cf *Kamasinski v Austria* A 168 (1989).

6 A 134 (1988). Cf *Helmers v Sweden* A 212-A (1991) (applicant had to be heard in person in a defamation appeal where the facts were disputed and his professional reputation and career were at stake).

7 A 212-B (1991) (road traffic offence admitted in its essentials). Cf *Fejde v Sweden* A 212-C (1991).

8 A 268-B (1993).

9 *Neumeister v Austria* A 8 (1968). 'Equality of arms' is 'an inherent element of a fair trial': *X v FRG No 1169/61*, 6 YB 520 at 574 (1963).

10 *Kaufman v Belgium No 10938/84*, 50 DR 98 at 115 (1986). This may include providing an accused with documents on the case file, even though they are not relied on in court: *Bendenoun v France* A 284 para 52 (1994). The Court adopted the above formula in the context of 'civil rights and obligations' in *Dombo Beheer v Netherlands* A 274 para 34 (1993), quoted below, p 209. Generally, the Court understood the principle as incorporating the idea of 'a "fair balance" between the parties': id, para 33.

11 This is most clearly the case with that in Article 6(3)(d), but it also applies to 'equality of arms' with the prosecution in respect of facilities (Article 6(3)(b)) and legal representation (Article 6(3)(c)).

12 *Ofner and Hopfinger v Austria* 6 YB 676 (1962) Com Rep para 46; CM Res (63) DHI.

Applying the principle in a criminal case, in *Borgers v Belgium*,[13] the Court held that the lack of equal standing between the Procureur General and the appellant before the Court of Cassation was in breach of Article 6(1). In particular, the Procureur General was entitled to state his opinion in open court as to whether the appellant's appeal in a criminal case should be allowed and then retire with the Court and take part (without a vote) in its discussion of the appeal. In contrast, the appellant or his lawyer could not respond to the Procureur General's opinion or retire with the judges. The decision reversed the European Court's earlier ruling to the contrary in the much criticised case of *Delcourt v Belgium*[14] and invalidated a century-old Belgian practice. In its reasoning, the Court accepted that the Procureur General was not a part of the prosecution and that his function was to give independent and impartial advice to the Court in the manner of an advocate general. However, once he had expressed an opinion on the merits of the appeal, he became the applicant's 'opponent', to whose arguments the applicant should have been able to respond. Similarly, and 'above all', the Procureur General's participation in the Court's private deliberations 'could reasonably be thought' to have afforded him an opportunity to reinforce his view that the appeal should be dismissed. In reaching its conclusion, the European Court emphasised the importance of 'appearances' and 'the increased sensitivity of the public to the fair administration of justice'.[15] The emphasis upon 'appearances', which echoes the English law doctrine that 'justice must be seen to be done', follows the use of the same idea in the Court's jurisprudence on the requirement of an 'independent and impartial' tribunal.[16] By requiring the applicant to show only a 'legitimate doubt', objectively justified, of a lack of procedural equality, rather than actual lack of such equality, the Court's reference to 'appearances' is to be welcomed as strengthening the principle of 'equality of arms'.

It is also a breach of the principle for an expert witness appointed by the accused not to be accorded equal treatment with one appointed by the trial court who has links with the prosecution.[17] It is permissible to exclude as evidence statements made by a third party favourable to the accused even though the accused's statements to the police are included, provided that the

---

13 A 214-B (1991). See Wauters, 69 RDIDC 125 (1992). Cf *Pataki and Dunshirn v Austria, Nos 596/59 and 789/60*, 6 YB 714 (1963) Com Rep; CM Res DH (63) 2, concerning a practice by which the Public Prosecutor could present arguments before the Austrian Criminal Court of Appeal when the accused had no right of audience. Austria changed its law following the Commission's finding against it. See also *Ofner and Hopfinger v Austria*, id, 676 (1962).

14 A 11 (1970). For criticisms, see Cappelletti and Jolowicz, *Public Interest Parties and the Active Role of the Judge in Civil Litigation*, 1975, p 31, Nadelmann 66 AJIL 509 (1972) and Velu, *L'Affaire Delcourt*, 1972.

15 A 214-B para 24 (1991). Cf the reasoning in *Brandstetter v Austria* A 211 (1991): see below, n 17.

16 See below, p 235. In the *Borgers* case, the Court confirmed the *Delcourt* case ruling that the Procureur General's role did not infringe that guarantee. For criticism of the Court's use of the 'appearances' doctrine in the *Borgers* case, see the dissenting opinion of Judge Martens.

17 *Bönisch v Austria* A 92 (1985). Contrast *Brandstetter v Austria* A 211 (1991) on the facts (no 'objective justification' for fear that a court-appointed expert not neutral).

accused can call the third party as a witness.[18] Nor does a period of time during which the prosecution may lodge an appeal that is marginally longer than that which is available to the accused infringe the principle.[19]

The principle also applies in 'civil rights and obligations' cases. Echoing the Commission's general formulation of the principle in earlier cases,[20] the Court stated in *Dombo Beheer v Netherlands*[1] that 'as regards litigation involving opposing private interests, "equality of arms" implies that each party must be afforded a reasonable opportunity to present his case – including his evidence – under conditions that do not place him at a substantial disadvantage vis-à-vis his opponent'. Thus in the *Dombo Beheer* case, in which it had to be proved that an oral agreement had been made by X and Y at a meeting which only they attended, there was a breach of the principle because the applicant was not allowed to call X to give evidence when the other party was allowed to call Y. Similarly, the principle was infringed in *Ruiz-Mateos v Spain*[2] when, in appeal proceedings before the Spanish Constitutional Court, the applicants were not allowed to reply to written submissions to the Court made by the Counsel for the State, their opponent in a civil case, on the constitutionality of a relevant law. The Court also invoked the principle of 'equality of arms' in *Stran Greek Refineries and Stratis Andreadis v Greece*.[3] There the Greek government put legislation through the national legislature that made 'inevitable' a decision against the applicant in his pending civil claim against the government. Finding a breach of Article 6(1), the Court stated that the 'principle of the rule of law and the notion of fair trial enshrined in Article 6 preclude any interference by the legislature with the administration of justice designed to influence the judicial determination of the dispute'. In other cases, the Court has indicated that 'equality of arms' requires that the parties to civil proceedings be permitted to cross-examine witnesses,[4] be informed of and so be able to challenge the reasons for an administrative decision[5] and be allowed access to facilities[6] on equal terms. The fact that a state authority against whose decision the applicant is appealing may be able to determine

---

18 *Blastland v UK No 12045/86*, 52 DR 273 (1987).
19 *U v Luxembourg No 10140/82*, 42 DR 86 (1985). Cf *Kremzow v Austria* A 268-B para 75 (1993). On 'equality of arms' in leave to appeal proceeding in the English Court of Appeal, see *Monnell and Morris v UK* A 115 (1987) and *Brown v UK No 11129/84*, 42 DR 269 (1985).
20 See above, p 207.
1   A 274 para 33 (1993). For other non-criminal cases on 'equality of arms', see *Feldbrugge v Netherlands* A 99 para 44 (1986) and *Van de Hurk v Netherlands* A 288 (1994).
2   A 262 (1993). The Court found a breach of the right to a 'fair hearing' by reference to the principle of 'equality of arms' and the right to an adversarial trial taken together. Cf *Brandstetter v Austria* A 211 (1991).
3   A 301-B paras 46 and 49.
4   *X v Austria No 5362/72*, 42 CD 145 (1972). Cf in criminal cases the specific guarantee in Article 6(3)(d). Claims to legal aid in civil litigation might in some cases be seen in terms of 'equality of arms' with the other party. On legal aid as a part of the right of access to a court, see above, p 198.
5   *Hentrich v France* A 296-A para 56 (1994).
6   See *Schuler-Zgraggen v Switzerland* A 263 (1993).

the order in which appeals are considered and thereby influence their outcome is not a breach of 'equality of arms' unless it can be shown that the particular applicant has suffered as a result.[7] Even though the facts show this the resulting unfairness may be corrected by an appellate court.[8]

c. Rules of evidence

The right to a fair hearing in Article 6(1) does not require that any particular rules of evidence are followed in national courts in either criminal or non-criminal cases; it is in principle for each state to lay down its own rules.[9] Such an approach is inevitable, given the wide variations in the rules of evidence in different European legal systems, with, for example, common law systems controlling the admissibility of evidence very tightly and civil law systems setting very few restrictions.[10] However, the Strasbourg authorities have set certain parameters within which a state must operate and have found that the use of a particular rule of evidence in any system may cause the trial to be unfair on the facts.

ADMISSIBILITY OF ILLEGALLY OBTAINED AND OTHER EVIDENCE

The Court has held that whereas a rule permitting the use of evidence obtained illegally under national law in a criminal prosecution is not in itself a breach of the right to a fair hearing, its application in a particular case may be. In *Schenk v Switzerland*,[11] there was no breach of Article 6(1) when an illegally obtained tape recording that incriminated the accused was admitted in evidence. This was because the defence had been able to challenge the use and authenticity of the tape and there was other evidence supporting the accused's conviction. The Court might have reached a different conclusion if the tape were the only or the main incriminating evidence and/or there were doubts as to its authenticity that could have been raised by the defence. It may also have been relevant that there was no suggestion of an abuse of police power, the tape having been handed over to the police by a private person. It is probable that the admission in court of evidence that is obtained by 'maltreatment with the aim of extracting a confession' is a breach of the right to a fair hearing.[12] During the investigation of a case, a confession or other statement by the accused must be given in the presence of the accused's lawyer or, in the absence of this, satisfactory procedures

---

7   *Schouten and Meldrum v Netherlands* A 304 para 71 (1994).
8   Ibid.
9   *Schenk v Switzerland* A 140 para 46 (1988). Thus, for example, rules as the burden of proof in civil proceedings are in principle for national courts: *G v France No 11941/86*, 57 DR 100 (1988).
10   See Schlesinger, Baade, Damaska and Herzog, *Comparative Law*, 5th edn, 1988, p 425.
11   A 140 (1988). Cf *Wischnewski v France No 12505/86*, 58 DR 106 (1988) and *Scheichelbauer v Austria No 2645/65*, 12 YB 156 (1969) DA; 14 YB 902 (1971) Com Rep; CM Res DH (71) 3.
12   See *Austria v Italy*, below, p 224, n 14 where it was stated that the admission of such evidence is a breach of Article 6(2).

be available at the trial to check that it has not been given under duress.[13] It is not a breach of Article 6 to admit evidence obtained by an undercover agent placed in prison to overhear conversations.[14] Evidence by an accomplice who has been promised immunity is admissible provided that the jury is made fully aware of the situation.[15] Consistently with the practice in a number of European criminal justice systems, it has been held in cases coming from such systems that it is not in breach of Article 6(1) for the court to be informed of the accused's criminal record during the trial[16] or for a conviction to be founded solely on circumstantial evidence.[17]

EVIDENCE OF A PERSON WHO DOES NOT APPEAR AS A WITNESS AT THE TRIAL

The right to a fair hearing may also be infringed in a criminal case[18] when written statements by a person who does not appear as a witness are introduced in evidence or when the evidence of such a person is recounted by another person who does appear as a witness.[19] The first in a series of cases concerning such evidence was *Unterpertinger v Austria*.[20] There the applicant's wife and daughter, whom he was accused of assaulting, exercised their privilege as family members under Austrian law not to give evidence. Their statements to the police were introduced by the prosecution in evidence and the accused's conviction was based 'mainly' on them.[1] The Court held that because the accused could not confront the witnesses, his defence rights were 'appreciably restricted' in breach of Article 6(1) taken together with the principles underlying Article 6(3)(d). The decision of a Chamber of the Court in the *Unterpertinger* case was followed by a decision of the plenary Court in *Kostovski v Netherlands*.[2] There, in breach of Articles 6(1) and (3)(d), the

---

13 *G v UK No 9370/81*, 35 DR 75 (1983). In this pre-PACE case, in which the accused had been questioned in the absence of a lawyer, the Commission was satisfied by the availability of *voir dire* proceedings and the fact that the prosecution had the burden of proving that the statement was voluntary.

14 *X v FRG No 12127/86*, 11 EHRR 88 (1989).

15 *X v UK No 7306/75*, 7 DR 115 (1976).

16 *X v Austria No 2676/65*, 23 CD 31 (1967).

17 *Alberti v Italy No 12013/86*, 59 DR 100 (1989).

18 The cases have been criminal ones. Reliance upon hearsay evidence in civil proceedings may also be suspect, although the differences between the two kinds of proceedings suggests a less rigorous rule.

19 The hearsay rule as it applies in the context of a jury system in English law has been stated to be 'in principle' not in breach of Article 6(1): *Blastland v UK No 12045/86*, 52 DR 273 (1987). In that case the exclusion of hearsay evidence sought to be introduced by the *accused* was not in breach of Article 6(1).

20 A 110 (1986). See Osborne, 1993 Crim LR 255. This and later cases were decided by the Court under Articles 6(1) and (3)(d) together. They are treated under Article 6(1) for convenience.

1 A 110 para 33 (1986).

2 A 166 (1989). Cf *Windisch v Austria* A 186 (1990) (court relied 'to a large extent' on missing witnesses' evidence: breach). See also *Barberà, Messegué and Jabardo v Spain* A 146 (1988). And see *Bricmont v Belgium* A 158 (1989), in which the Court found a breach of Articles 6(1) and 6(3)(d) even though the evidence of the missing witness was not the 'main' evidence leading to the conviction.

accused's conviction was to a 'decisive extent' based on statements before the court that had been made earlier by one witness to the police and by another to an examining magistrate. The two witnesses were allowed to remain anonymous and not give evidence in court because of their fear of reprisals by organised crime. The Court accepted that anonymous informants may be used during the investigation into an offence, above all when fighting organised crime.[3] But when their statements become evidence before a trial court, the defence is entitled to question them either during the investigation[4] or at the trial in order to test the credibility of the witness and the reliability of the evidence.[5] Whereas the two cases just discussed suggest that there is a breach of the Convention if the evidence in question is the 'main' or the 'decisive' evidence upon which the conviction is based, in *Asch v Austria*[6] a Chamber of the Court suggested that for there to be a breach, it must be the *only* item of evidence' on which the conviction is based. Although the Court sought to distinguish the *Unterpertinger* case on the facts, in that case the Court had expressly stated that the evidence of the missing witnesses was 'not the only evidence' before the court; although the conviction was based 'mainly' upon it, there was other corroborative evidence too. Since the Court found a breach on the facts of the *Unterpertinger* case, it would seem that the Court in the *Asch* case was applying a different, less demanding test. More recently, in *Artner v Austria*[7] another Chamber of the Court followed the *Asch* case, holding, by 5 to 4, that there was no breach of the Convention when the evidence of a missing witness was 'not the only evidence'. However, in *Lüdi v Switzerland*,[8] a differently composed Chamber found a breach when the evidence, although not the sole evidence, had 'played a part' in the conviction. Although these cases all have other particular facts that may have contributed to the decisions reached in them, it would appear from the general terms used in its judgments that the Court is at present not wholly consistent on the question whether the evidence of persons who do not appear as witnesses that is admitted must be the only evidence upon which the conviction is based or whether it is sufficient that it has played a crucial or significant part. The number of cases that have reached the Court suggests that such evidence is used a lot, so that the question is an important one in practice.

3   In *X v UK No 20657/92*, 15 EHRR CD 113 (1992) the screening of a witness in court so that he could not be seen by a person accused of a terrorist murder was not in breach of Articles 6(1) and (3)(d).

4   The same exception was allowed in the non-informer case of *Isgrò v Italy* A 194-A (1991). In that case there was no breach when the accused had been able to question the witness before the investigating judge.

5   The accused must request that the person be called as a witness at the trial: if he does not, his application will be inadmissible for non-exhaustion of local remedies: *Cardot v France* A 200 (1991).

6   A 203 para 30 (1991). No breach on the fact; there was other corroborative evidence.

7   A 242-A para 24 (1992). See also *Delta v France* A 191-A (1990) and *Saidi v France* A 261-C (1993) in which a breach was found where hearsay evidence was the only evidence. It does not necessarily follow from these judgments that there would not have been a breach if it was the 'main' but not the only evidence.

8   A 238 para 47 (1992).

DEFENCE ACCESS TO EVIDENCE

A fair hearing requires that the prosecution disclose to the defence 'all material evidence for or against the accused'; the failure to do so, which would otherwise be a breach of Article 6(1), will, however, be remedied where the effect of the non-disclosure on the outcome of the case before the trial court is properly considered by a court of appeal.[9] In a non-criminal case, it also requires that a party be permitted to consult relevant evidence at the disposal of the authorities[10] and to call and cross-examine witnesses on terms comparable to those that apply under Article 6(3)(d) in criminal cases.[11] The refusal of a court to order a report by an expert at the request of a party to a civil case may cause the hearing to be unfair, depending on the facts.[12]

ASSESSMENT OF EVIDENCE BY THE NATIONAL COURT

Just as the Strasbourg authorities regard the rules as to the admissibility of evidence as primarily a matter for national decision, so they will not generally review the assessment of evidence by a national court. However, in an exceptional case, looking at the proceedings as a whole, where no evidence of guilt was actually presented adversarially (witnesses having failed to identify the accused), in *Barberà, Messegué and Jabardo v Spain*[13] the Court was prepared to assess the weight of evidence actually before the national court when deciding whether the accused has had a fair hearing.

d. *Freedom from self incrimination*

The right to a fair hearing in a criminal case includes the right to freedom from self-incrimination. In *Funke v France*,[14] the applicant was convicted of an offence of failing to produce bank statements relevant to investigations into customs offences that might have been committed by him. Although no prosecution was eventually brought against him, the Court held that, by attempting to compel him to produce incriminating evidence, the state had infringed his right to remain silent. The decision is to be compared with the Commissions's opinion in *K v Austria*.[15] There the applicant was fined for refusing to give evidence in the trial of persons for drug trafficking on the ground that this would prejudice his defence in criminal proceedings pending against him for purchasing drugs from them. The Commission found that Article 6 did not apply to the case as the fine did not result from a 'criminal charge'. It did, however, find a breach of the applicant's freedom of speech under Article 10. The *Funke* case was followed by the Commission in

---

9   *Edwards v UK* A 247-B para 36 (1992). See further below, p 241.
10   *Feldbrugge v Netherlands* A 99 (1986).
11   As to Article 6(3)(d), see below, p 266.
12   *H v France* A 162-A (1989).
13   *Barberà, Messegué and Jabardo v Spain* A 146 para 68 (1988).
14   A 256-A (1993).
15   A 255-B (1993) Com Rep. F Sett before Court.

Saunders v UK.[16] There, on pain of a criminal sanction (including imprisonment), the applicant was required by law to answer questions put to him by Department of Trade and Industry inspectors in the course of their investigation into the conduct of a company takeover. The information that he gave was introduced as 'a not insignificant part of the evidence against him at his trial', at which the applicant was convicted and sentenced to imprisonment for offences involving commercial fraud. The Commission concluded, by 14 votes to 1, that the applicant's freedom from self-incrimination had been infringed. In the course of its report the Commission stressed that the freedom was 'an important element in safeguarding an accused from oppression and coercion during criminal proceedings' and noted that the freedom was closely linked with the presumption of innocence (Article 6(2)).[17]

The Court's reading of a guarantee of freedom from self-incrimination into Article 6, seemingly through the requirement of a fair hearing,[18] is welcome, if unexpected, as filling a gap in the Convention right to a fair trial that was not closed when the Seventh Protocol was drafted.[19] On its facts, the *Funke* case concerns only freedom from self-incrimination at the pre-trial stage and a breach in the form of conviction for non-co-operation with the authorities in the production of documents. The *Saunders* case goes further in that it concerns coercion in the form of a threat of a criminal sanction. It has yet to be established whether Article 6 prohibits rules that require a person to answer police questions or give evidence in court, although arguably it does, or that it permits certain inferences to be drawn by a judge or jury from a suspect's failure to mention certain facts or explain his presence at the time of arrest.[20] As with some other elements of the right to a fair hearing, the question whether non-compliance with the freedom from self-incrimination involves a breach of Article 6 will depend upon its effect upon the fairness of the proceedings in the particular case taken as a whole.[1]

e. Adversarial proceedings

A principle that underlies Article 6 as a whole is that judicial proceedings must be adversarial. This is most clearly illustrated by the specific guarantee in Article 6(3)(d) of the right to cross-examine witnesses in criminal cases,[2] a

---

16 *No 19187/91* (1994) Com Rep paras 69-75, unreported. Case pending before Court.
17 On the presumption of innocence aspect of the *Saunders* case, see below, p 243.
18 The Court just found a breach of Article 6(1) in the *Funke* case.
19 Freedom from self-incrimination is protected by Article 14(3)(e), ICCPR.
20 See the Criminal Justice and Public Order Act 1994, ss 34-39. In *Murray (John) v UK* (1994) Com Rep, pending before Court, the judge, applying Northern Irish law, drew adverse inferences from the fact that an accused charged with terrorist offences had refused to give evidence at his trial in response to a strong *prima facie* prosecution case against him based on circumstantial evidence. The Commission was of the opinion, by 15 votes to 2, that there was no breach of the right to silence in Article 6(1).
1 See the *Saunders* case, above, Com Rep para 73.
2 See also the right to an oral hearing in one's presence in Article 6(1) and the guarantees in Articles 6(3)(a) and (c).

right which is an element of a fair hearing in non-criminal cases also.[3] Generally, it means that 'all evidence must in principle be produced in the presence of the accused . . . with a view to adversarial argument'.[4] In *Kamasinski v Austria*,[5] compliance with the principle was treated as a distinct requirement, presumably as a part of the requirement of a fair hearing. In that case, there was a breach of Article 6(1) when an appeal judge obtained information over the telephone from the trial judge on the subject-matter of the appeal without the accused being informed or having an opportunity to comment on the trial judge's response.[6] However, it is permissible to prepare and discuss a draft judgment before the hearing.[7]

f.   A reasoned judgment

The requirement of a 'fair' hearing also supposes that a court will give reasons for its judgment. Whereas national courts are allowed considerable discretion as to the structure and content of their judgments, they must 'indicate with sufficient clarity the grounds on which they basis their decision' so that the 'accused may usefully exercise the right of appeal available to him'.[8] It is not necessary for the court to deal with every point raised in argument.[9] If, however, a submission would, if accepted, be decisive for the outcome of the case, it requires a 'specific and express outcome' by the court in its judgment.[10] In the case of a jury trial, given that such trials are not contrary to Article 6, the requirement to give reasons must be limited so as to take account of the way that jury trials operate. Further justifications for the need for a reasoned judgment, which applies in civil[11] as well as criminal cases, are the interest of a party to the case in knowing the reasons for any judgment concerning him and of the public in a

---

3 *X v Austria No 5362/72*, 42 CD 145 (1972).

4 *Barberà, Messegué and Jabardo v Spain* A 146 para 78 (1988). Cf *Feldbrugge v Netherlands* A 99 (1986); *Sanchez-Reisse v Switzerland* A 107 (1986); *H v Belgium* A 127-B (1987); and *Ruiz-Mateos v Spain* A 262 (1993). In the *Barberà* case, the Court found a breach of the fair hearing guarantee partly because various witness statements and documents on the investigation file were simply read into the record. As to exceptions for hearsay evidence, see above, p 211.

5 A 168 (1989). The Court in fact expressed itself in terms of a breach of the 'principle that contending parties should be heard (*le principe du contradictoire*)', para 102, which is essentially the same idea. Cf *Brandstetter v Austria* A 211 (1991) in which the principle was prominent in finding a breach of Article 6(1) when an accused was not given notice of submissions by the Senior Public Prosecutor relied on by the appeal court.

6 Cf the facts of *Jager v Switzerland No 13467/87* (1989), unreported, F Sett in which a conviction was based on reports obtained after the hearing unknown to the accused.

7 *Kremzow v Austria* A 268-B (1993).

8 *Hadjianastassiou v Greece* A 252 para 33 (1992). In criminal cases, the Article 6(1) guarantee of a reasoned judgment overlaps with Article 6(3)(b) 'facilities' guarantee in this regard: ibid. Reasons need not be given for a fine for abuse of process: *Les Travaux de Midi v FRG No 12275/86*, 70 DR 247 (1991).

9 *Van der Hurk v Netherlands* A 288 para 61 (1994).

10 *Hiro Balani v Spain* A 303-B para 28 (1994). Cf *Ruiz Torija v Spain* A 303-A para 30 (1994). Breaches in both cases.

11 *H v Belgium* A 127-B para 53 (1987).

democratic society in knowing the reasons given for judicial decisions in its name. These further justifications suggest that the right to a reasoned judgment applies to final appeal proceedings also, although the reasons given at this stage need not be so full.[12]

g. Legal representation

Whereas Article 6(3)(c) provides a specific guarantee of the right to be legally represented and to be granted legal aid where appropriate in criminal cases, there is no such guarantee in non-criminal cases. However, it has been established that Article 6(1) provides a guarantee, although a less extensive one, in the latter kind of case. This has been achieved by means of the right of access to a court, rather than the right to a fair hearing, so that the matter is dealt with under that heading.[13]

h. Prejudicial publicity

Where a jury trial occurs in a criminal case, the guarantee of a 'fair trial' may be infringed by a 'virulent press campaign against the accused', which influences the jurors.[14] However, the Commission has set several limits to the application of this principle which together help to explain why, despite the great publicity that sometimes attends trials, no case has been admitted on the merits on this basis. The test would appear to be a subjective one, requiring proof of a prejudicial effect upon a jury in fact, rather than just an indication that it is likely.[15] Moreover, where a national appeal court does not consider that the trial has been unfair, the Commission is unlikely to find otherwise.[16] It also has to be borne in mind that some press comment on a trial involving a matter of public interest must be expected.[17] Moreover, the effect of prejudicial comment may be countered by the judge's direction to the jury to discount it.[18] Finally, it may be that state involvement in the generation of the publicity is necessary for it to be responsibile for any resulting prejudice.[19]

12 *X v FRG No 8769/79*, 25 DR 240 (1981). In practice, many constitutional courts reject an appeal in very brief terms.

13 See above, p 198. In some cases, the Commission has referred to the 'fair hearing' requirement as well as the right of access: see eg *Webb v UK No 9353/81*, 33 DR 133 (1983). It has then considered whether there has been a 'fair hearing' in the circumstances of the case as a whole.

14 *X v Austria No 1476/62*, 11 CD 31 at 43 (1963) and *Berns and Ewert v Luxembourg No 13251/87*, 68 DR 137 (1991).

15 *X v Norway No 3444/67*, 35 CD 37 (1970).

16 See eg *X v UK No 3860/68*, 30 CD 70 (1969).

17 *X v Norway No 3444/67*, 35 CD 37 (1970). See also the *Sunday Times case*, below, p 392, in which a contempt of court decision in respect of comment on pending civil litigation was contrary to the guarantee of freedom of speech in Article 10.

18 *X v UK No 7542/76*, 2 Digest 688 (1978). Cf *Nielsen v Denmark* 4 YB 490 at 568 (1961) Com Rep; CM Res (61) 28.

19 *Ensslin, Baader and Raspe v FRG Nos 7572/76, 7586/76 and 7587/76*, 14 DR 64 at 112 (1978). The Commission's decision is unclear; it may be that it was saying ('particularly') only that there was a particularly strong case for establishing state responsibility where a state organ is involved. Cf *Hauschildt v Denmark No 10486/83*, 49 DR 86 (1986).

i. Other fair hearing requirements

In addition to the elements of the right to a 'fair hearing' identified above, a number of other particular points have been established in the jurisprudence of the Strasbourg authorities. In *Stanford v UK*,[20] the Court indicated that the state must provide a courtroom with good acoustics, since it follows from the right to 'participate effectively' in the proceedings that an accused must be able to hear and follow them. It is not a breach of Article 6 for an accused to be handcuffed in court[1] or to be placed in a glass cage for security reasons.[2] In *Kraska v Switzerland*[3] it was held that there is also a 'duty to conduct a proper examination of the submissions, arguments and evidence adduced by the parties'. There an appeal court judge had, as he remarked, not had time to read all of the appellant's memorial before the hearing; however, although the judge's remark was 'open to criticism', when the proceedings were considered as a whole it was not established that there had been an unfair hearing. On a separate matter, the Commission has left open the possibility that the right to a fair hearing requires that a person not be tried twice for the same offence.[4] The fact that freedom from double jeopardy (*ne bis in idem, autrefois acquit*) is guaranteed by the Seventh Protocol to the Convention for the parties thereto does not necessarily mean that it is not protected by Article 6(1) for the Convention parties as a whole.[5] Likewise, it is not established whether the trial of an accused who has been brought within the defendant's territory following an abduction for which it is responsible infringes his right to a fair hearing.[6] It is, however, clear that Article 6 does not contain a guarantee of a jury trial in criminal cases.[7]

On a more particular point, in *Colak v FRG*[8] it was held that the failure of a court to act in accordance with an informal, out of court statement by the presiding judge in a case that the accused would not be convicted of a particular offence did not render a hearing unfair; given the impossibility of establishing with certainty whether the conversation took place, the accused should have obtained formal confirmation. A similar disagreement as to what took place arose in *Pardo v France*.[9] There it was held that if an

---

20 A 280-A para 26 (1994). In this case there was no liability where neither the accused, who had impaired hearing, nor his lawyer informed the court officers that he could not hear the evidence. His complaint that the acoustics were unsatisfactory was rejected on the facts.

1 *Campbell v UK No 12323/86*, 57 DR 148 (1988).

2 *Auguste v France No 11837/85*, 69 DR 104 (1990) Com Rep; CM Res DH (91) 3.

3 A 254-B para 30 (1993).

4 See *X v Austria No 4212/69*, 35 CD 151 (1970). Article 6 does not prevent a prosecution in two states successively: *S v FRG No 8945/80*, 39 DR 43 (1983).

5 Cf the approach to appellate courts in the *Ekbatani* case: see below, p 240.

6 See *Stocké v FRG A 199* (1991) in which the Court was not satisfied that there had been state involvement on the facts.

7 *X and Y v Ireland No 8299/78*, 22 DR 51 (1980) and *Callaghan v UK No 14739/89*, 60 DR 296 (1989). The same must be true in civil cases. Where a jury trial occurs, the judge's summing up must be 'fair' (*X v UK No 5574/72*, 3 DR 10 (1975)) and Article 6 must be complied with generally. As to jury vetting and Article 6, see Gallivan and Warbrick, 5 HRR 176 (1980).

8 A 147 (1988). It may have been relevant that the presiding judge was not sitting alone.

9 A 261-B (1993).

accused wishes to argue that he was not allowed an opportunity as promised to develop his case on a later occasion, he must 'provide sufficient *prima facie* evidence of the accuracy of his version of events'.

iii. The right to a public hearing and the public pronouncement of judgment[10]

a. *The right to a public hearing*

Article 6(1) provides that 'everyone is entitled to a . . . public hearing'. The purpose of this guarantee is to 'protect litigants from the administration of justice in secret with no public scrutiny', thereby contributing also to the maintenance of confidence in the courts.[11] The presence of the press is particularly important in this latter regard.[12] Article 6(1) does not, however, require that the press be informed of a hearing or that a case be listed for the information of the press or the public generally: it is sufficient that they are not excluded.[13] The guarantee applies in criminal and non-criminal cases. In non-criminal cases involving compulsory arbitration the arbitration tribunal must hear the case in public.[14]

The right to a public hearing implies a right to an oral hearing at the trial court level.[15] A public hearing of the court's consideration of written pleadings does not make much sense. It also follows in criminal cases from the nature of the guarantees in Articles 6(3)(c), (d), (e). The right to an oral hearing must also apply when a court sits in camera, although in such cases the proper basis for it will be the right to a fair hearing in Article 6(1).

The right to a public hearing is subject to extensive restrictions. These follow from the text of Article 6(1) itself and its interpretation at Strasbourg, which has diluted the Convention guarantee. Article 6(1) expressly provides for restrictions in the following terms:

> '. . . the press and public may be excluded from all or part of the trial in the interests of morals, public order or national security in a democratic society, where the interests of juveniles or the private life of the parties so require, or to the extent strictly necessary in the

---

10 See Cremona, *Wiarda Mélanges*, 107.
11 *Pretto v Italy* A 71 para 21 (1983). Cf *Barberà, Messegué and Jabardo v Spain* A 146 para 89 (1988) in which a breach of the right to a public hearing was found because much of the evidence against the accused was made a part of the record without being adduced or read in court and hence not subjected to 'the watchful eye of the public'.
12 *Axen v FRG*, B 57 (1981) Com Rep para 77.
13 *X v UK No 6512/79*, 2 Digest 444 (1979). Stavros, p 190, suggests that, although not a breach of the public hearing requirement, the fact that a criminal case is unlisted might be relevant when deciding whether there has been a 'fair' hearing on the facts as a whole.
14 *Bramelid and Malmström v Sweden Nos 8588/79 and 8589/79*, 38 DR 18 (1983) Com Rep; CM Res DH (84) 4. In the case of voluntary arbitration, whereby the parties themselves choose to go outside the courts, Article 6 does not apply: ibid.
15 See *Fredin v Sweden* (No 2) A 283-A para 21 (1994).

opinion of the court in special circumstances where publicity would prejudice the interests of justice.'

In the interpretation of similar lists of restrictions to the rights guaranteed in Articles 8-11, the Strasbourg authorities have required that the restriction be a proportionate response to a pressing social need.[16] This interpretation is based upon the wording 'necessary in a democratic society' in those articles. Although the text of Article 6(1) does not contain this precise formula, there are the echoes of it and, in any event, such a balancing approach seems generally appropriate.[17]

In the interpretation of Articles 8-11, the Strasbourg authorities have also applied a margin of appreciation doctrine, by which the state is allowed a certain discretion in its assessment of the need for a restriction in a particular factual situation.[18] In the limited number of cases that have arisen, there is no case in which margin of appreciation language is used and the Commission and the Court have made their own assessment of the need for a restriction without indicating that any discretion is left to the defendant state. The wording of the 'interests of justice' restriction ('in the opinion of the court') most clearly invites a margin of appreciation approach.

One of the few cases in which the Court has applied any part of the list of restrictions in Article 6(1) is *Campbell and Fell v UK*.[19] In that case, it was held that prison disciplinary proceedings could be conducted in camera for 'reasons of public order and security'. The Court had in mind the problems of security that would result for the state in admitting the press and the public to the prison or in transporting convicted prisoners to court. Because of these considerations, a requirement that disciplinary proceedings be in public would 'impose a disproportionate burden on the authorities of the state'.[20] In terms of the categories of restriction permitted by Article 6(1), the Court would appear to have been relying upon the 'public order' restriction,[1] interpreting the term as having a wide public interest meaning, rather than one limited to public disorder.[2]

In other cases, the Commission has held that the exclusion of the public from the trial of an accused for sexual offences against children was justified

16 See below, Ch 8. As to the wording 'strictly necessary' in Article 6(1), see the standard set for 'absolutely necessary' in Article 2: above, p 47.
17 A proportionality test was used in effect in the context of the public hearing guarantee in *Campbell and Fell v UK*: see below at n 20.
18 See below, Ch 8.
19 A 80 (1984).
20 Id, para 87. Note, however, that with the abolition of the disciplinary role of Boards of Visitors in the UK system, convicted prisoners are now transported to the courts.
1 Although the Court refers to 'security' also, it seems unlikely that it would include the situation before it within the 'national security' restriction.
2 Cf *Le Compte, Van Leuven and De Meyere v Belgium* A 43 para 59 (1981). This public interest meaning is consistent with the French text of Article 6(1) which uses the term '*ordre public*'. Public disorder in the courtroom might be brought within the 'interests of justice' restriction.

under Article 6(1), without specifying which particular ground of restriction it was applying.[3] The exclusion of the public from divorce proceedings[4] and from medical disciplinary proceedings[5] has been considered permissible as being for the 'protection of the private life of the parties'. The 'interests of justice' may justify the giving of evidence by witnesses in camera in appropriate cases in order to ensure their safety.[6] It has, quite properly, not been held to justify the exclusion of the public on the ground that a hearing in camera would help reduce the court's workload.[7]

In addition to the restrictions listed in Article 6(1), it has been established that a public hearing is not required or limited in two other situations. Firstly, where the applicant waives his right to a public hearing, so long as the waiver is done 'in an unequivocal manner' and there is no 'important public interest' consideration that calls for the public to be present.[8] A waiver may be tacit, provided that it is clear from the facts that one is being made. An 'unequivocal' waiver was found to have been made in *Håkansson v Sweden*[9] when the applicant failed to ask for a public hearing before a court that by law conducted its proceedings in private unless a public hearing was considered by it to be 'necessary'. The judgment can be criticised as requiring the applicant to take the initiative to request the application of an exception to a general rule, when the general rule should itself, consistently with Article 6(1), provide for a public hearing.[10] The case may be distinguished from *H v Belgium*[11] where an applicant barrister was held not to have waived his right to a public hearing in disciplinary proceedings when he failed to request a public hearing where the practice was to hold such proceedings in private and there was 'little prospect' of a request for a public hearing succeeding. The cases in which a waiver has been established have concerned professional disciplinary proceedings or civil litigation; it is arguable that a stricter test should apply to criminal cases.

Secondly, the right is limited in its application to appeal proceedings. As in the case of the right to a hearing in person,[12] provided that there has been a public hearing before the trial court, 'the absence of "public hearings" before a second or third instance court may be justified by the special

---

3   *X v Austria No 1913/63*, 2 Digest 438 (1965). Several grounds, including the 'interests of juveniles', could have applied.
4   *X v UK No 7366/76*, 2 Digest 452 (1977).
5   *Guenoun v France No 13562/88*, 66 DR 181 (1990) and *Imberechts v Belgium No 15561/89*, 69 DR 312 (1991) (private lives of patients).
6   *X v UK No 8016/77*, 2 Digest 456 (1980) and *X v Norway No 3444/67*, 35 CD 37 (1970). Cf *X v UK No 20657/92*, 15 EHRR CD 113 (1992) (witness screened from accused in terrorist case).
7   *Axen v FRG*, B 57 (1981) Com Rep para 78. The Court has stated that the 'need for expeditious handling of the courts' workload' is a relevant consideration in deciding whether a case should be heard in public on appeal: see below at p 221.
8   *Håkansson v Sweden* A 171 para 66 (1990). See also *Schuler-Zgraggen v Switzerland* A 263 para 58 (1993) and *Zumtobel v Austria* A 268-A para 34 (1993).
9   Ibid. See also the *Schuler-Zgraggen* and *Zumtobel* cases, above, n 8.
10 Cf Judge Walsh dissenting.
11 A 127-B (1987).
12 See above, p 206.

features of the proceedings' concerned.[13] In particular, where the proceedings involve an appeal only on points of law,[14] an oral, and hence a public, hearing is not required. If, however, an appeal court is competent to decide questions of fact as well as law, an oral hearing in public may be required, depending on the facts.[15] In deciding the question on a case by case basis, the Court has emphasised that the need to ensure confidence in the courts through publicity must be balanced at the appellate level against such considerations as the right to trial within a reasonable time and the need to control an appeal court's workload.[16]

Finally, it should be noted that the absence of a public hearing has been a particular problem for administrative and other tribunals that are not 'classic' courts within the ordinary court system. As indicated later, in the case of such a tribunal, its failure to provide a public hearing will be remedied from the standpoint of Article 6 if the case is dealt with on appeal by a court that does satisfy the public hearing requirement.[17] In the case of a court 'of the classic kind', this will not be sufficient; the appellate court will need to quash the defective trial court decision.[18]

b. The right to the public pronouncement of judgment

In contrast with the right to a public hearing, the right to have judgment 'pronounced publicly' is not subject to any exceptions in the text of Article 6(1). In particular, the list of restrictions in the final sentence of Article 6(1) applies only to the hearing of the case.[19] Nor have the Strasbourg authorities as yet applied the idea of a waiver of rights to this second right. However, it has been interpreted restrictively in one respect. The text of Article 6(1) appears to require that judgment be pronounced orally in open court: '[j]udgment shall be pronounced publicly'.[20] In fact, the Court has not adopted this interpretation for all proceedings. Noting that the publication of at least some kinds of judgments by making them available to the public in the court registry, rather than by reading them out in court, is a long-standing tradition in many Council of Europe member states, the European Court ruled in *Pretto v Italy*[1] that 'the form of publicity to be given to the 'judgment' . . . must be assessed in the light of the special

---

13 *Ekbatani v Sweden* A 134 para 31 (1988). On the application of Article 6 to appellate proceedings generally, see below, p 240. An appellate court that cannot determine all questions of law and fact on a criminal appeal cannot by having a public hearing thereby make good the failure of the trial court to do so: *Weber v Switzerland* A 177 (1990). Cf *Le Compte, Van Leuven and De Meyere v Belgium* A 43 para 61 (1981).

14 *Axen v FRG* A 72 (1983) and *Sutter v Switzerland* A 74 (1984).

15 See the cases discussed above at p 207.

16 *Helmers v Sweden* A 212-A (1991).

17 See eg *Le Compte, Van Leuven and De Meyere v Belgium* A 43 para 51 (1981).

18 See the *De Cubber* case, below, p 240.

19 *Campbell and Fell v UK* A 80 (1984).

20 The French text – *'rendu publiquement'* – suggests the same: *Pretto v Italy* A 71 para 25 (1983).

1 Id, para 26. See the separate opinions of Judges Van Der Meersch and Pinheiro Farinho.

features of the proceedings in question and by reference to the object and purpose of Article 6(1)'. Thus in the *Pretto* case, the Court held that Article 6(1) was complied with when the judgment of the Italian Court of Cassation rejecting the applicant's appeal in a civil claim was made available to the public in the court registry without having been delivered orally in open court. The European Court noted that the Court of Cassation had jurisdiction to consider only points of law and to reject an appeal or quash a judgment, returning the case to the trial court, and that it had given its judgment after a public hearing. Bearing in mind the purpose of the 'pronounced publicly' requirement, which is to contribute to a fair trial through public scrutiny, publication via the registry was consistent in this situation with Article 6(1). In *Axen v FRG*,[2] the Court reached the same conclusion in a criminal case in respect of a similar practice of the German Federal Court of Justice, which again heard appeals on points of law only.[3]

Although the same practice of publishing judgments via the court registry is followed in some national courts at other levels, as yet the European Court has only had occasion to apply its ruling in the *Pretto* and *Axen* cases to final courts of appeal. In *Helmers v Sweden*,[4] however, the Commission considered that it was in accordance with the purpose of the 'public pronouncement' requirement that the judgment in the applicant's private criminal prosecution of another person for defamation was made available to the public in full in the trial court registry without being delivered in open court. In the different context of the functioning of Boards of Visitors in the former English system of prison disciplinary proceedings, the Court has accepted that a Board of Visitors award need not be pronounced in the presence of 'press and public' in view of the problem of prison security.[5] However, it found a breach of the 'pronounced publicly' requirement since no alternative arrangements had been made to publish the award subsequently.[6]

iv. The right to trial within a reasonable time

The purpose of the 'reasonable time' guarantee, which applies to criminal and non-criminal cases, is to protect 'all parties to court proceedings . . .

---

2 A 72 para 31 (1983).
3 In contrast with the Italian Court of Cassation in the *Pretto* case, the Federal Court of Justice in the *Axen* case did not hear argument on the appeal in public, dismissing the appeal as being without merit without a hearing. In *Sutter v Switzerland* A 74 (1984), it was sufficient in military disciplinary proceedings that a person who could establish an interest could consult or obtain a copy of a judgment in the court registry.
4 *No 11826/85*, 61 DR 138 (1989). See also *Crociani v Italy No 8603/79*, 22 DR 147 (1980), in which it was sufficient that the essential elements of the judgment, without the reasoning, were read out in court.
5 *Campbell and Fell v UK* A 80 (1984). The disciplinary function of Boards of Visitors has since been abolished.
6 Following the judgment, arrangements were made for the publication of Boards of Visitors awards in the local press.

against excessive procedural delays'.[7] As the Court stated in *H v France*,[8] the guarantee 'underlines the importance of rendering justice without delays which might jeopardise its effectiveness and credibility'. In criminal cases, it is also 'designed to avoid that a person charged should remain too long in a state of uncertainty about his fate.'[9] In such cases, the effect that being an accused has upon a person's reputation is relevant too.

In criminal cases, the reasonable time guarantee runs from the moment that an individual is subject to a 'charge'.[10] In non-criminal cases, it normally begins to apply from the initiation of court proceedings.[11] In both kinds of cases, the 'reasonable time' guarantee continues to apply until the case is finally determined.[12] If the defendant state has accepted the right of individual petition after Article 6 has begun to apply to a particular case, the 'reasonable time' guarantee will only begin to run as of the date of acceptance of the right of petition.[13] None the less, in assessing the reasonableness of the time that is taken to determine a case after the date of acceptance, 'account must be taken of the then state of proceedings'.[14] Thus, a decision as to whether a case has been treated with the necessary expedition after the date of acceptance will be influenced by the fact that the case has already been pending for a long time.[15] If proceedings are still pending in the national courts when an application is under consideration at Strasbourg, the reasonable time guarantee continues to apply until the final decision is taken in the case at Strasbourg.[16]

The reasonableness of the length of proceedings in both criminal and non-criminal cases depends on the particular circumstances of the case.[17] There is no absolute time limit. Factors that are always taken into account are the complexity of the case, the conduct of the applicant and the conduct of the competent administrative and judicial authorities.[18] No particular factor is conclusive; the approach must be to examine them separately and then to assess their cumulative effect. Although particular instances of delay attributable to the state may not seem unreasonable, they may be such when taken together.[19] No margin of appreciation doctrine is applied, at least expressly, when determining the reasonableness of the time taken; the

---

7   *Stögmüller v Austria* A 9 p 40 (1969).
8   A 162-A para 58 (1989).
9   *Stögmüller v Austria* A 9 p 40 (1969). Cf *Wemhoff v FRG* A 7 (1968).
10 As to the point at which this happens, see above, p 171.
11 See above, p 195, where certain exceptions to the normal rule are also indicated.
12 See above at pp 173 and 196.
13 *Foti v Italy* A 56 (1982). As to appeal proceedings, however, see the *Stamoulakatos* case, below, p 677. The date of entry into force of the Convention, which coincided with the date when the right of petition entered into force, was used in *Silva Pontes v Portugal* A 286-A para 38 (1994).
14 *Foti v Italy* A 56 para 53 (1982).
15 *Brigandi v Italy* A 194-B para 30 (1991).
16 *Neumeister v Austria* A 8 (1968) and *Nibbio v Italy* A 228-A (1992).
17 *König v FRG* A 27 para 99 (1978).
18 Ibid.
19 *Ruotolo v Italy* A 230-D (1992).

European Court simply makes its own assessment of the length of time taken.[20] When it does so, it must bear in mind that Article 6 can only require such expedition as is consistent with the proper administration of justice.[1]

As to the first of the three factors listed above, a case may be complicated for many reasons, such as the volume of evidence,[2] the number of defendants or charges,[3] the need to obtain expert evidence[4] or evidence from abroad,[5] or the complexity of the legal issues involved.[6]

With regard to the second factor, the state is not responsible for delay that is attributable to the conduct of the applicant. While an applicant is entitled to make use of his procedural rights, any consequential lengthening of proceedings cannot be held against the state.[7] Although an accused in a criminal case is not required 'actively to co-operate with the judicial authorities',[8] if delay results, for example, from his refusal to appoint a defence lawyer, this is not the responsibility of the state.[9] A state is responsible for its negligent delay in discontinuing proceedings against an accused: it cannot claim that the accused should have taken the initiative to remind it.[10] In civil litigation between private parties some municipal legal systems apply the principle that the parties are responsible for the progress of proceedings.[11] This does not, however, 'absolve the courts from ensuring compliance with the requirements of Article 6 concerning reasonable time';[12] the state must itself take appropriate steps to ensure that proceedings progress speedily. The responsibilities of the applicant in civil cases, whether such a principle applies or not, are only to 'show diligence in carrying out the procedural steps relevant to him, to refrain from using delaying tactics and to avail himself of the scope afforded by domestic law for shortening proceedings'.[13] Delay caused by the conduct of the applicant's legal aid lawyer is not attributable to the state: although he is

---

20 See eg *Casciaroli v Italy* A 229-C para 18 (1992), in which the Court simply disagreed with the defendant state's assessment of the complexity of the case. However, the fact that the Court's jurisprudence still contains cases where unexplained delays of a relatively modest degree have been tolerated, see below, p 230, may suggest that a margin of appreciation is being allowed in fact.
1 *Boddaert v Belgium* A 235-D (1992).
2 *Eckle v FRG* A 51 (1982).
3 *Neumeister v Austria* A 8 (1968).
4 *Wemhoff v FRG* A 7 (1968).
5 *Neumeister v Austria* A 8 (1968). If the delay is caused by the tardiness of the authorities of the state whose cooperation is needed to obtain the evidence, a claim may be brought against that state under Article 6 if it is a party to the Convention: *X v FRG No 9604*, 5 EHRR 587 (1983).
6 *Neumeister v Austria* A 8 (1968).
7 See eg *König v FRG* A 27 para 103 (1978) (changing lawyer, making appeals, calling new evidence) and *Buchholz v FRG* A 42 para 56 (1981) (method of pleading case).
8 *Eckle v FRG* A 51 para 82 (1982).
9 *Corigliano v Italy* A 57 (1982) .
10 *Orchin v UK No 8435/78*, 34 DR 5 (1982) Com Rep; CM Res DH (83) 14.
11 See *Buchholz v FRG* A 42 para 50 (1981). Cf *Martins Moreira v Portugal* A 133 para 46 (1988).
12 *Union Alimentaria Sanders SA v Spain* A 157 para 35 (1989).
13 Ibid. Cf *Deumeland v FRG* A 100 para 80 (1986).

publically appointed, such a lawyer acts for his client, not the state.[14] Nor is a state responsible for delay that results from the conduct of the defendant against whom the applicant brings a civil claim.[15] In criminal cases, where the applicant flees from the jurisdiction or disappears while subject to a 'charge', the time during which he is absent is not to be taken into account in determining the length of proceedings.[16]

The state is responsible, however, for delays that are attributable to its administrative or judicial authorities. In criminal cases, breaches of Article 6 have been found because of unjustified delays in the conduct of the preliminary investigation in a civil law system,[17] in entering a *nolle prosequi*,[18] in the commencement of court proceedings following the preferment of the indictment,[19] in transferring cases between courts,[20] in the communication of the judgment to the applicant,[1] and in the hearing of appeals.[2] Whereas it may be sensible to hear cases against two or more accused persons together, this cannot 'justify substantial delay' in the bringing of a case against any one of them.[3] Where the accused is acquitted and the prosecution does not appeal, the reasonable time guarantee continues to apply, engaging the responsibility of the state, until the time-limit for an appeal has expired.[4] In appropriate circumstances, a court may be justified in permitting a delay in order to allow political or other passions to cool.[5]

In non-criminal cases, states have been held responsible for delays in civil and administrative courts in performing routine registry tasks,[6] in the conduct of the hearing by the court,[7] in the presentation of evidence by the state,[8] for the adjournment of proceedings pending the outcome of another case[9] and for delays caused by lack of co-ordination between administrative authorities.[10]

---

14 *H v France* A 162-A para 54 (1989). Note, however, that in a criminal case there is a duty to provide effective legal aid under Article 6(3)(c): see below, p 264.

15 *Bock v FRG* A 150 para 41 (1989).

16 *Girolami v Italy* A 196-E (1991). In *Ventura v Italy No 7438/76*, 23 DR 5 at 91 (1980) the Commission suggested a possible exception where the accused flees for a 'sufficient reason'. Possibly it had in mind the situation where there would not be a fair trial.

17 *Eckle v FRG* A 51 (1982); *Foti v Italy* A 56 (1982); and *Corigliano v Italy* A 57 (1982).

18 *Orchin v UK No 8435/78*, 34 DR 5 (1982) Com Rep; CM Res DH (83) 14.

19 *Eckle v FRG* A 51 (1982).

20 *Foti v Italy* A 56 para 72 (1982).

1 *Eckle v FRG* A 51 (1982).

2 Ibid. See also *X v UK No 8323/78*, 26 DR 13 (1981) (15 weeks to decide on an application for leave to appeal not unreasonable).

3 *Hentrich v France* A 296-A para 61 (1994). Cf *Kemmache v France* A 218 para 70 (1991).

4 *Ferraro v Italy* A 197-A para 15 (1991). This provides a basis for reviewing the reasonableness of the period allowed for the appeal. As to the position in civil proceedings in Italy, where the responsibility for making the judgment final rests initially with the parties, not the state, see *Maciariello v Italy* A 230-A (1992).

5 *Foti v Italy* A 51 (1982).

6 *Guincho v Portugal* A 81 (1984).

7 *König v FRG* A 27 (1978).

8 *H v UK* A 120 (1987).

9 *König v FRG* A 27 (1978).

10 *Wiesinger v Austria* A 213 (1991).

Although the Court has emphasised the complexity of the case and the conduct of the applicant and the authorities when assessing the reasonableness of the length of proceedings, it has also referred to other factors where appropriate. One such factor is what is 'at stake' for the applicant.[11] Particular diligence is required in cases concerning the applicant's employment,[12] his civil status,[13] his mental health[14] or his title to land[15] or where he is a road accident victim.[16] It is also required where delay might render the proceedings pointless.[17] It may be relevant that the applicant has been charged interest on the sum in dispute while the case is pending.[18]

Criminal cases generally require more urgency than civil ones[19] and a more rigorous standard applies where the applicant is in detention pending the outcome of his case.[20] In a criminal case in which the accused is in detention, the reasonable time guarantee in Article 6(1) overlaps with that in Article 5(3), under which 'special diligence' is required.[1] However, since Article 5(3) ceases to apply once an accused is convicted, the reasonable time guarantee in Article 6(1) is the only one that protects a convicted person detained during his appeal. Thus in *B v Austria,*[2] a breach of Article 6(1) was found when it took two years and nine months for an appeal court judge to draw up the court's judgment after the hearing of an appeal by a convicted person in detention. Another factor concerns the practice in criminal justice systems by which the time spent awaiting trial is taken into account when deciding upon the sentence in a criminal case or ruling upon a civil claim. Although any reduction in sentence or other favourable outcome of proceedings will not take away from a breach of Article 6, it may mean that the applicant is not a 'victim' who is competent to bring an application.[3]

The factors considered so far are ones that the Strasbourg authorities take into account when considering whether the proceedings on the facts of a particular case have been conducted with sufficient expedition. There is,

---

11 Id, para 61.
12 *Buchholz v FRG* A 42 para 52 (1981) and *Obermeier v FRG* A 179 para 72 (1990).
13 *Bock v FRG* A 150 para 48 (1989). Delay in divorce proceedings largely because of the time taken to determine the applicant's mental competence to bring them.
14 Ibid.
15 *Poiss v Austria* A 117 para 60 (1987) and *Hentrich v France* A 296-A para 61 (1994).
16 *Silva Pontes v Portugal* A 286-A para 38 (1994).
17 *X v France* A 234-C (1992). In this case, 'exceptional diligence' was required in a civil claim by a haemophiliac against the state alleging a negligent blood transfusion causing AIDS in case he died. For other AIDS cases, see *Vallee v France* A 289-A (1994); *Karakaya v France* A 289-B (1994); and *Demai v France* A 289-C (1994) F Sett. Child custody cases must also be dealt with 'speedily': *Hokkanen v Finland* A 299-A para 72 (1994). Cf *H v UK* A 120 (1987) (parental access).
18 *Schouten and Meldrum v Netherlands* A 304 para 68 (1994).
19 *Baggetta v Italy* A 119 para 24 (1987).
20 *Abdoella v Netherlands* A 248-A para 24 (1992).
1 See above, p 143. Although not expressly stated in the *Abdoella* case, it would seem likely that the same 'special diligence' standard applies under Article 6(1).
2 A 175 (1990).
3 *Eckle v FRG* A 51 (1982); *Preikhzas v FRG* No 6504/74, 16 DR 5 (1978).

however, another dimension to the 'reasonable time' guarantee. The Convention places a duty on the contracting parties, which applies regardless of cost,[4] 'to organise their legal systems so as to allow the courts to comply with the requirements of Article 6(1)'.[5] It follows that a state may be held liable not only for any delay in the handling of a particular case in the operation of a generally expeditious system for the administration of justice, but also for a failure to increase resources in response to a backlog of cases and for structural deficiencies in its system of justice that cause delays.

As to a backlog of cases, in *Zimmermann and Steiner v Switzerland*,[6] the defendant state was held liable when administrative appeal proceedings of a straightforward kind before the Swiss Federal Court had taken nearly three and a half years, during most of which time the applicants' case had remained stationary. The agreed reason for the delay was that the Court was overworked and had for that reason given priority to urgent or important cases,[7] within neither of which categories the applicants' case fell. The Court's case-load had built up over several years and adequate steps to increase the number of judges and administrative staff or otherwise reorganise the court system to cope with what had become a permanent problem had not been taken to remedy the situation by the time that the applicants' appeal was heard. Similarly, a backlog defence was rejected in *Guincho v Portugal*[8] in which delays in the civil courts were attributed to the increase in litigation that resulted from the return to democracy, the increase in litigation resulting from the new constitution, the repatriation of nationals from Portuguese colonies and the 1970s economic recession. Portugal was found to be in breach of Article 6(l) because the resulting overloading had become a permanent problem by the time that the applicant's claim was brought and because it could, in some respects, have been foreseen.

However, in *Buchholz v FRG*,[9] it was held that a state will not be liable for delays that result from a backlog of cases that was not reasonably forseeable provided it takes 'reasonably prompt remedial action'. In that case, the defendant state was not in breach of Article 6 when the delay in the consideration of the applicant's claim for unfair dismissal was attributable to a backlog of cases that had developed suddenly with the economic recession of the mid-1970s and because prompt steps had been taken to increase the number of judges when the problem became apparent. Although these steps did not benefit the applicant, they were all that could reasonably be expected of the defendant state in the circumstances. Where the backlog results from a clearly temporary situation, no special measures

---

4 *Airey v Ireland* A 32 (1979).
5 *Zimmermann and Steiner v Switzerland* A 66 para 29 (1983).
6 A 66 (1983). Cf *X v Netherlands No 9193/80*, 6 EHRR 134 (1983).
7 Such a system of priorities is permissible as a short term measure: *Zimmerman and Steiner v Switzerland* A 66 (1983).
8 A 81 (1984). Backlog arguments were also rejected in *B v Austria* A 175 (1990); *Ruiz-Mateos v Spain* A 262 (1993); and *Hentrich v France* A 296-A para 61 (1994).
9 A 42 para 51 (1981).

may be required. Thus, in *Foti v Italy*,[10] delays were caused when the competent regional courts were flooded by several hundred prosecutions as a result of large-scale public disorder. It was held that delays in certain of the cases concerned were acceptable simply by reference to the temporary overloading of the courts that had occurred.

More delicate than the problem of delays resulting from a backlog of cases is the question whether a state can be required to restructure its administration of justice system to eliminate delays that are inherent in it. This question arose in *Neumeister v Austria*[11] in which much of the delay had occurred at the preliminary investigation stage. Under some civil law systems of criminal justice, including that in Austria, a person may spend a considerable length of time waiting for a 'charge' against him in the sense of Article 6 to be fully examined by an investigating judge when much of that examination is a repetition of work already done by the police in its investigation. If such a system, which has advantages in other respects, were altered to eliminate this overlap of time, the period during which an accused had a charge hanging over him would generally be reduced. In the *Neumeister* case, the Court confirmed that preliminary investigation systems of the kind described are not in themselves contrary to Article 6; the requirement is only that they be administered efficiently. It could not have been the intention of the drafting states that such a fundamental change in the legal systems of many of their number would be required.

The same question arose again in *König v FRG*[12] in the different context of the elaborate system of administrative courts in West Germany. Faced with one set of proceedings that had lasted nearly eleven years and were still pending, the Court first noted that it was not its function to comment on the structure of the courts concerned which, it conceded, was aimed at providing a full set of remedies for the individual's grievances. It added, however, that if efforts to this end 'resulted in a procedural maze, it is for the state alone to draw the conclusions and, if need be, to simplify the system with a view to complying with Article 6(1) of the Convention'. The implication is that if a case takes what is on the face of it an unreasonably long time, a state will not escape liability by providing that it has been dealt with efficiently within the limits of an unduly elaborate court structure.

It is interesting to consider what lengths of time are considered to be reasonable or unreasonable in the light of the above factors. Although consistently acting on the basis that each case must be considered on its facts, so that there is no objective limit to the length of time that can be taken, in all cases in which proceedings have taken over eight years or more, the Court has in fact almost always found a breach of Article 6(1).[13] At the

10 A 56 (1982).
11 A 8 (1968).
12 A 27 para 100 (1978).
13 For an exception, see *Katte Klitsche de la Grange v Italy* A 293-B (1994) (eight years for four levels of civil proceedings in a sensitive and complicated area of law not a breach). One of the worst cases was *Poiss v Austria* A 117 (1987) (19 years for land consolidation proceedings). The text above concerns the jurisprudence of the Court. For an account of the Commission's practice in reasonable time cases, see Stavros, p 105ff.

other extreme, in cases in which the facts suggested a particular need for
expedition, a period of two years has been held to be unreasonable.[14] In
between these extremes, the Court has found some cases that lasted six or
seven years not to involve a breach of Article 6(1) where there were
particular circumstances that justified this[15] and found proceedings lasting
three to five years in other cases to have taken an 'unreasonable' time.[16]

However, the length of proceedings by itself is only a part of the story. A
great deal depends on the number of stages involved in the case (preliminary
investigation, trial court, appeal court) and the impact of the relevant
factors already discussed (complexity of the case, what is 'at stake' for the
applicant, etc). For example, in *Zimmerman and Steiner v Switzerland*,[17]
nearly three-and-a-half years for a single court to hear a straightforward
appeal against an administrative decision was 'unreasonable'. In contrast, in
Ringeisen v Austria,[18] over five years from the commencement of the
preliminary investigation to the end of appeal proceedings to complete a
complicated fraud case in which the applicant's exercise of his procedural
rights caused considerable delay was not. It is noticeable that most of the
cases involving breaches of the 'reasonable time' guarantee come from civil
law jurisdictions and involve much longer periods of time than would
normally be found in common law courts.[19]

It is difficult to find consistent guidelines in the Court's jurisprudence that
provide assistance in predicting the outcome of cases. At one stage, the
Court followed an approach by which it looked to see whether the overall
time taken was such as to be *prima facie* unreasonable for the kind of
proceedings concerned. If it was, then the proceedings were examined in
detail and the onus was upon the defendant state to justify each element of
the time taken. Thus in *Guincho v Portugal*,[20] nearly four years for a
personal injuries claim that was still pending before the trial court was 'at
first sight' unreasonable for a single jurisdictional level and therefore

---

14 *H v UK* A 120 (1987) (parental access).
15 *Vernillo v France* A 198 (1991) (seven years: fault of the parties) and *Boddaert v Belgium* A
    235-D (1992) (six years: links between two cases justified their proceeding in parallel
    although slower). Contrast *Boddaert v Belgium* with *Kemmache v France* A 218 (1991) and
    Hentrich v France A 296-A para 61 (1994) in which two or more cases should have been
    separated to expedite proceedings. *Neumeister v Austria* A 8 (1968) is another cases in which
    over seven years to try a criminal case was not held to be 'unreasonable'. Part of the delay
    resulted from the time taken to obtain evidence from abroad that was the responsibility of
    other states. The case was also a very early one in which the Court had for the first time
    found a state in breach of any Convention provision (Article 5(3)). It is likely that the case
    would be decided differently now.
16 See eg *Foti v Italy* A 56 (1982) (three years).
17 A 66 (1983).
18 A 13 (1971).
19 The two UK cases in which a breach has been found are *H v UK*; see above, n 14, and
    Darnell v UK A 272 (1993) (claim for unfair NHS dismissal took nearly nine years). See also
    Ewing v UK No 11224/84, 56 DR 71 (1987) (nearly four years for a complicated criminal
    case not unreasonable, given diligence by the courts).
20 A 81 (1984) (breach found). Cf *Eckle v FRG* A 51 (1982); *Deumeland v FRG* A 100 (1986);
    and *Lechner and Hess v Austria* A 118 (1987).

required 'close examination'. Lately, the Court has not overtly used such a formula, preferring instead to look at each case on its merits.[1] Whatever the approach, one would expect that whenever a period of unjustifiable and other than *de minimis* delay can be attributed to the state, the Court would find a breach of Article 6. In fact, however, it does not always do so. Although it requires periods when little or nothing has happened in order find a breach,[2] the Court has been prepared to tolerate some proven instances of delay provided the overall length of the proceedings is not clearly excessive given the number of stages of proceedings in the case.[3]

v.   The right to an independent and impartial tribunal established by law

The right to a fair trial in Article 6(1) requires that cases be heard by an 'independent and impartial tribunal established by law'. The right applies equally to criminal cases and cases concerning 'civil rights and obligations'. As with other guarantees in Article 6, when evaluating the Strasbourg authorities' jurisprudence on the right to an independent and impartial tribunal, it is important to bear in mind whether the case was one concerning an ordinary court or a disciplinary or other special tribunal.

a.   A tribunal

A 'tribunal' was defined in *Belilos v Switzerland*[4] as follows:

> '. . . a "tribunal" is characterised in the substantive sense of the term by its judicial function, that is to say determining matters within its competence on the basis of rules of law and after proceedings conducted in a prescribed manner. . . .. It must also satisfy a series of further requirements – independence, in particular of the executive; impartiality; duration of its members' terms of office; guarantees afforded by its procedure – several of which appear in the text of Article 6(1) itself.'

This definition is overly comprehensive insofar as it contains organisational and procedural elements that, as the Court notes, are included or may be

---

1   The Commission continues to follow this approach: see eg *Minniti v Italy* No 9630/81, 59 DR 5 (1987) Com Rep; CM Res DH (89) 7. In some recent cases in which the overall length of proceedings has reached a clearly unacceptable level, the Court has, without abandoning its general position that there is no objective upper limit to a 'reasonable time', found a breach without finding it necessary to make any detailed assessment of the facts: see, eg, *Obermeier v Austria* A 179 (1990) (nine years).
2   See recently *Lombardo v Italy* A 249-C (1992); *De Moor v Belgium* A 292-A para 66 (1994); and *Beaumartin v France* A 296-B para 33 (1994).
3   See eg *Cesarini v Italy* A 245-B (1992) (delays amounting to three years out of six; three courts, lack of urgency by the applicant, etc).
4   A 132 para 64 (1988). Cf *Le Compte, Van Leuven and De Meyere v Belgium* A 43 para 55 (1981) and *H v Belgium* A 127-B para 50 (1987).

subsumed under other guarantees in Article 6(1). As to the functional element, an important feature of a tribunal is that it must be competent to take legally binding decisions; the capacity to make recommendations or give advice (even if normally followed) is not enough.[5] The fact that a body has other functions (administrative, etc) does not prevent it being a tribunal when exercising its judicial function.[6] As to membership, a tribunal may be composed predominantly, or even entirely, of persons who are not professional judges. Civil servants[7] and members of the armed forces[8] may be members of administrative and disciplinary tribunals respectively.

b. An independent tribunal

Most of the decided cases on the meaning of an 'independent' tribunal concern administrative or disciplinary tribunals, in which context the Strasbourg authorities have not imposed standards as high as might be applied to the ordinary courts of law. This is particularly true of such matters as the duration of office of tribunal members and their protection from outside pressures.

By 'independent' is meant 'independent of the executive and also of the parties'.[9] A court is not independent where it seeks and accepts as binding Foreign Office advice on the meaning of a treaty that it has to apply; in such a case it has surrendered its judicial function to the executive.[10] Clearly a member of the executive is not 'independent', so that a decision taken by him does not comply with Article 6(1), even though the particular function being exercised by him is 'of an essentially judicial nature'.[11] With regard to other bodies, in *Campbell and Fell v UK*,[12] the Court indicated the considerations it takes into account when assessing independence:

'In determining whether a body can be considered to be 'independent'
– notably of the executive and of the parties to the case – the Court has
had regard to the manner of appointment of its members and the

5   *Benthem v Netherlands* A 97 (1985). In *Van de Hurk v Netherlands* A 288 para 45 (1994), Article 6 was infringed because the government was empowered by law not to implement a court decision, even though the power was never exercised.
6   *Campbell and Fell v UK* A 80 paras 33, 81 (1984) and *H v Belgium* A 127-B para 50 (1987). In *H v Belgium*, the Commission had taken the opposite view: id, Com Rep para 95. Cf *Demicoli v Malta* A 210 (1991) Com Rep para 41 in which the Commission considered that the Maltese House of Representatives was not independent because it was a legislature as well as a court. The point was not considered by the Court.
7   *Ettl v Austria* A 117 para 38 (1987) (majority of members civil servants), following *Ringeisen v Austria* A 13 (1971).
8   *Engel v Netherlands* A 22 (1976).
9   *Ringeisen v Austria* A 13 para 95 (1971). It also means independence of Parliament: *Crociani v Italy No 8603/79*, 22 DR 147 at 221 (1980).
10 *Beaumartin v France* A 296-B para 38 (1994).
11 *Benthem v Netherlands* A 97 para 42 (1985).
12 A 80 para 78 (1984). Footnotes omitted. Cf *Langborger v Sweden* A 155 (1983). In the *Campbell and Fell* case, the Court did not question the membership of the prison Board of Visitors (magistrates and lay members).

duration of their term of office, the existence of guarantees against outside pressures and the question whether the body presents an appearance of independence.'

As far as 'manner of appointment' is concerned, appointment by the executive is permissible, indeed normal.[13] For a judge's independence to be challenged successfully by reference to his 'manner of appointment' it would have to be shown that the practice of appointment 'as a whole is unsatisfactory' or that 'at least the establishment of the particular court deciding a case was influenced by improper motives',[14] ie motives suggesting an attempt at influencing the outcome of the case. The arrangements for the selection or substitution of judges for a particular case from amongst the judiciary as a whole can give rise to questions of independence.[15]

With regard to the 'duration of their term of office', a very short term has been accepted as far as members of administrative or disciplinary tribunals are concerned. In *Campbell and Fell v UK*,[16] appointment for a term of three years as a member of a prison Board of Visitors acting as a disciplinary tribunal was sufficient, the Court being influenced by the fact that members were unpaid and might be hard to find for any longer duration. The appointment of a judge for a fixed term, so as to prevent dismissal at will, is a relevant factor,[17] although apparently not in itself required.[18]

As to 'guarantees against outside pressures', tribunal members must be protected from removal during their term of office, either by law or in practice.[19] In the *Campbell and Fell* case, the Court did not require any 'formal recognition' in law of the irremovability of a Board of Visitors member during his term of office; it was sufficient that this was 'recognised in fact and that the other necessary guarantees are present'.[20] This modest

---

13 *Campbell and Fell v UK* A 80 (1984) and *Belilos v Switzerland* A 132 (1988). Election by Parliament is also permissible: *Crociani v Italy No 8603/79*, 22 DR 147 (1983).

14 *Zand v Austria No 7360/76*, 15 DR 70 at 81 (1978) Com Rep; CM Res DH (79) 6. (No breach.) As to the appointment of judges by reference to their political views, see *Crociani v Italy No 8603/79*, 22 DR 147 at 222 (1980) (question seen in terms of impartiality).

15 *Barberà, Messegué and Jabardo v Spain* A 146 paras 53-59 (1988) (an impartiality case).

16 A 80 (1984). Cf *Sramek v Austria* A 84 (1984) (three years, no special factors indicated). Even in ordinary courts, appointment for life is not required: *Zand v Switzerland No 7360/76*, 15 DR 70 (1978) Com Rep; CM Res DH (79) 6.

17 See *Crociani v Italy No 8603/79*, 22 DR 147 at 221 (1980) and *Zand v Switzerland No 7360/76*, 15 DR 70 at 82 (1978).

18 See *Engel v Netherlands*, at n 20 below and *No 12839/87*, below, p 233. In *Dupuis v Belgium No 12717/87*, 57 DR 196 (1988), a one month appointment of the military members of a military tribunal was not questioned.

19 *Zand v Austria No 7360/76*, 15 DR 70 at 80 (1978). See also *Sramek v Austria* A 84 para 38 (1984). The requirement of a lengthy fixed term also serves to reduce outside pressures.

20 A 80 para 80 (1984). In practice, the Home Secretary would require the removal of a member 'only in the most exceptional circumstances': ibid. In *Engel v Netherlands* A 22 paras 30, 68, 89 (1976), the military members of the Netherlands Supreme Military Court were removable by Ministers at will. The Court would appear to have considered, without discussion, that their independence was not an issue in fact. In both cases, the possibility of removal by the executive without procedures for judicial review was not questioned. But see *X v Sweden No 5258/71*, 43 CD 71 (1973).

standard was applied by the Commission in *Eccles, McPhillips and McShane v Ireland*[1] to the Irish Special Criminal Court, which deals with terrorist offences. The independence of its judges was questioned because they could be dismissed at will and have their salaries reduced. Emphasising the need to look at the 'realities of the situation', the Commission found no evidence of any attempt by the executive to interfere with the Court's functioning on either basis and noted that the ordinary courts had powers to review the Court's independence. In other cases, the possibility of transferring tribunal members to other duties has also not been considered to present a problem.[2]

As far as other 'guarantees against outside pressure' are concerned, the Court requires that tribunal members be not subject to instructions from the executive, although here too it is sufficient that this is the case in practice.[3] In the *Greek* case[4] the extraordinary courts-martial during the regime of the Colonels were found not to be independent partly because their jurisdiction was to be exercised 'in accordance with decisions of the Minister of National Defence'. The secrecy of a tribunal's deliberations also affords protection against outside pressures.[5] Any authority given to the executive to grant an amnesty or a pardon must not be used so as to undermine the judicial function.[6]

Finally, the 'appearance of independence' consideration listed by the Court in the *Campbell and Fell* case relates to an objective test that has been developed by the Court.[7] It was found to have been infringed in *Sramek v Austria*[8] when a member of a tribunal was a civil servant whose immediate superior was representing the government party to the case. Without examining the superior's competence to give the member instructions, the Court held that this situation was in breach of Article 6(1) because it could give rise to a 'legitimate doubt' as to the member's independence of one of the parties. The objective test was also applied in *Belilos v Switzerland*,[9] in which the accused was convicted of a minor criminal offence by a Police Board composed of a single member, who was a lawyer from police headquarters and a municipal civil servant. The member sat in his personal

---

1 *No 12839/87*, 59 DR 212 (1988).
2 See *Sutter v Switzerland No 8209/78*, 16 DR 166 (1979). See also *Santschi v Switzerland No 7468/76*, 31 DR 5 at 43 (1981) Com Rep (an Article 5(1)(a) case).
3 See *Sramek v Austria* A 84 (1984) (law) and *Campbell and Fell v UK* A 80 (1984) (practice). Cf *Schiesser v Switzerland* A 34 (1979) (an Article 5(3) case).
4 12 YB (the *Greek* case) at 148 (1969); Com Rep CM Res DH (70) 1.
5 *Sutter v Switzerland No 8209/78*, 16 DR 166 (1979) DA.
6 12 YB (the *Greek* case) at 148 (1969) Com Rep; CM Res (70) 1.
7 Cf the objective test used in connection with the 'impartial' tribunal requirement, below, p 234.
8 A 84 (1984). Cf *Langborger v Sweden* A 155 (1989), considered below as an 'impartiality' case. Contrast the *Sramek* case with *Ringeisen v Austria* A 13 (1971) in which the Court held that it was permissible for a civil servant to be a member of a tribunal where he had no comparable relationship with a party. Cf *Ettl v Austria* A 117 (1987).
9 A 132 (1988).

capacity, took a different oath from other policemen, was not subject to orders and in principle could not be dismissed during his four-year term.[10] However, the ordinary citizen would, the Court considered, 'tend to see him as a member of the police force subordinate to his superiors and loyal to his colleagues', which was a situation that 'could legitimately have raised doubts as to the independence and organisational impartiality of the Police Board' and so was in breach of Article 6(1).[11] In contrast, the Court found no breach of the objective test in *Campbell and Fell v United Kingdom*. There a Board of Visitors served a dual role as a disciplinary tribunal and as a body independent of the government whose function was to monitor the administration of the prison in the interest of both prisoners and the public. However, it was argued that prisoners regarded the Board of Visitors as being too closely connected with the prison administration to be independent when exercising their role as a disciplinary tribunal. The Court held that this impression was not a reasonable one, so that the objective test had not been infringed.[12]

c.   An impartial tribunal

There is a close inter-relation between the guarantees of an 'independent' and an 'impartial' tribunal.[13] A tribunal that is not independent of the executive will not comply with the requirement of impartiality either in cases to which the executive is a party. Likewise, a tribunal member will be neither independent nor impartial if he has links with a private party to the case. For this reason, some of the cases treated by the Strasbourg authorities as raising questions of independence can be seen as cases of impartiality and vice versa.

'Impartiality' means lack of 'prejudice or bias'.[14] To satisfy the requirement, the tribunal must comply with both a subjective and an objective test:[15]

> 'The existence of impartiality for the purpose of Article 6(1) must be determined according to a subjective test, that is on the basis of the personal conviction of a particular judge in a given case, and also according to an objective test, that is ascertaining whether the judge offered guarantees sufficient to exclude any legitimate doubt in this respect.'

10 In fact, the member of this particular Prison Board could be transferred to other departmental duties.
11 Id, para 67.
12 The disciplinary function of Boards of Visitors was removed in 1992.
13 See *Demicoli v Malta* A 210 (1991) Com Rep.
14 *Piersack v Belgium* A 53 (1982)
15 *Hauschildt v Denmark* A 154 para 46 (1989). The test was first adopted in *Piersack v Belgium* A 53 (1982).

As to the subjective test, the question is whether it can be shown on the facts that a member of the court 'acted with personal bias' against the applicant.[16] In this connection, there is a presumption that a judge is impartial, 'until there is proof to the contrary.'[17] Given this presumption and the need to prove actual bias, rather than a 'legitimate doubt' as is the case under the objective test, it is not surprising that there has been no case in which a breach of the subjective test has been found. The closest was *Boeckmans v Belgium*[18] in which the President of a Court of Appeal described the accused's system of defence as 'mendacious', 'disgraceful' and 'distasteful', so much so that the sentence might have to be increased. Although the case resulted in a friendly settlement so that there was no final ruling, it is probable that there was sufficient proof of actual bias on these facts. In view of the robust remarks of some English judges, it is noticeable that no English case has been admitted on the merits. In one such case,[19] in which the judge had indicated very clearly that the accused was guilty and expressed his concern at the cost of the case for the legal aid fund, the application was declared inadmissible, the Commission emphasising that the trial had to be considered as a whole.

The objective test of 'impartiality' is comparable to the English law doctrine that 'justice must not only be done: it must also be seen to be done'. In this context, the Court emphasises the importance of 'appearances'.[20] As the Court has stated, '[w]hat is at stake is the confidence which the courts in a democratic society must inspire in the public and, above all, as far as criminal proceedings are concerned, in the accused'.[1] In applying the test, the opinion of the party to the case who is alleging partiality is 'important but not decisive'; what is crucial is whether the doubt as to impartiality can be 'objectively justified'.[2] If there is a 'legitimate doubt' as to a judge's impartiality, he must withdraw from the case.[3]

The Court has applied the objective test mostly in cases in which the trial judge in a criminal court has previously taken part in the proceedings at the

---

16 Id, para 47 (1989). Cf *De Cubber v Belgium* A 53 para 25 (no 'hostility or ill-will'). On the political sympathies of judges and their impartiality, see *Crociani v Italy No 8603/79*, 22 DR 147 at 222 (1980).

17 *Le Compte, Van Leuven and De Meyere v Belgium* A 43 para 58 (1981). Cf *Albert and Le Compte v Belgium* A 58 para 32 (1983) and *Debled v Belgium* A 292-B para 37 (1994).

18 *No 1727/62*, 8 YB 410 at 412 (1965) F Sett. In *Barberà, Messegué and Jabardo v Spain* A 146 (1988), the applicants' doubts concerning a judge's political connections (he wore a Francoist tie and cufflinks) were not substantiated.

19 *X v UK No 4991/71*, 45 CD 1 (1973). Cf *X v UK No 5574/72*, 3 DR 10 (1975) (accused had 'not a ghost of a chance'). In *Grant v UK No 12002/86*, 55 DR 218 (1988) the fact that an appellate court had formed a view of the case before the hearing on the basis of the file was not a problem.

20 See eg *Sramek v Austria* A 84 para 42 (1984). Cf *Borgers v Belgium* (an 'equality of arms' case), above, p 208.

1 *Fey v Austria* A 255-A para 30 (1993).

2 *Hauschildt v Denmark* A 154 para 48 (1989).

3 Ibid.

pre-trial stage in a variety of different capacities.[4] The Court has stated that 'the mere fact that a judge has also made pre-trial decisions in the case cannot be taken as in itself justifying fears as to his impartiality . . . What matters is the extent and nature of those decisions'.[5] In practice, the Court has found a 'legitimate doubt' in a number of cases, including some involving long-established national practices. In *Piersack v Belgium*,[6] the presiding trial court judge had earlier been the head of the section of the public prosecutor's department that had investigated the applicant's case and instituted proceedings against him. Although there was no evidence that the judge had actual knowledge of the investigation, the Court held there had been a breach of the objective test:

> '[I]f an individual, after holding in the public prosecutor's department an office whose nature is such that he may have to deal with a given matter in the course of his duties, subsequently sits in the same case as a judge, the public are entitled to fear that he does not offer sufficient guarantees of impartiality.'[7]

In *De Cubber v Belgium*,[8] the *Piersack* case was extended to the situation where a judge had earlier acted as an investigating judge. Although the investigating judge was, unlike a member of the public prosecutor's department, independent of the prosecution, he had links with that department and it could reasonably be supposed that he had already formed a view as to the accused's guilt before the trial, thereby giving rise to a 'legitimate doubt' as to his impartiality.

The position is normally different where pre-trial decisions are taken by a judge who is not a part of the investigation or prosecution process. In *Hauschildt v Denmark*,[9] a judge who had taken numerous pre-trial decisions as to detention on remand, solitary confinement and other ancillary matters, later served as the presiding judge at the accused's trial. Under the Danish system, the judge had taken no part in the preparation of the case for trial or the decision to prosecute. Instead, his role had been to act as an independent

---

4   For similar civil cases, see *Nordborg v Sweden No 13635/88*, 65 DR 232 (1990); *Jensen v Denmark No 14063/88*, 68 DR 177 (1991); and *S v Switzerland No 17722/91*, 69 DR 345 (1991). These cases were declared inadmissible because the earlier proceedings had involved less strict standards of proof.

5   *Fey v Austria* A 255 para 30 (1993).

6   A 53 (1982). A 'legitimate doubt' would also exist where the judge took over the role of the prosecution during the trial: *Thorgeir Thorgeirson v Iceland* A 239 (1992). See also *Kristinsson v Iceland* A 171-B (1990) Com Rep; F Sett before Court. There the chief of police was also a criminal court judge. The Commission found a breach, the limited number of qualified persons in a small population being no excuse. For a case on the other side of the line, see *D'Haese, Le Compte, Van Leuven and De Meyere v Belgium* 6 EHRR 114 (1983).

7   Id, para 30.

8   A 86 (1984). Cf *Pfeifer and Plankl v Austria* A 227 (1992) (breach of Article 6(1) – and national law – for an investigating judge to be the trial judge). Contrast *Fey v Austria* A 255 (1993) in which the trial judge had played a marginal interrogating role at the pre-trial stage (no breach).

9   A 154 para 50 (1989).

judge, taking decisions as bail, etc, in open court on the application of the police and after hearing the defence. The Court stated that the fact that a trial court judge has earlier taken pre-trial decisions in such a system does not give rise to a 'legitimate doubt' as to impartiality in the absence of 'special circumstances'. Unfortunately for the defendant state, the Court found that were such 'special circumstances' on the facts. These were that the judge's decisions to remand the accused in detention had been on a statutory ground that required him to be convinced that there was a 'particularly confirmed suspicion of guilt'. This, it might well be supposed, involved him in formulating a considered opinion on the applicant's guilt and contrasted with the normal situation in Danish law, which had not have raised a 'legitimate doubt' as to impartiality, in which the judge would be looking only for *prima facie* grounds for the police's suspicion. The *Hauschildt* case was followed in *Sainte Marie v France*.[10] There two members of an appeal court that sentenced the accused following his conviction on charges of possession of arms had earlier been members of a court that had refused his application for bail in criminal damage proceedings arising out of the same facts. Noting that the judges had played no part in the preparation of the case for trial, the Court stated that in such circumstances the 'mere fact that such a judge has already taken pre-trial decisions in the case, including decisions relating to detention on remand, cannot in itself justify fears as to his impartiality'. In the absence of 'special circumstances' such as those in the *Hauschildt* case, the Court found no breach of Article 6.

Another question is whether a judge can take part at more than one stage in the hearing of the merits of a case or other cases against the same accused. In many situations he can. In *Ringeisen v Austria*,[11] the Court indicated that 'it cannot be stated as a general rule resulting from the obligation to be impartial' that a case must be re-heard, having being referred back by an appellate court, by a tribunal with a totally different membership from that of the first hearing. In a later case, it has held that a judge should not take part in two different appellate stages of the same case.[12] Clearly, a judge may try two civil and/or criminal cases with different parties that happen to arise out of the same facts.[13]

The objective test is also infringed if the judge has a personal interest in the case. A financial interest will disqualify a judge as not being impartial,

10 A 253-A para 32 (1992). Cf *Padovani v Italy* A 257-B (1993); *Nortier v Netherlands* A 267 (1993); and *Saraiva de Carvalho v Portugal* A 286-B para 35 (1994). Contrast *Ben Yaacoub v Belgium* A 127 (1987) Com Rep; F Sett before Court, in which the Commission found a 'legitimate doubt' where the judge who took pre-trial decisions on remand was not independent of the investigation and prosecution. The confirmation of a provisional child care order by the judge who made the provisional order is not a breach of Article 6: *Nordborg v Sweden No 13635/88*, 65 DR 232 (1990).
11 A 13 para 97 (1968).
12 *Oberschlick v Austria* A 204 (1991). See also *G v Austria No 15975/90*, 71 DR 245 (1991).
13 *Gillow v UK* A 109 (1986). Similarly, he may judge two different cases concerning the same accused: *Schmid v Austria No 11831/85*, 54 DR 144 (1987). See also *Brown v UK No 11129/84*, 8 EHRR 272 (1985).

although there will be no breach of Article 6(1) if the interest is disclosed and the applicant given an opportunity to object.[14] Non-financial interests are also relevant. Thus in *Demicoli v Malta*,[15] the Maltese House of Representatives that tried the applicant for breach of parliamentary privilege was not impartial because two of its members who participated in the proceedings were the Members of Parliament who were criticised in the article that was the subject of the alleged offence. The objective test was also not satisfied in *Langborger v Sweden*,[16] in which lay members of a tribunal whose function was to adjudicate upon the continuation of a clause in a tenancy agreement were nominated by and had close links with organisations that had an interest in the removal of the clause. It did not matter that the tribunal was composed of two judges as well as the two lay members, with the presiding judge having the casting vote. The *Langborger* case may be contrasted with *Le Compte, Van Leuven and De Meyere v Belgium*,[17] in which the fact that the medical members of a professional tribunal had 'interests very close to' those of one of the doctors being disciplined. This fact was counterbalanced by the presence of an equal number of judges, one of which had the casting vote, so that there was no breach of Article 6(1).

The requirement of impartiality was applied to jury trials in *Holm v Sweden*.[18] There a breach of Article 6(1) was found because of the links between members of a jury[19] and the defendants in an unsuccessful private prosecution brought by the applicant for libel in a book commenting on right wing political parties.[20] A majority of the jury were active members of a political party that owned the first defendant (the publisher) and that had been advised by the second defendant (the author). Although it bears upon impartiality also, the question of the effect on a jury of prejudicial publicity has been considered by the Commission under the residual fair hearing guarantee.[1]

---

14 *D v Ireland No 11489/85*, 51 DR 117 (1986) (judge owned shares in defendant company). On waiver of the right to an impartial court, see further, below, p 239.

15 A 210 (1991).

16 A 155 (1989). A breach of both the independence and impartiality requirements was found. See also *Stallarholmens Platslageri O Ventilation v Sweden* 66 DR 111 (1990).

17 A 43 para 58 (1981). For more recent decisions in which professional disciplinary tribunals with a majority of professional members have been held to be 'impartial' on the basis of the fact that members sit in their professional capacity and the 'margin of appreciation' doctrine, see *Nyström v Belgium No 11504/85*, 58 DR 48 (1988) and *Versteele v Belgium No 12458/86*, 59 DR 113 (1989).

18 A 279-A (1993). In *X v Norway No 3444/67*, 35 CD 37 (1970), a jury member was the godchild of a person who had an interest in having the applicant convicted and in *X v Austria No 7428/76*, 13 DR 36 (1978) the jury foreman was employed by the organisation that owned the shop allegedly robbed by the accused. Both applications were declared inadmissible, the Commission noting that jury challenges had been made unsuccessfully.

19 The jury system was a special one used in freedom of the press cases. The jury panel consisted of 24 persons elected from politically active people by the competent local authority. The nine-man jury was chosen by lot. Each side could make four challenges.

20 In terms of Article 6(1), the case concerned the applicant's 'civil right' to a reputation.

1 See above, p 216.

As to other possible cases of lack of impartiality, the rules as to the appointment of arbitrators in compulsory arbitration proceedings may be such as to raise a 'legitimate doubt' as to whether the tribunal might favour one side.[2] However, the fact that a judge in a divorce case has a conversation with the applicant's wife immediately after the hearing does not by itself raise a 'legitimate doubt'.[3] Nor does the judge's mere membership of the same student association as one of the parties.[4]

Whereas the Commission has ruled that the right to an impartial tribunal may be waived,[5] the Court has left the question open. In *Pfeifer and Plankl v Austria*,[6] the Court stated that 'the waiver of a right guaranteed by the Convention – *in so far as it is permissible* – must be established in an unequivocal manner'. This was not true on the facts of the case; a purported waiver by the applicant of his right to challenge two judges as being disqualified in the absence of his lawyer was not 'unequivocal'. It is arguable that the impartiality (or independence) of the courts is a structural matter of general public interest which a particular party to court proceedings should not be permitted to waive.

d. A tribunal established by law

Article 6(1) requires that the tribunal is 'established by law'. The intention is that, with a view to ensuring its independence, 'the judicial organisation in a democratic society must not depend on the discretion of the Executive, but that it should be regulated by law emanating from Parliament'.[7] This does not mean that every detail of the court system must be spelt out in legislation: provided that the basic rules concerning its organisation and jurisdiction are set out by legislation, particular matters may be left to the executive acting by way of delegated legislation and subject to judicial review to prevent illegal or arbitrary action.[8] Article 6(1) does not prohibit the establishment of special courts if they have a basis in law.[9] 'Established by law' also means 'established in accordance with law', so that the requirement is infringed if a tribunal does not function in accordance with the particular rules that govern it.[10]

---

2 *Bramelid and Malmström v Sweden Nos 8588/79 and 8589/79*, 38 DR 18 (1983) Com Rep; CM Res DH (84) 4.

3 *X v Austria No 556/59*, 4 CD 1 (1960).

4 *Steiner v Austria No 16445/90* (1993) unreported.

5 *D v Ireland No 11489/85*, 51 DR 117 (1986).

6 A 227 (1992). Italics added. In the earlier case of *Oberschlick v Austria* A 204 (1991), in which a waiver was also found not to have occurred in the facts, the question of permissibility of waiver was not discussed.

7 *Zand v Austria No 7360/76*, 15 DR 70 at 80 (1978) Com Rep; CM Res DH (79) 6.

8 Ibid. Cf *Crociani v Italy No 8603/79*, 22 DR 147 at 219 (1980). In *Campbell and Fell v UK* A 80 (1984), no question was raised about the rules concerning prison Boards of Visitors, which were mostly in delegated legislation.

9 See *X and Y v Ireland No 8299/78*, 22 DR 51 (1980) (special criminal court to deal with terrorist offences). As to the extraordinary courts-martial in the *Greek* case, see above, p 233.

10 *Zand v Italy No 7360/76*, 15 DR 70 at 80 (1978) Com Rep; CM Res DH (79) 6. See also *Rossi v France No 11879/85*, 63 DR 105 (1989).

vi. The application of Article 6(1) to appeal proceedings

Article 6(1) does not guarantee a right of appeal from a decision by a court complying with Article 6 in either criminal or non-criminal cases.[11] If, however, a state in its discretion provides a right of appeal, proceedings before the appellate court are governed by Article 6(1).[12] The extent to which Article 6 (1) applies to appeal proceedings, however, depends upon the nature of the particular proceedings, including the function of the appeal court and the relationship of proceedings before it with those earlier in the case. For example, the requirement of a public hearing may not apply fully where the court hears an appeal on points of law only and where a public hearing has taken place on the merits in the trial court.[13] The exercise of a right of appeal may be subjected to reasonable time limits.[14]

Where the initial determination of 'civil rights' within the meaning of Article 6 is made by an administrative or professional authority or a jurisdictional organ of a professional association which does not comply with the right to a fair trial (eg no public hearing), Article 6 is satisfied if there is an appeal to a body with full jurisdiction that does comply with it.[15] The fact that Article 6 is complied with in cases heard initially by such special tribunals if at least one body, at first instance or on appeal, meets all of the requirements of Article 6 is a proper recognition of the 'demands of flexibility and efficiency'[16] that permit the use of such tribunals.

As the Court established in *De Cubber v Belgium*,[17] the same is not true in respect of 'courts of the classic kind', ie courts that are 'integrated within the standard judicial machinery of the country'. In the case of such courts, Article 6 must be fully complied with at the trial court stage and on any appeal. The fact that allowance may be made for special professional or disciplinary bodies 'cannot justify reducing the requirements of Article 6(1) in its traditional and natural sphere of application'. There is, however, a limit to this properly stringent rule. In a case in which the breach of Article 6 concerns the conduct of the first instance court, it may be that the appeal court can 'make reparation' for the breach, in which Article 6 will be complied with. For example, in *Adolf v FRG*,[18] there was no breach of

---

11 A right of appeal in criminal cases is provided by Article 2, Seventh Protocol: see below, p 566. The intepretation of the Article 6 guarantee concerning appeal courts is not to be influenced by the content (particularly the limitations) of the guarantee in the Seventh Protocol: *Ekbatani v Sweden* A 134 (1988).

12 *Delcourt v Belgium* A 11 (1970). This includes proceedings in which a court of appeal decides whether to grant leave to appeal in a criminal case: *Monnell and Morris v UK* A 115 (1987), but *semble*, according to the Commission, not in a civil case: *Porter v UK No 12972/87*, 54 DR 207 (1987).

13 See the cases discussed above, p 221.

14 *Bricmont v Belgium No 10857/84*, 48 DR 106 (1986).

15 *Le Compte, Van Leuven and De Meyer v Belgium* A 43 para 51 (1981) and *Albert and Le Compte v Belgium* A 58 para 29 (1983). See further on these cases, above, pp 192-195. Likewise, it is sufficient if there is such an appeal from a decision by an administrative authority.

16 *Le Compte* case, ibid.

17 A 85 para 32 (1984).

18 A 49 (1982). Cf *Edwards v UK* A 247-B (1992).

Article 6 when the appeal court corrected the impression given by the trial court that the accused was considered by it to be guilty in breach of the presumption of innocence. Likewise, in *Edwards v UK*,[19] there was no breach of Article 6 when the implications of the police's failure to disclose relevant information to the defence at the trial were examined by the Court of Appeal, which was competent to overturn the conviction on the basis of the evidence of non-disclosure. However, where the earlier defect is or cannot be remedied on appeal, the position is different. This is particularly likely to be true where the defect concerns the organisation of the trial court, rather than its conduct of the trial. Thus in the *De Cubber* case,[20] in which the trial court was not impartial because the judge had taken part in an earlier stage of the case, the 'defect involved matters of internal organisation and the Court of Appeal did not cure that defect since it did not quash on that ground the judgment of 29 June 1979 in its entirety'.[1]

4. ARTICLE 6(2): THE RIGHT TO BE PRESUMED INNOCENT IN CRIMINAL CASES

Article 6(2) provides that a person 'charged with a criminal offence shall be presumed innocent until proved guilty according to law'. It guarantees a right that is fundamental to both common law and, despite legend in the United Kingdom to the contrary,[2] civil law systems of criminal justice. The term 'criminal charge' has the same autonomous Convention meaning as it has in Article 6(1).[3] As a result, Article 6(2) does not apply to a person detained for a purpose (eg deportation or extradition) other than his prosecution for a criminal offence.[4] Nor does it benefit a person who is under suspicion of having committed an offence, but is not yet subject to a 'criminal charge'.[5] Article 6(2) continues to apply to the end of any appeal proceedings against conviction.[6] It does not apply to either trial or appellate proceedings insofar as they concern the sentencing of a convicted person; it 'deals only with the proof of guilt and not with the kind or level of

---

19 A 247B (1992). Cf *Schuler-Zgraggen v Switzerland* A 263 (1993).
20 A 86 para 33 (1984). Cf *Holm v Sweden* A 279 A para 33 (1993) (defect stemming from jury system could not be cured by appeal court because it was bound by the jury's verdict).
1 It was not clear whether the Court of Appeal had this power to quash.
2 See Allen, *Legal Duties*, 1993, p 253.
3 *Adolf v Austria* A 49 para 30 (1982). Accordingly, Article 6(2) applies to some disciplinary proceedings: *Albert and Le Compte v Belgium* A 58 (1983). Article 6(2) applies to a criminal prosecution in its entirety, so that it continues to apply to ancillary proceedings after the case on its merits is over: *Minelli v Switzerland* A 62 para 30 (1983) and *Sekanina v Austria* A 266-A para 24 (1993). And see the *Allenet de Ribemont* case, below, p 248.
4 *X v Austria No 1918/63*, 6 YB 484 (1963) (extradition); *X v Netherlands No 1983/63*, 8 YB 228 (1965) (deportation).
5 *X v FRG No 4483/70*, 38 CD 77 (1971).
6 *Nölkenbockhoff v FRG* A 123 (1987). It does not apply to cases referred to the English Court of Appeal under s 17(1)(a), Criminal Appeal Act 1968: *Callaghan No 14739/89*, 60 DR 296 (1989) (the *Birmingham Six* case). On the application to appeal proceedings of Article 6 generally, see above, p 240.

punishment'.[7] Accordingly, a court may take a person's criminal record and other factors into account when sentencing him even though they have not been introduced in evidence (and hence have not been open to challenge) during the trial.[8] Similarly Article 6(2) does not apply to an application by a convicted person for re-trial.[9] Article 6(2) does, however, apply to proceedings concerning the discontinuance of a case against an accused[10] or the award of costs or compensation for detention on remand following discontinuance or acquittal.[11] Such proceedings are a part of the determination of the charge against him. The obligation in Article 6(2) is independent of those in other Article 6 guarantees, so that there may be a breach of it even though the rest of Article 6 is respected.[12]

Article 6(2) operates mainly at the stage of court proceedings. It has been held not to apply to practices in the course of a criminal investigation such as the conduct of blood tests[13] or medical examinations[14] or an order to produce documents.[15] By analogy, Article 6(2) probably also does not apply to breathalyser tests, fingerprinting, searches of the person and of property[16] and identity parades.[17] Nor does it extend to the closure of a shop as a provisional measure or the offer of an 'out of court' fine.[18] A person may also be detained pending trial[19] and subjected to restrictions during such detention (eg as to clothing and correspondence)[20] without an issue arising under Article 6(2). However, prejudicial statements at the pre-trial stage about an accused who is subject to a criminal charge are controlled by Article 6(2).[1]

The fullest statement by the Court of the meaning of Article 6 (2) is found in *Barberà, Messegué and Jabardo v Spain:*[2]

> 'Paragraph 2 embodies the principle of the presumption of innocence. It requires, *inter alia*, that when carrying out their duties, the members of a court should not start with the preconceived idea that the accused

7 *Engel v Netherlands* A 22 (1976).
8 Ibid. Cf *Albert and Le Compte v Belgium* A 58 (1983).
9 *X v FRG No 914/60*, 4 YB 372 (1961).
10 *Adolf v Austria* A 49 (1982).
11 *Minelli v Switzerland* A 62 (1983).
12 *I and C v Switzerland No 10107/82*, 48 DR 35 (1985) Com Rep; CM Res DH (86) 11.
13 *X v Netherlands No 8239/78*, 16 DR 184 (1978).
14 *X v FRG No 986/61*, 5 YB 192 (1962).
15 *Funke v France* A 256-A (1993) Com Rep para 69.
16 The seizure of the property of an arrested person as security for costs is not a breach of Article 6(2): *X v Austria No 4338/69*, 36 CD 79 (1970).
17 Articles 8(2), 10(2), 11(2), Convention, support this view. For criticism of the limited interpretation of Article 6(2) in this regard, see Stavros, p 50.
18 *Deweer v Belgium* B 33 (1980). Com Rep para 64.
19 See Articles 5(1)(c) and 5(3).
20 *Skoogström v Sweden No 8582/72*, 5 EHRR 278 (1982). Cf *Englert v FRG* A 123 (1987) Com Rep para 47.
1 *Krause v Switzerland*, below, p 247. In *X v Austria No 9077/80*, 26 DR 211 (1981) the Commission left open the question whether the prohibition of prejudicial statements by public officials might apply before a person is subject to a charge.
2 A 146 para 77 (1989). See also *Austria v Italy* 6 YB 740 at 782-784 (1963) Com Rep; CM Res DH (63) 3.

has committed the offence charged; the burden of proof is on the prosecution, and any doubt should benefit the accused. It also follows that it is for the prosecution to inform the accused of the case that will be made against him, so that he may prepare and present his defence accordingly, and to adduce evidence sufficient to convict him.'

This confirms, in common law terms, that the presumption of innocence under Article 6(2) means, at least in part, that the general burden of proof must lie with the prosecution, or, in terms more appropriate for civil law systems, that the court, in its inquiry into the facts, must find for the accused in a case of doubt.[3] Although the matter has not been explored in the Strasbourg jurisprudence, it can be taken that the different approaches to the presumption of innocence in the accusatorial and inquisitorial systems of criminal justice in common and civil law systems respectively are both consistent with Article 6(2). The close link between the presumption of innocence and freedom from self-incrimination was noted by the Commission in *Saunders v UK*,[4] with the presumption reflecting 'the expectation that the state bear the general burden of establishing the guilt of an accused, in which process the accused is entitled not to be required to furnish any involuntary assistance by way of confession'.

Although the burden of proof must fall upon the prosecution, it may be transferred to the accused when he is seeking to establish a defence.[5] Similarly, Article 6(2) does not prohibit presumptions of fact or of law that may operate against the accused. However, it does require that states confine such presumptions 'within reasonable limits which take into account the importance of what is at stake and maintain the rights of the defence'. This was stated in the leading case of *Salabiaku v France*,[6] in which the applicant had been convicted of the strict liability customs offence of smuggling prohibited goods. The applicant had collected and taken through the 'green' customs exit at Paris airport a trunk that contained prohibited drugs, of which he claimed to have no knowledge. Under French law, a person who was in possession of prohibited goods in these circumstances was presumed to be guilty of smuggling them. Thus the case was not a straightforward one of strict liability for an act that the prosecution had proved that the accused had committed. Instead it was one in which the *actus reus* of smuggling had been presumed from the proven fact of possession. The Court found that, as applied to the applicant's case, this presumption of fact was not contrary to Article 6(2). Under French law, the

3 The question whether Article 6(2) incorporates the civil law principle *in dubio pro reo* was raised but not clearly answered in *Lingens and Leitgens v Austria No 8803/79*, 26 DR 171 (1981).
4 Loc cit at p 214, n 16, above, Com Rep para 72. There was no breach of Article 6(2) by the inferences drawn from the accused's refusal to give evidence in *Murray (John) v UK* (1994) Com Rep: see above, p 214. Case pending before the Court.
5 *Lingens v Austria*, above (burden of proof on defence in criminal defamation proceedings to show that statement is true; no breach of Article 6(2)).
6 A 141-A para 28 (1988). Cf *Pham Hoang v France* A 243 (1992) (presumption of fact not unreasonable in view of the defences open to the accused). See also *Duhs v Sweden No 12995/87*, 67 DR 204 (1990) (car-parking fine based just on ownership permissible).

applicant had a defence of *force majeure*, by which it was open to him to prove that it was impossible for him to have known of the contents of the trunk. This he failed to prove to the satisfaction of the trial court. The Court held that, having regard to the possibility of the *force majeure* defence, the Customs Code was not applied by the courts in a manner which conflicted with Article 6(2), despite what was 'at stake' (imprisonment and a substantial fine) for the applicant. In other cases it has been held that rebuttable presumptions that an accused was living knowingly off the earnings of a prostitute who was proved to be living with him or under his control[7] and that a company director was guilty of an offence committed by the company[8] were not inconsistent with Article 6(2).

As the *Salabiaku* case also decided, Article 6(2) does not prohibit offences of strict liability, which are a common feature of the criminal law of the Convention parties. An offence may thus be committed, consistently with Article 6(2), on the basis that a certain act has been committed, without it being necessary to prove *mens rea*. Provided a state respects the rights protected by the Convention, it is free to punish any kind of activity as criminal and to establish the elements of the offence in its discretion, including any requirement of *mens rea*.

As to the standard of proof, there is no clear statement that there is a requirement of proof of guilt beyond reasonable doubt. In *Austria v Italy* the Commission stated that Article 6(2) requires that a court find the accused guilty only on the basis of evidence 'sufficiently strong in the eyes of the law to establish his guilt'.[9] As to the kind of evidence that may be relied upon, this may be 'direct or indirect'.[10] Otherwise, apart from the obligation to exclude coerced statements (see below), no indication has been given other than that Article 6(2) requires the existence of probative evidence. What is clear is that, in accordance with their general policy of not acting as a *quatrième instance*,[11] the Strasbourg authorities do not regard themselves as competent to question findings of fact by the trial court that appear to be based upon probative evidence.[12]

Article 6(2) does, however, impose certain other obligations of an evidential kind. The accused must be allowed an opportunity to rebut the evidence presented against him.[13] In addition, a confession obtained by 'maltreatment' must not be admitted in evidence.[14] A statement may be

7 *X v UK No 5124/71*, 42 CD 135 (1972).
8 *G v Malta No 16641/90* (1991) unreported.
9 6 YB 740 at 784 (1963) Com Rep; CM Res DH (63) 3.
10 Ibid.
11 See above, p 15.
12 See *Albert and Le Compte v Belgium* A 58 (1983). See also the discussion of the rules of evidence requirements under Article 6(1), above, p 210.
13 *Austria v Italy* 6 YB 740 at 784 (1963) Com Rep; CM Res (63) 3. The Commission emphasised the words 'according to law' in Article 6(2). See also *Albert and Le Compte v Belgium* A 58 (1983) and *Schenk v Switzerland* A 140 (1988). Article 6(2) overlaps with Article 6(3)(d) in this respect.
14 *Austria v Italy* 6 YB 116 at 784 (1963) Com Rep; CM Res DH (63) 3. Cf *X v UK No 5076/71*, 40 CD 64 (pressure to plead guilty may be contrary to Article 6 (2)). There is an overlap here with the general 'fair hearing' requirement in Article 6(1): see above, p 210.

admitted, however, despite the fact that the accused has not been informed of his right to silence before making it.[15] A number of other claims concerning rules of evidence have also been rejected. Thus it is not contrary to Article 6(2) to reveal the accused's past criminal record to the court before his conviction.[16] In England, the accused's record is not revealed to the jury for fear of prejudice; it is available to the judge.[17] In civil law systems evidence of convictions is commonly given to the court (including any jury) as being indicative of the likelihood of the accused having committed the offence.[18] In accordance with its normal approach, the Commission is not prepared to find a practice that is followed by a significant number of Council of Europe members to be contrary to Article 6(2).[19]

Various other claims that the presumption of innocence has been infringed in the conduct of the trial other than in respect of the operation of the rules of evidence have been rejected. The handcuffing of the accused in front of the jury was consistent with Article 6(2) as a necessary security measure.[20] The arrest of a witness in the courtroom for perjury immediately after giving evidence for the accused was also permissible,[1] as also was the re-trial of the accused before a court that had earlier considered his application for bail.[2] A procedure by which a person may plead guilty to an offence, as a result of which the proceedings are limited to the question of sentencing, is not in breach of Article 6(2), provided that pressure has not been brought improperly to bear upon the accused to obtain the guilty plea.[3]

The Commission has on occasion considered the presumption of innocence requirement in terms of lack of judicial bias or partiality. Insofar as judicial bias is an aspect of Article 6(2), it overlaps with the 'impartial tribunal' requirement in Article 6(1) and might be better treated entirely under that provision.[4] Prejudicial comment by counsel or witnesses will only raise a question under Article 6(2) if failure to control it shows judicial bias.[5]

---

15 *X v FRG No 4483/70*, 38 CD 77 (1971).
16 *X v Austria No 2742/66*, 9 YB 550 (1966).
17 Coutts, op cit at p 165, n 6, above, p 12.
18 Id, pp 12-14.
19 *X v Austria No 2742/66*, 9 YB 550 (1966).
20 *X v Austria No 2291/64*, 24 CD 20 (1967).
1 *X v FRG No 8744/79*, 5 EHRR 499 (1983).
2 *X v FRG No 2646/65*, 9 YB 484 (1966).
3 *X v UK No 5076/71*, 40 CD 69 (1972). See also *Duhs v Sweden No 12995/87* (1990), 67 DR 204 (1990) (out of court car-parking fines).
4 For cases in which prejudicial comment by a judge has been considered under both Articles 6(1) and 6(2), see *Boeckmans v Belgium No 1727/62*, 8 YB 410 (1965) and *X v UK No 5574/72*, 3 DR 10 (1975).
5 See *Austria v Italy* 6 YB 740 Com Rep; CM Res DH (63) 3; *Nielsen v Denmark No 343/57*, 2 YB 412; *X, Y, Z v Austria No 7950/77*, 4 EHRR 270 at 274 (1980). In determining whether proceedings have been allowed to get out of hand to the prejudice of the accused, allowance may be made for different national temperaments and legal traditions: *Austria v Italy*, ibid.

As well as being a guarantee that concerns the rules of evidence and proceedings in courts, Article 6(2) is also infringed in certain circumstances in which a court or other public official indicates its view that the applicant is guilty of an offence when he has not been tried and found guilty of it. As far as pronouncements by a court are concerned, the question has arisen in the context of decisions to discontinue criminal proceedings against the applicant,[6] as to the payment of compensation for detention on remand following an accused's acquittal or the discontinuance of criminal proceedings against him[7] or as to the payment of costs by him.[8] The general rule insofar as it concerns judicial pronouncements was formulated in *Minelli v Switzerland*[9] as follows:

'. . . the presumption of innocence will be violated if, without the accused's having previously been proved guilty according to law and, notably, without his having had the opportunity of exercising his rights of defence, a judicial decision concerning him reflects an opinion that he is guilty. This may be so even in the absence of any formal finding; it suffices that there is some reasoning suggesting that the court regards the accused as guilty.'

In that case, a private prosecution against the applicant was discontinued because it had become statute-barred. A Swiss court thereupon ordered the applicant to pay part of the private prosecutor's and court costs on the basis that the applicant would 'very probably' have been convicted had the case gone to trial. The European Court held that Article 6(2) had been infringed. Although there was no formal decision as to guilt, the court's judgment as to costs 'showed that it was satisfied' of the accused's guilt, and this was sufficient.[10] Prior to the *Minelli* case, the Court had adopted the same approach in *Adolf v Austria*,[11] in which, in the judgment discontinuing proceedings against the accused for a petty assault, there was a passage that was 'well capable of being understood as meaning' that the accused had committed the offence. However, the Court found no breach of Article 6(2) because the passage had been corrected on appeal.

Where a court takes a decision in which it declares that there remain suspicions against the accused, but does not go so far as to suggest guilt, Article 6(2) will not be infringed if the proceedings against the accused have been discontinued without a final decision on the merits.[12] If, however, the

6 *Adolf v Austria* A 49 (1982).
7 See eg *Englert v FRG* A 123 (1987) (discontinuance) and *Sekanina v Austria* A 266-A (1993) (acquittal).
8 See eg *Minelli v Switzerland* A 62 (1983). It would also be contrary to Article 6(2) to revoke the suspension of a sentence because of another alleged offence: see the facts of *Grabbemann v FRG No 12748/87*, 63 DR 137 (1989) F Sett.
9 Id, para 38.
10 Cf *I and C v Switzerland No 10107/82*, 48 DR 35 (1985) Com rep; CM Res DH (86) 11.
11 A 49 para 39 (1982).
12 *Nölkenbockhoff v FRG* A 123 (1987); *Lutz v FRG* A 123 (1987); and *Englert v FRG* A 123 (1987). *A fortiori*, the mere refusal of costs or of compensation for detention on remand with no such remarks is not in breach of Article 6(2): ibid.

statement is made in a decision after the accused has been finally acquitted, Article 6(2) is infringed.[13] This is because while the 'voicing of suspicions regarding an accused's innocence is conceivable as long as the conclusion of criminal proceedings has not resulted in a decision on the merits of the accusation', once the acquittal is final such statements are 'incompatible with the presumption of innocence'.[14] But a statement by an appellate court of a convicted person's motives for committing an offence when the trial court has not identified them is not a breach of Article 6(2).[15]

The above cases concern judicial statements made in criminal cases, decisions that directly concern the applicant. Article 6(2) is not infringed when a court refers, in its judgment in criminal proceedings against another person, to the involvement of the applicant, who has yet to be tried, for the same offence where this is relevant in establishing the other person's guilt.[16] However, the rule in the *Minelli* case may apply to assertions of an accused's guilt in civil proceedings. Although such proceedings are not directly subject to Article 6(2),[17] an assertion by a court in a civil case that a person is guilty on a criminal charge that is pending against him is contrary to the presumption of innocence. But the mere suspension of civil proceedings pending the outcome of a criminal case is not a breach.[18] Article 6(2) requires that a civil court be bound by a finding as to criminal liability by a criminal court.[19] Although this is a common and desirable rule, it is difficult to see that it follows from Article 6(2) since the convicted person will no longer be subject to a criminal charge.

The approach in the *Minelli* case concerning judicial pronouncements applies also to public statements by public officials[20] of the guilt of a person prior to his conviction. In *Krause v Switzerland*,[1] the Commission stated:

'It is a fundamental principle embodied in this Article which protects everybody against being treated by public officials as being guilty of an offence before this is established according to law by a competent court. Article 6, paragraph 2, therefore, may be violated by public officials if they declare that somebody is responsible for criminal acts without a

13 *Sekanina v Austria* A 266-A (1993).
14 Id, para 30.
15 *Kremzow v Austria* A 268-B (1993). Nor is general reference to 'financial misdeeds', rather than to a specific offence, a breach: ibid.
16 *Gjerde v Norway No 18672/91* (1993) unreported.
17 *X v FRG No 6062/73*, 2 DR 54 (1974).
18 *Farragut v France No 10103/82*, 39 DR 186 (1984).
19 *X v Austria No 9395/81*, 30 DR 227 (1982).
20 This includes a member of a court other than the one that will try the accused: *C v UK No 10427/83*, 47 DR 85 (1986). *Quaere* whether a state is obliged by Article 6(2) to control by law assertions of guilt in the private press. See *Ensslin, Baader and Raspe v FRG* 14 DR 64 at 113 (1978); *X v UK No 3860/68*, 30 CD 70 (1969); *Crociani v Italy No 8603/79*, 22 DR 147 at 227 (1980). As to the obligation to control private conduct generally under the Convention, see p 19.
1 *No 7986/77*, 13 DR 73 (1978). The word 'formal' is best understood in the sense of 'official' in the light of the *Minelli* case. See also *X v Austria No 2343/64*, 10 YB 176 (1967); *X, Y, Z v Austria No 7950/80*, 19 DR 213 (1980); *RF and SF v Austria No 10847/84*, 44 DR 238 (1985).

court having found so. This does not mean, of course, that the authorities may not inform the public about criminal investigations. They do not violate Article 6, paragraph 2, if they state that a suspicion exists, that people have been arrested, that they have confessed, etc. What is excluded, however, is a formal declaration that somebody is guilty.'

In that case, the applicant was detained on remand pending trial for terrorist offences. When aircraft hijackers demanded her release, the Swiss Federal Minister of Justice stated on television that the applicant had 'committed common law offences' for which she must accept responsibility, although tempering this remark in a later television statement by the comment that he did not know whether she would be convicted. However, the Commission found that Article 6(2) had not been infringed on the facts because the Minister's remarks were an assertion of suspicion, not of guilt.[2] The same approach has since been adopted by the Court. In *Allenet de Ribemont v France*[3] a senior police officer, flanked by other officials who made supporting remarks, stated at a press conference that the applicant was one of the 'instigators' of a murder. The Court held that Article 6(2) applied and had been infringed. Although not yet charged, the applicant had been arrested and hence was 'charged' in the sense of Article 6(2).[4] As to the infringement:

> 'The Court notes that . . . some of the highest ranking officers in the French police referred to Mr Allenet de Ribemont, without qualification or reservation, as one of the instigators of a murder and thus an accomplice in that murder . . . This was clearly a declaration of the applicant's guilt which, firstly, encouraged the public to believe him guilty and, secondly, prejudged the assessment of the facts by the competent judicial authority.'[5]

Article 6(2) is not infringed when a public revenue authority exercises a right of pre-emption, whereby it buys real property from a person who has purchased it at a price that the authority considers below the market value. Although the pre-emption procedure may be aimed at preventing tax evasion, its exercise is not tantamount to a declaration of guilt.[6]

A violation of the presumption of innocence by a lower court may be made good by a higher court on appeal.[7] It may be, however, that 'the failure of the lower court to observe the principle of presumption of innocence has so distorted the general course of proceedings' that this is not possible.[8]

---

2 Cf *X v Austria* No 9077/80, 26 DR 211 (1981). And see *Berns and Ewert v Luxembourg* No 132351/87, 68 DR 137 (1991) and *Hayward v Sweden* No 14106/88 (1991), unreported.
3 A 308 paras 37, 41 (1995).
4 See above, p 241, n 3.
5 The Court noted that Article 6(2) entails a limit upon freedom of speech in this regard: id, para 38.
6 *Hentrich v France* A 296-A (1994).
7 *Adolf v Austria* A 49 (1982).
8 *Austria v Italy* 6 YB 740 at 784 (1966) Com Rep; CM Res DH (63) 3.

5. ARTICLE 6(3): FURTHER GUARANTEES IN CRIMINAL CASES

i. Article 6(3): Generally

Article 6(3) guarantees certain rights that are necessary to the preparation and conduct of the defence and to ensure that the accused is able to defend himself on equal terms with the prosecution. The rights listed are 'minimum rights'. They are elements of the wider concept of the right to a fair trial in Article 6(1).[9] Because of this the Strasbourg authorities sometimes decide cases on the basis of Article 6(1) *and* the relevant specific right in Article 6(3), emphasising the one or the other in different cases, or even on the basis of Article 6 as a whole.[10] There is also some overlap between the rights guaranteed within Article 6(3).[11]

The rights in Article 6(3) are guaranteed only to persons 'charged with a criminal offence'. This wording is identical to that in Article 6(2) and has the same autonomous Convention meaning as it has in that paragraph and in the equivalent wording in Article 6(1).[12] Article 6(3) does not protect a person who is suspected of a criminal offence but not yet charged with it in the sense of Article 6.[13] Nor does it benefit a person who is being extradited for prosecution in another jurisdiction.[14]

As the term has been interpreted in Article 6(1), mainly in connection with the trial within a reasonable time guarantee, a person is charged with a criminal offence from the moment that he is 'substantially affected' by the steps taken against him.[15] This will normally be when he is arrested or issued with a summons or when criminal proceedings against him are initiated to his knowledge in some other recognised way. However, the fact that a person is 'charged with a criminal offence' does not mean that each of the rights in Article 6(3) extends to him from the very moment of his being so charged. Just as, for example, the right to a public hearing in Article 6(1) applies only from the time that the court hearing begins, so a right in Article 6(3) may have no application at the pre-trial stage.

The extent to which Article 6(3)[16] applies to the pre-trial stage of criminal proceedings has been a matter of dispute, with a number of civil law contracting parties questioning in particular whether Article 6(3) applies to the preliminary investigation stage of their criminal justice systems. This argument was expressly rejected by the Court in *Imbrioscia v Switzerland*.[17]

---

9 On the relationship between Articles 6(1) and 6(3), see further above, p 202.
10 For an 'Article 6 as a whole' case, see *Vidal v Belgium* A 235-B (1992).
11 See below, pp 250 and 255.
12 See *Adolf v Austria* A 49 (1982). Cf *C v Italy No 10889/84*, 56 DR 40 (1988).
13 *X v FRG No 1216/61*, 11 CD 1 (1963) and *X v FRG No 4483/70*, 38 CD 77 (1971).
14 *X v Austria No 1918/63*, 6 YB 484 (1963) and *X v FRG No 4247/69*, 36 CD 73 (1970) (an Article 6(3)(c) case).
15 See above, p 171.
16 The same question arises for Article 6(1) and (2): see above, pp 171 and 242.
17 A 275 para 36 (1993).

Noting that the reasonable time guarantee in Article 6(1) applied at the pre-trial stage, the Court stated that:

> '[o]ther requirements of Article 6 – especially of paragraph 3 – may also be relevant before a case is sent for trial if and insofar as the fairness of the trial is likely to be seriously prejudiced by the initial failure to comply with them.'

The question whether each particular right, or part of a right, guaranteed in Article 6(3) applies at the pre-trial stage is considered in the appropriate section below. It is sufficient to note at this point that Articles 6(3)(b), (c) and (e) apply fully to the pre-trial stage and that Article 6(3)(a) may apply at least as of the issuing of the indictment in a civil law system. In contrast, Article 6(3)(d), concerning the examination of witnesses, generally has no application to the pre-trial stage. Although there have been few common law cases, the above conclusions that have been established in the context of civil law systems apply to pre-trial procedures in common law systems *mutatis mutandis*.

Article 6(3) applies to appeal proceedings, although its requirements at this level must be shaped by the function of the appellate court and its place in the proceedings as a whole.[18]

ii.   Article 6(3)(a): The right to be informed of the accusation

Article 6(3)(a) requires that a person charged with a criminal offence 'be informed promptly, in a language which he understands and in detail, of the nature and cause of the accusation against him'. It overlaps with Article 5(2), which provides a similarly worded guarantee for persons detained pending trial.[19] However, although both provisions respond to the legitimate claim of an individual to know why the state has acted against him, the purpose of the two guarantees is essentially different. Whereas Article 5(2) seeks to assist the arrested person in challenging his detention, Article 6(3)(a) is intended to give the accused person the information he needs to prepare his defence.[20] There is also an overlap between Article 6(3)(a) and Article 6(3)(b); compliance with the former is a necessary condition of compliance with the latter.[1]

It is not yet clearly established when Article 6(3)(a) begins to apply. In *Kamasinski v Austria*,[2] it was considered to do so, in the civil law system concerned, at the latest when the accused was indicted. Given the purpose of Article 6(3)(a) of assisting the accused in preparing his defence and the typically crucial role of the preliminary investigation stage in such systems, it

---

18 See eg *Artico v Italy* A 37 (1980) and *Kremzow v Austria* A 268-B para 58 (1993). On the application of Article 6 to appeal proceedings generally, see above, p 240.

19 See above, p 128.

20 *Bricmont v Belgium No 10857/84*, 48 DR 106 (1986).

1   *Ofner v Austria No 524/59*, 3 YB 322 at 344 (1960).

2   A 168 paras 78-81 (1989).

is arguable that Article 6(3)(a) begins to run as soon as a person is subject to a criminal charge in the sense of Article 6. The requirement that the information be given 'promptly', which has not been the subject of interpretation,[3] supports this view. The Commission has expressly left the question open.[4] In *Brozicek v Italy*,[5] a 'judicial notification' of the commencement of a preliminary investigation in the civil law system concerned was considered to contain enough detail to satisfy the requirements of Article 6(3)(a). Although neither the Commission nor the Court clearly decided in that case that Article 6(3(a) had to be complied with at that stage, they did not appear unsympathetic. In any event, the point at which the information required by Article 6(3(a) must be communicated to the accused is reduced in importance for a suspect who is under arrest because of the reasons available to him by virtue of Article 5(2) and the fact that the difference in the detail required under the two provisions is, as they have been interpreted, not great.

The accused must be informed of the 'nature' of the accusation against him, ie the offence with which he is charged, and also its 'cause', ie the material facts upon which the allegation is based.[6] The offence with which the accused is charged may be altered as the case proceeds provided that the accused is informed of the change.[7] What needs to be communicated to the accused will depend upon what he can be taken to know from the questioning he has undergone and from the other circumstances of the case.[8] Similarly, the accused must take advantage of what opportunities exist to learn of the accusation against him; if a prisoner fails to attend a preliminary hearing of a disciplinary charge against him at which he could have obtained further information, this will count against his claim of a breach of Article 6(3)(a).[9]

The words 'in detail' clearly suggest that the information to which a person is entitled under Article 6(3)(a) is 'more specific and more detailed' than that which he must receive under Article 5(2).[10] In practice, however, not a great deal of 'detail' has been required under Article 6(3)(a). The Commission has stated that it should 'contain the material enabling the accused to prepare his defence . . . without however *necessarily* mentioning the evidence on which the charge is based'.[11] In *Brozicek v Italy*,[12] the Court did not mention any

3 For its meaning in Articles 5(2) and (3), see above, pp 130, 134.
4 *X v Netherlands No 8361/78*, 27 DR 37 (1981).
5 A 167 (1989). See also *C v Italy No 10889/84*, 56 DR 40 (1988).
6 *Ofner v Austria No 524/59*, 3 YB 322 at 344 (1960).
7 Ibid. There was a breach of Article 6(3)(a) where the accused, having been acquitted of the initial charge, were convicted on a prosecution appeal of another offence of which they had not been given notice before the appeal hearing; *Chichlian and Ekindjian v France* A 162-B (1989) Com Rep; F Sett before Court. Cf *C v France No 15440/89* (1991), unreported. See also *Zimmerman v Austria No 8490/79*, 22 DR 140 (1981); 30 DR 15 (1982) F Sett.
8 *Kamasinski v Austria* A 168 paras 79-81 (1989).
9 *Campbell and Fell v UK* A 80 (1984).
10 *Neilsen v Denmark No 343/57*, 2 YB 412 at 462 (1959).
11 *X v Belgium No 7628/76*, 9 DR 169 (1977). Italics added. See also *Ofner v Austria No 524/59*, 3 YB 322 (1960); *Neilsen v Denmark No 343/57*, 4 YB 494 (1961); *G, S and M v Austria No 9614/81*, 34 DR 119 (1983).
12 A 167 para 42 (1989). Cf *X v Belgium No 1103/61*, 5 YB 168 (1962) ('You are accused of corruption' sufficient).

need to indicate the evidence against the accused and was satisfied with information that 'listed the offences of which he was accused, stated the place and the date thereof, referred to the relevant Article of the Criminal Code and mentioned the name of the victim'. Such a ruling leaves little room for the distinction that should exist between Articles 6(3)(a) and 5(2). Insofar as the amount of information required by Article 6(3)(a) may be reduced by the importance of giving some information to the accused 'promptly', this limitation on the rigour of Article 6(3)(a) is made good by the fact that Article 6(3)(b) requires further information ('facilities') to be made available later. In the light of the *Brozciek* case, it seems likely that the information that must be given to the accused under English criminal law in a warrant for arrest or in a summons or when a person is charged after arrest without a warrant meets the requirements of Article 6(3)(a).

Although the importance of the required information is such that it should normally be given in writing, this is not necessary to the extent that the accused has been given sufficient information orally or has waived his right to a written communication.[13]

The information must be given to the accused in a 'language which he understands'. Unless the authorities can prove or have reasonable grounds to believe that the accused has a sufficient command of the language in which the information is given to him, they must provide him with an appropriate translation.[14] Since the right is that of the defence as a whole, Article 6(3)(a) is complied with if the required information is given in a language that the accused *or* his lawyer understands.[15] If an interpreter is used to translate documents or statements in order to give the information required by Article 6(3)(a), the costs of interpretation must be met by the state under Article 6(3)(e).[16]

iii. Article 6(3)(b): The right to adequate time and facilities

Article 6(3)(b) guarantees a person charged with a criminal offence 'adequate time and facilities for the preparation of his defence'.

a. Adequate time

The guarantee in Article 6(3)(b) for an accused of adequate time to prepare his defence, which protects him against a 'hasty trial',[17] is the counterpoise to

---

13 *Kamasinski v Austria* A 168 paras 79-81 (1989).

14 *Brozicek v Italy* A 167 (1989). The case for a written translation of a key document such as an indictment is particularly strong: *Kamasinski v Austria* A 168 (1989).

15 *X v Austria No 6185/73*, 2 DR 68 (1975). The question was not ruled on in *Kamasinski v Austria* A 168 (1989), the applicant having requested that the indictment be sent to his lawyer. For the view that the information should be given in a language that the accused understands so that he can control his defence, see Stavros, p 174.

16 See below, p 270.

17 *Kröcher and Müller v Switzerland No 8463/78*, 26 DR 24 at 53 (1981). *Quaere* whether the power of the English courts to convict a person summarily for contempt in the face of the court, which is a criminal offence in English law, is consistent with Article 6(3)(b).

that in Article 6(1) by which an accused must be tried within a reasonable time.[18] The guarantee begins to run from the moment that a person is subject to a criminal charge. This will be from the moment that he is arrested or otherwise 'substantially affected'[19] or, in the context of prison disciplinary proceedings, when he is given notice of the charges against him.[20] Generally, the adequacy of the time allowed will depend upon the particular facts of the case. Relevant considerations are the complexity of the case,[1] the defence lawyer's workload,[2] the stage of proceedings[3] and the accused's decision to conduct his defence in person.[4] A legal aid lawyer must be appointed,[5] or the accused allowed to appoint his own lawyer,[6] in good time before the hearing. If a lawyer is replaced for good reason, additional time must be allowed for the new lawyer to prepare the case.[7]

In cases at the trial stage before the ordinary courts, the Commission has accepted that a period of seventeen days' notice of the hearing in a 'fairly complicated' case of misappropriation of funds[8] was sufficient on the facts. Five days' notice of a prison disciplinary hearing was also enough.[9] Remarkably, in the absence of any evidence of prejudice in fact, there was no breach of Article 6(3)(b) when the applicant had met and instructed his legal aid barrister only ten minutes before a trial that led to a sentence of seven years' imprisonment.[10] As this case demonstrates, Article 6(3)(b) requires actual prejudice, which may well be difficult for an applicant to prove. Generally, less time will be needed to prepare for an appeal than for a trial.[11] Where an accused considers that the time allowed is inadequate, he should, as a matter of local remedies, seek an adjournment or postponement of the hearing,[12] but there may be exceptional circumstances which make this unnecessary.[13]

18 See above, p 222.
19 See above, p 171. And see *X and Y v Austria No 7909/77*, 15 DR 160 (1978).
20 *Campbell and Fell v UK* A 80 (1984).
1 *Albert and Le Compte v Belgium* A 58 (1983).
2 *X and Y v Austria No 7909/77*, 15 DR 160 (1978).
3 *Huber v Austria No 5523/72*, 46 CD 99 (1974).
4 *X v Austria No 2370/64*, 22 CD 96 (1967).
5 *X and Y v Austria No 7909/77*, 15 DR 160 (1978). An accused cannot complain, however, to the extent that he is at fault for the late appointment of his lawyer: *X v Austria No 8251/78*, 17 DR 166 (1979).
6 *Perez Mahia v Spain No 11022/84*, 9 EHRR 145 (1985) (ten days sufficient).
7 See *Goddi v Italy* A 76 (1984) (decision under Article 6(3)(c), but in effect, a finding of a breach of Article 6(3)(b) also). See also the facts of *Samer v FRG No 4319/69*, 14 YB 322 (1971).
8 *X and Y v Austria No 7909/77*, 15 DR 160 (1978). See also *X v Austria No 2267/64*, 2 Digest 793 (1969) (one month's notice for accused's lawyer sufficient); *X v Austria No 2370/64*, 22 CD 96 (1967); and *X v Austria No 8251/78*, 17 DR 166 (1979).
9 *Campbell and Fell v UK* A 80 (1984). Cf *Albert and Le Compte v Belgium* A 58 (1983) (fifteen days sufficient for professional disciplinary hearing).
10 *X v UK No 4042/69*, 13 YB 690 (1970). Cf the *Murphy* case, below, n 12.
11 *Huber v Austria No 5523/72*, 17 YB 314 (1974) (fifteen days for a complicated case raised doubts, but not a breach). On the need for sufficient time to prepare an appeal, see *Kremzow v Austria*, below, p 256, n 18.
12 *Campbell and Fell v UK* A 80 (1984). In *Murphy v UK No 4681/70*, 43 CD 1 (1972), in which a legal aid barrister was allocated to the accused just minutes before a hearing, the application was rejected because an adjournment would have been granted if requested.
13 *Goddi v Italy* A 76 (1984).

b.   Adequate facilities

The accused's right to adequate facilities was explained in *Can v Austria*[14] as requiring that he has 'the opportunity to organise his defence in an appropriate way and without restriction as to the possibility to put all relevant defence arguments before the trial court'.

It includes the accused's right to communicate with his lawyer during the pre-trial period, as well as later, to the extent necessary to prepare his defence.[15] This has particular significance for persons in detention on remand pending the hearing.[16] A prisoner must be allowed to receive a visit from his lawyer out of the hearing of prison officers or other officials in order to convey instructions or to pass or receive confidential information relating to the preparation of his defence.[17] Restrictions upon visits by lawyers may be imposed if they can be justified in the public interest (eg to prevent escape or the obstruction of justice).[18] In the terrorist case of *Kröcher and Möller v Switzerland*,[19] a limit of two visits a week, a requirement of prior notice, a separating glass panel and a ban on tape recorders were permissible. In the same case, an initial complete ban on lawyers' visits for three weeks while the applicants were in solitary confinement was justifiable for security reasons.[20] A restriction by which a lawyer may not discuss certain evidence with his client may also be permissible to protect the identity of an informer.[1] A refusal to allow a prisoner to take his notes and annotated documents to an interview with his lawyer is not in breach of Article 6(3)(b).[2] In an early decision, the Commission held that an accused's lack of opportunity to discuss his appeal with his legal aid lawyer in person because the lawyer lived too far away was not a breach of the Convention in view of the possibility of correspondence.[3] It is for the accused who appoints his own lawyer to ensure that he speaks a language that the accused understands or to arrange for an interpreter; the state is under no obligation to provide an interpreter in such circumstances.[4]

14 A 96 (1985) Com Rep para 53 F Sett before Court.
15 *Campbell and Fell v UK* A 80 (1984); *Goddi v Italy* A 76 (1984).
16 Cf *Campbell and Fell v UK* (a prison disciplinary hearing case), A 80 (1984).
17 *Can v Austria* A 96 (1985) Com Rep paras 51-52, F Sett before Court, and *Campbell and Fell v UK* A 80 para 113 (1984). In the *Can* case, the Commission referred to the Council of Europe Standard Minimum Rules for the Treatment of Prisoners, Rule 93, CM Res (73) 5 and to Article 3(2), 1969 European Agreement Relating to Persons Participating in Proceedings of the European Commission and Court of Human Rights, 787 UNTS 244; ETS 67; UKTS 44 (1971), Cmnd 4699.
18 See the *Can* and *Campbell and Fell* cases, above, n 17.
19 For the exceptional facts, see above, p 69. The case pre-dates the *Can* case, in which the Commission spelt out strict limits to permissible restrictions.
20 The Commission noted that written communication was permitted. Cf *Bonzi v Switzerland No 7854/77*, 12 DR 185 (1978) and *Schertenleib v Switzerland No 8339/78*, 17 DR 180 (1979).
1   *Kurup v Denmark No 11219/84*, 42 DR 287 (1985).
2   *Koplinger v Austria No 1850/63*, 12 YB 438 (1968).
3   *X v Austria No 1135/61*, 6 YB 194 (1963).
4   *X v Austria No 6185/73*, 2 DR 68 (1975).

The right to communicate with one's lawyer extends to written as well as oral communication. In practice, questions concerning prison correspondence, in respect of which most problems of correspondence between accused persons and their lawyers concerning criminal proceedings[5] are likely to arise, have generally been considered under Article 8 (the right to respect for correspondence).[6] The right of access to a lawyer under Article 6(3)(b) overlaps with that in Article 6(3)(c).[7]

In any criminal case, the prosecution will have at its disposal the results of the police investigation or, in a civil law system, the preliminary investigation.[8] This includes evidence obtained by the use of forensic resources which the defence may well lack[9] or by questioning or searches backed by the power of the state. In this context, the primary purpose of Article 6(3)(b) is to achieve equality of arms between the prosecution and the defence by requiring that the accused be allowed 'the opportunity to acquaint himself, for the purposes of preparing his defence, with the results of investigations carried out throughout the proceedings'.[10] It would appear from *Edwards v UK*[11] that the onus is upon the prosecution authorities to 'disclose to the defence all material evidence for or against the accused' and that failure to do so can render a trial unfair. However, Article 6(3)(b) does not require that the prosecution reveal to the defence before the trial all of the evidence that it plans to introduce in court.[12] Nor does it imply a right to attend a hearing by an investigating judge of witnesses abroad when these will give evidence later at the trial.[13]

Article 6(3)(b) also extends to other facilities that the defence requires in order to plead its case at the trial so that, for example, time restrictions placed upon defence counsel[14] and the refusal of an adjournment[15] could be in breach of Article 6(3)(b). However, as is the case with breaches of the right to facilities generally,[16] actual prejudice might need to be shown.

5 As to prisoners' correspondence in civil proceedings and the right of access to a court, see above, p 197.
6 See eg *Schönenberger and Durmaz v Switzerland* A 137 (1988). For a case under Article 6(3)(c), see *McComb v UK No 10621/83*, 50 DR 81 (1986).
7 See eg *Goddi v Italy* A 76 (1984).
8 As to access in a civil law system to the complete case-file, see Stavros, pp 181-183. Since the right to inspect the file is that of the defence as a whole, it is sufficient that the accused's lawyer, not the accused, may inspect it: *Kamasinksi v Austria* A 168 para 88 (1989) and *Kremzow v Austria* A 268-B para 52 (1993).
9 For criticism of the limited access of the accused to forensic resources in England and Wales, see Justice Report, *Miscarriages of Justice*, 1989, p 20.
10 *Jespers v Belgium No 8403/78*, 27 DR 61 at 87 (1981) Com Rep; CM Res DH (82) 3.
11 See above, p 241. Although the *Edwards* case was decided under Articles 6(1) and 6(3)(d), the statement in the above sentence must apply to Article 6(3)(b) also.
12 *X v UK No 5282/71*, 42 CD 99 (1972). As to the late introduction of prosecution witnesses, see *X v UK No 5327/71*, 43 CD 85 (1972).
13 *X v FRG No 6566/74*, 1 DR 84 (1974). See also *Crociani v Italy No 8603/79*, 22 DR 147 (1980).
14 *X v FRG No 7085/75*, 2 Digest 809 (1976) (no breach).
15 *X v UK No 6404/73*, 2 Digest 895 (1975) (no breach).
16 Cf *Köplinger v Austria No 1850/63*, 12 YB 438 (1968); *X v FRG No 8770/79*, 2 Digest 405 (1981); and *F v UK No 11058/84*, 47 DR 230 (1986).

If there is a right of appeal against the trial court decision, Article 6(3)(b) requires that the accused be allowed sufficient facilities to prepare his appeal. Thus he must be informed of the reasons for the decision against him[17] and a copy of the pleadings[18] in good time.[19] If he is detained, the prison authorities must take reasonable steps to supply him with legal materials to prepare his appeal.[20]

iv. Article 6(3)(c): The right to defend oneself or to legal assistance

Article 6(3)(c) guarantees the right of a person charged with a criminal offence to:

'defend himself in person or through legal assistance of his own choosing or, if he has not sufficient means to pay for legal assistance, to be given it free when the interests of justice so require.'

The purpose of this guarantee is to ensure that proceedings against an accused 'will not take place without an adequate representation of the case for the defence'.[1] In terms of equality of arms, it is 'primarily to place the accused in a position to put his case in such a way that he is not at a disadvantage *vis-à-vis* the prosecution'.[2] The accused's lawyer may also serve as the 'watchdog of procedural regularity'[3] both in the public interest and for his client.

Article 6(3)(c) protects any person subject to a criminal charge.[4] It applies at the pre-trial stage as well as during the trial. Thus in *Quaranta v Switzerland*[5] Article 6(3)(c) required that the accused have the assistance of a legal aid lawyer in connection with his appearances before an investigating judge in the civil law system concerned as well as later in connection with his trial. The accused's right of private access to a lawyer guaranteed by Article 6(3)(c) also applies at the pre-trial stage.[6]

The question whether an accused's lawyer is entitled to be present during pre-trial questioning was raised in *Imbrioscia v Switzerland*.[7] There the applicant was questioned by the police and later the district prosecutor in the absence of his lawyer. The lawyer had neither been invited to attend the

---

17 *Hadjianastassiou v Greece* A 252 (1992).
18 *Kremzow v Austria* A 268-B (1993) (three weeks' notice of Attorney General's position paper ('*croquis*') sufficient).
19 As to the need to give notice of the date of the hearing, see *Goddi v Italy*, A 76 (1984).
20 *Ross v UK No 11396/85*, 50 DR 179 (1986).
1 *Pakelli v FRG A 64* (1983) Com Rep para 84.
2 *X v FRG No 10098/82*, 8 EHRR 225 (1984).
3 *Ensslin, Baader and Raspe v FRG Nos 7572/76, 7586/76 and 7587/76*, 14 DR 64 at 114 (1978).
4 As to the meaning of this term, see above, p 166.
5 A 205 (1991).
6 See *S v Switzerland*, below, p 264.
7 A 275 (1993). On the *Imbrioscia* case, see further, above, p 249.

initial interrogation sessions nor asked to attend. When the lawyer later complained that he had not been given notice of the sessions, he was invited to attend the remaining one. The Court held that Articles 6(1) and 6(3)(c) had not been infringed. What emerges from the case is that Article 6(3)(c) does not require a state to take the initiative to invite an accused's lawyer to be present during questioning in the course of the investigation. However, although the Court does not say this in so many words, it would appear from the tenor of its judgment that if the accused or his lawyer requests the latter's attendance, this must be allowed if, as is likely, there is a risk the information obtained will prejudice the accused person's defence. The question whether the accused must be asked if he wishes to have his lawyer present during questioning was not considered in the Court's judgment. Referring to *Miranda v Arizona*,[8] Judge De Meyer, dissenting, suggested that he should. The case concerned a civil law system. The Court's approach can be taken to apply to police questioning in a common law system also.[9]

As far as other stages of the proceedings are concerned, Article 6(3)(c) does not apply to proceedings concerning detention on remand; these come within Article 5(4), not Article 6.[10] Article 6(3)(c) does, however, apply to any appeal proceedings following the accused's conviction, although when assessing its requirements at the appellate level regard must be had to the special features of the appeal proceedings involved and the part they play in the case as a whole.[11] Thus in *Monnell and Morris v UK*,[12] an oral hearing of the applicant was not required in proceedings before the English Court of Appeal for leave to appeal; it was sufficient that he could present written submissions. The appointment of a legal aid lawyer for the hearing of an appeal will not remedy the absence of a lawyer at the trial stage where the appeal court lacks jurisdiction to consider the case again fully on the law and the facts.[13]

Although Article 6 does not generally apply to extradition proceedings, in *Soering v UK*,[14] the Court left open the possibility that an extraditing state may be liable under Article 6 where the trial in the requesting state involves a 'flagrant denial of a fair trial'. On the facts of that case, the claim under Article 6(3)(c) that the applicant would to some extent not be allowed legal aid in his trial in Virginia did not fall within this category.

---

8   384 US 436 (1966). *Miranda* also requires that an arrested person be informed of his rights.
9   In English law, an arrested person is entitled to have his lawyer present during police questioning and must be so informed: Code C, para 6.8, issued under s 67, PACE 1984. For a pre-1984 Act case, see *Di Stephano v UK No 12391/86*, 60 DR 182 (1989). In *Murray (John) v UK* (1994) Com Rep, see above, p 214, pending before Court, the police delayed the applicant's access to a solicitor for 48 hours because such access would interfere with police anti-terrorist operations. The Commission was of the opinion, by 13 votes to 4, that there was a breach of Articles 6(1) and 6(3)(c).
10 *Woukam Moudefo v France No 10868/84*, 51 DR 62 (1987). Article 5(4) does, however, require a judicial procedure: see above, p 146.
11 This is generally true under Article 6: see above, p 240.
12 A 115 (1987). The decision was taken under Article 6(1) and 6(3)(c) together.
13 *Quaranta v Switzerland* A 205 (1991).
14 See above, p 74.

Article 6(3)(c) guarantees the accused the right to 'defend himself in person or through legal assistance'. The right of the accused to defend himself in person has not been interpreted as allowing the accused a completely free choice. As the law of a number of Convention parties provides, the state may require that he be assisted by a lawyer in the interests of justice at the trial stage[15] or on appeal.[16] Moreover, if, in compliance with such a requirement, the accused chooses his own lawyer, the state may appoint another lawyer for him where this is called for in the interests of justice. If the state appoints a second lawyer contrary to the wishes of the accused, particularly in a legal system in which the accused will have to pay the additional lawyer's costs if convicted, the appointment will be 'incompatible with the notion of fair trial under Article 6(1) if, even taking into account a proper margin of appreciation, it lacks relevant and sufficient justification'.[17] Such justification may be found in the length and complexity of the proceedings and, insofar as the accused objects to the particular lawyer, the lack of any reason for the accused's objection and the unsuitability of any lawyer he proposes instead. The absence of any actual prejudice to the accused's defence is also a relevant consideration.[18]

In *Melin v France*,[19] the Court held that an accused who lawfully elects to defend himself in person, having 'thus deliberately waived his right to be assisted by a lawyer', is 'under a duty to show diligence'. Accordingly, there will be no breach of Article 6 by the state because of a deficiency in the proceedings that results from a lack of diligence that may reasonably be expected of the accused. Thus in the *Melin* case, Article 6[20] was not infringed when the accused, who was a lawyer, was not sent a copy of the judgment giving the reasons for his conviction in time for him to prepare his appeal. The Court held that, as a lawyer, the accused could have taken steps to have obtained the judgment in time. The duty to show diligence does not mean that any accused who defends himself should be held to the standards of a professional lawyer; account must be taken of the particular accused's capabilities and the knowledge and expertise that can be expected of him.

Article 6(3)(c) requires that an accused who does not wish to defend himself in person be able to have legal assistance through his own lawyer or, subject to certain conditions, by means of legal aid; the state cannot require him to defend himself in person.[1] Although not absolute,

> 'the right of everyone charged with a criminal offence to be effectively defended by a lawyer, assigned officially if need be, is one of the fundamental features of a fair trial.'[2]

---

15 *Croissant v Germany* A 237-B (1992).
16 *Philis v Greece No 16598/90*, 66 DR 260 (1990).
17 *Croissant v Germany* A 237-B para 27 (1992).
18 Id, para 31.
19 A 261-A para 25 (1993).
20 The case was decided under Articles 6(1) and 6(3)(b) and (c) together.
1 *Pakelli v FRG* A 64 (1983).
2 *Poitrimol v France* A 277-A para 34 (1993).

Where an accused is assisted by a lawyer, Article 6(3)(c) guarantees the accused's right to be present at the trial as well.[3] However, the right to legal representation is not dependent upon the accused's presence. Thus in *Campbell and Fell v UK*,[4] the Court held that Article 6(3)(c) had been infringed by the United Kingdom because a prisoner, who had refused to attend in person, was denied legal representation at a Board of Visitors hearing of a disciplinary charge against him.

The refusal of legal representation in *Campbell and Fell* resulted from the application of a rule by which representation was not permitted at Board of Visitors hearings generally; it was not a penalty imposed upon the applicant for failing to attend the hearing. The question of such a penalty was first considered in *Poitrimol v France*.[5] There the applicant was a convicted person who was not allowed to be represented in his absence at the hearing of his appeal, which he was under a legal obligation to attend, because he had absconded from the country. As the European Court stated, the refusal of legal representation had a coercive element, being designed to cause him to appear and be arrested under a warrant that had been issued after his conviction *in absentia*. The European Court held that on these facts there was a breach of Article 6(3)(c): although a state must be able to discourage the unjustified absence of an accused, it was 'disproportionate in the circumstances' to deny him legal representation. The matter was taken further in *Lala v Netherlands*,[6] in which a general rule was stated. There the Court held that, although it is 'of capital importance that the accused should appear at his trial, the fact that 'the defendant, in spite of having been properly summoned, does not appear, cannot – even in the absence of an excuse – justify depriving him of his right' to be defended by counsel under Article 6(3)(c). In the *Lala* case, the applicant, who was under no legal obligation to attend the hearing, had simply decided not to attend in person, leaving his interests in the hands of his lawyer.

When the accused elects to have legal assistance and to appoint his own lawyer, for whom he will pay, his choice of lawyer is not an absolute one. Regulations governing the qualifications and conduct of lawyers authorised to practise law in a state's legal system are obviously permissible, as are regulations concerning the practice in its courts of lawyers qualified in another legal system. Thus a lawyer may be excluded for failure to comply with professional ethics,[7] for refusal to wear robes,[8] for showing disrespect to

3   *FCB v Italy* A 208-B (1991). See also the guarantee in Article 6(1) of an oral hearing in one's presence, above, p 203. A breach of Articles 6(1) and 3(c) was found in the *FCB* case.
4   A 80 (1984).
5   A 277-A para 35 (1993). The decision was by 5 to 4. The case concerned an appeal that took the form of a full re-hearing of the facts. Hence the same considerations as to the importance of the accused's presence and of his representation applied as at the trial.
6   A 297-A para 33 (1994). Cf *Pellandoah v Netherlands* A 297-B para 40 (1994), in which the accused would have had to have returned from Mauritius, to which he had been expelled following his conviction. As in the *Poitrimol* case, both the *Lala* and *Pellandoah* cases involved full re-hearings on appeal.
7   *Ensslin, Baader and Raspe v FRG* Nos 7572/76, 7586/76 and 7587/76, 14 DR 64 (1978).
8   *X and Y v FRG* Nos 5217/71 and 5367/72, 42 CD 139 (1972).

the court[9] or because he is appearing as a witness for the defence.[10] In a case that raised the question of a barrister's personal interests, it was not a breach of Article 6(3)(c) to bar a barrister from representing his father on a charge of criminal damage caused while protesting against the treatment of his barrister son.[11] In another case it was held permissible to bar a lawyer from representing an accused because of his support for a criminal organisation to which the accused belonged and in circumstances in which a number of other lawyers nominated by the accused were permitted to act.[12] It has been said that 'the state has full discretion to exclude lawyers from appearing before the courts'.[13] In the case in which this very sweeping statement was made, the Commission rejected a complaint that an accused had not been allowed to appoint his own lawyer, apparently because of the lawyer's political interests. This, however, was a very early decision. The Commission has more recently stated that as a general rule the accused's choice of lawyer should be respected.[14] Although the state certainly has a general regulatory power, the Strasbourg authorities must retain the capacity to intervene if it is used improperly, eg by excluding a lawyer simply because of his willingness to represent an 'unpopular accused' or his opposition to the government.

The Commission has held that Article 6(3)(c) also does not permit the accused to appoint an unlimited number of lawyers to assist him; a restriction upon their number is permissible, so long as the defence is able to present its case on an equal footing with the prosecution.[15] Nor is a state liable if an accused is unable to find a lawyer who will act for him, provided that this failure is not the result of 'pressure or manoeuvres' by the state.[16] Article 6(3)(c) refers to 'legal assistance'. This can be taken to allow assistance by a person chosen by the accused who is not a qualified lawyer as well as assistance by a lawyer,[17] although the state no doubt has a regulatory power which it may exercise properly in respect of such persons.[18]

With regard to the conduct of the defence, given that lawyers are not state employees or agents they cannot, whether private or legal aid lawyers, directly engage the responsibility of the state under the Convention by their acts in the way, for example, that members of the armed forces can. However, there may be liability on the part of the state in extreme cases by virtue of the fact that Article 6(3)(c) guarantees a right to 'effective' legal assistance.[19]

9　*X v UK No 6298/73*, 2 Digest 831 (1975).
10　*K v Denmark No 19524/92* (1993) unreported.
11　*X v UK No 8295/78*, 15 DR 242 (1978).
12　*Ensslin, Baader and Raspe v FRG Nos 7572/76, 7586/76 and 7587/76*, 14 DR 64 (1978).
13　*X v FRG No 722/60*, 5 YB 104 at 106 (1962).
14　*Goddi v Italy* B 61 p 25 (1982).
15　*Ensslin, Baader and Raspe v FRG Nos 7572/76, 7586/76 and 7587/76*, 14 DR 64 (1978).
16　*X and Y v Belgium No 1420/62* et al, 6 YB 590 at 628 (1963).
17　The *travaux préparatoires* support this view; see below, p 265. See also *Engel v Netherlands* A 22 (1976) (representation in army disciplinary proceedings by a fellow conscript who was a lawyer in civilian life).
18　Cf the state's regulatory power over lawyers providing legal representation: see above, p 259.
19　See below, p 264.

In practice, most accused persons are indigent so that the guarantee of legal aid in Article 6(3)(c) is of particular importance. The right to legal aid is subject to two conditions. Firstly, the accused must lack 'sufficient means' to pay for legal assistance himself. The Convention contains no definition of 'sufficient means' and there is no case-law indicating the level or kind of private means that may be taken into account when deciding whether to award legal aid.[20] When seeking to establish a breach of Article 6(3)(c), the onus would appear to be upon the accused to show that he lacks 'sufficient means'. He need not, however, do so 'beyond all doubt'; it is sufficient that there are 'some indications' that this is so. This test was satisfied in *Pakelli v FRG*[1] on the basis that the applicant had spent two years in custody shortly before the case, had presented a statement of means to the Commission that led it to award him legal aid in bringing his Article 25 application and had offered to prove lack of means to the West German Federal Court.

The Commission has taken the view that Article 6(3)(c) does not prohibit a contracting party from requiring an accused upon conviction to pay the costs of any free legal assistance that he has been allowed if he then has the necessary means to do so.[2] The point was left open by the Court in *Luedicke, Belkacem and Koç v FRG*[3] in which it held that there was such a prohibition under Article 6(3)(e) with regard to the costs of an interpreter. The text of Article 6 supports the Commission's interpretation in that, in contrast with the right in Article 6(3)(e), the right to legal aid in Article 6(3)(c) is made conditional upon the accused's means. None the less, the possibility that an accused might have to repay the cost of legal aid could, as was recognised in the *Luedicke* case, cause him to defend himself in person rather than apply for legal aid in a case in which legal representation would be in the interests of a fair trial and hence of the object and purpose of the Convention. Moreover, the word 'given' in the English text can be read as meaning an irrevocable grant of free legal aid where the accused is without means at the time that the grant is made.

Secondly, legal aid need only be provided 'where the interests of justice so require'. This is to be judged by reference to the facts of the case as a whole, including those that may materialise after the competent national authority has taken its decision. Thus, in *Granger v UK*,[4] the refusal of legal aid should have been reviewed when it proved during the appeal proceedings that the case was more complicated than appeared earlier. Although an assessment of whether legal aid is required is in the first instance for the national authorities to make, the Strasbourg authorities are competent to review and disagree with their assessment. Whereas the Commission has tended to be

---

20 On the rules applicable to the grant of legal aid to applicants in order to allow them to bring a case to Strasbourg, see below, p 590.
1 A 64 para 34 (1983).
2 *Croissant v Germany* A 237-B (1992) Com Rep.
3 See below, p 270. It was left open by the Court again in *Croissant v Germany* A 237-B (1992).
4 A 174 (1990).

reluctant to question the decisions of national authorities,[5] the Court has shown a willingness to make its own determination on the facts rather than apply a margin of appreciation or 'no *quatrième instance*' approach.[6]

A number of criteria have been identified by the Court as being relevant when determining whether the 'interests of justice' call for legal assistance. Firstly, the more complicated the case, the more likely that legal assistance is required.[7] Secondly, regard must be had to the contribution that the accused would be able to make if he defended himself. In this connection, the test is the capacity of the *particular* accused to present his case.[8] A third consideration is the importance of what is 'at stake' for the applicant in terms of the seriousness of the offence with which he is charged and the possible sentence that could result.[9] This is a consideration that may by itself require legal aid to be granted. In *Quaranta v Switzerland*[10] the 'mere fact' that the possible sentence that could be imposed upon the accused for drugs offences was three years' imprisonment automatically meant that legal aid should have been provided.[11]

In appeal cases, it does not matter that the accused's chances of success are negligible. To the extent that the accused is granted a right of appeal by national law, he must be provided with legal aid if this is required for him to exercise it. In *Boner v UK*,[12] the applicant was refused legal aid on the statutory ground that he did not have 'substantial grounds for making the appeal'.[13] In holding that there had been a breach of Article 6(3)(c), the European Court focused on the fact that the accused would need the services of a lawyer in order to argue the point he wished to raise, as well as the importance of what was at stake for the applicant (an eight-year sentence). For these reasons, the 'interests of justice' required legal representation for the accused to exercise effectively the (admittedly wide)[14] right of appeal that Scots law allowed him; it did not matter that his chances of success were slight.

Finally, Fawcett[15] has argued that 'the interests of justice' might also require legal assistance for the accused where an issue of public

5   See eg *Bell v UK No 12322/86*, 11 EHRR 83 (1987).
6   See, in particular, *Quaranta v Switzerland* A 205 (1991).
7   *Granger v UK A 174* (1990); *Quaranta v Switzerland* A 205 (1991); and *Pham Hoang v France* A 243 (1992). And see, on this and other criteria, the *Airey* case in the context of civil proceedings: above, p 197.
8   See the *Granger* and *Quaranta* cases above, n 7.
9   The length of the sentences against which the applicant was appealing was an important factor in *Boner v UK* A 300-B para 41 (eight years) and *Maxwell v UK* A 300-C para 38 (1994).
10 A 205 para 34 (1991).
11 The Court emphasised the possible, rather than the likely, penalty. Cf *Pham Hoang v France* A 243 (1992).
12 A 300-B paras 41-44 (1994). Cf *Maxwell v UK* A 300-C paras 38-41 (1994).
13 Section 25(2) of the Legal Aid (Scotland) Act 1986. The applicant's solicitors refused to support his application for legal aid and counsel was not prepared to represent him because of a professional rule applicable to appeals which are considered to have no merit.
14 The defendant government stated in argument that a consequence of its losing the case might be the ending of the accused's unlimited right of appeal.
15 Fawcett, p 170. There may have been an element of this approach in the account taken in the *Pakelli* case of the fact that the case might have some value in the development of case-law.

importance is involved irrespective of whether a lawyer could assist the defence.

When applying the 'interests of justice' requirement, the test is not whether the absence of legal aid has caused 'actual prejudice' to the presentation of the defence. In *Artico v Italy*,[16] the Court stated that the test is a less stringent one, viz whether 'it appears plausible in the particular circumstances'[17] that the lawyer would be of assistance, as was true on the facts of that case. There the Court noted that a lawyer would have been more likely than the applicant to have emphasised a statute of limitations argument in the applicant's favour before the Court of Cassation and that only a lawyer was competent to request a hearing at which the defence could have replied to the Public Prosecutor's arguments against the appeal. On this basis, legal aid comes close to being generally required because a lawyer will nearly always, by virtue of his professional expertise, be able to add to the accused's defence.[18] In any event, the determination in the *Quaranta* case that legal aid should be provided in all cases involving a serious offence or a severe penalty means that it is likely to be required in the most important cases.

An accused cannot complain of lack of legal representation if he does not make use of the legal aid system that is provided.[19] However, the state is not required by Article 6(3)(c) to allow the accused any involvement in the appointment and functioning of his legal aid lawyer. He is not entitled to choose the lawyer who will represent him on legal aid,[20] to be consulted when the lawyer is chosen,[1] or to insist upon a particular line of defence which the lawyer considers untenable.[2]

The funding of legal aid is an expensive item for states. In the context of legal aid in civil proceedings, it has been held that it must be provided in accordance with Article 6(1) irrespective of the economic cost.[3] The same approach ought to apply to criminal cases under Article 6(3)(c), so that budgetary considerations should not prevent effective legal assistance for accused persons who otherwise qualify under Article 6(3)(c). However, the Commission has recognised that the need to 'ensure the most cost-effective use of the funds available for legal aid' might justifiably limit the number of consultations with an appellant.[4]

16 A 37 (1980). Cf *Alimena v Italy* A 195-D (1991).
17 A 37 para 35 (1980). Cf *Biondo v Italy No 8821/79*, 64 DR 5 (1983) Com Rep; CM Res DH (89) 30.
18 But for a case in which the 'interests of justice' did not require legal aid in respect of written appeal proceedings, see *X v FRG No 599/59*, 8 CD 12 (1961). See also *M v UK No 9728/82* 36 DR 155 (1983).
19 *Biondo v Italy No 8821/79*, 64 DR 5 (1983) Com Rep; CM Res DH (89) 30.
20 See eg *X v Netherlands No 846/60*, 3 YB 273 (1961); *X v UK No 9728/82*, 6 EHRR 345 (1983); *F v Switzerland No 12152/86*, 61 DR 171 (1989).
1 *X v FRG No 6946/75*, 6 DR 114 (1976). See also *Ostergren v Sweden No 13572/88*, 69 DR 198 (1991). The lawyer need not be known by the accused: *No 1807/63*, cited by Fawcett, p 194.
2 *No 9127/80*, 2 Digest 851 (1981). Cf *Kamasinski v Austria* A 168 (1989) Com Rep para 160. See also *X v UK No 8386/78*, 21 DR 126 (1980).
3 See the *Airey* case, discussed above, p 197.
4 *M v UK No 9728/82*, 36 DR 155 at 158 (1983).

The right in Article 6(3)(c) is to 'effective' legal assistance. In *Artico v Italy*,[5] the applicant was granted free legal aid under Italian law for his appeal to the Italian Court of Cassation. Unfortunately, the appointed lawyer never acted for the applicant, claiming other legal commitments and ill-health. Despite constant requests by the applicant, the Court of Cassation refused to appoint another lawyer to replace him. As a result, the applicant was forced to plead the case himself in circumstances in which legal assistance would have been of value. Noting that the right in Article 6(3)(c) was to 'assistance', not 'nomination', the European Court rejected an Italian argument that by appointing a lawyer for the accused the Court of Cassation had done sufficient to comply with Article 6(3)(c).

However, a 'state cannot be held responsible for every shortcoming on the part of a lawyer appointed for legal aid purposes'.[6] Instead, the 'competent national authorities are required by Article 6(3)(c) to intervene only if a failure by legal aid counsel to provide effective representation is manifest or sufficiently brought to their attention'.[7] The *Artico* case concerned legal aid. In *Imbrioscia v Switzerland*,[8] the Court applied exactly the same approach in the case of a private lawyer. The defendant state was not liable for failing to act when the lawyer did not ask to be present when the accused was questioned because the accused had not complained to the state authorities and the problem was not otherwise 'manifest'. There may be other shortcomings that are equally crucial to the accused's defence, eg the failure to call a vital witness or to appeal in good time, for which the state cannot be held responsible.

The right to effective legal assistance in Article 6(3)(c) includes a right of private access to a lawyer, both at the pre-trial stage and later. In *S v Switzerland*,[9] Article 6(3)(c) was infringed when the accused, who was in detention on remand, was not allowed to consult with his lawyer out of the hearing of a prison officer. As the Court stated, 'if a lawyer were unable to confer[10] with his client and receive confidential instructions from him without such surveillance, his assistance would lose much of its usefulness, whereas the Convention is intended to guarantee rights that are practical and effective'.[11] It may also be a breach of Article 6(3)(c) to tap the telephone conversations between an accused and his lawyer.[12] However, the

5   A 37 (1980).
6   *Artico v Italy* A 37 para 36 (1980).
7   *Kamasinski v Austria* A 168 para 65 (1989). See also *Stanford v UK* A 280-A (1994) and *Tripodi v Italy* A 281-B para 30 (1994).
8   A 275 (1993).
9   *S v Switzerland* A 220 para 48 (1991). Cf *Can v Austria* A 96 (1985) Com Rep; F Sett before Court.
10   The right of access also includes access by correspondence, although such cases are most commonly dealt with under Article 8: see eg *Campbell v UK* A 233 (1992). For an Article 6 case on correspondence with a lawyer in criminal proceedings, see *McComb v UK No 10621/83*, 50 DR 81 (1986) F Sett.
11   In support of this statement, the Court cited the Council of Europe documents referred to above, p 254, n 17.
12   *D v Austria No 16410/90* (1990) unreported.

Article 6(3)(c) guarantee of access to a lawyer may be subject to restrictions in the public interest.[13]

In guaranteeing a right of access to a lawyer, Article 6(3)(c) overlaps with Article 6(3)(b) which guarantees the accused 'adequate facilities' to prepare his defence, a phrase that has been interpreted to include the right of access.[14] But Article 6(3)(c) is wider than Article 6(3)(b) since it 'is not especially tied to considerations relating to the preparation of the trial but gives the accused a more general right to assistance and support by a lawyer throughout the whole proceedings'.[15]

A state will be in breach of the guarantee of 'effective' assistance if it fails to notify the accused's lawyer, whether his own or a legal aid lawyer, of the hearing with the result that the accused is not represented at it. In *Goddi v Italy*,[16] the applicant's prison sentence was increased after a hearing at which neither the applicant nor the legal aid lawyer who was acting for him in the appeal was present. Although it was not established on the facts that the applicant's absence was the state's fault, the appeal court was responsible for the absence of his lawyer. This was because it had sent notification of the hearing to the wrong lawyer. The error was not rectified by appointing a third lawyer on the day of the hearing who had no knowledge of the applicant or his case.

To be 'effective' a lawyer appointed to defend an accused must be qualified to represent the accused at the particular stage of proceedings for which his assistance is sought.[17] Whether assistance must be provided by a qualified lawyer or whether, for example, a 'McKenzie adviser' would suffice is not clear. The drafting history[18] and the object and purpose of Article 6(3)(c) suggests that professional qualifications are not necessary so long as the legal assistance provided is 'effective' in fact.[19] Frequent changes of lawyers

---

13 *S v Switzerland* A 220 (1991). See also *Can v Austria* A 96 (1985) Com Rep para 52, F Sett before Court, and *Egue v France No 11256/84*, 57 DR 47 (1988). As to the requirement of proportionality and the margin of appreciation that apply in such cases, see Stavros, pp 58-63. In English law, an accused is entitled to consult privately with his lawyer subject to certain restrictions: s 58 of the Police and Criminal Evidence Act 1984. For pre-1984 Act Strasbourg cases, see *G v UK No 9370/81*, 35 DR 75 (1983) and *Di Stephano v UK No 12391/86*, 60 DR 182 (1989).

14 See above, p 255.

15 *Can v Austria* A 96 (1985) Com Rep para 54, F Sett before Court. In *S v Switzerland* the Court focused on paragraph (c), not (b), seemingly because the restrictions on the applicant's communications with his lawyer were later lifted for a long enough period prior to the trial to permit the proper preparation of his defence, so that the facilities were 'adequate'.

16 A 76 (1984).

17 See *Biondo v Italy No 8821/79*, 64 DR 5 (1983) Com Rep; CM Res DH (89) 30.

18 In the drafting of Article 14, ICCPR, upon which Article 6 is based, the words 'qualified representative' were replaced by 'legal assistance' so that they 'did not necessarily mean a lawyer, but merely assistance in the legal conduct of a case': UN Doc E/CN.4/SR. 107, p 6.

19 In *X v FRG No 509/59*, 3 YB 174 (1960), it was held that assistance from a probationary lawyer undergoing training in the West German criminal system would qualify. The Commission stated that the word '*avocat*' in the French text should be understood not in the technical sense but in the sense of a person who actually gives legal assistance.

appointed for the defence may raise a problem of effectiveness,[20] as may the allowance of inadequate time for a defendant's lawyer, whether a legal aid lawyer or not, to prepare his case.[1] In the context of English law, a barrister appointed at the hearing to represent an accused without a solicitor having been instructed beforehand may none the less be able to give 'effective' assistance, depending on the circumstances.[2] It is also permissible to limit the role of the accused's lawyer, at least in army disciplinary proceedings, to the legal, as opposed to the factual, issues in the case where the facts were simple.[3]

In *Brandstetter v Austria*,[4] the Court introduced an extra dimension to Article 6(3)(c) by interpreting it as prohibiting state action impeding the exercise of the 'rights of the defence set forth in Article 6(3)(c)'. In the *Brandstetter* case, the accused had subsequently been prosecuted for defamation on the basis of false statements made by him at his trial for another offence. While finding against the accused on the facts, the Court accepted that 'the position might be different if it were established that, as a consequence of national law or practice in this respect being unduly severe, the risk of subsequent prosecution is such that the defendant is genuinely inhibited from freely exercising' his right to defend himself.[5]

v.   Article 6(3)(d): The right to call and cross-examine witnesses

Article 6(3)(d) guarantees a person charged with a criminal offence the right:

> 'to examine or have examined witnesses against him and to obtain the attendance and examination of witnesses on his behalf under the same conditions as witnesses against him.'

The right applies to the trial and any appeal proceedings. It does not apply generally at the pre-trial stage.[6] In particular, Article 6(3)(d) does not require that the accused or his lawyer be allowed to cross-examine a witness being questioned by the police[7] or an investigating judge[8] provided that he may be cross-examined at the trial.[9] The refusal by an investigating judge to hear a defence witness is likewise not a breach of Article 6(3)(d) if the witness may be called at the trial.[10]

---

20 See *Koplinger v Austria No 1850/63*, 9 YB 240 (1966).
1   Such cases have been considered under both Articles 6(3)(b) and 6(3)(c): see eg *X v UK No 4042/69*, 32 CD 76 (1970): *Murphy v UK No 4681/70*, 43 CD 1 (1972).
2   *Murphy v UK*, id. See also under Article 6(3)(b) ('adequate time' to prepare the defence).
3   *Engel v Netherlands* A 22 (1976).
4   A 211 para 51 (1991).
5   Id, para 53. See also *Melin v France* A 261-A (1993), discussed above, p 258.
6   See the general statements in *Can v Austria* A 96 (1985) Com Rep para 47; F Sett before Court, and *Adolf v Austria* B 43 (1980) Com Rep para 64.
7   *X v FRG No 8414/78*, 17 DR 231 (1979).
8   *Ferraro-Bravo v Italy No 9627/81*, 37 DR 15 (1984).
9   For the hearsay exception, see below, p 267.
10 *Schertenleib v Switzerland No 8339/78*, 17 DR 180 (1979).

The term 'witness' in Article 6(3)(d) has an autonomous Convention meaning. It includes expert witnesses called by the prosecution or the defence. An expert appointed by the Court may be regarded as a 'witness against' the accused for the purpose of Article 6(3)(d) if his evidence justifies his being so treated.[11] A person whose statements are produced as evidence before a court but who does not give oral evidence is none the less a 'witness' for the purposes of Article 6(3)(d).[12]

Neither the accused's right to cross-examine witnesses nor his right to call defence witnesses is absolute.[13] However, such limits as are set or occur must be consistent with the principle of equality of arms, the full realisation of which is the 'essential aim' of Article 6(3)(d).[14] The Commission applied this principle in *Bönisch v Austria*.[15] In that case, an expert appointed by the court consistently took a view opposed to that of the accused. The Commission concluded that the failure of the court to seek further expert opinion when it knew that other experts took a different view was inconsistent with equality of arms. So too was the lack of equal treatment of the court's expert and the expert witness called by the defence at the court hearing.[16]

The right of the accused to cross-examine witnesses against him is, of course, frustated to the extent that it is permissible for evidence to be introduced without the persons whose direct evidence it is being called as witnesses at the trial. Although Article 6(3)(d) in principle entitles the accused to confront persons giving prejudicial evidence, it has been interpreted as excusing persons from giving evidence in court in certain circumstances in accordance with European national practice. Thus a rule by which a member of an accused's family is not required to appear as a witness in recognition of a conflict of interests does not infringe Article 6(3)(d).[17] Likewise, a police informer need not be called as a witness in court; the system of police informers is necessary to the administration of justice and would be undermined by such a requirement.[18] However, in these and in other cases in which a person does not appear as a witness,[19] it will be a breach of Articles 6(1) and 6(3)(d) for a statement made by him to be admitted as evidence without the accused having had the opportunity to

---

11 *Bönisch v Austria* A 92 para 32 (1985) and *Brandstetter v Austria* A 211 (1991).
12 *Kostovski v Netherlands* A 166 (1989). A convicted co-accused whose statements at his own separate trial are introduced in the accused's trial is a 'witness': *Cardot v France* A 200 (1991) Com Rep para 51; case not considered by Court: non-exhaustion of local remedies.
13 *Engel v Netherlands* A 22 para 91 (1976).
14 Ibid. The obligation is to achieve equality in fact as well as in law: *Austria v Italy*, 6 YB 740 (1963) Com Rep; CM Res DH (63) 3. As to the equality of arms requirement in Article 6(1), see above, p 207.
15 A 92 (1985) Com Rep. The case was decided by the Court under Article 6(1). See also *Brandstetter v Austria* 211 (1991).
16 In particular, the defence was unable to cross-examine the court's expert.
17 *Unterpertinger v Austria* A 110 (1986).
18 Cf *Kostovski v Netherlands* A 166 (1989).
19 Cf the situation in which a prison doctor is not permitted to give evidence in court on the treatment of a prisoner for public interest reasons: see *L v Switzerland No 12609/86*, 68 DR 108 (1991) F Sett.

confront him during the preceding investigation where the statement is the only, or possibly, the main evidence against the accused.[20] Subject to certain safeguards, Article 6(3)(d) does not prevent the use of statements taken from witnesses abroad[1] or evidence from foreign court proceedings against the accused.[2]

As to the calling of witnesses for the defence, it is for the national courts, 'as a general rule, to assess whether it is appropriate to call witnesses'.[3] Although the national court's decision is subject to review under Article 6(3)(d), the Commission has generally adopted a relaxed approach to its role of monitoring the exclusion of witnesses, seldom questioning a national court's exercise of its discretion in the assessment of the relevance of the proposed evidence.[4] The Commission has justified its 'hands off' approach to the calling of witnesses on the ground that the text of Article 6(3)(d) refers to the calling of witnesses by the accused 'on his behalf' and not 'at his request'. Such an approach is also in accord with the *'quatrième instance'* doctrine[5] which the Strasbourg authorities generally apply when reviewing the decision of national courts. It may stem too from the difficulty presented by the great diversity in the laws of evidence of the contracting parties. A decision to exclude a defence witness under Article 6(3)(d) may, however, be a breach of the general fair hearing requirement in Article 6(1).[6]

The Commission has, however, stated that Article 6(3)(d) requires that 'a court must give the reasons for which it decides not to summon those witnesses whose examination has been expressly requested.'[7] The Court reached a similar conclusion in *Vidal v Belgium*.[8] There a court to which the applicant's case was remitted for a rehearing convicted him on the basis of the evidence in the case-file, without calling any witnesses, including four witnesses whom the defence had asked to be called. It gave no reasons for its refusal to hear the defence witnesses, an omission which, the European Court stated, was 'not consistent with the concept of a fair trial which is the basis of Article 6'. Although the Court's judgment emphasises the national

---

20 The Court's now extensive jurisprudence on this subject is considered under Article 6(1), above, p 211.
1   *X v FRG No 11853/85*, 10 EHRR 521 (1987). See also *X, Y and Z v Austria No 5049/71*, 43 CD 38 (1973).
2   *S v FRG No 8945/80*, 39 DR 43 (1983).
3   *Vidal v Belgium* A 235-B para 33 (1992). Cf *Engel v Netherlands* A 22 (1976). National courts are also permitted considerable discretion in controlling the accused's questioning of such defence witnesses as are called.
4   For typical cases, see *X v Austria No 753/60*, 3 YB 310 (1960) and *X v Sweden No 10563/83*, 8 EHRR 86 (1985). The Court adopted a similarly restrained approach in a civil case under Article 6(1): see *H v France* A 162-A (1989). But see *Payot and Petit v France No 16596/90* (1991) unreported (civil servant prohibited by statute from giving evidence; application declared admissible).
5   See above, p 15. The Commission has also invoked the 'margin of appreciation doctrine': see eg *X v Switzerland No 9000/80*, 28 DR 127 (1982) and *Payot and Petit v Switzerland No 16596/90* (1991) unreported.
6   *Wiechart v Switzerland No 1404/62*, 7 YB 104 (1964).
7   *Bricmont v Belgium* A 158 (1989). The Court did not consider the point.
8   A 235-B para 34 (1992). The case was decided on the basis of Article 6 generally.

court's failure to give reasons, the case can also be read as one in which the European Court questioned the decision itself to exclude the testimony of witnesses who might have given evidence helpful to an accused who was sentenced to four years' imprisonment for a serious offence.

A state is not liable under Article 6(3)(d) for the failure of defence counsel to call a particular witness.[9] Where witnesses are properly called by the defence, a court must take appropriate steps to ensure their appearance.[10] There is no breach of Article 6(3)(d), however, if a defence witness fails to appear for reasons beyond the court's control[11] or is called by the court at a time other than that requested by the accused unless this affects the presentation of the defence.[12]

Article 6(3)(d) recognises that at the trial court hearing 'it is in principle essential that an accused is present when witnesses are being heard in a case against him'.[13] Exceptionally, however, the interests of justice may permit the exclusion of the accused consistently with Article 6(3)(d) to ensure that a witness gives an unreserved statement provided that the accused's lawyer is allowed to remain and conduct any cross-examination.[14] A co-accused who makes a dock statement in respect of the case against himself is not a 'witness against' the accused if none of the evidence in the co-accused's statement may be taken into account by the court in deciding the accused's case. In such a case, a rule preventing the accused from cross-examining the co-accused on the latter's dock statement is therefore not in breach of Article 6(3)(d).[15]

In *Luedicke, Belkacem and Koç v FRG*,[16] the Court left open the question whether it would be a breach of Article 6(3)(d) for a state to require an accused to pay the costs associated with compliance with this provision (eg interpreters' costs in questioning witnesses) if convicted.

vi. Article 6(3)(e): The right to an interpreter

Article 6(3)(e) guarantees the right of a person charged with a criminal offence 'to have the free assistance of an interpreter if he cannot understand or speak the language used in court'. As in the case of other Article 6(3) rights, the guarantee protects persons once they are 'charged with a criminal

---

9 *F v UK No 18123/91*, 15 EHRR CD 32 (1992). As to the position under Article 6(3)(c), see above, p 260.

10 *X v FRG No 3566/68*, 31 CD 31 (1969); *X v FRG No 4078/69*, 35 CD 125 (1970).

11 *X v Austria No 4428/70*, 15 YB 264 (1972); *X v FRG No 4078/69*, 35 CD 125 (1970).

12 *X v UK No 5506/72*, 45 CD 59 (1973).

13 *Kurup v Denmark No 11219/84*, 42 DR 287 (1985). Cf *X v Denmark No 8395/78*, 27 DR 50 (1981). See also the cases under Articles 6(1) and 3(c), above, pp 204 and 259.

14 *Kurup v Denmark No 11219/84*, 42 DR 287 (1985). Cf *X v UK No 20657/92*, 15 EHRR CD 113 (1992) (permissible to screen a witness from the accused, but not his lawyer, in court in a terrorist case).

15 *X v UK No 10083/82*, 6 EHRR 142 (1983).

16 See below, p 270.

offence'.[17] It does not benefit suspects being questioned by the police prior to their being 'charged' in the sense of Article 6(1); it does apply to the pretrial stage of proceedings thereafter. Thus in *Kamasinski v Austria*,[18] an interpreter was required during police questioning and in the course of the civil law preliminary investigation in the case. As with Article 6 rights generally,[19] Article 6(3)(e) applies during any appeal proceedings.

The obligation to provide 'free' assistance is unqualified. It does not depend upon the accused's means; the services of an interpreter for the accused are instead a part of the facilities required of a state in organising its system of criminal justice. Nor can an accused be ordered to pay for the costs of interpretation if he is convicted, as was required by West German law in *Luedicke, Belkacem and Koç v FRG*.[20] The language of Article 6(3)(e) indicates 'neither a conditional remission, nor a temporary exemption, nor a suspension, but a once and for all exemption or exoneration'.[1] Any contrary interpretation would also be inconsistent with the object and purpose of Article 6, which is to ensure a fair trial for all accused persons, whether subsequently convicted or not, since an accused might forgo his right to an interpreter for fear of the financial consequences.[2]

The 'assistance' required by Article 6(3)(e) extends to the translations of documents as well as the provision of an interpreter at hearings.[3] However, Article 6(3)(e) does not require a 'written translation of all items of written evidence or official documents',[4] only those which are necessary for the accused to have a fair trial. A written translation of the indictment may not be necessary if sufficient oral information as to its contents is given to the accused.[5] In the *Luedicke* case, the Court stated that 'it does not at first sight appear excluded' that the costs of providing in translation the information required to be given to the accused by Articles 5(2) and 6(3)(a) are also covered.[6] The failure to provide the accused with a written translation of the

---

17 As to the meaning of this phrase, see above, p 166.
18 A 168 (1989). Proceedings concerning detention on remand are also included: *Luedicke, Belkacem and Koç v FRG* A 29 (1978). On the *Luedicke* case generally, see Duffy, 4 HRR 98 (1978).
19 See above, p 240.
20 A 29 (1978). The decision was followed in *Öztürk v FRG* A 73 (1984) and several Committee of Ministers cases: see eg *Zengin v FRG No 10551/83*, 63 DR 5 (1988) Com Rep; CM Res DH (89) 29.
1 A 29 para 40 (1978).
2 Id, para 42.
3 *Kamasinski v FRG* A 168 para 74 (1989). Cf *Luedicke, Belkacem and Koç v FRG* A 29 (1978), in which the Court preferred the meaning of the English text to the more limited wording of the French text (*à l'audience*) in accordance with the rules of interpretation that apply to the Convention; see above, p 6.
4 Ibid.
5 *Kamasinski v Austria* A 168 (1989). The question was in fact considered in terms of Article 6(3)(a). In the *Luedicke* case, it was a breach of Article 6(3)(e) to charge the accused with the cost of translating the indictment.
6 A 29 (1978). In the *Kamasinski* case, the requirement of providing a translation of the information required by Article 6(3)(a) was considered under that provision, not Article 6(3)(e).

judgment in his case is not in itself a breach of Article 6(3)(e); in the *Kamasinski* case, it was enough that the accused was given an oral indication of the outcome and of the court's reasoning sufficient on the facts to allow him, with the assistance of his German-speaking lawyer, to lodge an appeal against his conviction.[7]

Where, as is usually the case, the accused does not defend himself in person but is represented by a lawyer, it is not clear whether it is sufficient that the accused's lawyer (but not the accused) can understand or speak the language used in court or in the documents. In the *Kamasinski* case, the Court would appear to have supposed,[8] correctly it is believed, that the right to a fair trial requires that the accused personally be given a translation in order to be able to understand proceedings that concern him vitally and to inform his lawyer of any point that should be made in his defence. A related question is whether the accused must be provided with an interpreter, where necessary, in order to communicate with his lawyer. Although the Court has not clearly ruled upon this point, in the *Kamasinski* case it noted that Article 6(3)(e) extended beyond the 'trial hearing' to all 'statements . . . which it is necessary for him to understand in order to have a fair trial'.[9] This wording could be regarded as including communications between an accused and his lawyer in a legal aid case.[10] In such a case, the responsibility should lie with the state to appoint a lawyer who can communicate with his client or to provide an interpreter. Where, however, the accused is not entitled to legal aid and appoints his own lawyer, it must be for the accused to appoint a lawyer who can communicate with him if such a lawyer is available.[11]

Clearly, the interpreter who is provided must be competent. In this connection, the Court has stated that in order for the right guaranteed by Article 6(3)(e) to be 'practical and effective', the 'obligation of the competent authorities is not limited to the appointment of an interpreter but, if they are put on notice in the particular circumstances, may also extend to a degree of subsequent control over the adequacy of the interpretation provided'.[12]

It is arguable that the state's obligation should extend at the outset to informing an accused who appears in need of assistance to his right to an interpreter,[13] a right which he can then waive if he wishes.[14]

Whether the accused does not 'understand or speak' the language in which the proceedings against him are being conducted is a question of fact, the

---

7   Cf *X v FRG No 11169/84*, 8 EHRR 93 (1985) and *X v FRG No 3117/67*, 2 Digest 915 (1967).
8   The Court considered the applicant's arguments concerning the interpretation at the trial hearing on their merits even though the accused's English speaking lawyer was present at the hearing.
9   A 168 para 74 (1989).
10 The Commission had earlier ruled that Article 6(3)(e) applied only to the relations between the accused and the judge: *X v Austria No 6185/73*, 2 DR 68 (1975).
11 *X v FRG No 10221/82*, 6 EHRR 353 (1983).
12 *Kamasinski v Austria* A 168 para 74 (1989).
13 Cf Stavros, p 257.
14 The possibility of waiver of the right to an interpreter was established in *Kamasinski v Austria* A 168 para 80 (1989).

onus being upon the accused to prove that the national court's assessment of the situation is incorrect.[15] An accused who understands the language used in court cannot insist upon the services of a translator to allow him to conduct his defence in another language, including the language of an ethnic minority of which he is a member.[16]

6. CONCLUSION

Although Article 6 cases do not generally catch the headlines or raise questions of human rights theory as much as cases under some other articles, such as Articles 3 or 10, they are the staple diet of the Convention system. More than half of the cases decided at Strasbourg raise issues under Article 6. One reason for this is that it is in the administration of justice that the state is most likely to take decisions affecting individuals in the areas of conduct covered by the Convention.

Article 6 has been given an unexpectedly but commendably wide field of application. Although it does not yet extend to every situation in which an individual would benefit from a 'right to a court', Article 6 none the less has an extensive reach. It controls appellate as well as trial and some pre-trial proceedings. It applies to certain disciplinary and other proceedings before special tribunals. If this is good for the individual, it presents problems of uniform or differential interpretation of a text that was devised with the classical court of law in mind. Article 6 also requires states to provide a right of appeal from, or judicial review of, administrative decisions that are directly decisive for an individual's 'civil rights and obligations'. Should the Court's jurisprudence in this last regard appear confusing and in need of a coherent statement of principle, the result is still an extension of the rule of law into areas of administrative justice where it was sometimes lacking.

As to the meaning of a 'fair trial', Article 6 has, in certain respects, been imaginatively interpreted. A right of access to a court has been read into the text.[17] The recent emphasis upon 'objective justice' has given more bite to the guarantees of an 'independent and impartial tribunal' and 'equality of arms', leading in some cases to changes in longstanding national practices.[18] The residual right to a 'fair hearing' has proved fertile ground for the addition of further nominate rights[19] and has served as a means of dealing with cases on a flexible 'facts as a whole' basis[20] and with cases that cannot easily be categorised but that give rise on their facts to 'reasonable misgivings'.[1] But the most striking feature of Article 6 cases has been the

---

15 *X v FRG No 2465/65*, 24 CD 50 (1967); *X v UK No 8124/77*, 2 Digest 916 (1978).
16 *K v France No 10210/82*, 35 DR 203 (1983) and *Bideault v France No 11261/84*, 48 DR 232 (1986).
17 See the *Golder* case, above, p 196.
18 See the *Piersack* and *Borgers* cases, above, pp 236 and 208.
19 See eg the right to a hearing in one's presence, above, p 203.
20 See the *Barberà* case, above, p 203.
1   See *Kraska v Switzerland* A 254-B para 33 (1993).

long line of decisions involving violations of the right to trial 'within a reasonable time'. If one feature of the administration of justice in European states has been highlighted by the working of the Convention, it is the delay with which justice can be delivered. Proceedings in some cases have lasted an astonishing number of years.

As to the mechanics of the trial process, the Court has been far less intrusive. Given the great diversity of practice in European criminal justice systems concerning, for example, the rules of evidence, the Court has applied a very wide margin of appreciation as to the conduct of trials by national courts. One issue in respect of which it has taken a stand concerns the admissibility of hearsay evidence. Its decision in the *Unterpertinger* case[2] has precipitated a long line of cases, although in some of them there are signs that the Court may be having second thoughts. This example demonstrates clearly the choice that the Court has between leading and following national practice in the administration of justice. Whereas Article 6, like the US Constitution, should not be seen as a 'uniform code of criminal procedure federally imposed',[3] there are areas in which corrective action could properly be taken in respect of trial proceedings in the interests of human rights. It is fair to say that there remain aspects of the trial process, particularly in criminal cases, in which recognised standards of procedural justice have yet to be fully imposed by the Court.

2 See above, pp 211-212.
3 Frankfurter, *Law and Politics*, 1939, pp 192-193.

CHAPTER 7

Article 7: Freedom from retroactive criminal offences and punishment

'**Article 7**

1. No one shall be held guilty of any criminal offence on account of any act or omission which did not constitute a criminal offence under national or international law at the time when it was committed. Nor shall a heavier penalty be imposed than the one that was applicable at the time the criminal offence was committed.

2. This article shall not prejudice the trial and punishment of any person for any act or omission which, at the time when it was committed, was criminal according to the general principles of law recognised by civilised nations.'

Article 7 incorporates the principle of legality, by which, in the context of criminal law, a person should only be convicted and punished on a basis of law: *nullem crimen, nulla poena sine lege*.[1] Its general scope was indicated in *Kokkinakis v Greece*[2] as follows:

'The Court points out that Article 7(1) of the Convention is not confined to prohibiting the retrospective application of the criminal law to an accused's disadvantage. It also embodies, more generally, the principle that only the law can define a crime and prescribe a penalty (*nullum crimen, nulla poena sine lege*) and the principle that the criminal law must not be extensively construed to an accused's detriment, for instance by analogy; it follows from this that an offence must be clearly defined in law. This condition is satisfied where the individual can know from the wording of the relevant provision and, if need be, with the assistance of the courts' interpretation of it, what acts and omissions will make him liable.'

The meaning of Article 7 has been interpreted mostly by the Commission in decisions as to admissibility. Very few cases have been admitted for consider-

---

1 See *Kokkinakis v Greece* A 260-A (1993). On the principle of legality, see Hall, *General Principles of Criminal Law*, 2nd edn, 1960, pp 225 et seq. The principle is implicit in the 'rule of law' mentioned in the Convention preamble and in Dicey's understanding of the same concept: see Dicey, *An Introduction to the Study of the Law of the Constitution*, 10th edn, 1959, p 188. On the principle as interpreted in Article 7, see Cremona, *Pallieri Studies*, Vol 2, 1978, p 194.

2 A 260-A para 52 (1993).

ation on the merits under Article 7 and only two breaches of it have so far been found. The importance of the guarantee in Article 7(1) is recognised by the fact that it cannot be derogated from in time of war or public emergency.[3]

1. *EX POST FACTO* CRIMINAL OFFENCES

The wording of Article 7(1) is limited to cases in which a person is 'found guilty', ie convicted, of a criminal offence.[4] A prosecution that does not lead to a conviction cannot raise an issue under Article 7 – at least not by means of an individual application.[5] A state application under Article 24 may question the compatibility with Article 7 of a law *in abstracto*, so that not even a prosecution is required. Thus in *Ireland v United Kingdom*,[6] Ireland challenged the consistency of the Northern Ireland Act 1972 with Article 7, insofar as it could be read as making it an offence retroactively to fail to comply with an order issued by the security forces. The application was withdrawn when the UK Attorney-General gave an undertaking that the Act would not be applied retroactively. Article 7 does not prevent the retroactive application of laws in respect of such ancillary matters concerning criminal proceedings as detention on remand,[7] the refusal of legal aid or leave to appeal, or the entry of a conviction on a person's record,[8] since they do not involve a finding of guilt. However, it is arguable that a change in the rules of evidence (eg as to admissibility) to the detriment of the accused is so closely related to the finding of a person 'guilty of a criminal offence' that it is within Article 7.[9] Article 7 does not incorporate the principle *non bis in idem* (a person should not be tried twice for the same offence).[10] Since Article 7 applies only to criminal prosecutions, decisions to extradite a person to another jurisdiction,[11] to order the preventive detention of suspected terrorists[12] or to detain a person as a vagrant[13] are not controlled by it. Similarly, Article 7(1) does not apply to the imposition of a regime of civilian service upon a conscientious objector to military service[14] or to judicial decisions in civil, ie non-

---

3 See Article 15(2), Convention.
4 'Found guilty' in Article 7 has an autonomous Convention meaning: *X v Netherlands No 7512/76*, 6 DR 184 (1976).
5 *X v UK No 6056/73*, 3 Digest 21 (1973).
6 *No 5310/71*, 15 YB 76 (1972).
7 See Fawcett, p 202.
8 *X v FRG No 448/59*, 3 YB 254 (1960).
9 The only case that would appear to be relevant is *X v UK No 6683/74*, 3 DR 95 (1975). There it was held that a reference by the English Court of Appeal to a House of Lords decision on the law of evidence that post-dated the applicant's trial in order solely to confirm that his conviction involved no miscarriage of justice was not in breach of Article 7.
10 *X v Austria No 7720/76*, 3 Digest 32 (1978).
11 *X v Netherlands No 7512/76*, 6 DR 184 (1976). *Quaere*, however, whether extradition to face a real risk of conviction contrary to Article 7 might be a breach of that Article: see the *Soering* case, above, p 74.
12 *Lawless v Ireland (Merits)* A 3 p 54 (1961).
13 *De Wilde, Ooms and Versyp v Belgium* A 12 para 87 (1970).
14 *Johansen v Norway No 10600/83*, 44 DR 155 (1985).

criminal, law.[15] It would thus clearly not control the *ex post facto* application by a court of the United Kingdom War Damage Act 1965, by which the common law rule requiring compensation in certain circumstances for the wartime destruction of private property was reversed with retroactive effect.

The Commission decided in a number of early cases that offences that are classified as disciplinary offences under a state's law do not qualify as 'criminal' offences for the purposes of Article 7.[16] These decisions, which date from the 1970s, were linked to the then prevailing interpretation of the term 'criminal' in Article 6. Since then, however, it has been established by the Court in *Engel v Netherlands*[17] that disciplinary offences in national law may, exceptionally, qualify as 'criminal' offences for the purposes of Article 6. Given that the Court's reasoning applies equally to Article 7, it is probable that a disciplinary offence that meets the requirements of the *Engel* case would now be treated as coming within the autonomous Convention concept of a 'criminal' offence for the purposes of Article 7 as well.[18] Likewise, offences that are classified as regulatory offences or are otherwise non-criminal offences in national law but that are treated as 'criminal' offences for the purposes of Article 6[19] are probably to be regarded as 'criminal' for the purposes of Article 7 too.[20] In *Harman v UK*,[1] a solicitor had been found guilty of civil contempt of court because she allowed a journalist access to documents copied to her under the rules as to discovery of documents in civil proceedings. The application was admitted for consideration on the merits under Article 7, without the question whether civil contempt in English law was a 'criminal' offence for the purposes of that Article being considered. Given that civil contempt, although not classified as a crime in English law, does carry typically penal sanctions (imprisonment, fine),[2] it is properly regarded as 'criminal' in the sense of Article 7, despite the fact that its purpose is coercive (to enforce court orders and procedures) rather than punitive. As under Article 6, it is likely that an offence that is classified as a 'criminal' offence under the law of the state in which the person is found guilty is always to be regarded as such for the purposes of Article 7.

---

15 *X v Belgium No 8988/80*, 24 DR 198 (1981). The case involved a determination of bankruptcy by a commercial court. The Commission noted that under Belgian law a criminal court that tried an accused on a charge of negligent or fraudulent bankruptcy would not be bound by any decision taken by a commercial court in bankruptcy proceedings on the same facts. *Quaere* whether Article 7 might control a non-criminal court ruling (eg as to the presence of negligence) based upon an *ex post facto* law that would later be binding upon a criminal court when determining guilt.

16 See eg *X v FRG No 4274/69*, 13 YB 888 (1970) (civil service disciplinary proceedings).

17 See above, p 167.

18 On the drafting history of 'criminal' in Article 7, which supports a wide reading of the word, see Fawcett, pp 200-201.

19 See above, p 169.

20 In *X v Sweden No 11408/85*, 9 EHRR 244 (1985), it was held that Article 7 did not apply to penalties imposed for non-compliance with Swedish building regulations. See also *Pagmar v Sweden No 10728/83*, 9 EHRR 91 (1985). These cases would be unlikely to be 'criminal' for the purposes of Article 6 either.

1 *No 10038/82*, 38 DR 53 (1984). The case resulted in a friendly settlement: see 46 DR 57 (1986).

2 On the English law of civil contempt, see Miller, *Contempt of Court*, 2nd edn, 1989, Ch 14.

Article 7(1) refers to criminal offences 'under national or international law'. A conviction that results from the retroactive application of a national law will not be in breach of Article 7 if the conduct upon which the conviction is based is a crime 'under . . . international law' at the time that it occurs. This is particularly significant for a state if, and to the extent that, public international law is not a part of its national law. The question then arises as to the meaning of 'crimes under international law'. It is likely that this refers not to crimes under public international law that give rise to responsibility on the part of states (eg a breach of the prohibition of resort to aggression),[3] but to crimes in respect of which public international law permits individuals to be prosecuted by states under their national law on the basis solely of their custody of the alleged offender (universality jurisdiction). Such offences include, in customary international law, war crimes and piracy. They also include, for the states parties to the relevant treaties, drug trafficking, hijacking, the sabotage of aircraft, apartheid, attacks upon diplomats, the taking of hostages and torture.[4]

For Article 7(1) to be infringed, the act or omission on the basis of which a person is convicted must not 'constitute a criminal offence ... at the time when it is committed'. This clearly covers the position in which a new offence is introduced with retroactive effect by legislation[5] or at common law[6] after the accused's act or omission. It also includes the situation in which the existing law is newly interpreted or applied with the result that an act or omission not reasonably foreseeable as being criminal at the time of its occurrence becomes such later. What Article 7(1) prohibits in this second situation is the extension of existing offences 'to cover facts which previously clearly did not constitute a criminal offence.'[7] In contrast, 'it is not objectionable that the existing elements of the offence are clarified and adapted to new circumstances which can reasonably be brought under the original conception of the offence'.[8] The case in which these statements were made concerned the English law of blasphemy as interpreted in *Whitehouse v Lemon* (the Gay News case).[9] There the House of Lords had held that the required mens rea for the common law offence of blasphemous libel was only an intention to publish; there was no need to prove an intent to blaspheme. Given that there was no earlier case-law that had clearly required a specific

---

3 See Article 19, ILC Draft Articles on State Responsibility, YBILC, 1980, II (Part Two), p 32. The existence of criminal responsibility on the part of states is a matter of controversy: see Harris, *Cases and Materials on International Law*, 4th edn, 1991, p 463.

4 See Harris, op cit n 3, p 276. Some of these offences may also be subject to universality jurisdiction in customary international law.

5 With regard to the question whether statutory offences apply retroactively in English law, in *Waddington v Miah* [1974] 1 WLR 683 at 694, HL, Lord Reid stated that 'it is hardly credible that any government department would promote or that Parliament would pass retrospective criminal legislation'.

6 Judge-made offences are 'criminal offences' for the purposes of Article 7: *X Ltd and Y v UK No 8710/79*, 28 DR 77 (1982).

7 *X Ltd and Y v UK No 8710/79*, 28 DR 77 at 81 (1982). Cf *Gerlach v FRG No 11130/84*, 43 DR 210 at 212 (1985).

8 *X Ltd and Y v UK No 8710/79*, 28 DR 77 at 81 (1982).

9 [1979] AC 617.

intent to blaspheme, the Commission held that the House of Lords ruling on the necessary *mens rea* was not a change in the law but an 'acceptable clarification' of the existing law.[10]

Other Strasbourg cases have concerned other aspects of the need for certainty in the law. Thus in *Handyside v UK*[11] the crucial issue was whether the kinds of acts that would fall within an offence were sufficiently clearly indicated by the law. There it was argued that the offence of 'obscenity' in the Obscene Publications Acts 1959-64 'was so far-reaching and imprecise that it might be applied almost without limit'. While accepting that the principle *nullem crimen sine lege* 'includes the requirement that the offence should be clearly described by law', the Commission stated that 'the requirement of certainty in the law cannot mean that the concrete facts giving rise to criminal liability should be set out in the statute concerned'. The requirement was satisfied if, as in the case of the Obscene Publications Acts, a general definition was provided by law for the courts to apply.[12] A different aspect of the requirement of uncertainty was raised in *Prasser v Austria*.[13] There the applicant complained that although his health food was produced with a level of pesticides within the limit set by the pesticides law applicable to all foodstuffs, he had been convicted of offering adulterated products to the public under that law on the basis of a stricter standard for health foods that the competent regulatory authority had decided to apply to health foods that was not to be found in the pesticides law. The principle *nullem crimen sine lege* supposed, it was claimed, some more precise basis in law for the offence and less administrative discretion. Although the application was declared admissible, it was later withdrawn so that the Article 7 issue was not decided on its merits. Relevant considerations under Article 7 would be whether the agency was acting within its powers and whether its stricter standard was known to the public and not applied retroactively.[14]

Statements by the Commission[15] that Article 7 incorporates 'the principle of the restrictive interpretation of penal texts' are relevant to the interpretation of Article 7. In view of this generally recognised principle,[16]

---

10 For other cases of permissible clarification or reasonable interpretation, see eg *Enkelmann v Switzerland No 10505/83*, 41 DR 178 (1985) (interpretation of the requirement of 'approval' of violence was a clarification, not a 'substantial modification', of that element of an offence); *X v Austria No 1852/63*, 8 YB 190 (1965); *Murphy v UK No 4681/70*, 43 CD 1 (1972) (interpretation and application of the Theft Act 'reasonable') and *G v FRG No 13079/ 87*, 60 DR 256 (1989). The House of Lords ruling in *R v R*, [1991] 4 All ER 481, HL that, contrary to the long understood position, a husband may rape his wife is the subject of pending applications at Strasbourg alleging a breach of Article 7: see *SW v UK No 20166/92* and *CR v UK No 20190/92* (Article 31 reports adopted; pending before Court).
11 *No 5493/72*, 17 YB 228 at 290 (1974). For other unsuccessful claims of 'vagueness', see *X v Austria No 1747/62*, 6 YB 424 (1963) and *G v Liechtenstein No 10980/84*, 38 DR 234 (1984).
12 Cf *Gerlach v FRG No 11130/84*, 43 DR 210 (1985).
13 *No 10498/83*, 46 DR 81 (1986). Rule 54 Rep.
14 Cf *X v Austria No 8141/78*, 16 DR 141 (1978).
15 See eg *X v Belgium No 1103/61*, 5 YB 168 (1962).
16 Note, however, that in English law the presumption against retroactive criminal legislation is less consistently applied than previously: see Smith and Bailey, *The Modern English Legal System*, 2nd edn (by Bailey and Gunn), 1991, p 356.

it is reasonable for a person to suppose that an offence will be interpreted restrictively. Insofar as national courts develop their national law to such an extent as to present possible problems under Article 7,[17] a simple remedy would be for any judicial alteration to the criminal law to the detriment of an accused to apply prospectively only.[18]

For Article 7 to be complied with, the criminal law on the basis of which a person is convicted must also be 'accessible'.[19] Importing into Article 7 an idea that was first relied upon when interpreting the wording 'prescribed by law' in Article 10(2), the Commission has thus confirmed that in the context of this article too the law must be publicly available.

Article 7 extends to criminal offences that have been abrogated or have ceased to apply by reason of desuetude as well as to those newly introduced.[20] In both cases, a person is convicted of an offence that does not exist at the time that his act or omission occurs.

Article 7 applies where a change in the law occurs retroactively 'to the detriment of the accused.'[1] What it does not do is guarantee that the accused has the benefit of any alteration in the law to his advantage that takes place between his act or omission and his trial.[2]

A consequence of the Commission's approach to Article 7 is that it sometimes finds itself reviewing the interpretation of a state's law by its national courts. This is particularly noticeable when the Commission considers whether a state's law has been interpreted or applied in a manner that is reasonably foreseeable or whether it has become obsolete. Given that Article 7 requires that a state act in accordance with its national law, the Commission is called upon to check that it has done so, thereby departing from its general approach to national law, by which it does not question the interpretation and application of that law by national courts.[3] The exercise by the Commission of this 'supervisory function' is undertaken 'with

---

17 The most striking example of retroactive judicial lawmaking in criminal law by the English courts in recent times was the establishment of the offence of conspiracy to corrupt public morals: *Shaw v DPP* [1962] AC 220, HL. However, in *Knuller v DPP* [1973] AC 435, HL, the House of Lords denied that there was a judicial power to create new offences; the *Shaw* case was to be seen as the extension of an existing offence to new circumstances. Whether new in 1962 or not, the question concerning the offence that arises now under Article 7 is whether its scope is reasonably foreseeable. See *X v UK No 5327/71*, 43 CD 85 (1972) (conspiracy to bring illegal immigrants into the UK: no breach of Article 7).

18 This is sometimes done by the US Supreme Court when it changes its interpretation of the Constitution: see, eg *Linkletter v Walker* 381 US 618 (1965).

19 *X Ltd and Y v UK No 8710/79*, 28 DR 77 at 80 (1982). The Commission quoted a passage to this effect from the *Sunday Times (No 1)* case, see below, p 287, interpreting Article 10(2). Cf *G v FRG No 13079/87*, 60 DR 256 (1989).

20 *X v FRG No 1169/61*, 6 YB 520 at 5888 (1963). Cf *X v Netherlands No 7721/76*, 11 DR 209 at 211 (1977).

1 *Gerlach v FRG No 11130/84*, 43 DR 210 at 212 (1985).

2 *X v FRG No 7900/77*, 13 DR 70 (1978). See also *X v UK No 3777/68*, 31 CD 120 (1969). Contrast Article 15(1), ICCPR.

3 As to the '*quatrième instance*' doctrine, see above, p 15. For another context in which the Strasbourg authorities must also consider whether national law has been complied with, see Article 5: see above, p 104.

caution'[4] and has so far not led it to find that any state has infringed, through its courts, the principle of legality.

2. *EX POST FACTO* CRIMINAL PENALTIES

Article 7(1) also provides that there shall not be imposed a 'heavier penalty ... than the one that was applicable at the time the criminal offence was committed'. Much of what has been said above concerning *ex post facto* criminal offences applies to penalties also. Article 7(1) applies to any 'penalty', or sentence, imposed following conviction for a criminal offence. The meaning of 'penalty' was examined in *Welch v UK*.[5] The Court indicated that it had an autonomous Convention meaning. The measure in question must be one that is imposed following conviction for a criminal offence. Other factors that may be taken into account are 'the nature and purpose of the measure in question; its characterisation under national law; the procedures involved in the making and implementation of the measure; and its severity'. In the *Welch* case, the applicant was convicted of criminal offences involving drug trafficking. He was given a 22-year prison sentence and a confiscation order was made under the Drug Trafficking Offences Act 1986. The order was for the payment of £59,000, in default of which he would receive a further, consecutive two-year prison sentence. There was no dispute that the Act had been applied retroactively in the sense of Article 7 to an offence that had been committed before the Act came into force.[6] The only question was whether the confiscation order was a 'penalty' so that Article 7 applied. In deciding that it was, and that Article 7 had been infringed, the Court noted that it had been imposed following a conviction; that the measure had punitive as well as preventative and reparative aims; and that there were indications of a regime of punishment in the fact that:

(i) the amount of the order was related to the proceeds of drug dealing, not just the actual profits;
(ii) the amount could be affected by culpability; and
(iii) imprisonment might result in default of payment.

The removal from the jurisdiction of an illegal immigrant as an administrative measure is not a 'penalty' in the sense of Article 7.[7] An

---

4 *X v Austria No 1852/63*, 8 YB 190 at 198 (1965). Cf *X v FRG No 1169/61*, 6 YB 520 (1963).
5 A 307-A paras 27-35 (1995). Cf *Jamil v France* A 320 (1995) (term of imprisonment in default increased by law enacted after offence: breach of Article 7).
6 The case does not affect the 1986 Act insofar as it applies to crimes committed after it entered into force.
7 *Moustaquim v Belgium* A 193 (1991) Com Rep. Under Belgian law, the removal was a security, not a penal measure. The position under UK immigration law is similar. Whereas, under the Immigration Act 1971, s.24(1), illegal entry is a criminal offence punishable with a fine or imprisonment, the removal of an illegal immigrant is an administrative act: see Immigration Act 1971, Sch 2, para 8.

order for the preventive detention of a recidivist is probably not a 'penalty' in the sense of Article 7; even though it is made by a court following a conviction for a criminal offence, 'it is by definition a preventive measure imposed in view of possible future offences and not a sanction for criminal acts in the past'.[8] In another case, the Commission left open the question whether Article 7 applies where a convicted person is sent to a mental institution as mentally disordered.[9] Again, it would seem that Article 7 should not apply, since the purpose of committing a person to a mental institution is not to punish. The Commission has also left open the question whether the award of costs in criminal cases is a 'penalty'.[10] Article 7 applies only to the 'penalty' imposed, not to the manner of its enforcement. Hence it does not prevent any retroactive alteration in the law or practice concerning the parole or conditional release of a prisoner.[11] It may, however, apply to a retroactive change in the conditions of detention where the new conditions are 'essentially different' from those that would have applied previously.[12] A threat of a 'penalty' is not sufficient.[13]

With regard to the retroactive application of 'penalties', Article 7 extends both to the retroactive application of new laws establishing 'penalties' and, by analogy with the Commission's jurisprudence concerning *ex post facto* criminal offences, to their application to the detriment of the convicted person in a way that is not reasonably foreseeable. It does not prohibit the existence or harsh application of a tariff of possible 'penalties', unless the tariff is applied retroactively in either of the above senses. Nor does Article 7 prevent a court decision to convict a person of an offence carrying a higher, rather than a lower, sentence.[14] As with *ex post facto* criminal offences, the nature and severity of a 'penalty' is a matter within a state's discretion; considerations of proportionality arise under Articles 2 and 3, not Article 7.

3. GENERAL PRINCIPLES OF LAW EXCEPTION

Article 7(2) provides that Article 7 'shall not prejudice the trial and punishment of any person for any act or omission which, at the time when it was committed, was criminal according to the general principles of law recognised by civilised nations'. The phrase 'general principles of law recognised

---

8 *X v Austria No 9167/80*, 26 DR 248 (1981). The Commission expressed 'doubts' along these lines without finding the need to decide the point.
9 *Dhoest v Belgium No 10448/83*, 55 DR 5 (1987).
10 *X and Y v Austria Nos 5424/72 and 5425/72*, 43 CD 159 (1973).
11 See eg *Hogben v UK No 11653/85*, 46 DR 231 (1986) (stricter parole policy for prisoners serving life sentences not subject to Article 7).
12 *X v Austria No 7720/76*, 3 Digest 32 (1978).
13 *Barthold v FRG No 8734/79*, 26 DR 145 (1981). Cf the *Greek* case, 12 YB (the *Greek* case) 1 at 184 (1969) Com Rep; CM Res DH (70)1 (no penalty imposed).
14 *X v UK No 6679/74*, 3 Digest 31 (1975). Cf *Crociani v Italy No 8603/79*, 22 DR 147 at 228 (1980).

by civilised nations' is taken word for word from Article 38, Statute of the International Court of Justice, in which it identifies a third formal source of public international law. If there is no treaty binding upon the parties to a dispute and if no rule of customary international law based upon state practice applies, recourse may be had to 'general principles of law recognised by civilised nations', ie by the states members of the international community, to fill the gap. In the context of the Statute of the Court and, presumably, of Article 7 of the Convention, these are 'general principles of law' to be found in municipal legal systems. Interestingly, the text of Article 7 refers to 'nations' generally; it is not limited to the legal systems of the contracting parties, to which the Strasbourg authorities not infrequently refer when looking for standards in the context of other articles which make no reference to national law.[15]

The *travaux préparatoires* indicate that Article 7(2) is intended 'to make it clear that Article 7 does not affect laws which, under the very exceptional circumstances at the end of the Second World War, were passed to punish war crimes, treason and collaboration with the enemy, and does not aim at any legal or moral condemnation of those laws'.[16] In fact, the text is not so restricted and could be interpreted dynamically to cover other offences involving fundamentally immoral conduct that is generally regarded as criminal in national law. Article 7(2) will not be needed insofar as a conviction under national law can be justified under Article 7(1) as being for a 'crime . . . under international law' at the time of its commission. It might, however, be relevant to any conviction or sentence under a statute such as the United Kingdom War Crimes Act 1991, which confers on the British courts retroactive jurisdiction to try any individual on the universality jurisdiction basis described above for offences of murder, manslaughter or culpable homicide amounting to war crimes committed in Germany or a place under German occupation during the Second World War. Although it has since become clearly established that war crimes are 'crimes ... under international law' in the universality jurisdiction sense, so that a conviction under a 1991 statute that gave the British courts jurisdiction to try individuals for offences amounting to war crimes that took place in 1990 would not be contrary to Article 7(1), the existence during the Second World War of an international law rule permitting the exercise of universality jurisdiction in respect of war crimes was less certain.[17]

---

15 See above, p 9.
16 *X v Belgium No 268/57*, 1 YB 239 at 241 (1957). Translation in 3 Digest 34. Cf *De Becker v Belgium No 214/56*, 2 YB 214 at 226 (1958). Germany has made a reservation to Article 7(2) (text in 1 YB 40 (1955-58)) that in effect excludes the exception that Article 7(2) provides: see *X v FRG No 1063/61*, 3 Digest 36 (1962).
17 See Woetzel, *The Nuremberg Trials in International Law*, 1962, Ch 5.

CHAPTER 8
Articles 8-11: General considerations

1. INTRODUCTION

There are common features to and connections between Articles 8-11 which justify considering them together. Some of these are formal: Articles 8-11 are constructed in identical form, the first paragraph defining the protected rights, the second laying down the conditions upon which a state might legitimately interfere with the enjoyment of those rights. Others are substantive: Articles 9-11 protect 'freedoms', essentially liberties, against interference by the state with activities which an individual may or may not choose to engage in. However, the Articles are expressed in terms of 'rights' to the various freedoms, language which has enabled the Strasbourg authorities to interpret the protected rights beyond a mere guarantee of non-interference by the government. States have routinely, but unsuccessfully, argued that these are freedoms in the Hohfeldian sense of liberty, requiring only that the state not interfere with the exercise of the freedom by an individual.[1] Article 8 is unique in using the language 'right to respect' for various interests. It has sometimes been suggested that this formulation imposes a less onerous burden on the state but, again, the Strasbourg authorities have taken the opportunity to expand the obligations which flow from these words.[2] The substantive rights protected are both multiple and complex. Four rights are set out in Article 8, three in Article 9, two in Article 11. Certain of the rights are said to 'include' particular rights. For instance, the right to freedom of association in Article 11 includes the right to form and join trade unions.

Finally, as with other rights in the Convention, some of the rights in Articles 8-11 must be read in conjunction with those in other provisions. For instance, the right to respect for family life has, in some of its aspects, close relations with Article 12, on the right to marry and found a family, and with Article 5, Seventh Protocol, which protects the equality of spouses in private law. It may also overlap with the prohibition or inhuman of degrading treatment in Article 3.

---

1   See eg government arguments in *Lingens v Austria* A 103 para 37 (1986) and *Plattform 'Arzte für das Leben' v Austria*, Oral Argument, 21 March 1988, Corr/Misc (88) 71, pp 15-17.
2   See below, pp 320-335.

2. NEGATIVE AND POSITIVE OBLIGATIONS[3]

The classical conception of the fundamental right is that it imposes a duty on the state not to interfere with the enjoyment of the right. So the state must not torture anyone or, in the context of Articles 8-11, interfere with a person's exercise of his freedom of expression by preventing the publication of his writing. Important though it is, this wholly negative view of a state's responsibility towards the enjoyment of civil liberties is inadequate to secure the effective exercise of the individual's freedoms. Thus freedom of expression, if it be restricted to requiring the state to tolerate the enunciation of certain opinions by an individual, will be of little practical consequence if the state is under no obligation to interfere against a hostile group which wishes to prevent the dissemination of the message. The principle that the Convention protects the effective rather than the theoretical enjoyment of rights set out in *Golder v UK*[4] and *Airey v Ireland*[5] is of great importance here.

The Court has not determined any general theory of positive obligations and, accordingly, it will be necessary to consider the question in relation to each particular right.[6] However, it is worth noticing here what levels of obligation may be contained in each of the rights in Articles 8-11. In addition to the wholly negative obligation of non-interference already referred to, three other, inter-related, possibilities arise:

(i) the obligation of the authorities to take steps to make sure that the enjoyment of the right is effective;[7]

(ii) the obligation of the authorities to take steps to make sure that the enjoyment of the right is not interfered with by other private persons;[8] and

(iii) the obligation of the authorities to take steps to make sure that private persons take steps to ensure the effective enjoyment by other individuals of the right.

It is a characteristic of positive obligations that the duties they impose are seldom absolute. What is required of the state will vary according to the importance of the right and the resources required to be disbursed to meet any positive obligation. While the Strasbourg authorities have interpreted some positive obligations strictly, notably some of the state's obligations

---

3   On negative and positive obligations generally, see above, pp 19-22.

4   A 18 para 28 (1975).

5   A 32 para 24 (1979).

6   In general, see Clapham, *Human Rights in the Private Sphere*, 1993, Ch 7.

7   See the *Golder* and *Airey* cases, loc cit at nn 4 and 5 above. This general obligation includes the obligation to have in place laws that grant individuals the legal status, rights and privileges required to ensure, for example, that their family and private life is properly respected. See eg the family law regime for children born out of wedlock required by the *Marckx* case, below, pp 329-330. The obligations in (ii) and (iii) above can also be subsumed within the general obligation in (i), but are usually and helpfully separated out.

8   *X and Y v Netherlands* A 91 para 32 (1985).

under Article 6,[9] more generally, they have considered only whether the state has taken reasonable measures to safeguard the individual's enjoyment of his right.[10] Nor is the state's obligation uniform with respect to the three categories of positive obligation listed above which may arise in connection with a single right. Thus the Commission has been cool towards suggestions that the rights to enjoy the various freedoms in Articles 9-11 involve much by way of positive obligations to supply the means for the exercise of those freedoms.[11] It is more likely that the state will be required to act to protect the exercise of the freedom against interference by other private groups.[12] In contrast, and hardly surprisingly, the obligation on the state to require one private person to provide facilities for another to exercise his right (see (iii) above) is little more than a suggestion in the practice of the Strasbourg authroities.[13]

3. LIMITATIONS

The conditions upon which a state may interfere with the enjoyment of a protected right are set out in elaborate terms in the second paragraphs of Articles 8-11. These paragraphs have a common structure but differ in detail.[14] Limitations are allowed if they are 'in accordance with the law' or 'prescribed by law' and are 'necessary in a democratic society' for the protection of one of the objectives set out in the second paragraph.[15] The Court's usual practice is to consider those elements separately and in the order 'law', 'objective' and 'necessity'.

i. 'In accordance with the law'/'prescribed by law'

On the face of it, there is a significant difference between the formulation in Article 8(2), 'in accordance with the law' and the words used in Articles 9(2)-11(2), 'prescribed by law'. The first could carry the meaning 'not unlawful' whereas the second could imply that some specific authorisation is required. The difference would be of importance for the United Kingdom with its tradition of recognising the lawfulness of action (including action by the state) where such action is not specifically prohibited. However, the argument that there was a difference in meaning was abandoned by the British government in *Malone v UK*[16] and it was established by the Court in

9 See eg *Zimmermann and Steiner v Switzerland* A 66 para 29 (1983).
10 See eg *Plattform 'Arzte für das Leben' v Austria No 10126/82*, 44 DR 65 (1985) and *Rees v UK* A 106 paras 38-45 (1986).
11 *X and Association Z v UK No 4515/70*, 38 CD 86 at 88-89 (1971). For facts, see below, p 381.
12 Eg *Young, James and Webster v UK* A 44 paras 55-56 (1981).
13 *X v UK No 4515/70*, 38 CD 86 at 88 (1971).
14 Eg Article 8(2) alone permits restrictions for 'economic well-being'.
15 There are further special powers of limitation in the final sentences of Articles 10(1) and 11(2): see below pp 384-386 and 430-432.
16 B 67 (1983-5) Com Rep paras 118-9; cf oral argument, id, pp 201-203.

that case that both formulations are to be read in the same way.[17] They mean that, as a minimum, the defendant state must point to some specific legal rule or regime which authorises the interfering act it seeks to justify.[18] The rule need not be a rule of domestic law but may be a rule of international law or Community law so long as it purports to authorise the interference.[19] It may consist of a whole legal regime regulating the area of activity, including rules made by a delegated rule-making authority[20] and rules from more than one legal order.[1] If a state does indicate the legal basis for its action, the Court is reluctant in the extreme to accede to arguments that the national law has not been properly interpreted or applied by the national courts.[2]

Domestic legality is a necessary condition but it is not sufficient. The Court has said that the notion of 'law' is autonomous.[3] The Court has taken a wide view of what delegated powers are capable of generating 'law'[4] in a Convention sense and has recognised that unwritten law, most importantly judge-made law, will satisfy its understanding of 'law'.[5] Van Dijk and Van Hoof[6] embrace Alkema's criticism[7] that the Court has not paid enough attention to securing the democratic legitimacy of a rule as an essential ingredient of its character as 'law'. Thus, they cast doubt on the legislation of the European Communities[8] and yet they are content with the common law's 'firm democratic basis' on the wholly fictional ground that 'it is impliedly endorsed by Parliament'.[9] The fact is that delegated rule-making finds its authority in actual endorsement by a legislative superior and some legal challenge on grounds of *ultra vires* is often available as a check on unlawful rule-making. The democratic basis of the modern common law is problematic.[10] Extracting the 'right' amount of legislative input into a rule is probably an unnecessary complication.

17 A 82 para 66 (1984). The French text of each is identical, *'prévues par la loi'*.
18 *Silver v UK* A 61 para 86 (1983).
19 *Groppera Radio AG v Switzerland* A 173 para 68 (1990); Com Rep para 153. Note Judge Bernhardt dissenting on the importance of establishing that the legal effect of the international rule in the appropriate domestic legal order is to authorise the interference against the applicant.
20 *Barthold v FRG* A 90 paras 45-46 (1985).
1   *Groppera Radio AG v Switzerland* A 173 (1990) paras 65-68.
2   In *Malone v UK* A 82 para 69 (1984), the Court preferred the judgment of the English High Court in *Malone v Commissioner of Police* [1979] 2 All E.R. 620 Ch D, to the government's account of the position in national law.
3   *Sunday Times v UK* A 30 para 49 (1979).
4   *Barthold v FRG* A 90 para 46 (1985). A professional association's rules were 'law', being traditionally regarded as made by 'parliamentary delegation' and monitored by the state.
5   *Sunday Times v UK* A 30 para 47 (1979).
6   Van Dijk and Van Hoof, p 579. Cf *The Word 'Laws' in Article 30 of the ACHR*, Inter-Am Ct H Rts Rep, Series A 6; 7 HRLJ 231 (1986), Advisory Opinion.
7   Alkema, *Studies over Europese Grondrechten*, 1978, p 67.
8   The European Parliament's power of co-decision under Article 189 of the Rome Treaty as amended by the Maastricht Treaty removes most of the force from the argument concerning EC legislation.
9   Van Dijk and Van Hoof, p 580.
10 See Simpson, in Simpson, ed, *Oxford Essays in Jurisprudence* (Second Series), 1973, pp 77-99.

It is conceivable that the notion of 'law' here could include the element of propriety or absence of arbitrariness in terms of purpose which the Court has ascribed to it in other contexts,[11] but this is unlikely to be of consequence for it is hard to see how a manifestly arbitrary law could ever be 'necessary in a democratic society'. However, the Court has introduced the notion of arbitrariness in a different sense into its idea of 'law'. In *Sunday Times v UK*[12] the Court added two further criteria for a rule to be a 'law':

> 'Firstly, the law must be adequately accessible: the citizen must be able to have an indication that is adequate in the circumstances of the legal rules applicable to a given case. Secondly, a norm cannot be regarded as a "law" unless it is formulated with sufficient precision to enable the citizen to regulate his conduct.'

These are further guarantees against substantively arbitrary rules. Accessibility of course requires that the texts be available to an applicant[13] but it is accepted that understanding of the texts may require access to appropriate advice.[14] If texts or rules are relied on to establish the foreseeability of the law, for instance, to supplement the wide language of the primary, published rule, then they also must be available to the applicant. In *Silver v UK*,[15] the government conceded that some restrictions on prisoners' correspondence imposed on the basis of unpublished Prison Orders and Instructions that supplemented the relevant delegated legislation could not be used to establish that interferences had been 'in accordance with law'. In *Autronic v Switzerland*,[16] the Court allowed that the horrendously complicated regime which regulated international broadcasting was sufficiently accessible to those whose activities as broadcasters were regulated by it, with proper advice. The same is true about the common law, the true purport of which is available only through the medium of legal advice.[17]

The meaning of 'sufficient precision' is more difficult to ascertain. Wholly general, unfettered discretion will not satisfy the Convention, no matter what the formal validity of the delegating rule, the more particularly if the exercise of the delegated powers may be secret. Good examples of this are the judgments of the Court in *Kruslin v France*[18] and *Huvig v France*.[19] The

---

11 As to Article 5, see above, pp 105-106. See also *Council of Civil Service Unions v UK No 11603/85*, 50 DR 228 at 240-242 ('lawful' in Article 11(2)).

12 A 30 para 49 (1979).

13 *Silver v UK* A 61 paras 87-88 (1983).

14 *Sunday Times v UK* A 30 (1979) and *Markt intern Verlag v FRG* A 165 para 30 (1989) ('commercial operators and their advisers').

15 A 61 paras 87-88, 91 (1983).

16 A 178 paras 55, 59 (1990).

17 The Court accepts that there may be a wide division of opinion about what the common law is without that resulting in inaccessibility of the law but that wholly new developments in the common law may not satisfy the test, see below pp 288-289. Cf also the similar problem under Article 7, above, p 279.

18 A 176-A (1990).

19 A 176-B (1990).

Court accepted that there was in French law a legal basis for secret telephone tapping by the police to be found in Articles 81, 151 and 152 of the Code of Criminal Procedure and the case-law interpreting them.[20] However, the Court was not satisfied with the 'quality' of the French law. In the *Kruslin* case,[1] the Court said:

> 'Tapping and other forms of interception of telephone conversations represent a serious interference with private life and must accordingly be based on a "law" that is particularly precise. It is essential to have clear, detailed rules on the subject, especially as the technology available for use is continually becoming more sophisticated.'

The government argued that subsequent case-law and reasonable 'extrapolation' from the interpretation by the French courts of other, analogous provisions provided sufficient assurance against oppressive use of the interception powers, even in the absence of specific language in the Code of Criminal Procedure. The Court was not satisfied with this. Amongst other deficiencies, the law neither identified the persons whose telephones might be tapped nor imposed any limits of time during which the process could be carried out. Because the French law lacked the quality of 'law' in the Convention sense, the interference with the applicants' rights had not been in accordance with Article 8(2).[2] The test, the Court had said in *Silver v UK*,[3] was that where a law conferred a discretion, it must also indicate with sufficient clarity the limits of that discretion.

Other factors may serve to relax the degree of precision which is required of a national law. In *Müller v Switzerland*,[4] the Court acknowledged that obscenity laws could not be framed with 'absolute precision', not least because of the need to keep the law in accord with the prevailing views of society. It has taken a similar position about laws protecting against restraint of trade.[5] The meaning of widely drawn legal texts and rules of common law may be worked out and developed by courts without affecting their quality as 'law'. None the less, there is a limit to this process. In *Sunday Times v UK*,[6] the applicants argued that the House of Lords had introduced a novel principle into the English common law of contempt, which they could not have anticipated and, accordingly, could not have based their conduct upon. The Court rejected this claim and held:

---

20 *Kruslin* case, loc cit at p 287, n 18, above, paras 15-22.
1 Id, para 33.
2 Id, para 36.
3 A 61 para 80 (1983). See also *Leander v Sweden* A 116 paras 50-57 (1987).
4 A 133 para 29 (1988). Even here there must be some indication of what is comprehended by the law: it would not do to replicate Justice Stewart's famous dictum that, while he could not define obscenity, he knew it when he saw it!: *Jacobellis v Ohio* 378 US 184 (1964).
5 *Barthold v FRG* A 90 para 47 (1985). See also *Markt intern Verlag v FRG* A 165 para 30 (1989).
6 A 30 para 52 (1979). See also *Observer and Guardian v UK* A 216 para 53 (1991). Cf *Kruslin v France*, at p 287, n 18, above.

'. . . the applicants were able to foresee, to a degree that was reasonable in the circumstances, a risk that publication of the draft article might fall foul of the principle.'

The line between the reasonably foreseeable and the wholly novel is not an easy one to draw. In *Harman v UK*,[7] the Commission declared admissible an application in which it was argued that the English courts had introduced a wholly new category of contempt – a solicitor passing to a third party documents obtained by discovery but subsequently read out in court.[8] The case was settled, so no judgment on the merits was reached. The difficulties of the foreseeability test can be further illustrated by reference to *Open Door and Dublin Well Women Centre v Ireland*. Injunctions against the applicants had been issued by the national court forbidding them from circulating in Ireland information about the possibility of abortion outside Ireland. The injunctions had been issued to enforce a Constitutional Amendment which provided:

'The State acknowledges the right to life of the unborn and, with due regard to the equal right to life of the mother, guarantees in its laws to respect, and, as far as practicable, by its laws to defend and vindicate that right.'

The applicants argued that the language of the Amendment did not clearly reach their activities and that it was in any case unforeseeable that the courts would issue injunctions to prevent the commission of constitutional torts. A majority of the Commission took the view that the 'prescribed by law' requirement had been infringed because a lawyer could reasonably have concluded that no illegal act was being committed, particularly because there had been no previous attempts to take enforcement action since the passing of the Amendment. It said that 'in such a vital area' the law requires 'particular precision'.[9] Although the Court conceded that these arguments were not without their cogency, it took the view that in the light of the very high threshold of protection given to the unborn in Irish law, it was foreseeable that the courts would use their powers against the applicants, a conclusion reinforced by legal advice given to one of the applicants to that effect.[10]

ii. Legitimate aims

A defendant state must identify the objective(s) of its interference with an individual's protected right. It often identifies more than one. Applicants

7 *No 10038/82*, 38 DR 53 (1984); 46 DR 57 (1986) F Sett.
8 *Harman v Secretary of State for Home Dept* [1983] 1 AC 280, HL.
9 *Open Door and Dublin Well Woman Centre v Ireland* A 246 (1992) Com Rep para 52.
10 Id, Ct Jmt para 60.

have frequently challenged the aims asserted by the state as being no more than rationalisations of limitations imposed for quite different and impermissible purposes.[11] However, the breadth of most of the grounds for interference is so wide – for example, 'the protection of public order', 'the interests of national security', 'the prevention of disorder or crime'[12] – that the state can usually make a plausible case that it did have a good reason for interfering with the right. The applicant's claim is thus essentially that the reason given is not the 'real' reason, an allegation tantamount to bad faith on the part of the government. Not surprisingly, the Strasbourg authorities have not been willing to accept such a claim easily. Identification of the aim will be of importance, because an interference which might be appropriate to one aim will not necessarily be appropriate to another. There have been cases where the Court has not pursued this matter as vigorously as it might.[13] States sometimes cite more than one aim as the purpose for which they limit the enjoyment of a right. If the Court is satisfied that the measures are necessary for the protection of one of these aims, it has no need to go on and consider the others pleaded by the state, the absence of a violation having already been established. But if the Court is not convinced that the restriction is justified for one of the claimed purposes, it should go on and see if it may be justified for another. In the *Open Door* case,[14] the Court collapsed the alternative aims cited by the state – the protection of morals and the protection of the rights of others – into one enquiry: were the restrictions on the giving of advice about abortion necessary for the protection of morals? Although it found that the restrictions could properly be seen on the facts of the case as being for the protection of morals, it found a breach of Article 10 because they were disproportionate and hence not 'necessary'. Although this approach enabled the Court to avoid a difficult issue – was the unborn an 'other' whose rights the state could protect? – it may be doubted whether the Court did full justice to the government's arguments.

iii. 'Necessary in a democratic society': the margin of appreciation[15]

It is not enough that a state has *some* reason for interfering with an individual's right under Articles 8(2)-11(2) for one of the appropriate aims. It must show that the interference is 'necessary in a democratic society', a

---

11 Eg *Campbell v UK* A 233 paras 39-41 (1993), where the applicant prisoner alleged that the real reason for opening letters to him from his lawyer was to discover their contents. The Court accepted the government's claim that the interference was 'for the prevention of disorder or crime'.

12 In *Groppera Radio AG v Switzerland* A 173 para 70 (1990) and *Autronic v Switzerland* A 178 para 59 (1990) the Court accepted that prevention of disorder in the telecommunications regime was a legitimate aim within Article 10(2).

13 *Barfod v Denmark* A 149 paras 30-36 (1989) and *Observer and Guardian v UK* A 216 paras 55-56, 69 (1991).

14 A 246 para 67 (1992).

15 On the margin of appreciation doctrine, see the literature cited above, p 12, n 18.

phrase heavy with uncertainty. In *Handyside v UK*,[16] the Court explained the meaning of 'necessary' as follows:

'The Court notes . . . that, while the adjective "necessary" . . . is not synonymous with "indispensable", neither has it the flexibility of such expressions as "admissible", "ordinary", "useful", "reasonable" or "desirable".'

Having thus excluded excessively strict or generous interpretations of the term 'necessary', the Court has since settled upon a requirement of proportionality. In *Olsson v Sweden*,[17] it stated:

'According to the Court's established case-law, the notion of necessity implies that an interference corresponds to a pressing social need and, in particular, that it is proportionate to the legitimate aim pursued.'

In assessing whether an interference is 'proportionate to the legitimate aim' to which the government claims that it responds, the Court and Commission have relied on the principle of the 'margin of appreciation', which they concede to states when their institutions make the initial assessment of whether the interference is justified. In *Handyside v UK*[18] the Court stated:

'By reason of their direct and continuous contact with the vital forces of their countries, state authorities are in principle in a better position than the international judge to give an opinion on the . . . "necessity" of a "restriction" or "penalty" . . . it is for the national authorities to make the initial assessment of the reality of the pressing social need implied by the notion of "necessity" in this context.

Consequently, Article 10(2) leaves to the contracting states a margin of appreciation. This margin is given both to the domestic legislator ("prescribed by law") and to the bodies, judicial amongst others, that are called upon to interpret and apply the laws in force.

Nevertheless, Article 10(2) does not give the contracting states an unlimited power of appreciation. The Court, which, with the Commission is responsible for ensuring the observance of those states' engagements, is empowered to give the final ruling on whether a "restriction" or "penalty" is reconcilable with freedom of expression . . . The domestic margin of appreciation thus goes hand in hand with a European supervision. Such supervision concerns both the aim of the measure challenged and its "necessity"; it covers not only the basic legislation but also the decision applying it, even one given by an independent court.'

16 A 24 para 48.
17 A 130 para 67 (1988).
18 A 24 paras 48-49 (1976). Cf *Sunday Times v UK* A 30 para 59 (1979). Both of these are Article 10 cases; the Court's pronouncements apply to Articles 8-11 generally.

In principle, the doctrine of a 'margin of appreciation' , which applies in other areas of the Convention too,[19] is not a doctrine of judicial deference to the national decision, for the Convention authorities carry out their own fact-finding and apply the Convention law for themselves. Yet they have declined the role of a fully-fledged appeal mechanism from the national decision. Instead, the Court has said that the role of the Convention in protecting human rights is 'subsidiary' to the roles of the national legal systems.[20] This allows for a diversity of systems for the protection of human rights and even for different conceptions of the rights themselves and acknowledges the superiority of the organs of a state in fact-finding and in the assessment of what the local circumstances demand by way of limitation of rights.[1] However, the danger that excessive respect for national decision-making will result in the swamping of the individual right by national determinations of the public interest is apparent.

The question then is how the Convention organs are to preserve the quality of rights as worthy of special protection. As noted, the answer that the Court has given is that the idea of necessity implies that a state should demonstrate a 'pressing social need' that the right should be interfered with in the particular public interest identified by the state. In *Handyside v UK*,[2] the Court indicated that while the initial assessment was for the national authorities, it was its duty to review the national decision:

> 'in the light of the case as a whole [including the facts] and the arguments and evidence adduced by the applicant in the domestic legal system and then at the international level. The Court must decide, on the basis of the different data available to it, whether the reasons given by the national authorities to justify the actual measures of "interference" they take are relevant and sufficient . . .'

This was in answer to the government's claim that the review function of the Court was restricted to examining whether the authorities had acted in good faith in assessing what the Convention allowed. Good faith, even the good faith of an independent decision-maker like a court, will not be sufficient of itself.[3]

Putting the burden on the government to demonstrate a pressing social need for the interference preserves the superior character of the protected rights. On the other hand, it introduces a new dilemma for the Court: how is it to make its decisions in a principled manner so that its judgments do not appear to the states as the substitute of one discretion for another? The language of the Convention is so broad that the text alone will seldom dictate solutions, though it should be noticed that there are minor differences in the way Articles 8(2)-10(2) are drafted which allows

19 See above, pp 12-15.
20 *Handyside v UK* A 24 para 48 (1976).
1 *Müller v Switzerland* A 133 para 35 (1988).
2 A 24 para 50 (1976).
3 *Sunday Times v UK* A 30 para 59 (1979).

differences of approach to particular questions.[4] The Court has adopted a variety of principles to give some structure to its judgments in which it considers the exercise of the margin of appreciation by states. While they supplement the general language of the Convention, it is important not to ascribe to them too great a weight: they are not rules and must be applied as a whole to each case with which the Court is faced.[5]

a. The importance of the protected right

The Court has identified some rights or some aspects of some rights as being of more importance than others. For instance, in *Dudgeon v UK*,[6] which concerned the criminality of private, consensual, adult homosexual activity, the Court said:

'The present case concerns a most intimate aspect of private life. Accordingly, there must exist particularly serious reasons before interferences on the part of public authorities can be legitimate for the purposes of [Article 8(2)].'

In *Lingens v Austria*,[7] the Court stressed the freedom of the press as a particularly significant aspect of the 'right to receive and impart information and ideas. . .'. In *Campbell v UK*,[8] the Court confirmed a line of authorities which determined that a prisoner's correspondence with his legal adviser was of such importance as to entitle it to greater protection against interference than his correspondence in general. Where a strong right is invoked by the applicant, there will be a demanding burden on the state to demonstrate the pressing social need for limiting his enjoyment of it.

b. The character of 'democratic society'[9]

While an interference with a protected right must be 'necessary in a democratic society', the nature of democratic society may be a constraint on

---

4   The language of Article 10(2) is more open-ended in ascribing powers to the state to interference with the protected right than the other provisions – Article 8(2) 'There shall be no interference . . . *except such as is* . . .', Article 9(2) 'Freedom to manifest one's religion . . . shall be subject *only* to such limitations . . .', Article 11(2) 'No restrictions shall be placed on the exercise of these rights *other than* . . .' (emphasis added).

5   See Delmas-Marty, in Delmas-Marty, ed, *The European Convention for the Protection of Human Rights: International Protection Versus National Restrictions*, 1992, p 319. Macdonald, *European System*, Ch 6 at pp 123-124, states that 'the justification of the margin of appreciation is usually a pragmatic one', but argues that the maturing of the Convention system requires the Court to articulate 'the underlying reasons why a particular amount of deference is considered proper'.

6   A 45 para 52 (1981).

7   A 103 para 42 (1986).

8   A 233 paras 46-47 (1992).

9   See Jacot-Guillarmod, in *Democracy and Human Rights*, Thessaloniki Colloquy Proc, 1990, pp 43-66, especially pp 57-63.

the justification of some forms of interference. Again in *Dudgeon v UK*,[10] the Court spoke of 'tolerance and broad-mindedness' as two of the 'hallmarks' of democratic society, characteristics which inclined against the justifiability of interferences to protect the intolerance and narrowmindedness of others, however widely and strongly felt. The importance of political expression derives from its role in a properly functioning democracy.[11] In *Klass v FRG*,[12] the Court referred to the dangers of destroying democracy under the guise of trying to preserve it, so requiring the strictest supervision of the justification for interferences with rights which removed the normal protections of the law against abuses of power by the authorities. Freedom of association, particularly for trade unions and professional bodies, was likewise important to democratic societies to protect plural centres of power and influence,[13] though it has to be said that the Court has not given strong protection to the claims by trade unions to enjoy particular rights. These foundational features of the Court's conception of democratic society reinforce the special weight to be given to individual rights when assessing the legitimacy of an interference with a particular right. There have been hints in the practice of the Commission that the exercise of rights in the context of the Convention's own guarantee of democracy, Article 3 of the First Protocol, might also be worth stronger protection against limitation.[14]

c.   The European consensus

There might be little objection to the features isolated by the Court as characteristic of democratic society. However, that is in part because of their generality. If more precise guidance is to be obtained as to what is or is not necessary in a democratic society to interfere with protected rights, then the Court needs to look elsewhere for evidence one way or the other if it is not to be accused of simply substituting its judgment for the judgment of the state. One of the devices to which it has had recourse is to search for a 'European standard' among the national laws of the parties to the Convention.[15] It is an approach which requires some caution. Unless the case is particularly stark, the comparative investigation is likely to be complicated.[16] None the less, a European-wide standard of toleration may sometimes be established[17] and the burden on the state to justify its exceptional interference contrary to the

---

10 A 45 para 53 (1981).
11 *Barthold v FRG* A 90 para 58 (1985).
12 A 28 para 42 (1978).
13 *Le Compte, Van Leuven De Meyere v Belgium* A 43 para 65 (1981).
14 See *X v UK No 4515/70*, 38 CD 86 (1971).
15 See Macdonald, *European System*, Ch 6 at p 103.
16 Cf the search for a European standard against the criminalisation of adult homosexuality in *Dudgeon v UK* A 45 para 60 (1981) and that for the age of consent to homosexual activities, *Zukrigl v Austria No 17279/90* (1993), unreported.
17 The finding in the *Dudgeon* case, ibid, was confirmed in *Norris v Ireland* A 142 para 46 (1988).

consensus is increased.[18] This may be particularly useful where a developing consensus indicates a clear trend to isolate the state maintaining an interference, the unacceptability of which has gradually become recognised elsewhere. An example of this is *Marckx v Belgium*[19] where the Court found that the great majority of the Council of Europe states acknowledged the impermissibility of discrimination between the legitimate child and the illegitimate child in the law of affiliation. In the cases dealing with the criminalisation of male homosexuality, the Court has reinforced its findings that such an interference with an individual's right to respect for his private life may not be justified by noting 'the marked changes' in the laws of national states.[20] In *Modinos v Cyprus*,[1] the government sought to justify its law which criminalised homosexual behaviour in proceedings before the Commission, which found against it on the basis of an established European consensus. The government did not argue justification before the Court.

The establishment of the existence of a European consensus is not an arithmetical exercise of simply adding up the number of states participating in the practice, a certain number being sufficient to establish the threshold. The Strasbourg authorities have been criticised for not developing a more scientific concept of what the consensus consists.[2] Sometimes, the Court is presented with evidence of a consensus but finds no need to rely on it. In *Lingens v Austria*,[3] the Court relied on the disproportionality of an interference rather than on the extensive comparative evidence of its incompatibility with a consensus, presented by an intervenor.[4] Demonstrating a consensus may not be sufficient to establish the unjustifiability of the interference. In *Handyside v UK*,[5] the applicant argued that the book which had been condemned in England had circulated freely in the majority of member states of the Council of Europe. So, he said, it could not be necessary in a democratic society to ban it. The conclusion of the Court that, none the less, banning it in part of England was not a breach of Article 10 is not explicated. Judge Mosler dissented on this point, indicating that since it had not been found necessary to prohibit the circulation throughout the whole of the UK, it could hardly be necessary to forbid it in only a part of England – at least not without much stronger justification than was provided.[6] It is, therefore, open to a state to argue that, notwithstanding an

---

18 In the *Norris* case, ibid, the Court said: 'Yet the government have adduced no evidence which would point to the existence of factors justifying the retention of impinged laws which are *additional to or are of greater weight* than those present in the aforementioned *Dudgeon* case.' (Emphasis added.)
19 A 31 para 41 (1979).
20 See the *Dudgeon* and *Norris* cases, above.
1　A 259 (1993) Com Rep para 45.
2　See Helfer, 26 Corn ILJ 133 at 138-140 (1993). See also pp 9-11, above.
3　A 103 paras 43-47 (1986).
4　Written comments submitted by Interrights on behalf of the International Press Institute, Corr (85) 114.
5　A 24 paras 54-57 (1976).
6　In *Dudgeon v UK* A 45 paras 56-61 (1981) the majority of the Court did not accept the government's argument that different standards on so important an issue as the criminalisation of homosexual activity might apply in Northern Ireland and England and Wales.

established European consensus against the interference, there are reasons particular to its democratic society which are sufficiently strong to justify limiting an individual's rights there.

Being able to rely on a consensus among the laws of the European states is especially valuable to the Court if it is confronted with a fundamental moral issue where a solution favouring one outcome over another will appear to the disappointed side to depend entirely on the premise from which the argument starts – abortion, euthanasia, recreational use of drugs, homosexuality are among the questions of this kind. The Strasbourg authorities have shown themselves adept at avoiding taking them head-on. However, they cannot always be side-stepped. *Marckx v Belgium*, dealing with illegitimacy, and the *Dudgeon-Norris* cases, concerning adult homosexual relations, are examples where the Court has been able to rely on the consensus. To the contrary, where there is no consensus, the Court is the more likely to defer to the choice made by the state, unless there is a textual basis on which the Court may rely. The Court has largely conceded the powers of the state to regulate transsexuality in the absence of a widely received European resolution of these matters[7] and relied on a textual basis to find for the compatibility of Ireland's law excluding divorce, even in the face of a European standard to the contrary.[8]

d.   The interest to be protected by the interference

THE WEIGHT OF THE INTEREST

The reason for some interferences with rights is to protect the enjoyment of other rights protected by the Convention. Freedom of expression may be limited in favour of the right to a fair trial[9] or to take into account the right of others to exercise their freedom of religion.[10] In these cases, the interest which is sought to be protected is a strong one and usually an accommodation must be reached between the two competing rights, when the initial assessment by the state of how that accommodation should be made will carry great weight. The fact that the protection of a countervailing right is the object of the state's interference is relevant to the application of the general principle that limitation powers should be construed narrowly, but the state must take care not to give one of the rights total priority over the other.[11] Only if one of the rights is 'absolute' will it take complete

---

7   See below pp 324-325.
8   *Johnston v Ireland* A 112 paras 51-54 (1986).
9   *Observer and Guardian Newspapers v UK* A 216 (1991).
10 *Otto-Preminger-Institut v Austria* A 295-A para 47 (1994).
11 One of the weaknesses of the government's case in *Sunday Times v UK* A 30 para 65 (1979) was that the House of Lords' judgment gave practically no weight to the applicants' right to freedom of expression against the interest sought to be protected, the administration of justice. Ironically, the only reference the European Court made to Article 6 was to narrow the margin of appreciation of the state: see para 59.

priority over another right, subject to limitations, expressly or impliedly in the text.[12]

If even some interferences in the interest of protecting fundamental rights may not always be within the margin of appreciation, then it would follow that no other of the interests set out in the second paragraphs of Articles 8-11 are of overwhelming weight, for, if that were the case, the rights protected by the Convention would lose their fundamental status. Finally, it should be noted that it is not so much the denominated interest but the actual situation in which it is invoked which is important[13] – action for the prevention of crime may be directed against homicide or parking offences: the weight of each compared with the right sought to be limited is not the same.

THE OBJECTIVITY OF THE INTEREST

In *Sunday Times v UK*,[14] the Court suggested that the greater the prospect of obtaining an objective understanding of the content of the interest sought to be protected, the narrower the state's margin to determine what interferences are necessary to protect it. The Court drew a contrast between the relative objectivity of 'maintaining the authority and impartiality of the judiciary' and the 'protection of morals'. The former, objectively ascertainable, left a narrower margin to the state than the latter which was subject to a wide notion of what 'morals' were and, therefore, what was necessary to protect them. The actual example chosen by the Court has been challenged[15] but the principle seems well-established. It has been made to carry considerable weight in upholding limitations of individual rights. *Müller v Switzerland*[16] is an example. The Court held that the idea of 'morals' might be determined by the opinions within even a narrow locality, let alone from state to state. However, it has not gone so far as accepting states' claims that questions of morals are so subjective that the Court should simply defer to their conclusions. The Court's jurisprudence on the standard of objectivity is weak. It has easily found ways of avoiding its consequences if it deems it desirable to do so.[17] The Court shows no inclination to abandon reliance on the objectivity standard as an indication of the reach of the margin of appreciation with respect to different aims of interferences.[18] There are doubts though whether it adds anything to the calculations to be made about the necessity of interferences with protected rights.

12 Eg a state would have a duty, let alone a right, to interfere with a religious practice which constituted inhuman or degrading treatment.
13 *Handyside v UK* A 24 para 50 (1976).
14 A 30 para 59 (1979): 'The domestic law and practice of the contracting states reveal a fairly substantial measure of common ground in this area.'
15 *Weber v Switzerland* A 177 (1990), Swiss government, verbatim record, 23 Jan 1990, p 35.
16 A 133 paras 35-36 (1988).
17 In the homosexuality cases, above, p 294, nn 16, 17, the Court struck down serious interferences with rights which it regarded as of high importance even though the states claimed to be acting to protect morals and brought evidence that the relevant prevailing moral climate was opposed to the toleration of private homosexual activity.
18 *Otto-Preminger-Institut v Austria* A 295-A para 50 (1994).

THE JUSTICIABILITY OF THE INTEREST

In the *Greek* case,[19] the Commission rejected the argument that the assessment of the existence of an emergency within the terms of Article 15 was beyond its competence on grounds of non-justiciability. Given the difficulty and the sensitivity of the issue with which the Commission was faced, it is hard to see why, in principle, the assessment of whether there is evidence that any of the interests listed in Articles 8(2)-11(2) is in jeopardy is also not appropriate for the Strasbourg authorities. Even when action is taken 'in the interests of national security', they may insist that the state produce some evidence that there is a national security interest to be protected by the interference.[20] The mere assertion of a national security interest is not sufficient.[1]

There are, however, two kinds of fact-finding and assessment involved. The first relates to the facts of the particular case, for example, what was the content of a proscribed publication and could access to it plausibly threaten moral standards?[2] The second is what is sometimes called 'constitutional fact-finding', ie establishing the factual accuracy of general claims about the protected interest, for example, that the perpetual or long-term confidentiality of security information as a whole is necessary to protect the integrity of the security services and the efficacy of its operations.[3] Some of the questions which arise in the context of constitutional fact-finding are more intractable than others. They are questions which may arise about *any* protected interest, for example, whether the circulation of sexually explicit material has an impact on conduct, such that restrictions may be placed upon it to prevent crime or protect others, or whether immigration of aliens permitted in the exercise of the right to respect for family life may be limited because of the impact of such immigrants on the labour market and, hence, in the 'interests of . . . the economic well-being of the country'. In controversial matters, the Commission, especially, has been willing to accept the claims of defendant governments based on only scant evidence and not to engage in extensive constitutional fact-finding of its own.[4] The margin of appreciation here operates substantially in favour of the state.

---

19 12 YB (the *Greek* case) 1 at 72 (1969); CM Res DH (70) 1. See below p 494.
20 *Observer and Guardian v UK* A 216 para 69 (1991).
1   In *Observer and Guardian*, Judge Walsh, dissenting, para 4, suggested that the threat to national security was 'simply . . . an expression of opinion' and, therefore, inadequate to allow the state to rely on Article 10(2).
2   See eg *Müller v Switzerland* A 133 para 36 (1988) where the inclusion of a description of the painting in the judgment, para 16, was insisted upon by the government and the Court sustained the state's assessment of the need to punish the artist for the protection of morals for exhibiting the painting.
3   *Observer and Guardian v UK* A 216 paras 66-70 (1991).
4   Eg homosexual age of consent cases based on assertions of predatory promiscuity: *X v FRG No 5935/72*, 3 DR 46 at 55-56 (1975). In *X v UK No 7215/75*, 19 DR 66 at 75-78 (1978) Com Rep; CM Res DH (79) 5, the Commission considered the matter on the merits but deferred to the government's fact-finding.

THE SIGNIFICANCE OF THE INTERFERENCE

While some interferences are of themselves more significant than others – a term of imprisonment rather than a fine, prior censorship rather than post-publication punishment – in other cases, the significance of the interference may be closely related to the particular facts. The forfeiture orders of the Little Red School Book in *Handyside v UK*[5] were of less significance to a publisher who could reproduce the publication elsewhere and modify it for publication in England than the forfeiture order of his paintings against the artist in *Müller v Switzerland.*[6] The weight of the interference, then, must be assessed by considering its effects in the circumstances of the particular application, conceding though that some interferences will have a great impact, whatever the situation. In *Dudgeon v UK*[7] and the other homosexuality cases, the Court put some weight on the criminalisation of the applicants' private activities as an indication of the excessiveness of the interference. In *Observer and Guardian v UK*,[8] while rejecting the argument that Article 10 implied a complete proscription against prior censorship, the Court acknowledged that such an interference with freedom of expression called for 'the most careful scrutiny', especially for news media 'for news is a perishable commodity'.

e. The resolution of the conflict between the different factors

THE GENERAL APPROACH

It will be appreciated now that the inquiry into the exercise of a State's margin of appreciation may be complex, involving a variety of factors, not merely a simple balance between the rights of the individual and the interests of the State, however convenient it might be to express it in these terms. The explanation of how the Court resolves the various forces is complicated by a difference between its rhetoric and practice in some judgments. The basic principle remains that explicated in the *Handyside* case,[9] that the word 'necessary' means neither 'indispensable' at the strict end nor 'reasonable' at the lenient end, so far as the state is concerned. What is 'necessary' in a particular case will fall along a spectrum between those two extremes and it is better to understand the Court's approach as being a multifaceted one, rather than try to demarcate its decisions into groups of 'strict scrutiny'/ 'rational basis' or other categories, on the American constitutional model.[10] If, after treating all the appropriate factors considered already, the Court finds that the interference might conceivably have been 'necessary in a democratic society', it reaches the final resolution of forces by asking

5   A 26 paras 19, 22-23 (1976).
6   A 133 para 17 (1988).
7   A 48 paras 49, 60 (1981).
8   A 216 para 60 (1991).
9   A 24 para 48 (1976).
10 See Gunter, 86 Harv LR 1 (1972).

whether the restriction of the applicant's rights was 'proportionate' to the interest sought to be protected.[11]

ASSESSING PROPORTIONALITY[12]

Proportionality, it should be underlined, is the final factor the Strasbourg authorities take into account in determining whether an interference with a right is necessary. The practice of the Court has isolated various factors which are to be taken into account in determining the proportionality issue.

While the balance of factors in a close case may be difficult and, therefore, incline the Court to accept the balance struck by the state, manifest disproportionality will result in the Court finding that the measure of limitation is not necessary. An example of this may be seen in *Campbell v UK*[13] where the government claimed the right to open and inspect in-coming mail to prisoners from the European Commission to guard against the possibility that the Commission's envelopes might have been forged. The Court took the view that the eventuality was far-fetched and held the interference with the prisoner's right of correspondence unnecessary. Another way in which a lack of proportionality may be demonstrated is where there is an alternative, less intrusive way of protecting the public interest. The *Campbell* case also provides an example of this. The Court rejected a blanket right of the authorities to open and read a prisoner's letters to his legal advisers where they suspected that the letters contained illicit enclosures. The Court conceded only that a narrower rule, allowing inspection only on reasonable suspicion, with guarantees to the prisoner against abuse, such as opening letters in his presence, would satisfy the test of necessity.[14] In *Marckx v Belgium*,[15] though in a slightly different context, the Court pointed out that where there were alternative ways in which social policies might be pursued, the state was not entitled to choose a way which violated an individual's rights.

Interference with an individual's rights is disproportionate where it is purposeless, that is, where the object cannot be achieved by the interference. It is not necessary to interfere with freedom of expression on grounds of protecting confidential information where the confidence has been lost because of its publication elsewhere.[16] The proportionality requirement is not satisfied where the government does not provide evidence to show that the claim of necessity was made out. In *Kokkinakis v Greece*,[17] the government claimed the right to interfere with the applicant's right to religion

---

11 *Sunday Times v UK* A 30 para 67 (1979).
12 On the principle of proportionality, see Eissen, *European System*, Ch 7. See also pp 11-12, above.
13 A 233 para 62 (1993).
14 Id, para 48.
15 A 31 para 40 (1979).
16 *Weber v Switzerland* A 177 para 51 (1990) and *Observer and Guardian v UK* A 216 para 68 (1991).
17 A 260-A para 49 (1993).

because he had been attempting to convert others by 'improper means'. The Court held that because no evidence was presented to show that what he had done fell within 'improper means', the interference was not necessary.

Questions of proportionality involve some element of balancing one factor against another but it is not a scientific process, despite the metaphor. A state will be in a stronger position if the domestic institutions have themselves addressed the issue of proportionality of the interference with the applicant's right but, because of its ultimate responsibility, the Court will review, and may differ from, the results of even the most careful domestic scrutiny.[18]

4. CONCLUSION

Cases alleging violations of Articles 8-11 will raise a variety of questions to be disposed of for their determination. In general, the Court has adopted the practice of taking each item in an application successively, no matter how simple some of them may be. The stages are:

1. the identification of the right, including positive aspects of the right;
2. the identification of the interference;
3. consideration of whether the interference is prescribed by law, including both the internal and external (Convention) understanding of 'law';
4. determining what objectives are sought to be protected by the interference; and
5. deciding whether the interference is 'necessary in a democratic society', ie whether the state gives, and gives evidence for, relevant and sufficient reasons for the interference and those reasons are proportionate to the limitation of the applicant's enjoyment of his right, in which connection the margin of appreciation is most important.

While the Court has often used the same language in its judgments to explain what each of these various stages involves, the precedential value of previous judgments must be assessed against the changing social, technical and economic conditions as reflected in national laws and decisions. In carrying on its task, the Court is conscious of its 'subsidiary' role, recognising the quasi-federal nature of the Convention regime. The states may adopt a variety of solutions to similar problems and all or several of them may be compatible with the Convention.[19] The result is that the processes of arguing and deciding cases brought under these articles is seldom simple and the outcome is difficult to anticipate.[20]

18 See, eg *Beldjoudi v France* A 234-A (1992).
19 Frowein, 1-2 AEL 267 at 337-349 (1990) and Warbrick, 10 Mich JIL 698 (1989).
20 Macdonald, *European System*, Ch 6 at pp 160-161.

CHAPTER 9

Article 8: The right to respect for private and family life, home and correspondence

'**Article 8**
1. Everyone has the right to respect for his private and family life, his home and his correspondence.
2. There shall be no interference by a public authority with the exercise of this right except such as in accordance with the law and is necessary in a democratic society in the interests of national security, public safety or the economic well-being of the country, for the prevention of disorder or crime, for the protection of health or morals, or for the protection of the rights and freedoms of others.'

1. INTRODUCTION

Article 8 places on states the obligation to respect a wide range of personal interests. Those interests – 'private and family life, home and correspondence' – embrace a variety of matters, some of which are connected with one another, some of which overlap with others. In *Kroon v Netherlands*,[1] the Court stated that the 'essential object' of Article 8 was:

'. . . to protect the individual against arbitrary action by the public authorities. There may in addition be positive obligations inherent in "effective" respect for family life [and the other Article 8(1) values].'

The obligation not to engage in 'arbitrary action' is an obligation of the classic negative kind. The 'positive obligations inherent' in Article 8(1) include both those requiring the state to take steps to provide rights or privileges for individuals and those which require it to protect persons against the activities of other private individuals which prevent the effective enjoyment of their rights.[2] The source of these positive obligations is found in the language of Article 8(1). It protects the right '*to respect for*' each of the

1 A 297-C para 31 (1994).
2 See above, pp 284-285.

interests, not the right to private life, etc. If the intention in choosing this formulation, reinforced by the reference in Article 8(2) to 'interferences by a public authority', was to suggest a rather narrow duty not to interfere with the rights in Article 8,[3] the Strasbourg authorities have taken a different view, using the wording 'respect for' as a basis for expanding the duties in Article 8(1).[4] The Court has not perceived the rights in Article 8(1) in wholly negative terms – the right 'to be left alone'. Instead it has acknowledged the part they play in the confident exercise of liberty and, what is more, has found that the states must ensure the effective enjoyment of liberty so understood. The private sphere embracing the interests recognised in Article 8(1) is better understood as the personal rather than the secret.[5] Accordingly, if it is to respect private life (*not* privacy with its rather narrower connotations of the secrecy of information or seclusion), the state must not merely desist from the revelation or surveillance of activities that the individual would rather keep from public view. It must also allow and even facilitate the establishment of open relationships between individuals which make liberty worth having.[6]

None of the four interests referred to in Article 8(1) is entirely self-explanatory in meaning. Each of them is 'autonomous', so the Strasbourg authorities are not constrained by any national interpretation of them. Both the Commission and the Court have avoided laying down general understandings of what each of the items covers and, in some cases, they have utilised the co-terminancy of them to avoid spelling out precisely which is or are implicated when an applicant has invoked more than one of them in his claim that there has been a violation of the Convention.[7] This has allowed them to take advantage of the lack of precision of Article 8(1) to develop the case-law to take into account social and technical developments.[8] The disadvantage is the absence of a theoretical conspectus, which makes an account of the jurisprudence inevitably descriptive and prediction about its likely progress hazardous. Because so many separate issues may be involved in a single application and the margin of appreciation intrudes into the determination of some of them, the outcome of any particular case may not tell us much beyond its own facts. Such generalisations as are advanced in what follows are made cautiously.

As well as overlaps between the interests protected by Article 8(1), there are also connections between Article 8 and other articles of the Convention. Many Article 8 rights are 'civil rights' in the sense of Article 6 and decisions

---

3   For discussion of the preparatory work, see Velu, in Robertson, ed, *Privacy and Human Rights*, 1973, pp 12, 14-18.

4   See Connelly, 35 ICLQ 567 at 570-575 (1986) and Cohen-Jonathan, *European System*, Ch 14 at pp 409-415.

5   Louciades, 62 BYIL 176, especially 192-196 (1991).

6   On the legal concept of privacy, see Feldman, *Civil Liberties and Human Rights in England and Wales*, 1993, pp 353-380, which includes treatment of the Convention. See also Clapham, Ch 4.

7   Eg *Klass v FRG* A 28 para 41 (1978) (telephone conversations a part of 'private life,' 'family life' and 'correspondence').

8   *Rees v UK* A 106 para 47 (1986) and *Marckx v Belgium* A 31 para 40 (1979).

concerning them must be taken by a procedure which satisfies that Article.[9] Also, the effect of Article 8 may be to impose a duty on the state to take measures involving the limitation of another Convention right in order to secure the enjoyment of an Article 8 right. For example, to the extent that Article 8 protects one's reputation as a part of private life,[10] a total failure by the state to provide a remedy to an aggrieved individual would involve the responsibility of the state under Article 8(1). The state could provide some remedy without exceeding its powers under Article 10(2), although a law of defamation too respectful of individual reputations at the expense of freedom of expression will involve a breach of Article 10.[11] Because of this need to balance competing Convention rights, the margin of appreciation conceded to a state where there is a conflict of rights is likely to be wide, the more so because the applicant will be seeking the benefit of a positive obligation of the state.[12]

The following issues may arise within the course of a single application under Article 8:

1. What is the scope of the protected interest (eg what is 'private life')?
2. What is required of the state to 'respect' that interest?

Under Article 8(2):

3. Has there been an interference with the Article 8 right?
4. If there has,
    (a) is it 'in accordance with the law'?
    (b) is it for a legitimate aim?
    (c) is it necessary in a democratic society?

Each of these issues will be treated separately so that it will sometimes be necessary to follow the discussion through subsequent sections to discover the outcome of a particular case.

---

9 Eg *Golder v UK* A 18 (1976) (prisoner's correspondence with lawyer); *Airey v Ireland* A 32 (1979) (access to legal procedure for terminating obligations part of a family life); and *Olsson v Sweden (No 1)* A 130 (1988) (conditions of foster-care of children taken from natural parents).
10 See Velu, loc cit at n 3, above, pp 15-16, 42-43. In *Asociación de Aviadores de la República + Mata v Spain No 10733/84*, 41 DR 211 at 224 (1985), the Commission said that the right to honour and good name are not protected 'as such' by Article 8(1) but the inquiry undertaken by the Commission in *N v Sweden No 11366/85*, 50 DR 173 (1986) indicates that there is some protection for reputation implied in the requirement of respect for private life. See also Van Dijk and Van Hoof, p 369.
11 Eg *Lingens v Austria* A 103 (1986); *Times Newspapers v UK No 14631/89*, 65 DR 307 (1990);and *Tolstoy-Miloslavsky v UK No 18139/91* (1993) Com Rep (pending before the Court).
12 *Winer v UK No 10871/84*, 48 DR 154 at 169-171 (1986) and *N v Sweden No 11366/85*, 50 DR 173 at 175 (1986).

2. THE FOUR INTERESTS PROTECTED BY ARTICLE 8(1)

Because Article 8(1) protects the right to respect for private life, etc, it is necessary to determine first what is the content of each of the interests set out in Article 8(1). It is up to the applicant to characterise the interest which he seeks to protect or advance in the terms of the Commission's and Court's understanding of Article 8(1). A good example of this is *Gaskin v UK*,[13] where the applicant successfully convinced a majority in the Court that his interest in obtaining access to information in the hands of a local authority about his upbringing in public foster-care concerned his private and family life and not some general interest in access to information, which would not be protected by Article 8.

i. Private life

The Commission's practice concerning the meaning of private life has been distinguished neither by its clarity nor its discipline. The Commission has not been careful to distinguish the ambit of private life from the content of the state's obligation to respect private life. Nor has it kept separate the questions whether a state has failed to respect private life in breach of Article 8(1) and whether an interference with a right is justified under Article 8(2).[14]

Similarly, the Court in *Niemietz v Germany* case[15] was unwilling to attempt an exhaustive definition of private life, or even to isolate the values it protects. However, the Court did give some guidance as to the meaning or ambit of 'private life' for the purposes of Article 8 and other aspects of it emerge from the jurisprudence of both the Commission and the Court. In *Niemietz v Germany*,[16] the Court said:

> '. . . it would be too restrictive to limit the notion [of private life] to an "inner circle" in which the individual may live his own personal life as he chooses and to exclude therefrom entirely the outside world not encompassed within that circle. Respect for private life must also comprise to a certain degree the right to establish and develop relationships with other human beings.'

The Court thus endorsed a long practice of the Commission in which it had sought to extend the concept of private life beyond the narrower confines of the Anglo-American idea of privacy, with its emphasis on the secrecy of

---

13 A 160 paras 36-37 (1989).
14 For a particularly glaring example, the more regrettable given the seriousness of what was at stake, see *Bruggemann and Scheuten v FRG No 6959/75*, 10 DR 100 (1977) Com Rep; CM Res DH (78) 1. See Connelly, 35 ICLQ 567 at 586-588 (1986).
15 A 251-B para 29 (1992). Cf D'Oswald-Beck, 4 HRLJ 283 at 183-7 (1983) on earlier practice.
16 A 251-B para 29 (1992).

personal information and seclusion.[17] In *McFeeley v UK*,[18] the Commission underlined the importance of relationships with others, concluding that it applied to prisoners and required a degree of association for persons imprisoned. Freedom to associate with others is thus a further, social feature of private life. In *Niemietz v Germany*[19] the Court was even prepared to consider that some personal relations in business contexts might fall within 'private life'. In *X and Y v Netherlands*,[20] the Court established that 'private life' also covered 'the physical and moral integrity of the person', including, in that case, 'his or her sexual life'. This statement was relied on by the Commission in *Costello-Roberts v UK*,[1] when assessing corporal punishment inflicted on a pupil at a private school by a master. The Court conceded that there might be circumstances where Article 8 provided protection in relation to school discipline but, accepting also the government's view that not every measure which adversely affected an individual's physical or moral integrity necessarily involved an interference with his right to respect for his private life, decided that the punishment complained of here:

> 'did not entail adverse effects for his physical or moral integrity sufficient to bring it within the scope of the prohibition contained in Article 8.'[2]

These widening categories of 'private life', combined with a lack of rigour in classifying cases in practice, make an account of 'private life' difficult. The best that can be done is to identify the categories of interests and activities that the institutions have held to be within the ambit of 'private life'. These categories are not closed[3] and, doubtless, the cases could equally profitably be arranged under different heads.[4]

It must be said also that they hold out a promise of protection of individual interests which ultimately is rarely conceded by the Strasbourg authorities. The margins of appreciation allowed to the states to determine what is required by 'respect' and what interferences are 'necessary in a democratic society' mean that there are substantial burdens for an individual in making out his case successfully in Strasbourg even if he is able to identify his interest as falling within 'private life'.

---

17 *X v Iceland No 6825/74*, 5 DR 86 (1976).
18 *No 8317/78*, 20 DR 44 at 91 (1980).
19 A 251-B para 29 (1992).
20 A 91 para 22 (1985).
1   A 247-C Com Rep para 49 (1993).
2   The Court considered the matter principally under Article 3: see above p 86. See also *X v Belgium No 8707/79*, 18 DR 255 (1979) (regulation in interests of public safety not generally affecting private life (seat-belts)).
3   See Louciades, 62 BYIL 176 at 192 (1991) on the need to keep 'private life' in tune with moral and social developments.
4   For general surveys, see Duffy, 3 YEL 191 (1983); D'Oswald-Beck, 4 HRLJ 283 (1983); Connelly, 35 ICLQ 567 (1986); Louciades, 62 BYIL 176 (1991); Cohen-Jonathan, *European System*, Ch 16.

a. Personal identity

The fundamental interest within the sphere of private life is the capacity of the individual to determine his identity: to decide and then to be what he wants to be. Within the individual's power are matters like his choice of name, his mode of dress and his sexual identity.[5] There is not merely a right to a closet identity; he must be free to choose how he is to be regarded by the state and how to present himself to others.

This is what lies at the root of the transsexual cases. The central question – does the individual or does the state have the right to decide whether a person is male or female? – has not arisen. The cases do not decide what are the limits of the state's obligation to respect the self-identification of a transsexual. However, they do show that the decision lies within the sphere of private life and, furthermore, that the protection extends not just to the choice itself but to the identity by which transsexuals make themselves known to others: it is a right which goes beyond the 'inner circle'.[6]

An example of a case concerning 'private life' in the sense of personal identity from within the 'inner circle' is *Gaskin v UK*.[7] There the majority of the Court acknowledged the applicant's claim that the records of his upbringing in public foster-care were significant to him as part of what he was, as a substitute for the parental memory of children brought up within their own family. Determining whether a putative parent (usually the father) actually is the parent of a child or whether a child actually is the child of a particular adult (as may sometimes occur if a child has been adopted) is also a matter of private life.[8] It is an aspect of establishing the identity of the applicant in the full sense in which it is understood by the Court.

b. Moral or physical integrity

It has already been stated that the Court takes the view that while *some* interferences with the moral or physical integrity of an individual may impinge on the private life of that person, not all such actions will do so. In *Costello-Roberts v UK*,[9] the Court took into account both the relatively slight nature of the punishment and the fact that it had been inflicted in the not wholly personal context of school discipline, where it could readily be foreseen that some measures might be taken which would interfere with a pupil's physical or moral integrity. Both features were crucial to the decision

---

5   On names, see *Burghartz v Switzerland* A 280B (1994), violation in conjunction with Article 14 (the Court, unlike the Commission, did not refer to the applicant as 'Schnyder Burghartz', the very name to which it held him entitled!) and *Stjerna v Finland* 299-B (1994). Note also *Konstandinis v Stadt Altensteigstandsamt* C-168/91, ECtJ [1993] 3 CMLR 401. On prison dress, see *McFeeley v UK No 8317/78*, 20 DR 44 at 91 (1980) and *Sutter v Switzerland No 8209/78*, 16 DR 166 (1979) (haircut).

6   *B v France* A 232 para 62 (1992). As to the 'inner circle', see above, p 305.

7   A 160 paras 36-37 (1989).

8   *Rasmussen v Denmark* A 87 para 33 (1984) and *MB v UK No 22920/93*, 77-A DR 108 at 114-116 (1994).

9   A 247-C para 36 (1993).

because, in general, compulsory physical treatment of an individual will fall within the sphere of private life, however slight the intervention.[10] *X and Y v Netherlands*,[11] which concerned the sexual assault upon a mentally handicapped young woman by a man, shows that an unwelcome physical attack by one individual is capable of infringing the private life of another. Both the *Costello-Roberts* and *X and Y* cases concerned physical assaults of a traditional kind. In *Rayner v UK*,[12] the applicant argued that the intensity and persistence of aircraft noise interfered with his rights to respect for his private life and home. The government maintained that the claim fell outside Article 8(1) altogether but the Commission took the view that it covered,

> 'indirect intrusions which are unavoidable consequences of measures not directed against private individuals'

(the measures here being the operating of major airports), and, it went on,

> 'considerable noise nuisance can undoubtedly affect the physical well-being of a person and thus interfere with his private life.'

The significance of this opinion is that it opens the prospect for environmental claims to be brought within Article 8(1), although there will, of course, be further substantial obstacles to the individual actually making out his claim that an Article 8 right has been violated.[13] A successful claim of this kind was made in *Lopes Ostra v Spain*,[14] where the applicant was able to show that the failure by the state to act to prevent or to protect her from serious pollution damage – fumes from a waste disposal plant dealing with waste from a tannery – did constitute a failure to respect her home and her private and family life.

c.   Private space

When it considered the *Rayner* case and other aircraft noise cases, the Commission regarded the disturbance as potential violations of the Convention because of the physical harm which may be occasioned by severe noise. It is possible to look at the claims in another way, as an aspect of the right to be left alone, to enjoy one's private space free from unwelcome interferences. These interferences may be noisy or visible and apparent or covert. The various wire-tapping cases have proceeded on the assumption that secret surveillance will infringe upon the private life of an

---

10 *X v Austria No 8278/78*, 18 DR 154 at 156 (1979) (bloodtest); *Peters v Netherlands No 21132/93*, 77-A DR 75 (1994)(urine test) .
11 A 91 (1985).
12 *No 9310/81*, 47 DR 5 (1986). See also *Arrondelle v UK No 7889/77*, 26 DR 5 (1982) F Sett and *Baggs v UK No 9310/81*, 52 DR 29 (1987) F Sett.
13 See *Powell and Rayner v UK* A 172 Com Rep (1990).
14 A 303-C (1994). See further, below pp 323, 328.

individual.[15] Usually, of course, other aspects of Article 8(1) will be involved as well, such as 'home' or 'correspondence'. However, private space includes places such as hotel rooms or prison cells which are not 'home', and spying on the activities of an individual which could not be brought within the notion of 'correspondence' may interfere with a person's private life. The reason for this is that it is not enough just for the individual to be himself: he must be able to a substantial degree to keep to himself what he is and what he does, if he wishes to do so. This is the essence of the 'Anglo-Saxon' idea of privacy to which the Commission referred in *X v Iceland*.[16] That an individual should be able to keep to himself what books he reads or what pictures he hangs as part of his private life is hardly controversial. However, the expansion of the idea of private life to include the making and enjoyment of personal relations means that the idea of private space need not be confined to those areas in which the person has some exclusive rights of occupancy where secrecy or confidentiality can be maintained. Do activities in non-public places where the applicant has no such exclusive rights – for example, private beaches or private occasions in churches or restaurants – fall within the sphere of private life? The question whether such places or occasions fall within the sphere of 'private life' is of significance both for the collection of information by the state and for assessing what the state must do to ensure respect for private life against the intrusions of non-official persons like private detectives or the media. Clear guidance on this question, and on the further question whether 'private life' extends to what a person does in public places, is lacking in the Strasbourg jurisprudence. Where the intrusion is slight and foreseeable – being photographed in the street against one's wishes, say – the judgment in the *Costello-Roberts* case would suggest that that is no infringement of private life.[17] This was also the view of the Commission in *Friedl v Austria*,[18] in which it decided that there had been no interference with the applicant's rights under Article 8 by reason of his being photographed by the police during the course of a 'sit-in' as part of a political demonstration. However, the expanding understanding of private life set out in the *Niemietz* case indicates that a formal public/private division about the nature of the location will not always be decisive.

d. Collection and use of information

The collection of information by officials of the state about an individual without his consent will interfere with his right to respect for his private life. This is the case with an official census[19] and with fingerprinting and photography by the police.[20] The collection of medical data and the

---

15 *Klass v Germany* A 28 (1978) and *Malone v UK* A 82 (1984).
16 *No 6825/74*, 5 DR 86 (1976).
17 See D'Oswald-Beck, 4 HRLJ 283 at 293-295 (1983).
18 A 305-B (1994) Com Rep paras 48 and 51 F Sett.
19 *X v UK No 9702/82*, 30 DR 239 (1982).
20 *Murray v UK* A 300 paras 84, 85 (1994) and *McVeigh v UK No 8022/77*, 25 DR 15 at 49 (1981); CM Res DH (82) 1.

maintenance of medical records falls within the sphere of private life.[1] In *Hilton v UK*,[2] the Commission said that a security check *per se* did not interfere with respect for private life, but that it might do so if it involved the collection of information about a person's private affairs. This position is sustainable only if it takes account of the widening concept of private life as it is being developed by the Court.[3] It is more obviously so where the information is gained surreptitiously by telephone-tapping or reading a person's mail. There may be strong reasons why the authorities want to conduct covert surveillance but, equally, such powers are easily open to abuse. The Court has required that powers of secret surveillance be accompanied by appropriate safeguards.[4] However, as will be seen, since some secret surveillance may be justified under the Convention even though the individual is never informed about it, there is no invariable right of a person to know that information about him has been collected and retained.[5]

The obligation of the state to respect private life by controlling the intrusive activities of its agents and officials ought to extend also to similar operations by private persons, such as private detectives or newspaper reporters.[6] The precise content of the positive obligation here involved is subject to a wide margin of appreciation on the part of the state and, for the press at least, may involve consideration of other Convention rights, particularly freedom of expression.[7]

Interference with an individual's Article 8(1) right by collecting information about him will need to be justified under Article 8(2). The mere fact that the collection of information might be justified does not inevitably mean that its retention or use will be equally defensible. Thus

---

1   *Chare née Jullien v France No 14461/88*, 71 DR 141 at 155 (1991).
2   *No 12015/86*, 57 DR 108 at 117 (1988).
3   See above pp 305-306.
4   *Klass v FRG A 28* (1978). See also *Mersch v Luxembourg No 10439/8*, 43 DR 34 (1985).
5   On collection, *Leander v Sweden A 116* (1987); on retention if collected unlawfully, *Hewitt and Harman v UK No 20317/92* (1993), unreported (inadmissible) or rendered redundant, *Williams v UK No 19404/92* (1992), unreported (inadmissible).
6   Direct authority is lacking. In *A v France A 277-B* (1993), the government argued there was no interference because there was no state involvement (but the Court found that the state was implicated). In *Winer v UK No 10871/84*, 48 DR 154, 170 (1986), the Commission found that the absence of a right of privacy in English law did not show a failure to respect the applicant's right to private life in so far as it left him without a remedy against the publication of information he would rather have had kept secret in view of other remedies that existed: *quaere* whether the same would apply to the manner in which information was obtained, if that involved intrusion into the applicant's home. See further on the *Winer* case, below, p 326.
7   The complexity of data protection issues requires regulation of a more sophisticated kind than can be derived from the simple standards of the Convention. There has been a good deal of international co-operation on standards. See the Council of Europe Convention for the Protection of Individuals with regard to Automatic Processing of Personal Data 1981, ETS 108, UKTS 86 (1990), Cm 1329. See also the EC Draft Directive concerning the Protection of Individuals in Relation to the Processing of Personal Data Com (90) 314, (1990) OJ C277/3, on which, see H Pearson, 7 Computers Law and Practice 182 (1991).

fingerprints taken in the course of investigating crime should be destroyed when there are no longer suspicions about the defendant.[8] Where information may properly be retained, an individual has no general right of access to it. However, as *Gaskin v UK*[9] shows, a person may be able to demonstrate that the specific importance of information to him does create a positive obligation on the state to allow him to see it. But the significance of the information to the individual is only a factor to be taken into consideration: establishing this is a necessary but not sufficient condition of access. In *Leander v Sweden*,[10] the Court confirmed that the retention and use of information about an individual in connection with employment in national security sensitive jobs (which in the applicant's case resulted in his being denied employment) did not carry with it a positive obligation to allow the applicant to know the content of the files so that he might have the opportunity of refuting data that was damaging to him. It is necessary to rely on Article 8 rather than Article 10 in cases like this because the Commission is strongly of the view that Article 10 does not grant a right of access to information generated by others.[11] Finally, where the secret collection of information is at the core of an individual's complaint, the problems of proving that information has been collected about him and, more particularly, that it has been used to his disadvantage should not be underestimated.[12]

e. Sexual activities

Private life embraces not only individual, personal choices but choices about relationships with others. Some of these, whether strictly private or not, will be governed mainly by other articles in the Convention, such as Article 11 on the right of freedom of association. Other matters are mainly for Article 8, predominantly sexual relations. It is beyond doubt that sexual relations fall within the sphere of private life. In *Dudgeon v UK*,[13] where the activities were consensual homosexual ones between adult men in private, the Court described sexual life as being 'a most intimate aspect' of private life. Although it is an obscure decision, the Commission in *Bruggeman and Scheuten v FRG*[14] had earlier acknowledged the importance of untroubled sexual relations as a part of private life. There, it was the right of a woman to an abortion in the event of an unwanted conception. As will be seen, the Court has contributed to a process which has seen the toleration of private, adult, consensual, homosexual relationships become practically the

---

8 *Friedl v Austria* A 305-B Com Rep para 66 (1995) F Sett; *McVeigh v UK No 8022/77*, 25 DR 15 at 49 (1980); *Williams v UK No 19404/92* (1992), unreported (DNA Samples).
9 A 160 (1989).
10 A 116 (1987). See also *N v UK No 12327/86*, 58 DR 85 (1980).
11 See below, pp 379-380.
12 *Hilton v UK No 12015/86*, 57 DR 108 at 117, 119 (1988) and *G, H, I v UK Nos 18600-2/91*, 15 EHRR CD 41 (1993).
13 A 45 para 52 (1981).
14 *No 6959/75*, 10 DR 100 (1977); Com Rep; CM Res DH (78) 1.

universal condition in the Convention states.[15] However, consideration of the reach of private life is by no means concluded. The same matter already raised under 'private space' above arises here also – does the reach of private life include the manifestation of sexual relationships in public or non-private places? Of course, this does not mean that the state cannot forbid the performance of acts of sexual intercourse, whether homosexual or heterosexual, in a public place. In a case as stark as this, it probably is of no consequence whether public copulation is not regarded as part of private life or that the state may easily justify interference with it under Article 8(2). On the other hand, displays of affection, holding hands or kissing, may fall within the ambit of private life, at least when deciding on an issue of discrimination under Article 14.[16] Indulging in this kind of activity in public places can be seen as an aspect of the effective enjoyment of private life, once that notion is understood to embrace relationships with others. It is outside the 'inner circle' but within the meaning of private life approved of in the *Niemietz* case.

f. Social life; the enjoyment of personal relationships

While sexual activities may be the central element in the notion of personal relationships as part of private life, they do not exhaust it. Individual members of the Commission and judges of the Court have accepted a view of private life which encompasses the possibility of the effective enjoyment of a social life being an aspect of 'private life'. This involves the capacity by reason of cultural familiarity and linguistic facility to enter into social relationships with others. Judge Martens in his separate opinion in *Beldjoudi v France*[17] stresses the importance of a sphere of personal relationships beyond the 'inner circle' which are protected by the concept of 'private life'. The development of this idea is incomplete but it carries with it important possibilities for those who may be isolated from wider society by reason of cultural tradition or educational opportunity.

ii. Family life

The elaboration of the idea of 'family life' is one of the best examples of the way the institutions have interpreted the Convention to take account of social changes.[18] Family life is now understood as extending beyond formal

---

15 In addition to the *Dudgeon* case, see *Norris v Ireland* A 142 (1988) and *Modinos v Cyprus* A 259 (1993). See generally, Van Dijk, in Waaldijk and Clapham, eds, *Homosexuality: a European Community Issue*, 1993, p 184 at pp 185-193 and Helfer, 32 VJIL 157 (1991).

16 *Masterson v Holden* [1986] 3 All ER 39 (two men kissing in street convicted of insulting behaviour). See below, Article 14, p 479.

17 A 234-A (1992). See also Mr Schermers, id, Com Rep.

18 In contrast with the Court's jurisprudence, the *travaux* reveal an emphasis on the *father's* right to family life: see Opsahl, in Robertson, ed, *Privacy and Human Rights*, 1973, p 182 at 183-188. See now Seventh Protocol, Article 5, below, p 569. In general, see Douglas, 2 IJL Fam 101 (1988). For the right to marry, see Article 12, below, pp 436-438.

relationships and legitimate arrangements.[19] The Strasbourg authorities have taken into account increasingly the substance and reality of relationships, acknowledging developments in social practices and the law in European states. Scientific progress in methods of procreation is causing the Commission to consider whether and to what extent the Convention protects 'artificial' family life.[20] Although some of the problems thrown up by the possibilities of technology will be less tractable than those faced already, it is easy to predict that the same general approach will be followed – to look at the substance of the relationship and to provide for its effective enjoyment rather than to be confined to formal relationships and their equally formal enjoyment.

It should be noticed at the outset that the obligation on the state is to respect family life: it does not allow persons to claim a right to establish family life, eg by marrying or having the opportunity to have children,[1] nor a general right to establish family life in a particular jurisdiction.[2] However, the right to respect for one's family life may involve the recognition by the state of the reality of family life already established.[3] There is no right to formal termination of family life, in particular no right of partners to a formal marriage to a divorce,[4] though the effective enjoyment of family life may require that the state establish procedures which may result in the termination of some obligations of family life where that is necessary to protect some family members from the disruptive activities of another.[5]

While the Convention understanding of family life is not restricted to formal relationships, such arrangements represent the typical situation which will fall within Article 8. Despite the rise in *de facto* unions and the growth in the numbers of illegitimate children, most marriages are celebrated according to the formalities of the law and most children are the children of such arrangements. It is usually the case that formal marriages are accompanied by enough of substance for them to be regarded as constituting family life but a marriage subsisting in form only, for example, a sham marriage entered into for the purposes only of avoiding immigration controls or obtaining nationality, might fall outside Article 8 altogether.[6] If a relationship established in accordance with the forms

19 *Johnston v Ireland* A 112 (1986) and *Marckx v Belgium* A 31 (1979).
20 *G v Netherlands No 16944/90*, 16 EHRR CD 38 (1993) (refusal of access rights to biological father of child born by artificial insemination) (inadmissible).
1 See Article 12.
2 See below, pp 331-334 and Fourth Protocol, Article 3(2).
3 See below, p 333.
4 *Johnston v Ireland* A 112 paras 51-58 (1986), where, unusually in the interpretation of Article 8, the Court set little store by social developments.
5 *Airey v Ireland* A 32 para 33 (1979). The remedy here was judicial separation to relieve the wife of her duty to cohabit with an abusive husband.
6 In *Moustaquim v Belgium* A 193 Com Rep para 51 (1991), the government initially questioned whether there was a real family life between parents and an adolescent child: the link had been asserted purely for the purpose of relying on the Convention. See also *Benes v Austria No 18643/91*, 72 DR 271 (1992) (annulment of marriage entered into for the sole purpose of obtaining spouse's nationality interference with right to respect for family life but justified under Article 8(2)).

recognised by the national law ought ordinarily to fall within Article 8(1), then so ought marriages celebrated abroad but recognised by the national law, a matter of particular importance for polygamous unions.[7] Prospective relationships as husband and wife, that is to say, those between present fiancé and fiancée, may be regarded as family life if they are sufficiently established.[8] Where the union between partners is informal, it will depend on all the facts whether it constitutes family life. Stability of the relationship over a period and the intention of the parties are significant factors. It does not appear to be essential that the man and woman live together.[9]

In general, natural relationships between parents and young children will be accompanied by substantive relationships as well. The Commission has said:

> 'The question of the existence or non-existence of "family life" is essentially a question of fact depending upon the real existence in practice of close personal ties . . .'[10]

The Commission has found evidence of family life between an unmarried father and his child, but this is unlikely to be the case where there was only a casual encounter between father and mother. In other cases, the link of family life is established where the child is a child of a settled union and it may survive between the father and the child even where the union subsequently breaks down.[11] It is clear that as the child grows older, the maintenance of the link of family life will require a continuing substantive element to demonstrate its real existence.[12] While the natural connection between mother and child appears to be sufficient to establish 'family life' at birth, it does not necessarily do so for a father, possibly even though he is the formal husband of the mother at the time of birth if he has no contacts with the mother or child. It has been argued that the blood link should always be sufficient to establish family life[13] but technological developments, such as semen or egg donation, which make it possible for the natural parent to be totally remote from the child, indicate the need for caution in following this line.[14] On the other hand, states have an obligation not to prevent fathers from establishing a relationship with their children if they

---

7 See *Alam and Khan v UK* No 2991/66, 10 YB 478 (1967). There does not appear to be an obligation to recognise polygamous unions as formal marriages, although a family relationship between parties to such a union may be established as existing in substance: see *A and A v Netherlands* No 14501/89, 72 DR 118 at 121-123 (1992).
8 *Wakefield v UK* No 15817/89, 66 DR 251 at 255 (1990).
9 *Kroon v Netherlands* A 297-C para 30 (1994).
10 *K v UK* No 11468/85, 50 DR 199 at 207 (1986). See also *Marckx v Belgium* A 31 (1979)
11 *Keegan v Ireland* A 290 paras 42-44 (1994).
12 *Singh v UK* No 2992/66, 10 YB 478 (1967). See on this case, Van Dijk and Van Hoof, pp 380-381.
13 Mr Schermers, dissenting in *Kroon v Netherlands* A 297-C Com Rep (1994)
14 See *G v Netherlands*, above p 313, n 20.

seek to do so.[15] Matters such as the identification of children given for adoption by natural mothers and the tracing of their natural parents by adopted children are questions of private life as much as they are of family life.[16]

The central relationships of family life are those of husband and wife and parent and child. The Convention does not stop there: relationships between siblings[17] and between grandparents and grandchildren[18] are covered by it. The more remote the relationship, the less might be demanded of a state to respect it or the more easily might a state justify interfering with it,[19] but generalisations restricted to the formal closeness of the relationship are unhelpful. In each case, attention will have to be paid to the actual circumstances of the relationship as well.[20]

Family life may be terminated, say by divorce, between husband and wife,[1] or by adoption, between natural parent and child, just as it is, by the same process, established between adoptive parent and child. However, because a single family life might involve a number of relationships, the severance of one of them does not necessarily mean the end of all of them. In *Berrehab v Netherlands*,[2] the Court accepted that family life between a father and daughter had survived the divorce between the father and the mother. Although the latter had custody, the father maintained real contact with the girl, which the state was obliged to respect.

The law may allow the creation of formal relationships other than by marriage and the recognition of legitimate children. Adoption creates family life between the adoptive parents and the adopted child[3] and the same may be true of a relationship between foster-parent and foster-child although the content of family life will depend on the terms of the fostering arrangement.[4] The Court has extended the protection of the Convention to informal matrimonial unions and to the relationship between an illegitimate child and his mother.[5] The two situations may be combined so that a man who has a stable but informal living arrangement with a woman may enjoy family life

---

15 *Keegan v Ireland* A 290 para 50 (1994).
16 Cf Van Beuren, 58 MLR 37, 44-46 (1995), suggesting better prospects under the Convention for establishing a child's right to adoption records as an aspect of its family life rather than its private life.
17 *Moustaquim v Belgium* A 193 para 56 (1993).
18 *Marckx v Belgium* A 31 para 45 (1979) and *Price v UK No 12402/86*, 55 DR 224 at 237 (1988).
19 *Boyle v UK* A 282-B Com Rep (1994) (uncle-nephew), where the Commission divided by 14 to 4 on what was required to respect the interests in the custody of a child in this relationship compared to parents and child. A friendly settlement was reached which acknowledged the uncle's interest.
20 Duffy, 3 YEL 191 (1983), suggests that the content of family life might depend on the context in which it is being considered, drawing a contrast between domestic and immigration cases.
1 *Berrehab v Netherlands* A 138 para 21 (1988).
2 Id, para 59. See also *Hendriks v Netherlands No 8427/78*, 29 DR 5 (1982).
3 *X v France No 9993/82*, 31 DR 241 (1982).
4 *Gaskin v UK* A 160 para 49 (1989).
5 See above, pp 312-313.

with their illegitimate child in addition to that between mother and child.[6] Because there can be no formal criteria to rely on, the reality of the union or the parent-child connection must be demonstrated by its substance – the intensity and longevity of the relationship – and those details have both substantive and probative aspects to them.

One aspect of the proof of a relationship raises special problems. It is the matter of paternity. A presumption of paternity of the husband to a formal marriage whose wife has a child does not, of itself, contravene the Convention. However, the Court said in *Kroon v Netherlands*[7] that biological and social reality should prevail over legal presumptions and the quest for legal certainty of relations, so that any presumption of paternity must be effectively capable of being rebutted and not amount to a *de facto* rule. Voluntary testing to establish paternity of the non-married father to contradict the presumption remains controversial. Voluntary testing by a husband to disprove paternity or compulsory testing raises issues of private life rather than family life.[8]

The Commission has considered the claim of the father of a foetus that family life existed between him and the foetus. It rejected the specific claim that such a right to respect for family life included a right to be consulted as to whether the mother should have an abortion.[9] This may largely exhaust the content of family life for the father in such a case but it is possible that other matters, such as succession, could arise where the existence of family life between a father and a foetus would require reconsideration.

The essential ingredient of family life is the right to live together so that family relationships may 'develop normally'[10] and that members of the family may 'enjoy each other's company'[11] but the reach of this right cannot be considered separately from the specific duty on a state under Article 8, ie its duty to respect family life.[12]

The positions of members of a family with respect to one another are not identical. In particular, the idea of family life acknowledges some authority of parents over young children. In *R v UK*,[13] the Court said that the exercise of parental rights was a fundamental element of family life. In *Nielsen v Denmark*[14] the Court said that it was normally for the parent(s) to decide where the child should live and to take other decisions about him, for instance, on medical treatment. Article 2, First Protocol specifically recognises 'the rights of parents to ensure . . . education and teaching in conformity with their [viz the parents'] own religious and philosophical convictions . . . '.[15] Other possibilities arise implicitly, such as the right of

6 *Johnston v Ireland* A 112 para 75 (1986).
7 A 297-C para 40 (1994).
8 *Rasmussen v Denmark* A 87 para 33 (1984).
9 *X v UK No 8416/78*, 19 DR 244 at 253-54 (1980).
10 *Marckx v Belgium* A 31 para 31 (1979).
11 *Olsson v Sweden* A 130 para 59 (1988).
12 See below, pp 329-334.
13 A 121-C para 64 (1987).
14 A 144 para 61 (1988).
15 See below, pp 544-547.

parents to control the personal relationships and sexual activities of their children[16] or to require generally that their children are brought up in a particular religious tradition.[17] The exercise of this authority brings the possibility that the assertion of the group right of family life may conflict with the assertion of some autonomous individual right by the child, for instance, his right to respect for his private life or his right 'to freedom of thought, conscience and religion . . . ', which he wants to exercise differently to his parents. The burgeoning attention given to children's rights is bound to have an effect in diluting the weight to be given to parental authority as an aspect of family life.[18] This is the case also where the child is not able to express his wishes because he is too young. The state must act in the 'best interests' of the child. However, because of the importance of family life, it is incumbent upon the state to show that it is necessary to remove a child from its parents into public care. The Court attaches importance to the efforts a state makes to reunite parents and children and to securing the access of parents to the children while they are in care.[19] The requirements of family life in terms of the relationships between children and divorced or separated parents are yet more complicated. Although the 'best interests' phrase is used again, the Strasbourg authorities are in any event very cautious in reviewing considered decisions of national bodies, however harshly they may bear on a parent.[20]

The Commission does not accept that homosexual unions, whatever their stability, are entitled to protection within the family life provision of Article 8, although aspects of the relationship may fall within private life.[1]

iii. Home

In general, 'home' is where one lives on a settled basis. The French text uses the word '*domicile*'. It may be the case that not all living places are 'home',

---

16 *X v Netherlands No 6753/74*, 2 DR 118 (1974).

17 It is implicit in *Hoffmann v Austria* A 255-C paras 32, 33 (1993) that parents are normally entitled to bring up children in their own religion.

18 See *X v Denmark No 6854/74*, 7 DR 81 (1976). See also *Rieme v Sweden* A 226-B para 73 (1992) where the Court found that decisions of social workers as to the continuing placement of a child, founded predominantly on the child's wishes rather than the parent's, not incompatible with the Convention. The child's wishes were of substantial importance in the custody decision in *Hokkanen v Finland* A 299-A (1994). On children under the Convention, see Buquicchio-De Boer, *Wiarda Mélanges*, pp 73, 82-88.

19 See eg *Eriksson v Sweden* A 156 para 71 (1989) and *Andersson (M and R) v Sweden* A 226 paras 91-97 (1992).

20 See *Hendriks v Netherlands No 8427/78*, 29 DR 5 (1982) Com Rep; CM Res DH (82) 4. In *Rieme v Sweden* A 226-B paras 70-73 (1992), the Court endorsed a national decision against a separated parent seeking custody based on the 'best interests'of the child.

1 *S v UK No 11716/85*, 47 DR 274 (1986) and *B v UK No 16106/90*, 64 DR 278 (1990). As the attitude to homosexual unions changes in European national law, this matter may be reconsidered or, alternatively, raised under Article 14: see Van Dijk, loc cit at p 312, n 15, above, pp 189-192.

for example, 'holiday homes'[2] and work hostels might be exceptions. In *Gillow v UK*,[3] the Commission decided that 'home' could include a place where one intended to live, not confining 'home' to where one actually was living. The facts in *Gillow* were rather special. The applicants had built a house on Guernsey with a special licence and a licence to live on the island. After living there for five years, the Gillows lived in a variety of places for eighteen years as Mr Gillow's employment took him round the world. The couple also maintained a house in England. In the government's view, the object of the right to respect for one's home was the protection of the integrity of home life rather than the physical security of one's house and possessions. Because the Gillows had been absent from the house for so long, it was not their 'home' and so the refusal of the Guernsey authorities to grant a new residence permit did not conflict with any Convention right. In any event, if one of the Gillows' houses were their home, it was the one in England. The Commission rejected this argument and accepted that the applicants had always had an intention to return to the house in Guernsey. In these circumstances there was a right to (re-)establish home life in the government's sense in the particular house. When the case reached the Court, the government conceded that the applicants did not have a 'home' in England, a point to which the Court attached importance in reaching its conclusion that the Guernsey house was the applicants' 'home'.[4] However, it ought not to be ruled out that a person may have more than one home.

Recently, the Court has extended the notion of 'home' to cover some business premises. In *Niemietz v Germany*,[5] the Court, relying on the French text of Article 8 and on German law, decided that 'home' may extend, for example, to a professional person's office. This, the Court said, was consonant with the object of Article 8 to protect against arbitrary interference by the authorities. Because 'activities which are related to a profession or business may well be conducted from a person's private residence and activities which are not so related may well be carried on in an office or commercial premises', it 'may not always be possible to draw precise distinctions'. This conclusion does not seriously prejudice a state because it is still open to it to justify the interference and it would be easier for a state to do that where professional premises were involved than where the case concerned wholly domestic premises. The *Niemietz* case[6] was one where the professional's activities (he was a lawyer) could be carried on as easily at home as at his office. Equally, some businesses may be conducted from home. Some such possibility would appear to be essential for Article 8 protection to apply. Some interferences with wholly work premises might be

---

2   In *Kanthak v FRG No 12474/86*, 58 DR 94 (1988), the question whether a camping van could be a 'home' was raised, but not answered.
3   A 119 (1986) Com Rep paras 109-119.
4   A 109 paras 44, 46 (1986).
5   A 251-B para 30 (1992). See also *Chappell v UK* A 152-A (1989) Com Rep para 96 ('home' where part of premises used as residence and part for business purposes).
6   A 251-B paras 29-30 (1992).

protected against by relying on private life but surely not as an aspect of the right to respect for one's home.

Where it is established that premises are 'home', then the first protection is of a right of access and occupation,[7] and a right not to be expelled or evicted from them.[8] The property right in houses, is protected, if at all, by Article 1 of the First Protocol,[9] although the line is sometimes hard to draw. In *Howard v UK*,[10] the Commission decided that a compulsory purchase order for the house where the applicants lived interfered potentially with their rights under Article 8 as well as Article 1 of the First Protocol.

The interests protected by 'home' include the peaceful enjoyment of residence there. The various aircraft noise cases have established this[11] and the principle may be extended to both personal harassment and other forms of environmental interference with quiet enjoyment. Many aspects of home life will also be part of private life but the right to live one's life as one wishes, to adopt a particular life style, may have implications for the kind of home one wants.[12] There are some slight indications in the Commission's practice that, for example, the right to live in a mobile home might fall within Article 8, as an aspect of one's life style.[13]

There is no right *to* a home, not even a family home,[14] but the notion of 'home' is not seen entirely as the protection of a particular category of established property right. It includes a family home but it is not restricted to it. While its core idea is one of sanctuary against intrusion by public authorities, there are further connotations to the idea of 'home', in particular that the state will facilitate the right to live in one's home, rather than merely protect it as a possession or property right.[15]

Beyond the right to occupy one's home, the central protection afforded by the right to respect for one's home is against intrusion by the authorities of the state to arrest, to search, to seize or to inspect. The weight attached to the strong interest a person has in the sanctuary of his home puts the burden on the state to justify such interventions for good public purposes.

---

7 *Wiggins v UK No 7456/76*, 13 DR 40 (1978).
8 *Cyprus v Turkey Nos 6780/74 and 6950/75 (First and Second Applications)*, 4 EHRR 482 at 519-20 (1976); *Cyprus v Turkey No 8007/77*, 72 DR 5, 41-43 (1983); CM Res DH (92) 12.
9 *James v UK* A 98 (1986).
10 *No 10825/84*, 52 DR 198 (1985). See also *X v UK No 9261/81*, 28 DR 177 (1982).
11 Eg *Arrondelle v UK No 7889/77*, 26 DR 5 (1982) F Sett. See also *Lopes Ostra v Spain* A 303-C (1994).
12 *G and E v Norway Nos 9278/81 and 9415/81*, 35 DR 30 (1983) (the applicants were members of a minority).
13 Cases involving the right of gypsies to live in caravans against the UK have gone in different directions at the admissibility stage: see *Smith v UK No 18401/91* (1991) 18 EHRR CD 65 (1994) (inadmissible) and *Buckley v UK No 20348/92* (1994) 18 EHRR CD 123 (1994) (admissible), *Carol and Steven Smith v UK No 22902/93* (1994), unreported (admissible); *Carol and Walter Smith v UK No 23442/94* (1994), unreported (admissible).
14 *X v FRG No 159/56*, 1 YB 202 (1956) (no right to a decent ('*convenable*') home).
15 *Howard v UK No 10825/84*, 52 DR 198 (1987). The Commission has dealt with the denial of access to their homes in the north of Cyprus to Greek Cypriots under Article 8 and under Article 1, First Protocol: *Cyprus v Turkey Nos 6780/74 and 6950/75*, paras 208, 486; and id, *No 8007/77*, 72 DR 5, 42, 46-47; *Loizidou v Turkey No 15318/89*, paras 86-101.

iv. Correspondence

The right to respect for one's correspondence is a right to uninterrupted and uncensored communications with others. A letter-writer retains no right to respect for his correspondence once the letter is in the hands of the addressee[16] nor, it would seem to follow, would the right be violated if the contents of one's telephone conversations were revealed by the other party to them. That there may be expectations of confidentiality about the contents of a letter or telephone conversation, as, for instance, between lawyer and client or doctor and patient, suggests that the conclusion is not unqualified, though the protection of the individual's right to confidence is as likely to be a matter of respect for his private life as for his right to correspondence. In telephone-tapping cases, the literal meaning of 'correspondence' has been expanded to include telephone communications.[17] There is no reason why it should not keep pace with developments in technology which may bring other methods of communication into operation, although the appropriate level of protection required by 'respect' will have to take into account the techniques involved.[18] The protection is about the means of communication rather than its content (which will ordinarily fall to be considered under Article 10).[19] However, the content of a communication may be relevant to determining the limits of the right of the state to interfere with a letter or telephone call.[20] Equally, the identity of the sender or consignee of correspondence will play a part in determining what is required by Article 8. The Court has become increasingly solicitous in protecting letters between detained persons and their lawyers.[1] It is to persons in detention that the right of correspondence is of the greatest importance because for such people it is, visits apart, the only method of communication with others beyond the closed institution.

3. 'RESPECT'

Article 8(1) protects the right to *respect* for the various interests it lists. This makes it clear that not every act of a public authority which has an impact on the exercise of the interest will constitute an interference with the Article 8(1) right. So wide is the content of the interests that much state activity will

---

16 *AD v Netherlands No 21962/93*, 76A DR 157 (1994).
17 Eg *Klass v FRG* A 28 para 41 (1978) – telephone-tapping constitutes an interference with 'the applicant's right to respect for private life and family life and correspondence'.
18 There are not the same expectations of confidentiality for radio telephone conversations or open fax communications as there are for ordinary telephone calls because of the greater susceptibility of the former to interception.
19 *A v France* A 277-B paras 34-7 (1993), rejecting government's claim that telephone conversations about criminal activities fell outside Article 8(1).
20 See below, prisoners' correspondence, pp 345-346.
1   See more recently, *Campbell v UK* A 233 para 47 (1992) and *Herczegfalvy v Austria* A 242-B para 91 (1992).

have an incidental impact upon them. The criminal law on assault will, if it applies, have an impact on the exercise of parental discipline and hence on family life.[2] Road safety legislation requiring the wearing of seat-belts touches on private life (the 'right' to take risks as an element of one's personality).[3] This kind of incidental consequence is sometimes regarded by the Commission as not constituting a failure to respect an Article 8(1) interest and, therefore, not requiring justification under Article 8(2).[4]

The obligation on states is to 'respect' the interests set out in Article 8(1). States have argued that this is necessarily purely a negative obligation not to interfere (excessively) with those rights.[5] This limited conception of the obligation would condemn only interferences by the state with the protected interest, a conclusion buttressed by the language of Article 8(2) which says, 'There shall be no interference *by a public authority* with the exercise of this right . . . ' Thus a state would have a duty, for example, to desist from criminalising private sexual relations or from authorising arbitrary powers for social workers to separate members of a family or for policemen to enter private houses. However, it would not be responsible where, for example, the interference with private life was by a newspaper reporter or the disruption of family life was caused by another member of the family or the entry into a person's home was by a private detective. Such a narrow reading has not been acceptable to the Court. The principle was set out by the Court in *X and Y v Netherlands*[6] when it said:

'[Article 8] does not merely compel the state to abstain from . . . interference: in addition to this primarily negative undertaking, there may be positive obligations inherent in an effective respect for private and family life . . . These obligations may involve the adoption of measures designed to secure respect for private life even in the sphere of the relations of individuals between themselves.'

The identification of the circumstances in which the duty to respect an individual's interest involves positive action is not without its difficulties. In *Abdulaziz, Cabales and Balkandali v UK*,[7] the applicants argued that the state had a positive obligation to admit their alien husbands to join them when these men had no independent right to be admitted under immigration law. The Court said:

'. . . especially as far as those positive obligations are concerned, the notion of "respect" is not clear-cut: having regard to the diversity of

2   *Seven Individuals v Sweden No 8811/79*, 29 DR 104 at 114 (1982).
3   *X v Belgium No 8707/79*, 18 DR 255 (1979).
4   For other examples, see Louciades, 62 BYIL 176 at 193-194 (1991).
5   See, eg *Lingens v Austria* A 103 (1986).
6   A 91 para 23 (1985), as to which, see below, p 323. See also eg *Johnston v Ireland* A 112 para 55 (1986).
7   A 94 para 67 (1985).

practices followed and the situations obtaining in the Contracting states, the notion's requirements will vary considerably from case to case.'

It conceded a wide 'margin of appreciation' to states to decide what 'respect' required in the circumstances of a particular application. What the state has to do, the Court has said on several occasions, is to have regard,

'to the fair balance that has to be struck between the general interest of the community and the interests of the individual, the search for which balance is inherent in the whole Convention.'[8]

These generalisations do not take us very far, particularly since they concern the establishment of the primary obligations under Article 8(1) and not the justifications for derogating from them under Article 8(2). The legitimate aims of justifiable interferences in Article 8(2) have a 'certain relevance' for the inquiry under Article 8(1)[9] but they do not exhaust the matters of public interest which may have a bearing on the existence of a positive obligation. Although the Court has used the language of 'margin of appreciation', the inquiry is not identical to the one to be made in deciding whether an interference with a protected right 'is in accordance with law and is necessary in a democratic society' within Article 8(2). Under Article 8(2), the balance is struck between a right already established, which, formally at least, carries a special weight, and the countervailing interests which the state is seeking to protect. In reaching the balance in Article 8(1), the Court is determining the content of the protected right. It is thus incumbent on an applicant to establish the distinctive importance of the interest to him as it can be easy for the Court to underestimate this and there is no formal weight to attach to his claim as there would be if his interest were already acknowledged as a right.[10] The applicant in *Stjerna v Finland*[11] was not able to establish that the state had failed to respect his private life when it refused to allow him to register a change of surname in the official records nor was this refusal an 'interference' with his right as, the Court surmised, an order to him to change his surname might have been. As an interference, it would have been necessary that the state justify it under Article 8(2). It is likely that justification could have been shown in this case, but structuring the argument in this way can make a difference in other circumstances.[12]

So far we have considered the matter of positive obligations in Article 8 in circumstances where the applicant has suffered directly because of state inaction. In some cases it is possible for there to be interference with the

---

8 *Cossey v UK* A 184 para 37 (1990).
9 *Rees v UK* A 106 para 37 (1986).
10 See the transsexual cases and *Gaskin*, below, pp 324-326.
11 A 299-B para 38.
12 See, eg *Beldjoudi v France* A 234-A (1992) below pp 352-353. Note also Judge Wildhaber's concurring opinion in the *Stjerna* case suggesting that the Court treat breaches of negative and positive obligations in Article 8(1) in the same way.

enjoyment of one individual's rights by the activities of another individual.[13] It has been argued by states that conduct of this kind cannot implicate the state. Article 8(2) talks only of 'interference by a public authority'. The Court has rejected this contention. The matter of what kinds of interferences with Article 8(1) rights might be justified under Article 8(2) is independent of the question of what rights are protected by Article 8(1). In *Airey v Ireland*,[14] the Court said that 'there may be positive obligations inherent in an effective respect for private or family life . . . '. Here, the duty to respect family life included relieving partners to a marriage of their duty to live together in some circumstances. Ireland had failed to make its procedures for doing this effectively accessible to the applicant and had violated its positive obligation to respect her right to family life.

In *X and Y v Netherlands*,[15] the Court held that the positive obligation on the state extended to the circumstances of private activities. Here, there had been a sexual assault on a 16-year-old, mentally-handicapped girl by an adult male of sound mind. It had not been possible to bring a criminal charge against the man because of a procedural gap in Dutch law. The Court conceded that there was a wide margin of appreciation for a state to determine what steps it should take to intervene between individuals. The government's position was that there were civil remedies available to the girl and so she was not bereft of protection. However, affirming the *Airey* case, the Court found that the civil remedies were not without their practical drawbacks and that the absence of an effective criminal remedy in these circumstances constituted a failure by the Dutch authorities to respect Y's right to private life. In the *X and Y* case,

> 'fundamental values and essential aspects of private life are at stake. Effective deterrence is indispensable in this area and it can be achieved only by criminal law provisions . . .'

This is a strong statement of what the positive obligation entails. It is unusual, of course, for the Court to be so specific about the content of a state's obligation (and the state, even here, retains the discretion about the precise form of the criminal sanction to be provided). The very particular circumstances of this case, that there was an admitted gap in the law and the gap was procedural rather than substantive, might militate against too wide an obligation being imposed upon states to criminalise private activities. One can imagine relatively easy cases which would attract this positive obligation – the lack of a criminal remedy against the raping husband in English law before the judgment of the House of Lords in *R v R*[16] would

13 In *Lopes Ostra v Spain* A 303-C paras 52, 55-56 (1994), the Court seemed to discern elements of both kinds of positive duty to protect the applicant from environmental damage from a private plant built on public land.
14 A 32 para 32 (1979).
15 A 91 para 27 (1985).
16 [1991] 4 All ER 481. See now *SW v UK No 20166/92* and *CR v UK No 20190/92* (referred to Court).

seem to be an example. It is harder to predict whether the Court would find positive obligations to criminalise private surveillance or data collection which impinged upon an individual's rights to private life or correspondence, even if a state has a duty to provide civil remedies in such cases.[17] One factor which is likely to be of some influence in favour of an applicant is the existence of a widely adopted common position among the Convention states.

The positive obligation on a state with respect to private conduct may extend even to requiring positive action from private persons. States might be obliged to require that private data collection firms grant access to individuals to records kept about them or that the parent with custody of children allow access to the other parent or other relatives like grandparents.[18]

i.   Private life

The transsexual cases are good illustrations of the positive obligations which arise from the right to respect for one's private life. In none of the cases which have reached the Court did the state forbid the treatment which brought about the physical transformation of the applicant. Indeed, in the United Kingdom cases, the treatment was provided by the public health service. The governments, then, did not interfere with the applicants' rights. Rather, the applicants argued, the states had failed to respect their rights to private life by refusing to amend their birth certificates after they had undergone the transformation surgery. In *Van Oosterwijk v Belgium*,[19] the Court did not reach the merits but the Commission found that there was a violation because the state 'had refused to recognise an essential element of his personality' and the effect of its refusal to concede his request for rectification was to 'restrict the applicant to a sex which can scarcely be considered his own'. When a similar question arose in cases against the United Kingdom, the Court weighed the interest of the applicants in having the altered birth-certificate against the burden on the state substantially to reassess the system for registering births. It found the balance to be in favour of the state and, therefore, that the state had not failed to respect the applicant's private life.[20] The equation came out the other way in *B v France*,[1] where the majority held that the disadvantages for the applicant were greater in that there were more occasions when she was required to use documents indicating her sex in French practice than would have been the case in the United Kingdom, while the consequences for the state were less because entries on the birth certificate (and other official documents like her

17 See Clapham, *Human Rights in the Private Sphere*, 1993, pp 211-222.
18 See *Hokkanen v Finland* A 299-A Com Rep para 129-46 and Ct Jmt paras 58-62 (1994).
19 B 36 Com Rep para 52 (1979).
20 *Rees v UK* A 106 paras 42-46 (1986) and *Cossey v UK* A 184 para 39 (1990).
1 A 232-C paras 49-62 (1992).

driving licence about the non-rectification of which she also complained) were not contrary to the purpose of such documents as was the case in the United Kingdom where they were a record of the position at birth. In all three cases which reached the Court, the interest of the applicants was considered by the majority to be the rather mundane concern that their original sex be not revealed to others in the narrow variety of circumstances in which it was essential they rely on their birth certificates.

The difference in outcome between the British and French cases is explained both by the less significant consequences for the applicants in British law compared with those in French law and the greater consequences for the government of the reform which would be required in the administrative operation of the birth certificate regime in the United Kingdom compared with the changes necessary in France. However, if the position taken by the Commission in the *Van Oosterwijk* case and followed by the minority in the *Rees* and *Cossey* cases were to be adopted, the calculation of what may be required by the state to respect private life would change. These opinions emphasise the centrality of the legal recognition of the physical changes of the operations to the transsexuals' perception of themselves.[2] To such a deeply felt matter, the administrative inconveniences to the state should yield. The essence of private life is the expression of one's personality. The state has a correspondingly high positive obligation to ensure its effective enjoyment.

The characterisation of the interest of an applicant as of central importance to his private life determined the outcome in *Gaskin v UK*.[3] The applicant had been in public foster-care as a child. The local authority had maintained records about his care, some of it given on express or implied understandings of confidentiality. When he was an adult, Gaskin wished to obtain access to the files held about him. The authority would reveal only that for which it had obtained a release from its obligation of confidentiality from the person who had been the source of the information. The government emphasised the importance of confidential record-keeping for an effective system of child-care and argued that, if any positive obligation existed with respect to the applicant, it had been discharged by the measures the local authority had taken to obtain waivers of confidentiality. However, the majority of the Court shared the Commission's perception that this kind of information was of especial importance to the applicant. It said:

> '. . . persons in the position of the applicant have a vital interest, protected by the Convention, in receiving the information necessary to know and understand their childhood and early development.'

The majority concluded that the positive obligation on the state demanded a process before an independent adjudicator to decide whether the continued confidentiality of information was really necessary if the contributor refused

2   See especially Judge Martens, dissenting in the *Cossey* case.
3   A 160 para 48 (1989).

to waive confidentiality or was not able to be traced. The dissenting judges did not attribute any particular significance of the information to the applicant, though they were concerned about the consequences for the child-care system of the possible revelation of information given in confidence. Given a wide margin of appreciation, the balance, they determined, came down in favour of the state.[4]

These cases show that it is not enough to establish that the interest the applicant seeks to protect falls within private life, because some inconsequential interests may be easily defeated by considerations of the public interest, ie that 'respect' does not require the state to take positive measures in every case in which these are sought by the applicant. Thus in *Winer v UK*[5] the Commission found that the limited range of legal remedies available in English law to protect the applicant's reputation from both true and false statements about his and his wife's sexual relations that had been published in a book did not amount to a failure to respect his private life. There was a remedy in defamation in respect of the untrue statements, which he had indeed used and which had led to a settlement. The defamation remedy did not, however, extend to the statements that were true, the publication of which he claimed was an invasion of privacy. The Commission rather easily found that there was no positive obligation to provide additional remedies, in particular a remedy directly for invasion of privacy in the case of true statements. Explaining its cautious approach, the Commission noted that a positive obligation of the kind sought by the applicant would involve a limitation upon another Convention right, viz freedom of expression. Bearing this in mind and considering that on the facts 'the applicant's right to privacy was not wholly unprotected, as shown by his defamation action and settlement', the Commission found no breach of Article 8. What the *Winer* case does not decide is that there is no positive obligation to protect against invasions of privacy by the press or other private persons by the relevation of private information in a case in which there is no remedy at all on the facts. Nor does it address the situation where the interference with privacy takes the form of an intrusion (eg by electronic eavesdropping or photography) in search of information, in which case a limitation on freedom of expression or any other Convention right would not be directly involved.

The task of the Strasbourg authorities is not made any easier because, with regard to any particular interest, the facts of the case may have a determinative role in deciding the content of the positive obligation, as the contrast between the United Kingdom and French cases involving transsexuals demonstrates. It might be better, where this is a feasible course, if the existence of the positive obligation were established in relatively general terms and the facts of the application were taken into account to determine whether the state had justifiably interfered with the

---

4   Judges Ryssdal, Cremona, Gölcüklü, Matscher and Evans. Judge Walsh thought Article 8 did not apply at all, although there was an issue under Article 10.
5   *No 10871/84*, 48 DR 154 at 170-171 (1986).

enjoyment of the positive right under Article 8(2).[6] The practice of the Court is far from consistent. In *Kroon v Netherlands*,[7] the Court considered the case under Article 8(1) and found no need to take the matter further once it had found a violation of Article 8(1). In *Beldjoudi v France*[8] and *Keegan v Ireland*,[9] the Court did not expressly decide the Article 8(1) claim but went on to decide if the interference were justified under Article 8(2) – in each case, it decided that it was not. To some extent, the approach the Court takes will be determined by the pleadings of the government. If its argument is that there is no duty under Article 8(1), the government may offer no justification under Article 8(2) and so be without ground to stand on if the Court finds against it on its principal argument.

It has been indicated already that a state's duty to respect private life may require it to take positive action to intervene in the relations between individuals.[10] In the *X and Y* case, the Dutch government argued an obligation to criminalise private action would drive the legal regime from protection to paternalism. While the facts of that case made the contention somewhat unworthy, the claim in general is not without its merits. There is an obvious tension between those 'fundamental values and essential interests' of private life which require that the state desist from interference with a person's activities (for instance, the obligation not to criminalise adult, consensual homosexual activities in private) and others, such as those that were present in *X and Y*, where the positive obligation demands that the state does interfere to the point of criminalising private action. Where the activities are wholly consensual between adults, it might be expected that a state would be slow to intervene. However, where there are elements of duress or exploitation, then the state can be expected to take action. The primary responsibility for identifying which situations are which lies on the state but, as *X and Y* itself shows, the final assessment is for the Court.

The Commission utilised the notion of positive obligations in *Powell and Rayner v UK* in the context of deciding whether the applicants had an arguable claim for the purposes of Article 13.[11] Earlier cases involving aircraft noise had implicated the state directly as the operator of national airports but, by the time these applications came to be determined, the British Airports Authority had been privatised. It was therefore necessary to determine whether Article 8(1) imposed on the government an obligation to protect the applicants' enjoyment of their rights to private life and home

6 To the same end, see Judge Wildhaber, concurring, in *Stjerna v Finland* A 299-B (1994), arguing that, whether negative or positive obligations are involved, the Court should consider whether there has been an interference with an Article 8(1) right and, if there has, whether it may be justified under Article 8(2). Cf *B v UK No 16106/90*, 64 DR 278 (1990) (deportation of partner in homosexual union; claim considered under Articles 8(1) and (2); inadmissible on both counts). See also cases on family life, below, pp 329-330.

7 A 297-C para 40 (1994). See also *Marckx v Belgium* A 31 paras 36 and 37 (1979) and *Johnston v Ireland* A 112 para 75 (1986).

8 A 234-A para 79 (1992).

9 A 290 para 55 (1994).

10 See above, p 321.

11 See *Rayner v UK No 9310/81*, 47 DR 5 (1986).

against excessive noise from aeroplanes using the now privately owned airport. If there were such an obligation and that obligation had not been complied with, then it would have been open to the government to justify its interference under Article 8(2). The Court said that the 'applicable principles' were 'broadly similar' in each enquiry and it held that there was no violation of the Convention however the claim was framed.[12] The Commission's report, although it treats the matter more thoroughly, is scarcely more illuminating. It distinguished the two cases because the noise levels endured by Rayner were much higher than by Powell and affected far fewer people. The toleration of the conditions by the government amounted to a failure by it to respect Rayner's private and home life, albeit a failure which could be justified under Article 8(2) as being 'necessary in the interests of the economic well-being of the country'.[13] In *Lopes Ostra v Spain*,[14] the Court balanced the 'town's economic well-being' against the applicant's interests in home and private and family life to decide whether there had been a breach of Article 8(1) (which it determined that there had). The investigation, as the Court acknowledged, was not dissimilar to the one it would have made under Article 8(2) to see if an interference with an Article 8(1) right was necessary for the protection of the 'economic interests of the country' under Article 8(2).

While it may not have influenced these applications, it does seem to be important generally that the two tests under Articles 8(1) and 8(2) are not collapsed into a single one. For the government, the matter is simple: it ought not to be put to justifying that which is not in breach of a duty anyway. For an applicant, the establishment of the positive duty will be of significance in his dealings with the government in 'environmental' cases. While the margin of appreciation of the government under Article 8(2) is wide,[15] the range of solutions possible in many such circumstances is also wide – as the airport noise cases show, the responses of the government included measures of mitigation, damages, purchase of property, and planning changes.[16] Having a 'right' to rely on enhances the individual's position in reaching the appropriate accommodation which will usually be achieved through legislative and administrative measures in the national legal system. That environmental disputes are likely to be settled in these ways rather than by judicial means is partly a consequence of the limited remedial power of the Court: even the relatively simple measures the Court regarded as necessary to discharge the state's positive obligation in the *X*

12 *Powell and Rayner v UK* A 172 paras 37-46 (1990). Cf *Lopes Ostra v Spain* A 303-C Com Rep (1994) paras 47-58.
13 A 172 Com Rep paras 58-59 (1990).
14 A 303-C para 58 (1994).
15 Some environmental cases may be framed as interference with 'the right to the peaceful enjoyment of one's possessions' (First Protocol, Article 1) where the state has a wide margin of appreciation, see below, Ch 18.
16 *Powell and Rayner v UK* A 172 paras 22-30 (1990). See also *S v France No 13728/88*, 65 DR 250 at 263-64 (1990) (environmental damage, no violation because adequate compensation paid).

and Y and *Gaskin* cases are at the limit of what it can do. Clapham[17] suggests that both the reach and the content of the margin of appreciation differ depending upon whether what is at stake is an individual-state conflict or whether the state is fulfilling its positive duty to intervene in what is in its essence a wholly private dispute. His concession of a wider margin in the latter case is an acknowledgement of the greater complexity of the questions which arise once it is decided that the state has a positive duty to intervene in relationships between individuals for the protection of human rights.

ii. Family life

Extensive claims have been made about the reach of the state's duty to respect family life on the basis of the observation of the Court in *Marckx v Belgium*[18] that Article 8(1),

> 'does not merely compel the state to abstain from . . . interference: in addition to this primarily negative undertaking, there may be positive obligations inherent in an effective "respect" for family life.'

The Commission has interpreted this very widely. In one case, it said:

> 'In shaping the domestic law, the state must act in a manner calculated to allow those concerned to lead a normal family life . . . The Commission is of the opinion that this consideration applied not only to legislation regulating family relationships, but also to legislation regulating the use of property insofar as it interferes with the possibility to use this property for family purposes.'[19]

In the *Marckx* case[20] itself, the Court held that the state had a positive obligation to provide a system of domestic law which safeguarded the illegitimate child's integration into its family. By requiring further steps beyond mere registration at birth to establish maternal affiliation, Belgium had failed to respect the family life of the child and the mother. In the *Airey* case,[1] the state's failure consisted of the absence of an effective and accessible remedy for protection of one family member from the threats of violence of another. In *Hokkanen v Finland*,[2] the Court held that the non-enforcement of a father's right of access to his daughter against other persons (the maternal grandparents) who refused to comply with court orders did not respect his family life. In *Keegan v Ireland*,[3] the Court

17 *Human Rights in the Private Sphere*, 1993, pp 211-222, especially at p 216.
18 A 31 para 31 (1979). See also *Airey v Ireland* A 32 para 32 (1979).
19 *Z and E v Austria No 10513/83*, 49 DR 67 (1986).
20 A 31 para 36 (1979). See also *Johnston v Ireland* A 112 paras 73-76 (1986).
1 A 32 para 32 (1979).
2 A 299-A paras 58-62 (1994).
3 A 290 paras 49-51 (1994).

concluded that the failure to consult a natural father (who had been party to a relationship within 'family life' with the mother) before placing a child for adoption did not respect the father's family life. The Court did not decide whether natural fathers had 'an automatic but defeasible right to guardianship' where the mother was not able or willing to keep the child.[4] The Commission has on several occasions found that the natural father has no right to joint custody as against the mother.[5]

Where decisions are to be made about interfering with family relationships, such as placing children for adoption or taking children into care, the obligation to respect family life imposes procedural obligations on the state. Where the decision determines a 'civil right', the procedure must satisfy the requirements of Article 6(1), but Article 8(1) imposes obligations of its own. In *W v UK*,[6] the Court said that Article 8(1) requires that the procedure be sufficient to protect the interests of the family members; accordingly, parents should be actively involved in proceedings about their children. In *McMichael v UK*,[7] the Commission held that there was a right of access for parents to reports about their children in proceedings which potentially could lead to the children being freed for adoption.

The existence or non-existence of family life between a pair of individuals may be of great importance, since the conclusion will carry benefits and burdens for them. In *Marckx v Belgium*,[8] the Court held that the situation in Belgian law which faced an unmarried mother with the choice of either 'recognising' her child with certain disadvantages in the succession of property between mother and child, or avoiding these drawbacks at the expense of establishing a formal family tie between them was not consonant with Belgium's duty to respect the mother's right to family life. Where paternity is contested, there is an obligation to provide a procedure whereby the issue may be resolved. In *Rasmussen v Denmark*,[9] where the father was contesting paternity, the Court suggested that this was an aspect of private life, acceding to the government's claim that the right to respect for family life could not require a process to establish that there was no family life by reason of natural relationship. If the implication is that where the object of the process is to establish or confirm the natural relationship, then family life is necessarily involved, the point might be reconsidered. For a father or a child, the ultimate reason to know the reality of the relationship is at least as likely to be an issue of private life, of personality, which has no necessary connection with matters of family relations.[10]

---

4 Id, para 52. For a comparative study of the father's position, see Forder, 7 IJL Fam 40 at 73-77 (1993).
5 *N v Denmark No 13557/88*, 63 DR 167 at 170 (1989).
6 A 121 paras 64, 77-79 (1987).
7 A 307-B (1995) Com Rep paras 101-105 confirmed by Court, para 92.
8 A 31 para 36 (1979). See also *Johnston v Ireland* A 112 para 75 (1986).
9 A 87 para 33 (1984). The case was decided under Article 14, see below, p 463.
10 See Fortin, 57 MLR 296 (1994). Forder, loc cit at n 4, above, relies on the *Gaskin* case to establish the right of the child to know the identity of his father.

The state's positive obligation stops short of support for the substance of family life. The Commission rejected an application demanding financial support from the state so that one parent could stay at home to look after the children rather than the day-care offered so that both parents could work.[11] The state does have an obligation to assist serving prisoners to maintain contact with their families,[12] although only in exceptional circumstances will that duty extend to transferring a prisoner from one jail to another.[13] The duty may be more extensive between prisoners and their children than between prisoners and their spouses, who can ordinarily be expected to travel more easily to visit a prison.[14]

One developing aspect of the positive obligation of a state to respect family life concerns the position of family members who do not have an independent right to enter or to stay in a Convention state where other family members have a right to reside. The essence of family life is the right to live together. Initially, the Commission in *Agee v UK*[15] regarded the place where family life was to be enjoyed as the place where the father or husband had a right to reside. The Convention does not protect the right to live in a contracting state. Agee had no right to stay in the United Kingdom and it was not shown that his wife could not accompany him if he were deported from the United Kingdom. Accordingly, the United Kingdom would not fail to respect his right to family life if it expelled him from its territory. However, the Commission later accepted that there could be factors which bore on the possibility of effective family life if the other members of the family were compelled to follow the husband/father[16] which undermined the absoluteness of its original criterion. More fundamentally, the discriminatory quality of the test – why should the place of ordinary residence of the family be where the father may go rather than where the mother may – also reduced the impact of the *Agee* rule.

It should be recognised that imposing the obligation on a state to admit a person to its territory or to allow him to stay when he has no right of residence there is a sensitive matter. The Court acknowledged this in *Abdulaziz, Cabalas and Balkandali v UK*[17] when it said:

'The duty imposed by Article 8 cannot be considered as extending to a general obligation on the part of a contracting state to respect the

---

11 *Andersson and Kullman v Sweden No 11776/85*, 46 DR 251 (1986). Cf Duffy, 3 YEL 191 at 199 (1983) who suggests that it is 'very probable' that welfare benefits come within Article 8 and 'possible' that minimum welfare provision is a positive obligation to achieve effective respect for private and family life.
12 *X v UK No 9054/80*, 30 DR 113 (1982) and *McCotter v UK No 18632/91*, 15 EHRR CD 98 (1993).
13 *Campbell v UK Nos 7819/77*, Decision, 6 May 1978, paras 30-32, unreported.
14 *Ouinas v France No 13756/88*, 65 DR 265 at 277 (1990). See also *Wakefield v UK No 15817/89*, 66 DR 251 (1990) (fiancé imprisoned, private life rather than family life).
15 *No 7729/76*, 7 DR 164 (1976).
16 *Uppal v UK No 8244/78*, 17 DR 149 (1979).
17 A 94 para 68 (1985).

choice by married couples of the country of their matrimonial
residence and to accept the non-national spouses for settlement in
that country.'

In this case, the applicants had not shown that there were obstacles to
establishing family life in their own (the applicants were non-United
Kingdom national women with rights of residence there) or their husbands'
(their husbands were non-United Kingdom nationals with no right of
residence there) home countries.[18] If any future case could not be dealt with
on the basis of a conflict with the state's duties under Article 14 (as this case
was[19]), then the *Abdulaziz* case leaves it open to a woman or a child to show
why they could not enjoy family life in the country of their husband's or
father's residence. The strongest cases are where the Convention state
members of the family have no right in the law of the alien member state to
join him there. Equally, where the alien member is not able to return to his
own state because he is a refugee, there is good reason why Article 8(1)
should be interpreted to require the Convention state to allow him to join
the other members of his family, whether it is formally bound to do so under
refugee law or not.[20] Otherwise, the obstacles to the family members joining
the other outside the Convention state will have to be substantial –
economic or cultural disadvantage will generally be insufficient.[1] That
Convention rights would not be enjoyed there ought to be a more
compelling reason – whether a woman, unwilling to do so, would have to
submit to an Islamic regime in the place of her husband's right of residence
might be an example. In addition to drawbacks arising in the state of the
husband's residence, advantages not available there but available to family
members in the Convention state, such as imperative medical treatment,
might constitute an obstacle to establishing effective family life abroad.[2] It is
suggested that the Commission and Court ought to keep the test of
sufficient hardship distinct from that of Article 3, to take into account that
what is at stake is the family relationship and not just the likely treatment of
one individual.

The duty to respect family life may be stronger where family life has
already been established in the state and stronger still where it has been
established there for some time. Where the state then seeks to remove a
family member who has no right to stay, *he*, as well as the other members of

---

18 The Court found that there was a violation of Article 14 because men in the same position
    would have been entitled to have their wives join them.
19 See below, p 466.
20 Cohen-Jonathan, *European System*, Ch 14 at pp 436–437.
1   *Beldjoudi v France* A 234-A para 79 (1992), where making the wife follow her husband
    'might imperil the unity or even the very existence of the marriage'. The matter was
    considered under Article 8(2), below, p 352.
2   Note the friendly settlement in *Fadele v UK No 13078/87*, 70 DR 159 (1991) where an alien
    father was granted leave to return to the UK to join his children, who had rights of
    residence, after they had followed him to Nigeria and suffered hardship, including problems
    about medical treatment.

the family, will be able to assert a right to respect for his family life. If the deportation of the family member makes the maintenance of family life practically impossible, then the obligation to respect family life will exclude the removal of the applicant. In *Berrehab v Netherlands*,[3] the applicant was a Moroccan national whose right to stay in the Netherlands was dependent on him being the husband of a Dutch national. The Court decided that the failure of the Netherlands authorities to grant the applicant a residence permit after their divorce did not respect his family ties with his daughter, since contact with her at the level he had previously enjoyed would have been impracticable following his expulsion. The principle was extended in *Moustaquim v Belgium*[4] where a deportation order served on a young Moroccan national, who was a second generation immigrant in Belgium, was held to violate his right under Article 8(1). The applicant had been brought to Belgium by his parents as an infant and, besides his parents, seven brothers and sisters lived in Belgium. Moustaquim was able to demonstrate strong family attachments. It was not suggested that the remainder of the family depart with the applicant. Accordingly, his family life could be enjoyed only in Belgium and the unwillingness of the authorities to allow him to stay violated his right to respect for family life. Similarly in *Beldjoudi v France*,[5] the Court considered that the deportation from France of a long-settled Algerian national would fail to respect his family life enjoyed in France with his French national wife. The judgment gives special protection to aliens who have established family life in a Convention state and Judge Martens went so far as to suggest the assimilation of 'integrated aliens' and nationals.[6] The *Beldjoudi* case switches the relevance of the possibility of family life being enjoyed elsewhere to the assessment of the proportionality of any proposed removal under Article 8(2).[7] The right to respect for family life for an alien in a Convention state embraces a right to remain, dependent on the demonstration that he has a long and well established family life there. This right, it now appears to be the case, is independent of the conditions in the state to which removal is proposed.[8] The state's obligation to respect such well-established family life is to allow it to continue where it has been enjoyed. It is a different question whether it might justifiably interfere with the continued enjoyment of family life within the terms of Article 8(2) and it is here that the conditions in the state of destination become relevant.[9] Whilst it sometimes seems as though an applicant in this kind of case is complaining about an interference in breach of a negative obligation (the

3   A 138 (1988).
4   A 193 (1991).
5   A 234-A (1992).
6   See Judge Martens, concurring in the *Beldjoudi* case.
7   See below, pp 352-353.
8   Although they may be relevant to considering whether the decision to deport respects an applicant's right to private life: see above, p 312.
9   See below, p 352.

deportation order), what he is really seeking is a positive benefit, the right to stay in the state in order to enjoy his family life.[10]

iii. Home

Because the idea of 'home' has been interpreted relatively narrowly, positive obligations with respect to it are likely to be limited. The aircraft noise cases indicate that positive obligations to protect the quiet enjoyment of one's own home are to be found in Article 8(1).[11] Analogous interventions, say, harassment by private gangs or intrusions by journalists, are capable of raising the same issue.[12]

iv. Correspondence

The right to respect for one's correspondence is largely a right not to have one's communications interfered with. The Commission has rejected the claim that there is a positive obligation on the authorities to guarantee the perfect functioning of the postal service.[13] However, for people in detention, the possibility of corresponding with others will often depend on the provision of facilities by the authorities. In *Boyle v UK*,[14] the Commission said that while the general principle was that the state did not have to pay for a prisoner's letters, an obligation might arise where the prisoner's inability to pay severely limited or denied him altogether the possibility of correspondence. The applicant's circumstances did not bring him within the exception. In *Grace v UK*,[15] the Commission said that there were positive obligations on the prison authorities where correspondence was routed through the prison administration to make sure that letters were posted and delivered and that where there were difficulties with the postal service, for instance the return of an inadequately addressed letter, the prisoner had a right to be informed. There is a fine line between interference with the letters of a person in detention by a positive act of censorship, which will require justification under Article 8(2), and the effective organisation of the transmission of letters which are allowed by the authorities to be sent out. In

10 See also *Djeroud v France* A 191-B (1991) and *Lamguindaz v UK* A 258-C (1993) (friendly settlements). For the reaction of the French Conseil d'Etat, see Errera, (1993) PL 688 at 689-91. Cf for the UK, *Iye v Secretary of State for the Home Department* [1994] Imm AR 63 where the Court of Appeal declined to impose its understanding of what the Convention required on the Minister, even though it was presented with evidence that it was the Department's policy to comply with the Convention (Notes for Guidance on Family Reunion, DP/2/93).
11 Eg *Arrondelle v UK No 7889/77*, 26 DR 5 (1982) F Sett.
12 On private harassment, see *Whiteside v UK No 20357/92*, 76A DR 80 (1994).
13 *X v FRG No 8383/78*, 17 DR 227 (1979).
14 *No 9659/82*, 41 DR 90 at 94 (1985).
15 *No 11523/85*, 62 DR 22 at 41 Com Rep; CM Res DH (89) 21.

Herczegfalvy v Austria,[16] letters from a mental patient were sent to his guardian who decided whether they should be directed on to the addressees. The Court found the system not in accordance with the law and therefore not justifiable under Article 8(2) but it might have been considered to be a failure under Article 8(1) to establish a proper system for the effective respect for the applicant's right to correspondence.

4. ARTICLE 8(2): JUSTIFICATION FOR INTERFERENCE WITH ARTICLE 8(1) RIGHTS

i. Interference

Article 8(1) establishes some wide categories of interest which an individual has a right to have respected and the notion of respect imposes positive obligations on the state to further the enjoyment of those interests. However, the state has also the power to 'interfere' with Article 8(1) rights in accordance with the conditions in Article 8(2). That measures taken by it are an interference with a protected interest is often not disputed by the state: the question is instead whether they may be justified under Article 8(2). Examples are the storing and release of information on a secret police file,[17] the removal into public care of children from their parents,[18] stopping prisoners' correspondence[19] and searches of a person's home.[20]

It is for the applicant to establish the fact of interference. In *Campbell v UK*,[1] the government maintained that the applicant prisoner had not substantiated his claim that his right to respect for his correspondence had been interfered with because he could not show that any particular letter had been opened. The Court was satisfied that there had been an interference for the purpose of the Convention because the prevailing prison regime allowed for letters to be opened and read, a condition which had been specifically brought to the applicant's and his legal advisor's attention. The Court said:

> 'In these circumstances, the applicant can claim to be a victim of an interference claim with his right to respect for his correspondence under Article 8.'[2]

Tying together the questions of the status of 'victim' and the existence of an interference, however theoretically unsound,[3] does give an applicant

16 A 242-B para 91 (1992).
17 *Leander v Sweden* A 116 para 48 (1987).
18 *Olsson v Sweden* A 130 para 59 (1988).
19 *Campbell and Fell* v *UK* A 80 para 109 (1984).
20 *Chappell v UK* A 152-A para 51 (1989). The Court sometimes considers whether an Article 8(1) right is involved at all when looking at whether there is an interference, eg *Niemietz v Germany* A 251-B paras 27-33 (1992), but the two questions are distinct.
1   A 233 para 32 (1992).
2   Id, para 33.
3   Duffy, 3 YEL 191 at 201 (1983).

assistance in some circumstances in establishing that his rights have been interfered with. There are two separate situations. The first is where the applicant cannot establish the certainty of the material damage which would constitute the interference. As the *Campbell* case shows, if he can demonstrate that there is a sufficient degree of likelihood that the interference has occurred, that will be sufficient. The second situation is where the damage claimed by the applicant which amounts to the interference is not an actual, material effect upon him, such as a conviction, but psychological damage attributable to the threat that material interference will occur, such as the threat of prosecution. The two cases are distinct but they share the element of threat or risk of interference against which protection is required if an individual is to take effective advantage of his rights.

In *Dudgeon v UK*,[4] the government did not contest that the applicant, who was an adult, male homosexual, was a 'victim' for the purposes of Article 25, even though he had not been prosecuted or convicted of an offence. However, because he had not, the government said that his right under Article 8(1) had not been interfered with. The Commission conceded that, 'as a general rule', it was necessary to see how a law was applied in practice to determine if there was an interference with an individual's rights. Here, the prosecution of consenting adult males had not occurred for some time but the Commission noted that there was no guarantee that an action might not be started and the potential penalties were grave. The threat was not,

> 'illusory or theoretical or [had] no real or practical effect. It still has concrete effects on the private life of male homosexuals including the present applicant, even if the risk that it will be enforced in criminal proceedings is not great.'[5]

Accordingly, there was an interference with Dudgeon's right. This approach was endorsed by the Court:

> 'In the personal circumstances of the applicant, the very existence of this legislation continuously and directly effects his private life.'[6]

The Court was sustained in this view because there had been a criminal investigation into Dudgeon's activities. This was not the case in *Norris v Ireland*,[7] where the government first disputed the applicant was a victim. The Irish government argued next that there was no interference with his rights because the mere existence of legislation criminalising homosexual acts had no effect on Norris's ability to maintain 'an active public life side by side with a private life free from any interference on the part of the state and

---

4   A 45 para 40 (1981).
5   B 40 Com Rep para 95 (1980)
6   A 45 para 41 (1981).
7   A 142 para 37 (1988).

its agents'. The Court followed the same line as in the *Dudgeon* case and decided that his right had been interfered with.[8]

There were analogous difficulties for the applicants in *Klass v FRG*.[9] They complained about surreptitious state activity – wire-tapping – which in the nature of things they could not prove.[10] What the applicants could do, according to the Court in the *Klass* case, was 'claim to be a victim'.[11] Once this was established, the interference which they claimed was not dependent upon the actual interception of their calls (the government said that there had not been any):

> 'In the mere existence of the legislation itself there is involved, for all those to whom the legislation could be applied, a menace of surveillance . . .'[12]

While the individual will have to establish some reason for explaining why the legal regime *might* be applied to him, once he has done that, there has been an interference with his rights because of the threat to the effective enjoyment of them.

A different problem arises where the state maintains that the individual is directly responsible for the conditions about which he complains. In *McFeeley v UK*,[13] the Commission was faced with a wide variety of allegations of violations of the Convention during a protest in prison in Northern Ireland by prisoners claiming political status and certain privileges which would flow from that. The Commission held that there was no Convention guarantee of political status,[14] so it was not possible for the applicants to maintain that action taken by them could be justified as being in pursuit of Convention rights nor to attack the state's response to their action on the ground that it necessarily violated the Convention. Parts of the protest took the form of refusing to wear prison clothes and refusing to use lavatories. The applicants argued that the requirements that they use chamber pots in the presence of their cell-mates and that they take the pots for emptying dressed only in a blanket interfered with their right to respect for their private life. Since these conditions resulted directly from the prisoners' own decisions, there were no interferences with their rights for which the state was responsible.[15]

Where consent is normally required, as in the case of medical treatment, action without consent will not be an interference if the state can show that

---

8   See also *Modinos v Cyprus* A 259 paras 17-24 and Judge Pikis, dissenting (1993). Cf *Seven Individuals v Sweden No 8811/79*, 29 DR 104 at 113 (1982) where the threat was held insufficiently substantial to constitute an interference.
9   A 28 (1978).
10 Cf *Leander v Sweden* A 116 (1987).
11 A 28 para 38 (1978).
12 Id, para 41.
13 *No 8317/78*, 20 DR 44 (1980).
14 Id, p 77.
15 Id, pp 90-91.

the individual was not in a position to give informed consent. In *Herczegfalvy v Austria*,[16] the Court said it gave,

> 'decisive weight here to the lack of specific information capable of disproving the government's opinion that the hospital authorities were entitled to regard the applicant's psychiatric illness as rendering him entirely incapable of taking decisions for himself.'

It should not be without importance that the Court had earlier noted that the treatment of the applicant was in accord with 'psychiatric principles generally accepted at the time'.[17] The danger is that any 'irrational' unwillingness to consent will be classed as a failure to consent at all, thus undermining the individual's right to exercise his rights as he sees fit.

ii.   In accordance with the law

The question whether an interference with an Article 8 right is 'in accordance with the law' has been a prominent issue in three kinds of cases: secret surveillance, especially telephone-tapping; taking children into public care; and interfering with detained persons' correspondence.

a.   Secret surveillance

In *Malone v UK*,[18] the government failed to convince the Court that its power to intercept telephone conversations had a legal basis. At the relevant time, telephone-tapping was regulated by administrative practice, the details of which were not published. There was no specific statutory authorisation. As a national court had held, telephone tapping was lawful because it was not prohibited by law. The Court did not reject out of hand the government's arguments that there was a basis to be found in an amalgam of statutory provisions and actual practice, although if the Court had relied solely on the domestic judgment in the case,[19] it might have done. It is clear that an administrative practice, however well adhered to, does not provide the guarantee required by 'law'. The Court said that there was not sufficient clarity about the scope or the manner in which the discretion of the authorities to listen secretly to telephone conversations was exercised: because it was an administrative practice, it could be changed at any time. About the practice of 'metering', that is supplying details of numbers called and their time and duration, the Court was more forthright. It said:

---

16 A 242-B para 86 (1992).
17 Id, para 83.
18 A 82 para 79 (1984). See also *Hewitt and Harman v UK No 12175/86*, 67 DR 88 at 99-101 (1989) Com Rep; CM Res DH (90) 36 and *N v UK No 12327/86*, 67 DR 123 at 132-133 (1989) Com Rep; CM Res DH (90) 36.
19 *Malone v MPC* [1979] 2 All ER 620 at 635-638, 647-649.

'. . . apart from the simple absence of prohibition, there would appear to be no legal rules concerning the scope and manner of the exercise of the discretion enjoyed by public authorities.'[20]

It will not be enough to satisfy the Convention simply to write unlimited administrative power into formal law. The British response to the judgment in *Malone* is the Interception of Communications Act 1985, which provides a statutory basis for telephone-tapping, with the warrant of the Home Secretary. It sets up as well mechanisms for control of the power but it excludes the courts from this process. Individuals may make complaints to an independent tribunal, though, in the nature of things, they will find it difficult to provide evidence in support of their claims. An independent Commissioner, a senior judge, is charged with overall supervision of telephone-tapping. He reports to Parliament.[1] In *Christie v UK*,[2] the Commission declared inadmissible an application which asserted that these arrangements were not sufficient to secure against abusive recourse to the power to issue warrants. The Commission accepted that the scheme of the Interception of Communications Act satisfied the substantive as well as the formal requirements of 'law'.[3]

This was not true, however, of the French law under consideration in *Kruslin v France*.[4] There the French government relied on Article 81 of the Code of Criminal Procedure which provided:

'The investigation judge shall, in accordance with the law, take all investigative measures which he deems useful for establishing the truth.'

Its generality was supplemented by extensive case-law which showed that the French courts accepted that powers conferred by this provision included the power to order telephone-tapping. However, this formal legality was not sufficient to avoid the Court holding that the French law was defective as Convention 'law' because it did not provide guarantees against arbitrary use of the power it conferred. The need for protection here was strong because a particularly serious intrusion into private life and correspondence was involved. What was required were adequate safeguards against abuse. Whose telephones might be tapped? For what offences? For how long? How were results to be used? What were the rights of the defence of access to them? What happened to tapes and records at the end of the proceedings?[5]

---

20 A 82 para 87 (1984).
1   For a description of the Act, see L Lustgarten and I Leigh, *In From the Cold: National Security and Parliamentary Democracy*, 1994, pp 51-72.
2   *No 21482/93*, 78-A DR 119, 133-135.
3   The outcome confirmed the reluctant predicition of Lustgarten and Leigh, above, n 1, p 72. It is of some importance to the UK because similar patterns of supervision of clandestine activities have been adopted for the security services, see below, p 340.
4   A 176A para 17 (1990).
5   Id, para 34.

The French government had complained that the Court engaged in an abstract review of French law and was not confining its inquiries to the facts of Kruslin's application.[6] However, the Court said that its approach was inevitable: the requirement under Article 8(2) that the interference be in accordance with the law required that a state provide 'the minimum degree of protection to which citizens are entitled under the rule of law in a democratic society'.[7] In contrast, in another case the Commission found that Luxembourg law did satisfy the requirements of Article 8(2), both in terms of the detail and the control over the exercise of the power, with the ultimate safeguard that the Convention was itself directly applicable in Luxembourg law.[8] While the law had to be expressed with such a degree of particularity that the circumstances in which it would be applied were generally foreseeable, that obligation did not extend to providing advance warning to a person whose telephone might be tapped where that would threaten the object of the interception and the interception was otherwise compatible with the Convention. The precision in the law required here was only that which allowed a person to know in general when, say, the security forces might intercept telephone calls, not whether they were about to intercept his calls.[9]

The United Kingdom has enacted the Security Services Act 1989 and the Intelligence Services Act 1994 to provide a statutory basis for the operations of these services, which include, but are by no means restricted to, secret surveillance.[10] The 1989 Act meets the deficiency acknowledged in the *Hewitt and Harman* case[11] of the total lack of foundation for secret surveillance and was regarded by the Commission as 'law' of sufficient quality in the Convention sense despite the lack of operational detail in the legislation.[12]

b.   Children: public care

In *Eriksson v Sweden*[13] and *Olsson v Sweden (No 2)*,[14] the Swedish courts had found that there was a lacuna in the national child-care law because there was no legal basis for the conditions imposed by social workers restricting the access of parents to their children who were in public care. Swedish law was amended in 1990 but the European Court necessarily found that restrictions imposed before that date were not 'in accordance

6   Id, para 31.
7   Id, para 36. See also *A v France* A 277-B (1993).
8   *Mersch v Luxembourg Nos 10439/83*, 43 DR 34 at 93-99, 114-115 (1985).
9   *Leander v Sweden* A 116 para 51 (1987).
10 For the Security Services Act 1989, see Leigh and Lustgarten 52 MLR 801 (1989); for the Intelligence Services Act 1994, see Wadham 57 MLR 916 (1994).
11 Loc cit at p 338, n 18, above.
12 *Esbester v UK No 18601/91* (1993) 18 EHRR CD 72 (1994); *Hewitt and Harman v UK No 20317/92* (1993), unreported. This latter application concerned the retention of information collected by secret surveillance, see below, p 346.
13 A 156 para 67 (1989).
14 A 250 para 76 (1992).

with the law'. The usual complaint of applicants in cases like this is not that there is no national law but that the national law is too general in the scope of the powers that it confers on social workers to remove children from the custody of their parents or to take other decisions about children in public care. In *Olsson v Sweden (No 1)*,[15] Swedish law authorised the taking of children into care, *inter alia*, if:

'1. lack of care for him or any other condition in the home entails a danger to his health or development; or
2. the young person is seriously endangering his health or development by abuse of habit-forming agents, criminal behaviour or any other comparable behaviour . . .'

While acknowledging the 'rather general' terms of the Swedish law, the Court accepted that it satisfied the notion of 'law' in Article 8. The circumstances in which social workers needed to be able to act were so various that a general power, including a pre-emptive authority, was necessary. Protection against arbitrariness was to be found in the procedural protection which accompanied the general power, including judicial supervision.[16] The principle that the wider the power, the greater the procedural protection required is welcome but, as is sometimes the case when the Court looks at national remedies, the actual degree of supervision of the exercise of administrative power is less than the form of the law might suggest.[17]

c. Prisoners' correspondence

Several applications from prisoners in the United Kingdom have alleged that interferences with their correspondence were not 'in accordance with the law'. United Kingdom prison law is a complex arrangement of statute, delegated legislation, and several levels of administrative instruction to governors and prison staff, by no means all of them available to prisoners or their legal advisers.[18] In *Silver v UK*,[19] one of the applicant prisoners

---

15 A 130 (1988). For the law, see the Special Provisions on Care of Young Persons Act 1980, printed in para 37, judgment. See also the Child Welfare Act 1960, para 35, judgment. There have been sharp differences between the Commission and the Court on the question whether the requirements of 'law' have been satisfied in some child care cases. In *Andersson (M and R) v Sweden*, A 226 (1992), the Commission (id, Com Rep paras 89-104) unanimously found a violation because of impermissible 'uncertainty' as to both the content of the law and the scope of the social welfare authorities' decisions prohibiting parental access. The Court unanimously (id, Ct Jmt paras 80-85) found no such uncertainty.

16 Id, para 62.

17 See below, p 349.

18 For the present position, see Livingstone and Owen, *Prison Law*, 1993, pp 144-157.

19 A 61 paras 91, 93-95 (1983). Standing Order No 5, which regulates correspondence in England and Wales, has now been published and is available to prisoners: see Bailey, Harris and Jones, loc cit at n 18, above, p 698.

maintained that some of his letters had been stopped in accordance with Standing Orders and Circular Instructions, which were directions to governors not having the force of law. The Court accepted that these instruments, which filled in some details of the necessarily wide legal authority to intercept prisoners' mail, could be taken into account to determine whether the legal regime satisfied the Convention standard of foreseeability. However, this was acceptable only to the extent that the Orders and Instructions were accessible to a prisoner, which in general they were not. The result was that the stopping of several of Silver's letters had not been in accordance with the law. Where the authorities relied primarily on the Prison Rules as the basis for stopping the letters, the Court held that these were sufficiently available to prisoners through 'cell cards' and that the guidance they gave was adequate for the prisoner to be able to foresee how the Rules would be applied to his correspondence.

A similar problem arose in Scotland and was considered in *McCallum v UK*.[20] Although the Commission's report is not entirely clear, it found that the interference with the applicant's mail was not compatible with Article 8 because the government relied on 'management guidelines' to supplement the generalities of the law and those guidelines were not available to prisoners; it also found that the guidelines themselves were over-broad and so they authorised interference with correspondence which was not 'necessary for a democratic society'.[1] The Court confirmed these conclusions without comment.[2] In *Campbell v UK*,[3] the Court rejected a claim that stopping the applicant's letters was without legal foundation altogether in the national law because the claim was based on an interpretation of national law which had been rejected by the Scottish courts and which the European Court was not prepared to re-examine. In contrast, in *Herczegfalvy v Austria*[4] the requirement of foreseeability was held not to be satisfied by decisions under an Austrian law which allowed a mental patient's curator to decide whether his correspondence should be sent on. A curator's powers were set out in the most general terms and, the Court stated,

> '. . . in the absence of any detail at all as to the kind of restrictions permitted or their purpose, duration and extent or arrangements for their review, [these] provisions do not offer the minimum degree of protection against arbitrariness required by the rule of law in a democratic society.'

20 A 183 (1990).
1   Id, Com Rep para 45-48.
2   A 183 para 31 (1990).
3   A 233 para 37 (1992). See further, Cram, 13 Legal Studies 356 (1993). Note also *Boyle and Rice v UK* A 131 para 50 (1988) (breach because letter stopped when Rules not applied correctly).
4   A 244 para 91 (1992). Section 51(1) of the Austrian Hospitals Law simply said: 'Patients who are compulsorily detained . . . may be subjected to restrictions with respect to freedom of movement or contact with the outside world', id, para 51.

d. Summary

Although the formal tests for 'law' have been well established since the *Silver* case, their application does present some difficulties. The question cannot be resolved in the abstract but must take into account the nature of the applicant's right and the precise reasons for which the state seeks to interfere with it. The principal cause for uncertainty is the requirement that the national law protect against arbitrary exercise of any discretion that it confers. An applicant's complaint is unlikely to be that the law on its face authorises action which is contrary to the Convention. Rather, it will be that a wide and uncontrolled power *might* be used in an unacceptable way, which means essentially in a way contrary to the Convention. Inevitably this shades into consideration of whether an interference is necessary in a democratic society, though it is the risk rather than the actuality of incompatibility with the Convention which is at stake. That risk can be reduced by the provision of adequate safeguards of a procedural kind attached to the exercise of the power. In some cases, like *Leander v Sweden*[5] and *Hewitt and Harman v UK*,[6] the available safeguards have been considered under the 'in accordance with law' and the 'necessary in a democratic society' inquiries. Applicants have also raised the same question under Article 13 but where the Stasbourg authorities have been satisfied that there has been no breach of Article 8 by reason of procedural deficiency, they have also concluded that there has been no violation of Article 13. Until the jurisprudence is further refined, it is advisable for applicants to plead issues of substantive and procedural arbitrariness on too many, rather than too few, occasions.[7]

iii. The aim of the interference

It is for the state to identify the objective for which it is interfering with an applicant's Article 8(1) right. The list of legitimate aims in Article 8(2) is broadly similar to those in Articles 9(2)-11(2), except that Article 8(2) permits interference 'in the interests . . . of the economic well-being of country'. In some cases, the dispute between the applicant and the state turns on whether the state has 'respected' the individual's interest and when the Court has found against the state on this point, it has not sought to go on to try to justify the breach under Article 8(2).[8] In other cases, the Court has not needed to proceed with the justification offered by the state because it has concluded that the interference was not in accordance with the law.[9] When the Strasbourg authorities do reach the explanation given by a state justifying the interference, the state can rely on a long list of broad purposes.

---

5 A 116 paras 50-57, 61-67 (1987).
6 *No 20317/92* (1993), unreported.
7 See Strasser, *Wiarda Mélanges*, pp 595-604.
8 Eg *Gaskin v UK* A 160 (1989).
9 Eg *Malone v UK* A 82 (1984).

States have always been able to convince the Court that they were acting for a proper purpose, even where this has been disputed by the applicant.[10] Examples include the secret collection of information about an individual in the interests of national security,[11] the separation of children from their parents in the interests of the rights of others (viz of the children, when the parents are the applicants)[12] or the protection of health or morals (viz of the children, when the children themselves are the applicants),[13] and stopping prisoners' letters for the prevention of disorder (within the prison) or the prevention of crime,[14] likewise the deportation of aliens convicted of crimes.[15]

iv. Necessary in a democratic society

In the preceeding chapter, the complexity of the criteria to be taken into account in deciding whether an interference was necessary in a democratic society was underlined.[16] It is for the state to indicate the objective of its interference and to demonstrate the 'pressing social need' for limiting the enjoyment of the applicant's right. The Court recognises that some aspects of the various rights protected by Article 8 are more important than others. In *Dudgeon v UK*,[17] the Court identified the right to private enjoyment of sexual relations as requiring 'particularly serious reasons' to justify interference with it. In deciding that the criminalisation of adult, private, consensual male homosexual relations was not necessary, the Court was not deterred by the good faith of the United Kingdom's assessment to the contrary, nor by the claim that the existing position enjoyed wide support in Northern Ireland.[18] Instead, it relied on the developing European consensus towards removing criminal sanctions and the absence of any evidence that the practice of the Northern Ireland authorities in refraining from the implementation of the law had led to damage to moral standards in the province. These considerations led it to conclude that the legislation was not necessary in a democratic society.[19] The European consensus was important in *Norris v Ireland*,[20] where the Court, faced with the same issue in Ireland, had to

10 Eg *Andersson (M and R) v Sweden* A 226-A (1992).
11 *Leander v Sweden* A 116 (1987).
12 *Olsson v Sweden (No 1)* A 130 (1988).
13 *Andersson (M and R) v Sweden* A 226-A (1992).
14 *Campbell and Fell v UK* A 80 (1984).
15 *Moustaquim v Belgium* A 193 (1993).
16 See above pp 290-301.
17 A 45 para 52 (1981).
18 Id, paras 57-59.
19 Id, paras 60-61.
20 A 142 paras 43-46 (1988). In *Modinos v Cyprus* A 259 (1993) the government denied that there had been an interference with the applicant's rights but, when the Court found that there had, it made no attempt to justify the interference. The development of the jurisprudence from earlier Commission decisions such as *X v FRG No 5935/72*, 3 DR 46 (1975) and *B v UK No 9237/81*, 34 DR 68 (1983) is marked.

answer the government's claim that the assessment of what the protection of morals required was essentially reserved to the state. This conclusion was bolstered by reference to the qualities of tolerance and broadmindness as features of a democratic state: that people were shocked, offended or disturbed by homosexual practices was not sufficient justification for criminalising them.

The significance of the particular exercise of the right has been a feature in cases dealing with the right of correspondence of persons in detention, particularly convicted prisoners. The Court has accorded a high priority to the protection of their right to communicate with their legal advisers. In *Golder v UK*,[1] the Court rejected the government's claim that it was necessary to refuse to transmit a letter from a prisoner to his solicitor about the possibility of bringing a civil action against a prison officer 'for the prevention of disorder'. After the friendly settlement in *McComb v UK*,[2] new Standing Orders were introduced for English and Scottish prisons. The Standing Orders distinguish between correspondence with legal advisers about legal proceedings already instituted and other correspondence, including that about prospective legal proceedings.[3] Letters in the second category are liable to be opened and read. However, the Court in *Campbell v UK*[4] found that this infringed Article 8. The Court emphasised the 'general interest' that consultations with lawyers should be in conditions 'which favour full and uninhibited discussion'. No distinction could usefully be drawn between correspondence which related to instituted proceedings and those merely contemplated. All such letters were 'privileged', which meant that reasonable cause must be shown by the state for suspecting that a particular letter contained illicit material before it could be opened and that there must be guarantees to the prisoner that this limited power to intercept and read his correspondence was not being abused, for instance, by opening any letters in his presence.

The lawyer-client privilege is regarded by the Court as of high importance outside the context of prison. In holding in *Niemietz v Germany*[5] that, in the circumstances in which it had taken place, the search of a lawyer's office was not justified under Article 8(2), even though it was for the prevention of crime and the protection of the rights of others, the Court noted that:

> 'Where a lawyer is involved, an encroachment on professional secrecy may have repercussions on the proper administration of justice and hence on the rights guaranteed by Article 6 of the Convention.'

1 A 18 para 45 (1976).
2 *No 10621/83*, 50 DR 81 (1986).
3 See Livingstone and Owen, *Prison Law*, 1993, pp 144-157.
4 A 233 paras 46-48 (1992). On communication between a prisoner and the European Commission of Human Rights, see paras 61-64. Campbell's application had been introduced before the reforms following *McComb*. See also *R v Secretary of State for the Home Department, ex p Leech* [1993] 4 All ER 539 at 554-555.
5 A 251-B para 37 (1992). See also *Schonenberger and Durmaz v Switzerland* A 137 para 28 (1988) (not necessary to stop a letter from lawyer to remand prisoner advising prisoner to exercise his lawful right to remain silent).

While the same degree of solicitude for the confidentiality of correspondence is not required for prisoners' letters in general, the powers to intercept, scrutinise and prohibit correspondence must be related to some specific objection and not be couched in general terms which would unnecessarily catch letters of an unobjectionable kind.[6]

If some interests of individuals are given higher priority than others, the same is true about the interests the state seeks to protect by interfering with rights under Article 8. In *Klass v FRG*,[7] the Court accepted the government's claim that secret surveillance of telephone calls was undertaken in the interests of 'national security' and 'public safety'. The threats to these interests came from increasingly sophisticated foreign espionage and serious, internal terrorist activities. These were 'exceptional conditions' which could justify exceptional measures of secret surveillance. Similarly, in *Leander v Sweden*[8] the Court accepted the need of the state to collect information and maintain secret dossiers on candidates for employment in sensitive jobs, where there might be threats to national security. It was the state's responsibility to identify those exceptional conditions and special jobs. However, even when it had done so, the Court insisted on the provision of measures to protect against abuse of the powers asserted by the state. In each of these cases, the applicant could not demand protective powers of such scope as to undermine the purpose of the interference – there could be no right to prior notification that one's telephone was to be tapped, for instance. In the *Klass* case,[9] the Court accepted that parliamentary supervision and an independent board under the chairmanship of a person qualified to hold judicial office to review the exercise of the surveillance powers was an adequate protection against abuse, in all the circumstances. In the *Leander* case,[10] the Court accepted that the provision of several measures of control by bodies independent of the government were sufficient guard against abuse. In neither case did the Court require in all circumstances even *ex post facto* notification to an individual of the fact that his telephone had been tapped or that information continued to be held about him by the authorities.[11]

---

6   There has been a large number of cases from the UK, because law reform has not kept up with the progress of applications, see Jones, in 16th Report of the Standing Advisory Commission on Human Rights (Northern Ireland), 1990-1991 HC 488, pp 256-259.

7   A 28 para 48 (1978).

8   A 116 para 60 (1987). These considerations are closely similar to those which arise in deciding whether the national law is 'law' in the Convention sense: for a series of cases where the Court chose to deal with the absence of procedural protection as demonstrating a lack of proportionality rather than a failure of 'law', see *Funke, Crémieux, Miaihle v France* A/256 A, B, C (1993), below p 347.

9   A 28 para 56 (1978).

10   A 116 para 65 (1987).

11   For cases where the Commission has held the procedural safeguards adequate and interferences in accordance with them 'necessary in a democratic society, see *Mersch v Luxembourg No 10439/83*, 43 DR 34 (1985); *MS and PS v Switzerland No 10628/83*, 44 DR 175 (1985); *Spillmann v Switzerland No 11811/85*, 55 DR 182 (1988); *L v Norway No 13564/88*, 65 DR 210 (1990); for retention, *Hewitt and Harman*, see above, p 340, n 12.

However, the circumstances of cases like *Klass* and *Leander* are very special. More typically, interferences with private life or a person's home or correspondence will occur in the course of the enforcement of the ordinary criminal law. In this context, search warrants will generally require prior judicial authorisation if they are to be regarded as proportionate to their purpose by the Strasbourg authorities. In *Funke v France*,[12] the Court said about the very wide powers given to the customs authorities to institute searches of property:

'Above all, in the absence of any requirement of a judicial warrant the restrictions and conditions provided for in law . . . appear to be too lax and full of loopholes for the interferences with the applicant's rights to have been strictly proportionate to the legitimate aim pursued.'

In the *Funke* case, the customs authorities had searched the applicant's house in order to obtain information of his assets abroad and seized documents concerning foreign bank accounts in connection with customs offences which, under French law, were criminal offences. Under the law that applied at the time, the customs authorities had, as the Court noted with concern, 'exclusive competence to assess the expediency, number, length and scale of inspections'.[13] The customs officers were required by law to be accompanied during their search by a local municipal officer or, as on the facts, by a senior police officer. The Court held that the search and seizure was not justified under Article 8(2), emphasising particularly the absence of prior judicial authorisation. While judicial authorisation may ordinarily be required if search for and seizure of materials which interfere with an applicant's rights under Article 8(1) are to be justified under Article 8(2), the fact that a judicial warrant has been obtained will not always be sufficient. In *Niemietz v Germany*,[14] the Court found that a search of the premises of a lawyer in quest of documents to be used in criminal proceedings was disproportionate to its purposes of preventing crime and protecting the rights of others,[15] even though it took place under the authority of a warrant. The warrant was drawn in too broad terms and the search impinged on the professional secrecy of some of the materials which had been inspected. There were, in German law, no special procedural safeguards attending the exercise of search powers on the premises of lawyers.

---

12 A 256-A para 57 (1993). To the same effect, *Crémieux v France* A 256-B para 40 (1993) and *Miaihle v France* 256-C para 38 (1993).
13 A 256-A para 57 (1993).
14 A 251-B para 37 (1992).
15 The warrant extended to 'documents' that might reveal the identity of a third party to be prosecuted for the criminal offence of writing an insulting letter to a judge. The reason for searching the applicant's office was that it had been used as a post box for the political party for which the letter had been written. The police examined the contents of four filing cabinets.

The above cases concern searches in the context of criminal proceedings. In *Chappell v UK*,[16] the Court accepted that in civil proceedings the execution of an Anton Piller order in respect of the applicant's premises could be justified under Article 8(2) as being for the protection of the 'rights of others'. An Anton Piller order is one by which the English High Court may, without notifying or hearing the defendant, authorise the plaintiff in civil proceedings to enter the defendant's premises to search for and seize property that is the subject of civil proceedings, *inter alia*, to prevent its disappearance. The order is subject to certain restrictions as to the time of day and the number of persons who may execute it. The latter must include the party's solicitor, who is an officer of court and subject to its discipline. There is no right to forcible entry, but the defendant may be in contempt of court if he does not permit entry. In the *Chappell* case, the applicant was a video tape dealer who was being sued in breach of copyright by the plaintiffs who obtained an order to search for pirate videos. The order was executed in premises that served as the applicant's offices and, upstairs, his home. It was executed by five persons, including the applicant's solicitor. At the same time, as pre-arranged, eleven policemen executed a separate criminal search warrant for obsence videos. The Court held that the resulting interference with the applicant's privacy and his home could be justified under Article 8(2) as being to protect the plaintiff's copyright. While the manner of execution was, as the English Court of Appeal had said, 'disturbing' and 'unfortunate and regrettable', with a large number of persons invading the applicant's privacy, the issue and execution of the order was not disproportionate to that end.

Disclosure of personal information about an individual other than for the direct purpose for which it was legitimately collected may constitute an interference with the right to respect for private life and accordingly require justification under Article 8(2). In *TV v Finland*,[17] the Commission held that the disclosure that a prisoner was HIV-positive to prison staff directly involved in his custody and who were themselves subject to obligations of confidentiality was justified as being necessary for the protection of the rights of others.

The positive obligation to provide procedural safeguards against arbitrary treatment as a condition of justifying interference with Article 8 rights is also a feature of decisions to remove children from their parents in the interests of the children's welfare and to impose conditions upon the access of parents to their children who are in public care. In *W v UK*,[18] the decision to remove children from their parents and put them into foster-care was one which might ultimately have led (and did, in fact, lead) to the placing of children for adoption and, therefore, the severing of the family link between parents and children. This is, the Court said, 'a domain in which there is an even greater call than usual for protection against arbitrary interferences'. What was

16 A 152 (1989).
17 *No 21780/93*, 76A DR 140 at 150-151 (1994).
18 A 121 para 62 (1987). See also *H v UK, O v UK* A 120 (1987) and *B v UK, R v UK* A 121 (1987).

required was a process which, taken as a whole, involved the parents to a degree sufficient to provide protection of their interests. In the particular case, the parents had not been informed of a decision which arranged the legal basis of the foster-care seriously to the parent's disadvantage; they were not kept informed about the development of the long-term foster-care of their children and the possibility that it might lead to adoption; they were not consulted about the decision to deny them access to the children. There were significant delays in legal proceedings which were in part attributable to the authorities. The result eventually had been that the High Court issued an order as being in the best interests of the child that the parents' consent to his adoption be dispensed with. Even allowing for the margin of appreciation in the state about how such cases were managed, the Court found that this catalogue of exclusion and delay was not necessary for the protection of the rights of the child and that there was a violation of Article 8.[19]

In *W v UK*, the failures were stark, but that is not always the case and then the supervisory function of the Court is more difficult to discharge. Several of the cases have involved decisions of social services authorities in Sweden, where national law appears to give officials an unusual degree of authority to control relations between parents and children. Allegations of bad faith to one side (and they have been frequently made), the Court has not found it possible to review the general policy of the national law in the absence of any common European understanding about how far the state may legitimately interfere between parents and children. The test spelt out in *Olsson v Sweden (No 1)*[20] is whether, given the national policy that the state has decided upon, the authorities have 'relevant and sufficient reasons' for acting as they did in taking children into care and/or in deciding to continue it on the conditions which had been set. The confirmation of social workers' decisions by national courts is some support for the social workers' position if the case reaches Strasbourg but it is not conclusive as to whether the Convention has been complied with. Furthermore, there is a positive duty on the social workers to involve the parents in any decisions they take, however difficult that may be.[1] On the facts of *Olsson (No 1)*, the Court found that there were good and adequate explanations for the decisions of the authorities, save for placing two of the children in care a great distance away from their parents and their brother. Since the authorities had proceeded on the basis that the ultimate aim of the care was to reunite the parents and all the children, this decision was inimical to *that* policy and was not, therefore, necessary for any Convention objective.[2] The same dispute came back to the Court more than four years later by which time the

---

19 *W v UK* A 121, paras 62-65 (1987). Note the even more precise requirements of the separate opinion of Judges Pinheiro Farinha, Pettiti, De Meyer and Valticos. Cf also *McMichael v UK* A 307-B (1995) Com Rep para 105, where the Commission considered the procedural requirements of child-care decisions under Article 8(1); also Ct Jmt paras 89-93.

20 A 130 paras 74, 77 (1988).

1 Id, para 83.

2 Id, para 82. The Court detected also that the decisions had not been driven by considerations of the interests of the family but by administrative factors, which further inclined it to finding a violation. See Gomien, 7 Neth QHR 435 at 443-446 (1989).

reunification of the family had still not been achieved. The Court said that, in cases like this, there was a positive, but not absolute, duty on the state to take steps to bring about the reuniting of parent and child. What that duty involved in a particular case was subject to a margin of appreciation,

> 'whether the national authorities have made such efforts to arrange the necessary preparations for reunion as can *reasonably* be demanded under the special circumstances of each case.'[3]

Not least, this was because of the direct access to the parties which the national courts had, unlike the European Court which relied exclusively on the case-file.[4] The Court's conclusion, which suggests that the burden of proof in cases like this switches back to the applicant, was that:

> '... it has not been established that the social welfare authorities failed to fulfil their obligation to take measures with a view to the [reunification of the family].'[5]

In *Andersson (M and R) v Sweden*,[6] the Court did find a violation of Article 8, even despite the wide margin of appreciation. The basis for the conclusion was that the government had not shown that the conditions restricting access and communication between the parent and child while the child was in care were necessary. They 'had to be supported by strong reasons ... ', which suggests a different burden than the one imposed in *Olsson (No 2)*. In his dissent, Judge Lagergren recognised the inconsistencies:

> 'The full implications of the available margin of appreciation will be difficult to draw until a larger and more coherent body of law emerges.'[7]

He endorsed the government's suggestion that witnesses be called by the European Court if it were minded to review national decisions. That is likely to be unwelcome to the Court. However, his general position does accord with the approach of the Court in *Olsson (No 1)* and, in the absence of more widely accepted standards of the appropriate conduct for social workers, Judge Lagergren's prescription of greater deference to decisions of national authorities with necessary judicial supervision has much to commend it.[8]

---

3   *Olsson v Sweden (No 2)* A 250 para 90 (1992). Italics added.
4   Id, para 91 (1992).
5   Id, para 91. Compare Judge Pettiti, dissenting, who held that in the circumstances of this case, there were objective, European standards of what good social work practice required, which had been ignored by the Swedish authorities.
6   A 226 para 95 (1992).
7   Ibid.
8   See also *Rieme v Sweden* A 226-B paras 73, 74 (1992) where the Court found that the authorities had acted properly and reasonably. And see Mr Schermers, dissenting in *Eriksson v Sweden* A 156 Com Rep (1989), suggesting a procedural approach to questions of child-care and allowing a wide margin of appreciation to the states on the substance of decisions. And see Cohen-Jonathan, *European Supervision*, Ch 16 at p 440, urging judicial supervision of decisions *prior* to their implementation.

This approach would fix attention on the general procedures in the national law, not least the need for the appropriate degree of expedition, given the serious effects of delay on the substantive outcome of individual cases. It cannot be ruled out that the Court does not have full confidence in the effectiveness of the judicial supervision of the social work system in Sweden with respect to children in care as a result of the long-drawn out saga of the *Olsson* cases.

In *Hokkanen v Finland*,[9] the Court held that the transfer of custody rights from the father to the maternal grandparents was justifiable under Article 8(2), taking into account the girl's wishes and the length of time she had been in the *de facto* custody of her grandparents. This was so even though the authorities had failed to enforce court orders allowing the father custody and access against the recalcitrant grandparents. The interests of the child were elevated over those of the father and the Court emphasised the better position of national courts to assess the evidence upon which such decisions would be based. Given the emphasis placed by the family law of many states and in international human rights treaties[10] on the 'best interests of the child' in reaching decisions about him, it was to be anticipated that action justified by the state on this ground (as being necessary 'for the protection of the rights of others') would weigh particularly heavily in favour of the legitimacy of an act of interference with an Article 8(1) right. However, the Strasbourg institutions have been criticised for deferring too readily to the state's determination of what these best interests are in a particular case, to the detriment of the child's right to family life.[11]

There have been developments in the case-law on the justification for interfering with family life by removing from the jurisdiction a member of the family who has no right to stay. Given the established position that the right to respect for family life does not in general involve a positive obligation to allow the family to establish itself in a particular country, the state is entitled to remove an alien for a good reason under Article 8(2), usually for the protection of public order or the prevention of crime, even where it might be difficult for him thereafter to enjoy his family life. In *Berrehab v Netherlands*,[12] the Court took a new line. There, a previously married alien had lost his right to stay in the Netherlands after his divorce from his Dutch wife. Despite his continued close links with his daughter, the authorities proposed to deport him. What counted with the Court was the evidence of the strength of Berrehab's ties with his daughter, even after the divorce. Refusal to grant him a residence permit seriously threatened those ties. There was no suggestion that the child could travel with him and the

---

9   A 299-A paras 63-65 (1994). See also *Hendriks v Netherlands No 8427/78*, 29 DR 5 (1982) Com Rep; CM Res DH (82) 4. For criticism of the Commission majority in this case, see Gomien, 7 Neth QHR 435 at pp 440-443 (1989). These criticisms would apply also to the *Hokkanen* case.

10 See the Convention on the Rights of the Child, Article 3(1).

11 Gomien, above n 9, pp 449-450.

12 A 138 para 29 (1988). The Court gave practically no consideration to the interest of the state.

prospects of family life being maintained by his returning to the Netherlands from time to time were negligible. In these circumstances, the state had a positive obligation to allow him to stay and it was not necessary to depart from that duty because of any perceived need to protect the economic well-being of the country.

If the *Berrehab* case is relatively uncontroversial in the context of the development of the Convention (even if it were not so in the Netherlands), the extension of the principle which it establishes to cases involving second generation immigrants has been less easily accepted. In *Moustaquim v Belgium*,[13] the Court found that Belgium would interfere with the applicant's right to respect for his family life if it deported him to Morocco, his country of nationality. He had been brought by his parents as a young child with the rest of his family. As an adolescent, he had engaged in an intensive life of crime, much of it petty but some of it serious. Once it had been established that there were real and substantial ties between Moustaquim and his parents and brothers and sisters, the Court decided that his deportation would interfere with his family life and that that could not be justified as being necessary for the prevention of crime. The division between the majority and minority in the Court was solely about the seriousness of Moustaquim's criminal activities. Perhaps even more remarkably, the Court took the same position in *Beldjoudi v France*.[14] Here too the applicant had been brought to Europe from North Africa as an infant, in this case from Algeria to France. He retained his Algerian nationality. He had been educated in French and his close relatives had also lived in France for many years. Beldjoudi had been married to a Frenchwoman for twenty years. He was a professional criminal who had spent about half of his adult life in prison. There would have been severe practical and even legal obstacles to Beldjoudi's wife accompanying him to Algeria: it should be remembered that she was an applicant, too. The Court found that it would be disproportionate to the aims of preventing crime or preserving public order if he were deported for that 'might imperil the unity or even the existence of the marriage . . . ', for, though the Court does not say so expressly, the government continued to have the option of imprisoning Beldjoudi if he persisted with his criminal career. With different degrees of enthusiasm, some members of the Commission and Court have said that the case-law is tantamount to giving a second-generation alien with family ties in a state the right to stay.[15] Certainly, it is difficult to see that the mere seriousness of crime will be good reason for deportation. The state will have to show some additional impact on public order, as might arise in terrorist offences or drug trafficking. There were suggestions in *Beldjoudi* that an alien threatened with deportation might also

13 A 193 (1991).
14 A 234-A para 78 (1992).
15 In the *Beldjoudi* case, Judge Martens, concurring, assimilating settled aliens and nationals in the interests of legal certainty; Judge Pettiti, dissenting, regarding the power to deport aliens as a condition for accepting them at all.

demonstrate an interference with his right to private life if he had no connections with the territory to which he was to be removed, no facility in the local language and no prospect of developing there a social life.[16] If this proposal were acted upon, it would give a wider degree of protection against deportation based on conditions in the destination state than the claim that the treatment of the applicant there would violate the standards of Article 3.[17] The margin of appreciation of states in what they once would have regarded as a practically unfettered prerogative is gradually being reduced.

5. CONCLUSION

The complexity of Article 8(1) is twofold: the interests which it protects are wide and there is much scope for interpretation by the Strasbourg authorities, although the way in which these interests are protected – 'the right to respect' for them rather than 'the right' to them – allows some leeway to the states in determining what 'respect' requires. There is a dual focus on the state with regard to many aspects of Article 8(1). On the one hand, there is the concern to control the state's capacity to interfere in central matters of inter-personal relationships: consensual sexual activities, parent and child relations, conversation and correspondence, where the principal concern of the right-holder is keeping the state out. On the other hand, the state's assistance is called for to protect persons from harm inflicted by others: exploitative sexual conduct, children damaged by parents, communications which harass the recipient. The practice shows how hard the various balances are to strike but, even once struck, the Commission and the Court are faced with the more familiar problem under Articles 8-11 of supervising the power of the states to limit the exercise of the rights established under Article 8(1).

The Court is notoriously unwilling to elaborate general statements of rights. In relation to Article 8, this has had an advantage as well as the usual drawback of making it difficult for an account of the case-law to rise above the single instances before the Court. The advantage is that the Court has been able to develop the interests protected to take into account changing circumstances and understandings without being confined by an established theoretical framework. The expansion of the right to respect for private life to include personal relationships of a non-secret kind and to provide for an element of protection against environmental damage are examples of this. Equally, the extended notion of family life has enabled the Court to provide protection for the substance rather than the form of relationships in accordance with the developing practice and expectations of people. While the Court has seldom been confronted with widespread patterns of hostility

16 Judge Martens, ibid.
17 See above, pp 78-80; Errera, (1994) PL 656, reporting the decision of the Conseil d'Etat in *Bahri* (8 April 1994).

towards individuals, the prevalence of public and private animus to immigrants, including asylum-seekers and settled aliens, is likely to make the recent jurisprudence on the protection of family life of great significance. It is one thing to get states to comply with obligations which affect only a few people and which are on the periphery of political concerns: it is much more of a test to secure the co-operation of the authorities on matters of such central and prominent interest. Yet it is against such threats to human rights that the Convention was originally designed.

The Strasbourg authorities have made use of the term 'respect' in Article 8(1) to enhance rather than reduce the reach of states' obligations. Imposing positive obligations on states, whether to take action to enhance the enjoyment of a right or to take action to prevent interference with a right by non-state actors, presents further difficulties in giving an account of the law. Positive obligations are hardly ever absolute and the reach of obligations to stand between private actors remains largely unexplicated by the Court. Once again, recourse is made to the 'balance' metaphor but the problem is not so much in weighing the individual interest against the public interest as in deciding just what weight to attach to the individual interest. The characterisation of the interests of transsexuals in the rectification of their birth certificates, either as an essential ingredient in the confirmation of their new status or as a mere convenience, substantially determined which way the cases were decided. The Court is deciding here the rights that are protected by the Convention, not balancing an established right against the public interest as it does under Article 8(2). The 'margin of appreciation' doctrine, developed in the latter context, ought not to be relied on in the same way to determine what is necessary to 'respect' an individual's interest. Instead, the Court should welcome more argument on the real nature of the individual's interest before embarking on its balancing exercise against the countervailing demands of the public interest.

One thing which distinguishes the deportation cases is the willingness of the Court to review substantive decisions of national authorities, even though taken in accordance with national laws, laws furthermore which satisfy the Convention understanding of 'law'. Elsewhere, the Strasbourg authorities have been very reluctant to challenge substantive decisions, as in the child-care cases, or practically unwilling to do so, as in the wire-tapping cases. Great emphasis is put on formal legality and procedural guarantees and the Court has been able to establish a flexible due process standard to accommodate the variety of cases which fall within Article 8. First, there are very specific requirements for particular rights, such as the independent review required in *Gaskin* (there, under Article 8(1)). Then, there is the obligation to satisfy Article 13. What has been influential is the *Klass* case, which decided that the remedy required had to be tailored to the legitimacy of the state's power to interfere with the right rather than the right of the individual. If wire-tapping was, in some conditions, permissible, those conditions did not include a remedial system which undermined the effectiveness of a particular wire-tap. Where the authorities have been able to point to a lawful basis for wire-tapping and procedural protections which satisfy the *Klass* interpretation of Article 13, the institutions have never disputed that the interception was 'necessary in a democratic society'.

Finally, if the right protected by Article 8(1) is a 'civil right' within the terms of Article 6(1) and if the act of interference by the state has 'determined' the applicant's civil right, then the procedural protection which he is due is that established by Article 6(1), a fairly rigid standard, not as amenable as Article 13 to flexible interpretation. However, some aspects of Article 6 may be interpreted in ways related to the Article 8 character of the right, for instance, the need for special expedition in child-care cases. The procedural failure under Article 6(1) may also be a substantive failure under Article 8. If it seems a cautious conclusion that procedure will often prevail over substance, it is a reflection of the subsidiary role of the Convention in protecting rights. It is only in the exceptional case that the Court will reject a conclusion of state authorities which have addressed themselves, in substance at least, to the very question that comes before the Court.

CHAPTER 10

Article 9: Freedom of religion

'**Article 9**
1. Everyone has the right to freedom of thought, conscience and religion; this right includes freedom to change his religion or belief and freedom, either alone or in community with others and in public or private, to manifest his religion or belief, in worship, teaching, practice and observance.
2. Freedom to manifest one's religion or beliefs shall be subject only to such limitations as are prescribed by law and are necessary in a democratic society in the interests of public safety, for the protection of public order, health or morals, or for the protection of the rights and freedoms of others.'

Despite the importance and breadth of the interests protected by Article 9, relatively few applications have been made alleging violations of it and only a small proportion of those have given rise to successful claims. This may speak well of the protection given to Article 9 rights in national law, though to some extent it has been due to a cautious approach by the Commission to the interpretation of this provision.[1]

1. WHAT RIGHTS ARE PROTECTED?

Dealing with language in Article 18 of the ICCPR that is similar to that in Article 9 of the Convention, Partsch[2] points out that the 'diplomatic wording' was carefully chosen to mean many things to different groups:

1 See Goy, 107 RDP 5 (1991) and Shaw, *European System*, Ch 17. Although the ambit of 'freedom of thought, conscience and religion' has been given only limited consideration at Strasbourg, it has occasioned much attention in international human rights law generally. See, eg Humphrey, in Meron, ed, *Human Rights in International Law: Legal and Policy Issues*, Vol I, 1984, pp 174-181 and Dinstein, 20 Israeli YBHR 55 (1990). See also the UN Declaration on the Elimination of All Forms of Intolerance and Discrimination based on Religion or Belief, GA Res 36/55 (1981) and Sullivan, 82 AJIL 487 (1988).
2 In Henkin, ed, *The International Bill of Rights*, 1981, p 209 at p 210.

'Atheists may have been satisfied to see "thought" and "conscience" precede "religion". Libertarians may have been pleased to see all three freedoms on an equal level without preference to any one of them. Strongly religious people may have regarded "thought and conscience" as corresponding not only to religion generally but even to the only true religion, the one to which they adhere.'

The last words point to the great dilemma of the protection of strongly felt beliefs. Toleration of them is demanded because of the vital nature of the belief to the individual but unless attention is paid to the content of the belief, there is the danger that extreme beliefs, held with vehemence, may be accorded stronger protection than more reflective and contingent opinions. The Strasbourg authorities have not yet had to set the limits to the content of acceptable 'thought, conscience and religion',[3] although the Court has recently had to face the question whether a state may limit the manner of propagation of religious belief.[4]

Article 9 protects non-religious beliefs. In *Kokkinakis v Greece*,[5] the Court said that the values of Article 9 were at the foundation of democratic society:

'It is, in its religious dimension, one of the most vital elements that go to make up the identity of believers and their conception of life, but it is also a precious asset for atheists, agnostics, sceptics and the unconcerned.'

For the Court, Article 9 embraces another manifestation of tolerance and pluralism which runs through its conception of the values protected by the Convention. An illustration of the principle in the *Kokkinakis* case is found in *Arrowsmith v UK*[6] where the Commission accepted that pacifism fell 'within the ambit' of the right to freedom of thought and conscience because it was a 'philosophy'. The line between a philosophy and a political programme may yet be hard to draw. Van Dijk and Van Hoof[7] advocate not drawing it at all – 'in our opinion, Article 9 actually concerns any ideas and views whatever' – but the enquiry the Commission made in the *Arrowsmith* case makes it dubious whether so generous a view will prevail.[8]

Such a wide notion could be called in aid to avoid having to determine what is understood by 'religion'. In principle, the determination of whether

---

3 The matter was treated cursorily in *X v Italy No 6741/74*, 5 DR 83 (1976). In *Hoffmann v Austria* A 255-C para 32 (1993), the Court did not question that the belief of a Jehovah's Witness which precluded her from receiving blood transfusions and which would lead her to refuse blood transfusions for her children was a religious belief.
4 See below, p 367.
5 A 260-A para 31 (1993).
6 *No 7050/75*, 19 DR 5 (1978) Com Rep paras. 69-71; CM Res DH (79) 4.
7 Van Dijk and Van Hoof, p 397, n 1031.
8 See also *Revert and Legallais v France Nos 14331/88 and 14332/88*, 62 DR 309 (1989). And see Article 2, First Protocol, Ch 19, below ('religious and philosophical convictions').

a belief is religious or not may be made by the Strasbourg authorities. So far, it has not been necessary to decide whether a set of beliefs and practices is a 'religion'. In *X and Church of Scientology v Sweden*,[9] the Commission had to consider whether an advertisement by the Church was essentially for religious or commercial purposes. Having decided that it was for commercial purposes, so that it was not a manifestation of religion that was protected by Article 9, the Commission did not discuss the question whether Scientology was a religion. The Commission has likewise found no need on the particular facts to decide whether the Divine Light Zentrum[10] or Druidism[11] are religions.

In any case, it will be necessary for the applicant to show that he is, in fact, an adherent of the religion and, if necessary, that a particular belief or practice is an element of that religion.[12] In this regard, it should be easier for an applicant who claims that his 'thought' or 'conscience' is based on his own individual conception of a belief to establish the reality of his adherence to it and its content than for a person whose claim is based upon a 'religion' shared by others to do so. When the thought or conscience is the result of membership of a church or community, there are circumstances when the church or community may be a victim as well as individuals. This is more than mere representation of the interests of the members[13] because the church is capable of having interests of its own to protect.[14] One of its principal interests is the development and protection of its doctrine.

The rights protected by Article 9 may both overlap and conflict with others protected by the other Articles of the Convention. In general, and particularly for matters of religious belief, the protection of Article 9 appears superior to that afforded by Article 10, where the activity of the individual is both the manifestation of belief and the exercise of freedom of expression.[15] It will, therefore, usually be in the applicant's interest to characterise his claim as one arising under Article 9. However, in some cases, more precise protection is available elsewhere, such as the right of parents to have their children educated in accordance with the parents' religious or philosophical convictions, in which case it will be advantageous to rely on Article 2, First Protocol.[16] The Court sometimes resists applicants' attempts to raise under Article 9 issues which can be dealt

---

9 *No 7805/77*, 16 DR 68 at 72 (1979).
10 *Omkarananda and the Divine Light Zentrum v Switzerland No 8118/77*, 25 DR 105 (1981).
11 *Chappell v UK No 12587/86*, 53 DR 241 (1987).
12 The Commission has not backed away from deciding whether an applicant's conduct is required by his religion: see eg *X v UK No 8160/78*, 22 DR 27 at 35 (1981) and *D v France No 10180/82*, 35 DR 199 at 202 (1983). Note also the complaints in *Chauhan v UK No 11518/85*, 65 DR 41 at 44 (1990) F Sett, at the failure of the national court to assess fairly and accurately matters of religious belief.
13 *X and Church of Scientology v Sweden No 7805/77*, 16 DR 68 at 70 (1979) (reversing an earlier position).
14 *Chappell v UK No 12587/86*, 53 DR 241 at 246 (1987).
15 See below, pp 359, 367.
16 See below, Ch 19.

with under other provisions. In *Hoffmann v Austria*,[17] the Court regarded the matter of custody of children between their Jehovah's Witness and non-Jehovah's Witness parents as falling within the Article 8 right to respect for family life, rather than within Article 9. The Commission has decided that the right to marry is governed by Article 12 (and, therefore, by national law) so that, even though the applicant's religion permitted a lower age of capacity to marry than national law allowed, there was no violation of Article 9 by reason of the fact that this lower age was not recognised in national law or by virtue of the conviction of the applicant for unlawful sexual intercourse.[18] In *Johnston v Ireland*,[19] it was held that Article 9 could not provide the basis for a right to divorce that was not otherwise discoverable in the Convention.

Where there is a conflict between protected rights, the judgment of the Court in *Otto-Preminger-Institut v Austria*[20] speaks in favour of the strong regard to be had for religious beliefs (and therefore, Article 9 rights) in deciding priority between the competing rights. In that case, the state had interfered with the applicant's Article 10 right to freedom of expression by seizing and ordering forfeit a film found likely to offend the religious feelings of the Catholics who constituted the large majority of people in the region where the applicant proposed to show it. The Court upheld the interferences with the applicant's right as being necessary for the protection of 'the [religious] rights and freedoms of others'. In confirming that the interference had a legitimate aim, the Court said:

> '. . . the manner in which religious beliefs and doctrines are opposed or denied is a matter which may engage the responsibility of the state, notably its responsibility to ensure the peaceful enjoyment of the right guaranteed under Article 9 to the holders of those beliefs and doctrines . . .'

and, it went on,

> ' – in the context of religious opinions and beliefs – may legitimately be included an obligation [on individuals] to avoid as far as possible expressions which are gratuitously offensive to others . . .'.

This is a strong affirmation of the power and even the duty[1] of states to protect manifestations of religious belief. It strongly suggests that the Court would endorse the decision of the Commission in the *Gay News* case, that

17 A 255-C (1993).
18 *Khan v UK No 11579/85*, 48 DR 253 (1986).
19 A 112 paras 62, 63 (1986). But see Judge De Meyer, partly dissenting, arguing that an absolute prohibition on the dissolution of marriage motivated by religious considerations constitutes a violation of Article 9 for those who want to divorce, paras 5 and 6.
20 A 295 paras 47, 49 (1994).
1 See the term 'responsibility' in the first passage from *Otto-Preminger* quoted above.

the applicant's conviction for blasphemy against the Christian religion did not violate Article 10.[2] There might also be grounds for reconsidering the decision in *Choudhury v UK*[3] that the absence of a criminal sanction in English law against publications which offended against the religious beliefs of non-Christians was not a violation of Article 9. This conclusion, as surprising at it is regrettable, is out of line with the general practice of European states.[4]

In *Young, James and Webster v UK*,[5] the Court held that a national law which required the applicants to join a trade union against their will violated their rights under Article 11. It did not decide the applicants' claim that their rights under Article 9 were prejudiced also, even though objections based on personal convictions were among the reasons they resisted trade union membership. However, another implication of the *Otto-Preminger* case is that a closed-shop arrangement, otherwise compatible with Article 11, might be vulnerable to challenge where the applicant's reason for not joining is based on religious grounds. Equally, a trade union could not complain of an unnecessary violation of its rights if a religious exemption were provided by the law regulating its right to organise a closed-shop.

2. FREEDOM OF THOUGHT, CONSCIENCE AND RELIGION: THE RIGHT TO BELIEVE

Article 9(1) is divided into two parts: the right to freedom of thought, conscience and religion, or the right to believe – a right stipulated as including the right to change one's religion or belief – and the freedom to manifest one's religion or belief. It is only with respect to the latter that a state may interfere under Article 9(2) and only for a relatively restricted list of interests.[6] Freedom of thought, etc, then, is given very strong protection.

As to the guarantee of freedom to hold and to change one's religion or belief, in *Angelini v Sweden*,[7] the Commission said that this is a guarantee against 'indoctrination of religion by the state'. The Convention ought to protect against the indoctrination of any belief, whether religious or not. It has been suggested that such attempts at 'brainwashing' will involve violations of Article 3[8] but, as the *Angelini* case suggests, it is possible to envisage state activity which would fall within Article 9(1) without

---

2   *X Ltd and Y v UK No 8710/79*, 28 DR 77 (1982).
3   *No 17439/90*, 12 HRLJ 172 (1991). It may be significant, however, that the *Otto-Preminger* case concerned a majority religion, para 56, although para 47 refers to members of a religious 'majority or minority': see further, p 364, n 8, below.
4   See below, p 364.
5   A 44 (1981).
6   The protection given to freedom of thought etc. in the first part of Article 9(1) is such that Article 15 may not apply: Jacobs, p 144.
7   *No 10491/83*, 51 DR 41 at 48 (1986).
8   See Judge Martens, concurring, in *Kokkinakis v Greece* A 260-A (1993).

necessarily reaching the high threshold of Article 3. 'Indoctrination' involves some positive action directed against the individual. As long as he is free to hold his own beliefs, Article 9(1) will not be violated.

The maintenance of an established church, so long as membership is not compulsory, is compatible with Article 9.[9] Although public policy may be influenced by religious considerations, whether of an established church or otherwise, there will be no violation of Article 9 by this reason alone. In *Johnston v Ireland*,[10] the applicant could not demonstrate that any provision of the Convention provided a right to divorce. The proscription against divorce in the Irish Constitution can be attributed to the influence of the doctrine of the Roman Catholic church but that alone did not amount to indoctrination nor was the applicant able to show that any belief of his required him to divorce. As a result, he was not able to establish an independent right to a divorce under Article 9. At the same time, the fact that public policy is based on religious considerations will not, of itself, insulate the policy from review by the Strasbourg authorities. For example, the manifest religious basis of the Irish Supreme Court's judgment in the *Norris* case[11] upholding the criminalisation of male homosexuality did not prevent the European Court from deciding that the national decision was in violation of Article 8.[12]

The state may not consistently with Article 9 dictate what a person believes or take coercive steps to make him change his belief. Nor may it demand to know what he believes. The Commission takes the view that an order to fill a census form interferes with the respect for private life that is guaranteed by Article 8(1) but that the state can justify its interference as being necessary for the economic well-being of the country under Article 8(2).[13] As indicated earlier, this option of justifying an interference is not available with respect to the first part of Article 9(1) because Article 9(2) does not apply to it. If there are *some* circumstances when a state may not require an individual to reveal his beliefs because of Article 9(1), then that prohibition must apply to all circumstances.[14] Perhaps the explanation for this very strong protection of freedom of thought, conscience and religion is that there is no good reason why the state needs the information (though there are bad ones). If there were conceivably good reasons, possibly in the context of national security, for the state to know what a person believes, the resistance to giving it the power to do so reflects the shade of the Inquisition and the coercive investigations of modern totalitarian regimes. It remains to be seen if better protection of freedom of political belief may be found here than in Article 10(1), where the state may be able to justify its demand for the information under Article 10(2).[15]

---

9   *Darby v Sweden* A 187 (1991) Com Rep para 45. The Court decided this case under Article 1, First Protocol and Article 14, see below, p 465.
10 A 112 paras 53, 57 (1986).
11 *Norris v Attorney-General* [1984] IR 36.
12 *Norris v Ireland* A 142 (1988).
13 *X v UK No 8160/78*, 22 DR 27 at 36 (1981).
14 Van Dijk and Van Hoof, pp 397-398.
15 *X v FRG No 9228/80*, 30 DR 132 at 141 (1982) (the *Glasenapp* case).

According to the Court in the *Otto-Preminger* case,[16] the state has a responsibility to ensure the peaceful enjoyment of the right guaranteed under Article 9 to the holders of religious beliefs. The Court envisages positive obligations on the state to control activities of others which might inhibit those who hold religious beliefs from exercising their freedom to hold and express them. Positive obligations, then, may arise with respect to both parts of Article 9(1), holding beliefs as well as the manifestation of them. Indeed, as the facts of the *Otto-Preminger* case suggest, the state *may* have a duty (the issue was not directly in point) to regulate activities, where the mere knowledge that they are taking place is sufficient to anger or disturb those who hold religious inclinations to the contrary. The Court has not decided if the same strong protection applies also to those who might be affected in the holding of political or other non-religious beliefs.

Penalties imposed solely for holding a belief or for being a member of a church are probably outlawed by Article 9(1). Thus, when it first ratified the Convention, Norway made a reservation with respect to its constitutional exclusion of Jesuits from its territory.[17] The Commission will shortly have to consider whether penalties imposed for membership of a political party violate Article 9 since it has declared admissible several applications against Turkey in which individuals complain that they were punished for the beliefs they held and expressed by their membership of the Communist party.[18] In *Darby v Sweden*,[19] the Commission was of the opinion that the imposition of a church tax on a non-member interfered with his freedom of belief.

It is less certain that all forms of 'test' as a ground for holding public office are excluded. If the test is independent of the function of the job, the judgments of the Court in the *Kosiek* and *Glasenapp* cases[20] (which concerned Article 10) indicate that there is an inclination to treat such cases as claims for rights to the office, a right not protected by the Convention, rather than as cases involving restrictions upon Convention rights, such as freedom of religion. If the individual may preserve his belief at the expense of his public office, he may find himself wizhout protection under the Convention.[1] A minister of a church has no claim to be protected against his church under Article 9(1) in a dispute about doctrine. He is free to resign his position, to leave the church if need be, and to continue to hold to his version of his belief.[2] The Commission has set some store by the possibility of an individual adjusting his position so that he is then able to continue

---

16 A 295 para 47 (1994). For the facts of this case, see below, p 402.
17 The reservation was withdrawn when the Constitution was amended: see *Collected Texts*, p 100.
18 *H, H and A v Turkey Nos 16311-16313/90*, 72 DR 200 (1992).
19 A 187 (1991) Com Rep paras 57-60. The situation is different where there is a requirement on church members to pay a tax: *Gottesmann v Switzerland No 101616/83*, 40 DR 284 (1984).
20 *Glasenapp v FRG* A 104 (1986) and *Kosiek v FRG* A 105 (1986). See below, pp 381-382.
1 *Knudsen v Norway No 11045/84*, 42 DR 247 (1985). There is a suggestion that pressure to change one's views or face dismissal might raise a question under Article 9, id, p 258.
2 *Karlsson v Sweden No 12356/86*, 57 DR 172 (1988).

with his beliefs. This is a reflection of the nature of the 'right' under Article 9(1) principally as a freedom, rather than as a right *stricto sensu*. None the less, the tolerance of religious or political tests as a condition of office or employment has little to commend it. If, even *sub silentio*, the Court revises its approach to this question when it decides *Vogt v Germany* under Article 10,[3] the impact of the judgment could profitably be felt under Article 9 also and advantage taken of the Commission's dictum in *Knudsen*.

3. MANIFESTING RELIGION OR BELIEF IN WORSHIP, TEACHING, PRACTICE AND OBSERVANCE

The second part of Article 9(1) protects the right to the freedom 'to manifest' one's religion or belief, in public or in private, alone or with others. The manifestations to which it refers are 'worship, teaching, practice and observance', a catalogue of not wholly distinct activities. In *Arrowsmith v UK*,[4] the Commission indicated that the term 'practice' in this list 'does not cover each act which is motivated or influenced by a religion or belief'. In that case, the distribution of leaflets to soldiers advising them to go absent or to refuse to serve in Northern Ireland was held not to be the 'practice' of pacifist belief. The Commission gave as an example of an activity which would fall within Article 9(1) 'public declarations proclaiming generally the idea of pacifism and urging the acceptance of a commitment to non-violence . . .'.[5]

In drawing the line between religious and commercial advertisements in the *X and Church of Scientology v Sweden*,[6] the Commission said that those which were 'informational or descriptive' (presumably of the Church's beliefs) were capable of being manifestations of religion, but that the advertisements in question, being directed at the sale of devices produced by the Church, were not. If the manifestation of religion or belief involves the exercise of another Convention right – for example, religious processions as the exercise of freedom of assembly – the fact that it is the exercise of an Article 9 right may be of some importance for, as will be seen, the purposes for which an Article 9 right may be interfered with under Article 9(2) are narrower than those provided for elsewhere in the Convention.

As indicated above,[7] the judgment of the Court in *Otto-Preminger-Institut v Austria* envisages that states have a positive obligation under Article 9(1) to secure the peaceful enjoyment of religious freedom from hostile attacks by others. From this it may follow that the state is required to protect individual members of a religion, collective acts of public witness and church

3   *No 17851/91* (1993) Com Rep para 88 (referred to the Court).
4   *No 7050/75*, 19 DR 5 at 19 (1978) Com Rep; CM Res DH (79) 4.
5   Ibid.
6   *No 7805/77*, 16 DR 68 at 72 (1979).
7   See above, p 359.

property. Those exercising Article 9 religious freedoms are privileged in two ways over those whose analogous activities fall within Articles 10 and 11. On the one hand, the manifestation of religious belief is entitled to enhanced, positive protection. On the other hand, exercises of Article 10 or 11 freedoms which run counter to Article 9 rights are vulnerable to regulation and even expungement in the interest of protecting religious freedom. Two aspects of the *Otto-Preminger* case await further consideration. The first is whether the judgment is limited to the protection of religious rights of the majority.[8] The other is whether the associated freedoms of belief and conscience are to be protected equally. Given that the depth of religious conviction is not related to the number of believers and that political or atheistic beliefs may be quite as firm as articles of religious faith, the potential reach of the *Otto-Preminger* judgment is wide. Prioritising of belief-based ideas over secular opinion is not without substantial dangers.

While the state is precluded from interfering with a particular activity *because* it is a manifestation of religion or belief, it is not so restrained where a provision of the general law incidentally prohibits or restricts such a manifestation in pursuit of some other public interest. While the state must be circumspect about punishing people for fulfilling their religious callings, it is less constrained in its capacity to raise general taxation for projects to which a particular taxpayer objects on grounds of conscience.[9] The Commission was not prepared to hold that a Swedish law which criminalised parental chastisement of their children to be an interference with the parents' rights under Article 9 even though the parent-applicants maintained that their religious convictions required such measures of discipline.[10] Equally, in *Omkaranda and Divine Light Zentrum v Switzerland*,[11] the Commission found that an expulsion order made against an alien priest who had been convicted of serious public order offences was not in breach of Article 9(1). That would have been the case only if it could have been established that the order was directed against the religious activities of the priest and his church. But the state may be required to act to exempt a person from the operation of a general law where his objection to complying with it is based on considerations of conscience or belief.[12] In *X v UK*,[13] where the issue was the right of a Moslem school-teacher to attend prayers at the mosque during school hours in breach of his contract of employment, the Commission held that the decision of his state employers not to release

8   This would be one consideration in deciding whether the *Otto-Preminger* case gives protection to Muslims in the UK complaining about the publication of Salman Rushdie's *Satanic Verses*: see *Choudhury v UK*, p 360, n 3, above.
9   See below, p 368.
10   *Seven Individuals v Sweden No 8811/79*, 29 DR 104 at 114 (1982).
11   *No 8118/77*, 25 DR 105 at 118 (1981). See also *Holy Monasteries v Greece* A 301-A (1994) Com Rep para 93 (changes in law affected property of monasteries but did not affect religious practices).
12   See below, p 369.
13   *No 8160/78*, 22 DR 27 at 37-38 (1981).

him had given 'due consideration' to his right under Article 9(1), taking into account the extent of the religious obligation and the measures of accommodation offered by the employer. It was not conclusively established that he had a binding obligation to attend the mosque and the education authority had allowed him to be absent when the consequences for his school were not so great. Where what is required of the state is less disruptive than was the case in *X v UK* and/or where the impact on the applicant is clearer, the outcome of an application may be different. Compare *Prais v EC Council*,[14] a European Community case, where the plaintiff/applicant, who was a Jew, successfully complained that the holding of examinations on a Saturday for a week-day job, examinations which she could not sit because of her religious obligations, was a violation of her rights. This is another example of a positive obligation imposed on states by the Convention being subject to assessment rather than being regarded as imposing absolute requirements.

The obligation under this part of Article 9(1) includes desisting from interference with acts of worship and from rites associated with worship.[15] The state must allow 'teaching' of the religion and, within certain limits, this to the unconverted as well as to members of the church. In *Kokkinakis v Greece*,[16] the Court held the conviction of a Jehovah's Witness for proselytism to be incompatible with Greece's obligations under Article 9. The Court recognised the evangelical ambitions of some religions and decided that teaching with the object of obtaining converts was protected as a manifestation of the applicant's religious beliefs. The separate, concurring judgments of Judges Pettiti and Martens understood the freedom to teach as a very wide one indeed. Judge Pettiti specifically rejected the claim that attempting to make converts was an infringement of other people's rights. In complete contrast, Judge Valticos, one of three dissenting judges, regarded 'teaching' as a manifestation of one's beliefs as 'undoubtedly' referring to teaching in school or religious institutions. Such a view would favour orthodox, established religions but there is no suggestion in other practice that Article 9 is to be construed so restrictively.[17]

4. JUSTIFIABLE INTERFERENCES

It is worth reiterating that the power of the state to interfere under Article 9(2) with the exercise of an Article 9(1) freedom is confined to manifestations of religion or belief. Freedom of thought etc, including the

---

14 *Case 130/75* [1976] ECR 1589, ECJ.
15 *Chappell v UK No 12587/86*, 53 DR 241 (1987).
16 A 260-A paras 48-49 (1993).
17 Judges Foighel and Loizou also dissented, striking the balance required by tolerance in favour of the right to hold beliefs without being pestered rather than in favour of the right of evangelicals to propagate their beliefs.

freedom to change or abandon one's religion or belief, is immune from interference by the state.

Legitimate interferences must be 'prescribed by law'. This was an issue of some importance in the *Kokkinakis* case. The applicant had been convicted of the criminal offence of proselytism, which Greek law defined as:

> 'in particular, any direct or indirect attempt to intrude on the religious beliefs of a person of a different religious persuasion, with the aim of undermining those beliefs, either by any kind of inducement or moral support or material assistance, or by fraudulent means or by taking advantage of his experience, trust, need, low intellect or naivety.'

His first complaint was that the vagueness of the national law violated Article 7, a claim that was rejected by the Commission, not without hesitation, because of the clarifications introduced by the case-law of the Greek courts. The majority carried that reasoning over in deciding that Greek law satisfied the 'prescribed by law' requirement of Article 9(2).[18] The Court adopted practically the same reasoning but reversed the treatment of the two questions, relying on its finding that there had been an interference 'prescribed by law' under Article 9(2) for its decision that there had been no breach of Article 7.[19] While nothing turned on the difference in this case, in general the Commission's approach is to be preferred because a finding that some matter has been 'prescribed by law' is not necessarily determinative of the criminal nature of the law for the purpose of Article 7.

Under Article 9(2), the state may interfere with the manifestation of religion or belief in 'the interests of public safety, for the protection of public order, health or morals, or for the protection of the rights and freedoms of others'. There has been relatively little practice under Article 9(2), partly because the Commission has drawn the limits of Article 9(1) quite narrowly. Some of the decisions have been rather mechanical. The Commission held that denying a prisoner access to a religious book which contained a chapter on martial arts could be justified as being necessary for the protection of public order and the rights of others.[20] In another application, while it was prepared to concede that there was a practice of high caste Sikhs like the applicant not sweeping floors, the requirement that a Sikh prisoner clean the floors of his cell was held to be necessary for the protection of health.[1] A requirement that all motorcyclists wear crash-helmets was permissible for the protection of public safety, even as applied to Sikhs and even though, by the time the decision was given, the national law provided an exception in favour of Sikhs.[2]

---

18 A 260-A (1993) Com Rep paras 36-52, 58-61.
19 Id, paras 37-41, 51-53.
20 *X v UK No 6886/75*, 5 DR 100 (1976).
1   *X v UK No 8231/78*, 28 DR 5 at 38 (1982).
2   *X v UK No 7992/77*, 14 DR 234 (1978). For comment, see Fawcett, pp 248-249.

In only one case have the Strasbourg authorities held a restriction not to be justified. In *Kokkinakis v Greece*, the Commission unanimously[3] and the Court by 6 votes to 3[4] held that the application of the Greek law criminalising the proselytising activities of a Jehovah's Witness was not proportionate to the aim of protecting the rights of others. The Court accepted the distinction between evangelical witness and 'improper proselytism'. Evangelism was the essential mission of the Church and the responsibility of every Christian. 'Improper proselytism' was the attempt to convert by offering material or social benefits or taking advantage of the need or incapacity of others.[5] It concluded that the facts as found by the national court did not show evidence of any improper approach by the applicant. He had doubtless been persistent but he had done no more than try to persuade an adherent to another Christian religion of the virtues of his faith. Two of the concurring judges took a more robust line. Judge Pettiti was critical of the inadequacy of the reasoning of the majority judgment. His position was that the only limits on the right to expound one's beliefs,

> 'are those dictated by respect for the rights of others where there is an attempt to coerce the person into consenting or to use manipulative techniques.'

Judge Martens was even stricter. In his view, Article 9 requires that the state adopt a position of neutrality between religions, even, or perhaps especially, where one religion enjoys a privileged position in national law, as the Greek Orthodox Church does in Greece. 'Improper' proselytism was only that which offended against the general criminal law, perhaps only that which would violate Article 3.

The *Kokkinakis* case and the Commission decisions are concerned with the negative duty of the state not to interfere with an individual's right under Article 9. It might just be possible if one took the language of the dissenting judges in the *Kokkinakis* case to the limit to conclude that they would be in favour of a positive duty (as distinct from a power) on the state to protect persons from 'improper proselytism' so that they could effectively enjoy their right to hold their beliefs. However, there are no indications in the case-law of even more substantial general positive obligations on states, particularly to facilitate the exercise of rights of worship or practices, such as by providing churches or buildings for non-religious instruction.[6] The issue might fall within the 'ambit' of Article 9(1), so as to allow claims under

---

3   A 260-A (1993) Com Rep paras 69-74.
4   A 260-A paras 45-50 (1993).
5   Id, para 48.
6   *X v UK No 5947/72*, 5 DR 8 (1976) (government had acted 'as far as possible' to respect a prisoner's dietary requirements mandated by his religion). In *ISKCON v UK No 20490/92*, 76-A DR 90 at 107 (1994), the Commission decided that sufficient weight had been given to the applicants' Article 9 interests in a planning inquiry which rejected claims to extend the religious uses of their property.

Article 14 that rights to establish churches or to have access to premises had been protected on a discriminatory basis.

5. CONSCIENTIOUS OBJECTION

Judge Martens pointed out in the *Kokkinakis* case that the Greek anti-proselytism law was unique among the Convention states. A more pervasive problem is conscientious objection, an unwillingness to comply for reasons of conscience with obligations imposed by law. The Commission has taken a formalistic approach when applications asserting a right of conscientious objection under Article 9 have come before it. First of all, as indicated above, the application of a general law to someone who has reasons of conscience for not complying with it does not violate Article 9(1).[7] In *C v UK*,[8] the applicant was a Quaker who objected on religious grounds to a proportion of his taxes being disbursed on military purposes. He wished those funds to be redirected towards peaceful purposes. The Commission did not enquire whether this particular outcome was demanded by his faith. Instead, it emphasised the narrow reach of Article 9(1) as being restricted to the personal sphere. The general obligation to pay taxes raised no specific issue of conscience. The distribution of tax revenue was a political matter beyond the influence of any individual. The Commission so far has invariably found that refusals to comply with the general law are not direct exercises of religious or conscience-driven practices. If a state is not obliged to take note of a dissenter's objections, it may none the less choose to do so without violating the rights of others who are obliged to undertake burdens from which the state chooses to exempt the dissenter. Furthermore, if it does protect the conscientious objector as against others who fail to perform their obligations for other reasons, the acknowledgement of the former's dilemma will not violate Article 14 in connection with Article 9, for the state will have an objective and reasonable basis for the differentiation between him and those who had no comparable motivation for their default.[9]

Applicants have argued that even if the Convention does not provide an immunity for the conscientious objector, it does, where relevant, provide a right of substitute service for the oppressive obligation. The Commission has dealt with these claims relying on a literal reading of Article 4(3)(b) of the Convention. This excludes from its prohibition of 'forced or compulsory labour':

> 'any service of a military character or, in the case of conscientious objectors *in countries where they are recognised*, service extracted instead of compulsory military service' (emphasis added).

7 *Seven Individuals v Sweden No 8811/79*, 29 DR 104 (1982).
8 *No 10358/83*, 37 DR 142 at 147 (1983). For the Quaker position, see Forbes, in *Freedom of Conscience*, Leiden Seminar Proc, 1993, pp 123-128. See also *X v Netherlands No 10678/83*, 39 DR 267 (1984) (refusal to participate in a pension scheme).
9 *Suter v Switzerland No 11595/85*, 51 DR 160 (1986).

The Commission understands the italicised words to mean that a state may, but need not, recognise conscientious objectors, and only if it does should it consider providing an alternative obligation for them to the ordinary conscripted service.[10] If a state does take this option, it may take measures to enforce the civilian service without violating Article 9.[11] Where the state does provide for substitute service, it does not violate Article 9, alone or in conjunction with Article 14 if it provides for a longer period of civilian service than for military conscription.[12] In *N v Sweden*,[13] the Commission found also that an exception from even substitute service for those who object to it on religious grounds does not violate the Article 14 rights of others who are obliged to complete the civilian activities. However, the decision is a narrow one. Swedish law in fact granted total exemption only to Jehovah's Witnesses, a practice the Commission endorsed because of the all-embracing commitment of members of this religion to its prescriptions – a commitment which the Commission allowed 'creates a high degree of probability that exemption is not granted to persons who simply wish to escape service'.

The debate beyond the Convention about the respect which is due to the refusal on grounds of conscience to perform public obligations, especially military service, is not closed.[14] A recommendation of the Council of Europe's Committee of Ministers urges recognition of a right of conscientious objection[15] and the UN Commission on Human Rights continues to press its view that states are obliged to acknowledge the right.[16] The approach of the Commission, based on a literal reading of the Convention text, looks far from immutable in the light of these developments.

The Commission has been faced with a variety of other claims of conscientious objection outside the military service context. It has rejected them all.[17] As indicated earlier, the Court in *Hoffmann v Austria*[18] did not question the characterisation as a matter of religious belief the refusal by a Jehovah's Witness of life-saving blood transfusions. Indeed, because the national court had been substantially influenced by this consideration in deciding on the custody of children, the Court held the national judgment to be in breach of Article 14 in conjunction with Article 8 because the distinction between the mother and the father had been made 'on the ground of religion'. If the refusal of life-saving treatment is motivated by religious belief and is, therefore, protected by Article 9(1), which question the Court did not address directly in the *Hoffmann* case, it is not easy to see how a plausible claim could be made under Article 9(2) that the state is entitled to

10 *Grandrath v FRG No 2299/64*, 10 YB 626 at 674 (1966) Com Rep ; CM Res (67) DH 1 and *X v FRG No 7705/76*, 9 DR 196 (1977).
11 *Johansen v Norway No 10600/83*, 44 DR 155 (1985).
12 *Autio v Finland No 17086/90*, 72 DR 245 (1991).
13 *No 10410/83*, 40 DR 203 at 208 (1984).
14 See Vermulen, in *Freedom of Conscience*, loc cit, p 368, n 8, above. Cf also Rodata, id, pp 94-106.
15 CM Recommendation R(87)8, *Collected Texts*, p 338.
16 Resolution 1989/59.
17 See cases cited by Vermulen, in *Freedom of Conscience*, loc cit, p 368, n 8, above, p 85.
18 A 255-C para 33 (1994).

make him submit to treatment. Following cases under Article 8 which concern children,[19] it might be argued that the imposition of compulsory treatment was for the protection of health, but it is less obviously 'necessary in a democratic society' to resort to such measures over the objection of a sentient adult. The same would not be true for the hunger-striker who refused sustenance out of reasons of conviction because the refusal of food would not be required by his political belief but would be a means to achieving his political object, which would fall within the *Arrowsmith* limitation and, therefore, not be within Article 9(1) at all. Different considerations might apply in each case under Article 2, if the state were to argue that it had a positive obligation to protect life.[20]

6. CONCLUSION

The overall impression is that Article 9 has neither been interpreted to impose wide or substantial burdens on the states nor – perhaps partly for this reason – revealed any widespread and serious denials of Article 9 rights by the contracting parties. The full implications of the *Otto-Preminger* case may prove this assessment wrong if the Court insists on wide positive obligations on the state to ensure that those holding religious beliefs are not disturbed in their beliefs by the activities of others.

It may be complacent to think that Article 9 has seldom been successfully invoked for lack of need. The Convention is deficient compared with the ICCPR in not providing specific protection for minorities. An additional protocol to the Convention to put this right has been proposed but its adoption is not an immediate prospect.[1] However, a Framework Convention for the Protection of Minorities was adopted in 1994.[2] Many minorities identify themselves and are identified by others at least in part through their religious affiliations and practices.[3] It is in the context of protecting minority rights that Article 9 may have its greatest part to play. Aspects of religious practice are referred to in Articles 5-9 of the Framework Convention. Finding some interim protection within the existing provisions of the European Convention on Human Rights until a minorities protocol can be agreed will be difficult but not impossible. Much may depend upon whether the great regard the Court displayed for the religious susceptibilities of the majority of the population in the *Otto-Preminger* case were to be repeated where the strongly held beliefs of a minority were under attack. The content of the rights under Article 9 (in conjunction or not with Article 14) has not been exhausted. States are not able to ignore the problems presented by the increasing vehemence with which minority claims are

---

19 See *Andersson (M & R) v Sweden* A 226-A paras 86-87 (1992).
20 *Hoffmann v Austria* A 255-C paras 32-33 (1993).
1   The question of a Convention protocol on the social and cultural rights of minorities is at present under consideration by the Council of Europe Human Rights Steering Committee.
2   ETS 157; 2 IHRR 217 (1995).
3   See Rimanque, in *Freedom of Conscience*, loc cit at p 368, n 8, above, pp 144-165.

advanced and little will be gained by maintaining that the obligation of the state in these matters is one of lofty neutrality, a purely negative duty. It is in the possibilities of positive duties to protect the effective enjoyment of the rights of conscience and the manifestation of them that more pressing obligations for states are to be found. Even if the outcome of applications like *X v UK* and *Choudhury v UK* were to be the same, the basis on which they would be decided might well be different if the Strasbourg authorities were to claim a role in developing the rights of members of minorities. The steps that the Court has already taken to protect the rights of settled aliens under Article 8 are the indication that it does lie within its powers to make a contribution to the protection of minority rights.[4]

4 See above pp 351-353.

CHAPTER 11

Article 10: Freedom of expression

'**Article 10**
1. Everyone has the right to freedom of expression. This right shall include freedom to hold opinions and to receive and impart information and ideas without interference by public authority and regardless of frontiers. This Article shall not prevent States from requiring the licensing of broadcasting, television or cinema enterprises.
2. The exercise of these freedoms, since it carries with it duties and responsibilities, may be subject to such formalities, conditions, restrictions or penalties as are prescribed by law and are necessary in a democratic society, in the interests of national security, territorial integrity or public safety, for the prevention of disorder or crime, for the protection of health or morals, for the protection of the reputation or rights of others, for preventing the disclosure of information received in confidence, or for maintaining the authority and impartiality of the judiciary.'

1. INTRODUCTION

Given the objectives of the Council of Europe and the premises contained in the Preamble to the Convention,[1] it is obvious that freedom of expression is not only important in its own right but that it has a central part to play in the protection of other rights under the Convention.[2] Its pervasive influence raises two different problems: the one is that several other protected rights and freedoms have aspects of freedom of expression within their ambit, such as the overlap between expression and assembly;[3] the other is that freedom of expression may frequently conflict with other interests, indeed with other rights protected by the Convention, for instance the right to a fair trial,[4] the

1 In particular, the relationship between 'effective political democracy' and 'a common understanding and observance of human rights'.
2 On Article 10 generally, see Lester, *European Supervision*, Ch 18 and Bullinger, 6 HRLJ 339 (1985).
3 Eg *Ezelin v France* A 202-A (1991).
4 Eg *Sunday Times v UK* A 30 (1979).

right to respect for private life,[5] and the right to freedom of thought, conscience and religion.[6] Where what might be an expression interest can be assimilated under some other right protected by the Convention, the Strasbourg authorities have tended to consider the case under that other head, so the right to vote is regarded as an element of the state's obligations to hold fair elections and not as an exercise of freedom of expression.[7] Where there is a conflict between freedom of expression and some other interest, the Strasbourg authorities are inevitably engaged in some sort of weighing exercise to determine the priority of one over the other,[8] an undertaking amply provided for by Article 10 which, despite the importance of freedom of expression, is attended by more potential grounds of limitation than any other article of the Convention.

In *Handyside v UK*,[9] the Court, in a very well known passage, said:

> 'Freedom of expression constitutes one of the essential foundations of a [democratic] society, one of the basic conditions for its progress and for the development of every man. Subject to paragraph 2 of Article 10, it is applicable not only to "information" or "ideas" that are favourably received or regarded as inoffensive but also to those that offend, shock or disturb the state or any sector of the population. Such are the demands of that pluralism, tolerance and broadmindedness without which there is no "democratic society".'

The opening sentence embraces the two strongest theoretical bases for protecting expression – its essential part in the operation of the democratic political process[10] and its necessity for self-realisation of the individual.[11] However, as we shall see, the words in the second sentence, 'Subject to', carry much weight against the language strongly favouring expression interests.

'Freedom of expression' includes the negative freedom not to speak as well as the more usual freedom to speak. The former was relied on by the Commission in *K v Austria*[12] to protect the applicant against self-incrimination in connection with criminal proceedings, in circumstances where he could not rely on Article 6. Equally, while Article 10 protects the freedom to receive ideas and information, no one may be compelled to listen to another.

There appears to be no expression which is not protected at all by Article 10 because of its content. However, some anti-democratic sentiments might

5 Eg *Lingens v Austria* A 103 (1986) and *X v Sweden No 11366/85*, 50 DR 173 (1986).
6 Eg *Otto-Preminger-Institut v Austria* A 295-A (1994).
7 *X, Y, Z v FRG No 6850/74*, 5 DR 90 (1976).
8 See *Chorherr v Austria* A 266-B para 32 (1993) where the government justified its interference with expression by reference to its positive duties to protect the right of assembly under Article 11.
9 A 24 para 49 (1976).
10 See Schauer, *Free Speech: a Philosophical Enquiry*, 1982, pp 35-46.
11 Id, pp 60-72.
12 A 255-B (1993) Com Rep paras 45, 49. F Sett before Court. See also *Goodwin v UK No 17488/90* (1994) Com Rep para 48 (compelling journalist to reveal source was a breach of 'negative right').

be attacked directly under Article 17[13] and some expression, such as racist epithets, is regarded as particularly obnoxious and, therefore, only lightly protected against limitation by state.[14] None the less, the Court has not relied on Article 17 to justify interference with an expression interest, rather requiring that the legitimacy of interference must be justified under Article 10(2), even in relation to the most reviled expression. Article 17 will be an exception of almost last resort. Not every instance of thoroughly disapproved speech may properly be interfered with either under Article 10(2) or Article 17. In *Jersild v Denmark*,[15] a television journalist was convicted of aiding and abetting the dissemination of racial insults after a programme which he made was broadcast that included explicit and crude racial remarks by a disaffected group of young people. Even though the applicant had solicited the contributions and had edited them to give prominence to the most vehement of the racist opinions, the Court found that his conviction was not proportionate to the interest of protecting the rights of others, ie those foreigners against whom the hatred and contempt were expressed. The previous practice of the Commission,[16] which the Court endorsed,[17] of giving only scant protection to racist expression, was confined to the intentional propagation of racial hatred rather than the dispassionate presentation of the information that such sentiments were, as a matter of fact, held by others. The Court has given another illustration of expression which, while still protected by Article 10, it regards as of relatively little worth in *Otto-Preminger-Institut v Austria*.[18] There it said that gratuitously offensive remarks about the religious opinions of others 'do not contribute to any form of public debate capable of furthering progress in human affairs'.

The important matter for the present is that the exclusion of content considerations from the definition of expression allows an applicant to argue that the widest scope of ideas and information, furthermore transmitted by the widest range of media, are embraced by the notion of expression in the Convention, thereby putting on the state the obligation to justify interference with them. However, one consequence of the extensive ambit of expression is that a single generalisation about why particular exercises of freedom of expression should be protected and the extent to which a state might limit them is impossible to state. Instead it is necessary to take into account the 'kind' of expression – political, commercial, artistic – the medium through

---

13 On Article 17, see below, pp 510-513.
14 But note *Glimmerveen and Hagenback v Netherlands Nos 8384/78 and 8406/78*, 18 DR 187 (1979) (racist leaflets); *X v FRG No 9235/81*, 29 DR 194 (1982) (Nazi leaflets); *T v Belgium No 9777/82*, 34 DR 158 (1983) (Nazi pamphlet); *Kuhnen v FRG No 12194/86*, 56 DR 205 (1988) (Nazi pamphlet); *H, W, P and K v Austria No 12774/87*, 62 DR 216 (1989) (Nazi activities); *Purcell v Ireland No 15404/89*, 70 DR 262 at 278 (1991) (political support for terrorism): all manifestly ill-founded under Article 10. Contrast reports of the Commission in *Glasenapp v FRG No 9228/80* and *Kosiek v FRG No 9704/82*, see below, p 410. See further, McCrudden, in Birks, ed, *Pressing Problems in the Law*, Volume 1, 1995, Ch 12.
15 A 298 para 37 (1994).
16 See above, n 14.
17 A 298 para 35 (1994).
18 A 295-A para 49 (1994).

which it is delivered – personal or news media, press or television – and the audience to which it is directed – adults or children, the public at large or a special group – to calculate how extensive the protection is that the Strasbourg authorities give to a particular item of expression. Even the 'truth' of the expression will not be of uniform significance.

As in other areas of the Convention, the Strasbourg authorities have paid attention to national constitutional practice, including that of the United States. Because of the prolixity of the case-law, the intensity of comment upon it and the strong protection the Constitution gives to freedom of speech, it is not surprising that applicants use decisions of the United States Supreme Court in arguing cases in Strasbourg.[19] However, the structure of the First Amendment is markedly different from Article 10.[20] The Supreme Court's interpretation of the First Amendment[1] puts greater emphasis on what *is* 'freedom of speech, or of the press', with what is included enjoying great protection and what is not, no protection at all. Under the Convention, all expression, whatever its content, falls within Article 10(1) and the emphasis shifts to the justification for interference under Article 10(2).[2] Direct reliance upon American judgments must therefore be limited. The United States experience is useful in indicating the questions which might arise in a freedom of expression case. It is a less sure guide to their answers within the Convention context.[3] In any event, and this is true elsewhere in the Convention, national decisions from whatever jurisdiction may be of only limited utility to an international institution interpreting an international treaty. From time to time, the Court and Commission have found it helpful to refer to Articles 19 and 20 of the ICCPR[4] and Article 4 of the Racial Discrimination Convention.[5] This further differentiates Convention law from United States law.[6]

As will be seen, the Court has been forthright in announcing the importance and the reach of freedom of expression but the robustness of its language has often been tempered in its application to particular cases. If it is difficult to reconcile some of its judgments with its firmest remarks in favour of freedom of expression, that is because the Court is discharging its

19 Lester, loc cit at n 2 above, pp 472-473, appears to give too great a weight to US constitutional law in criticising the Convention case-law. But see Frowein, 1-2 AEL 267 at 336 (1990) (Convention becoming more and more comparable to case-law of US Supreme Court).

20 See Barendt, *Freedom of Speech*, 1985, especially pp 28-36.

1 'Congress shall make no law . . . abridging freedom of speech, or of the press.'

2 Eg 'obscene' expression is not expression for the purposes of the First Amendment, US Constitution and so receives no protection at all under it: *Roth v US* 354 US 476 at 485 (1957). In contrast, it is 'expression' within Article 10(1) of the Convention but may be controlled consistently with Article 10(2).

3 Errera, in Henkin and Rosenthal, eds, *Constitutionalism and Rights*, 1990, pp 63-93.

4 Eg *Müller v Switzerland* A 133 para 27 (1988).

5 Eg *Glimmerveen and Hagenback v Netherlands* Nos 8384/78 and 8406/78, 18 DR 187 (1979) and *Jersild v Denmark* A 298 (1994).

6 The US has attached a reservation to its ratification of the ICCPR concerning Article 20: see 14 HRLJ 123 (1993).

role as a 'subsidiary mechanism' for the protection of human rights and the development of this role has imposed upon it certain limits in reviewing state action on controversial issues, where there is something to be said on the state's side as well as on the applicant's. Moreover, the Court has frequently been deeply divided on freedom of expression issues and sometimes has differed widely from the Commission.[7] There are indications that the Court is at present more favourably inclined towards expression rights than it has been in the past, although the accuracy of this assessment is obscured by the number of judgments given by chambers of the Court and is challenged by the judgment in *Otto-Preminger-Institut v Austria*.[8]

The sensitivity of expression matters, perhaps beyond all others in working democratic systems, arises in large measure from their connection with the maintenance and exercise of political power. Governments are bound to take a close interest in media affairs because of the impact that they have on the political process.[9] Unlike other areas of the Convention, where violations might result from governmental and legislative indifference, on matters of expression contested claims are more likely to involve deliberate government acts. Further complications have arisen because the media are, at the same time, both important beneficiaries of the rights of expression, whose activities are essential if the values behind freedom of expression are to be effectively enjoyed, and yet capable of the most egregious violations of other interests. Attempts to control media conduct invariably face the criticism that they go too far and restrain proper news-gathering activities.[10] Furthermore, because the media are commercial operations, the state retains a legitimate interest in regulating the industries involved. There is a danger that the regulatory foot in the door may be used with the object or effect of interfering with the production and distribution of information.[11] In relation to broadcasting, the technical need to regulate the industries gives an opportunity to the authorities to do so in such a way as to enable the regulation of expression in ways which would be unacceptable for other media.[12]

What are involved are invariably matters of appreciation and, in the absence of 'bright lines',[13] the Strasbourg authorities have a role to play in making sure that the balance is not struck by the national authorities so that the essential purposes of the freedom of the press are not effectively undermined. A final complicating factor is the impact of technology: decisions cannot be final when the means of production and the techniques

---

7 Eg *Sunday Times v UK* A 30 (1979) (11 to 9 Court decision); *Markt intern Verlag v FRG* A 165 (1989), decision on casting vote of Court President differing sharply from the Commission; and *Groppera Radio AG v Switzerland* A 173 (1990), Commission 7-6 violation, Court 16-3 no violation.
8 A 295-A (1994).
9 See Barendt, *Broadcasting Law*, 1993, Ch VII.
10 See *Goodwin v UK No 17488/90* (1994) Com Rep para 64.
11 See below, on control of press concentration, p 383.
12 See below, on broadcasting, pp 384-386.
13 In *Observer and Guardian v UK* A 216 para 60 (1991), the Court would not commit itself unequivocally to the position that prior censorship of the press was inevitably in breach of the Convention, simply that prior restraints required 'the most careful scrutiny'.

of distribution are quickly changing, increasingly bringing international audiences within the technical and commercial reach of the news media.[14]

In comparison with the other articles of the Convention of a similar structure to Article 10, the Commission and Court have been proportionately less concerned with the definition of the protected right and the question whether it has been interfered with and more concerned with the justification for the interference.

2. FREEDOM OF EXPRESSION: WHAT IS PROTECTED?

It is a characteristic of freedom of expression that it protects activities which carry a risk of damaging or actually damage the interests of others or the public interest. Thus we tolerate the publication of some information which injures the reputation of an individual and risk that outrageous statements at public meetings cause distress or insult to those who hear them. Although there is no single basis for justifying the priority given to expression over other interests, it is widely accepted that the toleration of different views is an essential aspect of a democratic political system. At one level, the competition between the major political parties for governmental power is expressed in terms of ideas and programmes; at another, the unorthodox proposition has the chance to overturn the mistaken orthodoxy, however entrenched it has become. Because political controversy can touch practically any aspect of life, the subject-matter of the expression ought not to be a major consideration in determining whether it should be protected.[15] None the less, there have been arguments about whether particular kinds of undoubted 'expression', most widely conceived, fall within Article 10 However, as indicated above, none of these has been successful.

That political expression does is taken for granted.[16] Equally, the Court is of the view that artistic activities are protected by Article 10.[17] In *Markt intern Verlag v FRG*,[18] the government argued that information in a trade magazine fell outside Article 10, being directed to the promotion of the economic interests of a group of traders and, thus, an aspect of the right to carry on business. Failing this, it was expression at the very limit of Article 10's concerns. The Court described the item as 'information of a commercial

14 See *Groppera Radio AG v Switzerland* A 173 (1990) (cable radio) and *Autronic v Switzerland* A 178 (1990) (satellite television).
15 The Court has resisted an attempt to distinguish between 'high politics' and matters of general public interest: see *Thorgierson v Iceland* A 239 para 61 (1992).
16 *Lingens v Austria* A 103 para 42 (1986) and *Barthold v FRG* A 90 para 42 (1985).
17 *Müller v Switzerland* A 133 para 27 (1988), partly relying on Article 19, ICCPR.
18 A 165 para 25-26 (1989). Cf *Casado Coca v Spain* A 285-A paras 35-36 (1994) (argument that professional advertising not protected by Article 10 rejected) and *Hempfing v FRG No 14622/89*, 69 DR 272 (1991). It was not contested that professional advertising fell within Article 10 in *Colman v UK* A 258-D (1994) Com Rep. It was accepted by the government that commercial communications fell within Article 10(1) in *Jacubowski v Germany* A 219-A (1994). See also *X and Church of Scientology v Sweden No 7805/77*, 16 DR 68 (1979). On advertising generally, see Lester and Paninck, 1985 PL 349.

nature' but held that it was protected by Article 10 because that Article did not apply 'solely to certain types of information or ideas or forms of expression'. However, there have been suggestions that expression of 'no value' – abusive or inflammatory words, for instance[19] – or mere entertainment might not be covered by the Convention.[20] It seems unnecessary to try to draw the line between 'valuable' and 'valueless' expression because there are ample grounds under Article 10(2) for authorising state interference with 'valueless' expression if a state can demonstrate the necessity for doing so,[1] whereas excluding some 'expression' from the Convention would introduce difficult, possibly intractable, problems of drawing lines between that which lies within and that which lies without the scope of Article 10.[2] In *Autronic v Switzerland*,[3] the Court was confronted with the question whether the reception and demonstration of a satellite television signal for commercial purposes was protected by Article 10. The government argued that because the content of the programme was irrelevant to the company's purpose, which was to encourage the sale of satellite dishes, the applicant was seeking the protection of an economic right rather than a right protected by Article 10. In rejecting this submission, the Court said that Article 10 extended to the means of transmission or reception as well as to the content of information. It is, perhaps, significant that the government conceded that the Swiss decisions on the matter in 1982, when only Soviet satellite signals were available and were being used for demonstration purposes, would have been the same in 1989 when there was a variety of programmes in accessible languages available.[4]

'Expression' is not merely words, still less only spoken words, but extends to pictures,[5] images[6] and actions intended to express an idea or to present information.[7] Equally, the means of protected expression go beyond speech to print,[8] radio[9] and television broadcasting,[10] artistic creations,[11] film[12]

---

19 *Otto-Preminger-Institut v Austria* A 295-A para 49 (1994).
20 Light music not 'information and ideas': Judge Matscher concurring in *Groppera Radio AG v Switzerland* A 173 (1990). See Judge Valticos, ibid, for an even wider limitation.
1   *Handyside v UK* A 24 para 52 (1976) (information on sex in an otherwise political book directed to children); *Müller v Switzerland* A 133 para 36 (1988) (painting regarded by some judges as of dubious merit); *Barfod v Denmark* A 149 para 35 (1989) (defamatory criticism of judges). Contrast the US approach by which obscenity has no value and hence is not protected at all: see above, p 375, n 2.
2   *Groppera Radio AG v Switzerland* A 173 para 55 (1990).
3   A 178 para 44 (1990).
4   Id, para 47.
5   *Müller v Switzerland* A 133 (1988).
6   *Chorherr v Austria* A 266-B (1993).
7   *Stevens v UK No 11674/85*, 46 DR 245 (1986) (in some circumstances dress might fall within Article 10). But see *X v UK No 7215/75*, 19 DR 66 (1978) (homosexual activities not within Article 10).
8   *Handyside v UK* A 24 (1976).
9   *Groppera Radio AG v Switzeralnd* A 173 (1990).
10 *Autronic v Switzerland* A 178 (1983).
11 *Müller v Switzerland* A 133 (1988).
12 *Otto-Preminger-Institut v Austria* A 295-A (1994).

and, probably, electronic information systems. Because of this, what is protected is not only the expression itself but the means for its production and for its communication. Because the means of production, transmission and distribution of information and ideas are in many fields developing rapidly, it is particularly important that the Court's approach to interpretation, which takes into account economic and technological development, be kept in mind here.[13]

It should be noted at this stage that because all kinds (political, artistic, commercial), forms (words, pictures, sounds) and media (speech, print, film, television, etc) of expression may fall within Article 10, it does not follow that they must all be treated equally by the state. The wide powers of limitation which Article 10 allows may be applied differentially (but not discriminatorily).

Article 10 states that freedom of expression 'includes the freedom to hold opinions and to receive and impart information and ideas'. 'Holding opinions' is obviously a precondition for expressing them but it is hardly 'expression' itself. None the less, this part of Article 10 protects persons against adverse consequences of having opinions ascribed to them on the basis of their previous public expression and the negative freedom protects them against being compelled to reveal what opinions they hold.[14] There is no specific provision about the language of expression[15] and, to the extent the Strasbourg authorities have considered claims to use a particular language, they have found against the applicant under Article 8.[16] However, this is a coming problem as the Council of Europe turns its attention to the protection of minorities[17] and it cannot be excluded that the existing practice will be reconsidered.[18]

The Strasbourg authorities have not been receptive to the argument that Article 10 protects *access* to information on which to base an opinion or otherwise to exercise Article 10 freedoms more effectively. In *Leander v Sweden*,[19] the applicant sought confidential information in government files, on the basis of which he believed he had been denied a job, in order that he could effectively challenge the information but the Court concluded that Article 10 gave him no protection. Rather, the general duty on the state is not to obstruct access to information which is available.[20] There are other

13 See above, Ch 1, pp 7-9.
14 *Vogt v Germany No 17851/91* (1993) Com Rep (although it was the applicant's political activities which were the reason for her dismissal from her civil service post, there is no reason to think that the outcome would have been different if she had been dismissed for her political opinions).
15 As to which, see De Varennes, 16 HRQ 163 (1994).
16 *Fryske Nasjonale Partij v Netherlands No 11100/84*, 45 DR 240 (1985).
17 See the European Charter for Regional or Minority Languages 1992, ETS 148; 14 HRLJ 148 (1993).
18 See de Witte, in Dinstein and Tabory, eds, *The Protection of Minorities and Human Rights*, 1992, p 281, quoted in de Varennes, loc cit at n 15, above.
19 A 116 para 74 (1987). See also *Nederlandse Omroepprogramma Stichting v Netherlands No 13920/88*, 71 DR 126 (1991).
20 *Z v Austria No 10392/83*, 56 DR 13 (1988).

provisions of the Convention which do provide for a right of access to information in particular, limited circumstances. In deciding *Gaskin v UK*[1] in favour of the applicant, the Court noted though:

> 'This finding is reached without expressing any opinion on whether general rights of access to personal data and information may be derived from Article 8(1) of the Convention'

and that

> '. . . in the circumstances of the present case, Article 10 does not embody an obligation on the state concerned to impart the information in question to the individual.'

The information sought by the applicant was in records held by a public authority about the time he had been in public foster care. In reaching its decision, the majority gave more attention to what the information meant to Gaskin than to any use he might have wished to make of it, which explains why the case was decided under Article 8 rather than Article 10. It would be optimistic to read into the reference to Article 10 in the *Gaskin* case the possibility that it might guarantee access to information in other circumstances. There have been suggestions that the discriminatory denial of access to information might involve a breach of the Convention but it is discrimination with respect to recipients which is envisaged,[2] not discrimination with respect to classes of information and so these possibilities seem to be an aspect of the right to receive information rather than the right to have access to information in the hands of one unwilling to release it.[3]

Attention thus switches to the right to 'receive and impart'. In *Sunday Times v UK*,[4] the Court said that these were not simply the corollary of one another: there was a right to express opinions and there was an independent right of a willing hearer to hear such expression. The state may not stand between a speaker and his audience, each has a right to get to the other for it is only in this way that the purposes for which expression is protected can be realised.[5] While the right to receive information includes the right to seek it out, this right goes no further than the right to seek that which is available, ie with the consent of the producer or proposer of it. The right of access to information cannot be found here either.[6]

The right to impart information does not imply a right of access to the means of imparting information, such as newspaper space or television air

---

1   A 160 paras 37, 52 (1989). See also the right of defendants to obtain information required for their defence, above, p 213.
2   *X and Association Z v UK No 4515/70*, 38 CD 86 at 88 (1971).
3   See *De Geillustreede Pers v Netherlands No 5178/71*, 8 DR 5 at 13 (1976) Com Rep; CM Res DH (77) 1.
4   A 30 paras 65-66 (1979). The distinction between the two rights may become of significance when assessing the right of the state to interfere with them under Article 10(2). See below, pp 384-385.
5   *Groppera Radio AG v Switzerland* A 173 para 53 (1990) and *Casado Coca v Spain* A 285-A para 59 (1994).
6   See above, p 379, n 20.

time.[7] As already indicated, the Commission has made remarks that discriminatory denial of access to a medium of communication might raise a Convention issue.[8] The matter is troublesome because insisting on a right for a person to use another's facility for his expression of opinion seems to conflict with the freedom of expression of the proprietor of the means of communication.[9] The issue would be different where provision of access to third parties was a condition for the proprietor's own access to the means of communication, for instance a licence requirement that private broadcasting channels provide a certain amount of time to minority groups.[10] The same device might be used to impose right of reply obligations on a broadcaster but the Convention has not yet been interpreted to impose a duty on states so to use their licensing power.

Article 10 distinguishes between 'information' and 'ideas' and makes it clear that the freedom of expression is not restricted to verifiable, factual data.[11] It includes also opinions, criticism, speculation: for these latter instances, in particular, there is no room in general for the argument that Article 10 extends only to 'true' information.[12]

It is not enough for an application to fall within Article 10 that 'expression' in the sense so far explained is in some way affected by a decision of the state. Where the impact on expression is consequential upon or collateral to the exercise of authority for other purposes, the Court and Commission have been reluctant to consider the matter within Article 10, most particularly where the applicant's freedom of expression is not prohibited or punished, simply that conditions are imposed upon its exercise. In *Glasenapp v FRG*[13] and *Kosiek v FRG*,[14] the Court held that claims made by German teachers that conditions attaching to their employment by German *lander* interfered with their Article 10 rights were, in reality, claims of access to public employment, since the applicants held only temporary posts, a right not protected by the Convention. The applicants would have been free to express the opinions in question if they had not been in public employment. The characterisation of the applicants' claims in these cases was artificial and has an unhappy effect on the expression rights of public servants because it avoids the state having to show that the limitation imposed upon a particular civil servant's

7   *X and Association Z v UK No 4515/70*, 38 CD 86 (1971). See further, Barendt, *Broadcasting Law*, 1993, Ch VII.
8   Ibid.
9   Similar considerations apply to a 'right to reply'. See *Ediciones Tiempo v Spain No 13010/87*, 62 DR 247 at 253 (1989) where the Commission upheld a right to reply order as 'a guarantee of the pluralism of information which must be respected'. Article 14(1), American Convention on Human Rights includes a specific right of reply.
10 See above, p 379.
11 *Lingens v Austria* A 103 (1986).
12 Cf *Thorgierson v Iceland* A 239 (1992) (applicant expressing opinions and not facts, so obligation to prove their truth an interference) and *Castells v Spain* A 236 (1992) (applicant not allowed to prove truth of allegations as a defence to charge against him).
13 A 104 (1986).
14 A 105 (1986).

fundamental right is 'necessary in a democratic society'.[15] The Court will have the opportunity to consider the question of the treatment of established civil servants in *Vogt v Germany*,[16] where the Commission has held that the interference with the applicant's Article 10 right was not justifiable.

But there will be no violation where the interference with freedom of expression is the necessary (and unintended) corollary of some unrelated exercise of state authority, such as the expulsion of an alien.[17] An individual may also contract to limit his expression rights and the enforcement of the agreed restrictions will not amount to an interference with his rights under Article 10(1).[18] However, there is a positive duty on a state to take steps to ensure that the exercise of an employee's freedom of expression should not be subject to such restrictions as 'strike at [its] very substance'.[19] The more remote the restricted expression from the discharge of the employee's work duties the more likely it will be that a positive obligation on the state to protect him will arise from the effects of onerous conditions in his contract.

Freedom of expression is protected by Article 10(1) against 'interference by public authority'. The states continue to argue that this protection is restricted to prior censorship[20] and that the imposition of legal consequences as a result of the exercise of freedom of expression does not contradict Article 10.[1] The Court has been consistent in opposing this narrow understanding and has recognised that a wide variety of measures against persons who have exercised their freedom of expression constitute 'interference by public authorities'. Criminal[2] and civil[3] actions, forfeiture of items[4] and denial of licences[5] have all been held to amount to interference with expression already published. The impact of such post-publication sanctions on the future exercise of freedom of expression (whether by the applicant or others) is the justification for extending the reach of Article 10,[6]

---

15 The Commission has required states to justify interference with public servants' rights on a number of occasions. See Eg *B v UK No 10293/83*, 45 DR 41 (1985); *Morissens v Belgium No 11389/85*, 56 DR 127 (1988).

16 *No 17851/91* (1993) Com Rep para 49 (*permanent* civil servant, freedom of controversial expression protected).

17 *Agee v UK No 7729/76*, 7 DR 164 (1976) (effect of deportation). Cf *Piermont v France* A 314 paras 51-53 (1995) (expulsion and ban on re-entering).

18 *Vereiging Rechtswinkels Utrecht v Netherlands No 11308/84*, 46 DR 200 (1986).

19 *Rommelfanger v FRG No 12242/86*, 62 DR 151 at 161 (1989).

20 *Observer and Guardian v UK* A 216 (1991).

1 *Lingens v Austria* A 103 para 37 (1986) (government arguing post-publication penalty not disproportionate, given applicant had been able to exercise his freedom of expression).

2 *Barfod v Denmark* A 149 (1989).

3 *Lingens v Austria* A 103 (1986).

4 *Müller v Switzerland* A 133 (1988).

5 *Autronic v Switzeralnd* A 178 (1990).

6 *Lingens v Austria* A 103 para 44 (1986). It was argued in *Times Newspapers v UK No 14631/89*, 65 DR 307 (1990), that the size and unpredictability of libel awards was an unjustifiable interference with press freedom but, while the Commission conceded the argument in principle, it held that the newspaper was not a 'victim'. See also *Rantzen v Mirror Group* [1993] 4 All ER 975, CA (Article 10 taken into account to decide what is an 'excessive' award of damages in defamation under Courts and Legal Services Act 1990, s 8(1)) and the *Tolstoy* case, loc cit at p 387, below.

though whether the interference is prior to or after the publication will, in some cases, be a factor to be taken into account in deciding whether the interference was 'necessary' within the terms of Article 10(2).

While Article 10(1) speaks in terms of 'interference by public authority', it is clear that there are positive obligations on a state to take action where the material threat to an individual's freedom of expression comes from a private source. The reasoning in *Plattform 'Arzte für das Leben' v Austria*,[7] finding that there was an obligation on a state under Article 11 to prevent disruption of a demonstration by a hostile mob, would be applicable equally to Article 10 in equivalent circumstances. The precise content of the positive obligation is still in need of elaboration.[8] In what may have been an optimistic aside, the Commission suggested that there may be an obligation on states to take steps to guard against 'excessive press concentrations'.[9] Even in national law, this is a matter of great complexity and isolating the content of the duty, identifying who are 'victims' of its violation, and reducing claims to justiciable questions are each such problematic issues for the Convention regime that it is no surprise that the Commission's *obiter dictum* has not been the source of further applications. However, one value of positive duties is that they put an obligation on the state to show that it has done something. The minimum duty in the field of competition would be machinery where complaints of excessive concentration or restrictive practices could be tested and where Article 10 considerations would be relevant to the outcome of any applications. Another area where a similar approach would be appropriate is in relation to industry – established regulatory bodies, like the Advertising Standards Association or the Press Complaints Commission in the United Kingdom.[10] The possibility that the activities of this kind of body might 'chill' expression, otherwise lawful, suggests a positive obligation on the state to provide a remedial regime similar to that alluded to by the Commission in *Rommelfanger v FRG*.[11]

Establishing positive duties in Article 10 is of significance not just for this provision itself but also for fixing the duty on public authorities not to discriminate. However, the obligation may go beyond this if the wider interpretation of Article 14 is adopted.[12] When the state steps into the area of expression, even if it has no duty to do so, and acts within the ambit of Article 10, then it attracts a duty not to discriminate in its initiatives – an example might be the placing of advertising with newspapers on political rather than commercial grounds.[13]

7   A 139 (1988).
8   See Clapham, *European System*, Ch 9 at pp 188-193.
9   *De Geillustreede Pers v Netherlands No 5178/71*, 8 DR 5 (1976) Com Rep para 88; CM Res DH (77) 1. See also Coleman, 11 Eur Comp L 202 (1990).
10 For the application of judicial review to the decisions of these bodies, see *R v Advertising Standards Ass, ex p Vernons* [1992] 2 WLR 1289. See also *Wingrove v UK No 17419/90*, 76-A DR 26 (1994) (decision of British Board of Film Classification, a private body but here acting under legislation).
11 *No 12242/86*, 62 DR 151 (1989).
12 See below, p 468.
13 Cf *R v Derbyshire County Council, ex p Times Supplements* (1991) COD 129.

The final sentence of Article 10(1) is unique in the Convention. It reflected the actual arrangements in the member states when the Convention was being drafted and, for broadcasting and television, at least, there are still technical reasons for states to continue to regulate these operations, given the limited range of the transmitting spectrum, in order that there can be any effective use of these media at all. However, the inclusion of this provision in Article 10(1) rather than in Article 10(2), raises the possibility that the powers of the state are wider with respect to grounds upon which enterprises might be limited by their operating licences but narrower in the degree of supervision which the Convention authorities will exert over state decisions. None the less, the final sentence of Article 10(1) gives a power of limitation to the states the exercise of which lies within the capacity of the Strasbourg authorities to review.

It is one thing to say that the final sentence gives a wide power to the state to make technical or financial licensing decisions. It is another to decide what matters fall within this wider discretion. In its early decisions, the Commission was inclined to take the view that the maintenance of public service monopolies in broadcasting was compatible with the Convention.[14] Subsequently, it has retreated from that position,[15] a conclusion which has now been endorsed by the Court in *Informationsverein Lentia v Austria*.[16] Applications were brought against Austria by persons who wanted to establish cable television and radio stations in Austria. Because of the state monopoly in broadcasting, the applicants had either been refused permission to proceed or had been advised that their plans would not be allowed to be implemented. The Court said that the compatibility of a broadcasting monopoly was to be considered under Article 10(2) rather than under the final sentence of Article 10(1) and, on the basis of the judgment (in the applicant's favour), it can be anticipated that the Court will not easily be persuaded that the exclusion of other operators is 'necessary in a democratic society'.[17] At its narrowest, the final sentence of Article 10(1) permits the state to decide who shall have a licence to operate a radio or television station or a cinema and on what technical and financial conditions. As a consequence a state may take action against unlicensed operators without infringing any right of theirs under the Convention.[18] But the mere fact that the producer of information is unlicensed appears not to give the state the

14 *X v Sweden No 3071/67*, 26 CD 71 (1968) and *Sacchi v Italy No 6452/74*, 5 DR 43 at 50 (1976).
15 *Nydahl v Sweden No 17505/90*, 16 EHRR CD 15 (1993). For a review of Commission practice, see Kruger and Buquichio-De Boer, in Cassese and Clapham, eds, *Transfrontier Television in Europe: the Human Rights Dimension*, 1990, pp 97-112.
16 A 276 (1993). Note also the impact of European Community law: *Elliniki Radiophonia Tileorassi Anonimi Etairia v Dimotiki Etairia Pliroforissis*, C-260/89 1991-6 ECR 2925 (Broadcasting monopoly not compatible with EC law) and *EC Commission v Netherlands*, C-353/89 (not reported) (discrimination on ground of nationality in producers of broadcast programmes not justified on need to promote national culture).
17 As to this requirement, see below, pp 396-410.
18 *X v UK No 8266/78*, 16 DR 190 (1978) and *Radio X, S, W and A v Switzerland No 10799/84*, 37 DR 236 (1984).

right to interfere with the reception of his programmes.[19] It seems unlikely that the Court would review the licensing process, although the Commission has indicated that there might be occasion to do so, particularly in conjunction with Article 14.[20] Of more concern is whether the state may use its licensing powers to regulate the content of what a licensee may broadcast. While the Commission has previously been reluctant to interfere with decisions based on such terms,[1] recent judgments of the Court have given more thorough consideration to the limits of a state's power under the 'broadcasting' provision. The Court has acknowledged that the limited nature of the radio spectrum requires the regulation of television and radio in a way distinct from other sectors of the media but it has said that this power is not to be exercised for other than technical purposes and not in a way which interferes with freedom of expression (unless the interference can be justified under Article 10(2)). In the *Groppera* case,[2] the Court said:

'. . . the purpose of the third sentence of Article 10(1) of the Convention is to make it clear that states are permitted to control by a licensing system the way in which broadcasting is organised in their territories, particularly in its technical aspects. It does not, however, provide that licensing measures shall not otherwise be subject to the requirements of Article 10(2), for that would lead to a result contrary to the object and purpose of Article 10 taken as a whole.'

This is a substantial fetter on the licensing power and, indeed, since the state's regulatory function might easily be justified under Article 10(2), seems to empty the broadcasting provision of most of its content. What it does mean is that content-based restrictions on material to be transmitted cannot be founded on the licensing power alone but must be necessary for one of the purposes in Article 10(2).[3] This will supplement in important ways the limits of protection allowed from time to time by the Commission based on violations of Article 14. As the proliferation of broadcasters increases and as they escape from actual or *de facto* state control, the temptation for states to maintain influence over their activities will be high. While the Convention may provide some protection against the application of excessively onerous terms in licences, it may prove less effective in ensuring that decisions about whom to license are not made in ways which prejudice the right of expression under Article 10. Accordingly, while the

---

19 *Radio X, S, W and A v Switzerland No 10799/84*, 37 DR 236 (1984) and *A v Switzerland No 10248/83*, cited in Bullinger, loc cit at p 372, n 2, above, p 352. See also *Groppera Radio AG v Switzerland* A 173 para 61 (1990) (licensing power applies to technical aspects of 'broadcasting . . . *organised in their territories*') (emphasis added).
20 *Verein Alternatives Lokalradio Bern v Switzerland No 10746/84*, 49 DR 126 at 140-141 (1986).
1 *X and Association Z v UK No 4515/70*, 38 CD 86 (1971).
2 A 173 para 61 (1990). See also *Informationverein Lentia v Austria* A 276 para 32 (1993). Cf the more ambiguous language in *Autronic v Switzerland* A 178 para 61 (1990).
3 See *Purcell v Ireland No 15404/89*, 70 DR 262 (1989) and *Brind and McLaughlin v UK Nos 18714/91 and 18759/91*, 77-A DR 42 (1994).

danger that the prospect of non-renewal of a licence might influence the content of a broadcaster's programmes is all too easy to envisage, the possibilities of a remedy under the Convention are remote.[4]

The limited capacity of the radio spectrum for the air transmission of radio and television broadcasts not only requires that the state regulate the broadcasting industry from a technical point of view but it gives the state a legitimate interest in what is broadcast by those it licenses. It may and, arguably, must be concerned with programme content, taken as a whole, in the interests of pluralism and balance, considerations which do not bear to the same extent when the medium is open to all on market principles. The contrast is made between radio and television on the one hand and newspapers, books and magazines on the other. Developments in satellite and cable television technology are beginning to make the distinction of dubious worth. Satellite broadcasting brings within the reach of viewers television programmes originating from beyond the state's territory and over the content of which it has no control. Cable systems multiply without practical limit the number of channels which might be available to viewers and listeners.

States have a variety of reasons why they wish to use their licensing power in this burgeoning market to impose content-based conditions on operators: the need to protect the press,[5] the protection of national culture,[6] or an unwillingness to accept 'lower' standards of content-based limitations prevailing in other states.[7] Some of these issues must take into account the right in Article 10 to receive 'information and ideas . . . regardless of frontiers' and, for those states which are members of the European Union, their obligations not to discriminate against foreign enterprises. The Council of Europe has taken some steps towards establishing an international regime which takes properly into account human rights considerations.[8]

3.   INTERFERENCE WITH FREEDOM OF EXPRESSION

i.   The significance of the interference

Pre-publication censorship is particularly to be deprecated because it prevents the transmission of information and ideas to those who wish to

4   If 'the determination of a civil right' is involved, then the national licensing decision would fall within Article 6(1). See above, pp 178-179. Cf *R v Independent Television Commission, ex p TSW Broadcasting*, (1992) Times, 7 February.
5   See Lester, loc cit at p 372, n 2, above, Ch 18 at pp 483-484 at n 77.
6   See France's Freedom of Communication (Amendment) Act 1994 which provides for a state-owned company to make TV programmes promoting the French language. See also *X S A v Netherlands No 21472/93*, 76-A DR 129 (1994).
7   *R v Secretary of State for National Heritage ex p Continental Television B Vio* [1993] COD 421.
8   Hondius, 8 YEL 141 (1988). On the EC position, see Council Directive, OJ 1989 L 298, p 23. See also Wallace and Goldberg, 9 YEL 175 (1989); Schwartz, in Cassese and Clapham, loc cit at p 384, n 15, above, pp 165-188; and Van Loon, 4 Media Law and Practice 17 (1993). Although there have been developments since then, Bullinger, loc cit at p 372, n 2, above, pp 360-377, has an excellent summary of the problems presented by the new technologies of communication.

receive them and thus to make their own minds up about them and because it thwarts the self-expression justification which stands behind the right. Pre-publication measures such as licensing of outlets or journalists,[9] submission of copy to a public official[10] and court-ordered injunctions are subject to close scrutiny for their necessity. There is no 'bright-line' prohibition against such measures but the burden of establishing the need for them will be heavy.[11] In some instances, even temporary interference of this kind may destroy or substantially reduce the value of the information: the Court has noted the 'perishability' of news to the press and broadcasters.[12]

Post-publication sanctions include civil and criminal actions. The impact each may have will depend on the consequences for the applicant. On the face of it, a criminal punishment, especially if it involves loss of liberty, will be more severe, though in *Markt intern Verlag v FRG*,[13] the publisher was faced with the prospect of a penalty of 500,000 DM for failure to comply with a civil injunction. In *Tolstoy Miloslavsky v UK*,[14] the level and unpredictability of libel damages in English law is being challenged under Article 10. Penalties and costs of legal proceedings may reach such a level that the survival is put at risk of corporate persons which have exercised their right to freedom of expression and against which proceedings have been taken.[15] Another form of sanction, which may be a pre- or post-publication measure, is seizure and forfeiture of the means of communication or, in the case of works of art, the work itself. The interference here will have a different impact to penalties, limiting or prescribing altogether future access to the information. The confiscation of the pictures in *Müller v Switzerland*[16] was regarded by the Court as not in violation of the Convention for the technical reason that there was an unexplored avenue of appeal, but the Court did concede a 'special problem' about the seizure of original works of art. In *Otto-Preminger-Institut v Austria*, the Commission has said that 'very stringent reasons' were needed to justify the seizure of a film 'which excludes any chance to discuss [its] message . . .',[17] reasons the Commission found lacking in this case, although the Court did not.[18]

Even post-publication sanctions may have an impact on the publication of information other than that against which they are directed because of their 'chilling effect' on those responsible for the subsequent production of other

9 *De Becker v Belgium* A 4 (1962). See also *Compulsory Membership in an Association Prescribed by Law for the Practice of Journalism*, Inter-Am Ct H Rts Rep, Series A 5 (1985); 7 HRLJ 74 (1986).
10 Not, it seems, at present an issue. But note the licensing of films in the UK under the Cinemas Act 1985 and role of British Board of Film Classification: see Bailey, Harris and Jones, *Civil Liberties: Cases and Materials*, 3rd ed, 1991, pp 300-304.
11 *Observer and Guardian v UK* A 216 (1991).
12 Id, para 60.
13 A 165 para 15 (1989).
14 *No 18139/91*, Report, 6 Dec 1993, paras 45-55. The damages were £1.5m.
15 *Open Door and Dublin Well Woman Centre v Ireland* A 246 para 21 (1992).
16 A 133 para 43 (1988).
17 A 295-A (1994) Com Rep para 77.
18 A 295-A para 57 (1994).

materials. The prospect of future publishing policy being influenced by a post-publication sanction increases the suspicion with which the Court will approach interference with expression. The Court was disturbed by the effect of the civil action against the applicant in *Barthold v FRG*[19] because of its likely consequence for the participation of members of professions in debates about their work which were of general interest. The impact of libel actions like the one sustained by the Austrian courts against the journalist Lingens on the matter of reporting political events was regarded by the Court as a strong reason for finding a violation.[20]

ii.   Duties and responsibilities

The injunction in Article 10(2) that the exercise of freedom of expression carries with it 'duties and responsibilities' is unique in the limitative provisions of the Convention. Since it directly refers to the possibility of interferences with Article 10(1) rights, it carries the potential for restrictions of the exercise of expression rights going beyond those otherwise provided for by Article 10(2). At the very least, the phrase might legitimate otherwise discriminatory distinctions in interferences between people in different positions.[1] More widely, it might serve as justification for restricting 'irresponsible' expression by anybody. Governments have relied on the words as reinforcing the legitimacy of interferences they have made with expression rights.[2] The Strasbourg authorities have referred to the need to take into account 'duties and responsibilities' of persons in the same position as the applicant in terms suggesting an endorsement of these aims. The positions of soldiers[3] and civil servants[4] are among those carrying 'duties and responsibilities' which may justify interference with their freedom of expression on grounds particular to their status. But it might be thought that the powers of states to take action to restrict expression rights are quite wide enough within Article 10(2) and that it would be perfectly possible to take account of the particularities of the applicant's position as one item among the many which will be relevant to assessing whether an interference was 'necessary in a democratic society'.

In practice, the Commission and Court have adopted an approach to the interpretation of 'duties and responsibilities' which does serve the interests of freedom of expression rather more than might have been anticipated. Although seldom invoking the phrase directly, they have acknowledged that the position of applicants in particular categories is a reason for limiting rather than extending the power of the state to interfere with their right:

19 A 90 para 58 (1985).
20 *Lingens v Austria* A 103 para 44 (1986). See also *Jersild v Denmark* A 298 para 44 (1994).
1   *Engel v Netherlands* A 22 paras 102-103 (1976).
2   See *B v UK No 10293/83*, 45 DR 41 (1984).
3   *Engel v Netherlands* A 22 para 100 (1976). See also *Müller v Switzerland* A 133 para 34 (1988) (artists).
4   B v UK No 10293/83, 45 DR 41 (1984); *Morissens v Belgium No 11389/85*, 56 DR 127 (1988) (teacher); and *X v UK No 8010/77*, 16 DR 101 (1979) (teacher).

publishers,[5] journalists,[6] and politicians[7] have enjoyed this advantage. Their 'duties and responsibilities', it has been suggested, are to be understood in relation to their position in a 'democratic society'. In *Jersild v Denmark*,[8] the Court referred to the special responsibilities of television journalists compared to print journalists on account of the 'much more immediate and powerful effect' of television. In *Otto-Preminger-Institut v Austria*,[9] the majority of the Court said that those who make remarks critical of the religious predilections of others have 'an obligation to avoid as far as possible expressions that are gratuitously offensive'! Also, the Strasbourg authorities look increasingly at the details of the 'duties and responsibilities' and add them to the other factors to be taken into account under Article 10(2). A recent example is *Vereinigung Demokratischer Soldaten Osterreichs and Gubi v Austria*,[10] where a majority of the Court rejected a claim by the government to rely on *Engel v Netherlands* in deciding whether denial of facilities for the distribution of a magazine directed to soldiers could be sustained. The Court distinguished *Engel* because in that case there had been evidence of a threat to military order. Here, that had not been demonstrated. The Court made no distinction between the position of the publisher and the distributor, who was a soldier.[11] There is no reference in the judgment to 'duties and responsibilities' – if anything, the contrary for the Court drew attention to the fact that:

'Freedom of expression applies to servicemen *just as it does* to other persons within the jurisdiction of the contracting states . . .'[12]

It would be premature to say that the phrase has become a 'dead letter' – *Otto-Preminger* shows that – but its significance as a further source of justification for interferences with expression should not be exaggerated.

iii. Prescribed by law

The state must identify the national law which authorises or mandates the interference with an applicant's right. This has seldom been a difficulty for states in Article 10 cases[13] but it should be noted that in *Groppera Radio AG*

---

5 Eg *Observer and Guardian v UK* A 216 (1991).
6 Eg *Lingens v Austria* A 103 para 41 (1986). But note *Prager and Oberschlick v Austria* A 313 (1995) Com Rep para 65, where the Commission found that a reporter had 'failed to prove that he had applied the necessary diligence as a journalist', Ct Jmt, id.
7 Eg *Castells v Spain* A 236 para 42 (1992).
8 A 298 para 31 (1994).
9 A 295-A para 49 (1994).
10 A 302 (1994).
11 Id, paras 33-40, 48-49.
12 Id, para 27 (emphasis added), referring also to *Hadjianastassiou v Greece* A 252 para 39 (1992).
13 Delegation of rule-making authority to professional bodies by the general law does not prevent their rules being 'law' for the purposes of Article 10(2): *Barthold v FRG* A 90 para 46 (1985) and *Casado Coca v Spain* A 285-A para 46 (1994).

v Switzerland[14] and *Autronic v Switzerland*,[15] the Court allowed the state to rely on domestically applicable rules of public international law to satisfy this criterion. More problematic has been the adequacy of the national law when measured against the Convention standards of predictability and foreseeability. In three areas the precision of the national law has come under scrutiny. In the *Markt intern Verlag v FRG*[16] and *Barthold v FRG*[17] cases, the Court was satisfied that the German law on Unfair Competition Law 1909, s 1, which required 'honest practices', did satisfy Article 10(2). Absolute precision could not be achieved, especially in,

> 'spheres such as that of competition, in which the situation is constantly changing in accordance with developments in the market and in the field of communication . . .'.[18]

In addition, the Court noted, there was consistent case-law – 'clear and abundant' – which served to make the application of the general words sufficiently foreseeable.[19] The Court has exhibited a similar degree of flexibility with respect to obscenity laws. In *Müller v Switzerland*,[20] the Court referred to 'the need to avoid excessive rigidity and to keep pace with changing circumstances'. This language came from *Sunday Times v UK*[1] where the Court was faced with the common law rule on contempt of court. One issue here was whether a particular head of contempt, that the prohibited article was a prejudgment of an issue before the domestic court, was an unforeseeable development of the general common law rule or whether it was only an application of a general principle which might have been anticipated by the applicants. The Court took the latter view, holding that the application of the rule was foreseeable 'to a degree that was reasonable in the circumstances'.[2] Many of the cases indicate that the matter of foreseeability will be assessed in the light of the advice available to the applicant. It must be anticipated that the Court will expect the media to be properly advised on legally controversial matters. An unusual point arose in the *Open Door* case, where the applicants argued that it was not foreseeable that a provision in the Constitution would be a sufficient legal basis for proceedings against them. The Commission accepted this claim[3] but it was

14 A 173 para 68 (1990).
15 A 178 para 57 (1990).
16 A 165 para 30 (1989).
17 A 90 para 47 (1985).
18 *Markt intern Verlag v FRG* A 165 para 30 (1989).
19 Ibid.
20 A 133 para 29 (1988).
1   A 30 para 49 (1979).
2   Id, para 52. It was argued that an application of the law of contempt was not 'prescribed by law' in *Harman v UK No 10038/82*, 38 DR 53 (1984); ibid 46 DR 57 (1986) F Sett. The Commission expressed doubts about whether s 10 of the Contempt of Court Act 1981 satisfied the Convention standard of 'law' in *Goodwin v UK No 17488/90* (1994) Com Rep paras 56-57, but found it unnecessary to resolve them .
3   *Open Door and Dublin Well Woman Centre v Ireland* A 246 (1992) Com Rep paras 45-52.

rejected by the Court, a conclusion doubtless buttressed by the information, not available to the Commission, that the applicants had in fact had legal advice which adverted to the possibility that the Constitution did provide adequate authority for an action against them.[4]

iv. The aim of the interference

For an interference with freedom of expression to be permitted, it must have the legitimate aim of furthering one or more of the public interest purposes listed in Article 10(2) (the protection of 'national security', etc).

A number of cases have concerned restrictions on freedom of expression to safeguard the judicial process. Because of the requirements of Article 6(1), there may be circumstances in which the state has a duty to interfere with freedom of expression if the right of an individual to a fair trial would be prejudiced by the publication of information about the proceedings.[5] More generally, the reputation of the court system is a value of some importance. These considerations are recognised by Article 10(2), which permits interferences which have as their aim the protection of 'the rights of others', including an accused person, or 'for maintaining the authority and impartiality of the judiciary'.

The Court acceded to a state's claim that it was necessary to interfere with freedom of expression on this ground in *Barfod v Denmark*[6] where the applicant, writing in a magazine, had criticised in vigorous terms a court in Greenland which had decided a tax case of general importance to the local people. The decision went in favour of the authorities and Barfod wrote that two lay judges who were also local government employees had 'done their duty', which, the Danish Court held, implied that they had not discharged their judicial functions independently and impartially. The applicant maintained that his criticisms were directed at the tribunal rather than the individuals and that his article was part of a wider political debate about the tax. The European Court rejected this argument, partly because of the robust character of the applicant's criticism but mainly because it decided that he had directed imputations against the reputations of the judges and it was necessary to punish him in order to protect their rights. The government's explanation of the objective for which Barfod was punished was never clearly stated and the European Court rather took what it thought was its best point in order to reach its decision. The judgment is an indication that the identification of the objective for which the interference has been imposed may be crucial to the outcome of a case.

---

4 A 246 paras 59-60 (1992).
5 *Observer and Guardian v UK* A 216 paras 61-64 (1991).
6 A 149 paras 30-35 (1989). See also the *Observer and Guardian* case, below, p 394.

In *Sunday Times v UK*,[7] the defendant state was less successful. There the government argued that the publication of a newspaper article about the merits of pending litigation created the prospect of 'trial by newspaper' and that it was, therefore, necessary to restrain its publication in order to maintain public confidence in the courts. The majority rejected this argument for a variety of reasons, one of which was that measures 'for maintaining the authority and impartiality of the judiciary' protected an objectively determinable interest.[8] That being so, the margin of appreciation to the state was less. The Court reviewed the situation in great detail and, relying on a cumulation of factors, decided that there was no pressing social need for the injunction against the newspaper. Those factors were that the English court had not given proper weight to the *right* of freedom of expression, that the litigation was dormant, that there was substantial public interest in the case, that the article was moderately phrased and fairly balanced and that the injunction was cast in altogether too wide terms.[9] What is striking is not any particular item in this list but that the European Court was prepared to engage in so detailed a review because it deemed the margin of appreciation relatively slight, given the objectivity which it discerned in the aim of the interference. Certainly, once the Court embarked upon its inquiry and assessment, it gave no particular weight to the right to fair trial.[10] However, in *Channel Four v UK*[11] the Commission does seem to have been easily satisfied of the necessity of prohibiting contemporaneous reconstructions of a criminal appeal of a *cause célèbre* to be broadcast on television because the state deemed it necessary to protect the right to a fair trial ('the rights of others') and the reputation of the court ('the authority and impartiality of the judiciary').

One can contrast the narrowness of the margin of appreciation allowed in the *Sunday Times* case with cases where the state claims to act for the protection of morals. The Court does not regard 'morals' as having an objective content, nor is it helped by any European consensus on the question.[12] Accordingly, the Court has conceded a wide margin to the national decision-maker about what 'morals' are and what is necessary to

---

7   A 30 para 59 (1979). In terms of the English law of contempt, whereas the *Barfod* case was about 'scandalising the court' (a form of contempt that is no longer invoked), the *Sunday Times* cases concerned conduct calculated to prejudice a fair trial.

8   The 'objectivity' of 'maintaining the authority and impartiality of the judiciary' was challenged by the government in *Weber v Switzerland*, A 177 (1990) Verbatim Record, 23 January 1990, p 35.

9   A 39 paras 62-67 (1979). The judgment was by 11 to 9 and the dissenting judges also subjected the facts of the litigation to close scrutiny.

10   The Court did refer to this right in *Weber v Switzerland* A 177 para 51 (1990), but found the allegation without factual foundation.

11   *No 14132/88*, 61 DR 285 (1989). For a slightly stronger case in favour of the state where a trial before a jury was going on, see *Hodgson v UK Nos 11553/85 and 11685/85*, 51 DR 136 (1987). See also *Atkinson v UK No 13366/87*, 67 DR 244 (1990). And see Michael, (1993) CLP 190.

12   *Handyside v UK* A 24 para 48 (1976).

protect them: the first concession may be legitimate; the second is not obviously so. In the *Handyside* and *Müller* cases, the Court accepted that there was a pressing social need to punish expression for the protection of 'morals' of relatively small areas of population. It is true that, in both cases, the right of the state to intervene was enhanced because, in the one case, the material was aimed at children and, in the other, children were not excluded from the exhibition. Determining what 'morals' are may be peculiarly susceptible to local appreciation; determining what is necessary in a democratic society to protect them ought not to be, lest the same local prejudices which take a singular view of the content of morals also take the view that stringent measures are necessary to protect them.[13] In the *Open Door* case,[14] the Court acknowledged that it was primarily for the national authorities to assess the content of 'morals' but it subjected to scrutiny the claim that the action taken by the state to protect its own conception of morals was 'necessary in a democratic society'. The Court eventually concluded that the interference could not be justified.[15]

Other aims of repression are still less homogeneously 'objective' or 'subjective' but the classification will seriously influence the outcome of Strasbourg cases. This is convincingly demonstrated by the judgment in *Otto-Preminger-Institut v Austria*.[16] The Court held that the interference with the applicant's rights had been to protect the (religious) rights of others. There was, the Court said, no uniform conception of the significance of religion in society throughout Europe. Accordingly, the state had a wide margin of appreciation as to whether it was necessary to prevent the applicant from showing the film in order to protect the rights of the local people. The Court said:

'It is in the first place for the national authorities, who are better placed than the international judge, to assess the need for such a measure in the light of the situation obtaining locally at a given time. In all the circumstances of the present case, the Court does not consider that the Austrian authorities can be regarded as having overstepped the margin of appreciation in this respect.'

Article 10(2) also permits the state to interfere with expression for the prevention of 'disorder'. This concept is not restricted to 'public order', though it certainly includes that.[17] In *Groppera Radio AG v Switzerland*[18]

13 Note the order for the confiscation of the pictures in *Müller v Switzerland* A 133 paras 40-43 (1988).
14 A 246 paras 63, 68 (1992).
15 Id, paras 67-77.
16 A 295-A para 56 (1994).
17 See eg *Chorherr v Austria* A 266-B (1993). The need to protect public order in the face of terrorist threats is also regarded by the Commission as a significant basis for restricting freedom of expression: see p 385, n 3, above. See also the dissenting opinion in *Castells v Spain* A 236 (1992)
18 A 173 para 70 (1990).

and *Autronic v Switzerland*,[19] the Court said that the state could move against expression in the interest of preventing disorder in the international telecommunications order. In *Engel v Netherlands*,[20] the Court accepted that the prevention of disorder within the armed forces was a legitimate aim within Article 10(2). The same position was taken by the Commission in *Arrowsmith v UK*,[1] where the Commission found that the applicant's activities also threatened national security.

Considerations of national security raise a rather different obstacle to review by the Strasbourg authorities, that is the justiciability of the claim. It was a particularly troublesome matter in *Observer and Guardian Newspapers v UK*.[2] The Attorney-General obtained interlocutory injunctions in the English High Court against two newspapers to prevent them publishing information about the operation of the British security services from the manuscript of a proposed book, *Spycatcher*, written by a retired secret agent, Peter Wright. The interlocutory injunctions were granted in connection with a High Court application by the Attorney-General for a permanent injunction to prevent the applicant newspapers publishing material from *Spycatcher* on grounds of breach of confidence. They were granted under English law pending the outcome of the application of the proceedings for a permanent injunction to prevent the Attorney-General's claim in those proceedings being prejudiced by the prior publication of material that would be the very subject of any permanent injunction. The interlocutory injunctions were maintained by the House of Lords on 30 July 1987, despite the publication of the book in the meantime in the United States and the resulting circulation of copies in the United Kingdom.[3]

At Strasbourg, the government claimed initially that the interlocutory injunctions could be justified under Article 10(2) as having the aim of 'maintaining the authority of the judiciary'. When the case reached the Court, it also argued that they were necessary to safeguard the operation of the security service. The Court accepted these were both legitimate aims for the purposes during the whole period of the injunctions for the purposes of Article 10(2).

After publication of the book overseas and some distribution of it in the United Kingdom (by persons bringing it home), the newspapers argued that there was no need to continue the injunction while the substantive action was being decided because the government's right to keep the information secret had already been effectively undermined. None the less, the government persisted with the attempt to maintain the injunctions and the

---

19   A 178 (1990).
20   A 22 (1976). See also *Vereniging Democratischer Soldaten Osterreichs and Gubi v Austria* A 302 para 32 (1994).
1   *No 7050/75*, 8 DR 123 (1977); 19 DR 5 (1978) Com Rep; CM Res DH (79) 4.
2   A 216 (1991). Cf *Sunday Times v UK (No 2)* A 217 (1992).
3   The book was published in Australia and Ireland in October 1987. It was not published in the UK until after the Attorney-General's application for permanent injunctions was rejected in 1988 in *A-G v Guardian Newspapers Ltd (No 2)* [1990] 1 AC 109, HL.

English courts continued them until the end of the litigation when the House of Lords refused to grant permanent injunctions against the newspapers.[4]

The case is a difficult one because the government did not isolate a single aim in justification for the ban on publication of extracts from the book. Because national security was only indirectly in point, the specific Convention objective which the government said that the injunctions were protecting was based on the fact that Mr Wright's information has been received in confidence. Originally, the argument had been that the injunction was necessary 'for maintaining the authority and impartiality of the judiciary', to wit, to prevent the revelation of information during the course of a judicial hearing, the very purpose of which was to determine whether there was a legal right to keep that information confidential. To publish prematurely would have destroyed any right to confidentiality which the court might later find. When the information did get into the public domain as a result of its publication abroad, this argument lost its cogency. In consequence, the government relied upon a different aim. National security was to be protected by assuring third parties (for which read, allied states) of the effective protection of secret information by making it clear that officers who threatened to breach their life-long duty of confidentiality could be effectively prevented from doing so by legal action and that such action would, indeed, be taken.[5] The European Court did not attempt to assess whether this was a plausible national security objective, though it did comment on the transformation of the government's case,[6] because it found that, in any event, the continuance of the injunction was disproportionate to any need to protect the confidence interest.[7] Among the dissenting judges, Judge Walsh objected that the government had presented no evidence at all of the threat to national security – 'that cannot be invoked to gain a restriction simply by an expression of opinion on the part of the authorities . . .'. This was the same point taken by the two dissenting members of the Commission in *Arrowsmith v UK*.[8]

In the '*Bluf*' case,[9] the Commission was disposed to question the government's claim that it remained necessary to prevent the publication of information indicating that the security services had had an interest in the activities of certain political organisations some six years before. Its report suggests that claims of national security will not always be left unquestioned. While the Strasbourg authorities will remain unlikely to inquire into the appropriateness of measures to prevent the dissemination of

---

4   *A-G v Guardian (No 2)* [1988] 3 All ER 545. For a convenient account of the whole saga, see Feldman, *Civil Liberties and Human Rights in England and Wales*, 1993, pp 648-668. On the case in Strasbourg, see Leigh, 1992 PL 200.
5   A 216 para 59 (1991). See now the Official Secrets Act 1989, s 1.
6   Id, para 69.
7   Ibid. However, the Court held that there was no breach of Article 10 before the book was first published, in the US in July 1987; the injunctions were justified to protect national security and maintain the authority of the judiciary.
8   *No 7050/75*, 19 DR 5.
9   *Vereniging Weekblad 'Bluf' v Netherlands* A 306-A (1995) Com Rep para 47. The dissent said it was for the state to decide whether it was necessary to keep the information confidential.

information about battlefield strategy or weapons plans, they ought not to be so reluctant where the information is the tittle-tattle of intelligence. The claim that national security is at stake requires making out on the evidence, even if the burden is not a heavy one, and, even then, it is one item among those which the Court must consider on the necessity question, not necessarily the decisive one.

v.   Necessity of the interference[10]

The strong language in the *Handyside* and the *Sunday Times* cases in favour of the right of freedom of expression seeks to give expression a preferred status over other interests for the protection of which the state may seek to act. *Handyside v UK*,[11] with its reference to 'pressing social need', puts the burden on the state first to assert grounds for interfering with expression and then to demonstrate the existence of 'relevant and sufficient' grounds for doing so. These grounds, the Court reiterated in *Weber v Switzerland*,[12] must be 'convincingly established'. What is at stake, the majority said in the *Sunday Times* case,

> 'is not . . . a choice between two conflicting principles but with a principle of freedom of expression that is subject to a number of exceptions which must be narrowly interpreted . . .'.[13]

It will be seen that these powerful sentiments in favour of expression have not always been acted upon, none the less, they have enabled the Court, sometimes only by narrow majorities, to dispute on a number of occasions the necessity of measures taken by states which limited applicants' freedom of expression. Although the Court frequently resorts to the language of 'balance' between the expression and the public interest, its enquiries involve a multiplicity of considerations and over-simplification of its jurisprudence is unjustified. Furthermore, the 'balance' metaphor is apt to disguise the special consideration which is to be given to the right of freedom of expression.

a.   The importance of the expression interest

Since the Court has not excluded from the Convention understanding of expression anything which might plausibly be included within it, the categories of expression to which it has from time to time referred must relate to the different characteristics of each of them and, therefore, on establishing the necessity for interfering with any particular exercise of the freedom of expression. If this be right, not only must it be established how

10 See Macdonald, 1-2 AEL pp 104-124 (1990).
11 A 24 para 48 (1976).
12 A 177 para 47 (1990).
13 A 30 para 65 (1979).

the nature of one class of expression affects the state's right to interfere with it but also a preliminary judgment must be made to consign each example of expression to one category or another.

POLITICAL EXPRESSION

The three classes to which the case-law alludes are political, artistic and commercial expression. It may be that these groups do not embrace the whole spectrum of expression[14] but the Court's conception of the first is so wide that much will be included in it. The Court attaches the highest importance to the protection of political expression and, generally, requires the strongest reasons to justify impediments on the exercise of political speech. States, therefore, argue for the narrowness of this category but, at the level of general principle, it is an argument which has been lost.[15] The privileged position of political speech derives from the Court's conception of it as a central feature of a democratic society, both in so far as it relates to the electoral process and to day-to-day matters of public concern. Further, those qualities of 'tolerance and broadmindedness' which characterise a democratic society require not only that approved information and received ideas enter into circulation but that publications which 'offend, shock and disturb' do so also. The protection of the expression rights of politicians demands particular stringency, the more so for members of the opposition.[16] There is, though, a price to be paid: politicians are required to be tolerant of criticisms of themselves, even of sharp attacks, in the same democratic interest.[17] However, this high degree of concern for political expression is not, despite the urgings of governments, restricted to matters of high politics. In *Thorgierson v Iceland*, where the Court said,

'there is no warrant in its case-law for distinguishing between political discussion and discussion of other matters of public concern',[18]

the issue was police misconduct; in *Barfod v Denmark*,[19] the impartiality of a court; in *Barthold v FRG*,[20] the availability of an emergency veterinary service in a single German city: these were all issues of 'political speech' widely understood.

In the cases which have reached the Court, political speech has invariably involved questions of press freedom. The traditional fora of the political meeting or demonstration, where the speaker's message is delivered directly to his audience, have not raised problems which have come before the Court

14 Eg there are also scientific publications.
15 *Barthold v FRG* A 90 paras 42, 58 (1985).
16 *Castells v Spain* A 236 paras 42, 46 (1992).
17 *Lingens v Austria* A 103 (1986); *Oberschlick v Austria* A 204 (1991); and *Schwabe v Austria* A 242-B (1992).
18 A 239 para 64 (1992).
19 A 149 (1989). See also *Prager and Oberschlick v Austria* A 313 (1995) Com Rep.
20 A 90 (1985).

or, if they have, they have concerned other provisions than Article 10.[1] Also, typically these informal political actions involve fringe politics. The mainstream parties these days operate through and often also against the media. There is an intense relationship between government and the media, which the case-law of the Court acknowledges. The role of the press is that of 'public watchdog'[2] and,

> '. . . it is . . . incumbent on it to impart information and ideas on political issues just as on these other areas of public interest. Not only does the press have the task of imparting such information and ideas: the public also has a right to receive them. . .'.[3]

The press is not above the law but the Court sees the Convention as protecting the press against interferences which will impede its effective operation. The Commission has spoken with particular firmness about the right of a journalist to protect his sources. In *Goodwin v UK*,[4] a journalist was ordered by the national court to reveal the source of information to be included in an article he proposed to write. The information related to the affairs of a company, which alleged that it had been stolen. The national court ordered that the information should be revealed for the 'prevention of crime'.[5] The Commission said that the protection of sources was an 'essential means'[6] for the effective exercise of press freedom and a journalist could be compelled to reveal his sources only in 'exceptional circumstances', which these were not.[7] The Court has taken into account the commercial and practical realities of news-gathering and distribution.[8] While the Court is more likely to protect moderately expressed sentiments in established journals,[9] it has conceded the legitimacy of vigorous and even hostile reporting and comment, however much it may be resented by those against whom it is directed. Politicians, especially, are fair game, but the Court granted a wide latitude in respect of criticism of the police in *Thorgierson v Iceland*[10] and *Castells v Spain*.[11] It was less accommodating in *Barfod v Denmark*,[12] perhaps unnecessarily so, to a robust assault on some judges in a magazine article.

1 Eg *Ezelin v France* A 202-A (1991) (political demonstrations, Article 11).
2 *Observer and Guardian v UK* A 216 para 59(b) (1991).
3 *Lingens v Austria* A 103 para 41 (1986).
4 *No 17488/90* (1994) Com Rep. Pending before Court.
5 This was authorised by the Contempt of Court Act 1981, s 10.
6 *K v Austria No 16002/90*, A 255-B (1993) Com Rep para 64.
7 Id, para 69.
8 *Observer and Guardian v UK* A 216 para 60 (1991). The point was made even more strongly in the dissenting opinion of Judge Pettiti.
9 *Sunday Times v UK* A 30 para 63 (1979).
10 A 239 para 67 (1992). Cf the government's position at para 62.
11 A 236 paras 33-35 (1992).
12 A 149 paras 33-36 (1989). See also Judge Gölcüklü, dissenting. In *Prager and Oberschlick v Austria* A 313 (1995) but the Commission divided, 15 to 12, in finding no violation where journalists were punished for a strongly-worded attack on a judge; Ct Jmt, id.

Strong criticism, colourfully presented, has the advantage of drawing attention to political issues and serves the commercial aims of newspaper proprietors. However, the approach carries the risk of serious disadvantage and even damage to those who are unjustifiably pilloried by the press. In deciding where the line is to be drawn, the Court has leant in favour of the press. It has not expressly adopted the American 'public figure' doctrine (which limits remedies in defamation to allegations made with malice if the subject of them is a person in the public eye) in all its details[13] but, *sub silento*, that approach appears to have influenced the jurisprudence. In *Lingens v Austria*,[14] the applicant was a journalist who had published articles critical of the Austrian Chancellor (ie Prime Minister). The gravamen of his charge was that the Chancellor's political association with a politician accused of having a Nazi past made the Chancellor's attack on Simon Weisenthal, the prominent 'Nazi hunter', unacceptable. Lingens accused the Chancellor of being an 'opportunist'. He was convicted in the Austrian courts of a criminal offence of defamation but the European Court was unanimously of the view that the conviction violated Article 10. Noting the Chancellor's position and the importance of press criticism of public figures for the working of a democratic system, the Court found that the conviction of Lingens for not being able to prove the truth of what were matters of opinion was not necessary in a democratic society.

Where the reason for the condemnation of a press report is that it is untrue, the defendant must be given the opportunity to prove the truth of his allegations. This was the position in *Castells v Spain*,[15] where the applicant had complained about the manner of and lack of accountability for policing of the Basque country. Castells was a senator and a member of an extreme Basque nationalist party. His allegations were particularly serious: that the police were responsible for the murder of Basque activists and that they were protected by the authorities from prosecution. He had been convicted of criminal offences involving serious insults to the government and public servants. The Court was concerned about resort to the criminal law in a case like this. It said:

'. . . the dominant position which the government occupies makes it necessary for it to display restraint in resorting to criminal proceedings, particularly where other means are available for replying to the unjustified attacks and criticisms of its adversaries or the media.'

The Court found that the Spanish courts had denied Castells the opportunity he had requested to prove the truth of his allegations and held that it was not necessary to punish him for the publication of factual assertions which were/might be true.[16] Two concurring judgments suggested

13 See *New York Times v Sullivan* 376 US 254 (1964). See also Macdonald, *Wiarda Mélanges*, pp 361-372.
14 A 103 para 46 (1986).
15 A 236 para 46 (1992).
16 Id, para 48.

a test even more favourable to persons in the applicant's position. Judge Pekkanen regarded Castells's claims as matters of opinion, not susceptible to being proved true or not. Judge De Meyer said that since Castells was commenting on a matter of 'general interest', it made no difference whether he was right or wrong. Judge Pekkanen's position follows the *Lingens* and *Oberschlick* cases where the Court held that a law requiring the proof of truth of opinions held about political figures was not necessary in a democratic society.[17] This reasoning was adopted also in *Thorgierson v Iceland*.[18] The applicant had been convicted of defaming the police by publishing several articles severely critical of the conduct and discipline of the Reykjavik police force. Finding for the applicant, the Court decided that the strong language followed from the author's assessment of the allegations of others and the state of public opinion about police misbehaviour. *He* did not make any allegations which he should have been called upon to prove. He was writing about a matter of serious public concern and his vigorous copy was designed to serve his purpose of drawing attention to it.[19] Judge De Meyer's stand in the *Castells* case gathers support from the finding of a breach on Article 10 in *Schwabe v Austria* by both the Commission and the Court. Schwabe had been convicted of the offence of referring to a 'spent' conviction of another politician in the course of a political dispute, in which Schwabe suggested that the politician's previous conduct disqualified him from making critical remarks about Schwabe's colleagues. The Commission said that politicians must be prepared to accept criticism, even if far-fetched, but that such criticism must be founded on correct factual statements. It somewhat mitigated what correctness required when it said:

> '. . . in a short contribution to a discussion on the behaviour of politicians and the political morals, not every word can be weighed to exclude any possibility of misunderstanding.'[20]

The Court conflated the facts and opinion of Schwabe's article – they amounted to 'a value-judgment for which no proof of truth is possible. . .'.[1] On matters of general, political interest the Court is more inclined to regard comments as involving the statement of the author's opinion rather than as a statement of fact and, if of fact, to hold that their publication ought not to be interfered with if the allegations are made in good faith. There is room for further consideration about the burden of proof between applicant and government and about the weight to be given to the findings of the national court but the gradual movement towards the protection of a

---

17 *Lingens v Austria* A 103 para 46 (1986) and *Oberschlick v Austria* A 204 para 63 (1991).
18 A 239 para 65 (1992). The case shows how difficult it can be to draw the line between fact and opinion.
19 Id, para 67.
20 A 242-B (1992) Com Rep para 55.
1 A 242-B para 34 (1992).

realistic understanding of press freedom has been established by these recent cases.[2]

ARTISTIC EXPRESSION

The Court has been rather less inclined to stand out in favour of artistic expression. The sentiments expressed in *Handyside v UK* about the protection of Article 10 extending to expressions which 'offend, shock or disturb the state or any sector of the population'[3] would appear to have particular application to artistic works. Of course, the artist, like the journalist and newspaper owner, is not immune from the law but the artistic vocation as it is understood in liberal societies certainly extends to the radical and the challenging.[4] What one might, perhaps, anticipate is that the state's power to interfere with the production and display of works of art would be substantially limited compared with its power to deal with materials produced primarily for profit or entertainment. In *Müller v Switzerland*, the Commission identified precisely this point as one of the distinctions between democratic and undemocratic societies. It found that the conviction of Müller under s 204 of the Swiss Criminal Code which provides,

> 'anyone who makes or possesses . . . pictures . . . which are obscene with a view to . . . displaying them in public . . . shall be imprisoned or fined'

and the order that paintings done by him should be confiscated were violations of Article 10.[5] Müller, it should be stressed, was a serious artist, exhibiting at a public exhibition to celebrate the 500th anniversary of Fribourg's entry into the Swiss Confederation. He produced three large and spectacular paintings. One at least depicted a complex conglomeration of sexual activities involving homosexuality and bestiality, a description of which the Swiss government insisted be incorporated in the judgment.[6] The paintings were seen by a young girl, visiting the exhibition with her father.

---

2 Note also the reference in *Thorgierson v Iceland* A 239 para 66 (1992), rejecting the government's claim that the articles were intended as an attack on the police but accepting the applicant's position that they were a call for reform. In *Castells v Spain* A 236 para 46 (1992), the Court said, '. . . it remains open to the competent state authorities to adopt, in their capacity as guarantors of public order, measures, even of a criminal law nature, intended to react appropriately and without excess to defamatory accusations devoid of foundation or formulated in bad faith'.

3 A 24 para 49 (1976), quoted above at p 373, n 9.

4 Cf Lester, loc cit at p 372, n 2 above, p 471 n 35 – 'the inherently subversive nature of the artistic impulse'.

5 A 133 (1988) Com Rep para 70. See also *X Ltd and Y v UK No 8710/79*, 28 DR 77 (1982) (private prosecution and conviction of poet and publisher for blasphemous libel – no violation) and *Wingrove v UK No 17419/90*, (1995) Com Rep (decision of BBFC that video was blasphemous – violation).

6 A 133 para 16 (1988). See also oral argument, 25 Jan 1988, Court/Misc (88) 15 at 35.

There were no warnings about what was on offer. Her father did not shield her view but informed the prosecutor. The emphasis in the judgment of the European Court is on the 'duty and responsibilities' of the artist which the Court construed as imposing special considerations of restraint on the artist rather than special opportunities of freedom. Judge Spielmann's lone dissent is surely more faithful to the liberal tradition. The history of governmental interference with artistic works was not, he suggested, encouraging and the Court should require prudence of the states when interpreting their powers under Article 10(2). Recent decisions of the Commission have shown more regard for Judge Spielmann's position in *Müller* and, indeed, the Commission's own opinion.[7] However, a majority of the Court in *Otto-Preminger-Institut v Austria*[8] followed the general line in *Müller* when it upheld Austrian decisions to seize and then to order forfeit a film to be exhibited by the applicant institute, on the grounds that its showing would occasion 'justified indignation' among the local population, the religious opinions of whom were likely to be outraged by the blasphemous and lampooning character of the film. The minority[9] found that the state's action, which precluded the film from ever being screened in Austria, when the applicants had taken steps to ensure that no one came to the film unaware of its content and that no young people would be admitted, was disproportionate to any need to protect the religious feelings of even a majority of the population in the area. It is hard to know which aspect of the majority's judgment more threatens expression interests: that outrage of people based only on knowing of, not being confronted with, certain expression provides justification for interfering with the expression, or, this being the case, that the indignation of the people in a discrete, geographic area is sufficient to justify the interference across the entire state. In *Scherer v Switzerland*,[10] the Court was denied the opportunity to decide whether a line could be drawn between artistic expression and entertainment and, if so, what the appropriate level of protection for the latter should be, because of the discontinuance of a case following the death of the applicant. In that case, the Commission was of the opinion that the conviction of the proprietor of the sex shop for showing explicit videos violated Article 10, given that no one was likely to be confronted with them against their will and that only adults would be admitted.

COMMERCIAL EXPRESSION

The third category of expression to which reference may be found in the case-law of the Strasbourg authorities is commercial expression. The indications are that commercial expression is not regarded as so worthy of

7   *Otto-Preminger-Institut v Austria* A 295-A (1994) Com Rep paras 72, 77.
8   A 295-A paras 56-57 (1994).
9   Judges Palm, Pekkanen, Makarczyk.
10 A 287 (1993) Com Rep para 53 (no dispute that homosexual obscene video falls within Article 10(1)). The Court noted, judgment, paras 23-34, that decisions of Swiss courts and legislation had brought the law in line with the Commission's opinion.

protection as political or even artistic expression and that some considerations which make expression valuable in the political context may not apply in quite the same way in the commercial environment. This is particularly the case with truth: the state may insist on a requirement of truth as a condition of the legitimacy of commercial speech with a rigour which would be unacceptable for political speech. However, truth may not always be enough (as it usually, though not invariably, will be for political speech).

These distinctions are crucial but the identification of what constitutes commercial speech is not free from difficulty. It is not the commercial *value* of expression which is the touchstone because that would catch the entire commercial media. Rather, it is expression that is directed to furthering the economic interests of individuals and enterprises (whether by advancing their own interests or undermining those of their rivals), through the medium of expression, particularly 'advertising or other means of commercial information to consumers'.[11] A remarkable attempt to classify expression as commercial advertising and then to claim an extended right to regulate it was made by the German government in *Barthold v FRG*.[12] Barthold was the veterinary surgeon of last resort for the owners of a sick cat because he alone maintained an emergency service in Hamburg. He was interviewed by a local journalist who wrote a piece about this lacuna in the provision for animal welfare in the district. Barthold's fellow veterinarians instigated an action against him under unfair competition law alleging that 'he had instigated or tolerated publicity on his own behalf'. The European Court properly rejected the claim that this case was about commercial advertising rather than public discussion of a matter of general interest and it found the conviction of Barthold unjustified:

'Its application risks discouraging members of the liberal professions from contributing to public debate on topics affecting the life of the community if even there is the slightest likelihood of their utterances being treated as entailing, to some degree, an advertising effect. By the same token, application of a criterion such as this is liable to hamper the press in the performance of its task of purveyor of information and public watchdog.'

It is unnecessary to be dogmatic and say that a newspaper item could *never* be tantamount to advertising. Items which are based on public relations profiles may be scarcely distinguishable from commercial promotions. It is clear that professional advertising is a form of commercial expression, though one which is closely regulated in a number of European states. In a recent case, *Colman v UK*,[13] the Commission was divided by 11 votes to 8 in

---

11 See *Jacubowski v Germany* A 291-A para 26 (1994) and id, Com Rep para 69.
12 A 90 para 50 (1985).
13 A 258-D (1993) Com Rep para 39. The case was settled, the rule concerned having been amended.

holding that a restriction on advertising by a doctor (who wished to bring to potential patients' attention his expertise in homoeopathic medicine) was justified within the terms of Article 10(2). The majority said:

> '. . . the Convention organs should not substitute their own evaluation for that of the competent medical authorities in the present case where those authorities, on reasonable grounds, had considered the restrictions to be necessary at the material time. . .'

This approach was endorsed by the Court in *Casado Coca v Spain*[14] (in which the Commission had found that there was a violation of Article 10 only on the casting vote of the President).[15] This case concerned the distribution of advertising material by a barrister which had resulted in disciplinary proceedings against him. The Court found that the penalty imposed, whilst an interference with his Article 10 rights, could be justified under Article 10(2) because *some* regulation of barristers' advertising was legitimate and, in the absence of a common European standard of what this should be, there was nothing to suggest that this restriction fell outside the wide margin of appreciation which states had on this matter.[16]

The Commission in *Colman v UK* cited *Markt intern Verlag v FRG*[17] where the Court upheld an injunction against a trade magazine prohibiting it from publishing information about an enterprise operating in its market sector as compatible with Article 10(2). The *Markt intern* judgment is notable for its apparent retreat from the fundamental principle of the *Handyside* and *Sunday Times* cases that an interference with expression is necessary only if the state presents convincing evidence of a pressing social need for it. The Court was equally divided and the judgment in favour of the government was given on the casting vote of the President. The various dissenting judgments all take this point and, for Judge Pettiti, the economic context of this case was no ground at all for extending the state's margin of appreciation. He said:

> 'Only in the rarest cases can censorship or prohibition of publication be accepted . . . This is particularly true in relation to commercial advertising or questions of economic or commercial policy . . . The protection of the interests of users and consumers in the face of dominant positions depends on the freedom to publish even the harshest criticisms of products . . .'

The majority in the Court conceded that Markt intern was not a competitor in the sector about which it reported but that it did intend to protect the

14 A 285-A (1994).
15 Id, Com Rep para 66.
16 Id, para 55.
17 A 165 (1989). The Commission had found a violation by 12 votes to 1 in the *Markt intern* case.

interests of one group in that sector, the retail purchasers of products of a manufacturer. Its articles raised doubts about the commercial reliability of the manufacturer. The Court determined that this was commercial expression and that commercial expression was subject to different standards of control than other kinds. For instance, it said:

'. . . even the publication of items which are true and describe real events may under certain circumstances be prohibited: the obligation to respect privacy of others or the duty to respect the confidentiality of certain commercial information are examples.'[18]

However, neither these examples nor any of the others that the majority gave seem to have had much bearing on the information actually at stake in this case, information about individual retailers' experiences in dealing with the manufacturer in response to a request from the magazine. The Court then concluded:

'It is obvious that opinions may differ as to whether the [German] court's reaction was appropriate or whether the statements made in the specific case by Markt intern should be permitted or tolerated. However, the European Court of Human Rights should not substitute its own evaluation for that of the national courts in the instant case, where those courts, on reasonable grounds, had considered the restrictions to be necessary.'[19]

The judgment is remarkable not only for its deference to the national decision[20] but also for the brevity with which the applicant's arguments were treated, notably the claim that the German decision, because of the exceptional stringency of its Unfair Competition Law, was out of line with the standards in other European states.[1]

Concern that the judgment in the *Markt intern* case departed from the 'pressing social need' criterion was justified by *Jacubowski v Germany*.[2] The applicant was the editor of a news agency who had been dismissed by his employer who had issued a press release which cast aspersions on his professional competence. The applicant circulated a document which answered the criticisms and contained newspaper cuttings reflecting badly on the employer. The circular was addressed to clients of the employer and he regarded it as an attempt by Jacubowski to further his own economic prospects at the expense of the employer who would in the future be Jacubowksi's competitor. The employer's analysis was accepted by the German courts, which injuncted further distribution of Jacubowski's

18 Id, para 35.
19 Id, para 47. For doubts about the majority judgment, see Eissen, *European System*, Ch 7 at pp 145-146.
20 Cf *Barfod v Denmark* A 149 (1989).
1 See Lester, loc cit at p 372, n 2 above, p 480 at n 65.
2 A 219-A (1994).

circular as being an act of unfair competition, and by a majority in the European Court.[3] The minority[4] in the European Court complained precisely that the majority had abandoned the privileged position for freedom of expression established by the Convention and engaged in the mere balancing of the equally valued interests of expression and the protection of commercial reputation. Although these judges do not use the language of *Markt intern*, their criticism is that the Court was satisfied that the action of the German courts was 'not unreasonable', and that the state had not established a 'pressing social need' for the interference. In defence of *Markt intern*, Clapham[5] explains the wider margin of appreciation as reflecting the private nature of the litigation and for it to have reviewed the judgment of the German court,

> 'it would have essentially been operating as a court of final appeal for private disputes'

(not that this would distinguish *Markt intern* in its essential character from cases like *Lingens* or *Thorgierson*). Even if, or perhaps especially if, the Court is reluctant to interfere with a national decision, there is no reason why it should not stipulate that the test that the national decision-maker should apply must be more strictly weighted in favour of expression than the one applied by the German court in this case.

Markt intern is the leading authority on commercial speech and it would appear to leave substantial leeway to national authorities in regulating or even barring certain kinds of advertising, say, about individual products, like tobacco, or individual subjects, like political advertising, or through particular techniques, like 'knocking copy'. The recent judgments of the Court confirm that states have a wide margin of appreciation in regulating professional advertising in ways which interfere with the advertiser's freedom of expression.[6]

b. The medium and manner of communication

It has already been explained that the Court attaches great importance to the role of press and television in assuring the effective enjoyment of the right to receive ideas and information on matters of political and public concern. If the cases considered by the Court so far have involved newspapers rather than television and radio, it is because there is no licensing regime of a kind applicable to the press and it is free from many of the constraints such as balance and taste which are applied to television, especially to public monopoly broadcasters. A further distinction is the

---

3 Id, para 28.
4 Judges Walsh, Macdonald, Wildhaber.
5 *Human Rights in the Private Sphere*, 1993, p 224.
6 *Jacubowski v Germany* A 219-A (1994) and *Casado Coca v Spain* A 285-A (1994).

relationship between the consumer and producer of the expression. Television and radio are more likely to impinge upon the unwilling or reluctant consumer than books and newspapers.

The Court does take the 'audience' or 'market' into account in deciding whether an interference with expression is justified. In *Muller v Switzerland*,[7] one factor which weighed with the Court was that access to the exhibition where Müller was painting was open to the public and there was no warning of the kind of art that was on view: hence the confrontation between the young girl and Müller's shocking picture. In the *Otto-Preminger* case, where a film the content of which was distressing to some people was to be shown, the Commission accepted the applicant's point that access to the showing of the film was limited in fact because his specialised cinema was directed only to the 'specially interested' public and, 'most important of all', a warning had been given in public announcements about the contents of the film. This did not satisfy the Court which used the warnings that the applicant had given to prevent innocent attendance as evidence of how local people would know that the film was to be shown and, in consequence, would be so outraged that the state was entitled to prevent the performance, even though no person who would be distressed was likely to attend and children were unable to gain admittance.[8] In *Handyside v UK*,[9] where the intended audience was children and the book was produced and marketed in ways designed to appeal to children, the Court held that the forfeiture of copies of the book could be justified. The Commission has distinguished the necessity of interfering with pornographic videos sold to the general public where there was a risk that children would see them, when prohibition was justified, and where they were to be shown at a private club where the risk was non-existent, when prohibition was not justified.[10] The *Otto-Preminger* case aside, there is a general reluctance on the part of the Court to uphold interferences with the communication of ideas and information between willing producers and adult consumers.[11] This is no more clearly illustrated than in *Jersild v Denmark*,[12] where one reason why the journalist's conviction could not be justified under Article 10(2) was that the item was part of a serious news programme and was intended for a well informed audience. It is not, then, so much the particular medium of communication that will determine whether an interference is justified, as the degree of access that the medium gives to consumers who may be unwilling to accept the message or are held to be in need for protection from it.

---

7   A 133 para 36 (1988).
8   A 295-A para 54 (1994).
9   A 24 para 52 (1976).
10   *Scherer v Switzerland* A 287 (1993) Com Rep paras 59-62 and *X and Y v Switzerland No 16564/90* (1991), unreported.
11   See *Open Door and Dublin Well Woman Centre v Ireland* A 246 paras 44, 55 (1992) (a wide notion of 'victim').
12   A 298 para 34 (1994).

c. Character of democratic society

One central facet of freedom of expression is its relationship with the political process. While the electoral process itself falls to be considered under Article 3 of the First Protocol, expression in the course of an election may attract particular protection. In *X v UK*,[13] the Commission suggested that the normal position, that individuals had no right of access to the media to express their ideas or convey information, might yield an exception where there was discriminatory denial of access to television to political parties during an election campaign. In *Castells v Spain*,[14] the Court indicated the special value of freedom of expression to members of the opposition. It said:

> 'In a democratic system the actions or omissions of the government must be subject to close scrutiny not only of the legislative and judicial authorities but also of the press and public opinion. Furthermore, the dominant position which the government occupies makes it necessary to display restraint in resorting to criminal proceedings, particularly where other means are available for replying to the unjustified attacks and criticisms of its adversaries or the media.'

This general commitment to discussion and debate as the means of airing and resolving matters of public concern requires a state wishing to curtail political debate to show very strong reasons for doing so: it should be hard for a state to show that it is 'necessary in a democratic society' to proscribe the process of democracy.[15]

This strong obligation on states will protect mainstream orthodox debate. Another characteristic of democratic society identified by the Court – 'tolerance' – requires respect for the marginal or the unorthodox. Here, though, the Strasbourg authorities have been less assiduous in protecting expression. The Court did not follow through on its vigorous affirmation of the need for tolerance in *Handyside v UK*[16] because, even if it were accepted that he had a controversial political agenda of anti-authoritarianism, Handyside had directed his message through the medium of an obscene publication to an audience of children whom the state could justifiably act to protect. Other marginal groups, even where they have directed their expression to less vulnerable audiences than did Handyside and even in the context of political demonstrations, have fared little better. The Commission upheld broadcasting bans on members of political parties that supported the aims of terrorist organisations which the state characterised as undemocratic.[17] In *Arrowsmith v UK*,[18] over the strong dissents of Messrs Opsahl and

---

13 *No 4515/70*, 38 CD 86 at 88 (1971). See more generally, Boyle, 1986 PL 562.
14 A 236 para 46 (1992).
15 But see Article 17, below, pp 510-513.
16 A 24 para 52 (1976).
17 *Purcell v Ireland No 15404/89*, 70 DR 262 (1991) and *Brind and McLaughlin v UK Nos 18714 and 18759/91*, 77-A DR 42 (1994). The banning orders challenged unsuccessfully in these applications have been withdrawn.
18 *No 7050/75*, 19 DR 5 (1978) Com Rep; CM Res DH (79) 4.

Klecker, the Commission found that the conviction and imprisonment of a woman who had been distributing leaflets to soldiers advising them about ways to avoid serving in Northern Ireland were necessary to protect national security. In *Chorherr v Austria*,[19] where the Commission divided equally on the merits and found a violation only on the casting vote of the President, the Court, by 6 votes to 3, upheld the right of the state to interfere with the 'unpopular' expression of protestors 'because of the commotion that [their] behaviour was beginning to engender among the spectators who wished to attend the parade peaceably'. The Court suggested that Chorherr had brought the restraint upon himself.[20] The interest of decorum appeared to assert itself over tolerance. Nor, beyond the political sphere, have the Commission and Court imposed onerous burdens on states to require tolerance for unpopular and disturbing expression against moral or religious sensibilities.[1]

The Strasbourg authorities have in their case-law put another limit on what tolerance requires. Where the expression is directed at the undermining of democracy and human rights themselves, the state is not obliged to confer the same protection on it as would be the case if it were orthodox political speech. In the (now probably obsolete) *German Communist Party* case,[2] the Commission upheld the state's right to interfere decisively with the applicant's right (the right to organise in Article 11), the interference being proscription of the organisation. The basis for doing so was Article 17. The same approach was adopted more recently in a different context in *Glimmerveen and Hagenback v Netherlands*.[3] The protection of Article 10 was denied to the applicants who had been convicted of possessing leaflets which were an incitement to racial discrimination. In *Kuhnen v FRG*,[4] the Commission relied on Article 17 to establish that the conviction of the applicant for advocating the reinstitution of the Nazi Party was justified under Article 10(2) in the interests of national security and public order and the protection of the rights of others. Whether relied upon on its own or in conjunction with Article 10(2), the importance of Article 17 is that it allows content-based restrictions on freedom of expression. The difference between the two approaches is slight because the Commission did not refer to any evidence that it was necessary to repress Kuhnen's publications because, say, there was a threat to public safety.

The Commission was deeply divided in two cases involving controversial speech by West German civil servants who had lost their public service jobs because it had been decided that their political opinions were incompatible with the requirement of their employment that they respect the West

19 A 266-B para 31 (1993).
20 Id, para 33.
1 See *Müller v Switzerland* A 133 (1988); *Otto-Preminger-Institut v Austria* A 295-A (1994); and *X Ltd and Y v UK No 8710/79*, 28 DR 77 at 82-83 (1982).
2 *KPD v FRG No 250/57*, 1 YB 222 (1957).
3 *Nos 8384/78 and 8406/78*, 18 DR 187 (1979). See also Article 3, First Protocol, Ch 21, below.
4 *No 12194/86*, 56 DR 205 (1988).

German Constitution. In *Kosiek v FRG*,[5] the applicant was a university teacher who had been active in extremist right-wing politics. In *Glasenapp v FRG*,[6] the applicant was a kindergarten teacher who had publicly supported a project initiated by a Maoist group. The Commission found that there was no violation of Article 10 in the *Kosiek* case (by 10-7) but that there was in the *Glasenapp* case (by 9-8).[7] The decision that there was no pressing social need to dismiss Glasenapp was partly based on the ambiguity of her relationship with the Maoist party[8] and also because it was not established that the opinions 'were in themselves' a threat to the democratic order.[9] Kosiek was unequivocally associated with the extremist views by reason of his active membership of the party and because of his authorship of certain books. Furthermore, 'such views may well be regarded as a threat to the basic assumption of democratic states . . .' so that the interference with Kosiek's rights was, correspondingly, necessary 'for the protection of the rights of others and in the interests of national security'.[10] Europe's past and present experiences and the obligations which states have under Article 20 of the ICCPR and Article 4 of the Racial Discrimination Convention serve to underpin the distinction made in the outcome of these applications. There has been no inclination by the Commission to expand the range of content-based restrictions on expression. The *Glasenapp* and *Kosiek* cases show that cases like this can be dealt with under Article 10(2). It has already been explained that the mere fact that racist speech is involved does not inevitably mean that measures to interfere with it will be justified. In *Jersild v Denmark*,[11] the Court placed emphasis on the news value of the information of the programme containing the contested language, a question primarily for professional journalists to decide. It was for the journalists also to determine how the programme should be presented. It was not a question here of special tolerance being required for obnoxious ideas (the speakers themselves were punished for what they had said) but of allowing the media to carry out its role as 'public watchdog'. While some expression, by reason of its content alone may seriously threaten democratic values, the language or images must be examined in their context: the very seriousness of the

---

5   A 104 (1986) Com Rep.
6   A 105 (1986) Com Rep.
7   The Commission did not rely on Article 17 in these cases. The defendant state invoked it in the *Kosiek* case only. The Article 10 question was not considered by the Court in either case because it took the view that the cases concerned the right to access to the public service, not freedom of expression.
8   A 105 (1986) Com Rep para 226.
9   Id, para 228.
10 A 104 (1986) Com Rep para 115. In *Vogt v Germany No 17851/91* (1993) Com Rep para 81, the Commission said that the seriousness of the threat to democracy from East Europe and the Soviet Union had evidently declined before 1991 when the collapse of the communist regimes was complete and, accordingly, the need to impose restrictions on communist sympathisers had much diminished.
11 A 298 para 31 (1994). The distinction between expression itself and debate about the expression has not always been noted by the Commission: cf *X, Y, Z v Belgium Nos 6782/74, 6783/74, 6784/74*, 9 DR 13 at 19-20 (1977).

perceived threat is a reason why the phenomenon of racist speech may in a democratic society be properly subject to dispassionate investigation.

d. *Margin of appreciation*[12]

IN GENERAL

Here, as elsewhere in Articles 8-11, the Court concedes a margin of appreciation to the states in assessing whether an interference with a protected right is 'necessary in a democratic society'. It is for the state to show that there is a 'pressing social need' for the interference, given that the rights protected by Article 10 carry a particular weight. Enough has been said in Chapter 8 and the immediately preceding sections to indicate the wide range of factors the Strasbourg authorities may be called upon to take into account to decide whether the state has stayed within or has exceeded its margin of appreciation. Nothing is gained by trying to reduce this process of assessment to a few words or phrases. However, it is worth noting that the issue of proportionality of the interference to its objective has come to play a prominent part in the disposition of freedom of expression cases.

PROPORTIONALITY

Scarcely a recent case on freedom of expression has been decided without the Court referring to the proportionality of the interference.[13] Although all issues of proportionality involve the Strasbourg authorities in some 'balancing' exercise, in practice they can be divided into two groups: those where the finding is that the restriction is disproportionate because there is practically no need at all for it, when a review of the national decision will be readily undertaken; and those where there is room for different assessments of the breadth of a restriction or the feasibility of alternative for the state, where the margin of appreciation conceded to the state is, other things being equal, likely to be greater.

The defendant state will be held to have acted disproportionately where it fails to produce evidence for its claims of the necessity to interfere with expression. In *Autronic v Switzerland*,[14] the government claimed that it was necessary to interfere with the reception of uncoded, direct-broadcast satellite signals because it was not possible to distinguish confidential signals, which the government had a duty to protect. However, the government could not show that dishes of the kind used by the applicant could receive

---

12 See McGregor, Report to the Sixth International Colloquy on the European Convention on Human Rights, Seville, 1985, in 6 HRLJ 384 (1985).
13 See *Casado Coca v Spain* A 285-A para 56 (1994); *Jacubowski v Germany* A 291-A para 29 (1994); *Otto-Preminger-Institut v Austria* A 295-A para 57 (1994) (though not in para 56); and *Jersild v Denmark* A 298 para 37 (1994).
14 A 178 para 63 (1990). In *Goodwin v UK No 17488/90* (1994) Com Rep paras 65-67, the Commission found that the third party involved had not suffered the damage, the prevention of which was the object of the interference.

confidential signals. In *Informations verein Lentia v Austria*,[15] the Court
found that the technical basis on which the government argued for the
continuation of a public monopoly in broadcasting could not be sustained on
the evidence, as was the case also with an economic argument which claimed
that a market the size of Austria's would not support public and private
systems. Where the information, publication of which is being restricted, is
available elsewhere, the Court is strongly of the view that the continuation of
the restriction, even if once necessary, would be disproportionate. In *Weber v
Switzerland*,[16] the information about the court action to which a contempt
order related had already been made public by the applicant some time
before. It was unnecessary, therefore, to punish him for his later statements.
In the *Spycatcher* case,[17] the Court made a distinction between the situation
before the book was published in the United States (and began to be brought
into England), when the injunction against publishing extracts was
compatible with the Convention, and the position after that date when the
alternative availability of the information rendered the continuation of the
injunction unnecessary. The fact that the information provided by the
applicants in *Open Door Counselling and Dublin Well Women Centre v
Ireland*[18] was available from other sources in Ireland, albeit not as readily nor
as comprehensively, was a factor in the Court finding the injunction issued in
that case as being unnecessary. Combined with the wide right to receive
information produced abroad, particularly through direct-broadcast satellite
programmes, this approach makes the justification for the continuation of
prior restraints on publication vulnerable. However, there is a danger that
this development of the case-law will encourage states to interfere as widely
as possible to prevent the circulation of information they think should be
restricted. The trans-frontier television example shows that this might not
always be feasible. But, for example, the British government could have
taken more stringent measures to prevent the import of *Spycatcher*. The Irish
government could have criminalised travel abroad to obtain an abortion and
sought to justify the restrictions considered in *Open Door* on the grounds that
they were necessary for the prevention of crime. In the '*Bluf*' case[19] the
matter which weighed most heavily with the Commission was that the
government had not taken effective action to prevent the information which
it sought to protect being reprinted and circulated quite widely. It is,
therefore, not impossible that it if had moved with more vigour and more
urgency against the applicant, then its claims that the interference were
necessary would have been upheld.

The claim of 'over-breadth' was made by the applicants in the *Open Door*
case.[20] The Court said that it was:

---

15 A 276 paras 39, 42 (1993).
16 A 177 (1990).
17 *Observer and Guardian v UK* A 216 para 69 (1991).
18 A 246 para 76 (1992). See also *Vereinigung Demokratischer Soldaten Osterreichers and Gubi
v Austria* A 302 (1994) Com Rep paras 50, 83.
19 *Vereniging Weekblad 'Bluf' v Netherlands* A 306-A (1995) Com Rep para 50; Ct Jmt para 45.
20 A 246 para 73 (1992).

'struck by the absolute nature of the Supreme Court injunctions which imposed a "perpetual" restraint on the provision of information to pregnant women concerning abortion facilities abroad, regardless of age or state of health or their reasons for seeking counselling on the termination of pregnancy.'

The reaction of the Irish courts in a case arising during the hearing of the *Open Door* case showed the unsustainability of the position. On 'that ground alone' the Court said, the injunction was 'over broad and disproportionate'.[1] In *Barthold v FRG*,[2] the Court held that the injunction against the applicant was disproportionate to the need to protect the rights of his fellow veterinarians to fair competition because it reached matters which were properly ones of public concern.

In the *Spycatcher* case,[3] the Court resisted the government's claim that the continuation of the injunction against the applicant newspapers remained necessary after the publication of the book in the United States because of the need to protect confidence in the security services. This was so because there were alternatives, some of which were being pursued by the government, such as actions against Wright himself, which did not involve interference with the rights of the applicants. One criticism which may be made of the Court in the *Markt intern* case is that the majority judgment did not pay enough attention to the possibility of other ways of protecting the rights to fair competition of the producer, notably individual actions against retailers who had supplied the magazine with its information. The 'alternative means' factor can also be applied to the position of an applicant. In *Jacubowski v Germany*,[4] one factor which divided the majority and minority opinions was the possibility of the applicant using means to defend his reputation other than the one prohibited by the German courts, the distribution of a circular. The majority emphasised that he retained the right to defend himself by other, albeit unspecified, means and so the interference with his freedom of expression could not be said to be disproportionate to its purpose in protecting the rights of his previous employer. The minority[5] thought that there was no other way, either in means – the distribution of the circular – or in substance – the imputations against his employer – by which Jacubowski could have protected his own reputation. Müller, the artist, could have protected himself by suitable warning notices at the entrance to the exhibition, warning visitors of what they might expect. His failure to do so contributed to the legitimacy of the state's enforcement of its obscenity law against him.[6] It is something of an

1 Id, para 74.
2 A 90 para 58 (1985).
3 *Observer and Guardian v UK* A 216 para 69 (1991).
4 A 291-A para 29 (1994) (the German court had refused a request for a comprehensive injunction against Jacubowski which would have forbidden all criticism of his ex-employers).
5 Judges Walsh, Macdonald and Wildhaber.
6 *Müller v Switzerland* A 133 para 36 (1984).

irony that the advertisements for the film which was the subject of the application in *Otto-Preminger-Institut v Austria*,[7] part of the purpose of which was to warn people of the nature of the film, lest they were taken unawares, was regarded by the Court as bringing to the attention of the local population the possibility that it would be distressed simply by knowing such a film were to be shown, distress sufficient for the state to be justified in preventing the showing of the film and ordering its forfeiture.

4. CONCLUSION

In contrast with many other areas of the Convention, the Strasbourg authorities have enunciated an overall theoretical position to explain the policies which underline freedom of expression. Informed discussion of matters of public concern is of high value because of its role in the working of a democratic society. Self-expression is important because of its centrality to the effective liberty of the individual. 'Expression' has been interpreted widely and all the means for engaging in expression have been brought within the ambit of Article 10(1). However, this wide right is not an absolute right, Article 10(2) permitting certain interferences. The Court has struggled with the conflict between the individual right and the public interest. The rhetoric of its judgments in support of freedom of expression is strong and it has been through Article 10 cases that the requirements of 'law' as the basis for interference have been elaborated and the demand for 'a pressing social need' to justify interference was first set down. If it cannot be shown that the Court has wholeheartedly followed the spirit of this language in individual decisions, there are two grounds on which this can be explained. Firstly, the very wide reach of the Article 10(1) right brings in expression of different worth. It is clear that the Court ascribes a hierarchy of value, first to political expression, widely understood, then to artistic expression and finally to commercial expression. Accordingly, the interference that is permitted will depend upon the character of the expression involved. The requirement of a 'pressing social need' to limit political speech puts a high burden upon the state to show that its action was necessary, but for advertising it appears to be sufficient that its restrictions were not unreasonable.

It would be a mistake, though, to imagine that the characterisation of the kind of expression would alone be enough to decide whether interferences were legitimate. Many factors related to the vigour of the expression, the means by which it is communicated and the audience to which it is directed will be relevant in each case. The inquiries which must be made are wide and the process by which the information must be assessed is complicated. The second reason why the application of Article 10(2) has sometimes seemed weaker than the strong language of the judgments would suggest arises

7   A 295-A para 54 (1994).

directly from the necessity of assessing these diverse factors. The question is whether these different decisions are best taken in the national legal system or by the Strasbourg authorities? The fact that there have been such differences between the Court and Commission and within each of these institutions is partly attributable to different perceptions of the degree of deference to be given to a national decision in which the Convention issue has been directly addressed. While the fact that there has been such a decision is no guarantee that the Court will not overturn it, it will carry some weight in encouraging the Court to sustain the position taken by the state and so to endorse the legitimacy of its interference with freedom of expression. In this connection, a significant factor that encourages the Court to review a national decision is the existence of a 'European' standard more favourable to expression than the national law. The 'European' standard is one adopted in national laws and practice by a wide spectrum of Convention states.[8]

However interventionist the Strasbourg authorities may be, the Convention will not resolve all the problems which arise in the field of expression. Neither the language of Article 10 nor the resources of the Court are adequate to deal with the conflicts which arise out of the dual role of the media. Press and television companies claim strong rights of effective newsgathering. These are rights that are necessary to fulfil their special responsibilities, but that also allow them to trespass on the rights and interests of individuals. In this connection, there is always the danger that the commercial interests of the media will predominate over the disinterested pursuit of information for the purposes of public discussion.[9] Equally, the legitimate interest of the state to control the commercial operations of the media and to regulate technologically complex industries provides the opportunity for disguised interference with the output of newspapers and television.[10] One could go further: the Convention does not provide standards to arbitrate on matters of taste,[11] on the legitimacy of measures to protect cultural identity, on the conflict between concentration and pluralism of media outlets, among many issues of current concern.[12] The margins of appreciation here will be very wide but the jurisprudence of the Court reminds states that their powers are not unlimited. Because many of these issues are both multinational and economic, for those Convention states which are members of the European Union it is encouraging that the development of European Community law has paid attention to the

---

8 For the view that there are widely held standards on press freedom, see Coliver, in *Press Law and Practice: an Article 19 Report*, 1993, p 255.

9 Barendt, (1991) CLP 63.

10 See Bullinger, loc cit at p 372, n 2, above and Barendt, loc cit at p 375, n 20, above, especially Ch V. For the UK position, see Gibbons, *Regulating the Media*, 1991.

11 See Coleman, 1993 PL 488 at 512-513, who criticises vagueness and unpredictability.

12 The Council of Europe Steering Committee on the Mass Media engages in an extensive programme which deals, *inter alia*, with many of these issues. See CE H Rts Inf Sheet No 30, pp 93-94. See also Committee of Ministers 1982 Declaration on the Freedom of Expression and Information, *Collected Texts*, p 327.

standards of the Convention. The result is that the resolution of industry-dominated questions is not based on economic and integrationist considerations alone, with regard also being had to the importance of the right of freedom of expression.[13]

---

13 Directive 89/552/EEC, OJ 1989 L 298, p 23. See Winn, *European Community and International Media Law*, 1993, pp 61-65. The Commission has said that the Directive is in need of revision to take into account technological developments and the French government has expressed concern about the adequacy of powers to protect cultural objectives: Europe No 6206 (NS) 8 April 1994, p 6. See also, Hitchens, 57 MLR 585 (1994) and Barendt, 1 MJ 41 (1994).

CHAPTER 12

Article 11: Freedom of assembly and association

'**Article 11**

1. Everyone has the right to freedom of peaceful assembly and to freedom of association with others, including the right to form and to join trade unions for the protection of his interests.
2. No restrictions shall be placed on the exercise of these rights other than such as are prescribed by law and are necessary in a democratic society in the interests of national security or public safety, for the prevention of disorder or crime, for the protection of health or morals or for the protection of the rights and freedoms of others. This article shall not prevent the imposition of lawful restrictions on the exercise of these rights by members of the armed forces, of the police or of the administration of the state.'

Article 11 protects the two distinct, if sometimes connected, freedoms of peaceful assembly and association.[1] They are sufficiently different to be treated separately but they share the objective of allowing individuals to come together for the expression and protection of their common interests. Where those interests are political in the widest sense, the function of the Article 11 freedoms is central to the effective working of the democratic system. In particular, it provides for the creation and operation of political parties, interest groups and trade unions which serve as diverse centres of power, and for the propagation of ideas and programmes, from among which others may choose and by which influence may be exerted on the holders of public power for the time being. Equally, Article 11 protects the right of individuals to assemble and to associate for the furtherance of their personal interests, be they economic, social or cultural. The same ends are sought: the effective enjoyment of a diversity of interests. Article 11 makes specific reference to trade unions, the roles of which overlap considerably between the political and the economic interests of their members. The Court and Commission regard the rights of trade unions as being embraced within the general freedom of association but, since certain matters particular to trade unions have arisen in the case-law, they will be treated separately.

---

1 See Tomuschat, *European System*, Ch 19, pp 493-513 and Lewis-Anthony, in *Freedom of Association*, Rekjavik Seminar Proc, reprinted in 33A YB 27 (1994).

1. FREEDOM OF PEACEFUL ASSEMBLY

The holding of public meetings and the mounting of demonstrations through marches, picketing and processions has played a significant part in the political history of European states. The recent events in Eastern Europe show the potency of these activities. It is true that much orthodox politics has moved to the private meeting and the orchestrated occasion, the impact of which depends upon transmission through the news media. However, public meetings and demonstrations are a tool for those outside the established parties, whose direct access to the media is limited but who may be able to gain attention by staging '*évènements*' which capture the television and newspaper headlines. The Convention protects their right to organise political demonstrations as a 'fundamental right'.[2] It covers 'private meetings and meetings in public thoroughfares'.[3] It includes marches as well as meetings.[4] The content of the message which the organisers wish to project is not, of itself, a reason for regarding the occasion as being outside the scope of Article 11. The only limitation is that the assembly must be 'peaceful'. Disruption incidental to the holding of the assembly will not render it 'unpeaceful', whereas a meeting planned with the object of causing disturbances will not be protected by Article 11.[5] The line between the two may not be clear. Acknowledging the importance of freedom of assembly, the Commission has said it ought not to be interpreted restrictively. It held that a non-violent sit-in, blocking the entrance to American barracks in Germany, did count as 'peaceful assembly', so interference with it required justification under Article 11(2).[6]

For the authorities, freedom of assembly raises a number of problems, especially where public meetings and marches are involved. These pose threats to public order through the disruption of communications, the prospect of confrontation with the police and the danger of violence with rivals, they claiming, of course, their own freedom to demonstrate. It is this last situation which raises particular difficulties under Article 11(1).

The Commission and Court have confirmed that there are positive duties on a state to protect those exercising their right of freedom of peaceful assembly from violent disturbance by counter-demonstrators.[7] Because both sides may claim to be exercising Article 11 rights, initially this may be a duty to hold the ring between rival meetings or processions, but if one of them is aimed at disruption of the activities of the other, the obligation of the authorities is to protect those exercising their right of peaceful assembly. The threat of disorder from opponents does not of itself justify interference

---

2   *Rassemblement Jurassien Unité Jurassienne v Switzerland No 8191/78*, 17 DR 93 at 119 (1979).
3   Ibid.
4   *Christians against Racism and Fascism v UK No 8440/78*, 21 DR 138 at 148 (1980).
5   Id, p 150.
6   *G v FRG No 13079/87*, 60 DR 256 at 263 (1989).
7   *Plattform 'Arzte für das Leben' v Austria No 10126/82*, 44 DR 65 at 72 (1985); id, A 139 para 32 (1988).

with the demonstration.[8] The requirements of this positive duty do leave a good deal to the discretion of the authorities. The fact that action may have to be taken in anticipation of possible disturbances or, in other cases, that policing measures must be taken at short notice leaves a wide margin of appreciation to the state to decide what Article 11(1) requires in a particular case.[9] One matter, yet untested by European Convention practice, which has been of concern in the United States, is whether there is a positive obligation on a state to require private individuals to allow the exercise of peaceful assemblies by others on their properties. As a freedom, in principle peaceful assembly confers no obligations on, say, owners of private halls, to hire them to political groups for meetings. However, the growth of quasi-public spaces, formally held as private property, such as shopping malls, excludes them as the arenas for the effective exercise of freedom of assembly if it is a right which may be exercised only in public places. Similar considerations apply to areas, once public, which have been privatised. In the United States, the question has been resolved in favour of the property right.[10] Reliance on the kind of positive duty alluded to by the Commission in *De Geillustreede Pers v Netherlands*[11] means that the apparatus is there for a contrary outcome under the Convention if the Strasbourg authorities were so inclined.

Because the threats to public order from the exercise of the right of peaceful assembly are real, the authorities demand a variety of powers to meet or to mitigate them. Interferences with peaceful assembly range from requirements of prior authorisation and authorisation subject to conditions to complete bans. Criminal penalties may be imposed for participation in assemblies held in defiance of such regulation or for offences committed in the exercise of the right. The Court has rejected the contention that post-demonstration penalties do not amount to an interference with freedom of assembly.[12] Requirements of notification or permission will not normally be regarded as interferences[13] but bans, because of the seriousness of the interference, will require justification under Article 11(2).

The interference must be 'prescribed by law'. The Commission has always been satisfied that this condition has been met, although it avoided an interesting question in *Rassemblement Jurassien Unité Jurassienne v Switzerland*[14] where one of the government claims was that a ban had been imposed on the basis of an unexpressed constitutional principle of 'the general police clause'. The Commission found enough alternative legal

---

8 *Christians against Racism and Fascism v UK No 8840/78*, 21 DR 138 at 148 (1980).
9 *Plattform 'Ärzte für das Leben' v Austria No 10126/82*, 44 DR 65 at 74 (1985). The Court in this case held that there was not even an 'arguable' claim that the authorities had failed in their positive duty sufficient to raise an issue under Article 13: A 139 paras 34-39 (1988).
10 *Pruneyard Shopping Centre v Robins* 447 US 74 (1980).
11 *No 5178/71*, 8 DR 5 (1976) Com Rep; CM Res DH (77) 1; see above, p 383.
12 *Ezelin v France* A 202 para 39 (1991).
13 *Rassemblement Jurassien Unité Jurassienne v Switzerland No 8191/78*, 17 DR 93 at 110 (1979).
14 Id, pp 114, 119.

authority not to have to examine this. The aims of government interferences permitted by Article 11(2) are 'the prevention of disorder or crime' and 'the protection of the rights and freedoms of others'. They have given rise to no serious difficulties.[15] The Strasbourg authorities have spoken inconsistently about the fundamental quality of the Article 11 rights and, hence, the need to interpret them widely, while conceding a 'fairly broad' margin of appreciation to states to assess the necessity of any limitation of peaceful assembly. In both the *Rassemblement Jurassien* case and *Christians against Racism and Fascism v UK*,[16] the Commission found that total bans on marches were justified under Article 11(2). In the first case, it pointed to the relatively narrow area and short time for which the ban had been imposed, against the evidence of tension in the area and the government's expectation of trouble. In the second case, a blanket ban on processions in London was directed principally at marches by the National Front, a racist group whose demonstrations had frequently been attended by violence. The applicants, against whom no aspersions were made, were simply caught in a wide ban imposed on the whole of London for two months which was framed in such terms to prevent its circumvention by the National Front. For the Commission, that was sufficient justification for the interference. Further, it said, the applicants were not precluded from holding meetings to press their point during the period of the ban on marches. In *Friedl v Austria*,[17] the Commission declared the application manifestly ill-founded after considering in detail the circumstances of a sit-in organised by the applicant in a busy square, where there was evidence of disruption of the progress of passers-by. The 'manifestation' had continued day and night for a week, after which the authorities ordered its dispersal. The Commission confirmed that the decison to do this fell within the margin of appreciation for the prevention of disorder.

Only in *Ezelin v France*[18] has a violation of Article 11 been established. The applicant had taken part in a demonstration directed against the courts and individual judges in Guadeloupe. Ezelin attended in his capacity as lawyer and trade union official, carrying an inoffensive placard. The march disintegrated into violence. Ezelin did not leave the demonstration when this happened and he refused to answer police questions in an inquiry into the events. He was reprimanded by the Court of Appeal exercising its disciplinary function over lawyers for 'breach of discretion' in not disassociating himself from the march and for not cooperating with the police. No allegations of unlawful conduct during the march were made against Ezelin. The European Court held by 6 votes to 3 that there had been

---

15 Except in the *Greek* case, 12 YB (the *Greek* case) 1 at 171 (1969); CM Res DH (70)1. In *Ezelin v France* A 202 para 47 (1991) the applicant claimed that proceedings had been taken against him because of his opinions and trade union affiliation but Court was satisfied that the action was for 'the prevention of disorder'.

16 *No 8440/78*, 21 DR 138 at 150-151 (1980).

17 *No 15225/89* (1992), unreported.

18 A 202 paras 52-53 (1991).

a lack of proportionality between the imposition of the sanction and the need to act in the interests of the prevention of disorder. A 'just balance' must not discourage persons from making their beliefs peacefully known. The judgment is a strong one in favour of freedom of assembly, given the relatively insignificant punishment imposed on the applicant. However, if the demonstrators resort to conduct which is independently criminal, like the sit-in in *G v FRG*,[19] even if it is done with the purpose of drawing attention to the cause, Article 11(2) is unlikely to protect them against prosecutions and conviction.

2. FREEDOM OF ASSOCIATION

The right of freedom of association embraces a complex of ideas, not all of which are fully worked out in the practice under the Convention. It involves the freedom of individuals to come together for the protection of their interests by forming a collective entity which represents them. This 'association' is capable of enjoying fundamental rights against the state[20] and will generally have rights against and owe duties to its members. An individual has no right to become a member of a particular association so that an association has no obligation to admit or continue the membership of an individual.[1] Equally, an individual cannot be compelled to become a member of an association nor disadvantaged if he chooses not to do so.[2] This last arrangement, the so-called 'negative' freedom of association, is not specifically spelled out in Article 11(1), as it is in Article 20(2) of the Universal Declaration of Human Rights. None the less, it is settled that this is the proper interpretation of Article 11(1).[3]

The notion of 'association' has an autonomous Convention meaning. As a result, the fact that a substantive coordination of activities of individuals is not recognised in the national law as an 'association' will not necessarily mean that freedom of association is not at stake under Article 11. Whereas association in the sense of the right to 'share the company' of others does not qualify as 'association' for the purposes of Article 11,[4] informal, if also stable and purposive, groupings will fall within its scope.[5] However, the mere existence of separate legal status for an institution beyond that of its individual members will not necessarily implicate Article 11(1). On several occasions, the Strasbourg authorities have decided that professional associations, established by law and requiring membership of all practising

---

19 *No 13079/87*, 60 DR 256 at 263 (1989). For the facts, see above, p 418.
20 *Plattform 'Ärzte für das Leben' v Austria No 10126/82*, 44 DR 65 at 72 (1985).
1 *Cheall v UK No 10550/83*, 42 DR 178 at 185 (1985).
2 *Young, James and Webster v UK* A 44 para 55 (1981).
3 See below, p 427.
4 *McFeeley v UK No 8317/78*, 20 DR 44 at 98 (1980) (concerning contact between prisoners).
5 See, however, Tomuschat, *European System*, Ch 19 at p 494, requiring 'an organisational structure'.

professionals, are not 'associations' within the meaning of Article 11(1).[6] Amongst other things, this means that the issue of compulsory membership in such associations does not present a difficulty under the Convention. The autonomous meaning of 'association' is vital here too, because the question whether an institution is a professional association will not finally be decided by its classification in the national law.[7] In an important article, Alkema[8] has considered whether the distinction between public and private associations can be sustained in the way that the professional association cases have suggested. He is in favour of a wider Convention notion of 'association' and argues that greater efforts should be made to reconcile the concepts of 'association' in Article 11, entitlement to fair trial for legal persons in Article 6 and the 'non-governmental victim' in Article 25. His concern is that the freedom of association may not be effectively enjoyed if there are serious obstacles to the association acting for its members by bringing legal actions in national law or applications to the Commission in its own name. While the mere fact of incorporation under a general law mainly directed at facilitating economic enterprises is not enough to make the resulting corporate body an association, use of the corporate structure by associations whose principal purposes are the furtherance of the non-economic interests of their members will not take them outside Article 11.[9]

Associations may have a wide variety of different purposes. They include political parties,[10] although Article 17 allows a state to impose a restraint upon the programmes they may pursue.[11] There is no right to associate for a purpose that is illegal in national law but there ought to be a right to associate to campaign for a change in the law, however difficult it may be to draw the line between the two.[12] Associations for the promotion of the cultural and recreational interests of their members also fall within Article 11. Tomuschat[13] raises the difficult question whether minorities may claim to be 'associations'. If an association through which a minority acts were to do so in other than a representational capacity, this would assume the existence of collective minority rights, a matter which has proved

6   Eg *Le Compte, Van Leuven and De Meyere v Belgium* A 43 paras 64-65 (1981) and *A v Spain* No 13750/88, 66 DR 188 (1990).

7   *Sigurjonsson v Iceland* A 264 paras 30-31 (1993).

8   *Freedom of Association*, loc cit at p 417, n 1, above, pp 55-86 at 72-82.

9   Cohen-Jonathan, *La Convention Européenne des Droits de l'Homme*, 1989, p 515, would restrict 'association' to non-profit-making bodies. Tomuschat, *European System*, Ch 19 at p 495, instead distinguishes between non-economic (protected) and economic (not protected) activities of institutions.

10 *KPD v FRG* No 250/57, 1 YB 222 (1957) (*German Communist Party* case). Other cases, like *Van der Heijden v Netherlands* No 11002/84, 41 DR 264 (1985), are not quite clear on this point.

11 *KPD v FRG* No 250/57, 1 YB 222 (1957). See also *X v Italy* No 6741/74, 5 DR 83 (1976). Note the powers under the UK Prevention of Terrorism (Temporary Provisions) Act 1989, s 1 to proscribe organisations involved in terrorism connected with Northern Ireland.

12 *Lavisse v France* No 14223/88, 70 DR 218 at 234-239 (1991) (interference justified anyway under Article 11(2)).

13 *European System*, Ch 19 at p 496.

controversial under the ICCPR, which has a specific minority provision.[14] The Commission is likely to be extremely cautious of introducing the idea of collective minority rights under the cover of Article 11. The matter is one more properly dealt with by a tailor-made protocol to the Convention[15] and the other minorities programmes of the Council of Europe.

The first duty of a state is to interfere neither with individuals who seek to exercise their freedom of association nor with the essential activities of any established association. However, although it is conceivable that informal associations will satisfy the aspirations of individuals, the effective exercise of their freedom will be enhanced by the provision of a legal basis for the formation and recognition of associations, both so that individuals may be certain of what is required of them to set up an association and also so that the resulting body has legal personality and is able to act in an independent way to further the interests of its members. While an absolute, positive obligation on a state to institute a legal framework for every form of association that might be envisaged by groups of individuals goes beyond what Article 11 demands,[16] the Convention states invariably do provide some options for association which lead to legal personality. Individuals have the right to avail themselves of the power to form associations and to have these actions recognised by the state.[17]

Once the association is set up, the essential relationships are between this body and its members and the body and non-members. There are indications from the trade union cases that members have a limited right to remain as members but, in general, neither they nor non-members may claim a right to membership over the objection of the association.[18] Because we are here dealing with the relationships between individuals or between individuals and the association, another aspect of the positive obligation of states intrudes: what is a state's duty to regulate these private relationships in the interest of the effective enjoyment of Article 11 rights? This is perhaps the most pressing context in which the question whether a state has a positive obligation under the Convention to control private action that infringes other individuals' rights arises.[19] Since the important practice concerns trade unions, it will be dealt with separately below. The association will have rights of its own, for which the right to operate effectively provides

14 Article 27, which is expressed in terms of the rights of individual members of a minority. For a summary of the practice of the Human Rights Committee on Article 27, see McGoldrick, 40 ICLQ 658 (1991).

15 See Parl Ass Recommendation 1201 (1993) on an Additional Protocol on the Rights of National Minorities to the European Convention on Human Rights, text in 14 HRLJ 145 (1993), which is expressed in terms of individual rights.

16 Eg, it is not conceivable that the Convention protects the right to associate with limited liability or charitable status: *Association X v Sweden No 6094/73*, 9 DR 5 (1977).

17 This may be inferred from the trade union cases: see, eg, *Young James and Webster v UK* B 39 Com Rep para 160 (1979). In *Le Compte, Van Leuven and De Meyere v Belgium* A 43 para 65 (1981), the Court emphasised that while medical practitioners were obliged to be members of the *public* association, they were quite free to establish private associations for the protection of their interests, so no violation of Article 11 had been demonstrated.

18 *Cheall v UK No 10550/83*, 42 DR 178 (1985).

19 See Clapham, *Human Rights in the Private Sphere*, 1993, pp 232-240.

a general rubric. Again, the trade union cases to one side, the practice lacks specificity as to what these rights might be. In practice, it is less likely that the association will claim rights not provided for in the local law than that it will claim that the state has obstructed it in the exercise of those rights it has. Interferences with Article 11(1) rights to freedom of association must find their justification under Article 11(2). The trade union cases apart, there is little practice on the impact of Article 11(2) on freedom of association generally. However, in *Vogt v Germany*,[20] the Commission found that the dismissal of a state-employed school teacher because she was an active member of an extreme but lawful left-wing political party was not proportionate to the aims of protecting national security and the prevention of disorder. In *Hazar, Hazar and Acik v Turkey*,[1] the Commission has declared admissible applications alleging that convictions for membership of the Communist Party violate Article 11.

3. FREEDOM TO FORM AND JOIN TRADE UNIONS[2]

The right to the freedom to form and to join trade unions is a sub-division of freedom of association, not some special and independent right.[3] The state must allow the establishment of trade unions at the wish of individuals. In particular, it is not permitted to establish or to favour a single trade union in which membership of the appropriate individuals is compulsory. In the professional association cases, the Court has made it clear that the right to set up these comprehensive public law bodies must not be at the expense of the private right to establish other associations for the promotion of the interests of those professionals who elect to join and which can provide a different perspective to the government-required body.[4] The state, then, may breach Article 11 either by instituting too restrictive a regime of association or by using its public powers to interfere with associations set up under a more liberal arrangement.

In the area of industrial relations, the government may appear in another guise, that of employer. States have tried to argue that in this role a government's activities are not susceptible to regulation under Article 11. This narrow interpretation was rejected in the *Swedish Engine Drivers Union* case[5] and *Schmidt and Dahlstrom v Sweden*.[6] In the former case, the Court said:

20 *No 17851/91* Com Rep para 89 (1993), unreported. Pending before Court.
1 *Nos 16311/90-16313/90*, 72 DR 200 (1992).
2 See Forde, 31 AJCL 301 (1983); Hepple, in *Freedom of Association*, loc cit at p 417, n 1, above, p 162; and Morris, in Ewing et al, eds, *Human Rights and Labour Law: Essays for Paul O'Higgins*, 1994, pp 28-55.
3 *National Union of Belgian Police* case A 19 para 38 (1975). Tomuschat, *European System*, Ch 19 at p 501, argues for equal rights for *employers'* associations if the interpretation of the rights of trade unions gives them privileges additional to other associations.
4 *Le Compte, Van Leuven and De Meyere v Belgium* A 43 (1981). See also *Young, James and Webster v UK* B 39 (1979) Com Rep para 160 – 'a trade union monopoly is excluded'.
5 A 20 para 37 (1976).
6 A 21 para 33 (1976).

'The Convention nowhere makes an express distinction between the functions of a contracting state as holder of public power and its responsibilities as employer . . . Article 11 is accordingly binding upon the 'State as employer', whether the latter's relations with its employees are governed by public or private law.'

Given that decision, it would hardly be consistent to regard the activities of private employers, who, *vis-à-vis* the individual worker, are hardly in a different case from the government, as not subject to Article 11. It is here that the matter of the state's positive obligations to ensure that private persons do not infringe the rights under Article 11 of other private persons becomes crucial. In *Young, James and Webster v UK*,[7] the Court said:

'Although the proximate cause of the events giving rise to this case was the 1975 agreement between British Rail and the railway unions, it was the domestic law in force at the relevant time that made lawful the treatment of which the applicants complained.'

The state's positive obligation in this regard was not infringed in *Cheall v UK*.[8] This was an inter-union membership dispute case in which the applicant had been expelled from his current union in response to a request from his previous union in implementation of a membership-protection agreement to which both unions were parties. The Commission said that while matters of admission to membership and expulsion were for the union rules and that there was no general right of an individual to be admitted nor not to be expelled,

'None the less for the right to join a union to be effective the state must protect the individual against any abuse of a dominant position by trade unions . . . such abuse might occur, for example, where exclusion or expulsion was not in accordance with union rules or where the results were wholly arbitrary or where the consequences of exclusion or expulsion resulted in exceptional hardship such as job loss because of a closed shop.'

On the facts of this application, the Commission found nothing arbitrary or unreasonable about the decision and, it went on:

'. . . the expulsion of the applicant from [the union] must be seen as the act of a private body in the exercise of Convention rights under Article 11. As such, it cannot engage the responsibility of the respondent government.'

---

7 A 44 para 49 (1981). The Court said that it did not have to decide whether the employer, British Rail, a nationalised industry, was part of the state, so that its acts implicated the state directly.
8 *No 10550/83*, 42 DR 178 at 186 (1985).

In a case arising out of a dispute between an employee and his private employer considered by the Court in *Sibson v UK*,[9] the employee-applicant argued that the decision of his employer to transfer him to another depot (in accordance with the terms of his contract) was arbitrary in the sense referred to by the Commission in the *Cheall* case because it had been motivated by a desire to appease a trade union which the applicant had decided to leave. The employer's decision had been taken as a result of trade union pressure after the applicant had resigned from it and joined another one (as he was entitled to do under his contract). The members of his original union had refused to work with the applicant, which was the reason for the offer of work at the other depot. Accordingly, the applicant argued, the government's failure to provide him with a remedy against the decision was a violation of Article 11. The Court rejected the applicant's case. It found by a majority of 7 to 2 that because he had no strong reason for refusing to join *any* union and because he was not threatened with the loss of his job,

> '[he] was not subjected to a form of treatment striking at the very substance of the freedom of association guaranteed by Article 11.'[10]

A strongly-worded dissent by Judge Morenilla[11] focused on the applicant's right under Article 11 rather than on the contractual arrangements to which the majority had given such weight. In his view, pressure, admittedly private pressure, had been brought on the applicant requiring him to regain his original union membership if he wished to retain his original job. Since he did not want to rejoin, the government had a positive obligation to protect his negative freedom, his freedom not to become a member of an association when he did not want to. On the face of it, this represents a serious division between the majority and Judge Morenilla but a closer examination reveals that the difference is less profound. For both, the issue was whether the state had failed in its positive duty to protect the applicant against private interference with the negative freedom of association. For Judge Morenilla, that was all that was in issue. For the majority, the negative right of the trade union not to associate with Sibson was to be considered also.[12] Neither were absolute entitlements. The question was not whether the state had refused to give him protection against the unreasonable decision of his employer but whether it had struck a reasonable (or, at least, not unreasonable) balance between the competing interests of Sibson and the trade union.

---

9 A 258-A (1993).
10 Id, para 29.
11 Judge Russo joined him in his dissent.
12 The Court has always left open whether the guarantee of negative freedom of association under Article 11 is 'on the same footing' as the protection of the positive freedom: see *Young, James and Webster v UK* A 44 para 55 (1981). The situation must be different where the state is mediating between conflicting fundamental rights and where it is interfering with a fundamental right in the public interest.

How that balance is to be reached was first considered in *Young, James and Webster v UK*.[13] The case concerned a post-entry closed shop, ie an agreement between employer and union that all employees must be union members, including those already employed who were not members, on pain of dismissal. The Court rejected the government's arguments that the *travaux* showed that the drafting states did not intend to protect the negative freedom of association at all and, in particular, did not intend to inhibit a state's right to impose or permit closed shops. The Court carefully avoided generalities. It was not prepared to endorse the position that every closed shop arrangement was compatible with Article 11. Equally, compulsion to join a union was not always prohibited. The test was whether the compulsion 'strikes at the very substance of the freedom guaranteed by Article 11'.[14] On the facts, the Court said that it did because the closed shop was addressed to workers already in employment who had strong objections to union membership (which touched, even if they were not considered directly, interests under Articles 9 and 10) and the consequence of holding to their position was the very serious one of dismissal. Furthermore, in practice there was no choice open to the applicants as to which union to join and they were not in a position to form their own union.[15]

In the *Young, James and Webster* case, the government was not prepared to seek to justify the arrangements under Article 11(2)[16] but, as the case of *Sigurjonsson v Iceland*[17] shows, justification will be difficult. In the case, the Court found that a requirement in law that a taxi licence-holder be a member of an association of taxi-drivers was in violation of Article 11.[18] The Court found that international legal developments were increasingly favouring the individual against closed-shop arrangements and referred to a finding of the European Social Charter Committee of Independent Experts that Iceland's practice was not in accordance with the Charter. Again, what appeared to weigh most with the Court was that the consequences for the applicant were so severe: if he was not a member of the association, he could not earn his living as a taxi-driver. Furthermore, the applicant had at all times objected to becoming a member of the association and had held a licence at a time when membership was not required.[19] His objections were based on strongly held beliefs. When the Court turned to the government's case under Article 11(2), it found the reasons advanced, mainly that the arrangement facilitated the administration of the taxi service in the public interest, to be 'relevant but not sufficient'. The objective could have been

---

13 A 44 para 52 (1981). See also id, B 39 (1979-82) Com Rep para 166.
14 A 44 para 55 (1981).
15 Id, para 56.
16 There had been a change of government during the progress of the application and the new Conservative government was not prepared to rely on Article 11(2). See Forde, 11 ILJ 1 (1982).
17 A 264 paras 36, 37 (1993).
18 The Court said that it did not need to decide whether the association was a trade union.
19 The Commission more explicitly makes the point that this was a post-entry closed shop case: id, Com Rep para 57.

achieved at not significantly greater cost whether membership were compulsory or not. The government could demonstrate expediency but not a pressing social need.[20]

The closed-shop cases are about the negative freedom of association. A separate question is whether the positive freedom of individuals to form and join a trade union carries with it the right to form and join a body that may organise and function effectively for their benefit. Focusing on the words 'for the protection of his interests' in Article 11(1), in the *National Union of Belgian Police* case[1] the Court answered this question in the affirmative in the following terms:

> 'These words, clearly denoting purpose, show that the Convention safeguards freedom to protect the occupational interests of trade union members by trade union action, the conduct and development of which the state must both permit and make possible ... What the Convention requires is that under national law trade unions should be enabled, in conditions not at variance with Article 11, to strive for the protection of their members' interests.'

Despite this language, trade unions have enjoyed little success in claims that they or their members have brought under Article 11. In the closed-shop cases, the emphasis in the Court's approach was on freedom of association as an individual right, not as a collective right of trade unions. And in a group of cases in the 1970s, the Court simply did not support claims brought by unions or union members alleging that state restrictions upon trade union activities had infringed Article 11. In these cases, the Court noted that Article 11 is phrased in very general terms and 'does not secure any particular treatment of trade unions or their members'.[2] Apart from the specified rights to form and to join trade unions, Article 11 demanded of states only that they protect rights 'that [are] indispensable for the effective enjoyment of trade union freedom'.[3] The Court took a very narrow view of what rights were indispensable. In the *National Union of Belgian Police* case,[4] it conceded that they included a right to be heard by the employer on behalf of their members in order to function effectively. This did not, however, suppose a right to be consulted, which the applicants claimed and which in Belgium was allowed only to certain large trade unions. Similarly, in the *Swedish Engine Drivers' Union* case[5] the Court held that the right to be

---

20 A 264 para 41 (1993). A variety of UK cases involving compulsion to join a union have been the subject of friendly settlements: see, eg, *Reid v UK No 9520/81*, 34 DR 107 (1983); *Eaton v UK Nos 8476/79-8481/79*, 39 DR 11 (1984); and *Conroy v UK No 10061/82*, 46 DR 66 (1986) (the applicant was expelled from his union and then dismissed by his employer in compliance with a closed shop agreement).
1 A 9 para 39 (1975)
2 This wording is found, eg, *Swedish Engine Drivers' Union* case A 20 para 39 (1976).
3 Ibid.
4 A 19 para 39 (1975).
5 A 20 (1976)

heard, which remains the only indispensable right so far recognised, did not entail that the applicant trade union be allowed to enter into a collective agreement with an employer. In the Swedish system of industrial relations the terms and conditions of work of state employees, including railway engine drivers, were governed by a collective agreement entered into with four large federations of trade unions to which the applicant union was not affiliated, the resulting agreement then being applied to its members. Although these arrangements limited the power of the applicant union to protect its members' interests, there was no breach of Article 11. In both of the above cases, the Court stated that Article 11(1) allowed the state 'a free choice of means' as to how it ensured the right to be heard, and that these means might involve the right to bring claims or make representations rather than the specific right that was claimed.[6] Neither of the claimed rights were 'indispensable' or to be found generally in the 'national law and practice' of the contracting parties.[7]

Finally, in *Schmidt and Dahlstrom v Sweden*,[8] the Court held that it was not a breach of Article 11 for the applicant non-striking members of a striking trade union to be denied by the state as employer the retroactive benefit of the eventual collective agreement, when the agreement was applied retroactively to the benefit of members of non-striking unions. Referring both to the obligation of states to facilite trade union action[9] and to the 'free choice of means' that states are allowed when complying with it, the Court commented on the right to strike as follows:

'The grant of the right to strike represents without any doubt one of the most important of these means, but there are others. Such a right, which is not expressly enshrined in Article 11, may be subject under national law to regulation of a kind that limits its exercise in certain instances. The Social Charter of 18 October 1961 only guarantees the right to strike subject to such regulation, as well as to 'further restrictions' compatible with its Article 31 . . .'

The facts of the *Schmidt and Dahlstrom* case were considered by the Court to involve a permissible 'regulation' of the applicants' right to strike. It has yet to be established whether the right to strike in its essentials is a specific right that a state is required to secure under Article 11. Whereas the tone of the judgment in the *Schmidt and Dahlstrom* case is not sympathetic to the right to strike, given that it is generally recognised in the law of European states, that it has been given strong protection under the European Social

---

6 A 9 para 39 and A 20 para 40. In the *Swedish Engine Drivers' Union case*, the Court also noted that, although not able to conclude an agreement, the applicant union was permitted to negotiate.

7 A 9 para 38 and A 20 para 39

8 A 21 (1976).

9 The Court cited its statement of principle in the *National Union of Belgian Police* case quoted above.

Charter[10] and that the freedom to withdraw one's labour is crucial to the proper balance of power in industrial relations in a democratic society, it can be strongly argued that the right to strike should be protected under Article 11 as 'indispensable'.[11]

Although the judgments in the 1970s cases just discussed do create the appearance that Article 11(1) guarantees only the barest minimum of implied rights for trade unions, it is the case that in each application the trade union or its members had extensive rights in the national legal system concerned which could be seen cumulatively as allowing for the effective exercise of the positive right to organise. What the applicants were complaining about was the absence of a specific right or a specific restriction. It remains the case that a state which conceded only the bare minimum of rights to organised labour could not be confident that it was complying with Article 11, although the opaque language of the Court may make it difficult for an applicant to demonstrate that the state is in dereliction. If Article 11 is ultimately interpreted as offering little or nothing by way of protection for the collective right to organise,[12] the only remedies available at the international level will be the less effective ones under the European Social Charter and the International Covenant on Economic, Social and Cultural Rights and within the procedures of the ILO.[13]

4. RESTRICTIONS ON PUBLIC SERVICE EMPLOYEES

The second sentence of Article 11(2) reads:

'This article shall not prevent the imposition of lawful restrictions on the exercise of these rights by members of the armed forces, of the police or of the administration of the state.'

This provision was considered by the Commission in *Council of Civil Service Unions v UK* (the *GCHQ* case).[14] The British government had decreed that

10 Various restrictions upon the right to strike have been found to be contrary to Article 6(4) of the Charter: see Harris, *The European Social Charter*, 1984, p 77.
11 The second sentence of Article 11(2) would provide a basis for allowing exceptions for members of the armed forces, the police and at least some civil servants. This sentence was not relied on by the Court in the *Schmidt and Dahlstrom* case, in which one of the applicants was in the armed forces (the other was a state-employed university lecturer).
12 As far as a trade union's right to organise its affairs is concerned, the Commission acknowledges that the right to form trade unions does includes the right to draw up and enforce union rules: see *Cheall v UK No 10550/83*, 42 DR 178 at 185 (1985) and *Johansson v Sweden No 13537/88*, 65 DR 202 at 205 (1990). There may be difficult questions, going to the tension between the individual and collective aspects of the right to organise, when trade unions mobilise or discipline their members.
13 Neither the Charter nor the Covenant offer a right of petition. The ILO system of petitions does not lead to legally binding decisions, which is one reason why its adverse ruling in the *GCHQ* case has simply been ignored.
14 *No 11603/85*, 50 DR 228 (1987). See Burrows, in Jaspers and Betten, eds, *25 Years European Social Charter*, 1988, pp 38-44; and Morris, loc cit at p 424, n 2, above, pp 45-49.

civil servants working at a telecommunications interception station should cease to have the right to belong to a trade union. Instead, they were allowed membership only of an approved staff association. Previously, staff had been members of trade unions which operated at the station to represent their interests. The Commission decided that the staff fell within the second sentence of Article 11(2) as 'members of the administration of the state'. In particular, it noted that GCHQ was a 'special institution' with functions associated with those of the military and the police. It held that the term 'lawful' in the second sentence meant firstly that the restrictions must be imposed in accordance with national law and, secondly, that, the restriction should not be arbitrary. Both of these requirements were met on the facts. As to the second, the Commission read 'restrictions' as encompassing a complete ban and concluded that the decision to impose such a ban, though 'drastic', was within the power of the state under the second sentence of Article 11(2).[15] The decision has been criticised as permitting the government to go beyond the power in Article 11(2) to impose 'restrictions on the exercise' of Article 11 rights because here the freedom to associate was removed altogether.[16] In consequence, it has been suggested that the Convention be amended, at least to exclude from the final sentence of Article 11(2) the reference to 'members . . . of the administration of the state'.[17] The same conclusion as that of the Commission was reached by the Committee of Independent Experts under the European Social Charter.[18] A different conclusion was reached by the ILO Freedom of Association Committee, a conclusion endorsed by the ILO Governing Body. However, the wording of the ILO Freedom of Association Convention is different to that in Article 11.[19] The decision of the Commission reflects the general attitude of deference of the Strasbourg authorities to the choices made by the states in the field of trade union rights and freedoms, a position doubtless enhanced in this case because of the general reluctance of the Strasbourg authorities to review determinations of the states made in the interests of national security. None the less, it is a matter of regret that an application affecting the rights of 8,000 workers, raising novel questions under Article 11, did not reach the Court. The only other form of protection available against too ready resort to this exception lies in the determination

---

15 *Council of Civil Service Unions v UK*, id, pp 241-242. Although the decision was not based on the first sentence of Article 11(2), it was clearly of significance that the government's case was based on the need to act in the interests of national security. Now see *Groppera Radio*, above, p 385, on the third sentence of Article 10(2).

16 Hepple, loc cit at p 424, n 2, above, p 173.

17 Zanghi, in *Freedom of Association* loc cit at p 417, n 1, above, p 149.

18 Conclusions of the Committee of Independent Experts, Eleventh Cycle, Part I, 1989, p 80. See also Morris, loc cit at p 424, n 2, above, pp 48-49.

19 Article 9(1) of the ILO Convention on Freedom of Association reads: 'The extent to which the guarantees provided for in this Convention shall apply to the armed forces and the police shall be determined by national law or regulations.' In contrast with Article 11(2), it makes no special allowance for 'the administration of the state'. A further decision of the ILO Freedom of Association Committee in the case is imminent. See also Corby, 15 ILJ 161 (1986).

of who are 'members of the administration of the state'. In *Vogt v Germany*,[20] the Commission said that German school teachers were not 'members of the administration of the state'.

5. CONCLUSION

The unwillingness of the Commission and the Court to find greater protection for trade unions and their members within Article 11 has been criticised.[1] The restraint of the Strasbourg authorities affects both the identification of rights under Article 11(1) and the upholding of restrictions under Article 11(2). The Court has retained with respect to the first a narrow view of the positive obligations of the state which may be found under Article 11(1) to prevent private interference with individual freedoms. Under Article 11(2), it has allowed a wide margin to the states, not least in deciding how conflicts of rights under Article 11(1) should be resolved. It has been urged that the Court should take a more active role in protecting the collective interest if the application raises an issue under Article 11(2). There is a danger that too great a concentration on the position of the dissenting individual – the person who will not join a union or the member who will not submit to majority decisions – will weaken the fundamental right of association of others and the effective capacity of the association to protect their interests.[2]

Indeed, in *Gustafsson v Sweden*[3] the Commission recently declared admissible a case in which the applicant argued that effective trade union action against his business violated his negative freedom of association (not to be a member of the employers' association with which the trade union dealt) under Article 11 and his right to enjoyment of his possessions under Article 1 of the First Protocol. At the same time, in *Englund v Sweden*,[4] the Commission held inadmissible an application by employees of the applicant in the *Gustafsson* case. They were not members of the trade union taking action against him and had not authorised the union to act on their behalf. They said that the union action interfered with their right to conclude employment contracts on terms agreed by them with their employer and, if he had acceded to the union's demand, there would have been an interference with their negative freedom of association because they would have been bound to accept the terms of the collective agreement. The Commission did not decide the government's main point that Article 11 did not apply at all but, assuming that it did, said that it had not been violated because the employer's refusal to give in to the unions meant that the

---

20 *No 17851/91* (1993) Com Rep, para 88. Pending before Court.
1 Leader, 20 ILJ 39 at 57 (1991).
2 Ibid. See also the dissenting opinion of Judge Soerensen, joined by Judges Thór Vilhjálmsson and Lagergren in *Young, James and Webster v UK*.
3 *No 15573/89* (1994), unreported. Commission found breach. Pending before Court.
4 *No 15533/89*, 77-A DR 10 at 18-19 (1994).

applicants could remain unorganised employees and the conditions of their employment were not affected. This last point may have seemed somewhat academic to the applicants because the business had been sold due to the effectiveness of the industrial action and they had lost their jobs.

The references to standards of 'unreasonableness' and 'arbitrariness'[5] as those that are applicable when deciding whether the state's positive obligation to protect private persons from interferences with their Article 11 rights by others do not indicate a willingness by the Strasbourg authorities to subject national laws and decisions to intensive scrutiny.[6] For some labour lawyers, this is an acceptable outcome.[7] Many of the conflicts are essentially between trade unions and members or non-members or between trade unions and employers. In the field of industrial relations, not only do the states adopt a variety of ways of managing these matters but they frequently acknowledge that considerable degrees of economic and social pressure are legitimate instruments in industrial conflict.[8] The Court has recognised this too. In the *National Union of Belgian Police* case,[9] it found no Convention violation where the pattern of union organisation favoured by the state was leading to a loss of the applicant's members to bigger unions. In *Schmidt and Dahlstrom v Sweden*,[10] it was similarly dismissive of a complaint by strikers that they were treated less favourably than non-strikers in a pay settlement. It is a realistic attitude. The European Court cannot write a comprehensive trade union law on the narrow basis of Article 11. It has declined to use international labour law as a substitute, although it has frequently referred to other international instruments. These have included the key ILO Conventions,[11] the European Social Charter and European Community law.[12] The treatment of them has not been consistent. In the *Swedish Engine Drivers' Union* case,[13] the Court used the European Social Charter as evidence that precise trade union rights were not protected by the Convention. More recently in *Sigurjonsson v Iceland*,[14] it relied on developments in international labour law to confirm its earlier judgment in *Young, James and Webster v UK*[15] that closed shop agreements may not be compatible with Article 11. However, the Commission did not

---

5 See *Cheall v UK No 10550/83*, above at p 425.
6 But see Mr Busuttil, dissenting in *Sibson v UK* A 258-A (1993) Com Rep, who was effectively reviewing the judgment of the Court of Appeal.
7 See Forde, loc cit at p 424, n 2, above, pp 330-332.
8 See Baglioni and Crouch, eds, *European Industrial Relations*, 1990, particularly Ch 1 by Baglioni.
9 A 19 para 41 (1975).
10 A 21 para 40 (1976).
11 Freedom of Association Convention 1948 (ILO 87), 48 UNTS 17; Cmd 7638, and the Right to Organise and Collective Bargaining Convention 1949 (ILO 98), 96 UNTS 257; Cmd 7852.
12 See the EC Charter on the Fundamental Social Rights of Workers, Article 11, European Commission 23rd General Report, 1989, p 187.
13 A 20 para 39 (1976).
14 A 264 para 35 (1993). The instruments referred to included the EC Charter of the Fundamental Rights of Workers. Iceland is not a member of the European Union.
15 A 44 para 42 (1981).

refer to arguments based on the ILO Conventions in the *GCHQ* case, although in that case there was the complication that the ILO itself had the incident under review at the same time.[16]

---

16 See *Council of Civil Service Unions v UK No 11603/85*, 50 **DR** 228 at 236-237 (1987).

CHAPTER 13

Article 12: The right to marry and to found a family

'**Article 12**
Men and women of marriageable age have the right to marry and to found a family, according to the national laws governing the exercise of this right.'

1. INTRODUCTION

The text of Article 12 asserts a relatively narrow right (or, possibly, rights) to marry and to found a family, subject to a wide power on the part of states to regulate the exercise of the right. The interpretation of Article 12 by the Strasbourg authorities has not greatly expanded its scope. Although closely connected with the notion of 'family life' in Article 8, which has been interpreted imaginatively, the Commission and Court have not been so receptive to developing the content of Article 12.[1] This has a particularly inhibiting effect on the right to found a family. The original understanding of Article 12 appears to have been, as its text suggests ('this right'), that it set out a single right of men and women to marry and found a family.[2] Although the Commission has allowed that the right to marry is protected in circumstances where there is no intention or no possibility of procreation,[3] neither it nor the Court has been willing to admit that the right to found a family can arise in the absence of a marriage.[4] If an unmarried couple do have a family, their various rights will be protected under Article 8 but there is no decision (as perhaps there will be) giving them equal right to that of a married couple to found a family under Article 12 and, accordingly, any differentiation the national law makes between married and unmarried couples in this respect will not fall to be considered under Article 14. The qualificatory clause – 'according to the national laws' – in Article 12 is of a

---

1 See *Marckx v Belgium* A 31 para 67 (1979) and *BR and J v FRG No 9639/82*, 36 DR 130 at 140 (1984).
2 Contra, Fawcett, p 285, 'two distinct rights are involved', but there is 'a close conjunction of the two rights', id, p 288.
3 See *Hamer v UK No 7114/75*, 24 DR 5 at 16 (1979) Com Rep; CM Res DH (81) 5.
4 *Rees v UK* A 106 para 49 (1986), although the case concerned the right to marry, not to found a family, on its facts.

quite different kind from those in Articles 8-11. While it does provide a wider margin of appreciation to states, the words are not to be read literally for that would deprive Article 12 of all meaning at the international level. National 'laws' must satisfy a European standard as to the meaning of a 'law' and must not so interfere with the enjoyment of the right that they empty of it of all substance.[5] The limitation on the reach of the national law is sometimes bolstered by reference to the words 'governing the *exercise* of this right' to indicate that the national laws may not go so far as to prohibit or exclude the right altogether.[6] National laws on marriage and the right to found a family must not breach Article 14.[7]

2. THE RIGHT TO MARRY

i.   Generally

It is for the national law to fix such matters as form and capacity, including marriageable age, prohibited degrees and so on.[8] The Convention limits the freedom of a state's 'national laws' to settle these issues only if its standards are arbitrary or rob the right of its content. In *Van Oosterwijk v Belgium*[9], the majority in the Commission said that the reference to national law in Article 12 did not authorise a state 'completely to deprive a person or category of persons of the right to marry'. It is for the state to decide on what the content of its conflict rules should be and whether to apply them.[10] There is no duty to allow marriage in any particular form, including polygamous unions or according to particular religious ceremonies.[11] The question of the recognition of foreign marriages, whether of a different kind to national ones or not, will generally arise under Article 8 rather than Article 12.

Marriage is a consensual union between the parties and ordinarily the state will have no positive obligations to facilitate the celebration of a marriage. However, where there are collateral circumstances which prevent willing parties from entering into what otherwise would be a lawful marriage, the state may have a duty to mitigate or eliminate these obstacles. The Commission considered this in two cases involving prisoners in the United Kingdom. There was no specific rule of English law preventing prisoners from marrying but the Marriage Act 1949 required that marriages be celebrated only at certain places outside prisons and the prison

---

5 Id, para 50.
6 *Hamer v UK*, loc cit at n 3 above.
7 Opsahl, in Robertson, ed, *Privacy and Human Rights*, 1973, pp 182, 190-91.
8 *Hamer v UK*, loc cit at n 3, above, p 14 and *F v Switzerland* A 128 para 32 (1987).
9 A 40 (1980) Com Rep para 56.
10 *X v UK No 3898/68*, 35 CD 102 at 108 (1970); *X v Switzerland No 9057/80*, 26 DR 207 (1981) (in each case reference was made to the personal law of the applicant to establish that he was already married); and *Khan v UK No 11579/85*, 48 DR 253 (1986) (marriageable age).
11 *X v FRG No 6167/73*, 1 DR 64 (1974).

authorities would not allow the applicants temporary release to be married outside the prison. In *Hamer v UK*,[12] the prisoner's opportunity to be married would have been delayed for a period until he obtained parole. In *Draper v UK*,[13] the prisoner was serving a life sentence and had no foreseeable date when he would be released on licence and be able to marry. The Commission decided that there was a violation in each case, an assessment confirmed by the Committee of Ministers. Considerations of security did not preclude the state from making some arrangement which would have allowed the prisoners to marry. The effect of the law and the decision of the authorities was to cause such delay in the prisoners' opportunity to be married as to infringe the substance of their right to marry. As a result of these cases, the government introduced legislation to allow prisoners to be married in prison.[14]

It seems unlikely that a state would be obliged to admit to its territory an alien solely for the purpose of contracting a marriage.[15] It is most probable in such a case that the parties would wish to live together in the state, which would give rise to a claim under Article 8 rather than Article 12.

In *F v Switzerland*,[16] a Swiss court ordered that the applicant could not marry again for three years after a divorce in which the court found him solely responsible for the breakdown of the marriage. After the divorce, the applicant was a single man and wanted to remarry. He was, the majority in the European Court said, entitled to remarry 'without unreasonable restrictions'. The condition imposed by the Swiss court was unreasonable because the reasons the government gave for it were inappropriate (to protect the future spouse) or its effects on others were disproportionate (the chance that children would be born out of wedlock). The judgment was by the narrowest majority, 9 to 8. The dissenting judges thought that this regulation fell within the wide power of the state to legislate for the exercise of the right to marry: it did not affect the essence of the right. However, the majority judgment confirms the decisions of the Commission in the *Hamer* and *Draper* cases that the imposition of delay in the exercise of the right to marry between two people who are ready to do so will be regarded as a serious infringement of their interests and a breach of Article 12.

One of the government's arguments in the *Draper* and *Hamer* cases was that there was no opportunity for cohabitation and consummation of the marriage. To that, the Commission said:

'The essence of the right to marry . . . is the formation of a legally binding association between a man and a woman. It is for them to

12 *No 7114/75*, 24 DR 5 at 16 (1979) Com Rep; CM Res DH (81) 5.
13 *No 8186/78*, 24 DR 72 at 81 (1980) Com Rep; CM Res DH (81) 4.
14 Marriage Act 1983, s 1, which also allows marriages for some mental patients in their institutions and for house-bound persons at home.
15 *Abdulaziz, Cabales and Balkandali v UK* A 94 (1985) which concerned the right of persons settled in the UK to have their alien spouses join them was not argued under Article 12 and, in any event, turned on the discrimination point: see below, p 466.
16 A 128 paras 30-40 (1987).

decide whether or not they wish to enter an association in circumstances where they cannot cohabit.'[17]

There is no positive duty on a state to provide the material conditions to make the right to marry effective: if there were an obligation of this kind, it would not arise under Article 12 but under Article 8.[18] A state may foster marriage by granting benefits to married couples which it denies to single cohabitees but it is not obliged to do so.[19] Indeed, it is not under a duty to guarantee that married couples are no worse off than cohabitees in a similar position to them.[20] Van Dijk and Van Hoof[1] suggest that there are circumstances when the state would be obliged to protect married persons against action by private persons – they give as an example the discharge of employees on the sole grounds of their marital status. In view of the general reluctance of the Strasbourg authorities to protect persons against collateral consequences of the exercise of their rights, particularly in a case where what is at issue is the 'right' to a job, this suggestion, however worthy, must be treated with circumspection.

ii.   Transsexuals

The question whether marriage is limited to unions between a man and woman has arisen in two situations: unions between a transsexual and another; and unions between homosexuals.

For the transsexual, the complaint is that a state which denies the transsexual the right to marry a person of the *now* opposite sex is inconsistent with the words in the *Draper* and *Hamer* cases, that marriage is the association between a man and woman. However, some states insist that the original gender of the transsexual survives whatever transformation surgery and treatment have taken place: marriage is then denied on the basis that the proposed union is between two people of the same sex. In *Rees v UK*,[2] the Commission was evenly divided on the reasons (although unanimous on the outcome) why the denial of the claim of a transsexual to the right to marry did not violate Article 12. For half of the Commission, the issue was a formal one: the denial of the change of status following transformation surgery was a violation of Article 8; once the state had repaired that violation, the applicant would have the new sex he/she sought. There would then be no impediment to the applicant marrying someone of

---

17   *Hamer v UK*, loc cit at p 435, n 3, above, p 16. Cf *Draper*, loc cit at p 437, n 13, above, p 81.
   There is no right of prisoners to conjugal relations with their spouse: *X and Y v Switzerland No 8166/78*, 13 DR 241 (1978).
18   See above, p 331.
19   *Marckx v Belgium* A 31 (1979).
20   *Kleine Staarman v Netherlands No 10503/83*, 42 DR 162 (1985) (loss of benefit on marriage) and *Lindsay and Lindsay v UK No 11089/84*, 49 DR 181 at 193 (1986) (married couple taxed more heavily than cohabitees).
1   Van Dijk and Van Hoof, p 446.
2   A 106 (1986) Com Rep paras 52-55.

the (now) opposite sex. The remainder of the Commission took the position that the substance of a marriage 'includes the physical capacity to procreate' and that a state was, therefore, entitled to disqualify transsexuals from marrying. The outcome was confirmed unanimously by the Court:

'. . . the right to marry guaranteed by Article 12 refers to the traditional marriage between persons of opposite biological sex. This appears also from the wording of the Article which makes it clear that Article 12 is mainly concerned to protect marriage as the basis of the family.'[3]

On the same question, in *Cossey v UK*,[4] the Commission held, by a majority of ten to six, that there *was* a violation of Article 12, rejecting the conjunction between the right to marry and the capacity to found a family. The Court,[5] by 14 votes to 4, confirmed its judgment in *Rees*. Although there were some states in which a marriage between a transsexual and another person of the now opposite sex was permitted, there was no 'general abandonment' of the traditional notion of marriage propounded in *Rees*.

iii. Homosexuals

The Commission has decided that homosexual unions do not concern 'family life' for the purposes of Article 8.[6] It is, therefore, unsurprising that it has taken the position that homosexuals do not have the right to marry one another. In his dissent in *W v UK*,[7] Mr Schermers hinted that such a right should be recognised. This would be a step beyond allowing a transsexual the right to marry under Article 12 for, as the Commission report in *Cossey* explains, those unions may be regarded as associations between a man and a woman. In the case of homosexuals, it would be the substance of the proposed union rather than the character of the participants in it which would decide whether it was a 'marriage'.[8]

iv. Divorce

Article 16 of the Universal Declaration of Human Rights provides that parties to a marriage have equal rights 'during marriage and its dissolution'.

3 A 106 para 49 (1986).
4 A 184 (1990) Com Rep.
5 A 184 para 46 (1990). See also *W v UK No 11095/84*, 63 DR 34 (1989) Com Rep (note Mr Schermers's dissent at p 48); CM Res DH (89) 27 and *Eriksson and Goldschmidt v Sweden No 14573/89*, 63 DR 213 (1989).
6 *S v UK No 11716/85*, 47 DR 274 (1986).
7 Loc cit at n 5, above. Mr Schermers took the view that Article 12 protects two rights and his decision was directed mainly to the right to found a family. See also Van Dijk, in Waaldijk and Clapham, eds, *Homosexuality: a European Community Issue*, 1993, p 179 at 198-199.
8 See Nielsen, 4 IJL Fam 297 at 299 (1990), explaining that Danish law allows a formal relationship between homosexuals to be recognised but the 'registered partnership' 'attracts to it more of the legal effects of marriage', without being marriage.

There is no reference to the dissolution of marriage in Article 12. After a review of the *travaux préparatoires*, the Commission in *Johnston v Ireland*[9] decided that the omission was deliberate. The drafting states did not intend the Convention to grant a right to divorce. The Court held that the prohibition on divorce in the Irish Constitution did not infringe the Convention and that a different conclusion would not be reached by taking into account developments in other European states which had established a very wide right to divorce, because:

> '. . . the Court cannot, by means of an evolutive interpretation, derive from [the Convention and the Protocols] a right which was not included therein at the outset. This is particularly so here, where the omission was deliberate.'[10]

The Court found that Article 5 of the Seventh Protocol also had been drafted in such a way as to avoid the implication that a right to divorce was contained in the Convention.[11] The consequences of the judgment are less serious because of the requirement of a protective remedy between husband and wife[12] and the steps the Court has taken to ameliorate the position of illegitimate children under Article 8,[13] but it does not sit happily with the importance the Court attached to the right to remarry to avoid children being born out of wedlock in its judgment in *F v Switzerland*.[14]

3. THE RIGHT TO FOUND A FAMILY

The judgments in *Rees* and *Cossey*[15] indicate that the Court regards the two parts of Article 12 as being closely related. However, while this may be important when determining the meaning of 'marriage', it need not necessarily restrict the right to found a family to persons who are married. The most obvious interferences with the right to found a family are programmes of compulsory sterilisation or abortion.[16] Voluntary sterilisation or abortion by one partner to a marriage clearly has an impact on the interests of the other partner but, however serious this may be, it is hard to see that the Strasbourg authorities would find a positive obligation on a state to regulate a private decision of the above kind except in circumstances where some other right under the Convention was more

9   A 112 (1986) Com Rep paras 92-102.
10 A 112 para 53 (1986).
11 See below pp 569-570. Article 7 refers to equality of spouses 'during marriage and *in the event* of its dissolution' (emphasis added).
12 *Airey v Ireland* A 32 (1979).
13 See *Marckx v Belgium* A 31 (1979) and pp 312-313, above.
14 A 128 para 36 (1987).
15 *Rees v UK* A 106 paras 49-50 (1986) and *Cossey v UK* A 154 para 43 (1990). See also Fawcett, p 288. But see above, p 435, for unmarried couples.
16 The Commission has sometimes described the right to found a family as an 'absolute right' in the sense that Article 12 gives no grounds for the state to interfere with it: see *X v UK No 6564/74*, 2 DR 105 at 106 (1975).

directly implicated, such as that in Article 2 or Article 8.[17] While the states have the power to encourage the legitimate family, they have no positive obligation to do so. Article 12 cannot be made the vehicle for requiring positive social programmes from the state in support of the family.[18] We have already seen that couples have the right to marry even in the absence of a prospect of cohabitation. In these circumstances, the state has no duty to facilitate opportunities for the couple to found a family by allowing for consummation of the marriage.[19] Where the separation is the result of a deportation decision which removes one party to the marriage or proposed marriage from the jurisdiction or an immigration order which prevents a party to a marriage or proposed marriage from entering a state, any Convention remedy will arise under Article 8, not Article 12.[20] It is perhaps unlikely that a right of a partner to a marriage or a proposed marriage to stay in or to be admitted to a state in order to found a family can be found in Article 12 if it cannot be found in Article 8.[1]

While Article 12 protects couples from interference by the state with their right to found a family, for some couples the chance will be an empty one because of their incapacity to procreate. States commonly provide for adoption and allow for artificial techniques of producing children to be used. Adoption does fall within Article 12 and so conditions on the right of a couple to adopt imposed by the national law are subject to scrutiny by the Commission.[2] There is no indication that a state has an obligation to provide a system of adoption, still less any particular form of adoption.[3]

More recently, attention has switched to artificial reproduction. The state may be implicated at two levels. It has first to decide whether and what techniques of artificial reproduction may be used and to whom they should be available. It does not seem likely that the Convention imposes any limits on what choices a state may make and it is probably premature to decide that the Convention imposes a positive obligation on a state to legislate to allow any particular technique. However, as the acceptability of those measures which are closest to natural reproduction (eg IVF) increases, states may find themselves having an increasingly heavy burden to explain why married persons may not avail themselves of them.[4] It is much less likely that a positive duty will be placed on the state to provide the appropriate treatment.

---

17 Cf *X v UK No 8416/78*, 19 DR 244 (1980).
18 Cf *Andersson and Kullmann v Sweden No 11776/85*, 46 DR 251 (1986).
19 *X v UK No 6564/74*, 2 DR 105 (1975) and *X and Y v Switzerland No 8166/78*, 13 DR 241 (1978).
20 See eg *Beldjoudi v France* A 234A (1992). See further p 333, above.
1 *X v Switzerland No 7031/75*, 6 DR 124 (1976) (which concerns the right to marry) might be reconsidered now in the light of the developments with respect to expulsion of aliens under Article 8: see above, pp 331-334.
2 *X and Y v UK No 7229/75*, 12 DR 32 at 34 (1977) and *X v Netherlands No 8896/80*, 24 DR 176 at 177-178 (1981).
3 In *X and Y v UK*, id, the Commission said that a state was not obliged to recognise a foreign adoption.
4 For a more cautious position, see Liu, *Artificial Reproduction and Reproductive Rights*, 1991, pp 27-31.

4. NON-MARRIED PERSONS

In *Marckx v Belgium*,[5] the mother of an illegitimate child claimed a right 'not to marry', that is to say, that her right to found a family should not be inhibited by disadvantages which she and her child would suffer by reason only of the fact that the mother had chosen not to marry the father of the child. The Court held that there was no legal obstacle confronting the mother 'in the exercise of the freedom to marry or to remain single' and that the disadvantage to which she referred did not constitute an interference with that legal opportunity such as to violate Article 12. In *B, R and J v FRG*,[6] the Commission confirmed that a state could treat the legitimate family more favourably than the illegitimate one, provided that its treatment of the latter did not violate Article 8. The 'full protection' of German family law extended only to the legitimate family. Here, an unmarried father and mother were living in a stable relationship with their child. A parental link was recognised by German law between the father and his child but the law would not allow him to obtain custody of the child. Just as he could not rely on Article 8, the Commission said that he could not find the right to custody in Article 12, so long as the couple remained unmarried. In *X v Belgium and Netherlands*,[7] the Commission decided that an unmarried person could assert no right to adoption under Article 12. The British government has taken the view that Article 12 'has no application' where single women seek access to techniques of artificial fertilisation.[8] Article 14 claims associated with this kind of application are bound to fail once the position is taken that it is Article 12 itself which authorises the limitation of the right to found a family to married couples. If any change is to be brought about, it will be through an alteration in the understanding of who can marry (transsexuals, homosexuals)[9] but this will still leave the unmarried and the single person without a remedy where the right to found a family depends upon adoption or artificial reproduction.

---

5 A 31 para 67 (1979).
6 *No 9639/82*, 36 DR 130 (1984).
7 *No 6482/14*, 7 DR 75 (1975).
8 Health Minister (Mrs Bottomley), HC Debs, Vol 184, Col 1029, 20 June 1990, quoted in Douglas, Hebenton and Thomas, 142 NLJ 537 (1992).
9 *Kerkhoven v Netherlands No 15666/89* (1993), unreported. For the position in English law, see Sandland (1993) JSWL 321.

CHAPTER 14

Article 13: The right to an effective national remedy

'**Article 13**

Everyone whose rights and freedoms as set forth in this Convention are violated shall have an effective remedy before a national authority notwithstanding that the violation has been committed by persons acting in an official capacity.'

Article 13 is central to the cooperative relationship between the Convention and national legal systems. In conjunction with Article 26, it means that the Convention requires both the provision of effective national remedies and that individuals make use of them before commencing an application at Strasbourg. In this way, the primary responsibility of the states to secure the enjoyment of human rights is enhanced and the effective discharge of the subsidiary role of the institutions is facilitated. The more comprehensive the national remedies, the less the need for applications to be made to the Commission; the less the pressure of cases on the Convention bodies, the better and quicker they are able to deal with the cases they must decide; the more considered the case-law of the institutions, the clearer it is to the national authorities what is required of them.

Despite its importance, the language and objective of Article 13 are far from clear: two judges have called it the 'most obscure' provision of the Convention.[1] The approaches to its interpretation by the Strasbourg authorities have oscillated, now demanding more of the state,[2] now less,[3] as they have sought an understanding of Article 13 which fits into the whole structure of the Convention. If the general principles which it embodies are now tolerably clear, they are not free from criticism.[4] Nor is their application to the facts of an individual case always easy; in particular, the development of remedies in a national legal system over time may mean that previous judgments of the Court or decisions of the Commission

---

1   Judges Matscher and Pinheiro Farinha, partly dissenting in *Malone v UK* A 82 (1984).
2   Eg *Plattform 'Arzte für das Leben' v Austria* A 139 (1988).
3   Eg *Leander v Sweden* A 116 (1987).
4   See Van Dijk and Van Hoof, pp 528-531.

finding them to be inadequate must be revised.[5] It is important to emphasise at the beginning that the application of Article 13 to the facts of a particular case must take all these matters into consideration. Generalisations are rarely useful.

1. A PRE-EMPTIVE REMEDY

One of the early uncertainties of Article 13, Fawcett[6] suggests, was whether it was intended to promote the pre-emptive, domestic protection of individual rights – to provide an avenue open to the individual in the domestic legal system to test whether his Convention rights had been violated and to remedy them if they had – or whether it was designed instead to impose an obligation to establish a means of redress open to the individual in the domestic legal system to obtain the enforcement of a judgment he had won at Strasbourg. The ambiguity arose because of the words 'Everyone whose rights and freedoms . . . *are violated* shall have an effective *remedy* . . .' (emphasis added). It has been clearly resolved in favour of the former understanding. In *Klass v FRG*[7] the Court said:

> 'Thus Article 13 must be interpreted as guaranteeing an "effective remedy before a national authority" to everyone who *claims* that his rights and freedoms under the Convention have been violated.'

Similarly, in *Soering v UK*[8] it stated:

> 'Article 13 guarantees the availability of a remedy at national level to enforce the substance of the Convention rights and freedoms in whatever form they may happen to be secured in the domestic legal order . . .'

In view of this interpretation, certain questions arise as to the inter-relationship between Article 13 and the rule in Article 26 that an applicant must exhaust local remedies before bringing an Article 25 application. If there is no Article 13 remedy, then there can be no obligation to have recourse to it[9] for the purposes of Article 26 (although an individual may be advised to test whether a particular process satisfies Article 13, even if he has

---

5 An example is the development of judicial review in the UK, where the prospects of review of official action against the substantive standards of the Convention, if not its provisions themselves, have been enhanced, although perhaps not quite to the extent the Court imagines: see the *Soering* case, below, pp 452-453.

6 Fawcett, pp 289-291.

7 A 28 para 64 (1979). Emphasis added.

8 A 161 para 120 (1989).

9 *Warwick v UK No 9471/81*, 60 DR 5 at 19 (1989) (no remedy to test parent's claim that lawful school beating of daughter violated Article 2, First Protocol). But see below, p 454.

doubts whether it does). However, because the notion of 'remedy' in Article 13 is wider than that in Article 26,[10] failure to have recourse to a remedy that meets the requirements of Article 13 will not necessarily amount to a failure to exhaust domestic remedies in the sense of Article 26. If there is an Article 13 remedy, then an individual will need to go on to Strasbourg only where the process has failed to reach a result satisfactory to him. That may be the case because what Article 13 requires is the opportunity to test the substance of a claim that the Convention has been violated, not a guarantee that the national decision-maker will reach the right result on the Convention question.[11]

Article 13 imposes in two senses a minimum obligation for states. Firstly, in some instances the Convention fixes on states a more stringent procedural obligation to provide a remedy in particular contexts than that required by Article 13: see Articles 5(4), 5(5) and 6(1). In such cases, the 'context-specific' remedy required by the article concerned is what the Convention requires, not the less rigorous Article 13 remedy. For example, any claim to an Article 13 remedy is absorbed by the claim that a detained person has the *habeas corpus* remedy required by Article 5(4).[12] Secondly, states may choose to provide in their national law a higher standard of procedural protection for a right than either Article 13 or any specific provision of the Convention requires. For example, as will be seen, there is no obligation under Article 13 to provide for the judicial review of legislation.[13] However, if such a remedy is provided, the local remedies rule in Article 26 requires that an applicant uses it as a precondition for the admissibility of any substantive claim.[14] However, no issue arises under Article 13 about the effectiveness of this particular channel of review,[15] because there could be no issue about its absence altogether.

2. AN AUXILIARY REMEDY

Given that Article 13 imposes an obligation to provide a pre-emptive remedy, the question arises whether Article 13 is auxiliary to claims that other articles of the Convention have been violated or whether it has an independent role. The answer is clearly the former, for Article 13 does not guarantee a remedy against all kinds of illegality in the national legal order, but only illegal acts related to the enjoyment of Convention rights. The Court has regarded Article 13 obligations as auxiliary in other ways also. Firstly, the effectiveness of the remedy required may be conditioned by the

10 *Golder v UK* A 18 para 33 (1975). And see below, pp 608-612.
11 *Silver v UK* A 61 para 113 (1983).
12 Eg *Campbell and Fell v UK* A 80 para 123 (1984) (Article 6(1)) and *de Jong et al v Netherlands* A 77 para 60 (1984) (Article 5(4)).
13 See below, pp 458-459.
14 See above, p 610.
15 Eg that the *locus standi* rules are too strict.

character of the Convention right to which it is sought to attach it, the suggestion being that more important rights require more stringent remedies.[16] Secondly, the effectiveness of any remedy that Article 13 requires may be limited by virtue of the nature of the state power the exercise of which is being questioned.[17] Thirdly, the Court has narrowed the obligation to provide a remedy to claims of a violation which pass a threshold of 'arguability', a notion which is determined by Convention procedural standards and not by any independent substantive character of Article 13.[18] These developments have been criticised, in some cases roundly,[19] but they seem too well entrenched to be easily abandoned and remedies for the perceived deficiencies must be sought by other strategies. Even with these limitations, Article 13 has an important function, requiring states to provide effective national remedies to test claims that the Convention has been violated. This achieves quicker resolution of disputes and, where a violation is established, allows for a remedy with immediate and wide effect in the national legal system and, in consequence, removes the need for applicants to have to take their cases to Strasbourg.[20]

3. THE REQUIREMENT OF A 'CLAIM' OF A CONVENTION VIOLATION

The wording of the English text of Article 13 could be read as giving it a very narrow meaning indeed: it could require a remedy only where Convention rights 'are violated'. Had this literal interpretation been adopted, no cases would reach Strasbourg against a contracting party that complied fully with Article 13, because they would all have been taken care of in the national legal system. Alternatively, all cases reaching Strasbourg would be a combination of Article 13 claims and claims that another article had been violated and a breach of Article 13 would be found only when a violation of the other article had been established, making the Article 13 obligation of little consequence. However, the literal interpretation was rejected by the Court in *Klass v FRG*[1] in a well known passage:

'. . . Article 13 requires that where an individual considers himself to have been prejudiced by a measure allegedly in breach of the

16 *Klass v FRG* A 28 para 55 (1979).
17 Id, para 72 and *Leander v Sweden* A 116 para 84 (1987). In these cases the Court accepted that remedies against secret surveillance for national security reasons would inevitably be restricted.
18 *Powell and Rayner v UK* A 172 para 33 (1990).
19 Van Dijk and Van Hoof, pp 528-531.
20 But see Thune in Gomien, ed, *Broadening the Frontiers of Human Rights: Essays in Honour of Asbjorn Eide*, 1993, pp 91-92, arguing that Article 13 is 'not a good tool' for ensuring more efficient enforcement of the Convention at the national level, especially compared to incorporation of the Convention in domestic law.
1   A 28 para 64 (1979). The Court's decision was facilitated by the use of the word *'recours'* for 'remedy' in the French text: Raymond, 5 HRR 161 at 165-167 (1980).

Convention, he should have a remedy before a national authority in order both to have his claim decided and, if appropriate, to obtain redress. Thus, Article 13 must be interpreted as guaranteeing an "effective remedy before a national authority" to everyone who *claims* that his rights and freedoms under the Convention have been violated.'

Article 13 thus applies when an applicant claims a violation of the Convention. If an applicant sustains his claim before the national authority, he will have no need to resort to Strasbourg. Even if he loses, he may, in some cases, be persuaded by the reasoning of the national authority that there is little point in making an application to the Commission.

As indicated earlier, Article 13 does not embrace an obligation to give domestic effect to the Convention. Accordingly, where a state has not done that, the individual will not be able to rely on it directly to argue his claim before the national authority. What is required is that he be able to put the substance of his Convention claim to the national decision-maker.[2]

4. AN 'ARGUABLE' CLAIM

The *Klass* case establishes that the applicant must claim that *some* Convention right of his has been violated: there will, for example, be no violation of Article 13 if an applicant alleges a denial of his right to health care or to a passport, no matter how well-founded his claim on the facts, because no Convention right is implicated by the claim. But if a Convention right is asserted, will any claim, no matter how self-evidently misconceived or how patently unsupported by the evidence, give an individual a right to an Article 13 remedy? In *Silver v UK*,[3] the Court held that the Article 13 obligation arises only where the applicant has an 'arguable' claim that he is a victim of a violation of the Convention. 'Arguability' is hardly a self-evident term. From what has already been said, it is less demanding than establishing that a violation has occurred. Thus, in *Leander v Sweden*,[4] the Court accepted that the applicant had had an arguable claim even though the Court was eventually persuaded that no violation of another article had been made out. The question of how much lower the arguability threshold might be is bound up with the Commission's admissibility functions under Article 27. It is obliged by that provision to determine whether an application is 'manifestly ill-founded', which involves taking a position on

2 See *Soering v UK* A 161 para 122 (1989) and *Vilvarajah v UK* A 215 paras 117-127 (1991). Cf Judges Walsh and Russo, dissenting in the *Vilvarajah* case. See also *Council of Civil Service Unions v UK No 11603/85*, 50 DR 228 at 242-243 (1987). In *Warwick v UK No 9471/81*, 60 DR 5 at 18 (1989), the Commission found that there was a breach of Article 13 because the civil court did not apply the criteria of Article 3 to decide if school beating violated the Convention. And see below, p 454.
3 A 61 para 113 (1983). See also *Verein Altenatives Lokalradio, Bern v Switzerland No 10746/84*, 49 DR 126 at 143 (1986).
4 A 116 para 79 (1987).

the legal and/or factual merits of a claim.[5] The Commission had been inclined to hold that some claims of a violation of a substantive article, while manifestly ill-founded in themselves, were, none the less, 'arguable' for the purposes of Article 13. In *Plattform 'Arzte für das Leben' v Austria*,[6] the Commission found the applicant's Article 11 claim was manifestly ill-founded and inadmissible but none the less decided that the claim had been 'arguable', so the allegation that Article 13 had been violated was admissible. The Court has taken a different view. In *Boyle and Rice v UK*,[7] it said that 'it is difficult to conceive how a claim that is "manifestly ill-founded" can nevertheless be "arguable", and *vice versa*.' Subsequently, in *Powell and Rayner v UK*,[8] the Court concluded that the tests of 'arguability' in Article 13 and 'manifestly ill-founded' were the same, when it said:

> 'Article 13 and Article 27(2) are concerned within their respective spheres with the availability of remedies for the enforcement of the same Convention rights and freedoms. The coherence of this dual system of enforcement is at risk of being undermined if Article 13 is interpreted as requiring a national law to make available an "effective remedy" for a grievance classified under Article 27(2) as being so weak as not to warrant examination on its merits at the international level.'

Despite its plausibility, the judgment has been criticised as being based on a misconception of the Commission's practice in examining the admissibility of applications.[9] The Commission, it is argued, does not understand all claims that it considers to be 'manifestly ill-founded' for the purposes of declaring an application inadmissible under Article 27 as ones which are groundless in law or utterly unsustainable on the evidence as the Court appeared to suppose. On the contrary, 'some serious claims might give rise to a *prima facie* issue but, after "full examination" at the admissibility stage, ultimately be rejected as manifestly ill-founded notwithstanding their arguable character'.[10] In such cases, the Commission may decide that an application is inadmissible when '*on balance*'[11] it concludes that there is clearly no violation of the substantive provision. This outcome is possible where the Commission must assess whether a clear interference with a right may be justified under an exception clause. This was the case, for example, in *Powell and Rayner v UK*[12] itself, where the Commission concluded, after a full review of the facts, that failure to respect the right to private life by not

5   See below, pp 627-628.
6   *No 10126/82*, 44 DR 65 (1985). The Court did not deal with this point because it revised the Commission's finding that the claim had been 'arguable': A 139 para 39 (1988).
7   A 131 para 54 (1988).
8   A 172 para 33 (1990).
9   Hampson, 39 ICLQ 891 (1990).
10 *Powell and Rayner v UK* A 172 para 32 (1990). This is the Court's summary of the Commission's position.
11 Hampson, loc cit at n 9 above, p 896. Emphasis added.
12 A 172 para 32 (1990).

controlling aircraft noise was justified under Article 8(2). Similarly, in cases involving complex factual issues the Commission conducts an extensive inquiry as part of the admissibility process which, if the Commission reaches a conclusion adverse to the applicant, will result in the application being declared manifestly ill-founded even though, from the standpoint of Article 13, the claim might be thought to be arguable.[13] However, the Court has gone the other way and equated manifestly ill-foundedness with unarguability.

The Commission itself has generally been strict in regarding manifestly ill-founded claims as not involving claims that are 'arguable' for the purposes of Article 13.[14] This makes all the more remarkable a recent decision that deeply divided the Commission in which it found that an application that it had not rejected as 'manifestedly ill-founded' did *not* involve an 'arguable' claim under Article 13. In *Friedl v Austria*[15] the Commission declared admissible a claim under Article 8(1) but, having examined it on the merits, found that there was no violation. It said, further, that there was no breach of Article 13 because the claim was not 'arguable'. Rather more persuasively, the dissenting Commissioners said:

'. . . when a claim has been declared admissible and, only after detailed consideration, the Commission has found that there was no violation, it cannot be said that such a claim was not "arguable".'

5.   A REMEDY BEFORE A NATIONAL AUTHORITY

The remedy required by Article 13 need not be judicial.[16] In ordinary circumstances, a judicial remedy will satisfy the Convention. However, in the exceptional conditions of the *Greek* case,[17] the Commission conceded the applicants' claims that the courts in post-coup Greece were not independent and impartial and for that reason failed to comply with Article 13. If the national remedy need not be judicial, still less need it satisfy all the criteria of Article 6(1). Such a conclusion would absorb Article 13 within Article 6(1) and would have the effect of making all Convention rights 'civil rights' within its terms, an interpretation rejected by the Court in *Golder v UK*.[18] A variety of non-judicial authorities have been accepted as satisfying Article 13, including parliamentary and executive bodies.[19] It is not the

13 See eg *McCallum v UK* A 183 (1990) Com Rep para 26. In such a case, there may be an 'arguable' view of the facts which ultimately the Commission does not accept.
14 See eg *C Ltd v UK No 14132/88*, 61 DR 285 (1989).
15 A 305-B (1994) Com Rep. F Sett before Court.
16 See eg *Leander v Sweden* A 116 para 77 (1987) and *M and EF v Switzerland No 12573/86*, 51 DR 283 (1987).
17 12 YB (the *Greek* case) 1 at 174 (1969); CM Res DH (70) 1.
18 A 18 para 33 (1975).
19 See eg *Klass v FRG* A 28 para 21 (1979) ('G10 Commission' (parliamentary)) and *Silver v UK* A 61 para 53 (1983) (Home Secretary (executive)).

formal position of the national authority which matters so much as its capacity to provide an effective remedy in fact.[20] However, while the Court is prepared to be flexible in special cases, for instance those involving national security, it is influenced by the judicial model in determining the question of the effectiveness of the remedy.[1]

6.   AN EFFECTIVE REMEDY

Effectiveness has four elements to it, though each may impact on the others: institutional, substantive, remedial and material effectiveness. Effectiveness is to be assessed in relation to the alleged violation of the substantive article and is to be calculated taking into account the cumulation of procedures available in the national law.

i.   The elements of an effective remedy

a.   *Institutional effectiveness*

Institutional effectiveness requires that the decision-maker be 'sufficiently independent'[2] of the authority alleged to be responsible for the violation of the Convention.[3] There is relatively little guidance on this elusive standard in the cases, which have seldom turned on it alone. The fact that the official to whom the appeal lies is under the authority of the body that took the decision does not by itself render a remedy ineffective; it would need to be shown by the applicant that the appeal body simply endorses decisions without making its own independent examination of the facts.[4] In *Silver v UK*,[5] the Court accepted that a right of petition to the Home Secretary against a decision by the prison authorities applying his directives on the censorship of prisoners' correspondence could be an effective remedy. A body which is independent for the purposes of Article 6(1), like Prison Boards of Visitors,[6] would doubtless be independent for the purposes of Article 13 also.

---

20 See eg *Leander v Sweden* A 116 para 81 (1987) ('The Chancellor of Justice . . . may likewise be regarded as being, *at least in practice*, independent of the government . . .' (emphasis added)).

1   A judicial-like process makes it more likely that matters like access, independence, binding and enforceable decisions will be part of the process: see eg *Soering v UK* A 161 (1989) and *Andersson v Sweden (M and R)* A 226 (1992).

2   *Silver v UK* A 61 para 116 (1983).

3   *Leander v Sweden* A 116 para 81 (1987).

4   *M and EF v Switzerland No 12573/86*, 51 DR 283 (1987). *Quaere* whether this approach is consistent with the Court's jurisprudence on the need for justice to be seen to be done: see above, pp 235-237.

5   A 61 para 116 (1983). If the appeal involved a challenge to the legality of his directions, the Home Secretary would not be sufficiently independent since he would in effect be a judge in his own cause: ibid.

6   *Campbell and Fell v UK* A 80 para 81 (1984).

b. Substantive effectiveness

Neither the Convention as a whole nor Article 13 in particular imposes an obligation on states to give direct effect in their national legal systems to the provisions of the Convention.[7] Where a state does choose to do so, the precise Convention point may be raised directly before the national courts. Where a state does not incorporate the Convention into its law, it cannot be maintained that the requirement of substantive effectiveness requires that the Convention point itself be raised before a national authority, for that would result in some kind of direct effect.[8] Rather, it is the possibility of canvassing the substance of the Convention argument which is required as the minimum condition of substantive effectiveness.[9] A provision of national law, which, though narrower than the applicable Convention article, allows the applicant to make the specific argument that he might make at Strasbourg would be sufficient. It should not be assumed that because the Convention has been given some status in domestic law that a violation of Article 13 is impossible. The exact place of the Convention in the domestic hierarchy of laws, matters of standing and justiciability may serve to deny an effective remedy in a particular case.[10] However, the unwillingness of a constitutional tribunal to exercise a discretion to undertake a review of the Convention question will not involve a violation of Article 13.[11]

This matter is of some importance in United Kingdom law. There remains a degree of uncertainty about the extent to which the United Kingdom courts may rely on the Convention.[12] The courts may not challenge the clear words of primary legislation.[13] Where they find that the meaning of legislation or the position at common law is clear, there is no national remedy to test the substance of the claim that the statutory or the common law rule has been applied contrary to the Convention. There is authority that the English courts may hear argument about what the Convention requires when they are required to resolve ambiguities in legislation (Acts of Parliament or delegated legislation) or in the common law.[14] In *Malone v UK*,[15] however, the national judge was not prepared to construct a common law right to privacy which would have allowed the substance of the Convention argument to be decided. The Commission found that the remedies suggested by the government – criminal and civil actions against persons responsible for telephone-tapping not under warrant – did not reach

7 *Ireland v UK* A 25 para 239 (1978).
8 For the view that such an outcome is desirable, see Thune, loc cit at p 446, n 20, above.
9 *Soering v UK* A 161 para 121 (1989).
10 See Polaciewicz and Jacob-Foltzer, 12 HRLJ 65, 125 (1991).
11 *VDSO and Gubi v Austria* A 302 paras 54-55 (1994).
12 For the fullest judicial consideration, see Balcombe LJ in *Derbyshire County Council v Times Newspapers* [1992] 2 All ER 65 at 77-78, CA.
13 Eg *Azam v Home Secretary* [1974] AC 18, HL.
14 On the position in Scotland, see Murdoch, 1991 PL 40.
15 [1979] 2 All ER 620 at 642-644 Ch D (no right to privacy at common law).

the substance of Malone's complaint under the Convention that the interception, which was based on a warrant, violated his Article 8 rights. As a result, Article 13 had been violated.[16] The Court did not decide this question.[17] The approach taken by the Commission had been regarded as the correct one on the Article 13 point but it has now been modified by the Court in *Murray v UK*.[18] The applicant claimed that the taking and retention of photographs of her by the police violated her rights under Article 8 and that she had no means of raising this claim in the domestic court because the police simply relied on the argument that they were not forbidden to do what they had done because it was not prohibited at common law or by statute, exactly the claim of the authorities in *Malone*. However, in contrast to *Malone*, the Court characterised her claim as a challenge to primary legislation, a claim which did not require to be tested by an effective national remedy.[19]

The approach of the English courts may be developing in favour of more receptiveness to arguments based upon the Convention. However, in *R v Secretary of State for the Home Department, ex p Brind*,[20] the House of Lords decided that those invested with ministerial powers under legislation (and the same would apply to prerogative powers) have no obligation to take the Convention into account when exercising a discretion which Parliament has conferred upon them. Accordingly, no action lies in the domestic courts to challenge in judicial review proceedings the exercise of a power on the ground that it is contrary to the Convention. It is, therefore, surprising that the European Court has accepted that the substance of some Convention claims may be brought within the ordinary grounds of judicial review in United Kingdom law so that, with respect to these at least, the possibility of judicial review of an administrative decision will be a substantively effective remedy for the purposes of Article 13. *Soering v UK*[1] is an example. Soering's substantive claim was that the decision of the Home Secretary to extradite him to the United States would violate his rights under Article 3 of the Convention. He claimed that he could not put this argument to the English court to challenge the extradition decision so that there was a violation of Article 13 also. This claim was accepted by the Commission[2] but unanimously rejected by the European Court,[3] which concluded that the argument that the extradition of a person to another jurisdiction where he was likely to suffer treatment in breach of Article 3 was an argument which could have been put to the English court under the

16 *Malone v UK* B 67 (1982) Com Rep, paras 155-157.
17 *Malone v UK* A 82 (1984) (although the conclusion that the interference with the applicant's right was not 'in accordance with the law' points strongly in the direction that there was a breach of Article 13 as well).
18 A 300-A paras 100-101 (1994).
19 Cf paras 39 and 40 of the judgment. See also id, Com Rep, Sir Basil Hall, dissenting in part, para 11. See now *Air Canada v UK* A 316 paras 57-62 (1995).
20 [1991] 1 AC 696, HL.
1 A 161 (1989).
2 Id, Com Rep paras 158-168, especially para 166.
3 Id, paras 116-124 (1989).

'irrationality' head of *Wednesbury* and *GCHQ*.[4] The efficacy of judicial review for the purposes of Article 13 was endorsed by the Court in the similar deportation case of *Vilvarajah v UK*,[5] again in contradiction of the opposite view of the Commission.[6] The domestic cases[7] here were more strongly in point than they had been in *Soering* but, even so, the Court was satisfied with a very limited degree of scrutiny by the national court so long as the substantive argument might have been put to it.[8] It is clear that claims of the disproportionality of official action may not be raised in judicial review proceedings,[9] so, to this extent at least, judicial review would seem to be substantively ineffective for the purposes of Article 13. Some of the uncertainty about the effectiveness of judicial review for the purposes of Article 13 arises because of the way in which *Soering* reached the Court. The British government had not pleaded that the applicant had failed to exhaust local remedies by not applying for judicial review (which he had not done because he thought that it would not be substantively effective) and so there was no argument at the admissibility stage as to what the English courts would have done. As a result, the European Court was free to speculate that the English courts would have heard the substance of Soering's Convention argument.[10] Some help may be on the way if the English courts do accede to the arguments of some judges that they should pay more attention to the Convention in deciding domestic cases.[11] However, full relief will be obtained only if *Brind* is reconsidered by the House of Lords or *Soering* is reconsidered by the European Court. In any event, judicial review can only provide a remedy where the decision-maker has a discretion which is open to review. If the decision-maker and, therefore, the reviewing court is bound by

4 *Associated Provincial Picture Houses v Wednesbury Corpn* [1948] 1 KB 223 and *CCSU v Minister for the Civil Service* [1985] AC 374, HL. The Extradition Act 1989, s.13(6), makes express provision for judicial review of the decision to extradite. The decision of the Commission in *Colman v UK* A 258-D (1993) Com Rep para 47 that judicial review is an effective remedy for freedom of expression cases is even more puzzling.
5 A 215 paras 124-126 (1991). The decision was by 7 to 2.
6 Id, Com Rep paras 114-160. Note that the Commission has not always been willing to accept the effectiveness of judicial review as a remedy for the purposes of local remedies rule in Article 26: see eg *Wingrove v UK No 17419/90*, 76-A DR 26 (1994).
7 Particularly *R v Secretary of State for the Home Department, ex p Bugdaycay* [1987] 1 All ER 940.
8 The applicants in *Vilvarajah* had sought judicial review of the decision to deport them but the decision had been upheld: *R v Home Secretary, ex p Sivakamuran* [1988] 1 All ER 193. It seems likely also that judicial review does not operate uniformly across Convention rights: *Soering* and *Vilvarajah* concerned Articles 2 and 3; *Brind*, where the relevance of the Convention argument was denied, concerned Article 10.
9 *R v Secretary of State for the Home Dept, ex p Brind* [1991] 1 AC 696, HL, per Lord Ackner. If other judges were more sympathetic to the introduction in the future of proportionality as a discrete head of review, they did not undermine Lord Ackner's specific conclusion. However, note Craig, *Administrative Law*, 3rd edn, 1994, p 421 predicting that it is 'highly likely' that proportionality will be recognised as an independent ground of review.
10 For the admissibility decision, see 58 DR 219 (1988). The fact that the British government did not argue that Soering had failed to exhaust domestic remedies by not seeking judicial review suggests that it was of the view that judicial review would not have been effective.
11 Lord Bingham MR, 109 LQR 390 (1993) and Lord Browne-Wilkinson, 1992 PL 397.

a rule of law on the matter in dispute, then judicial review is not a substantively effective remedy. If, in that situation, there is no alternative avenue through which the issue may be pursued, there will be a breach of Article 13.

As with judicial review, the Court has also been more willing than the Commission to accept that Convention arguments might be substantively effective in civil actions in the English courts. In *Costello-Roberts v UK*,[12] the Commission found that the applicant had an arguable claim that Article 3 had been violated, even though it reached the conclusion ultimately that there had been no violation. It held that there had been a violation of Article 8. In respect of each claim, there was no substantively effective national remedy as required by Article 13. However, the Court's judgment (which found no violation of Articles 3 or 8) very much dilutes the requirement of substantive effectiveness. It refers only to the possibility of the remedial effectiveness of the civil action, not whether the substance of the Convention arguments would be properly considered by the English court. It attached great importance to the fact that the standard of English law was one of 'reasonable' chastisement and said that 'it is not for the Court to speculate as to what decision the English courts would have reached'.[13]

In the *Costello-Roberts* case and in *Y v UK*,[14] the Commission followed its decision in *Warwick v UK*[15] and held that a civil action offered no realistic hope of success to a plaintiff seeking to challenge school beatings as being contrary to Article 3. What is remarkable is that *Warwick*, *Y* and *Costello-Roberts* were all declared admissible by the Commission in the face of the government's arguments that local remedies had not been exhausted because the Commission was of the view that the actions had no hope of success.[16]

c.   Remedial effectiveness

It is not necessary that an individual obtain a favourable decision on the substance of his Convention claim for Article 13 to be complied with. What is required is that if the applicant's substantive arguments are accepted by the national authority, it will be in a position to grant him a remedy.[17] In *Murray v UK*,[18] the Court said that the 'feeble prospects of success' on the facts of the case did not detract from the effectiveness of a remedy which could, on stronger facts, have afforded the applicant relief. The prospect of a wholly discretionary response, either from the national authority or by another national decision-maker to the national authority's decision, will

---

12 A 247-C (1993) Com Rep para 59.
13 A 247-C para 40 (1993). The Court found that there was no arguable claim that *any* beating was contrary to English law, para 39.
14 A 247-A (1992) Com Rep para 56.
15 *No 9471/81*, 60 DR 5 (1989); CM Res DH (89) 5.
16 See eg *Warwick v UK*, 36 DR 49 (1983).
17 *Soering v UK* A 161 para 120 (1989) and *Council of Civil Service Unions v UK No 11603/85*, 50 DR 228, 243 (1987).
18 A 300-A para 100 (1994).

not be enough to satisfy the requirement of remedial effectiveness.[19] But the practice on this matter is not quite so simple. A judicial discretion will not undermine the effectiveness of proceedings before a court, as those judgments of the Court accepting the adequacy of judicial review show.[20] However, a remedy by dint of the exercise of political discretion will not suffice. For this reason, a petition to the Home Secretary by prisoners contesting the compatibility of Prison Rules with the Convention, rules made by him and amendable by him but only in the discharge of his political function, was not an effective remedy.[1] Bodies whose powers are limited to advising the ultimate decision-maker do not offer a remedially effective remedy for the purposes of Article 13:[2] some element of enforceability is generally required.[3] Yet in some cases the Court has been prepared to say that a consistent, even if not formally mandatory, practice of national bodies responding to the decisions of a national authority does constitute an adequate guarantee of remedial effectiveness.[4]

There are circumstances (eg deportation or extradition) where an individual will require some interim relief while his Article 13 remedy is being pursued.[5] In *Soering*, the applicant argued that judicial review was not an adequate remedy for the purposes of Article 13, even if it might ultimately have led to the decision to extradite him being quashed, because the absence of interim relief against the Crown meant that the Secretary of State might have ordered his removal before the hearings had been completed. The European Court responded:

'. . . there is no suggestion that in practice a fugitive would ever be surrendered before his application to the Divisional Court and any eventual appeal therefrom had been determined.'[6]

19 Eg an English prisoner's right of complaint to the Parliamentary Commissioner was not remedially effective because a finding in the prisoner's favour was merely reported to an individual Member of Parliament or, exceptionally, to Parliament as a whole: *Silver v UK* A 61 paras 54, 115 (1983) and *Campbell and Fell v UK* A 80 paras 51, 126 (1984).
20 *Vilvarajah v UK* A 215 para 126 (1991).
1 *Silver v UK* A 61 para 116 (1983). See also *Malone v UK* A 82 (1984) Com Rep para 156, where the Commission was not satisfied that the power of a judge to act on his own initiative and to report to the Prime Minister about possible misuse of powers to intercept telephone calls was, by reason of the judge's status, remedially effective.
2 Eg the Unit Review Board and the Standing Committee on Difficult Prisoners: *McCallum v UK* A 183 (1990) Com Rep para 80.
3 Eg Prison Boards of Visitors: *Silver v UK* A 61 para 116 (1983).
4 In *Leander v Sweden* A 116 para 82 (1987) the Court conceded that neither the Ombudsman nor the Chancellor of Justice could make a binding decision but that their opinions 'command by tradition great respect in Swedish society and in practice are usually followed', para 82. In *Klass v FRG* A 28 para 71 (1979), the Court included an action for a declaration among the national remedies which satisfied Article 13.
5 Eg *Cruz Varas v Sweden* A 201 (1991).
6 *Soering v UK* A 161 para 123 (1989). See also *Vilvarajah v UK* A 215 para 153 (1991). Note that the Commission has no power to make binding interim orders under Rule 36 of its Rules of Procedure and that no right to interim protection may be found in Article 25: see the *Cruz Varas* case, above, para 102.

There remains, then, a good deal of uncertainty as to how far a consistent practice of compliance may compensate for the non-mandatory quality of the national decision. If an applicant gains his non-binding remedy in the national legal system but it is not, despite past practice, complied with, that ought to be a demonstration that the national remedy is not remedially effective and enable him to establish a breach of Article 13. His position should be even stronger where he alleges that the breach of the Convention will result in irreparable damage, usually because of his removal from the jurisdiction of a Convention state. Then the need for the national remedy to be binding and suspensive should be seen as elements of its remedial effectiveness.[7] Where the 'practice' argument has been accepted by the Court in respect of compliance with the opinions of non-judicial bodies, it has been in cases where the Court has taken a narrow view of what Article 13 requires in the light of its understanding of what substantive violation is alleged.[8]

d.   Material effectiveness

It is not enough that an effective remedy is available in the national legal system. The applicant must be able to take effective advantage of it. The principle in the *Airey* case that rights in the Convention must be effective and not theoretical applies here. The issue arose in *Andersson (M and R) v Sweden*.[9] The applicants were mother and son who claimed that the removal of the child to public care and the conditions of the care violated Article 8. Although there were remedies available in Swedish law to challenge the decisions, the child could take advantage of them only through his guardian, his mother. It was argued that the conditions of the separation of mother from child made it impossible for her to take effective action to protect the child's rights. By a narrow majority (5 to 4), the Court found that the claim was not made out on the facts. The principle is an important one for vulnerable or isolated individuals, such as prisoners and mental patients. In *Vilvarajah v UK*, the Commission decided that an appeal on the merits against the refusal of asylum which could be exercised only after the individual had left the United Kingdom (which usually, as in this case, would mean that he had been returned to the state from which he was fleeing) was not an effective remedy to test a claim that return would violate Article 3, however viable it might be in the abstract.[10] The Court did not address this point because it had already decided that judicial review was an adequate remedy satisfying the terms of Article 13 and that an individual would not be removed during the judicial review process.[11]

---

7   Such an interpretation of Article 13 would go some way to repairing the interpretation of Article 25 in the *Cruz Varas* case; this Article 13 claim was not put to the Commission.
8   Eg *Leander v Sweden* A 116 para 84 (1987).
9   A 226 paras 98-103 (1992).
10 A 215 (1991) Com Rep para 153. In *Re M* [1993] 3 All ER 537, where a refugee-applicant had been removed despite assurances given to the court that he would not be, the House of Lords held that there was a power to issue injunctions, even against Ministers, to prevent this.
11 A 215 para 125 (1991).

e. Effectiveness based on the cumulation of remedies in the national system

In *Silver v UK*,[12] the Court said that the cumulation of possible channels of redress in the national legal system must be taken into account when deciding whether an applicant has an effective remedy for the purposes of Article 13, rather than examining any or each procedure in isolation. In either of two senses, this proposition is unproblematic. Firstly, where an appeal lies to a sufficiently independent body from the decisions of one which is not independent, then the applicant must use this opportunity, which will satisfy Article 13.[13] Secondly, where an applicant makes different kinds of complaint, the national remedies must be effective with respect to each kind. So in *Silver v UK*,[14] the Court distinguished between complaints about the application of the Prison Rules (was it within the Rules to stop this letter?), for which the possibility of a petition to the Home Secretary was an effective remedy, and complaints about the Rules themselves (was a Rule which authorises the stopping of letters to a legal adviser about litigation compatible with the Convention?), in which case a petition to the Minister was not effective because he was not sufficiently detached to review his own rule-making.

However, a problem arises with the Court's assertion in the *Silver* case that an aggregation of remedies might together be an effective remedy for a single complaint, even though none would be if taken on its own and none can be seen as appeal from another. In that case, the Court assessed four possible remedies: application to the Board of Visitors; application to the Parliamentary Commissioner for Administration; petition to the Home Secretary; and application to the courts for judicial review. It concluded that 'the aggregate of remedies available' was sufficient to satisfy Article 13 where the complaint concerned the application of the Prison Rules rather than the Rules themselves. However, the Court had decided already that applications to the Board of Visitors and the Parliamentary Commissioner were not effective remedies because, *inter alia*, they could not give decisions binding on the prison authorities. On the other hand, a petition to the Minister was effective because it held out the possibility of a reversal of a lower level decision in the application of the Rules. Although the judgment refers to the cumulation of remedies, in fact, it appears one of them (petition to the Home Secretary) by itself was effective in that case; it met the requirements of Article 13, compliance with which did not depend in any way on the availability of the others.[15]

The dangers of the Court's approach were made apparent in *Leander v Sweden*.[16] Again, four remedies in the national legal system were indicated

---

12 A 61 para 118 (1983).
13 Eg the possibility referred to in *Klass v FRG* A 28 para 70 (1979) of raising some questions before the Constitutional Court.
14 A 61 para 118 (1983). See also *Lithgow v UK* A 102 paras 206-207 (1986), where the Court talks about 'aggregate' remedies, when what was involved was different remedies for different claims.
15 A 61 para 116 (1983).
16 A 116 paras 80-82 (1987).

by the Swedish government: appeal to the government from refusal to appoint to the post; request to the National Police Board for access to its secret register, with appeal to the courts in the event of refusal; complaint to the Chancellor of Justice; and complaint to the Ombudsman. The majority inclined to the view that the last two might have been effective remedies, even though neither the Chancellor nor the Ombudsman could give a binding decision, but held that, in any event, appeal to the government was capable of providing a remedy. In language similar to that in the *Silver* case, the Court said:

> 'Even if, taken on its own, the complaint to the government was not considered sufficient to ensure compliance with Article 13, the Court finds that the aggregate of the remedies . . . satisfies the conditions of Article 13 in the particular circumstances of the instant case . . .'[17]

It is not made clear how each of the remedies reinforces any other. If any of them individually was adequate to satisfy Article 13, then no reference need be made to the others. On the other hand, if none of them individually were sufficient, as the dissenting judges thought, and none were appeals from another, then aggregating the series of inadequate measures would not be satisfactory to an applicant in the absence of an explanation of how the deficiencies of one were made up by the advantages of another, which the Court did not give.[18] Until the Court is able to demonstrate the effective operation of the aggregation approach in an actual case, a degree of caution is appropriate in assessing a government's claim that this is the case.

ii. Limitations on the effectiveness principle

a. Primary legislation

If Article 13 required that a national remedy be available to determine a claim that statutory law violated the Convention, it would practically amount to a demand that the Convention be incorporated into the national legal order. The only alternative would be the establishment of a national system of judicial review by which national legislation could be struck down under a constitutional bill of rights.[19] In principle, there is no reason why Article 13 should not be interpreted in this way but there is a long and well established practice to the contrary. In *Leander v Sweden*,[20] the Court said:

---

17 Id, para 84.
18 For further comment, see Drzemczewski and Warbrick 7 YEL 364-367 (1987).
19 Eg *Klass v FRG* A 28 para 66 (1979).
20 A 116 para 77 (1987). See also *James v UK* A 98 para 85 (1986). In *Young, James and Webster v UK* A 44 (1981) Com Rep para 177, the Commission explained this limitation by reference to the text of Article 13, somewhat unconvincingly. Cf Messrs Opsahl and Trechsel, dissenting.

'Article 13 does not guarantee a remedy allowing a contracting state's laws as such to be challenged before a national authority on the ground of being contrary to the Convention or equivalent domestic norms.'

This puts some importance on determining what are 'laws as such'. While primary legislation is obviously included, in *Abdulaziz, Cabales and Balkandali v UK*,[1] the British government argued that the Immigration Rules, which are *sui generis* as a form of legislation[2], were covered by the *Leander* principle. The Court rejected this argument, even though the result of its judgment was that the Rules themselves were incompatible with the Convention. Since there was no domestic channel for testing the applicant's claim that the Rules were incompatible with the Convention, there had been a breach of Article 13 also. Given that the general principle of the non-applicability of Article 13 to legislation is an anomaly in the Convention scheme, this approach of the Court in narrowing its impact by reference to the formal status of the legislation can be justified. The Commission has held also that Article 13 does not require a remedy against a decision of the final court in the national system.[3]

b. The 'special' nature of the right in issue

In *Klass v FRG*,[4] the Court held as compatible with Article 8 of the Convention a German law allowing secret surveillance of individuals by the state, naturally without prior notification to the target but sometimes even without *ex post facto* notification. The applicants maintained that unless persons were told that their telephone calls had been intercepted, then they had no opportunity to challenge the surveillance as being contrary to their Convention rights and, accordingly, that there had been a breach of Article 13. Since there could be *no* remedy, *a fortiori* there could not be an effective one. If this argument had prevailed, there would have been an incompatibility with the decision under Article 8. The Court avoided this by saying:

'. . . an effective remedy under Article 13 must mean a remedy that is as effective as can be having regard to the restricted scope for recourse inherent in any system of secret surveillance.'[5]

The Court held on the facts that Article 13 was satisfied. In cases where there was later notification, the individual could go to the courts in the ordinary way. Where there was no notification, the process was supervised

1   A 94 paras 92-93 (1985).
2   *R v Secretary of State for the Home Department, ex p Hosenball* [1977] 1 WLR 766. See Evans, *Immigration Law*, 2nd edn, 1983, pp 399-407.
3   *Crocianietal v Italy Nos 8603, 8722, 8723, 8729/79*, 22 DR 147 at 223-4 (1981); *Verein Alternatives Lokalradio, Bern v Switzerland No 10746/84*, 49 DR 126 at 142 (1986).
4   A 28 para 58 (1979).
5   Id, para 69.

by an independent committee, which was, in the circumstances, the best that could be done. The Court found for the defendant state in much the same terms as in *Leander v Sweden*,[6] where the applicant was unable to gain access to secret information which he might have wished to challenge. Again, in circumstances involving the protection of national security, the Court held that Article 13 could not guarantee a right to a remedy which undermined a state's rights to take action established elsewhere under the Convention.[7] While the impact of this approach is limited because there is only a narrow range of situations where there will be a need to rely on wholly secret processes, given the seriousness of what is at stake, the Court's conclusions are strong confirmations of the subsidiary character of the Article 13 obligation.[8] The Convention must be interpreted as a whole: other provisions of the Convention may limit what is required of a state under Article 13 but there are no indications that Article 13 may be used to improve the lot of individuals in the exercise of their substantive rights.[9]

7. THE 'STATE ACTION' PROBLEM

Article 13 imposes an obligation to provide a remedy 'notwithstanding that the violation has been committed by persons acting in an official capacity'. It has been argued that this wording acknowledges that there may be violations of Convention rights by individuals, with respect to which the state has an obligation under Article 13 to provide an effective national remedy.[10] The alternative is to read the words as denying effect to national laws which provide immunity to public officials or the state for some wrongful acts.[11] The first alternative would go beyond the possibility of indirect responsibility of the state arising out of positive duties to take action to prevent violations by individuals of the human rights of others. It would be of particular importance where the Convention has been given the force of domestic law and cases could, therefore, arise between individuals.[12] To reach the conclusion that this was required by the Convention in all cases[13] (as distinct from being a choice made by the domestic court) would mean

---

6 A 116 para 59 (1987).
7 Id, paras 80-84. The UK has taken advantage of this in the Interception of Communications Act 1985, s 7, the Security Service Act 1989, s 5 and the Intelligence Services Act 1994, s 9. In *Esbester v UK No 18601/91* (1993), 18 EHRR CD 72 (1994), the Commission held that the remedial provisions of the Security Services Act satisfied Article 8(2) and that there was no 'arguable' claim requiring a further Article 13 remedy. See also *Christie v UK No 21482/93*, 78-A DR 119 (1994), to the same effect about the Interception of Communications Act 1985.
8 For criticism of this line of case-law, see Van Dijk and Van Hoof, pp 528-531.
9 Another example is that Article 13 cannot be used to give a right of appeal not otherwise required by another provision (here, Article 6(1)): *Z and E v Austria No 10153/82*, 49 DR 67, 74 (1986).
10 See Clapham, *Human Rights in the Private Sphere*, 1993, pp 240-244.
11 See Raymond, loc cit at p 446, n 1, above, pp 168-170.
12 See above, p 21.
13 This position is strongly pressed by Clapham, loc cit at n 10 above, p 243, n 198.

resolving the still open-ended question of the third-party effect of the Convention. As an aspect of the subsidiary character of Article 13, it is better that its interpretation should follow the interpretation of the substantive obligations under the Convention: only where they impose a positive obligation on a state with respect to private action should the state be obliged to provide a remedy under Article 13. Only if its positive obligation is extended to providing a private law remedy should it be obliged by Article 13 to provide an effective remedy between individuals.[14]

8. CONCLUSION

Article 13 is of autonomous but subsidiary character. While a breach of Article 13 does not depend on establishing a breach of another article, what the obligations of a state are under Article 13 can be established only by taking the exact nature of each Convention claim into consideration. None the less, this does not reduce the importance of Article 13 in securing cooperation between national legal systems and the Convention regime. The more effective and embracing the scheme of national remedies, particularly if the national authorities are sensitive to the developments in the Convention case-law, the more likely it is that Convention cases may be decided without recourse to the Strasbourg authorities. This is, after all, one of the primary goals of the Convention system and it is, therefore, surprising that the Court has not been more consistent in interpreting Article 13 in a way which enhances the effectiveness of national remedies. The most effective cooperation is the incorporation of the terms of the Convention into national law but Article 13 has not been read to impose an obligation to do this on contracting states. Where all public power derives from specific rules of law and where its exercise may be challenged in national courts, then Article 13 may be readily satisfied. For the United Kingdom, the non-implementation of the Convention in its national law, its limited indirect effect therein and the discretionary or residuary nature of much public power combined with relatively unintrusive judicial control, mean that Article 13 has a particularly important role to play.[15] It is not surprising that so many of the cases on Article 13 originate from the United Kingdom.

14 Eg *X and Y v Netherlands* A 91 (1985) (obligation to provide a criminal remedy) and *Gaskin v UK* A 160 (1989) (obligation to provide an administrative remedy). There ought to be an Article 13 procedure to test whether there is an arguable claim that there is a right to a discrete remedy like these.
15 Which is not to say that the English courts might not do better, Warbrick, 19 ELR 34 (1994).

CHAPTER 15

Article 14: Freedom from discrimination in respect of protected rights

'**Article 14**
The enjoyment of the rights and freedoms set forth in this Convention shall be secured without discrimination on any ground such as sex, race, colour, language, religion, political or other opinion, national or social origin, association with a national minority, property, birth or other status.'

Protection against discrimination and the promotion of equality have been prominent items in the international human rights agenda.[1] The UN Charter makes the promotion and encouragement of respect for human rights 'without distinction as to race, sex, language or religion' one of the purposes of the organisation.[2] The International Covenants have elaborate provisions dealing with non-discrimination and equality[3] and the UN has sponsored international agreements aimed at protecting against discrimination on specific grounds.[4] The increasingly detailed regulation of the subject at the international level is not only an acknowledgement of its importance but reflects the experience of national legal systems that the complexity of non-discrimination and equality as legal ideas requires special attention to be given to them if the values they embody are to be protected effectively.[5]

Non-discrimination does not have the same, specific, foundational designation in the Statute of the Council of Europe or Preamble to the Convention as it does in the UN Charter. Nor is there an equivalent to

---

1 See Lauren, *Power and Prejudice: the Politics and Diplomacy of Racial Discrimination*, 1988, pp 135-165, 233-267; McKean, *Equality and Discrimination under International Law*, 1983; and Bayefsky, 11 HRLJ 1 (1990).

2 UN Charter, Article 1(3).

3 See Ramcharan, Sohn, in Henkin, ed, *The International Bill of Rights: the Covenant on Civil and Political Rights*, 1981, Chs 10 and 11 respectively; and McGoldrick, *The Human Rights Committee*, 1991, pp 163-166, 282-285.

4 International Convention on the Elimination of All Forms of Racial Discrimination 1966, 60 UNTS 195; UKTS 77 (1969), Cmnd 4108 and the International Convention on the Elimination of Discrimination against Women 1979, UKTS 2 (1989), Cm 643. See Meron, *Human Rights and Law-making in the United Nations*, 1986, p 5.

5 For the UK, see McCrudden, in McCrudden and Chambers, eds, *Individual Rights and the Law in Britain*, 1994, pp 409-455.

Article 26 of the ICCPR, which provides comprehensive protection against discrimination in all those activities which the state chooses to regulate by law.[6] Instead, the reach of Article 14 of the Convention[7] is restricted to protecting persons against discrimination only with respect to the rights and freedoms set out elsewhere in the Convention:[8] it is thus a parasitic provision and not a general proscription against every kind of discrimination. However, as some compensation, the list of specific grounds on the basis of which discrimination in the area of a Convention right is prohibited is a long one and not exhaustive. The grounds on the list are examples ('any ground such as . . .') and the final one ('or other status') is open-ended.

What is understood by 'discrimination' is not explicated in Article 14. It should be noted, however, that it protects against discrimination rather than promoting equality. While it is sometimes said that non-discrimination and equality are simply different ways of expressing the same idea,[9] the obligation of equal protection carries more readily the notion of positive obligations than does that of non-discrimination. While this may appear to be of less consequence under the Convention because the existence of a positive obligation will primarily be determined by the substantive provision within the ambit of which the unlawful differentiation has taken place, the interpretation of what Article 14 requires may be influenced by the standard of non-discrimination/equal protection which is to be applied. 'Discrimination' is not to be equated with mere 'differentiation', despite the language of the French text of Article 14 which reads '*sans distinction aucune*'. Different treatment of persons in similar situations may be justified by the state and, therefore, not be forbidden by Article 14. This includes the possibility of states taking positive measures, ie providing advantages for members of a group to deal with factual inequalities between them and others.[10] The practice of the Court and Commission can best be explained by considering each of the elements in Article 14 separately. They have an impact on each other and must be approached together when considering a particular case.

The case in which the Court set out most clearly its approach to Article 14 is *Rasmussen v Denmark*.[11] There a husband complained that the fact that he was subject to time-limits to contest the paternity of a child born during the marriage whereas his wife could institute paternity proceedings at any time

6 Article 26 reads: 'All persons are equal before the law and are entitled without any discrimination to the equal protection of the law. In this respect, the law shall prohibit any discrimination and guarantee to all persons equal and effective protection against discrimination on any ground such as race, colour, sex, language, religion, political or other opinion, national or social origin, property, birth or other status.' For the case-law, see McGoldrick, loc cit at n 3, pp 163-166.
7 On Article 14 generally, see Partsch, *European Supervision*, Ch 23.
8 Those Protocols to the Convention which contain new substantive rights all provide that they shall be regarded as additional rights to the Convention itself and, accordingly, persons are protected by Article 14 in the enjoyment of them: Article 5, First Protocol; Article 6(1), Fourth Protocol; Article 6, Sixth Protocol; Article 7(1), Seventh Protocol.
9 Bayefsky, loc cit at n 1 above, pp 1-2.
10 See below, pp 485-486.
11 A 87 (1984).

was a violation of the Convention as a breach of Article 14 in combination with Articles 6 and 8. The Court decided that:

1. the allegations of violation of Article 14 fell 'within the ambit' of Articles 6 and 8;
2. there was a difference of treatment between a husband and a wife (and, since the list of categories of discrimination in Article 14 was not exhaustive, it was not necessary to determine the basis for this different treatment);
3. it was not necessary in this case to decide whether the husband and the wife were in 'analogous situations', though it proceeded on the assumption that they were; and
4. there was an 'objective and reasonable' justification for the difference in treatment of individuals in analogous positions, relying on the Danish state's margin of appreciation: in particular, the discrimination was proportionate to the legislator's aims of ensuring legal certainty and protecting the interests of the child, a conclusion reinforced by the absence of 'common [European] ground' as to how paternity proceedings should be regulated.

As a result, the Court decided in the *Rasmussen* case that there was no violation of the Convention.

1. THE RELATION BETWEEN THE OBLIGATION OF NON-DISCRIMINATION AND THE ENJOYMENT OF THE RIGHTS AND FREEDOMS IN THE CONVENTION

Article 14 imposes an obligation on states to secure the non-discriminatory enjoyment of the rights and freedoms protected by the Convention. Where a right falls outside the Convention, such as the right of access to civil service employment,[12] a state has no obligation to avoid discrimination. In practice, this is a significant restriction because a great deal of discrimination law is concerned with the enjoyment of economic and social rights, such as rights to employment or to pay and working conditions or to housing, none of which are concerns of the European Convention on Human Rights.[13] Some provisions of the Convention have 'equality' obligations[14] built into them and the Strasbourg authorities have shown an inclination to subsume allegations of discrimination into the obligation of the state under the

---

12 *Glasenapp v FRG* A 104 para 53 (1986) and *Kosiek v FRG* A 105 para 39 (1986).
13 Such rights are protected by the European Social Charter, which has a non-discrimination provision in its Preamble. See also Additional Protocol to the European Social Charter, Article 1 (Right to equal opportunities and equal treatment in matters of employment and occupation without discrimination on the grounds of sex). Article 8 of the Convention has some application to housing.
14 Eg Article 5, Seventh Protocol.

substantive standard.[15] The Commission has considered some incidents of discrimination as elements in deciding whether there has been a breach of Article 3.[16] However, Article 16 and, by implication, Article 17 allow discrimination.[17]

There are several possible approaches which the Strasbourg authorities might have taken about the relationship between Article 14 and the substantive provisions of the Convention and the Protocols. They have rejected the claim that there can be no violation of Article 14 *unless* there is a violation of another article as leaving no practical function for Article 14.[18] Accordingly, an applicant may establish a violation of Article 14, *even though* he cannot show or does not even claim a violation of another article. In the latter case, the applicant's claim is of discrimination alone. *Inze v Austria*[19] is an example. The applicant did not allege that his rights under Article 1 of the First Protocol had been infringed by an Austrian law affecting succession to 'hereditary' farms, which was designed to preserve farms as economically viable units. He did argue that the Austrian law which gave priority to legitimate over illegitimate heirs as to who should succeed to an entire farm was a violation of Article 14 in combination with Article 1 of the First Protocol. The test, the Court said, was not whether Article 1 of the First Protocol had been violated but whether the applicant's claim fell within its 'ambit'.[20] There was a dispute about this: the government argued that Inze was seeking a right *to acquire* possessions (which Article 1 of the First Protocol does not protect); the applicant said that he was already the co-owner of a yet undivided share in the estate, his complaint being that he was discriminated against in obtaining the exclusive right to one part of it, the hereditary farm. The Court agreed with the applicant and found that his Article 14 complaint could properly be brought because it fell within the ambit of Article 1 of the First Protocol.[1]

As the *Inze* case indicates, for an Article 14 claim to succeed, there will sometimes be scope for argument as to whether a claim falls within the ambit of another provision. One source of doubt, though not strictly an 'ambit' issue, has been cleared up. Article 14 extends not only to those elements of a right that a state is obliged by the Convention to guarantee, but also those other elements of the right that it chooses to guarantee and

15 *Mathieu-Mohin and Clerfayt v Belgium* A 113 paras 58-59 (1987); *Tete v France No 11123/84*, 54 DR 52 (1987); and *Airey v Ireland* A 32 (1980), on which see below, p 473.
16 See above, pp 81-82.
17 See below, pp 508-509 and 512.
18 *Belgian Linguistic* case B 3 Com Rep para 400 (1965). Cf the Court judgment in A 6 (1968).
19 A 126 (1987).
20 Id, para 36. See also *Van der Mussele v Belgium* A 70 para 43 (1983).
1   *Inze v Austria* A 126 paras 43-45 (1987). Cf *Kleine Staarman v Netherlands No 10503/83*, 42 DR 162 (1985) and *Vos v Netherlands No 10971/84*, 43 DR 190 (1985), deciding on a close examination of the national law that pensions were not possessions. Since they did not come within the 'ambit' of Article 1 of the First Protocol, no Article 14 question could arise. See also *Claes v Belgium No 11285/84*, 54 DR 88 (1987). Identifying the Article within the ambit of which a claim falls may not be easy: see *Darby v Sweden* A 187 (1990) (Commission deciding it was Article 9 and Court deciding it was Article 1, First Protocol).

which are thereby subject to Convention control.[2] Thus in the *Belgian Linguistics* case[3] one of the complaints was about the right of access to language-based state education. The Convention does not require a state to provide *any* system of education but, if it does, it may not restrict access to it on a discriminatory basis.[4] Similarly, in *Abdulaziz, Cabales and Balkandali v UK*,[5] the United Kingdom allowed resident, alien husbands who had a right to remain to be joined by their wives, even though the women had no independent right to stay. There was no obligation on the United Kingdom under the Convention to allow them to do so. The same privilege was not given to resident, alien women to have their husbands join them. The Court considered that the question fell within the ambit of the right to respect for family life and that it could assess whether the differential treatment was discriminatory. In contrast, in *Family K and W v Netherlands*,[6] the Netherlands allowed the alien wives, but not husbands, of Dutch citizens to obtain Dutch nationality. Although the distinction was important in that a spouse who had Dutch nationality could not be separated from his or her family by expulsion, the Commission held that Article 14 did not apply because the case concerned the right to nationality, which was not a Convention right. The 'ambit' test, for all its uncertainty, ensures that there is an independent basis for Article 14, regardless of whether there is an associated violation of another, substantive Article.

In its early decisions, when the Commission was searching for a practical role for Article 14, it suggested that there was a distinct place for Article 14 where a state exercised a power to limit its primary obligations.[7] While a state's power to interfere with an individual's rights might satisfy, say, Article 11(2) because it could demonstrate a 'pressing social need' for the action it had taken, if that action had been taken on a discriminatory basis, then it could, independently, violate Article 14. Consider *Christians against Racism and Fascism v UK*.[8] The applicants argued that their right of freedom of assembly had been violated by a ban imposed on their marches. The Commission held that the ban was necessary to protect public order and so satisfied Article 11(2). The applicants contended further that some other marches had not been subject to the same regulation. Consequently, that was a breach of Article 14. The Commission held that there were rational grounds for distinguishing between the marches so that Article 14 had not been violated. But suppose the decision had been that the other marches posed an identical threat to public order to that arising out of the applicant's demonstrations? It is difficult to imagine an objective and rational justification for prohibiting some of these marches but not others. As

---

2 See *Delcourt v Belgium*, above, p 240.
3 A 6 para 9 (1968).
4 Ibid.
5 A 94 paras 65, 71-72 (1985). Judge Fitzmaurice, dissenting, paras 23-26, in *Marckx v Belgium* A 31 (1979), warned against too ready a conclusion that another right is implicated.
6 *No 11278/84*, 43 DR 216 (1985).
7 *Belgian Linguistic* case B 3 para 400 (1965).
8 *No 8440/78*, 21 DR 138 (1980).

against the applicants, this would constitute a violation of Article 14 (but not of Article 11). The state would have a choice of means in putting the situation right – it might tolerate threats to public order from both or it might prohibit both but its obligation under Article 14 would exclude banning one set of marches and tolerating the other. It can be anticipated that the state would argue that the situations were not analogous, the difference between them being such that it was not necessary to move against activities other than those of the applicants.[9]

The requirement of a rational basis for differential treatment which, as will be seen, is the approach the Court takes under Article 14, is very close to the test of a 'pressing social need' under Articles 8(2)–11(2).[10] In *Rasmussen v Denmark*,[11] the government's arguments that there was an objective and reasonable justification for the different treatment of husband and wife could equally have been put under Article 6(1) (whether the positive obligation to assure effective access to a tribunal had been satisfied) and Article 8(2) (whether the action was necessary to protect the rights of others, the mother and the child). This is not the case with other limitation provisions in the Convention. Article 12 protects the right to marry 'according to the national law'. The Strasbourg authorities have conceded a wide margin of appreciation to states in deciding what their law should be. Similarly, the protection of the right to the enjoyment of one's possessions in Article 1 of the First Protocol is subject to 'the right of a state to enforce such laws as it deems necessary to control the use of property . . .'. Again, the review function under the Convention is subject to a wide margin of appreciation in the states to determine what laws are necessary. The burden on a state to justify its laws under Article 12 and Article 1 of the First Protocol, is less than the need to show an objective and reasonable justification for differential treatment under Article 14. For matters which fall within the ambit of Article 12 or Article 1 of the First Protocol, a national law which subjects members of different groups to different regimes must satisfy the objective and rational justification test: for example, a law which forbids miscegenous, or inter-racial, unions[12] or which singles out one property developer from a group of them for unfavourable treatment will violate Article 14 in conjunction with Article 12 or Article 1 of the First Protocol, even if it does not violate them standing alone.[13] While it might be argued that it can never be 'necessary to control the use of property' in a discriminatory way, just as it could be argued that it can never be 'necessary

---

9   Id, at pp 151-152. Note also Judge Thór Vilhjálmsson, concurring in the *Fredin v Sweden* A 192 (1991), conceding a wide margin of appreciation to states in making such decisions.
10 See below, pp 476-483.
11 A 87 para 39 (1984). In *W v FRG No 11564/85*, 45 DR 291 (1985) the Commission held that because the denial of legal aid had not been unreasonable under Article 6(1), it could not be discriminatory under Article 14.
12 Cf *Johnston v Ireland* A 112 (1986), below, pp 473-474. Note that such an egregious rule might be regarded as precluded by Article 12 alone: see *Hamer v UK No 7114/75*, 24 DR 5 (1979) Com Rep; CM Res DH 81(5).
13 *Pine Valley Developments Ltd v Ireland* A 222 paras 61-64 (1991).

in a democratic society' to interfere in a discriminatory way with protected rights in Articles 8–11, cases like *Pine Valley* show that the Court is disinclined to collapse the two inquiries into one.

The Court has rejected the claim that there can be no violation of Article 14 *if* there is a breach of another article. If Article 14 were to be interpreted in this way, the effect would be always to elevate the substantive violation above any allegation of discrimination. Experience has shown that, in some cases, the breach of Article 14 is at least as significant to the applicant as the breach of the substantive provision. Accordingly, the Court has not taken the position that a finding of a violation of another article invariably pre-empts a finding that Article 14 has been violated as well.[14]

However, the Court by no means always goes on to decide the Article 14 point if it has already determined that another provision of the Convention has been infringed. The test that it applies in deciding whether to do so is whether 'a clear inequality of treatment in the enjoyment of the right in question is a fundamental aspect of the case.'[15] While one can point to the cases where the Court has decided the discrimination complaint is a 'fundamental aspect' of the application and those where it has not, explaining how the line is to be drawn is difficult. There appears to be a strong inclination to avoid the Article 14 question where another violation has been established (and even to consider that the other violation precludes the Article 14 question[16]). In *Dudgeon v UK*,[17] the Court decided that its ruling that the criminalisation of adult, private male homosexual acts was a breach of Article 8 absolved it from the need to adjudicate on the applicant's Article 14 allegations. It said that these concerned 'the same complaint, albeit from a different angle' as that underlying the Article 8 claim and that there was 'no useful legal purpose' in deciding them.[18] In *Norris v Ireland*,[19] which raised practically the same issues as those in the *Dudgeon* case, the Article 14 arguments did not even reach the Court. In contrast, in *Marckx v Belgium*[20] the Court did find that there were breaches of Article 14 as well as of Article 8 and Article 1 of the First Protocol. The Court gave no explanation for doing so. Simply, the allegations had been made, arguments had been heard and the Court disposed of them. The Court's approach to this problem in *VDSO and Gubi v Austria*[1] is even more puzzling. The claim of one of the applicants, a magazine publisher, was that the military authorities had violated its rights under Article 10 and under Article 14 in conjunction with Article 10 by refusing to distribute its journal in the mail to soldiers when they did distribute other, similar publications. The Court held that there was a violation of Article 10 and that there was no need to

---

14 *Marckx v Belgium* A 31 (1979). See below, p 469.
15 *Airey v Ireland* A 32 para 30 (1980). Cf *Dudgeon v UK* A 45 para 67 (1981).
16 See *Airey v Ireland* A 32 paras 29-30 (1980).
17 A 45 para 69 (1981).
18 But see Judge Matscher, dissenting, arguing that the point should have been decided.
19 A 142 (1988).
20 A 31 (1979).
1   A 302 para 56 (1994).

consider the Article 14 point. This seems misplaced. If *no* journals had been distributed in this way, the applicant would have had no Convention right to have its journals sent out alone: the distinction that the authorities made between its journal and the others was an essential ingredient of its claim.

The 'fundamental aspect' criterion derives from the judgment in *Airey v Ireland*.[2] As will be explained below, the Court had strong reasons for wishing to avoid the Article 14 complaint and to subsume it under that made about Article 6. If the *Airey* case had been decided before the *Marckx* case, the Court would have had to explain in *Marckx* what there was about the case which required the disposition of the charges of discrimination. One factor on which it might have relied was the seriousness of the badge of discrimination in the *Marckx* case: illegitimacy. The development of social attitudes to discrimination on grounds of sexual orientation might yet bring the Article 14 issues in the *Dudgeon* and *Norris* cases into the same category.

What the *Marckx* case does establish is that there is no bar to a judgment on the discrimination complaint merely because there has been a finding of an associated breach of a substantive provision. The reluctance of the Court to take the discrimination question is symptomatic of its cautious approach to Article 14. What is at work here is a policy of judicial abstention rather than any rule of law which prohibits simultaneous findings of violations of Article 14 and another article by reason of the same conduct of the state.

Finally, discrimination, whether within the terms of Article 14 or not, may be relevant to establishing the violation of another article of the Convention. Where a state has a duty not to act, for example, not to subject a person to treatment contrary to Article 3, the fact that the duty has been breached with a discriminatory motive or effect will not alter the responsibility of the state under Article 3. If the allegation of discrimination is central to the complaint, there may also be a violation of Article 14.[3] However, the fact of discrimination may be enough to bring treatment, not otherwise severe enough, within Article 3.[4] Nor need the discriminatory treatment be in connection with another Article of the Convention if it is severe enough to breach Article 3.[5]

---

2   A 32 para 30 (1979).
3   In *Tyrer v UK*, the applicant had argued that judicial corporal punishment, ultimately held to be in breach of Article 3, was in breach of Article 14 because (i) it could be imposed only on young males, and (ii) was primarily pronounced on persons from financially and socially deprived homes. The first argument was not proceeded with by the Commission in its Report (B 24 (1976) Com Rep paras 41-44), the second was withdrawn at the admissibility stage (17 YB 356 at 364 (1974)).
4   Cf *Costello-Roberts v UK* A 247-C (1993) where the Court held that the beating by a master of a boy at a private school had not been sufficiently severe to constitute a breach of Article 3. A similar punishment in a state school would have been unlawful under the Education (No 2) Act 1986, s 47. The discrimination point was not argued in the *Costello-Roberts* case (the application was introduced before the change in the law). *Quaere* whether the discriminatory element is enough to bring the treatment within Article 3 or to amount to a breach of Article 14, even in the absence of a breach of Article 3.
5   See the *East African Asian* cases, above, pp 81-82, concerning racial discrimination.

2. DIFFERENTIAL TREATMENT AND ANALOGOUS SITUATIONS

In the typical discrimination claim, the applicant will claim that he has been treated differently from others who, though in a similar position to him, are treated better.[6] Often the applicant will argue that the basis for the different treatment is that he is a member of one group, while the better treated are members of another group, whereas in reality the members of both groups are in the same position.[7] Identifying the 'badge' on the basis of which the differential treatment is made, in addition to identifying the differential treatment, is sometimes necessary where the forbidden 'badges' of differentiation are limited.[8] This is not the case under Article 14. It contains a long, and apparently non-exhaustive,[9] list of characteristics which might render differential treatment discriminatory. These identified 'badges' are supplemented by an open-ended 'other status' category. The Strasbourg authorities have characterised a large number of 'other statuses', including sexual orientation, marital status, illegitimacy, status as a trade union, military status, conscientious objection, professional status, and imprisonment as falling within this residual category. Since classification according to some characteristics raises a *prima facie* case, at least, that the members of each group are in analogous situations and that very good reasons are needed for distinguishing between them, it can be of significance for the applicant to establish that he has been treated differently on one basis rather than another.[10] Although the questions of difference in treatment and comparability of situations are closely related, it is necessary to consider them separately.

i.   Differential treatment

An applicant usually has no difficulty identifying how he has been treated less favourably than others. Interference with the enjoyment of possessions, criminalisation of sexual activities, obligations to provide free services are instances where the complaint relates to positive action by the state to the disadvantage of the applicant. In other cases, the complaint is about the denial of opportunities afforded to others, for example the right to bring civil actions or to be tried by an ordinary criminal court or to exercise the same freedom of expression. If, ordinarily, this question is not troublesome, there are circumstances where the applicant and the state dispute what is

---

6   *Van der Mussele v Belgium* A 70 para 46 (1983).
7   *Marckx v Belgium* A 31 (1979).
8   *Mandla v Dowell-Lee* [1983] 2 AC 458 (necessary to decide whether Sikhs were a religious or racial group because UK law prohibited only racial discrimination).
9   The text reads 'any ground such as'. See further on the question of a limit to the 'badges of discrimination', below, p 472.
10 See below, pp 481-482, on 'suspect categories'.

different treatment. In *Schmidt v Germany*,[11] the applicant was a man who had had to pay a levy as an alternative obligation to serving in his local fire brigade. All men were potential firemen but women were not. Accordingly, women never had a obligation to pay the levy. Schmidt's complaint was that he was a victim of different treatment on the basis of his sex. But what was the different treatment? A majority of the Court, taking into account the fact that no man was ever obliged to serve in a fire brigade because the fire service was never short of volunteers, considered that the different treatment was the payment of the levy. There was no justification for taxing men and women differently by reason of their sex alone.[12] That being the case, it is somewhat surprising that these judges thought that Schmidt had been discriminated against with respect to Article 4(3)(d), work or service which forms part of normal civic obligations, rather than with respect to Article 1 of the First Protocol, which protects the right to property.[13] Two of the dissenting judges said that the different treatment was with respect to the obligation to serve in the fire service. The distinction the state made was not primarily between men and women but between those who were fit to serve and those who were not.[14]

Furthermore, the state may contest the claim of differential disadvantage where an applicant complains of only an isolated aspect of his conditions and neglects to take account of advantages which he enjoys compared with others. In *Nelson v UK*,[15] the complaint by a convicted juvenile prisoner was that he did not enjoy the privilege of remission for good behaviour granted to adults. The government pointed out that, *inter alia*, the sentencing court had indicated that had the applicant been older he could have anticipated a much severer sentence. The Commission decided that the aim of establishing a more flexible sentencing regime for children provided an objective and reasonable basis for differentiating them from adults and that the omission of remission of sentence from the regime for children was not disproportionate to the objective.

ii. Analogous situations

The applicant will argue that his position (and the position of people like him) is similar to, 'analogous' to, the situation of people in the group he has identified as enjoying more favourable treatment. In *Van der Mussele v Belgium*,[16] the applicant, who was a trainee barrister, claimed that he had been treated less favourably (by being made to provide free legal services) than apprentices in other professions, who were not obliged to work for nothing, even though their positions were analogous to his. Alternatively, an

11 A 291-B (1994).
12 Id, para 28.
13 Ibid.
14 Judge Spielmann and Gotchev, dissenting.
15 *No 11077/84*, 49 DR 170 at 174 (1986).
16 A 70 para 45 (1983). The Court did not find the situations analogous, see below p 474.

applicant may contend that he has been discriminated against by being treated differently from the way other members of his group have been treated. An example of this is *Pine Valley Developments Ltd v Ireland*[17] where two of the applicant property developers argued successfully that their rights under Article 1 of the First Protocol had been breached in connection with Article 14. Their claim was that remedial legislation, introduced to correct a misapplication of the planning law, had been drafted in such a way as to exclude them but not other holders of permissions in the same categories as theirs from the benefit of the law.[18]

The identification of the 'badge', ie the criterion on the basis of which the difference in treatment has been meted out, is the obligation of the applicant. The list of 'badges' in Article 14 is long and not exclusive. The question is whether it is limited at all. In *Dudgeon v UK*[19] one of the applicant's claims of discriminatory treatment was that the law in Northern Ireland which criminalised his homosexual activities was different from that in England and Wales and that, therefore, the Court should consider whether this difference was compatible with Article 14. The British government maintained that a difference of this kind, different laws in different law areas, was generically distinct from the list of badges in Article 14, all of which referred to some sort of personal characteristic of a victim.[20] The Court did not decide upon Dudgeon's Article 14 complaints, regarding them as effectively disposed of by the judgment in his favour under Article 8. The Court did not advert to the government's position but, in a dissenting opinion, Judge Matscher said that:

'The diversity of domestic laws, which is characteristic of a federal state, can in itself never constitute a discrimination, and there is no necessity to justify diversity of this kind.'[1]

There is something to be said for this position but, where fundamental rights are at stake, diversity is not the primary virtue. A violation of a guaranteed right in one state of a federal union remains a violation, whatever the position in other states. Since Article 14 does not protect the right to be treated equally, where the claim is that people in other states of the federation are treated better (but the applicant is not treated in a way which violates one of his Convention rights), there will not be an issue under Article 14 if Judge Matscher's position prevails, even though the treatment falls within the ambit of Article 14. Equally, where one state relies on the power of limitation, even though other states do not, that will not amount, of itself, to a violation of the primary article or of Article 14. The test is

17 A 222 (1991).
18 Id, paras 14-17, 61.
19 A 45 (1981).
20 Note of the Hearing, 23 April 1981, Cour/Misc (81)47 pp 57-58.
1   A 45 (1981). See also *Nelson v UK No 11077/84*, 49 DR 170 at 174 (1986) (different penal regimes in Scotland and England 'not in anyway related to the personal status of the applicant' and therefore not discrimination).

whether the restriction is 'necessary in a democratic society', as to which the position in other states is, at best, only evidence.[2]

While it may be the case that practically any personal characteristic of the applicant may form the foundation of a claim of discriminatory treatment, a question mark remains over financial status. This is a characteristic that has not been rejected peremptorily by the Court but it did show some reluctance to address the claim in *Airey v Ireland*[3] that the applicant had been discriminated against by reason of her poverty. Article 14 forbids discrimination on the ground of 'property'. This is the most problematic of categories.[4] On the one hand, it seems quite wrong that the enjoyment of fundamental rights should depend upon financial resources. On the other hand, in capitalist societies at least, the acceptance of even wide inequalities based on wealth is a central characteristic of a market system. One would anticipate that the institutions would be reluctant to admit a separate violation of Article 14 on this ground alone but that they would rather consider, as the Court did in the *Airey* case, whether there had been a violation of a substantive provision. As indicated below, in *Johnston v Ireland*,[5] the Court found that a lack of financial resources was not in fact the basis on which the applicants had been treated differently from others.

Whichever way the question of differentiation on the basis of a geographical or federal unit category is resolved, and however the Court decides the financial status question, an applicant has a very wide range of factors from which he may isolate the basis for his distinctive situation. In some cases, this will be clear on the face of the law: the sexual activities of Dudgeon and Norris were criminalised because they were homosexual; Belgian child and inheritance law on its face drew a distinction between legitimate and illegitimate children and families. In other cases, the applicant must explain how the law differentiates him from comparable others. In the *Pine Valley* case,[6] the applicants showed that the interpretation of the remedial legislation had the effect of excluding them and only them from its benefits from among those who had been affected by the misapplication of the law. The burden on the applicant is to show that the badge he identifies is the basis for the differential treatment. In *Johnston v Ireland*,[7] the applicants, unable to marry because one of them could not obtain a divorce in Ireland where both were resident, maintained that they were discriminated against on the ground of their financial status because they could not travel abroad to obtain a divorce, as could richer Irish residents. The Court held that the true badge of distinction was between

---

2 The Court has conceded that the maintenance of different standards in different regions of the same state may be 'necessary in a democratic society': *Handyside v UK* A 24 para 57 (1976) and *Müller v Switzerland* A 133 para 36 (1988).
3 A 32 paras 29-30 (1980).
4 See Thornberry, 29 ICLQ 250 (1980) (on the *Airey* case). More generally, see Michelman, 83 Harv LR 7 (1969).
5 A 112 paras 59-61 (1986).
6 A 222 paras 61-64 (1991).
7 A 112 para 60 (1986).

persons who were domiciled in Ireland (who could not obtain a divorce which would be recognised in Ireland) and those who were domiciled abroad (who, if they obtained a divorce there lawfully, were entitled to have it recognised in Ireland). The applicants' position as poor residents was not, the Court said, 'analogous' to non-Irish domiciliaries.

There are other cases that illustrate the application of the 'analogous situation' test. In *Van der Mussele v Belgium*,[8] the applicant sought to compare himself (and apprentice barristers like him) with members of other professions, including other legal professionals, who were paid for taking part in the same legal aid cases the apprentices had to take for free. The Court's dismissal of his claim to comparability was cursory. It relied on the Commission's disposition of the issue but this was scarcely more informative, complaining about lack of evidence to support the applicant's claims and running together considerations of comparability with those of justification for differential treatment.[9] In two similar cases from the United Kingdom, the applicants complained that they had been discriminated against because they were suffering from AIDS. They argued that the discrimination was in respect of mitigation of sentence[10] or compassionate release from jail.[11] They claimed that their medical conditions were the same as those of people who would benefit from sentencing or release discretions. The Commission's view was that they were not as ill as those who would be so treated: their positions were not analogous.

In *Fredin v Sweden*,[12] the applicants argued that the revocation of a licence to extract gravel had been discriminatory because they were in the same position as other licence-holders who had been allowed to continue operating (they were all commercially viable) and they were not like those whose licences had been terminated on environmental grounds (whose operations were not commercially successful). The Court said that it was for the applicant to establish that his situation 'can be considered similar' to those who had been treated better. The most that the applicants were able to do was to demonstrate that they were not like the others whose licences had been withdrawn: ie that they were an exceptional case. The Court did not accept that this had the effect of putting the obligation on the government to show that the applicants were different from the enterprises whose licences continued. The applicants had established only that they were not entirely like those whose licences had been called in. That was not the same as showing that they were similar to the surviving operators. Accordingly, the government was under no obligation to explain why it had treated them differently.[13]

The *Fredin* and *Pine Valley* cases show how hard it can be to separate the questions whether situations are analogous and whether there is different

8 A 70 (1983).
9 B 77 (1983) Com Rep paras 125-128.
10 *R M v UK No 22761/93*, 77-A DR 98 (1994).
11 *Grice v UK No 22564/93*, 77-A DR 90 (1994).
12 A 192 para 60 (1991).
13 Id, para 61.

treatment. In both of these cases, the applicants were claiming to be excluded from groups, where the badge of distinction was the way in which they had (or had not) been treated. They did not claim that they had been treated in the way that they had for any particular reason.

When the badge of differentiation has been isolated, there may be a call for further inquiries as to whether the distinction relied upon is founded in fact. This inquiry shades into the justification for the differential treatment and will be considered further below.[14]

Finally, if it is established that the situations are not analogous, then there is no obligation on the state to justify the differential treatment (though the institutions have sometimes examined the explanations given). In *S v UK*,[15] the Commission decided that a stable lesbian union was not entitled to protection as 'family life' within the Convention and that such arrangements were not analogous to family life. There was no need to consider why the state had excluded parties to lesbian unions from the benefits of succession to leasehold accommodation granted to members of families (though, in a desultory way, the Commission did look at the reasons given). Contrast this with the *Marckx* case, where the initial question was whether illegitimate relations were protected as 'family life'. Once it was decided that they were, the analogous situation of legitimate and illegitimate families was established and the state had to try to justify the distinction between them that it had made.[16]

3. THE CONCEPT OF DISCRIMINATION

i. The test in the *Belgian Linguistic* case[17]

The Court had to deal with the concept of discrimination in Article 14 in one of its earliest judgments, the *Belgian Linguistic* case.[18] The language it used then has stood up to the various challenges made to it since and still represents the core of the Convention meaning of discrimination.

Firstly, the Court rejected the argument made on the basis of the French text that every difference of treatment in the exercise of Convention rights is excluded. Such a conclusion, the Court said, would be 'absurd'.[19] It recognised the existence of a wide variety of national legislative and administrative regimes based on differential treatment which could well be seen to be for a good reason. As a result, a test had to be formulated to allow the distinction to be drawn between permissible differentiation and unlawful discrimination.

---

14 See pp 476-483.
15 *No 11716/85*, 47 DR 274 (1986).
16 A 31 para 39 (1979). Consideration of whether the situations were analogous drifted into deciding whether treating them differently had objective and reasonable justification.
17 See Verhoeven, 23 RBDI 353 (1990).
18 (Merits) A 6 (1968).
19 Id, p 34.

The Court said:

> 'It is important . . . to look for the criteria which enable a
> determination to be made as to whether or not a given difference in
> treatment, concerning of course the exercise of one of the rights and
> freedoms set forth, contravenes Article 14. On this question the Court,
> following the principles which may be extracted from the legal practice
> of a large number of democratic states, holds that the principle of
> equality of treatment is violated if the distinction has no reasonable
> and objective justification. The existence of such a justification must be
> assessed in relation to the aim and effects of the measure under
> consideration, regard being had to the principles which normally
> prevail in democratic societies. A difference of treatment in the exercise
> of a right laid down in the Convention must not only pursue a
> legitimate aim: Article 14 is likewise violated when it is clearly
> established that there is no reasonable relationship of proportionality
> between the means employed and the aim sought to be realised.'[20]

Although the matter has not been free from controversy, it now appears that
this test embraces two elements, the identification of a legitimate aim for the
different treatment, which is the obligation of the state, and a 'reasonable
relationship of proportionality' between the different treatment and the aim
pursued, where it is for the applicant to 'clearly establish' the lack of
proportionality.[1]

The general principle against discriminatory treatment was thus
established at the European level but it had to be applied to situations in
national societies, one of the differences between which was the choice they
made in establishing legal and tolerating factual inequalities between
members of different groups. With this in mind, in the *Belgian Linguistic*
case, the Court also noted[2] that its role was not to put itself in the place of
the national law-maker but to exercise its subsidiary role of ensuring that
national determinations were not incompatible with the Convention.
Accordingly, it conceded to states a 'margin of appreciation' in making
their assessments of what different treatment was proportionate to the
legitimate objective they had chosen.

ii.   Discrimination: justification for differential treatment

The differentiating characteristic relied on by the state may be, and in
practice under the Convention so far usually is, overt or direct. There is no
room for confusion as to why a state is distinguishing between people or
groups. However, the 'badge' of differentiation relied on in the legislation or

20 Ibid.
1   See Eissen, *European Supervision*, Ch 7 at p 141.
2   A 6 p 34.

decision by the state may be challenged by the applicant as not being the 'real' reason for distinguishing him from others. Some of the disputes of this kind may be relatively simple, consisting merely of a difference between the state and the applicant as to whether the different treatment of the applicant was actually based on the 'badge' or not. In *Hoffmann v Austria*,[3] the applicant was a Jehovah's Witness. She alleged that the decision of the Austrian courts to award custody of her child to her husband was taken largely on the basis of her religious beliefs. The government argued that the decision had been made in the interests of the child. The European Court examined the national judgments and decided that the final judgment had been taken on grounds of religion.

Other kinds of disputes about the 'real' reason are not so easy to resolve. While the different treatment based on the apparent categorisation may be rationalised in terms acceptable to the Court, if the 'real' reason for it were addressed, so the argument goes, the Court would not be able to conclude that there was proper justification for differentiation on those grounds. *Abdulaziz, Cabales and Balkandali v UK*[4] is an example. The applicants argued that the explanations given by the British government for subjecting them as women to a different regime from that for men in the matter of the immigration rights of their partners – for the protection of the labour market and the protection of public order – disguised the racial motivation behind the Rules. The Court gave the claim short shrift, as it has other claims attributing covert and discreditable motives to governments.[5]

Persuasively demonstrating a hidden motive behind official decisions is often a difficulty in the way of the effective implementation of non-discrimination standards in whatever legal system it arises. Another problem is that of indirect discrimination. This is discrimination that results from a rule or practice that in itself does not involve impermissible discrimination but that disproportionately and adversely affects members of a particular group. An obvious example would be a rule that required all motorcyclists to wear a crash helmet, which would have a disproportionate effect upon Sikhs. Regardless of any intention to discriminate, such a requirement would be unacceptable as indirect discrimination because of its effects unless it could be shown to be justified on public safety or other recognised grounds.[6] Indirect discrimination may fall within Article 14,[7] but the burden upon the applicant to establish that it exists is severe. Again, the leading case is *Abdulaziz*. The Immigration Rules allowed a woman to join her husband or fiancé in the United Kingdom even though she had no independent right of entry. For intended marriages, one disqualifying circumstance was where the prospective partners had never met. The

---

3   A 255-C paras 33, 36 (1993).
4   A 92 para 84 (1985).
5   Id, paras 85-86. See also eg *Handyside v UK* A 24 paras 52, 66 (1976).
6   The legal origin of this idea is *Griggs v Duke Power Co* 401 US 424 (1971). See the UK Sex Discrimination Act 1975, s 1(1)(b) and Race Relations Act 1976, s 1(1)(b).
7   It would appear to be recognised in the passage quoted from the *Belgian Linguistic* case, above, p 476, 'aims *and effects*'.

applicants in this case were women who were settled in the United Kingdom who argued that they had a right to have their non-British husbands or fiancés join them. If they had no right to this under Article 8 alone, then they did so under Article 14 in combination with Article 8 because of the different treatment of men (who in similar circumstances to the applicants would have been entitled to be joined by their partners). Disqualifying prospective partners who had not met their fiancés affected very largely persons wishing to marry men from the Indian sub-continent, where arranged marriages were a familiar institution, as they were practically nowhere else. A dissenting opinion in the Commission concluded that the rules 'by their practical side effect, in the short term and their very purpose were indirectly racist'.[8]

The Court denied that the 'previous meeting' rule was 'an indication of racial discrimination'[9] (and, in any event, this was not an issue raised by the applications). The handling of the issue can be criticised for the Court avoided addressing specifically the indirect discrimination question by running together the applicants' claims that this was the effect of the Immigration Rules with the government's explanation of the purpose of the rule (to avoid their evasion by bogus marriages). There ought to have been more intense scrutiny of the applicants' claim that the indirect effect of the rules was discriminatory. If they had made it out, it ought not to be enough that the government had some non-racial purpose in mind when introducing the rule. The issue of the proportionality of the provision should have been considered, the more particularly since what would have been involved was a particularly invidious badge of differentiation.[10]

While there is more to be done to establish whether indirect discrimination is effectively excluded by Article 14, the *Abdulaziz* case is informative in focusing attention on the burden of proof associated with the application of the *Belgian Linguistic* test in the case of all kinds of discrimination within Article 14. To have had their case reach this stage, applicants will have to have identified the article within the ambit of which the differential treatment falls and they will have to have established that they are receiving less favourable treatment than others in an analogous situation. It is then for the government to show that there is an objective and reasonable justification for making the differentiation. In this connection, the Court has often used the term 'legitimate aim' of the regulation but this is only another form of words for 'objective justification'.[11] If the government does not

---

8 B 77 (1983-85) Com Rep p 46. Mr Carrillo, joined by Messrs Melchior and Weitzel.

9 A 94 para 85 (1985).

10 In *Ireland v UK* A 25 paras 224-229 (1978), the Court found no breach of Article 14 combined with Article 5, even though the application of detention provisions had resulted entirely in the arrest of Republican (and no Loyalist) suspects. The government successfully maintained that the explanation was found in the different ways the activities of the two groups were conducted and not in the discriminatory application of the law.

11 *Darby v Sweden* A 187 para 31 (1990), where the Court said: '. . . a difference in treatment of one of these individuals will be discriminatory if it "has no objective and reasonable justification", that is if it does not pursue a "legitimate aim" and if there is no "reasonable relationship between the means employed and the aim sought to be realised".'

plead any justification, the applicant's claim of a violation will be made out. If it does suggest an explanation, the justification which the government gives must have a rational basis and an evidential foundation. The danger of a state being able to rationalise as acceptable differentiation what is in reality egregious discrimination is reduced if the Court insists upon a rigorous evidential burden on the state to prove the factual basis of its claim. This is the case whether the allegation is of direct or indirect discrimination. There should be an opportunity to contest the 'constitutional facts' on which the claim of inequality is made. This was the case in the *Abdulaziz* case, where the applicants were able to show that the supposed reason for distinguishing between men and women, that they had a different effect on the labour market, was without factual basis.[12]

In some of the early applications challenging laws which criminalised male homosexuality on the ground of its discriminatory nature, the states argued that the differential treatment of male and female homosexuals was justified because 'masculine homosexuals often constitute a distinct socio-cultural group with a clear tendency to proselytise adolescents . . .'.[13] This was based on evidence submitted by the government which satisfied the Commission. There is no indication in the decision of any evidence brought in response by the applicant. In a later decision on the same question, the Commission rejected an attack on the different ages of consent to male homosexual activities on the one hand and to heterosexual and female homosexuality on the other. It accepted the evidence of reports of public inquiries relied on by the government to reach its conclusion that the situations were not analogous: 'Heterosexualism and lesbianism do not give rise to comparable social problems [to male homosexuality].'[14] The evidence on which this judgment was reached was hardly compelling. Conceding even a wide margin of appreciation to the state in the evaluation of the evidence ought not to absolve the state from the obligation from providing proper evidence in the first place.

States are usually able to satisfy the Court that their regulations have a rational aim: in the *Belgian Linguistic* case, to achieve the effective implementation of the policy of developing linguistic unity of the two large language regions;[15] in the *Marckx* case, to support and encourage the traditional family;[16] and in the *Abdulaziz* case, to protect the labour market and the protection of public order.[17] Often these assertions by the government will be unchallenged but the applicant may contest the authenticity of the government's explanation and the Court must adjudicate upon its argument. In the *Abdulaziz* case, it rejected the

12 A 94 paras 74-80 (1985). Cf the summary way in which a similar claim was dealt with by the Commission in *A and A v Netherlands No 14501/89*, 72 DR 118 (1992).
13 *X v FRG No 5935/72*, 3 DR 46 at 56 (1975), on which see Fawcett, pp 302-304. See also *X v UK No 7215/75*, 19 DR 66 (1977).
14 *Johnson v UK No 10389/83*, 47 DR 72 at 77-78 (1986).
15 A 6 para 7 (1968).
16 A 31 para 40 (1979).
17 A 94 paras 75-76 (1985).

applicant's claim that the Immigration Rules were racially motivated.[18] Given that the state must show a 'reasonable' objective and taking into account the margin of appreciation conceded to the state, it is not surprising that government arguments about the aims of its regulations have largely been accepted by the Court.[19] Occasionally, states have not offered any justification for the different treatment and, when they do not, the applicant will succeed. *Darby v Sweden*[20] is an example. The explanation for treating resident and non-resident non-nationals differently for the purposes of a religious tax was administrative convenience, which the state declined to put by way of excuse to the Court.

However, establishing the aim of the legislation or decision is only the first part of the enquiry. As the Court stated in the *Belgian Linguistic* case,[1] what is required also is that the differences in treatment between the members of the groups 'strike a fair balance between the protection of the interests of the community and respect for the rights and freedoms safeguarded by the Convention'. In the *Belgian Linguistic* case, with a single exception,[2] the Court found that the policies adopted by Belgium for promoting the language regions could be justified and did not impinge excessively on the rights of individuals.[3] In the *National Union of Belgian Police* case,[4] the denial of consultation rights to a trade union (made on the basis of its small size compared to unions given consultation rights) was justified as striking a reasonable balance between the rights of the union and the interests of the employers in ensuring a 'coherent and balanced staff policy'. In contrast, the Court in the *Marckx* case found that the reasons for treating the 'illegitimate' mother and child differently from the legitimate mother and child were not sufficiently supported in fact or, even if generally true, imposed too big a burden on those 'illegitimate' mothers and children who did not fit the state's stereotype. In relation to the different processes by which legitimate and 'illegitimate' mothers had to establish the affiliation of their children, the government said, *inter alia*, that they were justified because legitimate mothers were more likely to accept the responsibilities of motherhood than 'illegitimate' mothers. The Court found this unsustain-

---

18 Id, paras 85-86.
19 The problems encountered by applicants in this regard is a reflection of the Court's failure to provide an adequate evidential framework for dealing with complaints of indirect discrimination: see above, p 478. Note also the cursory review in *Angelini v Sweden No 10491/83*, 51 DR 41 (1986).
20 A 187 para 33 (1990).
1 A 6 p 44 (1968). See also *G v Netherlands No 11850/85*, 51 DR 180 (1987), upholding a longer period of compulsory service for conscientious objectors than the period of military service for conscripts, to avoid too much opting out.
2 The Court held that there was no objective and reasonable justification for allowing Dutch-speaking children resident in the French language region to have access to Dutch language schools in the bilingual zone while French-speaking children resident in the Dutch language area were denied access to French language schools in the same zone: A 6 pp 68-71 (1968).
3 Id, pp 42-44, 49-51, 55-56, 60-61 and 85-87.
4 A 19 para 48 (1975).

able. The government had provided no evidence to support its general assertions and it clearly was not true that all 'illegitimate' mothers were susceptible to abandoning their children.[5]

As noted earlier, assessing where the balance is properly struck or whether the difference in treatment is disproportionate to the objective of the state is subject to the state's margin of appreciation. As a guide to deciding whether that margin of appreciation has been exceeded, the Court has relied on some general propositions. The first is the identification of discrimination on the basis of certain badges as particularly serious, making them the equivalent of 'suspect categories' in United States constitutional law.[6] On the basis of the *East African Asians* cases[7] and the *Abdulaziz* case,[8] one can infer that discrimination on grounds of race is an example. More explicitly in the *Abdulaziz* case,[9] the Court established that discrimination on grounds of sex is such a category. It said that:

> '. . . the advancement of the equality of the sexes is today a major goal in the member states of the Council of Europe. This means that very weighty reasons would have to be advanced before a difference of treatment on the ground of sex could be regarded as compatible with the Convention.'

The Court relied on this language in reaching the same conclusion about different treatment on the ground of illegitimacy.[10] As the quotation indicates, the function of the 'suspect category' is to put a heavy burden on the state to identify a difference between men and women which would allow a state rationally to adopt a policy of treating men as a whole and women as a whole in different ways.[11] Differential treatment of groups or individuals who advocate racial hatred and associated ideas is, in contrast, particularly easy for a state to justify. The burden is slight on a state to explain why measures which discriminate against them compared with others who hold different political opinions are necessary.[12]

The criteria by which 'suspect categories' are identified are not clear. The Commission in the *Abdulaziz* case noted that:

> '. . . the elimination of all forms of discrimination against women is an accepted general principle in the member states of the Council of

---

5   A 31 paras 38-39 (1979).
6   Ely, *Democracy and Distrust: A Theory of Judicial Review*, 1980, pp 145-170. Reliance on 'suspect categories' may not only subject differential treatment to an especially high burden of justification but may be a strong reason justifying positive discrimination in the subject category's favour.
7   3 EHRR 76 (1976). See also *Patel v UK No 4403/70*, 36 CD 92 at 117 (1970).
8   B 77 para 113 (1983), endorsed by the Court: A 94 para 85 (1985).
9   A 94 para 78 (1985).
10 *Inze v Austria* A 126 para 41 (1987).
11 *Burghartz v Switzerland* A 280-B paras 25-30 (1994) (discrimination against men).
12 Eg *HWP and K v Austria No 12774/87*, 62 DR 216 at 220-221 (1989).

Europe, confirmed in domestic legislation, and regional and international treaties.'[13]

In seeking to establish the special character of sex discrimination, the applicants relied on the UN General Assembly Declaration on the Elimination of Discrimination against Women[14] (and then only to establish the appropriate remedy under Article 50).[15] The Court referred to no evidence at all. In *Inze v Austria*,[16] the Court referred to the 1977 European Convention on the Legal Status of Children Born out of Wedlock[17] (to which there were then nine parties, including Austria). So far, only race, sex and illegitimacy have been identified as suspect categories. Extending the list will not be easy.[18] The mere existence of an international agreement prohibiting discrimination on a particular ground may not be enough. On the other hand, clear evidence of a European consensus on this point is likely to be influential. One might compare the 'suspect category' under Article 14 with the special weight given to certain interests (eg privacy in sexual matters) falling within the sphere protected by a Convention right. The identification of a (developing) European standard is a significant indicator of both statuses.[19]

The same is true of the Court's assessment of the state's exercise of its margin of appreciation generally. The less evidence there is that the state's differential treatment departs from a common standard in the Convention states, the less likely is the Court to condemn it. In *Rasmussen v Denmark*,[20] there was evidence that a Danish law distinguishing between husbands and wives in the matter of time-limits applicable to paternity proceedings was not different to that in some other European states. Accordingly, the Court found that making the distinction did fall within the state's margin of appreciation.

In many cases, the national situation will be peculiar to that state and the search for European standards will be fruitless. Here, the Court relies on the

---

13 B 77 (1983) Com Rep para 102. *Schuler-Zgraggen v Switzerland* A 263 (1993) was a particularly strong sex discrimination case. The Court reviewed an evidential question in the national proceedings, governed by Article 6(1), a course it takes only in exceptional cases: see above, p 181. See also *Schmidt v FRG* A 291-B (1994) Com Rep paras 45-51, emphasising that as 'suspect categories' emerge, reasons for differentiation which once would have been 'objective and reasonable' may cease to be so. To the same effect but with less consequence for the judgment, see the Court id, A 291-B paras 24-28 (1994).
14 GA Res 2716. Now reliance would be placed on the Convention on the Elimination of All Forms of Discrimination against Women 1979, to which there are 135 parties, including most members of the Council of Europe.
15 Memorial of the Applicants, Cour (84) 85, p 38.
16 A 126 para 41 (1987).
17 ETS 85; UKTS 43 (1981), Cmnd 8287.
18 See Wintemute, *Sexual Orientation and Human Rights*, 1995 (forthcoming), arguing that discrimination on grounds of sexual orientation is a form of discrimination on grounds of sex and, therefore, protected as a 'suspect category'.
19 Cf *Dudgeon v UK* A 45 para 52 (1981) and *Inze v Austria* A 126 para 41 (1987).
20 A 87 para 41 (1984). See Helfer, 65 NYULR 1044 at 1075-1100 (1990), for a thorough investigation of the European standard in this context.

notion of 'proportionality' to assess the lawfulness of the differential treatment. The equation is between the 'means employed', that is the different treatment, and the 'aim sought to be realised', that is the explanation the state gives for the different treatment of what (by now) has been established to be analogous cases.[1] The Commission concedes a wide margin to the state in making this assessment and its decisions often do little more than endorse the state's conclusion.[2] One factor in assessing proportionality is the possibility of alternative means for achieving the same end. That an applicant can identify an alternative will not be decisive evidence that the state has acted excessively. According to the Court in the *Rasmussen* case, its margin of appreciation extends to choosing between alternatives.[3] However, where serious discrimination is at stake, a practical alternative to the 'means unemployed' will be evidence of the disproportionality of the state's choice of means.[4] Even so, unless the case is clear, the margin of appreciation doctrine will stand as a protection for the state at this stage of the argument. As the Court has consistently asserted, it is not its function to substitute itself for the national decision-maker.[5] The fact that some schemes will have even a marked disparity in their impact on separate individuals will not be conclusive that the arrangements are disproportionate if the overall effect is achieved with reasonable tolerance. In *James v UK*,[6] a scheme of leasehold enfranchisement aimed at protecting disadvantaged leaseholders in general produced windfall benefits for some tenants and large losses for some landlords but these exceptional cases were not sufficient for the Court to condemn the whole deal.

iii. Positive obligations to protect against discrimination

According to Article 14, the enjoyment of the rights and freedoms in the Convention 'shall be secured' without discrimination. This replicates the language of the guarantee in Article 1[7] and emphasises that states may have positive obligations under Article 14 as well as the negative obligation not to discriminate in its official acts.[8] The first kind of positive obligation a state may have is the duty to ensure effective enjoyment of the non-discrimination

---

1 *James v UK* A 98 paras 76-77 (1980).
2 Eg *Autio v Finland No 17086/90*, 72 DR 245 (1992) (longer period of substitute service for conscientious objectors than period of military conscription).
3 A 87 para 41 (1984).
4 *Inze v Austria* A 126 para 44 (1987).
5 *Belgian Linguistic* case A 6 p 35 (1968) and *National Union of Belgian Police* case A 19 para 47 (1975). Even where there is room for serious disagreement, the Commission's decisions on proportionality are frequently cursory: see eg *B v UK No 16106/90*, 64 DR 278 (1990) (discrimination in immigration laws between partners to informal heterosexual and homosexual unions).
6 A 98 para 77 (1980).
7 See above, p 19.
8 See *Belgian Linguistic* case B 3 para 400 (1965).

protection. There is no express positive obligation under Article 14 so any obligation of this kind must be implied. The judgment in the *Belgian Linguistics* case makes it clear that positive differentiation is not incompatible with Article 14,[9] although it does not decide whether some positive steps may be a matter of obligation. In *Airey v Ireland*,[10] it was the applicant's claim that she was entitled to positive discrimination in her favour to enable her to enjoy an effectively equal right of access to the courts as was available to people who, unlike her, could afford to employ a barrister. The Court's answer was to find the existence of the positive obligation under Article 6(1) and, in the light of having done so, to decide that it was not necessary to pursue the claim under Article 14. The pattern is for the Court to absorb a positive discrimination claim in the finding that there is a positive obligation in the relevant substantive article or to reject it if it finds that there is no substantive positive obligation. It is an approach which comports with Article 14 as a protection against discrimination rather than as a guarantee of equality.

The obligation of the state to take action to protect against private acts of discrimination which affect the enjoyment of Convention rights could embrace matters like membership of private associations or the right to be freed from privately imposed discriminatory fetters, like restrictive covenants on property rights. The inference to be drawn from *Young, James and Webster v UK*[11] and *Sigurjonsson v Iceland*[12] is that a state does have a duty to prevent private action which compels a person to be a member of an association. On the other hand, there cannot, in general, be a duty to compel a private club to accept a member because that would violate the freedom of association of the club. Yet, if the reason for the exclusion were discriminatory, it is arguable that the state should have a positive duty to disallow it.[13] Like other positive obligations, that duty will be qualified. The egregiousness of the badge of differentiation, the 'closeness' of the society, the impact of the decision on the individual (membership of a trade union might be more important than participation in a social club), and the rationality of the exclusion (restricting political associations to supporters, churches to believers) will all weigh in assessing the compliance with a positive duty with respect to private action once one is established. It has been considered already that a state might justify as having an objective and reasonable justification action taken against some kinds of expression or some kinds of association (without necessarily relying on Article 14 or Article 17).[14] The Convention may impose some positive obligations on states to take action against expression which gratuitously insults religious feelings.[15]

---

9   A 6 (1968).
10   *Airey v Ireland* A 32 para 30 (1979).
11   A 44 para 57 (1981).
12   A 264 para 37 (1993).
13   The UK Race Relations Act 1976, s 25, which prohibits discrimination in respect of membership of private clubs, would comply with such a duty.
14   See above, p 374.
15   *Otto-Preminger-Institut v Austria* A 295-A para 49 (1994).

It remains to be seen whether a like obligation can be found in other substantive articles to restrain racially inflammatory speech or associations.[16] As a strong European consensus about the unacceptability of such opinions or activities develops, it cannot be ruled out that the Court would imply into Article 14 a positive obligation on the state to take action against private speech or action to ensure the effective enjoyment of other Convention rights of those against whom the sentiments were directed.[17]

Finally, although it will concededly be a rare example, the Commission has envisaged that there may be circumstances where there is a positive obligation on the state to secure access to private facilities, ie a positive obligation to impose and enforce a positive duty on private individuals. An example is the suggestion that, while there was in general no right of access under Article 10 for private persons to broadcasting facilities, there might be in connection with Article 14, 'if one party was excluded from broadcasting facilities at election time while other parties were given broadcasting time'.[18]

iv. Reverse discrimination

Reverse discrimination involves 'programmes designed to favour or promote the interests of disadvantaged groups'.[19] A state may engage in reverse discrimination within the ambit of Convention right without being in breach of Article 14. The Court acknowledged this in the *Belgian Linguistic* case[20] when it noted generally that not all instances of differential treatment are unacceptable and that 'certain legal inequalities tend only to correct factual inequalities'. Thus a protected quota of university student places for members of a particular racial group would be discrimination within the ambit of a Convention right (the right to education, Article 2 of the First Protocol), but would not be in breach of Article 14 if it had the 'objective and reasonable justification' of increasing the disproportionately low percentage of members of that disadvantaged group in the university student population.[1] However, given the parasitic nature of Article 14, there can be no *legal obligation* on the part of states derived from that Article to engage in a policy or act of reverse discrimination; any such obligation would stem from a positive obligation in another article guaranteeing a Convention right. As noted above, in the *Airey* case the Court held that the

---

16 Cf Article 20(1), ICCPR and Article 4, Racial Discrimination Convention. On the *power* to limit race hate speech, see the *Jersild* case, above, p 374.
17 Such other Convention rights include the rights in Articles 10 and 11.
18 Cf *X and Assn Z v UK No 4515/70*, 38 CD 86 at 88 (1971). In this application, the access envisaged was to public broadcasting. What is considered here is access to private stations.
19 Parekh, in Hepple and Szyszczak, eds, *Discrimination: The Limits of Law*, 1992, Ch 15 at p 261.
20 A 6 para 10 (1968).
1 Cf *DG and DW Lindsay v UK No 11089/84*, 49 DR 181 at 190-191 (1986) (a tax advantage for married women, which fell within the ambit of the right to property, Article 1, First Protocol, had 'an objective and reasonable justification in the aim of providing positive discrimination' to encourage married women back to work).

applicant was entitled to legal aid on the basis of Article 6 and did not examine her Article 14 claim. If there was an Article 14 claim on the facts of that case, it stemmed from the positive obligation in Article 6 to provide a 'fair hearing' coupled with Article 14, not from any reverse discrimination claim based upon Article 14 by itself. Positive obligations of a reverse discrimination kind commonly exist in European law in the form of various kinds of assistance for the poor, although legal aid is exceptional in falling within the ambit of a Convention right.[2] The absence of a widespread policy of reverse discrimination in European national law in key areas such as racial and sex discrimination[3] suggests that reverse discrimination obligations in these two areas would not be easily read into the few Convention rights that are relevant.

4. CONCLUSION

The development of these implied positive duties in Article 14 will depend upon the general approach the Court takes to this article. Quite apart from criticism of the technical way in which the Court has approached its interpretation, its judgments have been criticised as being too favourable to states.[4] If, as seems to be the case, Article 14 has not played as prominent a part in furthering the protection of Convention rights as might have been expected, given the significance of non-discrimination in other areas of human rights,[5] the responsibility is not wholly the Court's. The drafting of Article 14 narrows its potential impact by excluding from its field of operation economic and social rights, with regard to which arise some of the most pervasive discrimination questions.[6] National non-discrimination law is often more elaborate than the brief language of Article 14. The Court's conception of its role as one 'subsidiary' to the national legal system is of importance. The margin of appreciation intrudes at several stages in the process of deciding whether Article 14 has been violated. The Court needs to defer to the state on only one of these calculations and the application will fail. Finally, the Court is aware of the limitations of its remedial capacity. Striking down one regime as discriminatory does not put another in its place. In *Dudgeon v UK*, declaring the total criminalisation of male homosexual activities incompatible with the Convention (there under

---

2   Social welfare benefits, for example, would not.
3   Eg reverse discrimination is generally prohibited in UK discrimination law: see Pitt, in Hepple and Szysczak, op cit at p 485, n 19, above, Ch 16.
4   Van Dijk and Van Hoof, pp 545-547. For a more sympathetic view of the Court's jurisprudence, see Merrills, *The Development of International Law by the European Court of Human Rights*, 2nd edn, 1993, pp 169-175. See also Partsch, loc cit at p 463, n 7, above, pp 591-592.
5   See McKean, loc cit at p 462, n 1, above.
6   Cf *Zwaan-de Vries v Netherlands* (182/1984), 2 SDHRC 209; 9 HRLJ 256 (1988) (sex discrimination in social security law).

Article 8 rather than Article 14) while conceding the legitimacy of some regulation of homosexual practices, put the burden on the state to introduce new provisions dealing with matters of the age of consent,[7] the limits of privacy, the position of 'sensitive' professions, as well as removing the blanket criminal proscription. The difficulty in drafting a whole new regime to replace one condemned by the Court is illustrated by the reaction of Belgium to the *Marckx* judgment. It was given in 1979 and yet, in 1991, the Court found Belgium in violation of the same provisions on similar facts, Belgian law not having been reformed until 1987.[8]

The limitations and deficiencies of Article 14 have been given particular currency by the concerns for the protection of minorities in Europe. Although Article 14 cites 'association with a national minority' as a specific 'badge' of forbidden discrimination, the Convention provides only partial and indirect obligations in favour of minorities.[9] The thrust of the Convention is the securing of individual rather than group rights.[10] Minorities themselves have no status under the Convention and minority organisations may assert rights of their own only if they are, *mutatis mutandis*, like individual rights, such as the right of a political party to a free and fair election. Some compensation may be found in the development of positive obligations for states so that individual members of a minority may enjoy their rights effectively, for instance in matters of religion or education. However, it is difficult to demonstrate the existence of such obligations and relatively easy for a state to show that it has satisfied them.[11] Nor does the Convention serve only to *protect* minority rights. States may insist, indeed may have a duty to insist, that minorities respect the rights of others guaranteed by the Convention.[12] Finally, many minorities' concerns fall outside the Convention altogether, so neither as individual rights nor as an aspect of Article 14 protection do they fall within the competence of the Strasbourg authorities.[13] The attention of the Council of Europe is fixed on

---

7 The UK Criminal Justice and Public Order Act 1994, s 145, reduces the age of consent for male homosexual relations to 18 in England and Wales. The age of consent for heterosexuals is 16. Before the Act came into force, the Commission had communicated to the government an application alleging a breach of Article 14 because of the difference between the then existing age of consent for heterosexual and homosexual activities (16 as opposed to 21), *X v UK No 22382/93* (1994), unreported. See also *X v UK No 7215/75*, 19 DR 66 (1978) Com Rep; CM Res DH (79) 5 (no violation of Article 8 alone or in conjunction with Article 14 by reason of different ages of consent for heterosexual and homosexual activities).
8 *Vermiere v Belgium* A 214-C para 24 (1991).
9 Gilbert, 23 NYIL 57 at 81-93 (1992).
10 See *48 Kalderas Gipsies v FRG and Netherlands Nos 7823/77 and 7824/77*, 11 DR 221 (1977) (the applicants were *individual* gipsies).
11 As demonstrated by the almost complete lack of success of the applicants in the *Belgian Linguistic* case A 6 (1968).
12 Poulter, 36 ICLQ 589 at 614-615 (1987). Although making a strong plea for tolerance and pluralism, the author accepts the limits imposed by international human rights obligations.
13 This includes economic and social rights, where the prospects of oblique protection relying on *Airey v Ireland* A 32 (1979), are not encouraging. See eg *X v UK No 8160/78*, 22 DR 27 (1981).

new instruments for minorities' protection, including the elaboration of a Protocol to the Convention on minorities' rights which would take advantage of the Convention machinery.[14]

14 See Malinverni, 12 HRLJ 265 (1992). The Council of Europe has adopted the Framework Convention for the Protection of National Minorities 1994, ETS 157. Consideration is being given also to including in a Protocol a right to equality of women and men and to amending Article 14 to guarantee equality before law and the equal protection of the law. Generally, see Hillgruber and Jestaedt, *The European Convention on Human Rights and the Protection of National Minorities*, 1994.

CHAPTER 16

Article 15: Derogation in time of war or other public emergency

'**Article 15**

1. In time of war or other public emergency threatening the life of the nation any High Contracting Party may take measures derogating from its obligations under this Convention to the extent strictly required by the exigencies of the situation, provided that such measures are not inconsistent with its other obligations under international law.

2. No derogation from Article 2, except in respect of deaths resulting from lawful acts of war, or from Articles 3, 4 (paragraph 1) and 7 shall be made under this provision.

3. Any High Contracting Party availing itself of this right of derogation shall keep the Secretary General of the Council of Europe fully informed of the measures which it has taken and the reasons therefor. It shall also inform the Secretary General of the Council of Europe when such measures have ceased to operate and the provisions of the Convention are again being fully executed.'

1. INTRODUCTION[1]

Article 15 allows states in some exceptional circumstances to take measures which interfere with the enjoyment of the rights protected by the Convention and the Protocols (with the exception of the Sixth Protocol[2]).

1　The literature on emergency derogations is extensive. The principal items are Higgins, 48 BYIL 281 (1976-77); Questiaux, *Study of the Implications for Human Rights of Recent Developments concerning situations known as State of Siege or Emergency* (E/CN.4/Sub.2/ 1982/15); International Commission of Jurists, *States of Emergency: Their Impact on Human Rights*, 1983; Ergec, *Les Droits de l'homme à l'épreuve des circonstances exceptionelles: Etude sur l'article 15 de la Convention Européenne des droits de l'homme*, 1987; Chowdhury, *Rule of Law in State of Emergency: The Paris Minimum Standards of Human Rights Norms in a State of Emergency*, 1989; Oraa, *Human Rights in States of Emergency in International Law*, 1992 (which has an extensive bibliography); Klein, *Protection des droits de l'homme et circonstances exceptionelles*, 1-2 AEL 91 (1992); Fitzpatrick, *Human Rights in Conflict: the International System for Protecting Human Rights during States of Emergency*, 1994.

2　Article 3, Sixth Protocol.

National constitutions usually contain equivalent provisions.[3] Where they do not, some doctrine of necessity is relied on as an alternative legal basis for taking extraordinary action.[4] At the international level, instruments for the general protection of civil and political rights usually[5] have a derogation clause. They are closely similar in their terms, and the practice of international institutions under other international human rights treaties[6] is potentially more useful in the interpretation of Article 15 than anywhere else in the European Convention. The dilemma posed by derogation clauses is as easy to state as it is hard to resolve. Once the necessity for derogation is conceded, it becomes difficult to control abusive recourse to the power of suspending rights that the provision permits. In many cases, the effective use of the power will require expedition. The evidence on which recourse to the power is based may be extensive but at the same time sensitive. The determination of the propriety of particular measures of derogation, once the existence of an emergency has been established or conceded, is a matter of practical judgment rather than refined analysis. Any review is inevitably open to the criticism that fraught decisions made at a time of crisis are being subjected to considered re-evaluation with the comfort of hindsight. It has been suggested that the value of judicial intervention in the exercise of what is essentially a political power is limited – and that the more narrowly the power of derogation is confined, that is to say, the more serious the circumstances must be before it may be relied upon, the less the room for judicial review.[7] However, the experience of abusive recourse to the derogation power is extensive enough for an abstentionist approach to be highly undesirable. In the nature of things, the national judicial means of redress will often have been undermined, so the responsibility of international institutions is the more compelling.

The Strasbourg authorities have rejected the claims of states that questions arising under Article 15 are beyond their competence altogether but they have approached cases before them rather cautiously, some say too cautiously.[8] Happily, the number of occasions on which European states have relied on Article 15 has been small, although the result is that the jurisprudence is underdeveloped and several of the points which follow are expressed with varying degrees of tentativeness.

2.   THE GENERAL PATTERN OF ARTICLE 15

The language of Article 15 seeks to balance the formidable power given to states by subjecting its exercise to various kinds of limitation. The first are

---

3   See the examples in Int Com Jur *States of Emergency*, op cit at n 1, above.
4   For the United States, see *Korematsu v US*, 323 US 81 (1943).
5   The Universal Declaration of Human Rights and the African Charter of Human and Peoples' Rights have no express emergency clauses.
6   See Oraa, op cit at n 1, above.
7   Alexander, 5 HRLJ 1 (1984).
8   See below, p 495.

textual limitations, confining the power to 'time of war or other public emergency threatening the life of the nation' and allowing states to take only such action as is 'strictly required by the exigencies of the situation'. That two levels of questions are involved – the existence of the emergency and the strict necessity of the derogations – means that in principle at least two different standards of review may be appropriate at Strasbourg. Next, the power to derogate is subject to substantive restrictions: no derogation is permitted in the case of the specific articles of the Convention referred to in Article 15(2)[9] and the derogating state must not contravene its other international law obligations (Article 15(1)). It has been argued that there are other Articles of the Convention which operate as substantive restrictions on the power of derogation.[10] Finally, there are procedural conditions in Article 15(3) which attend recourse to the derogation power and which have the important consequence of drawing attention to these special situations and which are also a source of information which will be useful in the pursuit of any applications in Strasbourg. Not many such applications have been initiated and it is worth noticing just how high a proportion of the few inter-state cases have involved Article 15 questions.

These several limitations and conditions which control the exercise of the power of derogation in Article 15 provide the basis for any review by the Strasbourg authorities. Compliance with some of them is manifestly capable of objective assessment. Even if doubts about the justiciability of particular questions are maintained, it should be noted that some cases have proceeded on the basis that the parties are agreed about them. This was true, for example, of the question of the existence of a public emergency in *Ireland v UK*.[11] Supposing no such agreement, there may still be clear cases on the facts in which the Strasbourg authorities may properly reach an objective decision rejecting a claim put by the defendant state. However wide the margin of appreciation allowed to states, it would go too far to say that any question is inherently non-justiciable. In the appropriate case, the last word will lie with the Strasbourg authorities.

3.   'IN TIME OF WAR OR OTHER PUBLIC EMERGENCY THREATENING THE LIFE OF THE NATION'

It is for the Strasbourg authorities to interpret each element in Article 15, including what can constitute a 'public emergency'.[12] Although it has been argued that 'war' should both be read narrowly and serve so as to limit the kinds of 'other' public emergencies which are envisaged by Article 15, the practice of the Strasbourg authorities has established that such a restricted

---

9   The rights affected are the right to life, the right not to be tortured etc, the right not to be enslaved and the right not to be subjected to retrospective criminal penalties.

10   See below, p 504.

11   A 25 para 205 (1978).

12   *Greece v UK No 176/56*, 2 YB 176 (1958) Com Rep; CM Res (59) 12 and *Lawless v Ireland* A 3 para 28 (1961).

understanding is not the proper one. They have not limited 'other' public emergencies to 'war'-like situations, ie those where there is an external threat to the state.[13] Even if 'war' were to be confined to its international legal meaning, 'other public emergency' covers other incidents of serious violence. Civil war and insurrection are the main categories but it has been conceded that Article 15 goes further and allows a state to derogate from its human rights obligations in the face of low-intensity, irregular violence. In *Ireland v UK*,[14] the Irish government accepted that conditions in the province were sufficiently exceptional for Article 15 to apply. The period involved was from 1970 to 1976, which included the most violent period in the continuing disturbances in Northern Ireland. From August 1971 to March 1972, more than 200 people were killed and nearly 30,000 injured in over 3,000 bombings and shooting incidents.[15] Even so, it has been questioned whether the Court was correct to endorse the applicant government's acceptance that there was a public emergency without making its own inquiries and assessment. That there ought to be this obligation on the Court is explained by the nature of the rights in the Convention: since they are the rights of individuals, they ought not to be capable of being diminished by the unilateral act of a state.[16] While it is not suggested that an independent inquiry by the Court would have resulted in a different outcome in *Ireland v UK*, the possibility of unjustifiable reliance on Article 15 increases as the level of violence diminishes. In *Brannigan and McBride v UK*,[17] the applicants accepted that there was a public emergency in Northern Ireland but the Commission said that it had to make its own assessment of the situation, 'albeit [a] limited [one]'. It was very limited, the Commission concluding on the basis of cumulative government statistics[18] that the situation remained 'very serious'.[19] The brief of one of the intervening parties, the NGO 'Liberty', argued that there was not an emergency of sufficient seriousness for Article 15 to be relied upon.[20] The Court briefly endorsed the Commission's conclusion,

> '. . . making its own assessment, in the light of all the material before it as to the extent and impact of terrorist violence in Northern Ireland and elsewhere in the United Kingdom . . . the Court considers that there can be no doubt that such a public emergency existed at the relevant time.'[1]

---

13 *Lawless v Ireland* A 3 (1961).
14 A 25 paras 20-77 (1978).
15 Id, para 48.
16 Van Dijk and Van Hoof, pp 552-553.
17 A 258-B (1993) Com Rep para 45.
18 Id, paras 26-27.
19 Id, para 49.
20 A 258-B para 45 (1993).
1   Id, para 47.

This degree of scrutiny is hardly different from accepting the parties' own view of the situation. None the less, the Court said that it had made its own assessment and it may be that the Court would feel obliged to give a fuller account of why it accepted that there was an emergency if the issue was contested by the applicant. However, it cannot be asserted that the margin of appreciation allowed to a state on the question of the existence of the emergency is anything but wide. The reliance on cumulative figures, which necessarily do not give an accurate picture of the seriousness of the circumstances at a particular time, is an indication that the Strasbourg authorities accept a view of some emergencies as 'campaigns' or continuing events which involves some reconsideration of the derogation power as a temporary expedient. Where there is an organised campaign of violence resulting in deaths at whatever low level among the security forces and civilians it is now hard to see how the Strasbourg authorities could avoid confirming a state's claim that there is a public emergency within Article 15.

Although the cases which have reached the Court on Article 15 have all concerned threats to internal security arising from the use of armed force, the concept of public emergency will cover other kinds of crisis such as economic dislocation or natural disaster.[2] If it be thought that construing Article 15 in this way would go too far, an important element of limitation is to be found in the words 'threatening the life of the nation' in Article 15(1). In *Lawless v Ireland*,[3] the Court adopted the language of the Commission:

'[the words] refer to an exceptional situation of crisis or emergency which affects the whole population and constitutes a threat to the organised life of the community of which the state is composed.'

The requirement that the consequences of the emergency be plenary in their effects and, what is more, be 'exceptional' is a significant block against too wide a reading of Article 15(1). That it has not always served this purpose with regard to terrorist violence is a measure of the seriousness with which the phenomenon has been regarded in Western Europe. In the *Lawless* case,[4] the Court found the existence of the emergency to be 'reasonably deduced' from a combination of three factors, the violent operations of a secret army, the fact that its cross-border activities threatened Ireland's relations with the United Kingdom and the escalation of terrorist activities during the period under review, culminating in a particularly serious incident which triggered the introduction of emergency legislation.

The 'public emergency' must 'threaten the life of the nation'. In the *Lawless* case,[5] the Court referred to a 'crisis or emergency which affects the whole population' but, in practice, this standard has been relaxed or, put another way, it has been accepted that the whole population may be affected

2 Oraa, loc cit at p 489, n 1, above, p 31.
3 A 3 para 28 (1961).
4 Ibid.
5 Id, para 28.

by events in only part of a state and that the derogation may be restricted to that part. In its first Article 15 derogation notices, the United Kingdom alluded to the situation in particular overseas colonies to which it had extended the Convention's application under Article 63. It could hardly be said that these examples of distant disorder affected the population of the United Kingdom as a whole.[6] In *Ireland v UK*, the notice of derogation[7] in point made reference only to the relevant circumstances in Northern Ireland and no objection to it was taken by the Irish government or by the Court. Since no objection was taken either to the colonial declarations, where, at the least, political considerations of self-determination might have argued in favour of a narrow interpretation of Article 15, it is unlikely that disturbances of sufficient intensity within any part of a single European state would be held to fall outside Article 15.

In none of the terrorist cases considered so far was there much dispute about the facts: rather there was disagreement about what facts counted and how serious a situation they revealed.[8] In the *Greek* case[9] this was not so. The government's argument was that there had been a decline in public order for a number of months bringing the country to the brink of anarchy, such that the government had had to take action (including emergency derogations) to pre-empt an armed Communist takeover of Greece. The Commission said that its task was 'to examine on the evidence before it' whether there was a situation of such scope and intensity that it constituted an actual or imminent threat to the life of the Greek nation.[10] The Commission concluded that there was no evidence of such a situation, the only case in which one of the Strasbourg authoritites has not endorsed the government's claim that there was an emergency.[11] Three dissenting opinions differed from this conclusion. They relied on the 'margin of appreciation' of the authorities, an idea introduced in the first *Cyprus* case when the Commission said (in a slightly different context):

'the government should be able to exercise a certain measure of discretion in assessing the extent strictly required by the exigencies of the situation.'[12]

The views of the dissenting Commissioners in the *Greek* case, though different in emphasis, gave weight to the difficulty, close to impossibility, of a review of the evidence and the assessment of its significance by the Commission.[13] Deference to the government's calculations was, therefore,

6   Oraa, loc cit at p 489, n 1, above, pp 28-29.
7   For text, see 14 YB 32 (1971).
8   Eg the Commission divided by 9 votes to 5 on these questions in *Lawless v Ireland* B 3 (1965) Com Rep pp 81-102.
9   12 YB (the *Greek* case) 1 (1969); CM Res DH (70) 1.
10 Id, para 157.
11 Id, paras 159-165.
12 *Greece v UK No 176/56*, 2 YB 174 at 176 (1956); CM Res (59) 12.
13 12 YB (the *Greek* case) 1 at 76-93 (1969).

practically a matter of necessity. There is little sign of any deference in the decision of the majority, whose conclusion was simply different to the government's.[14] On the matter of principle, the Court has come closer to the approach of the dissenting Commissioners in the *Greek* case. In a well known passage in *Ireland v UK*,[15] it said:

'It falls in the first place to each contracting state, with its responsibility for "the life of [its] nation", to determine whether that life is threatened by a "public emergency" and, if so, how far it is necessary to go in attempting to overcome the emergency. By reason of their direct and continuous contact with the pressing needs of the moment, the national authorities are in principle in a better position than the international judge to decide both on the presence of such an emergency and on the nature and scope of derogations necessary to avert it. In this matter Article 15(1) leaves the authorities a wide margin of appreciation.'

Commentators have resisted the extension of such a wide margin of appreciation to the determination of the existence of an emergency. Higgins writes that 'the question whether a threat to the life of a nation exists is capable of objective answer'.[16]

While this may be true in some circumstances – an armed attack by another state or, in the light of practice, a campaign of terrorism – it is not so obviously the case where the state makes the claim that the emergency is imminent rather than actual, more particularly where the evidence of the threat is sensitive intelligence, the production of which may cause problems for a state and the assessment of which may stretch the capacity of the Commission and the Court. In such cases, the Strasbourg authorities may be properly cautious about disputing the conclusions of the national authorities (as suggested by the minority in the *Greek* case) but need not defer absolutely to them in cases where there is no credible evidence on which to base the claims that there is an Article 15 emergency.

In inter-state cases, the question whether there is a public emergency will be joined with the merits,[17] but in an individual application the matter may be disposed of at the admissibility stage, at least if the Commission has a judgment of the Court on the same point to rely on.[18] If the alleged emergency is being examined by the Commission for the first time, it is more likely that the Commission would inquire into its existence at the merits stage.

14 Id, pp 71-76.
15 A 25 para 207 (1978).
16 48 BYIL 281 at 299 (1976-7). See also Oraa, loc cit at p 489, n 1, above, p 32.
17 *Greece v UK* 2 YB 182 at 184 (1956); CM Res (59) 12; *France, Norway, Denmark, Sweden, Netherlands v Turkey* Nos 9940-9944/82, 35 DR 143 at 170 (1983); 44 DR 31 (1985) F Sett.
18 *X, Y and Z v UK* Nos 5727/72, 5744/72, 5857/72, 14 DR 5 (1978).

4. 'MEASURES . . . TO THE EXTENT STRICTLY REQUIRED BY THE EXIGENCIES OF THE SITUATION . . .'

It is apparent that states have not resorted to Article 15 in every conceivable circumstance in which they might have done. There are a variety of reasons why this is so. In general, states will wish to avoid relying on Article 15, especially in cases of internal disorder, where there is the risk that the government's opponents will use the emergency derogation as evidence of the effectiveness of their campaign against the authorities. Article 15(2) makes it clear that some measures of derogation are impermissible whatever the emergency, so that some options which the state might wish to take advantage of are absolutely forbidden to it. Other articles of the Convention have express limitation clauses in them which allow measures of derogation in most of the circumstances which fall within 'public emergency': so it may be 'necessary in a democratic society' for a state to interfere with, say, freedom of expression to preserve public order to a greater extent in time of emergency than it would be in settled conditions.[19] In *Klass v FRG*,[20] the Court said:

> 'Democratic societies nowadays find themselves threatened by highly sophisticated forms of espionage and by terrorism, with the result that the state must be able, in order to counter such threats, to undertake the secret surveillance of subversive elements operating within its jurisdiction.'

The Court held that the measures here were justified under Article 8(2), falling within a wider necessity occasioned by the special threat to national security posed by urban terrorism. While this approach might not reach every measure a state might wish to take in limitation of a protected right,[1] it leaves a good measure of leeway on which a state might rely before having to contemplate invoking Article 15.

In practice, the consequence is that the measures of derogation most likely to be implemented under the authority of Article 15 will be ones that involve derogation from Articles 5 and 6. Typically, emergency legislation is directed to extending the powers of the executive to arrest and detain persons suspected of engagement in forbidden activities, who would normally rely on Article 5 and 6 to protect them. States have argued that special regimes to meet emergency circumstances, while deviating from the ordinary standards of domestic law, do not violate the Convention because the ordinary rules are above the minimum standards of Articles 5 and 6 and the exceptional measures do not fall below these levels.[2] Although the Court

---

19 Eg *Brind v UK No 18714/91*, 77-A DR 42, 53-53 (1994).
20 A 28 para 48 (1978).
1   Eg *McVeigh v UK No 8022/77*, 25 DR 15 at 53 (1981) Com Rep; CM res DH (82) 1.
2   This was the argument in *Klass v FRG* A 28 (1978). See also Diplock Report of the Commission to Consider Legal Procedures to Deal with Terrorist Activities in Northern Ireland, Cmnd 5185 para 16.

has acknowledged the relevance of exceptional circumstances of disorder to the interpretation of Articles 5 and 6, it has been reluctant to give decisive weight to them. In *Lawless v Ireland*,[3] the Court declined to interpret Article 5(1)(c) in a manner wide enough to embrace the measures of preventive detention used in Ireland. In *Brogan v UK*,[4] a majority of the Court was not persuaded that the background of terrorism justified extended periods of post-arrest detention in the absence of judicial supervision. As Judge Evans, dissenting, pointed out, despite the admitted intensity of the threat to public order in Northern Ireland, the majority was not prepared to countenance as compatible with the Convention periods of detention hardly greater than those it accepted as satisfying Article 5(3) in ordinary times. There was no support for Judge Martens's dissenting opinion which sought to establish a wider margin of appreciation for states faced with terrorist campaigns. Although not expressly, his opinion seeks to introduce the *Klass* principle into the interpretation of Article 5. It has been strongly criticised as creating a middle category of 'quasi-emergency' not justified by the Convention.[5] However, the Court did take rather more notice of the background of terrorism in *Fox, Campbell and Hartley v UK*,[6] when it said:

> 'Certainly Article 5(1)(c) of the Convention should not be applied in such a manner as to put disproportionate difficulties in the way of the police authorities of the contracting states in taking effective measures to counter organised terrorism . . . .'.

None the less, *some* evidence of 'reasonable suspicion' to justify an arrest has to be produced to satisfy Article 5(1)(c). In the *Fox* case, the Court held that there had been a breach because no evidence had been produced. In contrast, in *Murray v UK*[7] there was sufficient evidence from national court proceedings to satisfy the Court's discounted 'reasonable suspicion' test in terrorist cases. These judgments go some way towards sparing a state from having to make an Article 15 declaration in the face of a terrorist campaign.[8]

At the time the *Brogan* case was decided, the United Kingdom had withdrawn its notice of derogation with respect to Northern Ireland.[9] Following the judgment on 29 November 1988, the government submitted another notice of derogation on 23 December 1988,[10] referring to the legislation providing for extended periods of post-arrest detention and explaining the need for it by reference to 'the background of the terrorist campaign and the

3   A 3 para 15 (1961).
4   A 145-B paras 55-62 (1988). The judgment was by 12 votes to 7.
5   Van Dijk and Van Hoof, pp 587-588.
6   A 182 para 34 (1990).
7   A 300-A paras 47, 63 (1994).
8   See Vercher, *Terrorism in Europe: an International Comparative Legal Analysis*, 1994, pp 342-350.
9   21 CE Inf Bull Legal Activities 2 (1985).
10 For the text, see 31 YB 15 (1988). The note is restricted to events connected with Northern Ireland but the extended power of detention is available for 'international' terrorism. See Walker, *The Prevention of Terrorism in British Law*, 2nd edn, 1992, pp 166-167.

overriding need to bring terrorists to justice'. The justification for the measures of derogation was challenged unsuccessfully in *Brannigan and McBride v UK*,[11] *inter alia* on the ground that the extended detention provisions, during which the person arrested was not brought before a judge, were not strictly required by the exigencies of the emergency in Northern Ireland.

As to the interpretation of 'strictly required', the language of Article 15(1) suggests a test more demanding than 'necessary' in, for example, Article 10(2), which requires that the state show a 'pressing social need' for its measures of limitation. The Court has worked out a series of factors to be taken into account to determine whether measures are strictly required. The first inquiry is into the necessity for the measures at all by examining why the ordinary law or action otherwise compatible with the Convention is not adequate to meet the emergency and why the exceptional measures are. In *Lawless v Ireland*,[12] the Court accepted that neither ordinary nor special courts in Ireland were able to meet the dangers to public order occasioned by the secret, terrorist character of the IRA, in particular the near impossibility of obtaining evidence necessary to convict suspects by judicial proceedings. Internment or detention without trial did have the effect of meeting this problem. In *Ireland v UK*,[13] the Court held that 'the British government was reasonably entitled to consider' that the ordinary criminal procedure was inadequate to meet the 'far-reaching and acute danger' presented by the 'massive wave of violence and intimidation', characterising the IRA's activities in Northern Ireland. Extrajudicial deprivation of liberty, even for the purposes of interrogating witnesses – otherwise contrary to Article 5(1) – and the removal of procedural guarantees to regulate deprivation of liberty – otherwise in violation of Article 5(4) – were necessary to meet the emergency situation.[14] In *Brannigan and McBride v UK*,[15] the Court acceded to the government's argument that, in a common law system, it was not feasible to introduce a judicial element into the detention process at an early stage. It accepted also that extended detention was necessary to investigate successfully terrorist crimes when some of the suspects would have been given training in resisting interrogation and where extensive forensic checks might be required. Detention without judicial supervision was thus 'strictly required by the exigencies of the situation'.

As indicated above, in practice, the emergency situations which have reached the Court have involved continuing campaigns of irregular, terrorist violence.[16] Inevitably, the question arises whether a state can justify the

11 A 258-B (1993).
12 A 3 para 36 (1961).
13 A 25 para 212 (1978).
14 Id, paras 214, 220.
15 A 258-B paras 56-59 (1993). The Court found that the government's position had been supported by the various independent inquiries into the situation in Northern Ireland, but there is little analysis of the evidence or assessment of its worth in the judgment. For comment, see Marks, 52 CLJ 360 (1993); 150 JLS 69 (1995).
16 'Terrorist' and 'terrorism' are used for convenience and because they are used by the Strasbourg authorities. They are not legal terms of art and are unhelpful in some circumstances, for instance, in considering the application of international humanitarian law.

continuance of measures, which may be a proper response to the most intense periods of violence and disorder, during periods of relative calm, albeit possibly temporary ones. The exact point has not been decided by the Court but in view of what has been said about its recognition that emergencies may consist of prolonged campaigns, if the state can bring evidence to show that it reasonably believes the campaign to be continuing, it will be difficult to say that the more stringent measures are no longer strictly required.[17] Equally, the fact that a government modifies and mitigates the measures on which it relies under Article 15 during the course of a campaign against the authorities is not, of itself, evidence that the measures were not strictly required at some earlier stage.[18] In *Brannigan and McBride v UK*,[19] a similar point arose. The applicants argued that the extended detention power could not be strictly required because the government had previously withdrawn its derogation notice. That was because, the government responded, it had taken the view that the detention power was compatible with Article 5 and that no derogation was necessary. The withdrawal of the notice did not show that there was no emergency, nor that it was not one for which the power was strictly required. The Court agreed. It rejected by a majority the arguments that because there had been no increase in the intensity of the emergency in the time between the withdrawal of the notice and the judgment in *Brogan* there was no power to rely on Article 15, the real purpose being to avoid the effect of the *Brogan* judgment.[20] The British government's claim was that the *power* of extended detention had always been necessary and that the dispute hinged only on the appropriate legal basis for it.

Establishing the necessity for the emergency measures will not always be sufficient to demonstrate that they are strictly required. The Strasbourg authorities may go on to inquire into the proportionality between the need and the response.[1] The greater the need – eg, the 'very exceptional situation' in Northern Ireland, acknowledged by the Court in *Ireland v UK* – the greater the permissible derogation – eg, detention of a person not suspected of an offence for the purposes of the investigation.[2] Proportionality does not imply some arithmetic calibration. Instead, the Court takes into account whether the measure is less draconian than others which might have been contemplated. In the *Lawless* case,[3] the Court considered that one alternative – sealing the border between Ireland and Northern Ireland as

---

17 Oraa, loc cit at p 489, n 1, above, p 30, says, 'The institution of states of emergency is by its very nature temporary . . .' but that does not necessarily mean brief. See also Judge Makarczyk, dissenting in *Brannigan and McBride v UK* A 258-B (1993).

18 *Ireland v UK* A 25 para 213 (1978).

19 A 258-B paras 47, 51 (1993).

20 Van Dijk and Van Hoof, pp 557-558, maintain that the events demonstrated the bad faith of the British government and called on the Committee of Ministers to exercise its powers under Article 54.

1 *De Becker v Belgium*, B 4 (1962) Com Rep para 271.

2 A 25 para 212 (1978).

3 A 3 para 36 (1961).

a means of combating cross-border raids – would have gone beyond the exigencies of the emergency in Ireland, thus reinforcing the proportionality of the government's lesser reaction. Many of the contested measures of derogation have involved the removal of safeguards against abuse of powers of arrest or detention, usually the removal of the judicial element. In establishing the proportionality of the response, the Court also looks at the alternative mechanisms of supervision introduced by the state. Thus the system of administrative detention examined in the *Lawless* case was accompanied by detailed and continuous supervision by Parliament and a detainee could make representations to a tribunal, the 'Detention Commission'.[4] In *Ireland v UK*,[5] the judicial control of detention was replaced by non-judicial advisory committees and there remained a residuary and, in the view of the Court, not a wholly illusory possibility of access to the courts. In *Brannigan and McBride v UK*,[6] the British government succeeded in rebutting the claim that there were no effective safeguards against abuse of the extended detention power. The actual arrest itself remained challengeable by *habeas corpus* in the ordinary courts. There was a right to see a solicitor after 48 hours of detention, a right the interference with which could be contested by judicial review, and a detainee was entitled to have other persons informed about his detention and have access to a doctor. These, the Court decided, were sufficient basic safeguards against abuse. While it may not be possible to draw the absolute conclusion that the suspension of *habeas corpus* may never be justified under Article 15, the importance the Court attaches to the provision of safeguards against abuse of exceptional powers makes it unlikely that the Court would consider that powers of executive detention which were not accompanied by some measure of independent control as 'strictly required', even if that measure were not formally *habeas corpus*.[7]

The judgment in the *Brannigan* case is open to the criticism that it did not answer sufficiently the concerns of Amnesty International in its intervention that, in the particular circumstances, safeguards were necessary not only to protect against unnecessarily prolonged detentions but also to protect detainees who might be detained *in communicado* during the first 48 hours of detention. The evidence world-wide of abuse of persons detained without supervision during interrogation is strong.[8]

In *Ireland v UK*,[9] the Irish government maintained that the measures adopted by the authorities in Northern Ireland had manifestly failed in their

4 Id, para 67.
5 A 25 paras 218-219 (1978).
6 A 258-B paras 61-65 (1993).
7 Cf *Habeas Corpus in Emergency Situations (Articles 27(2), 25(1), ACHR)*, Inter-Am Ct H Rts Rep, Series A 8 (1987); 9 HRLJ 94 (1988) Advisory Opinion.
8 See Amnesty International in *Brannigan and McBride v UK* A 258-B para 61 (1993). See also Judge Pettiti, dissenting, id; *Ireland v UK* A 25 paras 165-168 (1978); *Tomasi v France* A 241-A paras 114-115 (1992) and id, Com Rep paras 99-100. See further, Report of the European Committee on the Prevention of Torture: Northern Ireland, 1994, para 110.
9 A 25 para 214 (1978). See also Judge Makarczyk, dissenting, in *Brannigan and McBride v UK* A 258-B (1993).

purpose because the period during which they had been in operation had seen an increase in terrorist violence and, eventually, the British government had abandoned administrative detention. In principle, the argument about effectiveness has much to recommend it: how can an interference with human rights which does not contribute to some other good end be 'strictly required'? Indeed, one might go further and argue that, because of what is at stake, the government should be called upon to demonstrate the effectiveness of the measures it has introduced. The difficulty is not of principle and desirability but of practicability and justiciability. Debates about the removal of emergency legislation in the United Kingdom have often addressed this very question: the opposition to renewal argues that the continuation of terrorist activities shows the ineffectiveness of the measures; the government maintains that without the special legislation, things would be much worse. The debates have hardly been conclusive.[10] The alternative of independent reviews of the operation of anti-terrorist legislation,[11] though perhaps more convincing, does not resemble the judicial process of the Convention. It is easy to conclude that in 'evident cases of inefficacy . . . the conditions of Article 15 have not been satisfied'[12] but much less easy to demonstrate that a particular case is an 'evident' one.

In the case of each of these tests and cumulatively the Court accepts that the state has a margin of appreciation in assessing whether the measures which it has taken were 'strictly required'. This means that the decision about what measures to adopt, whether to modify them, whether to continue or discontinue them, so long as they otherwise satisfy Article 15, is for the state. Matters of prudence or expediency are not for the Court.[13] While the Court did not refer explicitly to the margin of appreciation in the *Lawless* case, it did rely on the idea in *Ireland v UK*,[14] when it said, in somewhat curious language, that internment could 'reasonably have been considered strictly required' by the emergency. The words used in *Brannigan and McBride v UK*,[15] couched in the negative, further underline the primacy of the state's assessment of what is strictly required. At one stage, the Court noted that, 'The Commission was of the opinion that the government had *not overstepped* their margin of appreciation . . .' and it said that, '. . . it *cannot be said* that the government *have exceeded* their margin of appreciation . . .'[16] and again, '. . . the Court takes the view that the government have *not exceeded* their margin of appreciation . . .'.[17] This essentially negative review, which takes into account matters of evidence, necessity, proportionality, adequacy of safeguards, individually and

10 Walker, *The Prevention of Terrorism in British Law*, 2nd edn, 1992, pp 244-261.
11 For references to the Shackleton, Jellicoe and other reports, see Bailey, Harris and Jones, *Civil Liberties: Cases and Materials*, 3rd edn, 1991, Ch 4.
12 Van Dijk and Van Hoof, p 554.
13 *Ireland v UK* A 25 paras 207, 214 (1978).
14 Id, para 213.
15 A 258-B paras 57 (1993). Emphasis added.
16 Id, para 60. Emphasis added.
17 Id, para 66. Emphasis added.

together, does not amount to a particularly intrusive form of review, despite the strong words of Article 15(1).[18] What it does do is force the state into a public justification for its actions but there are some doubts whether this is enough.[19]

5. OTHER INTERNATIONAL LAW OBLIGATIONS

Even if measures of derogation can be justified under Article 15, a state is precluded from relying on them if their introduction would breach other international law obligations of the state. This specific provision reinforces the general principle of Article 60.[20] The obvious sources of treaty obligations are the ICCPR[1] and the Geneva Red Cross Conventions.[2] It is conceivable that the European Union treaties could contain obligations which would be relevant to emergency measures, especially if the emergency were economic or industrial in character. While the terms of Article 15(1) do not preclude obligations under customary international law, these are unlikely to raise any questions in practice because of the wide participation of the European states in the Covenant and the Conventions. In all these cases, it will be necessary for the European Court to interpret the other treaty to identify the state's obligation. In practice, this provision has been of little significance. In *Lawless v Ireland*[3] and *Ireland v UK*,[4] the Court decided that the measures of derogation did not conflict with the defendant state's obligations, if any, under international law. In *Brannigan and McBride v UK*,[5] it was argued that the more stringent provisions of Article 4 of the ICCPR – that the existence of the emergency be 'officially proclaimed' – had not been satisfied. There was a dispute between the applicants and the government about what Article 4 required.[6] The Court disclaimed any responsibility to resolve it authoritatively but was satisfied that parliamentary statements by a British Minister were sufficient in terms of their certainty and publicity to comply with Article 4.[7] The Court said

---

18 The Court's approach is endorsed by Merrills, *The Development of International Law by the European Court of Human Rights*, 2nd edn, 1993, pp 139-140.

19 *Brannigan and McBride v UK* A 258-B (1993), Judge Martens, concurring, Judges Pettiti and Walsh dissenting. See also Marks 15 OJLS 69, 84-95 (1995).

20 Article 60: 'Nothing in this Convention shall be construed as limiting or derogating from any of the human rights and fundamental freedoms which may be ensured under the laws of any High Contracting Party or *under any other agreement to which it is a Party*' (emphasis added).

1 All the Convention parties except Greece, Liechtenstein and Turkey are parties to the Covenant.

2 All the Convention parties are parties to the 1949 Geneva Conventions.

3 A 3 para 41 (1961). The Court undertook this inquiry *proprio motu*.

4 *Ireland v UK* A 25 para 222 (1978) (*Geneva Conventions*).

5 A 258-B para 68 (1993).

6 See McGoldrick, *The Human Rights Committee*, 1991, p 306, on the lack of guidance on this point from the Human Rights Committee.

7 *Brannigan and McBride v UK* A 258-B paras 73-74 (1993).

that it was obliged to examine the applicants' argument but it found it was without 'any plausible basis'.[8] Article 4 does contain a longer list of non-derogable provisions than Article 15(2). It is a convincing argument that a state which is a party to the Convention and the ICCPR is precluded from derogating under the Convention from those rights listed in Article 4 that are not in Article 15(2), viz the right not be imprisoned for the non-fulfilment of a contractual obligation, the right to be recognised as a person before the law, and the right to freedom of thought, etc.[9]

One of the arguments put to the Commission by the applicant government in *Cyprus v Turkey*[10] was that Turkey was not entitled to avail itself of Article 15 because its military action in Cyprus was an aggressive war in breach of its obligations under the UN Charter. The Commission found that Turkey was not entitled to rely on Article 15 in any event because there was no declaration of derogation with respect to northern Cyprus[11] and did not address the 'aggressive war' claim. This was perhaps as well. Such matters are for the UN Security Council and the consideration of them by the Strasbourg authorities would raise enormously complicated problems of fact-finding and intricate legal questions. If the Security Council had determined that a state was the aggressor, then perhaps the Strasbourg authorities could draw legal conclusions from this finding, which, on an *ex turpi causa* basis, might include denying the government the right to take advantage of Article 15.

6. ARTICLE 15(2): THE NON-DEROGABLE PROVISIONS

Whatever the seriousness of the emergency and however convincing the case a state might make that a derogation was strictly required, in no circumstances may a state depart from its obligations under Articles 2, 3, 4(1) and 7, nor from Article 3 of the Sixth Protocol. These limitations are not equally the absolute prohibitions they might at first appear. Article 15(2) itself makes an exception for deaths resulting from lawful acts of war and Article 2 contains exceptions, some of which, such as the right to use force resulting in death to suppress an insurrection, are clearly relevant to some kinds of emergency.[12] Derogation under Article 15 from the Sixth Protocol – which abolishes the death penalty – is prohibited (Article 3, Sixth Protocol), but Article 2 of that Protocol allows states to make provision for the death penalty for acts committed in time of or under imminent threat of war, another exception which would be applicable in certain kinds of

8 Id, para 72.
9 Van Dijk and Van Hoof, pp 554-555.
10 4 EHRR 482 at 552 (1976) Com Rep; CM Res DH (79) 1.
11 Id, p 556.
12 Cases involving the use of force which has resulted in death in Northern Ireland have been argued under Article 2 and, although the force has been exceptional, there has been no finding of a violation: see above, pp 46-54.

emergency. The exception in Article 7 of the Convention to the proscription against retrospective criminal penalties – acts 'criminal according to the general principles of law recognised by civilised nations' – also may be applicable in some emergency situations, notably international armed conflicts. There are no limitations in Articles 3 and 4(1) and these, it has been pointed out, are the only true absolute obligations in the Convention.[13]

Although there is no specific reference to them in Article 15, there are other provisions of the Convention which may have an impact on the legality of measures of derogation. One example is Article 14. In *Ireland v UK*,[14] the Court examined the Irish government's complaint that internment had been applied discriminatorily to Republican/Nationalist suspects in conjunction with Article 5. It held that there were objective and reasonable differences between Republican/Nationalist and Loyalist/Unionist violence, notably the much greater extent of the former. Furthermore, the authorities had found it easier to proceed in the ordinary courts against Loyalist/ Unionist defendants. There was, accordingly, no breach of Article 14 combined with Article 5 and, thus, no need to consider the matter separately under Article 15. Judge Matscher, who dissented on this matter, raised but did not answer the question whether a breach of Article 14 could be strictly necessary within the terms of Article 15(1). He alluded to this again in *Brannigan and McBride v UK*.[15] Given the flexible operation of the doctrine of the margin of appreciation in establishing whether there are objective and reasonable grounds for differentiation within Article 14, it is hard to see circumstances when such grounds could not be established and yet it could be said that the discriminatory treatment was strictly required by the emergency.[16]

The American Convention on Human Rights prohibits the suspension of a list of numerated substantive rights and also 'the judicial guarantees essential for the protection of such rights' (Article 27(2)). Relying on these words, the Inter-American Court has advised that states may not suspend the rights to a judicial remedy to test the lawfulness of detention (Article 7(6)) and the general right of judicial protection (Article 25). The Inter-American Court recognised that the right of emergency derogation was not unlimited and that, both in the scope and application of emergency measures, national courts had a role to play in guaranteeing that the emergency powers were not exceeded.[17] While this argument cannot be made in precisely the same terms, given the language of Article 15 of the European Convention, it does enhance the position taken by the Court that the proportionality of derogation measures will ordinarily require a process for their supervision to prevent or reduce the possibility of abuse.

---

13 Higgins, loc cit at p 489, n 1, above, p 306.
14 A 25 paras 225-232 (1978).
15 A 258-B (1993).
16 There is also conceivably room for the application of Articles 17 and 18 as limitations on a state's powers under Article 15: cf Van Dijk and Van Hoof, p 555.
17 Loc cit at p 500, above.

7. THE PROCEDURAL REQUIREMENTS: ARTICLE 15(3)

The specific requirement of Article 15(3) is that a state relying on the right of derogation shall keep the Secretary General fully informed of the measures it has taken and the reasons for doing so. The importance of this safeguard is that the Secretary General informs the other parties to the Convention about the notice of derogation.[18] If the idea that the Convention contains a collective guarantee is to mean anything at all, it surely ought to apply when exceptional measures of interference with human rights are introduced. The other parties to the Convention are thus put on notice that there is a situation which demands their consideration. As mentioned already, Article 4 of the ICCPR requires a public proclamation of the emergency. In *Cyprus v Turkey*,[19] the Commission said that some formal and public declaration of the state of emergency (unless special circumstances prevented it) was a pre-condition for reliance on Article 15(1).

The obligation under Article 15(3) is not necessarily one of prior notification, that is to say, prior to the date from which the state wishes to execute the measures of derogation, at least if the state can give reasons why this should be so. In *Ireland v UK*,[20] the British government explained that its notifications (communicated on 20 August 1971) had been delayed until after the implementation of internment (9 August 1971) so that no persons whom it was desired to detain might have notice and escape. In accepting the adequacy of this justification,[1] the Court relied on the *Lawless* case,[2] where a twelve-day delay in notification was accepted as having been made 'without delay'. In the *Greek* case,[3] the Commission concluded that Greece had 'not fully met the requirements of Article 15(3)'. In particular, while the Commission did not find that Article 15(3) required the state to identify the provisions from which it was derogating, the respondent government had failed to communicate to the Secretary General the texts of some of its emergency legislation and had not provided full information on the administrative measures taken, especially measures for the detention of persons without a court order; the provision of information to the Commission in the course of the proceedings in the application brought against the state was not a substitute for its obligation to communicate the required information to the Secretary General. In addition, it had not informed the Secretary General of the reasons for the measures of derogation for more than four months after they had been taken. Since the *Greek* case, notices of derogation have generally appeared adequate for

---

18 The Secretary General circulates notices of derogation to other member states: CM Res (56) 16. See also the *Greek* case, 12 YB (the *Greek* case) 1 at 42 (1969).
19 4 EHRR 482 (1976) Com Rep para 527; CM Res DH (79)1. But note the dissent of Mr Sperduti in *Cyprus v Turkey* and the judgment of the Court in *Lawless v Ireland* A 3 para 47 (1961).
20 A 25 para 80 (1978).
1 Id, para 223.
2 A 3 para 47 (1961).
3 12 YB (the *Greek* case) 1 at 41-42 (1969); CM Res DH (70) 1.

the purpose of Article 15(3) and to have been delivered without delay.[4] The exception has been Turkey's unwillingness to accept responsibility under the Convention for the acts of its forces in northern Cyprus, which has led it not to make any formal declaration applicable there.[5] Turkey maintained that it had no jurisdiction over any part of Cyprus, which was exercised in the northern part of the island by the Turkish Cypriot authorities.[6] The Commission took the view that Turkey is responsible under the Convention for acts which can be attributed to its armed forces, wherever they may be.[7]

Because the Commission found that there was no emergency in the *Greek* case, it had no need to consider what were the legal consequences of a violation of Article 15(3). While it might be salutary if the Strasbourg authorities regarded a deficiency in notification as rendering the declaration a nullity, the seriousness of what is at stake if the state demonstrates the existence of an emergency at the appropriate time may equally make it appear too draconian a sanction and one which is likely to be of little efficacy. Higgins[8] suggests that failure to notify in reasonable time might be evidence of bad faith which would be a matter to be taken into account in deciding whether Article 15(1) was satisfied.

Article 15(3) requires that the Secretary General be notified when the derogation measures have been terminated. The Court has said that Article 15(3) implies an obligation to keep the need for emergency measures under permanent review, an obligation implicit in the proportionality of any measures of derogation.[9] Action taken under measures justified only by the emergency may not be continued after the emergency has ended.[10]

8. THE FRENCH RESERVATION

When France ratified the Convention, it made the following reservation to Article 15(1):

> 'Firstly, that the circumstances specified in Article 16 of the Constitution regarding the implementation of that Article, in section 1 of the Act of 3 April 1878 and the Act of 9 August 1849 regarding proclamation of a state of siege, and in section 1 of Act No 55-385 of 3 April 1955 regarding proclamation of a state of emergency, and in

---

4 Oraa, loc cit at p 489, n 1, above, p 85.
5 *Cyprus v Turkey*, 4 EHRR (1976) 482 at 555-556; CM Res DH (79) 1 and id, *No 8007/77*, para 67, 72 DR 5 at 24 (1992).
6 *Cyprus v Turkey*, 2 DR 125 at 130 (1975). See Necatigil, *The Cyprus Question and the Turkish Position in International Law*, 1989, pp 94-100.
7 4 EHRR 482 at 509 (1982); CM Res DH (79) 1 and id, *No 8077/77*, 72 DR 5 at 23 (1992). The Commission declined also to accept Turkey's argument that its Article 15 declaration for parts of its national territory could be taken into account with respect to its treatment of Greek Cypriots taken to Turkey. See now *Loizidou v Turkey*, below, p 643.
8 Loc cit at p 489, n 1, above, p 291.
9 *Brannigan and McBride v UK* A 258-B para 54 (1993).
10 *De Becker v Belgium* B 2 (1962) Com Rep 271.

which it is permissible to apply the provisions of those texts, must be understood as complying with the purpose of Article 15 of the Convention and that, secondly, for the interpretation and application of Article 16 of the Constitution of the Republic, the terms "to the extent strictly required by the exigencies of the situation" shall not restrict the power of the President of the Republic to take "the measures required by the circumstances".[11]

The validity of the reservation has never been an issue in any application.[12] It surely could not be maintained that, if the French government found it necessary to resort to treatment which violated Article 2 or Article 3 to meet an emergency, the effect of the reservation would be to preclude consideration of a case challenging the action. In *France, Norway, Denmark, Sweden and the Netherlands v Turkey*,[13] Turkey argued that the terms of the reservation precluded France contesting emergency measures taken by Turkey under Article 15(1). The Commission rejected this, relying on the objective nature of the obligation under the Convention.

---

11 17 YB 4 (1974).
12 Van Dijk and Van Hoof, p 611, argue that it 'conflicts' with the Convention. On the status of France's equivalent reservation to the International Covenant on Civil and Political Rights, see McGoldrick, *The Human Rights Committee*, 1991, pp 304-305.
13 *Nos 9940-9944/82*, 35 DR 143 at 168-169 (1983) Com Rep; 44 DR 31 (1985) F Sett. DR 31 (1985). See below, p 607.

CHAPTER 17

Articles 16-18: Other restrictions upon the rights protected

1. ARTICLE 16: RESTRICTIONS ON THE POLITICAL RIGHTS OF ALIENS

'Article 16

Nothing in Articles 10,11 and 14 shall be regarded as preventing the High Contracting Parties from imposing restrictions on the political activities of aliens.'

Article 16 allows potentially wide-ranging interference with the political rights of aliens. It runs counter to the basic principle of Article 1 that rights in the Convention are to be enjoyed by 'everyone within [the state's] jurisdiction'.[1] It applies specifically to Articles 10 and 11 but there is no indication that the reference to Article 14 is confined to restrictions imposed on aliens' rights under those articles. Rather, it appears that the state may take advantage of Article 16 with respect to discriminatory rules within the ambit of any of the Convention's provisions. This includes rights under Article 3 of the First Protocol involving the right to vote.[2] Draconian though such a power would be, it must not be forgotten that a state has the ultimate remedy of deportation against an alien to whose activities it objects and the Convention provides no direct protection[3] against the use of that power, even if it is because of the political activities of the person expelled.[4] The right to vote in national law is frequently confined to citizens. Article 25 of the ICCPR also protects the right to vote expressly for citizens only and the United Nations Declaration on the Human Rights of Individuals who are not Nationals of the Country in which They Live[5] does not afford any protection for the political rights of aliens.

---

1 Distinctions are drawn between nationals and aliens with respect to freedom of movement, see Articles 3 and 4 of the Fourth Protocol, below, pp 562-563, and, formally at least, there is different protection for national and alien-owned property under Article 1 of the First Protocol: see below, pp 530-532.
2 *Mathieu-Mohin v Belgium* A 113 para 54 (1987).
3 Indirect protection may be provided by Article 3 (likely treatment in destination state) or Article 8 (family ties in expelling state).
4 See *Agee v UK No 7729/76*, 7 DR 164 (1976).
5 GA Res 40/53.

The reference to 'aliens' in Article 16 originally caught all non-nationals of the Convention state claiming to act under it. There was no special protection for nationals of other Convention states. As far as nationals of European Union states are concerned, this position may survive the introduction of European Union citizenship under the Maastricht Treaty,[6] although the Commission's Report in the *Piermont* case (see below) makes this conclusion less likely. It is ironic that the rights to vote given to Union citizens in elections in Union states of which they are not nationals are elections to which Article 3 of the First Protocol does not apply,[7] ie municipal elections and elections to the European Parliament[8].

In *Piermont v France*,[9] which was the first case in which it has had to give serious consideration to Article 16, the Commission indicated that it regards the provision as expressing an outdated view of the rights of aliens. Both because the Commission took notice of developments outside the Council of Europe and because Article 16 is a limitation provision which ought to be construed strictly, the Commission was able to reach a conclusion in favour of the applicant.[10] She was a member of the European Parliament, elected in Germany, who had been invited to French overseas territories in the South Pacific by groups opposed to the French government's nuclear testing policy. She went to French Polynesia and took part in demonstrations against the government. She was formally expelled from the territory and forbidden to re-enter. One of her claims was that the action violated her rights of expression under Article 10, either alone or in conjunction with Article 14. One of the answers the government gave was that the interference, if not otherwise justified under the Convention, could be excused by relying on Article 16.[11] Relying on the applicant's status as a Member of the European Parliament, on the fact that the people of French Polynesia voted in European elections and that she was there in her official capacity, the Commission concluded she could not be regarded as an 'alien' within Article 16.[12] The case was, therefore considered under Article 10 alone, with a narrow majority of the Commission finding that the interference with the applicant's rights was disproportionate to the protection of any interest under Article 10(2).[13]

If the *Piermont* decision is extended to citizens of the European Union as well as MEPs, it will be, in an appropriate case, an important advance because there is very little opportunity for the Strasbourg authorities to control resort to the Article 16 power otherwise. However, it does apply

6 EC Treaty, Article 8(1).
7 See below, p 553.
8 EC Treaty, Article 8b.
9 A 313 (1995) Com Rep para 58 (pending before Court): '. . . those who drafted [Article 16] were subscribing to a concept that was then prevalent in international law, under which a general, unlimited restriction of the political activities of aliens was thought legitimate'; also Ct Jmt paras 60-64.
10 Ibid, paras 59-69.
11 Ibid, paras 54-56.
12 (1994) Com Rep para 69.
13 Ibid, para 77.

expressly only to the 'political activities' of aliens and the Strasbourg authorties might be persuaded to interpret these words narrowly to include only matters directly part of the political process: the setting up and the operation of political parties; expression in connection with the programmes and campaigns of these parties; and participation in elections which fall within Article 3 of the First Protocol. Even so, there remains the possibility that a state could take advantage of Article 16 to inhibit the political activities of expatriate groups, the opportunities for which increase as European states become more cosmopolitan communities. The Parliamentary Assembly has called for the deletion of Article 16.[14]

2.   ARTICLE 17: RESTRICTIONS ON ACTIVITIES SUBVERSIVE OF CONVENTION RIGHTS

'Article 17
Nothing in this Convention may be interpreted as implying for any state, group or person any right to engage in any activity or perform any act aimed at the destruction of any of the rights and freedoms set forth herein or at their limitation to a greater extent than is provided for in the Convention.'

Article 17 is unusual in the Convention in that it may be invoked both by an individual against a state and by a state to justify its interference with the rights of an individual. Its function is 'to protect the rights enshrined in the Convention by safeguarding the free functioning of democratic institutions . . .'.[15]

When relied upon by a state, it is intended as a safeguard against the threat of totalitarianism, especially in circumstances where the threat has not reached such proportions that the state could rely on Article 15 and where there might be difficulties in showing that an interference with an individual's rights was otherwise justified under the Convention. The Commission held that an order banning the German Communist Party could be founded on Article 17 because the programme of the Party inevitably envisaged a period of dictatorship by the proletariat in which rights under the Convention would be destroyed, a conclusion reached at the admissibility stage without a full consideration of the merits.[16] The power in Article 17 is available to exclude groups from participation in elections if they are not committed to the democratic process or if a plank of their political programme involves an interference with human rights. In *Glimmerveen and Hagenback v Netherlands*,[17] the Commission relied on

14 Recommendation 799 (1977) on the Political Rights and Position of Aliens, CE Parl Ass, 28th Ord sess, 3rd Pt, Texts Adopted.
15 *KPD v FRG No 250/57*, 1 YB 222 at 223 (1957).
16 Ibid. The Party was disbanded effectively for the beliefs it held rather than for 'engaging in any activity or performing any act' aimed at Convention freedoms.
17 *Nos 8348/78 and 8406/78*, 18 DR 187 (1979).

Article 17 to justify interference with the rights of the applicants under Article 10 and Article 3 of the First Protocol where the applicants had been convicted for distributing racist pamphlets and had been excluded from participating in an election on a racist platform. Article 17 allows the state to act in cases like this without confronting obstacles under Article 14, ie allegations that its action is discriminatory. The approach in the *Glimmerveen and Hagenback* case has been approved by the Court in *Jersild v Denmark*[18] without specific reference to Article 17. While the original threat to which Article 17 was directed was Communist manipulation of political rights,[19] more recently the focus has switched to racist and xenophobic groups.[20] It is conceivable that terrorist groups and their supporters also could find their rights limited by reliance by the state on Article 17. However, in many cases, the necessity for a state to act could be assessed elsewhere under the Convention as, in principle, it ought to be, so that Article 17 becomes an instrument of last resort.[1] Even where reliance on Article 17 is appropriate, the state's power must be exercised,

> 'to an extent strictly proportionate to the seriousness and duration of [the threat to the democratic system] . . .'.[2]

It has been suggested that a further protection against unnecessary recourse to Article 17 should be found by the Commission considering the state's arguments on the merits and not peremptorily dismissing applications as manifestly ill-founded.[3]

Article 17 allows action to be taken against an individual where he seeks to use his Convention rights in a subversive way. Such a person does not, however, become an outlaw, deprived of all his Convention rights. In *Lawless v Ireland*,[4] the Court held that, even if the applicant, who was accused of being a member of a terrorist organisation, could have been deprived of some of his rights under the Convention, the state was not, by

---

18 A 298 para 35 (1994).
19 '. . . an agitator who pursues communist, fascist, national socialist or, generally, totalitarian aims . . .': *Lawless v Ireland* B1 (1959) Com Rep para. 141. In *Vogt v Germany No 17851/91* (1993) Com Rep (pending before the Court), the Commission noted that the collapse of communist regimes in Eastern Europe had reduced the threat of a communist takeover of governments in Western Europe. It did so in the course of assessing whether there was a 'pressing social need' for interfering with the applicant's Article 10 right to freedom of expression.
20 See *Kühnen v FRG No 12194/86*, 56 DR 205 (1988).
1   Cf *Purcell v Ireland No 15404/89*, 70 DR 262 at 278 (1991). The Commission used Article 17 in the *Purcell* case and in the *Kühnen* case, loc cit at n 20, above, to reinforce its conclusion that an interference with freedom of expression is justified under Article 10(2).
2   *De Becker v Belgium No 214/56 B 2* (1960) Com Rep para 279.
3   Van Dijk and Van Hoof, pp 564-565.
4   A 3 para 7 (1961). In *Open Door Counselling and Well Women Centre v Ireland* A 246 paras 78-79 (1992), the Court rejected an argument by the government based on Article 17 and Article 60 that Article 10 should not be interpreted to limit the right to life. The Court said that it was Irish law which made any limitation of the right to life possible (by allowing women to travel abroad to obtain abortions), not the interpretation of Article 10.

that reason alone, entitled to deprive him of his rights under Articles 5 and 6. He was complaining about being interned, ie detained by order of the executive without any demonstration of a reasonable suspicion that he had committed an offence. The object of Article 17, the Court said, was to make it impossible for individuals to take advantage of a Convention right with the aim of destroying the enjoyment by other people of the rights in the Convention. Here, Lawless was not seeking to take advantage of his rights under Articles 5 and 6 in order to subvert the rights of others. The result is that Article 17, whether in conjunction with Article 14 or otherwise, is most likely to be called in aid by a state when it acts to restrict rights under Articles 8, 10 and 11 and under Article 3 of the First Protocol.[5]

Article 17 applies to states as well as to individuals and groups. It serves to control the powers of the state, as well as to enhance them in the manner just discussed. The nature of the complaint by an applicant will be that the state has used its powers to interfere with rights for a purpose or in a manner beyond those permitted by the Convention. It is essentially an allegation of bad faith against the state because it is hardly conceivable that a limitation of a right which, on its face, could otherwise be justified under the Convention, would be excluded by Article 17.[6] Thus, when relied on by an individual, the applicant frequently couples his complaint that Article 17 has been violated with an allegation that there has been a breach of Article 18 also. Bad faith to one side – and there are always the greatest difficulties in demonstrating this – Article 17 thus becomes subsidiary to the determination that interferences with Convention rights by the state are, in any event, not compatible with the Convention. It explains why, even in the relatively few cases in which it has been called upon to consider Article 17 as applied against a state, the Court has found no need to deal with the question.

In the *Greek* case,[7] the applicant states argued that the government of Greece could not under Article 17 limit the exercise of individual rights in order to consolidate its hold on power. They said that Article 17 was directed against 'totalitarian conspiracies' and that the Greek government was one of these. The majority of the Commission found no need to decide this question because it had already decided that the government could not base its actions on Article 15, there being no emergency. Mr Ermacora found the derogation to be impermissible under Article 17, accepting the applicants' argument and pointing out that the government had shown no inclination to comply with its obligation to hold free and fair elections.[8] Mr Busuttil allowed that there might be circumstances when a revolutionary government might have to rely on Article 17 while it set about restoring

5   There was a suggestion in *Retimag SA v FRG No 712/60*, 4 YB 384 (1961), that Article 17 could apply to interferences with the right to property under First Protocol, Article 1 but the question was not reached. For comment, see Jacobs, pp 210-211.
6   See *Engel v Netherlands* A 22 para 108 (1976) and *Lithgow v UK* A 102 (1986) Com Rep para 448 (the Article 17 point was not argued before the Court).
7   12 YB (the *Greek* case) 1 at 111-112 (1969); CM Res DH (70) 1.
8   Id, pp 102-103.

democracy; it was entitled to a 'reasonable period' to prove that this was its objective, an obligation manifestly not met by the Greek regime.[9]

Allegations that Article 17 should be applied to state activities have been rare and, even where the Commission has been prepared to look at them, the Court has managed to avoid reaching a decision.[10] Article 17 confers a power on states to act,[11] not a positive duty.[12] On the one hand, in what will be a narrow range of circumstances, Article 17 legitimates action by a state which, as a matter of routine, cannot be brought within any of the ordinary exceptions of the Convention when circumstances sufficient to give a wider power to derogate under Article 15 have not arisen. On the other, it provides some protection against states, where the individual shows that the state is interfering with his rights other than for the good (in Convention terms) reason it claims.

3. ARTICLE 18: PROHIBITION OF THE USE OF RESTRICTIONS FOR AN IMPROPER PURPOSE

'**Article 18**
The restrictions permitted under this Convention to the said rights and freedoms shall not be applied for any purpose other than those for which they have been prescribed.'

Article 18 has no independent character: it may be invoked only by an applicant who asserts that a restriction permitted by the Convention on the enjoyment of his rights has been used for some purpose other than the one for which it is authorised. For instance, in *Engel v Netherlands*,[13] two of the applicants argued that disciplinary proceedings against them for writing in an army magazine were taken to inhibit them in the exercise of their trade union activities and not, as maintained by the state, for the prevention of disorder in the camp. The Court did not accede to those claims. Article 18 gives protection against misuse of powers or breaches of the principle of good faith. In *Kamma v Netherlands*,[14] the Commission said:

'Article 18, like Article 14 of the Convention, does not have an autonomous role. It can only be applied in conjunction with other Articles of the Convention. There may, however, be a violation of Article 18 in connection with another Article, although there is no violation of that Article taken alone'.

---

9 Id, p 119.
10 Eg *Sporrong and Lönnroth v Sweden* A 52 para 76 (1982). For the Commission, see id, B 46 (1980) Com Rep paras 122-123.
11 Warbrick, 32 ICLQ 82 at 91-93 (1983).
12 But see Fawcett, pp 275-276, suggesting that in some circumstances there may be a positive obligation to discriminate against a group whose activities are covered by Article 17.
13 A 22 paras 104-108 (1976).
14 *No 4771/71*, 1 DR 4 at 9 (1974) Com Rep; CM Res DH (75) 1.

Article 18 is to be read as an integral part of all the various limitation clauses of the Convention[15] but it can have no application where the right is not subject to restrictions.[16]

In *De Becker v Belgium*,[17] the Commission said that Article 18 was a bar to relying on derogations legitimately made under Article 15 once the emergency had passed, a matter conceded by the government. The concession was not without importance because allegations of breaches of Article 18 will impugn the good faith of the state or cast serious doubts on the efficiency of its administration and the system of its democratic remedies for dealing with them. In *Bozano v France*,[18] the Commission was not prepared to accept an allegation of unlawful collusion between the police authorities of France and Switzerland which had been considered and found to be without foundation by a Swiss court. On the other hand, it did accept that there had been an abuse of power by the French police, prior to the applicant's expulsion from France, on the basis of a judgment to that effect by a French court.[19] The evidential barrier is often the greatest obstacle to sustaining claims of violations of Article 18. In the *Kamma* case,[20] the applicant could show no more than that, while he was properly detained on suspicion of committing one offence, the police questioned him about his involvement in another. While there was an ambiguity about the ground on which he was being held, the Commission held that this did not demonstrate a breach of Article 18 and that, since one of the grounds on which he was detained could be justified, he had not been held contrary to the Convention. In *Engel v Netherlands*,[1] the applicants were not able to prove the motive of the authorities, nor in *Handyside v UK*[2] could the applicant show that his books were seized for political reasons rather than for 'the protection of morals' of a child audience. Some claims have failed where the applicant has not demonstrated an abuse of the power, even on his version of the facts.[3] The Strasbourg authorities should be alive to the possibility of the rationalisation of the reasons for interfering with an individual's rights, presented only when the state is required to explain itself in Strasbourg. A legitimate reason for so acting must have been *the* reason for acting.[4] However, unless there is something of a shift in the burden of proof, an

15 *X v Austria No 753/60*, 4 CD (1960).
16 *Kamma v Austria* loc cit at p 513, n 14, above, p 10.
17 *No 214/56* B 2 Com Rep para 271 (1960).
18 *No 9990/82*, 39 DR 119 at 142 (1984).
19 Id, p 141.
20 Loc cit at p 513, n 14, above, pp 11-12.
1   A 22 (1976).
2   B 22 Com Rep para 175 (1976). See also *X v FRG No 6038/73*, 44 CD 115 at 119 (1973) and *McFeeley v UK No 8317/78*, 20 DR 44 at 102 (1980).
3   *Bozano v Switzerland No 9909/80*, 39 DR 58 at 70 (1984) (state obliged to extradite, no matter how person came in to its territory) and *Bozano v Italy No 9991/82*, 39 DR 147 at 157 (1984). Both cases might be reconsidered in the light of developments in situations where an accused is brought unlawfully to a state's territory: see *Stocke v Germany* A 199 (1991) (where the claim failed on the facts).
4   *K v France No 18580/91*, 16 EHRR CD23 (1993).

applicant is unlikely to be able to prove that this is not the case in only the most exceptional case.

Where the institutions have found a violation by reason of a failure to comply with the specific limits of a restriction provision, the Court has been unwilling to go on to decide whether Article 18 has been breached also.[5] If this turns out to be invariably the case, Article 18 will serve little purpose.

5 *Sporrong and Lönnroth v Sweden* A 52 para 56 (1982) and *Bozano v France* A 111 para 61 (1986). On the reluctance of the Court to proceed under Article 18, see Sudre, 91 RGDIP 533 at 580-583 (1987).

CHAPTER 18

Article 1, First Protocol: The right to property

'**Article 1, First Protocol**
Every natural or legal person is entitled to the peaceful enjoyment of his possessions. No one shall be deprived of his possessions except in the public interest and subject to the conditions provided for by law and by the general principles of international law.

The preceding provisions shall not, however, in any way impair the right of a state to enforce such laws as it deems necessary to control the use of property in accordance with the general interest or to secure the payment of taxes or other contributions or penalties.'

1. INTRODUCTION

It proved exceedingly difficult to reach agreement on a formulation of the right to property when the European Convention was being drafted.[1] A proposed article based on Article 17 of the Universal Declaration of Human Rights was not acceptable.[2] Eventually, it was one of the provisions left over until the First Protocol. Even then, the differences between states were considerable and the provision finally adopted guarantees only a much qualified right, allowing the state a wide power to interfere with property.[3] The United Kingdom and Sweden in particular were concerned that no substantial fetter be placed on the power of states to implement programmes of nationalisation of industries for political and social purposes.[4] In its final

1 See Robertson, 28 BYIL 359 (1951) and Peukert, 2 HRLJ 37 at 38-42 (1981). On Article 1 generally, see Sermet, *La Convention européenne des droits de l'homme et le droit de propriété*, Dossiers sur les droits de l'homme No 11, 1991; Van Der Broek, (1986) LIEI 52; and Frowein, *European System*, Ch 20.
2 See 2 TP 132. The question was dealt with intermittently in the debate in the Consultative Assembly: id, pp 56-132. Article 17 of the Universal Declaration reads: '1. Everyone has the right to own property alone as well as in association with others. 2. No one shall be arbitrarily deprived of his property.' On the Declaration, see Alfredsson, in Eide et al, *The Universal Declaration of Human Rights*, 1992, pp 252-262.
3 For the main items in the preparatory work, see 3 TP 92-96, 106-108 (Consultative Assembly) and 134-136 (Secretary General's Memorandum). The text was eventually approved by the Consultative Assembly: 8 TP 168.
4 6 TP 140, 200.

form, Article 1 of the First Protocol contains no express reference to a right to compensation at any level in the event of interference with property, save any that might be found in the reference to 'the general principles of international law'. The Court has made frequent reference to the drafting history of Article 1 of the First Protocol and its influence has been substantial in confirming the wide latitude states have in interfering with the right.

The right of 'Every natural or legal person . . .' is protected, wording which provides specific recognition of the general position that corporate bodies have rights under the Convention. It is necessary that the applicant be the real 'victim', ie the corporation if its rights are affected, the shareholder if his rights have been interfered with.[5]

The English language text uses the word 'possessions' to describe the protected interest but any suggestions that it should be read narrowly is refuted by the word '*biens*' in the French text which indicates that a wide range of proprietorial interests were intended to be protected.[6] It embraces immoveable and moveable property and corporal and incorporeal interests, such as shares[7] and patents.[8] Contractual rights,[9] including leases,[10] and judgment debts[11] are possessions. The essential characteristic is the acquired economic value of the individual interest. Expectations do not have the degree of concreteness to bring them within the idea of 'possessions'.[12] Initially, the ascription and identification of property rights is for the national legal system[13] and it is incumbent on an applicant to establish the precise nature of the right in the national law and his entitlement to enjoy it.[14] However, the mere fact that the national law does not acknowledge as a legal right a particular interest or does so in terms which do not result in it being recognised as a property right does not conclusively determine that the interest is not a 'possession' for the purposes of Article 1, First Protocol. The concept of 'possession' is autonomous and the demonstration of an

---

5　*X v Austria No 1706/62*, 21 CD 34 (1966) (substantial majority shareholder 'victim' when company injured); *Yarrow v UK No 9266/81*, 30 DR 155 at 185 (1983) (shareholders not 'victims' by reason of damage to company which affects only the value of their shares); *Company S and T v Sweden No 11189/84*, 50 DR 121 (1986).

6　*Wiggins v UK No 7456/76*, 13 DR 40 at 46 (1978).

7　*Bramelid and Malmström v Sweden Nos 8588/79 and 8589/79*, 29 DR 64 (1982).

8　*Smith Kline and French Laboratories v Netherlands No 12633/87*, 66 DR 70 at 79 (1990).

9　*A, B and Company AS v FRG No 7742/76*, 14 DR 146 at 168 (1978) and *Association of General Practitioners v Denmark No 12947/87*, 62 DR 226 at 234 (1989).

10　*Mellacher v Austria* A 169 para 43 (1989).

11　*Stran Greek Refineries and Stratis Andreadis v Greece* A 301B paras 61-62 (1994) – arbitral award.

12　*Batelaan and Huiges v Netherlands No 10438/83*, 41 DR 170 at 173 (1984).

13　There are few restrictions upon what a state may regard as capable of being owned – perhaps only individuals because of freedom from slavery in Article 4. But the fact that something is capable of being owned in one legal system (eg human blood or organs) is not a reason why it must be capable of being owned in another.

14　*S v UK No 11716/85*, 47 DR 274 at 279 (1986) (occupation of property without legal right not 'possession') and *Agneessens v Belgium No 12164/86*, 58 DR 63 (1988) (claims to a debt rejected by court not a 'possession').

established economic interest by an applicant may be sufficient to establish a right protected by the Convention. In *Tre Traktörer Aktiebolag v Sweden*,[15] the Court rejected the government's argument that because a liquor licence conferred no rights in national law, it could not be a 'possession' for the purposes of Article 1, First Protocol. It was essential to the successful conduct of the applicant's restaurant and its withdrawal had adverse effects on the goodwill and value of the business.

As indicated in an earlier chapter,[16] the right to a fair trial in Article 6 applies to the determination of 'civil rights and obligations'. This is a term with an autonomous Convention meaning that has been interpreted as including pecuniary rights.[17] The coherence of the Convention as a whole demands that the autonomous concept of 'possessions' in Article 1 of the First Protocol be no less a category than the concept of pecuniary rights for the purposes of Article 6: the reasoning about the essence of the interest measured by its nature and importance to an individual should apply to its formal protection (Article 6(1)) and its substance (Article 1, First Protocol) alike.[18] The minimum in each case is that the applicant shows that he is entitled to some real, if yet unattributed, economic benefit. This is relevant to the treatment of pensions as property. While the Commission has said that there is no general right to a pension to be found in Article 1 of the First Protocol,[19] it has allowed that for the purposes of Article 1 a person has a protected right in a contributory pension scheme.[20] What is required is that the applicant demonstrate that he has a legal right to some benefit if he satisfies certain conditions, rather than that he seeks to ensure that a discretion is exercised in his favour. While he may be entitled under Article 6(1) to a fair hearing to determine whether the conditions are satisfied, if they are not, the applicant will have no right to the benefit and the state will not be put to justifying why the benefit does not accrue.[1] It is necessary to separate clearly the questions of the existence of a property right and the justification for interfering with it. As far as the second question is concerned, the flexibility of the 'fair balance' test[2] is such that no great damage is done by widening the 'property right'. So, for example, the

---

15 A 159 para 53 (1984). See also *Van Marle v Netherlands* A 101 para 41 (1986) (a clientele built up by the applicants' efforts an asset (cf business goodwill) that qualified as a possession).

16 See above, pp 177-178.

17 See, eg, *Beaumartin v France* A 296-B para 28 (1994), discussed above, p 180 (compensation agreement negotiated by France for its nationals concerned the applicant's pecuniary rights so that Article 6 applied even though no legal right in French law; right to compensation should likewise be treated as a 'possession' under Article 1, First Protocol).

18 *Feldbrugge v Netherlands* A 99 paras 37-40 (1986) and *Deumeland v FRG* A 100 paras 71-71 (1986). To similar effect, see Rosas, in Rosas and Helgesen, eds, *The Strength of Diversity: Human Rights and Pluralist Democracy*, 1992, pp 150-151.

19 *X v FRG No 2116/64*, 23 CD 10 (1966).

20 *Müller v Austria No 5849/72*, 3 DR 25 (1975) Com Rep; CM Res DH (76) 2.

1 *C v France No 10443/83*, 56 DR 20 at 34 (1988) seems to accept that the pension right was a possession. However, on the facts there was no interference with a property right because a condition for the pension had not been met.

2 See below, p 522.

distinction between contributory and non-contributory[3] pensions may be dealt with by assessing the legitimacy of interferences with them rather than deciding whether either is protected by Article 1, First Protocol.[4]

The Convention protects an applicant's existing possessions against interference. It is not a right to be put into the possession of things one does not already have, however strong the individual's interest in doing so may be. In *Marckx v Belgium*,[5] the Court said that Article 1 of the First Protocol 'does not guarantee the right to acquire possessions whether on intestacy or through voluntary dispositions'. There is no right to have food or to have shelter, whatever one's destitution, under this provision.[6] This confirms that the protection offered by Article 1 of the First Protocol is much closer to the origins of property rights as civil rights than to modern ideas of economic rights, even though it is now to the defence of economic interests that the provision is directed.[7]

The specific right protected by Article 1 of the First Protocol is the right to the 'peaceful enjoyment' of possessions: the right to have, to use, to dispose of, to pledge, to lend, even to destroy one's possessions. As the Court said in the *Marckx* case,[8] 'Article 1 is in substance guaranteeing the right of property'. Enjoyment is protected principally against interference by the state. Interference may be in the forms specifically referred to in Article 1 of the First Protocol – deprivation or control of use – but it is a wider category. So in *Sporrong and Lönnroth v Sweden*,[9] where there was a long delay between an initial decision indicating that property was likely to be expropriated and its execution, the Court held that there had been an interference with the applicants' right to the enjoyment of their possessions even though the interference was neither a seizure nor a measure of control. The state will be responsible under Article 1 of the First Protocol only for interferences which affect the economic value of property. Accordingly, claims about interferences with the aesthetic or environmental qualities of possessions are protected, if they be protected at all, elsewhere in the Convention. In *S v France*[10] the Commission looked at the effects on the value of property as a result of noise pollution but did not consider, as the

---

3 *G v Austria No 10094/82*, 38 DR 84 at 86 (1984).

4 *T v Sweden No 10671/83*, 42 DR 229 (1985) and *Stigson v Sweden No 12264/86*, 57 DR 131 (1988) could certainly have been decided in this way, with the same result. On the difficulties of classifying the rights in pensions in English law, see R Nobles, 14 Legal Studies 345 (1994).

5 A 31 para 50 (1979). Cf *Inze v Austria* A 126 para 38 (1987).

6 Cf Cassese, 1 EJIL 141 (1991) with discussion of *Van Volsem v Belgium No 14641/89* (1990), unreported.

7 *Van der Mussele v Belgium* A 70 para 48 (1983) and *Linde v Sweden No 11628/85*, 47 DR 270 (1986).

8 A 31 para 63 (1979).

9 A 52 para 60 (1982). See also *Erkner and Hofauer v Austria* A 117 para 74 (1987); *Poiss v Austria* A 117 para 64 (1987); *Argrotexim Hellas v Greece No 14807/89* Com Rep (1994) (pending before the Court).

10 *No 13728/88*, 65 DR 250 at 261 (1990) and *Rayner v UK No 9310/81*, 47 DR 5 at 14 (1986) (Article 1, First Protocol 'does not, in principle, guarantee a right to the peaceful enjoyment of possessions in a pleasant environment').

French court also had not considered, amenity loss of the rural aspect from the property, resulting from industrial development nearby.

In principle, positive obligations on the state to protect the enjoyment of possessions are included in Article 1 of the First Protocol, including obligations to prevent private interferences, but there is little practice to indicate when the state is obliged to act. It is clear that it is not obliged to act to prevent loss of value as a result of market factors.[11] Such case-law as there is suggests that positive obligations may arise in some circumstances when a state interferes with the enjoyment of possessions. Such obligations include obligations to provide compensation, expeditious processes and, where the interferences lead to the determination of a civil right, a process which fully satisfies Article 6(1).[12]

In *Loizidou v Turkey*,[13] the Commission had to deal with what it characterised as an issue of access to property in order that the property owner could exercise her rights. The facts of the case are complicated by the political background to the application, which concerns the Turkish occupation of northern Cyprus.[14] The applicant claimed that the defendant state had interfered with her rights under Article 1 of the First Protocol because, directly or indirectly, it had responsibility for her, a Greek Cypriot, being denied access to her real property in northern Cyprus. A majority of the Commission held that the complaint was really about the applicant's freedom of movement, the denial of which had the effect of preventing her physical access to the land. It said that 'the right of peaceful enjoyment of one's possessions does not include, as a corollary, the right of freedom of movement'.[15] In two separate dissenting opinions, Messrs Rozakis and Pellonpää took a much wider view of the content of the right to enjoy one's possessions. In Mr Rozakis's words, it includes:

> '. . . the possibility to repair an immoveable good; or the possibility usefully to exploit the possession; or the possibility to exchange a possession through the free acquisition of another one, etc . . .'[16]

There is force in this argument: alien property owners may have no right of entry to a state to visit their property but the rights they have in respect of their property which do not require their presence should not be interfered with. Nor should they be deprived of their property by reason of their absence alone. Apart from the very particular circumstances of this

11 Nor to protect against the effects of inflation, *X v FRG No 8724/79*, 20 DR 226 (1980).
12 See below, pp 526-527.
13 *No 1531/89* Com Rep (1993) (pending before the Court).
14 See *Chrysostomos, Papachrysostomou* and *Loizidou v Turkey Nos 15299/89*, 15300/89, 15318/89, 68 DR 216 (1991) (admissibility decision).
15 *Loizidou v Turkey*, Com Rep para 98 (1993) (pending before the Court on merits).
16 At p 19. Mr Rozakis found the need to dissent in these terms in a case concerning restrictions upon entry into the territory of a state in which one's property is located. If one if lawfully within the territory, one should, subject to the terms of a tenancy agreement and any public health or other recognised public interest considerations, be allowed access to one's property to effect repairs, etc.

application, the position of the majority might be explained by the way the case was pleaded, because matters of freedom of movement as aspects of the applicant's right to liberty featured prominently in her claims.[17]

2. THE STRUCTURE OF ARTICLE 1, FIRST PROTOCOL AND THE INTER-RELATIONSHIP OF ITS PROVISIONS

The Court has broken down Article 1 of the First Protocol into its component parts and has gradually established the relationship between them. Its language has become familiar by frequent repetition. In *Sporrong and Lönnroth v Sweden*,[18] the Court stated:

> '. . . this provision comprises three distinct rules. The first rule, set out in the first sentence of the first paragraph, is of a general nature and enunciates the principle of peaceful enjoyment of property; the second rule, contained in the second sentence of the same paragraph, covers deprivation of possessions and makes it subject to certain conditions; and the third rule, stated in the second paragraph, recognises the contracting states are entitled, amongst other things, to control the use of property in accordance with the general interest. The three rules are not 'distinct' in the sense of being unconnected: the second and third rules are concerned with particular instances of interference with the right to peaceful enjoyment of property and should therefore be construed in the light of the general principle enunciated in the first rule . . .'

The three sentences in Article 1 of the First Protocol will henceforth be referred to as Article 1/1/1, Article 1/1/2 and Article 1/2.

It follows from the above passage that Article 1/1/1 is not only a statement of principle. It also provides a third, separate basis for regulating interferences with the 'peaceful enjoyment of possessions' that do not qualify as a deprivation of a person's possessions subject to Articles 1/1/2 or a control of the use of property subject to Article 1/2. For example, in the *Sporrong and Lönnroth* case itself, the Court found that the grant of expropriation permits, which did not fall within Article 1/1/2 or 1/2, was subject to control under Article 1/1/1 as an interference with the peaceful enjoyment of the houses concerned.

When considering whether Article 1/1/1 has been complied with, the Court applies a 'fair balance' test. In the *Sporrong and Lönnroth* case,[19] the Court stated:

17 See paras 29 and 30.
18 A 52 para 61 (1982). Cf *James v UK* A 98 para 37 (1986).
19 A 52, para 69 (1982).

'For the purposes of [Article 1/1/1] . . . the Court must determine whether a fair balance was struck between the demands of the general interest of the community and the requirements of the protection of the individual's fundamental rights. The search for this balance is inherent in the whole of the Convention and is also reflected in the structure of Article 1.'

On the facts of the *Sporrong and Lönnroth* case[20] the Court found that there had been a breach of Article 1/1/1 because the grant of the expropriation permits, which adversely affected the property rights of the applicants, did not involve a 'fair balance' between the public and the private interests concerned.[1] In terms of the structure of Article 1, what is important to note is that, as the passage from the judgment quoted in the preceding paragraph suggests, the Court has since applied its 'fair balance' test – which was devised particularly to provide a criterion by which to assess compliance with Article 1/1/1 – when deciding cases under Articles 1/1/2 and 1/2 also. Indeed, although cases may still be dealt with by reference to Article 1/1/2 or 1/2 separately, and may focus upon the particular language of these sentences when this is done, there is a tendency for the Court to decide cases simply by reference to its 'fair balance' test whatever sentence, if any, it identifies as being the one within which the case might technically fall.

When applying the 'fair balance' test, the Court generally leaves it to the state to identify the community interest; claims made by the state will seldom be reviewed. The balancing process thereafter may be complex and will always involve acts of judgment of a political (or policy) kind. It is hardly surprising that the Court has conceded a wide margin of appreciation to a state in reaching its decision that the community interest outweighs the individual's claims. This is true whether the case falls within Article 1/1/1 or Article 1/1/2 or 1/2, although the language of these last two sentences indicates a little further what factors the state ought to take into account. To that extent, an applicant may enjoy a certain advantage if he is able to persuade the Court to consider the matter under these provisions rather than under the general principle, but the benefits will be marginal only. For instance, under Article 1/1/2, a foreign owner of property could always be assured of the minimum protection of general international law, even if a state were able to persuade the Court that the fair balance did not import equivalent protection for national owners.

As will be apparent, it may be very difficult to determine within which sentence of Article 1 a particular case falls. This may be illustrated by reference to the treatment in *Papamichalopoulos v Greece*[2] of the question whether there was a *de facto* deprivation of property that brought Article 1/1/2 into play. In that case there were three sets of separate opinions in the Commission's report, all reaching the same conclusion but each for different

---

20 See further, below, pp 523-524.
1   See further below, p 526, on the *Sporring and Lönnroth* case.
2   A 260-B (1993) Com Rep. On *de facto* deprivation, see further, below, p 528.

reasons. The applicants' land in Greece had been occupied by a public body for public purposes but without legal sanction. The Greek courts had upheld the applicants' title to the land but it, or land of equivalent value, had not been returned to them. The applicants had been denied access to the land and were effectively precluded from dealing with it in any way, even though they remained formally the owners. In its opinion, a unanimous Commission decided the case under Article 1/1/1 and found a breach of the applicants' right to peaceful enjoyment of their possessions because of the failure of the state to provide an expeditious procedure to determine and grant appropriate compensation.[3] Four members of the Commission said in a concurring opinion that there was a continuing *de facto* expropriation of the applicants' land because they had been denied all use of it and all means of dealing with it. Here, there was a violation of Article 1/1/2 because the deprivation was not according to law nor had any compensation been made.[4] Three other members of the Commission were of the view that there had been a *de facto* deprivation of the applicants' property once a law had been passed granting them a claim only to compensation *in lieu* of the restoration of the land. The violation here was a breach of Article 1/1/1 in that their claim to compensation remained unsatisfied for a very long period (six-and-a-half years) after it had been recognised by the authorities.[5] The Court's judgment is clearer, not least because it was unanimous, in that it held that there had been a *de facto* expropriation of the applicants' property which had not been remedied.[6] What is remarkable, however, is that the Court did not identify the particular sentence within which the case fell. Although it concluded that the *de facto* interference was serious enough to amount to an expropriation of the property, which would suggest that technically Article 1/1/2 was the relevant sentence, the Court does not mention any particular sentence, merely deciding that there had been a breach of Article 1.

3. ARTICLE 1/1/1: INTERFERENCE WITH THE PEACEFUL ENJOYMENT OF POSSESSIONS

As noted, the origin of the Court's opinion that Article 1/1/1 provides a ground for regulating interferences with a person's possessions that is separate from and additional to those in Articles 1/1/2 and 1/2 is the judgment in *Sporrong and Lönnroth v Sweden*. There the applicants' properties had been affected by expropriation permits granted to the City of Stockholm for the purposes of redevelopment of the city centre. The expropriations had not been executed but, while the permits were in force, the owners were prohibited from construction on the sites and were subject

3 Id, para 48.
4 Id (Messrs Frowein, Trechsel, Busuttil and Rozakis).
5 Ibid (Messrs Pellonpää and Schermers and Mrs Liddy).
6 A 260-B para 45 (1993).

to planning blight. The permits and prohibition orders remained in place in one case for 23 and 25 years and in the other for 8 and 12 years.

The prohibitions on construction were clearly measures of control of use within Article 1/2. However, the Court decided that neither the expropriation permits as a matter of form nor the actual consequences as a matter of substance amounted to a deprivation within Article 1/1/2.[7] Instead, there had been an 'interference' with the applicants' enjoyment of their possessions under Article 1/1/1. Since the *Sporrong and Lönnroth* case there have been others involving an interference with the peaceful enjoyment of possessions against which Article 1/1/1 provides protection where there is neither a deprivation nor a control of property. For instance, in *Stran Greek Refineries and Stratis Andreadis v Greece*,[8] the Court (somewhat surprisingly) decided that the making null and unenforceable by legislation of an arbitral award in the applicants' favour was an 'interference' within Article 1/1/1 rather than (as contended by the applicants) a *de facto* deprivation or, even a *de iure*, deprivation within Article 1/1/2.

Where there has been an interference with the peaceful enjoyment of possessions in the sense of Article 1/1/1, the Court must consider whether there has been a fair balance between 'the demands of the general interest of the community and the requirements of the protection of the individual's fundamental rights'.[9] Even though the Court in *Sporrong and Lönnroth* was prepared to concede a wide margin to the state in 'complex and difficult' matters of city centre planning, when deciding whether a 'fair balance' had been struck, it did not find acceptable the 'inflexibility' of the Swedish arrangements which left the property owners in a state of great uncertainty over an extensive period, without any effective remedy for their concerns. The applicants, the Court said, had borne

'an individual and excessive burden which could have been rendered legitimate only if they had the possibility of seeking a reduction of the time-limits or of claiming compensation'.[10]

What is interesting about this approach is the suggestion that the *way* in which the national authorities strike the balance may be a factor in deciding whether in *substance* they have struck the balance compatibly with the Convention's requirements.[11] Further, the provision of compensation as an element in striking the right balance can arise other than in cases of outright deprivation which would fall within Article 1/1/2.[12] Similar considerations motivated the Court in finding that the administration of a scheme for the

7 Id, paras 62-65.
8 A 301-B para 67 (1994).
9 Id, para 69.
10 Id, para 73. The Court found no need to go on to consider the question of the construction prohibitions.
11 In *Erkner and Hofauer v Austria* A 117 para 76 (1987), the Court noted that the passing of time for the purposes of the balance in Article 1/1/1 was independent of the 'reasonable time' required by Article 6(1).
12 A 52 (1982).

consolidation of agricultural holdings in the interest of their economic exploitation was in violation of Article 1/1/1.[13] The scheme had not been brought to a conclusion sixteen years after it had been implemented against the applicants' land and there was no means of redress for their interim losses up to the time it was implemented.

The 'fair balance' principle or test laid down in the *Sporrong and Lönnroth* case finds its authority in two complementary sources. The first is the general balance which the Court holds to be pervasive throughout the Convention between the enjoyment of individual rights and the protection of the public interest.[14] The second is in the substantive content of 'law' as understood by the Strasbourg authorities to include protection against the arbitrary and disproportionate effects of an otherwise formally valid national law.[15] The first provides the elements for the balancing equation. The second gives more precise guidance as to how the weight of the factors in the balance are to be assessed. One important aspect of the insistence that interferences with possessions be found in an identified legal source in the national legal system is that the law will generally provide an indication of the factors motivating the measures of interference and the application of the law will be evidence of how the state has assessed the competing interests. While the state's conclusions are not the last word, since the Strasbourg authorities claim the ultimate power of review,[16] they none the less carry great weight because the language of Article 1 suggests a wide measure of discretion for the state and because many factors have to be taken into account, some of which are not amenable to objective assessment.

The clear tendency in the jurisprudence has, as suggested, been to assimilate the assessment of all interferences with the peaceful enjoyment of possessions under the single principle of fair balance set out in the *Sporrong and Lönnroth* case, this despite the language of Article 1 of the First Protocol suggesting distinct standards for measures which deprive a person of his property and measures which seek to control property. There are two reasons for this. The first is, as already indicated, that the Court has isolated a third head of interference with the peaceful enjoyment of possessions in the *Sporrong and Lönnroth* case, a category which has assumed greater importance because of the reluctance of the Court to expand the notion of 'deprivation' to cover *de facto* deprivations of property beyond all but the most clear cases. The Court has subsumed other, extensive but less absolute measures affecting property under the *Sporrong and Lönnroth* head. The second reason is that the Court has had to spell out the conditions upon which an interference in the sense of Article 1/1/1 could be properly exercised. These conditions are both substantive and procedural and are elaborated in such a

---

13 *Erkner and Hofauer v Austria* A 117 (1987) and *Poiss v Austria* A 117 (1987). The cases are examples in which the Court did consider the facts in terms of each of the three particular sentences in Article 1. After concluding that the cases did not fall within either Article 1/1/2 or 1/2, it decided that there was a breach of Article 1/1/1.

14 *Belgian Linguistic* case A 6 p 32 (1968).

15 See above, pp 285-289.

16 *Sporrong and Lönnroth v Sweden* A 52 para 69 (1982).

way that has proved useful with respect to the express powers of interference in the second and third sentences of Article 1, First Protocol. The applicants succeeded in the *Sporrong and Lönnroth* case because there was no procedure by which they could challenge the long-continued application of the expropriation permits which were blighting their property nor were they entitled to any compensation for the loss that this situation had brought about.[17] These matters are of general importance because neither of the express grounds of interference, deprivation or control of use, is expressly accompanied by either procedural conditions or compensatory obligations (save as may be required by 'the general principles of international law') for its use.[18] The Court has relied on the *Sporrong and Lönnroth* principle to import similar considerations into cases falling under either head.[19] This is not to say that the detailed application of the 'fair balance' test will be the same in all circumstances[20] but that it provides the framework for resolving issues whatever the characterisation of the interference. The protection the 'fair balance' test gives is that the burden of promoting a community interest should not fall excessively on a property owner and that he should have some process to challenge whether this is the case, a process which can take into account not just the balance of advantage but which can consider whether the public good pursued could otherwise have been achieved than by trespassing on the individual rights of the property owner.[1] In the *Stran Greek Refineries* case,[2] the Court made reference to the position in public international law (even though it had no formal relevance because the case involved the government of Greece and two Greek nationals) as one element in deciding whether the state had struck a 'fair balance' between the rights of the applicants and the interests of the community.

The 'fair balance' will sometimes require the payment of compensation for the interference with property rights. The *Sporrong and Lönnroth* case does not establish clearly the nature and extent of this obligation. While we know the extent of the 'just satisfaction' ordered by the Court under Article 50, the judgment, typically, does not enunciate the principles upon which the award was made.[3] The identification and assessment of the loss endured by the

---

17 One of the factors which counted against the applicant in *Katte Klitsche de la Grange v Italy* A 293-B (1993) was that he had not used a procedure available to him, para 46.

18 See below, pp 530-532, on 'the general principles of international law'.

19 Eg deprivation of property (*Tre Traktörer Aktiebolag v Sweden* A 159 para 59 (1984)) and control of use of property (*Allan Jacobsson v Sweden* A 163 para 55 (1989)).

20 Eg in *Gillow v UK* A 109 (1986) Com Rep para 148 the Commission suggested that the application of the proportionality principle is different in cases involving deprivation and cases involving control of use.

1   Many interferences with the enjoyment of possessions will involve the 'determination of a civil right' and therefore the individual will be entitled to an Article 6(1) procedure: *Sporrong and Lönnroth v Sweden* A 52 paras 84-87 (1982). However, this will not always be the case, eg for taxation.

2   *Stan Greek Refineries and Stratis Andreadis v Greece* A 301-B para 72 (1994).

3   (Article 50) A 88 (1984). In *Erkner and Hofauer v Austria* (Article 50) A 124-D (1987) and *Poiss v Austria* (Article 50) A 124-E (1987), the Court approved friendly settlements which involved elements of compensation. There is much more detail in *Pine Valley Developments v Ireland* (Article 50) A 246-B (1993).

applicants was difficult. Because a central element of their claim was that there had been no national process to make even a tentative evaluation of it, the Court was without any guidance from the national authorities, still less decisions, to which it could defer. It is not possible to discern whether the measures of 'just satisfaction' represent a different valuation of the loss suffered by the applicants or a proportion of the loss, the proportion required to satisfy the balance between the public interest in urban planning and the burden which should fall on any property owner. If the state had decided the question of compensation differently from that awarded by the Court by way of satisfaction, it does not follow that the Court would have found a violation of Article 1/1/1, given the wide margin conceded to the state to fix the fair balance. The measure of compensation required by the fair balance test has been considered in cases concerning deprivations under Article 1/1/2 and measures of control under Article 1/2.

4. ARTICLE 1/1/2: DEPRIVATION OF PROPERTY

i. What is a deprivation?

In principle, there will be a deprivation of property only where all the legal rights of the owner are extinguished by operation of law or by the exercise of a legal power to the same effect.[4] However, not all such incidents are deprivations. The Court has treated some seizures of property as an aspect of the control of property.[5] For there to have been a deprivation of his property, the applicant must, of course, demonstrate that he had title to it.[6] In the *Holy Monasteries* case, the government argued that the creation of a presumption in favour of state ownership of disputed land was merely a procedural device to allow the settlement of such disputes and not an interference with established titles. In any event, no steps had been taken to implement the provisions of any law which might have transferred title from the applicants. The Court found that the presumption effectively vested an unchallengeable title in the state because the monasteries were not in a position to prove their own superior title, relying as they did on ancient, adverse possession. The Greek law was, the Court said, a substantive provision, the effect of which was to transfer ownership to the state.[7] The fact that the law had not yet been implemented was no guarantee that it

---

4   Eg *Lithgow v UK* A 102 (1986). Acts in accordance with the condition upon which property is held are not interferences and, *a fortiori*, not deprivations of property: *Fredin v Sweden* A 192 (1991).

5   *Allegemeine Gold-und Silberscheideanstalt [AGOSI] v UK* A 108 (1986). See below, p 536.

6   In *Holy Monasteries v Greece* A 301A (1994), the applicants divided into two groups: those which had made an agreement with the state about their property (which they now appeared to regret) and those who had not. The Court held that there had been no interference with the former's rights, para 78, whereas there had with the latter's, para 66.

7   Id, paras 57-61.

would not be.[8] Taking both matters together, there had been a deprivation of the applicants' property.[9]

In the absence of a formal extinction of the owner's rights, the Court has been very cautious about accepting that a *de facto* deprivation of property qualifies as a 'deprivation' for the purpose of Article 1/2.[10] *De facto* takings are generally understood to occur when the authorities interfere substantially with the enjoyment of possessions without formally divesting the owner of his title. In the *Sporrong and Lönnroth* case the Court held that the facts did not amount to a *de facto* deprivation of property so that Article 1/1/2 did not apply.[11] Only in the *Papamichalopoulos* case[12] has the Court conceded that the physical occupation of land was so extensive and the possibility of dealing with it in any way so remote that there was a *de facto* expropriation, though even here the Court did not say expressly that there had been a 'deprivation'. In *Hentrich v France*,[13] the applicant claimed that there had been a *de facto* expropriation, even though the effect of the national decision was to transfer ownership from the individual to the state. The act of interference complained of in the *Hentrich* case was the exercise of a right of pre-emption by the tax authorities over property bought by the applicant at a price the tax authorities considered to be below its market value. No allegation of fraud was necessary to trigger the right. An independent procedure to recover any lost tax revenue was available. If the right of pre-emption were exercised, the purchaser was paid his purchase price plus 10 per cent.[14] The Court did not explicitly endorse the applicant's claim that there had been a *de facto* taking, although it did agree that there had been a deprivation of property. Its treatment of the lawfulness of the deprivation entirely in terms of the substantive qualities of the French law indicates that the Court regarded the taking as *de iure*. Real instances of *de facto* takings will be rare and will be in breach of the Convention because they will not have been 'provided for by law'. There has been little support so far for Professor Pellonapää's suggestion that the test should be whether the interference amounts to a taking under international law.[15]

It may be formally necessary to determine whether an interference is a deprivation of property or an extensive control of the use of property because, in principle, they are governed by different provisions. If ownership is seen as a bundle of rights, the fact that an owner has been deprived of one

8 Id, para 65.
9 Id, para 66.
10 Eg *Stran Greek Refineries and Stratis Andreadis v Greece* A 301-B para 67 (1994).The Court noted without comment that the treatment of the applicant was not regarded by the national law as a *de facto* expropriation (and that, therefore, he was not entitled to compensation) in *Katte Klitsche de la Grange v Italy* A 293-B para 47 (1993).
11 Ibid, paras 62-63. For criticism of the judgment, see Higgins, 176 *Hague Recueil* 260 at 343-357, 367-368 (1982). The judgment was by 10 votes to 9 but the dissenting judges did not regard this as a case of *de facto* deprivation of property either.
12 A 260-B (1993). See above, p 253.
13 A 296-A paras 34, 35 (1994).
14 Id, paras 20-21.
15 Concurring in *Papamichalopoulos v Greece* A 260-B (1993) Com Rep.

right will not usually be sufficient to say that he has been deprived of ownership: rather it is a control of the use of property.[16]

ii. In the public interest

For a 'deprivation' of property to be consistent with Article 1/1/2, it must be 'in the public interest'. The identification of the objective of a deprivation of property and its characterisation as being 'in the public interest' is primarily for the state. It is difficult to imagine circumstances in which the Court would dispute the purpose alleged by the government or to contest its assertion that the measure was in the public interest.[17] In *Lithgow v UK*,[18] the Court said that the 'public interest' factor 'relates to the justification and motives for the actual taking'. In that case, the applicants strongly, but unsuccessfully, contested the desirability of measures for the nationalisation of the ship building industry. In *James v UK*,[19] they challenged the characterisation as being in the public interest of a legislative programme designed to transfer property rights from one individual to another for the purpose of enfranchising long lease-holders. The applicants relied on the French text – '*pour cause d'utilité publique*' – and the practice of some European states to narrow the notion of public interest to 'community interest'. The Court rejected this claim, maintaining that the object and purpose of Article 1 of the First Protocol was to protect against *arbitrary* confiscation of property. Accordingly:

> 'The taking of property in pursuance of a policy calculated to enhance social justice within the community can properly be described as being "in the public interest".'[20]

Even penal confiscations might be explained as being in the public interest. In such a case, the most an applicant would be able to establish would be a lack of due process if the deprivation were decided to be in the determination of a criminal charge against him and Article 6 were not satisfied. In many cases, deprivations of property will be under acts of legislation by Parliament. Any 'civil' right that the applicant may have had will have been removed by the legislation and there will be no place for Article 6(1).[1] If, therefore, the expropriation is to be attacked successfully, it

---

16 *Banér v Sweden No 11763/85*, 60 DR 128 at 140 (1989).
17 In *Hentrich v France* A 296-A para 39 (1994), the Court accepted the first (the prevention of tax evasion) of two reasons the state had given for interfering with the applicant's property and then found no need to consider the other (regulation of the property market).
18 A 102 para 109 (1986).
19 A 98 para 41 (1986). See also *Holy Monasteries v Greece* A 301-A (1994) Com Rep para 76. In most cases under Article 1/1/2, the public interest will be, in a wide sense, a planning objective.
20 Id, para 49. See also *Holy Monasteries v Greece* A 301A, paras 67-69 (1994).
1 Id, para 81.

must be on the conditions which attach to it rather than for the reason for which it was done.

iii. Subject to the conditions provided for by law

In the context of the Convention, 'provided for by law' means the state must have a basis in national law for its act of deprivation and that the law concerned must be both accessible and sufficiently certain. The identification of the legal basis for confiscations and the satisfaction of the criteria of accessibility and certainty have seldom posed difficulties for the Strasbourg authorities.[2] Beyond this, the law must provide protection against arbitrariness. The Court in the *Hentrich* case[3] found that a right to take property by way of pre-emption, vested in the tax authorities but exercised by them according to an unexplicated policy, did not satisfy the standard of foreseeability and that there were no procedural safeguards to prevent the unfair use of the power. The Court went on to find that the level of compensation was inadequate.[4] The safeguards against arbitrariness are implied conditions on the power of the state to deprive an owner of his property. What is required in each case will be determined by the application of the 'fair balance' test.[5]

iv. The general principles of international law

It is necessary first to consider the reference in Article 1/1/2 to the 'general principles of international law'. General international law protects *alien* property against arbitrary expropriation and against nationalisation without compensation.[6] Both the compensation standard for and the methods of valuation of property taken are controversial[7] and, arguably, they have changed considerably since the Convention was drafted.[8] The content of the 'general principles' to one side, reference to them in Article 1/1/2 allows two possible interpretations of their effect. The first is that the

---

2   *Papamichalopoulos v Greece* A 260-B (1993) might be explained on the basis that there was no law authorising the taking of the property.
3   A 296-A para 42 (1994).
4   Id, para 48.
5   Above, p 522.
6   Oppenheim, *International Law*, Volume I (9th edn, Jennings and Watts), pp 910-927.
7   Portugal made the following reservation (now withdrawn) on becoming a party to the Convention (21 YB 16-17 (1978)): '. . . expropriation of large landowners, big property owners and entrepreneurs or shareholders may be subject to no compensation under conditions to be laid down by the law', to which France, Germany and the UK responded: 'The general principles of international law require the payment of prompt, adequate and effective compensation in respect of the expropriation of foreign property' 22 YB 16-20 (1979).
8   Christie, 38 BYIL 307 (1962); Aldrich, 88 AJIL 585 (1994); *ELSI* case (*US v Italy*) (1989) ICJ Rep 15 at 67-71.

reference benefits only alien property holders, since they are, if only indirectly, the only beneficiaries under international law.[9] On this interpretation, what the Convention does is give such persons a tribunal where they, as individuals, may bring claims against a nationalising state without the intervention of their governments.[10] The alternative is that the Convention incorporates the *standards* of general international law in this particular case for the benefit of all persons protected by the Convention, thereby establishing a right to compensation for all persons deprived of their property with the compensation payable being defined by the 'general principles of international law'.[11]

In *James v UK*,[12] relying on the *travaux*, the Court said that it was not the intention of the parties to extend the protection of general international law to nationals. In fact, practically all cases arising under Article 1 of the First Protocol, have involved the property of nationals. Whether reference to international law will ever be given much effect is doubtful if the view of the Commission in the *Gasus* case prevails.[13] A German company was deprived of its property which had been in the possession of a Dutch company, sold by the former to the latter under a reservation of title agreement by which title was not to pass to the purchaser until the final purchase price had been paid in full. On the bankruptcy of the Dutch company, the property had been seized by the Dutch authorities for the settlement of the company's tax debts. The Commission found no violation of Article 1/1/2, the seizure being in the public interest, according to Dutch law, and not disproportionate to the purpose of protecting creditors. This was a case where the nationality of the property owner might have been of consequence. However, the Commission said only:

'... the deprivation of property which occurred cannot be compared to these measures of confiscation, nationalisation or expropriation in regard to which international law provides special protection to foreign citizens and companies.'[14]

Whether this really represents the condition of international law is open to doubt. Lump sum settlements commonly include isolated items of property taken or destroyed by a state as well as those seized under nationalisation programmes.[15] Indeed, it appears to be the case that if, under the international minimum standard, there is any liability for interference with

9   See *Beaumartin v France* A 296-B (1994).
10 *James v UK* A 98 para 62 (1986).
11 Ibid, para 61.
12 Ibid, paras 58-66. The Court made extensive reference to the preparatory work, para 64. The judgment confirms the long-established position of the Commission: see *Gudmundsson v Iceland No 511/59*, 4 CD (1960). See also *Lithgow v UK* A 102 paras 111-119 (1986).
13 *Gasus Dosier-und Fördertechnik v Netherlands* A 306-B (1995) Com Rep.
14 Ibid, para 63. The finding of no violation was only on the casting vote of the President but the dissenting opinions place practically no importance on the nationality of the applicant.
15 Eg *Yeager v Iran*, Iran-US Claims Tribunal, 17 Iran-US CTR92 (1987).

alien property then it will involve the ordinary responsibility to make reparation. It is the nationalisation case which may be different in this respect, where the compensatory element of reparation is subject to special conditions more favourable to the expropriating state. Still, if the Commission position prevails, even more attention will be focused on the 'fair balance' test to establish the incidence and content of the obligation to provide compensation in the event of a deprivation of property.[16] In the *Gasus* case, the Court did not need to address this question because it found the case to be governed by Article 1/2 (to secure the payment of taxes) rather than Article 1/1/2.[17]

v. Compensation

While it is clearly established that under the Convention nationals may not take advantage of the substance of 'the general principles of international law' to protect them against the consequences of deprivations of their property by their own state, the Court has not left such people bereft of protection. What it has said is that the need for a 'fair balance' between the public and the private interest that runs through Article 1 of the First Protocol requires, in all but the exceptional case,[18] *some* compensation.[19] Even interferences in protection of strong public interests may require some compensation. In the *Stran Greek Refineries* case,[20] the Court was unanimously of the view that the cancellation of an arbitration award by legislation, rendering it unenforceable, in pursuit of the policy of rectifying distorted arrangements entered into by the former military dictatorship in Greece, was a disproportionate interference with the applicants' rights. The effect of the national law was that they had lost the entire award, which was an assessment of the compensation due to the applicants as a result of the termination of their contractual rights. The Court effectively deferred to the arbitral tribunal's judgment that this was the proportionate level of compensation by ordering the state to pay the full amount of the award plus interest as satisfaction under Article 50. The compensation requirement was also infringed in the *Holy Monasteries* case where there were strong

---

16 A further reason why this is desirable is that it provides a proper standard of protection under the Convention for aliens, even if the development of the rules of general international law diminishes their entitlement: Frowein, at p 516, n 1, above, p 522.

17 See below, p 537.

18 An exceptional case might be the uncompensated seizure of property in time of war, eg. War Damage Act 1965; in *Holy Monasteries v Greece* A 301A (1994), the Commission thought that an uncompensated taking was proportionate on the facts, Com Rep paras 78-83 but the Court disagreed, para 75.

19 *Lithgow v UK* A 102 para 120 (1986). The state will be vulnerable where there is *no* right to *any* compensation in national law: *Katte Klitsche de la Grange v Italy* A 293B (1994) Com Rep paras 86-93 ; the Court appears to have accepted the conclusion of the national authorities that there had been no expropriation (and so, no violation), para 47.

20 A 301-B paras 80-83; also Com Rep paras 85, 88 (1994).

public interest considerations as well.[1] The law which the Court found deprived the monasteries of their lands effectively made no provision for compensation, providing only a discretionary power for use by a public body if a monastery was left with insufficient land to support its monks. The law as a whole failed to provide a fair balance between the rights of the applicants and the public interest.

The level of compensation must be 'reasonably related' to the value of the property taken. However, Article 1/1/2 requires neither full compensation[2] nor the same level of compensation for every category of deprivation.[3] In *James v UK*,[4] the Court said that where the state was pursuing economic reform or social justice, less reimbursement was due to the dispossessed owners than full market value. The state enjoys a wide margin in assessing the appropriate level of compensation and, indeed, in estimating the value of the property in the first place. Where the amounts are fixed by reference to objective standards with the possibility of representation for those deprived of property in the process, intervention by the European institutions is unlikely.

In *Lithgow v UK*, the legislation established alternative methods for valuing the ship building companies nationalised under the Aircraft and Shipbuilding Industries Act 1977, depending on the position of the companies to be nationalised. One method relied on the market value of the shares in quoted companies; the other, for shares in unquoted companies, was based on an assumed 'base value'. The value of all shares was assessed during a 'reference period' before the election after which the legislation was enacted, on the assumption that this was a period when the value would be influenced by market factors alone and not by political considerations like the prospect of nationalisation. Other methods of valuation, claimed by the applicants to be more appropriate, were nominated by them but the Court held that those adopted by the government were not inconsistent with Article 1/1/2.[5] The Court held to this conclusion even though the effects of the scheme in the legislation, both generally and in relation to individual firms, resulted in levels of compensation quite different from those claimed by the firms. Once the Court had accepted the rationality of the method itself, it was in no case persuaded that assessments were inconsistent with Article 1/1/2 by reason of the application of the general scheme.[6] Because the disparities between the companies' own valuations and the amounts of compensation

---

1 A 301A para 74-75 (1994). The amount of satisfaction under Article 50 has not been decided: the total amount claimed by the eight monasteries exceeds seven trillion drachmas, in the region of £200 billion.

2 Contrast Frowein, at p 516, n 1, above, p 525 – '. . . it would seem that under normal circumstances for the expropriation of private property the full value must be paid to assure fair compensation.'

3 *Lithgow v UK* A 102 para 121 (1986), rejecting the applicants' claim that the measure of compensation in nationalisation cases should be the same (ie market value) as for compulsory purchase of land.

4 A 98 para 54 (1986).

5 A 102 paras 125-136 (1986).

6 Ibid, paras 137-151. For extensive comment, see Mendelson, 58 BYIL 33 at 52-63 (1987).

awarded under the Act and approved by the European Court were so great – for instance, one company received £1.8m in compensation when its cash assets alone totalled £2.2m – it is difficult to envisage the circumstances when the Court would find a breach of Article 1/1/2 by reason of the level of compensation alone.

In *Hentrich v France*,[7] the government's interference took the form of the exercise of a right of pre-emption over the applicant's property. The Court measured the proportionality of the government's action against its objective, the prevention of tax evasion. *One element* in the equation was the level of compensation. The Court found that the action was arbitrary in that the right of pre-emption was not exercised systematically, that there were other methods available for dealing with tax evasion which were not so burdensome on the individual *and* the level of compensation was inadequate. It was 'all these factors' which resulted in the conclusion that the applicant bore an 'individual and excessive burden'. While the judgment suggested that the matter might have been put right by procedural changes, it did not suggest that enhanced compensation would have done the same in the absence of procedural changes.[8] The guiding principle remains the 'fair balance', reliance upon which is necessary to establish *any* right to compensation for nationals. It is also a principle which leaves a wide margin of appreciation to the state to determine what the level of compensation should be.

5.   ARTICLE 1/2: CONTROL OF USE

If the provisions of Article 1/1 do not appear in practice to impose a substantial fetter on interference with property rights, the language of Article 1/2 is even more favourable to the state. Article 1/2 is said 'not . . . in any way to impair' the right of a state to *control the use* of property. The strong implication is that Article 1/2 is not to be read subject to Article 1/1. Instead any protection for an individual must be found in the 'in accordance with the general interest' limitation in the text of Article 1/2.[9] A state may thus control the use of property, but may do so only 'in accordance with the general interest'. That the limitation upon state authority that flows from this wording will be narrow is confirmed by the phrase 'as it [the state] deems necessary', which suggests an unfettered discretion.[10] However, the Court has moved to the position that Article 1/2 is merely one of the three, not unconnected, rules in Article 1, all of which must be read in the light of the general principle of 'fair balance'.[11] Given the narrow reading ascribed

7   A 296-A paras 47-49 (1994).
8   Id, para 49.
9   There is no significant difference between the way the Court regards 'general interest' in Article 1/2 and 'public interest' in Article 1/1/2, see above, p 529.
10   *Handyside v UK* A 24 para 62 (1976) (states as the 'sole judges' of necessity; Court to supervise the lawfulness and purposes of the restriction). The power of review extends also to proportionality of the measures taken to their purpose: Peukert, above, p 516, n 1, p 64.
11   Eg *Allan Jacobsson v Sweden* A 163 para 55 (1989).

to 'deprivation' of property, the notion of 'control' of property is a correspondingly wider one[12] but, as the *Sporrong and Lönnroth* case shows, not every interference short of deprivation will be an act of controlling the use of property.[13]

The power of the state to intervene in cases of control that fall within Article 1/2 is a wide one. The Court has been notably unsympathetic to those who have taken development risks and who have failed to make any gains as a result of action or inaction by the state.[14] Given that the power of the state is so wide, an applicant may be driven to seeking protection elsewhere in the Convention: whatever the powers under Article 1/2, they may not be used discriminatorily;[15] there may be specific protections for some kinds of possessions, like one's private life or home[16] or means of communication;[17] and there may be procedural requirements under Article 6(1) or Article 13 which should accompany the exercise of Article 1/2 powers.[18]

A state may effect 'control' by requiring positive action by individuals,[19] as well as by imposing restrictions upon their activities. Restrictions of the latter kind might result from planning controls,[20] environmental orders,[1] rent control,[2] import and export laws,[3] economic regulation of professions,[4] the seizure of property for legal proceedings[5] or inheritance laws.[6]

While the state must indicate what general interest is being served by the interference, it is unlikely to have its claim that the measure is necessary to secure it successfully challenged. But because Article 1/2 has been brought under the 'fair balance' umbrella, the Strasbourg authorities may go on to investigate the lawfulness and the proportionality of the controlling measure. Apart from the formal lawfulness in national law of the measures of control, the state must show that the fair balance is satisfied, ie that in the

---

12 Eg *Pine Valley Developments v Ireland* A 222 paras 55-56 (1991), where the Court held that the failure to re-validate a planning permission nullified by the courts, resulting in very substantial reduction in the value of land, was not a *de facto* deprivation but a control of use.

13 A 52 (1982). In other cases of interference falling short of 'deprivation', the 'fair balance' requirement of Article 1/1/1 will need to be satisfied.

14 *Allan Jacobsson v Sweden* A 163 (1989); *Pine Valley Developments v Ireland* A 222 (1991); *Håkansson and Sturesson v Sweden* A 121 para 55 (1990).

15 *Pine Valley Developments Ltd v Ireland* A 222 paras 61-64 (1991) (Article 14).

16 *Niemietz v Germany* A 251-B (1992) and *Gillow v UK* A 109 (1986) (Article 8).

17 Cf *Müller v Switzerland* A 133 (1988) where the Article 1 of the First Protocol argument was not even put to the Court (although, in the end, the Article 10 claim failed).

18 In *Allan Jacobsson v Sweden* A 163 para 62 (1989), the Court found that there were adequate procedural avenues through which the applicant could have raised his complaints.

19 *Denev v Sweden No 12570/86*, 59 DR 127 (1989) (obligation on landowner to plant trees in interests of environmental protection).

20 Eg *Allan Jacobsson v Sweden* A 163 (1989); *Pine Valley Developments v Ireland* A 222 (1991).

1 Eg *Fredin v Sweden* A 192 (1991).

2 Eg *Mellacher v Austria* A 169 (1989).

3 Eg *AGOSI v UK* A 108 (1986).

4 Eg *Karni v Sweden No 11540/85*, 55 DR 157 (1988).

5 Eg *G, S and M v Austria No 9614/81*, 34 DR 119 (1983).

6 Eg *Inze v Austria* A 126 (1987).

light of the public good underlying the control, the burden which falls on the individual is not excessive[7] and that the measures are not disproportionate, that is to say, that the public end cannot be satisfied other than by imposing this cost on the applicant. The fact that a generally satisfactory scheme may impose greater costs on some individuals than others will not be an objection to it unless those suffering the greater burden can demonstrate a discriminatory interference with the enjoyment of their possessions.[8] While the last word remains with the Strasbourg authorities, evidence that the substance of the 'fair balance' test has been applied by a national body will be helpful to a state in demonstrating that it has remained within the wide margin of appreciation conceded to it.[9]

An important sub-set of measures which the Court regards as being for the control of property are forfeiture provisions for the enforcement of laws relating to the use or possession of property. In *Handyside v UK*,[10] the Court said that the destruction of books after a finding of obscenity had been made was justified under Article 1/2. In *AGOSI v UK*,[11] gold Krugerrands (bullion coins) belonging to the applicants were confiscated by United Kingdom customs after third parties had tried unlawfully to import them into the country. The Court characterised the prohibition against importation as a control of the use of property and the forfeiture order as 'a constituent element of the procedure for the control of the use' of the Krugerrands, to be dealt with under Article 1/2 rather than as a deprivation of property within Article 1/1/2. The Court resorted again to the 'fair balance' test, the particular issue here being whether confiscation was justified as a measure of enforcement against an innocent owner. The 'fault' or otherwise of the owner was only one of the factors to be taken into account in reaching the fair balance, according to the Court. One other factor was a procedure by means of which the owner could put his case before seizure of his goods was confirmed. In United Kingdom law, the procedure was an administrative one before the Commissioners of Customs and Excise, whose decisions were subject to judicial review. These processes were sufficient. AGOSI had not established that reasonable account had not been taken of its behaviour in reaching the decision to order the forfeiture of its property.[12] If the general interest is strong enough, even preventative seizures and confiscation may be justified.[13] The *AGOSI* case is further confirmation of the importance of procedural avenues to aggrieved parties

---

7　The Commission has suggested that a requirement of compensation is less likely to be required for a fair balance under Article 1/2 than under Article 1/1/2, *Banér v Sweden No 11763/85*, 60 DR 128 at 142 (1989).
8　*Mellacher v Austria* A 169 paras 54-56 (1989).
9　Eg *ISKCON v UK No 20490/92*, 76-A DR 90 (1994).
10　A 24 para 63 (1976).
11　A 108 para 54 (1986).
12　Ibid, paras 55-60. See also *Air Canada v UK* A 316-A (1993) Com Rep (endorsed by Court) (forfeiture of 'jumbo jet' bringing drugs into UK in its cargo, later reduced to £50,000 payment, not a breach of Article 1/2).
13　*Raimondo v Italy* A 281-A paras 26-30 (1994).

in establishing the fair balance. Procedures must not only be effective to test an applicant's claims[14] but must be expeditious,[15] so that there is no unacceptable collateral impact on the enjoyment of his property while the exercise of the control measures takes place.[16]

Finally, Article 1/2 concedes a practically unlimited power on states 'to enforce such laws as it deems necessary . . . to secure the payment of taxes or other contributions or penalties'. Because the powers of the state under this provision are very wide, it is a matter of significance whether an interference with the enjoyment of possessions falls within it or not. For example, in *Gasus Dosier-und Fördertechnik v Netherlands*,[17] the Court decided that the seizure by the tax authorities of property in the possession of a tax debtor in which title had been retained by the vendor was not a deprivation of the latter's possessions to be assessed under Article 1/1/2 but a measure for securing the payment of taxes falling within Article 1/2.

The power to secure the payment of taxes is not a separate matter but a specific aspect of the state's right to control the use of property. The 'fair balance' will require procedural guarantees to establish the applicant's liability to make the payments but the state is largely unconstrained about the levels of taxation, the means of assessment and the manner of exaction to fulfil those liabilities. However, the formal power of the state to raise taxes is not totally unlimited. The Commission has said that a taxation scheme may 'adversely affect the guarantee of ownership if it places an excessive burden on the taxpayer or fundamentally interferes with his financial position'.[18] However, the state's power of appreciation is wide and it would be an exceptional case indeed where the institutions would declare a tax programme contrary to the Convention.[19] As far as the enforcement of the resulting tax obligations is concerned, the Court said in the *Gasus* case[20] that it 'will respect the legislature's assessment in such matters unless it is devoid of reasonable foundation'. In determining that the Dutch law was not beyond this considerable margin, the Court deferred to the legislature's position that security rights of the kind preserved by reservation of title clauses were not 'true' ownership. In the circumstances of this case, the applicant could not have expected otherwise than that the question would have been governed by this Dutch law and that, appreciating that there was some risk (hence the reservation of title clause), the applicant should have

14 *M v Italy No 12386/86*, 70 DR 59 at 101-102 (1991).
15 Preventative measures must be brought rapidly to an end when the need for them has ceased: *Raimondo v Italy* A 281-A paras 34-36 (1994) and *Vendittelli v Italy* A 293-A paras 38-40 (1994).
16 *Allan Jacobsson v Sweden* A 163 para 63 (1989).
17 A 306-B para 59 (1995).
18 *Svenska Managementgruppen v Sweden No 11036/84*, 45 DR 211 (1985) and *Wasa Liv Omsesidigt v Sweden No 13013/87*, 58 DR 163 at 185-187 (1988).
19 Cf *Darby v Sweden* A 198 paras 32-33 (1990), where the violation was of Article 14 in connection with Article 1, First Protocol, and *Schmidt v Germany* A 291-B para 28 (1994), although the Court considered that case under Article 4(3)(d) rather than Article 1, First Protocol.
20 A 306-B para 60 (1995).

appreciated the risk of seizure of the property by the tax authorities and taken measures to protect itself against this eventuality. There had, then, been no failure of proportionality in the measures taken by the Netherlands to secure the payment of the tax debtor's obligations.[1] The state will be constrained by Article 6 insofar as it seeks to use the criminal process to enforce tax obligations.[2] The *Hentrich* case[3] shows that Article 1 of the First Protocol itself imposes some limitations upon the methods a state may use to enforce its tax policies but they arise under Article 1/1/1 and 1/1/2 rather than under this part of Article 1/2.

6. CONCLUSION

Article 1/1 both establishes the right to the peaceful enjoyment of one's possessions and expressly allows a state a wide power to interfere with the right in the public interest. Although there is specific language to regulate the deprivation and control of the use of property under Articles 1/1/2 and 1/2 respectively, these are not the only occasions when interference by the state may be justified. Nor does the different language of these two sentences indicate much substantial difference in the way the Court approaches claims that Article 1 has been violated. The 'fair balance' between the public interest identified by the state and the burden on the individual applicants affected by the interference set out in the *Sporrong and Lönnroth* case is pervasive throughout Article 1 of the First Protocol cases. It is noticeable how more recent cases proceed straight to the application of the fair balance test, while earlier ones dissected the language of Article 1 of the First Protocol in some detail.[4] The Court also makes reference to cases arising under this Article regardless of the particular issue before it and the issue considered in the other cases.[5]

The reference to a general 'fair balance' standard of protection against interference under Article 1/1/1 in the *Sporrong and Lönnroth* case avoids the need to break down and classify complex combinations of fact and laws which have had an impact on an applicant's enjoyment of his possessions.[6] The justiciability of many of the factors to be taken into account in striking a balance is problematic and the Court has deferred extensively to the decisions of national bodies. The language of review here is not that of 'pressing social need' but whether the applicant has shown that the state measures are 'manifestly unjustified'. In cases where the state has addressed

1 Id, paras 65-74.
2 See *Funke v France* A 256-A (1993).
3 A 296-A paras 47-49 (1994).
4 Cf *James v UK* A 98 (1986) and *Tre Traktörer Aktiebolag v Sweden* A 159 (1984).
5 Eg in *Pine Valley Development v Ireland* A 222 para 59 (1991), the Court relied on *Håkansson and Suresson v Sweden* A 121 (1990), an Article 1/1/2 case, and *Fredin v Sweden* A 192 (1991), an Article 1/2 case, for the same point.
6 Eg *Agrotexim Hellas v Greece* No 14807/89 Com Rep para 65 (1994) (pending before the Court).

the issues, either in establishing the legal basis for interference, which is always required to comply with Article 1 of the First Protocol, or in applying a general legislative scheme, the Court has generally confirmed that the state was acting within its powers under Article 1, First Protocol.

The wide margin of appreciation allowed to states may prove of importance to the states of Eastern Europe, while they implement far-reaching economic reform and are confronted with property claims which go back to the Communist era. The recognition in *James v UK* that states have a wide power to interfere with property rights in the general social and economic interest,[7] even where the benefits fall to the advantage of particular individuals, will conceivably be of wide significance. Where the Court does find that a state has exceeded its powers under Article 1 of the First Protocol, the financial consequences can be severe. In the *Sporrong and Lönnroth* case, the defendant state was ordered to pay approximately £100,000 in compensation; in the *Pine Valley* case, it was approximately £1 ¼ million; and in *Stran Greek Refineries*, the order was for approximately £15 million plus £9 million interest.

7   A 98 (1986).

CHAPTER 19

Article 2, First Protocol: The right to education

'**Article 2, First Protocol**
No person shall be denied the right to education. In the exercise of any functions which it assumes in relation to education and teaching, the state shall respect the right of parents to ensure such education and teaching in conformity with their own religious and philosophical convictions.'

1. INTRODUCTION

The right to education consists of a variety of rights and freedoms for parents and children and of different duties for the state.[1] At the international level, it is protected in a number of human rights instruments. It is at once an 'economic, social and cultural' right[2] and a 'civil and political' right.[3] The state is in the paradoxical position of (usually) being the chief provider of education, which involves not only the necessity of committing substantial resources to the education system but of regulating it in the interests of efficiency and fairness, while at the same time it has a duty not to use its powerful position as provider to promote one set of opinions or perspectives to the exclusion of all others: it must educate but it may not indoctrinate. This duty to facilitate pluralism within the curriculum of its schools extends to the regulation of teaching, so that individual teachers must not be allowed to depart from the prescribed standards by inculcating their own ideas in their students. The state may insist that children be educated and may impose duties on the parents to make sure that they attend. As far as higher education is concerned, the state may impose a condition of capacity to benefit for admission to any such education which it provides. In neither case is it strictly correct to speak about a right to education.

---

1 See Opsahl, in Robertson, ed, *Privacy and Human Rights*, 1973, pp 220-243 and Wildhaber, *European System*, Ch 21.
2 International Covenant on Economic, Social and Cultural Rights 1966, Article 13.
3 Article 2, First Protocol. On the international right to education generally, see Delbruck, 35 GYIL 92 (1992).

Such rights to education as there are will ordinarily be the rights of the pupil or student.[4] When the pupil is young, his right may have to be exercised by his parents but, as the child grows up, he will develop the capacity to assert his own rights.[5] For higher education, the appropriate rights will be the rights of the student. Parents may have, and under the Convention do have, certain rights of their own about the way in which their child is educated.

The right to education had a 'stormy genesis'[6] in the Convention. It was possible to reach an agreed text only in the First Protocol[7] and, even then, an unusually large number of states have appended reservations to Article 2 in their ratifications of the Protocol.[8] The Court has made frequent reference to the preparatory work in its judgments. The text was transmuted from its original form – 'every person has the right to education' – to its present one – 'No person shall be denied the right to education' – to avoid what some states anticipated might be excessively burdensome, positive obligations.[9] The result is that the resourcing and the organisation of public education is for the state and the rights that individuals have in the state system are only those which the state, in its discretion, provides.

Article 2 of the First Protocol extends to all forms of education provided or permitted by the state, although its focus is on primary education.[10] Individual rights with respect to one level of education may not be the same for another: while a state, if it establishes a state schooling system, may be obliged to provide *universal* primary – and, it may be supposed, secondary – education, it is, as noted above, permitted to restrict access to higher education to those with the ability to benefit from whatever it provides.[11] Although 'education' includes higher education, it does not extend to vocational training.[12]

'Education' and 'teaching' are differentiated in the text of Article 2 of the First Protocol. On this distinction the Court has said:

'. . . the education of children is the whole process whereby, in any society, adults endeavour to transmit their beliefs, culture and other

4 Convention on the Rights of the Child 1989, UKTS 44 (1992), Cm 1976; 28 ILM 1448 (1989), Article 28(1).
5 Mr Kellberg, in *Kjeldsen, Busk Madsen and Pedersen v Denmark* B 21 (1975) p 50. In *Campbell and Cosans v UK* A 48 para 40 (1982), the Court described the right not to be denied access to education as 'the right of the child'.
6 Opsahl, loc cit at p 540, n 1, above, p 221.
7 Robertson, 28 BYIL 359 at 362-364 (1951).
8 For the reservation texts, see *Collected Texts*, p 121ff. For a brief summary of the reservations, see Wildhaber, loc cit at n 1 above, p 551. On the Swedish reservation, see *Angeleni v Sweden No 10491/83*, 51 DR 41 at 46-47 (1986).
9 Robertson, loc cit at n 7, above, p 362 and Clarke, 22 Ir Jur 28 at 34-41 (1987).
10 *X v UK No 5962/72*, 2 DR 50 (1975) (right to education is concerned 'primarily with elementary education') and *15 Foreign Students v UK No 7671/76*, 9 DR 185 (1977).
11 *X v UK No 8844/80*, 23 DR 228 (1980) and *Glazewska v Sweden No 11655/85*, 45 DR 300 (1985).
12 *X v UK No 8844/80*, 23 DR 228 (1980). Cf Convention on the Rights of the Child 1989, Article 28(1)(b).

values to the young, whereas teaching or instruction refers in particular to the transmission of knowledge and to intellectual development.'[13]

The implication of drawing the distinction this way appears to be that the state may not step between a child or student and a private provider of 'education' outside the school system, such as religious bodies or cultural institutions, lest otherwise a person be 'denied the right to education' in this wide sense. If it wished to intervene, the state would have to rely on its implied power to regulate educational activities.

There is nothing in the Convention to identify any particular substantive objectives of education and teaching, comparable, for instance, to Article 26(2) of the Universal Declaration of Human Rights which reads:

> 'Education shall be directed to the full development of the human personality and to the strengthening of respect for human rights and fundamental freedoms. It shall promote understanding, tolerance and friendship among all nations, racial or religious groups, and shall partner the activities of the United Nations for the maintenance of peace.'[14]

Indeed, as will be seen, the Convention demands only a negative quality, that students be not subjected to the indoctrination of a single point of view.[15]

2.   THE BASIC OBLIGATION

According to the Court in the *Belgian Linguistic* case,[16] the rights protected by the first sentence of Article 2 of the First Protocol, are:

1.   a right to access to educational institutions existing at a given time;
2.   a right to an effective education; and
3.   a right to official recognition of the studies a student has successfully completed.

None of these rights is absolute. The state must regulate them all and, while it may take into account 'the needs and resources of the community and of

---

13   *Campbell and Cosans v UK* A 48 para 33 (1982). See Robertson, loc cit at n 1 above, p 363, drawing attention to the French text of Article 2, First Protocol.
14   See Pentti Arajärvi, in Eide et al, eds, *The Universal Declaration of Human Rights: A Commentary*, 1992, pp 405-428, looking also at other international instruments which prescribe the content of education. In the absence of a positive statement of this kind, it is not easy to see how *excluding* a topic from the curriculum would raise an issue under Article 2, First Protocol. See in this connection the Local Government Act 1988, s 28 which prohibits 'the teaching of the acceptability of homosexuality as a pretended family relationship'.
15   The state will have the power under Article 17 to prohibit education in values which fall within its scope: Opsahl, at p 540, n 1, above, pp 235-237.
16   A 6 (1968). Cf *Campbell and Cosans v UK* A 48 paras 40-41 (1982).

individuals', the regulation must 'never injure the substance of the right to education nor conflict with other rights enshrined in the Convention'.[17] While the first and third rights are expressly alluded to in the judgment, the second can be inferred generally from the language the Court used in terms appropriate to the facts before it. It said:

'. . . the right to education would be meaningless if it did not imply in favour of its beneficiaries the right to be educated in the national language or in one of the national languages, as the case may be.'[18]

The education provided must not be useless: how effective need it be? The answer to this question is also to be found in the *Belgian Linguistic* case.[19] In another passage in its judgment, the Court stated that the states did not accept, and so the Convention did not require, an understanding of the right to education that,

'. . . would require them to establish at their own expense, or to subsidise, education of any particular type or at any particular level'.

Where the challenge to the effectiveness of education depends upon resources or the organisation and pattern of the system set up by the state, this negative formulation would provide the state with a sufficient answer.[20]

The state may require that children be educated and enforce a duty against parents to ensure that children attend school or receive adequate education at home.[1] It may allow private systems of education or permit children to be educated by their parents. If it does so, it has no obligation to fund or subsidise these alternatives.[2] The text of Article 2 of the First Protocol does not make it clear whether there is a right to establish schools outside the state system. Opsahl is adamant that there is such a right (and that it is not dependent on the second sentence of the Article).[3] The Commission in *Kjeldsen, Busk Madsen and Pedersen v Denmark*[4] took the opposite view. The judgment of the Court is not clear,[5] but in the *Jordebo* case[6] the Commission interpreted the Court's words to mean that there is a

17 *Belgian Linguistic* case A 6 p 32 (1968).
18 Id, p 31.
19 Ibid. Parents have no right to single-sex schools or to selective schools: *W & DM and M & HI v UK Nos 10228/82 and 10229/82*, 37 DR 96 (1984); *Rosengren v Sweden No 9411/81*, 29 DR 224 (1982); and further cases in Wildhaber, loc cit at p 540, n 1, above, p 535, n 19.
20 *Simpson v UK No 14688/89*, 64 DR 188 (1989).
1 *Family H v UK No 10233/83*, 37 DR 105 (1984).
2 *W and KL v Sweden No 10476/83*, 45 DR 143 at 148-149 (1985).
3 Loc cit at p 540, n 1, above, p 230. In *Kjeldsen, Busk Madsen and Pedersen v Denmark* B 21 p 53 (1975), he took the view that such a right was the inevitable consequence of a parent's right to withdraw his child from the state system. See also Lester and Pannick, *Independent Schools and the European Convention on Human Rights: A Joint Opinion*, 1982.
4 B 21 (1975) Com Rep paras 151-153.
5 A 23 para 50 (1976).
6 *Ingrid Jordebo Foundation of Christian Schools and Ingrid Jordebo v Sweden No 11533/85*, 51 DR 125 at 128 (1987).

right to start and run a private school. This is a right of the parents alone, not the school: in the *Jordebo* case the Commission held that the applicant foundation which ran the school was not a 'victim' of the state's refusal to allow it to carry on certain educational activities. The state has the power and duty to regulate private as well as public education. It may not use its regulatory power to injure the substance of the right, that is to say in this case, to make it impossible to establish private schools.[7] Even if the original inclination of the Commission were the right one, ie that there is no right under the first sentence of Article 2 of the First Protocol to run private schools, the requirements of the second sentence, that the state respect the religious or philosophical convictions of parents, probably creates a practical imperative to permit the operation of *some* private schools.[8]

3. RESPECT FOR PARENTS' RELIGIOUS AND PHILOSOPHICAL CONVICTIONS

The second sentence in Article 2 of the First Protocol must be read together with the first sentence. It is to the fundamental right to education that the right of parents[9] for respect for their religious and philosophical convictions is attached.[10] This right applies to all the systems of education in the state, public and private, and to all the functions the state exercises in connection with education, whether academic or administrative.[11] It is principally a protection against indoctrination by the state[12] and teachers[13] in the schools but it covers as well administrative matters, such as the manner of maintaining discipline, insofar as they are capable of conflicting with parents' convictions. There are two protections for the state against this potentially wide-ranging right of parental influence in the education system. These are that the convictions which are to be taken into account are to be interpreted narrowly and that the burden on the parent to demonstrate their relevance to his stand is heavy.

If it is relatively easy to identify what is a 'religious' conviction, it is not so simple to set the limits of 'philosophical' convictions.[14] About the latter, the Court said they comprehend:

---

7 Ibid.
8 This is the main thrust of Opsahl's approach, loc cit at p 540, n 1, above, p 230.
9 The parent's right continues when the child is in care (*Aminoff v Sweden No 10554/83*, 43 DR 120 at 144 (1985)), but it will cease if the child is adopted (*X v UK No 7626/76*, 11 DR 160 (1977)). If the child is in the custody of one parent, it will cease for the other: *X v Sweden No 7911/77*, 12 DR 192 (1977).
10 *Kjeldsen, Busk Madsen and Pedersen v Denmark* A 23 para 56 (1976).
11 *Campbell and Cosans v UK* A 48 paras 33-36 (1982).
12 *Kjeldsen, Busk Madsen and Pedersen v Denmark* A 23 para 53 (1976).
13 Implied by *X v UK No 8010/77*, 16 DR 101 at 102 (1979).
14 They do not include convictions as to the language of instruction: *Belgium Linguistic* case A 6 p 32 (1968). See also Robertson, loc cit at p 541, n 7, above, p 362.

'... such convictions as are worthy of respect in a "democratic society" ... and are not incompatible with human dignity; in addition, they must not conflict with the fundamental right of the child to education. . .'.[15]

The individual parent must show the basis for and the content of the belief;[16] that it is a belief he holds; that holding it is the reason for his objection to what the state is doing;[17] and that he has brought the reason for his objection to the attention of the authorities.[18]

If the applicant can satisfy these tests, the next measure of protection for the state is that mere incidental treatment in lessons of matters about which religious and philosophical convictions may be held will not raise an issue under the second sentence of Article 2, First Protocol. As the Court said in *Kjeldsen, Busk Madsen and Pedersen v Denmark*,[19] this provision does not permit a parent to object to the integrated teaching of religious or philosophical information, a right that would have disruptive consequences for the organisation of teaching. All the parent is entitled to is that this information, like any other, be conveyed 'in an objective, critical and pluralistic manner'. As the *Kjeldsen* case[20] showed, this is an injunction which is easier to articulate than to apply. There, Danish law required the teaching of sex education as an integral part of the curriculum for 9 to 11-year-olds. Children at state schools were not excused from the lessons. A claim by parents that this was a violation of their right to have their religious and philosophical convictions respected was rejected by 6 votes to 1 by the Court. For the majority, the crucial point was that the teaching programme was principally a matter of conveying information. There was no attempt to indoctrinate a particular moral attitude towards sexual activities, especially concerning contraception. Judge Verdross's dissent conceded that the teaching was not indoctrination but argued that the proper distinction to be drawn was between the biological science of reproduction and 'sexual practices'. Parents could, for reasons of religious conviction, properly object to information about the latter being given to their children, even in an objective manner.[1]

If the *Kjeldsen* case shows the difficulty of deciding the limits of the parents' concern on academic matters, *Campbell and Cosans v UK*[2] raised the same problem about administrative matters, here school discipline maintained by corporal punishment over the parents' objections. The Court

---

15 *Campbell and Cosans v UK* A 48 para 36 (1982).
16 *Campbell and Cosans v UK* B 42 Com Rep para 93 (1980).
17 *Warwick v UK No 9471/81*, 60 DR 5 at 18 (1986).
18 *B and D v UK No 9303/81*, 49 DR 44 at 50 (1986).
19 A 23 para 53 (1976).
20 For a case going the other way under the ICCPR where atheistic parents complained about religious education in state schools, see *Hartikainen v Finland* (40/1975), A/36/40 p 147.
1   The Commission divided and the minority shared Judge Verdross's opinion that the mere provision of information could infringe a parent's right. For the English law on religious worship and education in state schools, see Poulter, 2 Education and the Law 1 (1990).
2   A 48 para 36 (1982). Judge Evans, dissenting, relied on the *travaux* to establish that the parents' convictions protected by Article 2, First Protocol extended only to the subject-matter of what was taught and not to how the school was administered.

decided that the parents' objections were 'philosophical' because they attained 'a certain level of cogency, seriousness, cohesion and importance'. It was surely not without significance that the practice complained about raised a serious question of the violation of a fundamental Convention provision – Article 3 – even if on the facts the Court held that Article 3 had not been breached.[3] It is less likely that the Court would reach the same conclusion about, say, obligations to wear school uniform or the fixing of the school starting and leaving ages, however strongly parents might feel about such things, unless another Convention right were implicated. This is not so remote as might once have seemed likely, given the controversy over the exclusion of Muslim girls wearing the chador, or head scarf, from France's secular state schools.[4]

If the parents' objection is sufficiently well founded on a religious or philosophical conviction, the state's duty is to 'respect' their right. There is something of a hiatus here between the qualified connotation of 'respect' and the strong right of parents 'to ensure' appropriate teaching. The qualified nature of the duty 'to respect' has prevailed.[5] It is a conclusion reinforced by the nature of the duty in the first sentence: it is the state which determines and finances the provision of education.[6] The state will respect the parents' right if it allows the children to be excused from the offending lessons or removed from the disapproved institution. However, the child retains his right to education and, if the state cannot arrange public education in a way which is sensitive to the convictions of all parents, it must permit them to establish private schools which do meet their needs or allow them to educate their children themselves.[7] The state has a right and, arguably, a duty to ensure that these alternative systems of education are of adequate efficiency. It does not, however, have a duty to subsidise private institutions.[8] The burdens on a dissenting parent may be, as the Court has acknowledged, severe.[9] If the burdens cannot be sustained by parents, perhaps then the state must consider alternatives but not to the extent that it must finance the private schools itself, unless there is no other way of resolving the problem.[10] In *Campbell*

3 On school corporal punishment under Article 3, see above, pp 86-87.
4 See *Kherovan*, 2 November 1992, decision of the French Conseil d'Etat, digested in (1993) PL 198, and The Economist, 8 October 1994, p 51. In the *Kherovan* case, a school rule prohibiting the head scarf was quashed by the Conseil d'Etat. As to religious objections against wearing school uniform or religious duties to wear particular clothes in the UK, see Lonbay, 46 MLR 345 at 347 (1983).
5 In *Kjeldsen, Busk Madsen and Pedersen v Denmark* A 23 para 54 (1976) the government's claim to have respected the parents' convictions was doubtless assisted by the fact that private schools were available for their children, which enjoyed a substantial public subsidy.
6 *W & DM and M & HI v UK Nos 10228/82 and 10229/82*, 37 DR 96 (1984). For cases on respect for the convictions of parents of handicapped children, see *PD and LD v UK No 14135/88*, 62 DR 292 (1989) and *Graeme v UK No 13887/88*, 64 DR 158 (1990).
7 *X v UK No 7782/77*, 14 DR 179 (1978).
8 *W and KL v Sweden No 10476/83*, 45 DR 143 (1985).
9 *Kjeldsen, Busk Madsen and Pedersen v Denmark* A 23 para 50 (1976).
10 Following *Airey v Ireland* A 32 (1979), the state has a choice of means to respect the parents' rights and a general reservation may not preclude a particular solution if it be the only one available.

and Cosans v UK, the government argued that the duty to respect the wishes of parents who objected to the corporal punishment of the children could be met only by setting up a dual system of schools, with some schools permitting corporal punishment and others not. This, the government said, was excluded by its reservation to Article 2 of the First Protocol, because it would lead to unreasonable expenditure. However, the Court suggested other solutions, instancing the possibility of exemptions for individual pupils, which, it said, did not have the same financial consequences.[11] The Court's treatment of this matter follows from its view of the subsidiary nature of the second sentence obligation in relation to the fundamental obligation of the first sentence.

4. DISCRIMINATION AND MINORITY RIGHTS

On the face of it, a state is well protected with defences to claims that it is in violation of Article 2 of the First Protocol so long as it runs and finances an efficient system of education which is in some way sensitive to the most heart-felt concerns of parents. Many of their wishes can be met by tolerating a system of private education.

However, while the general provision of education by European states may be sound, some individuals or groups of individuals may find themselves at particular disadvantages compared with the majority of parents and children. At the international level, discrimination with respect to educational provision has long been a matter of concern and claims for special treatment for minority education are familiar.[12] The *Belgian Linguistic* case[13] remains the core authority on Article 2 of the First Protocol, but it also addressed concerns of the applicants under Article 14. The parents of French-speaking children alleged that several of the schooling arrangements differentiated between their children and Dutch-speaking children and that, because there was no reasonable and objective justification for the differences, they constituted discrimination in breach of the Convention. The Court condemned only one, relatively minor, practice as contravening Article 14, where Dutch-speaking children in a particular area were allowed to be educated in Dutch-speaking schools in a bilingual district outside the neighbourhood, whereas French-speaking children in an equivalent Flemish area could not attend the French-speaking schools in the same bilingual district but were compelled to attend their local Dutch-language schools. The narrow effect the Court gave to Article 14 was in part because it endorsed as a legitimate policy the Belgian state's objective of

11 A 48 para 37 (1982). The government regarded as unacceptable a situation in which some, but not all children at the same school were subject to corporal punishment. The Education (No 2) Act 1986, s 47 abolished corporal punishment in all state schools in England and Wales and the Education (Scotland) Act 1980, s 48A did so for Scotland.

12 See Cullen, IJFL 143 at 146-151 (1993). See also the UNESCO Convention against Discrimination in Education 1960, 429 UNTS 93; UKTS 23 (1969), Cmnd 3894.

13 A 6 (1968).

securing unilingual regions in the bulk of the country. That this policy disadvantaged members of linguistic minorities was not discrimination and the children's rights had not been violated. Nor, because language, rather than religious or philosophical convictions, was the badge of distinction could the parents find any protection in the second sentence of Article 2, First Protocol.[14]

The Court's approach to the Article 14 issue has not escaped criticism.[15] The tolerance the judgment shows for assimilative policies, albeit in discrete regions, is out of line with its insistence on pluralism on other matters. The state, it is thought, may neither discriminate in the access to the educational system it provides nor establish segregated educational systems, although it may have to tolerate separate schools if that is necessary to respect the religious and philosophical convictions of parents.[16] To this extent, parents who are members of religious or philosophical minorities have the right to establish their own schools. It has been argued[17] that, where this is the case, the state must support these schools to a similar extent to which it supports state schools. Given the Court's interpretation of the first sentence of Article 2 of the First Protocol – no obligation to provide any particular form of education – and the relationship between the first and second sentences of this provision – the second subsidiary to the first – this looks an optimistic view except, perhaps, where the state can find no other way of satisfying the parents' right and that failure is interpreted as a failure 'to respect' their rights.[18] However, the position will be different where the state grants subsidies to *some* schools established in respect of parents' religious and philosophical convictions. There may first be a question as to whether a state should be subsidising denominational education at all. Since, in fact, several European states do so, here it may be argued that under Article 14 it may do so but that it may not discriminate between such groups by subsidising some schools for some groups but not others. In the United Kingdom, the power to support grant-maintained schools has been exercised only in favour of Christian and Jewish schools; the government has rejected applications from Muslim schools. In the absence of a reasonable and objective justification for the decision, this would appear to be incompatible with Article 14, subject to the United Kingdom reservation.[19] In a case from Northern Ireland,[20] the Commission held manifestly unfounded a claim by a parent that differential funding between

14 Ibid.
15 See Cullen, loc cit at p 547, n 12, above, pp 171-172 (1993).
16 *Kjeldsen, Busk Madsen and Pedersen v Denmark* A 23 para 53 (1976) and *Karnell and Hardt v Sweden No 4733/71*, 14 YB 664 (1971). The *Karnell and Hardt* case was settled: *Council of Europe, Stock-Taking 1954-1984*, pp 149-150.
17 Van Dijk and Van Hoof, p 473.
18 For doubts as to whether this could ever be necessary if the rights of children to a non-indoctrinating education are respected, see Clarke, 35 ICLQ 271 at 300-301 (1986).
19 Cumper, 139 NLJ 1067 (1989). In its most recent rejection of an application by an Islamic group, the government cited the surplus of school places in the district as the reason for refusing the application, a reason which has some relevance to the UK reservation.
20 *X v UK No 7782/77*, 14 DR 179 (1978).

state schools and 'maintained' schools in which private bodies could exercise a degree of control over the school violated Article 14 in conjunction with Article 2, First Protocol. The different treatment was justified because the amount of state subsidy to maintained schools was large (85 per cent of capital costs and 100 per cent of running costs) and the advantages to the private trusts were considerable (a controlling interest in the governors and the vesting of the school property in them).

Even if the obligation to support minority schools goes as far as has been argued, it applies only to those catering for religious or philosophical minorities. Linguistic minorities are certainly excluded and it would appear that groups claiming educational rights on cultural, ethnic or regional grounds would also fall beyond the scope of Article 2, First Protocol. The national minorities Protocol proposed by the Parliamentary Assembly requires the state to provide mother-tongue education in schools in areas with substantial numbers of minority children and/or to allow private schools teaching in the minority language.[1] The Council of Europe's 1994 Framework Convention for the Protection of National Minorities[2] sets obligations on States to take measures in the field of education to foster understanding of minority (and majority) culture, to recognise the rights of persons belonging to national minorities to set up and manage their own education departments (though this involves no right to state financial support) and to recognise the right of persons belonging to national minorities to learn their national language and, in minority areas, to endeavour to provide instruction in the minority language.

---

1 See Parl Ass Recommendation 1201 (1993), Parl Ass 44th Ord Sess, Texts Adopted, for the draft ECHR protocol text.
2 ETS 157, Articles 12-14.

CHAPTER 20

Article 3, First Protocol: The right to free elections

'**Article 3, First Protocol**
The High Contracting Parties undertake to hold free elections at reasonable intervals by secret ballot, under conditions which will ensure the free expression of the opinion of the people in the choice of the legislature.'

In the *Greek* case,[1] the Commission said that Article 3 of the First Protocol[2] 'presupposes the existence of a representative legislature, elected at reasonable intervals, as the basis of a democratic society'. This opinion fixes the place of political democracy in its relationship with human rights. It is one of the conditions for the protection and enjoyment of human rights but it is not the only one: as the Court said in *Mathieu-Mohin v Belgium*,[3] it is, '*a* characteristic principle of democracy'. It almost goes without saying that an accommodation has to be made between the demands of human rights standards and the acts of even a properly elected legislature: human rights are a limit on majoritarianism, however legitimately constituted. The ultimate objective, as the Commission indicated in the *Greek* case,[4] is not 'democracy' but 'a democratic society'. In a 'democratic society', the majority has regard to the interests of all groups and people in the state, not merely those of its supporters.[5]

The language of Article 3 of the First Protocol is rather different to that of the other substantive articles of the Convention and its Protocols, being expressed as an obligation imposed on states, rather than as a right of individuals. The Court has declined to treat this difference as indicative of an intention to exclude individual rights from Article 3, First Protocol. In *Mathieu-Mohin v Belgium*,[6] it said:

1   12 YB (the *Greek* case) 1 at 179 (1969); CM Res DH (70) 1.
2   On Article 3, see De Meyer, *European System*, Ch 22. See also the Concluding Document, Copenhagen Meeting on Human Dimension of CSCE, para 7, text in 11 HRLJ 232 (1990).
3   A 113 para 47 (1987). Italics added.
4   See further, Jacot-Guillarmod, in *Democracy and Human Rights, Proceedings of the Colloquy organised by the Government of Greece and the Council of Europe*, 1987, pp 43-66. See generally, Rosas and Helgesen, eds, *The Strength of Diversity: Human Rights and Pluralist Democracy*, 1992.
5   See below, p 557.
6   A 113 para 50 (1987).

'The reason would seem to lie rather in the desire to give great solemnity to the commitment undertaken in the fact that the primary obligation in the field concerned is not one of abstention or non-interference, as with the majority of the civil and political rights, but one of adoption by the state of positive measures to "hold" democratic elections.'

While there are, then, individual rights in Article 3 of the First Protocol, their identification encounters a number of obstacles. The first is the uncertainty which attends the notion of a 'democratic' election. Some states were doubtful about the inclusion of this provision at all in the Convention.[7] None of them intended that their institutional version of democracy should be impugned against the standard finally adopted.[8] Anomalies such as the hereditary second chamber in the United Kingdom[9] and systemic differences such as those between 'first past the post' and proportional representation methods of voting were regarded as being compatible with what was agreed. These differences reflect both respect for entrenched tradition (which might be thought not to count for much against the requirements of human rights) and genuine divisions about the objective of an electoral system. Conflicts between the representativeness of an assembly and its political effectiveness (especially where there is a direct link between the assembly and the government) may be resolved in quite distinct ways.[10] The choices states make are reflected in the details as well as the generalities of their electoral systems and so, if it be conceded that Article 3 of the First Protocol leaves a generous margin of appreciation to a state in the selection of the latter, a similarly wide discretion should be allowed in the implementation of the basic scheme it selects.

Finally, despite the importance of questions about elections, the justiciability of issues arising out of them often gives even national tribunals pause before they embark upon a review of matters which are of such direct concern to the legislature.[11] There is, however, a contrary view that because of legislative self-interest or inertia, the toleration of unfair election practices is likely and redress by the legislature thus elected remote. There is, it is said, a more compelling than usual obligation on the courts to intervene when it

---

7 Robertson, 28 BYIL 359 at 364 (1951).
8 8 TP 130, 202, 210.
9 In *Mathieu-Mohin v Belgium* A 113 para 53 (1987), the Court said that Article 3 of the First Protocol, applied to elections to the legislature 'or at least one of its chambers if it has two or more . . .'. In his concurring opinion, Judge Pinheiro Farinha said that the statement was gratuitous and 'inadequate and dangerous'. He said the statement should have been, 'or at least one of its chambers if it has two or more, on the two-fold condition that the majority of the membership of the legislature is elected and that the chamber or chambers whose members are not elected does not or do not have greater powers than the chamber that is freely elected by secret ballot'.
10 Ibid, para 54. See also Imbert, in *Democracy and Human Rights*, loc cit at n 4 above, pp 74-75.
11 Kommers, *The Constitutional Jurisprudence of the Federal Republic of Germany*, 1989, pp 199-200 ('Contested Elections').

has been established that the legislature cannot or will not put things right.[12] At present, the Strasbourg authorities stand between these positions: they have established the right to intervene but they have been most reluctant to exercise it to condemn national decisions. *Mathieu-Mohin v Belgium*[13] is the only case to have reached the Court, which found no violation.

Furthermore, the states have adopted such different arrangements that decisions about one national electoral system may have little significance for another. *Mathieu-Mohin v Belgium* is a case in point. It arose out of the highly complex arrangements which regulate elections in Belgium, necessary to satisfy the national and local aspirations of the Flemish and Walloon communities. While the state is largely divided into Dutch and French language regions, the existence of the French-speaking area of Brussels in the Flemish region has required special provisions to treat the population there fairly. Drawing the boundaries of the capital district has not been easy. One area, Halle-Vilvoorde was in the French district for national elections and the Flemish district for elections to the regional council. The council exercised such extensive powers that the Court held that it was a 'legislature' within Article 3, First Protocol. A French-speaker elected for Halle-Vivoorde was confronted with the dilemma of having to choose whether to be a member of the French group in the national assembly, and thus being excluded from the regional council, or surrendering his influence on behalf of his language group at the national level so that he could participate in the consideration of regional affairs which affected Halle-Vilvoorde. The applicants in the *Mathieu-Mohin* case argued that the potential consequences of decisions at the national level, which included constitutional affairs, were so important that a representative was effectively compelled to associate himself with his language group in the assembly. The result was that there was no representation of the interests of the French-speakers of Halle-Vilvoorde in the regional council. In finding that there was no violation of the Convention, the majority of the Court endorsed the government's claim that to be allowed the choice at all was a concession to elected French-speakers, itself not required by any consideration of fairness, given the electoral arrangements as a whole. The dissenting minority in the Court regarded this so-called privilege as a right of the French-speaking voters to effective representation. The majority, it said, had practically reduced the margin of appreciation to a good faith test. While the judgment is important for the general principles it enunciates, the details which it addressed are of no concern to other national systems. Only in a wholly egregious situation such as that in the *Greek* case,[14] where elections had been suspended and there was no immediate prospect of them being re-introduced, is it easy to say that the Convention standards have been transgressed.

---

12 See most notably, Ely, *Democracy and Distrust*, 1980. See also Bell, *French Constitutional Law*, 1992, pp 205-209.
13 A 113 (1987).
14 12 YB (the *Greek* case) 1 at 179-180 (1969); CM Res DH (70)1.

Article 3 of the First Protocol applies to 'the choice of legislature'. It is for each state to make its own constitutional arrangements allocating legislative power. It is for the state to decide on how many chambers the legislature should have, how they are related and whether to adopt a federal or unitary system.[15] While the Strasbourg authorities have nothing to say about these arrangements, they must determine whether any particular body is a 'legislature' and thus within Article 3, First Protocol. The test is whether the national body has an independent power to issue decrees having the force of law. So in *Mathieu-Mohin v Belgium*[16] the Court decided that regional councils in Belgium were constituent parts of the legislature, in addition to both houses of the national Parliament. The Commission has reached the same conclusion without any argument about the legislatures of the German[17] and Austrian *Lander*.[18] But it was not satisfied that English metropolitan county councils were legislatures in the Convention sense, despite their power to issue bye-laws, because the power was delegated by the national Parliament, which could not only define the power but completely abolish the councils.[19]

Until now, the Commission has not been willing to regard the European Parliament as a 'legislature' on the grounds that it does not have an identifiable legislative function, although it has been able to avoid taking a definitive stand on the question.[20] The Commission has acknowledged that the power of the Parliament is developing[1] and has been urged to revise its opinion.[2] This question might matter less when uniform rules for elections to the European Parliament are finally adopted.[3] For instance, in *Lindsay v UK*,[4] the applicant complained that the adoption of different voting systems by the United Kingdom for European Parliament elections for Northern Ireland and Great Britain was in breach of Article 14 in conjunction with Article 3, First Protocol. The Commission found that there was no breach, but this kind of claim would be unnecessary if there were common, European-wide standards for the elections. The potential responsibility of a state party to the Convention arises because it may not plead the provisions of a subsequent international agreement as the reason for not fulfilling its Convention duties.[5] In the meantime, the post-Maastricht EC Treaty[6]

---

15 *Moureaux v Belgium No 9276/81*, 33 DR 97 at 128-129 (1983).
16 A 113 para 53 (1987).
17 *X, Y and Z v FRG No 6850/74*, 5 DR 90 (1976).
18 *X v Austria No 7008/75*, 6 DR 120 (1976).
19 *Booth-Clibborn v UK No 11391/85*, 43 DR 236 (1985). This application was challenging the abolition of the councils.
20 See, eg *Lindsay v UK No 8364/78*, 15 DR 247 (1979) and *Tete v France No 11123/84*, 54 DR 52 (1987).
1 *Tete v France No 11123/84*, 54 DR 52 at 68 (1987) and *Fournier v France No 11406/85*, 55 DR 130 at 140 (1988).
2 De Meyer, *European System*, Ch 22 at p 554.
3 See EEC Treaty, Article 138(3).
4 *No 8364/78*, 15 DR 247 (1979).
5 *X v FRG No 235/56*, 2 YB 256 at 300 (1958).
6 Article 8b(2).

provides a right for Union citizens to stand for election to and to vote in elections for the European Parliament.

According to the Commission, referenda are not within the terms of Article 3 of the First Protocol,[7] a decision which has also been criticised.[8] The criticism is apt if the direct outcome of the referendum is the enactment of law but it is hardly compelling if applied to a referendum like that held in the United Kingdom in 1975 about continued membership of the European Community. That referendum was advisory and if the outcome had been in favour of withdrawal, the requisite legislation would still have had to have been enacted by Parliament.

Article 3 of the First Protocol does not require popular participation in the selection of the government[9] nor the head of state, no matter what its or his powers.[10] It requires no particular form of separation of powers or of control of the government by the elected legislature.

There are collective and individual aspects to the states' obligations under Article 3, First Protocol. The duty to hold free and fair elections at reasonable intervals is one which is owed to people collectively and individually. It is appropriate for an inter-state complaint or for an individual application. However, the state has a wide margin to decide which system it will adopt because the object to 'ensure the free expression of the opinion of the people' is sufficiently indeterminate to encompass a variety of electoral systems. Such positive duties as states have to ensure 'fairness' appear to relate only to formal matters like candidature and voting. There is no suggestion that states have duties to compensate parties or candidates for economic disadvantage in the election process, either by subsidising parties or by imposing limits on contributions. However, if a state chooses to provide public financing, it is not precluded from doing so by the Convention.[11] The matters of contribution-capping or imposing restrictions on candidates' expenditure of even their own resources have not yet been canvassed before the Commission.[12] Furthermore, the Strasbourg authorities have said that each system must be considered in the light of political conditions in the state, so that measures which are adopted, say, to protect a minority in one state might not be appropriate in another with a more homogeneous population.[13] The dissenting judges in *Mathieu-Mohin v Belgium*[14] did find a violation of Article 3 of the First Protocol, in that there was an effective bar to the representation of a minority in a regional council which exercised important legislative functions. This might suggest positive obligations to provide for

7   *X v FRG No 6742/74*, 3 DR 98 (1975) and *X v UK No 7096/75*, 3 DR 165 (1975).
8   De Meyer, *European System*, Ch 22 at p 556.
9   Id, p 557.
10 *Habsburg-Lothringen v Austria No 15344/89*, 64 DR 210 at 219 (1989).
11 *Association X, Y and Z v FRG No 6850/74*, 5 DR 90 at 94 (1976).
12 On US law, see *Buckley v Valeo* 424 US 1 (1976). See also *Australian Capital Television v Commonwealth of Australia* (1992) 177 CLR 106. For a discussion of these questions, see Garber, *Transforming Free Speech*, 1991.
13 *Lindsay v UK No 8364/78*, 15 DR 247 at 251 (1979).
14 A 113 (1987). See also *Liberal Party, R and P v UK No 8765/79*, 21 DR 211 at 225 (1980).

minority representation, independently of any question of discrimination. The fact that states adopt an electoral system which, even foreseeably, disadvantages certain political parties will not, of itself, contravene Article 3, First Protocol. In the *Liberal Party* case,[15] the complaint was that the United Kingdom's electoral system of 'first past the post' inevitably lead to a significant dissonance between the proportion of votes cast for a small national party and the proportion of seats it obtained in the legislature. The Commission said that the United Kingdom system was overall an acceptable system for elections to the legislature and it did not become unfair by reason of the results obtained under it.[16] An electoral system which routinely excluded from all effective influence a discrete minority would raise a different question. However, if one relies on the existing case-law, it is likely that a remedy, as for other matters touching minorities, must be found elsewhere in the Council of Europe system, conceivably even through a Protocol to the Convention.[17] The 1994 Council of Europe Framework Convention for the Protection of National Minorities[18] imposes only a general obligation in this respect. Article 15 states:

'The parties shall create the conditions necessary for the effective participation of persons belonging to national minorities in cultural, social and economic life and in public affairs, in particular those affecting them.'

Apart from the several rights that each individual enjoys to a fair electoral system, individuals have discrete rights with respect to the system, identified originally by the Commission and now confirmed by the Court as the rights to vote and to stand for election.[19] The rights are not absolute for the state has an implied power to exclude some individuals from the right to vote[20] or to stand as candidates or to impose conditions on their doing so.[1] While prohibitions on voting or standing are not ruled out on grounds of age, for instance, they must not thwart 'the free expression of the opinion of the people'.[2] Article 16 allows discrimination against aliens in the exercise of political activities, so that qualifications for voting based on nationality are

---

15 Loc cit at p 554, n 14. In the 1979 General Election, the Liberal Party gained 13.8 per cent of the votes but only 1.7 per cent of the seats: see the *Liberal Party* case, loc cit at n 35 above, p 213.
16 Id, pp 224-225.
17 See Hillgruber and Jestaedt, *The European Convention on Human Rights and the Protection of National Minorities*, 1994, pp 52-76.
18 ETS 157.
19 *Mathieu-Mohin v Belgium* A 113 para 51 (1987), relying on *W, X, Y and Z v Belgium Nos 6745/74, 6746/74*, 2 DR 110 (1975).
20 *H v Netherlands No 9914/82*, 33 DR 242 (1979) (convicted prisoners may be disenfranchised) and *X v UK No 7730/76*, 15 DR 137 (1979) (restriction on citizen resident abroad permissible).
1 *Fryske Nasjonale Partij v Netherlands No 11100/84*, 45 DR 240 (1985) (language requirement for registration). See further, De Meyer, *European System*, Ch 22 at pp 562-563.
2 *W, X, Y and Z v Belgium Nos 6745/74, 6746/74*, 2 DR 110 at 116 (1975).

not forbidden. Where voting or candidature is subject to conditions, these conditions must not impair the essence of the right by making its exercise burdensome or practically impossible. In *Mathieu-Mohin v Belgium*,[3] the Court said that the Convention did not require that states adopt systems which gave equal weight to votes cast in the same election, which essentially would have required constituencies of approximately equal electoral populations. In *Purcell v Ireland*,[4] the Commission said that the rights of individual voters protected by Article 3 of the First Protocol did not include the right that all political parties be granted equal coverage by the broadcasting media or, indeed, any coverage at all.

Political parties have interests of their own, independent of their members or supporters, to participate and campaign effectively in elections for the legislature and they should, in appropriate cases, be protected by the Convention.[5] The possibility of parties bringing their own applications might account for the somewhat narrow view of the Commission in *Purcell v Ireland*[6] that individual voters could not be disadvantaged by restrictions imposed on a party which the applicants did not support. If this is the explanation, for it might be thought that all voters had an interest in an election which was fair to all parties, the Commission might profitably reconsider its reluctance to accept the political party as an independent applicant evinced in its decision in the *Liberal Party* case. States may be entitled to prohibit the activities of certain political parties under Article 17 but, given the importance attached to the electoral process as the legitimation of political opinion, it is a power which should be used only as the last resort. There has been a suggestion that political parties are entitled to some positive protection in respect of access to radio and television during elections because of concern about discrimination between political parties during the campaign.[7] Political parties are not guaranteed a successful outcome to a fair electoral process. If the system adopted by the state excludes from the legislature parties not passing a minimum threshold of votes[8] or does not allocate seats in proportion to votes,[9] then the disadvantaged parties have no redress under the Convention.

It cannot be maintained that Article 3 of the First Protocol, has so far been interpreted as imposing burdensome obligations on states.[10] Its language reflects the reservations of some of the original parties to including a provision on elections at all. It is 'an extraordinarily weak formulation'[11]

---

3 A 113 para 54 (1987). See also the *Liberal Party* case (where the differential weights of votes were stark: see p 555, n 15, above) and *X v Iceland No 8941/80*, 27 DR 145 (1981).
4 *No 15404/89*, 70 DR 262 (1991).
5 The Commission avoided the question whether a political party was a proper applicant in the *Liberal Party* case, loc cit at p 555, n 15, above. It did not even refer to a problem of this kind in *Fryske Nasjonale Partij v Netherlands No 22200/84*, 45 DR 240 (1985).
6 *No 15404/89*, 70 DR 262 (1991).
7 *X and Association Z v UK No 4515/70*, 38 CD 86 (1971).
8 *Tete v France No 11123/84*, 54 DR 52 (1987).
9 *Liberal Party* case, loc cit at p 555, n 15, above.
10 See Rawlings, *Law and the Electoral Process*, 1988, pp 61-62.
11 Novak, *UN Covenant on Civil and Political Rights: A Commentary*, 1993, p 437.

which interpretation has done little to bolster. Such caution is out of sympathy with recent developments outside the Convention system which have emphasised the importance of effective political democracy.[12] Judge de Meyer[13] has hinted that more might be done by relying on the idea of (internal) self-determination to strengthen Article 3 of the First Protocol. The development of this idea implies, amongst other things, that the political arrangements of a state will guarantee not only the fair election of a majority legislature but that the influence of the minority, particularly permanent and discrete minorities, will not be without effect on the political process. Because such an outcome might be achieved other than through the way the legislature is elected, Article 3, First Protocol is not an entirely adequate tool for imposing this standard on states.[14] The Convention parties have, of course, encountered few substantial problems about protecting their electoral systems but, as Franck[15] has pointed out, it is precisely such states which should set examples of how the same result shall be achieved in more perilous conditions. However, it would be a bold prediction to suggest that the Convention will in future be interpreted to intrude substantially into the way that states conduct elections to the legislature.[16]

---

12 Rosas, in Rosas and Helgesen, eds, *Human Rights in a Changing East-West Perspective*, 1990, pp 17-57; Steiner, 1 Harv HRYB 77 (1988); and Franck, 86 AJIL 46 (1992).
13 *European System*, Ch 22 at p 556.
14 See Thornberry, Rosas, in Tomusachat, ed, *Modern Law of Self-Determination*, 1993, pp 101-138, 225-252 respectively.
15 Loc cit at n 12 above, p 90.
16 The straws in the wind are in the cases referred to at p 556, n 3, above.

CHAPTER 21

Rights protected by the Fourth, Sixth and Seventh Protocols to the Convention

As yet there has been only a small amount of jurisprudence on the rights added by the Fourth Protocol and just a handful of cases in which the Sixth or Seventh Protocols have been considered. Reasons for this include the fact that these Protocols have not been ratified by all of the parties to the Convention and the Sixth and Seventh Protocols in particular have only been in force for a limited period of time.[1]

1. ARTICLE 1, FOURTH PROTOCOL: FREEDOM FROM IMPRISONMENT FOR NON-FULFILMENT OF A CONTRACTUAL OBLIGATION

Article 1 of the Fourth Protocol reads:

'No one shall be deprived of his liberty merely on the ground of inability to fulfil a contractual obligation.'

It extends to a failure to fulfil a contractual obligation of any kind. It may thus include non-delivery, non-performance and non-forbearance, as well as the non-payment of debts.[2] Article 1 is limited in its application by the words 'merely on the ground of inability to fulfil' an obligation. Deprivation of liberty is not forbidden if there is some other factor present, as where the detention is because the debtor acts fraudulently or negligently or for some other reason refuses to honour an obligation that he is able to comply with. Thus, where a person was detained on the request of a creditor for refusing to make an affidavit in respect of his property, Article 1 of the Fourth Protocol did not apply.[3] Other examples given in the Explanatory Report to the Protocol[4] are where a person, knowing that he does not have the money

1 For details, see above, p 2.
2 Explanatory Reports on the Second to Fifth Protocols, H(71)11 (1971), p 39. Explanatory Reports or Memoranda accompanying Council of Europe treaties provide guidance as to their meaning but are not an authorative source of interpretation.
3 *X v FRG No 5025/71*, 14 YB 692 (1971).
4 Loc cit at n 2, above, pp 39-40.

to pay, orders food in a restaurant; through negligence, fails to supply goods under contract; or is preparing to leave the country in order to avoid his contractual obligations.

The term 'deprivation of liberty' is that found in Article 5 of the Convention and can be taken to have the meaning that it has there.[5] Under Article 5(1)(b) of the Convention, a person may be deprived of his liberty for 'non-compliance with a lawful order of a court'. This could include a court order that results from the failure to fulfil a contractual obligation. The effect of Article 1 is that, for parties to the Fourth Protocol, the detention of a person for failure to comply with such a court order merely because that person is unable to comply with the contractual obligation concerned is prohibited.[6]

In practice, Article 1 of the Fourth Protocol is unlikely to present a problem for parties in post-Dickensian Europe.

2. ARTICLE 2, FOURTH PROTOCOL: FREEDOM OF MOVEMENT WITHIN A STATE AND FREEDOM TO LEAVE ITS TERRITORY

Article 2 of the Fourth Protocol reads:

'1. Everyone lawfully within the territory of a state shall, within that territory, have the right to liberty of movement and freedom to choose his residence.
2. Everyone shall be free to leave any country, including his own.
3. No restrictions shall be placed on the exercise of these rights other than such as are in accordance with law and are necessary in a democratic society in the interests of national security or public safety, for the maintenance of *ordre public* for the prevention of crime, for the protection of health or morals, or for the protection of the rights and freedoms of others.
4. The rights set forth in paragraph 1 may also be subject, in particular areas, to restrictions imposed in accordance with law and justified by the public interest in a democratic society.'

For the purposes of Article 2 as a whole, a territory to which the Fourth Protocol is extended by declaration is a separate territory from a state's metropolitan territory, so that freedom of movement, etc, applies only within the non-metropolitan territory concerned (Article 5(1), Fourth Protocol). A state's embassy abroad is not a part of its territory for the purposes of the Fourth Protocol generally.[7]

5 See above, p 97.
6 For the view that Article 5(1)(b) does not in any event permit detention in the circumstances covered by Article 1 of the Fourth Protocol, thereby rendering the latter superfluous, see Trechsel, *European System*, p 278.
7 *V v Denmark No 17392/90*, 15 EHRR CD 28 (1992).

i.   Freedom of movement within a state's territory

Article 2(1) of the Fourth Protocol provides that 'everyone lawfully within the territory of a state shall, within that territory, have the right to liberty of movement and freedom to choose his residence'. 'Everyone' includes aliens, ie nationals of other states and stateless persons,[8] although, as is well established, an alien has no right under the Convention 'to enter, reside or remain in a particular country'.[9] The term 'lawfully' was inserted to take into account the sovereign power of states to control the entry of aliens.[10] An alien who infringes the conditions attaching to his entry into a state's territory is not 'lawfully' within it.[11] Article 3 of the Fourth Protocol expressly guarantees the right of a national of a state to enter and remain in its territory.

A person's right to 'liberty of movement' within a state's territory that is protected by Article 2(1) of the Fourth Protocol has to be distinguished from the right not to be 'deprived of his liberty' that is protected by Article 5(1), Convention. The latter involves a severe form of restriction on freedom of movement and is subject to the different and more rigorous regime in Article 5. The point at which the line is drawn is considered in the context of that Article.[12] As to the freedom to choose one's place of 'residence', the restrictions upon the applicants' residence in their home in *Gillow v UK*,[13] which would appear to raise an issue under Article 2, were not considered by the Court because the Fourth Protocol had not been ratified by the defendant state.

The rights protected by Article 2(1) of the Fourth Protocol are not absolute; they are curtailed by the restrictions contained in Articles 2(3) and (4), the structure and content of which are similar to that of Articles 8-11, Convention. Article 2(3) requires that a restriction be 'necessary in a democratic society' for one or more of the following reasons: for 'national security or public safety, for the maintenance of *ordre public*', 'for the prevention of crime, for the protection of health or morals, or for the protection of the rights and freedoms of others'. These grounds for restriction can be taken to have the meaning that they have been given under Articles 8-11, Convention.[14] Article 2(4) adds to them a further ground for restriction that is not found in Articles 8-11, viz 'public interest'. The Explanatory Report[15] indicates that the intention was to permit restrictions that might not come within the concept of *ordre public*'. The term 'public interest' was preferred to 'economic welfare', which was considered and

---

8   Cf below, p 563, n 18.
9   *Paramanathan v FRG No 12068/86*, 51 DR 237 at 240 (1986).
10 Explanatory Report, loc cit at n 2, above, p 40.
11 *Paramanathan v FRG*, above.
12 See above, p 98.
13 A 109 para 42 (1986). There was a breach of the Article 8, Convention right to respect for the applicants' 'home' in that case: see above, p 318. As to whether an order withdrawing a liquor licence that affects a person's place of residence is an interference with the right of residence, see the facts of *X v Belgium No 8901/80*, 23 DR 237 (1980).
14 See above, Ch 8.
15 Loc cit at n 2, above, pp 46-48.

rejected. None the less, the term 'public interest', is potentially very wide, and could be read as covering 'economic welfare'.[16]

The restrictions permitted by Articles 2(3) and (4) are clearly subject to the principle of proportionality developed under Articles 8-11 of the Convention and to the doctrine of a 'margin of appreciation'.[17] Applying Article 2(3) to restrictions upon freedom of movement, the Commission has upheld a condition that a bankrupt should not absent himself from the district without prior authorisation on the grounds of '*ordre public*' and the 'rights and freedoms of others'.[18] Likewise, restrictions upon freedom of movement may be imposed upon an accused person released on bail[19] or a person suspected of mafia activities on the ground of 'prevention of crime'.[20] The withdrawal of a liquor licence following a person's conviction for running a disorderly house that affects his place of residence can be justified as being both 'for the prevention of crime' and the 'protection of health or morals'.[1] The '*ordre public*' restriction has also been used to justify the removal of families from one mobile home site to another.[2] The phrase 'particular area' in Article 2(4) has not been interpreted as yet; the Explanatory Report[3] indicates that the intention was not to limit it to any particular geographical or administrative unit; any 'well defined area' would qualify. It might include an urban area within which it is thought necessary to control residential development.

Both Articles 2(3) and (4) require that a restriction be 'in accordance with law'. This wording can be taken to have the autonomous Convention meaning that it has been given in other provisions.[4] The Article 2(3) requirement was infringed in *Raimondo v Italy*[5] when a person who was suspected of mafia activities was made the subject of a court supervision order by which he was required not to leave his home without informing the police. The Court found that the case fell within Article 2 of the Fourth Protocol – not Article 5 of the Convention – and that the restriction upon the applicant's freedom of movement could be justified under Article 2(3) as being necessary 'for the maintenance of "*ordre public*"' and for the 'prevention of crime'. However, the applicant was not informed of the judicial revocation of the order for 18 days, during which time he continued to be restricted in his movements. The Court held that during this period the restrictions had not been 'in accordance with law'.

---

16 See Van Dijk and Van Hoof, p 492, who suggest that 'public interest' would permit a restriction on residence to persons with an economic connection with the area: see the facts of the *Gillow* case, above, p 318.
17 Article 2(4) requires that a restriction be 'justified', but not 'necessary' in a democratic society, which is the standard and seemingly stricter formula in Article 2(3).
18 *X v Belgium No 8988/80*, DR 24 198 (1981). It also interfered with his right to leave the country.
19 *Schmid v Austria No 10670/83*, 44 DR 195 (1985).
20 *Raimondo v Italy*, see below, at n 5, and *Ciancimino v Italy No 12541/86*, 70 DR 103 (1991).
1 *X v Belgium No 8901/80*, 23 DR 237 (1980).
2 *Van de Vin v Netherlands No 13628/88*, 3 HRCD 93 (1992).
3 Loc cit at p 558, n 2, above, p 46.
4 See above, p 285.
5 A 281-A paras 39-40 (1994).

ii.   Freedom to leave a state's territory

Article 2(2) states that 'everyone shall be free to leave any country, including his own'. The freedom extends to nationals and aliens. The freedom is subject to the same 'in accordance with law' requirement and the same restrictions in Article 2(3) as apply to the guarantee of freedom of movement within a state's territory in Article 2(1). These limitations are discussed above under Article 2(1) and the same considerations apply under Article 2(2) as apply there. Thus, as far as Article 2(3) restrictions are concerned, an accused may be detained in prison[6] or refused a passport[7] in connection with pending criminal proceedings on grounds of '*ordre public*' or 'the prevention of crime'. In *Piermont v France*,[8] the Commission declared admissible an application by an MEP who claimed that her expulsion from the Republic of French Polynesia, which she had entered lawfully, for speaking out against nuclear tests there, restricted her freedom of movement between Tahiti and another island within the Republic where she was to address another meeting. Freedom to leave a country is a personal right which does imply a right to transfer one's possessions out of it.[9]

3.   ARTICLE 3, FOURTH PROTOCOL: THE RIGHT OF A NATIONAL NOT TO BE EXPELLED FROM AND TO ENTER A STATE'S TERRITORY

Article 3 of the Fourth Protocol reads:

'1.   No one shall be expelled, by means either of an individual or of a collective measure, from the territory of the state of which he is a national.

2.   No one shall be deprived of the right to enter the territory of the state of which he is a national.'

An expulsion occurs when a person is 'obliged permanently to leave the territory of a state of which he is a national without being left the possibility of returning later'.[10] Extradition of nationals is outside the scope of Article 3, Fourth Protocol. Thus, a request from the East German authorities for the extradition of a West German national from West Germany was not covered by Article 3, Fourth Protocol.[11] Article 3 only protects nationals of the

---

6   *X v FRG No 7680/76*, 9 DR 190 (1977). See also *X v FRG No 3962/69*, 13 YB 688 (1984).
7   See *Schmid v Austria No 10670/83*, 44 DR 195 (1985) and *M v FRG No 10307/83*, 37 DR 113 (1984).
8   *Nos 15773/89 and 15774/89*, 15 EHRR CD 76 (1992). The claim was later rejected unanimously by both the Commission and the Court: Judgment of 27 April 1995.
9   *S v Sweden No 10653/83*, 42 DR 224 (1985).
10   *X v Austria and FRG No 6189/73*, 46 CD 214 (1974).
11   *Brückmann v FRG No 6242/73*, 17 YB 458 (1974). As to extradition under Article 3 of the Convention, see above, p 73.

expelling state.[12] The fact that a person has an application for the nationality of the expelling state under consideration by its authorities is not sufficient for Article 3 to apply; if he is granted nationality later, he will be able to return as a national.[13] Neither the Explanatory Report nor any Strasbourg jurisprudence as yet explores the meaning of the term 'national' for the purposes of Article 3. Although the classification of an individual as a national under a particular state's law will generally be decisive, the term presumably has an autonomous Convention meaning that would permit the Strasbourg authorities to take into account the limited controls to which general international law subjects states when granting or withdrawing nationality.[14] As to the withdrawal of nationality, although the principle was accepted, it was thought too difficult to include in Article 3 a provision prohibiting a state from withdrawing a person's nationality in order to expel him.[15]

A person who is required to leave his national state's embassy abroad is not expelled from its 'territory', as an embassy is not territory for the purposes of the Fourth Protocol.[16]

As with Article 2 (see above), a non-metropolitan territory to which the Fourth Protocol is extended is a separate unit for the purposes of Article 3 (Article 5(1), Fourth Protocol).

Article 3(2) provides that 'no one shall be deprived of the right to enter the territory of the state of which he is a national'. As was noted by Mr Fawcett in his separate opinion in the *East African Asians* cases,[17] the right of entry guaranteed for nationals by it does not exclude the possibility that the failure to admit nationals may be a breach of Article 3, Convention.

4. ARTICLE 4, FOURTH PROTOCOL: FREEDOM OF ALIENS FROM COLLECTIVE EXPULSION

Article 4 of the Fourth Protocol reads:

'Collective expulsion of aliens is prohibited.'

Aliens are understood to include stateless persons.[18] 'Expulsion' can be taken to have the same meaning as it has under Article 3, Fourth Protocol (above). Article 4 does not prohibit individual cases of expulsion; this is a matter dealt with by Article 1 of the Seventh Protocol instead (below). The phrase 'collective expulsion' refers to 'any measure of the competent authority

---

12 See eg *X v Sweden No 3916/69*, 32 CD 51 (1969).
13 *L v FRG No 10564/83*, 40 DR 262 (1984). See also *X v FRG No 3745/68*, 31 CD 107 (1969).
14 As to nationality in international law, see Oppenheim, *International Law*, Vol 1, 9th edn (by Jennings and Watts), 1992, pp 851ff.
15 Explanatory Report loc cit at n 2, above, p 48.
16 *V v Denmark No 17392/90*, 15 EHRR CD 28 (1992).
17 3 EHRR 76 (1973) Com Rep para 242; CM Res DH (77) 2.
18 Explanatory Memorandum, loc cit at n 2, above, p 50.

compelling aliens as a group to leave the country, except where such measure is taken after and on the basis of a reasonable and objective examination of the particular cases of each individual alien of the group'.[19] The fact that a number of aliens from the same country had all been refused asylum in similar terms did not mean that they had been collectively expelled when there was evidence that each of them had received individual, reasoned decisions.[20] However, an issue may arise in such a case under Article 3, Convention.[1]

5. SIXTH PROTOCOL: FREEDOM FROM THE DEATH PENALTY

Article 1 of the Sixth Protocol reads:

'The death penalty shall be abolished. No one shall be condemned to such penalty or executed.'

The Sixth Protocol revises, for the parties to it, Article 2 of the Convention, which expressly permits the death penalty.

The inter-relationship between the Sixth Protocol and Articles 2 and 3 of the Convention, which was discussed in the *Soering* case, is considered above.[2] Significantly, applying *Soering* reasoning, the Commission has held that it can be a breach of the Sixth Protocol to extradite a person to another state where there is a real risk that the death penalty will be imposed.[3]

The text of the Sixth Protocol makes it clear that it is not sufficient that the death penalty is not used in practice. A party to the Protocol must abolish the death penalty, if it still exists in its law, and must not re-introduce it. Moreover, quite apart from the law, 'no one shall be condemned to such penalty or executed' by the state in fact. This wording is intended to create a 'subjective right', ie one that a person is able to enforce in the national courts.[4] The prohibition is limited to peacetime.[4a] A party to the Protocol may make provision in its law for the death penalty in time of war and may carry the penalty out in accordance with, and subject to, the limits of its law (Article 2). The prohibition in the Sixth Protocol may not be derogated from under Article 15 (Article 3). Exceptionally, a state may not make a reservation to the Sixth Protocol (Article 4).

---

19 *Becker v Denmark No 7011/75*, 4 DR 215 at 235 (1975).
20 *A v Netherlands No 14209/88*, 59 DR 274 (1988).
1   See above, p 73 and see *A, B and C v France No 18560/91*, 15 EHRR CD 39 (1992).
2   Above, p 46.
3   *Aylor-Davis v France No 22742/93*, 76A DR 164 (1994).
4   Explanatory Memorandum to the Sixth Protocol, CE Doc H (83) 3, p 6.
4a The Parliamentary Assembly has proposed a further protocol prohibiting the death penalty in wartime also, see above, p 34, n 14.

6. ARTICLE 1, SEVENTH PROTOCOL: FREEDOM FROM EXPULSION OF INDIVIDUAL ALIENS

Article 1 of the Seventh Protocol reads:

'1. An alien lawfully resident in the territory of a state shall not be expelled therefrom except in pursuance of a decision reached in accordance with law and shall be allowed:
   a. to submit reasons against his expulsion,
   b. to have his case reviewed, and
   c. to be represented for these purposes before the competent authority or a person or persons designated by that authority.
2. An alien may be expelled before the exercise of his rights under paragraph 1, a, b and c of this Article, when such expulsion is necessary in the interests of public order or is grounded on reasons of national security.'

This guarantees that an alien 'lawfully resident in the territory of a state shall not be expelled except in pursuance of a decision reached in accordance with law' and only, in most cases, after specified procedural rights have been respected. In contrast with Article 4 of the Fourth Protocol, it concerns cases of individual, rather than collective, expulsion. However, unlike Article 4, it requires only that the rule of law be complied with; it is not a prohibition on expulsion.

Article 1 applies only to aliens who are lawfully 'resident' in a state's territory. It therefore does not include aliens who have not passed through immigration, those in transit, those admitted for a non-residential purpose or those awaiting a decision on residence.[5] The term 'lawful' refers to national law and excludes a person who has gained admission illegally, whose permit has expired or who has infringed other conditions of his permit.[6] 'Expulsion' can be taken *mutatis mutandis* to have the meaning that it has under Article 3 of the Fourth Protocol,[7] so that, *inter alia*, it does not include extradition. The requirement that the expulsion be 'in accordance with law' can likewise be taken to have the autonomous meaning that it has in other Convention provisions.[8] Where Article 1 applies, the applicant must be allowed '(a) to submit reasons against his expulsion, (b) to have his case reviewed, and (c) to be represented for these purposes before the competent authority or a person or persons designated by that authority' (Article 1(1)). Exceptionally, an alien may be expelled before he has exercised these procedural rights where the expulsion is 'necessary in the interests of public order or is grounded on reasons of national security' (Article 1(2)). In both

5 Explanatory Memorandum on the Seventh Protocol, CE Doc H (83) 3, p 7. An alien in this context can be taken to include a stateless person: see above, at p 563, concerning Article 4, Fourth Protocol.
6 Ibid.
7 See above, p 562.
8 See above, p 285.

of these cases, the Explanatory Memorandum suggests, the exceptions should be applied taking into account the principle of proportionality[9] and the rights set out in Article 1(1) should be available after expulsion.[10]

According to the same Memorandum, the alien's right to submit reasons against his expulsion applies 'even before being able to have his case reviewed'.[11] As to the right to have the expulsion decision 'reviewed', this 'does not necessarily require a two-stage procedure before different authorities'; it would be sufficient for the 'competent authority' that took the decision to consider the matter again.[12] The 'competent authority' does not have to give the alien or his representative an oral hearing; a written procedure would suffice. Nor does it have to have a power of decision; it is enough that it may make a recommendation to the body that does take the final decision. Clearly, the 'competent authority' does not itself have to be a judicial body that complies with Article 6, Convention.[13] As a result, although Article 1 offers an alien at least the possibility of having his arguments against expulsion taken into account by the executive, if the above interpretation suggested in the Explanatory Memorandum is adopted, it offers only a modest guarantee of procedural due process. As noted earlier, however, the Memorandum does not have to be followed by the Commission or the Court.

7. ARTICLE 2, SEVENTH PROTOCOL: THE RIGHT TO REVIEW IN CRIMINAL CASES

Article 2 of the Seventh Protocol reads:

'1. Everyone convicted of a criminal offence by a tribunal shall have the right to have his conviction or sentence reviewed by a higher tribunal. The exercise of this right, including the grounds on which it may be exercised, shall be governed by law.

2. This right may be subject to exceptions in regard to offences of a minor character, as prescribed by law, or in cases in which the person concerned was tried in the first instance by the highest tribunal or was convicted following an appeal against acquittal.'

The 'exercise of this right, including the grounds on which it may be exercised, shall be governed by law'. Article 2 supplements Article 6,

9 However, whereas a state relying upon 'public order' should have to show that it was necessary in the particular case or kind of case to dispense with the Article 1(1) rights, in a 'national security' case an assertion to this effect should be conclusive: id, p 9. If this interpretation were followed in the latter case, the margin of appreciation allowed to states would become far too wide.
10 Ibid.
11 Ibid.
12 Ibid.
13 As the Explanatory Memorandum, loc cit at n 5, above, notes, a decision to deport an alien is not subject to Article 6: see above, p 183.

Convention. Whereas Article 6 has been interpreted as controlling any right of appeal in criminal cases that a state in its discretion may provide under its law,[14] it does not require that there be such a right. Article 2 of the Seventh Protocol now does this for the parties to it. The term 'tribunal' is used to indicate that Article 2 'does not concern offences which have been tried by bodies which are not tribunals within the meaning of Article 6 of the Convention'.[15] For example, someone who is convicted of a disciplinary offence which qualifies as a 'criminal offence' for the purposes of Article 2 has no right to review under Article 2.[16] It is submitted that the fair trial requirements in Article 6 of the Convention, as they apply to appeal proceedings,[17] must be respected by the 'higher tribunal' when it conducts its review of the tribunal decision for Article 2 to be complied with.

The guarantee in Article 2(1) of the Seventh Protocol is in certain respects limited in its impact by Article 2(2). This provides that the right of appeal 'may be subject to exceptions in regard to offences of a minor character, as prescribed by law, or in cases in which the person concerned was tried in the first instance by the highest tribunal or was convicted following an appeal against acquittal'. As to the meaning of 'minor' offences, the Explanatory Memorandum[18] suggests that 'an important criterion is whether the offence is punishable by imprisonment or not'. The Memorandum[19] also suggests that where a person pleads guilty at his trial, his right of review is limited to his sentence. The same Memorandum also states that the same right is satisfied by leave to appeal proceedings where leave is not given[20] and, as the Commission has confirmed,[1] that it is not necessary for the appeal to be on points of fact and law; the state concerned may decide to limit it to one or the other.

8. ARTICLE 3, SEVENTH PROTOCOL: RIGHT TO COMPENSATION FOR MISCARRIAGES OF JUSTICE

Article 3 of the Seventh Protocol reads:

'When a person has by a final decision been convicted of a criminal offence and when subsequently his conviction has been reversed, or he has been pardoned, on the ground that a new or newly discovered fact

---

14 See above, p 240. As to the effect of Article 2 of the Seventh Protocol, on the interpretation of Article 6 of the Convention, see the *Ekbatani* case, above, p 16.
15 Explanatory Memorandum, loc cit at n 5, above, p 9.
16 But if the offence is a 'criminal' one in the sense of Article 6, that provision requires at least an appeal to an Article 6 tribunal. In that case, Article 2 of the Seventh Protocol requires a right of review of the second, Article 6 tribunal, decision. See further Van Dijk and Van Hoof, p 508.
17 For the application of Article 6 to appeal proceedings, see above, p 240.
18 Loc cit at n 5, above, p 9.
19 Ibid.
20 Ibid.
1 *T v Luxembourg No 19715/92*, 15 **EHRR CD** 107 (1992).

shows conclusively that there has been a miscarriage of justice, the person who has suffered punishment as a result of such conviction shall be compensated according to the law or the practice of the state concerned, unless it proved that the non-disclosure of the unknown fact in time is wholly or partly attributable to him.'

Article 3 provides for a right to compensation for miscarriages of justice in the circumstances and subject to the conditions that are set out. The person must have been convicted of a criminal offence by a final decision and suffered consequential punishment. A decision will be final when it is *res judicata*. The Explanatory Memorandum states that this will be the case where it 'is irrevocable, that is to say when no further ordinary remedies are available or when the parties have exhausted such remedies or have permitted the time-limit to expire without availing themselves of them'.[2] Article 3 does not apply where a charge has been dismissed or an accused person is acquitted by the trial court or by a higher court on appeal. The conviction must have been overturned or a pardon granted because new or newly discovered facts show conclusively that there has been a miscarriage of justice, by which is meant 'some serious failure in the judicial process involving grave prejudice to the convicted person'.[3] The Explanatory Memorandum states that the procedure to be followed to establish a miscarriage of justice is a matter for national law.[4] Article 3 provides that there is no right to compensation if the non-disclosure of the unknown fact in time is wholly or partly attributable to the person convicted. It is for the state concerned to determine the compensation to be paid in accordance with its law and practice, although presumably the Strasbourg authorities are competent to ensure that it is not totally insufficient.

9. ARTICLE 4, SEVENTH PROTOCOL: *NE BIS IN IDEM*

Article 4(1) of the Seventh Protocol reads:

'No one shall be liable to be tried or punished again in criminal proceedings under the jurisdiction of the same state for an offence for which he has already been finally acquitted or convicted in accordance with the law and penal procedure of that state.'

Article 4 of the Seventh Protocol incorporates the principle *ne bis in idem*. In other terms it protects freedom from double jeopardy. The question whether freedom from double jeopardy is guaranteed by Article 6 of the Convention

---

2 Loc cit at p 565, n 5, above. The Memorandum is quoting the Explanatory Report of the European Convention on the International Validity of Criminal Judgments 1970, p 22.
3 Loc cit at p 565, n 5, above, p 10.
4 Ibid.

has been left open by the Commission.[5] Article 4 is restricted to acts within the same jurisdiction; it does not prevent a person being convicted of the same offence in different jurisdictions. Nor does it prevent a person being made the subject of proceedings of a different character, eg disciplinary proceedings, as well as criminal proceedings within the same jurisdiction. The term 'criminal' will presumably be given the meaning that it has under Article 6 of the Convention.[6] Article 4 applies only in respect of 'final' convictions, the meaning of which has been considered above under Article 3, Seventh Protocol. Exceptionally, a case may be re-opened consistently with Article 4(1), 'in accordance with the law and penal procedure of the state concerned, if there is evidence of new or newly discovered facts, or if there has been a fundamental defect in the previous proceedings, which could affect the outcome of the case' (Article 4(2)). No derogation from Article 4 is permitted under Article 15, Convention (Article 4(4), Seventh Protocol).

10. ARTICLE 5, SEVENTH PROTOCOL: EQUALITY OF RIGHTS OF SPOUSES

Article 5 of the Seventh Protocol reads:

> 'Spouses shall enjoy equality of rights and responsibilities of a private law character between them, and in their relations with their children, as to marriage, during marriage, and in the event of its dissolution. This Article shall not prevent states from taking such measures as are necessary in the interests of the children.'

This provision relates to the rights and responsibilities of spouses under private law only. The Explanatory Memorandum[7] states that it 'does not apply to other fields of law, such as administrative, fiscal, criminal, social, ecclesiastical or labour law'. Accordingly, the state's obligation under Article 5 involves essentially a positive obligation to provide a satisfactory framework of law by which spouses have equal rights and obligations concerning such matters as property rights and their relations with their children. Article 5 does not protect the partners to any relationship outside marriage, and specifically excludes the period preceding marriage. Article 5 does not concern the 'conditions of capacity to enter into marriage provided by national law'; the words 'as to marriage' relate instead to the 'legal effects connected with the conclusion of marriage'.[8] Although Article 5 refers to the

---

5   See above, p 217. The fact that freedom from double jeopardy is now expressly protected by the Seventh Protocol, which has not been ratified by all Convention parties, does not mean that it is not required by Article 6, Convention: ibid.
6   See above, p 167.
7   Loc cit at p 565, n 5, p 12.
8   Ibid. As to the capacity to marry, see Article 12, Convention, above, p 436.

'dissolution of marriage', the Explanatory Memorandum states that this does not 'imply any obligation on a state to provide for dissolution of marriage'.[9] The Memorandum also suggests that Article 5 does not prevent the national authorities 'from taking due account of all relevant factors when reaching decisions with regard to the division of property in the event of dissolution of marriage'.[10] The final sentence of Article 5 enters the caveat that Article 5 does not prevent state legislative or administrative action that results in the spouses not having equal private law rights and responsibilities in their relations with their children where this is necessary in the 'interests of the children'. As the Explanatory Memorandum[11] notes, the need to take the interests of the children into account is already reflected in the Strasbourg jurisprudence under Articles 8 and 14, as is the basic principle of equality of treatment between spouses.

9   Ibid.
10 Ibid.
11 Ibid.

CHAPTER 22

The European Commission of Human Rights: Practice and procedure

The European Commission of Human Rights first met in 1954 and has since evolved into one of the world's busiest and most important international human rights tribunals.[1] All individual and inter-state complaints are filed with the Commission which is the Convention's obligatory pathway to the European Court of Human Rights. While its primary role is to identify those cases which satisfy the admissibility criteria set out in Articles 25-27 of the Convention, it is also the Convention's main fact-finding organ. Its increasingly important friendly settlement procedures have, over the years, led to legislative and administrative changes in many different European countries, often achieved silently and efficiently beyond the glare of publicity. In admissible cases its reasoned opinions as to whether there has been a breach of the Convention have played a crucial role in developing and shaping the case-law of the Convention. The procedures it has established in handling large numbers of cases, together with its voluminous case-law on questions of admissibility and the merits, entitle it to be regarded as the corner-stone of the Convention system.

As shall be seen below, the Commission's multi-faceted role under the Convention marks it out as being not only complementary to the role of the European Court of Human Rights but in many respects a quite distinct and unique legal forum in its own right.

1. COMPOSITION, ELECTION AND INDEPENDENCE

According to Article 20 of the Convention, the Commission is composed of as many members as there are contracting parties (at present 30). No two members may be nationals of the same state. There is, however, no rule limiting membership to nationals of contracting states although this has usually been the case up until now. In practice, therefore, as was doubtless intended by the drafters of the Convention, each contracting party numbers one of its nationals as a member of the Commission. Since the Commission's business is essentially concerned with observance of the

---

1 On the Commission generally, see Fribergh and Villiger, *European System*, Ch 25 and Krüger and Nörgaard, id, Ch 28.

Convention by the national authorities of the contracting parties the usefulness of such an arrangement is obvious in that it ensures the presence in the Commission of at least one member familiar with the domestic legal system of the contracting party concerned.[2] Membership of the Commission ends automatically when the contracting party either denounces the Convention (Article 65(1))[3] or ceases to be a member of the Council of Europe which has the effect of disengaging the state from the Convention (Article 65(3)). During their term of office members of the Commission, like members of the Court, cannot be removed against their will.

The members are elected by the Committee of Ministers of the Council of Europe by an absolute majority of votes from a list of candidates drawn up by the Bureau of the Parliamentary Assembly of the Council of Europe on the proposal of the Assembly representatives of the states concerned (Article 21(1)). In practice, national members of the Assembly prepare a list of three candidates for each vacancy in order of preference which is then transmitted to the Committee of Ministers.

Members are elected for terms of six years and are eligible for re-election (Article 22(1)).[4] Election of half of the members takes place every three years.[5] A member elected to replace a Commissioner whose term of office has not expired shall hold office for the remainder of his predecessor's term (Article 22(5)). Members hold office until they are replaced. After being replaced, they continue to deal with such cases as they already have under consideration (Article 22(6)).

Originally, the Convention contained no provision concerning the qualifications of Commission members. This lacuna was remedied by the Eighth Protocol which entered into force on 1 January 1990. Article 21(3) now provides that 'candidates shall be of high moral character and must possess the qualifications required for appointment either to high judicial office or be persons of recognised competence in national or international law'. Members are either law professors, judges or practising lawyers. There are two women members.[6]

As regards the independence of the Commission, Article 23 provides that members sit in their individual capacity, ie not as representatives of the contracting parties in respect of which they are elected. Consequently, in the discharge of their duties they may not receive instructions either from governments or from any institution (such as the Council of Europe) or any private party. This individual independence is reinforced by the manner of appointment – elections in which parliamentarians participate, rather than governmental nomination – and by their irremovability during the term of office. It was further reinforced by the Eighth Protocol, which added to

2 For a list of members of the Commission, see Appendix 1.
3 As was the case with Greece: 13 YB 33 (1970). The denunciation took effect on 13 June 1990.
4 The first election took place on 18 May 1954. The first meeting of the Commission was held on 12 July 1954. At that time eleven states had ratified the Convention.
5 See Article 22(2)-(4) for details of the triennial replacement of members.
6 They are Jane Liddy (Irish) and Gro Hillestad Thune (Norwegian).

Article 23 the requirement that '[d]uring their term of office they shall not hold any position which is incompatible with their independence and impartiality as members of the Commission or the demands of this office'.[7] A further guarantee of independence is provided by the entitlement of members to the privileges and immunities provided for in Article 40 of the Statute of the Council of Europe and the agreements made thereunder. These are specified in the Second Protocol to the General Agreement on Privileges and Immunities of the Council of Europe.[8] They encompass *inter alia*, while members are exercising their functions, immunity from arrest and detention and from seizure of personal baggage; inviolability of all papers and documents and – most important of all to secure their freedom of speech and independence in the discharge of their duties – immunity from legal process of every kind in respect of 'words spoken or written and all acts done by them' in their official capacity (Article 3). Before taking up his duties, each member must solemnly declare that he will exercise his duties, *inter alia*, 'impartially and conscientiously'.[9]

In addition, the Rules of Procedure provide that a member may not take part in the consideration of an application before the Commission (a) where he has a personal interest in the case, or (b) where he has participated in any decision on the facts on which the application is based as adviser to any of the parties or as a member of any tribunal or body of enquiry. In such circumstances withdrawal would be automatic. Where there is a doubt or where there are other circumstances which appear to affect the impartiality of members in their examination of an application, the Commission shall decide.[10]

2. ROLE OF THE COMMISSION

The pivotal position of the Commission can be seen from the variety of roles that are conferred on it by the Convention. In the first place, all applications, be they from individuals under Article 25 or by states under Article 24, begin their life with the Commission. It falls to the Commission to determine whether the applications are admissible in the light of the admissibility requirements set out in Articles 25-27 (cases brought by individuals) or Article 24 (inter-state complaints). Thus, its routine work involves a determination of such questions as the 'victim' status of the

---

7 Thus members must be not only independent and impartial but they must be able fully to assume all the duties inherent in membership of the Commission: see the Explanatory Report on the Eighth Protocol, para 29; 7 EHRR 339 (1985).
8 *Collected Texts*, p 204. In *Zoernsch v Waldock* [1964] 2 All ER 256 the English Court of Appeal held, in an action for damages against the President and the Secretary to the Commission, that they enjoyed immunity from legal process under the International Organisations (Immunities and Privileges) Act 1950 and an Order in Council made thereunder which reproduced the provisions of the Second Protocol.
9 Rule 3 of the Commission's Rules of Procedure, *Collected Texts*, p 171.
10 Rule 20(1), (2).

applicant, exhaustion of domestic remedies, whether the case has been lodged in time or whether it is incompatible with the provisions of the Convention or manifestly ill-founded. In this way the Commission filters out from a large and ever-growing number of individual applications a limited number of admissible applications for eventual decision by the Court or by the Committee of Ministers. The importance of this activity can be seen from Commission statistics and the high percentage of cases rejected as inadmissible.[11]

However, the description of the Commission as a filter inadequately characterises the complexity of its role. In a true sense, the Commission can be regarded as the spinal cord of the Convention system. Thus, in respect of cases which have been declared admissible, the Commission has three further functions. The first is that of *establishing the facts* of the case (Article 28(1)). In most cases this can be done on the basis of the national decisions or other documents furnished by the parties. In others it may require an on-site investigation or the holding of witness hearings. In this regard, the Court has emphasised that under the structure of the Convention the establishment and verification of the facts is essentially a task for the Commission.[12] It is thus on the basis of the facts set out in the Commission's Article 31 report that the case will be examined by the Court, although the Court is not bound by the Commission's findings.

The Commission has the further role of *conciliation* between the parties. After a case has been declared admissible it places 'itself at the disposal of the parties concerned with a view to securing a friendly settlement of the matter on the basis of respect for human rights as defined in [the] Convention' (Article 28(1)(b)). This friendly settlement function has evolved considerably during the life of the Commission and has proved its worth with important results in a large number of cases. Informal settlements have also taken place in a number of cases *prior* to the determination of admissibility.[13]

The third task is that of preparing a *legal opinion* as to whether or not there has been a violation of the Convention in cases where no settlement has been reached (Article 31(1)). The Commission draws up a report and transmits it to the Committee of Ministers. It may attach to the report 'such proposals as it thinks fit' (Article 31(3)). The report is also sent to the state or states concerned, who are not at liberty to publish it (Article 31(2)). The Commission's opinion is, of course, not binding on the state concerned. If the case is subsequently referred to the Court under Article 48 the report, with its findings of fact and detailed legal opinion on the issues involved, becomes a central document in the case. A delegate of the Commission will appear in the proceedings before the Court to explain and defend the opinion.

11 See below, p 580.
12 See below, p 678.
13 See below, p 602.

The heterogeneous nature of these successive functions makes it difficult to attempt any neat, conceptual classification of the Commission.[14] As can be seen from above, its role comprises, at the same time, administrative, quasi-judicial, investigative, conciliatory, representative and advisory functions. The only feature it lacks to be regarded as an international court in its own right is the power to give binding decisions.

3. ORGANISATION AND FUNCTIONING OF THE COMMISSION[15]

The seat of the Commission is in Strasbourg, although the Commission may decide that an investigation be carried out elsewhere (Rule 15). It has evolved over the years to become almost a full-time body which meets for eight two-weekly sessions a year (Rule 16). Given the amount of session time throughout the year, membership of the Commission has become the main professional activity of members. There is, however, no requirement to reside in Strasbourg.

Prior to the entry into force of the Eighth Protocol (1 January 1990) the Commission could only meet in plenary sessions. However, it became clear from the increasing numbers of applications and the growing backlog of cases in the Commission's docket that a more flexible structure was needed to enable it to deal more expeditiously with complaints. Accordingly, the Eighth Protocol created the possibility for the Commission to establish Chambers and also Committees of Three.[16] The respective roles of the plenary Commission, Chambers and Committees are described below.

i. Plenary Commission

The plenary Commission is composed of all members of the Commission. It has a quorum of at least the number of members equal to the majority of members of the Commission (Rule 23(1)). However, seven members constitute a quorum when the Commission examines an application submitted under Article 25 and decides to communicate it to the respondent government or to reject it without further examination (Rule 23(2)). Decisions are taken by majority vote (Article 34). The President has a casting vote if the voting is equal (Rule 18). While the plenary Commission is competent to decide all cases, Article 20(5) of the Convention provides that only it can:

---

14 Some of these functions may, in fact, be exercised at the same time. For example, most hearings before the Commission concern both the admissibility and the merits of the case.
15 See Fribergh and Villiger, *European System*, pp 605-610.
16 See Explanatory Report on the Eighth Protocol, paras 13-22, 7 EHRR 339 (1985), for the background to this development.

(1) examine inter-state applications,
(2) decide to bring a case before the Court under Article 48(a), and
(3) draw up the rules of procedure.

The plenary Commission also retains the prerogative of ordering the transfer to it of any petition referred to a Chamber or Committee.

ii. Chambers

The Commission is empowered to set up 'Chambers', each composed of at least seven members (Article 20(2)).[17] It has so far constituted two Chambers and with the growing number of contracting parties is likely to establish a third in 1995-1996. The President and Vice-President of the Chamber are elected by each Chamber voting separately.[18] The composition of the Chamber is determined by the Commission. At present, the Chambers have thirteen and fourteen members respectively, chosen by an alternating attribution of members, in order of precedence, to each Chamber. They have a quorum of seven members. The President of the Commission does not sit in a Chamber. The member who is a national of a respondent state has a right to sit in the Chamber to which the petition has been referred (Article 20(2) *in fine*). In this way, the national member's knowledge of domestic law is fully utilised. The Chamber may at any time relinquish jurisdiction in favour of the plenary Commission. The latter may also order relinquishment at any time (Article 20(4)).[19]

Article 20(2) of the Convention provides that Chambers may examine individual complaints which can be dealt with on the basis of established case-law or which raise no serious questions affecting the interpretation or application of the Convention. However, due to the constantly increasing case-burden of the Commission these criteria have been loosely interpreted. The work of the Commission is increasingly being done by Chambers. In 1994, for example, 90 per cent of all decisions declaring cases admissible were taken by Chambers. The figures for the adoption of Article 31 reports (85 per cent) and decisions declaring applications inadmissible (80 per cent) are almost as high. The amount of work done by Chambers has more than doubled in recent years.[20]

In practice, cases which are not rejected by a Committee of Three will be first examined by a Chamber which will decide *inter alia* whether they should be communicated to the government. In this way, the Commission is

---

17 Chambers are constituted for three years as soon as possible following the election of the President of the Commission: Rule 24(3).
18 For terms of office, see Rule 6(5).
19 The Commission may make special arrangements concerning the constitution of Chambers as it sees fit: Rule 24(4). There is thus a wide latitude to organise the Chamber system flexibly.
20 Statistics provided by the secretariat of the Commission.

able to utilise fully the decision-making capacity conferred on it by the introduction of the Chamber system.[1]

iii. Committees[2]

Article 20(3) provides that the Commission may set up Committees of three members, with the power, exercisable by unanimous vote, to reject or strike a case from its list. Committees are thus designed to dispose of straightforward cases *de plano* which are clearly inadmissible. Where there is a difference of opinion between members of the Committee the case is referred in practice to the Chamber for decision. A Committee may at any time relinquish jurisdiction in favour of the plenary Commission (Article 20(4)). To date the Commission has appointed six Committees which meet during Commission sessions (Rule 29). The Rules of Procedure provide that they shall be constituted once a year by the drawing of lots (Rule 27(1)). The most senior member acts as President of the Committee (Rule 7(3)).

In practice, it falls to the *Rapporteur* who has been assigned a particular case to propose whether it should first be dealt with by a Chamber or Committee or the plenary Commission. It is open to any member, after inspection of the list of cases and their attribution, to propose (prior to the examination of the case) that a case be dealt with by a Chamber rather than a Committee or by the plenary Commission rather than a Chamber. In the latter event the plenary Commission shall decide whether it will deal with the case.

iv. The Presidency

The Commission elects its President following the periodical elections of members provided for in Article 22(1) of the Convention.[3] The term of office is three years. Each Chamber elects its President and Vice-President as soon as the Chambers have been constituted. Elections are by secret ballot and by an absolute majority of either the Commission or the Chamber. The President of the Commission directs the work of the Commission and presides at its plenary sessions. The Secretary of the Commission exercises responsibility for the work of the secretariat under his general direction. In case of urgency (eg expulsion cases) when the Commission is not in session the President of the Commission or the President of either Chamber may take any necessary action on the Commission's behalf. The President may also indicate interim measures to the parties under Rule 36 of the Rules of Procedure.[4] He may delegate certain functions to the President of either Chamber. If he is unable to carry out his duties or if the office is vacant, the

---

1   For the operation of Chambers generally, see Rules 24-26.
2   See Rules 27-29. For the method of appointment, see Rules 28(2)-(3).
3   See Rules 6-12 and Addendum, Rule 3(4) and (7).
4   See below, p 589.

President of a Chamber shall take his place according to order of precedence.

v. Secretariat

The Commission is assisted by a legal secretariat composed of a large number of permanent or temporary lawyers from different countries working in an independent capacity. The Secretary of the Commission is responsible for the work of the secretariat. Rule 13 of the Rules of Procedure provides *inter alia* that he shall be the channel for all communications concerning the Commission and shall have custody of its archives. Both the Secretary and Deputy Secretary are appointed by the Secretary General of the Council of Europe on the proposal of the Commission. The other officials are appointed by the Secretary General with the agreement of the President of the Commission.[5]

The legal activities of the secretariat are central to the work of the Commission. They are responsible for drafting decisions and reports under the supervision of a member of the Commission (*Rapporteur*), responding to inquiries, preparing cases for examination and investigating issues of national and Convention law relevant to the Commission's work. Given the large volume of cases handled by the Commission and the fact that Commission members are not based permanently in Strasbourg, the role of the secretariat is undoubtedly influential. At the same time, their work is subject to hierarchical supervision within the secretariat itself, by the *Rapporteur* with whom they work in close cooperation and ultimately by the Commission, in all of its compositions, which is responsible for decision-making.

Article 37 of the Convention states that the 'secretariat of the Commission shall be provided by the Secretary General of the Council of Europe'. It is clear, however, from the constant practice of the Commission that 'providing' a secretariat does not mean the same as 'having authority' over it. The Commission is an independent body created by international treaty and not in application of the Statute of the Council of Europe. The independence of the Commission as a quasi-judicial body requires that its own secretariat be autonomous in the performance of the work of assisting the Commission. Somewhat at odds with this need for autonomy the Secretary General, the holder of an elective office which is in many respects political, is responsible to the Committee of Ministers for the work of the secretariat of the Council of Europe. However, it has been clearly established over the years that the secretariat is primarily responsible to the Commission and that this line of authority has been respected and indeed reinforced by successive Secretary Generals.

---

5   Rule 12(2)-(3).

vi. The confidential character of the Commission's proceedings

The general rule laid down by the Convention is that 'the Commission shall meet in camera' (Article 33). This applies not only to deliberations – which is normal in the case of a judicial body – but also to hearings. Thus, hearings before the Commission are not open to the public or to the press. Furthermore, the contents of all case-files, including the written and oral pleadings, are confidential, with the consequence that not even the parties are at liberty to make disclosures.[6] There is not, however, a total press 'blackout' as the obligation of secrecy concerns only the application as such and does not prevent an applicant from giving basic information to the press, prior to the lodging of the case, about the factual and legal basis of his complaint, particularly if the case is already in the public domain because of a national court decision. Moreover, the Secretary to the Commission is empowered to issue press releases at any stage of the procedure.[7] In practice, brief press releases concerning cases considered by the Commission are issued after each session. Admissibility decisions are available to the public – and, if of sufficient interest, published in printed form – with the identity of the applicant and other persons concerned being protected where necessary. On the other hand, Article 31 reports on the merits of admissible applications are confidential, at least initially. Friendly settlement reports, however, are published (Article 28(2)). Following reference of a case to the Court, the Commission's Article 31 report, any other documents in the Commission's case-file produced to the Court as well as the applicant's identity, become public unless the Court decides otherwise. In cases which stay with the Committee of Ministers, Article 31 reports are not published until after the Committee takes its decision under Article 32.

Leaving aside the Commission's friendly settlement procedure which is undoubtedly facilitated by the absence of media coverage, the explanation for the confidential character of the procedure before the Commission is that it was part of the price paid for the right of individual petition when the Convention was being drafted. The states consented in the form of an optional clause to granting individuals access to the Commission but subject to the condition that the Commission should not serve as a public forum for the expression of grievances.[8] Confidentiality was the means to protect states against abusive or ill-intentioned applications brought for publicity purposes. As the system has matured the question has been repeatedly asked whether the public or the private interest would be so adversely affected if the doors of the Commission were less securely closed.[9]

---

6 Rule 17(1) and (2) and Rule 37(1).
7 Rule 17(3). Press releases are also issued after each hearing following consultation of the parties.
8 See 4 TP 132-144, 178-180, 194-198, 212-214, 228, 232, 252, 264, 284 and 288.
9 The Eleventh Protocol answers this question negatively. In the single Court, hearings shall be public and documents shall be accessible to the public: new Article 40, Convention. See below, Ch 26.

4. RIGHT OF INDIVIDUAL PETITION

The importance of the right of individual petition under the Convention system resides in the wide variety of legal issues in practically every sphere of state activity that have been raised with the Commission. By the end of 1994 the Commission had registered more than 25,000 cases and had taken decisions, since its inception in 1955, in more than 22,000 applications against many different contracting parties. The number of cases to have been declared admissible was 2,027.[10] In terms of the impact on national law and practice and the steady growth of a corpus of European human rights law, the right of individual petition has proved to be the most dynamic feature of the system – much more so than inter-state proceedings.

Under Article 25 of the Convention the Commission may receive petitions from any person, non-governmental organisation or group of individuals claiming to be a victim of a violation of the Convention 'provided that the High Contracting Party against which the complaint is lodged has declared that it recognises the competence of the Commission to receive such petitions'. The Commission's competence was thus not an automatic consequence of ratification but depended on a further declaration by the state concerned. This was also seen as an essential part of the compromise by states to secure agreement to permit individuals to complain to an international tribunal. It is a telling reflection of the extent to which the Convention has taken root in the emerging legal culture of Europe that, at the present time, acceptance of the right of individual petition has become a political obligation of membership of the Council of Europe.[11]

i. Limitations to Article 25 declarations

Some states have accepted the right of individual petition indefinitely, others for a fixed period subject to express or tacit renewal. It is common for the state expressly to limit its acceptance to acts or events which occur subsequent to the date of deposit of the instrument of acceptance.[12] The only restriction expressly permitted by Article 25 is temporal.[13] Attempts to limit

---

10 *Survey of Activities and Statistics: European Commission of Human Rights*, Council of Europe, 1994. More than 80,000 provisional files have been opened since records were first kept in 1973. The number of cases dealt with by the Commission increases every year. Thus in 1994, 582 applications were declared admissible and 1,790 cases were declared inadmissible. In the same period, 9,968 provisional files were opened, of which only a fraction will ultimately be registered. See Appendix II for further details.

11 The right of individual petition has been accepted by all 30 parties to the Convention.

12 See *Collected Texts*, Council of Europe, 1987 edn, p 73 for details. The declaration under Article 25 also extends to the substantive provision of the First and Sixth Protocols (Articles 5 and 6 of the First and Sixth Protocols respectively). The Fourth and Seventh Protocols, however, require separate declarations (Articles 6 and 7 of the Protocols respectively). The Fourth and Seventh Protocols enable the state to limit the declaration to certain provisions.

13 Article 25(2) provides: 'Such declarations may be made for a specific period.'

acceptance to a particular territory or to particular rights (or the manner in which they should be interpreted) have been deemed impermissible.

The question arose in cases concerning the Turkish declaration of 28 January 1989, in which that state accepted the right of individual petition subject to a series of limitations *ratione loci, ratione materiae* and *ratione temporis*.[14] In *Chrysostomos v Turkey*,[15] which concerned, *inter alia*, complaints arising out of the arrest and detention of the applicants by Turkish military forces in the northern part of Cyprus, the Commission found that, apart from the temporal limitation, the limitations were invalid. This view was ratified by the Court in *Loizidou v Turkey* (Preliminary Objections)[16] where it held that neither Articles 25 nor 46 permitted restrictions other than of a temporal nature. The Court held specifically that the restriction *ratione loci* attached to Turkey's Article 25 and 46 declarations was invalid. In reaching this view it noted that if substantive or territorial restrictions were permissible under Articles 25 and 46, contracting parties would be free to subscribe to separate regimes of enforcement of Conventions obligations depending on the scope of their acceptances. Such a system would enable states to qualify their consent under the optional clauses and would seriously weaken the role of the Commission and Court in the discharge of their functions. It would also diminish the effectiveness of the Convention as a constitutional instrument of European public order. In addition, it also noted that where the Convention permitted states to limit their acceptance under Article 25, there is an express stipulation to this effect (for example, Article 6(2) of the Fourth Protocol and Article 7(2) of the Seventh Protocol). In the Court's view, the consequences for the enforcement of the Convention and the achievement of its aims would be so far-reaching that a power to this effect should have been expressly provided for.[17] This approach was confirmed, the Court stated, by the subsequent practice of contracting parties under these provisions. Since the entry into force of the Convention almost all of the 30 parties to the Convention, apart from Turkey, had accepted the competence of the Commission and Court to examine complaints without restrictions *ratione loci* or *ratione materiae*.[18]

14 The limitation *ratione loci* reads as follows: 'The recognition of the right of petition extends only to allegations concerning acts and omissions of public authorities in Turkey performed within the boundaries of the territory to which the constitution of the Republic of Turkey is applicable.' For the full text of the declaration, see *Chrysostomos v Turkey Nos 15299/89, 15300/89 and 15318/89*, 68 DR 216 at 228-229 (1991). The restrictions were rejected by Greece, Belgium, Denmark, Luxembourg, Norway; Sweden and the CE Secretary General, as depositary, reserved their positions: id, p 243. The restrictions *ratione materiae* were later removed in the Turkish declaration of 28 January 1993. On the Turkish declaration, see Cameron, 37 ICLQ 887 (1988) and Tomuschat, *Ermacora Festschrift*, p 119.
15 68 DR 216 (1991).
16 A 310 paras 65-89 (1995). Decision by 16 votes to 2. The case had been disjoined from *Chrysostomos* and referred to the Court by Cyprus.
17 Id, para 75.
18 Id, para 79. On the use of subsequent practice in the interpretation of a treaty, see Article 31(3)(b) of the Vienna Convention on the Law of Treaties which the Court relied on: id, para 73. The Cypriot Article 25 declaration of 9 August 1988 contained a restriction *ratione materiae* which was withdrawn on 22 December 1994: see id, paras 30-32.

The Court noted that Article 46 of the Convention had been modelled on Article 36 of the Statute of the International Court of Justice which has been interpreted as permitting restrictions. It considered, however, that the fundamental difference in the role and purpose of the tribunals, coupled with the existence of a practice of unconditional acceptance under the Convention, provided a compelling basis for distinguishing Convention practice from that of the International Court. In this context, it observed that the International Court was called on, *inter alia*, to examine any legal dispute between states that might occur in any part of the globe with reference to principles of international law and that the subject-matter of a dispute may relate to any area of international law. Moreover, unlike the Convention institutions, the role of the International Court was not exclusively limited to direct supervisory functions in respect of a law-making treaty such as the Convention.[19]

Finally, the Court also rejected the argument that the application of Article 63(4), by analogy, provided support for the claim that a territorial restriction was permissible under Articles 25 and 46. The argument was based on the premise that if the Convention (ie Article 63(4)) enabled the right of petition to be extended to Article 63 territories, it must also permit the state to impose limitations on its application to acts outside its own metropolitan territory. The Court responded to this argument as follows:[20]

> 'The Court first recalls that in accordance with the concept of "jurisdiction" in Article 1 of the Convention, state responsibility may arise in respect of acts and events outside state frontiers. It follows that there can be no requirement, as under Article 63(4) in respect of the overseas territories referred to in that provision, that the Article 25 acceptance be expressly extended before responsibility can be incurred.
>
> In addition, regard must be had to the fact that the object and purpose of Article 25 and Article 63 are different. Article 63 concerns a decision by a Contracting Party to assume full responsibility under the Convention for all acts of public authorities in respect of a territory for whose international relations it is responsible. Article 25, on the other hand, concerns an acceptance by a Contracting Party of the competence of the Commission to examine complaints relating to the acts of its own officials acting under its direct authority. Given the fundamentally different nature of these provisions, the fact that a special declaration must be made under Article 63(4) accepting the competence of the Commission to receive petitions in respect of such territories, can have no bearing, in the light of the arguments developed above, on the validity of restrictions *ratione loci* in Article 25 and 46 declarations.'

19 Id, paras 82-85.
20 Id, paras 87-88.

Having found the restriction *ratione loci* to be invalid, the Court found that it could be severed from the Article 25 and 46 declarations leaving intact the acceptance of the optional clauses in these provisions.[1]

The *Loizidou* judgment prompts several observations. While the Court has struck down the territorial restriction, it is clear from the terms of the judgment that the optional clauses do not permit restrictions of any kind apart from those of a temporal nature. The judgment thus contains a statement of principle which is crucial to the integrity of the system at a time when the Convention is being ratified by an increasing number of Eastern and Central European states, although there has been no indication so far that these new signatories have sought to condition their acceptances. The Court must have had these states in mind when it stated that:

'The inequality between Contracting States which the permissibility of such qualified acceptances might create would run counter to the aim, as expressed in the Preamble to the Convention, to achieve greater unity in the maintenance and further realisation of human rights.'[2]

Further, the Court evidenced its concern to maintain the effectiveness of the Convention as 'a constitutional instrument of European public order'. Moreover, in its interpretative approach to Articles 25 and 46, it also emphasised that it must have regard 'to the special character of the Convention as a treaty for the collective enforcement of human rights'.[3] There can be no doubt that as a result of the *Loizidou* judgment the key concept of collective enforcement and the notion of the Convention as a European bill of rights have gained an extra (and indispensable) foothold in the developing human rights culture of the new Europe. Finally, it is these very concepts which explain the boldness of the Court's approach in finding that the territorial restriction was severable from the declarations under Articles 25 and 46 notwithstanding firmly worded statements by Turkish officials that the declarations must be accepted in their entirety. In this extremely delicate and political terrain the Court appears to have given

1 Id, paras 90-98. Turkey had submitted to the Court that if her restrictions were not recognised to be valid the declarations were to be considered null and void in their entirety: id, para 90. The Court considered that Turkey, in view of the consistent practice of states to accept unconditionally the competence of the Commission and Court, must have been aware that the restrictions were of questionable validity and might be deemed impermissible. Moreover as early as 1967 and 1976 in pleadings to the Court in the *Belgian Linguistics* and *Kjeldsen, Busk Madsen and Pederson* cases (A5 and 23 respectively) the Commission had already expressed the opinion that Article 46 did not permit any restrictions. The Court concluded that, against this background, the *ex post facto* statements by Turkish representatives could not be relied upon to detract from the government's basic intention to accept the competence of the Commission and Court and that the clauses did not form an integral and inseparable part of them: id, paras 95-98. See also *Belilos v Switzerland* A 132 para 60 (1989) where the Court found that Switzerland was still bound by the Convention after having struck down an interpretative declaration because it did not conform to the Article 64 requirements for reservations: see above, p 22.
2 Id, para 77.
3 Id, paras 70, 75 and 93.

priority to the effectiveness of the system over the express intentions of a contracting party.[4] Its reasoning comes close to *caveat emptor*. In a system which is completely dependent on the consent of contracting parties, it remains to be seen whether the Court's version of what Turkey consented to when it accepted the optional clauses continues to be endorsed through her participation in proceedings before the Commission and Court.

ii.   Effective exercise of right of individual petition

States which have made a declaration under Article 25 also undertake not to hinder in any way the effective exercise of the right of petition. It is now clear from the Court's judgment in *Cruz Varas v Sweden*[5] that an applicant can complain of a violation of this procedural provision independently from complaints concerning infringement of substantive rights. *Cruz Varas* is the only case where the Commission has found a breach of this provision. It did so because of Sweden's expulsion of the applicant to Chile notwithstanding a Rule 36 indication by the Commission that the expulsion should be suspended pending examination of the case. In these circumstances the Commission considered that the deportation of the applicant frustrated the examination of the case and rendered his right of petition ineffective even though it later concluded that there had been no violation of Article 3.[6] The Court, however, considered that there had been no breach and found that, in fact, the degree of hindrance had not been significant. Cruz Varas remained at liberty on his return to Chile. He was free to leave the country and counsel had been able to represent him and his family fully before the Commission.[7]

In most of the cases where a complaint of hindrance has been made the Commission has followed an approach similar to that of the Court in *Cruz Varas* noting that, notwithstanding the restriction in question, the applicant had been free to present his case and thus no further action was called for. Arguably, this approach has been followed by the Commission because of a certain doubt, which has now been dispelled by *Cruz Varas*, as to whether a separate breach of the Convention could be found on this basis. However, where hindrance has occurred, to base the finding as to whether this requirement in Article 25 was infringed on a conclusion that, ultimately, the obstruction had not succeeded, is not entirely convincing. Further questions need to be addressed. Under what conditions would the application have been brought and examined by the Commission in the absence of hindrance? How does this compare with the manner in which the case was actually

4   See the joint and separate dissenting opinions of Judges Gölcüklü and Pettiti.
5   A 201 para 99 (1991). For discussion, see p 668.
6   A 201 (1991) Com Rep, pp 51-52. See also *Mansi v Sweden No 15658/89*, 64 DR 253 (1990) F Sett, where the applicant was also expelled in the face of a Rule 36 request. The government, in a friendly settlement, expressed regrets and paid compensation to the applicant. He was also allowed to reside permanently in Sweden.
7   A 201 para 104 (1991).

brought? Has the hindrance rendered it significantly more difficult for the applicant to prove and present his case? Is the form the hindrance has taken in breach of the applicant's substantive rights? Should it ever be acceptable under this provision to punish a person because he has lodged an application? In the latter regard it should be recalled that, although control of prisoners' mail which does not involve censorship or delays is permissible,[8] the opening of mail from the Commission is not.[9] Other issues that have arisen under this provision have concerned abnormal delays in sending correspondence to the Commission;[10] the seizure of correspondence;[11] impeding access to relevant files or documents;[12] imposing disciplinary sanctions on an applicant because of complaints to the Commission[13] or other forms of pressure to withdraw a complaint.[14]

5. INTER-STATE APPLICATIONS

Article 24 of the Convention provides that any contracting party may refer to the Commission any alleged breach of the Convention by another contracting party. The right to bring a case flows directly from the ratification of the Convention and is not subject to any other conditions.

In bringing an application the state is fulfilling its role as one of the collective guarantors of Convention rights. As the Commission indicated in *Austria v Italy*,[15] Convention obligations are essentially of an objective character being designed to protect 'the fundamental rights of individual human beings from infringement by any of the High Contracting Parties rather than to create subjective and reciprocal rights for themselves'. From this characterisation of the nature of the Convention, the Commission deduced that a contracting party could refer to the Commission any alleged breach of the Convention, regardless of whether the victims were its nationals or whether its own interests were at stake. It is not exercising a right of action for the purpose of enforcing its own rights but rather to bring before the Commission an alleged violation of the public order of Europe.[16]

---

8 *Campbell v UK* A 233 paras 42-54 (1992) and 63 DR 174 (1989). See also *G v Austria No 12976/87*, 71 DR 45 (1991).
9 *Campbell v UK* A 233 paras 55-64 (1992).
10 *X v FRG No 892/60*, 4 YB 241 (1961).
11 *X v FRG No 2137/64*, 7 YB 311 (1964).
12 *Herczegfalvy v Austria No 10533/83* (1989), decn admiss, para 14, reproduced as Appendix III, Com Rep.
13 *No 1753/63*, 8 YB 175 (1965).
14 *X v UK No 5265/71*, 3 DR 5 (1975). See also Article 3(2) of the European Agreement relating to Persons Participating in Proceedings before the European Commission and European Court of Human Rights, concerning the freedom to correspond with the Commission and Court: *Collected Texts*, p 155.
15 *No 788/60*, 4 YB 112, 140 (1961).
16 Ibid. See also *Ireland v UK* A 25, pp 90-91 (1978) and *Cyprus v Turkey No 8007/77*, 13 DR 85 (1978).

It follows from this notion of the collective guarantee of the Convention that the principle of reciprocity is subordinated to the states' right to take enforcement action. Thus in *Austria v Italy*[17] the Commission accepted that Austria could file a complaint against Italy concerning matters arising before Austria became a party. It appears to follow that an applicant state would not be prevented from complaining under Article 24 because it had entered a reservation to the provision allegedly violated by the respondent state or because the right concerned is protected by a Protocol which the applicant state has not ratified.[18] Nor is it relevant that the applicant government has not been recognised by the respondent government.[19]

Inter-state complaints under Article 24 differ from individual complaints in the following respects.

1. Under Article 24, states may refer 'any alleged' breach of the Convention to the Commission while individual applicants can only complain of a violation of the rights and freedoms in the Convention.[20]
2. The state can challenge a legislative measure *in abstracto* where the law is couched in terms sufficiently clear and precise to make the breach apparent or with reference to the manner in which it is interpreted and applied *in concreto*.[1] The individual must show that he is a 'victim' of the measure complained of.
3. The only formal admissibility requirements are the local remedies and six-months rule (Article 26). The rules contained in Article 27 apply to individual complaints only.[2]
4. An inter-state application is automatically communicated to the respondent government for observations on admissibility. The Commission has no discretion in this respect. Moreover, unlike the procedure in individual cases, there are separate proceedings on questions of admissibility and the merits (Rule 45 of the Rules of Procedure).

---

17 *No 788/60*, 4 YB 117 (1961).
18 These specific issues have not yet arisen in an inter-state case. However in *France, Norway, Denmark, Sweden and the Netherlands v Turkey Nos 9940-9944/82*, 35 DR 143 at 168-169 (1983) the Commission found, with reference to the objective character of the Convention system, that France was not barred from bringing a case against Turkey under Article 24 which gave rise to a consideration of issues under Article 15 to which France has entered a reservation: see below, p 506. If such an issue were to be referred to the Court a question of reciprocity might arise under the terms of the respondent state's Article 46 declaration.
19 *Cyprus v Turkey No 8007/77 (Third Application)*, 13 DR 85 (1978). The constitutional propriety of the state's right to bring the complaint was discussed in the first two *Cyprus v Turkey* cases, *Nos 6780/74 and 6950/75*, 2 DR 125 (1975). The Commission, in finding that the applicant state had *locus standi*, based itself on the fact that the Government was and continued to be internationally recognised by states and international organisations as the government of the Republic of Cyprus.
20 See above, p 585.
1 *Ireland v UK* A 25 paras 239-240 (1978) and *Denmark, Norway, Sweden and the Netherlands v Greece*, 12 YB (the *Greek* case) 134 (1969).
2 See below, pp 604-605.

In practice there have been few inter-state complaints.[3] In most of the cases that have been brought, the applicant state has had a political interest to assert in the proceedings. Often they have concerned allegations of violations of human rights on a large scale. The reality is that European states will be reluctant to have recourse to legal action under the Convention to resolve their disputes. In the close-knit community of like-minded states in the Council of Europe, contracting parties will be reluctant to jeopardise their good diplomatic relationships with other parties and undoubtedly prefer negotiation to a legal process which may be lengthy, counter-productive and ultimately ineffective.[4]

6.   PROCEDURE BEFORE THE COMMISSION[5]

The procedure before the Commission involves two principal phases:

(1) the *pre-admissibility* procedure involving the dismissal of large numbers of applications for non-compliance with the conditions of admissibility and the retention of a small number of admissible applications; and

---

3   So far, eleven inter-state cases have been brought before the Commission: *Greece v UK Nos 176/56 and 299/57*, 2 YB 176 (1958) Com Rep; CM Res (59) 12 and (59) 32 (two applications relating to UK conduct in Cyprus emergency; cases settled after Zurich agreement on Cypriot indpendence); *Austria v Italy No 788/60*, 4 YB 113 (1961) Com Rep; CM Res (63) DH 3 (criminal trial connected with events in South Tyrol); *Denmark, Norway, Sweden and the Netherlands v Greece Nos 3321-3/67, 3344/67*, 11 YB-II 691 (1968) and 12 YB (the *Greek* case) 1 (1969) Com Rep; CM Res DH (78) 1 (wide-scale violations of human rights under the Greek dictatorship); *Denmark, Norway, Sweden v Greece No 4448/70*, 13 YB 109 (1970) (*Second Greek* case: trial of 34 persons before a court-martial in Athens; withdrawn after Greece re-entered the Council); *Ireland v UK Nos 5451/72*, 41 CD 82 (1972) (case withdrawn after UK undertaking); *Ireland v UK* A 25 (1978) (interrogation techniques and emergency powers in Northern Ireland; the only inter-state case to have been referred to the Court); *Cyprus v Turkey Nos 6780/74 and 6950/75 (First and Second Applications)*, 2 DR 125 (1975); 4 EHRR 482 (1976); Com Rep; CM Res DH (79) 1 (consequences of the Turkish military intervention in northern Cyprus in 1974); *Cyprus v Turkey No 8007/77 (Third Application)*, 13 DR 85 (1978); 13 HRLJ 154 (1992) Com Rep; CM Res (92) 12 (facts as above); *France, Norway, Denmark, Sweden and the Netherlands v Turkey Nos 9940-9944/82*, 35 DR 143 (1983) and 44 DR 31 (1985) F Sett (the *Turkish* case; consequences of the military takeover in Turkey in 1980).

4   Consider, eg the *Cyprus v Turkey* dispute. The Commission's report in the first two applications was forwarded to the Committee of Ministers in 1976. The Committee took formal note of the report as well as a memorial of the Turkish government, urged the parties to resume inter-communal talks, and 'found that events which occurred in Cyprus constitute violations of the Convention' without attaching direct responsibility. It took until 31 August 1979 for the case documentation (including the Commission's report) to be declassified (Resolution DH (79) 1 of 20 January 1979). In the third case the Commission's report of 4 October 1983 remained pending before the Committee of Ministers until 2 April 1992 when it was decided to publish it. The Committee of Ministers resolved that the decision to publish completed its consideration of the case under Article 32 (Resolution DH (92) 12).

5   See Clements, *European Human Rights: Taking a Case under the Convention*, 1994, pp 40-64.

(2) the *post-admissibility* procedure involving the establishment of the facts, friendly settlement negotiations where applicable and the drawing up of the Commission's Article 31 report.

Both phases take place against the background of various procedural rules of a general nature which take their source in the Rules of Procedure and the practice of the Commission. The procedures involved in both of the above phases (as well as the general rules) are set out below. The Commission's case-law on admissibility is dealt with in the following chapter.

i.   General rules and practice

a.   *Language and representation*

The official languages of the Commission are English and French although the President has authorised the secretariat to employ other national languages in its correspondence with applicants.[6] The presence in the secretariat of a lawyer from each jurisdiction means that in practice applicants can file their complaint in their own language.[7] Where communications are received in some other language the applicant may be asked to show that he is unable to present his claim in one of the official languages or in one of the authorised languages. Where there is a hearing, interpretation into English and French will be provided by the Commission. The applicant's lawyer will normally be permitted to address the Commission in his own language.[8] Decisions and reports of the Commission are produced in the official languages only.

It is not necessary for applicants to be represented by a lawyer; they may present and conduct their own applications. However, in many cases, given the complexity and importance of the issue, or the disadvantageous position of the applicant (prisoners, mental patients, etc) the secretariat may inform an applicant that legal representation is advisable for the proper presentation of his case. If an application is presented by a lawyer or other person, a power of attorney or simple written authorisation is required.[9] Parents, guardians and persons *in loco parentis* are entitled to introduce applications on behalf of children in their care.[10] Normally, representatives should be chosen from persons residing in the territory of a Convention country. The Commission reserves the right to supervise representation and has on occasion refused

---

6 Rule 30(4). A Commission member may also be authorised by the President to speak another language during meetings: Rule 30(2).
7 In practice the President has authorised the secretariat to communicate in the national languages of contracting parties, in particular, Bulgarian, Danish, Dutch, Finnish, German, Greek, Italian, Hungarian, Norwegian, Portuguese, Polish, Spanish, Swedish and Turkish. This is to be contrasted with the practice in the registry of the Court where no such rule exists – see below, p 658.
8 Rule 30(3). Documents may also be submitted in an original language: ibid.
9 Rule 43(3).
10 See below, p 658.

further communication from individuals whose conduct was regarded as unacceptable.[11] When an application is brought by an NGO or group of individuals, the Commission will require documentary proof that the signatories of the application are competent to act in a representative capacity, in accordance with domestic law.[12]

b. *Amicus curiae*

The Commission's Rules of Procedure make no provision for the submission of *amicus* briefs since the case-file and the proceedings are confidential. There is, however, no reason why an applicant's lawyer could not incorporate, as part of his written submissions, opinions on relevant questions of comparative law prepared by an outside agency.[13]

c. *Interim measures*[14]

Rule 36 provides that:

> 'The Commission, or when it is not in session, the President may indicate to the parties any interim measure the adoption of which seems desirable in the interest of the parties or the proper conduct of the proceedings before it.'

Applications lodged with the Commission do not have any suspensive effect. Consequently, in general it is not open to the Commission to grant an injunction to restrain the state from enforcing a particular measure. Nevertheless the practice has developed, in cases concerning expulsion or extradition to a country (usually a non-Convention country) where the applicant runs the risk of being treated contrary to Article 3 of the Convention, of indicating to the state interim measures under Rule 36.[15] The President of the Commission may request the state that it is desirable, in the interests of the proper conduct of the proceedings, not to proceed with the expulsion until the Commission has had an opportunity of examining the application. Once this has taken place the Commission may decide, after an evaluation of the extent of the risk involved, to maintain the

11 *A v UK* ('Northern Irish' cases), 36 CD 1 at 37 (1970). The Commission decided not to receive any further submissions from the applicants' lawyer (an attorney from the USA) on the grounds of erroneous and unjustified accusations against the Secretary of the Commission which were considered to transgress the limits 'for the proper conduct of the proceedings and not serving the interests of the applicants'. See also *Foti v Italy* A 56 para 38 (1982)

12 Rule 43 § 2. See *Times Newspapers Ltd v UK No 6538/74*, 2 DR 90 (1975).

13 This occurred in *Farrell v UK No 9013/80*, 30 DR 96 (1982); 38 DR 44 (1984) F Sett.

14 For a description of the Commission's practice see, Nørgaard and Krüger, *Ermacora Festschrift*, pp 109-117 (1988). See also *Cruz Varas v Sweden* A 201 paras 52-55 (1991).

15 As of 3 November 1993, a total of 800 requests for interim measures under Article 36 had been made. 166 requests had been granted (statistical information provided by the Secretariat of the Commission). See also *Cruz Varas v Sweden* A 201 para 55.

request or to remove it. The practice of the Commission is restrictive and is limited to cases where 'irretrievable' damage would occur if the person was expelled prior to the Commission's decision.[16] A request for interim measures must be accompanied by material which substantiates as far as possible the risk of ill-treatment that is alleged.

States normally comply with Rule 36 requests. In *Cruz Varas v Sweden* the Commission found that Sweden had hindered the effective exercise of the right of individual petition in breach of Article 25(1) *in fine* by refusing to comply with a Rule 36 indication.[17] The Court, however, subsequently found that Rule 36 indications, as their cautious wording already suggested, do not give rise to a binding obligation on contracting parties. Moreover, in the absence of a specific interim measures provision in the Convention, such an obligation could not be derived from the state practice of almost total compliance with Rule 36 indications. Such practice was characterised by the Court of amounting to no more than 'good-faith compliance'. Notwithstanding the *Cruz Varas* judgment, Rule 36 indications, limited to serious and deserving cases, are still normally complied with. The judgment has, however, revealed a serious gap in the Commission's armoury and its ability to ensure that the right of application remains an effective and useful procedure in such cases.

d. Legal aid

Legal aid is, in certain circumstances, available in proceedings before the Commission. The Scheme, in force since 1964,[18] is governed by the Addendum to the Rules of Procedure. Rule 2 of the Addendum provides that it shall only be granted where the Commission is satisfied that it is essential for the proper discharge of the Commission's duties and that the applicant has not sufficient means to meet all or part of the costs involved. Legal aid is not granted for the purpose of presenting an application to the Commission. It only becomes available where the Commission invites the government to submit written observations and, in practice, will only be granted when these observations have been submitted.[19] In order to show financial need, the applicant must complete a declaration, providing details

---

16 Interim measures have occasionally been granted by the Commission in cases other than expulsion or extradition. Eg in *Patane v Italy No 11488/85* unreported, the Commission requested the Italian government to take all necessary measures to preserve the applicant's health (she was suffering from severe depression in prison) either by transferring her to an institution better suited for her health or by granting her provisional release. See also *Baader, Ensslin and Raspe v Germany Nos 7572/76, 7586/76 and 7587/76*, 14 DR 64 (1978) (use of Rule 36 to send a Commission delegation to visit Stammheim prison to establish the facts). Rule 36 indications have also been given to applicants – see *Altun v FRG No 10308/83*, 36 DR 209 (1983) (if released pending extradition proceedings, to remain at the disposal of the German authorities).

17 A 201 (1991). See above, p 584 and Cohen-Jonathan, 3 RUDH 205 (1991).

18 CM Res (63) 18.

19 Rule 1(a) of the Addendum. It is also available where the application has been declared admissible (Rule 1(b)).

about his income and capital assets, and this must be certified by an appropriate national authority. The certified declaration of means is submitted to the government concerned for its comment after which the Commission decides whether legal aid will be granted.[20] The scale of fees paid is roughly based on a composite of the average rates of legal aid available in contracting parties, and is usually significantly lower than the sums available within the domestic system. It is not calculated to cover the costs in their entirety but only to contribute to them. The grant of legal aid covers a fee for counsel, travel and subsistence allowances for up to two lawyers and the applicant, and other incidental outlays. The grant will only cover fees for a lawyer who is a barrister, solicitor or professor of law or professionally qualified person of similar status. A fee or compensation for loss of income cannot be obtained by an unrepresented applicant. It is fixed at each stage of the procedure by agreement between the Secretary of the Commission and the lawyer concerned.[1]

e. Death of the applicant

The death of the applicant does not lead automatically to the termination of the Convention proceedings. The Commission accepts that the application may be pursued by the applicant's heirs or personal representatives if they have a sufficient legal interest of their own. Complaints considered by the Commission to be 'untransferable' have included claims concerning the length of criminal proceedings[2] and the risk of inhuman treatment in the event of extradition.[3] On the other hand, the Commission has recognised the right of heirs or next-of-kin to pursue claims concerning a prisoner's conditions of detention,[4] fair trial[5] and detention of a mentally-ill patient.[6] Where the next-of-kin expresses no interest in continuing the proceedings the Commission will examine whether the continued examination of the case is required by the general interest. If not, the case will be struck off the list.[7]

---

20 Rule 3(1)-(3) of the Addendum. In England and Wales the national certifying authority is the Legal Aid Assessment Office, DHSS and, in Scotland, the Scottish Legal Aid Board.

1 Fees are paid in respect of the following items: (1) preparation of the case; (2) drafting of observations in reply; (3) drafting of written submissions on the merits; (4) oral pleadings before the Commission; (5) written observations on the Commission's report; (6) participation in friendly settlement negotiations. For legal aid before the Court see below, p 664.

2 *Kofler v Italy No 8261/78*, 30 DR 5, 9 (1982). Case struck off list. The Commission stated that 'the heirs of a deceased applicant cannot claim a general right that the examination of the application' introduced by the *de cujus* 'be continued by the Commission'. The case had previously been declared admissible. See also *Björkgren and Ed v Sweden No 12526/86*, 68 DR 104 (1991).

3 *Altun v FRG No 10308/83*, 36 DR 236 (1983) (also an admissible application).

4 *Baader, Ensslin and Raspe v FRG Nos 7572/76, 7586/86 and 7587/76*, 14 DR 64 (1978).

5 *Nölkenbockhoff v FRG No 10300/83*, 40 DR 180 (1984).

6 *X v UK* B 40 Com Rep, p 16 (1980).

7 *X v FRG No 7060/75*, 9 DR 47 (1977). In *Kofler v Italy*, n 2, above, at pp 9-10, the Commission indicated that a question of general interest might arise where an application concerned 'the legislation, or a legal system or practice of the defendant state'.

ii.   Pre-admissibility procedure

a.   Registration

A member of the secretariat opens a provisional file for each application, corresponds with applicants, and points out obvious grounds of inadmissibility such as failure to comply with the six-month rule or with the exhaustion of domestic remedies rule. The secretariat is authorised by the Commission to discourage applications that are obviously inadmissible although it cannot refuse to register an application against the wish of an applicant. If a case warrants registration or if the applicant insists on having his case examined by the Commission he will be sent an application form to be completed which will constitute the basis for the Commission's examination of the case.[8] When the completed form is received the case will be registered and attributed an application number. The date of the introduction of the case (of relevance for the six-month rule) shall be the date of the first communication from the applicant setting out, even summarily, the object of the application.[9] While additional information is being gathered a considerable time may have elapsed between the first communication and the registration of the application.

b.   Preliminary examination[10]

Following registration, a member of the Commission is assigned to the case as the *Rapporteur* by the Commission's Secretary in the exercise of powers delegated to him by the President. The *Rapporteur's* role is to examine the application with a view to proposing how the case should be dealt with. If the case-file is incomplete he may request further information from the applicant or the defendant state.[11] Information obtained from the state will be forwarded to the applicant for his comments. At this stage the *Rapporteur*, assisted by a lawyer from the secretariat, will prepare a report for a Chamber proposing either to declare the application inadmissible, or to communicate it to the government for observations on admissibility and the merits. He may also propose that the case, if obviously inadmissible, should be referred to a Committee of Three; alternatively that the case be dealt with by the plenary Commission on the grounds that it raises a serious

8   Rule 44(1) provides that the application shall set out: (a) the name, age, occupation and address of the applicant; (b) the same details for his representative; (c) the name of the respondent state; (d) the object of the application and the provision[s] of the Convention allegedly violated; (e) a statement of facts and arguments; (f) any relevant documents, particularly judicial decisions concerning the case. Rule 44(2) provides *inter alia* that applicants shall furnish information showing that the conditions in Article 26 have been satisfied. Failure to comply with the requirements in Rule 44(1) and (2) may result in the application not being registered (Rule 44(3)).
9   Rule 44(4): The Commission can decide to give precedence to a particular application. Otherwise it deals with applications in the order in which they become ready for examination (Rule 33). It may also order the joinder of two or more applications (Rule 35).
10 See generally Rules 45-52.
11 Rule 47(2).

question affecting the interpretation or application of the Convention (Article 20(2) of the Convention). Cases which are not referred to a Committee of Three are first dealt with by a Chamber and only where new points are raised by the plenary Commission.[12] As already noted, a Chamber or Committee of Three may relinquish jurisdiction in favour of the plenary Commission. The plenary Commission may also order the transfer to it of any petition referred to a Chamber or Committee of Three (Article 20(4) of the Convention).

The case may then be either declared inadmissible by the Commission (Chamber or plenary Commission) or communicated to the government for observations.[13] The observations will normally address issues of fact, admissibility issues and arguments on the merits. Reasoned requests from a party that the application should be referred to the plenary are considered by the plenary Commission.[14] Where the Commission is awaiting the outcome of a case before the Court it can also decide to communicate a case raising a similar question without asking for observations.

Where a case is communicated to the government,[15] the *Rapporteur* will prepare a second report for the Commission, in the light of the parties' written pleadings, proposing either to invite the parties to a hearing or to reject the application as inadmissible.

c. Oral hearings

Hearings, in the limited number of cases that have reached this stage, will take place in private before the plenary Commission or a Chamber. In recent years they have been considerably streamlined. Normally the parties are allocated 30 minutes for a first round of addresses and fifteen minutes for a reply. Members may ask questions during or after the presentation. Following the hearings, the Commission deliberates *in camera* and decides whether the case is admissible.[16] It also takes a provisional vote on the merits of the case (if one can be adopted at this stage) which may be intimated to the parties, on a confidential basis, in order to focus their attention on the possibility of reaching a friendly settlement.[17]

---

12 Rule 49(1).
13 Rule 48(2)(b). Exceptionally the Commission may either adjourn its consideration of the case or request information from the parties (Rule 48(2)(a)).
14 Rule 49(3). The parties used to be consulted for their views as to whether a case should be dealt with by a Chamber or the plenary Commission. This practice has been discontinued.
15 The government is usually requested to submit its observations within ten weeks. The applicant is given four weeks to file his comments.
16 Following the *Rapporteur's* analysis of the case and a general discussion, members are asked to state their views of the admissibility and merits of the case. Thereafter a vote on admissibility is taken. If admissible, a provisional vote is usually taken on the question of violation. In exceptional cases this may be postponed to a later session.
17 The parties are informed of the admissibility decision as soon as possible by telephone. A press release is also issued by the Secretary (Rule 17(3)). He also prepares a verbatim record of the oral submissions which is forwarded to the representatives of the parties for correction.

iii. Post admissibility procedure

If no friendly settlement can be reached the Commission must then ascertain the facts of the case (Article 28(1)(b)). Both the applicant and the government are invited to submit additional written observations on the merits of the case if they so wish in the light of the admissibility decision. Exceptionally a hearing on the merits may be held if no previous hearing has taken place. From time to time the Commission has delegated to one or more of its members the task of carrying out an investigation on the spot and/or hearing witness testimony. In cases declared admissible it is open to the Commission, at this stage, to reverse its admissibility decision in the light of new information which may have come to its attention (Article 29). However, a two-thirds majority is required.[18]

The Commission is then required under Article 31 to prepare a report setting out the facts as they have been established and stating its opinion as to whether there has been a violation of the Convention.[19] The report may contain separate opinions. Once the report has been adopted it is transmitted to the Committee of Ministers together with any proposals the Commission thinks fit under Article 31(3).[20] In practice where the Commission has found a violation it informs the Committee of Ministers in general terms that just satisfaction should be awarded to the applicant, reserving its position as to the precise amount to be paid.[1] A copy of the Article 31 report is also communicated to the government which is not at liberty to publish it. The applicant is merely informed at this stage that the report has been adopted.[2]

The Commission's Article 31 report, although fully reasoned and containing findings on questions of law and fact, is not a 'decision' or a 'judgment'. It merely expresses the opinion of the Commission and does not bind the parties. It is, however, an authoritative document which will usually be published if the case is decided by the Committee of Ministers under Article 32. If the case is sent to the Court the report will become the centrepiece of the proceedings. It will also usually be published by the Court.[3]

---

18   Article 29 provides that the Commission 'may nevertheless decide . . . to reject the petition if, in the course of its examination, it finds that the existence of one of the grounds for non-acceptance provided for in Article 27 has been established'. Because of the difficulty in securing the requisite majority – prior to the Eighth Protocol it required unanimity – only one case has been rejected under this provision – *Donnelly v UK Nos 5577-5583/72*, 4 DR 4 (1975). See also Rule 56.

19   See Rules 57-62 concerning the Report of the Commission.

20   According to the Committee of Ministers' Rules, where the Commission does not find a violation it is not entitled to make such proposals – see Committee of Ministers' Rules for the Application of Article 32, Rule 6, *Collected Texts*, p 315.

1   Where the Committee of Ministers decide that there has been a violation of the Convention it will request the Commission to complete its proposals – see below, p 699.

2   As from 3 October 1994 (entry into force of the Ninth Protocol) applicants are informed that they have the right to refer the case to the Court and are forwarded a copy of the Commission's report. See below, p 661.

3   When a case is referred to the Court the report is sent to the applicant by the Commission on a confidential basis. For the publication of the report by the Court, see below, p 656.

a. Discontinuance of proceedings

Article 30(1) of the Convention states in part:

> 'The Commission may at any stage of the proceedings decide to strike a petition out of its list of cases where the circumstances lead to the conclusion that:
>
> (a) the applicant does not intend to pursue his petition, or
> (b) the matter has been resolved, or
> (c) for any other reason established by the Commission, it is no longer justified to continue the examination of the petition . . .'[4]

It shall continue its examination, however, if 'respect for Human Rights . . . so require' ie if there is an important reason relating to the general interest for doing so.[5]

The Commission may also strike an *admissible* petition out of its list. This may occur where the parties have reached an informal settlement *inter se* or where the applicant shows no interest in pursuing his complaint.[6] In this case the Commission draws up a report provided for under Article 30(2) which is transmitted to the parties and the Committee of Ministers and may be published by the Commission. The report contains a statement of the facts and the strike-out decision together with the reasons therefor.[7]

b. Fact-finding, evidence and proof[8]

In reality the process of fact-gathering and fact-proving will have begun at an earlier stage when the secretariat compiles the relevant documents in correspondence with the applicant or his lawyer. Thus, in most cases, the facts will have been established at the admissibility stage. In many cases the facts will have been clearly set out in relevant national decisions and will be undisputed.

The Commission may be called on to determine different types of factual issues in its examination of an application: the facts invoked by the applicant in a dispute (eg allegations of ill-treatment in prison); background facts relating to the case (eg the political situation in a particular country); facts concerning a government defence (eg the existence of a public

---

4 For example where the applicant has died and the heirs do not have a sufficient legal interest to justify further examination.
5 In *Tyrer v UK* A 26 para 21 (1978), where the applicant complained of the use of the birch as a form of judicial corporal punishment, the Commission decided that it could not grant the applicant's request for withdrawal since the case raised important questions of general interest.
6 See below p 602.
7 Article 30(3) provides that the Commission may decide to restore a petition to its list of cases if it considers that the circumstances justify such a change.
8 See generally Rogge, *European Supervision*, Ch 29; Loucaides, in *Mélanges Velu*, pp 1431-1443; and Trechsel, in *Troisième Colloque du Départment des Droits de l'Homme de l'Université Catholique de Louvain*, pp 121-143 (1977).

emergency under Article 15) and questions concerning the content of domestic law. If the facts cannot be adequately established from the documents submitted by the parties it may be necessary to organise an on-site investigation involving, in particular, the visiting of localities and the hearing of witnesses in Strasbourg or elsewhere. Rule 34(2) provides that the Commission may delegate one or more of its members *inter alia* 'to hear witnesses or experts, to examine documents or to visit any locality'. Rule 34(1) provides that:

> 'The Commission may, *proprio motu* or at the request of a party take any action which it considers expedient or necessary for the proper performance of its duties under the Convention.'

These powers of investigation have most frequently been used in inter-state cases, although they have also been used in numerous individual applications, particularly concerning treatment in prison. On the spot investigations were also conducted by delegates of the Commission in the *First Cyprus* case,[9] the *Greek* case[10] and *Cyprus v Turkey (First and Second Applications)*.[11] In *Ensslin, Baader and Raspe v FRG* a Commission delegation carried out an on-the-spot visit under Rule 36 of the Commission's Rules of Procedure prior to admissibility for the purpose of securing evidence.[12] The applicants had been found dead in their prison cells in suspicious circumstances. In *Marcella and Robert Sands v UK*[13] a delegation visited a dying hunger-striker in the Maze prison in Northern Ireland with a view to determining whether he was willing to confirm an application brought in his name by his sister. The visit took place after a telegram had been received from his sister complaining of conditions of detention against a background of mounting communal tension generated by the hunger strike campaign.

On several occasions the Commission has had recourse to expert medical testimony. For example, in *Cruz Varas v Sweden*[14] the Commission heard a medical expert who had worked with torture victims in order to evaluate the first applicant's allegation that he had been tortured in Chile. In the *Greek*

---

9   *Greece v UK No 176/56*, 2 YB 176 (1958) (the investigation concerned the existence of a state of emergency).

10   12 YB (the *Greek* case) 1 (1969) (hearing of witnesses on the state of emergency and a practice of torture by the Athens security police).

11   *Nos 6780/74, 6950/75*, 2 DR 125 (1975); 4 EHRR 482 (1976) (Commission delegation took evidence in Cyprus and visited refugee camps). In *Ireland v UK* A 25 (1978), more than 100 witnesses were heard in Strasbourg, Norway and the United Kingdom. In *France, Norway, Denmark, Sweden and the Netherlands v Turkey Nos 9940-9944/82*, 44 DR 31 at 36-37 (1985), the Commission sent a delegation to Turkey to gather first-hand information concerning the 'present' situation in Turkey in connection with friendly settlement discussions. Witnesses and experts are protected by the Agreement relating to Persons Participating in Proceedings of the European Commission and Court of Human Rights 1969: *Collected Texts*, p 155.

12   See above, p 589.

13   *No 9338/81* unreported (1981) – the case was later struck off the list and Mr Sands did not join in the application.

14   A 201 (1990) Com Rep paras 77-83.

case[15] medical experts examined eight alleged victims of torture, and in *Ireland v UK*[16] the Commission stressed the objective character of undisputed medical findings when compared with the evidence of security force witnesses and the complainants (most of whom had a personal interest in the outcome of the case). Equally important, it adopted the rule that the burden of proof shifted to the respondent government where the alleged victims were in the custody of the security forces at the relevant times.

Witness hearings usually take place in the presence of the parties and *in camera*, although in the *Greek* case[17] the respondent government objected to the presence of the applicant governments during the sub-Commission's on-site investigation in Greece on the basis that it was not necessary and could create difficulties. The verbatim record of the hearings in the absence of the parties was nevertheless communicated to the parties for their observations. The principle that evidence which is obtained shall be communicated to the parties for their observations has been followed scrupulously by the Commission in its practice. At the same time the parties are obliged to cooperate with the Commission in the carrying out of its investigation. Article 28(1)(a) of the Convention provides that the Commission, when accepting an application, shall 'undertake . . . if need be . . . an investigation, for the effective conduct of which the state concerned shall furnish all necessary facilities, after an exchange of views with the Commission.' The Court in *Ireland v UK*[18] and *Artico v Italy*[19] has stressed the importance of this duty of cooperation with the Convention institutions in order to arrive at the truth. Failure on the part of an applicant to cooperate with the Commission could lead it to conclude that he was no longer interested in pursuing his application.[20]

In *Chrysostomos v Turkey*, the Commission filed an interim report with the Committee of Ministers requesting it to urge Turkey to participate in the Commission's examination of the merits of the case. Subsequently the Committee of Ministers adopted a resolution to this effect following which Turkey proposed witnesses and participated in a hearing in Strasbourg before a delegation of the Commission.[1] However, it should be noted that when a respondent state refuses to co-operate with the Commission or decides not to participate at all in the investigation, there is no question of a finding automatically in favour of the other party. Such a situation occurred in the first *Cyprus v Turkey* cases[2] when the respondent government refused

15 12 YB (the *Greek* case) 1 (1969).
16 B 23-I Com Rep, pp 412-413 (1976).
17 12 YB (the *Greek* case) at 13 et seq (1969).
18 A 25 para 148 (1978).
19 A 37 para 30 (1980).
20 Article 30 of the Convention.
1 CM Res DH (91) 41. For the Commission's interim report, see 68 DR 216 (1991).
2 *(First and Second Applications)* 4 EHRR 482 Com Rep, para 57 (1976). Although the Commission was entitled to consider the government's failure to cooperate as corroborating the relevant complaints, it refrained from drawing adverse conclusions. For criticism of this approach see Loucaides, at p 595, above, pp 1441-1442. Cf the approach of the International Court of Justice, *Nicaragua v USA*, ICJ Reports (1986) paras 28-31.

to participate in the proceedings on the merits although it had participated at the admissibility stage. The Commission's delegation was refused entry into Turkey and cooperation by Turkey or the Turkish Cypriot authorities for an investigation in the north of Cyprus. The Commission considered that such a policy of non-cooperation should not hinder it in accomplishing its task of ascertaining the facts. Relying on its practice in the *First* and *Second Greek* cases, it stated as follows:

'If this were not so, the respondent Party might find it too easy and might even feel encouraged to evade its obligations under the Convention by not entering an appearance before the Commission. . . . The Commission would, however, in such circumstances have to satisfy itself that the information before it is sufficient to express a well-founded opinion. There could be no question of automatically finding in favour of the applicant irrespective of the circumstances of the case.'

At the admissibility stage the applicant need only present facts which are supportive albeit not conclusive of his allegations or a 'beginning of proof' (*commencement de preuve*). There should be enough factual elements to allow the Commission to conclude that his contentions are not completely groundless.[3] At the merits stage, however, apart from a duty to cooperate with the Commission, the applicant does not bear the burden of proving his allegations since at this stage it falls to the Commission under Article 28 of the Convention to establish the facts. In this process the proceedings are governed by the principle of the free admission and assessment of evidence.[4] The Commission has no fixed rules of evidence concerning illegally obtained evidence, privileged documents or perjury. The rare problems that might occur in these respects will be dealt with on a case-by-case basis.

Neither the Convention nor the Rules of Procedure prescribe a particular standard of proof. However, the Commission has consistently held that facts constituting a violation of the Convention must satisfy a reasonable doubt standard:

'A reasonable doubt means not a doubt based on a merely theoretical possibility or raised in order to avoid a disagreeable conclusion, but a doubt for which reasons can be given drawn from the facts presented.'[5]

In expulsion or extradition cases raising an Article 3 issue, the Court has indicated that '*substantial grounds*' must be shown for believing the existence

---

3 See below, p 627 (manifestly ill-founded section). In inter-state cases the applicant is under no obligation to prove allegations at the admissibility stage, the merits of the case being reserved for examination post-admissibility – see below, p 605.

4 See Trechsel, above at p 595, at 132, 134 and 136.

5 The *Greek* case, 12 YB (the *Greek* case) at p 196. Proof beyond reasonable doubt 'may follow from the coexistence of sufficiently strong, clear and concordant inferences or of similar unrebutted presumptions of fact': *Ireland v UK* A 25 para 161 (1978).

of a risk of treatment contrary to Article 3.[6] The assessment of the risk of ill-treatment will be made with reference to those facts which were known or ought to have been known to the contracting party at the time of the expulsion. The Court, however, has stated that it may also have regard to information which comes to light subsequent to the expulsion.[7]

iv. Friendly settlement[8]

While the Commission is ascertaining the facts, under Article 28(1)(b) it is also required to 'place itself at the disposal of the parties concerned with a view to securing a friendly settlement on the matter on the basis of respect for human rights as defined in this Convention'.[9] In practice when a case has been declared admissible, the Secretary of the Commission is authorised to intimate to the parties, on a confidential basis, the provisional opinion of the Commission on the merits of the case. This unusual step is taken to focus the minds of the parties on the possibility of reaching a settlement. They will then be requested to submit in writing any friendly settlement proposals they may wish to make. It will become clear at this stage from the reaction of the parties whether or not there is any interest in pursuing the matter. If there is not, the Commission, after giving them an opportunity to submit further observations on the merits, will proceed to draw up its Article 31 report. If there is interest, a meeting may be arranged between the parties, often involving the Secretary as intermediary (and on occasions a member of the Commission), with a view to brokering a satisfactory solution. In some cases the parties enter into direct contact and will inform the Commission when they reach agreement on the terms of the settlement. At the outset of this process the Commission, through its secretariat, plays an entirely passive role limited to facilitating an exchange of proposals. However, if the

---

6 Eg *Soering v UK* A 161 para 88 (1989). At the admissibility stage the standard of proof for such a complaint will be lower. The applicant must produce evidence to show that there is a concrete and serious risk that he will be exposed to treatment of the kind prohibited by Article 3: *Kalema v France No 12877/87*, 53 DR 254 at 264 (1987). A lesser degree of probability is required for an interim measure under Rule 36: see Rogge, above, at p 595, pp 688-689. And see above, p 589.

7 *Cruz Varas v Sweden* A 201 para 75 (1991) and *Vilvarajah v UK* A 215 para 107 (1991).

8 See generally Kiss, *European Supervision*, Ch 30; Krüger and Nørgaard, in *Wiarda Mélanges*, pp 329-334; also in Imbert and Pettiti, eds, *La Convention européenne des droits de l'homme*, 1995; and Opsahl and Dollé, 'Settlement based on respect for Human Rights under the ECHR', written communication to the 6th International Colloquy on the ECHR, Seville, 1985. Under Article 47 of the Convention the Court can only deal with a case after the Commission has acknowledged the failure of efforts for a friendly settlement.

9 Friendly settlement has become increasingly important in recent years. Thus, for example, between 1965 and 1980 there were 19 settlements; whereas there were 21 between 1981 and 1985, 56 between 1986 and 1990 and 98 from 1991 to the end of June 1994. In 1994, there were 32 settlements. As of 31 December 1994, a total of 211 settlements under Article 28 were reached as compared to 2,027 admissible applications. As regards informal settlements (see below, p 602) no statistics are available. See *Survey of Activities and Statistics*, and CE Human Rights News Press Release, 5 January 1995, pp 18-19 loc cit at p 580, n 10, above.

positions are not too far apart, direct negotiations will take place and the Secretary (assisted by the member of the secretariat dealing with the case) will assume a more active mediation role, in the course of joint or separate discussions with the parties, until a compromise has been reached. In general the submission of observations on the merits is suspended during the negotiations. However, the Commission is careful to ensure that friendly settlement negotiations should not have the effect of unnecessarily delaying the proceedings and may exert pressure on the parties by indicating to them that, notwithstanding the negotiations, they should submit their observations on the merits within a certain period.

Both sides may have a strong motivation to reach a settlement if the Commission finds a breach. The government may be concerned to limit the political damage that an unfavourable and much publicised judgment of the Court might give rise to and perhaps to limit the costs involved in continuing to defend a lost cause. It may even welcome the opportunity to change the law and to be able to attribute responsibility for this to the decisions of an international tribunal. On the other hand, the principal consideration for an applicant is likely to be the possibility that the Court might not agree with the opinion of the Commission; whereas a settlement would normally cover lawyers' costs and provide speedy vindication. The Commission also has an interest in adopting a settlement which addresses the wider issues affecting many other potential complainants and, at the same time, enables it to reduce its heavy case-load. Friendly settlement is thus a process which provides reason for satisfaction and perhaps contentment on all sides but which formally terminates the proceedings with neither winners nor losers.

The terms of the settlement are subsequently set out in an exchange of letters between the parties. The government might formally undertake, for example, to pay compensation and cover domestic and Strasbourg costs, amend an administrative practice or undertake to seek a change in offending legislation.

Often it may add a clause indicating that the proposals are being made without prejudice to their submission that there has been no breach of the Convention. In response, applicants will declare that they accept the government's proposals as being a full and final settlement of their claims under the Convention. They may also undertake to pursue no other domestic or international proceedings in relation to the dispute. Naturally the terms will vary considerably in accordance with the features of the dispute. Settlements may involve, for example, individual measures such as compensation and costs[10] coupled with general measures to ensure that

---

10 According to Krüger and Nørgaard, in Imbert and Pettiti, above, at p 599, nn 28-29, 72 settlements refer in some way or other to legal costs and 95 involve the grant of compensation. See eg *Stoutt v Ireland No 10978/84*, 54 DR 43 (1987) F Sett (both individual and general measures) and *Conroy v UK No 10061/82*, 46 DR 66 (1986) F Sett (compensation). Individual measures may also involve specific decisions concerning domestic proceedings, eg to grant a conditional release or pardon (*Nagel v FRG No 7614/76*, 12 DR 97 (1978) F Sett) or to suspend the execution of a sentence (*Widmaier v Netherlands No 9573/81*, 48 DR 14 (1986) F Sett). For a detailed analysis of the content of settlements, see Krüger and Nørgaard, id.

similar problems will not occur in the future. Where legislative measures are concerned, the government is usually unable to give an undertaking that specific measures will be passed by Parliament because of the uncertainty of the legislative process. They can usually only undertake to submit a Bill to Parliament proposing a particular amendment.[11] Other general measures have included drawing the attention of the courts to the case-law of the Commission and Court, enacting appropriate delegated legislation, issuing circular instructions to administrative bodies or undertaking to introduce organisational changes.[12]

As the wording of Article 28(1)(b) ('on the basis of respect for human rights') indicates, the settlement must be approved by the Commission, which has special responsibility to have regard to the general interest. In essence it must ensure, as far as possible, that the agreement is not merely a bargain between the parties which leaves the basic underlying human rights problems unresolved. This important feature will, of course, have been drawn to the attention of the parties by the Secretary of the Commission in the course of friendly settlement discussions. Depending on the nature of the case, however, individual measures may be sufficient. This can involve difficult questions of judgment. For example, in *Farrell v UK*,[13] which concerned the shooting of the applicant's husband by soldiers in Northern Ireland, the Commission accepted a settlement involving the payment of £37,500 to the applicant. Although the case raised questions concerning the use of lethal force by the security forces, the Commission, in endorsing the settlement, stressed the government's statement that the shooting was an 'unfortunate mistake'. No case has yet arisen where the Commission has refused to accept a settlement.

In the case of *Denmark, France, the Netherlands, Norway and Sweden v Turkey*[14] the settlement negotiated by the parties, with the active participation of a delegation of the Commission, assigned a role to the Commission itself. Provision was made in the terms of the settlement for a series of reports by Turkey to the Commission 'of the measures by which the internal law and practice of Turkey ensures the effective implementation of Article 3 of the Convention (including conditions and procedures of

---

11 *Harman v UK No 10038/82*, 46 DR 57 (1986) F Sett and *Baggs v UK No 9310/81*, 52 DR 29 (1987) F Sett.

12 *Reed v UK No 7630/76*, 25 DR 5 (1981) F Sett (amendment of Prison Rules); *McComb v UK No 10621/83*, 50 DR 81 (1986) F Sett (circular instruction that correspondence between a legal adviser and a prisoner should not be opened); *A v UK No 6840/74*, 20 DR 5 (1980) F Sett (refurbishment of the Intensive Care Unit in Broadmoor).

13 *No 9013/80*, 38 DR 44 (1984) F Sett. The Commission was certainly influenced by the large amount of compensation offered and acceptable to the applicant. The questions of principle, however, did not go away and have been raised in subsequent cases: see above, Ch 2 (Article 2).

14 The *Turkish* case *Nos 9940-9944/82*, 44 DR 31 at 38-39 (1985) F Sett. The dialogue was carried out by correspondence and by meetings with a Commission delegation. The delegates were able to make comments to representatives of the Turkish government, on a confidential basis, on the information received. For criticism of the settlement, see, Van Dijk and Van Hoof, pp 127-128.

detention)'. The reports were to be followed by a dialogue with a delegation of the Commission terminating with a common final report. This exceptional follow-up role for the Commission was in all probability a *conditio sine qua non* of the settlement and provided it with an opportunity to contribute to the development of human rights in Turkey in a crucial and sensitive area.

After approval of the settlement, the Commission adopts a Report which is confined to a brief statement of the facts of the case and of the solution reached. It is then transmitted to the states concerned, the Committee of Ministers and to the Secretary General of the Council of Europe for publication. The parties are not at liberty to disclose the Commission's provisional opinion or details of the friendly settlement negotiations even where the negotiations are unsuccessful. The entire negotiation phase is considered by the Commission to have been conducted on a 'without prejudice' basis.[15] Thus where the case is later sent to the Court the parties are not free in their written and oral pleadings to divulge offers made or positions taken during settlement discussions.

No supervisory machinery has been provided for in the Convention for the implementation of settlements. Practice in this area reveals that, notwithstanding occasional bureaucratic delays in executing the terms of the settlement, states fulfil their obligations. In jurisdictions where the Convention is regarded as part of national law the terms of a settlement may be directly enforceable before domestic courts as a contract that has been entered into between the state and the individual.[16] The fact that a settlement has been reached between the parties, however, does not exclude the Commission from subsequently examining a complaint lodged by the same or another applicant concerning an identical issue. Nor is the Commission estopped in later cases from verifying the conformity with the Convention of legislative measures adopted pursuant to a settlement.[17]

Mention must also be made in this context of informal settlements which have been reached directly by the parties without the intervention of the Commission and which lead to a strike-off under Article 30 as opposed to the formal adoption by the Commission of a friendly settlement under Article 28. In essence the parties have resolved the dispute by themselves and the applicant indicates that he seeks to withdraw the case. Such agreement may be reached either prior to admissibility or post admissibility. A typical example of this type of unofficial settlement is where the state agrees to permit an applicant who is subject to an expulsion order to remain in the country or where the state effectively removes the basis of the Convention

---

15 Krüger and Nørgaard, in Imbert and Pettiti, above, at p 599.
16 As eg in Belgium and the Netherlands. See, in this connection, Velu and Ergec, pp 915-916.
17 Cf *McComb v UK No 10621/83*, 50 DR 81 (1986) F Sett and *Campbell v UK* A 233 (1992) – both concerning the opening of letters by the prison authorities between a prisoner and his lawyer. See also *Peschke v Austria No 8289/78*, 25 DR 182 (1981) F Sett; *Kremzow v Austria* A 268-B (1993); and *Kamasinski v Austria* A 168 (1989) concerning, *inter alia*, the personal appearance of an accused at an appeal hearing before the Supreme Court.

complaint.[18] The Commission could refuse to accept the withdrawal in this situation also if it considered that any reason of a general character affecting the observance of the Convention required further examination of the application.[19] Where an admissible case has been resolved in this way a report which is confined to the facts and the reasons for the strike-off is communicated to the Committee of Ministers.

7. CONCLUSION

In recent years, important changes have occurred in the work of the Commission. Its work-load continues to increase dramatically and the entry into the Convention community of Eastern and Central European states has begun to make its mark. As a result, the Commission has increased in membership and its secretariat is correspondingly larger. More important for the consistency and quality of the Commission's case-law, the locus of decision-making has moved, within the short space of two years, from the plenary Commission to the first and second Chambers.[20] In addition, a steady flow of cases is being registered against the new contracting parties from Eastern and Central Europe.[1] While none of these cases has yet been declared admissible, they represent a trend which continues to evolve and which provides a glimpse of the future work of the Commission and Court and, ultimately, of the new single Court. There can be no doubt that the vast experience of the Commission in handling large numbers of applications from many different backgrounds, in both its plenary, chamber and Committee compositions, forms an essential part of the *acquis conventionel* to be inherited by the new single Court when it comes into operation.

18 See, *inter alia, Karnell and Hardt v Sweden No 4733/71*, 14 YB 664 (1971) where the applicants who were members of the Evangelical-Lutheran Church of Sweden objected to compulsory religious education for their children under Article 2 of the First Protocol. The government introduced a change in the rules which enabled exemptions to be granted. The applicants subsequently withdrew their complaint: Commission Report of 28 May 1973. Cf *Vampel v Austria No 4465/70*, 2 DR 4 (1975) and *Brückmann v FRG No 6242/73*, 6 DR 57 (1976), where the applications were also withdrawn.

19 This has only occurred on one occasion in a case not involving a settlement: *Tyrer v UK* B 17 Com Rep, p 12 and A 26 (1978). See below, p 682.

20 See above, pp 575-576.

1 In 1993-94, 18 cases were registered against Bulgaria; 68 against the Czech Republic; 107 against Hungary; 200 against Poland; and 40 against the Slovak Republic. In 1994, 9 cases were registered against Romania and 33 provisional files were opened in respect of Slovenia. By way of comparison with another recent contracting party, 102 cases were registered against Finland in 1993-94 and 5 cases were declared admissible. See *Survey of Activities and Statistics*, loc cit, at p 580, n 10, above.

CHAPTER 23
Admissibility of applications

The determination of questions of admissibility is the principal role of the Commission under the Convention.[1] Over the years it has established an impressive body of case-law interpreting and applying the various conditions of admissibility set out in Articles 25-27 and selecting from the large volume of registered cases those that deserve closer examination on the merits. The Commission's case-law, for example, on exhaustion of domestic remedies has made an important contribution to international law where the rule is of general application. The Court has also participated in this process through the examination of preliminary objections, although to a lesser extent. The increasing number of applications before the Commission has required it to develop summary procedures which enable it to reject worthless complaints with an economy of effort and to concentrate on the more deserving cases. Moreover, in most cases which are selected for the hearing of oral argument, questions of admissibility and the merits are examined together for reasons of convenience. Most of the admissibility requirements are procedural in nature such as the six-month and exhaustion of domestic remedies rules; but some, such as 'manifestly ill-founded' and 'incompatibility', direct the Commission to assess the merits of the complaint at this preliminary stage. Undoubtedly many cases which were rejected on these grounds twenty years ago would, in the light of the developing jurisprudence, be clearly admissible cases today. In many respects the history of the Convention system can thus be described in terms of the gradual receding of the shifting boundaries defined by the concept of admissibility. As will be seen below, this process has involved the examination of many thousands of cases, most of which have been rejected as inadmissible.

1. APPLICATION OF ADMISSIBILITY REQUIREMENTS TO INTER-STATE CASES

It is clear from the terms of Article 27(1)-(3) that, apart from conditions *ratione materiae*, *personae*, *loci* and *temporis*,[2] the only admissibility

1 See Zwart, *The Admissibility of Human Rights Petitions: the Case Law of the European Commission of Human Rights and the Human Rights Committee*, 1994.
2 See below, pp 629-647.

requirements applicable to inter-state cases are those set out in Article 26, namely the requirement to exhaust domestic remedies and the six-month rule.[3] In the third *Cyprus v Turkey* case[4] the Commission explicitly refused to reject the application on the basis that it was 'substantially the same as a matter which has already been examined by the Commission' and contains 'no relevant new information' on the grounds that Article 27(1)(b) was not applicable to an inter-state case and that rejection would imply a preliminary examination of the merits of the case – an examination which in Article 24 cases is entirely reserved for the post-admissibility stage.

The Commission has also consistently refused to assess the merits of an inter-state case at the admissibility stage. Thus an Article 24 application cannot be rejected under Article 27(2) as manifestly ill-founded. In *France, Norway, Denmark, Sweden, the Netherlands v Turkey*,[5] for example, the Turkish government submitted that the applicant states had failed to adduce *prima facie* evidence of their allegations of multiple breaches of the Convention. They supported their argument with reference to the rules and practice on questions of admissibility of the International Court of Justice and the Inter-American Commission of Human Rights. The European Commission noted that the text of Article 24 ('may refer to the Commission . . . any alleged breach'), in particular the French text *'qu'elle croira'*, made it clear that the applicant state can submit 'allegations' for examination. It was thus not the Commission's role to 'carry out' a preliminary examination of the merits.[6] Moreover, Article 27 constitutes a specific regulation of admissibility in Convention proceedings which takes precedence over general rules of international law. At the same time the Commission stated that an application submitted under Article 24 could be declared inadmissible 'if it is clear, from the outset, that it is wholly unsubstantiated, or otherwise lacking the requirements of a genuine allegation in the sense of Article 24 . . . '.[7] Thus, apart from this unlikely situation, the merits of an inter-state case escape scrutiny at the admissibility phase. The application of this principle means, therefore, that in Article 24 cases the defence of derogation from the Convention under Article 15 will only be examined at the merits stage.[8]

It has also been argued in various inter-state cases that the application should be rejected as 'abusive' on the grounds that it was politically inspired or that it consisted of accusations of a political nature designed to further a propaganda campaign. In *Denmark, Norway, Sweden and the Netherlands v Greece*[9] the Commission found that even if the allegations had a political element it was not such as to render them 'abusive' in the general sense of

---

3 For reasons of convenience the application of Article 26 to inter-state complaints will be examined under the general heading of exhaustion of domestic remedies.
4 *No 8007/77*, 13 DR 85 at 154-155 (1978). See also *Ireland v UK* B 23-I Com Rep, p 670.
5 *Nos 9940-9944/82*, 35 DR 143 at 160-162 (1983).
6 Id, p 161.
7 Id, p 162.
8 Id, p 170.
9 11 YB 764 (1968).

the term. In both this case and *Cyprus v Turkey*,[10] the Commission held that the 'abuse of the right of petition' ground of inadmissibility was restricted under Article 27(2) to cases brought by individuals. It left open, however, the issue as to whether an Article 24 application could be rejected on the basis of a general principle of international law that proceedings before an international tribunal must not be abused.

The Commission's competence to deal with inter-state applications is not optional, as it is for individual applications under Article 25, but follows automatically from ratification of the Convention. In other terms, the sole condition for the Commission's competence *ratione personae* in respect of both applicant and respondent states is ratification. The capacity to sue under Article 24 – as well as the liability to be sued – is thus limited to those member states of the Council of Europe which have become contracting parties to the Convention.[11] This is natural in view of the fact that the machinery of protection set up under the Convention is grounded in the concept of a collective enforcement by like-minded states of the guaranteed rights. An applicant state, unlike an individual applicant, does not have to claim to be a 'victim' in any way of the alleged breach. Article 24 is therefore wider than Article 25 in that the applicant state does not have to justify a special interest in the subject-matter of the complaint; in particular, it is not a condition that the matter complained of should have affected or prejudiced one of its nationals.[12] As the Commission explained in the case of *Austria v Italy*,[13] the enforcement mechanism provided in Article 24 reflects the objective character of the engagements assumed by the contracting parties under the Convention:

> '. . . the obligations undertaken by the High Contracting Parties in the Convention are essentially of an objective character, being designed rather to protect the fundamental rights of the individual human being from infringement by any of the High Contracting Parties than to create subjective and reciprocal rights for the High Contracting Parties themselves; . . . it follows that a High Contracting Party, when it refers an alleged breach of the Convention to the Commission under Article 24, is not to be regarded as exercising a right of action for the purpose of enforcing its own rights, but rather as bringing before the Commission an alleged violation of the public order of Europe. . . .'

Accordingly, as a matter of law, inter-state proceedings are taken in the common interest of all the contracting parties and have the objective and purpose of securing observance of common standards of conduct in the field of human rights. Hence a state may take proceedings under Article 24 not only in support of the rights of its own nationals but also on behalf of the

---

10 *No 8007/77 (Third Application)*, 13 DR 85 at 156 (1978).
11 Article 66(1), Convention.
12 *Ireland v UK* A 25 para 239 (1978).
13 *No 788/60*, 4 YB 140 (1961) (*Pfunders* case).

nationals of the respondent state and indeed on behalf of any person, regardless of nationality and regardless of whether the alleged breach particularly affects its own national interests.

It follows from this conception of the inter-state case and the objective character of the Convention that the principle of reciprocity does not apply to inter-state cases examined by the Commission. Thus in *France, Norway, Denmark, Sweden and the Netherlands v Turkey*[14] the Commission concluded that France was not barred from bringing a case against Turkey which concerned issues that might be covered by the French reservation under Article 15. In addition, the non-recognition of the applicant government by the respondent government cannot remove the right to bring a case under Article 24. As the Commission held in *Cyprus v Turkey*,[15] 'to accept that a government may avoid "collective enforcement" of the Convention under Article 24, by asserting that they do not recognise the government of the applicant state, would defeat the purpose of the Convention'. At the same time, in deciding whether Cyprus had *locus standi* to bring the case against Turkey, the Commission based its approach on international practice, particularly of the Council of Europe, as regards the status of the government. It observed that:

'. . . the applicant government have been, and continue to be, recognised internationally as the government of the Republic of Cyprus and that their representation and acts are accepted accordingly in a number of contexts of diplomatic and treaty relations and of the working of international organisations.'

Reference to international practice was also relied upon to rebut the argument that the applicant government had acted unconstitutionally in bringing the application.[16]

The absence of a 'victim' requirement means that a contracting party may, unlike an individual applicant, challenge a law or practice *in abstracto*, without having to adduce evidence as to actual prejudice of the application of the law or practice. The Court stated in *Ireland v UK*[17] that such a complaint will be possible where the alleged breach 'results from the mere existence of a law which introduces, directs or authorises measures incompatible with the rights and freedoms guaranteed'. The judgment, however, added a proviso:

14 *Nos 9940-9944/82*, 35 DR 143 at 168-169 (1983).
15 *(Third Application) No 8007/77*, 13 DR 85 at 146-147 (1978).
16 Id at p 146. It was argued that the applicant government was not the government of Cyprus but only the leaders of the Greek Cypriot community who, in 1963, had assumed control of the state in violation of the London and Zurich Agreements of 1959, the Treaty of Guarantee of 1960 and the Constitution of Cyprus of 1960. This argument had been previously rejected in the first *Cyprus v Turkey* case – *Nos 6780/74 and 6950/75*, 2 DR 125 at 135-136 (1975). It was also argued that, in lodging the case with the Commission, the government had acted unconstitutionally since the decision had not been taken by the competent organ under Article 54 of the Constitution of Cyprus of 1960: 13 DR 85 at 148 (1978).
17 A 25 para 240 (1978).

'Nevertheless, the institutions established by the Convention may find a breach of this kind only if the law challenged pursuant to Article 24 is couched in terms sufficiently clear and precise to make the breach immediately apparent; otherwise, the decision of the Convention institutions must be arrived at by reference to the manner in which the respondent state interprets and applies *in concreto* the impugned text or texts.'

2. EXHAUSTION OF DOMESTIC REMEDIES

Article 26 provides that:

'The Commission may only deal with the matter after all domestic remedies have been exhausted, according to the generally recognised rules of international law . . . '.

This rule is founded on the principle of international law that the state must first have the opportunity to redress the wrong alleged.[18] In many cases, since the violation can no longer be eliminated with retrospective effect, the only means of redress will be compensation. The rule reflects the general norm of the system of human rights protection that the task of securing Convention rights is, in the first place, the responsibility of contracting states and that the Convention is subsidiary to the national system.[19] Since a high percentage of cases will be rejected *de plano* for failure to comply with the exhaustion rule, it also serves the pragmatic purpose of reducing the mass of complaints to more manageable proportions.

i.   The general requirements of the rule

The exhaustion rule, as it has been interpreted and applied by the Convention institutions, requires that normal use be made of remedies which are likely to be adequate and effective to provide redress for the alleged wrong.[20] Accordingly, if an applicant complained of police brutality he would be required to bring civil proceedings for damages against the police or, in some jurisdictions (eg France), criminal proceedings to which he could be joined as a civil party. The lodging of a criminal complaint in

---

18 See, *inter alia*, *Van Oosterwijck v Belgium* A 40 para 34, (1980). For a survey of the voluminous case-law under Article 26, including country-to-country references, see 5 Digest 5-296. See also indexes of Decisions and Reports series, Vols 1-20, 21-40, 41-60.

19 *Handyside v UK* A 24 para 48 (1976).

20 *Donnelly v UK Nos 5577-5583/72*, 4 DR 4 at 64 (1975) and *Drozd and Janousek v France and Spain No 12747/88*, 64 DR 97 (1989). Failure to exhaust cannot be invoked against someone who, at the time a remedy was available, could not have thought that he was adversely affected by the situation – *Farmakopoulos v Belgium No 11683/85*, 64 DR 52 (1990) and *Kolompar v Belgium No 11613/85*, 65 DR 75 (1990).

such jurisdictions is regarded as an effective and sufficient remedy. Where there is no follow-up to the complaint, the victim is not required to bring additional civil proceedings for compensation or to challenge the decision not to pursue the complaint.[1]

The remedies available under national law to which recourse must be had will depend on the nature of the breach alleged. Thus if an applicant complains of unlawful detention he must show that he has brought proceedings for *habeas corpus* or for damages for false imprisonment. Similarly, a complainant alleging that he will be subjected to ill-treatment contrary to Article 3 if, for example, he is deported from the United Kingdom, must seek to challenge the exercise of discretion by the Secretary of State in judicial review proceedings. On the other hand, if such proceedings or their equivalent in other jurisdictions do not have suspensive effect, they would not be seen as providing an effective remedy.[2] In *M v UK*[3] the Commission rejected a complaint for non-exhaustion by an applicant who claimed that if he was deported to Iran he would be executed because of his involvement in drugs dealing. He had not sought to introduce judicial review proceedings, having been advised by his lawyer that these offered no prospects of success. After reviewing national case-law to the effect that the courts will scrutinise such decisions strictly since the right to life is at stake and noting that these proceedings had suspensive effect, the Commission rejected the claim that the remedy was ineffective.

In this case it was still open to the applicant to bring judicial review proceedings and prevent the apprehended harm from occurring; but what if this had not been possible? Is this not a situation where the strict application of the exhaustion rule could, in fact, give rise to irreparable harm? In such circumstances where there may be an imminent danger to life it is certainly arguable that the protection of non-derogable rights, such as those in Articles 2 and 3, should, in a human rights treaty, be given priority over the standard application of a procedural admissibility requirement.[4]

An applicant is only required to have recourse to remedies which are capable of providing an effective and sufficient means of redressing the alleged wrong. Thus, actions to obtain a 'favour' such as a petition to the Queen or a request to re-open proceedings need not be availed of. But procedures that involve the vindication of a right must be tried.[5] Normally,

---

1 *M v France No 10078/82*, 41 DR 103 (1984); *Sargin and Yagci v Turkey Nos 14116-7/88*, 61 DR 250 (1989); and *Erdagöz v Turkey No 17128/90*, 71 DR 275 (1991).
2 *X v FRG No 7216/75*, 5 DR 137 (1976) and *X v Denmark No 7465/76*, 7 DR 153 (1976).
3 *No 12268/86*, 57 DR 136 (1988).
4 It is arguable that in this situation there are 'special circumstances' which ought to absolve the Commission from applying the rule strictly as opposed to 'special circumstances' which absolve the applicant from exhausting – a quite separate issue. For the 'special circumstances' rule, see below at p 620.
5 See, *inter alia*, *Greece v UK No 299/57*, 2 YB 186 at 192 (1957) and *De Becker v Belgium*, id, pp 236-238. Extraordinary remedies such as petitions for a re-opening of proceedings or, in extradition cases, requests for a new decision, are not regarded as effective and sufficient remedies – see the cases in 5 Digest 170-173 and *Altun v FRG No 10308/83*, 36 DR 209 (1983).

but not necessarily, these will be judicial procedures. In certain situations they may also be administrative procedures. Thus, for example, complaints by prisoners in the United Kingdom that the Prison Rules are not being observed should first be raised in a petition to the Home Secretary.[6]

In legal systems with a written constitution, a constitutional action must be taken to challenge the law or administrative practice alleged to be in breach of the Convention. Thus in Germany and in Spain, complaints must, where possible, be pursued to the Constitutional Court.[7] Similarly in Ireland the constitutionality of the law or practice must be challenged before the courts.[8] Where legal aid is not available to bring such proceedings, it may be arguable that the remedy is inaccessible and ineffective on the grounds of cost.[9] How realistic is it to expect an impecunious applicant or even an average salary earner to mount expensive constitutional proceedings?

In principle, the complainant must appeal to the highest court of appeal against an unfavourable decision at first or second instance. Mere doubts as to the prospects of success of national proceedings do not absolve the applicant from the obligation to exhaust.[10] But applicants are not obliged to make use of remedies which, according to 'settled legal opinion' existing at the relevant time, do not provide redress for their complaints.[11] A well reasoned opinion from counsel which sets out the position under national law may provide evidence of 'settled legal opinion'. In *McFeeley v UK*[12] the applicants were able to show with reference to counsel's opinion that no remedy existed under Northern Ireland law in respect of their complaints concerning the continuous imposition of disciplinary punishments by the prison governor as well as their general prison conditions and treatment by the prison authorities. However, despite counsel's opinion to the contrary, the Commission rejected for non-exhaustion a United Kingdom case where the applicants had not sought to appeal to the House of Lords against an unfavourable Court of Appeal decision. The Court of Appeal had refused leave to appeal and the applicants were advised that petitioning the House of Lords directly for leave would be to no avail. The Commission was not satisfied that the state of the law on the issue in question was clear and observed that, in a subsequent case on similar facts, leave to appeal to the House of Lords had in fact been granted by the Court of Appeal.[13] In a later case, where there were conflicting Court of Appeal decisions concerning the possibility of a wife obtaining an injunction against her husband on grounds

6   See 5 Digest 142-145 for case references.
7   *X v FRG No 8499/79*, 21 DR 176 (1980) and *Castells v Spain* A 236 paras 24-32 (1992).
8   *McDonnell v Ireland No 15141/89*, 64 DR 203 (1990). For the case-law as regards different legal systems, see 5 Digest 83-148.
9   This was argued unsuccessfully in *Van Oosterwijck v Belgium* A 40 para 38 (1980). The Court found that he had supplied no proof of financial difficulties and had not actually sought legal aid. See also *Airey v Ireland* A 32 passim (1979).
10 *Donnelly v UK Nos 5577-5583/72*, 4 DR 4 (1975) and *McDonnell v Ireland No 15141/89*, 64 DR 203 (1990).
11 *De Wilde, Ooms and Versyp v Belgium* A 12 p 33 (1971) (the *Vagrancy* cases).
12 *No 8317/78*, 20 DR 44 at 71-76 (1980).
13 *K, F and P v UK No 10789/84*, 40 DR 298 (1984).

of harassment, the Commission held that in a common law system it was incumbent on an aggrieved individual to allow the domestic courts the opportunity to develop existing rights by way of interpretation.[14]

Nevertheless, the existence of a remedy must be sufficiently certain not only in theory but also in practice. If it appears, for example, on the basis of established case-law that pursuit of a particular remedy would be futile, it need not be exhausted. Thus in *Johnston v Ireland*[15] the government submitted that the applicants could have raised their complaint concerning the discriminatory legal position of a child born out of wedlock before the Irish courts. The Irish government made similar pleas in the later cases of *Open Door and Dublin Well Woman v Ireland*[16] and *Keegan v Ireland*[17] concerning certain of the applicants' complaints. The Court rejected these submissions with reference to the established case-law of the Irish courts on the ground that the remedies in question offered no prospects of success. As the Court held in *Johnston v Ireland*,[18] the government had not established with any degree of certainty the existence of an effective remedy.

Where analysis of the national case-law reveals a dispute in the domestic courts as to what the relevant legal rules are, the situation may be different. In such a situation, as we have seen, an applicant may be required to bring proceedings in order to assert his version of the appropriate rule.[19] In *Van Oosterwijck v Belgium*[20] the applicant transsexual had chosen not to appeal against the decision of the Brussels Court of Appeal to the Court of Cassation, notwithstanding the fact that the Convention, and Article 8 in particular, was directly applicable under Belgian law. He had maintained that a further appeal had no real likelihood of success under national law. The Court rejected his complaint for non-exhaustion on the basis that he could have relied on Article 8 before the Belgian courts on the same basis as he relied on it before the Convention institutions. It found that he did not even plead in substance the complaint he later made in Strasbourg. He thus denied the courts precisely that opportunity which the exhaustion rule is designed to afford to states, namely the opportunity to put right the violations alleged against them. In deciding that there were no special

---

14 See *Whiteside v UK No 20357/92*, 76-A DR 80 (1994); *No 18760/91* (1993), unreported; *No 20075/92* (failure to appeal to the House of Lords from a decision of the Court of Session in Scotland); and *No 20946/92* (1994), unreported.

15 A 112 para 44 (1986).

16 A 246 para 47 (1992).

17 A 291 para 39 (1994).

18 A 112 para 46 (1986). See also *Purcell v Ireland No 15404/89*, 70 DR 262 (1991).

19 See above p 610.

20 A 40 paras 30-41 (1980). The last point concerning the *ex officio* powers of the Court of Cassation was criticised by Judge Martens in his dissent in *Cardot v France* A 200 (1991), on the grounds that, as regards human rights cases it is too strict where the Convention can be applied *ex officio*: 'It unnecessarily disregards the protection which a national law that requires its judiciary to apply the Convention *ex officio* intends to afford to those who . . . should be assumed to be victims . . .' The rule was applied by the Commission in *Braithwaite v UK No 15123/89*, 70 DR 252 (1991) (impugned confession statement made to the police must be challenged during the trial).

circumstances which absolved the applicant from the exhaustion rule, the Court noted that the case-file did not disclose on what precise grounds his lawyers had considered an appeal to be futile and, more importantly, that the fact that the courts could have examined the case of their own motion under the Convention did not dispense him from pleading the Convention or 'arguments to the same or like effect' before them.

The terms of the Convention need not be pleaded directly before the domestic courts provided that the substance of the complaint has been raised by the applicant in compliance with the formal requirements and time-limits laid down in domestic law. Accordingly, a failure to lodge an appeal or an action in time will, in the absence of special circumstances, lead to a finding of non-exhaustion.[1]

The Court has observed, notwithstanding the importance of the rule, that Article 26 must be applied with 'some degree of flexibility and without excessive formalism'.[2] In *Castells v Spain*,[3] for example, the question arose whether the applicant had actually formulated his complaint before the Constitutional Court in terms of an interference with freedom of expression. The government claimed that in his *amparo* appeal he had referred to the relevant provision of the Spanish constitution only indirectly and had made no mention of Article 10 of the Convention. The Court was satisfied, however, after scrutiny of the pleadings before the national courts, that, both before the Supreme Court and the Constitutional Court, he had raised in substance his Convention complaint. On the other hand, in a decision which departed from the Commission's finding, the Court held that the applicant in *Cardot v France*[4] had failed to raise his complaint in substance before the French courts. The applicant had alleged a violation of the rights of the defence (Article 6(3)(d)) since he had been convicted of drugs charges on the basis of evidence given by former co-defendants in proceedings to which he had not been a party and that he had not had an opportunity, either at his trial or on appeal, to challenge their testimony. The Court rejected the case under Article 26 on the grounds that before the trial court he had not expressed any wish to hear evidence from the co-defendants or made an application to the Court of Appeal for such evidence to be heard. Moreover, his pleadings to the Court of Cassation were too vague to draw that court's attention to his real complaint under Article 6(3)(d). As to the former point, the Court stressed, with reference to international practice, that recourse must be had to any procedural means which might prevent a breach of the Convention.

1   See the cases in 5 Digest 241-253; *Cardot v France* A 200 para 34 (1991); and *J v Switzerland* No *13467/87*, 62 DR 269 (1989).
2   *Cardot v France*, ibid.
3   A 236 paras 24-32 (1992). See also *Endagoz v Turkey No 17128/90*, 71 DR 275 (1991) – even in a state where the Convention is directly applicable the applicant may raise equivalent arguments before the national authority instead of invoking a specific Convention provision.
4   A 200 paras 32-35 (1991). See also the dissenting opinion of Judges Macdonald, Martens and Morenilla (pp 21-24). The Commission considered that the applicant had raised his complaint in substance before the Court of Cassation since he complained that he had not received a fair trial: A 200 Com Rep para 31 (1991).

ii. Domestic remedies and inter-state cases

The Commission has consistently held that, in principle, the exhaustion rule applies in inter-state cases. In *Austria v Italy*[5] it rejected the Austrian argument that Article 26 did not apply since there was no injury to the state itself and since, by initiating proceedings, it was merely enforcing the collective guarantee embodied in the Convention system. In *Greece v UK*[6] the Commission found that the requirement was not satisfied in respect of various allegations of torture where the identity of the accused was known. However, it held that the court remedies were ineffective in cases where the identity of the interrogators had been withheld. Further, in *Ireland v UK*[7] the Commission rejected complaints concerning the killing by the army of 22 persons in Northern Ireland on the basis that domestic remedies had not been exhausted. It also found that the Irish government had not offered 'substantial evidence' of an administrative practice in breach of Article 2 so as to waive the exhaustion requirement. In *Cyprus v Turkey*,[8] the respondent government had complained that the alleged victim had made no use of remedies before the courts in Turkey or before the courts in 'the Turkish Federated State of Cyprus'. The Commission considered that any remedies before domestic courts in Turkey could not be regarded, in respect of complaints concerning the violation of human rights of Greek Cypriots in Cyprus, as 'both practicable and normally functioning in such cases'. The same view was expressed in respect of remedies in the northern part of Cyprus which Greek Cypriots were not permitted to enter.

It is settled case-law that the rule does not apply to inter-state complaints concerning legislative measures or where 'substantial evidence' is provided of an administrative practice in breach of the Convention.[9] The dispensation as regards legislative measures 'must be seen as a consequence of the absence, in many countries, of legal remedies against legislation'.[10] It must also be seen as the corollary of the state's right under the Convention to complain of an incompatibility of legislation with Convention standards without being required to show that it is adversely affected or to point to particular victims.[11]

In *France, Norway, Denmark, Sweden and the Netherlands v Turkey* (the *Turkish* case),[12] the Turkish government contended that the applicant states

5   *No 788/60*, 4 YB 116 (1961).
6   *No 299/57*, 2 YB 186 (1957).
7   *Nos 5310/71 and 5451/72*, 41 CD 3 at 85 (1972).
8   *Nos 6780/74 and 6950/75 (First and Second Applications)*, 2 DR 125 at 137-138 (1975); *No 8007/77*, 13 DR 85 at 150-153 (1978).
9   *Greece v UK No 299/57*, 2 YB 186 at 192 (1957); the *Greek* case 11 YB-II 690 at 726 (1968); *Second Greek* case *No 4448/70*, 13 YB 109 at 134 (1970); *Ireland v UK Nos 5310/71 and 5451/72*, 41 CD 3 at 84 (1972); *Cyprus v Turkey No 8007/77 (Third Application)*, 13 DR 85 at 151-152 (1978); *France, Norway, Denmark, Sweden, the Netherlands v Turkey Nos 9940-9944/82*, 35 DR 143 at 162 (1983).
10 *France, Norway, Denmark, Sweden, the Netherlands v Turkey*, id, p 163.
11 See above, p 607.
12 Loc cit at n 9 above, pp 162-168.

had not furnished substantial evidence of an administrative practice of torture or ill-treatment of prisoners. In particular, they referred to cases where those responsible for ill-treating prisoners had been successfully prosecuted. The issue for examination thus concerned the level of proof of a practice that must be offered by the complaining state.

The concept of administrative practice, which applies to individual cases[13] in the same way as to inter-state applications, involves: (1) a repetition of acts; and (2) official tolerance. The Court in *Ireland v UK*[14] described the first criterion as 'an accumulation of identical or analogous breaches which are sufficiently numerous and inter-connected to amount not merely to isolated incidents or exceptions but to a pattern or system'.

Official tolerance means that superiors, though cognisant of acts of ill-treatment, refuse to take action to punish those responsible or to prevent their repetition; or that a higher authority manifests indifference by refusing any adequate investigation of their truth or falsity; or that in judicial proceedings a fair hearing of such complaints is denied. In this regard the conduct of the higher authority must be on a scale which is sufficient to put an end to the repetition of acts or to interrupt the pattern or system.[15]

The significance of the concept of administrative practice as far as local remedies are concerned was highlighted by the Commission in the *Greek* case:[16]

> 'Where . . . there is a practice of non-observance of certain Convention provisions, the remedies prescribed will of necessity be side-stepped or rendered inadequate. Thus, if there was an administrative practice of torture or ill-treatment, judicial remedies prescribed would tend to be rendered ineffective by the difficulty of securing probative evidence, and administrative inquiries would either be not instituted, or, if they were, would be likely to be half-hearted and incomplete . . . '

In the *Turkish* case[17] the Commission was confronted with the paradox that, while at the admissibility stage there is no requirement on the state to make out a *prima facie* case of its allegation of violations of the Convention, the 'substantial' evidence test as regards an administrative practice appeared to suggest a degree of proof appropriate only to the merits stage of the examination. It resolved this difficulty by holding that at the admissibility stage only *prima facie* evidence of a practice was required. It went on to find this standard of proof to have been satisfied as regards both a repetition of acts and official tolerance. In particular it held that the efforts of the authorities to prevent violations of Article 3 on a considerable scale were not sufficient judging by the large number of complaints lodged with the

13 *Donnelly v UK Nos 5577-83/72*, 4 DR 64 (1975).
14 A 25 para 159 (1978).
15 12 YB (the *Greek* case) at 196 (1969) Com Rep.
16 Id, p 194.
17 *France, Norway, Denmark, Sweden and the Netherlands v Turkey Nos 9940-9944/82*, 35 DR 143 at 162-168 (1983).

competent national bodies which indicated a degree of tolerance at the level of direct superiors of those immediately responsible. The rule of exhaustion of local remedies thus did not apply.

The uncomfortable and inescapable proximity of issues concerning the existence of an administrative practice to the merits of the case is clearly reflected in the remarks of the Court in *Ireland v UK*:[18]

> 'It is inconceivable that the higher authorities of a state should be, or at least should be entitled to be, unaware of the existence of such a practice. Furthermore, under the Convention those authorities are strictly liable for the conduct of their subordinates; they are under a duty to impose their will on subordinates and cannot shelter behind their inability to ensure that it is respected.'

The practice of the Commission in this area suggests that a better resolution of the above difficulty would be to join the issue of remedies to the merits stage where an administrative practice is pleaded in an Article 24 application. On the other hand, an individual applicant should be required to show some evidence of a practice at this stage, since Article 27(2) requires at least a threshold case to be made out as regards the merits of the case.

iii. Burden of proof

Prior to the communication of an application to the state for observations, the applicant must provide information to show that the requirements of Article 26 have been satisfied (Rule 44(2) of the Rules of Procedure). The Commission will examine the matter *ex officio* at this stage and will reject for non-exhaustion if it appears that an appropriate remedy has not been availed of. Where the case is formally communicated for observations, the state bears the burden of showing that there exist available and sufficient remedies in respect of each complaint.[19] If it fails to raise the issue prior to admissibility it will be estopped from raising it before the Court.[20] It may, of

18 A 25 para 159 (1978). Interestingly, in the *Greek* case the Commission did not consider as 'substantial evidence' (which on its face suggests a higher standard of proof than *prima facie* evidence) of an administrative practice the detailed material submitted by the applicant governments consisting of statements by former prisoners, press reports and other publications, the authenticity and veracity of which it had not then had occasion to examine – 11 YB-II 690 at 770 (1968). On the other hand in *Ireland v UK Nos 5310/71* and *5451/72*, 41 CD 3 at 86-87 (1972), the Commission found an administrative practice of the five interrogation techniques based on statements by detainees, medical evidence and the report of a Committee of Inquiry.

19 See, *inter alia*, *De Wilde, Ooms and Versyp v Belgium* A 12 para 50 (1971) (the *Vagrancy* cases); *Johnston v Ireland* A 112 para 45 (1986); and *Smith Kline & French Laboratories Ltd v Netherlands No 12633/87*, 66 DR 70 (1990).

20 See below, p 675. The government could seek to raise an issue of non-exhaustion before the Commission at the post-admissibility stage of the proceedings, but its acceptance by the Commission requires a two-thirds majority (Article 29). Prior to the entry into force of the Eighth Protocol it required unanimity – see above, p 594.

course, expressly waive the right to rely on the rule.[1] In the absence of an express waiver the Commission reserves the right to examine the matter. In the case of *Deweer v Belgium*[2] the government had *inter alia* relied on 'other remedies' which the applicant could have availed of without specifying their nature. The Court took the view that it would be straying outside its role were it to set about identifying the remedies the government had in mind.

If the state is able to point to domestic remedies, the burden shifts to the applicant to show that these remedies are not adequate or effective to provide redress in respect of his complaints.[3] The same apportionment of the burden of proof applies in inter-state cases. Thus in *Cyprus v Turkey*[3a] the Commission stressed that it was for the respondent government to show that the remedies available in domestic courts in Turkey or before Turkish military courts in Cyprus were effective and sufficient.

iv. Adequacy and effectiveness of remedies

Although in the Commission's case-law a certain overlap exists between the notions of the 'adequacy' and 'effectiveness' of a given remedy, appropriate distinctions between the two concepts can be drawn. Thus an adequate remedy is one which is sufficient to provide redress for the applicant's complaints. In *Lawless v Ireland*[4] the Commission did not consider an Internment Commission to constitute an adequate remedy since it could only recommend the applicant's release and was unable to award damages. In the case of *Donnelly v UK*[5] the question arose whether compensation obtained through a civil action before the courts could constitute an adequate remedy in respect of an allegation of torture. The applicants submitted that compensation was not sufficient where there was allegedly an administrative practice and that a state could not pay for the right to violate Article 3. The Commission considered that, in general, compensation will constitute an adequate remedy since it is likely to be the only means whereby redress can be given to the individual for the wrong he has suffered. At the same time:

> 'Compensation could not . . . be deemed to have rectified a violation in a situation where the state had not taken reasonable measures to comply with its obligations under Article 3. The obligation to provide a remedy does not constitute a substitute for or alternative to those obligations, but rather an obligation to provide redress within the

1   The state is entitled under the generally recognised principles of international law to waive reliance on the rule: *Van der Mussele v Belgium No 8919/80*, 23 DR 244 (1981) and *57 Inhabitants of Louvain v Belgium No 1994/63*, 7 YB 252 (1964).
2   A 35 para 26 (1980). See also *Foti v Italy* A 56 para 48 (1982): vague assertions as to the existence of remedies.
3   *Donnelly v UK Nos 5577-83/72*, 4 DR 64 (1975). See 5 Digest 79 for other cases.
3a   See above, p 613.
4   *No 332/57*, 2 YB 308 at 326 (1958).
5   *No 5577-83/72*, 4 DR 4 at 78-79 (1975).

domestic system for violations which may, inevitably, occur despite measures taken to ensure compliance with the substantive provisions of Article 3. Thus, if conduct which contravened Article 3 were to be authorised by domestic law, even if the law also provided for the payment of compensation to the victims of such conduct, such compensation would not constitute a remedy which could be deemed to rectify the violation of Article 3. Similarly, if the higher authorities of the state pursued a policy or administrative practice whereby they authorised or tolerated conduct in violation of Article 3, compensation would not of itself constitute an adequate remedy. The protection afforded by Article 3 of the Convention is, as the applicants have submitted, an absolute one and a state cannot escape from its obligations thereunder merely by paying compensation. Compensation machinery can only be seen as an adequate remedy in a situation where the higher authorities have taken reasonable steps to comply with their obligations under Article 3 by preventing, as far as possible, the occurrence or repetition of the acts in question.'

After examining the steps taken by the authorities to prevent the occurrence or repetition of the acts complained of, the Commission was of the opinion that the applicants had not been victims of an administrative practice of ill-treatment tolerated by the higher authorities which could have had the effect of rendering compensation inadequate as a remedy. In a separate analysis of the effectiveness in practice of actions for compensation in times of civil strife, the Commission had regard to such factors as:

1.   whether the applicants were subject to harassment or reprisals by the security forces because of their allegations;
2.   the impartiality of judges and juries;
3.   the length of the proceedings before the courts;
4.   the extent to which the security forces were willing to cooperate in obtaining evidence; and
5.   offers of a settlement by the authorities by way of *ex gratia* payments in order to circumvent investigation.[6]

Examples of remedies which the Commission has considered inadequate to provide redress include a complaint to the French Ombudsman or other organs which supervise the administration;[7] an application to a court with power to order disclosure of records containing personal data to a medical or legal adviser, in respect of a privacy complaint concerning the inability of the applicant to have first hand access;[8] applications to a court which, though capable of highlighting an error in the impugned decision, could not

6   Id, pp 67-77.
7   *Montion v France No 11192/84*, 52 DR 227 (1987). See also *X v Sweden No 3893/68*, 13 YB 620 (1970).
8   *Gaskin v UK No 10454/83*, 45 DR 91 (1986).

annul it;[9] appeals limited to questions of lawfulness where the complaint concerns the facts or the law itself;[10] an action for breach of confidence under United Kingdom law, taken alone or in conjunction with an action for defamation, in respect of complaint about an interference in private life by the publication of a book;[11] claims for compensation in respect of a complaint under Article 5(3) concerning the length of detention on remand;[12] an application to the court by the accused to accelerate proceedings as regards an Article 6 complaint concerning the length of criminal proceedings;[13] an action for compensation or for a declaratory judgment recognising a violation of the Convention as regards complaints concerning length of civil proceedings.[14]

Remedies must not only be adequate or sufficient but they must also be capable in practice of providing redress in respect of the complaint. The Commission reserves the right to appreciate whether any given remedy is, in the light of its particular attributes, effective. Thus, as noted above,[15] the Commission in the cases brought by *Cyprus v Turkey* did not consider that the courtroom remedies in mainland Turkey or in the 'Turkish Federated State of Cyprus' were effective in practice to remedy complaints by aggrieved Cypriot nationals. In *Kuijk v Greece*[16] the Commission considered that remedies brought to the attention of a foreign detainee, without legal representation, were not accessible. Moreover with regard to allegations of ill-treatment in prison, an action for damages, which could only lead to a determination by the courts that the special rights of persons imprisoned for debt had been breached but not to compensation for the breach of her rights under Article 3, was not regarded as an effective remedy. Court or administrative proceedings involving undue delay may be regarded as ineffective remedies too.[17] Applicants must also be able to initiate the procedures

9   *Van der Slujis, Zuiderveld, Klappe v Netherlands Nos 9362/81*, 9363/81 and 9387/81, 28 DR 212 (1982).
10 *S v UK No 10741/84*, 41 DR 226 (1984) (Lands Tribunal in Northern Ireland).
11 *Winer v UK No 10871/84*, 48 DR 154 (1986). The applicant, who had been 'smeared' by passages in a book providing intimate details of his life, had complained of the absence of a remedy under English law for invasion of privacy.
12 *Woukam Moudefo v France No 10868/84*, 51 DR 62 (1987) and *Egue v France No 11256/84*, 57 DR 47 (1988). The Commission noted that the right to obtain release from detention and the right to obtain compensation for breaches of Article 5 are two separate rights. The legal remedy of seeking compensation is not directed at the termination of detention. This approach was followed by the Court in *Tomasi v France* A 241-A para 79 (1992).
13 *Orchin v UK No 8435/78*, 26 DR 5 at 18 (1982). The Commission stressed that the conduct of a criminal prosecution is the exclusive responsibility of the prosecution and an accused is under no obligation to renounce his procedural rights or to cooperate in proceedings against him. In any event a request to the court to speed up the proceedings could not provide any concrete redress if they have been unduly delayed (p 20). See also *D v Belgium No 12686/87*, 66 DR 105 (1990) (in civil proceedings it will be relevant to the substance of the length of the complaint).
14 *Guincho v Portugal No 8990/80*, 29 DR 129 (1982).
15 See above, p 613.
16 *No 14986/89*, 70 DR 240 at 250-251 (1991).
17 *X v UK No 7161/75*, 7 DR 100 (1976) and *Tomasi v France No 12850/87*, 64 DR 128 (1990). See also Article 5(2)(b) of the First Optional Protocol of the ICCPR.

directly and not be dependent on the favourable intervention of a public official. Thus the fact that the Belgian Attorney-General could, at the request of the Minister of Justice, report abuses of power by the Bar authorities to the Court of Cassation was not considered a relevant remedy for the purpose of Article 26 since the complainant could not initiate the procedure himself.[18] However, where individuals have not direct access to a constitutional court but are dependent on the issue being referred by an ordinary court, they may be required to raise the constitutional point before the ordinary courts.[19] In several cases the Commission has not considered special appeal procedures which are dependent on the discretion of officials, to be effective remedies. Under Irish law, the Attorney-General can grant a certificate in criminal cases permitting an appeal to the Supreme Court on a point of law of 'exceptional public importance'. Taking into account that the certificate could be sought at any time (even many years later) after dismissal of an appeal by the Court of Appeal and was not regarded as part of the normal hierarchy of judicial procedures following conviction, the Commission did not regard it as an effective remedy.[20]

A question has arisen in several cases as to the moment at which the availability of remedies is to be assessed. It is clear from the Court's judgment in *Ringeisen v Austria*[1] that applicants may lodge an application with the Commission before remedies have been exhausted provided that a final decision has been taken before the Commission rule on admissibility. In the *Vagrancy* cases,[2] for example, counsel for the government relied before the Court on judicial developments which had occurred subsequent to the admissibility hearings before the Commission. According to new judicial developments, recourse to the Conseil d'Etat against the orders of a magistrate to detain vagrants had become possible. The Court held that the applicants could not be reproached for failing to appeal to the Conseil d'Etat since, according to settled legal opinion up to a time subsequent to the decision on admissibility, such a remedy offered no prospects of success. In any event the applicants could not have benefited from the new development since the relevant time-limits had expired. The Commission has subsequently stated that it must normally decide the question whether remedies have been exhausted by reference to the situation prevailing at the date of its decision on admissibility. Thus in *Fell v UK*[3] it found that it would have been open to the applicant to seek an order of *certiorari* against an adjudication of the Board of Visitors, following the judgment of the Court of Appeal in *Ex parte St Germain*[4] of 3 October 1978, which was

18 *H v Belgium No 8950/80*, 37 DR 5 (1984).
19 *Sacchi v Italy No 6452/74*, 5 DR 43 (1976).
20 *X v Ireland No 9136/80*, 26 DR 242 (1981). See also *X v Denmark No 8395/78*, 27 DR 50 (1981).
1 A 13 paras 90-93 (1971). See also *Ventura v Italy No 7438/76*, 12 DR 38 (1978) and *Deschamps v Belgium No 13370/87*, 70 DR 177 (1991).
2 *De Wilde, Ooms and Versyp v Belgium* A 12 pp 60-62 (1971).
3 *No 7878/77*, 23 DR 102 (1981). See also *Campbell v UK No 7819/77*, 14 DR 186 (1978).
4 *R v Hull Prison Board of Visitors, ex p St Germain*, [1979] 1 All E.R. 701.

given subsequent to the filing of his complaint to the Commission in March 1977. In its *Campbell and Fell* judgment[5] the Court found, however, that it would be unjust to reject Campbell's complaint for non-exhaustion since recourse to *certiorari* was no longer open to him. He was thus entitled to rely on the Commission's decision of May 1978 (ie pre-*St Germain*) rejecting the non-exhaustion plea.

In many cases the relevant time for assessing the existence of a remedy will be the moment of the act giving rise to the complaint since national time-limits may well preclude any effort to avail of subsequent jurisprudential developments. Moreover an applicant could not be expected to bring fresh proceedings if he has already had recourse to a remedy and failed. Applicants need only make normal use of the effective remedies open to them. Thus where numerous remedies exist which are likely to be adequate and effective it is enough that the applicant has had recourse to one of them. In *Cremieux v France*[6] the applicant had made use of the appropriate legal remedies up to the Court of Cassation to challenge the lawfulness of searches and seizures by customs officials. The Commission rejected the government's argument that he had not availed of other remedies which would have enabled him to claim damages against the state. Similarly, in *Leander v Sweden*[7] the applicant appealed to the government requesting *inter alia* that he be given access to secret information concerning him which he believed had prevented him from obtaining employment. His request was unsuccessful. The Commission stressed that an applicant does not need to have recourse to other remedies which, although theoretically of a nature to constitute a remedy, in reality offer no chance of redressing the alleged breach and which would be a repetition of remedies already sought by him.

v.   Special circumstances and exemption from obligation to exhaust

It has been recognised by the Commission that there may be special circumstances where an applicant is absolved from the requirement to exhaust even adequate and effective domestic remedies. As noted above, where an applicant alleges that there exists an administrative practice and is able to show that there is official tolerance at the highest level of the state, he will be absolved from exhausting remedies since there will be an assumption that they will be ineffective in practice. Where the administrative practice involves official tolerance at the middle or lower levels of command it will be a question of fact to be resolved in each case whether the remedies are still effective and sufficient.[8]

The Commission has also recognised that there may be circumstances where it would be unreasonable to apply the exhaustion rule strictly. In *Reed*

5   A 80 paras 60-63 (1984).
6   *No 11471/85*, 59 DR 67 (1989). See also *L v Switzerland No 12609/86*, 64 DR 84 (1990).
7   *No 9248/81*, 34 DR 78 (1983).
8   *Donnelly v UK Nos 5577-5583/72*, 4 DR 4 (1975). See above, p 614.

v UK[9] the applicant, who had complained of ill-treatment in prison, was not permitted for more than two years to consult a solicitor with a view to initiating civil proceedings because of a prison rule that an internal investigation should take place first. The Commission considered it to be of fundamental importance that an existing remedy be immediately available, particularly in cases of alleged maltreatment. The fact that he could still bring the action after the two-year period was not considered an answer to the impediment. A similar view was taken in *Hilton v UK*[10] where the applicant prisoner had made two unsuccessful requests to the Secretary of State to see a solicitor in respect of alleged ill-treatment in prison. He was absolved from making further requests on the ground that it would doubtless have been ineffective.

The plea of 'special circumstances' has, however, been rarely accepted by the Commission. It has refused to absolve the applicant, for example, on the grounds that he was a mental patient or had lack of legal knowledge[11] or because he had doubts as to the prospects of success[12] or had no legal aid[13] or was old and sick or depressive.[14] When legal aid is not available to bring costly national proceedings such as a constitutional action, it may be questioned, as noted above, whether the remedy is an effective one in practice. The case-law, however, suggests that the rule is to be applied strictly even in such circumstances. The Court's remarks in *Cardot v France*[15] that Article 26 should be applied with some degree of flexibility and without excessive formalism should perhaps be taken to heart by the Commission in this context.

3. THE SIX-MONTH RULE

Article 26 further provides that the Commission 'may only deal with the matter . . . within a period of six months from the date on which the final decision was taken'. The *ratio legis* of the rule is the desire of contracting parties to prevent past decisions being constantly called into question.[16] It marks out the temporal limits of supervision carried out by the Convention

---

9 *No 7630/76*, 19 DR 113 (1979). But contrast *Campbell v UK No 7819/77*, 14 DR 186 (1978), where the Commission accepted a delay of thirteen months, when the applicant who complained of ill-treatment by prison officers was refused permission to seek legal advice for the purpose of suing them. The *Campbell* case was considered in *Reed*: see 19 DR at 133-134.

10 *No 5613/72*, 4 DR 177 (1976).

11 *X v UK No 6840/74*, 10 DR 5 (1977).

12 *Garcia v Switzerland No 10148/82*, 42 DR 98 (1985) and *McDonnell v Ireland No 15141/89*, 64 DR 203 (1990).

13 *Van Oosterwijck v Belgium* A 40 para 38 (1980) (although he had not made an application for legal aid).

14 *No 289/57*, 1 YB 148 (1957). See also *B v Belgium No 16301/90*, 68 DR 290 (1991) (depressive state did not exempt the applicant from applying to the Belgium Conseil d'Etat to have an expulsion order quashed).

15 A 200 para 34 (1991).

16 *X v France No 9587/81*, 29 DR 228 (1982).

institutions and signals to both individuals and state authorities the period beyond which such supervision is no longer possible.[17] As such the rule has been described as an element of legal stability and legal certainty. It applies to both inter-state[18] and individual applications.

Given the importance of the provision in enabling the Commission to avoid the examination of 'historic' complaints, it is not surprising that it has held that the state cannot waive the application of the rule on its own authority.[19] In the case of *X v France*[20] the Commission found that it was competent to examine complaints arising between the date of ratification of the Convention by France (in 1974) and the date of the Article 25 declaration, in the light of the terms of the declaration (in 1981), which did not contain the usual provision limiting the Commission's competence to subsequent acts or events. The Commission, however, found that the six-month rule was applicable in view of the notion of 'legal stability'. It then applied the six-month rule with reference, not to the date of the Article 25 declaration, but to the date of the final domestic decision which pre-dated the declaration. Prescient French applicants who were in a position to anticipate France's acceptance of the right of individual petition were thus required to have made their complaints at a moment when the Commission had no competence to examine them. In this way, the Commission was able to neutralise the effects of a retrospective Article 25 declaration, although the practicality of its decision is rather dubious.

In principle, the time-limit is interrupted by the first letter setting out summarily the substance of the applicant's complaints as opposed to the date of receipt in the secretariat or the date of registration of the complaint.[1] The mere filing of documents, unaccompanied by a clear statement of complaint, is not enough.[2] However, the Commission may decide to reject an application where the letter of introduction has been followed by a substantial period of inaction before the applicant submits further information. Delays in pursuing an application may be acceptable where the applicant is in the process of exhausting domestic remedies[3] but a long and unjustified silence may lead the Commission to reject the case as being out of time.[4] Indeed the practice of the secretariat is to warn applicants that

---

17 *K v Ireland No 10416/83*, 38 DR 158 (1984).
18 Eg *Cyprus v Turkey No 8007/77 (Third Application)*, 13 DR 85 (1978).
19 *X v France No 9587/81*, 29 DR 228 (1982). See also *K v Ireland No 10416/83*, 38 DR 158 (1984) and *Bozano v France No 9990/82*, 39 DR 119 (1984).
20 *No 9587/81*, 29 DR 228 (1982).
1 *X v Ireland No 8299/78*, 22 DR 51 (1980). See also Rule 44(4) of the Rules of Procedure.
2 *N v FRG No 9314/81*, 31 DR 200 (1982).
3 *Colozzo and Rubinat v Italy Nos 9024/80 and 9317/81*, 28 DR 138 (1982) and *Deschamps v Belgium No 13370/87*, 70 DR 177 (1991).
4 *Mercier de Bettens v Switzerland No 12158/86*, 54 DR 178 (1987). In this case eight years had elapsed before the applicant wrote again to the secretariat. Her reasons (voluminous case-file and the fact that she had seen no reason to send documentary evidence before completing the application form) were not considered sufficient to justify suspension of the time-limit. See also *Deschamps v Belgium No 13370/87*, above at n 3.

their failure to pursue the case may lead to rejection in the absence of special circumstances justifying the delay.

The 'final decision' for purposes of Article 26 will normally be the final domestic decision rejecting the applicant's claim. Where no adequate and effective remedy is available, the 'final decision' will be the act or decision complained of. In *X v UK*,[5] for example, the applicant complained that the British Railways Act 1968 had deprived him of certain property he would have obtained following the closure of a railway line. The Commission found that since the Act could not be challenged in court, the date of the entry into force of the Act should be considered as the 'final decision'. In another case, concerning a prohibition of a public procession against which there was no judicial remedy, the Commission found that the relevant date was the time when the applicant was actually affected by the measure, ie the date of the planned procession.[6] Similarly, in cases concerning the amount of compensation granted after the nationalisation of a business, the six-month period was held to run, not from the date of the enabling legislation, but from the moment when the level of compensation to shareholders was determined.[7]

Where a judgment is not pronounced in open court the time-limit will be calculated from the date on which the judgment is served. It is for the state, which invokes the six-month rule, however, to establish the date on which the applicant learned of the final decision.[8] In one application against Switzerland concerning the length of proceedings the applicant had filed proceedings more than six months after he had received the operative provisions of the Federal Court's judgment. The Commission found that the relevant date ought to be considered as the date on which he received the full text of this decision since it was only this which would have enabled him to decide whether an application was likely to succeed and to provide reasons for his Convention claim.[9]

The time-limit only starts to run from the final decision resulting from the exhaustion of remedies which are adequate and effective to provide redress in respect of the matter complained of. The six-month rule and the exhaustion requirement are thus intertwined in this respect. It follows that the time-limit will not run from the date of decisions resulting from extraordinary remedies such as requests for a pardon or applications to re-open the proceedings.[10]

---

5 *No 7379/76*, 8 DR 211 (1976).
6 *Christians against Racism and Fascism v UK No 8440/78*, 21 DR 138 (1980).
7 *Scotts of Greenock Ltd v UK No 9599/81*, 42 DR 33 (1985) and *Yarrow v UK No 9266/81*, 30 DR 155 (1983).
8 *X v France No 9908/82*, 32 DR 266 (1983). See also *Gama Da Costa v Portugal No 12659/87*, 65 DR 136 (1990).
9 *P v Switzerland No 9299/81*, 36 DR 20 (1984) and *Aarts v Netherlands No 14056/88*, 70 DR 208 (1991) (period runs from the date when lawyer learns of decision notwithstanding the fact that applicant became aware later).
10 *X v Ireland No 9136/80*, 26 DR 242 at 244 (1981). The remedy concerned an application to the Attorney-General for a certificate to appeal to the Supreme Court on a point of law of exceptional importance. Since, *inter alia*, the remedy could be sought at any time subsequent to a criminal conviction it was not considered effective. See also *X and Church of Scientology v Sweden No 7805/77*, 16 DR 68 (1979) and *R v Denmark No 10326/83*, 35 DR 218 (1983).

The six-month rule does not apply to continuing situations where the alleged violation takes the form of a state of affairs as opposed to a specific act or decision. This will be the case where the alleged violation stems from a legislative provision which constantly impinges on or restricts particular activities.[11] Thus in *De Becker v Belgium*[12] the Commission did not consider that the rule applied to the continuing restrictions on De Becker in the exercise of his profession as a journalist which flowed from a criminal conviction for collaborating with the enemy. Similarly in *McFeeley v UK*[13] repeated disciplinary punishments for persistent refusal to obey the prison rules was considered to amount to a continuing situation. The rule will start to apply, however, when the continuing situation comes to an end.

On the other hand, acts of expropriation depriving a person of his property are not usually seen as involving a continuing situation of lack of property.[14] In the same vein, trial proceedings leading to imprisonment are not regarded as leading to a continuing deprivation of liberty in respect of a complaint concerning the fairness of proceedings.

Finally, the running of the period may be interrupted by 'special circumstances' which absolve the applicant from the strict application of the rule. The burden of establishing such circumstances falls on the applicant. In *K v Ireland*[15] the applicant maintained that his mental state rendered him incapable of lodging a complaint within the time-limit. The Commission rejected the claim notwithstanding the fact that the government did not contest the existence of special circumstances. It noted laconically that his state of mind did not appear to hinder the pursuit of numerous appeals before the Irish courts and, further, that Ireland could not waive the requirement in this way. While preventing a prisoner from writing to the Commission would undoubtedly constitute a special circumstance, error or ignorance of the law would not.[16]

4. OTHER GROUNDS OF INADMISSIBILITY

Article 27 provides in part:

1. The Commission shall not deal with any petition submitted under Article 25 which:
    (a) is anonymous; or

---

11 *Tete v France No 11123/84*, 54 DR 52 (1987). The applicant complained about provisions of French electoral law concerning election to the European Parliament.

12 *No 214/56*, 2 YB 214 at 230-234 (1958).

13 *No 8317/78*, 20 DR 44 (1980) and *Gama Da Costa v Portugal No 12659/87*, 65 DR 136 (1990).

14 *X v UK No 7379/76*, 8 DR 211 (1976). Cf *Chrysostomos v Turkey Nos 15299/89, 15300/89 and 15318/89*, 68 DR 216 (1991).

15 No 10416/83, 38 DR 158 at 160 (1984). See also *X v Austria No 6317/73*, 2 DR 87 (1975).

16 *Bozano v France No 9991/82*, 39 DR 147 (1984). See also the cases in 5 Digest 328-332. The plea of 'special circumstances' has been accepted by the Commission in very few cases.

(b) is substantially the same as a matter which has already been examined by the Commission or has already been submitted to another procedure of international investigation or settlement and if it contains no relevant new information.

2. The Commission shall consider inadmissible any petition submitted under Article 25 which it considers incompatible with the provisions of the present Convention, manifestly ill-founded, or an abuse of the right of petition.

Unlike the non-exhaustion and six-month rule these requirements, as is clear from the wording of Article 27, do not apply to inter-state cases. The Commission has, however, left it open that an inter-state complaint could be rejected as abusive in the light of general principles of international law.[17] The question of inadmissibility on the ground that the application is 'incompatible with the provisions of the present Convention' (Article 27(2)) is considered separately below.[18]

i. Anonymity (Article 27(1)(a))

In practice this is not an important ground of inadmissibility since applicants are required to disclose their identity when completing the application form.[19] The Commission's secretariat would not register an anonymous application. It is, however, open to applicants to request that their identity not be made public. Their wishes in this regard will be respected by the Commission in any publication of the decision or report in their case.

In an application brought by a Church or by an association concerning an infringement of its rights, it is not necessary to reveal the identity of members. The Commission has held, for example, that a Church is capable of possessing and exercising Article 9 rights in its own capacity as a representative of its members.[20] In one case,[1] however, the Commission rejected a complaint brought by a Federation of Medical Trade Unions which had complained of breaches of its members' rights. The Commission noted that the Federation did not claim to be a victim but had stated that it acted as representatives of unnamed individuals who were. Under the Rules of Procedure the association was required to identify the victims and show that they had received specific instructions from each of them.

---

17 See above, p 606; *Cyprus v Turkey Nos 6780/74 and 6950/75*, 2 DR 125 at 138 (1975); and ibid *No 8007/77*, 13 DR 85 (1978). As has the Court, in *Loizidou v Turkey* A 310 (1995).
18 See below, p 629.
19 Older cases have been rejected on this basis – eg *No 361/58*, reported in 5 Digest 334-5.
20 *X and Church of Scientology v Sweden (1979) No 7805/77*, 16 DR 68 (1979) and *Omkarananda and Divine Light Zentrum v UK No 8118/77*, 25 DR 105 (1981).
1 *Confederation des Syndicats Medicaux Français v France No 10983/84*, 47 DR 225 (1986). See also Rule 43(3) of the Rules of Procedure.

ii. Substantially the same (Article 27(1)(b))

The Commission will reject an application under this head if the factual basis of the new application is the same as that of an application which has previously been rejected by the Commission. It makes no difference if the second application contains new legal arguments.[2] The situation is different, however, where new information is provided which alters the factual basis of the complaint. For example, an application which has been rejected for non-exhaustion of domestic remedies may be re-examined after the applicant has had recourse to the remedy.[3] Similarly it is open to applicants complaining of length of proceedings or of the length of detention on remand to bring a second application if the proceedings have still not terminated or if the detention continues.[4] In such cases, although the Convention complaint remains the same, the facts have evolved.

Complaints concerning the same act or decision or subject-matter would not normally be rejected under this head where they are brought consecutively by different applicants, although in such a situation the secretariat of the Commission would draw the applicant's attention to a previous rejection of the case and discourage pursuit of the complaint.[5] It is not unusual for numerous complaints concerning the same matter (eg censorship of prisoners' correspondence or arrest and detention under the UK Prevention of Terrorism Acts) to be registered. Their examination may be adjourned pending the decision of the Court in a pilot case.

The second limb of Article 27(1)(b) has not been the subject of much case-law. The purpose of the provision is to prevent a duplication of examination by different international bodies. The term 'international investigation or settlement' is rather vague but has been interpreted as encompassing organs such as the ICCPR's Human Rights Committee, other enforcement agencies set up within the UN system (such as ILO bodies) and the Court of Justice of the European Union. In applying the rule the Commission has not considered it relevant to take into account that many of these bodies cannot give binding decisions. In the *GCHQ* case[6] the government had drawn the Commission's attention to the fact that an identical complaint had been examined by ILO organs. The Commission did not consider that the applicant was substantially the same since the ILO complaint had been brought by the Trades Union Congress on its own behalf whereas the *GCHQ* case had been brought by the Council of Civil Service Unions and six individual applicants. It is implicit in the Commission's decision, however, that Article 27(1)(b) would have been applied had the applicant been the TUC. In a subsequent case, *Martín and 22 Others v Spain*[7] the Commission rejected an

---

2   *X v UK No 8206/78*, 25 DR 147 (1981). See generally 5 Digest 336-352.
3   *No 361/58*, 5 Digest 334-335.
4   *W v FRG No 10785/84*, 48 DR 102 (1986) and *Vallon v Italy No 9621/81*, 33 DR 217 (1983).
5   The issue turns on whether the second applicant has a personal interest in bringing the case: *X v FRG No 9028/80*, 22 DR 236 (1980) and *Ensslin v FRG Nos 7572/76, 7586/76 and 7587/ 76*, 14 DR 64 (1978).
6   *Council of Civil Service Unions v UK No 11603/85*, 50 DR 228 (1987).
7   *No 16358/90* (1992), unreported.

Article 11 complaint that the applicants had been dismissed because of trade union activities on the basis that the same complaint had been made and examined by the Committee of Freedom of Association provided for under ILO Convention No 87. Although the ILO complaint had been brought by a major trade union body, it had been joined by the union branches representing the applicants. In the Commission's view, the European Convention complaint had been brought by essentially the same applicants. Complaints that have been lodged with the ICCPR's Human Rights Committee have also been rejected on this basis even where the applicant had filed his Convention complaint first and had sought an adjournment of the United Nations procedure. For the Commission what counted was the situation which existed at the moment of its examination of admissibility. The fact that an identical case was pending before the Human Rights Committee and had not been withdrawn brought Article 27(1)(b) into play.[8]

iii. Manifestly ill-founded (Article 27(2))

This provision requires the Commission to examine the merits of an application and decide whether it deserves further examination. It is thus essential to the screening role of the Commission. In the Commission's case-law the term has been broadly interpreted as encompassing cases which have no merit, because the applicant has failed to substantiate his allegations, to cases where the Commission considers that no *prima facie* violation of the Convention has been made out.[9] This spectrum of standards, ranging from totally unmeritorious to no *prima facie* breach, means in effect that the qualification 'manifestly' may not always be applied and that cases will be rejected on the grounds that the Commission considers them to be 'ill-founded'. This is possibly the only provision in the Convention where the Commission, in its practice, has departed from the literal and ordinary meaning of the words employed. Occasionally, the practice of the Commission in this regard has given rise to criticism on the grounds that there is an excessive tendency to reject cases that might not survive scrutiny by the Court but which certainly are deserving of full examination on the merits. In recent years cases like *McFeeley, GCHQ, Kelly* and *Purcell*[10] have

8 *No 17512/90* (1992), *No 8464/79* (1979), and *No 17230/90* (1991), all unreported.
9 The Commission frequently uses this ground for dismissing *de plano* applications which make numerous unsupported or worthless complaints. Such cases will be rejected by Committees using the so-called 'global formula' which reads: 'An examination of this case by the Commission as it has been submitted does not disclose any appearance of a violation of the rights and freedoms set out in the Convention.'
10 *McFeeley v UK No 8317/78*, 20 DR 44 (1980); *Council of Civil Servants Union v UK No 11603/85*, 50 DR 228 (1987); *Kelly v UK No 17579/90* (1993), unreported (a case concerning the use of lethal force); and *Purcell v Ireland No 15404/89*, 70 DR 262 (1991). See also *Iversen v Norway No 1468/62*, 6 YB 278 (1963) where six members considered the case to be manifestly ill-founded, four members dissented and the majority of six set out their reasons in 20 pages. In the present practice of the Commission an indication may be given in the admissibility decision as to whether it was unanimous or by a majority: Rule 52(2) of the Rules of Procedure. For many years no indication was given.

been regarded as falling into this category. These cases sit ill with the Commission statement in, for example, *Klass v Germany*[11] that applications raising complex questions of law, which are also of a general interest, cannot be regarded as manifestly ill-founded. They prompt the following question. How can a case be rejected as *manifestly* ill-founded after extensive legal argument, often involving an oral hearing, and a *lengthy* fully reasoned opinion of the Commission with which not all members agree? It might be true that the Court would not find a breach in such cases. However, this ignores the general European interest in having important issues of interpretation of the Convention examined at the highest level. It is certainly open to question whether the practice can be justified for reasons of procedural economy linked to the Commission's heavy case-load.

In *Boyle and Rice v UK*,[12] where the applicants had complained of the absence of effective remedies in respect of complaints arising from their imprisonment, the Commission maintained that although it had rejected various complaints as manifestly ill-founded this did not mean that they were not 'arguable' complaints for the purpose of Article 13. Such a stance was, of course, perfectly consistent with the Commission's practice in this area. The Court, however, viewed the argument with a different eye:

> '. . . rejection of a complaint as "manifestly ill-founded" amounts to a decision that "there is not even a *prima facie* case against the respondent state" . . . . On the ordinary meaning of the words, it is difficult to conceive how a claim that is "manifestly ill-founded" can nevertheless be "arguable", and vice versa.'

In other words, if the Commission considers complaints to be 'arguable' they should not be rejected under Article 27(2). As already noted, an inter-state case cannot be rejected on this basis.[13]

iv. Abuse of the right of petition (Article 27(2))

Dismissal on this ground is a rare occurrence and is mostly reserved for applicants who file multiple complaints which have no foundation. Since the introduction of the Committee system, which enables the Commission to dispose summarily of groundless complaints, rejection on this ground has become unnecessary. Nevertheless the Commission has from time to time asserted the right to police the petition system by considering applications to be abusive. In particular it has stressed that it is not its task to examine a succession of ill-founded and querulous complaints which create unnecessary work and hinders it in fulfilling its real function.[14] The persistent use of

---

11 *No 5029/71*, 1 DR 20 (1974).
12 A 131 paras 53-54 (1988).
13 But see the Commission's observations in the *Turkish* case, above at p 614.
14 *M v UK No 13284/87*, 54 DR 214 (1987).

insulting, provocative and threatening language may also be considered abusive, particularly where the applicant has been warned of the possible consequences.[15] On the other hand, an application is not considered abusive merely by the fact that it is motivated by the desire for publicity or propaganda unless the allegations are groundless or outside the purview of the Convention. The Commission so held in the case of *McFeeley v UK*[16] which had been brought by convicted IRA members engaged in an acrimonious protest at the requirement that they wear prison uniform. In another case, however, it stressed that it might be otherwise if the primary object of the case was to exert pressure or engage in political propaganda, alien to the purpose and spirit of the Convention.[17] Misleading the Commission deliberately or failing to reply to requests for information have also been construed as abusive in the past practice of the Commission although care should be taken not to visit the sins of lawyers on unsuspecting applicants.[18]

In one case the applicant, who had gone into hiding, complained about the length of extradition proceedings. The Commission rejected his case as an abuse of the right of petition, adding that while occasions

'. . . may arise where an alleged violation of the rights and freedoms guaranteed by the Convention may excuse an applicant from compliance with the rule of law . . . the applicant's proposed extradition to the United Kingdom to face trial in the jurisdiction of another member state of the Council of Europe does not justify the applicant's flight from domestic law enforcement.'[19]

This approach was not, however, followed in subsequent cases brought by applicants complaining of an unfair trial. They had failed to attend appeal hearings fearing that they would be arrested and the courts had refused to hear representations from their lawyers before affirming their convictions.[20]

5. INCOMPATIBILITY AND THE COMPETENCE OF THE COMMISSION

This head of admissibility concerns the competence of the Commission to examine individual or inter-state complaints. In the practice of the Commission questions of competence are examined as issues of admissibility under Article 27(2). They concern questions such as who can bring a case and against whom (*ratione personae*), the subject-matter of the

15 See 5 Digest 398-399 for details of cases.
16 *No 8317/78*, 20 DR 44 (1980). See also *McQuiston v UK No 11208/84*, 46 DR 182 (1986).
17 *Foti, Lentini and Cenerini v Italy Nos 7604/76, 7719/76 and 7781/77*, 14 DR 133 (1978).
18 See 5 Digest 393, 397.
19 *X v Ireland No 9742/82*, 32 DR 251 at 254 (1983).
20 *Lala v Netherlands* A 297-A (1994) Com Rep and *Pelladoah v Netherlands* A 297-B (1994) Com Rep.

application (*ratione materiae*) and the time and place of the alleged violation (*ratione temporis* and *ratione loci*).

i. Competence *ratione personae*

Complaints under the Convention can only be brought by a 'person, non-governmental organisation or group of individuals claiming to be the victim of a violation' of a Convention right (Article 25). While 'non-governmental organisations' and 'groups of individuals' are broad categories they do not cover, for example, municipalities, other local government organisations or semi-state bodies.[1] Complaints can only be brought against the state concerning action of the state itself or of state bodies such as the courts, the security forces or local government. An individual cannot complain of the actions of a private person or body such as a lawyer or newspaper.[2] Actions by private individuals or bodies may, however, give rise to state responsibility in certain circumstances since the state may have a positive obligation to secure particular rights, for example, the right to form and join trade unions or the right to education.[3] In *Costello-Roberts v UK*,[4] the question arose whether the state was responsible under the Convention for corporal punishment in private schools alleged to be in breach of Articles 3 and 8. In reaching the conclusion that there was responsibility the Court noted that:

(1) the state has an obligation to secure to children their right to education under Article 2 of the First Protocol and that a school's disciplinary system fell within the ambit of the right to education;
(2) in the United Kingdom independent schools co-exist with a system of public education, the right to education being guaranteed equally to pupils in both types of school;
(3) the state cannot absolve itself from responsibility by delegating its obligations to private bodies or individuals.

In *Van der Mussele v Belgium*,[5] the latter argument was the basis for finding Belgium responsible for its free legal aid system, the operation of which had been conferred by the state on the Bar Association. Of course, in both *Costello-Roberts* and *Van der Mussele* the complaints were in fact directed against the state's failure to intervene with third-parties in order to secure the protection of a Convention right.

---

1 *Rothenthurm Commune v Switzerland No 13252/87*, 59 DR 251 (1988) and *Ayuntamiento de M v Spain No 15090/89*, 68 DR 209 (1991).
2 A lawyer, even if officially appointed, does not incur the liability of the state under the Convention: *W v Switzerland No 9022/80*, 33 DR 21 (1983).
3 See *Young, James and Webster v UK* A 44 (1981). On positive obligations, see above, pp 19-22.
4 A 247-C paras 25-28 (1993). The finding has clear implications as regards the privatisation of certain sectors of government such as prisons or the provision of postal services.
5 A 70 paras 28-30 (1983). See also *Artico v Italy* A 37 paras 31-38 (1980).

In *Nielsen v Denmark*[6] the Court rejected the applicant's Article 5 complaint as incompatible *ratione personae* on the basis that his hospitalisation in a child psychiatric ward of a state hospital was not a deprivation of liberty by the state but a reasonable exercise by his mother of her custodial rights in the interest of the child. The Court accepted that the rights of the holder of parental authority were not unlimited and that the state must provide safeguards against abuse. However, it went on to find that the restrictions imposed on the child in hospital were normal requirements for the case of a sick child.

The judgment of the Court and the dissenting opinions reveal the difficulties of defining a boundary line between parental responsibility and state responsibility. At what point should the state intervene with the holder of parental rights to protect the interests of the child and at what point should it remain on the sideline in order to respect parental rights under Article 8? The resolution of this conflict of interests does not admit of any easy answers. It is, however, central to the effective protection of the rights of the child under the Convention.

Difficult questions of state responsibility under the Convention also arise in respect of the acts of public corporations or other public bodies. The Commission, for example, has left open the question whether the United Kingdom is responsible for the acts of the BBC or whether the actions of British Rail are imputable to the state.[7] In answering such questions factors such as the degree of state control or independence of the body are relevant. Is the body dependent only on the state for financial support exercising *de facto* autonomy in the running of its affairs or does the state exercise a constant and pervasive influence in its daily operation?

Individual complaints against states which have not ratified the Convention (or its Protocols) or accepted the right of individual petition will also be rejected on this ground. Although Article 27(2) does not apply to inter-state complaints, it is clear that the right of action under Article 24 presupposes that the applicant and defendant states have ratified the Convention. Complaints against the European Union will also be rejected as incompatible *ratione personae* until at such time as the Union adheres to the Convention. In *CFDT v European Communities*,[8] the Commission rejected the applicants' complaint (1) against the Communities; and (2) against the member states jointly and severally. It considered that the member states, by

---

6   A 144 paras 58-73 (1988). The majority of the Commission had found that the final decision to hospitalise the child was taken not by his mother but by the chief physician of the psychiatric ward (para 62). The Court's decision was taken by 9 votes to 7, with dissenting opinions by Judges Thór Vilhjálmsson, Pettiti, Russo, Spielmann, De Meyer, Carillo and Valticos, see above, pp 100-101.

7   *Hilton v UK No 12015/86*, 57 DR 108 at 117-118 (1988): question of the state's responsibility under Article 8 for an act of the BBC in carrying out a security check left open; *Young, James and Webster v UK* A 44 paras 48-49 (1981) and B 39 Com Rep, para 169 (1979). See also *X v UK No 8295/78*, 15 DR 242 (1978) – where the Commission also left open the question of state responsibility for an organ of the English Bar.

8   *No 8030/77*, 13 DR 231 (1978).

taking part in a decision of the Council of the European Communities, had not exercised their 'jurisdiction' within the meaning of Article 1 of the Convention. Insofar as the complaint was directed against the states jointly it was rejected on the basis that it was essentially a complaint against the Council of the European Communities. Insofar as the complaint was directed against the states severally the complaint against France was held to be incompatible *ratione personae* since France had not yet accepted the right of individual petition. The remaining eight member states, by voting in the community institutions, were considered to have been acting outside the purview of their 'jurisdiction' for purposes of the Convention.

Article 25 requires that the applicant claim to be a victim of a violation of one of the rights in the Convention. He must thus claim to be directly affected in some way by the matter complained of.[9] This provision has been characterised by the Court in the *Klass* case[10] as one of the keystones in the machinery of enforcement since it determines the individual's access to the Commission. The Court has also indicated in *Klass* that the 'procedural provisions of the Convention must, in view of the fact that the Convention and its institutions were set up to protect the individual, be applied in a manner which serves to make the system of individual applications efficacious'. In that case it held that an individual may, under certain conditions, claim to be the victim of a violation occasioned by the mere existence of secret measures or of legislation permitting secret measures, without having to allege that such measures were in fact applied to him.[11] Since all users or potential users of the postal and telecommunication services in the state were directly affected by legislation which provided for secret surveillance, they fell into the category of victim.[12] In subsequent cases, however, the Commission has narrowed the breadth of this ruling. It has held that where such legislation provides for notification of surveillance to a person concerned he cannot generally claim to be a victim of a violation of Article 8 unless he has received such notification.[13] Where the legislation affects all users and does not provide for notification, anyone may claim to be a victim. In *Hilton v UK*[14] the applicant had learned that she had previously been the subject of a security check by the secret service. She complained of the compilation and retention of personal information about

9   For details of the voluminous case-law of both the Commission and Court, see 4 Digest 358-415. See also Rogge in *Wiarda Mélanges*, pp 539-545.
10 *Klass v FRG* A 28 para 34 (1978).
11 The relevant conditions are to be determined in each case according to the Convention rights alleged to have been infringed, the secret character of the measures objected to, and the connection between the applicant and those measures. See also *Hewitt and Harman v UK No 12175/86*, 67 DR 88 (1989) Com Rep; CM Res DH (90) 36.
12 Even though in the hearing before the Court, the Agent of the government stated that none of the applicants had been subject to the surveillance measures in question: ibid at para 37.
13 *Mersch v Luxembourg Nos 10439-41/83, 10452/83, 10512-3/83*, 43 DR 34 (1985). See also *MS and PS v Switzerland No 10628/83*, 44 DR 175 (1985).
14 *No 12015/86*, 57 DR 108 (1988) (no reasonable likelihood made out). In another case concerning a person whose offer of a job in a company involved in defence contracts was withdrawn following a security service check, the Commission held that there was a reasonable likelihood: *N v UK No 12327/86*, 58 DR 85 (1988).

her. The Commission distinguished the *Klass* case on the basis that the category of persons likely to be affected by security checks was significantly narrower than all users of postal and telecommunications services. It considered that applicants must be able to show that there was a reasonable likelihood that the security service had compiled and retained personal information about them. To hold otherwise would have the consequence that anyone in the United Kingdom could claim to be a victim when it was not reasonable to suppose that they were – which would be tantamount to an *actio popularis*. Inevitably, however, the category of persons affected by a particular issue may be very broad. Thus in *Open Door and Dublin Well Woman v Ireland*,[15] which concerned a Supreme Court injunction against the provision of information by the applicant companies concerning abortion facilities outside Ireland, the Commission and Court considered that women of child-bearing age could claim to be victims since they belonged to a class of women which may be adversely affected by the restriction.

In *Leigh, Guardian Newspapers Ltd and Observer Ltd v UK*,[16] on the other hand, the applicants complained of the impact of a House of Lords decision that documents, which had been obtained by way of discovery in court proceedings, were confidential and could not be made available to journalists even when they had been read out in open court.[17] They maintained that the possibility of proceedings being brought against them for contempt of court had a 'chilling effect' on their right to freedom of expression. The Commission was not prepared to interpret the concept of 'victim' as encompassing every newspaper or journalist in the United Kingdom who might conceivably be affected by the decision of the House of Lords. The form of detriment required must be of a less indirect and remote nature. Nor did it consider the journalist who had actually inspected the documents in the case to be a victim since he had been able to publish the article based on the information he had received without proceedings being brought against him. However, the Commission indicated in *Times Newspapers Ltd v UK*[18] that a newspaper publisher could claim to be the victim of a breach of Article 10, even though no defamation proceedings have been brought against any of its newspapers, when the law is too vague to allow the risk of prosecution to be predicted.[19] This and the *Open Door* and *Leigh* decisions demonstrate the elasticity of the notion of victim in the Commission's case-law as well as the uncertain and shifting boundaries between those directly affected by a particular measure and those remotely affected.[20]

It is, however, clear that the Convention does not provide for applications in the form of an *actio popularis*. Thus it is not open to a citizen to complain

15 A 246 para 41 (1992).
16 *No 10039/82*, 38 DR 74 (1984).
17 *Home Office v Harman* [1981] 1 All ER 532.
18 *No 14631/89*, 65 DR 307 (1990).
19 Ibid.
20 In respect of certain complaints (eg the right to vote or to stand in an election or to free elections generally in Article 3 of the First Protocol) an application could be brought by any citizen eligible to vote or arguably by any political party: see *Liberal Party, Mrs R and Mr P v UK No 8765/79*, 21 DR 211 (1980).

in general of the provisions of abortion legislation unless he can show that he is in some way affected.[1] On the other hand, an individual can complain of an administrative practice in breach of the Convention if he brings *prima facie* evidence of such practice and of his being a victim of it.[2] Professional associations and non-governmental organisations, to be regarded as victims, must show that they are in some way affected by the measure complained of. They can only act on behalf of their members if they identify them and provide evidence of authority to represent them. In *Norris v Ireland*,[3] for example, the Commission did not regard the National Gay Federation as a victim of the law prohibiting homosexual acts. Churches, newspapers and trade unions may of course be directly affected in their own right.[4] Companies can also claim to be victims of violations of, for example, property rights or the right to have proceedings heard within a reasonable time. However, not all the rights in the Convention are of relevance to them.[5] In *Pine Valley v Ireland*[6] the Court upheld the status of victim of the two applicant companies even though one had been struck off the register of companies and a receiver had been appointed for the other. The Court considered that the companies were no more than vehicles through which the third applicant (Mr Healy) had sought to implement a property development for which outline planning permission had been granted. To draw a distinction between the applicants was thus regarded as artificial. In addition the company that had been dissolved had initiated the national proceedings and obtained the planning permission. This was considered sufficient to permit a claim to be made on its behalf. Insolvency was also considered immaterial to the Article 25 issue. In *Neves e Silva v Portugal*[7]

---

1   *X v Austria No 7045/75*, 7 DR 87 (1976). See also the cases in 5 Digest 382-389.

2   *Donnelly v UK Nos 5577-83/72*, 43 CD 122 at 145-146 (1975).

3   *No 10581/83*, 44 DR 132 (1985) See also *Asociación de Aviadores de la Republica v Spain No 10733/84*, 41 DR 211 (1988) and *CFDT v EC No 10983/84*, 47 DR 225 (1986). Similarly the applicant unions in *Purcell v Ireland No 15404/89*, 70 DR 262 (1991) were not considered victims of broadcasting restraints affecting their members.

4   *X and Church of Scientology v Sweden No 7805/77*, 16 DR 68 (1979); *Church of Scientology and 128 members v Sweden No 8282/78*, 21 DR 109 (1980); and *Council of Civil Service Unions v UK No 11603/85*, 50 DR 228 (1987).

5   Eg a company could not claim to be a victim of a violation of, *inter alia*, Article 2 (right to life) or Article 3 (freedom from torture, inhuman or degrading treatment) or Article 8 (private life). In *Open Door and Dublin Well Woman and Others v Ireland* A 246 (1992) the Commission found that the Open Door clinic could not make a privacy complaint on behalf of its clients (pp 60-61). The issue was left open by the Court (paras 81-83).

6   A 222 paras 40-43 (1991). But cf *Mendes Godinho e Filhos v Portugal No 11724/85*, 64 DR 72 (1990).

7   A 153-A para 39 (1989). But see *Yarrow v UK No 9266/81*, 30 DR 155 (1983) where the Commission held that minority shareholders will not usually have a personal interest sufficient to entitle them to qualify as 'victims' of any alleged violation in respect of acts directed against the company: the effects of such acts were considered too indirect and the shareholders' interests were adequately protected by the company itself being able to lodge an application. Majority shareholders were considered to have a direct personal interest in the complaint since they were, in reality, individuals carrying on their business through the medium of the company. See also *X v Austria No 1706/62*, 9 YB 112 at 130 (1966) and *Kaplan v UK No 7598/76*, 21 DR 5 at 23-24 (1980) Com Rep: CM Res DH (1981) 1.

the Court also considered as irrelevant, for purposes of a 'reasonable time' complaint under Article 6(1), the fact that the applicant was only a minority shareholder of a company.

Both the Commission and the Court have accepted that individuals can complain of legislation, in the absence of a measure of implementation, if they run the risk of being directly affected by it. In *Johnston v Ireland*[8] and *Marckx v Belgium*[9] the applicants risked being directly affected by provisions of succession legislation concerning children born out of wedlock. In *Dudgeon v UK* and *Norris v Ireland* the Court considered that the very existence of legislation prohibiting private homosexual acts continuously and directly affected the applicants' private life – either they respected the law and refrained from the prohibited behaviour or they engaged in such acts and became liable to criminal prosecution.[10] A similar approach, *mutatis mutandis*, was applied by the Commission concerning complaints by women against abortion legislation[11] and by parents against a Swedish law forbidding them from corporally punishing their children.[12] In *Campbell and Cosans v UK*[13] the Commission accepted that the applicants' children had a direct and immediate personal interest in complaining about corporal punishment by virtue of attending a school where it was practised even though they had not actually been punished. But a person cannot claim to be a victim of a violation of the right to a public hearing before a professional disciplinary body, if he has not asserted that right.[14]

In a number of cases the Court has indicated that the concept of victim refers to a person who is directly affected even though he may not be prejudiced by the act or omission in issue. In *Eckle v FRG*,[15] for example, the applicant had complained under Article 6(1) of the length of two sets of criminal proceedings. However, the prosecution had been discontinued in one of them, on account of the excessive length of the proceedings, and in the

8 A 112 para 42 (1986).
9 A 31 para 27 (1979).
10 A 45 para 41 (1981) and A 142 paras 28-34 (1988). In both cases there had been no prosecution; but there was no stated policy *not* to enforce the law. There was thus a risk of prosecution. A similar approach was followed by the Court in *Modinos v Cyprus*, A 259 paras 17-24 (1993), as regards the question whether there was an interference with the applicant's rights under Article 8 where the law had been described as a 'dead letter' because of its incompatibility with constitutional provisions. See also the dissenting opinion of Judge Pikis in the *Modinos* case.
11 *Brüggemann and Scheuten v FRG No 6959/75*, 5 DR 103-115 (1976). The applicants had not claimed to be pregnant or to have been refused an abortion or to have been prosecuted for unlawful abortion. The Commission considered that the legal regulation of abortion is an interference with private life. The decision has been criticised for its width since not all women are in fact liable to be affected by the legislation: see Rogge, loc cit at n 149 above, p 541 (n 15).
12 *7 individuals v Sweden No 8811/79*, 29 DR 104 at 109 (1982) – the parents had not been prosecuted.
13 A 48 (1982) Com Rep, paras 116-117.
14 *Guenoun v France No 13562/88*, 66 DR 181 (1991).
15 A 51 paras 64-70 (1982). The approach of the Court in *Eckle* has been followed by the Commission in length of proceedings cases: see *S v FRG No 10232/83*, 35 DR 213 (1983) and *Conrad v FRG No 13020/87*, 56 DR 264 (1988).

other the sentence had been mitigated. The Court stated that the existence of prejudice was not a pre-condition to the finding of a breach and was only relevant when it came to assessing just satisfaction under Article 50. It accepted, however, that an applicant would be deprived of his status of 'victim' where the national authorities had acknowledged, either expressly or in substance, the breach of the Convention and then afforded redress for it.

This approach was followed in *Lüdi v Switzerland*[16] where the applicant's sentence had been reduced to what his lawyer had suggested at the trial. He had complained *inter alia* under Article 8 of the activities of an undercover agent whose evidence had led to his conviction on drug charges. The Court rejected the argument that he was no longer a victim since the authorities, far from acknowledging a violation, had expressly decided that the actions of the undercover agent were in fact compatible with the Convention.

The Commission's approach to this issue has, on the other hand, been less strict. It has taken the view that victim status requires the applicant to have been harmed in some way. If the basis of the grievance has been remedied he can no longer claim to be a victim. In *X v Denmark*,[17] for example, the applicant had complained of the state of Danish law which did not permit a natural father to have the custody of his child without the mother's consent. In the course of the proceedings Danish law was amended to reinforce the legal status of the father of a child born out of wedlock. The Commission considered that, since the applicant's complaint was effectively met by the new legislation, he could no longer claim to be a victim. The grievance had thus been removed by an intervening event. This decision, however, can be criticised on the grounds that the national authorities had not recognised that there had been a breach in the applicant's case and that in such circumstances he ought not to be deprived of a ruling on a complaint which raised important Convention issues of general interest. Other decisions of the Commission in this area are also problematic. For example, should a favourable settlement of a labour dispute with a state body deprive an applicant of victim status in respect of a quite separate Convention complaint concerning the length of the proceedings?[18] Should compensation be considered sufficient to remove the victim status of a person alleging torture?[19] On the other hand, there can be no quarrel with decisions which

---

16 A 238 para 34 (1992). See also *Adolf v FRG* A 49 para 37 (1982); *De Jong v Netherlands* A 77 paras 40-41 (1984); *Duinhof and Duif v Netherlands* A 78 paras 36-37 (1984); *Groppera v Radio AG v Switzerland* A 173 paras 46-51 (1990).

17 *No 7658/76*, 15 DR 128 (1978). See also *Pitarque v Spain No 13420/87*, 62 DR 258 (1989) (non-enforcement of criminal conviction and the granting of a pardon – not considered to be a victim).

18 *Preikhzas v FRG No 6504/74*, 16 DR 5 (1978) Com Rep; CM Res DH (78) 8 (the Commission found that the applicant could no longer claim to be a victim). The Commission does not consider either acquittal or a civil judgment in one's favour to exclude a complaint under Article 6(1) concerning the length of proceedings: *Mlynek v Austria No 11688/85*, 62 DR 120 (1988) Com Rep; CM Res DH (1989) 19. See above, Ch 6.

19 *Donnelly v UK No 5577-83/72*, 4 DR 4 at 64 (1975). Surely the general interest in investigating such claims ought to prevent such a complaint from being 'bought off'? – see above, pp 616-617.

find that the applicant is not a victim where a deportation order has been lifted[20] or where an applicant complaining of a breach of due process rights under Article 6(3) is acquitted[1] or where adequate compensation has been paid to a person dismissed from employment for belonging to a trade union[2] or where the specific complaint has been examined and remedied satisfactorily by the authorities.[3] Where a settlement has been reached the adequacy of its terms and the strength of the applicant's bargaining position are factors to be taken into account.[4]

The Commission has rendered Convention proceedings more effective by permitting applications not only by the person immediately affected (the direct victim) but also by an indirect victim.[5] For example, in respect of alleged violations of the right to life (Article 2) close relatives such as spouses or parents will be regarded as indirectly affected. In one case a widow was considered to be an indirect victim of the terrorist killings of her husband and unmarried brother and a direct victim of the continuing situation in Northern Ireland as regards her own security.[6] Family members of those who have been detained or relatives of physically or mentally incapable victims such as young children, hospital patients and persons of unsound mind – may also be seen as indirect victims.[7] Broadly speaking the concept of indirect victims encompasses those who are also prejudiced by the violation as well as those who may have a valid personal interest in having the violation established such as parents or persons *in loco parentis*. Conceptually, the indirect victim is to be distinguished from the representation of a direct victim by a third party (where there is no personal link) or the continuation of Convention proceedings by an heir or personal representative.[8] A person may also be able to claim that he is directly affected as a consequence of a violation of the rights of someone else (eg spouse or parents of a person liable to be deported or a wife complaining that damage to her husband's property also affected her own property).[9] As can be seen from the above examples, the different categories of victimhood often shade into one another.

---

20 *No 7706/76*, 4 Digest 409.
1 *X v Austria No 5575/72*, 1 DR 44 (1974) and *Reed v UK No 7630/76*, 19 DR 113 at 142 (1979).
2 *Frederiksen v Denmark No 12719/87*, 56 DR 237 (1988).
3 *X v UK No 7826/77*, 14 DR 197 (1978) and *A, B, C and D v FRG No 8290/78*, 18 DR 176 (1979).
4 See, for example, *Inze v Austria* A 126 paras 30-34 (1987).
5 See the cases in 4 Digest 390-395.
6 *Mrs W v UK No 9348/81*, 32 DR 190 (1983). See also *Amekrane v UK No 5961/72*, 16 YB 356 (1973); *Mrs W v Ireland No 9360/81*, 32 DR 211 (1983); *Wolfgram v FRG No 11257/84*, 49 DR 213 (1986); and *Stewart v UK No 10044/82*, 39 DR 162 (1984).
7 *Paton v UK No 8416/78*, 19 DR 244 at 248 (1980) (a prospective father alleging a denial of the right to life on behalf of the foetus following the termination of his wife's pregnancy was considered to be so closely affected that he was a 'victim').
8 See above, p 591.
9 *X and Y v Belgium No 1478/62*, 6 YB 591 at 618-620 (1964) and *Abdulaziz, Cabales and Balkandali v UK Nos 9214/80, 9473/81, 9474/81*, 29 DR 176 at 181-182 (1982).

In cases concerning imminent deportation or extradition it is clearly established that an applicant can claim to be a victim of an alleged violation of Article 3 even though the act has not yet taken place. Such an approach is linked to the imperative of seeking to protect an applicant from harm that may be irremediable.[10] In *Vijayanathan and Pusparajah v France*,[11] however, the Court found that the applicants who had been ordered to leave the country could not claim to be victims since they had not yet been served with an expulsion order. In reality their expulsion from France was not imminent since it was open to them to challenge an eventual expulsion order before the courts with suspensive effect.

ii. Competence *ratione materiae*

The competence of the Commission only extends to examining complaints concerning the rights and freedom contained in the Convention and its Protocols. Complaints concerning rights not covered by the Convention are dismissed as incompatible *ratione materiae*. Thus, for example, the Convention does not guarantee, as such, a right to asylum[12] or a right to acquire a particular nationality[13] or a right to be detained in a particular prison,[14] or the right to work[15] or to diplomatic protection.[16] Nor does it guarantee a right to settle in a foreign state[17] or financial assistance from the state to maintain a certain standard of living.[18] The list is far from exhaustive. However, the fact that a particular right is not contained in the Convention does not necessarily mean that all Convention protection is excluded. For example, while the right to asylum is not guaranteed, expulsion or extradition to a country where there are substantial reasons to fear that the person may be subjected to inhuman and degrading treatment may amount to a breach of Article 3 by the sending state.[19] Similarly, while the Convention does not guarantee a right of appeal in criminal cases, the national authorities must respect the rights contained in Article 6 where an appeal is in fact possible.[20] The Commission has also stated that it cannot examine errors of law or fact that may have been committed by national courts. In this sense it is not a tribunal of fourth instance. It does, however, have competence under Article 6 to examine whether the national

10 *Soering v UK* A 161 (1989) Com Rep, para 199.
11 A 241-B para 46 (1992). Curiously the applicants had not challenged the effectiveness of this court remedy (which must be exercised within 48 hours) under Article 13.
12 Nor does it guarantee an alien a right to enter or to reside in a particular country: *inter alia*, *K and W v Netherlands No 11278/84*, 43 DR 216 (1985).
13 Ibid.
14 *McQuiston v UK No 11208/84*, 46 DR 182 (1986).
15 *X v Denmark No 6907/75*, 3 DR 153 (1975).
16 *Bertrand Russell Peace Foundation Ltd v UK No 7597/76*, 14 DR 117 (1978) and *Kaplan v UK No 12822/87*, 54 DR 201 (1987).
17 *C v UK No 10427/83*, 47 DR 85 (1986).
18 *Andersson and Kullman v Sweden No 11776/85*, 46 DR 251 (1986).
19 See above, pp 73-80.
20 See above, Ch 6.

proceedings complied with the requirements of a fair procedure.[1] It is also free to consider whether the interpretation of national law and its application to the facts of the case infringes a substantive provision of the Convention.[2]

An interesting distinction arises, in this context, between the Commission's competence to examine individual cases under Article 25 as opposed to inter-state cases under Article 24. Article 25 limits the Commission examination to 'a violation by one of the High Contracting Parties of the rights set forth in [the] Convention'; whereas Article 24 enables a contracting party to refer to the Commission 'any alleged breach of the provisions of the Convention by another High Contracting Party'. A state could therefore complain under Article 24 that another contracting party had failed under Article 28(1)(a) to 'furnish all necessary facilities' to enable the Commission to carry out its post-admissibility investigation or of breaches of other obligations under the Convention (eg Article 57)[3] other than the duty to secure rights and freedoms. In *Cruz Varas v Sweden*,[4] however, the Court had no difficulty in accepting that an individual could complain under Article 25(1) of a breach of the state obligation not to hinder the effective exercise of the right of individual petition. According to the Court:

'Such an obligation confers on an applicant a right of a procedural nature distinguishable from the substantive rights set out under Section I of the Convention or its Protocols. However, it flows from the very essence of this procedural right that it must be open to individuals to complain of alleged infringements of it in Convention proceedings. In this respect also the Convention must be interpreted as guaranteeing rights which are practical and effective as opposed to theoretical and illusory.'

The same argument suggests that an individual could also complain of a breach of the Article 28 obligation to 'furnish all necessary facilities' to assist the Commission's examination of his petition since such cooperation is essential to a proper investigation of his case.

Complaints concerning rights in respect of which the state has filed a reservation under Article 64 will also be rejected on this basis. The

1　The so-called 'Fourth Instance' doctrine (see above, p 15). See, *inter alia*, *X v Belgium No 8417/78*, 16 DR 200 (1979) and *D v FRG No 10812/84*, 44 DR 211 (1985). See also *Barberà, Messegué and Jabardo v Spain* discussed above at p 203.
2　For example, a determination by a national court that the use of lethal force by the security forces was 'reasonable' in the circumstances, while an important factor to be taken into account by the Commission, would not prevent it from applying Convention standards to the examination of the issue – see the *Stewart* and *Kelly* cases discussed above at p pp 47, 51.
3　Article 57 requires the state, on a request by the Secretary General of the Council of Europe, to furnish an explanation of the manner in which its internal law ensures the effective implementation of any Convention provision. See above, p 5.
4　A 201 para 99 (1991). The Commission had frequently examined this issue in its case-law but usually decided that no further action was called for – see eg *Campbell v UK No 12323/86*, 57 DR 148 (1988) and *X v UK No 5265/71*, 3 DR 5 (1975).

Convention institutions are, however, competent to examine whether the reservation is in conformity with Article 64.[5]

iii. Competence *ratione temporis*

The Commission has no competence to examine complaints concerning matters which take place before the entry into force of the treaty or the date of ratification by the state in question. The temporal effect of the Convention will also depend on the declaration accepting the right of individual petition. In most cases the declaration will limit the Commission's competence to acts or events which occur subsequent to the declaration. Where the declaration is silent on this point, the Commission's competence to examine petitions, in accordance with a principle of international law, dates back to the date of ratification of the treaty. The Commission, however, has tempered the effects of this principle in the case of *X v France*[6] where it held that the applicant was bound to apply to the Commission within six months of the date of the final domestic decision even if this occurred before the date of the Article 25 declaration.

The notion of a continuing situation may be of relevance in this context. In *De Becker v Belgium*,[7] for example, the applicant's conviction for treason had taken place before Belgium had ratified the Convention. However, his complaint to the Commission concerned the continuing restrictions on his freedom of expression as a result of his punishment. This situation continued after Belgium had ratified. Similarly, in *X v Belgium*[8] the Commission considered that the decision of a military court in 1948 to deprive the applicant of the right to vote gave rise to a continuing situation.

Does the Commission have competence to examine a complaint which takes its origin in events prior to the Article 25 declaration but ends with a court decision subsequent to that date? In *Ventura v Italy*[9] the applicant was detained on remand from 1971-1976. The Italian authorities had recognised the right of petition in respect of acts subsequent to 31 July 1973. The Commission considered that it had no competence *ratione temporis* prior to this date. However, in examining the length of detention undergone subsequently it could take account of the stage which the proceedings had reached. To that extent it could have regard to the previous detention in appreciating the length of the later period. This approach has been endorsed by the Court in many cases.[10] In *X v Italy*,[11] the Commission held that it was

5 For discussion on reservations under the Convention see above, p 22.
6 *No 9587/81*, 29 DR 228 (1982) – see above, p 622.
7 *No 214/56*, 2 YB 215 at 234 (1958).
8 *No 8701/79*, 18 DR 250 (1979).
9 *No 7438/76*, 12 DR 38 (1978).
10 *Foti v Italy* A 56 para 53 (1982); *Milasi v Italy* A 119 para 14 (1987); *Martins Moreira v Portugal* A 143 para 43 (1988); *Neves e Silva v Portugal* A para 153-A 40 (1989); and *Moreira de Azevedo v Portugal* A 189 para 70 (1990).
11 *No 8261/78*, 18 DR 150 (1979) and *X, Y and Z v Switzerland No 6916/75*, 6 DR 107 at 111 (1976).

competent to examine appeal proceedings which had occurred subsequent to the date of acceptance but not the proceedings at first instance which pre-dated the acceptance.

The Court's judgment in *Stamoulakatos v Greece*,[12] however, modifies the Commission's approach concerning appeal proceedings somewhat. The applicant was convicted *in absentia* of three separate criminal offences in proceedings prior to Greece's acceptance on 19 November 1985. In 1986 he appealed against the judgment effectively seeking a re-hearing of the charges against him. He had argued before the Convention institutions that the appeals could give rise to a violation of Article 6 in their own right. The Court considered that, although the appeals were lodged after the 'critical' date of 19 November 1985, they were closely bound up with the proceedings that led to his conviction. In the appeal proceedings he had attacked the unlawfulness of the summonses and of the service of the judgments given *in absentia*. In the Court's judgment, to divorce the appeals from the events which gave rise to them would be 'tantamount to rendering Greece's declaration nugatory'. It remains to be seen whether the *ratio* of *Stamoulakatos* is limited to cases concerning trial *in absentia* where the appellant seeks a re-trial or whether the logic of the Court's approach can be broadly applied to all appeal proceedings. Since an appeal procedure is necessarily 'closely bound up' with the trial proceedings a wider application of the principle appears defensible. On the other hand, where it is evident that the breach of the Convention occurs before the appeal courts themselves (for example, non-observance of the rights of the defence) the complaint should be seen as coming after the declaration.

As regards inter-state cases, the position is different with regard to events occurring before ratification by the applicant state. The Commission established, in *Austria v Italy*,[13] that Austria's complaint was not inadmissible *ratione temporis* because it related to facts which had occurred prior to Austria's ratification of the Convention. Given the objective character of Convention obligations, the principle of reciprocity was held to be inapplicable. Finally, questions of the Commission's competence *ratione temporis* arose in the *Second Greek* case[14] which had been submitted between the date of denunciation of the Convention by Greece and the date on which the denunciation took effect six months later (Article 65(1) and (2). The Commission held that it was competent to examine the matter since in the light of Article 65(2) Greece was still bound by the Convention at the time of the complaint.

---

12 A 271 paras 29-34 (1993).
13 *No 788/60*, 4 YB 116 at 142 (1961).
14 *No 4448/70*, 13 YB 108 at 120 (1970). The case was later struck off the list in 1976 at the request of the applicant states, Greece having re-joined the Convention fold.

iv. Competence *ratione loci*

a.   The concept of 'jurisdiction' in Article 1

The Commission has consistently held that the notion of 'jurisdiction' in Article 1 is not confined to acts within the national territory. Were it otherwise the acts of the state abroad would be immune from Convention control. In *Cyprus v Turkey*[15] it held that state responsibility may be incurred by acts of the authorised agents of the state, including diplomatic or consular agents and members of the armed forces, which produced effects outside the national territory. Such agents remain under the state's jurisdiction when abroad and bring persons and property within the 'jurisdiction' to the extent that they exercise authority over them. Turkey's responsibility was thus engaged on the grounds that members of the Turkish armed forces in Cyprus exercised authority over persons and property there. The Commission rejected the claim that responsibility could only be incurred if Turkey had annexed Cyprus or established military or civil government there. In *Hess v UK*,[16] on the other hand, the Commission did not consider that the United Kingdom's participation in the 'four power' agreement responsible for the administration of Spandau prison, where Hess was imprisoned, was a matter within the 'jurisdiction' of the United Kingdom. It was of the view that the joint authority could not be divided into four separate jurisdictions for purposes of Convention responsibility although it attached considerable weight to the fact that the agreement had been entered into prior to the government's ratification of the Convention. However, in *X and Y v Switzerland*[17] the Commission found that the exercise by Switzerland of special treaty responsibilities on behalf of Liechtenstein brought all those to whom they applied under Swiss jurisdiction for the purposes of Article 1.

This approach, however, had not been extended to read into Article 1 a right to diplomatic protection or intervention. It was argued in the case of *Bertrand Russell Peace Foundation Ltd v UK*[18] that the government should have intervened diplomatically with the Soviet authorities in order to protect the applicant's mail which was not being delivered by the Soviet postal authorities. The Commission considered that Article 1 could not be interpreted so as to give rise to any obligation on the contracting parties to ensure that non-contracting states respect the rights guaranteed by the Convention. The fact that the 'victim' resided in the United Kingdom was not enough to give rise to an issue within the United Kingdom's jurisdiction. However, the Commission appears to have left open the question whether there might be a positive obligation under Article 8 on diplomatic authorities abroad to protect family life. In one case the consular authorities

---

15 *Nos 6780/74 and 6950/75 (First and Second Applications)*, 2 DR 125 at 136-137 (1975).
16 No 6231/75, 2 DR 72 (1975) (cf *CFDT v France*, see above, pp 631-632).
17 *Nos 7289/75 and 7349/76*, 9 DR 57 (1977) – the applicants complained of a prohibition of entry by the Swiss Federal aliens' police with effect for Swiss and Liechtenstein territory.
18 *No 7597/76*, 14 DR 117 at 124 (1978). See also *Mrs W v UK No 9348/81*, 32 DR 190 (1983).

of the United Kingdom were held to have done all that could reasonably be expected of them to assist a British national whose child had been abducted by her Jordanian husband.[19] Against the background of both of these cases, it is conceivable that in certain circumstances diplomatic authorities, while not obliged to intervene diplomatically to protect individuals from the acts of a non-contracting state, may be obliged to take other forms of positive action to fulfil their own substantive Convention obligations.

The above interpretation of the territorial reach of the Convention was approved by the Court in *Drozd and Janousek v France and Spain*,[20] where it found that neither respondent state could be held liable for the acts of Andorra, and in *Loizidou v Turkey* (Preliminary Objections).[1] In the latter case, which concerned the acts of Turkish armed forces in northern Cyprus, the Court addressed the question of 'jurisdiction' where military intervention was involved. Departing from the notion that 'jurisdiction' required the direct intervention of a state agent, which characterises the Commission's approach, it held that: 'the responsibility of a contracting party may also arise when, as a consequence of military action – whether lawful or unlawful – it exercises effective control of an area outside its national territory'. The obligation to secure, in such an area, the rights and freedoms set out in the Convention, 'derives from the fact of such control whether it be exercised by a state directly, through its armed forces, or through a subordinate local administration'.[2] The Court went on to note that it was not in dispute that the applicant's loss of control of her property stemmed from the occupation of northern Cyprus by Turkish troops and that the applicant was prevented by those troops from gaining access to her property. In the Court's view such acts were 'capable of falling within Turkish "jurisdiction" within the meaning of Article 1'.[3]

The above statement of the basis of responsibility goes further than that developed by the Commission. Whereas the Commission emphasises control over persons and property, the Court has introduced the test of 'effective control of an area outside its national territory'. It has now been placed beyond doubt that the Convention is applicable to army operations abroad

19 *X v UK No 7547/76*, 12 DR 73 (1977).
20 A 240 paras 91-98 (1992). See Lush, 42 ICLQ 897 (1993).
1   A 310 paras 56-64 (1995)
2   Id, para 62.
3   Id, para 64. The judgment was limited to preliminary objections, *inter alia, ratione loci*, which had been raised by the Turkish government. The Court made it clear that it was not called at that stage of its procedure to examine whether Turkey was actually responsible under the Convention or to establish the principles that govern state responsibility under the Convention in a situation like that obtaining in the northern part of Cyprus. These questions belonged to the merits phase of the procedure. The Court's inquiry was limited to determining whether the matters complained of (prevention of access to property in northern Cyprus) 'are capable of falling within the "jurisdiction" of Turkey even though they occur outside her national territory': id, para 61. In this connection, the applicant had argued for the application of principles of state responsibility under international law, namely automatic accountability for violations or rights occurring in territories over which the state had physical control: id, para 57.

and, more subtly, to any subordinate administration that results from such activities. The approach is thus of great significance for the writ of the Convention system. The effect of *Loizidou v Turkey* (Preliminary Objections) is that the state cannot insulate itself from the Convention scrutiny either by operating beyond state frontiers,[4] by qualifying its acceptance of the optional clauses by a limitation *ratione loci*,[5] or by setting up surrogate administrations.

While a contracting party cannot be held responsible for acts committed by private parties or by other states in another country, the act of surrendering a person, either by deportation or extradition, may give rise to responsibility under Article 3 of the Convention. It is clear from the Court in *Soering v UK*[6] that in assessing that responsibility the situation in the country to which the person would be subjected if expelled will be appreciated in the light of Article 3 standards. The same may be true in the reverse situation. In the *Drozd and Janousek* case,[7] the question arose whether France's detention of the applicants was lawful under Article 5(1). The applicants had been convicted in Andorra and, on the basis of long-standing customary arrangements between the two countries, imprisoned in France. Ought France to have satisfied herself that the trial in Andorra was conducted in conformity with Article 6 requirements? The Court did not consider that France's Convention obligations went that far. It did, however, state that contracting parties are obliged to refuse their cooperation if it emerges that the conviction is the result of a 'flagrant' denial of justice. Accordingly, in their cooperation with other states, contracting parties are not free to turn a blind eye on 'flagrant' infringements of Convention standards by other countries.

b.   Article 63

Article 63(1), commonly referred to as the 'colonial clause', provides that a state may declare that 'the present Convention shall extend to all or any of the territories of whose international relations it is responsible'. Article 63(3) provides that:

---

4   Cf *Sale v Haitian Centers Council* (113 S Ct 2549 (1993)) where the US Supreme Court held that the principle of 'non-refoulment' of refugees in Article 33 of the 1951 Convention Relating to the Status of Refugees did not apply to acts of the coast guard on the high seas.
5   See above, pp 580–584.
6   A 161 para 91 (1989). The Court stated: 'The establishment of such responsibility inevitably involves an assessment of conditions in the requesting country against the standards of Article 3 of the Convention. None the less, there is no question of adjudicating on or establishing the responsibility of the receiving country, whether under general international law, under the Convention or otherwise . . . ' Notwithstanding this disclaimer, a judgment of a situation in another country is still being made and is doubtless perceived as such abroad.
7   A 240 paras 108-111 (1992). The notion of 'flagrant' is unclear – contrast with the Court's statement in *Soering* that an issue might exceptionally be raised under Article 6 by an extradition decision in circumstances where the fugitive has suffered or risks suffering a flagrant denial of a fair trial – A 161 para 113 (1989).

'The provisions of this Convention shall be applied in such territories with due regard . . . to local requirements'.

In a 1961 case brought against Belgium, it was argued that since, at the time of the events complained of, the Belgian Congo formed an integral part of the national territory, Article 63 was inapplicable. The Commission held that, whatever the exact status of the Congo, it clearly came within the category of territories referred to in Article 63. In the absence of a special declaration, the Commission thus lacked competence *ratione loci.*[8] However, it should not be inferred from this case that Article 63 applies to all overseas territories, whatever their status, if they are situated outside the European continent. The determining factor is the status given to the territory under domestic law: as a dependent territory of the kind intended to be covered by Article 63 or as an integral part of the national territory. France, for example, has chosen to treat a number of overseas territories, the '*départements d'outre mer*' (DOM),[9] on the same footing as metropolitan '*départements*' and not at all as dependent territories. The Convention institutions should arguably respect that choice and regard those overseas '*départements*' as coming within the ordinary jurisdiction of France and not as being covered by Article 63. France would seem to have opted for a different solution with regard to its '*térritoires d'outre mer*',[10] which have a slightly different status leaving a greater degree of autonomy to the local authorities.[11]

On the other side of the coin, Article 63 has been recognised as applying to dependent territories situated in Europe and having no special cultural or development differences in comparison with the metropolitan territory of the contracting state concerned. Such recognition has been given by the Court in cases against the United Kingdom concerning the Isle of Man and Guernsey.[12] Here again decisive importance was attached to the intention of the respondent state. In the *Gillow* case,[13] the Court relied on a statement issued in 1950 by the United Kingdom government to the effect that Guernsey was to be regarded as a territory for the international relations of which the United Kingdom is responsible, in order to hold that an express declaration of extension under Article 4 of the First Protocol (the equivalent

8 *X v Belgium No 1065/61*, 4 YB 260 at 264-268 (1961).
9 Guadeloupe, Guyana, Martinique and Réunion.
10 Antarctic territories, New Caledonia, Pacific territories, Saint Pierre and Miquelon. See also *Piermont v France* A 314 (1995).
11 In the French instrument of ratification of 3 May 1974 it was stated: 'The government of the Republic further declares that the Convention shall apply to the whole territory of the Republic, having due regard, where the overseas territories are concerned, to local requirements, as mentioned in Article 63 . . . ' (*Collected Texts*, p 93). This declaration introduces an element of ambiguity since it alludes to Article 63 without including an express declaration of extension as such. Arguably it is tantamount to an express and separate declaration. For a list of Article 63 declarations, see *Collected Texts*, pp 88 ff.
12 *Tyrer v UK* A 26 (1978) and *Gillow v UK* A 109 paras 60-62 (1986).
13 *Gillow v UK*, ibid. The United Kingdom had originally argued the case before the Commission and Court on the mistaken assumption that the Protocol applied to Guernsey. The mistake was discovered eight months after the oral hearing before the Court.

of Article 63 of the Convention) was necessary for the application of the Protocol to the island. Nevertheless it must be questioned whether the Isle of Man and Guernsey, given the closeness of their links to the metropolitan territory and the fact that they are situated in Europe, ought to require a special declaration of a type intended for the colonial territories.

The question has arisen whether responsibility under the Convention could arise through the exercise of 'jurisdiction' in respect of a territory which had not been the subject of an Article 63 declaration. In *Bui Van Thanh v UK*[14] the applicant 'boat people' were detained in Hong Kong pending expulsion to Vietnam where they feared persecution. The United Kingdom had not made a declaration under Article 63(1) extending the Convention to the territory of Hong Kong. The applicants argued that the Commission had jurisdiction to examine their complaints since the policy of repatriation of Vietnamese refugees was in reality the policy of the United Kingdom and since the Hong Kong authorities exercised their functions on the basis of decisions taken by the United Kingdom. The Commission considered that it was an essential part of the scheme of Article 63 that a declaration extending the Convention be made before the Convention applied either to acts of the defendant government or to policies formulated by the government of a contracting party in the exercise of its responsibilities in relation to such territories. It concluded that even if the acts of the Hong Kong authorities were based on United Kingdom policy, it had no competence to examine the application.

The Commission's reasoning in this case is copper-fastened by the United Kingdom's declaration of acceptance of the right of individual petition which contains the following statement:

> 'This declaration does not extend to petitions in relation to anything done or occurring in any territory in respect of which the competence of the European Commission of Human Rights to receive petitions has not been recognised by the government of the United Kingdom or to petitions in relation to anything done or occurring in the United Kingdom in respect of such a territory or of matters arising there.'[15]

It is submitted that in the light of the Commission and Court's interpretation of 'jurisdiction' in Article 1, neither the above decision nor the above declaration would exclude direct responsibility for the actions of authorised agents of the state (eg armed forces) in matters unconnected with the government of the dependency.

---

14 *No 16137/90*, 65 DR 330 (1990).
15 Instrument of acceptance of the right of individual petition of 14 January 1966 (9 YB 8 (1966)) incorporated by reference in the United Kingdom's most recent renewal of 14 January 1991. It could be argued that insofar as this clause refers to Article 63 territories it is unnecessary. On the other hand, insofar as it purports to limit the United Kingdom's responsibility to acts occurring within the national territory, it is open to question as to its validity; see above *Loizidou v Turkey*, pp 581–583.

In *Tyrer v UK*[16] (birching in the Isle of Man), the Court stated:

'The system established by Article 63 was primarily designed to meet the fact that, when the Convention was drafted, there were still certain colonial territories whose state of civilisation did not, it was thought, permit the full application of the Convention.'

The 'local requirements' referred to in paragraph 3 of Article 63 may therefore permit a lower standard of compliance with the Convention's requirements in dependent territories. There are, however, limits. Thus, the Court held in the *Tyrer* case that no requirement relative to the maintenance of law and order would entitle any contracting state, under Article 63, to make use of an 'inhuman or degrading punishment' (Article 3) in any territory, whatever its state of development. It is also difficult to see how a European self-governing territory such as the Isle of Man could have any 'local requirements' allowing for a different application of the Convention from the rest of Europe. In addition, there must be proof of 'local requirements' before the Commission or the Court can have regard to them; beliefs and local public opinion do not on their own constitute such proof.[17]

16 A 26 para 38 (1978).
17 Ibid. In *Piermont v France* A 314 (1995), the Court did not consider a 'tense local political' atmosphere in French Polynesia during an election campaign to be 'local requirements' justifying an interference with Article 10 rights. These were thought to be 'circumstances and conditions' rather than 'requirements' (see paras 55-59).

CHAPTER 24

The operation of the European Court of Human Rights

The European Court of Human Rights has established itself so firmly in the constitutional landscape that it may be appropriate to regard it, at least in human rights matters, as Europe's Constitutional Court.[1] It was set up together with the Commission under Article 19 of the Convention to 'ensure the observance of the engagements undertaken by the High Contracting Parties'. It came into being on 21 January 1959 after eight states had made declarations recognising its compulsory jurisdiction. It is a measure of both the stature of the Court and the growing importance of the Convention system in the new Europe that its jurisdiction has now been accepted by all current contracting parties to the Convention. Indeed, acceptance of the Court's jurisdiction (and the right of individual petition to the Commission) by the new democracies from Eastern and Central Europe is regarded by the Council of Europe authorities as a 'political' obligation flowing from membership of the Council of Europe.

The Court has an advisory jurisdiction conferred on it by the Second Protocol which has never been availed of. On the other hand, in the exercise of its contentious jurisdiction it has handed down more than 500 judgments. The explosion in the number of cases occurred in the course of the 1980s as the Convention system became better known and as lawyers in different European countries came to realise that it gave the possibility of not only providing a remedy for their clients but also of bringing about important legal change. In 1990, for example, the number of referrals (61) almost equals the total number of cases dealt with by the Court in the first 24 years of its existence.[2]

States have undertaken to abide by the decision of the Court in any case to which they are parties (Article 53). Judgments are not, however, binding *erga omnes*. Nevertheless, Court judgments on specific issues provide a clear indication to other contracting parties as to whether their law and practice is in conformity with the Convention. It is not unusual for states not directly

---

1   See Ryssdal, in Clapham & Emmert, op cit at p 1, n 1, above and Mahoney and Prebensen, *European System*, Ch 26.
2   For statistical information concerning the Court's activities, see *Survey of Activities of the European Court of Human Rights 1959-1991*, Council of Europe, 1992, and updates for 1992, 1993 and 1994.

involved in a case to seek to bring their law into line with the Court's judgment.[3] Judgments are declaratory in nature. The Court has refrained from stipulating what corrective measures should be introduced by the state found to have breached a Convention provision or from making any other type of consequential order.[4] This remains a matter for state discretion in the light of the terms of the judgment. It falls to the Committee of Ministers of the Council of Europe to supervise the execution of the judgment of the Court (Article 54).[5]

The Convention has wisely left it to the Court to organise its own working methods (Article 55). Questions of procedure and organisation of the Court's business are thus governed by the Rules of Court.[6] The Rules, originally based on those of the International Court of Justice, do not have to be approved by any other body such as the Committee of Ministers of the Council of Europe – in contrast with the rules of the Court of Justice of the European Communities.[7] The first Rules were adopted by the Court on 18 September 1959 and have since undergone revision on various occasions. The most important changes were made in the revised rules which came into force on 1 January 1983.[8] The Rules currently in force are dated 1 February 1994. On the entry into force of the Ninth Protocol on 1 October 1994 a separate set of Rules, setting out the procedure governing reference of a case to the Court by an individual, non-governmental organisation or group of individuals came into force in respect of those states which have ratified the Protocol.[9]

1. COMPOSITION AND INDEPENDENCE OF THE COURT

Unlike the Commission, which consists of a number of members equal to that of parties to the Convention (Article 20), the Court consists of a number of members equal to that of members of the Council of Europe (at present 34). It is thus possible for a judge to be elected in respect of a state which has not yet ratified the Convention. In an early draft of the Convention prepared by the Parliamentary Assembly in 1940 a Court of seven members had been envisaged. This was rejected by the Committee of Governmental Experts on the basis that it would operate to the detriment of small states which were less likely to be represented in it. The eventual

---

3   See the examples given above, p 31.
4   See below, p 684.
5   See below, Ch 25.
6   On the Rules of Court, see Eissen, 5 AFDI 618 (1959) and Mahoney, 3 YEL 127 (1983).
7   The Rules of Court of the Court of Justice of the European Communities must be approved by the Council of Ministers: Article 188, EEC Treaty.
8   See Mahoney, loc cit at n 6, passim. For details of other amendments see Rules of Court A and B, as to which, see next footnote.
9   Rules of Court B adopted on 27 May 1993. The Rules of Court applicable to States that have not ratified the Ninth Protocol are referred to as Rules of Court A. References throughout this book are to Rules of Court A unless otherwise stated. For the text of both sets of Rules, see *Collected Texts*, pp 213-295.

compromise was to envisage a Court operating in Chambers of seven judges (now nine) but composed of a number of judges equal to that of member states.[10]

No two judges may be nationals of the same state (Article 38) although a judge need not be a national of a Council of Europe state. The present Court has currently 31 judges including those elected in respect of recent members of the Council of Europe such as Hungary, Poland, Bulgaria, Slovenia, Estonia, Lithuania and the Czech and Slovak Republics.[11]

Judges are elected by the Parliamentary Assembly of the Council of Europe (by a majority of the votes cast) from a list of candidates nominated by member states.[12] Each member shall nominate three candidates, of whom two at least shall be its nationals (Article 39(1)). Article 40 provides that judges shall be elected for nine years and are eligible for re-election. Candidates must be 'of high moral character and must either possess the qualifications required for appointment to high judicial office or be jurisconsults of recognised competence' (Article 39(3)). In practice judges are (or have been) either members of the judiciary in their own countries, professors or practising lawyers. At present there is only one woman member. Judges sit in the Court in their individual capacity and during their term of office 'they shall not hold any position which is incompatible with their independence and impartiality as members of the Court or the demands of this office' (Article 40(7)).[13] This latter provision was added by the Eighth Protocol to the Convention and reflects Rule 4 of the Rules of Court which provides that 'a judge may not exercise his functions while he is a member of a government or while he holds a post or exercises a profession which is incompatible with his independence and impartiality'. Where problems arise the plenary Court decides (Rule 4). In addition, a judge may not take part in the consideration of any case in which he has a personal interest or has previously acted as agent, advocate or adviser of a party or of a person having an interest in the case, or as a member of a tribunal or commission of inquiry, or in any other capacity (Rule 24(2) of the Rules of Court). Withdrawal of a judge from a Chamber on the ground that he has

---

10 See Velu and Ergec, pp 927-929.

11 For details of members of the Court, see Appendix I.

12 To avoid the terms of the first judges that were elected to the Court ending at the same time, Article 40 provided that four judges be elected for three-year terms and four more for six-year terms. Article 40 was subsequently amended by the Fifth Protocol to provide for an orderly three-year rotation of judges. Article 40(3) provides as follows: 'In order to ensure that, as far as possible, one third of the membership of the Court shall be renewed every three years, the Consultative Assembly may decide, before proceeding to any subsequent election, that the term or terms of office of one or more members to be elected shall be for a period other than nine years but not more than twelve and not less than six years.' A judge elected to replace a judge whose term of office has not expired shall hold office for the remainder of his predecessor's term (Rule 2(2)). An elected judge holds office until his successor has taken the oath. Thereafter he can continue to deal with cases in connection with which hearings or deliberations had already begun (Rule 2(3)).

13 Before taking up his duties each elected judge takes an oath or makes a solemn declaration that he will exercise his functions as a judge 'honourably, independently and impartially and that [he] will keep secret all deliberations' (Rule 3(1)).

sat as a judge in the national proceedings occurs from time to time.[14] In such circumstances an *ad hoc* judge is nominated.[15]

Neither the Convention nor the Rules of Court impose an age limit although the Parliamentary Assembly has requested its members not to vote for candidates who have not given an undertaking to retire when they reach the age of 75.[16] The Assembly has also requested governments to nominate candidates who are less than 70 years of age and who are prepared to give a formal undertaking that they will retire on reaching the age of 75.[17] Notwithstanding these recommendations, the Assembly has proceeded to elect judges who have not been willing to undertake to retire on reaching the age of 75. It is perhaps understandable that some judges consider it to run counter to the concept of judicial independence to give such an undertaking and prefer to leave it to the discretion of the Assembly whether or not to elect them. On the other hand, and in contrast with the position in the International Court of Justice and the Court of Justice of the European Communities, the Convention does not prevent judges from exercising any other profession outside their function as judges, providing of course that it is not incompatible with their independence and impartiality.

The independence of the judges is further secured by their entitlement under the Fourth Protocol to the General Agreement on Privileges and Immunities of the Council of Europe, *inter alia*, to immunity from personal arrest or detention and from seizure of personal baggage while exercising their functions and during official journeys. They are also entitled to immunity from legal process of every kind 'in respect of words spoken or written and all acts done by them in their official capacity' (Article 2(a)). The latter immunity from legal process continues when members have ceased to discharge their duties (Article 5).[18] The Fifth Protocol to the General Agreement on Privileges and Immunities provides that members of the Court shall be exempt from taxation on salaries, emoluments and allowances paid to them by the Council of Europe.[19]

14 See eg the withdrawal of Judge Walsh in *Pine Valley Developments Ltd v Ireland* A 222 para 3 (1991) and in *Open Door and Dublin Well Woman v Ireland* A 246 para 3 (1992) and of Judge Loizou in *Modinos v Cyprus* A 259 para 3 (1993).
15 If a judge is unable to sit or withdraws or if the Court does not include an elected judge having the nationality of a Party, the President of the Court invites the state to nominate an *ad hoc* judge (Rule 23(1)).
16 Resolution 655, Texts Adopted 1977, 29th Ord Sess, Part I. The Assembly also requested its members not to vote for candidates who have not given an undertaking to resign from government functions.
17 Recommendation 809, Texts Adopted 1977, Parl Ass, 29th Ord Sess. Governments were also requested to nominate candidates who are prepared to give a formal undertaking that they will resign from any government-dependent position they may hold.
18 Article 4 of the Fourth Protocol to the General Agreement on Privileges and Immunities provides that the documents and papers of the Court, judges and Registry, insofar as they relate to the business of the Court, shall be inviolable. Official correspondence and other official communications of the Court may not be held up or censored. The privileges and immunities granted by the Protocol can only be waived by the Court sitting in plenary session (Article 6). During the exercise of his mandate an *ad hoc* judge enjoys the same immunities as an elected judge (Article 1). The Fourth Protocol entered into force in 1961.
19 In force 1991. It has been ratified by only eight states.

The expenses of the Court are borne by the Council of Europe (Article 58). Judges receive an allowance for each day of duty and an annual retainer. The Court has its seat in Strasbourg and meets for weekly sessions (or more) at the end of every month. It elects its President and Vice-President by secret ballot for a term of three years (Rule 7). It is assisted by a registry coming under its direct control. The Registrar is responsible for the organisation and activities of the registry under the authority of the President and is elected by the Court for a renewable seven-year term of office after having consulted the Secretary General of the Council of Europe. The Registrar and the legal staff of the registry play an important role in the work of the Court, notably in organising cases for hearing, attending deliberations and preparing draft judgments in the light of the Court's deliberations.[20]

2. THE REFERRAL OF CASES TO THE COURT AND ACCEPTANCE OF COMPULSORY JURISDICTION

Under Article 48 of the Convention, cases may be brought before the Court by the following: the Commission; the contracting party whose national is alleged to be a victim; the contracting party which referred the case to the Commission and the contracting party against which the complaint has been lodged. Most of the cases considered by the Court have been referred by the Commission. Only two states (Germany and Cyprus) have availed themselves of the right to refer a case to the Court in proceedings to which they had not been a party and which concerned one of their nationals (*Soering v UK*[1] and *Loizidou v Turkey*[2]). The *Soering* case had also been referred by the Commission and the United Kingdom. Germany was thus able to take full part in the proceedings before the Court as a party arguing its point of view on an equal footing with the United Kingdom. *Ireland v UK*[3] is the only inter-state case which has been referred to the Court.

Cases cannot be brought directly before the Court. They must first of all have been brought before the Commission and declared admissible. Moreover, the Court can only examine a case after the Commission has acknowledged the failure to reach a friendly settlement and within a period of three months following the transmission of the Commission's report to the Committee of Ministers (Article 47). The contracting party concerned must also have recognised the jurisdiction of the Court by a special declaration recognising it as compulsory *ipso facto* and without special agreement, 'in all matters concerning the interpretation and application of [the] Convention' (Article 46). A state can also give its consent to a

---

20 See Rules 11-14 concerning the election of the Registrar and Deputy Registrar, the functions of the Registrar and the appointment of other officials of the Registry.
1   A 161 (1989).
2   A 310 (1995).
3   A 25 (1978).

particular case being brought before the Court which falls outside the terms of a declaration or in the absence of an Article 46 declaration. Recognition of the Court's jurisdiction 'may be made unconditionally or on condition of reciprocity on the part of several or certain other High Contracting Parties' or for a specified period (Article 46(2)).

As mentioned above, all current contracting parties have accepted the Court's compulsory jurisdiction.[4] Some states have accepted the jurisdiction of the Court for an indefinite period as in the cases of Ireland and Switzerland. Others have accepted for specified time periods (three or five years), in some cases automatically renewed in the absence of an indication to the contrary (eg Poland, Portugal). Many states have imposed a condition of reciprocity although this has not given rise to any difficulties in practice since the Court has only been called on once to examine an inter-state dispute.[5] Other conditions may be problematical. Turkey's Article 46 declaration,[6] for example, relates 'to the exercise of jurisdiction within the meaning of Article 1 of the Convention, performed within the boundaries of the national territory of the Republic of Turkey, and provided further that such matters have previously been examined by the Commission within the power conferred upon it by Turkey'. In the case of *Chrysostomos v Turkey*,[7] which concerned the actions of Turkish soldiers in the northern part of Cyprus, the Commission decided that a similar territorial restriction attached to Turkey's acceptance of the right of individual petition was not permissible under Article 25 of the Convention. The related case of *Loizidou v Turkey*, which raises questions concerning access to the applicant's property in northern Cyprus, was referred to the Court by the government of Cyprus and is pending before it on the merits.[8] The Turkish government filed *inter alia* a preliminary objection challenging the Court's jurisdiction *ratione loci* on the basis of their Article 46 declaration. In its judgment of 23 March 1995, limited to Turkey's preliminary objections, the Court upheld the Commission's opinion and found that the restriction *ratione loci* in the Article 25 and 46 declarations was invalid.[9] In a ruling of importance to the continued effectiveness of the Convention's enforcement machinery, the Court held that neither Article 25 nor Article 46 permitted restrictions other than of a temporal nature. It went on to find that the restriction *ratione loci* could be severed from the text of the declarations leaving a valid acceptance *inter alia* of the Court's jurisdiction.[10] The Court observed that there existed a practice of accepting restrictions to the acceptance of the jurisdiction of the International Court of Justice under Article 36 of the Statute and that

4   See *Collected Texts*, p 86, for details concerning Article 46 declarations. The current UK declaration is for five years until 14 January 1996.
5   Acceptance of the Court's jurisdiction in respect of the rights set out in the Fourth and Seventh Protocols requires a specific statement – see Articles 6(2) and 7(2) of these Protocols respectively.
6   Dated 22 January 1993 in respect of acts subsequent to 29 January 1990.
7   68 DR 216 (1991). See above, p 581.
8   Mrs Loizidou was one of the applicants in the *Chrysostomos* case.
9   A 310, paras 65-89.
10   See above, p 583.

Article 46 of the Convention had been modelled on Article 36 of the Statute. However, it considered that there was a fundamental difference in the role and purpose of the international tribunals which provided a 'compelling basis for distinguishing Convention practice from that of the International Court'.[11] The Court also re-affirmed and developed the Commission's case-law on the meaning of 'jurisdiction' under Article 1 and the question whether there is state responsibility for acts of the authorities outside the national territory.[12]

3. RELINQUISHMENT OF JURISDICTION: CHAMBERS, GRAND CHAMBERS AND PLENARY

Article 43 of the Convention provides that cases shall be dealt with by a Chamber composed of nine judges.[13] If the President finds that two cases concern the same state and raise similar issues he may refer the second case to the Chamber already constituted or, if there is none, constitute one Chamber to consider both cases (Rule 21(6)).[14] He may subsequently order that the proceedings in both cases be conducted simultaneously with the possibility of their eventual joinder by the Chamber (Rule 37(3)).

The President (or, failing him, the Vice-President) and the national judge sit as *ex officio* members of the Chamber.[15] The remaining members, including four substitutes, are drawn by lot by the President in the presence of the Registrar (Rule 21(4)). The Rules of Court also provide for the appointment of an *ad hoc* judge where the Court does not include an elected judge having the nationality of the defendant state or if the national judge is unable to sit or withdraws (Rule 23). The participation of a national judge in proceedings before the Court reflects a standard requirement in international tribunals.[16] His presence is considered necessary to guide the other members of the Court through the thicket of national laws and remedies and to field any questions that arise concerning the domestic context of the dispute. This guidance has become an essential feature of the Court's practice although,

11 See above, pp 581-584.
12 See above, p 642.
13 Originally there were only seven judges in a Chamber. The number was increased to nine by the Eighth Protocol which entered into force on 1 January 1990. As the Court had grown larger it was considered that the Chamber of seven had become progressively less representative of the full Court leading to an increase in the frequency of relinquishments of jurisdiction in favour of the plenary Court: Explanatory Report on the Eighth Protocol, para 45, Council of Europe, 1985.
14 There have been no cases of joinder by the Court. Various cases have been joined at the Commission stage of the procedure, eg *Drozd and Janousek v France and Spain* A 240 (1992). In *Colozza and Rubinat v Italy* A 89 (1985) the Court disjoined a case where joinder had been ordered by the Commission and gave two separate judgments.
15 This rule was introduced in 1961 to ensure that the President was able to preside in cases. The first President of the Court, Lord McNair, had been unable to sit in any case since his name had not been chosen by lot. It may be queried whether the present rule is compatible with the Article 43 requirement that members of a Chamber be chosen by lot.
16 See, for example, Article 31 of the Statute of the International Court of Justice.

unlike the Commission, it does not have a *Rapporteur* system.[17] The substitute judges, who may be called upon at any stage in the proceedings to replace a full member who is unable to sit, are present at the hearings and deliberations – in which they frequently participate – although they do not have a vote.

Prior to an amendment of the Rules of Court in 1993, if a case raised serious questions affecting the interpretation of the Convention, the Chamber relinquished jurisdiction in favour of the plenary Court. However, with the increasing number of judges that were being elected to the Court it became obvious that a forum more appropriate to thorough discussion and effective decision-making was necessary to assume the functions of the plenary. Accordingly, the Court decided to amend the Rules of Court to provide for a reduced plenary or Grand Chamber with a fixed composition of nineteen judges, to deal with such cases.[18] At the same time it was decided that the Grand Chamber could, in its turn, 'exceptionally, when the issues raised are particularly serious or involve a significant change of existing case-law' relinquish jurisdiction in favour of the plenary Court (Rule 51(5)).

Relinquishment to the Grand Chamber is optional where a case raises serious questions affecting the interpretation of the Convention but obligatory where there is the possibility of departure from previous case-law of the Court (Rule 51(1)). The Grand Chamber may either retain jurisdiction over the whole case or refer the case back to the Chamber having decided the question that gave rise to the relinquishment (Rule 51(2)). After finding a violation, the Grand Chamber may also refer a case back to the Chamber to decide the question of just satisfaction (Rule 54(3)). Reasons need not be given for the decision to relinquish and, in practice, are not (Rule 51(1)). Where the Grand Chamber relinquishes jurisdiction in favour of the plenary Court similar provisions apply (Rule 51(5) and Rule 54(3)).[19] Prior to the establishment of the system of Grand Chambers, 87 cases had come before the plenary Court.[20] Compulsory relinquishment is rare. In some cases relinquishment has occurred following

17 For an indication of the voting record of national and *ad hoc* judges, see Eissen (1986) RDPSP, 1563, 1598. The record reveals an impressive percentage of judges voting against their own countries.

18 The Grand Chamber is composed of: (a) the President and the Vice-President(s) of the Court; (b) the other members of the Chamber which has relinquished jurisdiction; (c) additional judges appointed by means of a separate drawing of lots immediately after the Chamber has relinquished jurisdiction. The quorum of the Grand Chamber is seventeen judges; see Rule 51(1)-(3).

19 The plenary Court has sole competence *inter alia* to adopt or modify the Rules of Court (Article 55 of the Convention); to elect its President or Vice-President (Rule 7(1)); to elect the Registrar and Deputy Registrar (Rules 11 and 12); to give an advisory opinion (Article 3(1), Second Protocol); to waive the privileges and immunities of judges and the Registrar and Deputy Registrar (Fourth Additional Protocol to the General Agreement on Privileges and Immunities of the Council of Europe, Articles 6 and 7(3)).

20 Out of 487 cases decided by the Court up to October 1993. See *Survey of Activities of the European Court of Human Rights 1959-1991*, p 68 and the 1992 and 1993 Updates, for cases where the Chamber has relinquished jurisdiction. The Chamber has also relinquished jurisdiction in favour of the Grand Chamber in the cases of *Loizidou v Turkey*, *Jersild v Denmark* and *Murray v UK: Survey of Activities*, loc cit, 1993 Update, pp 21-26.

the oral hearing in the case thereby giving rise to the unusual situation that the matter will be decided by judges who have not been present during the hearing. In such cases the practice of the Court has been to ask those appearing before it whether they have any objection to the case being considered by the plenary Court.[1]

It is through relinquishment (of which there is no mention in the Convention) that the Court ensures the consistency of its case-law and satisfies the objective of legal certainty. Although the Court is not formally bound by its previous decisions, in practice it scrupulously adheres to previous case-law unless there are strong grounds for departing from it.[2]

4.   PROCEDURE BEFORE THE COURT

i.   Public nature

The procedure before the Court is adversarial in nature[3] and involves both a written and an oral phase although, with the consent of those appearing before the Court, the written procedure may be dispensed with by order of the President (Rule 37(1)).[4] In stark contrast with the confidentiality of the proceedings before the Commission and the Committee of Ministers, the procedure before the Court is essentially an open and public one, although the Convention is silent on this point. Thus the report of the Commission – initially confidential as required by Article 31(2) of the Convention – is made public by the Registrar as soon as possible after the case has been brought before the Court unless the President decides otherwise (Rule 29(3)).[5] Similarly the pleadings (memorials, supplementary memorials,

1   Ibid, for details of cases where relinquishment took place after the hearing.
2   In *Cossey v UK* A 184 (1990), the Court, in considering whether it should depart from *Rees v UK* A 106 (1986), stated as follows (para 35): 'It is true that . . . the Court is not bound by its previous judgments; indeed, this is borne out by Rule 51(1) of the Rules of Court. However, it usually follows and applies its own precedents, such a course being in the interests of legal certainty and the orderly development of the Convention case-law. Nevertheless, this would not prevent the Court from departing from an earlier decision if it was persuaded that there were cogent reasons for doing so. Such a departure might, for example, be warranted in order to ensure that the interpretation of the Convention reflects societal changes and remains in line with present-day conditions.' In *Borgers v Belgium* A 214-B paras 22-29 (1991), the Court departed from its earlier judgment in the *Delcourt* case, A 11 (1970), on the grounds that the concept of fair trial had undergone a considerable evolution in the Court's case-law in respect of the importance attached to appearances and to the increased sensitivity of the public to the fair administration of justice. See further above, p 18.
3   It must be borne in mind that technically neither the applicant nor the Commission are regarded as 'parties' to the procedure – Rule 1(h) – although in practice they are treated as if they are. The Rules of Court consider only applicant or respondent states to be 'parties'. It is only therefore in inter-state cases that the procedure can be described as wholly adversarial *stricto senso*.
4   The Court can derogate from the Rules of Court 'after having consulted the party or parties, the Delegates of the Commission and the applicant' (Rule 26).
5   The practice of the Court is to release the report one week after informing the applicant and the government that the case has been brought before the Court.

Article 50 claims and verbatim record) as well as third-party interventions are public and may be obtained on application to the Registrar.[6] The hearings are also held in public unless the Court 'in exceptional circumstances' decides otherwise (Rule 18). On one occasion the President of the Court – in order to protect the interests of children in five British child-care cases – directed that the Commission's report and the written pleadings should not be made accessible to the public. The Court also directed that the oral hearings be held *in camera*.[7]

ii. Stages of proceedings: written and oral

When a contracting party intends to refer the case to the Court it must file an application indicating:

1. the parties to the proceedings before the Commission;
2. the date on which the Commission adopted its report;
3. the date on which the report was transmitted to the Committee of Ministers;
4. the object of the application;
5. the name and address of the person appointed as Agent.

When a case is brought by the Commission it must file a request containing the information set out in (a) to (d) together with the name and address of the Commission's Delegate (Rule 32(1) and (2)). It not infrequently occurs that a case will be brought to the Court by both the Commission and the respondent state, particularly in cases raising complex or controversial issues of interpretation. The request or application is subsequently transmitted to the judges, the relevant contracting party or parties mentioned in Article 48, the Commission and the applicant (usually through his lawyer) as well as the Committee of Ministers through the Secretary General of the Council of Europe. Where the case has been referred by the Commission the respondent state is requested to nominate an Agent who will be the source of all communications to the Court from the government throughout the proceedings. Any other state party that has a right to bring the case to the Court under Article 48 is invited to inform the Registrar if it wishes to avail of this right. The applicant is also asked to indicate whether he wishes to take part in the proceedings and, if so, to provide particulars of his legal representative (Rule 33(3)(d)).

The registry will then proceed to make contact with the Agent, the Delegate of the Commission and the applicant's lawyer with a view to fixing

---

6 That such documents may be publicly accessible is based on the combined reading of Rule 14(4) (which makes the Registrar responsible for requests for information) and Rule 56 (which indicates which documents may be published).

7 See the cases of *O, H, W, B, and R v UK* A 120 and 121 (1987). Following the judgment the President ordered the documents in the case to be made public subject to taking steps to protect the identity of the applicants. In *Kamasinski v Austria* A 168 para 8 (1989) part of the applicant's submissions were heard *in camera*.

time-limits (usually three months) for the submission of written memorials and for the oral hearing. The Delegate will be afforded an opportunity to file a reply to the parties' memorials. Normally the government and the applicant comment on each other's memorials – the occasion for doing this being provided by the oral hearing. The authorisation of the President is required for the submission of any document after expiry of the memorial time-limit (Rule 37(1)). Permission is normally given where there is good cause for the late submission and the opposing side and the Commission's Delegate have an adequate opportunity to study and comment on the documents in question. It not infrequently happens that the President affords an opportunity to forward written comments on a late submission within a specified time-limit subsequent to the oral hearing.

The Rules of Court provide that any claims which the applicant wishes to make under Article 50 (just satisfaction) must be set out in his memorial or, if he does not submit one, in a special document filed at least one month before the hearing (Rule 50(1)). The state must also raise any preliminary objections not later than the expiry of the time-limit for the filing of their memorial (Rule 48). Leave may also be granted to a state or to an interested party to submit written observations to the Court.

The President will usually fix the date for the hearing (Rule 38) at the same time as the organisation of the written proceedings. He also directs the hearings and prescribes the order in which those appearing before the Court shall be called on to speak. As a general rule, they last for half a day. The order of address will be formally determined by the President at a meeting he holds with the 'parties' immediately before the hearing takes place, although the registry will have already discussed this matter informally with the representatives beforehand. Generally, following an introduction by the Delegate of the Commission, the Court will hear the applicant first and then the government. However, where the Commission has found a violation the government may be authorised to speak before the applicant.

The written and oral proceedings are generally conducted in one of the official languages – English and French – although leave to use a non-official language may be granted by the President (Rule 27(2)). Where such permission is granted at the request of a state it shall be responsible for the interpretation into the official languages of the pleadings of its legal team and bear the other incidental extra expenses. Where leave is granted to an applicant the Registrar shall make the necessary arrangements for interpretation or translation of their pleadings into English or French (Rule 27(1)-(3)). A verbatim record of the hearing in both official languages is prepared and sent to the 'parties' for correction. It should be noted, however, that interpretation or translation of documents or pleadings into a non-official language is not provided for. To that extent therefore participation in the proceedings before the Court requires at least a passive knowledge of English and French.[8]

8   With the ratification of the Convention by countries from Eastern and Central Europe a case can perhaps be made out for increasing the number of official languages.

The Chamber will normally deliberate a few days after the oral hearing and, in most cases, reach a provisional conclusion. A drafting committee of two or more judges, assisted by the national judge, will then be constituted by the President in the light of the deliberations. The Convention requires that reasons shall be given for the Court's judgment (Article 51). A preliminary draft judgment, prepared by the registry, will be submitted to the drafting committee for discussion and modification. The resulting draft judgment is put before the Chamber (or Grand Chamber) for a second deliberation, the adoption of the text of the judgment and the taking of final votes. Separate concurring or dissenting opinions may be expressed by any member of the Chamber (Rule 53(2)).

The judgment is read out by the President at a public hearing in one of the two official languages. However, he may direct that notification shall count as delivery in respect of a judgment striking a case out of the list or an Article 50 (just satisfaction) judgment (Rule 54(2)). All judgments are given in English and in French. Unless the Court decides otherwise, both texts shall be authentic (Rule 27(5)). The judgment is communicated to all those concerned and transmitted by the President to the Committee of Ministers (Rule 55(3) and (4)) which has responsibility under Article 54 of the Convention to supervise its execution.

iii. Position of the individual before the Court[9]

a. The practice up to 1994

One of the paradoxes of the Convention system is that the individual, until very recently, had no right to bring his case before the Court and is not a party to the proceedings as such. The right of the individual to refer his case to the Court was originally contained in the Draft Convention drawn up by the European Movement in July 1949. It was eventually rejected by member states on the basis that the interests of the individual would always be defended by the Commission.[10] What could be more striking in a treaty concerned with individual rights including equality of arms and non-discrimination? Articles 44 and 48 make it clear that only contracting parties (and the Commission) can bring a case before the Court. Indeed, the French text of Article 44 appears to be even more restrictive of the individual's rights than the English text. Read literally it seems as if the individual was meant to play no further part in the procedure following the reference of the case to the Court.[11] The silence of the text on this point is undoubtedly a reflection of the reluctance of many states at the time of the drafting of the Convention to accept the creation of a Court of Human Rights to protect the rights of individuals. Many questions such as how the individual's case was to be pleaded before the Court were thus left unresolved. Was it open to

9 See Mahoney, p 649, n 6, above, pp 129-135.
10 Explanatory Report to the Ninth Protocol, Council of Europe, 1992; 12 HRLJ 51 (1991).
11 The French text of Article 44 reads: 'Seules les Hautes Parties contractantes et la Commission ont qualité pour se présenter devant la Cour.'

the Commission to forward its confidential report to the applicant and ask for his observations on it? Could the Commission develop and explain the applicant's comments to the Court?

Both of the above questions were raised before the Court in its first case – *Lawless v Ireland*.[12] The Irish government had submitted that it was not open to the Commission to forward its report to the applicant since it was confidential. The Court considered that, in view of the importance of the proceedings before the Court for the individual applicant, it was open to the Commission to communicate its report to him with the proviso that it must not be published and that the Commission had not exceeded its powers in this respect. The Court also rejected the Irish government's submission that the individual was, in effect, excluded entirely from the Court's proceedings. Recalling that it was the applicant who instituted the proceedings before the Commission and that he would be directly affected by any decision on the substance of his case, the Court considered that it:

> 'must bear in mind its duty to safeguard the interests of the individual . . . whereas, accordingly, it is in the interests of the proper administration of justice that the Court should have knowledge of and, if need be, take into consideration, the applicant's point of view.'[13]

In its judgment on the merits in the *Lawless* case, the Court subsequently acknowledged that the Commission has:

> '. . . all latitude, in the course of debates and insofar as it believes they may be useful to enlighten the Court, to take into account the views of the applicant concerning either the Report or any other specific point which may have arisen since the lodging of the Report.'[14]

It was also accepted that the Delegate of the Commission could be assisted during the proceedings before the Court by the applicant or a person of his choice. The Court decided that the Commission was entirely free to decide by what means it wished to establish contact with the applicant and give him an opportunity to make known his views to the Commission.[15]

In 1970 this practice was developed further when the Commission in the *Vagrancy* cases[16] sought to be assisted by the applicant's lawyer and requested that he be permitted to address the Court on specific points. The Court explicitly allowed this, against the objections of the Belgian government, but stated that the person assisting the Delegates must restrict himself in his submissions to the points indicated to him by the Delegates and was subject to their control and responsibility. From this point on, until

12 *Lawless v Ireland* (Preliminary Objections and Questions of Procedure), A 1 pp 12-16 (1960).
13 Ibid, p 15.
14 *Lawless* A 2 p 24 (1961).
15 Ibid.
16 *De Wilde, Ooms and Versyp v Belgium* (Question of Procedure) A 12 p 7 (1970).

the revision of the Rules of Court in 1982, the applicant's lawyer appeared at Court hearings to 'assist' the Delegates and was given an increasingly broad liberty to address the Court on those points he saw fit. In addition, the practice developed that the Delegates would transmit the applicant's written observations to the Court in the form of a Commission document often appended to the Delegate's memorial. In this way the procedural limitations which hampered the applicant's full participation in the proceedings were steadily eroded by the useful but paternalistic fiction that his views were expounded by the Commission.

By 1982 it had become apparent that the applicant's full legal representation before the Court had long ceased to give rise to any objections on behalf of governments and that the time was ripe to confer in effect a party status on the applicant in order to respect, as far as possible, the notion of equality of arms. The revised Rules of Court introduced in 1983 thus provided for the establishment of direct relations between the Court and the applicant and for the separate representation of the applicant once a case had been referred to the Court. As a result, the applicant is now treated by the Rules as if he was a party to the proceedings notwithstanding the limitations in Articles 44 and 48. Accordingly, he is invited to indicate whether he wishes to take part in the proceedings before the Court; is consulted by the President on the different aspects of the procedure to be followed; is sent copies of documents filed and of the judgment and is given various notifications. He may also request the adoption of interim measures or measures for obtaining evidence, file written pleadings, appear at oral hearings, claim just satisfaction under Article 50 and negotiate friendly settlements.

Apart from being unable to lodge preliminary objections and to file a request for revision or interpretation of the Court's judgment, the applicant has thus been placed on an equal procedural footing with the states following reference of the case to the Court. The Ninth Protocol to the Convention, which entered into force on 1 October 1994 after ratification by ten states, has partially completed the logic and the equity of these developments by enabling the individual to refer his case to the Court subject to a leave to appeal procedure.

b. *The Ninth Protocol and the screening procedure*

The Ninth Protocol to the Convention amends Article 48 of the Convention by providing *inter alia* that 'the person, non-governmental organisation or group of individuals having lodged the complaint with the Commission' may now refer a case to the Court (Article 5(1)(e) of the Protocol).[17] The

---

17 The Ninth Protocol has been ratified by seventeen parties: see p 2, n 9, above. No provision has been included in the Protocol concerning its application to petitions which, at the moment of entry into force, are pending before the Commission. The Explanatory Report, para 34, suggests that the Protocol should apply to such petitions provided that the three-month period in Article 32 has not already begun.

Protocol provides that where a case is referred only by an individual it shall first be submitted to a Screening Panel of three members of the Court. If it does not raise 'a serious question affecting the interpretation or application of the Convention and does not for any other reason warrant consideration by the Court', the Panel may, by a unanimous vote, decide that it shall not be considered by the Court (Article 5(2), second sub-paragraph). In that event it will be decided by the Committee of Ministers (Article 5(2)). The judge elected in respect of the respondent contracting party sits as an *ex officio* member of the Panel.

According to the Explanatory Report to the Ninth Protocol, cases could be regarded as not giving rise to a serious question affecting the interpretation or the application of the Convention where *inter alia* there is an already established case-law developed by the Court with respect to the alleged violation or where the dispute relates mainly to the facts of the case.[18] Cases concerning length of criminal or civil proceedings or censorship of prisoners' correspondence (where there is a wealth of case-law) certainly fall into the first category. On the other hand, one could imagine cases where the dispute relates mainly to the facts, such as *Stocké v FRG*,[19] which raise important issues concerning the application of the Convention.

The second limb of Article 5(2) ('not for any other reason warrant consideration . . .') confers an unqualified discretion on the Panel to refuse cases. The Explanatory Report suggests that the Panel could take into account, for example, the fact that the state concerned has indicated that it accepts the conclusions reached by the Commission or the fact that the question of just satisfaction could be solved by a resolution of the Committee of Ministers.[20] Where the state concedes that there has been a violation and is prepared to make full reparation there is no need for a further determination by the Court unless there are reasons relating to the public interest for doing so.[1] This might be the case where an important and novel point is involved. While the balance between the public and private interests involved should tilt in favour of the individual in order to secure the aims of the Protocol, difficult questions are bound to arise. For example, should the Panel allow the Court to be seised where the case appears to be trivial[2] or where the concession that there has been a breach is only partial or where the offending law or administrative practice has been changed in the meantime[3] or where

---

18 Explanatory Report, para 25. See also the Explanatory Report to the Eleventh Protocol, loc cit at p 706, n 1, for interpretation of similar language.

19 A 199 p 46 (1991). See below, p 678.

20 Explanatory Report, para 26.

1   See eg *McCallum v UK* A 183 (1990) and *Darnell v UK* A 272 (1993). In both cases the government conceded that there had been a violation. In *Ireland v UK* A 25 (1978) the government accepted that various interrogation techniques were in breach of Article 3. The Court, however, considered that it was in the public interest to continue its examination.

2   See eg *Adolf v Austria* A 49 (1982), and *Hennings v Germany* A 251-A (1992) as examples of arguably trivial cases.

3   In *Fox, Campbell and Hartley v UK* A 182 (1990), the law had been changed by the time the case was examined by the Commission.

the applicant has died?[4] The fact that the Panel can only refuse a case by a unanimous vote suggests, however, that many of these problems are likely to be resolved in the applicant's favour.

In preparation for the entry into force of the Protocol the Court modified its procedure by way of new Rules of Court which will apply to cases concerning states bound by the Ninth Protocol. These new Rules (Rules of Court B) regulate the operation of the Panel.[5] They also embody a series of consequential amendments to the Rules in the light of the newly acquired 'party' status of the individual.

Rule 26 provides for the setting up of the Panel composed of the national judge and the first two judges designated by the drawing of lots for the composition of a Chamber. If one of the judges is unable to sit or withdraws he shall be replaced by one of the remaining members of the Chamber in accordance with the order determined by the drawing of lots.[6] As noted above, the national judge is automatically a member of the Panel.[7]

Where a private party intends to refer a case to the Court he must file an application with the registry indicating *inter alia* the object of the application and the serious question affecting the interpretation or application of the Convention which the case raises or the other reasons for which the case warrants consideration.[8] He need not be legally represented before the Panel.[9] As soon as it becomes established that the case has been referred to the Court solely by the individual the Panel shall proceed to examine the application. However, it shall do so only on the basis of the existing case-file.[10] It is thus not envisaged that the Panel actually hear the private party or accept further written submissions.[11] The Panel may decide by a unanimous vote to decline consideration of the case on the grounds provided for under the Protocol. In that event it shall deliver a briefly reasoned decision.[12] Where the Panel decides not to decline consideration of the case the Registrar shall immediately transmit a copy of the application to the contracting party and the Commission and inform them, as well as the Committee of Ministers, of its decision.[13] The Panel having completed its task at this point, the usual procedures in examining a case referred to the Court are then followed.

4 The Court's practice is to continue its examination of a case where the personal representative so requests: see *Deweer v Belgium* A 35 para 7 (1980) and *Brannigan and McBride v UK* A 258-B para 2 (1993).
5 They came into force in October 1994 after the entry into force of the Ninth Protocol (Rule 70 of Rules of Court B). The Rules referred to in this section are, Rules of Court B.
6 Rule 26(3).
7 Rule 26(2). Failing him an *ad hoc* judge.
8 Rule 34(1) and 34(1)(a).
9 Rule 31(1).
10 Rule 34(3).
11 Interim measures would seem possible during this phase (see Rule 38(1) and (2)) but the rule concerning friendly settlements and discontinuance seems on its face to be limited to cases which have been accepted by the Panel and where a Chamber has been constituted (Rule 51).
12 Rule 34(4).
13 Rule 35(2).

c. Representation and legal aid

Rule 30(1) of the Rules of Court provides that the applicant shall be represented by an advocate authorised to practise in any of the contracting states and resident in the territory of one of them or by any other person approved by the President. The applicant may be given leave to present his own case, subject 'if need be' to his being assisted by an advocate. The person representing or assisting the applicant must have an adequate knowledge of either English or French, the official languages of the Court. While the term 'advocate' is wide enough to encompass both solicitors and barristers, the President's permission must be sought if an applicant seeks to be represented by a person residing outside one of the contracting states or by a lawyer who is not a qualified practitioner.[14] On several occasions permission has been granted to applicants to be represented by lawyers from the United States. However, in such a situation there is a risk that the Court, in assessing just satisfaction under Article 50 where there has been a finding of a violation, might find that the expenses incurred in having recourse to a lawyer from a non-Council of Europe jurisdiction were not 'necessarily' incurred.[15]

Where the applicant has been granted legal aid[16] before the Commission, the grant shall continue in force for the purposes of his representation before the Court.[17] Legal aid may be granted at any time by the President where he is satisfied that the applicant lacks sufficient means to meet all or part of the costs involved and such a course is necessary for the proper conduct of the case before the Court.[18] Needless to say, where legal aid has been granted before the Commission and due to changed circumstances the above conditions are no longer satisfied, the grant of legal aid may be discontinued.[19] As in the procedure before the Commission, the applicant is asked to complete and have certified a declaration of means form when he has not been in receipt of legal aid during the Commission proceedings.[20] Before the President takes his decision he requests comments from the Agents of the parties and the Delegates of the Commission.[1] Legal aid covers not only fees for representation but also travelling and subsistence expenses and other necessary out-of-pocket expenses. The amounts are fixed by the Registrar in accordance with a scale of fees, approved by the Council of Europe, applicable to each phase of the procedure (preparation of memorial, attendance at hearing, etc).[2]

---

14 See eg *X v UK* A 46 (1981); *Kamasinski v Austria* A 168 (1989); and *Open Door and Dublin Well Woman v Ireland* A 246 (1992).
15 See below, p 687.
16 See Rules on Legal Aid to Applicants, Addendum to the Rules of Court.
17 Rule 3(1) (Addendum).
18 Rule 4(2) (Addendum).
19 Rule 5 (Addendum).
20 Rule 4(3) (Addendum).
1   Rule 4(4) (Addendum).
2   Rule 6(2) and (3) (Addendum).

Compared with the amounts offered by way of legal aid in many national systems the money offered in respect of fees are meagre, if not derisory, and it may be asked whether this operates to discourage lawyers from bringing cases to Strasbourg. Fortunately for applicants, in many cases lawyers are not motivated by the prospect of financial gain when they agree to appear in proceedings before the Court. Moreover it should not be overlooked that the shortfall between real costs and legal aid may, in a successful case, be recovered under the head of just satisfaction.

iv. The role of the Commission before the Court

When a case is referred to the Court, the Commission appoints a Delegate or Delegates to represent it during the proceedings. Although not a party to the proceedings under the Rules of Court, the Commission, through its Delegate, is consulted on various procedural questions that may arise in the course of the proceedings. Thus, for example, his views may be elicited where there is a request for evidence to be taken or for interim remedies to be granted or where the Chamber decides to relinquish jurisdiction following a hearing (Rules 48(1), 36(2), 51).

More important, however, the Delegate may submit his written comments on the memorials submitted by the 'parties' both as regards the merits and on the question of just satisfaction under Article 50.[3] He will also appear before the Court at the hearing to explain and defend the opinion of the Commission on the questions of fact and law raised by the case and provide any explanation that may be required of him by the Court concerning the Commission's report which will be the centrepiece of the proceedings. Where evidence is taken the Delegate may also be given the opportunity to cross-examine witnesses.[4] The Delegate will also be asked for his comments on any friendly settlement or arrangement that may be reached between those appearing before the Court[5] or on a request by a state which has brought the case before the Court to discontinue the proceedings.[6]

As the above examples show, the practice of the Court reflects a constant concern to permit the Commission, as defender of the public interest, to express its view at every stage of the proceedings. The Delegate's role of *amicus curiae* has been likened to that of an Advocate General before the Court of Justice of the European Communities although the latter has arguably more influence than a Delegate. During the hearing of the *Lawless* case Sir Humphrey Waldock described the Commission's role before the Court in the following terms:

'The Commission, however, does not understand its function before the Court to be to defend the interests of the individual as such. The

---

3 It is increasingly rare for the Delegate to file written comments.
4 Rule 45(2).
5 Rule 49(2).
6 Rule 49(1).

Commission's function is that stated in Article 19, namely to ensure the observance of the engagements undertaken by the Contracting Parties in the Convention; when it refers a case to the Court, it does so in order that the Court may give a decision as to whether or not the Convention has been violated. The Commission will, it is true, have expressed an opinion on that point, in the Report transmitted to the Ministers. But that opinion has the character not of a legal decision, but of an expert opinion to provide the basis for a legally binding decision either by the Ministers or by the Court. The function of the Commission before the Court, as we understand it, is not litigious: it is ministerial. It is not our function to defend before the Court, either the case of the individual as such, or our own opinion simply as such. Our function, we believe, is to place before you all the elements of the case relevant for the determination of the case by the Court. We perform this function, Mr President, primarily by placing before the Court our own Report on the case, together with all the material on which our Report is based. In the Report, the Commission not only has stated the opinions of its members on the facts, and the law, but has also set out with considerable fullness the contentions of both sides, of the individual and of the government.'[7]

The Court stressed the independent role of the Commission in proceedings before it in its judgment in the *Lawless* case. The Irish government had requested the Court to find that Rule 76 of the Commission's Rules of Procedure which authorised communication of the Commission's confidential report to the applicant was incompatible with the Convention. Rejecting the request, the Court noted that the Convention had assigned specific roles to the Commission and Court, the Commission's chief function being to carry out an independent inquiry, to seek a friendly settlement and, if need be, to refer a case to the Court. It added:

' . . . once this has been done, the Commission's main function is to assist the Court, and it is associated with the proceedings; whereas, however, even at this stage its action is determined not by a decision of the Court, but directly by the terms of the Convention.'[8]

The Court concluded that its competence under Article 45 of the Convention was limited to the specific cases referred to it and that it could not take decisions such as to delete a rule from the Commission's Rules of Procedure since this would amount to having power to make rulings on matters of procedure or to render advisory opinions.[9]

In practice the role of the Delegate has evolved considerably over the years and has become much less activist as the number of cases before the

7   *Lawless v Ireland* B 1, pp 261-262.
8   *Lawless* case (Preliminary Objections and Questions of Procedure) A 1, p 11 (1960).
9   Ibid.

Court and the concomitant burdens on the Commission have increased. It was not uncommon, for example, in the past for the Commission to appoint two Delegates to represent it, particularly where the case raised novel and important questions of interpretation and to defend its opinion with tenacity.[10] The Delegate, while respecting the views of the Commission, exercised a much broader freedom to respond to the arguments developed by states or applicants before the Court. The current practice has become somewhat mechanical and the question may be raised whether the Commission is performing its role as *amicus curiae* to the best of its abilities. Delegates rarely file written comments on the memorials submitted by the 'parties' and their oral pleadings tend to be limited to a bare restatement of the Commission's opinion carefully tailored to avoid expressing any view on issues which the Commission as a whole has not had an opportunity to consider. While the explanation for this undoubtedly lies in the enormous case burden which the Commission has been required to assume, leaving both Delegates and the secretariat with little time to devote to Court proceedings, a re-evaluation of the present practice seems called for.

v. Interim measures

As is the case with individual applications before the Commission, the institution of proceedings before the Court does not have the effect of requiring states to suspend actions which are feared will give rise to a breach of the Convention. However, Rule 36 of the Rules of Court provides that the President of the Court may, before the constitution of a Chamber, indicate to the state or to the applicant 'any interim measure which it is advisable for them to adopt'. This may be done at the request of a state, of the Commission, of the applicant or of any other person concerned or of his own motion. Notice of such measures shall be immediately given to the Committee of Ministers.[11] Rule 36 also provides that, where the Commission has already indicated an interim measure, its maintenance shall remain recommended unless the President or the Chamber decide otherwise.

In the *Soering* case,[12] the Court applied Rule 36 and indicated to the United Kingdom government that 'it would be advisable not to extradite the applicant to the United States of America pending the outcome of proceedings before the Court'. In the case of *Vijayanathan and Pusparajah v France*,[13] which concerned a decision to expel the applicant Tamils to Sri Lanka, the Court reminded the government that the Commission's interim measures not to remove the applicants, remained recommended.

---

10 Eg *Sunday Times v UK* (No 1) A 30 (1979) and *Young, James and Webster v UK* A 44 (1981).
11 Rule 36(1) *in fine*.
12 A 161 para 4 (1989).
13 A 241-B para 2 (1992). A request for interim measures was, however, refused in *Kremzow v Austria* A 268-B para 5 (1993).

In *Cruz Varas v Sweden*[14] the Court held that interim measures granted by the Commission had no binding force under the Convention. Although the Court was concerned with the Commission's procedure in *Cruz Varas*, its reasoning, which lays emphasis on the absence of an interim measures provision in the Convention,[15] applies with equal force to its own interim measures under Rule 36. As the Court noted in *Cruz Varas*, the cautious language in Rule 36 ('may indicate any interim measure the adoption of which seems desirable') already suggests that such measures are not binding.[16] Accordingly, as the dissenting judges pointed out, the Court lacks the power – which the dissenters believe to be implicit in the Convention – to require the parties to abstain from a measure which might not only give rise to serious and irreversible harm but which might also nullify the result of the entire procedure under the Convention.[17]

Given the narrow majority in *Cruz Varas*, which was adopted by a vote of 10 to 9, it remains to be seen whether a differently constituted Court will follow this view. However, the Court has already indicated in another context that it will follow its own precedents, in the interests of legal certainty and of the orderly development of Convention case-law.[18] It would thus seem that such a change of view concerning the powers of the Convention institutions is an unlikely development. An amending Protocol, to ensure the effectiveness of the Convention in deportation and other cases and to protect the integrity of the petition procedure, is thus urgently required.[19]

vi. Third-party intervention[20]

The Court's receptiveness to intervention by third parties has evolved considerably over the years. In *Winterwerp v Netherlands*[1] the Court had refused the United Kingdom government permission to address the Court on the interpretation of Article 5(4) which had implications for English

14 A 201 (1991). See above, p 589.
15 Contrast with Article 41 of the Statute of the International Court of Justice; Article 63 of the American Convention on Human Rights 1969 and Articles 185 and 186 of the EEC Treaty. Nevertheless a failure to comply with an indication of interim measures by the Court could give rise to the finding of an aggravated breach: *Cruz Varas v Sweden* A 201 para 103 (1991). While the concept of an aggravated breach of the Convention has not been elucidated by the Court it could arguably provide the basis for an award of punitive damages. In addition the fact that notice of interim measures is given to the Committee of Ministers (Rule 36(1)) suggests that the Committee should supervise, if need be, state compliance with the request.
16 A 201 para 98 (1991).
17 Dissenting opinion of Judges Cremona, Thór Vilhjálmsson, Walsh, Macdonald, Bernhardt, De Meyer, Martens, Foighel and Morenilla.
18 See *Cossey v UK*, above, p 656, n 2.
19 It is disappointing that provision is not made for binding interim measures in the Eleventh Protocol – see below, Ch 26.
20 See Lester, *Wiarda Mélanges*, pp 341-351. For details of cases where *amicus* briefs were authorised or refused see *Survey of Activities of the European Court of Human Rights 1959-1991*, pp 70-71 and 1992 and 1993 Updates, pp 26 and 29 respectively.
1 A 33 para 7 (1979).

mental health law. However, it subsequently accepted a memorial from the government submitted through the Delegate of the Commission. In contrast, in *Young, James and Webster v UK*,[2] the Court permitted a representative of the Trades Union Congress to be heard as a witness and also to submit a written memorial on various factual matters. This procedure had become necessary in that case since the government had not put forward any arguments seeking to justify the closed shop under Article 11(2) of the Convention.

These and other cases revealed the need to make provision in the Rules of Court for the possibility of third-party intervention. This was done in the revised Rules of Court (1 January 1983). Rule 37(2) now provides that the President may, in the interest of the proper administration of justice, invite or grant leave to any contracting state, not a party to the proceedings, to submit written comments on specific issues. He may also grant leave 'to any person concerned other than the applicant'. Leave is restricted to the submission of written comments and is entirely within the discretion of the President of the Court although in practice he will consult the Chamber for its views. Permission to submit an *amicus curiae* brief may be subject to the requirements that only specific matters be addressed relating, for example, to national or international standards concerning a particular provision and that the brief does not take the form of pleadings as such (which are the responsibility of the 'parties'). In addition, third parties are often requested to submit the brief in both official languages and to be as succinct as possible. Legal aid is not available for this purpose.

Individuals or groups must not only show that they have a discernible interest in the case but also that intervention is in the interest of the proper administration of justice. Thus, for example, leave was granted in *Soering v UK*[3] (which concerned the death row phenomenon in the United States) to Amnesty International – an NGO committed to the abolition of the death penalty. In *Brannigan and McBride v UK*[4] leave was granted to the Northern Ireland Standing Advisory Commission for Human Rights as well as to Amnesty International, Interights, Liberty and the Committee on the Administration of Justice, the latter three human rights NGOs making a joint submission. All of these organisations have been involved in different capacities with the protection of human rights in Northern Ireland. Similarly in *Open Door and Dublin Well Woman v Ireland*[5] permission was granted to the Society for the Protection of Unborn Children, which had originally instituted the injunction proceedings against the applicant agencies before the Irish courts, as well as 'Article 19' – an English-based organisation concerned with free speech. In *Hokkanen v Finland*[6] the third party in

2 A 44 (1981).
3 A 161 (1989).
4 A 258-B (1993). Permission has also been granted in *McCann v UK* (pending before the Court) to Amnesty, (and jointly) Liberty, Committee on the Administration of Justice and Inquest.
5 A 246 (1992).
6 A 295 (1994).

question – the grandparents – had a direct and personal interest in the dispute concerning the applicant's access to and custody of his child. On the other hand, permission was refused to the International Gay and Lesbian Association which had sought to file submissions in *Modinos v Cyprus*[7] – a case concerning the continued prohibition of homosexual relations between adults under Cypriot law. In that case third-party intervention was presumably considered unnecessary in the light of the Court's established case-law.

While the Court's judgment is only binding on the respondent state, the interpretation of a particular Convention provision may have important implications for other jurisdictions. In *Ruiz-Mateos v Spain*,[8] for example, the Court was called on to consider the applicability of Article 6 to proceedings before the Spanish Constitutional Court. Given the relevance of this question to the procedure before their own constitutional courts, both Germany and Portugal were granted leave to intervene in the proceedings.

Third-party intervention enables the Court to have regard to and perhaps take into account a wider range of legal arguments on Convention issues. At the same time the Court exercises care to ensure that *amicus* briefs are confined to the issues before it by prescribing the points that intervenors should address. Undoubtedly the Court has been assisted in its deliberations by interventions in certain cases. At the same time additional written memorials place an extra burden on all those participating in the proceedings. Not surprisingly governments will often feel obliged to respond to new lines of argument. On occasions they have requested the Court to review its policy of granting leave in view of what they consider to be irrelevant or erroneous submissions.[9] The practice of granting leave has not, however, opened the floodgates to excessive requests. The Court's policy is sensibly grounded on the premise that NGOs and other outside bodies have an interest in contributing to the legal debate on the interpretation of the Convention and that the proper administration of justice is thereby facilitated.[10] The educational benefits to third parties

7 A 259 (1993).
8 A 262 (1993).
9 See eg verbatim record of the hearing of 24 November 1992, *Brannigan and McBride v UK* p 16 – where the government states as follows: 'The comments lodged by these two sets of organisations appear to us not only to be far wider in ambit than was contemplated by the Court in granting leave, but to be made without any regard to the nature and scope of the claim actually advanced by these applicants and considered by the Commission in its decision on admissibility and in its report. It is our respectful submission that much of what is contained in the comments is wholly inappropriate, coming as it does from organisations which are not parties to the proceedings but have been permitted to lodge comments in what are and remain individual applications.'
10 Rule 37(2) *inter alia* restricts leave to contracting states. There is no reason, however, why leave could not be given to a non-contracting state with the consent of the Court and those appearing before it – see Rule 26 with respect to derogations from the Rules of Court. The situation could have risen in the *Soering* case had the United States of America sought to intervene. Unless the President were to decide otherwise, there is no reason why an *amicus* brief should not be treated as a public document. See Mahoney, p 649, n 6, above, pp 144-145, for discussion as to whether third parties enjoy the immunities and facilities provided for under the European Agreement relating to Persons Participating in the Proceedings of the Commission and Court of Human Rights.

participating in proceedings before the Court and the impact that this might have in furthering the aims of the Convention are also arguments which militate in favour of a liberal policy.

Under Rule 41(1) third parties who have been granted leave may request the Court to take evidence and may also be heard by the Chamber in this connection. The Chamber may also obtain evidence at the request of a party, the Delegate, the applicant or *proprio motu*. The Rule empowers the Court to hear 'as a witness or expert or in any other capacity any person whose evidence or statements seem likely to assist it in the carrying out of its task'.[11] To date, however, this provision has not been availed of as regards third parties, and the practice of the Court so far has been to authorise the making of written submissions only.

5. JURISDICTION OF THE COURT

i. Extent of jurisdiction

The Court's jurisdiction extends to 'all cases concerning the interpretation and application of [the] Convention which the High Contracting Parties or the Commission shall refer to it in accordance with Article 48' (Article 45). Accordingly, as noted above, in contentious cases jurisdiction is dependent on the respondent state having recognised the compulsory jurisdiction of the Court either by lodging a declaration to this effect under Article 46 or accepting jurisdiction *ad hoc* (Article 48) and on the case having been declared admissible by the Commission.[12]

It is the Commission's decision declaring the application admissible that governs the Court's jurisdiction since 'it is only within the framework so traced that the Court, once a case is duly referred to it, may take cognisance of all questions of fact or of law arising in the course of the proceedings'.[13] Thus complaints which have been rejected as inadmissible by the Commission cannot, as a general rule, be examined by the Court.[14] Nor can fresh complaints be entertained. For example, in *Schiesser v Switzerland*[15] the applicant raised before the Commission a complaint under Article 5(4) after the application had been declared admissible under Article 5(3). In its report the Commission considered that the applicant had not exhausted domestic remedies in respect of this complaint but it requested the Court to decide whether Article 5(4) could nevertheless be invoked. The Court

---

11 Witnesses or experts may use their own language (Rule 27(4)).

12 See *Tyrer v UK* A 26 para 23 (1978) where the government consented to the Court having jurisdiction *ad hoc* even though their declaration recognising the jurisdiction of the Court in respect of the Isle of Man had expired. See also Rule 34 of the Rules of Court.

13 *Ireland v UK* A 25 para 157 (1978).

14 But see *Handyside v UK* A 24 para 41 (1976) where the Court examined an Article 14 complaint which had been declared inadmissible by the Commission.

15 A 34 paras 39-41 (1979).

considered that the allegation amounted to a separate complaint which went beyond the framework of the case and that the remark in the Commission's report amounted, in substance, to an implicit decision of inadmissibility. Similarly in *Open Door and Dublin Well Woman v Ireland*[16] the Court found that it had no jurisdiction to examine fresh complaints made by Dublin Well Woman and two counsellors that the injunction of the Irish Supreme Court also breached their privacy rights under Article 8. It has also refused to allow applicants to resuscitate complaints which had been expressly withdrawn before the Commission on the grounds that they should not be permitted to circumvent the machinery established for the examination of petitions.[17]

On the other hand, a necessary distinction has been drawn between fresh complaints which the Commission has not had an opportunity to examine and new submissions in support of an existing complaint. Thus in the *Open Door and Dublin Well Woman* case[18] the government had submitted that the applicants were making a new complaint, in respect of which local remedies had not been exhausted, by seeking to introduce evidence concerning abortion and the impact of the Supreme Court's injunction on women's health that had not been examined by the Irish courts. The Court took the view that the applicants were merely developing their submissions in respect of their existing Article 10 complaint concerning the restriction on the provision of information to pregnant women.

Although reticent to examine new complaints which have not been looked at by the Commission, the Court has stressed in earlier cases that once a case is referred to it, it may take cognisance of:

'. . . every question of law arising in the course of the proceedings and concerning facts submitted to its examination by a contracting state or by the Commission. Master of the characterisation to be given in law to these facts, the Court is empowered to examine them, if it deems it necessary and if need be *ex officio*, in the light of the Convention and the Protocols as a whole.'[19]

It is therefore the facts as declared admissible by the Commission which are decisive for the Court's jurisdiction and not the legal characterisation of those facts by those appearing before it.[20] It is this approach which explains why the Court has on occasion examined issues *ex officio* or looked at issues

---

16 A 246 paras 39-40 (1992). See also *Le Compte, Van Leuven and De Meyere v Belgium* A 43 para 38 (1981) where the applicants sought to rely on an Article 10 complaint which had already been rejected for non-exhaustion by the Commission.
17 *Brogan v UK* A 145-B paras 45-47 (1988).
18 A 246 paras 47-49 (1992). See also *Campbell and Cosans v UK* A 48 para 40 (1982) and *Handyside v UK* A 24 para 41 (1978).
19 *Handyside v UK*, ibid.
20 See, *inter alia*, *Schiesser v Switzerland* A 34 para 41 (1979); *Le Compte, Van Leuven and De Meyere v Belgium* A 43 para 38 (1981); *Campbell and Cosans v UK* A 48 para 40 (1982); *Barthold v FRG* A 90 para 61 (1985); and *James v UK* A 98 para 80 (1986).

from a different Convention angle.[1] It also provides the basis for the Court's constant focus on the specific facts of the case as opposed to the broader problems which they exemplify.[2]

However, the dividing line between complaints based on the facts as declared admissible and new complaints beyond the framework of the case is not always easy to draw. Consider, for example, new complaints concerning discrimination contrary to Article 14. Should they be considered fresh complaints or are they inextricably linked to the facts declared admissible? The case can be argued either way.[3] It is clear that the Court's general approach to its jurisdiction enables it to examine legal issues which have not been addressed by the Commission, provided that they emerge from admissible facts. In practice, however, the Court will rarely stray from the issues examined in the Commission's report.

The Court, in this context, has also made it clear that it is competent, in the interests of economy of procedure, to have regard to new facts which occur subsequent to the decision on admissibility in so far as they constitute a continuation of the facts underlying the admissible complaints. Thus in *Olsson v Sweden (No 1)*[4] the Court found that the Commission could have regard to various decisions concerning children taken into care in respect of which domestic remedies had not been exhausted at the date of its admissibility decision. On the other hand, it will not have regard to such new facts where they have given rise to further proceedings which are pending before the Commission.[5]

Should the Court decline jurisdiction where the government concedes that there has been a violation? In *Ireland v UK*[6] the respondent government, having given an undertaking that particular interrogation techniques would not be reintroduced, argued that the Court should decline to exercise its jurisdiction where the objectives of an application had been accomplished or where adjudication of an application would be devoid of purpose. The government no longer contested that there had been a breach of Article 3. The Court considered that it should nevertheless rule on the allegations on the grounds that:

'The Court's judgments in fact serve not only to decide those cases brought before the Court but, more generally, to elucidate, safeguard

1 *Guzzardi v Italy* A 39 para 63 (1980): 'The Commission and Court have to examine in the light of the Convention as a whole the situation impugned by an applicant. In the performance of this task, they are, notably, free to give to the facts of the case, as found to be established by the material before them (. . .) a characterisation in law different from that given to them by the applicant.' See also *Darby v Sweden* A 187 paras 25-28 (1990).
2 See eg *Young, James and Webster v UK* A 44 para 53 (1981) and *Malone v UK* A 82 para 63 (1984) – where the Court refrained from examining the compatibility with the Convention of the closed shop and telephone-tapping in general.
3 This problem arose in *Open Door and Dublin Well Woman v Ireland* A 246 paras 81-83 (1992). The Court left the issue open.
4 A 130 paras 54-57 (1988).
5 See *Weeks v UK* A 114 paras 36-37 (1987) and *Olsson v Sweden (No 1)* A 130 para 57 (1988).
6 A 25 para 154 (1978). See also *McCallum v UK* A 183 paras 30-31 (1990).

and develop the rules instituted by the Convention, thereby contributing to the observance by the states of the engagements undertaken by them as Contracting Parties.'

In this regard it is of interest to note that the Explanatory Report to the Ninth Protocol suggests that the Screening Panel should take into account that the state has accepted the Commission's findings in a case in deciding whether to allow it to be considered by the Court.[7] Nevertheless the Court's remarks concerning the general interest in elucidating Convention obligations applies with equal force to cases referred to it by individuals where the issues raise important questions of interpretation.

Lastly, the Court in *Belilos v Switzerland*[8] confirmed its jurisdiction to examine the validity of reservations made under Article 64 which qualifies the power to make reservations and prohibits reservations of a general character. Although the Court's competence had not been disputed in that case, the Court noted that its jurisdiction to determine the validity of a reservation or, when appropriate, of an interpretative declaration, was apparent from Articles 19, 45 and 49 of the Convention and its case-law.

ii.   Preliminary objections to jurisdiction and admissibility

Rule 48(1) of the Rules of Court provides that states must file preliminary objections within a specific time-limit.[9] Failure to do so will lead the Court to reject the objection even if it had been raised before the Commission.[10] The filing of a preliminary objection does not have the effect of suspending the proceedings on the merits (Rule 48(2)) unless the Chamber decides otherwise.[11] The Court will normally proceed to hear the case in its entirety and answer the objection in its judgment. The objection, however, may be joined to the merits where the issues are closely linked to one another and considered after the merits of the case have been addressed. For example, in *Pfeifer and Plankl v Austria*[12] the applicant had claimed that he had not been tried by an impartial tribunal because two of the trial judges had also acted

---

7   Explanatory Report, paras 25-26.
8   A 132 para 50 (1988). See above, p 22. The Court in *Olsson v Sweden (No 2)* A 250 paras 93-94 (1992), has implicitly accepted that it has jurisdiction to examine a complaint that the state has not abided by a decision of the Court in breach of Article 53, see below, p 703.
9   Not later than the time when the party informs the President of its intention not to submit a memorial, or, alternatively, not later than the expiry of the time-limit for the filing of its first memorial. An objection raised before the Commission but not repeated before the Court may not be examined by the Court of its own motion: *Moreira de Azevedo v Portugal* A 189 para 60 (1990).
10 See *Olsson v Sweden* A 130 para 56 (1988) and *Open Door and Dublin Well Woman v Ireland* A 246 paras 45-46 (1992).
11 In *Loizidou v Turkey* A 310 (1995) the Court's hearing of 22 June 1994 was confined to the preliminary objections challenging the Court's jurisdiction *ratione temporis* and *ratione loci*.
12 A 227 paras 31-34 (1992). See also *Sibson v UK* A 258-A paras 24-27 (1993) and *Kremzow v Austria* A 268-B para 42 (1993).

as investigating judges in his case. The government objected that Mr Pfeifer had not exhausted his remedies since the defence had not challenged the judges in question. The Court considered that the objection related to the question of waiver of rights under Article 6(1) and was thus inextricably linked to the merits of the complaint under that provision.

Preliminary objections must have been raised first before the Commission to the extent that their character and circumstances permit; otherwise there is estoppel. This requirement is considered by the Court to result from the general economy of the Convention and the proper administration of justice. The situation may be different if the reason prompting the objection only comes to light post-admissibility, for example, where there has been a reversal of domestic case-law or the formulation of a new complaint whose admissibility the government have had no opportunity to test.[13]

A government will also be estopped from raising objections before the Court which are inconsistent with the position it has adopted before the national courts. Thus in *Pine Valley Developments Ltd v Ireland*[14] it was not open to the government to argue before the Court that the applicants could have brought proceedings before the Irish courts seeking the benefit of certain provisions of planning law when they had maintained in the national proceedings that the applicants were excluded from these provisions. This approach extends also to pleas which are inconsistent with arguments developed before the Commission. Thus if the government submits before the Commission that the applicant is not a 'victim' it is estopped from subsequently transforming this submission before the Court into one of non-exhaustion.[15]

The Court has consistently held, since the *Vagrancy* cases, that it can review the Commission's decision that a complaint is admissible under any head and, particularly, on the ground that domestic remedies have been exhausted. This view is based on the broad language of Article 45 which confers jurisdiction on 'all cases concerning the interpretation and application of the . . . Convention'. According to the *Vagrancy* cases,[16] where Articles 46, 47 and 48 have been complied with, 'the Court is endowed with *full* jurisdiction and may thus take cognisance of *all* questions of fact and of law which may arise in the course of the consideration of the case' (emphasis added).

This all-encompassing view of the Court's jurisdiction has been roundly criticised by various judges, by the Commission and by academic commentators. Their arguments are based on both law and policy. As regards

---

13 See, *inter alia, Artico v Italy* A 37 paras 23-28 (1980); *Guzzardi v Italy* A 39 para 67 (1980); *Van Oosterwijck v Belgium* A 40 para 26 (1980); *Johnston v Ireland* A 112 para 42 (1986); and *Barberà, Messegué and Jabardo v Spain* A 146 para 56 (1988).

14 A 222 para 47 (1991). See also *Kolompar v Belgium* A 235-C para 32 (1992).

15 *Pine Valley Developments Ltd v Ireland* A 222 para 45 (1991). There is also estoppel where the government makes a passing reference to a ground of inadmissibility but does not deal with the point in argument (ibid). See also *Otto-Preminger-Institut v Austria* A 295-A paras 36-37 (1994).

16 A 12 paras 49-50 (1971).

legal interpretation, they point out that Article 45 should not be read in isolation, and that Articles 24-27 and considerations relating to the economy of the Convention system, suggest that questions of admissibility are the exclusive preserve of the Commission. Furthermore, structurally the Court has not been designed as a court of appeal empowered to quash such decisions. As Judge Martens has pointed out in a dissenting opinion:

'It does not fit in with this system that (as is possible under the Court's doctrine) in one and the same case the Commission should reject the preliminary objection, accept the petition and express the opinion that there has been a violation, while the Court should find that objection well-founded and therefore hold that it is unable to take cognisance of the merits of the case. It is not to be assumed that the Convention makes it possible for a case to end with two contradictory decisions.'[17]

As regards policy it has been pointed out that the Court's approach builds a disparity into the system since governments are able to appeal against admissibility decisions but applicants, for whom a decision declaring their case inadmissible is final, are not so empowered. Moreover, governments are encouraged to seek to re-open questions of admissibility thereby increasing the burdens on a hard-pressed Court at a time when the number of cases it has to examine is increasing rapidly.[18]

Notwithstanding such criticism, the Court has not seen fit to depart from its constant case-law in this regard although in recent years it has been repeatedly invited to do so by the Commission.[19] However, in practice, it rarely disagrees with the Commission's admissibility decision. It has, for example, only accepted a plea of non-exhaustion of domestic remedies in two cases (*Van Oosterwijck v Belgium* and *Cardot v France*).[20] Moreover, as its case burden has developed over the years, the Court has tended to dismiss preliminary objections after only a very brief examination.

The Court is not obliged to examine the issue of non-exhaustion of domestic remedies *ex officio* and the burden rests on the government to indicate sufficiently clearly the remedies to which they are alluding, to prove their existence and to show that they are adequate and effective.[1] The Court will not cure any want of precision or shortcoming in the government's arguments.[2] Nor can the government resuscitate before it an argument

---

17 In *Brozicek v Italy* A 167 (1989). For a compilation of academic criticism see footnote 12 of the opinion of Judge Martens. See also the joint dissent of Judges Martens and Morenilla in *Cardot v France* A 200 (1991).

18 Judge Martens' dissent: 'The time and energy spent on these questions should be devoted to the specific task of ensuring the observance of the rights and freedoms guaranteed in the Convention.'

19 Eg *Pine Valley Developments Ltd v Ireland* A 222 paras 38-39 (1991).

20 A 40 paras 27-41 (1980) and A 200 paras 32-36 (1991) respectively.

1 *Duinhof and Duijf v Netherlands* A 79 para 30 (1984) and *Holy Monasteries v Greece* A 301-A para 51 (1994).

2 *Bozano v France* A 111 para 46 (1986) and *Stran Greek Refineries and Stratis Andreadis v Greece* A 301-B paras 31-36 (1994).

based on non-exhaustion which it had abandoned or waived before the Commission.[3] In addition the Court applies Article 26 'with some degree of flexibility and without excessive formalism'.[4] It is enough that the Convention complaint should have been raised by an applicant at least in substance (not necessarily couched in Convention terms) and in compliance with the formal requirements and time-limits laid down in domestic law.[5] In *Drozd and Janousek v France and Spain*[6] the Court upheld the objection that it lacked jurisdiction to examine the applicant's Article 6 complaints on the grounds that the Convention did not apply to the territory of Andorra despite having been ratified by France and Spain. It also upheld the plea of lack of jurisdiction *ratione personae* on the basis that the independent exercise of judicial functions in Andorra by French and Spanish magistrates did not engage the responsibility of either France or Spain; and in *Stamoulakatos v Greece*[7] it accepted the plea that it lacked jurisdiction *ratione temporis* to examine a fair trial complaint having regard to the date of Greece's recognition of the right of individual petition.

The Court has also affirmed its competence to review whether the applicant was a 'victim' within the meaning of Article 25 and whether the petition is substantially the same as a matter already examined by the Commission (Article 27(1)(b)).[8] However, questions of whether the complaint is manifestly ill-founded (Article 27(2)) or incompatible with the provisions of the Convention *ratione materiae* are generally considered to belong to the merits of the case. In *Airey v Ireland*[9] the Court stated that the distinction between finding an allegation manifestly ill-founded and finding no violation is devoid of interest for the Court whose task it is to determine whether there has been a breach of the treaty. Similarly, in *Glasenapp v FRG*[10] the Court considered the government's claim that there was no right of access to the public service and that the case was incompatible *ratione materiae* to require an examination of the point on the merits. The question was whether the revocation of the applicant's

---

3 *De Wilde, Ooms and Versyp v Belgium* A 12 para 55 (1971) (the *Vagrancy* cases).
4 *Cardot v France* A 200 para. 34 (1991).
5 *Castells v Spain* A 236 paras 25-32 (1992). The applicant had raised the substance of his freedom of expression complaint but had only briefly referred to the equivalent provision of the Spanish Constitution (Article 20). See also *De Geouffre de la Pradelle v France* A 253-B paras 24-26 (1992) where the applicant had not relied on the Convention in express terms but had raised his complaint in substance and *Hentrich v France* A 296-A paras 32-33 (1994) where the government had not shown that reliance on a particular argument before the Court of Cassation would have made any difference.
6 A 240 paras 84-90, 91-98 (1992). See also *Holy Monasteries v Greece* A301-A paras 48-49 (1994).
7 A 271 (1993).
8 On the 'victim' question see *Klass v FRG* A 28 paras 30-38 (1978); *Tomasi v France* A 241-A paras 80-81 (1992) (where the applicant had already obtained a measure of compensation); *Vijayanathan and Pusparajah v France* A 241-B paras 43-46 (1992); and *Ludi v Switzerland* A 238 paras 31-34 (1992). See above, p 630.
9 A 32 paras 16-18 (1979).
10 A 104 paras 40-41 (1986). See also *Kosiek v FRG* A 105 para 32 (1986) and *Bozano v France* A 111 para 42 (1986).

appointment amounted to an interference with her freedom of expression. Such a complaint was not considered to fall clearly outside the provisions of the Convention.

6. ESTABLISHING THE FACTS AND THE BURDEN OF PROOF[11]

In fact the Court has recognised, with reference to Articles 28(1) and 31 of the Convention, that under the Convention system the establishment and verification of the facts is primarily a matter for the Commission and that it is only in exceptional circumstances that the Court will use its powers in this area. In *Stocké v FRG*,[12] for example, it refused the applicant's request to hear witnesses, preferring to adopt the factual findings of the Commission. In that case the question arose whether the German government had been implicated in arranging the applicant's return to Germany against his will where he was sought in connection with fraud offences. The Commission had concluded, after hearing extensive evidence, that the German authorities had not been involved in bringing Mr Stocké back to Germany.

At the same time the Court has made it clear that it is not bound by the Commission's findings of fact and remains free to make its own appreciation in the light of all the material before it. In *Cruz Varas v Sweden*,[13] which concerned an applicant's expulsion to Chile, the Commission had taken evidence from a medical expert that the applicant had previously been subjected to inhuman and degrading treatment. According to the Commission the only plausible explanation for this treatment was that it was carried out by persons for whom 'the then Chilean regime' was responsible. While accepting the medical testimony, the Court did not consider that there was any direct evidence that the Chilean authorities had been involved. It went on to find that the applicant's allegations in this respect lacked credibility because he had not mentioned them to the Swedish police until more than eighteen months after his first interrogation.[14]

The Court has only heard witnesses under Rule 41(1) in one case – *Brozicek v Italy*.[15] The applicant, who lived in Germany, had complained under Article 6(3)(a) that he had not been informed of the charges against him in a language he could understand and that he had been convicted in his

---

11 See Eissen in *La Présentation de la preuve et la sauvegarde des libertés individuelles*, Bruxelles, 1977, pp 143-213.
12 A 199 para 53 (1991). For the Commission's evaluation of the evidence, see id, Com Rep paras 170-204. See also *Messina v Italy* A 257-H para 31 (1993).
13 A 201 para 77 (1991).
14 Id, paras 78-82.
15 A 167 paras 5-8 (1989). In *Young, James and Webster v UK* A 44 para 8 (1981), a representative of the TUC was heard as a 'witness' on certain questions of fact during the hearing. In fact the representative (Lord Wedderburn) addressed the Court on a much broader basis.

absence. At both the government's and the applicant's request, witnesses were heard by two judges appointed by the Chamber with a view to determining, *inter alia*, the applicant's linguistic competence and whether he had acknowledged receipt of a notification that charges had been brought against him. The Chamber had also sought the opinion of a handwriting expert on this latter point.[16]

The Court has also steered clear of the concept of the burden of proof. In *Ireland v UK*[17] it indicated that its approach was rather to examine 'all the material before it, whether originating from the Commission, the parties or other sources' and, if necessary, to obtain material *proprio motu*. It subsequently refused to accept submissions that the burden of proof should be borne by one or other of the two governments concerned. Accordingly at this stage of the proceedings the applicant does not have the burden of proving the factual basis underlying the admissible complaints. This will have been done to some extent at the Commission stage. *Ireland v UK* was an inter-state case. In *Artico v Italy*[18] it held that this approach applied 'just as much or even more to a case deriving from an application made pursuant to Article 25 since neither the individual applicant nor the Commission has the status of party before the Court'. The Court also stressed that contracting states have a duty to co-operate with the Convention institutions in establishing the truth. The applicant in that case had succeeded in providing *prima facie* evidence of allegations that his lawyer before the Court of Cassation had not provided effective assistance and that he had brought this problem to the attention of the authorities. It rejected the argument that the applicant should bear the burden of proof, observing that it was not enough for the government to formulate reservations about documents submitted by him, when the prison authorities had kept a record of them in their files and the government had claimed that they were unable to supply them to the Court.

The position is different, however, with injuries sustained during detention. In *Tomasi v France*[19] the Court found that the applicant had been ill-treated by the police in breach of Article 3 during two days' police custody notwithstanding the findings of the French courts that there was no case to answer. It inferred that the police were responsible for his injuries from medical evidence substantiating them and the absence of any alternative explanation. In effect, where injuries are sustained during a period of police custody, the burden of proving that they were not inflicted by the police shifts to the state.

16 For the position as regards costs, see Rule 41(3).
17 A 25 para 160 (1978).
18 A 37 para 30 (1980). The Court found a breach of Article 6(3)(c).
19 A 241-A paras 104-116 (1992). The principle, however, has not been applied to confrontations with the police in the course of an arrest procedure. See *Klaas v FRG* A 269 para 30 (1993), which is distinguished from *Tomasi v France* 'where certain inferences could be made from the fact that Mr Tomasi had sustained unexplained injuries during 48 hours spent in police custody'. See, however, the dissenting opinions of Judges Pettiti and Walsh on this point.

It has also adopted a flexible approach to the question of standard of proof, preferring, in most cases, to carry out a global assessment of the evidence without reference to any particular standard. In *Ireland v UK*,[20] however, it accepted that allegations of ill-treatment should be established 'beyond reasonable doubt' but added, in response to an argument that the standard was too high, that:

> 'Such proof may follow from the coexistence of sufficiently strong, clear and concordant inferences or of similar unrebutted presumptions of fact. In this context, the conduct of the parties when evidence is obtained had to be taken into account.'

In extradition or deportation cases raising Article 3 issues, the Court has stated that substantial grounds must be shown for believing the existence of a real risk of Article 3 treatment and that it will assess the issue in the light of all the material before it or material obtained *proprio motu*. In both *Cruz Varas v Sweden*[1] and *Vilvarajah v UK*[2] the Court further indicated that it was not precluded from having regard to information which comes to light subsequent to the expulsion since it may be of value in confirming or refuting the assessment of the risk of ill-treatment that had been made by the state or the well-foundedness or otherwise of an applicant's fears.

Finally the Court has made it clear that it will rely, as a general rule, on the findings of fact by domestic courts. It has stated that it will not substitute its own assessment of the facts for that of the local courts which have had the benefit of hearing and observing the witness at first hand.[3] Nevertheless it retains a general power to reach its own conclusions where, for example, the assessment of evidence is arbitrary or where the evidence was improperly obtained.[4] In several cases, for example, concerning freedom of expression issues it has stated that the national courts must have based themselves on an acceptable assessment of the relevant facts.[5]

7. FRIENDLY SETTLEMENT AND DISCONTINUANCE[6]

The Court may strike a case out of the list by way of a judgment where there has been a friendly settlement either on the merits of the case or on the residual question of just satisfaction or where the applicant seeks to withdraw his case or appears to have lost interest in pursuing it.

20 A 25 para 161 (1978).
1   A 201 para 76 (1991). See above, p 78.
2   A 215 para 107 (1991).
3   See *Edwards v UK* A 247-B para 34 (1992); *Vidal v Belgium* A 235-B pp 32-33 (1992); and *Klaas v Germany* A 269 paras 20-30 (1993).
4   See *Schenk v Switzerland* A 140 (1988).
5   *Oberschlick v Austria* A 204 para 60 (1991) and *Schwabe v Austria* A 242-B para 29 (1992).
6   See Berger, in *Wiarda Mélanges*, pp 55-65. For details of cases which have been settled see *Survey of Activities of the European Court of Human Rights 1959-1991*, p 48 and 1992 and 1993 Updates, pp 17 and 18 respectively.

Interestingly the Convention makes no reference to the possibilities of a settlement before the Court. However, it is clear from experience that the desire for settlement may assert itself at any stage of the proceedings. Moreover control of settlements is an inherent part of the judicial function. At the Court phase governments, anxious to avoid public condemnation, may be prepared to make more attractive settlement offers to weary applicants harassed by immediate money needs and the fear of losing the case.[7] As with out-of-court settlements before national courts, friendly settlements under the Convention ideally satisfy the interests of all the participants – the applicant, the government, the Commission – as well as the public interest. Indeed the public interest must be satisfied if the Court is to approve the settlement and Rule 49 § 4 of the Rules of Court makes it clear that the Chamber may, 'having regard to the responsibilities of the Court under Article 19 of the Convention', proceed with the consideration of the case notwithstanding friendly settlement or a notice of discontinuance.

How does the Court satisfy itself that there are no reasons of public policy (*ordre public*) why the case should not be struck out of the list when informed of a settlement? Settlements usually involve an offer to pay compensation coupled with a promise to amend the offending law or administrative practice in return for an agreement by the applicant to withdraw his case from the Court and to renounce any further claims before a national or international court. It is extremely rare for governments to concede in the text of the agreement that there has in fact been a violation of the Convention.[8] Where the issue of principle raised by the case has been resolved the Court will usually have no difficulty in endorsing a settlement. Thus, for example, in *Lamguindaz v UK*[9] which concerned the expulsion of the applicant to Morocco because of his criminal record, the Court adopted a settlement which proposed that the deportation order be revoked and the applicant be granted indefinite leave to remain in the United Kingdom. Similarly in *Ben Yaacoub v Belgium*[10] the Court noted that the Court of Cassation had re-assessed its case-law that permitted the judge who commits the case for trial to be a member of the trial court.

Government undertakings to change the law have not always been free of difficulties. In *Skoogström v Sweden*[11] the Delegate of the Commission submitted that the Court should not endorse the settlement on the grounds that the government's promise to amend the law provided no indication of the substance of the amendment or when it would come into force. The Court rejected his proposal that the case be adjourned so that more

---

7 Friendly settlement negotiations in cases before the Court do not usually involve the participation of members of the registry in contrast with the procedure before the Commission. See above, p 599.

8 But see *Vallon v Italy* A 95 paras 21-23 (1985) where the government acknowledged that there had been a violation of the Convention (length of detention on remand (Article 5(3)) and of criminal proceedings (Article 6(1)).

9 A 258-C (1993).

10 A 127-A (1987). See also *Colman v UK* A 258-D (1993); *Hurtado v Switzerland* A 280-A (1994); *Boyle v UK* A 282-B (1994) and *Diaz Ruano v Spain* A 285-B (1994).

11 A 83 paras 22-25 (1984).

information could be obtained, stating that there was no cause to believe that the settlement did not reflect the free will of the applicant and finding that the general interest was satisfied. In a dissenting opinion Judges Wiarda, Ryssdal and Ganshof Van Der Meersch agreed with the Delegate's position and added that the Court should have enlightened the Swedish legislature by ruling on the merits of the case.[12] In other cases (eg length of detention on remand or of civil or criminal proceedings) the Court has considered the general interest to be satisfied by compensation taking into account that previous case-law has already clarified the scope of the obligations undertaken by contracting states in the particular area.[13]

Rule 49(2) speaks of a 'friendly settlement, arrangement or other fact of a kind to provide a solution of the matter'. In *Owners' Services Ltd v Italy*[14] the applicant company informed the Court of its wish to 'withdraw'. The Court, while noting that the applicant's decision was not strictly speaking a withdrawal since it was not taken by a party to the case in view of the fact that the Ninth Protocol has not yet come into force, considered that it was in any event a 'fact of a kind to provide a solution of the matter'. In *Tyrer v UK*,[15] however, the Court was very wary of the applicant's desire to withdraw his case and refused a strike-off. It observed that the Commission had never examined the circumstances surrounding the applicant's request and that the Court had not been supplied with any further information of a nature to satisfy it that the declaration of withdrawal was a fact 'of a kind to provide a solution of the matter'.

8. JUST SATISFACTION UNDER ARTICLE 50[16]

i. Background

Article 50 provides as follows:

12 See also the joint concurring opinion of Judges Matscher and Pinheiro Farinha in *Can v Austria* A 96 p 12 (1985), where they stated that 'there is no room in a judgment striking a case out of the list for the inclusion of any observations on what the Court's opinion might have been if it had had to determine the merits of the case, or on the opinion it had expressed in similar cases . . . '.

13 Eg *Woukam Moudefo v France* A 141-B (1988); *Oliveira Neves v Portugal* A 153-B (1989); and *Clerc v France* A 176-C (1990).

14 A 208-A para 10 (1991). See also *Farmakopoulos v Belgium* A 235-A para 19 (1993) where the case was struck off the list on account of the applicant's complete failure to cooperate with the Court. The Court considered that there had been an implied withdrawal and thus 'a fact of a kind to provide a solution of the matter'. And see *MR v Italy* A 245-E (1992). A similar finding was made where the applicant had died and no heirs could be discovered – *FM v Italy* A 245-A (1992). Cf *De Becker v Belgium* A 4 (1962) and *Kjeldsen, Busk Madsen and Pedersen v Denmark* A 23 (1976).

15 A 26 paras 24-27 (1978). See also *Bunkate v Netherlands* A 248-B paras 18-19 (1993) where the Court refused to discontinue the case after the government decided not to proceed with it in the light of another judgment of the Court.

16 See Sharpe, in Imbert and Petitti, eds, *La Convention européenne des droits de l'homme*, 1995; Enrich Mas, *European System*, Ch 34; and Sansonetis, id, Ch 33.

'If the Court finds that a decision or a measure taken by a legal authority or any other authority of a High Contracting Party is completely or partially in conflict with the obligations arising from [the] Convention, and if the internal law of the said party allows only partial reparation to be made for the consequences of this decision or measure, the decision of the Court shall, if necessary, afford just satisfaction to the injured party.'

In the *Vagrancy* cases,[17] the Court explained that Article 50 owes its origin and its curious wording to certain clauses which appear in arbitration treaties such as the German-Swiss Treaty on Arbitration and Conciliation of 1921 and the Geneva General Pact for the Pacific Settlement of Disputes of 1928. Such clauses were intended to deal with the situation where the state, though willing, was unable for constitutional reasons to fulfil its international obligations. They conferred on the arbitral tribunal the power *inter alia* to award damages to the injured party. The language of Article 50 thus reflects the general principle of international law that the state must first be given an opportunity to provide redress.

Rule 50(1) of the Rules of Court provides that claims under Article 50 must be set out in the applicant's memorial or (if there is none) in a special document filed at least one month before the hearing. In this way the question will be ready for decision when the Court decides on the merits of the case (Rule 54(1)). In the past Article 50 claims were frequently dealt with in a separate judgment with a consequent increase in the length of the proceedings. In most cases today the issue will be ready for decision at the same time as the substantive issue although in cases, such as *Sporrong and Lönnroth v Sweden*[18] and *Pine Valley Developments Ltd v Ireland*,[19] where the claims for just satisfaction were substantial and the issues complex, a separate procedure was necessary. Where the matter is reserved, the Court will set a time-limit for the filing of submissions (Rule 54(1)) and will invite the parties to inform it of any settlement they may conclude. If there is a settlement the Court must be satisfied that it is equitable and, if so, the case will be struck off the list by means of a judgment. The Committee of Ministers is also entrusted with the supervision of the execution of such a judgment (Rules 54(4) and 49(3)). Where no settlement is reached a separate judgment on Article 50 will eventually be handed down.[20]

On the finding of a breach of the Convention the Court's powers are limited to awarding compensation. In the draft Convention presented by the Congress of the European Movement to the Committee of Ministers in 1949 it was envisaged that the Court should be able not only to prescribe measures of monetary compensation but also to require that the state

17 A 14 para 16 (1972) (Article 50).
18 A 88 (1984) (Article 50).
19 A 246-B (1993) (Article 50). See also *Papamichalopoulos v Greece* A 260-B (1993).
20 In respect of an Article 50 judgment or a judgment striking a case off the list, the President may direct that notification shall count as delivery (Rule 55(2)).

concerned take penal or administrative action in regard to the person responsible for the infringement and require the 'repeal, cancellation or amendment' of the act complained of. These broad powers did not meet with favour by the Committee of Experts entrusted with the drafting of the treaty and it was decided to limit the Court's power to awarding damages.[1]

ii.   Conditions of entitlement

In keeping with this drafting history, the Court has held on various occasions that it will only award pecuniary compensation and that it has no jurisdiction to make 'consequential orders' in the form of directions or recommendations to the state. Thus, for example, in *Ireland v UK*[2] it refused the request by the Irish government to direct that criminal prosecutions be brought against those responsible for ill-treatment in breach of Article 3. On other occasions, it has rejected invitations to require the state to undertake that children will not be corporally punished or to take steps to prevent similar breaches in the future.[3] Nor will the Court award compensation *ex officio* since the question of the application of Article 50 is not a question of 'public policy'.[4] The applicant must thus make a claim for just satisfaction. In one case the Court disallowed a claim for costs which had been made at too late a stage in the procedure.[5] In another, where only reimbursement of costs had been originally sought, it refused to consider whether to make an award for non-pecuniary damage.[6]

Awards will only be made to the 'injured party' as the person directly affected by the act or omission. Claims by the applicant's lawyer in respect of fees have thus been rejected on the ground that he cannot seek just satisfaction on his own account.[7] On the other hand an award may be made to heirs or to an estate in respect of pecuniary damage or costs and expenses. Compensation for non-pecuniary or moral damage cannot, however, be claimed by heirs unless they can also claim to have suffered damage.[8]

Article 50 provides that the Court should grant compensation 'if necessary'. There is thus no entitlement to an award and the Court's discretion is guided by the particular circumstances of each case having regard to equitable considerations. On many occasions the Court has held that no award should be made since the finding of violation constituted

---

1   See Sharpe, p 682, above, n 16. Contrast Article 63 of the American Convention on Human Rights.
2   A 25 para 187 (1978).
3   *Campbell and Cosans v UK* A 60 para 16 (1983) and *McGoff v Sweden* A 83 para 31 (1984). See also *Dudgeon v UK* A 59 para 15 (1983) and *Gillow v UK* A 124-C para 9 (1987). See generally Sharpe, p 682, above, n 16.
4   *Sunday Times v UK* A 38 para 14 (1980) (Article 50).
5   *Brogan v UK A* 152-B para 7 (1989) (Article 50).
6   *Sunday Times v UK* A38 para 14 (1980) (Article 50).
7   Eg *Delta v France* A 191-A para 47 (1990).
8   *X v UK* A 55 paras 18-19 (1982) (Article 50); *Colozza and Rubinat v Italy* A 89 para 38 (1985); *Deumeland v FRG* A 100 para 97 (1986); and *Gillow v UK* A 124-C para 23 (1987).

sufficient just satisfaction.[9] While the Court's judgments give little guidance as to how this discretion is exercised, the applicant's conduct, the criminal offences he has committed and the limited nature of the breach appear to be relevant factors. Thus, in *Campbell v UK*[10] the Court was unwilling to award damages to a life prisoner who had successfully claimed that correspondence with his lawyer was interfered with in breach of Article 8. Nor were damages awarded in *Modinos v Cyprus*[11] where the applicant was making a general complaint concerning the criminalisation of homosexual conduct in Cyprus. On the other hand substantial moral damages were awarded to the applicant in *Tomasi v France*[12] who had complained of the length of civil and criminal proceedings in connection with his claim that he had been ill-treated by the police during detention. Similarly, in *Pine Valley Developments Ltd v Ireland*[13] the applicant property developer was awarded *inter alia* substantial non-pecuniary damages having regard to personal difficulties which the Court accepted were linked to the breach of the Convention.

The application of Article 50 is dependent on the establishment of a violation of the Convention and the absence of full domestic reparation. The latter requirement has not, however, been interpreted as requiring the successful applicant to exhaust domestic remedies on this question before the Court can make an award.[14] In *Barberà, Messegué and Jabardo v Spain*[15] the Article 50 proceedings were suspended while the national courts set aside the applicants' convictions and a new trial was held resulting in their acquittal. The Court rejected the government's argument that they should pursue another remedy under Spanish law which made it possible to obtain compensation for a malfunctioning of the system of justice. It considered that, if the applicants were required to exhaust remedies a third time, the total duration of the proceedings would be hardly consistent with the effective protection of human rights.

Nor does it require an applicant to initiate a fresh procedure before the Commission under Article 25.[16] In its earliest cases on Article 50 the Court had considered that it need not look at the possibility of bringing domestic proceedings where the nature of the injury made *restitutio in integrum* impossible. This has been held to be the position, for example, in respect of an unlawful deprivation of liberty, an interference with freedom of expression, excessive length of administrative or criminal proceedings and a breach of Article 5(4).[17]

---

9 This doctrine was applied in 42 of the 108 cases considered by Sharpe, p 682, above, n 16.
10 A 233 paras 68-70 (1992).
11 A 259 paras 28-30 (1993).
12 A 241-A paras 127-130 (1992).
13 A 246-B paras 16-17 (1993) (Article 50).
14 *Vagrancy* cases A 14 paras 15-16 (1972) (Article 50).
15 A 285-C para 17 (1994) (Article 50).
16 *Ringeisen v Austria* A 15 paras 15-16 (1972) (Article 50).
17 See *Guzzardi v Italy* A 39 para 113 (1980); *Sunday Times v UK* A 38 para 13 (1980) (Article 50); *König v FRG* A 36 para 15 (1980); and *Vagrancy* cases A 14 paras 15-16 (1972) (Article 50).

In the *Vagrancy* cases[18] the Court considered that 'neither the Belgian internal law, nor indeed any other conceivable system of law, can make it possible to wipe out the consequences of the fact that the three applicants did not have available to them the right, guaranteed by Article 5(4), to take proceedings before a court in order to have the lawfulness of their detention decided'. The position may, however, be different where the state can show that national law permits damages to be sought in respect of a violation found by the Court or where the domestic proceedings could bring about a result as close to *restitutio in integrum* as possible.[19] In any event the availability of some measure of domestic reparation may be taken into account in the assessment of compensation.

iii. Awards

The Court awards just satisfaction under two heads: (1) pecuniary and non-pecuniary damage, and (2) costs and expenses.

Pecuniary damage has covered, for example, loss of past and future earnings (as in the *Young, James and Webster* case)[20] attributable to the violation found, fines or (as in the *Pine Valley* case)[1] a reduction in the value of property.[2] Many claims have been rejected on the latter basis.

For example, in *Ruiz-Mateos v Spain*[3] the Court found a violation of Article 6(1) on the grounds that the applicant could not participate in the proceedings before the Spanish Constitutional Court concerning the expropriation of assets and that the proceedings had not been conducted within a reasonable time. The Ruiz-Mateos family claimed two thousand billion pesetas for the damage allegedly deriving from the violation of their right to a fair hearing. The Court held that:

'There is nothing to suggest that, in the absence of these violations, the Constitutional Court would have declared the infringed law void and the European Court cannot speculate as to the conclusion which the national court would have reached.'

In some cases, however, where the Court has found a breach of the rights of the defence, it has awarded compensation on the grounds that the victim must have sustained a certain loss of opportunities. This notion of 'lost opportunities' is firmly rooted in the Court's case-law and is frequently

18 A 14 para 20 (1972).
19 See eg *Clooth v Belgium* A 225 (1991) where the Court noted the possibility under Belgian law of instituting proceedings for damages in respect of breaches of Article 5. On the other hand in *De Cubber v Belgium* A 124-B para 21 (1987) (Article 50) the Court considered that the violation had not been redressed by the state since the Court of Cassation did not order a retrial.
20 A 55 (1982) (1993).
1 A 246-B (1993).
2 See, *inter alia*, *E v Norway* A 181-A para 70 (1990) and *Huber v Switzerland* A 188 para 46 (1990). See Sharpe, p 682, above, n 16, para 187 for list of cases.
3 A 262 paras 69-70 (1993).

resorted to in other areas where the applicant is considered to have sustained pecuniary damage which is difficult to quantify or assess. In *Weeks v UK*[4] the Court decided that the applicant's inability under English law to challenge the lawfulness of his re-detention was in breach of Article 5(4). The Court's finding was as follows:

'It cannot be entirely excluded that he might have been released earlier and, in view of his age, might have obtained some practical benefit. Consequently, Mr Weeks may be said to have suffered a loss of opportunities by reason of the absence of such proceedings, even if in the light of the recurrence of his behavioural problems the prospect of his realising them fully was questionable.'

Non-pecuniary damage (or moral damage) has been awarded in respect of anxiety, distress, loss of employment prospects, feelings of injustice, deterioration of way of life and other varieties of harm and suffering. While the applicant is still required to substantiate his allegations in this respect and to show a link of causality with the breach found, the Court has sensibly recognised that such matters as pain and distress cannot always be the object of concrete proof and has concluded in some cases that such damage must have occurred.[5] On the other hand the Court has so far refused to award aggravated or exemplary damages.[6] Where appropriate, however, interest may be added.[7]

To be entitled to an award of costs and expenses under Article 50, the injured party must satisfy the Court that they were (1) actually incurred, (2) necessarily incurred, and (3) were reasonable as to quantum. As to (1) the applicant must produce bills of costs or similar evidence and must be under a legal liability to pay.[8] In the *Dudgeon* case part of the amount claimed for lawyers' fees was paid by agreement on a contingency basis. Since such an agreement was unenforceable under Northern Ireland law the Court made no award for these costs on the grounds that the applicant was under no obligation to pay them and, in fact, they had already been settled on his behalf.[9] However, when legal aid payments have been made under the

---

4 A 145-A para 13 (1988) (Article 50). See, *inter alia, Goddi v Italy* A 76 para 35 (1984); *Bönisch v Austria* A 103 para 11 (1986) (Article 50); and *Barberà, Messegué and Jabardo v Spain* A 285-C paras 15-20 (1994). See also Sharpe, p 682, above, n 16, paras 34-35 for further details.

5 *Abdulaziz, Cabales and Balkandali v UK* A 94 para 96 (1985).

6 See *B v UK* A 136-D paras 7-12 (1988) (Article 50). In *Zander v Sweden* A 279-B paras 30-35 (1994), however, it gave a lot more than had been awarded in similar cases.

7 See *Pine Valley v Ireland* A 246-B (1993) and *Stran Greek Refineries and Stratis Andreadis v Greece* A 301-B (1994). In the latter case the Court made its highest award ever under Article 50 for pecuniary damage (approximately 116 million drachmas plus $16 million plus 614 thousand French francs, plus simple interest at 6% from February 1984 to December 1994).

8 See *Öztürk v FRG* A 85 para 8 (1984) (Article 50) where the Court noted that there was nothing in the file to show that the applicant was bound to pay his lawyer since no documents had been furnished in substantiation. As to costs and expenses under Article 50 generally, see Sansonetis, p 682, above, n 16.

9 *Dudgeon v UK* A 59 paras 20-21 (1983) (Article 50).

Council of Europe's legal aid scheme the Court will now assume, in the absence of proof to the contrary, that the applicant is under an obligation to pay his lawyer additional fees in respect of the Convention proceedings.[10]

As regards (2) the Court will make an award in respect of national proceedings or other steps undertaken to avoid, prevent or seek redress for a violation. The domestic action taken, however, must relate to the breach established by the Court. Costs and expenses incurred at all the various stages of the Strasbourg proceedings (including the Article 50 stage) may also be recovered. However, appropriate reductions may be made in respect of costs referrable to unsuccessful complaints where the Court has found there to be a breach in only some respects.[11] The Court will also disallow claims for costs which it considers excessive or unnecessary.

As regards the requirement that costs and expenses must be 'reasonable as to quantum', the Court is not bound by domestic scales or by the relatively modest rates offered by the Council of Europe's legal aid scheme. It has on occasion awarded costs in excess of the domestic scale where the amount was not unreasonable.[12] In general the problem is resolved by making an assessment which is considered to be equitable in all the circumstances of the case.

9. INTERPRETATION AND REVISION OF A JUDGMENT

Although Article 52 of the Convention provides that 'the judgment of the Court shall be final', the Court has indicated that the sole object of this provision 'is to make the Court's judgment not subject to any appeal to another authority'. It does not prevent the Court from exercising its inherent jurisdiction to consider a request for interpretation of a judgment.[13] Such a request has been held by the Court not to constitute an appeal. It is governed not by the Convention but by Rule 57 of the Rules of Court.

A request for interpretation may be made by a party (ie a contracting party) or the Commission within a period of three years following delivery of the judgment (Rule 57(1)). It cannot be made by an individual. The request shall be communicated to the Commission and to the applicant and, as appropriate, to any other state, for further comments (Rule 57(3)). It shall be considered by the Chamber which gave the judgment which shall, as far as possible, be composed of the same judges (Rule 57(4)). The matter shall be decided by means of a judgment (Rule 57(5)).

In the history of the Court only one request for interpretation has been made. It was made by the Commission following the Court's Article 50 judgment in *Ringeisen v Austria*. The Court in that case had awarded the

---

10 See *Koendjbiharie v Netherlands* A 185-B para 35 (1990) and *Brandstetter v Austria* A 211 para 73 (1991).
11 Eg *Allan Jacobsson v Sweden* A 163 para 85 (1989) and *Mats Jacobsson v Sweden* A 180 para 46 (1990).
12 *Lingens v Austria* A 103 para 53 (1986) and *Granger v UK* A 174 para 55 (1990).
13 *Ringeisen v Austria* A 16 para 13 (1973) (Interpretation of Judgment of 22 June 1972).

applicant compensation in German marks for non-material or moral damage pursuant to a finding that his detention infringed Article 5(3). In its judgment it had left 'to the discretion of the Austrian authorities' the question as to whether the money should be paid directly to Ringeisen or to his trustee in bankruptcy. It noted, however, that under Austrian law compensation for detention was exempt from seizure. The Austrian government paid the money into court after several of the applicant's debtors had claimed it. The Court held that it had intended that the award be payable to the applicant personally in West Germany where he was then resident and that it should be free of attachment as it was compensation for non-material damage. What had been entrusted to the discretion of the authorities was 'the practical execution of the measures ordered by the Court in conformity with this principle'.[14] It remains unclear whether awards for pecuniary loss may be subject to attachment.

Rule 58 of the Rules of Court provides that a contracting party or the Commission may, in the event of the discovery of a fact which might by its nature have a decisive influence and which, when judgment was delivered, was unknown (both to the Court and to the party or the Commission), request the Court to revise its judgment.[15] The request must be made within six months after learning of the new fact (Rule 58(1)). It is communicated to the relevant state, the Commission and the applicant for written observations (Rule 58(3)). The request is considered by a Chamber which decides whether the above requirements are satisfied. If so, the matter shall be referred for judgment to the Chamber which gave the original decision (Rule 58(4) and (5)). To date no requests for revision of a judgment have been received by the Court.

10. ADVISORY OPINIONS[16]

The Second Protocol to the Convention confers on the Court an extremely restricted competence to give advisory opinions 'on legal questions concerning the interpretation of the Convention and the Protocols thereto' at the request of the Committee of Ministers. Article 1(2) of the Protocol provides that:

'Such opinions shall not deal with any question relating to the content or scope of the rights or freedoms . . . or with any other question which

14 Id, paras 12-15. The Court has refused requests for a declaration that awards in respect of non-pecuniary damage and costs be free from attachment on the ground that the question was hypothetical or that it was not in a position to make the declaration: *De Cubber v Belgium* A 124-B paras 34-35 (1987) and *Philis v Greece* A 209 para 79 (1991).

15 In the light of the entry into force of the Ninth Protocol an individual can now file requests for interpretation or revision of a judgment – see Rules 59 and 60 of Rules of Court B which provide that the requests be considered by a screening panel and rejected by unanimous vote.

16 See, for an account of the drafting history of the Second Protocol, Robertson and Merrills, *Human Rights in Europe*, 3rd edn, 1993, pp 315-319.

the Commission, the Court or the Committee of Ministers might have to consider in consequence of any such proceedings as could be instituted in accordance with the Convention.'

The Court has never been called on to give an advisory opinion.[17] The drafting history to the Second Protocol explains the narrow confines of the Court's competence in terms of a desire not to interfere with the Court's essential mission, namely to examine cases which arise in contentious proceedings. In the light of such restrictive terms of reference it is not an easy task to imagine an issue of any importance which could be raised under the Protocol. Possible questions could concern, for example, whether Article 43 would permit the meeting of several Chambers simultaneously or the scope of the privileges and immunities of members of the Court and Commission (Article 59).

Questions concerning the sufficiency of measures taken by a state in the light of a Court judgment, while important, are probably excluded by the terms of the Protocol since such measures would certainly fall for consideration by the Committee of Ministers in the exercise of its functions under Article 54.

Given the importance of the Convention to the emerging democracies in Eastern and Central Europe, and their concern to reflect Convention standards in new legislation, there is much to be said for recasting the Second Protocol and granting the Court a wider advisory jurisdiction. Article 64 of the American Convention on Human Rights which has so far yielded a rich jurisprudence of the American Court of Human Rights could serve as a model. Under this provision, requests for an advisory opinion may be made to the American Court of Human Rights by (1) member states of the Organisation of American States (OAS), whether or not they are parties to the Convention, regarding the interpretation of the Convention or of other treaties concerning the protection of human rights in the American states or regarding the compatibility of any of their domestic laws with these instruments, and (2) within their sphere of competence, by the relevant organs of the OAS in like manner.[18]

---

17 See Rules 59-67 of the Rules of Court for the procedure envisaged for a request for an advisory opinion.
18 See Buergenthal, 79 AJIL 1 (1985).

CHAPTER 25

The role of the Committee of Ministers

The Committee of Ministers is the executive organ of the Council of Europe.[1] According to the Statute of the Council,[2] the Committee shall consider the action required to further the Council's aim including the conclusion of Conventions or agreements and the adoption by governments of a common policy with regard to particular matters. It is composed of the Ministers of Foreign Affairs of member states. In practice, however, it only meets twice a year at ministerial level. Most of the Committee's business is carried out by Ministers' Deputies who are the permanent representatives of member states at the Council of Europe, ie career diplomats.[3]

The Committee of Ministers is also an organ of the Convention which has entrusted to it the election of members of the Commission (Article 21 of the Convention); deciding whether or not there has been a violation of the Convention in cases which have not been referred to the Court (Article 32); and supervising the execution of judgments of the Court (Article 54).[4] It also votes the budget *inter alia* for the operation of the Commission and Court.

1. DECISION-MAKING UNDER ARTICLE 32[5]

Article 32 provides as follows:

1 See generally on the role of the Committee of Ministers under the Convention, Hondius, in *Wiarda Mélanges*, pp 245-258 and Ravaud, *European Supervision*, Ch 27.
2 See Articles 13, 15 and 16.
3 See Article 14, Statute of the Council of Europe and Article 2 of the Rules of Procedure for the Meetings of the Ministers' Deputies. It is no longer questioned that the Ministers' Deputies can perform the role conferred on the Committee by the Convention: see Ravaud, loc cit at n 1 above, p 648.
4 The Committee also has responsibility to supervise the obligations undertaken by member states 'to accept the principles of the rule of law and of the enjoyment by all persons within its jurisdiction of human rights and fundamental freedoms . . .' (Article 3 of the Statute). Any member which has seriously violated Article 3 may be suspended from its rights of representation and requested by the Committee to withdraw (Article 8).
5 See Leuprecht, in *Ermacora Festschift*, pp 95-108, and Drzemczewski, *European System*, Ch 32. The texts of the Committee of Ministers' Resolutions adopted under Article 32 are printed in *Collection of Resolutions adopted by the Committee of Ministers in Application of Articles 32 and 54 (1959-1989)* and *(1990-1992)*, Council of Europe, 1993 and (post-1992 resolutions) the periodic Information Sheets published by the Council of Europe.

'1. If the question is not referred to the Court in accordance with Article 48 of this Convention within a period of three months from the date of the transmission of the report to the Committee of Ministers, the Committee of Ministers shall decide by a majority of two-thirds of the members entitled to sit on the Committee whether there has been a violation of the Convention.

2. In the affirmative case the Committee of Ministers shall prescribe a period during which the High Contracting Party concerned must take the measures required by the decision of the Committee of Ministers.

3. If the High Contracting Party concerned has not taken satisfactory measures within the prescribed period, the Committee of Ministers shall decide by the majority provided for in paragraph 1 above what effect shall be given to its original decision and shall publish the report.

4. The High Contracting Parties undertake to regard as binding on them any decision which the Committee of Ministers may take in application of the preceding paragraphs.'

That decision-making powers under the Convention were conferred on a political body such as the Committee of Ministers is a consequence of the refusal of certain governments to accept the compulsory jurisdiction of the Court when the Convention was being drafted. Because of this, a decision-making role had to be given to some other body for cases that were not referred to the Court and the Committee was conveniently available and acceptable to states. As has been stressed by commentators,[6] the political character of the Committee does not absolve it from the requirement to exercise its judicial functions with reference to legal considerations as opposed to political expediency.

i.   Categories of cases left for decision by the Committee of Ministers

As indicated, the Committee's competence only relates to cases which have not been referred to the Court in accordance with Article 48 by either the Commission, the defendant state or the state whose national is an applicant.[7] In practice, although with episodic exceptions, cases in the following categories are left by the Commission for decision by the Committee:

1. where the Commission has found no violation and the case does not raise an important Convention issue;[8]

6   Robertson and Merrills, *Human Rights in Europe*, 3rd edn, 1993, p 329, and Leuprecht, loc cit at n 5 above, p 101.

7   For developments under the Ninth Protocol, see above, p 661.

8   *Temeltasch v Switzerland No 9116/80*, 31 DR 120 (1982) Com Rep; CM Res DH (83) 6 is an obvious exception where there was an important issue (validity of reservation).

2.   where the Commission has found a violation but *either* the case raises issues which are already the subject of established Court case-law *or* the government has intimated that it accepts the Commission's finding and is willing to take the necessary consequential measures.

ii.   Procedure

In the exercise of its quasi-judicial functions under Article 32, the Committee of Ministers has adopted a series of Rules[9] to provide guidance on the various substantive and procedural questions that it has been confronted with since the Commission communicated its first Article 31 report in 1958 (*Greece v UK*).[10] The Rules have been regularly revised over the years. Although the Commission's reports form the basis of its deliberations, the Committee is not bound by the Commission's conclusion.

It is clear from Rule 1 that the Committee 'is entitled to discuss the substance of any case on which the Commission has submitted a report, for example, by considering written or oral statements of the parties and hearing of witnesses'. At the same time the Committee has recognised that it is not well equipped to take evidence and ought not normally undertake to do so.[11] Following an examination of this question by a Council of Europe Committee of Experts in 1967 the Committee of Ministers decided that it could:

1.   invite the Commission to undertake these tasks on its behalf if the Commission agreed;
2.   take evidence itself or appoint a sub-committee for the purpose;
3.   avail itself of Article 17 of the Statute of the Council of Europe which empowers it to set up advisory and technical committees for specific purposes.

It further decided to leave the choice open for a decision *ad hoc* should the need arise.[12] Although the rules in this respect reveal the Committee's awkwardness as a political body charged with a quasi-judicial role, in practice it has never sought to take evidence or to question the establishment of the facts set out in the Commission's report.

The Committee meets *in camera* and its deliberations on particular cases are confidential.[13] The individual applicant and his legal representative are specifically excluded from the Committee's procedure. The Committee has decided that they have no right to be heard by it or to have any written communication considered by the Committee.[14] The Secretary General is

9   Rules for the Application of Article 32, *Collected Texts*, pp 315-321.
10   See above, p 585.
11   See Rule 4.
12   Appendix to the Rules, point 2.
13   Access can be granted to certain confidential Council of Europe documents after 30 years – see Hondius, loc cit at n 1 above, pp 246-247.
14   Appendix to the Rules, point 3(c).

instructed to explain to the applicant that any submission he makes cannot be considered as a document in the case.[15] Nor is a copy of the Commission's report communicated to the applicant except for the purposes of receiving submissions on the question of just satisfaction after the Committee has taken its decision on the question whether there has been a violation.[16] The individual's lack of party-status is in stark contrast to the right of the defendant state to play a full part in the proceedings, 'to make submissions and deposit documents' and to take part in the vote.[17] Indeed the representative of any member state on the Committee can participate in the proceedings even if that state has not yet ratified the Convention.[18] This is clear from the wording in Article 32 that the Committee of Ministers 'shall decide by a majority of two-thirds of the members entitled to sit on the Committee whether there has been a violation of the Convention'.

In the large majority of cases the Committee has no difficulty in endorsing the conclusions in the Commission's report. Undoubtedly this is made easier by the fact that most of the cases will either concern uncontroversial issues that have already been examined by the Court (eg censorship of prisoners' correspondence) or issues that do not give rise to important or complex questions of interpretation.

The procedure described in paragraph 2 of Article 32 whereby the Committee, after having found a violation, may 'prescribe a period during which the High Contracting Party concerned must take the measures required by the decision of the Committee of Ministers', has remained largely theoretical, although in recent years it has been used to secure the payment of compensation where the state had refused to do so (see below). In almost all cases where the Commission has found a violation, the state decides what corrective measures are needed and informs the Committee of the steps taken. This enables the Committee, in a telescoped procedure, to find that there has been a breach of the Convention, to take note of the measures adopted by the state and to conclude that no further action is called for. Normally, when the Committee has adopted a resolution in the case, it authorises (without voting) the publication of the Commission's report.[19] Although the Committee is also responsible for supervising the implementation of its own decisions, it must be observed that a procedure which treats in one single operation the questions whether there is a violation, as well as the state's response to it, is not well adapted to ensuring that the corrective measures taken by the state are a sufficient response to the Commission's report.

15 Appendix to the Rules, point 3(d).
16 Appendix to the Rules, point 3(a).
17 Rule 3.
18 Rule 2.
19 Rule 9. Paragraph 2 of this rule provides that the Committee of Ministers 'may, by way of exception and without prejudice to Article 32, paragraph 3, decide not to publish a report of the Commission or part thereof upon a reasoned request of a contracting party'. As a rule, Commission reports under Article 31 are published. See Drzemczewski, loc cit at n 5 above, pp 745-746. But see the 'non-decisions' referred to below.

iii. Cases in which no decision is taken

Although there has been no individual case where the Committee has reached an opposite conclusion from the Commission, there have been a number of cases where the Committee has in fact taken no decision. Such non-decisions fall into three specific categories. The first category consists of cases in which the Committee, in the vote under paragraph 1 of Article 32, did not attain the majority of two-thirds of the members entitled to sit in favour of violation or non-violation. It appears that in these cases various governments abstained from exercising their vote, no doubt because of effective lobbying by the respondent government.

Such non-decisions have been soundly criticised by commentators as amounting to a denial of justice as well as a failure by the Committee to comply with its Convention obligations under Article 32(1) to decide whether there has been a violation.[20] As a former Director of Human Rights in the Council of Europe has pointed out:

'The attitude of the respondent state has an important and often decisive influence on the position of other states; some find it much easier and less embarrassing to vote in favour of a violation if the respondent state itself does so or at least does not openly oppose the findings of the Commission. Such an approach is, of course, hardly a judicial one.'[1]

Non-decisions in this group have occurred on five occasions: *Huber v Austria*,[2] *East African Asians v UK*,[3] *Dores and Silveira v Portugal*,[4] *Dobbertin v France*[5] and *Warwick v UK*.[6] In the *East African Asians* cases the applicants, who were British passport holders, had complained of the refusal of the United Kingdom to admit them into Great Britain or permit them to remain permanently there. The Commission, in its report of 14 December 1973, found that Article 3 had been violated in the cases of 25 applicants and that Article 8 and 14 had been violated in the cases of three applicants. It also found no violation of Article 3 in six cases and no violation of Article 5 considered in isolation and in conjunction with Article 14. After noting various measures that had been adopted by the government to facilitate the entry to the United Kingdom of British passport holders and that all 31 applicants were settled in the United Kingdom, the Committee followed the Commission's report as regards the findings of no violation but

---

20 See the views of Frowein and Peukert, and Velu cited by Leuprecht, loc cit at n 5 above, pp 101-102.
1 Ibid, p 101.
2 Res DH (75) 2. The case concerned the length of criminal proceedings (Article 6(1)).
3 Res DH (77) 2.
4 Res DH (85) 7 (length of civil proceedings).
5 Res DH (88) 12. The applicant complained under Article 5(3) of the length of detention in police custody and that he had not been brought promptly before a judge.
6 Res DH (89) 5.

failed to attain a two-thirds majority either way as regards the findings of a violation.[7] It then decided that no further action was called for and removed the examination of the case from its agenda. Although the Commission's vote appeared in the resolution, the Commission's report (as in all of the above cases) was not published.[8] In *Warwick v UK*, which concerned corporal punishment at school, the Committee failed to attain the requisite majority on whether there had been breaches of Articles 3 and 13 of the Convention. However, having been informed by the government that it accepted that there had been breaches of Article 2 of the First Protocol and Article 13, it was able to adopt a vote confirming breaches of these provisions. It also took note of information that the Education (No 2) Act 1986 provided for the abolition of corporal punishment in state schools and that the respondent government did not consider that the punishment inflicted on the child applicant attained a sufficient level of seriousness to be regarded as degrading within the meaning of Article 3.[9]

The *Warwick* resolution is a good illustration of the most criticised features of the Committee's procedures. The resolution in effect reveals that, subsequent to the judicial proceedings before the Commission, political forces were permitted to become the masters of procedure. Agreement was reached only on those points where the government in question was prepared to accept the Commission's finding. A power of veto was exercised as regards those findings of the Commission which did not meet with favour. In their place the resolution carried and gave weight to the state's view, undoubtedly expounded at length but previously rejected by the Commission, that there had been no breach of Article 3. The principle, essential to the integrity of any adjudicatory process, *nemo iudex causa sua*, was thus defeated by a voting procedure which permitted states to reflect their own political interests.

Fortunately for the system as a whole, such aberrations have occurred in only a few cases. In an effort to reduce the possibility of non-decisions, the Committee adopted Rule 9 *bis* (in December 1990) which requires a second and final vote to be taken at one of the next three meetings of the Committee where the first vote fails to secure the majority required. A more effective solution, however, was found in the Tenth Protocol[10] which amends Article 32(1) so that a simple majority of the members entitled to sit will be sufficient to decide whether there has been a violation.

The second category of non-decisions concerns either those cases where the Committee considers that it is unnecessary to vote on the question of violation because the state has already introduced corrective measures or where the applicant has accepted an out-of-Committee settlement of the

7   Res DH (77) 2. The resolution was adopted nearly four years after the Commission's report.
8   Extracts were published unofficially in 3 EHRR 76 in 1981. The full Commission report was only published by the Council of Europe in 1994! See text in 15 HRLJ 232 (1994).
9   Res DH (89) 5.
10 20 of the 30 parties to the Convention have ratified the Tenth Protocol. All of the Convention parties must ratify it for the Protocol to enter into force.

case. *Eggs v Switzerland*[11] and *Inhabitants of Fourons v Belgium*[12] are examples of the former.[13] As regards the latter, the most illustrious examples are the two inter-state cases brought by Greece against the United Kingdom concerning events in Cyprus.[14] When the Commission's report on the first case was pending before the Committee a political settlement of the Cyprus problem was concluded in the Zurich and London agreements of 1959. As a result both the Greek and British governments proposed to the Committee that no further action was called for. The second case was then terminated by the Commission without examination of the merits and forwarded to the Committee which decided that no further action was called for.[15] In other cases the Committee has taken no action since, due to the applicant's acceptance of redress by the government, the Commission had found that he could no longer claim to be a victim under Article 25. In *Pannetier v Switzerland*,[16] for example, the applicant complained of the length of criminal proceedings brought against him by the Swiss authorities which subsequently acknowledged and afforded redress for the damage suffered by the applicant. The Commission, which had declared the case admissible, had found in its Article 31 report that in these circumstances the applicant could no longer claim to be a victim. This decision was endorsed by the Committee.

The third category of cases concern politically sensitive inter-state disputes. In the *Greek* case, for example, after having endorsed the Commission's findings that the military dictatorship bore responsibility for multiple violations of the Convention, the Committee noted that Greece had denounced the Convention. It considered that these circumstances clearly established that the Greek government was not prepared to comply with its continuing obligations under the Convention and that the Committee was called upon to deal with the case in conditions which were not precisely those envisaged in the Convention. It then concluded that there was no basis for further action under Article 32(2) and decided to publish the report.[17]

In the first two *Cyprus v Turkey* cases[18] the Committee, by decision of 21 October 1977 and in a vague and non-committal statement, found 'that events which occurred in Cyprus constitute violations of the Convention'. It further urged the parties to resume intercommunal talks. It resumed consideration of the matter on 20 January 1979 and expressed the view *inter alia* that intercommunal talks 'constitute the appropriate framework for

11 Res DH (74) 1.
12 Res DH (79) 7.
13 The political expediency of not attempting to reach a decision by vote in these cases where remedial measures had been introduced has been criticised as a contravention of the Committee's obligations under Article 32: see Leuprecht, p 691, above, n 5, p 103.
14 Res (59) 2 and (59) 32. See above, p 585.
15 See Robertson and Merrills, p 692, above, n 6, pp 334-335 and Ch 7. The case had previously been declared admissible by the Commission which decided to refer it to the Committee of Ministers although it did not fall exactly within Article 30 or Article 31.
16 Res DH (86) 3.
17 See Res DH (70) 1.
18 *Nos 6780/74 and 6950/75*, 2 DR 125 (1975); 4 EHRR 482 (1976).

reaching a solution of the dispute'. The Committee viewed this decision as completing its consideration of the case.[19] In the third *Cyprus v Turkey* case,[20] the report of the Commission was communicated to the Committee in late 1983 and remained on its agenda without any decision being taken until 2 April 1992 when the Committee decided to make it public, adding that the decision completed its consideration of the present case.[1]

While the handling of the *Greek* case can be seen as an example of the triumph of political realism over the legal obligations contained in Article 32(2), the *Cyprus v Turkey* cases are more serious in their implications. They demonstrate that the political sensitivities are such that the Committee of Ministers prefer to deal with the issues in the case as a political question. This is perhaps inevitable given the intractable nature of the underlying political problems reflected in the cases and the natural gravitation of a political body to such an approach. Unfortunately, apart from raising questions concerning compliance with Article 32(2) and (3),[2] it reveals the limits of the concept of collective enforcement under the Convention in disputes concerning allegations of widespread violations, damages the reputation of the Committee and undermines the integrity of the Convention system as a whole.

iv. Friendly settlements

A friendly settlement may also intervene at the Committee of Ministers stage, although it is a rare occurrence. A new Rule 6 *bis* (introduced in 1987) provides that:

> 'The Committee of Ministers may be informed of a friendly settlement, arrangement or other fact of a kind to provide a solution of the matter. In that event, it may decide to discontinue its examination of the case, after satisfying itself that the solution envisaged is based on respect for human rights as defined in the Convention.'

In the case of *Sargin and Yagci v Turkey*[3] the Committee was informed, during the examination of the case, that a settlement had been reached between the parties involving important legislative improvements to the Code of Criminal Procedure in areas related to the applicants' complaint concerning their treatment in prison. The applicants were also awarded

---

19 Res DH (79) 1. It also decided to declassify the documentation, including the Commission's report, on 31 August 1979. The decision of 21 October 1977 had not been made public until then. It appears from the declassified material that both governments had filed memoranda with the Committee on the question of human rights in Cyprus.

20 *No 8007/77*, 13 DR 85 (1973).

1 Res DH (92) 12. See further on the three *Cyprus v Turkey* cases, above, p 585.

2 See Van Dijk and Van Hoof, p 203; Velu and Ergec, pp 1116-1117 and Robertson and Merrills, p 692, above, n 6, p 337.

3 *No 14116/88*; Res DH (93) 59. It was also decided not to publish the Commission's report.

substantial sums by way of just satisfaction. After having satisfied itself that the terms of the settlement had been executed, the Committee found that the solution was based on respect of human rights and decided to discontinue its examination of the case.

The Committee takes no initiative, however, and does not get involved in negotiations to reach a settlement. It confines itself to ratifying the agreement reached between the parties and satisfies itself that the terms have been respected.[4]

v. Just compensation

Prior to 1987, *mirabile dictu*, the Committee of Ministers did not award compensation in cases where it had found a violation. There thus existed a flagrant difference of treatment in comparison with applicants whose cases were decided by the Court. To fill this lacuna, Rule 5 was adopted enabling the Committee to make non-binding 'suggestions or recommendations' to the state which, according to Rule 5, did not constitute 'decisions' within the meaning of Article 32(4). Subsequently, in cases where it had found a violation, the Commission would recommend to the Committee that just satisfaction be awarded without specifying the amount. A practice then developed whereby the Commission's report is communicated by the Committee to the applicant or his lawyer on a confidential basis and the Commission is invited to formulate specific proposals.[5] The Commission invites the applicant to set out his claims and the government to comment on them. It then draws up proposals and submits them to the Committee of Ministers for decision and inclusion in the resolution on the case. In preparing proposals on just satisfaction the Commission appears to be guided by the Court's case-law on Article 50.

The limitations of Rule 5 became apparent in a number of cases against Italy concerning the length of civil and criminal proceedings. The government expressed the view that the recommendations to pay just satisfaction were not binding on it and thus could not under Italian law provide a basis for the payment of compensation. The Committee's response was to delete Rule 5 and rely on its largely untapped powers in Article 32(2).[6] It now takes a 'decision' that the state is to pay the amounts awarded within a fixed time-limit and invites the government to inform it of the measures taken in consequence of this decision having regard to its obligation under Article 32(4) to abide by it. Before adopting the resolution under Article 32, it satisfies itself that the compensation has been paid.[7]

---

4 For other examples of settlements see *Hewitt, Harman and N v UK* Res DH (90) 36; *P v Austria* DH (91) 33; and *Garzarolli v Austria* DH (91) 34.

5 Appendix to the Rules, point 3(b).

6 *Azzi, Lo Giacco, Savoldi, Van Eesbeeck, Sallustio and Minniti v Italy*, Res DH (92) 2-7. For an account of the procedure in these cases, see Leuprecht, *European Supervision*, Ch 35 at 796.

7 See eg *S v Sweden* Res DH (93) 58.

2. SUPERVISING THE EXECUTION OF THE COURT'S JUDGMENTS (ARTICLE 54)[8]

The second important role of the Committee of Ministers under the Convention is to 'supervise' the execution of judgments of the Court under Article 54. Judgments of the Court are final (Article 52) and binding (Article 53). The latter provision states that 'the High Contracting Parties undertake to abide by the decision of the Court in any case to which they are parties'. It follows that the Court's judgments give rise to a legal, as opposed to a moral, obligation of compliance under international law but only on states which are parties to a particular case. They are not binding *erga omnes*.[9] Judgments are declaratory in nature. In themselves they do not have the effect of quashing national decisions or striking down provisions of national legislation which have been found to breach a provision of the Convention. The Court, moreover, has constantly rejected requests from applicants to require the state to take particular measures such as annulling a national court decision or instituting criminal or disciplinary proceedings.[10] As it indicated in *Marckx v Belgium*[11] the judgment 'leaves to the state the choice of the means to be utilised in its domestic system for performance of its obligations under Article 53'. This constant refusal by the Court to widen its jurisdiction to embrace the making of consequential orders has been re-affirmed in more than 30 judgments.[12] It illustrates a sensible division of powers in the Convention system which appropriately leaves it to a political body – with power to suspend or expel a state from the Council of Europe – to ensure that states comply faithfully with judgments of the Court.

Where a legislative provision or administrative practice is at issue the state must ensure that the appropriate corrective measures have been taken. Where the breach resides in a decision of a national court which has become *res judicata* the situation is more problematic since contracting states are not under an obligation to provide for review proceedings before national courts, although some states have introduced such measures.[13] In other cases states would be expected to use other means to achieve the desired result such as the granting of a pardon or release from prison. In short, the state must put an end to the violation found, make reparation for its consequences and prevent the re-occurrence of similar violations.

Where the Court finds a violation of the Convention and awards just satisfaction, the supervisory role of the Committee extends to ensuring that

---

8 See generally Leuprecht, loc cit at n 6 above; Robertson and Merrills, p 692, above, n 6, pp 338-343; and Velu and Ergec, pp 1123-1128. For the texts of Committee of Ministers' Resolutions adopted under Article 54, see the Collection of Resolutions and Information Sheet documents referred to above.

9 For the effects of judgments on non-parties to the case see above, p 31.

10 See above, p 31.

11 A 31 para 58 (1979).

12 Contrast Article 63(1) of the American Convention on Human Rights 1969 which confers extensive powers on the Inter-American Court.

13 For the enforcement of judgments under domestic law, see above, p 26.

the state not only takes the general measures that are required by the terms of the decision but also that the amounts awarded under Article 50 have been paid.[14] The Committee's role also extends to ensuring that the terms of friendly settlements reached in proceedings before the Court have been complied with.[15]

The procedure adopted by the Committee is laid down in Rules for the application of Article 54.[16] In brief, following the judgment of the Court the case is inscribed on the agenda of the Committee 'without delay' (Rule 1). The state is then invited to inform the Committee of the measures it has taken in consequence of the judgment having regard to its obligation under Article 53 (Rule 2). Where no measures have been taken, the case is automatically inscribed on the agenda of a Committee meeting taking place not more than six months later (Rule 2(b)). Rule 3 provides that the Committee shall not regard its functions under Article 54 as having been exercised until it has taken note of the information supplied by the state and, when just satisfaction has been afforded, until it has satisfied itself that the state has paid the sums involved to the injured party. The decision takes the form of a resolution which marks the end of the Committee's role. The Committee normally appends to the resolution a summary of the information which the state has provided.

It is evident from the terms of the resolutions adopted under Article 54 that the Committee interprets its function of supervision as extending not merely to individual measures but also to measures of a general nature. Clearly a failure by the Committee of Ministers to be concerned with the wider questions associated with the general interest would not be supervision based on 'respect for human rights' as that notion has been interpreted by all three institutions in the field of friendly settlements. The propriety of the Committee's concern for general measures appears to have arisen in the case of *Luedicke, Belkacem and Koç v FRG* where the respondent government studiously avoided providing the Committee with information concerning amending legislation that they had in fact passed and which they had declared, during the proceedings before the Court, they intended to enact. It has been surmised that the government had argued before the Committee that its only function under Article 54 was that of ensuring that the position of the applicant had been remedied. In its resolution[17] the Committee declared that it had exercised its functions under Article 54 'being aware of the current position under the laws of the Federal Republic of Germany in the sector affected by the Court's judgment'. This allusion to the general measures adopted by the government may be

---

14 For details of corrective measures including legislative changes that have been made following judgments of the Court, see *Collection of Resolutions*, p 691, above, n 5, and *Survey of Activities of the European Court of Human Rights 1959-1991*, pp 50-60, and the 1992 and 1993 Updates thereto, pp 18-19 and 20-23 respectively.
15 Friendly settlements before the Court are effected by means of a judgment of the Court – Rule 49 para 3 of the Rules of Court.
16 *Collected Texts*, pp 322-323.
17 Res DH (87) 4.

interpreted as a diplomatic insistence that the Committee is not prepared to limit its role to that of merely taking note of the information provided by governments but will also expect to examine the colour of remedial legislative changes where appropriate.[18] In the *Brogan* case[19] it appears to have been argued that the derogation entered by the United Kingdom following the Court's judgment could amount to execution of that judgment. The Committee wisely side-stepped this curious suggestion and noted that it was not for it to pronounce on the validity of a derogation. Had it not done so it would have expressly pre-empted the legal questions associated with the validity of a contested derogation. The Committee discontinued its examination of the case after taking note of the government's information that the derogation had to remain in place since it had not been possible to identify a satisfactory alternative procedure to detention of terrorist suspects for up to seven days without bringing them before a judge. The derogation was subsequently upheld by the Court in *Brannigan and McBride v UK*.[20]

While it is clear from the terms of Article 54 that the Committee has no power to make consequential orders, the question is fittingly asked to what extent it is qualified, as a political body composed of diplomatic representatives, to assess the legal issue of whether remedial legislation or amendments to administrative practices are sufficient to comply with the terms of the Court's judgment. As Leuprecht has pointed out, the practical application of Article 54 places a heavy responsibility on the shoulders of the Directorate of Human Rights whose duty it is to 'assist and advise' the Committee. The 'uncomfortable' task of pointing out the shortcomings of proposed legislation or probing, together with government departments, the fine print of the information provided falls to the Directorate.[1] In the light of the numerous administrative and legislative changes that are recorded in Article 54 resolutions, it is evident that the quiet influence that has been brought to bear has been well directed.

The level of state compliance with judgments of the Court is generally recognised to be exemplary. It is also one of the reasons why the Convention system is held in such high esteem as an effective mechanism for the international enforcement of human rights. Nevertheless, on occasions there have been important delays in the introduction of remedial legislation which have threatened to bring the enforcement system into disrepute. For example, it took the Belgian authorities almost eight years to introduce legislation amending 'various legal provisions relating to affiliation' in response to the *Marckx* judgment.[2] In the meantime a further application based on the previous legislation was lodged with the Commission culminating in the Court's judgment in the case of *Vermeire v Belgium*[3] in

18 See Bartsch, in *Wiarda Mélanges*, p 47.
19 Res DH (90) 23.
20 A 258-B. See above, Ch 16.
1   Leuprecht, p 700, above, n 6, p 798 and Drzemczewski, 11 HRLJ 89 (1990).
2   Res DH (88) 3.
3   A 214-C (1991).

which a further violation was found. Important delays also occurred in the enforcement of the *Sporrong and Lönroth v Sweden*[4] judgment (six years) and that of *Norris v Ireland*[5] (four years).

Although these instances of delay must be seen in the context of more than 187 Article 54 resolutions, they raise several important questions of principle. In the first place, although it must be recognised that the amendment of national legislation may take some time and may be subject to the vagaries of national politics, proper 'supervision' of execution of the Court judgments presupposes that the Committee take firm and resolute action with recalcitrant states. The absence at present of a more effective procedure to cajole states into speedier compliance casts a shadow over the integrity of the enforcement system.

The second issue concerns the question whether the Committee of Ministers possesses exclusive competence in the field of enforcement. Is it open, for example, to the applicant to complain that the state is in breach of its obligations under Article 53 to abide by the Court's judgment, and would the Commission and the Court have competence to examine such a claim in proceedings instituted by an individual? The Commission has made a clear statement that it has no competence as regards the supervision of the Court's judgments. Following the *Sunday Times*[6] case, the Contempt of Court Act 1981 was enacted. The Sunday Times subsequently claimed that the new Act and its subsequent interpretation by the House of Lords could not be seen as full implementation of the state's obligation arising from the Court's judgment. A request to invite the Committee to review the matter was rejected in December 1982. The Commission rejected a fresh application by finding that it had no competence in the matter and that, after the adoption of its report under Article 31, 'it cannot examine subsequent developments in the case, nor can it assume any function in relation to the supervision of the Court's judgment'.[7] It was barred from examining the new development in relation to the facts of the former case by Article 27(1)(b) of the Convention.

The issue came before the Court in *Olsson v Sweden (No 2)*.[8] The applicants complained that despite the Court's judgment in the first *Olsson* case[9] (where a violation had been found concerning the implementation of a care order), the Swedish authorities had continued to prevent their reunion with their children. The Court considered that no separate issue arose under Article 53 since the fresh complaint raised a new issue which had not been determined by the *Olsson* judgment. Judge Martens, on the other hand, has forcefully argued that complaints under Article 53 should not be decided by the Committee of Ministers but by the Court since: (1) the interpretation of its own judgments is better left to the Court than to a gathering of

4   A 52 (1982).
5   A 142 (1988) and Res (93) 62.
6   Res (81) 2.
7   *Times Newspapers Ltd v UK No 10243/83*, 41 DR 123 at 129 (1985).
8   A 250 (1992).
9   A 130 (1988).

professional diplomats who are not necessarily trained lawyers possessing the qualifications enunciated in Article 39(3) of the Convention; and (2) the Committee cannot be regarded as a 'tribunal': its members are under the direct authority of their internal administration; the representative of the state concerned is not excluded from the deliberations and may even vote; the Committee may be unable to reach a decision because of the requirements of a two-thirds majority; it sits in private and applicants are excluded from participation in its proceedings.[10] A further argument in support of this position is that the Convention does not provide for sanctions against a respondent state for non-execution of a judgment. It is thus imperative that the question of non-execution be examined and authoritatively determined.

The Court's approach in *Olsson (No 2)* has been vigorously defended by Judge Ryssdal[11] who points out that:

> 'The correct approach in Convention logic was to determine, as the Court did in *Olsson (No 2)*, whether the further interference that occurred with the Olssons' family life in the later period was itself justified under Article 8 – rather than first investigating whether the later facts complained of were in some way or another a consequence of the execution or non-execution of the first *Olsson* judgment. Indeed I even have some doubts as to whether the statement in *Olsson (No 2)* that no separate issue arises under Article 53 was necessary. Was there any issue *at all* under Article 53?'

Whatever the outcome of further Court cases where this point is argued, it seems logical that the Convention system ought to be able to examine and rule on a claim that a contracting party is in violation of its obligations under Article 53 by either failing to give effect to the Court's judgment or introducing corrective measures which are insufficient. Where the breach resides in a clear-cut refusal to comply (eg to introduce individual and/or general measures) it falls, under the scheme of the Convention, to the Committee of Ministers under Article 54 to take cognisance of such refusal. The Court's jurisdiction could perhaps be asserted when it has become clear, for example, from a persistent refusal that there has been a *déni de justice*. However, where the case concerns a continuing situation (as in access, custody or other child care cases), where the facts continue to evolve after the Court has given judgment, it seems more appropriate to examine the new situation on its merits.[12] Likewise where it is being claimed that the

---

10 Martens, 'Individual complaints under Article 53 of the ECHR', *Essays in honour of H G Schermers*, Vol III, 1994, pp 253-293.

11 Ryssdal, 'The enforcement system set up under the ECHR', *Symposium in honour of H G Schermers*, Leiden, 1994.

12 Judge Ryssdal, ibid, suggests that Article 57 could possibly be combined with Article 53 so as to enable the Secretary General to ask a respondent State for an 'explanation' as to the measures taken to execute a judgment although he concedes that there are considerable political and diplomatic difficulties in seeking to use Article 57 in this way.

measures are insufficient (as in the *Sunday Times* case), although in this situation an ideal solution might be to confer an advisory jurisdiction on the Court.[13] In any event, it is not difficult to imagine cases where Article 53 ought to have a bearing on the level of just satisfaction awarded.[14]

As has been noted above, no sanctions against a respondent state for non-execution are specifically provided for under the Convention in contrast to the provisions (Article 32(2) and(3)) governing the execution of the Committee of Ministers' own decisions under Article 32. The Statute of the Council of Europe, on the other hand, provides that a serious violation of the principles of the rule of law and human rights may lead to a state having its right of representation suspended and being requested by the Committee of Ministers to withdraw from the Council of Europe (Articles 8 and 3 of the Statute). The likelihood, however, of such a severe sanction being employed for non-compliance with a judgment of the Court is remote.

3. CONCLUSION

The criticisms of the role of the Committee of Ministers under Article 32 have been strident. Commentators have expressed their dissatisfaction with a system which entrusts an essentially political body with the task of taking judicial decisions under Article 32. It will undoubtedly be seen as a paradox that the Committee, which permits full rein to political considerations in the exercise of its function under Article 32, has been able in the vast majority of cases to adopt the conclusions set out in the Commission's report. Nevertheless it is reflective of the maturing of the Convention system that the Article 32 role of the Committee has not been retained by the Eleventh Protocol.[15]

In contrast, the record of the Committee of Ministers under Article 54, judged by the wealth of legal reform that it has presided over, can be seen as more than satisfactory. The fact that its own authority as a political institution is involved in this process makes it well suited to perform such a role. This perhaps provides an important insight into its success. It is not surprising that this supervisory function has been retained by the Eleventh Protocol in respect of judgments of the proposed Single Court. However, further consideration will need to be given to the establishment of procedures which deal with the episodic problem of delay in introducing remedial legislation, as well as the often complex issues concerning the adequacy and sufficiency of such measures when measured against the judgment of the Court that has provoked them.

13 For the Court's very restricted advisory jurisdiction – see above, p 689.
14 See above, pp 682ff.
15 See below, Ch 26.

CHAPTER 26

Reforming the Convention: Eleventh Protocol

1. THE BACKGROUND TO THE ELEVENTH PROTOCOL[1]

The success of the Convention has inevitably highlighted its weaknesses and amplified the pressure for reform.[2] Under the present system it takes on average more than five years for a case to be finally determined by the Court or the Committee of Ministers. The increasing work-load of the Commission and the Court throughout the 1980s had already given rise to some discussion concerning the possibility of a merger of both institutions as a way of shortening the length of proceedings. However, after 1989, with the growing number of states joining the Council of Europe and ratifying the Convention, the question of reform became a priority issue within the Council of Europe and with member states.

The number of applications registered annually with the Commission increased from 404 in 1981 to 2,037 in 1993. At the end of January 1994 the Commission's backlog stood at 2,672 cases, of which more than 1,487 had not yet been examined by the Commission.[3] The increase in the number of cases referred to the Court has also increased dramatically[4] and, since the changes brought about by the Eighth Protocol[5] have already enabled the Commission to deal more rapidly with cases, this trend is likely to continue.

---

1 See the Explanatory Report to the Eleventh Protocol, Council of Europe, 1994, pp 5-17; reprinted in 17 EHRR 514 (1994); 15 HRLJ 86 (1994); and 1-3 IHRR 206 (1994).
2 See Golsong, 13 HRLJ 265 (1992); Guillarmod, ed, 8 HLRJ, pp 1-244 (1987) (proceedings of the Neuchatel conference); Meyer-Ladevig, *European System*, Ch 40; Peukert, 4 RUDH 217 (1992); and Petzold and Sharpe, in *Wiarda Mélanges*, pp 471-509. See also Reform of the Control System of the ECHR, Council of Europe Doc H (92)14, printed in 14 HRLJ 31-48 (1993).
3 Explanatory Report, paras 20-21. The number of provisional files opened annually increased from 2,000 in 1976 to 3,007 in 1984, to 4,108 in 1988, 4,942 in 1990 and 9,323 in 1993 – *Survey of Activities and Statistics of the European Commission of Human Rights*, Council of Europe, 1993.
4 Explanatory Report, para 21.
5 See above, p 575.

Coinciding with these developments, the number of states parties to the Convention from Eastern and Central European countries has continued to grow. It is currently estimated that by the year 2000 there may well be 35 to 40 contracting parties to the Convention.

Against this background it became clear that reform of the control machinery of the Convention was imperative and that failure to address realistically the problem of delay would undermine the achievements of the system and public confidence in it. One remedy that was mooted was the merger of the Commission and the Court. In the course of discussions by the committees of experts seized of the question,[6] it became clear that opinions were divided as to the desirability of such a merger. Several governments[7] proposed a two-tier system, converting the Commission into a court of first instance and the Court into a court of appeal. It was argued that this could be done with a minimum of dislocation of the existing system by simply making the opinions of the Commission under Article 31 binding on the state concerned and according states a right of appeal to the Court. The Court would be spared deciding on questions of admissibility as well as on cases which raised no difficult questions of interpretation. It would thus be free to control the flow and quality of cases coming to it for decision and concentrate on problems of interpretation raised by mainstream human rights cases. This proposal also had the advantage of retaining the possibility of having cases examined at two levels, thereby enhancing the quality and authority of the final decision - essential features for continuing state confidence in the system. The main disadvantage, it was feared, was that such a system was unlikely to facilitate the handling of cases within a reasonable time since it was to be foreseen that states would want to exercise their right of appeal as a matter of principle. If this assumption were correct, two levels of jurisdiction would still be involved in examining cases which had already been examined by two or more national courts.

Eventually the idea of a single Court gained ground and in 1992 the Parliamentary Assembly of the Council of Europe recommended that the Committee of Ministers 'give clear preference to the proposal to create a single court as a full-time body in place of the existing Commission and Court'.[8] The emphasis was on the need for supervisory machinery which eliminated time-consuming duplication of procedures and which could maintain the authority and quality of the case-law in the future. The proposal of a single court was then finally endorsed in the Vienna Declaration of 9 October 1993 at a meeting of the Council of Europe's heads of state and government.[9]

---

6 The Council of Europe's Steering Committee on Human Rights (CDDH), and the Committee of Experts for the Improvement of Procedures for the Protection of Human Rights (DH-PR). These consist of representatives of Council of Europe member states.
7 The Dutch-Swedish initiative. See the Explanatory Report, paras 15-17.
8 Recommendation 1194 (1992).
9 Explanatory Report, para 23.

The resulting Eleventh Protocol was opened for signature on 11 May 1994.[10] In addition to creating a single Court[11] the opportunity was taken to introduce various other improvements to the Convention system. Thus under the Protocol the right of individual petition ceases to be optional.[12] Accordingly, individuals for the first time have automatic access to an international tribunal. Further, the decision-making role of the Committee of Ministers under the present Article 32 is abolished, although its supervisory role under the present Article 54[13] in respect of judgments of the single Court is retained.

The Protocol will enter into force one year after the ratification by all states' parties and the terms of office of the present judge and members of the Commission will then expire.[14] Detailed transitional provisions are set out which provide for the orderly transfer of cases from the present system to the new Court.[15]

2. THE OPERATION OF THE NEW SINGLE COURT

The new Court will sit in Committees, Chambers and a Grand Chamber

10 The Eleventh Protocol replaces Articles 19-56 of the Convention and the Second Protocol thereto (advisory opinions by the Court). References in this chapter to 'Articles', are to the new Articles of the Convention set out in the Eleventh Protocol, unless otherwise stated. For commentary and description of the Protocol, see Bernhardt, 89 AJIL 145 (1995); Drzemczewski and Meyer-Ladevig, 15 HRLJ 81 (1994); Finnie (1994) SLT 389; Mowbray (1994) PL 54; and Schermers, 19 ELR 367 (1994). The Explanatory Report provides a detailed statement by the drafters of the Protocol of their conception as to how the new Court should operate and how the provisions of the Protocol should be interpreted. The normal proviso, to the effect that the report does not constitute an instrument providing an authoritative interpretation of the Protocol, does not appear in the text. It has been argued by one commentator that since the legal status of the report has not been clarified it could be seen as an indispensable element in the proper understanding, interpretation and application of the Protocol: see Drzemczewski, 144 NLJ 644 at 645 (1994).

11 Article 19.

12 Article 34. The inter-state jurisdiction continues to be mandatory: Article 33. The optional character of the right of individual petition has, however, been retained in respect of territories 'for whose international relations a state is responsible': Article 56, based on Article 63 of the present text.

13 See the new Article 46(2).

14 Articles 4 and 5(1), Protocol. At present 8 of the 30 parties to the Convention have ratified the Eleventh Protocol.

15 Article 5, Protocol. Cases pending before the Commission at the time of the entry into force of the Eleventh Protocol will be handled under the new procedure unless they have been already declared admissible. The Commission will have a year in which to draw up reports on cases that have already been declared admissible. Where a report is adopted within the twelve-month period, the case may be referred to the Court or decided by the Committee of Ministers under the old provisions. Where it is referred to the Court, the panel of the Grand Chamber will determine whether the case will be decided by a Chamber or the Grand Chamber. If the case is decided by a Chamber, the judgment of the Chamber shall be final. If a report is not prepared within a year, the case will be dealt with as an admitted case under the new procedure. Cases pending before the Court or the Committee of Ministers when the Protocol enters into force will be decided by them, with cases pending before the Court being decided by the Grand Chamber.

comprising three, seven and seventeen judges respectively.[16] The plenary Court will be responsible for *inter alia* appointing the Presidents of Chambers, constituting Chambers, adopting rules of procedure and the election of Presidents and Vice-Presidents of the Court.[17] It shall not hear cases. The new Court, in its various case-handling compositions, will have responsibility for determining all aspects of the admissibility and merits of registered applications. It thus combines the functions of the current Commission and Court and the decision-making role of the Committee of Ministers.[18]

The procedure for the consideration of applications under the new system will be as follows. Once an application is registered, a judge *Rapporteur* will be assigned to it by a Chamber. The application will then be considered by a Committee of Three judges, including the judge *Rapporteur*. The Committee may, by a unanimous vote, declare individual cases inadmissible *de plano* or strike cases off the list.[19] If no such decision is taken by a Committee, the application will be referred to a Chamber, which will decide on the admissibility and merits of the case.[20] All inter-state cases must be decided by a Chamber.[1] Decisions on admissibility will be taken separately unless the Court in exceptional cases decides otherwise.[2] Reasons must be given.[3] The criteria of admissibility remain unchanged.

As under the present system, when a case has been declared admissible the Court shall pursue the examination of the case and place itself at the disposal of the parties with a view to securing a friendly settlement.[4] It is the intention of the drafters of the Protocol that the new Court inherit the valuable friendly settlement practice established by the Commission. How this is to be done and, in particular, whether it would be open to the Court to follow the Commission's practice of informing the parties of its provisional opinion in order to stimulate interest in a settlement, is left to

16 Article 27. Committees and Chambers are set up by the Chambers (new Article 27(1)) and the plenary Court (Article 26(b)) respectively for fixed periods. The national judge is *ex officio* a member of the Chamber and Grand Chamber in a case to which his state is a party: Article 27(2).
17 Article 26. It will also elect the Registrar and Deputy Registrar.
18 The jurisdiction of the Court (Article 32, Convention) and its power to give advisory opinions (Articles 47-48, Convention) remain unchanged.
19 Article 28. Not all cases need be examined by a Committee. The judge *Rapporteur* could consider that an application should be sent immediately to a Chamber: Explanatory Report, paras 75-76.
20 Article 29(1).
1 Article 29(2).
2 Article 29(3).
3 Article 45 provides that reasons must be given for judgments as well as admissibility and inadmissibility decisions. The Explanatory Report, para 105, suggests that reasons may be given in summary form. This ought not to call into question the continued use of the 'global formula' which has enabled the Commission to reject unmeritorious cases with an economy of procedure. A practice by the new Court which requires a more detailed rejection of worthless cases, or indeed a more reasoned acceptance of deserving cases, would certainly lead to substantial delays in dealing with the large number of registered applications.
4 Articles 38 and 39.

the Court to decide.[5] To create conditions favourable to reaching a settlement, the Protocol specifically provides that friendly settlement proceedings shall be confidential.[6]

At any time before giving judgment, the Chamber may in certain circumstances relinquish to the Grand Chamber its jurisdiction in a case pending before it. In particular, it may do so where a case raises a serious question affecting the interpretation of the Convention or where the resolution of a question before the Chamber might have a result inconsistent with a judgment previously delivered by the Court.[7] However, relinquishment cannot take place if one of the parties to the case (ie the applicant or the state) objects.[8] The Protocol also provides for the possibility of a re-hearing of the case before the Grand Chamber. Within a period of three months from the date of judgment of the Chamber *any party* may, 'in exceptional cases', request that the case be referred to the Grand Chamber.[9] This request shall be considered by a panel of five judges of the Grand Chamber and accepted 'if the case raises a serious question affecting the interpretation or application of the Convention or the Protocols thereto, or a serious issue of general importance'.[10] The judgment of the Grand Chamber shall be final.[11] The judgment of a Chamber thus only becomes final: (a) when the parties declare that they will not request that the case be referred to the Grand Chamber; or (b) three months after the date of the judgment if referral has not been requested; or (c) when the panel rejects a referral request.[12] Supervision of the judgment of the Court rests with the Committee of Ministers.[13]

Judges of the new Court will still be elected by the Parliamentary Assembly,[14] although the number of judges will now be equal to that of parties to the Convention rather than members of the Council of Europe.[15] In addition they will be full time[16] and elected for six-year terms rather than

5   The Explanatory Report, para 78, indicates that the Chamber may provide the parties with an indication of its provisional opinion on the merits.

6   Article 38(2).

7   Article 30.

8   Ibid. See below, p 712.

9   Article 43(1).

10 Article 43(2). According to the Explanatory Report, p 46, serious questions of *interpretation* are raised: (1) when a question of importance not yet decided by the Court is at stake; (2) when the decision is of importance for future cases and for the development of the Court's case-law; (3) when the judgment concerned is not consistent with a previous judgment of the Court. A serious question of *application* may be at stake when a judgment necessitates a substantial change to national law or administrative practice but does not itself raise a serious question of interpretation. A serious issue considered to be of *general importance* could involve a substantial political issue or an important question of policy.

11 Article 44(1).

12 Article 44(2).

13 Article 46(2).

14 Article 22.

15 Article 20. The criteria for office remain largely the same as with the existing Court except that during their term of office judges may not engage in any activity incompatible with the full-time character of their office: Article 21.

16 See Articles 19 and 21(3).

the present nine years.[17] An express power of dismissal has also been introduced conditional on a majority of two-thirds of the Court that the judge has ceased to fulfil the required conditions.[18] There is no longer a prohibition on two judges having the same nationality, so smaller countries with limited legal resources will no longer have to look for candidates from countries that have not ratified the Convention. Their terms of office will expire when they reach the age of 70.[19] Following the model of the European Court of Justice, the Court will be assisted by both a registry and legal secretaries.[20]

3. ASSESSMENT

The Protocol introduces various improvements to the existing system. Firstly, the new Court will function on a full-time basis. This will greatly influence who is elected and how the Court will function in practice and thus the effectiveness of the institution. The risk of judges becoming detached from their national setting by virtue of their residence in Strasbourg is, judged by the experience of the European Court of Justice, a small one. Secondly, the mandatory acceptance of the right of individual petition has the advantage of opening the door for the new Court to examine complaints against those Eastern and Central European countries, which are not yet members of the Convention community, automatically upon ratification; there will be no need for them to make an Article 25 declaration. Indeed the fear of non-renewal of the right of individual petition by any of the contracting parties is thus a thing of the past.[1] In terms of the impact of the Convention on legal developments in the new signatory countries, this aspect of the reform may well prove to be a watershed. Thirdly, the role of the Committee of Ministers will now be limited to supervising the execution of judgments of the Court. This development can only enhance the credibility of the Convention as a judicial system whose decision-making competence is no longer shared by a political body. Fourthly, the friendly settlement procedure has not been compromised by the fact that cases are decided by a Court. There is every reason to suppose that the wide experience of the Commission in this area, as well as the attachment of contracting parties to the possibility of settlement, will exercise an important influence in this respect. Fifthly, the Convention now provides expressly for third-party interventions. Rule 37(2) of the present Rules of Court has been elevated to a Convention provision. The new Article 36(2) provides more explicitly than the existing rules that the President may invite contracting

17 Article 23(1).
18 Article 24.
19 Article 23(6).
20 Article 25. The relationship between the existing secretariat and the legal secretaries is unclear and is left to be determined by the new Court: see the Explanatory Report, paras 3 and 67.
1 There is still, however, the possibility of denouncing the Convention under Article 65.

parties and individuals not only to submit written comments but also to take part in hearings. The Protocol thus endorses the value and worth of *amicus* briefs as a method of assisting the Court in its deliberations. Sixthly, the reduction of the composition of Chambers to seven judges will make for greater flexibility than before by enabling more than one Chamber to sit at the same time.[2] This will permit the new Court to deal more rapidly with the backlog it will inherit from the Commission and with its own case-load.[3] Lastly, the new system will be more open and transparent. Hearings before the Chambers and the Grand Chamber will be in public and the principle of confidentiality that governs the Commission's proceedings and those of the Committee of Ministers under Article 32 has, apart from friendly settlement proceedings, been abandoned.[4] This will undoubtedly lead to greater media coverage of the system and in turn greater public awareness and an increase in the number of cases.

At the same time, the new system has various questionable features which are the product of the compromise reached between the states supporting a two-tier structure and those in favour of a single Court. Under the new Article 30 of the Convention the parties to a case are given the right to veto the Chamber's relinquishment of jurisdiction to the Grand Chamber. This is an essential component of the 'compromise' in the sense that it is designed to ensure that the possibility of a re-hearing of a case by the Grand Chamber after a judgment by a Chamber will be preserved. Nevertheless, it is a most unusual encroachment on what should be the Court's prerogative to ensure the quality and consistency of its case-law. Apart from the risk that the provision will be used strategically by the parties to the case to create for themselves the possibility of an appeal in the event of an unfavourable outcome, it is likely to give rise to unnecessary delays in the handling of cases.

In addition, the procedure for an internal re-hearing before the Grand Chamber has no parallel in any other international tribunal. It is open to criticism on the grounds that the composition of the Grand Chamber will include the President of the Chamber and the national judge,[5] both of whom will have already taken part in the case. It also has the unusual consequence that judgments of the Chamber are suspended for a period of up to three

2   Under the present practice, Chambers do not sit at the same time. Article 43 of the present Convention, which provides that judges are to be drawn by lot, combined with a Chamber membership of nine full members and four substitutes renders the organisation of collateral sittings difficult. The view has also been expressed, based on a very formalistic reading of Article 43, that such an arrangement would be impermissible under this provision.
3   The backlog is likely to be substantial since cases will continue to be registered with the Commission during the period of one year between ratification by all states parties and the entry into force of the Protocol.
4   See generally Article 40. This expressly provides that documents deposited with the Registrar shall be accessible to the public unless the President of the Court decides otherwise. Parties to friendly settlement proceedings will not be at liberty to disclose to anyone the nature and content of any communication made with a view to and in connection with a friendly settlement: see the Explanatory Report, para 93.
5   Article 27(2), (3).

months pending a decision as to whether there is to be a re-hearing. Further, if not restricted to 'exceptional cases', it could give rise to substantial delays and recreate the duplication of procedures that exist under the present system. It could also be a source of division within the new Court itself if differences of opinion between the Chamber and the Grand Chamber were frequent. Much will depend on the exercise of discretion by the panel of five judges of the Grand Chamber which will have the final responsibility for selecting exceptional cases worthy of a re-hearing in accordance with the criteria set out in both paragraphs 1 and 2 of Article 43.[6]

Finally, Article 35(4), which enables the Court to reject an application as inadmissible at any stage of the proceedings, will encourage states to pursue admissibility at the merits phase of the procedure before the Chamber and possibly the Grand Chamber. It lacks the safeguard currently contained in Article 29 of the Convention which requires a majority of two-thirds to reverse a decision admitting an application. While regulation may be possible by the application of an estoppel rule, the new Court will inherit the same difficulties of repetitive invocation of arguments as to inadmissibility that is a criticised feature of the present system.

The Eleventh Protocol has been carefully fashioned to provide an enforcement system which takes over from the existing institutions. It is not meant to be a fresh start but rather the continuation of the Convention system with more efficient machinery to handle an ever-increasing case-load against the background of a growing number of contracting parties. For example, the Commission's extensive case-law on admissibility and the accumulated jurisprudence of the Commission and Court will be applied by the new Court. It has been argued by a member of the Commission[7] that states should be hesitant to ratify the Protocol since it is unlikely that a new institution will be able to deal with cases as efficiently as predicted due to the inherited backlog from the Commission and the inevitable teething problems of a new institution; the existing system should rather be given more resources to enable the changes in the working methods of the Commission brought about by the Eighth Protocol (Committees and Chambers) to be exploited with more productive effect.

The above arguments reflect the debate waged between those in favour of the two-tier system as opposed to a single Court. In their support, it should be acknowledged that, with Committees and Chambers meeting at the same time, the Commission has indeed been able to bring about substantial improvements in its productivity. The weakness of the above arguments lies in the fact that even with a more productive Commission important cases would still have to be examined by two institutions in separate and time-consuming proceedings. With a single Court eliminating the present duplication of procedures, for all but exceptional cases where there might

6 With the large volume of cases that the new Court will be expected to handle it can perhaps be predicted that the panel will give a strict interpretation to the notion of 'exceptional cases'.
7 See Schermers, p 708, above, n 10, pp 377-382.

be an internal appeal, there is a greater likelihood of a significantly more efficient examination of cases. Nevertheless, the new Court will only achieve its goals if there is a strong element of continuity between the old and the new in terms of membership of the single Court, personnel experienced in the operation of the previous system and a successful transfer of the working methods and procedural know-how of the existing institutions. Together with Convention case-law these represent the '*aquis conventionnel*' which must be preserved and built upon if the Eleventh Protocol is to make the Convention a fitting instrument of human rights protection for the new Europe.

European Commission of Human Rights and European Court of Human Rights members on 31 December 1994

EUROPEAN COMMISSION OF HUMAN RIGHTS

Mr Carl Aage NØRGAARD, President	(Danish)
Mr Stefan TRECHSEL, President of the Second Chamber	(Swiss)
Mr Albert WEITZEL, President of the First Chamber	(Luxemburger)
Mr Felix ERMACORA	(Austrian)
Mr Edwin BUSUTTIL	(Maltese)
Mr Gaukur JÖRUNDSSON	(Icelandic)
Mr A Seref GÖZÜBÜYÜK	(Turkish)
Mr Jean-Claude SOYER	(French)
Mr Henry G SCHERMERS	(Dutch)
Mr Hans DANELIUS	(Swedish)
Mrs Gro Hillestad THUNE	(Norwegian)
Mr Luis Fernando MARTINEZ RUIZ	(Spanish)
Mr Christos L ROZAKIS	(Greek)
Mrs Jane LIDDY	(Irish)
Mr Loukis LOUCAIDES	(Cypriot)
Mr Jean-Claude GEUS	(Belgian)
Mr Matti Paavo PELLONPÄÄ	(Finnish)
Mr Benedikt MARXER	(Liechtensteiner)
Mr Giordano Bruno REFFI	(San Marinese)
Mr Marek A NOWICKI	(Polish)
Mr Ireneu CABRAL BARRETO	(Portuguese)
Mr Benedetto CONFORTI	(Italian)
Mr Nicolas BRATZA	(British)
Mr Imre BÉKÉS	(Hungarian)
Mr Jiři MUCHA	(Czech)
Mr Emil KONSTANTINOV	(Bulgarian)
Mr Daniel ŠVÁBY	(Slovakian)
Mr Georg RESS	(Germany)

EUROPEAN COURT OF HUMAN RIGHTS

Mr Rolv RYSSDAL, President	(Norwegian)
Mr Rudolf BERNHARDT, Vice-President	(German)
Mr Thór VILHJÁLMSSON	(Icelandic)
Mr Feyyaz GÖLCÜKLÜ	(Turkish)
Mr Franz MATSCHER	(Austrian)
Mr Louis-Edmond PETTITI	(French)
Mr Brian WALSH	(Irish)
Mr Ronald MACDONALD[1]	(Canadian)
Mr Carlo RUSSO	(Italian)
Mr Alphonse SPIELMANN	(Luxemburger)
Mr Jan DE MEYER	(Belgian)
Mr Nicolas VALTICOS	(Greek)
Mr Sibrand Karel MARTENS	(Dutch)
Mrs Elisabeth PALM	(Swedish)
Mr Isi FOIGHEL	(Danish)
Mr Raimo PEKKANEN	(Finnish)
Mr Andreas Nicolas LOIZOU	(Cypriot)
Mr José Maria MORENILLA	(Spanish)
Mr Federico BIGI	(San Marinese)
Sir John FREELAND	(British)
Mr András BAKA	(Hungarian)
Mr Manuel Antonio Lopes ROCHA	(Portuguese)
Mr Luzius WILDHABER	(Swiss)
Mr Giuseppe Mifsud BONNICI	(Maltese)
Mr Jerzy MAKARCZYK	(Polish)
Mr Dimitar GOTCHEV	(Bulgarian)
Mr Bohumil REPIK	(Slovakian)
Mr Peter JAMBREK	(Slovenian)
Mr Karel JUNGWIERT	(Czech)
Mr Pranas KŪRIS	(Lithuanian)
Mr Uno LÕHMUS	(Estonian)

1 Elected as the judge in respect of Liechtenstein.

Table of applications in 1993/94

	Provisional files opened		Applications registered		Applications inadmissible or struck off		Applications admissible	
	1993	1994	1993	1994	1993	1994	1993	1994
Austria	245	238	161	154	121	161	29	23
Belgium	128	212	70	78	87	47	4	5
Bulgaria	35	48	6	12	3	6	–	–
Cyprus	8	12	3	21	10	6	–	–
Czech Republic	90	111	16	52	–	32	–	–
Denmark	80	92	19	25	18	17	1	2
Finland	73	109	41	61	14	27	2	3
France	1383	1637	399	439	335	338	38	63
Germany	672	836	148	188	112	140	1	4
Greece	73	118	111	48	25	43	2	103
Hungary	127	184	51	56	28	35	–	–
Iceland	6	7	3	4	1	1	–	–
Ireland	29	43	5	18	12	7	–	1
Italy	3032	1858	142	507	87	107	90	298
Liechtenstein	–	–	3	–	4	1	–	–
Luxembourg	21	21	10	11	7	5	1	–
Malta	7	7	5	6	3	4	1	–
Netherlands	171	192	93	104	86	102	10	8
Norway	31	34	18	16	21	6	2	2
Poland	630	979	39	161	7	66	–	–

	Provisional files opened		Applications registered		Applications inadmissible or struck off		Applications admissible	
	1993	1994	1993	1994	1993	1994	1993	1994
Portugal	89	121	38	51	23	28	14	26
Romania	119	597	–	9	–	–	–	–
San Marino/Saint-Marin	1	6	–	8	1	–	–	–
Slovak Republic	36	100	4	36	–	18	–	–
Slovenia	–	33	–	–	–	–	–	–
Spain	228	254	90	138	94	125	5	1
Sweden	242	360	106	161	77	108	3	2
Switzerland	181	229	123	156	100	140	–	6
Turkey	104	130	128	187	46	78	8	19
United Kingdom	648	946	205	236	226	141	10	16
Other or not stated	834	454	–	1	–	1	–	–
TOTAL	9323	9968	2037	2944	1547	1790	218	582

Index